CONTENTS

INTERNATIONAL MARKETING

INTERNATIONAL MARKETING

Michael R. Czinkota, Ilkka A. Ronkainen and Gilbert Zvobgo

SOUTH-WESTERN
CENGAGE Learning

Australia • Brazil • Japan • Korea • Mexico • Singapore • Spain • United Kingdom • United States

International Marketing
Michael R. Czinkota, Ilkka A. Ronkainen
and Gilbert Zvobgo

Publishing Director: Linden Harris

Publisher: Brendan George

Development Editor: Annabel Ainscow

Editorial Assistant: Helen Green

Content Project Editor: Lucy Arthy

Production Controller: Eyvett Davis

Marketing Manager: Vicky Fielding

Typesetter: KnowledgeWorks Global, India

Cover design: Design Deluxe

For product information and technology assistance,
contact **emea.info@cengage.com**.
For permission to use material from this text or product,
and for permission queries,
email **clsuk.permissions@cengage.com**.

The Author has asserted the right under the Copyright, Designs and Patents Act 1988 to be identified as Author of this Work.

This work is adapted from *International Marketing* 8e by Czinkota and Ronkainen published by Cengage South-Western, a division of Cengage Learning, Inc. © 2007.

British Library Cataloguing-in-Publication Data
A catalogue record for this book is available from the British Library.

ISBN: 978-1-4080-0923-9

Cengage Learning EMEA
Cheriton House, North Way, Andover, Hampshire SP10 5BE
United Kingdom

Cengage Learning products are represented in Canada by Nelson Education Ltd.

For your lifelong learning solutions, visit
www.cengage.co.uk

Purchase your next print book, e-book or e-chapter at
www.cengagebrain.com

Printed by R R Donnelley, China
1 2 3 4 5 6 7 8 9 10 – 13 12 11

To Ilona and Margaret Victoria – MRC
To Susan, Sanna and Alex – IAR
To Mabel, Simbarshe and Nyasha – GZ

BRIEF CONTENTS

CASES 2   280

CASES 3   413

PREFACE

Thank you for reading our book! Practising international marketing and writing a text on the subject have much in common. The focus is on delighting the customer; it is a lot of work; the competition is tough; and it's fun to succeed. It is therefore with great pleasure that we present the EMEA edition *International Marketing* to you. We have made significant revisions in this edition, but our goals continue to be excellence and relevance in content, combined with user-friendliness for both the student and the lecturer. We have greatly streamlined the text, which now comprises 18 chapters. We have done so to balance the workload for the reader but without taking shortcuts. We have combined topics, eliminated redundancies and tightened content wherever possible. The result is a shorter, crisper text of better quality.

We now address in depth controversies surrounding issues such as globalization, terrorism and international aid. We paint a broader picture of the implications of a market orientation and highlight ethical concerns. We discuss the shortcomings encountered in corporate transparency and executive veracity. We also provide much deeper data analysis and support. For example, in addition to discussing the leading economic regions, we offer comparative benchmarks from China, Australia, Kenya and Brazil.

Here are the key features that make this book stand out:

- We cover the full spectrum of international marketing, from start-up operations to the formation of virtual alliances. We offer a thorough discussion of the operations of multinational corporations, but also present a specific focus on the activities of small and medium-sized firms, which are increasingly major players in the international market and will be the employers of many students.

- We provide a hands-on analysis of the growing interaction between government and business. We have served in government positions and advised international organizations. We know what role governmental considerations can play for the international marketer. This policy orientation greatly enhances the managerial relevance of this book.

- We cover both the theory and the application of international marketing. Based on our personal research record and business experience, we can offer research insights from around the globe and show how corporations are adjusting to the marketplace realities of today.

- We acknowledge and give clear examples of how the world has changed in an era of terrorism, hostility and distrust. We look at the marketing repercussions of these changes on people management, sourcing policies, cargo security, inventory management, and port utilization. However, we also draw on our work with corporations to find new forms of collaboration and network building without compromising safety or security.

- We address the concerns of emerging and developing markets throughout the text. We present the issue of underserved markets, with a population of four billion, and also suggest how these people and countries can become greater participants in marketing efforts.

- We examine international marketing from a truly global perspective. By addressing, confronting and analysing the existence of different environments, expectations and market conditions, we highlight the need for awareness, sensitivity and adaptation.

- We integrate the e-commerce and web impact on the international marketer. We discuss the revolutionary changes in communication between firms and their customers and suppliers, and present the latest consequences for international market research and market entry.

PERSONAL SUPPORT

Most important, we personally stand behind our product and we will work hard to delight you. Should you have any questions or comments on this book, you can contact us, talk to us and receive feedback from us.

Michael R. Czinkota
+1 202 687 4204
czinkotm@georgetown.edu

Ilkka A. Ronkainen
+1 202 687 3788
ronkaii@georgetown.edu

Gilbert Zvobgo
+44 121 444 2170
zvobgog@lsbu.ac.uk

ORGANIZATION

The text is designed primarily for the advanced undergraduate student with prior exposure to the marketing field. Due to its in-depth coverage, it also presents an excellent challenge for graduate instruction and executive education.

The text is divided into four parts. In Part I the core concepts of international marketing are outlined, and the environmental forces that the international marketer has to consider are discussed. Part II focuses on international market entry and development. We cover strategic planning for internationalization, organizing for implementation, preparing through research and executing the entry. Part III addresses the elements of the marketing mix that are most important for firms at an initial level of the international experience. Part IV discusses the marketing management issues most relevant to the expanded global operations of multinational corporations. We conclude with an appendix of international employment opportunities.

Both the instructor and the student can work with this text in two ways. One alternative is to cover the material sequentially, progressing from the initial international effort to multinational activities. In this way, marketing dimensions such as distribution, promotion and pricing are covered in the order in which they are most relevant for the particular level of expertise within the firm. Another approach is to use the text in a parallel manner, by pairing comparable chapters from Parts II, III and IV. In this way, the primary emphasize can be placed on the functional approach to international marketing.

KEY FEATURES

The European edition reflects the needs of the target audience, and is distinct from the previous editions. Its readership is mainly Europe, the Middle East and Africa (EMEA). Most of the cases and international marketplaces are based on the EMEA region in order to limit the American 'feel'. The text also reflects the highly dynamic nature of the international marketplace. We offer a perspective on the shift from marketplace to market space, and the impact of this revolution on international marketers in terms of outreach, research and competition. Our International Marketplace vignettes reflect state-of-the-art corporate practices. We have included links to the websites of companies, data sources, governments, international organizations and monitors of international marketing issues.

Our focus on the physical environment and geography is strong. Updated maps provide context in terms of social and economic data. An appendix directly addresses the relationship between geography and international marketing. New text components, marketplaces and cases specifically focus on the environment and the opportunities, challenges and ambiguities that it poses to international marketers.

This edition gives increased attention to developing economies and economies in transition. In Part I, international organizations such as the World Bank, the World Trade Organization, the International Monetary Fund and the United Nations are covered, along with the public debate surrounding these institutions. In particular, we focus on the evolving role of the World Trade Organization and the push for the conclusion of the Doha Round. A case later in the book (see page 564) highlights the controversies surrounding the United Nations' Oil for Food Programme. We have increased the focus on ethics and corporate citizenship in this section and strengthened our discussion of intellectual property rights.

We broaden our discussion of emerging markets by systematically addressing the issue of dealing with markets at the bottom of the income pyramid. Our revised strategy section is now linked directly with organization, implementation and research concerns. We have completely recast the chapter on market entry and expansion to include a wider variety of ways in which firms go global. All of these strategies are now integrated into one chapter, organized around our model of the internationalization process.

The marketing mix discussions now include new technologies and their impact. For example, we present the effect of consumer generated media (such as blogs) and new opportunities presented by m-payments through mobile devices. We offer specific sections on outsourcing by involving partners in research and design, on the effect of terrorism on international transportation and the reconfiguration of web-based services. New also is the focus on how local companies can defend against global players and win, and our emphasize is on sponsorship and ambush marketing. The final appendix of international employment opportunities helps students prepare for the implementation steps yet to come.

INNOVATIVE LEARNING TOOLS

Contemporary realism

Each chapter includes International Marketplace boxes. They focus on real marketing situations and help students understand and absorb the presented materials. The instructor can highlight the boxes to exemplify theory or use them as mini-cases for class discussion.

Research emphasis

A special effort has been made to provide current research information and data from around the world. Chapter notes are augmented by lists of relevant recommended readings incorporating the latest research findings. In addition, a wide variety of sources and organizations that provide international information are offered in the text. These materials enable the instructor and the student to go beyond the text when desired.

Internet focus

The internet, electronic commerce and the World Wide Web affect all of international marketing. We highlight how the way of reaching customers and suppliers has changed given the new technology. We explain the enhanced ability of firms to position themselves internationally in competition with other larger players. We offer insights into the electronic marketing research process and present details of how companies cope with new market realities. Whenever appropriate, we direct readers to internet resources that can be useful in updating information. Each chapter also provides several internet questions in order to offer training opportunities that make use of the internet.

Geography

This edition contains several maps covering the social, economic and political features of the world. In addition, several chapters have maps particularly designed for this book, which integrate the materials discussed in the text and reflect a truly 'global' perspective. These maps enable the instructor to visually demonstrate concepts such as socioeconomic variables or exposure to terrorism. An appendix, dealing specifically with the impact of geography on international marketing, is part of Chapter 1.

Cases

Following each part of the text are a variety of cases, some of which are new in this edition, that present students with real business situations. All cases cover a broad geographic spectrum. Challenging questions accompany each case, permitting in-depth discussion of the materials covered in the chapters.

ACKNOWLEDGMENTS

We are deeply grateful to all the professors, students and professionals using this book. Your interest demonstrates the need for more knowledge about international marketing. As our market, you are telling us that our product adds value to your lives. As a result, you add value to ours. Thank you!

We also thank the many reviewers for their constructive and imaginative comments and criticisms, which were instrumental in this edition. They are:

Joel Arnott, *University of Sunderland*

Mike Cant, *University of Pretoria*

Roger Dace, *University of Portsmouth*

Noel Dennis, *Teesside University*

Jens Graff, *Solbridge International School of Business*

Dr Finola Kerrigan, *Kings College London*

Siobhan Magner, *Dublin Business School*

Prof. Rauni Seppola, *University of Vaasa*

Prof. Reiner Springer, *Vienna University of Economics and Business*

We also thank the colleagues who have generously written new cases to contribute to this new edition of our book. They are Helmut Kohlert and Alex Verjovsky.

Foremost, we are grateful to our families, who have truly participated in our labours. Only the patience, understanding, and love of Ilona and Margaret Victoria Czinkota and Susan, Sanna and Alex Ronkainen, and Mabel Zvobgo enabled us to have the energy, stamina and inspiration to write this book.

Michael R. Czinkota
Ilkka A. Ronkainen
Gilbert Zvobgo

London
May 2010

ABOUT THE AUTHORS

Michael R. Czinkota teaches international marketing and business at the Graduate School and the Robert Emmett McDonough School of Business at Georgetown University, Washington, DC. He has held professorial appointments at universities in Asia, Australia, Europe and the Americas.

Dr Czinkota served in the US government as deputy assistant secretary of commerce. He also served as head of the US delegation to the OECD Industry Committee in Paris and as senior advisor for export controls.

Dr Czinkota's background includes eight years of private-sector business experience as a partner in a fur trading firm and in an advertising agency. His research has been supported by the US government, the National Science Foundation, the Organization of American States and the American Management Association. He was listed as one of the three most published contributors to international business research in the *Journal of International Business Studies,* and has written several books, including *Best Practices in International Marketing* and *Mastering Global Markets* (Cengage).

Dr Czinkota served on the global advisory board of the American Marketing Association, the global council of the American Management Association, and the board of governors of the Academy of Marketing Science. He is on the editorial boards of *Journal of the Academy of Marketing Science, Journal of International Marketing*, and *Asian Journal of Marketing*. For his work in international business and trade policy, he was named a distinguished fellow of the Academy of Marketing Science, a fellow of the Chartered Institute of Marketing, and a fellow of the Royal Society of Arts in the United Kingdom. He has been awarded honorary degrees from the Universidad Pontificia Madre y Maestra in the Dominican Republic and the Universidad del Pacifico in Lima, Peru.

Dr Czinkota serves on several corporate boards and has worked with corporations such as AT&T, IBM, GE, Nestlé, and US WEST. He advises the Executive Office of the President of the United States, the United Nations and the World Trade Organization. Dr Czinkota is often asked to testify before the United States Congress.

Dr Czinkota was born and raised in Germany and educated in Austria, Scotland, Spain and the United States. He studied law and business administration at the University of Erlangen-Nürnberg and was awarded a two-year Fulbright Scholarship. He holds an MBA in international business and a PhD in logistics from the Ohio State University.

Ilkka A. Ronkainen is a member of the faculty of marketing and international business at the School of Business at Georgetown University, Washington, DC. From 1981 to 1986 he served as associate director and from 1986 to 1987 as chairman of the National Centre for Export-Import Studies. Currently, he directs Georgetown University's Hong Kong Programme.

Dr Ronkainen serves as docent of international marketing at the Helsinki School of Economics. He was visiting professor at HSE during the 1997–88 and 1991–92 academic years and continues to teach in its Executive MBA, International MBA and International BBA programmes. He is currently the chairholder at the Saastamoinen Foundation Professorship in International Marketing.

Dr Ronkainen holds a PhD and a master's degree from the University of South Carolina as well as an MS (Economics) degree from the Helsinki School of Economics.

Dr Ronkainen has published extensively in academic journals and the trade press. He is a coauthor of a number of international business and marketing texts, including *Best Practices in International Marketing* and *Mastering Global Markets* (Cengage). He serves on the review boards of the *Journal of Business Research, International Marketing Review,* and *Journal of Travel Research,* and has reviewed for the *Journal of International Marketing* and the *Journal of International Business Studies.* He served as the North American coordinator for the European Marketing Academy, 1984–90. He was a member of the board of the Washington International Trade Association from 1981 to 1986 and started the association's newsletter, *Trade Trends.*

Dr Ronkainen has served as a consultant to a wide range of US and international institutions. He has worked with entities such as IBM, the Rand Organization and the Organization of American States. He maintains close relations with a number of Finnish companies and their internationalization and educational efforts.

Gilbert Zvobgo is a lecturer in marketing at London South Bank University, England. He has been teaching international marketing, marketing research, retailing marketing, advertisement and promotion, business ethics, small business and enterpreneurship and management in context since 2001.

Dr Zvobgo was a visiting professor at the University of Birmingham, UK from 2000–2002 and at Birmingham City University from 2002–2009.

Dr Zvobgo is also an online MBA instructor for Laurette Education BV, an e-learning partner of the University of Liverpool. He teaches corporate strategy, marketing management, strategic organization and organizational behaviour, and also supervises MBA dissertations.

Dr Zvobgo holds a PhD in industrial and business studies from the University of Warwick, an MBA in international business from the University of Birmingham and a BSc (Hon) in politics and administration from the University of Zimbabwe. He also holds a postgraduate diploma in personnel management and training management, online teaching and a PGCE in post compulsory education. He is currently in the dissertation stage of an MEed e-learning with the University of Hull, UK.

Dr Zvobgo was guest speaker at Middle Georgia College, Cochran, Georgia, US in 2006. He has reviewed books for the *Journal of Management Studies*, published conference papers and is a reviewer for the Academy of Marketing and and a reviewing editor for the *Journal of Business and Retail Management Research.*

SUPPLEMENTS

INSTRUCTOR RESOURCES

Instructor's Manual The text is accompanied by an in-depth Instructor's Manual, devised to provide major assistance to the professor. This is available on the password-protected instructor's resource website, and the material in the manual includes the following:

- *How to Use the Book* consisting of a simple course outline detailing how and when to use chapters and sections of the text.

- *End-of-chapter questions* Each question is fully developed in the manual to accommodate different scenarios and experience horizons. In addition, each chapter has internet-based exercises in order to offer students the opportunity to explore the application of new technology to international marketing on their own.

- Answers to all case study questions are provided.

ExamView testbank Available on the password-protected instructor's resource website, the ExamView testbank includes a variety of multiple choice, true/false questions, and cases, which emphasize the important concepts presented in each chapter. The testbank questions vary in levels of difficulty so that instructors can tailor their testing to meet their specific needs.

PowerPoint presentation slides Available on the password-protected instructor's resource website, the PowerPoint lecture presentation enables instructors to customize their own multimedia classroom presentations. The package includes select figures and tables from the text, as well as outside materials to supplement chapter concepts. Material is organized by chapter, and can be modified or expanded for individual classroom use. PowerPoint presentations are also easily printed to create customized transparency masters.

STUDENT RESOURCES

The following student resources accompany the text:

- Internet exercises with supporting answers
- Flashcards and key terms, to show key concepts
- Surf the net

WALK THROUGH TOUR

The international marketplace shows international marketing practice in real life situations.

Key terms are highlighted throughout the text and listed at the end of each chapter.

Summary captures the most important concepts in the chapter in a condensed form.

Questions for discussion at the end of each chapter, there are questions for discussion to reinforce the understanding of the chapter. They widen knowledge of the subject by pulling ideas and experiences from the reader.

Internet exercises provide further exercises in reinforcing the material introduced in the chapter. Most of the exercises are on contemporary examples.

Recommended readings these provide additional readings in terms of the concepts introduced in the chapter.

Notes these are sources of material which show the reliability of the source of information, so that the reader can check for more information.

Cases at the end of each Part there are cases at the end of each part to develop analytical and problem solving skills and allow application of theoretical knowledge in solving real life examples. These cases are generally related to the theme in each part of the text.

ABOUT THE WEBSITE

About the website

All of our Higher Education textbooks are accompanied by a range of digital support resources. Each title's resources are carefully tailored to the specific needs of the particular book's readers. Examples of the kind of resources provided include:

- A password protected area for instructors with, for example, a testbank, PowerPoint slides and an instructor's manual.
- An area for students including, for example, multiple choice questions and weblinks.

To discover the dedicated digital support resources accompanying this textbook please go to:

www.cengage.co.uk/crzim

For students

- Internet exercises
- Flashcards and key terms
- Surf the net

For lecturers

- Instructor's manual
- PowerPoint slides
- ExamView testbank

THE INTERNATIONAL MARKETING ENVIRONMENT

Part I introduces the international trade framework and environment. It highlights the need for international marketing activities and explores recent developments in world trade and global markets, including an overview of regional and international trade agreements. These chapters are largely devoted to macroenvironmental forces that firms and managers must be aware of when conducting business internationally. In order to be successful, the marketer must adapt to foreign environments and must be able to resolve conflicts stemming from differences in cultural, economic, political, and legal factors.

CHAPTER 1

THE GLOBAL MARKETING IMPERATIVE

THE INTERNATIONAL **MARKETPLACE 1.1**

International marketing: Bringing peace, fighting terrorism

One really big surprise of the post-war era has been that historic enemies, such as Germany and France or Japan and the United States, have not had the remotest threat of war from each other since 1945. Why should they? Anything Japan has that the United States wants can be bought, and on very easy credit terms, so why fight for it? Why should the Japanese fight the United States and lose all those profitable markets? France and Germany, linked intimately through marketing and the European Union, are now each other's largest trading partners.

Closed systems build huge armies and waste their resources on guns and troops; open countries spend their money on new machines to crank out Barbie dolls or some other consumer products. The bright young people of open countries figure out how to run machines or provide services, not how to fire the latest missile. For some reason, they not only get rich fast but also lose interest in military adventures. Japan, that peculiar superpower without super-guns, confounds everyone simply because no one has ever seen a major world power that got that way by selling you to death, not shooting you to death.

Freedom is about options. A true option provides the opportunity to make a meaningful decision, to exercise virtue. International marketing contains the freedom of almost unlimited growth potential. However, the cost of freedom is rising. Terms like free trade or free choice are misleading because they come with a price. We are all paying a higher price due to global terrorism. Marketers pay the higher cost of preparing their shipments, scrutinizing their customers, and conforming to government regulations. Local participants, employees and investors pay with their suffering and economic loss after a terrorist attack.

In most instances, terrorism is not an outgrowth of choice, but rather the lack of it. Terrorists do not succeed in increasing their free-dom through their actions, but only decrease the freedom of others. International marketers in turn can invest in the world's poorest markets and increase their own revenue while decreasing poverty. The expansion of trade creates jobs, improves health and education standards, and raises overall standards of living in impoverished regions – all of which bring a new sense of hope that turns aside the false appeal of terrorism. The slashing of tariffs on Pakistani textiles by the European Union is an example of the might of international marketing.

However, much effort continues to be required from the global community. Trade-based progress toward global wealth must include extensive health-care and environmental aid, massive debt write-offs, and substantial tariff and quota reductions for steel, textile, and agri-cultural exports from impoverished regions.

SOURCES: Czinkota, Michael R., 'On Freedom and International Marketing', *Congressional Record,* May 9, 2005; Farmer, Richard N., 'Would You Want Your Daughter to Marry a Taiwanese Marketing Man?', *Journal of Marketing* 51 (October 1987): 114–115.

You are about to begin an exciting, important, and necessary task: the exploration of international marketing. International marketing is exciting because it combines the science and the art of business with many other disciplines. Economics, anthropology, cultural studies, geography, history, languages, jurisprudence, statistics, demographics and many other fields combine to help you explore the global market. Different business environments will stimulate your intellectual curiosity, which will enable you to absorb and understand new phenomena. International marketing has been compared by many who have been active in the field to the task of mountain climbing: challenging, arduous and exhilarating.

International marketing is important because the world has become globalized. Increasingly, we all are living up to the claim of the Greek philosopher Socrates, who stated, 'I am a citizen, not of Athens or Greece, but of the world'. International marketing takes place all around us every day, has a major effect on our lives, and offers new opportunities and challenges. After reading through this book and observing international marketing phenomena, you will see what happens, understand what happens, and, at some time in the future, perhaps even make it happen. All of this is much better than to stand by and wonder what happened.

International marketing is necessary because, from a national standpoint, economic isolationism has become impossible. Failure to participate in the global marketplace assures a nation of declining economic capability and its citizens of a decrease in their standard of living. Successful international marketing, however, holds the promise of an improved quality of life, a better society, more efficient business transactions, and even a more peaceful world, as *The International Marketplace 1.1* highlights.

This chapter is designed to increase your awareness of what international marketing is about. It describes current levels of world trade activities, projects future developments and discusses the repercussions on countries, institutions and individuals worldwide. Both the opportunities and the threats that spring from the global marketplace are highlighted, and the need for an international 'marketing' approach on the part of individuals and institutions is emphasized.

This chapter ends with an explanation of the major organizational thrust of this book, which is a differentiation between the beginning internationalist and the multinational corporation. This theme ties the book together by taking into account the concerns, capabilities and goals of firms that will differ widely based on their level of international expertise, resources and involvement. The approach to international marketing taken here will therefore permit you to understand the entire range of international activities and allow you easily to transfer your acquired knowledge into practice.

WHAT INTERNATIONAL MARKETING IS

In brief, international marketing is the process of planning and conducting transactions across national borders to create exchanges that satisfy the objectives of individuals and organizations. International marketing has forms ranging from export–import trade to licencing, joint ventures, wholly owned subsidiaries, turnkey operations and management contracts.

As this definition indicates, international marketing very much retains the basic marketing tenets of 'satisfaction' and 'exchange'. International marketing is a tool used to obtain improvement of one's present position. The fact that a transaction takes place across national borders highlights the difference between domestic and international marketing. The international marketer is subject to a new set of macroenvironmental factors, to different constraints, and to quite frequent conflicts resulting from different laws, cultures and societies. The basic principles of marketing still apply, but their applications, complexity and intensity may vary substantially. It is in the international marketing field where one can observe most closely the role of marketing as a key agent of societal change and as a key instrument for the development of societally responsive business strategy. When we look, for example, at the emerging market economies of China and Russia, we can see the many new challenges confronting international marketing. How does the marketing concept fit into these societies? How can marketing contribute to economic development and the improvement of society? How should distribution systems be organized? How can we get the price mechanism to work? Similarly, in the international areas of social responsibility and ethics, the international marketer is faced with a multicultural environment with differing expectations and often inconsistent legal systems when it comes to monitoring environmental pollution, maintaining safe working conditions, copying technology or trademarks, or paying bribes.[1] In addition, the long-term repercussions of marketing actions need to be understood and evaluated in terms of their societal impact. These are just a few of the issues that the international marketer needs to address. The capability to master these challenges successfully affords a company the potential for new opportunities and high rewards.

The definition also focuses on international transactions. The use of the term recognizes that marketing internationally is an activity that needs to be pursued, often aggressively. Those who do not participate in the transactions are still exposed to international marketing and subject to its changing influences. The international marketer is part of the exchange, and recognizes the constantly changing nature of transactions. This need for adjustment, for comprehending change, and, in spite of it all, for successfully carrying out transactions, highlights the fact that international marketing is as much art as science.

To achieve success in the art of international marketing, it is necessary to be firmly grounded in its scientific aspects. Only then will individual consumers, policymakers and business executives be able to incorporate international marketing considerations into their thinking and planning. Only then will they be able to consider international issues and repercussions and make decisions based on answers to questions such as:

- Should I obtain my supplies domestically or from abroad?
- What marketing adjustments are or will be necessary?
- What threats from global competition should I expect?
- How can I work with these threats to turn them into opportunities?
- What are my strategic global alternatives?

If all these issues are integrated into each decision made by individuals and by firms, international markets can become a source of growth, profit, needs satisfaction and quality of life that would not have existed for them had they limited themselves to domestic activities. The purpose of this book is to aid in this decision process.

THE IMPORTANCE OF WORLD TRADE

World trade has assumed an importance heretofore unknown to the global community. In past centuries, trade was conducted internationally but never before did it have the broad and simultaneous impact on nations, firms and individuals that it has today. Within five years, world trade in merchandise has expanded from $6.2 trillion in 2000 to over $9 trillion in 2005. World trade in services has expanded from $1.5 trillion to $2.1 trillion in the same period of time. That represents a growth of nearly 150 per cent for trade in both merchandise and services![2] Such economic growth is exceptional, particularly since, as Exhibit 1.1 shows, trade growth on a global level has usually outperformed the growth of domestic economies in the past few decades. As a result, many countries and firms have found it highly desirable to become major participants in international marketing.

The Iron Curtain has disintegrated, offering a vast array of new marketing opportunities – albeit amid uncertainty. Firms invest on a global scale, with the result that entire industries shift their locations. International specialization and cross-sourcing have made production much more efficient. New technologies have changed the way we do business, allowing us to both supply and receive products from across the world by using the internet. As a result, consumers, union leaders, policymakers and sometimes even the firms themselves are finding it increasingly difficult to define where a particular product was made. There are trading blocs such as the European Union in Europe, NAFTA in North America, Mercosur in Latin America, and ASEAN in Asia. These blocs encourage trade relations between their members, but, through their rules and standards, they also affect the trade and investment flows of non-member countries.

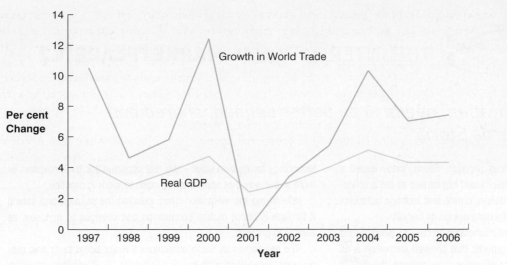

EXHIBIT 1.1

Growth of world output in trade (1997–2006)

Source: *International Monetary Fund, World Economic Outlook 2005, Statistical Appendix*, 205, 233.

Individuals and firms have come to recognize that they are competing not only domestically but also globally. World trade has given rise to global linkages of markets, technology and living standards that were previously unknown and unanticipated. At the same time, it has deeply affected domestic policy-making and has often resulted in the emergence of totally new opportunities as well as threats to firms and individuals. *The International Marketplace 1.2* provides an example.

Global linkages

World trade has forged a network of global linkages that bind us all – countries, institutions and individuals – much more closely than ever before. These linkages were first widely recognized during the worldwide oil crisis of 1970, but they continue to increase. A drought in Brazil and its effect on coffee production and prices are felt around the world. The 2004 tsunami in the Indian Ocean resulted in massive casualties in South Asia, caused worldwide disruptions in manufacturing and trade and devastated the tourism industry of many countries. For example, in the Maldives, which are located more than 2500 kilometres (1.6 kilometres = 1 mile) from the quake's epicentre, tourism is the largest industry, contributing 30 per cent of its GDP of $1.25 billion.[3] The industry is estimated to have suffered at least $100 million of damage in addition to another $250 million in business losses as an indirect result of the tsunami.[4] In total, the UK government has allocated the equivalent of around £290 million for disaster relief and reconstruction in the affected countries.[5]

These linkages have also become more intense on an individual level. Communication has built new international bridges, be it through music or international programmes transmitted by the BBC, Al Arabiya and other networks. New products have attained international appeal and encouraged similar activities around the world – where many of us wear jeans, dance to the same music on our iPods, and eat kebabs, curry and sushi. Transportation linkages let individuals from different countries see and meet each other with unprecedented ease. Common cultural pressures result in similar social phenomena and behaviour – for example, more dual-income families are emerging around the world, which leads to more frequent, but also more stressful, shopping.[6]

World trade is also bringing about a global reorientation of corporate processes, which opens up entirely new horizons. Never before has it been so easy to gather, manipulate, analyze and disseminate information – but never before has the pressure been so great to do so. Ongoing global technological innovation in marketing has direct effects on the efficiency and effectiveness of all business activities. Products can be produced more quickly, obtained less expensively from sources around the world, distributed at lower cost, and customized to meet

THE INTERNATIONAL **MARKETPLACE 1.2**

Outsourcing 'innovation' needs to be better defined, shared and implemented, warns Steria[7]

Major European IT services provider, Steria, today issued a wake-up call to IT suppliers and customers to get a collective grip on how they define, create and manage outsourcing innovation or run the risk of missing out on its benefits.

The warning follows a recent roundtable debate to which Steria invited customers and industry experts, that showed innovation is all too often viewed as the preserve of senior management, the duty of the supplier and reliant solely on new technology, rather than improved working practice. As a result, businesses are innovating in isolation and with limited long-term success.

'Innovation inside outsourcing' is the first of a series of white papers Steria has developed as a result of the roundtable that was facilitated by Bloor analyst and outsourcing expert, Dr Richard Sykes. In addition to poor understanding of the meaning of innovation in practice, the findings pointed to an inability to harness the input of grass-roots staff and a persistent failure to agree, and ultimately meet, expectations on innovation.

Summarizing the debate, Martin Waters, Head of Commercial Operations, Steria said: 'Businesses need to expand not only their definition of innovation, but also spread the responsibility for delivering it. The outsourcing landscape is changing, and so too must the customer and supplier dynamic. Innovation, whether in outsourcing or otherwise, is not a commodity to be delivered by the supplier to the customer. Genuine and long-lasting innovation relies on "co-creation" between the two and a mutual understanding of each other's business needs, objectives and capabilities.

'Innovation also needs to be disenfranchised from the boardroom. The key to delivering practical solutions that are fit-for-purpose is to take a "bottom-up" approach and involve frontline staff – on both the supplier and customer side – who know where innovation is most needed and best implemented in practice.

'Most importantly, innovation should not be viewed as an end in itself, nor a solely technological undertaking. It's not just about new technology for its own sake – the real opportunities for innovation lie more in the way that application is made to work in practice.

'Identifying the innovation need, creating the solution and seeing it through is about mutual cooperation and changes to mindsets as well as to process.'

The call comes as Steria announces a major boost to its own outsourcing capabilities with the acquisition of UK IT services provider, Xansa. The move brings significant BPO expertise into the business and creates a truly integrated global delivery model, combining Steria's established European onshore and near-shore model with Xansa's proven integrated UK-India delivery platform.

The outsourcing deal – a practical agenda for innovation

In order to embed a practical agenda for innovation in outsourcing, Steria recommends the following:

1 *Intimacy*: Select an outsourcing supplier that has a strong knowledge of the customer's business model, offering and market – the 'intimacy' test.

2 *Co-creation:* Recognize that innovation is best created through agreed and shared processes (co-creation) tightly aligned to the delivery of both the customer and supplier performance objectives.

3 *Frontline input*: Acknowledge that practical and relevant innovation is often best triggered by those staff who work at the 'coal face' of the business – be open about process and targets, encourage innovation in delivery and reward success.

SOURCE: Helen Bloxham, 'Outsourcing "innovation" needs to be better defined, shared and implemented, warns Steria'. Online. Available **http://www1.steria. co.uk/cms/ukweb.nsf/docs/BCFE97A52E5AB626802573A90046A78C/$file/ Steria_Press_Release_Bloor_innovation_20071205.pdf** (Accessed 15/01/08).

diverse clients' needs. As an example, only a decade ago, it would have been thought impossible for a firm to produce parts for a car in more than one country, assemble the car in yet another country and sell it in still other nations. Today, such global investment strategies coupled with production and distribution sharing are becoming a matter of routine. Of course, as *The International Marketplace 1.2* explains, these changes increase the level of global competition, which in turn makes it an ongoing effort to stay in a leadership position.

Advances in technology also allow firms to separate their activities by content and context. Firms can operate in a 'market space' rather than a marketplace[8] by keeping the content while changing the context of a transaction. For example, a newspaper can now be distributed online globally rather than house-to-house on paper, thereby allowing outreach to entirely new customer groups.

The level of global investment is at an unprecedented high. The shifts in financial flows have had major effects. They have resulted in the build up of international debt by governments, affected the international value of currencies, provided foreign capital for firms, and triggered major foreign direct-investment activities. For example, in response to the lack of skilled workers in certain sectors, the EU introduced the EU Blue Card which would allow skilled migrants from outside the European Economic Area (EEA) and Switzerland to live and work in any EU member state that adopts the relevant legislation.[9] In response to the question on the percentage of contracts awarded to foreign companies for the 2012 London Olympic Games, the Minister for the Olympics said it was the UK's policy to 'encourage competition, locally, nationally and internationally through actively promoting tendering opportunities, to promote as wide and as vigorous a competition as can be achieved'.[10] These examples make us more and more dependent on one another.

This interdependence, however, is not stable. On almost a daily basis, realignments taking place on both micro and macro levels make past trade orientations at least partially obsolete. For example, during its colonial days, the UK traded mainly with its colonies. Today it has widened its trade to Europe, the US and the rest of the world.

Not only is the environment changing, but the pace of change is accelerating as well. Atari's Pong was first introduced in the early 1980s; today, action games and films are made with computerized humans. The first office computers emerged in the mid-1980s; today, home computers have become commonplace. Email was introduced to a mass market only in the 1990s; today, many students hardly ever send personal notes using a stamp and envelope.[11]

These changes and the speed with which they come about significantly affect countries, corporations and individuals. One change is the role participants play. For example, the British market took over 15 per cent of Indian exports during the 1950s, but less than 10 per cent by the late 1960s. British firms provided 80 per cent of India's private foreign investment stock in 1948, but their share had fallen to less than 40 per cent by 1970.[12]

The way countries also participate in world trade is shifting. In the past two decades the role of primary commodities in international trade has dropped precipitously, while the importance of manufactured goods has increased. The increase in the volume of services trade has been even higher. In a few decades, international services went from being a non-measured activity to a global volume of more than $2.1 trillion in 2005.[13] Exhibit 1.2 shows how substantial the growth rates for both merchandise and services trade have been. Most important, the growth in the overall volume and value of both merchandise and services trade has had a major impact on firms, countries and individuals.

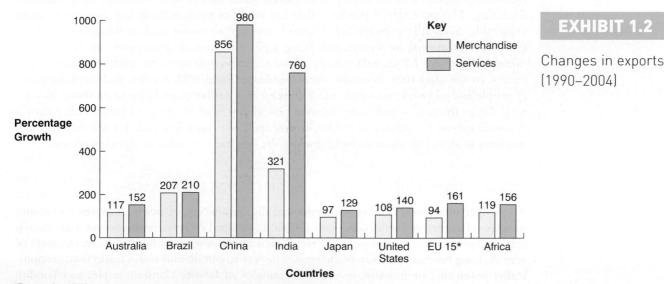

EXHIBIT 1.2

Changes in exports (1990–2004)

*Report for 2003

Source: WTO Statistics Database, accessed November 20, 2005.

Domestic policy repercussions

The effects of closer global linkages on the economics of countries have been dramatic. Policymakers have increasingly come to recognize that it is very difficult to isolate domestic economic activity from international market events. Decisions that once were clearly in the domestic purview have now become subject to revision by influences from abroad, and domestic policy measures are often cancelled out or counteracted by the activities of global market forces.

A lowering of interest rates domestically may make consumers happy or may be politically wise, but it quickly becomes unsustainable if it results in a major outflow of funds to countries that offer higher interest rates. Agricultural and farm policies, which historically have been strictly domestic issues, are suddenly thrust into the international realm. Any policy consideration must now be seen in light of international repercussions due to influences from global trade and investment.

To some extent, the economic world as we knew it has been turned upside down. For example, trade flows traditionally have been used to determine currency flows and therefore the level of the exchange rate. In the more recent past, currency flows took on a life of their own. Independent of trade, they set exchange rates, which are the values of currencies relative to each other. These exchange rates in turn have now begun to determine the level of trade. Governments that wish to counteract these developments with monetary policies find that currency flows outnumber trade flows by 100 to 1. Private-sector financial flows also vastly outnumber the financial flows that can be marshalled by governments, even when acting in concert. Similarly, constant rapid technological change and vast advances in communication permit firms and countries to quickly emulate innovation and counteract carefully designed plans. As a result, governments are often powerless to implement effective policy measures, even when they know what to do.

Policymakers therefore find themselves with increasing responsibilities yet with fewer and less effective tools to carry out these responsibilities. At the same time that more parts of a domestic economy are vulnerable to international shifts and changes, these parts are becoming less controllable. The global market imposes increasingly tight limits on national economic regulation and sovereignty.

To regain some of their power to influence events, policymakers have sought to restrict the impact of global trade and financial flows by erecting barriers, charging tariffs, designing quotas and implementing other import regulations. However, these measures too have been restrained by international agreements that regulate trade restrictions, particularly through the World Trade Organization (WTO) (**http://www.wto.org**). Global trade has therefore changed many previously held notions about nation-state sovereignty and extraterritoriality. The same interdependence that has made us more affluent has also left us more vulnerable. Since this vulnerability is spread out over all major trading nations, some have credited international marketing with being a pillar of international peace, as *The International Marketplace 1.1* showed. Clearly, closer economic relations can result in many positive effects. At the same time, however, interdependence brings with it risks, such as dislocations of people and economic resources and a decrease in a nation's capability to do things its own way. Given the ease – and sometimes the desirability – of blaming a foreign rather than a domestic culprit for economic failure, it may well also be a key task for the international marketer to stimulate societal thinking about the long-term benefits of interdependence.

Opportunities and challenges in international marketing

To prosper in a world of abrupt changes and discontinuities, of newly emerging forces and dangers, of unforeseen influences from abroad, firms need to prepare themselves and develop active responses. New strategies need to be envisioned, new plans need to be made, and the way of doing business needs to be changed. The way to obtain and retain leadership, economically, politically, or morally, is – as the examples of Rome, Constantinople, and London have amply demonstrated – not through passivity but rather through a continuous, alert adaptation to the changing world environment. To help a country remain a player in the world economy, governments, firms and individuals need to respond aggressively with innovation, process improvements and creativity.[14]

The growth of global business activities offers increased opportunities. International activities can be crucial to a firm's survival and growth. By transferring knowledge around the globe, an international firm can build and strengthen its competitive position. Firms that heavily depend on long production runs can expand their activities far beyond their domestic markets and benefit from reaching many more customers. Market saturation can be avoided by lengthening or rejuvenating product life cycles in other countries. Production sites once were inflexible, but now plants can be shifted from one country to another and suppliers can be found on every continent. Cooperative agreements can be formed that enable all parties to bring their major strengths to the table and emerge with better products, services, and ideas than they could produce on their own. In addition, research has found that multinational corporations face a lower risk of insolvency and pay higher wages than do domestic companies.[15] At the same time, international marketing enables consumers all over the world to find greater varieties of products at lower prices and to improve their lifestyles and comfort.[16]

International opportunities require careful exploration. What is needed is an awareness of global developments, an understanding of their meaning, and a development of capabilities to adjust to change. Firms must adapt to the international market if they are to be successful.

One key facet of the marketing concept is adaptation to the environment, particularly the market. Even though many executives understand the need for such an adaptation in their domestic market, they often believe that international customers are just like the ones the firm deals with at home. It is here that many firms commit grave mistakes that lead to inefficiency, lack of consumer acceptance, and sometimes even corporate failure. As *The International Marketplace 1.3* explains, there are quite substantial differences in this world between consumer groups.

THE INTERNATIONAL **MARKETPLACE 1.3**

Global consumers in the new century

One of the drivers behind the move toward global marketing strategies has been the notion that consumer needs are becoming more alike around the world. Yet drastic differences in the development of various regions of the world remain, and they are bound to continue well into the new century.

Such differences warrant differentiation in both marketing and pricing strategies. Here are just a few examples of what a baby in the western world and a baby in the less-developed world may face upon birth.

The western baby:

- In Switzerland she will live to the age of 83, while he will live to the age of 77.

- In the Netherlands there is a 100 per cent chance that she will use adequate sanitation.

- In the United States her family's income will likely be around $36,110 per annum.

- In Canada he will share one square mile with eight other people.

- In Italy she will be living in a city, as 90 per cent of the population does.

The baby of the less-developed world:

- In Sierra Leone she will live to the age of 36, while he will live to the age of 34.

- In Niger there is a 20 per cent chance that she will use adequate sanitation.

- In Uganda her family income is likely to be about $1,360.

- In China he will share one square mile with 352 other people.

- In India she will be living in a rural area, as 72 per cent of the population does.

SOURCE: Population Reference Bureau, *Data Finder,* **http://www.prb.org/** (Accessed March 4, 2005).

International trade as a percentage of gross domestic product

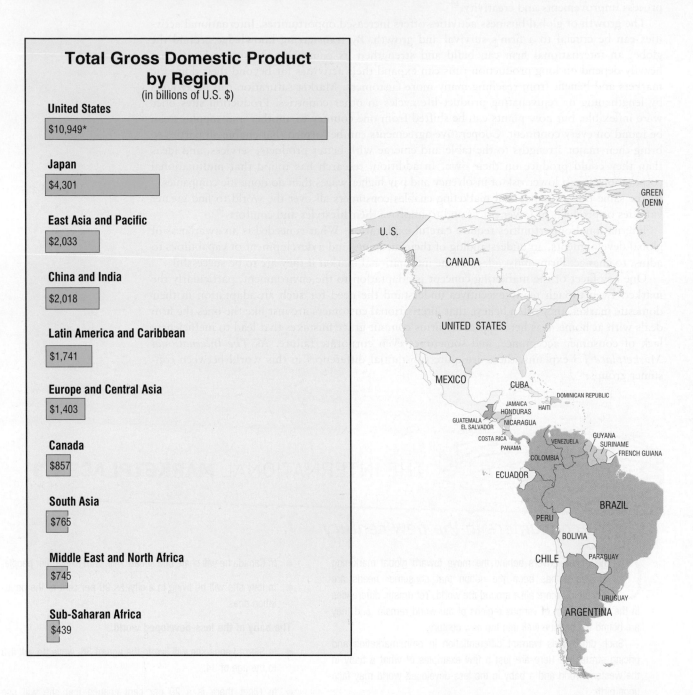

Total Gross Domestic Product by Region
(in billions of U.S. $)

United States
$10,949*

Japan
$4,301

East Asia and Pacific
$2,033

China and India
$2,018

Latin America and Caribbean
$1,741

Europe and Central Asia
$1,403

Canada
$857

South Asia
$765

Middle East and North Africa
$745

Sub-Saharan Africa
$439

Source: Based on *The Little Data Book 2002*, The World Bank.

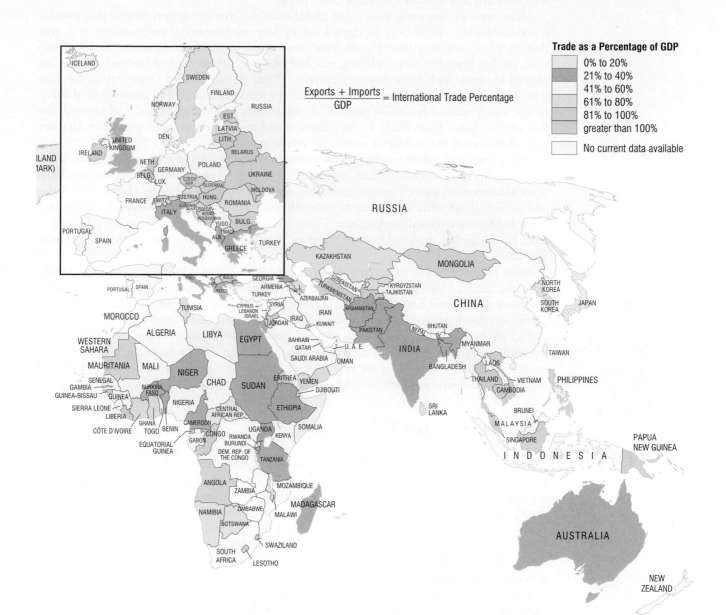

$$\frac{\text{Exports} + \text{Imports}}{\text{GDP}} = \text{International Trade Percentage}$$

Trade as a Percentage of GDP

- 0% to 20%
- 21% to 40%
- 41% to 60%
- 61% to 80%
- 81% to 100%
- greater than 100%

No current data available

Firms increasingly understand that many of the key difficulties encountered in doing business internationally are marketing problems. Judging by corporate needs, a background in international marketing is highly desirable for business students seeking employment, not only for today but also for long-term career plans.

Many firms do not participate in the global market. Often, managers believe that international marketing should only be carried out by large multinational corporations. It is true that there are some very large players from many countries active in the world market. However, smaller firms are major players, too. For example, 50 per cent of German exports are created by firms with 19 or fewer employees.[17] Over 95 per cent of Organization for Economic Co-operation and Development (OECD) members are small and medium-sized enterprises, which account for 60–70 per cent of employment in most countries.[18] Increasingly we find smaller firms, particularly in the computer and telecommunications industries, that are born global, since they achieve a worldwide presence within a very short time.[19]

Those firms and industries that are not participating in the world market have to recognize that in today's trade environment, isolation has become impossible. Willing or unwilling, firms are becoming participants in global business affairs. Even if not by choice, most firms and individuals are affected directly or indirectly by economic and political developments that occur in the international marketplace. Those firms that refuse to participate are relegated to react to the global marketplace and therefore are unprepared for harsh competition from abroad.

Some industries have recognized the need for international adjustments. Farmers understand the need for high productivity in light of stiff international competition. Car producers, computer makers and firms in other technologically advanced industries have learned to forge global relationships to stay in the race. Firms in the steel, textile and leather sectors have shifted production, and perhaps even adjusted their core business, in response to overwhelming onslaughts from abroad. Other industries have been caught unaware and have been unable to adjust. The result is the extinction of firms or entire industries, such as VCRs and coal mining and steel smelting in other countries.

THE GOALS OF THIS BOOK

This book aims to make you a better, more successful participant in the international marketplace by providing information about what is going on in international markets and by helping you to translate knowledge into successful business transactions. By learning about both theory and practice, you can obtain a good conceptual understanding of the field of international marketing as well as become firmly grounded in the realities of the global marketplace. Therefore, this book approaches international marketing in the way the manager of a firm does, reflecting different levels of international involvement and the importance of business–government relations.

Firms differ widely in their international activities and needs, depending on their level of experience, resources and capabilities. For the firm that is just beginning to enter the global market, the level of knowledge about international complexities is low, the demand on time is high, expectations about success are uncertain and the international environment is often inflexible. Conversely, for a multinational firm that is globally oriented and employs thousands of people on each continent, much more leeway exists in terms of resource availability, experience and information. In addition, the multinational firm has the option of responding creatively to the environment by shifting resources or even shaping the environment itself. For example, the heads of large corporations have access to government ministers to plead their case for a change in policy, an alternative that is rarely afforded to smaller firms.

To become a large international corporation, however, a firm usually has to start out small. Similarly, to direct far-flung global operations, managers first have to learn the basics. The structure of this text reflects this reality by presenting initially a perspective of the business environment, which covers national marketing and policy issues and their cultural, economic, financial, political and legal dimensions.

Subsequently, the book discusses in detail the beginning internationalization of the firm. The emphasize is on the needs of those who are starting out and the operational questions that are crucial to success. Some basic yet essential issues addressed are:

- What is the difference between domestic and international marketing?

- Does the applicability of marketing principles change when they are transferred to the global environment?

- How do marketers find out whether there is a market for a product abroad without spending a fortune in time and money on research?

- How can the firm promote its products in foreign markets?

- How do marketers find and evaluate a foreign distributor, and how do they make sure that their firm gets paid?

- How can marketers minimize government red tape yet take advantage of any governmental programmes that are of use to them?

These questions are addressed both conceptually and empirically, with a strong focus on export and import operations. We will see how the international commitment is developed and strengthened within the firm.

Once these important dimensions have been covered, we make the transition to the multi-national corporation. The focus is now on the transnational allocation of resources, the coordination of multinational marketing activities and the attainment of global synergism. Finally, emerging issues of challenge to both policymakers and multinational firms, such as countertrade, marketing to economies in transition and the future outlook of the global market, are discussed.

All the marketing issues are considered in relation to national policies so as to familiarize you with the divergent forces at play in the global market. Governments' increased awareness of and involvement with international marketing require managers to be aware of the role of governments and also to be able to work with them in order to attain marketing goals. Therefore, the continued references in the text to business–government interaction demonstrate a vital link in the development of international marketing strategy. In addition, we give full play to the increased ability of firms to communicate with a global market. Therefore, we develop and offer, for firms both small and large, our ideas and strategies for viable participation in electronic commerce.

We expect that this gradual approach to international marketing will permit you not only to master another academic subject, but also to become well versed in both the operational and the strategic aspects of the field. The result should be a better understanding of how the global market works and the capability to participate in the international marketing imperative.

SUMMARY

Over the last few decades, international trade in merchandise has expanded at astounding rates to reach over $9 trillion in 2005. In addition, trade in services has grown at particularly high rates within the last decade to reach $2.1 trillion in 2005. As a result, nations are much more affected by international business than in the past. Global linkages have made possible investment strategies and marketing alternatives that offer tremendous opportunities. Yet these changes and the speed of change also can represent threats to nations and firms.

On the policy front, decision makers have come to realize that it is very difficult to isolate domestic economic activity from international market events. Factors such as currency exchange rates, financial flows, and foreign economic actions increasingly render the policymaker powerless to implement a domestic agenda. International interdependence, which has contributed to greater affluence, has also increased our vulnerability.

Both firms and individuals are greatly affected by international trade. Whether willing or not, they are participating in global business affairs. Entire industries have been threatened in their survival as a result of international trade flows and have either adjusted to new market realities or left the market. Some individuals have lost their workplace and experienced reduced salaries. At the same time, global business

changes have increased the opportunities available. Firms can now reach many more customers, product life cycles have been lengthened, sourcing policies have become variable, new jobs have been created and consumers all over the world can find greater varieties of products at lower prices.

To benefit from the opportunities and deal with the adversities of international trade, business needs to adopt the international marketing concept. The new set of macroenvironmental factors has to be understood and responded to in order to let international markets become a source of growth, profit and needs satisfaction.

Key terms

currency flows
exchange rates

global linkages
international marketing

Questions for discussion

1 What are the recent trends in world trade? Will expansion of world trade in the future follow these trends?

2 Does increased world trade mean increased risk?

3 What impact do global linkages have on firms and consumers?

4 Can you think of examples of international marketing contributing to world peace?

5 Describe some opportunities and challenges in international marketing created by new advances in information technology.

Internet exercises

1 Using World Trade Organization data (http://www.wto.org) identify the top ten exporting and importing countries in world merchandise trade (examples: Germany, China, USA, Japan, the Netherlands, France, Italy).

2 Identify the top ten exporting and importing countries of commercial services (examples: USA, UK, Germany, Japan, France, Italy).

Recommended readings

Friedman, Benjamin. *The Moral Consequences of Economic Growth*. New York: Knopf, 2005.
Friedman, Thomas. *The World Is Flat*. New York: Farrar, Straus, and Giroux, 2005.

Prestowitz, Clyde. *Three Billion New Capitalists: The Shift of Wealth and Power to the East*. New York: Basic Books, 2005.
Stiglitz, Joseph. *Globalization and Its Discontents*. New York: W.W. Norton, 2003.

Notes

1 Robert W. Armstrong and Jill Sweeney, 'Industrial Type, Culture, Mode of Entry, and Perceptions of International Marketing Ethics Problems: A Cross-Culture Comparison', *Journal of Business Ethics* 13(10): 775–785.

2 World Trade Organization, **http://www.wto.org**, Statistics Database (Accessed November 20, 2005).

3 UNEP 2005 (quoted in **http://student.ulb.ac.be/~nroeck/index_files/Page2550.html**) (Accessed October 17, 2005).

4 Department for International Development (2009), 'Tsunami: One Year On . . . what has been spent?'. Online. Available from: **http://www.dfid.gov.uk/news/files/emergencies/tsunami-oneyearon/oneyearon-funding.asp** (Accessed 15/1/08).

5 Eugene H. Fram and Riad Ajami, 'Globalization of Markets and Shopping Stress: Cross-Country Comparisons', *Business Horizons* (January–February 1994): 17–23.

6 CIA, *The World Factbook,* **http://www.cia.gov/cia/publications/factbook/index.html** (Accessed December 1, 2005).

7 Bloxham, H. (2007), 'Outsourcing "innovation" needs to be better defined, shared and implemented, warns Steria'. Online. Available from: **http://www.steria.co.uk/assets/4_ASSETS/pdf/00044.pdf** (Accessed 15/01/08).

8 John J. Sviokla and Jeffrey F. Rayport, 'Mapping the Marketspace: Information Technology and the New Marketing Environment', *Harvard Business School Bulletin* 71 (June 1995): 49–51.

9 Workpermit.com (2008), 'Spotlight: The European Union Blue Card'. Online. Available from: **http://www.workpermit.com/news/2008-11-21/europe/spotlight-european-union-blue-card.htm** (Accessed 15/01/08).

10 House of Commons (2008), 'Olympic Games 2012: Foreign Companies'. Online. Available from: **http://www.publications.parliament.uk/pa/cm200708/cmhansrd/cm080703/text/80703w0012.htm** (Accessed 15/1/08).

11 Michael R. Czinkota and Sarah McCue, *The STAT-USA Companion to International Business,* Economics and Statistics Administration (U.S. Department of Commerce, Washington, DC, 2001), 16.

12 Tomlinson, B.R. (2002), 'The "erosion of a relationship"? Indo-British economic connections, 1950–1970'. Online. Available from: **https://eprints.soas.ac.uk/26/1/TRANS3.pdf** (Accessed 15/01/08).

13 World Trade Organization, International Trade Statistics 2005, **http://www.wto.org**.

14 Peter R. Dickson and Michael R. Czinkota, 'How the U.S. Can Be Number One Again: Resurrecting the Industrial Policy Debate', *The Columbia Journal of World Business* 31(3) (Fall 1996): 76–87.

15 Howard Lewis III and J. David Richardson, *Why Global Commitment Really Matters* (Washington, DC: Institute for International Economics, 2001).

16 Czinkota, Michael R., 'Freedom and International Marketing: Janis Joplin's Candidacy as Patron of the Field', *Thunderbird International Business Review*, 47(1), January–February 2005: 1–13.

17 *Cognetics,* Cambridge, MA, 1993.

18 Benney, A. (2000), 'Banking on small business'. Online. Available from: **http://www.oecdobserver.org/news/fullstory.php/aid/394.html** (Accessed 15/1/08).

19 Michael Kutschker, 'Internationalisierung der Wirtschaft', *Perspektiven der Internationalen Wirtschaft,* Wiesbaden, Gabler GmbH, 1999: 22.

APPENDIX A

BASICS OF MARKETING

This appendix provides a summary of the basic concepts in marketing for the reader who wishes to review them before applying them to international marketing. The American Marketing Association defines marketing as 'an organizational function and a set of processes for creating, communicating, and delivering value to customers, and for managing customer relationships in ways that benefit the organization and its stakeholders'.[1]

It is useful to focus on the definition's components to fully understand its meaning. Marketing as an *organizational function* interprets it as part of a thrust that gives direction to a unit. *Set of processes* highlights the idea that the activity goes beyond a single transaction. *Creating, communicating and delivering* emphasizes that the marketing discipline takes leadership in its activities from beginning to end and that the art and the practical implementation dimensions of the discipline are crucial in their simultaneity. *Value to customers* indicates the core focus of marketing. Physicians have as their overriding principle the Hippocratic Oath 'do no harm'. Marketers should consider any action under the prism of 'are customers better off?' *Managing customer relationships* in turn indicates the dyadic aspects of marketing – there is an interaction between the firm and the customers, as well as the relationships among the customers themselves. It is marketing's responsibility to handle both types of relationship. Customers need to be content in their assessment of the rapport they have with the firm. However, they also continue to be part of a network that is defined by their interaction with fellow customers. Since marketers will be major influencers on this relationship they need to take into account the repercussions that their actions are likely to have on these linkages. The term *relationship* is key, since it is indicative of the fact that actions build upon each other and are instrumental in forging bonds and inflaming disagreements. The marketer therefore cannot see any product or effort as an isolated event. Rather, it has to be understood as a component of an entire series of steps that define the bridge between entities. Using this perspective, marketing has a very broad mission. The discipline is not narrowly confined to relationships that emerge when money is exchanged for goods. Rather, marketing has its application just as well when there is performance of a service (say, coaching Manchester United or fundraising for a charity) in exchange for obtaining a good feeling and a sense of fulfilment.

The fact that marketing is to *benefit the organization* is critical. Marketing needs to be seen, after all, in the context of a planned and purposeful activity. It seeks a definite, favourable outcome for the institution conducting the marketing pursuit. Again, it is important to recognize that this benefit need not be seen strictly in terms of mammon. Rather, the organization itself is the one that defines what it determines to be beneficial. Therefore, there is ample room for both macro benefits such as 'more positive images of our country', as well as micro benefits such as 'increase desire to go to work', in addition to the business benefits customarily seen to be in the purview of organizations. As a result, marketing finds a full range of applicability in not-for-profit areas, such as medicine, the arts, or government areas typically wrongfully excluded from the need for marketing. The use of the term stakeholder is also indicative of this breadth of marketing in that it gives recognition to others who have an interest in either the process or the outcome of marketing activities.

As you can see, this definition packs a lot of punch, and lets marketing make a major contribution to the welfare of individuals and organizations. Nevertheless, based on our view of marketing, we will expand this definition on several dimensions. First, we believe that the terms *create*, *deliver* and *value* overemphasize transactions as one-time events. Therefore, we add the terms *maintain* and *value stream* to highlight the long-term nature of marketing that encourages customers to continue to come back. We also believe that, as the scope of marketing is broadened, societal goals need to be added to individuals and organizations, properly reflecting the overarching reach and responsibility of marketing as a social change agent that responds to and develops social concerns about the environment, technology and ethics. Equally important is the need to specifically broaden our marketing understanding beyond national borders. Today, sourcing and supply linkages exist around the globe, competition emerges from all corners of the earth and marketing opportunities evolve worldwide. As a result, many crucial dimensions of marketing need to be re-evaluated and adapted in a global context.

Based on these considerations, our expanded definition of marketing is 'an organizational function and a set of processes for creating, communicating, delivering, and maintaining value streams to customers and for managing customer relationships in ways that benefit the organization, its stakeholder, and society in the context of a global environment'.[2]

The concepts of satisfaction and exchange are at the core of marketing. For an exchange to take place, two or more parties must come together in person, through the mail, or through technology and they must communicate and deliver things of perceived value. Potential customers should be perceived as information seekers who evaluate marketers' efforts in terms of their own drives and needs. When the offering is consistent with their needs, they tend to choose the product; if it is not, they choose other alternatives. A key task of the marketer is to recognize the ever-changing nature of needs and wants. Increasingly, the goal of marketing has been expanded from sensing, serving, and satisfying individual customers to taking into consideration the long-term interests of society.

Marketing is not limited to business entities but involves governmental and nonbusiness units as well. Marketing techniques are applied not only to goods but also to ideas (for example, the 'Made in the United Kingdom' campaign) and to services (for example, international advertising agencies). The term *business marketing* is used for activities directed at other businesses, governmental entities and various types of institutions. Business marketing accounts for well over 50 per cent of all marketing activities.

STRATEGIC MARKETING

The marketing manager's task is to plan and execute programmes that will ensure a long-term competitive advantage for the company. This task has two integral parts: (1) the determining of specific target markets and (2) marketing management, which consists of manipulating marketing mix elements to best satisfy the needs of individual target markets.

Target market selection

Characteristics of intended target markets are of critical importance to the marketer. These characteristics can be summarized by eight Os: occupants, objects, occasions, objectives, outlets, organization, operations and opposition.[3]

Occupants are targets of the marketing effort. The marketer must determine which customers to approach and also define them along numerous dimensions, such as demographics (age, sex and nationality, for example), geography (country or region), psychographics (attitudes, interests and opinions), or product-related variables (usage rate and brand loyalty). Included in this analysis must be the major influences on the occupants during their buying processes.

Objects are what is being bought at present to satisfy a particular need. Included in this concept are physical objects, services, ideas, organizations, places and people.

Occasions are moments when members of the target market buy the product or service. This characteristic is important to the marketer because a product's consumption may be tied to a particular time period – for example, imported beer and a festival.

Objectives are the motivations behind the purchase or adoption of the marketed concept. A computer manufacturer markets not hardware but solutions to problems. Additionally, many customers look for hidden value in the product they purchase, which may be expressed, for example, through national origin of the product or through brand name.

Outlets are places where customers expect to be able to procure a product or to be exposed to messages about it. Outlets include not only the entities themselves but also location within a particular place. Although aseptic packaging made it possible to shelve milk outside the refrigerated area in supermarkets, customers' acceptance of the arrangement was not automatic: the product was not where it was supposed to be. In the area of services, outlet involves (1) making a particular service available and communicating its availability, and (2) selecting the particular types of facilitators (such as brokers) who bring the parties together.

Organization describes how the buying or acceptance of a (new) idea takes place. Organization expands the analysis beyond the individual consumer to the decision-making unit (DMU). The DMU varies in terms of its size and its nature from relatively small and informal groups like a family, to large groups (more than ten people), to formal buying committees. Compare, for example, the differences between a family buying a new home-entertainment centre and the governing board at a university deciding which architectural firm to use. In either case, to develop proper products and services, the marketer should know as much as possible about the decision-making processes and the roles of various individuals.

Operations represent the behaviour of the organization buying products and services. Increasingly, industrial organizations are concentrating their purchases with fewer suppliers and making longer-term commitments. Supermarkets may make available only the leading brands in a product category, thereby complicating the marketer's attempts to place new products in these outlets.

Opposition refers to the competition to be faced in the marketplace. The nature of competition will vary from direct product-type competition to competition from other products that satisfy the same need. For example, Wilson tennis rackets face a threat not only from other racket manufacturers but also from any company that provides a product or service for leisure-time use. Competitive situations will vary from one market and from one segment to the next. Gillette is number one in the European market for disposable razors. In the long term, threats may come from outside the industry in which the marketer operates. As an example, digital watches originated in the electronics industry rather than the watch industry.

Analysing the eight Os, and keeping in mind other uncontrollable factors in the environment (cultural, political, legal, technological, societal and economic), the marketer must select the markets to which efforts will be targeted. In the short term, the marketer has to adjust to these environmental forces; in the long term, they can be manipulated to some extent by judicious marketing activity. Consumerism, one of the major forces shaping marketing activities, is concerned with protecting the consumer whenever an exchange relationship exists with any type of organization.

Manifestations of the impact of consumerism on marketing exist in labeling, product specifications, promotional campaigns, recycling expectations and demands for environmentally friendly products.

As every marketer operates in a corporate environment of scarcity and comparative strengths, the target market decision is a crucial one. In some cases, the marketer may select only one segment of the market (for example, motorcycles of 1000+ cc) or multiple segments (for example, all types of motorized two-wheeled vehicles), or the firm may opt for an undifferentiated product that is to be mass-marketed (for example, unbranded commodities or products that satisfy the same need worldwide, such as Coca-Cola).

MARKETING MANAGEMENT

Having analyzed the characteristics of the target market(s), the marketing manager is in a position to specify the mix of marketing variables that will best serve each target market. The variables the marketing manager controls are known as the elements of the marketing mix, or the four Ps: product, price, place and promotion.[4] Each consists of a submix of variables, and policy decisions must be made on each.

Product policy is concerned with all the elements that make up the good, service, or idea that is offered by the marketer. Included are all possible tangible characteristics (such as the core product and packaging) and intangible characteristics (such as branding and warranties). Many products are a combination of a concrete product and the accompanying service; for example, in buying an Otis elevator, the purchaser buys not only the product but an extensive service contract as well.

Pricing policy determines the cost of the product to the customer – a point somewhere between the floor created by the costs to the firm and the ceiling created by the strength of demand. An important consideration of pricing policy is pricing within the channel of distribution; margins to be made by the middlemen who assist in the marketing effort must be taken into account. Discounts to middlemen include functional, quantity, seasonal and cash discounts, as well as promotional allowances. An important point to remember is that price is the only revenue-generating element of the marketing mix.

Distribution policy covers the place variable of the marketing mix and has two components: channel management and logistics management. Channel management is concerned with the entire process of setting up and operating the contractual organization, consisting of various types of middlemen (such as wholesalers, agents, retailers and facilitators). Logistics management is focused on providing product availability at appropriate times and places in the marketing channel.[5] Place is the most long term of all the marketing mix elements; it is the most difficult to change in the short term.

Communications policy uses promotion tools to interact with customers, middlemen and the public at large. The communications element consists of these tools: advertising, sales promotion, personal selling and publicity. Since the purpose of all communications is to persuade, this is the most visible and sensitive of the marketing mix elements.

Blending the various elements into a coherent programme requires trade-offs based on the type of product or service being offered (for example, detergents versus fighter aircraft), the stage of the product's life cycle (a new product versus one that is being revived) and resources available for the marketing effort (money and personnel), as well as the type of customer at whom the marketing efforts are directed.

THE MARKETING PROCESS

The actual process of marketing consists of four stages: analysis, planning, implementation and control.

Analysis begins with collecting data on the eight Os and using various quantitative and qualitative techniques of marketing research. Data sources will vary from secondary to primary. The data are used to determine company opportunities by screening a plethora of environmental opportunities. The company opportunities must then be checked against the company's resources to judge their viability. The key criterion is competitive advantage.

Planning refers to the blueprint generated to react to and exploit the opportunities in the marketplace. The planning stage involves both long-term strategies and short-term tactics. A marketing plan developed for a particular market includes a situation analysis, objectives and goals to be met, strategies and tactics, and cost and profit estimates. Included in the activity is the formation of a new organizational structure or adjustments in the existing one to prepare for the execution of the plan.

Implementation is the actual carrying out of the planned activity. If the plans drawn reflect market conditions, and if they are based on realistic assessments of the company's fit into the market, the implementation process will be a success. Plans must take into account unforeseeable changes within the company and environmental forces and allow for corresponding changes to occur in implementing the plans.

For this reason, concurrently with implementation, control mechanisms must be put into effect. The marketplace is ever dynamic and requires the monitoring of environmental forces, competitors, channel participants and customer receptiveness. Short-term control tools include annual plan control (such as comparing actual sales to quota), profitability control and efficiency control. Long-term control is achieved through comprehensive or functional audits to make sure that marketing is not only efficient (doing things right) but that it is also effective (doing the right things). The results of the control effort provide valuable input for subsequent planning efforts.

These marketing basics do not vary, regardless of the type of market one is planning to enter or to continue operating within. They have been called the 'technical universals' of marketing.[6] The different environments in which the marketing manager must operate will give varying emphases to the variables and will cause the values of the variables to change.

Key terms

analysis

control mechanisms

implementation

marketing

place

planning

price

product policy

promotion tools

Notes

1   Marketing Definitions, **http://www.marketingpower.com/content4620.pho** (Accessed May 11, 2006).

2   Michael R. Czinkota and Kotabe Masaaki, *Marketing Management* 3rd edn, (Cincinnati: Atomic Dog Publishing), 2005, 4–5.

3   Philip Kotler presents the eight Os in the eighth edition of *Marketing Management: Analysis, Planning, and Control* (Englewood Cliffs, NJ: Prentice-Hall, 1994), 174–175.

4   The four Ps were popularized originally by E. Jerome McCarthy. See William Perreault and E. Jerome McCarthy, *Basic Marketing: A Global Managerial Approach* 15th edn, (Burr Ridge, IL: Irwin/McGraw-Hill, 2005).

5   Bert Rosenbloom, *Marketing Channels: A Management View* 7th edn, (Mason, OH: Thomson Business & Professional Publishing, 2003).

6   Robert Bartels, 'Are Domestic and International Marketing Dissimilar?' *Journal of Marketing* 36 (July 1968): 56–61.

GEOGRAPHICAL PERSPECTIVES ON INTERNATIONAL MARKETING

The globalization of business has made geography indispensable for the study of international marketing. Without significant attention to the study of geography, critical ideas and information about the world in which business occurs will be missing.

Just as the study of business has changed significantly in recent decades, so has the study of geography. Once considered by many to be simply a descriptive inventory that filled in blank spots on maps, geography has emerged as an analytical approach that uses scientific methods to answer important questions.

Geography focuses on answering 'Where?' questions. Where are things located? What is their distribution across the surface of the earth? An old aphorism holds, 'If you can map it, it's geography'. That statement is true, because we use maps to gather, store, analyze, and present information that answers 'Where?' questions. Identifying where things are located is only the first phase of geographic inquiry. Once locations have been determined, 'Why?' and 'How?' questions can be asked. Why are things located where they are? How do different things relate to one another at a specific place? How do different places relate to each other? How have geographic patterns and relationships changed over time? These are the questions that take geography beyond mere description and make it a powerful approach for analysing and explaining geographical aspects of a wide range of different kinds of problems faced by those engaged in international marketing.

Geography answers questions related to the location of different kinds of economic activity and the transactions that flow across national boundaries. It provides insights into the natural and human factors that influence patterns of production and consumption in different parts of the world. It explains why patterns of trade and exchange evolve over time. As a geographic perspective emphasizes the analysis of processes that result in different geographic patterns, it provides a means for assessing how patterns might change in the future.

Geography has a rich tradition. Classical Greeks, medieval Arabs, enlightened European explorers and contemporary scholars have organized geographic knowledge in many different ways. In recent decades, however, geography has become more familiar and more relevant to many people because emphasize has been placed on five fundamental themes as ways to structure geographic questions and to provide answers for those questions. Those themes are (1) location, (2) place, (3) interaction, (4) movement and (5) region. The five themes are neither exclusive nor exhaustive. They complement other disciplinary approaches for organizing information, some of which are better suited to addressing specific kinds of questions. Other questions require insights related to two or more of the themes. Experience has shown, however, that the five themes provide a powerful means for introducing students to the geographic perspective. As a result, they provide the structure for this discussion.

Note: This Appendix was contributed by Thomas J. Baerwald. Dr. Baerwald is a senior science advisor and geography programme director at the National Science Foundation in Arlington, Virginia. He is co-author of *Prentice-Hall World Geography* – a best-selling geography textbook.

Source: Darrell Delamaide, *The New Superregions of Europe* (New York: Dutton, 1994); Joel Garreau, *The Nine Nations of North America* (New York: Houghton Mifflin Co.,1981).

LOCATION

For decades, people engaged in real estate development have said that the value of a place is a product of three factors: location, location and location. This statement also reflects the importance of location for international marketing. Learning the location and characteristics of other places has always been important to those interested in conducting business outside their local areas. The drive to learn about different areas, especially their resources and potential as markets, has stimulated geographic exploration throughout history. Explorations of the Mediterranean by the Phoenicians, Marco Polo's journey to China and voyages undertaken by Christopher Columbus, Vasco da Gama, Henry Hudson and James Cook not only improved general knowledge of the world but also expanded business opportunities.

Assessing the role of location requires more than simply determining specific locations where certain activities take place. Latitude and longitude often are used to fix the exact location of features on the Earth's surface, but to simply describe a place's coordinates provides relatively little information about that place. Of much greater significance is its location relative to other features. The city of Singapore, for example, is between 1 and 2 degrees North latitude and is just west of 104 degrees East longitude. Other locational characteristics are far more important if you want to understand why Singapore has emerged as such an important locale for international business. Singapore is at the southern tip of the Malay Peninsula near the eastern end of the Strait of Malacca, a critical shipping route connecting the Indian Ocean with the South China Sea. For almost 150 years, this location made Singapore an important centre for trade in the British Empire. After it attained independence in 1965, Singapore's leaders diversified its economy and complemented trade in its bustling port with numerous manufacturing plants that export products to nations around the world. Singapore quickly became one of the world's leading manufacturers of disk drives and other electronic components, using its pivotal location on global air routes to quickly ship these light-weight, high-value goods around the world. The same locational advantages have spurred its rise in recent decades as a business and financial services centre for eastern Asia.

An understanding of the way location influences business therefore is critical for the international marketing executive. Without clear knowledge of an enterprise's location relative to its suppliers, to its market and to its competitors, an executive operates like the captain of a fogbound vessel that has lost all navigational instruments and is heading for dangerous shoals.

Place

In addition to its location, each place has a diverse set of characteristics. Although many of those characteristics are present in other places, the ensemble makes each place unique. The characteristics of places – both natural and human – profoundly influence the ways that business executives in different places participate in international economic transactions.

Natural features

Many of the characteristics of a place relate to its natural attributes. Geologic characteristics can be especially important, as the presence of critical minerals or energy resources may make a place a world-renowned supplier of valuable products. Gold and diamonds help make South Africa's economy the most prosperous on that continent. Rich deposits of iron ore in southern parts of the Amazon Basin have made Brazil the world's leading exporter of that commodity, while Chile remains a pre-eminent exporter of copper. Coal deposits provided the foundation for massive industrial development in the Rhine river basin of Europe, in western Russia and in northeastern China. Due to the abundant pools of petroleum beneath desert sands, standards of living in Saudi Arabia and nearby nations have risen rapidly to be among the highest in the world.

The geology of a place also shapes its terrain. People traditionally have clustered in lower, flatter areas because valleys and plains have permitted the agricultural development necessary to feed the local population and to generate surpluses that can be traded. Hilly and mountainous areas may support some people, but their population densities are invariably lower. Terrain also plays a critical role in focusing and inhibiting the movement of people and goods. Business leaders throughout the centuries have capitalized on this fact. Just as feudal masters sought control of mountain passes in order to collect tolls and other duties from traders who traversed an area, modern executives maintain stores and offer services near bridges and at other points where terrain slows down travel.

The terrain of a place is related to its hydrology. Rivers, lakes and other bodies of water influence the kinds of economic activities that occur in a place. In general, abundant supplies of water boost economic development, because water is necessary for the sustenance of people and for both agricultural and industrial production. Locations like Saudi Arabia and Los Angeles have prospered despite having little local water, because other features offer advantages that more than exceed the additional costs incurred in delivering water supplies from elsewhere. While sufficient water must be available to meet local needs, over-abundance of water may pose serious problems, such as in Bangladesh, where development has been inhibited by frequent flooding.

The character of a place's water bodies is also important. Smooth-flowing streams and placid lakes can stimulate transportation within a place and connect it more easily with other places, while waterfalls and rapids can prevent navigation on streams. The rapid drop in elevation of such streams may boost their potential for hydroelectric power generation, however, thereby stimulating development of industries requiring considerable amounts of electricity. Large plants producing aluminium, for example, are found in Québec and British Columbia in Canada. These plants refine materials that originally were extracted elsewhere, especially bauxite and alumina from Caribbean nations like Jamaica and the Dominican Republic. Although the transport costs incurred in delivery of these materials to the plants is high, those costs are more than offset by the presence of abundant and inexpensive electricity.

Climate is another natural feature that has profound impact on economic activity within a place. Many activities are directly affected by climate. Locales blessed with pleasant climates have become popular recreational havens, attracting tourists whose spending fuels the local economy. The Côte d'Azur of France, the Crimean Peninsula of Ukraine, and the 'Gold Coast' of northeastern Australia are just a few examples of popular tourist destinations whose primary attribute is a salubrious climate. Agricultural production is also influenced by climate. The average daily and evening temperatures, the amount and timing of precipitation, the timing of frosts and freezing weather and the variability of weather from one year to the next all influence the kinds of crops grown in an area. Plants producing bananas and sugar cane flourish in moist tropical areas, while cooler climates are more conducive for crops such as wheat and potatoes. Climate influences other industries as well. The aircraft manufacturing industry developed largely in warmer, drier areas, where conditions for test flights were more beneficial throughout the year. In a similar way, major rocket-launching facilities have been placed in locations where climatic conditions are most favourable. As a result, the primary launch site of the European Space Agency is not in Europe at all, but rather in the South American territory of French Guiana. Climate also affects the length of the work day and the length of economic seasons. For example, in some regions of the world, the construction industry can build only during a few months of the year because permafrost makes construction prohibitively expensive the rest of the year. Construction demand can be spurred by climate-related disasters, for example, raising the cost of insurance premiums for properties as a result of expectations for rising flood risk in developed countries, as happened in the UK in 2007.[1]

Variations in **soils** have a profound impact on agricultural production. The world's great grain-exporting regions, including the Prairie Provinces of Canada, the 'Fertile Triangle' stretching from central Ukraine through southern Russia into northern Kazakhstan, the Pampas of northern Argentina, all have been blessed with mineral-rich soils made even more fertile by humus from natural grasslands that once dominated the landscape. Soils are less fertile in much of the Amazon Basin of Brazil and in central Africa, where heavy rains leave few nutrients in upper layers of the soil. As a result, few commercial crops are grown.

The interplay between climate and soils is especially evident in the production of wines. Hundreds of varieties of grapes have been developed in order to take advantage of the different physical characteristics of various places. The wines fermented from these grapes are shipped around the world to consumers, who differentiate among various wines based not only on the grapes but also on the places where they were grown and the conditions during which they matured.

Human features

The physical features of a place provide natural resources and influence the types of economic activities in which people engage, but its human characteristics also are critical. The **population** of a place is important because farm production may require intensive labour to be successful, as is true in rice-growing areas of eastern Asia. The skills and qualifications of the population also play a role in determining how a place fits into global economic affairs. Although blessed with few mineral resources and a terrain and climate that limit agricultural production, the Swiss have emphasized high levels of education and training in order to maintain a labour force that manufactures sophisticated products for export around the world. In recent decades, Japan and smaller nations such as South Korea and Taiwan have increased the productivity of their workers to become major industrial exporters.

As people live in a place, they modify it, creating a **built environment** that can be as important as or more important than the natural environment in economic terms. The most pronounced areas of human activity and their associated structures are in cities. In nations around the world, cities grew dramatically during the twentieth century. Much of the growth of cities has resulted from the migration of people from rural areas. This influx of new residents broadens the labour pool and creates vast new demand for goods and services. As urban populations have grown, residences and other facilities have replaced rural land uses. Executives seeking to conduct business in foreign cities need to be aware that the geographic patterns found in their home cities are not evident in many other nations. For example, in the United Kingdom, wealthier residents generally have moved out of cities, and as they established their residences, stores and services followed. Residential patterns in the major cities of Latin America and other developing nations tend to be reversed, with the wealthy remaining close to the city centre while poorer residents are consigned to the outskirts of town. A store-location strategy that is successful in one country therefore may fail miserably if transferred directly to another nation without knowledge of the different geographic patterns of that nation's cities.

Interaction

The international marketing professional seeking to take advantage of opportunities present in different places learns not to view each place separately. The way a place functions depends on the presence and form of certain characteristics as well as the interactions among them. Fortuitous combinations of features can spur a region's economic development. The presence of high-grade supplies of iron ore, coal and limestone powered the growth of Germany's Ruhr Valley as one of Europe's foremost steel-producing regions, just as the proximity of the fertile Pampas and the deep channel of the Rio de la Plata combined to make Buenos Aires the leading economic centre in southern South America.

Interactions among different features change over time within a place, and as they do, so does that place's character and economic activities. Human activities can have profound impacts on natural features. The courses of rivers and streams are altered as dams are erected and meanders are straightened. Soil fertility can be improved through fertilization. Vegetation is transformed, with naturally growing plants replaced by crops and other varieties that require careful management.

Many human modifications have been successful. For centuries, the Dutch have constructed dikes and drainage systems, slowly creating polders – land that once was covered by the North Sea but that now is used for agricultural production. However, other human activities have had disastrous impacts on natural features. A large area in Ukraine and Belarus was rendered uninhabitable by radioactive materials leaked from the Chernobyl reactor in 1986. In countless other places around the globe, improper disposal of wastes has seriously harmed land and water resources. In some places, damage can be repaired but in other locales, restoration may be impossible. At times, human activity can have counterproductive results for unforeseen reasons. In large parts of Bangladesh and the West Bengal state of India, arsenic concentrations in drinking water drawn from wells is far above acceptable levels, and increasing numbers of residents are exhibiting signs of arsenic poisoning. Ironically, the wells were drilled to provide a supposedly safer alternative to the highly polluted surface water on which residents previously relied.

Growing concerns about environmental quality have led many people in more economically advanced nations to call for changes in economic systems that harm the natural environment. Concerted efforts are under way, for example, to halt the destruction of forests in the Amazon Basin, thereby preserving the vast array of different plant and animal species in the region and saving vegetation that can help moderate the world's climate. Cooperative ventures have been established to promote selective harvesting of nuts, hardwoods, and other products taken from natural forests. Furthermore, an increasing number of restaurants and grocers are refusing to purchase beef raised on pastures that are established by clearing forests.

Market mechanisms have also been developed to try to facilitate environmentally friendly practices. Emissions trading has emerged as an administrative approach that can be instituted by a central unit to limit the overall level of pollution that is released in the area under that administrative unit's authority. The administrative unit can be a local government, state, nation, or even a set of nations. Based on historical patterns and other factors, maximum emission levels are established for subunits in the area. If some subunits expect to exceed the upper limits established for them, they can purchase credits from other subunits whose emissions are below their limits. This system provides incentives for subunits that have higher emissions levels to reduce their pollution in order to reduce costs, while other subunits may seek to reduce their emissions even more in order to reap income from the sale of additional credits. The system has been implemented across a range of geographic scales. The European Union's 27 member nations instituted a greenhouse gas emission trading scheme in 2005 to limit overall emissions across Europe. Emissions trading is envisioned as a way to help the world's nations stabilize atmospheric greenhouse gas concentrations in accordance with the terms of the **Kyoto Protocol**, which was signed in 1997. This protocol called for reductions in the emission of carbon dioxide and five other greenhouse gases. Opponents of the Kyoto Protocol, for example Australia and the US, argue that this places an unfairly heavy economic burden on them, particularly onto the US, which emits about one quarter of the world's greenhouse gases.

As with so many other geographical relationships, the nature of human–environmental interaction changes over time. With technological advances, people have been able to modify and adapt to natural features in increasingly sophisticated ways. The development of air conditioning has permitted people to function more effectively in torrid tropical environments, thereby enabling the populations of cities such as Rio de Janeiro and Jakarta to multiply many times over in recent decades. Owners of winter resorts now can generate snow artificially to ensure favourable conditions for skiers. Advanced irrigation systems now permit crops to be grown in places such as northern Africa and Israel. The use of new technologies may cause serious problems over the long run, however. Extensive irrigation can seriously deplete groundwater supplies. In central Asia, the diversion of river water to irrigate cotton fields in Kazakhstan and Uzbekistan has reduced the size of the Aral Sea by more than one-half since 1960. In future, business leaders may need to factor into their decisions the additional costs associated with the restoration of environmental quality after they have finished using a place's resources.

Other business leaders may have to deal with issues associated with social, ecological and ethical issues associated with genetically modified foods and organisms. These products are created by combining genes from different organisms in order to achieve certain desirable qualities. In 2003, one study estimated that seven million farmers in 18 countries grew genetically altered crops, especially herbicide- and insecticide-resistant soybeans, corn, cotton and canola. Other crops have been engineered to have greater nutritional value. The rapid growth in genetic modification of crops has led to concerns regarding potential introduction of new allergens, the unintended transfer of genes through cross-pollination and potentially adverse impacts on other organisms. As a result, some nations have prohibited their own farmers from producing genetically modified crops as well as banning the importation of such products grown elsewhere. The need for accurate labelling of products so that consumers know what kinds of products they are buying will be an issue that international marketers will need to address in the future.

Movement

Whereas the theme of interaction encourages consideration of different characteristics within a place, movement provides a structure for considering how different places relate to each other. International marketing exists because movement permits the transportation of people and goods and communication of information and ideas among different places. No matter how much people in one place want something found elsewhere, they cannot have it unless transportation systems permit the good to be brought to them or allow them to move to the location of the good.

The location and character of transportation and communication systems long have had powerful influences on the economic standing of places. Especially significant have been places on which transportation routes have focused. Many ports evolved to be prosperous cities because they channelled the movement of goods and people between ocean and inland waterways. In eastern Asia, Hong Kong grew as British traders used its splendid harbour as an exchange point for goods moving in and out of southern China.

Businesses also have succeeded at well-situated places along overland routes. The fabled oasis of Timbuktu has been an important trading centre for centuries because it had one of the few dependable sources of water in the Sahara. The growth of towns in Europe between the tenth and thirteenth centuries was a combination of population relocation and growth, because of social, economic and environmental factors, and changes in the structure of society, with the breakdown of the feudal system which caused a fundamental shift in the order of society. This started a process creating a new environment where larger numbers of people could coexist under their own control and governance and enabled new legal, trade and transport systems to develop (**http://www.histrenact.co.uk**).[2]

In addition to the business associated directly with the movement of people and goods, other forms of economic activity have become concentrated at critical points in the transportation network. Places where transfers from one mode of transportation to another were required often were chosen as sites for manufacturing activities. Nineteenth-century London was transformed by the coming of the railways. A new network of metropolitan railways allowed for the development of suburbs in neighbouring counties from which middle-class and wealthy people could commute to the centre. While this spurred the massive outward spread of the city, the growth of greater London also exacerbated the class divide, as the wealthier classes emigrated to the suburbs, leaving the poor to inhabit the inner city areas.[3]

Global patterns of resource refining also demonstrate the wisdom of careful selection of sites with respect to transportation systems. Some of the world's largest oil refineries are located at places like Bahrain and Houston, where pipelines bring oil to points where it is processed and loaded onto ships in the form of gasoline or other distillates for transport to other locales. Massive refinery complexes also have been built in the Tokyo and Nagoya areas of Japan and near Rotterdam in the Netherlands to process crude oil brought by giant tankers from the Middle East and other oil-exporting regions. For similar reasons, Grangemouth, on the mouth of Carron, is now the UK's third largest oil refinery[4] supplying 40 per cent of the UK's oil and gas.[5] Some of the most active aluminium works in Europe are beside Norwegian fjords, where abundant local hydroelectric power is used to process imported alumina.

Favourable location along transportation lines is beneficial for a place. Conversely, an absence of good transportation severely limits the potential for firms to succeed in a specific place. Transportation patterns change over time, however, and so does their impact on places. Some places maintain themselves because their business leaders use their size and economic power to become critical nodes in newly evolving transportation networks. London's experience provides a good example of this process. London became the United Kingdom's foremost business centre in the early nineteenth century because it was ideally situated for water transportation. As railroad networks evolved later in that century, they sought London connections in order to serve its massive market. During the twentieth century, a complex web of roadways and major airports reinforced London's supremacy in the United Kingdom. In similar ways, Moscow and Tokyo reasserted themselves as transportation hubs for their nations through successive advances in transport technology.

Failure to adapt to changing transportation patterns can have harmful impacts on a place. For about 30 years during the middle part of the twentieth century, airports at Gander (Newfoundland, Canada) and Shannon (Ireland) became important refueling points for transatlantic flights. The development of planes that could travel nonstop for much longer distances returned those places to sleepy oblivion.

Continuing advances in transportation technology have effectively 'shrunk' the world. Just a few centuries ago, travel across an ocean took harrowing months. As late as 1873, readers marvelled when Jules Verne wrote of a hectic journey around the world in 80 days. Today's travellers can fly around the globe in less than 80 hours, and the speed and dependability of modern modes of transport have transformed the ways in which business is conducted. Modern manufacturers have transformed the notion of relationships among suppliers, manufacturers and markets. Automobile manufacturers, for example, once maintained large stockpiles of parts in assembly plants that were located near the parts plants or close to the places where the cars would be sold. Contemporary auto assembly plants now are built in places where labour costs and worker productivity are favourable and where governments have offered attractive inducements. They keep relatively few parts on hand, calling on suppliers for rapid delivery of parts as they are needed when orders for new cars are received. This 'just-in-time' system of production leaves manufacturers subject to disruptions caused by work stoppages at supply plants and to weather-related delays in the transportation system, but losses associated with these infrequent events are more than offset by reduced operating costs under normal conditions.

The role of advanced technology and its effect on international marketing are even more apparent with respect to advances in communications systems. Sophisticated forms of telecommunication that began more than 150 years ago with the telegraph have advanced through the telephone to facsimile transmissions and electronic mail networks. As a result, distance has practically ceased to be a consideration with respect to the transmission of information. Whereas information once moved only as rapidly as the person carrying the paper on which the information was written, data and ideas now can be sent instantaneously almost anywhere in the world.

These communication advances have had a staggering impact on the way that international marketing is conducted. They have fostered the growth of multinational corporations, which operate in diverse sites around the globe while maintaining effective links with headquarters and regional control centres. International financial operations also have been transformed because of communication advances. Money and stock markets in London, Tokyo and secondary markets such as Frankfurt and Hong Kong are now connected by computer systems that process transactions around the clock. As much as any other factor, the increasing mobility of money has enabled modern business executives to engage in activities around the world.

Region

In addition to considering places by themselves or how they relate to other places, regions provide alternative ways to organize groups of places in more meaningful ways. A region is a set of places that share certain characteristics. Many regions are defined by characteristics that all of the places in the group have in common. When economic characteristics are used, the delimited regions include places with similar kinds of economic activity. Agricultural regions include areas where certain farm products dominate, for example, wheat, corn and rice. Regions where intensive industrial production is a prominent part of local economic activity include the manufacturing belts of northwestern Europe and southern Japan.

Regions can also be defined by patterns of movement. Transportation or communication linkages among places may draw them together into configurations that differentiate them from other locales. Studies by economic geographers of the locational tendencies of modern high-technology industries have identified complex networks of firms that provide products and services to each other. Due to their linkages, these firms cluster together into well-defined regions. The 'Western Crescent' on the outskirts of London, and the 'Technopolis' of the Tokyo region all are distinguished as much by connections among firms as by the economic landscapes they have established.

Economic aspects of movement may help define functional regions by establishing areas where certain types of economic activity are more profitable than others. In the early nineteenth century, German landowner Johann Heinrich von Thunen demonstrated how different costs for transporting various agricultural goods to market helped to define regions where certain forms of farming would occur. Although theoretically simple, patterns predicted by von Thunen can still be found in the world today. Goods such as vegetables and dairy products that require more intensive production and are more expensive to ship are produced closer to markets, while less demanding goods and commodities that can be transported at lower costs come from more remote production areas. Advances in transportation have dramatically altered such regional patterns. Once, city residents in Europe enjoyed fresh vegetables and fruits only in the summer and early autumn when producers brought their goods to market. Today, city residents buy fresh produce year-round, with new shipments flown in daily from all over the world during the colder months.

Governments have a strong impact on the conduct of business, and the formal borders of government jurisdictions often coincide with the functional boundaries of economic regions. The divisive character of these lines on the map has been altered in many parts of the world in recent decades. The formation of common markets and free trade areas in Western Europe, North America, and other parts of the world has dramatically changed the patterns and flows of economic activity, and similar kinds of formal restructuring of relationships among nations likely will continue into the next century. As a result, business analysts increasingly need to consider regions that cross international boundaries.

Some analysts have identified regional structures that transcend national boundaries. Darrell Delamaide divided Europe into ten regions based on economic, cultural and social affinities that have evolved over centuries. His vision of Europe challenges regional structures that persist from earlier times. Seen by many as a single region known as Eastern Europe, the formerly communist nations west of what once was the Soviet Union are seen by Delamaide as being part of five different 'superregions': 'The Baltic League', a group of nations clustered around the Baltic Sea; 'Mitteleuropa', the economic heartland of northern Europe; 'The Slavic Federation', a region dominated by Russia with a common Slavic heritage; 'The Danube Basin', a melange of places along and near Europe's longest river; and 'The Balkan Peninsula', a region characterized by political turmoil and less-advanced economies.

In his book *The Nine Nations of North America*, Joel Garreau identified a set of regions based on economic activities and cultural outlooks. Seven of Garreau's nine regions include territory in at least two nations. In the Southwest, 'Mexamerica' recognized the bicultural heritage of Anglo and Hispanic groups and the increasingly close economic ties across the US–Mexican border that were spurred by the maquiladora and other export-oriented programmes. The evolution of this region as a distinctive collection of places has been accelerated by the decade-long operation of the North American Free Trade Agreement (NAFTA). Another cross-national region identified by Garreau was 'The Islands', a collection of nations in the Caribbean for which Miami has become the functional 'capital'. Many business leaders seeking to tap into this rapidly-growing area have become knowledgeable of the laws and customs of those nations. They often have done so by employing emigres from those nations who may now be US citizens but whose primary language is not English and whose outlook on the region is multinational. The establishment of the Central American Free Trade Agreement (CAFTA) linking the United States, Guatemala, El Salvador, Honduras, Costa Rica, Nicaragua and the Dominican Republic will likely further strengthen links across many of the nations in this region.

The ideas posed by Delamaide and Garreau have been controversial, but the value of their ideas is measured not in terms of the 'accuracy' of the regional structures they presented, but rather by their ability to lead more people to take a geographic perspective of the modern world and the way it functions. The regions defined by Delamaide and Garreau are not those described by traditional geographers, but they reflect the views of many business leaders who have learned to look across national boundaries in their search for opportunities. As marketing increasingly becomes international, the most successful entrepreneurs will be the ones who complement their business acumen with effective application of geographic information and principles.

For online activities, visit the following websites:

http://www.bis.gov.uk/

http://www.feast.org/organisations/551

Key terms

built environment

Climate

geologic characteristics

hydrology

Kyoto Protocol

population

soils

terrain

Notes

1   *The Guardian* (2008), 'Insurers agree flood protection deal'.
     Online. Available from: **http://www.guardian.co.uk/money/
     2008/jul/11/homeinsurance.insurance** (Accessed 15/01/
     08).

2   Debono, D. (2002), 'On Accounting for the growth of towns in
     Europe between 1000 and 1300'. Online. Available from:
     http://www.histrenact.co.uk/articles/towns.htm
     (Accessed 15/01/08).

3   Wikipedia (2008), 'History of London'. Online. Available from:
     http://en.wikipedia.org/wiki/History_of_London
     (Accessed 15/01/08).

4   Macleod, A. and Lister, D. (2008), 'Fears grow of further
     strikes at Grangemouth oil refinery'. Online. Available from:
     **http://www.timesonline.co.uk/tol/news/uk/scotland/
     article3835794.ece** (Accessed 15/01/08).

5   Pals, F. (2008), 'BP shuts pipeline on strike, cutting UK oil
     output (Update5)'. Online. Available from: **http://
     www.bloomberg.com/apps/news?pid=20601085
     &refer=news&sid=a7vmbr4Mk5xQ** (Accessed 15/1/08).

CHAPTER 2
TRADE INSTITUTIONS AND TRADE POLICY

THE INTERNATIONAL **MARKETPLACE 2.1**

A trade negotiator's glossary: What they said and what they really meant

'An ambitious proposal'
(It is unlikely to get any support)
'An innovative proposal'
(This one really is out of the trees)
'This paper is unbalanced'
(It does not contain any of our views)
'This proposal strikes a good balance'
(Our interests are completely safeguarded)
'I should like to make some brief comments'
(You have time for a cup of coffee)
'We will be making detailed comments at a later stage'
(Expect that your posting will be over before you hear from us)
'This paper contains some interesting features'
(I am going to give you some face-saving reasons why it should be withdrawn)

'The paper will provide useful background to our discussions'
(I haven't read it)
'We need transparency in the process'
(I am worried that I won't be included in the back-room negotiations)
'English is not my mother tongue'
(I am about to give you a lecture on a fine point of syntax)
'The delegate of . . . spoke eloquently on this subject'
(I haven't the faintest idea what he or she means)
'A comprehensive paper'
(It's over two pages in length and seems to have an awful lot of headings)

SOURCE: Anonymous

The international environment is changing rapidly. Firms, individuals and policymakers are affected by these changes. These changes offer new opportunities but also represent new challenges. Although major economic and security shifts will have a profound impact on the world, coping with them successfully through imagination, investment and perseverance can produce a new, better world order and an improved quality of life.

This chapter begins by highlighting the importance of trade to humankind. Selected historical developments that were triggered or influenced by international trade are delineated. Subsequently, more recent trade developments are presented, together with the international institutions that have emerged to regulate and facilitate trade. As *The International Marketplace 2.1* shows, the attempts by nations to negotiate trade terms and regulate international trade can be tedious and bureaucracy-ridden.

The chapter will analyze and discuss the country position in the world trade environment and explain the impact of trade. Various efforts undertaken by governments to manage trade by restricting or promoting exports, imports, technology transfer, and investments will be described. Finally, the chapter will present a strategic outlook for future developments in trade relations.

THE HISTORICAL DIMENSION

Many nations throughout history have gained pre-eminence in the world through their trade activities. Among them were the Etruscans, Phoenicians, Egyptians, Chinese, Spanish and Portuguese. To underscore the role of trade, we will take a closer look at some selected examples.

One of the major world powers in ancient history was the Roman Empire. Its impact on thought, knowledge and development can still be felt today. Even while expanding their territories through armed conflicts, the Romans placed primary emphasize on encouraging international business activities. The principal approaches used to implement this emphasize were the Pax Romana, or the Roman Peace and the common coinage. The Pax Romana ensured that merchants were able to travel safely on roads that were built, maintained and protected by the Roman legions and their affiliated troops. The common coinage, in turn, ensured that business transactions could be carried out easily throughout the empire. In addition, Rome developed a systematic law, central market locations through the founding of cities, and an excellent communication system that resembled an early version of the Pony Express; all of these measures contributed to the functioning of the international marketplace and to the reduction of business uncertainty. As a result, economic well-being within the empire rose sharply compared to the outside.

Soon, city-nations and tribes that were not part of the empire wanted to share in the benefits of belonging. They joined the empire as allies and agreed to pay tribute and taxes. Thus, the immense growth of the Roman Empire occurred through the linkages of business rather than through the marching of its legions and warfare. Of course, the Romans had to engage in substantial efforts to facilitate business in order to make it worthwhile for others to belong. For example, when pirates threatened the seaways, Rome, under Pompeius, sent out a large fleet to subdue them. The cost of international distribution, and therefore the cost of international marketing, was substantially reduced because fewer goods were lost to pirates. As a result, goods could be made available at lower prices, which, in turn, translated into larger demand.

The fact that international business was one of the primary factors holding the empire together can also be seen in its decay. When 'barbaric' tribes overran the empire, it was not mainly through war and prolonged battles that Rome lost ground. The outside tribes were actually

Ancient Roman coinage, dated May 11, 330 AD

attacking an empire that was already substantially weakened, because it could no longer offer the benefits of affiliation. Former allies no longer saw any advantage in being associated with the Romans and willingly cooperated with the invaders, rather than face prolonged battles.

In a similar fashion, one could interpret the evolution of European feudalism to be a function of trade and marketing. As farmers were frequently deprived of their harvests as a result of incursions by other (foreign) tribes, or even individuals, they decided to band together and provide for their own protection. By delivering a certain portion of their 'earnings' to a protector, they could be assured of retaining most of their gains. Although this system initially worked quite well in reducing the cost of production and the cost of marketing, it did ultimately result in the emergence of the feudal system, which, perhaps, was not what the initiators had intended it to be.

Interestingly, the feudal system encouraged the development of a closed-state economy that was inwardly focused and ultimately conceived for self-sufficiency and security. However, medieval commerce still thrived and developed through export trade. In Italy, the Low Countries, and the German Hanse towns, the impetus for commerce was provided by East–West trade. Profits from the spice trade through the Middle East created the wealth of Venice and other Mediterranean ports. Europe also imported rice, oranges, dyes, cotton and silk. Western European merchants in turn exported timber, arms and woollen clothing in exchange for these luxury goods. A remaining legacy of this trade is found in the many English and French words of Arabic origin, such as divan, bazaar, artichoke, orange, jar and tariff.[1]

The importance of trade has not always persisted, however. For example, in 1896, the Empress Dowager Tz'u-hsi, in order to finance the renovation of the summer palace, impounded government funds that had been designated for Chinese shipping and its navy. As a result, China's participation in world trade almost came to a halt. In the subsequent decades, China operated in almost total isolation, without any transfer of knowledge from the outside, without major inflow of goods, and without the innovation and productivity increases that result from exposure to international trade.

International marketing and international trade have also long been seen as valuable tools for foreign policy purposes. The use of economic coercion – for example, by nations or groups of nations – can be traced back as far as the time of the Greek city-states and the Peloponnesian War or, in more recent times, to the Napoleonic wars. Combatants used blockades to achieve their goal of 'bringing about commercial ruin and shortage of food by dislocating trade'.[2] In the 1990s, the Iraqi invasion of Kuwait resulted in a trade embargo of Iraq by the United Nations, with the goal of reversing the aggression. Following government suppression of civil protests in Uzbekistan, the European Union imposed a ban on the sale of arms by any EU nation to Uzbekistan, beginning November 26, 2005.[3] Although such deprivations of trade do not often bring about policy change, they certainly have a profound impact on the standard of living of a nation's citizens.

Global division

After 1945, the world was sharply split ideologically into West and East, a division that had major implications for trade relations. The Soviet Union, as the leader of the Eastern bloc, developed the Council for Mutual Economic Assistance (CMEA or COMECON), which focused on developing strong linkages among the members of the Soviet bloc and discouraged relations with the West. The United States, in turn, was the leading proponent of creating a 'Pax Americana', or American peace, for the western world, driven by the belief that international trade was a key to worldwide prosperity. Many months of international negotiations in London, Geneva and Lake Success (New York) culminated on 24 March, 1948, in Havana, Cuba, with the signing of the charter for an International Trade Organization (ITO).

This charter, a series of agreements among 53 countries, was designed to cover international commercial policies, domestic business practices, commodity agreements, employment and reconstruction, economic development and international investment, and a constitution for a new United Nations agency to administer the whole. In addition, a General Agreement on Tariffs and Trade (GATT) was initiated, with the purpose of reducing tariffs among countries, and international institutions such as the World Bank and the International Monetary Fund were created.

Even though the International Trade Organization incorporated many farsighted notions, most nations refused to ratify it, fearing its power, its bureaucratic size, and its threat to national sovereignty. As a result, the most forward-looking approach to international trade never came about. However, other organizations conceived at the time are still in existence and have made major contributions toward improving international trade.

TRANSNATIONAL INSTITUTIONS AFFECTING WORLD TRADE

World Trade Organization (WTO) (http://www.wto.org)

The World Trade Organization has its origins in the General Agreement on Tariffs and Trade, to which it became the successor organization in January of 1995. In order to better understand the emergence of the WTO, a brief review of the GATT is appropriate. The GATT has been called 'a remarkable success story of a post-war international organization that was never intended to become one'.[4] It began in 1947 as a set of rules for non-discrimination, transparent procedures, and settlement of disputes in international trade. One of the most important tools is the Most-Favoured Nation (MFN) clause, which calls for each member country of the GATT to grant every other member country the most favourable treatment it accords to any other country with respect to imports and exports. In effect, MFN is the equal opportunity clause of international trade. Over time, the GATT evolved into an institution that sponsored successive rounds of international trade negotiations with a key focus on a reduction of prevailing high tariffs.

Early in its existence, GATT achieved the liberalization of trade in 50,000 products, amounting to two-thirds of the value of the trade among its participants. In subsequent years, special GATT negotiations such as the Kennedy Round and the Tokyo Round further reduced trade barriers and developed improved dispute-settlement mechanisms, better provisions dealing with subsidies, and a more explicit definition of rules for import controls.

In spite of, or perhaps because of, these impressive gains, GATT became less effective over time. Duties had already been drastically reduced. Further reductions were therefore unlikely to have a major impact on world trade. Most imports either enter member countries duty free or are subject to low tariffs. The highest tariffs apply mainly to imports of agri-food and tobacco products, as well as clothing, textiles and footwear. In these industries, tariffs tend to increase with the degree of processing.[5]

Many nations developed new tools for managing and distorting trade flows, non-tariff tools that were not covered under GATT rules. Examples are 'voluntary agreements' to restrain trade, bilateral or multilateral special trade agreements such as the multifibre accord that restricts trade in textiles and apparel, and other non-tariff barriers. GATT, which was founded by 24 like-minded governments, was also designed to operate by consensus. With a membership of 144, this consensus rule often led to a stalemate of many GATT activities.

After many years of often contentious negotiations, the Uruguay Round accord was finally ratified in January of 1995. As part of this ratification, a new institution, the World Trade Organization, was created, which now is the umbrella organization responsible for overseeing the

implementation of all the multilateral agreements negotiated in the Uruguay Round and those that will be negotiated in the future.[6] The GATT has ceased to exist as a separate institution and has become part of the WTO, which is also responsible for the General Agreement on Trade in Services (GATS), agreements on trade-related aspects of intellectual property rights (TRIPS), and trade-related investment measures (TRIMS) and administers a broad variety of international trade and investment accords. As of December 2005, the WTO had 149 members, with Saudi Arabia being the newest, as can be seen in *The International Marketplace 2.2.*

The creation of the WTO has greatly broadened the scope of international trade agreements. Many of the areas left uncovered by the GATT, such as services and agriculture, are now addressed at least to some degree by international rules, speedier dispute settlement procedures have been developed, and the decision-making process has been streamlined. Even though the WTO will attempt to continue to make decisions based on consensus, provisions are now made for decisions to be made by majority vote if such consensus cannot be achieved.

The WTO makes major contributions to improve trade and investment flows around the world. However, a successful WTO may well infringe on the sovereignty of nations. For example, more streamlined dispute settlements mean that decisions are made more quickly and that nations in violation of international trade rules are confronted more often. Negative WTO decisions affecting large trading nations are likely to be received with resentment. Some

THE INTERNATIONAL **MARKETPLACE 2.2**

Accessing the hallowed halls of the WTO

On 11 November, 2005, after 12 years of negotiation, the General Council of the World Trade Organization officially accepted Saudi Arabia, making it the 149th member of the WTO on 11 December, 2005. The road to accession, with many challenges along the way, is by no means an easy one. The legal texts constituting Saudi Arabia's membership were over 600 pages! The Russian Federation, after the election of Vladimir Putin in 1999, began to actively pursue WTO membership; at the time of this publication, the negotiations are still ongoing.

Becoming a member of the WTO requires compliance with WTO policies that span a broad spectrum of government and private sectors alike. For example, among many other considerations, Saudi Arabia had to ensure that her producers of natural gas earn a 'reasonable profit', eliminate export subsidies on agricultural goods, review her banned imports list annually, allow up to a 70 per cent foreign equity ownership in the telecommunications sector, and allow foreign insurance companies to operate within the country. The restriction on the imports of goods was a particularly important issue. The government retains a vested interest in banning certain goods in order to protect public morals (recall that Saudi Arabia is a conservative Muslim nation). For Russia, the issue of subsidized domestic energy prices has been a sticking point in the negotiations.

While compliance with WTO standards may be initially costly, it can have great payoffs in the long run. First, states that become members of the WTO are granted Most-Favoured Nation (MFN) status

which gives them equal treatment with all other members of the Organization. Second, companies looking to locate part of their operations abroad can expect certain legal guarantees from WTO members. For example, members of the WTO are required to adopt the Agreement on Trade-Related Aspects of Intellectual Property Rights (TRIPS). TRIPS covers topics such as how intellectual property rights should be applied, how countries should enforce intellectual property laws, and how members of the WTO should settle disputes regarding intellectual property. In an age of rampant privacy and copyright infringements, corporations are increasingly wary of countries with poor intellectual property protection. In addition, both consumers and corporations are guaranteed certain health guidelines, because member nations must adopt agreements on sanitary and phytosanitary measures (sanitary measures relate to human and animal health, while phytosanitary measures apply to plants). These regulate things such as the maximum allowable pesticide residues in crops and salmonella levels in chicken. Outbreaks of mad cow disease and avian flu have highlighted the need for countries to have a uniform procedure for dealing with food and livestock emergencies.

SOURCES: Global Trade Negotiations Home Page, **http://www.cid.harvard. edu/cidtrade/gov/russiagov.html** (Accessed December 3, 2005); 'WTO General Council Successfully Adopts Saudi Arabia's Terms of Accession', **http://www.wto.org/english/news_e/pres05_e/pr420_e.htm** (Accessed December 3, 2005).

governments intend to broaden the mandate of the WTO to also deal with social causes and issues such as labour laws, competition, and emigration freedoms. Since many nations fear that social causes can be used to devise new rules of protectionism against their exports, the addition of such issues may become a key reason for divisiveness and dissent within the WTO.[7] Outside groups such as non-governmental organizations and special interest alliances believe that international trade and the WTO represent a threat to their causes.

In 2001, a new round of international trade negotiations was initiated. As the agreement to do so was reached in the city of Doha (Qatar), the negotiations are now called the 'Doha Round'. The aim was to further hasten implementation of liberalization, particularly to help impoverished and developing nations. In addition, the goal was to expand the role of the WTO to encompass more of the trade activities in which there were insufficient rules for their definition and structure. This was due to either purposeful exclusion of governments in earlier negotiations or new technology changing the global marketplace. Examples include trade in agricultural goods, antidumping regulations, and electronic commerce. The latest session of negotiations to conclude the Doha Round took place in Hong Kong in December 2005. The negotiations were largely marked by disagreement between developed and developing countries. The most divisive issue continued to be agricultural tariffs and subsidies. While the negotiations began slowly and with much disagreement, a last-minute compromise was reached on the final day. Negotiators agreed to eliminate export subsidies on agricultural goods by 2013, for rich countries to eliminate export subsidies on cotton by 2006, and called for reforms in the banking and insurance sectors.[8] While the results of the negotiation fell short of expectations, they represented a step forward from negotiations in Cancun in 2003, where developing nations walked out because they felt their interests were not being addressed. A conclusion of the Doha Round was expected by 2007. In July 2008, a mini Ministerial meeting was abandoned in Geneva. The Doha Round can be concluded in late 2009.[9]

Unless trade advocates and the WTO are supported by their member governments and other outside stakeholders in trade issues, there is unlikely to be major progress on further liberalization of trade and investment. It will therefore be important to have the WTO focus on its core mission, which is the facilitation of international trade and investment, while ensuring that an effective forum exists to afford a hearing and subsequent achievements for concerns surrounding the core.

International Monetary Fund (IMF) (http://www.imf.org)

The International Monetary Fund (IMF), conceived in 1944 at Bretton Woods in New Hampshire, was designed to provide stability for the international monetary framework. It obtained funding from its members, who subscribed to a quota based on expected trade patterns and paid 25 per cent of the quota in gold or dollars and the rest in their local currencies. These funds were to be used to provide countries with protection against temporary fluctuations in the value of their currency. Therefore, it was the original goal of the IMF to provide for fixed exchange rates between countries.

Perhaps the not so unintended result of using the US dollar as the main world currency was a glut of dollar supplies in the 1960s. This forced the United States to abandon the gold standard and devalue the dollar and resulted in flexible or floating exchange rates in 1971. However, even though this major change occurred, the IMF as an institution has clearly contributed toward providing international liquidity and to facilitating international trade.

Although the system has functioned well so far, it is currently under severe pressure. In the 1980s, some of this pressure was triggered by the substantial debts incurred by less-developed countries as a result of over-extended development credits and changes in the cost of energy. Since the 1990s, major additional pressure has resulted from the financial requirements of the former socialist countries, which search for funds to improve their economies. In addition, 12 former Soviet republics joined the IMF. Beyond the needs of these new members, major currency fluctuations among old customers have stretched the resources of the IMF to the limit. For example, on 6 September 2002, the International Monetary Fund approved Brazil's request for a 15-month standby credit of US$30.4 billion to support the country's economic and financial programme through December 2003.[10] As a result of all these global financial needs, the future role of the IMF may be very different. If the institution can mobilize its members to provide the financial means for an active role, its past accomplishments may pale in view of the new opportunities. In 2005 the IMF agreed to write off $3.3 billion of debt owed to it by virtually all of the world's 20 poorest nations.[11] Proponents of debt write-off, for example, Jubilee Debt Campaign[12], cite that mounting national debts in developing countries prevent investment into crucial areas such as social services, which improve the likelihood of decreasing poverty. However, with the already strained budget of the IMF, it is unclear what impact these write-offs will have on future lending.

At the same time, however, the new orientation will also require a rethinking of the rules under which the IMF operates. For example, it is quite unclear whether stringent economic rules and performance measures are equally applicable to all countries seeking IMF assistance. New economic conditions that have not been experienced to date, such as the privatization of formerly centrally planned economies, may require different types of approaches. In addition, perhaps the link between economic and political stability requires more and different considerations, therefore magnifying but also changing the mission of the IMF.

World Bank (http://www.worldbank.org)

The World Bank, whose official name is the International Bank for Reconstruction and Development, has had similar success. It was initially formed in 1944 to aid countries suffering from the destruction of war. After completing this process most successfully, it has since taken on the task of aiding world development. With more and more new nations emerging from the colonial fold of the world powers of the early twentieth century, the bank has made major efforts to assist fledgling economies to participate in a modern economic trade framework. More recently, the bank has begun to participate actively with the IMF to resolve the debt problems of the developing world and may also play a major role in bringing a market economy to the former members of the Eastern bloc.

A major debate, however, surrounds the effectiveness of the bank's expenditures. In the 1970s and 1980s, major funds were invested into infrastructure projects in developing countries, based on the expectation that such investment would rapidly propel the economies of these nations forward. However, in retrospect, it appears that many of these funds were squandered by corrupt regimes, and that many large projects have turned into white elephants – producing little in terms of economic progress. In addition, some projects have had major negative side effects for the recipient nations. For example, the highway through the rain forest in Brazil has mainly resulted in the migration of people to the area and an upsetting of a very fragile ecological balance. The World Bank is now trying to reorient its outlook, focusing more on institution building and the development of human capital through investments into education and health. 'Under its current President, Robert B. Zoellick, the World Bank strengthens its dedication to helping people overcome poverty with a new emphasize on transparency and increased cooperation and communication with private sector organizations and investors.'[13]

Regional institutions

The WTO, IMF and World Bank operate on a global level. Regional changes have also taken place, based on the notion that trade between countries needs to be encouraged. Of particular importance was the formation of **economic blocs** that integrated the economic and political activities of nations.

The concept of regional integration was used more than 100 years ago when Germany developed the Zollverein. Its modern-day development began in 1952 with the establishment of the European Coal and Steel Community, which was designed to create a common market among six countries in coal, steel, and iron. Gradually, these nations developed a Customs Union and created common external tariffs. The ultimate goal envisioned was the completely free movement of capital, services and people across national borders and the joint development of common international policies. Over time, the goals have been largely attained. The European Union (EU) now represents a formidable market size internally and market power externally, and the well-being of all EU members has increased substantially since the bloc's formation.

Similar market agreements have been formed by other groups of nations. Examples are the North American Free Trade Agreement (NAFTA), the Mercosur in Latin America and the Gulf Cooperation Council (GCC). These unions were formed for different reasons and operate with different degrees of cohesiveness as appropriate for the specific environment. They focus on issues such as forming a customs union, a common market, an economic union or a political union. Simultaneous with these economic bloc formations, the private sector has begun to develop international trade institutions of its own. Particularly when governments are not quick enough to address major issues of concern to global marketers, business has taken the lead by providing a forum for the discussion of such issues. One example is the Transatlantic Business Dialogue, which is a non-governmental organization composed of business leaders from Europe and the United States. Recognizing the inefficiency of competing and often contradictory standards and lengthy testing procedures, this group is working to achieve mutual recognition agreements on an industry basis. The executives of leading international firms that participate in this organization attempt to simplify global marketing by searching for ways to align international standards and regulations in the pharmaceutical and telecommunication sectors.

The activities of all these institutions demonstrate that the joining of forces internationally permits better and more successful international marketing activities, thereby resulting in an improved standard of living and an effective counterbalance to large economic blocs. Just as in politics, trade has refuted the old postulate of 'the strong is most powerful alone'. Nations have come to recognize that trade activities are of substantial importance to their economic well-being. Over the long term, the export activities of a nation are the key to the inflow of imports and therefore to the provision of choice, competition and new insights. In the medium and long run, the balance of payments has to be maintained. In the short run, 'an external deficit can be financed by drawing down previously accumulated assets or by accumulating debts to other countries. In time, however, an adjustment process must set in to eliminate the deficit'.[14]

The urgency of the adjustment will vary according to the country in question. Some countries find it very hard to obtain acceptance for an increasing number of IOUs. Others, like the United Kingdom, can run deficits of hundreds of billions of pounds and are still a preferred borrower because of political stability and perceived economic security. Such temporary advantages can change, of course.

TRADE POSITIONS COMPARED

Over the years, international trade positions have changed substantially when measured in terms of world market share. For example, in the 1960s, British exports of manufactured goods comprised 53 per cent of total world exports. Since then, this share has declined precipitously. As other trade partners entered the picture and aggressively obtained a larger world market share for themselves, British export growth was not able to keep pace with total world export growth.[15] Exhibit 2.1 shows the world share of exports and imports of various trading countries and regions. Notable is the degree to which US imports exceed exports.

Another important development is the rise of China's trade position. In just over a decade China nearly doubled its exports as a percentage of GDP from 19.5 per cent in 1992 to 40.2 per cent in 2004.[16] In addition, within three years (2001 to 2004), China surpassed Japan with its trade as a percentage of world total.

The impact of international trade and marketing on individuals is highlighted when trade is scrutinized from a per capita perspective. Exhibit 2.2 presents this information on a comparative basis. From this table, in both China and Japan the exports per capita continue to greatly exceed the imports per capita. It is important to note that statistics for the European Monetary Union (EMU) have been changing drastically in recent years, mainly due to the addition of new countries with economies of varying strengths.

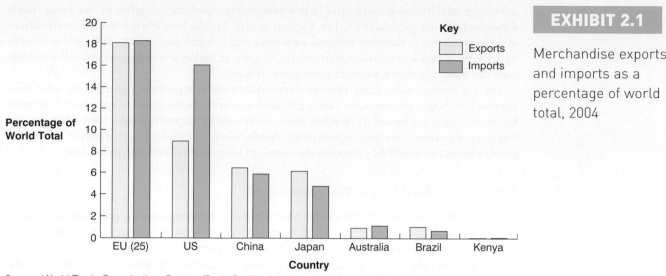

Source: World Trade Organization, Country Trade Profiles, http://www.wto.org, accessed December 15, 2005.

EXHIBIT 2.1

Merchandise exports and imports as a percentage of world total, 2004

Country	Exports per Capita	Imports per Capita
EMU*	$3,582	$3,651
Australia	$5,527	$6,709
Brazil	$548	$459
China	$506	$488
Japan	$5,172	$4,607
Kenya	$109	$158
United States	$3,874	$6,083

*Excludes intra-EMU trade

Source: Based on World Trade Organization, Statistics Database, Country Profiles, http://www.wto.org, accessed January, 5, 2006.

EXHIBIT 2.2

Exports and imports of goods and services per capita for selected countries, 2004

THE IMPACT OF TRADE AND INVESTMENT

The effect of trade

Exports are important in a macroeconomic sense, in terms of balancing the trade account. Exports are special because they can affect currency values and the fiscal and monetary policies of governments, shape public perception of competitiveness, and determine the level of imports a country can afford. A steady erosion of exports results in a merchandise trade deficit. Similarly, an increase in exports results in a reduced trade deficit.

These trade deficits have a major impact on a country and its citizens. They indicate that a country, in its international activities, is consuming more than it is producing. As indicated above, one key way to reduce trade deficits is to increase exports. Such an approach is highly beneficial for various reasons. For example, one billion dollars worth of exports supports the creation, on average, of 11,500 jobs.[17]

Equally important, through exporting, firms can achieve economies of scale. By broadening its market reach and serving customers abroad, a firm can produce more and do so more efficiently. As a result, the firm may achieve lower costs and higher profits both at home and abroad. Through exporting, the firm also benefits from market diversification. It can take advantage of different growth rates in different markets and gain stability by not being overly dependent on any particular market. Exporting also lets the firm learn from the competition, makes it sensitive to different demand structures and cultural dimensions, and proves its ability to survive in a less-familiar environment in spite of higher transaction costs. All these lessons can make the firm a stronger competitor at home.[18]

On the import side, firms become exposed to new competition, which may offer new approaches, better processes, or better products and services. In order to maintain their market share, firms are forced to compete more effectively by improving their own products and activities. Consumers in turn receive more choices when it comes to their selection. The competitive pressures exerted by imports also work to keep quality high and prices low.

The effect of international investment

International marketing activities consist not only of trade but also of a spectrum of involvement, much of which results in international direct investment activities. Such investment activities can be crucial to a firm's success in new and growing markets.

For decades, the United Kingdom was among the leading foreign direct investors in the world. British multinationals and subsidiaries sprouted everywhere. Of late, however, international firms increasingly invest in the United Kingdom. At the same time, investment continues to expand around the globe, following attractive factor conditions and entering new markets.

Foreign direct investment is a widely used entry strategy by many multinational corporations. However, foreign ownership is not equally distributed across all industries. Foreign direct investment tends to be concentrated in specific sectors, where the foreign investors believe they are able to contribute the best and benefit the most from their investment. For example, in the United Kingdom, foreign direct investment is biggest in the manufacturing industry.[19] The United Kingdom is also the EU's most favoured destination for foreign direct investment.[20]

Many of these investments take place in the industrialized nations and are carried out by industrialized nations. Exhibit 2.3 shows the geographic distribution of foreign direct investment.

To some extent, these foreign direct investments substitute for trade activities. As a result, firms operating only in the domestic market may be surprised by the onslaught of foreign competition and, unprepared to respond quickly, may lose their domestic market share.

EXHIBIT 2.3

FDI stock as percentage of world total, 2004

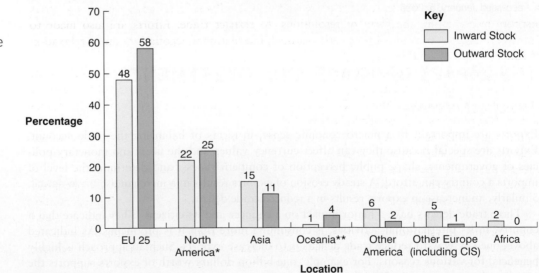

*Canada, Mexico, US
**Australia, New Zealand, and islands classified as "Oceania" (such as Fiji)
Totals may not equal 100% due to rounding

Source: FDI Database, United Nations Conference on Trade and Development, http://www.unctad.org, accessed January 17, 2006.

However, the substitution for trade is far from complete. In many instances, foreign affiliates themselves are major participants in trade. They may import raw materials or components and export some of their output.

Even though theory suggests an open investment policy that welcomes foreign corporations, some degree of uneasiness exists about the rapid growth of such investment. Therefore, many countries review major incoming investment projects as to their effect and desirability. For example, in the United Kingdom, the government review is done by the UK Trade & Investment and by the French National Council on Statistical Information (CNIS), in France.[21] These committees primarily scrutinize foreign investment activities from the standpoint of their impact on the national security and occasionally deny them. For example, in 2005, France came under criticism for its protectionist stance against foreign investors. In 2005, the French government acted to prevent Aventis, a pharmaceutical company, from being acquired by Swiss-owned Novartis.[22] Some countries do not welcome foreign direct investment. For example, Japan in is the most closed investment market for foreign direct investment.[23]

A general restriction of foreign investments might well be contrary to the general good of a country's citizens. Domestic industries may be preserved, but only at great peril to the free flow of capital and at substantial cost to consumers. A restriction of investments may permit more domestic control over industries, yet it also denies access to foreign capital and often innovation. This in turn can result in a tightening up of credit markets, higher interest rates, and a decrease in willingness to adapt to changing world market conditions.

POLICY RESPONSES TO TRADE PROBLEMS

The word *policy* implies that there is a coordinated set of continuous activities in the legislative and executive branches of government to attempt to deal with international trade. Unfortunately, such concerted efforts only rarely come about. Policy responses have consisted mainly of political ad hoc reactions, which over the years have changed from deep regret to protectionism.

Restrictions of imports

In light of persistent trade deficits, growing foreign direct investment, and the tendency by some firms and industries to seek legislative redress for failures in the marketplace, countries institute measures, in the form of resolutions, to restrict trade. Efforts are also made to improve international trade opportunities through international negotiations and a relaxation of rules, regulations and laws.

A trend has also existed to disregard the achievements of past international negotiations. There has also been a tendency to seek short-term political favours domestically in lieu of long-term international solutions. Trade legislation has become increasingly oriented to specific trading partners and specific industries.

Although the United States is still one of the strongest advocates of free trade, to which its large volume of imports and ongoing trade deficit attest, it has become very creative in designing and implementing trade barriers, examples of which are listed in Exhibit 2.4.

One typical method consists of 'voluntary' import restraints that are applied selectively against trading partners. Such measures have been used mainly in areas such as textiles, automobiles and steel. Voluntary restrictions, which are, of course, implemented with the assistance of severe threats against trading partners, are intended to aid domestic industries to reorganize, restructure and recapture their trade prominence of years past. They fail to take into account that foreign importers may not have caused the economic decline of the domestic industry.

The steel industry provides a good example. World steel production capacity and supply clearly exceed world demand. This is the result both of overly ambitious industrial development projects motivated by nationalistic aspirations and of technological innovation. However, a closer look at the steel industries of developed nations shows that demand for steel has also been reduced. In the automobile industry, for example, fewer automobiles are being

The global environment: A source of conflict between developed and less-developed nations

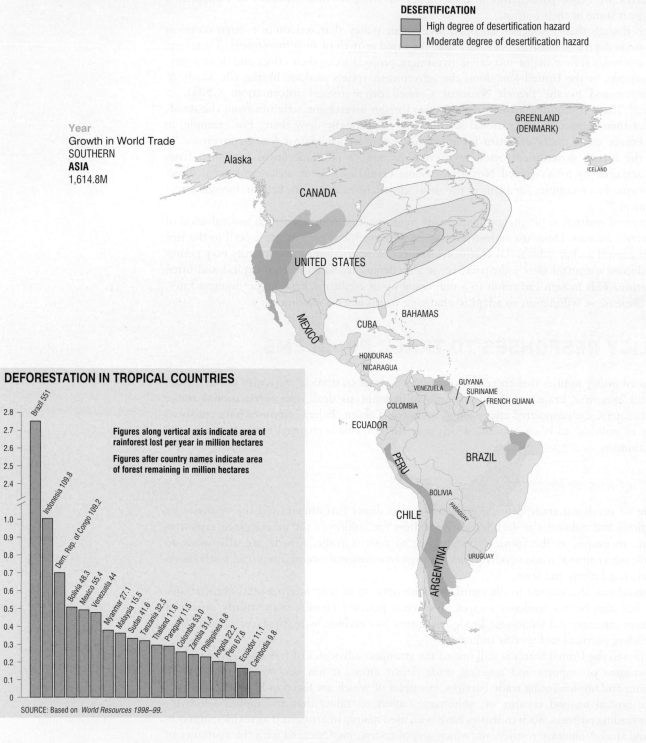

DESERTIFICATION
- High degree of desertification hazard
- Moderate degree of desertification hazard

Year
Growth in World Trade
SOUTHERN
ASIA
1,614.8M

GREENLAND
(DENMARK)

ICELAND

Alaska

CANADA

UNITED STATES

MEXICO

BAHAMAS

CUBA

HONDURAS

NICARAGUA

VENEZUELA

GUYANA

SURINAME

FRENCH GUIANA

COLOMBIA

ECUADOR

PERU

BRAZIL

BOLIVIA

PARAGUAY

CHILE

URUGUAY

ARGENTINA

DEFORESTATION IN TROPICAL COUNTRIES

Figures along vertical axis indicate area of
rainforest lost per year in million hectares

Figures after country names indicate area
of forest remaining in million hectares

Brazil 551
Indonesia 109.8
Dem. Rep. of Congo 109.2
Bolivia 48.3
Mexico 55.4
Venezuela 44
Myanmar 27.1
Malaysia 15.5
Sudan 41.6
Tanzania 32.5
Thailand 11.6
Paraguay 11.5
Colombia 53.0
Zambia 31.4
Philippines 6.8
Angola 22.2
Peru 67.6
Ecuador 11.1
Cambodia 9.8

SOURCE: Based on *World Resources 1998–99.*

RAINFOREST DESTRUCTION
Present distribution of forest area
Former extent of rainforest

ACID DEPOSITION
Estimated acidity of precipitation in the Northern Hemisphere
Slightly acid rain
Acid rain
Very acid rain

Source: Bassed on *Environment Atlas*

EXHIBIT 2.4

Trade barriers

There are literally hundreds of ways to build a barrier.
The following list provides just a few of the trade barriers that exporters face.

- Special Import authorization
- Restrictions on data processing
- Voluntary export restraints
- Advance import deposits
- Taxes on foreign exchange deals
- Preferential licencing applications
- Excise duties
- Licencing fees
- Discretionary licencing
- Trade restriction on e-commerce
- Anti-competitive practices
- Lack of intellectual property protection

- Country quotas
- Testing, labeling
- Seasonal prohibitions
- Health and sanitary prohibitions
- Certification
- Foreign exchange licencing
- Barter and countertrade requirements
- Customs surcharges
- Stamp taxes
- Consular invoice fees
- Taxes on transport
- Export subsidies

Source: Adapted from Office of the United States Trade Representative, 2005 National Trade Estimate Report on Foreign Trade Barriers, Washington. DC , March 30, 2005.
For more information, refer to http://www.ustr.gov/

produced, and they are being produced differently than ten years ago. Automobiles are more compact, lighter, and much more fuel efficient as a result of different consumer tastes and higher oil prices. The average automobile today weighs 700 pounds less than in the 1970s. Accordingly, less steel is needed for its production. In addition, many components formerly made of steel are now being replaced by components made from other materials such as plastic. Even if imports of steel were to be excluded totally from the markets of industrialized nations, the steel industries could not regain the sales lost from a substantial change in the automotive industry.

If countries do not use the subtle mechanism of voluntary agreements, they often resort to old-fashioned tariffs. For example, Japanese heavy motorcycles imported into the United States were assessed a duty of 49.4 per cent. This regulation kept the last US producer of motorcycles, the Harley-Davidson Company, in business. Even though these tariffs have since been removed – one year early – and the firm keeps on producing heavy motorcycles, one can rightfully question whether the cost imposed on US consumers who preferred foreign products during the four years of tariff imposition was justified. Even though tariffs have been substantially reduced on average, their specific application can still have a major effect on trade flows.

A third major method by which trade has been restricted is through non-tariff barriers. Typically, these barriers are much more subtle than tariffs. Compared with tariffs or even subsidies, which are visible and at least force products to compete for market acceptance on dimensions other than price, some non-tariff barriers are much more difficult to detect, prove and quantify. For example, these barriers may be government or private-sector 'buy domestic' campaigns, which affect importers and sometimes even foreign direct investors. Other non-tariff barriers consist of providing preferential treatment to domestic bidders over foreign bidders, using national standards that are not comparable to international standards, placing emphasize on design rather than performance, and providing for general difficulties in the market entry of foreign products. Most famous in this regard are probably the measures implemented by France. To stop or at least reduce the importation of foreign video recorders, France ruled in 1983 that all of them had to be sent through the customs station at Poitiers. This customs house is located in the middle of the country, was woefully understaffed and was open only a few days each week. In addition, the few customs agents at Poitiers insisted on opening each package separately in order to inspect the merchandise. Within a few weeks, imports of video recorders in France came to a halt. The French government, however, was able to point to international agreements and to the fact that officially all measures were in full compliance with the law.

The primary result of all of these trade restrictions is that many actions are taken that are contrary to what we know is good for the world and its citizens. Industries are preserved, but only at great peril to the world trade framework and at substantial cost to consumers. The direct costs of these actions are hidden and do not evoke much public complaint because they are spread out over a multitude of individuals. Yet, these costs are real and burdensome and directly affect the standard of living of individuals and the competitiveness of firms. For example, if agricultural subsidies and tariffs were eliminated in the Doha Round of trade negotiations, the gains to the world economy by 2015 have been estimated to be $287 billion annually! These gains do not necessarily mean that prices would decrease. The elimination of artificial distortions would increase the prices for some agricultural goods. For example, projections show that cotton prices would increase by 21 per cent, but the increase would primarily benefit the countries of Sub-Saharan Africa, currently one of the poorest regions in the world.[24]

Export promotion efforts

Many countries provide export promotion assistance to their firms. Key reasons for such assistance are the national need to earn foreign currency, the encouragement of domestic employment, and the increase in domestic economic activity. Many forms of export promotion can also be seen as government distortion of trade since government support simply results in a subsidization of profitability or reduction of risk. Yet, there are instances where such intervention may be justified. Government support can be appropriate if it annuls unfair foreign practices, increases market transparency and therefore contributes to the better functioning of markets,[25] or helps overcome, in the interest of long-term national competitiveness, the short-term orientation of firms.[26]

Governments provide companies with an impressive array of data on foreign trade and marketing developments. In the United Kingdom, the Department of Trade and Commerce provides a link with UK businesses in terms of information flow and market assistance. Efforts are made to coordinate the activities of diverse federal agencies. As a result of these efforts, a national network of export assistance centres has been created, capable of providing one-stop shops for exporters in search of export counselling and financial assistance. The DTI's Small Business Services, HMRC, Defra and Business Link have joined forces to create the UK International Trade Single Window (UK ITSW).[27]

A STRATEGIC OUTLOOK FOR TRADE AND INVESTMENT POLICIES

All countries have international trade and investment policies. The importance and visibility of these policies have grown dramatically as international trade and investment flows have become more relevant to the well-being of most nations. Given the growing links among nations, it will be increasingly difficult to consider domestic policy without looking at international repercussions.

An international perspective

From an international perspective, trade and investment negotiations must continue. In doing so, trade and investment policy can take either a multilateral or bilateral approach. Bilateral negotiations are carried out mainly between two nations, while multilateral negotiations are carried out among a number of nations. The approach can also be broad, covering a wide variety of products, services, or investments, or it can be narrow in that it focuses on specific problems.

In order to address narrowly defined trade issues, bilateral negotiations and a specific approach seem quite appealing. Very specific problems can be discussed and resolved expediently. However, to be successful on a global scale, negotiations need to produce winners. Narrow-based bilateral negotiations require that there be, for each issue, a clearly identified winner and loser. Therefore, such negotiations have less chance for long-term success, because no one wants to be the loser. This points toward multilateral negotiations on a broad scale, where concessions can be traded off among countries, making it possible for all participants to emerge and declare themselves as winners. The difficulty lies in devising enough incentives to bring the appropriate and desirable partners to the bargaining table. One area that would benefit greatly from multilateral negotiations is the regulation of e-commerce and the internet as described in *The International Marketplace 2.3* (for more on e-commerce, see Chapter 9).

Policymakers must be willing to trade off short-term achievements for long-term goals. All too often, measures that would be beneficial in the long term are sacrificed to short-term expediency to avoid temporary pain and the resulting political cost. Given the increasing links among nations and their economies, however, such adjustments are inevitable. In the recent past, trade and investment volume continued to grow for everyone. Conflicts were minimized and adjustment possibilities were increased manyfold. As trade and investment policies must be implemented in an increasingly competitive environment, however, conflicts are likely to increase significantly. Thoughtful economic coordination will therefore be required among the leading trading nations. Such coordination will result to some degree in the loss of national sovereignty.

THE INTERNATIONAL **MARKETPLACE 2.3**

The trade reality of e-commerce

The internet presents an opportunity for businesses and individuals to collaborate and communicate faster and cheaper than ever before. However, the new technology also poses challenges to modern policymakers, businesses and consumers. As more information is stored online and more people purchase with their computers, security is becoming a major problem. Hackers have been able to use security holes in websites and databases to steal information, including credit card and social security numbers. They have also attacked personal, corporate and government computers connected to the internet by exploiting weaknesses in the operating system and browser security. With the globalization of technology, hacking becomes much more than a simple break-in and entry. Who has the legal jurisdiction in these cases? Is it the country in which the computer that was hacked into is located? The country from which the hacker is attacking? Or the country in which the company is based? Many nations have yet to develop laws regarding Internet crimes and the existing laws vary greatly between nations.

In the past, consumers were able to buy foreign products through distributors and retailers in their home country. Today, they can skip intermediaries entirely and buy the product directly from the manufacturer over the internet. But what happens if a consumer buys a product from a relatively little known company and the product is defective, or the consumer is hurt by the product? Many countries have fairly extensive consumer protection laws, but many do not. Can the consumer sue based on the laws of his or her country, or on the laws of the country where the company is headquartered? Given the differences in legal theories and damage awards, should corporations be concerned about lawsuits from every country in the world?

Not only has the international community not agreed on matters of legal jurisdiction, but it has not even been able to agree on more simple issues such as who controls domain names (such as yahoo.com) on the internet. Currently, a non-profit organization, called the International Corporation for Assigned Names and Numbers (ICANN), is in charge of issuing such names, country codes, and internet Protocol addresses. However, in 2005 there was an unsuccessful move to bring the internet under more international oversight.

Even after the burst of the so-called 'dot-com bubble', we know that e-commerce is here to stay. In 2004, business-to-business and business-to-consumer sales worldwide topped $6.7 trillion. Yet, countries have still to agree on whether e-commerce should be classified as a good or service under the World Trade Organization framework. E-commerce does not even feature as a separate issue in global trade talks.

SOURCES: Global Reach, **http://glreach.com/eng/ed/art/2004.ecommerce. php3** (Accessed December 16, 2005); Global Business Dialog on Electronic Commerce, **http://www.gbde.org/trade.html** (Accessed December 16, 2005).

New mechanisms to evaluate restraint measures will also need to be designed. The beneficiaries of trade and investment restraints are usually clearly defined and have much to gain, whereas the losers are much less visible, which will make coalition building a key issue. The total cost of policy measures affecting trade and investment flows must be assessed, must be communicated, and must be taken into consideration before such measures are implemented.

The affected parties need to be concerned and join forces. The voices of retailers, consumers, wholesalers and manufacturers all need to be heard. Only then will policymakers be sufficiently responsive in setting policy objectives that increase opportunities for firms and choice for consumers.

SUMMARY

International trade has often played a major role in world history. The rise and fall of the Roman Empire and the emergence of feudalism can be attributed to trade. Since 1945, the western nations have made concerted efforts to improve the trade environment and expand trade activities. In order for them to do so, various multinational organizations, such as the WTO, the IMF and the World Bank were founded. In addition, several economic blocs such as the EU, NAFTA and Mercosur were formed. Many of these organizations have been very successful in their mission, yet new realities of the trade environment demand new types of action.

Recall from Chapter 1 that the last few decades have been marked by tremendous growth in world trade. In addition, there have been significant changes in the trade positions of many countries. For example, the United Kingdom's share of world exports has declined precipitously from 25 per cent in the 1950s, while China's share in world trade has risen substantially in the last few years alone. Furthermore, foreign direct investment has come to play an important role in the world economy.

The WTO has increasingly become a forum for trade disputes and negotiations. The 2005 negotiations that took place in Hong Kong highlighted the tensions between developed and developing countries, particularly in the sphere of agriculture.

Despite calls for trade liberalization, some policymakers intend to enhance trade performance by threatening the world with increasing protectionism. The danger of such a policy lies in the fact that world trade would shrink and standards of living would decline. Protectionism cannot, in the long run, prevent adjustment or increase productivity and competitiveness. It is therefore important to improve the capability of firms to compete internationally and to provide an international trade framework that facilitates international marketing activities.

Key terms

bilateral negotiations

economic blocs

economies of scale

foreign affiliates

foreign direct investment

multilateral negotiations

non-tariff barriers

pax Romana

trade deficit

Questions for discussion

1 Why is international trade important to a nation?

2 Give examples of the effects of the 'Pax Americana'.

3 Discuss the role of 'voluntary' import restraints in international marketing.

4 Provide examples of multilateral versus bilateral trade agreements.

5 How have consumer demands changed international trade?

6 Discuss the impact of import restrictions on consumers.

7 Does foreign direct investment have an effect on trade?

Internet exercises

1   What is the major role played by the World Bank today? Check **http://www.worldbank.org** to report on key projects.

2   Determine the latest exports per capita for a country of your choice not listed in Exhibit 2.2 (use data from **http://www. imf.org** and **http://www.un.org**).

Recommended readings

Diamond, Jared. *Guns, Germs, and Steel*. New York: W.W. Norton Company, 1999.

Finger, Michael J. *Institutions and Trade Policy*. Northampton, MA: Edward Elgar, 2002.

Letterman, Gregory G. *Basics of Multilateral Institutions and Multinational Organizations: Economics and Commerce*. Ardsley, NY: Transnational, 2002.

McCue, Sarah. *Farce to Force: Building Profitable E-Commerce Strategies*. Mason, OH: Cengage Higher Education, 2006.

Messerlin, Patrick A. *Measuring the Costs of Protection in Europe: European Commerical Policy in the 2000s*. Washington, DC: Institute for International Economics, 2001.

Odell, John (ed.) *Negotiating Trade : Developing Countries in the WTO and NAFTA*. Cambridge, England: Cambridge University Press, 2006.

Notes

1   Henri Pirenne, *Economic and Social History of Medieval Europe* (New York: Harcourt, Brace, and World, 1933), 142–146.

2   Margaret P. Doxey, *Economic Sanctions and International Enforcement* (New York: Oxford University Press, 1980), 10.

3   UK Department of Trade and Industry: Export Control Organisation, **http://www.dti.gov.uk/export.control/ notices/2005/notice1905.htm** (Accessed December 15, 2005).

4   Thomas R. Graham, 'Global Trade: War and Peace', *Foreign Policy* (Spring 1983): 124–137.

5   WTO Trade Policy Review of the United States 2001, WTO Secretariat Summary, Press Release, September 17, 2001. **http://www.wto.org/wto** (Accessed September 3, 2002).

6   *Business Guide to the Uruguay Round,* International Trade Centre and Commonwealth Secretariat, Geneva, 1995. **http://www.intracen.org**.

7   Michael R. Czinkota, 'The World Trade Organization – Perspectives and Prospects', *Journal of International Marketing* 3 (no. 1, 1995): 85–92.

8   Kurtenbach, Elaine, 'WTO Negotiators Agree on Farm Subsidies', Associated Press, ABC News, **http:// abcnews.go.com/Business/wireStory?id=1419446** (Accessed January 6, 2006).

9   **http://www.thehindubusinessline.com/2008/12/18/ stories/2008121851220800.htm.**

10 **www.imf.org/external/np/sec/pr/2002/pr0240.htm**.

11 IMF Backs Poverty Debt Write-off', BBC News, December 21, 2005, **http://news.bbc.co.uk/2/hi/business/ 4550778.stm** (Accessed January 21, 2009).

12 **http://www.jubileedebtcampaign.org.uk/ download.php?id=611**.

13 World Bank, 'Statements on Confirmation of Paul Wolfwitz as Tenth World Bank President', March 31, 2005, **http:// www.worldbank.org** (Accessed January 20, 2009).

14 Mordechai E. Kreinin, *International Economics: A Policy Approach,* 5th ed. (New York: Harcourt Brace Jovanovich, 1987), 12.

15 **http://books.google.co.uk/books?id=CpSvK3An 3hwC&pg=PA109&lpg=PA109&dq=Total+ British+exports+in+the+1950s&source= web&ots=Eph_bNr-wd&sig=EP2S3L9qB0311x 39EkVusGWYxzs&hl=en&sa=X&oi=book_ result&resnum=8&ct=result**

16 World Bank 2005 World Development Indicators, Washington, DC, 2005.

17 *U.S. Jobs Supported by Exports of Goods and Services,* U.S. Department of Commerce, Washington, DC.

18 Michael R. Czinkota, 'A National Export Development Strategy for New and Growing Businesses', remarks delivered to the National Economic Council, Washington, DC, August 6, 1993.

19 **http://www.berr.gov.uk/files/file49953.pdf**.

20 **http://www.euractiv.com/en/science/uk-top- destination-foreign-rd-investment/article-159798**

21 **http://www.cnis.fr/doc/rapports/RAP_0037.HTM**.

22 Erich Marquardt and Federico Bordonaro, 'Economic Brief: French Protectionism', *Power and Interest News Report,* September 15, 2005, **http://www.pinr.com/report. php?ac=view_report&report_id=367& language_id=1** (Accessed January 21, 2009).

23 **http://europa.eu/rapid/pressReleasesAction.do? reference=SPEECH/08/210&guiLanguage=en**

24   Kym Anderson, Will Martin, and Dominique van der
     Mensbrugghe, *Distortions to World Trade: Impacts on
     Agricultural Markets and Farm Incomes* (Washington, DC:
     World Bank, November 30, 2005).

25   *Die Aussenwirtschaftsförderung der wichtigsten
     Konkurrenzländer der Bundesrepublik Deutschland – Ein
     internationaler Vergleich* (The export promotion of the most
     important countries competing with the Federal Republic of
     Germany – An international comparison) (Berlin: Deutsches
     Institut für Wirtschaftsforschung, June 1991).

26   Masaaki Kotabe and Michael R. Czinkota, 'State
     Government Promotion of Manufacturing Exports: A Gap
     Analysis', *Journal of International Business Studies* (Winter
     1992): 637–658.

27   **http://www.sitpro.org.uk/policy/singwin/
     uksingwin.html**.

CHAPTER 3
THE CULTURAL ENVIRONMENT

Where Brits are the new imperialists

Multinationals that trample on other people's cultures. In Dublin's fair city, Tesco, Boots, the *Sun* and Walkers crisps are taking over. Whatever would Eamon de Valera make of it? Isn't that cultural imperialism?

Much has been written in the past decade about the economic miracle of the 'Celtic tiger'. The Republic of Ireland has been transformed in many respects – it has become more confident, greedy and anti-clerical – but its consumer habits and the face of its cities have also changed. This is because much of the business in the country is now British-owned.

Take a walk through the city of Dublin. I start off at Tesco in Baggot Street. Heading west, I nip in to a shop to purchase a packet of Walkers crisps and a copy of the *Irish Sun* or *Irish Mirror*, before taking in a pint of Guinness (British-owned) at the bar of the renowned Shelbourne Hotel (British-owned). Refreshed, I continue, turning right into Dawson Street, where I amble around Waterstone's and Hodges Figgis (both British-owned bookshops). Then a left into Nassau Street and another left to Grafton Street, to purchase a CD from the HMV store (British) before getting my groceries from Marks & Spencer.

While the homogenization of the British high street has been taking place since the 1960s, the Anglification of the Irish high street has been much more recent. Its most visible manifestation is the remarkable penetration of Tesco, or 'Tesco Ireland', as it brands itself. I remember my Auntie May dragging me along, as a child in the 1980s, to help her with her Saturday shopping at Quinns-worth or H Williams. Both chains have now vanished, the latter having folded

in 1987, the former having been purchased by Tesco ten years later. Today, Tesco Ireland is the largest food retailer in the republic, with more than 79 branches, employing more than 10,000 people. It has total sales of £1.22 billion and remains in rude health: its growth rate in 2002–2003 was 7.8 per cent.

Back in the 1980s, a great treat for an English lad on his summer holidays was tucking into a packet of greasy Tayto crisps. Tayto is perceived to be as Irish as the Blarney Stone. The firm has since come under acute competition from Walkers, which started in 2000 and rapidly made its mark in the crisps market, now second only to Tayto. Its aim is to take top spot, and it has the funds to do so, spending £581,000 a year on advertising, compared to Tayto's £528,000.

Tesco's good fortune has been mirrored by that of Boots the Chemist, which opened its first Irish branch in 1998. Having purchased the HCR chain, it is now the leading chemist chain in the republic, employing 1200 staff across 28 branches. More modest inroads have been made by Marks & Spencer, which has four stores. Considering, however, the difficulties M&S is having at home, not to mention its retreat from other foreign markets, it is surprising that it has any presence at all in Ireland. Elsewhere, both HMV and Virgin have opened outlets, providing competition for the country's independent record shops and its indigenous chain Golden Discs. BT's progress has been even more impressive. It acquired the Esat Group in 2000, renaming itself 'Esat BT', and is now second only to Eircom in the country's telecommunications industry. For a company that is manifestly British, this is no mean feat.

© Mike Clarke/AFP/Getty Images

Yet perhaps these developments are not so new. After all, since the creation of the Irish Free State in 1922, its people have remained resiliently British in their cultural appetites. The attempted Gaelicization of the country was a dismal failure. Newspapers such as the *News of the World* and the *Observer* continued to muster a substantial number of Irish readers, and the BBC came to be regarded as an honorary home broadcaster, while Manchester United, Liverpool and Celtic are perceived as honorary domestic clubs. This is not something that many of an Anglophobic disposition have been keen to admit, indulging instead in what Freud called the 'narcissism of minor differences': exaggerating trivial distinctions in order to mask very obvious similarities.

Far from the ties with British culture gradually withering after independence, as the founders of the Irish Free State hoped, the reverse has taken place. There are now more than 180 British companies operating in the republic. British cultural imperialism makes the two countries ever more similar, and not just in where people go to shop and what they buy. Thanks to the British media invasion, it also involves what they read and thus how they think. The success of Express Newspapers' Irish edition of the *Daily Star* in the 1990s prompted Trinity Mirror and News International to rebrand their

Dublin editions as the *Irish Daily Mirror* and the *Irish Sun*. The *Irish News of the World* followed, while the Dublin edition of the *Sunday Times* commands a big readership.

The repackaging has been a triumph for all three media organizations, with the *Mirror* selling 200,000 a day and the *Sun* close to 300,000 – easily outselling the *Irish Times* and *Irish Independent*. Although these titles do address domestic issues there is still substantial coverage of British affairs. If this development leads to better service and cheaper prices for the consumer, surely it is not all bad. From a cultural perspective, market forces are helping to bring the two nations closer together. It's not as if the traffic were all one-way. Dunnes Stores has several outlets in the north of England, Eason owns a 50-strong chain of bookshops in Britain and the *Independent* is Irish-owned.

It should serve as a reminder to those in Britain with an anti-American fixation, who deplore the idea of taking their children to McDonald's to drink Coca-Cola, that when it comes to cultural imperialism, Uncle Sam is not the only culprit.

SOURCE: West, P. (2004), 'Where Brits are the new imperialists'. Online. Available from: **http://www.newstatesman.com/200409130019** (Accessed 15/1/08).

The ever-increasing level of world trade, opening of markets, enhanced purchasing power of customers, and intensifying competition all have allowed and even forced marketers to expand their operations. The challenge for the marketing manager is to handle the differences in values and attitudes, and subsequent behavioural patterns that govern human interaction, on two levels: first, as they relate to customer behaviour and, second, as they affect the implementation of marketing programmes within individual markets and across markets.

For years, marketers have been heralding the arrival of the global customer, an individual or entity that would both think and purchase alike the world or region over.[1] These universal needs could then be translated into marketing programmes that would exploit these similarities. However, if this approach were based on the premise of standardization, a critical and fatal mistake would be made. Success in global markets is very much a function of cultural adaptability: patience, flexibility, and tolerance for others' beliefs.[2]

To take advantage of global markets or global segments, marketers are required to have or attain a thorough understanding of what drives customer behaviour in different markets, and to detect the extent to which similarities exist or can be achieved through marketing efforts. For example, no other group of emerging markets in the world has as much in common as those in Latin America. They largely share a Spanish language and heritage; the Portuguese language and heritage are close enough to allow Brazilians and their neighbours to communicate easily. Tapping into the region's cultural affinities through a network scale approach (e.g., regional hubs for production and pan-Latin brands) is not only possible but advisable.[3] As appliance makers such as Whirlpool study the habits and preferences of consumers in different countries, they develop specialized appliances (e.g., grinders for coffee and spices) and features (e.g., a fifth burner for ranges). Interestingly, as cooking habits have extended to include food from other cultures – from pizza to pot roast to tortillas – the new features have found new adopters. For example, non-Latinos want griddle cook tops for pancakes as well as fajitas.[4]

In expanding their presence, marketers will acquire not only new customers but new partners as well. These essential partners, whose efforts are necessary for market development and penetration, include agents, distributors, other facilitating agents (such as advertising agencies and law firms), and, in many cases, the government. Expansion will also mean new employees or strategic alliance partners whose motivations will either make or break marketing programmes. Thus understanding the hot buttons and turnoffs of these groups becomes critical.

In the past, marketing managers who did not want to worry about the cultural challenge could simply decide not to do so and concentrate on domestic markets. In today's business environment, a company has no choice but to face international competition. In this new environment, believing that concern about culture and its elements is a waste of time often proves to be disastrous. An understanding allows marketers to determine when adaptation may be necessary and when commonalities allow for regional or global approaches, as seen in *The International Marketplace 3.1*. Understanding culture is critical not only in terms of getting strategies right but also for ensuring that implementation by local operations is effective.

Cultural differences often are the subject of anecdotes, and business blunders may provide a good laugh. Cultural diversity must be recognized not simply as a fact of life but as a positive benefit; that is, differences may actually suggest better solutions to challenges shared across borders. Cultural competence must be recognized as a key marketing skill.[5] Adjustments will have to be made to accommodate the extraordinary variety in customer preferences and work practices, by cultivating the ability to detect similarities and to allow for differences. Ideally, this means that successful ideas can be transferred across borders for efficiency and adapted to local conditions for effectiveness. For example, in one of his regular trips to company headquarters in Switzerland, the general manager of Nestlé Thailand was briefed on a promotion for a cold coffee concoction called Nescafé Shake. The Thai group swiftly adopted and adapted the idea. It designed plastic containers to mix the drink and invented a dance, the Shake, to popularize the product.[6] Cultural incompetence, however, can easily jeopardize millions of pounds in wasted negotiations, potential purchases, sales and contracts, and customer relations. Furthermore, the internal efficiency of a firm may be weakened if managers, employees, and intermediaries are not 'on the same wavelength'.

This chapter will first analyze the concept of culture and its various elements and then provide suggestions for meeting the cultural challenge.

CULTURE DEFINED

Culture gives an individual an anchoring point – an identity – as well as codes of conduct. Of the more than 160 definitions of culture analyzed by Alfred Kroeber and Clyde Kluckhohn, some conceive of culture as separating humans from non-humans, some define it as communicable knowledge, and some see it as the sum of historical achievements produced by humanity's social life.[7] All the definitions have common elements: Culture is learned, shared, and transmitted from one generation to the next. Culture is primarily passed on by parents to their children but also by social organizations, special-interest groups, the government, the schools, and the church. Common ways of thinking and behaving that are developed are then reinforced through social pressure. Geert Hofstede calls this the 'collective programming of the mind'.[8] Culture is also multidimensional, consisting of a number of common elements that are interdependent. Changes occurring in one of the dimensions will affect the others as well.

For the purposes of this text, culture is defined as an integrated system of learned behaviour patterns that are distinguishing characteristics of the members of any given society. It includes everything that a group thinks, says, does, and makes — its customs, language, material artifacts, and shared systems of attitudes and feelings. The definition therefore encompasses a wide variety of elements, from the materialistic to the spiritual. Culture is inherently conservative, resisting change and fostering continuity. Every person is encultured into a particular culture, learning the 'right way' of doing things. Problems may arise when a person encultured in one culture has to adjust to another one. The process of acculturation — adjusting and adapting to a specific culture other than one's own — is one of the keys to success in international operations.

Edward T. Hall, who has made some of the most valuable studies on the effects of culture on business, makes a distinction between high and low context cultures.[9] In high context cultures, such as Japan and Saudi Arabia, context is at least as important as what is actually said. The speaker and the listener rely on a common understanding of the context. In low context cultures, however, most of the information is contained explicitly in the words. Western European cultures engage in low context communications. Unless we are aware of this basic difference, messages and intentions can easily be misunderstood. If performance appraisals of marketing personnel are to be centrally guided or conducted in a multinational corporation, those involved must be acutely aware of cultural nuances. One of the interesting differences is that the UK system emphasizes the individual's development, whereas the Japanese system focuses on the group within which the individual works. In the United Kingdom, criticism is more direct and recorded formally, whereas in Japan it is more subtle and verbal. What is not being said can carry more meaning than what is said.

Few cultures today are as homogeneous as those of Japan and Saudi Arabia. Elsewhere, intracultural differences based on nationality, religion, race or geographic areas have resulted in the emergence of distinct subcultures. The international manager's task is to distinguish relevant cross-cultural and intracultural differences and then to isolate potential opportunities and problems. An example is the Flemish and the Walloons in Belgium. The international business entity will act as a change agent by introducing new products or ideas and practices. Although this may consist of no more than shifting consumption from one product brand to another, it may lead to massive social change in the manner of consumption, the type of products consumed and social organization.

The example of Kentucky Fried Chicken in India illustrates the difficulties marketers may have in entering culturally complex markets. Even though the company opened its outlets in two of India's most cosmopolitan cities (Bangalore and New Delhi), it found itself the target of protests from a wide range of opponents. KFC could have alleviated or eliminated some of the anti-western passions by taking a series of preparatory steps. First, rather than opting for more direct control, KFC should have allied with local partners for advice and support. Second, KFC should have tried to appear more Indian rather than using high-profile advertising with western ideas. Indians are quite ambivalent toward foreign culture, and ideas usable elsewhere do not work well in India. Finally, KFC should have planned for reaction by competition that came from small restaurants with political clout at the local level.[10]

In some cases, the international marketer may be accused of 'cultural imperialism', especially if the changes brought about are dramatic or if culture-specific adaptations are not made in the marketing approach. There is a growing fear among many countries that globalization is bringing a surge of foreign products across their borders that will threaten their cultural heritage. In 2005, the United Nations Educational, Scientific and Cultural Organization passed the Convention on the Protection and Promotion of Diversity of Cultural Expressions, which declares the right of countries to 'maintain, adopt and implement policies and measures that they deem appropriate for the protection and promotion of music, art, language and ideas as well as cultural activities, goods and services'.[11] Some countries, such as Brazil, Canada, France and Indonesia, protect their cultural industries through restrictive rules and subsidies. France's measures include, for example, 'prix unique du livre', a limitation on the per cent of discount on books (to support small publishing houses and help maintain small bookstores); quotas on non-French movies on French TV channels and mandatory financing of films by TV channels (as a provision in their licence) as well as for French music on radio channels; and 'avance sur recettes' or 'fonds de soutien', a State financial advance on all French films.[12] Such subsidies have allowed the French to make 200 films a year, twice as many as the United Kingdom. Similar measures have been taken to protect geographic indications; for example, signs on goods that have a specific geographic origin and possess qualities or a reputation due to that place of origin (as seen in *The International Marketplace 3.2*). Some countries have started taking measures to protect their traditions in areas such as medicine, in which the concern is biopiracy of natural remedies.[13]

THE INTERNATIONAL MARKETPLACE 3.2

Protecting Feta and Mozzarella

The Trade-Related Aspects of Intellectual Property Rights (TRIPS) agreement[14] protects geographic indications (GIs, which are goods with distinct quality, reputation or characteristics). Members shall provide the legal means for interested parties to prevent the use of any means in the designation or presentation of a good that indicates or suggests that the good in question originates in a geographical area other than the true place of origin in a manner which misleads the public as to the geographical origin of the good.[15] In October 2005, the European Court of Justice brought to a close one of the most controversial disputes over geographic indications, removing the right of any non-Greek EU producers to use the name Feta for cheese. The Court decided that Feta fulfilled the requirements of a destination of origin because the name referred to an agricultural product from a defined geographical area and reflected characteristics specific to that area and its processing and preparation. By 2007 all other non-Greek Feta producers had changed the name of their cheese.

If European negotiators in the World Trade Organization get their way, food names associated with specific regions – Parma ham from Italy, Stilton cheese from the United Kingdom and Marsala wine from Italy – would be reserved solely for companies located in the respective regions. EU officials argue that Mozzarella, for example, is made according to exacting standards only in that particular part of Italy.

The EU Commission summarized the European point of view in this way: 'Geographical indications offer the best protection to quality products which are sold by relying on their origin and reputation and other special characteristics linked to such an origin. They reward investment in quality by our producers. Abuses in other countries undermine the heritage of EU products and create confusion among consumers'. Furthermore, Europeans fear that they may not be able to use their own names selling abroad in the future. A company in Canada, for example, could trademark a product named for a European place, preventing the rightful European originator from selling his goods in that market. The European Union has adopted geographic-indication laws governing over 600 products sold inside the EU. Now the EU wants to expand such a list worldwide and establish a multilateral register to police it.

For many, the European idea is bald-faced protectionism and has no merit on protecting cultural values. 'This does not speak of free trade; it is about making a monopoly of trade', said Sergio Marchi, Canada's ambassador to the WTO. 'It is even hard to calculate the cost and confusion of administering such a thing'. Others argue that the Europeans are merely trying to cover up for inefficient production practices. Some even make the argument that multinational companies are the ones who have built up the value of many of the product names on the list – not the small producers in the regions in question.

The debate is far from over. The definition of geographic indications is not altogether clear in that some countries want to protect the adjectives found on product labels (such as 'tawny' or 'ruby' to describe Portuguese port wine)... Other countries have their own lists as well; for example, India wants basmati rice to be protected even though 'basmati' is not a place name.

SOURCES: 'Greek Cheese Gets EU Protection', *Marketing News,* November 15, 2005, 15; 'Food Fight!' *Time Europe,* September 8, 2003, 32–33; 'WTO Talks: EU Steps Up Bid for Better Protection of Regional Quality Products', *EU Institutions Press Releases,* August 28, 2003, DN:IP/03/1178; 'Ham and Cheese: Italy Wins EU Case', *CNN.com,* May 20, 2003; 'Europe Says, "That Cheese is No Cheddar!"' *The Wall Street Journal,* February 13, 2003, B1; 'USTR Supports Geographic Indications for Drinks', *Gourmet News,* January, 2003, 3. See also **http://www.geographicindications.com**

Even if a particular country is dominant in a cultural sector, the commonly suggested solution of protectionism may not work. Although the European Union has a rule that 40 per cent of the programming has to be domestic, anyone wanting a US programme can choose an appropriate channel or rent a video. Quotas will also result in behaviour not intended by regulators. US programming tends to be scheduled during prime time, while the 60 per cent of domestic programming may wind up being shown during less attractive times. Furthermore, quotas may also lead to local productions designed to satisfy official mandates and capture subsidies that accompany them. Recently, a question has been raised of whether movies produced by foreign-owned companies in the US would be eligible for government subsidies.

Western European countries have had a dominant position worldwide in many areas, such as pop music and musicals. For example, the United Kingdom exported 3795 hours of television programming in 2004 as compared to the Netherlands' 2569 and the United States' 2236.[16] Furthermore, no market is only an exporter of culture. Given the ethnic diversity in the United Kingdom (as in many other country markets), programming from around the world is made readily available. Many of the greatest successes among cultural products in the United Kingdom have been imports; e.g., in television programming, *Disney* is an American concept as is McDonald's in fast food. In cartoons, Pokémon hails from Japan. Global marketers and media have made it possible for national and regional artists to break into worldwide markets, especially the US and European markets. Thailand's Tata Young has been signed by SONY BMG to be groomed for global stardom.[17]

The worst scenario for marketers is when they are accused of pushing alien behaviours and values – along with products and promotions – into other cultures, which can result in consumer boycotts and even destruction of property. McDonald's, KFC, Coca-Cola, Disney and Pepsi, for example, have all drawn the ire of anti-American demonstrators for being icons of globalization. Similarly, noisy boycotts and protests targeted many multinational companies in the wake of the situation of Iraq. In the United States, those protests were aimed at French and Germans, while opponents of the war focused on US companies.[18] The French and the Germans were targeted because they supported the Iraq war through military provisions.

THE ELEMENTS OF CULTURE

The study of culture has led to generalizations that may apply to all cultures. Such characteristics are called cultural universals, which are manifestations of the total way of life of any group of people. These include such elements as bodily adornments, courtship, etiquette, family gestures, joking, mealtimes, music, personal names, status differentiation and trade.[19] These activities occur across cultures, but their manifestation may be unique in a particular society, bringing about cultural diversity. Common denominators can indeed be found, but the ways in which they are actually accomplished may vary dramatically. Even when a segment may be perceived to be similar across borders, such as in the case of teenagers and the affluent, cultural differences make marketers' jobs challenging.

Observation of the major denominators summarized in Exhibit 3.1 suggests that the elements are both material (such as tools) and abstract (such as attitudes). The sensitivity and adaptation to these elements by an international firm depends on the firm's level of involvement in the market – for example, licencing versus direct investment – and the product or

		EXHIBIT 3.1
Language	Manners and customs	
• Verbal	Material elements	Elements of culture
• Non-verbal	Aesthetics	
Religion	Education	
Values and attitudes	Social institutions	

service marketed. Naturally, some products and services or management practices require very little adjustment, whereas others have to be adapted dramatically.

Language

A total of 6912 known living languages exist in the world, with 311 being spoken in the United States, 2269 in Asia (with 241 in China alone) and 239 in Europe.[20] The European Union has 20 official languages for its bureaucracy. Language has been described as the mirror of culture. Language itself is multidimensional by nature. This is true not only of the spoken word but also of what can be called the non-verbal language of international business. Messages are conveyed by the words used, by the way the words are spoken (for example, tone of voice), and by non-verbal means such as gestures, body position, and eye contact.

Very often, mastery of the language is required before a person is acculturated to a culture other than his or her own. Language mastery must go beyond technical competency, because every language has words and phrases that can be readily understood only in context. Such phrases are carriers of culture; they represent special ways a culture has developed to view some aspect of human existence.

Language capability serves four distinct roles in international marketing.[21]

1 Language aids in information gathering and evaluation efforts. Rather than rely completely on the opinions of others, the manager is able to see and hear personally what is going on. People are far more comfortable speaking their own language, and this should be treated as an advantage. The best intelligence on a market is gathered by becoming part of the market rather than observing it from the outside. For example, local managers of a multinational corporation should be the firm's primary source of political information to assess potential risk.

2 Language provides access to local society. Although English may be widely spoken, and may even be the official company language, speaking the local language may make a dramatic difference. For example, firms that translate promotional materials and information are seen as being serious about doing business in the country.

3 Language capability is increasingly important in company communications, whether within the corporate family or with channel members. Imagine the difficulties encountered by a country manager who must communicate with employees through an interpreter.

4 Language provides more than the ability to communicate. It extends beyond mechanics to the interpretation of contexts.

The manager's command of the national language(s) in a market must be greater than simple word recognition. Consider, for example, how dramatically different English terms can be when used in the United Kingdom, Australia or the United States. In negotiations, for US delegates 'tabling a proposal' means that they want to delay a decision, whereas their British counterparts understand the expression to mean that immediate action is to be taken. If the British promise something 'by the end of the day', this does not mean within 24 hours, but rather when they have completed the job. Additionally, they may say that negotiations 'bombed', meaning that they were a failure; to a US manager, this could convey exactly the opposite message. Similar challenges occur with other languages and markets. Swedish is spoken as a mother tongue by 8 per cent of the population in Finland, where it has idioms that are not well understood by Swedes. Goodyear has identified five different terms for the word *tires* in the Spanish-speaking Americas: *cauchos* in Venezuela, *cubiertas* in Argentina, *gomas* in Puerto Rico, *neumaticos* in Chile, and *llantas* in most of the other countries in the region.[22]

An advertising campaign presented by Electrolux highlights the difficulties in transferring advertising campaigns between markets. Electrolux's theme in marketing its vacuum cleaners,

'Nothing Sucks Like an Electrolux', is interpreted literally in the United Kingdom, but in the United States, the slang implications would interfere with the intended message. The danger exists of translingual homonyms; an innocent word may have a strong resemblance to another word not used in polite company in another country. For example, global elevator maker Kone wanted to ensure correct pronunciation of its name and added an accent (Koné) to its name in French-speaking countries to avoid controversy. Toyota Motor Corp. behaved similarly in changing its MR2 model to Spider. Other features of language have to be considered as well. In a Lucky Goldstar ad, adaptation into Arabic was carried out without considering that Arabic reads from right to left. As a result, the creative concept in this execution was destroyed.

The role of language extends beyond that of a communications medium. Linguistic diversity often is an indicator of other types of diversity. In Québec, the French language has always been a major consideration of most francophone governments because it is one of the clear manifestations of the identity of the province that separates it from the English-speaking provinces. The Charter of the French Language states that the rights of the francophone collectivity are, among others, the right of consumers to be informed and served in French. The Bay, a major Québec retailer, spends $8 million annually on its translation operations. It even changed its name to La Baie in appropriate areas. Similarly, in trying to battle English as the *lingua franca,* the French government has tried to ban the use of any foreign term or expression wherever an officially approved French equivalent exists (e.g., *mercatique,* not *un brainstorming*).[23] This applies also to websites that bear the '.fr' designation; they have to be in the French language. Similarly, the Hong Kong government is promoting the use of Cantonese rather than English as the language of commerce.

Other countries have taken similar measures. Germans have founded a society for the protection of the German language from the spread of 'Denglish'. Poland has directed that all companies selling or advertising foreign products use Polish in their advertisements, while some people in India – with its 800 dialects – scorn the use of English as a lingua franca since it is a reminder of British colonialism.[24]

Despite the fact that English is encountered daily by those on the internet, the 'e' in e-business does not translate into 'English'. In a survey, European users highlighted the need to bridge the culture gap. One third of the senior managers said they will not tolerate English online, while less than 20 per cent of the German middle managers and less than 50 per cent of the French ones believe they can use English well. Fully three-quarters of those surveyed considered that being forced to use non-localized content on the internet had a negative impact on productivity.[25] A truly global portal works only if online functions are provided in a multilingual and multicultural format.

Dealing with the language problem invariably requires the use of local assistance. A good local advertising agency and a good local market research firm can prevent many problems. When translation is required, as when communicating with suppliers or customers, care should be taken in selecting the translator or translation software. One of the simplest methods of control is back-translation – the translating of a foreign language version back to the original language by a different person from the one who made the first translation. This approach may help to detect only omissions and blunders, however. To assess the quality of the translation, a complete evaluation with testing of the message's impact is necessary.[26] In essence this means that international marketers should never translate words but emotion, which then, in turn, may well lead to the use of completely different words.

Language also has to be understood in its historic context. In Germany, Nokia launched an advertising campaign for the interchangable covers for its portable phones using the theme '*Jedem das Seine*' ('to each his own'). The campaign was withdrawn after the American Jewish Congress pointed out that the same slogan was found on the entry portal to Buchenwald, a Nazi-era concentration camp.[27] The Indian division of Cadbury-Schweppes incensed Hindu society by running an advertisement comparing its Temptations chocolate to war-torn Kashmir. The ad carried a tag line: 'I'm good. I'm tempting. I'm too good to share. What am I? Cadbury's Temptations or Kashmir?' The ad featured a map of Kashmir to highlight the point, and it also first appeared on August 15th, Indian Independence Day.[28]

Non-verbal language

Managers must analyze and become familiar with the hidden language of foreign cultures.[29] Five key topics – time, space, material possessions, friendship patterns, and business agreements – offer a starting point from which managers can begin to acquire the understanding necessary to do business in foreign countries. In many parts of the world, time is flexible and not seen as a limited commodity; people come late to appointments or may not come at all. In Hong Kong, for example, it is futile to set exact meeting times, because getting from one place to another may take minutes or hours depending on the traffic. Showing indignation or impatience at such behaviour would astonish an Arab, Latin American or Asian.

In some countries, extended social acquaintance and the establishment of appropriate personal rapport are essential to conducting business. The feeling is that one should know one's business partner on a personal level before transactions can occur. Therefore, rushing straight to business will not be rewarded, because deals are made not only on the basis of the best product or price, but also on the entity or person deemed most trustworthy. Contracts may be bound on handshakes, not lengthy and complex agreements – a fact that makes some, especially western, businesspeople uneasy.

Individuals vary in the amount of space they want separating them from others. Arabs and Latin Americans like to stand close to people they are talking with. If a British executive, who may not be comfortable at such close range, backs away from an Arab, this might incorrectly be taken as a negative reaction. In addition, westerners are often taken aback by the more physical nature of affection between Slavs – for example, being kissed by a business partner, regardless of sex.

International body language must be included in the non-verbal language of international business. For example, a British manager may, after successful completion of negotiations, shake hands, while a US manager impulsively gives a finger-and-thumb OKAY sign. In southern France, the manager will have indicated that the sale is worthless, and in Japan that a little bribe has been asked for; the gesture is grossly insulting to Brazilians. An interesting exercise is to compare and contrast the conversation styles of different nationalities. Northern Europeans are quite reserved in using their hands and maintain a good amount of personal space, whereas Southern Europeans involve their bodies to a far greater degree in making a point.

Religion

In most cultures, people find in religion a reason for being and legitimacy in the belief that they are part of a larger context. To define religion requires the inclusion of the supernatural and the existence of a higher power. Religion defines the ideals for life, which in turn are reflected in the values and attitudes of societies and individuals. Such values and attitudes shape the behaviour and practices of institutions and members of cultures, and are the most challenging for the marketer to adjust to. When Procter & Gamble launched its Biomat laundry detergent in Israel, it found Orthodox Jews (15 per cent of the population) a challenge since they do not own traditional media such as television sets. The solution was to focus on the segment's core belief that they should aid those less fortunate. A Biomat truck equipped with washing machines travelled around key towns. People would donate their clothing, and Biomat would wash and distribute them to the needy. As a result, the brand's share has grown 50 per cent among the segment.[30]

Religion provides the basis for transcultural similarities under shared beliefs and behaviour. The impact will vary depending on the strength of the dominant religious tenets. While religion's impact may be quite indirect in Protestant Northern Europe, its impact in countries where Islamic fundamentalism is on the rise (such as Algeria) may be profound. The impact of these similarities will be assessed in terms of the dominant religions of the world: Christianity, Islam, Hinduism, Buddhism and Confucianism. Other religions may have smaller numbers of followers, such as Judaism with 14 million followers around the world, but their impact is still significant due to the many centuries during which they have influenced world history. While some countries may officially have secularism, such as Marxism–Leninism, as a state belief (for example, China, Vietnam and Cuba), traditional religious beliefs still remain a powerful force in shaping behaviour. International marketing managers must be aware of the differences not only among the major religions but also within them. The impact of these divisions may range from hostility, as in Sri Lanka, to barely perceptible but long-standing suspicion, as in many European countries where Protestant and Catholic are the main divisions. With some religions, such as Hinduism, people may be divided into groups, which determines their status and to a large extent their ability to consume.

Christianity has the largest following among world religions, with more than 2 billion people. While there are many significant groups within Christianity, the major ones are Catholicism and Protestantism. A prominent difference between them is their attitude towards making money. While Catholicism has questioned it, the Protestant ethic has emphasized the importance of work and the accumulation of wealth for the glory of God. At the same time, frugality is stressed and the residual accumulation of wealth from hard work has formed the basis for investment. It has been proposed that this is the basis for the development of capitalism in the western world, and for the rise of predominantly Protestant countries to world economic leadership in the twentieth century.

Major holidays are often tied to religion. Holidays will be observed differently from one culture to another, and the same holiday may have different connotations. Christian cultures observe Christmas and exchange gifts on either December 24 or 25, with the exception of the Dutch, who exchange gifts on St Nicholas Day, December 6. Tandy Corporation, in its first year in the Netherlands, targeted its major Christmas promotion for the third week of December with less than satisfactory results. The international marketing manager must see to it that local holidays, such as Mexico's Dìa De Los Muertos (October 31 to November 2), are taken into account in the scheduling of events ranging from fact-finding missions to marketing programmes.

Islam, which reaches from the west coast of Africa to the Philippines and across a wide band that includes Tanzania, central Asia, western China, India and Malaysia has more than 1.2 billion followers.[31] Islam is also a significant minority religion in many parts of the world, including Europe. It plays a pervasive role in the life of its followers, referred to as Muslims, through the *shari'ah* (law of Islam). This is most obvious in the five stated daily periods of prayer, fasting during the holy month of Ramadan, and the pilgrimage to Mecca, Islam's holy city. While Islam is supportive of entrepreneurship, it nevertheless strongly discourages acts that may be interpreted as exploitation. Islam also lacks discrimination, except for those outside the religion. Some have argued that Islam's basic fatalism (that is, nothing happens without the will of Allah) and traditionalism have deterred economic development in countries observing the religion.

The role of women in business is tied to religion, especially in the Middle East, where women are not able to function as they would in the West. The effects of this are numerous; for example, a firm may be limited in its use of female managers or personnel in these areas, and women's role as consumers and influencers in the consumption process may be different. Except for food purchases, men make the final purchase decisions.[32] Access to women in Islamic countries may only be possible through the use of female sales personnel, direct marketing, and women's specialty shops.[33]

Religion affects the marketing of products and service delivery. When beef or poultry is exported to an Islamic country, the animal must be killed in the *halal* method and certified appropriately. Recognition of religious restrictions on products (for example, alcoholic beverages) can reveal opportunities, as evidenced by successful launches of several non-alcoholic beverages in the Middle East. Other restrictions may call for innovative solutions. A challenge for the Swedish firm that had the primary responsibility for building a traffic system to Mecca was that non-Muslims are not allowed access to the city. The solution was to use closed-circuit television to supervise the work. Given that Islam considers interest payments usury, bankers and Muslim scholars have worked to create interest-free banking products that rely on lease agreements, mutual funds, and other methods to avoid paying interest.[34]

Hinduism has 860 million followers, mainly in India, Nepal, Malaysia, Guyana, Suriname and Sri Lanka. In addition to being a religion, it is also a way of life predicated on the caste, or class, to which one is born. While the caste system has produced social stability, its impact on business can be quite negative. For example, if one cannot rise above one's caste, individual effort is hampered. Problems in workforce integration and coordination may become quite

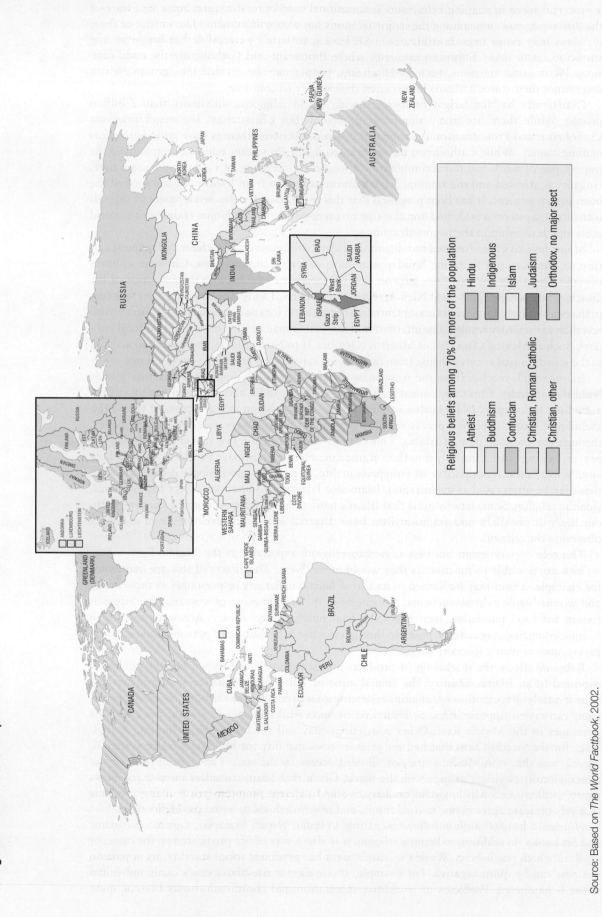

Religions of the world: A part of culture

Religious beliefs among 70% or more of the population

Atheist		Hindu
Buddhism		Indigenous
Confucian		Islam
Christian, Roman Catholic		Judaism
Christian, other		Orthodox, no major sect

Source: Based on *The World Factbook*, 2002.

severe. Furthermore, the drive for business success may not be forthcoming because of the fact that followers place value mostly on spiritual rather than materialistic achievement.

The family is an important element in Hindu society, with extended families being the norm. The extended family structure will have an impact on the purchasing power and consumption of Hindu families. Market researchers, in particular, must take this into account in assessing market potential and consumption patterns.

Buddhism, which extends its influence throughout Asia from Sri Lanka to Japan, has 360 million followers. Although it is an offspring of Hinduism, it has no caste system. Life is seen as an existence of suffering, with achieving nirvana, a state marked by an absence of desire, as the solution to suffering. The emphasize in Buddhism is on spiritual achievement rather than worldly goods.

Confucianism has over 150 million followers throughout Asia, especially among the Chinese, and has been characterized as a code of conduct rather than a religion. However, its teachings that stress loyalty and relationships have been broadly adopted. Loyalty to central authority and placing the good of a group before that of the individual may explain the economic success of Japan, South Korea, Singapore and the Republic of China. It also has led to cultural misunderstandings: in western societies there has been a perception that the subordination of the individual to the common good has resulted in the sacrifice of human rights. The emphasize on relationships is very evident when developing business ties in Asia. The preparatory stage may take years before the needed level of understanding is reached and actual business transactions can take place.

Values and attitudes

Values are shared beliefs or group norms that have been internalized by individuals.[35] Attitudes are evaluations of alternatives based on these values. The Japanese culture raises an almost invisible – yet often unscalable – wall against all *gaijin,* foreigners. Many middle-aged bureaucrats and company officials, for example, feel that buying foreign products is unpatriotic. The resistance therefore is not so much against foreign products as it is against those who produce and market them. As a result, foreign-based corporations have had difficulty in hiring university graduates or midcareer personnel because of bias against foreign employers. Dealing in China and with the Chinese, the international marketing manager will have to realize that marketing has more to do with cooperation than competition. The Chinese believe that one should build the relationship first and, if that is successful, transactions will follow. The relationship, or *guanxi,* is a set of exchanges of favours to establish trust.[36]

The more rooted values and attitudes are in central beliefs (such as religion), the more cautiously the international marketing manager has to move. Attitude toward change is basically positive in industrialized countries, whereas in more tradition-bound societies, change is viewed with great suspicion, especially when it comes from a foreign entity.

To counter the perceived influence of Mattel's Barbie and Ken dolls on Iranian values, a government agency affiliated with Iran's Ministry of Education is marketing its own Dara and Sara dolls. The new products, a brother and sister, are modelled on Iranian schoolbook characters. Sara is dressed in a white headscarf covering black or brown curls. A popular outfit is a full-length, flower-dotted chador, which covers the doll from head to toe. One toy seller explained that playing with Mattel's golden-haired, skimpily dressed Barbie may lead girls to grow up into women who reject Iranian values.[37]

Cultural attitudes are not always a deterrent to foreign business practices or foreign goods. Japanese youth, for instance, display extremely positive attitudes toward western goods, from popular music to Nike trainers to Louis Vuitton haute couture to Starbuck's lattes. Even in Japan's faltering economy, global brands are able to charge premium prices if they are able to tap into cultural attitudes that revere imported goods. Pokémon cards, Hello Kitty, and Sony's tiny minidisc players are examples of Japanese products that caught on in the United States almost as quickly as in Japan.[38]

While products that hit the right cultural buttons can be huge successes in foreign markets, not all top brands will translate easily from one culture to another. For example, while the Disneyland concept worked well in Tokyo, it had a tougher time in Paris. One of the main reasons was that while the Japanese have positive attitudes toward American pop culture, the Europeans are quite content with their own cultural values and traditions.[39]

Manners and customs

Changes occurring in manners and customs must be carefully monitored, especially in cases that seem to indicate narrowing of cultural differences between peoples. Phenomena such as McDonald's and Coke have met with success around the world, but this does not mean that the world is becoming westernized. Modernization and westernization are not at all the same, as can be seen in Saudi Arabia, for example.

Understanding manners and customs is especially important in negotiations, because interpretations based on one's own frame of reference may lead to a totally incorrect conclusion. To negotiate effectively in global markets, one needs to read correctly all types of communication. European executives often interpret inaction and silence as a negative sign, so Japanese executives tend to expect their European counterparts to lower prices or sweeten the deal if they just say as little as possible. Even a simple agreement may take days to negotiate in the Middle East, because the Arab party may want to talk about unrelated issues or do something else for a while. The abrasive style of Russian negotiators, and their usual last-minute change requests, may cause astonishment and concern on the part of ill-prepared negotiators. In addition, consider the reaction of a British businessperson if a Finnish counterpart were to propose the continuing of negotiations in the sauna. Preparation is needed not only in the business sense but in a cultural sense as well. Some of the potential areas in which marketers may not be prepared include: (1) insufficient understanding of different ways of thinking; (2) insufficient attention to the necessity of saving face; (3) insufficient knowledge and appreciation of the host country – history, culture, government and image of foreigners; (4) insufficient recognition of the decision-making process and the role of personal relations and personalities; and (5) insufficient allocation of time for negotiations.[40]

One instance when preparation and sensitivity are called for is in the area of gift giving. Exhibit 3.2 provides examples of what to give and when. Gifts are an important part of relationship management during visits and a way of recognizing partners during holidays. Care should be taken with the way the gift is wrapped; for example, it should be in appropriately coloured paper. If delivered in person, the actual giving has to be executed correctly; in China, this is done by extending the gift to the recipient using both hands.[41]

Managers must be concerned with differences in the ways products are used. For example, General Foods' Tang is positioned as a breakfast drink in the United States; in France, where

---

EXHIBIT 3.2

When and what to give as gifts

China	India	Japan	Mexico	Saudi Arabia
Chinese New Year (January or February)	*Hindu Diwali festival (October or November)*	*Oseibo (Jan. 1)*	*Christmas/ New Year*	*Id al-Fitr (December or January)*
✓ Modest gifts such as coffee table books, ties, pens	✓ Sweets, nuts, and fruit; elephant carvings; candleholders	✓ Scotch, brandy, Americana, round fruit such as melons	✓ Desk clocks, fine pens, gold lighters	✓ Fine compasses to determine direction for prayer, cashmere
✗ Clocks, anything from Taiwan	✗ Leather objects, snake images	✗ Gifts that come in sets of four or nine	✗ Sterling silver items, logo gifts, food baskets	✗ Pork and pigskin, liquor

✓ recommended
✗ to be avoided

Source: Kate Murphy, "Gifts without Gaffes for Global Clients," Business Week (December 6, 1999): 153.

orange juice is not usually consumed at breakfast, Tang is positioned as a refreshment. The questions that the international manager must ask are: 'What are we selling?'; 'What are the use benefits we should be providing?'; and 'Who or what are we competing against?' Campbell Soup has targeted China as one of the markets with the strongest growth potentials for soup. However, homemade soups account for 99 per cent of the consumption. With this in mind, Campbell's prices have been kept at an attractive level and the product is promoted on convenience. Care should be taken not to assume cross-border similarities even if many of the indicators converge. For example, a jam producer noted that the Brazilian market seemed to hold significant potential because per capita jelly and jam consumption was one-tenth that of Argentina, clearly a difference not justified by obvious factors. However, Argentines consume jam at tea time, a custom that does not exist in Brazil. Furthermore, Argentina's climate and soil favour growing wheat, leading it to consume three times the amount of bread Brazil does.[42]

Package sizes and labels must be adapted in many countries to suit the needs of the particular culture. In Mexico, for example, Campbell sells soup in cans large enough to serve four or five because families are generally large. In Britain, where consumers are more accustomed to ready-to-serve soups, Campbell prints 'one can makes two' on its condensed soup labels to ensure that shoppers understand how to use it.

Approaches that might be rarely taken in Europe could be recommended in other regions; for example, Conrad Hotels (the international arm of Hilton) experienced low initial occupancy rates at its Hong Kong facility until the firm brought in a feng shui man. These traditional 'consultants' are foretellers of future events and the unknown through occult means and are used extensively by Hong Kong businesses, especially for advising about where to locate offices and how to position office equipment.[43] In Conrad's case, the suggestion was to move a piece of sculpture to outside the hotel's lobby because one of the characters in the statue looked like it was trying to run out of the hotel.[44] At Disneyland Hong Kong, the feng shiu master rotated the front gate, repositioned cash registers, and ordered boulders set in key locations to ensure the park's prosperity.[45]

Meticulous research plays a major role in avoiding these types of problems. Concept tests determine the potential acceptance and proper understanding of a proposed new product. Focus groups, each consisting of eight to twelve consumers representative of the proposed target audience, can be interviewed and their responses used to check for disasters and to fine-tune research findings. The most sensitive types of products, such as consumer packaged goods, require consumer usage and attitude studies as well as retail distribution studies and audits to analyze the movement of the product to retailers and eventually to households. H.J. Heinz Co. uses focus groups to determine what consumers want in ketchup in the way of taste and image. European consumers go for a spicier variety of ketchup. In Central Europe and Sweden, Heinz sells a hot ketchup in addition to the classic variety. In addition to changes in the product, the company may need to promote new usage situations. For example, in Greece this may mean running advertisements showing how ketchup can be poured on pasta, eggs and cuts of meat. While some markets consider Heinz's US origin an advantage, there are others where it has to be played down. In Northern Europe, where ketchup is served as an accompaniment to traditional meatballs and fishballs, Heinz deliberately avoids reminding consumers of its heritage. The messages tend to be health related.[46] In-depth studies are also used to study consumer needs across markets. Intel, for example, has a team of 10 ethnographers travelling the world to find out how to redesign existing products or to come up with new ones to fit different cultures and demographic groups.

The adjustment to cultural variables in the marketplace may have to be long term and accomplished through trial and error. For example, the warehouse atmosphere should suit the local environment. When Office Depot reduced the size of its Tokyo store by a third and crammed the merchandise closer together, sales remained at the same level as before.[47]

Material elements

Material culture results from technology and is directly related to the way a society organizes its economic activity. It is manifested in the availability and adequacy of the basic economic, social, financial and marketing infrastructures. The basic economic infrastructure consists of transportation, energy, and communications systems. Social infrastructure refers to housing, health and educational systems. Financial and marketing infrastructures provide the facilitating agencies for the international firm's operation in a given market in terms of, for example, banks and research firms. In some parts of the world, the international firm may have to be an integral partner in developing the various infrastructures before it can operate, whereas in others, it may greatly benefit from their high level of sophistication.

The level of material culture can be a segmentation variable if the degree of industrialization of the market is used as a basis. For companies selling industrial goods, such as General Electric, this can provide a convenient starting point. In developing countries, demand may be highest for basic energy-generating products. In fully developed markets, time-saving home appliances may be more in demand.

While infrastructure is often a good indicator of potential demand, goods sometimes discover unexpectedly rich markets due to the informal economy at work in developing nations. In Kenya, for example, where most of the country's 30 million population live on less than a dollar a day, more than 10 000 people have signed up for money transfer services by mobile phone during the last two years; wireless providers are scrambling to keep up with demand.[48] Leapfrogging older technologies, mobile phones are especially attractive to Kenya's thousands of small-business entrepreneurs – market stall owners, taxi drivers and even hustlers who sell on the sidewalks. For most, income goes unreported, creating an invisible wealth on the streets. Mobile phones outnumber fixed lines in Kenya, as well as in Uganda, Venezuela, Cambodia, South Korea and Chile. This development is attractive for marketers as well, given the expense of laying land lines.

Again, however, the advent of new technologies must be culturally calibrated, as seen in *The International Marketplace 3.3*. Voicemail, while available, is not used to any significant degree in China. On the one hand, many Chinese do not comprehend the need to return phone calls or to respond to customers. Chinese workers tend to be away from their desks most of the day, conducting business in the traditional, face-to-face Asian style. On the other hand, Chinese do not leave messages either, expecting to talk to a live person.[49]

Technological advances have probably been the major cause of cultural change in many countries. For example, the increase in leisure time so characteristic in western cultures has been a direct result of technological development. Workers in Germany are now pushing for a 35-hour work week. Increasingly, consumers are seeking more diverse products – including convenience items – as a way of satisfying their demand for a higher quality of life and more leisure time. For example, a 1999 Gallup survey in China found that 44 per cent of the respondents were saving to buy electronic items and appliances, second only to saving for a rainy day.[50] Marketers able to tailor and market their products to fit the new lifestyle, especially in emerging markets, stand to reap the benefits. Consumers around the world are showing greater acceptance of equipment for personal use, reflected in increased sales of mobile phones and small computers as well as increased internet use. With technological advancement also comes cultural convergence. Black-and-white television sets extensively penetrated the European and Japanese markets. With colour television, the lag was reduced to five years. With video cassette recorders, the difference was only three years. With the compact disc, penetration rates were even after only one year. Today, with MTV available by satellite around the world, no lag exists at all.[51]

Material culture – mainly the degree to which it exists and how much it is esteemed – will have an impact on marketing decisions. Many exporters do not understand the degree to which US consumers are package-conscious; for example, cans must be shiny and beautiful. On the other hand, packaging problems may arise in the exporting countries due to lack of certain materials, different specifications when the material is available, different line-fill machinery, and immense differences in quality and consistency of printing ink, especially in developing markets. Even the ability of media to reach target audiences will be affected by ownership of radios, television sets and personal computers.

Aesthetics

Each culture makes a clear statement concerning good taste, as expressed in the arts and in the particular symbolism of colours, form and music. What is and what is not acceptable

THE INTERNATIONAL **MARKETPLACE 3.3**

Mobile payments across the globe?

Mobile payment services (m-payments) enable consumers to pay for goods and services from their bank account using their mobile phone. These services have evolved over time from using voice or short message services (SMS) to initiate and settle a transaction to the present-day use of a phone for one-step instant purchases. The convenience for consumers is significant in that they avoid using cash or credit cards, and, with prepaid services, avoid monthly bills. Services are secure in that an alphanumeric password is required for authentication. In addition, direct payments from the customer's account means that spending power is not limited to the amount of credit available on the phone account.

However, while analysts predicted that m-payments would account for as much as $15 billion a year, they have only reached $3 billion a year by 2005. M-payments have taken off in Japan and Korea but failed to reach estimated potential within the European Union and the United States. Reasons for this can be found in the lack of readiness in existing technology, unwillingness of the various stakeholders (banks, credit card issuers, handset makers, and telecommunication companies) to collaborate, as well as cultural variables in terms of existing usage patterns and perceptions of risk and relative advantage of a new technology.

The chief driver of mobile innovation in Japan is NTT DoCoMo. Its market power is so significant that it can impose new systems from the top down, as it did with the introduction of the i-mode (which allowed consumers to use their phones for everything from trading stocks and checking movie times to playing games, instant messaging and downloading Hello Kitty characters). While the i-mode did not include m-payments, it laid the groundwork for that continuous innovation. M-payment capability was added by using SONY's contactless chips, which allow payment by passing the phones over a sensor. Subscriptions to this service were estimated to exceed 10 million by the end of 2005. The key to success is NTT DoCoMo's dominance in the market. Customers have transitioned easily to adding making payments with their phones. Merchants wanted to tap into the large and growing market, especially when they were subsidized by NTT DoCoMo in buying the needed new technology. In Korea, the three big operators (SK Telecom, KTF and LG Telecom) have collaborated with credit card companies, which are taking care of the financing and operations.

In the European Union and the United States, payment cards are already deeply embedded in consumer behaviour; consumers may not be eager to move away from a familiar system, and they may not have thought of using phones as payment devices. In markets where mobile diffusion is high (such as the Nordic countries) or in countries where cash still accounts for a majority of retail transactions (e.g., Germany and Central Europe), chances may be better. In Central Europe merchants may be eager to switch to cashless systems at the expense of handling currency. At the same time, all of the stakeholders need to demonstrate to mobile phone users that m-payments are much more attractive than other familiar payment schemes. The bundle of convenience items (safe, secure, available, fast, transparent) needs to be packaged and sold to target groups.

None of the North American or European players have the market power of their Asian counterparts. Cooperation among banks, credit card issuers, handset makers and retailers will be essential. One such attempt, SIMPAY, an alliance set up by Orange, Vodafone, T-Mobile and Telefónica Móviles, to allow consumers to charge small purchases to their mobile phone bills, closed in 2005 after 18 months of operation. One of the main reasons was the lack of sufficient volume to cover collection costs.

Despite uneven global acceptance, Arthur D. Little predicted a tenfold increase in mobile payment transactions, to reach $37 billion by 2008.

SOURCES: Roman Friedrich, Johannes Bussman, Olaf Acker and Niklas Dietrich, 'Making Mobile Payment Work for Everyone', *Strategy and Business Resilience Report,* September 22, 2005, available at **http://www.strategy-business.com**; Lucy Sherriff, 'Simpay Halts Mobile Commerce Project', *The Register,* June 27, 2005, available at **http://www.theregister.co.uk/2005/06/27/simpay_halts_ project/**; 'M-payments Making Inroads', *Arthur D. Little's Global M-payment Update 2005,* Boston, MA: Arthur D. Little, 2005; 'M-payments Predicted to Be Worth £20 billion in 2008', *New Media Age,* August 5, 2004, 11; Malte Krueger and Gérard Carat, 'M-payments and the Role of Telcos', *Electronic Payment Systems Observatory Newsletter,* number 2, 2000, 4–7. See also **http://www. nttdocomo.com/corebiz/interconnected/felicaContent.html**.

may vary dramatically even in otherwise highly similar markets. Sex in advertising is an example. In an apparent attempt to preserve the purity of Japanese womanhood, Japanese advertisers frequently turn to blonde, blue-eyed foreign models to make the point. In introducing the shower soap Fa from the European market to the North American market, Henkel also extended its European advertising campaign to the new market. The main difference was to have the young woman in the waves wear a bathing suit rather than be naked, as in the German original.

Colour is often used as a mechanism for brand identification, feature reinforcement, and differentiation. In international markets, colours have more symbolic value than in domestic markets. Black, for instance, is considered the colour of mourning in Europe, whereas white has the same symbolic value in Japan and most of the Far East. A British bank interested in expanding its operations to Singapore wanted to use blue and green as its identification colours. A consulting firm was quick to tell the client that green is associated with death there. Although the bank insisted on its original choice of colours, the green was changed to an acceptable shade.[52] Similarly, music used in broadcast advertisements is often adjusted to reflect regional differences.

International firms have to take into consideration local tastes and concerns in designing their facilities. They may have a general policy of uniformity in building or office space design, but local tastes may often warrant modifications. Respecting local cultural traditions may also generate goodwill toward the international marketer. For example, McDonald's painstakingly renovated a seventeenth-century building for its third outlet in Moscow.

Education

Education, either formal or informal, plays a major role in the passing on and sharing of culture. Educational levels of a culture can be assessed using literacy rates and enrolment in secondary or higher education, information available from secondary data sources. International firms also need to know about the qualitative aspects of education, namely, varying emphases on particular skills, and the overall level of the education provided. Japan and the Republic of Korea, for example, emphasize the sciences, especially engineering, to a greater degree than do western countries.

Educational levels will have an impact on various business functions. Training programmes for a production facility will have to take the educational backgrounds of trainees into account. For example, a high level of illiteracy will suggest the use of visual aids rather than printed manuals. Local recruiting for sales jobs will be affected by the availability of suitably trained personnel. In some cases, international firms routinely send locally recruited personnel to headquarters for training.

The international marketing manager may also have to be prepared to fight obstacles in recruiting a suitable sales force or support personnel. For example, the Japanese culture places a premium on loyalty, and employees consider themselves to be members of the corporate family. If a foreign firm decides to leave Japan, employees may find themselves stranded mid-career, unable to find a place in the Japanese business system. University graduates are therefore reluctant to join all but the largest and best known of foreign firms.[53]

If technology is marketed, the level of sophistication of the product will depend on the educational level of future users. Product adaptation decisions are often influenced by the extent to which targeted customers are able to use the product or service properly.

Social institutions

Social institutions affect the ways in which people relate to each other. The family unit, which in western industrialized countries consists of parents and children, in a number of cultures is extended to include grandparents and other relatives. This will have an impact on consumption patterns and must be taken into account, for example, when conducting market research.

The concept of kinship, or blood relations between individuals, is defined in a very broad way in societies such as those in sub-Saharan Africa. Family relations and a strong obligation to family are important factors to be considered in human resource management in those regions. Understanding tribal politics in countries such as Nigeria may help the manager avoid unnecessary complications in executing business transactions.

The division of a particular population into classes is termed social stratification. Stratification ranges from the situation in Northern Europe, where most people are members of the middle class, to highly stratified societies such as India, in which the higher strata control most of the buying power and decision-making positions.

An important part of the socialization process of consumers worldwide is reference groups. These groups provide the values and attitudes that become influential in shaping behaviour. Primary reference groups include the family, co-workers, and other intimate groupings, whereas secondary groups are social socializations in which less-continuous interaction takes place, such as professional associations and trade socializations. Besides socialization, reference groups develop an individual's concept of self, which manifests itself, for example, through the use of products. Reference groups also provide a baseline for compliance with group norms through either conforming to or avoiding certain behaviours.

Social organization also determines the roles of managers and subordinates and the way they relate to one another. In some cultures, managers and subordinates are separated explicitly and implicitly by various boundaries ranging from social class differences to separate office facilities. In others, cooperation is elicited through equality. For example, Nissan USA has no reserved parking spaces and no private dining rooms, everyone wears the same type of white coveralls, and the president sits in the same room with a hundred other white-collar workers. The fitting of an organizational culture for internal marketing purposes to the larger context of a national culture has to be executed with care. Changes that are too dramatic may cause disruption of productivity or, at the minimum, suspicion.

While western business practice has developed impersonal structures for channeling power and influence through reliance on laws and contracts, the Chinese emphasize getting on the good side of someone and storing up political capital with him or her. Things can get done without this capital, or *guanxi,* only if one invests enormous personal energy, is willing to offend even trusted associates, and is prepared to see it all melt away at a moment's notice.[54] For the Chinese, contracts form a useful agenda and a symbol of progress, but obligations come from relationships. McDonald's found this out in Beijing, where it was evicted from a central building after only two years despite having a twenty-year contract. The incomer had strong *guanxi,* whereas McDonald's had not kept its relationships in good repair.[55]

Sources of cultural knowledge

The concept of cultural knowledge is broad and multifaceted. Cultural knowledge can be defined by the way it is acquired. Objective or factual information is obtained from others through communication, research, and education. Experiential knowledge, on the other hand, can be acquired only by being involved in a culture other than one's own. A summary of the types of knowledge needed by the international manager is provided in Exhibit 3.3. Both factual and experiential information can be general or country-specific. In fact, the more a manager becomes involved in the international arena, the more he or she is able to develop a meta-knowledge, that is, ground rules that apply to a great extent whether in Kuala Lumpur, Malaysia, or Asunción, Paraguay. Market-specific knowledge does not necessarily travel well; the general variables on which the information is based do.

In a survey on how to acquire international expertise, managers ranked eight factors in terms of their importance, as shown in Exhibit 3.4. These managers emphasized the

	Type of Information	
Source of Information	**General**	**Country-Specific**
Objective	Examples:	Examples:
	• Impact of GDP	• Tariff barriers
	• Regional integration	• Government regulations
Experiential	Example:	Examples:
	• Corporate adjustment to internationalization	• Product acceptance
		• Program appropriateness

EXHIBIT 3.3

Types of international information

EXHIBIT 3.4

Managers' rankings of factors involved in acquiring international expertise

Factor	Considered Critical %	Considered Important %
1. Assignments overseas	85	9
2. Business travel	83	17
3. Training programs	28	57
4. Non-business travel	28	54
5. Reading/web	22	72
6. Graduate courses	13	52
7. Pre-career activities	9	50
8. Undergraduate courses	0.5	48

Source: Data collected by authors from 110 executives by questionnaire, February, 2003. Original study by Stephen J. Kobrin, *International Expertise in American Business* (New York: Institute of International Education, 1984), 38.

experiential acquisition of knowledge. Written materials were indicated to play an important but supplementary role, very often providing general or country-specific information before operational decisions must be made. Interestingly, many of today's international managers have pre-career experience in government, the Peace Corps, the armed forces, or missionary service. Although the survey emphasized travel, a one-time trip to Bejing with a stay at a large hotel and scheduled sight-seeing tours does not contribute to cultural knowledge in a significant way. Travel that involves meetings with company personnel, intermediaries, facilitating agents, customers, and government officials, on the other hand, does contribute.

However, from the corporate point of view, the development of a global capability requires experience acquisition in more involved ways. This translates into foreign assignments and networking across borders, for example through the use of multicountry, multicultural teams to develop strategies and programmes. At Nestlé, for example, managers shuffle around a region (such as Asia or Latin America) at four- to five-year intervals and may have tours at headquarters for two to three years between such assignments. This allows these managers to pick up ideas and tools to be used in markets where they have not been used or where they have not been necessary up to now. In Thailand, where supermarkets are revolutionizing consumer-goods marketing, techniques perfected elsewhere in the Nestlé system are being put to effective use. These experiences will then, in turn, be used to develop newly emerging markets in the same region, such as Vietnam.

Various sources and methods are available to the manager for extending his or her knowledge of specific cultures. Most of these sources deal with factual information that provides a necessary basis for market studies. Beyond the normal business literature and its anecdotal information, specific country studies are published by governments, private companies and universities. The Economist Intelligence Unit's (**http://www.eiu.com**) *Country Reports* cover 180 countries. *Culturegrams* (**http://www.culturegrams.com**), which detail the customs of peoples of 187 countries, are published by the Centre for International and Area Studies at Brigham Young University. Many facilitating agencies – such as advertising agencies, banks, consulting firms and transportation companies – provide background information on the markets they serve for their clients: for example, Runzheimer International's (**http://www.runzheimer.com**) international reports on employee relocation and site selection for 44 countries, the Hong Kong and Shanghai Banking Corporation's (**http://www.hsbc.com**) *Business Profile Series* for 22 countries in the Asia-Pacific, and *World Trade* magazine's (**http://www.worldtrademag.com**) 'Put Your Best Foot Forward' series, which covers Europe, Asia, Mexico/Canada and Russia.

Many of the marketer's facilitators are equipped for advising the marketer on the cultural dimensions of their efforts. Their task is not only to avoid cultural mistakes but also to add culture as an ingredient of success in the programme. An example of such services is provided in Exhibit 3.5.

EXHIBIT 3.5

An example of culture consulting

Blunders that could have been avoided with factual information about a foreign market are generally inexcusable. A manager who travels to Taipei without first obtaining a visa and is therefore turned back has no one else to blame. Other oversights may lead to more costly mistakes. For example, in designing shelves for global retailing, the height of the local consumer should be taken into consideration.

International business success requires not only comprehensive fact finding and preparation, but also an ability to understand and fully appreciate the nuances of different cultural traits and patterns. Gaining this interpretive knowledge requires 'getting one's feet wet' over a sufficient length of time.

CULTURAL ANALYSIS

To try to understand and explain differences among cultures and subsequently in cross-cultural behaviour, the marketer can develop checklists and models showing pertinent variables and their interaction. An example of such a model is provided in Exhibit 3.6. This model is based on the premise that all international business activity should be viewed as innovation and as producing change processes.[56] After all, exporters and multinational corporations introduce, from one country to other cultures, marketing practices as well as products and services, which are then perceived to be new and different. Although many question the usefulness of such models, they do bring together, into one presentation, all or most of the relevant variables that have an impact on how consumers in different cultures may perceive, evaluate and adopt new behaviours. However, any manager using such a tool should periodically cross-check its results with reality and experience.

The key variable of the model is propensity to change, which is a function of three constructs: (1) cultural lifestyle of individuals in terms of how deeply held their traditional beliefs and attitudes are and also which elements of culture are dominant; (2) change agents (such as multinational corporations and their practices) and strategic opinion leaders (for example, social elites); and (3) communication about the innovation from commercial sources, neutral sources (such as government), and social sources, such as friends and relatives.

It has been argued that differences in cultural lifestyle can be accounted for by four major dimensions of culture.[57] These dimensions consist of (1) individualism (e.g., 'I' consciousness versus 'we' consciousness), (2) power distance (e.g., level of equality in a society), (3) uncertainty avoidance (e.g., need for formal rules and regulations) and (4) masculinity (e.g., attitudes toward achievement, roles of men and women). Exhibit 3.7 presents a summary of twelve countries'

EXHIBIT 3.6   A model of cross-cultural behaviour

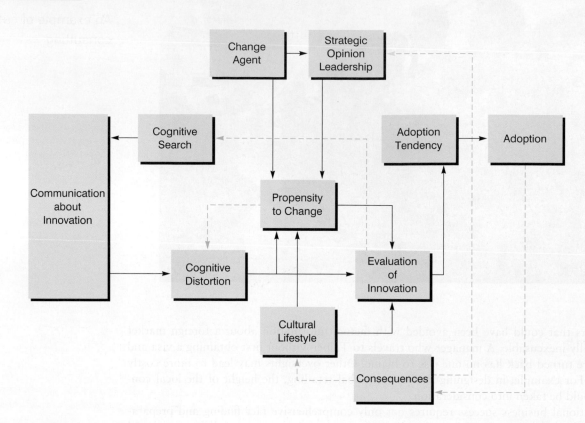

Source: Adapted by permission of the publisher from "A Theory of Cross-Cultural Buying Behavior," by Jagdish N. Sheth and S. Prakash Sethi, in *Consumer and Industrial Buying Behavior,* eds. Arch G. Woodside, Jagdish N. Sheth, and Peter D. Bennett, 1977, 373. Copyright 1977 by Elsevier Science Publishing Co., Inc.

positions along these dimensions. A fifth dimension has also been added to the list to distinguish cultural differences: long-term versus short-term orientation.[58] All the high-scoring countries on this fifth dimension (not shown in the Exhibit) are Asian (e.g., China, Hong Kong, Taiwan, Japan and South Korea), while most western countries (such as Germany and Great Britain) have low scores. Some have argued that this cultural dimension may explain the Japanese marketing success based on market-share (rather than short-term profit) motivation in market development.

Knowledge of similarities along these four dimensions allows us to cluster countries and regions and establish regional and national marketing programmes.[59] An example is provided in Exhibit 3.8, in which the European market is segmented along cultural lines for the development of programmes. Research has shown that the takeoff point for new products (i.e., when initial sales turn into mass market sales) is six years on average in Europe. However, in Northern Europe new products take off almost twice as fast as they do in Southern Europe. Culturally, consumers in Cluster 1 are far more open to new ideas. Cluster 2, consisting of Southern Europe, displays the highest uncertainty avoidance and should therefore be targeted with risk-reducing marketing programmes such as extended warranties and return privileges.[60] It is important to position the product as a continuous innovation that does not require radical changes in consumption patterns.[61] Since the United Kingdom highly regards individualism, promotional appeals should be relevant to individual empowerment. In addition, in order to incorporate the lower power distance, messages should be informal and friendly. In opposite situations, marketing communications must emphasize that the new product is socially accepted. However, if the product is imported, it can sometimes utilize global or foreign cultural positioning. For example, in China, individualism is often used for imported products but almost never for domestic ones.[62] Similarly, channel choice is affected by cultural factors. Firms in societies emphasizing individualism are more likely to choose channel partners based on objective criteria, whereas firms at the opposite end would prefer

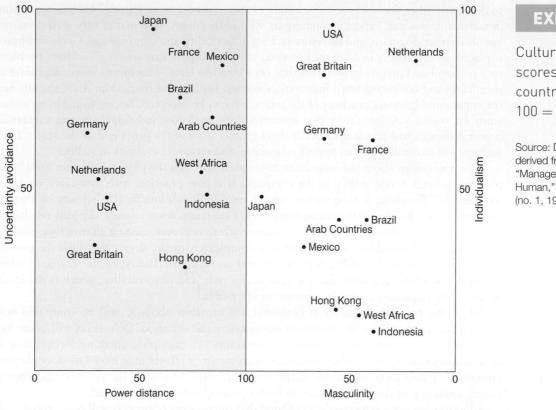

EXHIBIT 3.7

Culture dimension scores for twelve countries (0 = low; 100 = high)

Source: Data for the figure derived from Geert Hofstede, "Management Scientists Are Human," *Management Science* 40 (no. 1, 1994): 4–13.

EXHIBIT 3.8   Culture-based segmentation

			Cultural Characteristics			
	Size (Million)	Power Distance	Uncertainty Avoidance	Individualism	Masculinity	*Illustrative Marketing Implications*
Cluster 1 Austria, Germany, Switzerland, Italy, Great Britain, Ireland	203	Small	Medium	Medium-High	High	Preference for "high-performance" products, use "successful-achiever" theme in advertising, desire for novelty, variety and pleasure, fairly risk-averse market.
Cluster 2 Belgium, France, Greece, Portugal, Spain, Turkey	182	Medium	Strong	Varied	Low-Medium	Appeal to consumer's status and power position, reduce perceived risk in product purchase and use, emphasize product functionality.
Cluster 3 Denmark, Sweden, Finland, Netherlands, Norway	37	Small	Low	High	Low	Relatively weak resistance to new products, strong consumer desire for novelty and variety, high consumer regard for "environmentally friendly" marketers and socially conscious firms.

Source: Sudhir H. Kale, "Grouping Euroconsumers: A Culture-Based Clustering Approach," *Journal of International Marketing* 3 (no. 3, 1995): 42. Reprinted by permission.

to deal with other firms whose representatives they consider to be friends.[63] When negotiating in Germany, one can expect a counterpart who is thorough, systematic, very well prepared, but also rather dogmatic and therefore lacking in flexibility and compromise. Great emphasize is placed on efficiency. In Mexico, however, the counterpart may prefer to address problems on a personal and private basis rather than on a business level. This means more emphasize on socializing and conveying one's humanity, sincerity, loyalty and friendship. Also, the differences in pace and business practices of the region have to be accepted. Boeing found in its annual study on world aviation safety that countries with both low individualism and substantial power distances had accident rates 2.6 times greater than at the other end of the scale. These findings will naturally have an impact on training and service operations of airlines.

Communication about the innovation takes place through the physical product itself (samples) or through a new policy in the company. If a new practice, such as quality circles or pan-regional planning, is in question, results may be communicated in reports or through word-of-mouth by the participating employees. Communication content depends on the following factors: the product's or policy's relative advantage over existing alternatives; compatibility with established behavioural patterns; complexity, or the degree to which the product or process is perceived as difficult to understand and use; trialability, or the degree to which it may be experimented with and not incur major risk; and observability, which is the extent to which the consequences of the innovation are visible.

Before the product or policy is evaluated, information about it will be compared with existing beliefs about the circumstances surrounding the situation. Distortion will occur as a result of selective attention, exposure and retention. As examples, anything foreign may be seen in a negative light, another multinational company's efforts may have failed, or the government may implicitly discourage the proposed activity. Additional information may then be sought from any of the input sources or from opinion leaders in the market.

Adoption tendency refers to the likelihood that the product or process will be accepted. Individualism has a significant positive relationship and uncertainty avoidance a negative relationship with acceptance and diffusion rates of new products.[64] Similar findings have been reached on the penetration of e-commerce in different markets.[65] If an innovation clears the hurdles, it may be adopted and slowly diffused into the entire market. An international manager has two basic choices: adapt company offerings and methods to those in the market or try to change market conditions to fit company programmes. In Japan, a number of western companies have run into obstructions in the Japanese distribution system, where great value is placed on established relationships; everything is done on the basis of favouring the familiar and fearing the unfamiliar. In most cases, this problem is solved by joint venturing with a major Japanese entity that has established contacts. On occasion, when the company's approach is compatible with the central beliefs of a culture, the company may be able to change existing customs rather than adjust to them. Initially, Procter & Gamble's traditional hard-selling style in television commercials jolted most Japanese viewers accustomed to more subtle approaches. Now the ads are being imitated by Japanese competitors. However, this should not be interpreted to mean that Japanese advertising will adapt necessarily to the influence of western approaches. The emphasize in Japan is still on who speaks rather than on what is spoken. That is why, for example, Japan is a market where Procter & Gamble's company name is presented, as well as the brand name of the product, in the marketing communication for a brand rather than using only the product's brand name, which is customary in the European markets.[66]

Although models like the one in Exhibit 3.7 may aid in strategy planning by making sure that all variables and their linkages are considered, any analysis is incomplete without the basic recognition of cultural differences. Adjusting to differences requires putting one's own cultural values aside. James E. Lee proposes that the natural self-reference criterion – the unconscious reference to one's own cultural values – is the root of most international business problems.[67] However, recognizing and admitting this is often quite difficult. The following analytical approach is recommended to reduce the influence of one's own cultural values:

1 Define the problem or goal in terms of domestic cultural traits, habits or norms.

2 Define the problem or goal in terms of foreign cultural traits, habits or norms. Make no value judgements.

3   Isolate the self-reference criterion influence in the problem and examine it carefully to see how it complicates the problem.

4   Redefine the problem without the self-reference criterion influence and solve for the optimal goal situation.

This approach can be applied to product introduction. If Kellogg Co. wants to introduce breakfast cereals into markets where breakfast is traditionally not eaten or where consumers drink very little milk, managers must consider very carefully how to instill this new habit. The traits, habits and norms of breakfast are quite different in the United Kingdom, France and Brazil, and they have to be outlined before the product can be introduced. In France, Kellogg's commercials are aimed as much at providing nutrition lessons as they are at promoting the product. In Brazil, the company advertised on a soap opera to gain entry into the market because Brazilians often emulate the characters of these television shows.

Analytical procedures require constant monitoring of changes caused by outside events as well as the changes caused by the business entity itself. Controlling ethnocentricism – the belief that one's own culture is superior to others – can be achieved only by acknowledging it and properly adjusting to its possible effects in managerial decision making. The international manager needs to be prepared and able to put that preparedness to effective use.[68]

THE TRAINING CHALLENGE

International managers face a dilemma in terms of international and intercultural competence. Lack of adequate foreign language and international business skills by many British firms has resulted in lost contracts, weak negotiations and ineffectual management. It has been suggested that neither the British nor the French have taken the time to understand the culture of the Middle East going back to the time before T.E. Lawrence.[69]

The increase in overall international activity of firms has increased the need for cultural sensitivity training at all levels of the organization. Today's training must take into consideration not only outsiders to the firm but interaction within the corporate family as well. However inconsequential the degree of interaction may seem, it can still cause problems if proper understanding is lacking. Consider, for example, the date 11/12/06 on a message; a European will interpret this as the eleventh of December, but it might also be read as the twelfth of November in another country.

Some companies try to avoid the training problem by hiring only nationals or well-travelled executives for their international operations. This makes sense for the management of overseas operations but will not solve the training need, especially if transfers to a culture unfamiliar to the manager are likely. International experience may not necessarily transfer from one market to another.

To foster cultural sensitivity and acceptance of new ways of doing things within the organization, management must institute internal education programmes. These programmes may include (1) culture-specific information (e.g., data covering other countries, such as videopacks and culturegrams); (2) cultural general information (e.g., values, practices and assumptions of countries other than one's own); and (3) self-specific information (e.g., identifying one's own cultural paradigm, including values, assumptions and perceptions about others).[70] One study found that many companies use mentoring whereby an individual is assigned to someone who is experienced and who will spend the required time squiring and explaining. Talks given by returnees and by visiting lecturers hired specifically for the task round out the formal part of training.[71] At Samsung, several special interest groups were formed to focus on issues such as Japanese society and business practices, the Chinese economy and changes in Europe. In addition, groups also explored cutting-edge business issues, such as new technology and marketing strategies. And for the last few years, Samsung has been sending the brightest junior employees abroad for a year.[72]

The objective of formal training programmes is to foster the four critical characteristics of preparedness, sensitivity, patience and flexibility in managers and other personnel. These programmes vary dramatically in terms of their rigour, involvement and, of course, cost.[73] A summary of these programmes is provided in Exhibit 3.9.

Cross-cultural training
methods

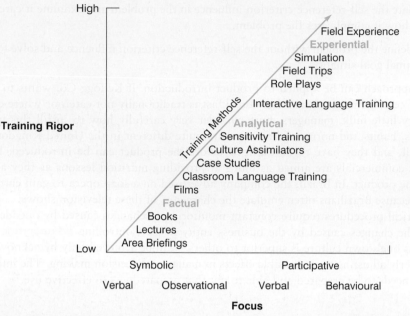

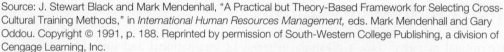

Source: J. Stewart Black and Mark Mendenhall, "A Practical but Theory-Based Framework for Selecting Cross-Cultural Training Methods," in *International Human Resources Management,* eds. Mark Mendenhall and Gary Oddou. Copyright © 1991, p. 188. Reprinted by permission of South-Western College Publishing, a division of Cengage Learning, Inc.

Environmental briefings and cultural orientation programmes are types of area studies programmes. These programmes provide factual preparation for a manager to operate in, or work with people from, a particular country. Area studies should be a basic prerequisite for other types of training programmes. Alone, they serve little practical purpose because they do not really get the manager's feet wet; in other words, action learning is the key.[74] Other, more involved programmes contribute the context in which to put facts so that they can be properly understood.

The cultural assimilator is a programme in which trainees must respond to scenarios of specific situations in a particular country. These programmes have been developed for the Arab countries, Iran, Thailand, Central America and Greece. The results of the trainees' assimilator experience are evaluated by a panel of judges. This type of programme has been used in particular in cases of transfers abroad on short notice.

When more time is available, managers can be trained extensively in language. This may be required if an exotic language is involved. Sensitivity training focuses on enhancing a manager's flexibility in situations that are quite different from those at home. The approach is based on the assumption that understanding and accepting oneself is critical to understanding a person from another culture. While most of the methods discussed are best delivered in face-to-face settings, web-based training is becoming more popular, as seen in *The International Marketplace 3.4.*

Finally, training may involve field experience, which exposes a manager to a different cultural environment for a limited amount of time. Although the expense of placing and maintaining an expatriate is high (and, therefore, the cost of failure is high), field experience is rarely used in training. One field experience technique that has been suggested when the training process needs to be rigorous is the host-family surrogate. This technique places a trainee (and possibly his or her family) in a domestically located family of the nationality to which they are assigned.[75]

Regardless of the degree of training, preparation and positive personal characteristics, a manager will always remain foreign. A manager should never rely on his or her own judgement when local managers can be consulted. In many instances, a manager should have an interpreter present at negotiations, especially if the manager is not completely bilingual. Overconfidence in one's language capabilities can create problems.

THE INTERNATIONAL **MARKETPLACE 3.4**

Online cultural training

The internet can play an important role in preparing marketing people for the international marketplace. While it cannot replace real-life interaction as an experiential tool, it does provide a number of benefits, including comparisons of behaviour in different cultures, and can provide an opportunity to develop the skills needed to interact successfully with people from other cultures. Many companies use online learning as an addition to existing instructor-led programmes. When time is at a premium (due to a fast-approaching assignment/project or to a manager's overall schedule), the role of this learning approach becomes even more critical.

Companies typically rely on the following elements in designing web-based training:

1 **Detailed scenarios.** Much of the training material consists of a detailed, realistic story that is tied into elements of the learner's background; i.e., the session becomes more than a briefing. It becomes a narrated experience full of learning moments for participants. This is made possible by the ability of the web to store and circulate a lot of information instantaneously around the world.

2 **Gradual delivery.** The ability to control the flow of information to the participant supports the learning process in a number of ways. First, the participant is allowed to fit the training into his or her schedule. Second, the real-life flow of information is mimicked and a higher degree of realism is achieved.

3 **Support.** A set of detailed materials is provided to the participants 24 hours a day. At any hour and at any location, participants can check their perceptions against the materials, reinforce learning from a dimly recalled lesson, or seek feedback on an important point or issue.

4 **Relevant exercises.** Participants can be provided topical exercises and activities, the level of which can be adjusted depending on how the participant has invested in the training.

5 **Online discussions.** Sessions can be simulcast to hundreds of participants around the world. The lack of face-to-face interaction can be remedied by having discussion groups where participants can share their experiences with one another. The pooled learning experience is stronger than the experience with one solitary participant.

The following case highlights some of the points made:

Joe Schmed is a marketing representative for a pharmaceutical company. His company has just undertaken a joint venture with a pan-Asian pharmaceutical company based in Kuala Lumpur. In order to develop a successful sales plan, over the next six months Joe will travel to South East Asia at least eight times. The first trip will be in two weeks. However, Joe lacks the time to take two full days out of his schedule for a traditional training programme. Since his undergraduate major was in Asian studies, Joe feels that his cultural understanding is quite adequate. Nevertheless, he would like to brush up on some of his knowledge and gain a better understanding of Asian business. Logging on, he enters a training course, completing parts of it as he finds time – on airplanes and after work, for example.

Online cross-cultural programmes focus on preparing international managers for the host of business scenarios encountered overseas. Training is often specific to a location, priming managers for posts in the Asia-Pacific, Latin America, Europe or the Middle East. Using a range of training tools, from case studies to web-based activities and exercises, programmes cover such topics as intercultural adaptation, recognizing differences in communication styles, negotiation strategies, and practical information aspects of business and daily life.

SOURCES: Mike Bowler, 'Online Learning is Fastest Growing Segment of Higher Education', *Knight Ridder Tribune Business News,* August 17, 2003, 1; 'On-Line Learning', Special Advertising Section, *Fortune*, July 1, 2002, S1–S19; Peter T. Burgi and Brant R. Dykehouse, 'On-Line Cultural Training: The Next Phase', *International Insight*, Winter 2000, 7–10. See also **http://www.runzheimer.com** and **http://www.iorworld.com**.

MAKING CULTURE WORK FOR MARKETING SUCCESS

Culture should not be viewed as a challenge but as an opportunity that can be exploited.[76] This requires, as has been shown in this chapter, an understanding of the differences and their fundamental determinants. Differences can quite easily be dismissed as indicators of inferiority or approaches to be changed; however, the opposite may actually be the case. Best practice knows no one particular origin, nor should it acknowledge boundaries. The following rules serve as a summary of how culture and its appreciation may serve as a tool to ensure marketing success.

- **Embrace local culture.** Many corporate credos include a promise to be the best possible corporate citizens in every community operated in.[77] For example, in 3M's plant near Bangkok, Thailand, a Buddhist shrine, wreathed in flowers, pays homage to the spirits that Thais believe took care of the land prior to the plant's arrival. Showing sensitivity to local customs helps local acceptance and builds employee morale. More importantly, it contributes to a deeper understanding of the market and keeps the marketer from inadvertently doing something to alienate constituents.

- **Build relationships.** Each market has its own unique set of constituents which need to be identified and nurtured. Establishing and nurturing local ties at the various stages of the market-development cycle develops relationships that can be invaluable in expansion and countering political risk. 3M started its preparations for entering the China market soon after President Nixon's historic visit in 1972. For ten years, company officials visited Beijing and entertained visits of Chinese officials to company headquarters in Minneapolis–St. Paul. Such efforts paid off in 1984, when the Chinese government made 3M the first wholly-owned venture in the market. Many such emerging markets require long-term commitment on the part of the marketer.

- **Employ locals to gain cultural knowledge.** The single best way to understand a market is to grow with it by developing human resources and business partnerships along the way. Of the 7500 3M employees in Asia, fewer than ten are from the United States. Of the 34 000 3M employees outside the United States, fewer than 1 per cent are expatriates. The rest are locals who know local customs and the purchasing habits of their compatriots. In every way possible, locals are made equals with their US counterparts. For example, grants are made available for 3M employees to engage in the product-development process with concept and idea development.

- **Help employees understand you.** Employing locals will give a marketer a valuable asset in market development; that is, in acculturation. However, these employees also need their own process of adjustment (i.e., 'corporatization') to be effective. At any given time, more than 30 of 3M's Asian technicians are in the United States, where they learn the latest product and process advances while gaining insight into how the company works. Also, they are able to develop personal ties with people they may work with. Furthermore, they often contribute by infusing their insights into company plans. Similar schemes are in place for distributors. Distributor advisory councils allow intermediaries to share their views with the company.

- **Adapt products and processes to local markets.** Nowhere is a company's commitment to local markets as evident as in its product offering. Global, regional and purely local products are called for, and constant and consistent product-development efforts on a market-by-market basis are warranted to find the next global success. When the sales of 3M's famous Scotchbrite cleaning pads were languishing in South East Asia, company researchers interviewed housewives and domestic help to determine why. They found that traditionally floors are scrubbed with the help of the rough shells of coconuts. 3M responded by making its cleaning pads brown and shaping them like a foot. In China, a big seller for 3M is a composite to fill tooth cavities. In the United States, dentists pack a soft material into the cavity and blast it with a special beam of light, making it as hard as enamel in a matter of seconds. In China, dentists cannot afford this technology. The solution was an air-drying composite that hardens in a matter of minutes, but at a reasonable expense to the dental customer.

- **Coordinate by region.** The transfer of best practice is critical, especially in areas that have cultural similarities. When 3M designers in Singapore discovered that customers used its Nomad household mats in their cars, they spread the word to their counterparts throughout Asia. The company encourages its product managers from different parts of Asia to hold regular periodic meetings and share insights and strategies. The goal of this cross-pollination is to come up with regional programmes and 'Asianise', or even globalize, a product more quickly. Joint endeavours build cross-border esprit de corps, especially when managers may have their own markets' interests primarily at heart.[78]

SUMMARY

Culture is one of the most challenging elements of the international marketplace. This system of learned behaviour patterns characteristic of the members of a given society is constantly shaped by a set of dynamic variables: language, religion, values and attitudes, manners and customs, aesthetics, technology, education and social institutions. In order to cope with this system, an international manager needs both factual and interpretive knowledge of culture. To some extent, the factual can be learned; the interpretation comes only through experience.

The most complicated problems in dealing with the cultural environment stem from the fact that we cannot learn culture – we have to live it. Two schools of thought exist in the business world on how to deal with cultural diversity. One is that business is business the world around, following the model of Pepsi and McDonald's. In some cases, globalization is a fact of life; however, cultural differences are still far from converging.

The other school proposes that companies must tailor business approaches to individual cultures. Setting up policies and procedures in each country has been compared to an organ transplant; the critical question centres on acceptance or rejection. The major challenge to the international manager is to make sure that rejection is not a result of cultural myopia or even blindness.

Successful global companies all share an important quality: patience. They have not rushed into situations but rather built their operations carefully by following the most basic business principles. These principles are to know your challenger, your audience and your customer.

Key terms

acculturation

area studies

back-translation

change agent

cultural assimilator

cultural convergence

cultural knowledge

cultural universals

culture

ethnocentricism

experiential knowledge

factual information

field experience

focus groups

high context cultures

in-depth studies

infrastructures

interpretive knowledge

low context cultures

reference groups

self-reference criterion

sensitivity training

social stratification

Questions for discussion

1   Comment on the assumption, 'If people are serious about doing business with you, they will speak English'.

2   You are on your first business visit to Germany. You feel confident about your ability to speak the language (you studied German in school and have taken a refresher course) and you decide to use it. During introductions, you want to break the ice by asking *'Wie geht's?'* and insisting that everyone call you by your first name. Speculate as to the reaction.

3   What can a company do to culture-sensitize its staff?

4   What can be learned about a culture from reading and attending to factual materials? Given the tremendous increase in international marketing activities, where will companies in a relatively early stage of the internationalization process find the personnel to handle the new challenges?

5   Management at a UK company trying to market tomato paste in the Middle East did not know that, translated into Arabic, tomato paste is 'tomato glue'. How could they have known in time to avoid problems?

6   Give examples of how the self-reference criterion might be manifested.

Internet exercises

1   Various companies, such as GMAC Global Relocation Services, are available to prepare and train international marketers for the cultural challenge. Using their website (**http://www.gmacglobalrelocation.com**), assess its role in helping the international marketer.

2   Compare and contrast an international marketer's home pages for presentation and content; for example, Coca-Cola (**http://www.coca-cola.com**) and its Japanese version (**http://www.cocacola.co.jp**). Are the differences cultural?

Recommended readings

Axtell, Roger E. *Do's and Taboos around the World.* New York: John Wiley & Sons, 1993.

Brett, Jeanne. *Negotiating Globally: How to Negotiate Deals, Resolve Disputes, and Make Decisions across Cultures.* New York: Jossey-Bass, 2001.

Brislin, R.W., W.J. Lonner and R.M. Thorndike, *Cross-Cultural Research Methods.* New York: John Wiley & Sons, 1973.

Carte, Penny and Chris Fox. *Bridging the Culture Gap: A Practical Guide to International Business Communication.* New York: Kogan Page, 2004.

Cellich, Claude and Subhash Jain. *Global Business Negotiations.* Mason, OH: Thomson South-Western, 2003.

Copeland, Lennie and L. Griggs. *Going International: How to Make Friends and Deal Effectively in the Global Marketplace.* New York: Random House, 1990.

Hall, Edward T. and Mildred Reed Hall. *Understanding Cultural Differences.* Yarmouth, ME: Intercultural Press, 1990.

Hoecklin, Lisa. *Managing Cultural Differences.* Wokingham, England: Addison-Wesley, 1995.

Hofstede, Geert. *Culture's Consequences: Comparing Values, Behaviours, Institutions and Organizations across Nations.* London: Sage Publications, 2003.

Kenna, Peggy and Sondra Lacy. *Business Japan: Understanding Japanese Business Culture.* Lincolnwood, IL: NTC, 1994.

Lewis, Richard D. *When Cultures Collide.* London: Nicholas Brealey Publishing, 2000.

Marx, Elizabeth. *Breaking through Culture Shock: What You Need to Succeed in International Business.* London: Nicholas Brealey Publishing, 1999.

O'Hara-Devereux, Mary and Robert Johansen. *Global Work: Bridging Distance, Culture, and Time.* San Francisco: Jossey-Bass Publishers, 1994.

Parker, Barbara. *Globalization and Business Practice: Managing across Boundaries.* London: Sage Publications, 1999.

Terpstra, Vern, and K. David. *The Cultural Environment of International Business.* Cincinnati, OH: South-Western, 1992.

Trompenaars, Fons and Charles Hampden-Turner. *Riding the Waves of Culture.* New York: Irwin, 1998.

Notes

1   Ernest Dichter, 'The World Consumer', *Harvard Business Review* 40 (July–August 1962): 113–122; and Kenichi Ohmae, *Triad Power – The Coming Shape of Global Competition* (New York: The Free Press, 1985), 22–27.

2   'Rule No. 1: Don't Diss the Locals', *Business Week,* May 15, 1995, 8.

3   Alonso Martinez, Ivan De Souza and Francis Liu, 'Multinationals vs Multilatinas', *Strategy and Business* (Fall, 2003): 56–67.

4   'Melting Pots', *The Washington Post,* January 6, 2006, H1, H4.

5   Mary O'Hara-Devereaux and Robert Johansen, *Global Work: Bridging Distance, Culture, and Time* (San Francisco: Jossey-Bass Publishers, 1994), 11.

6   Carla Rapoport, 'Nestlé's Brand Building Machine', *Fortune,* September 19, 1994, 147–156.

7   Alfred Kroeber and Clyde Kluckhohn, *Culture: A Critical Review of Concepts and Definitions* (New York: Random House, 1985), 11.

8   Geert Hofstede, 'National Cultures Revisited', *Asia-Pacific Journal of Management* 1 (September 1984): 22–24.

9   Edward T. Hall, *Beyond Culture* (Garden City, NY: Anchor Press, 1976), 15.

10   Marita von Oldenborgh, 'What's Next for India?' *International Business,* January 1996, 44–47; and Ravi Vijh, 'Think Global, Act Indian', *Export Today,* June 1996, 27–28.

11   'U.N. Body Endorses Cultural Protection', *The Washington Post,* October 21, 2005, A14.

12   'French Movies', **http://www.understandfrance.org/France/FrenchMovies.html**; 'Subsidy Wars', *The Economist,* February 24, 2005, 76.

13   'India Digitizes Age-Old Wisdom', *The Washington Post,* January 8, 2006, A22.

14   **http://www.wto.org/english/tratop_e/trips_e/t_agm0_e.htm**

15   **http://www.eurunion.org/newsweb/HotTopics/GIbackgrounder-4-24-08.doc**.

16   'Britannia Rules the Airwaves', *Foreign Policy,* July/August 2005, 19.

17   'Asian Pop Stars Struggle to Find Cross-Cultural Groove', *The Wall Street Journal,* March 31, 2005, B1, B2.

18   'Multinational Firms Take Steps to Avert Boycotts Over War', *The Wall Street Journal,* April 4, 2003, A1, A4.

19   George P. Mundak, 'The Common Denominator of Cultures', in *The Science of Man in the World,* ed Ralph

Linton (New York: Columbia University Press, 1945), 123–142.

20 **http://www.ethnologue.com**.

21 David A. Ricks, *Blunders in International Business* (Malden, MA: Blackwell Publishers, 2000), Chapter 1.

22 David A. Hanni, John K. Ryans and Ivan R. Vernon, 'Coordinating International Advertising: The Goodyear Case Revisited for Latin America', *Journal of International Marketing* 3 (no. 2, 1995): 83–98.

23 'We Are Tous Québécois', *The Economist,* January 8, 2005, 39; 'France: Mind Your Language', *The Economist,* March 23, 1996, 70–71.

24 'A World Empire by Other Means', *The Economist,* December 22, 2001, 65.

25 Rory Cowan, 'The **e** Does Not Stand for English', *Global Business,* March 2000, L/22.

26 Margareta Bowen, 'Business Translation', *Jerome Quarterly* 8 (August–September 1993): 5–9.

27 'Nokia Veti Pois Mainoskampanjansa', *Uutislehti 100,* June 15, 1998, 5.

28 'Sticky Issue', *The Economist,* August 24, 2002, 51.

29 Edward T. Hall, 'The Silent Language of Overseas Business', *Harvard Business Review* 38 (May–June 1960): 87–96.

30 'Anywhere, Anytime', *The Wall Street Journal,* November 21, 2005, R6.

31 *World Almanac and the Book of Facts* (Mahwah, NJ: Funk & Wagnalls, 2001), 721.

32 Nora Fitzgerald, 'Oceans Apart, but Closer than You Think', *World Trade,* February 1996, 58.

33 'Out from Under', *Marketing News,* July 21, 2003, 1, 9.

34 'Islamic Businesses Emerge From the Shadows', *European Business Forum,* Winter, 2005, 58–61.

35 Roger D. Blackwell, Paul W. Miniard and James F. Engel, *Consumer Behavior* (Mason, OH: Thomson, 2001), Chapter 10.

36 Y. H. Wong and Ricky Yee-kwong, 'Relationship Marketing in China: Guanxi, Favoritism and Adaptation', *Journal of Business Ethics* 22 (no. 2, 1999): 107–118; and Tim Ambler, 'Reflections in China: Re-Orienting Images of Marketing', *Marketing Management* 4 (no. 1, 1995): 23–30.

37 'Iran Unveils Islamic Twin Dolls to Fight Culture War', *AP Worldstream,* March 5, 2002.

38 Douglas McGray, 'Japan's Gross National Cool', *Foreign Policy,* May/June 2002, 44.

39 Earl P. Spencer, 'EuroDisney – What Happened?' *Journal of International Marketing* 3 (no. 3, 1995): 103–114.

40 Sergey Frank, 'Global Negotiations: Vive Les Differences!' *Sales & Marketing Management* 144 (May 1992): 64–69.

41 See, for example, Terri Morrison, *Kiss, Bow, or Shake Hands: How to Do Business in Sixty Countries* (Holbrook, MA: Adams Media, 1994), or Roger Axtell, *Do's and Taboos around the World* (New York: John Wiley & Sons, 1993). For holiday observances, see **http://www.religioustolerance. org/main_day.htm#cal** and **http://www.yahoo.com/ society_and_culture/holidays_and_observances**.

42 James A. Gingrich, 'Five Rules for Winning Emerging Market Consumers', *Strategy and Business* (second quarter, 1999): 68–76.

43 'Feng Shui Strikes Chord', available at **http://www.cnnfn.com/1999/09/11/life/q_fengshui/**.

44 'Feng Shui Man Orders Sculpture out of the Hotel', *South China Morning Post,* July 27, 1992, 4.

45 'Year of the Mouse', *The Economist,* September 30, 2005, 58; 'The Feng Shui Kingdom', *The New York Times,* April 25, 2005, A14.

46 'The New Life of O'Reilly', *Business Week,* June 13, 1994, 64–66; and 'Heinz Aims to Export Taste for Ketchup', *The Wall Street Journal,* November 20, 1992, B1, B10.

47 'U.S. Superstores Find Japanese Are a Hard Sell', *The Wall Street Journal,* February 14, 2000, B1, B4.

48 **http://www.guardian.co.uk/money/2007/mar/20/ kenya.mobilephones**

49 'Why the Chinese Hate to Use VoiceMail', *The Wall Street Journal,* December 1, 2005, B1, B5.

50 The results of the Gallup study are available in 'What the Chinese Want', *Fortune,* October 11, 1999, 229–234.

51 Kenichi Ohmae, 'Managing in a Borderless World', *Harvard Business Review* 67 (May–June 1989): 152–161.

52 Joe Agnew, 'Cultural Differences Probed to Create Product Identity', *Marketing News,* October 24, 1986, 22.

53 Joseph A. McKinney, 'Joint Ventures of United States Firms in Japan: A Survey', *Venture Japan* 1 (no. 2, 1988): 14–19.

54 Peter MacInnis, 'Guanxi or Contract: A Way to Understand and Predict Conflict between Chinese and Western Senior Managers in China-Based Joint Ventures', in Daniel E. McCarthy and Stanley J. Hille, eds, *Multinational Business Management and Internationalization of Business Enterprises* (Nanjing, China: Nanjing University Press, 1993), 345–351.

55 Tim Ambler, 'Reflections in China: Re-Orienting Images of Marketing', *Marketing Management* 4 (Summer 1995): 23–30.

56 Jagdish N. Sheth and S. Prakash Sethi, 'A Theory of Cross-Cultural Buying Behavior', in *Consumer and Industrial Buying Behavior,* eds Arch G. Woodside, Jagdish N. Sheth and Peter D. Bennett (New York: Elsevier North-Holland, 1977), 369–386.

57 Geert Hofstede, *Culture's Consequences: International Differences in Work-Related Values* (Beverly Hills, CA: Sage Publications, 1984).

58 Geert Hofstede and Michael H. Bond, 'The Confucius Connection: From Cultural Roots to Economic Growth', *Organizational Dynamics* 16 (Spring 1988): 4–21.

59 'When Will It Fly?' *The Economist,* August 9, 2003, 51.

60 Sudhir H. Kale, 'Grouping Euroconsumers: A Culture-Based Clustering Approach', *Journal of International Marketing* 3 (no. 3, 1995): 35–48.

61 Jan-Benedict Steenkamp and Frenkel ter Hofstede, 'A Cross-National Investigation into the Individual and National Cultural Antecedents of Consumer Innovativeness', *Journal of Marketing* 63 (April 1999): 55–69.

62 Hong Cheng and John C. Schweitzer, 'Cultural Values Reflected in Chinese and U.S. Television Commercials', *Journal of Advertising Research* 36 (May/June 1996): 27–45.

63 Sudhir H. Kale, 'Distribution Channel Relationships in Diverse Cultures', *International Marketing Review* 8 (no. 3, 1991): 31–45.

64 Sengun Yeniyurt and Janell Townsend', Does Culture Explain Acceptance of New Products in a Country? An Empirical Investigation', *International Marketing Review* 20 (number 4, 2003): 377–397.

65 'Is E-Commerce Boundary-less? Effects of Individualism-Collectivism and Uncertainty Avoidance on Internet Shopping', *Journal of International Business Studies* 35 (number 6, 2004): 545–560.

66 'Exploring Differences in Japan, U.S. Culture', *Advertising Age International,* September 18, 1995, 1–8.

67 James A. Lee, 'Cultural Analysis in Overseas Operations', *Harvard Business Review* 44 (March–April 1966): 106–114.

68 Peter B. Fitzpatrick and Alan S. Zimmerman, *Essentials of Export Marketing* (New York: American Management Organization, 1985), 16.

69 **http://www.finextra.com/fullfeature.asp?id=673**

70 W. Chan Kim and R.A. Mauborgne, 'Cross-Cultural Strategies', *Journal of Business Strategy* 7 (Spring 1987): 28–37.

71 Mauricio Lorence, 'Assignment USA: The Japanese Solution', *Sales & Marketing Management* 144 (October 1992): 60–66.

72 'Special Interest Group Operations', available at **http://www.samsung.com**; and 'Sensitivity Kick', *The Wall Street Journal* (December 30, 1996), 1, 4.

73 Rosalie Tung, 'Selection and Training of Personnel for Overseas Assignments', *Columbia Journal of World Business* 16 (Spring 1981): 68–78.

74 Maureen Lewis, 'Why Cross-Cultural Training Simulations Work', *Journal of European Industrial Training* 29 (number 7, 2005): 593–598.

75 Simcha Ronen, 'Training the International Assignee', in *Training and Career Development,* ed. I. Goldstein (San Francisco: Jossey-Bass, 1989), 426–440.

76 Nadeem Firoz and Taghi Ramin, 'Understanding Cultural Variables is Critical to Success in International Business', *International Journal of Management* 21 (number 3, 2004): 307–324.

77 See, for example, Johnson & Johnson's credo at **www.jnj.com/our_company/our_credo/index.htm**.

78 3M examples are adopted from John R. Engen, 'Far Eastern Front', *World Trade,* December 1994, 20–24.

CHAPTER 4

THE ECONOMIC ENVIRONMENT

And now for the next one billion consumers

During the first fifty years of the info-tech era, more than one billion people have come to use computers, the vast majority in the developed markets of Europe, North America and Australia. Those markets have become increasingly saturated and do not provide the needed growth. Computer sales are expected to increase a mere 6 per cent per year between 2005 and 2008. The next billion consumers have to be found in the emerging markets of the twenty-first century: China, India, Russia, South Africa and Brazil. Sales in info-tech are expected to increase by 11 per cent per year over the next five years, fuelled mostly by the burgeoning ranks of millions of middle-class consumers. These newly wealthy consumers are showing preferences for fashionable brands as well as for features every bit as sophisticated as their developed-country counterparts.

The challenges of succeeding in the emerging markets are forcing the established global players to come up with innovative new approaches. Areas in which fundamental rethinking is required include the following:

- *Design.* Solutions have to be simpler and more durable. TVS Electronics, an Indian printer manufacturer, is producing devices for India's 1.2 million small shops. They are an all-in-one computer, cash register and inventory-management system. They can be operated with icons, because many of the clerks are illiterate. They have to be robust to withstand the elements, such as heat and dust.

- *Innovation.* Marketers have to innovate for the peculiarities of emerging markets. Electricity may often be unavailable and unreliable. Hewlett-Packard adjusted to this by designing a small solar panel to charge digital printers for itinerant photographers in India. In South Africa, HP is working with a solar fabric that is cheaper and less fragile.

- *Business development.* Old strategies may have to be adjusted. IBM believes that it can do well in China only by supplying technology to local companies. It developed a low-cost, $12 microprocessor and a simple network computer for China's Culturecom, which is selling computers and internet access services in the country's rural areas.

- *Competition.* Companies such as Cisco, Dell and Microsoft dominate global markets. However, many new challengers are using their low costs and intimate knowledge of local, or similar emerging markets, to expand their businesses. Chinese network systems company Huawei can charge 50 per cent less than Cisco and has made sales in markets in Africa and Europe.

- *Pricing.* Pressure on prices can lead to innovative solutions in financing. Poland needed to modernize its motor vehicle driver's licencing system but could not afford it. Hewlett-Packard agreed to install Poland's new computer system in exchange for a cut of the fees drivers pay each time they get a new licence or renew an old one.

While the first billion customers may have created a sector with annual revenues of more than $1 trillion, sales for the second billion will not reach the same level. Lower prices in these markets may put pressure on prices everywhere. However, staying out of these markets is not an option.

SOURCES: Tarun Khanna, Krishna Palepu and Jayant Sinha, 'Strategies that Fit Emerging Markets', *Harvard Business Review* 83 (June 2005): 63–76; and 'Tech's Future', *Business Week,* September 27, 2004, 82–89.

The assessment of a foreign market environment should start with the evaluation of economic variables relating to the size and nature of the markets. Due to the large number of worthwhile alternatives, initial screening of markets should be done efficiently yet effectively enough, with a wide array of economic criteria, to establish a preliminary estimate of market potential. One of the most basic characterizations of the world economy is provided in Exhibit 4.1, which incorporates many of the economic variables pertinent to marketers.

The Group of Five – listed in Exhibit 4.1 as the United States, Britain, France, Germany and Japan – consists of the major industrialized countries of the world. This group is sometimes expanded to the Group of Seven (by adding Italy and Canada) and to the Group of Ten (by adding Sweden, the Netherlands and Belgium). It may also be expanded to encompass the members of the Organization for Economic Cooperation and Development, OECD (which consists of 30 countries: Western Europe, the United States, Australia, Canada, Czech Republic, Hungary, Japan, Mexico, New Zealand, Poland, Slovakia, South Korea and Turkey).

Important among the middle-income developing countries are the newly industrialized countries (NICs), which include Singapore, Taiwan, Korea, Hong Kong, Brazil and Mexico (some propose adding Malaysia and the Philippines to the list as well). Some of these NICs will earn a new acronym, RIC (rapidly industrializing country). Over the past 20 years, Singapore has served as a hub, providing critical financial and managerial services to the South East Asian markets. Singapore has successfully attracted foreign investment, mostly regional corporate headquarters and knowledge-intensive industries, and has served as one of the main gateways for Asian trade. Its exports have reached well over 300 per cent of GDP.[1]

The major oil-exporting countries, in particular the eleven members of the Organization of Petroleum Exporting Countries (OPEC) and countries such as Russia, are dependent on

EXHIBIT 4.1   The global economy

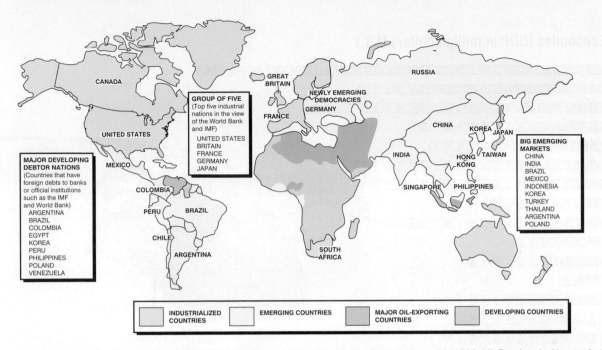

Source: Adapted and updated from "The Global Economy," *The Washington Post,* January 19, 1986, HI. Reprinted with permission.

the price of oil for their world market participation. A relatively high dollar price per barrel (as high as $70 in 2006) works very much in these countries' favour.

Many of the emerging economies will depend on the success of their industrialization efforts in the years to come, even in the case of resource-rich countries that may find commodity prices being driven down by human-made substitutes. China has become the world's largest exporter of textiles since beginning to increase production in the 1980s. Despite an image of hopeless poverty, India has nearly 300 million middle-class consumers, more than Germany. A special group in this category consists of the countries saddled with a major debt burden, such as Egypt and Peru. The degree and form of their participation in the world market will largely depend on how the debt issue is solved with the governments of the major industrialized countries and the multilateral and commercial banks. However, as shown in *The International Marketplace 4.1*, these countries, which constitute the majority of the world's population, may also provide the biggest potential market opportunity for marketers in the twenty-first century.[2]

In less-developed countries, debt problems and falling commodity prices make market development difficult. Africa, the poorest continent, owes the rest of the world $375 billion, an amount equal to three-quarters of its GNP and nearly four times its annual exports. Another factor contributing to the challenging situation is that only 1 per cent of the world's private investment goes to sub-Saharan Africa.[3]

In the former centrally planned economies, dramatic changes have been under way for the last 15 years. A hefty capital inflow has been key to modernizing the newly emerging democracies of both Central and Eastern Europe. They are crippled by $60 billion in foreign debt and decades of Communist misrule. Desperately needed will be western technology, management and marketing know-how to provide better jobs and put more locally made and imported consumer goods in the shops. Within the groups, prospects vary: The future for countries such as Hungary, the Baltics, the Czech Republic and Poland looks far better than it does for Russia, as they reap the benefits of membership in the European Union.[4]

Classifications of markets will vary by originator and intended use. Marketers will combine economic variables to fit their planning purposes by using those that relate directly to

Economic strength

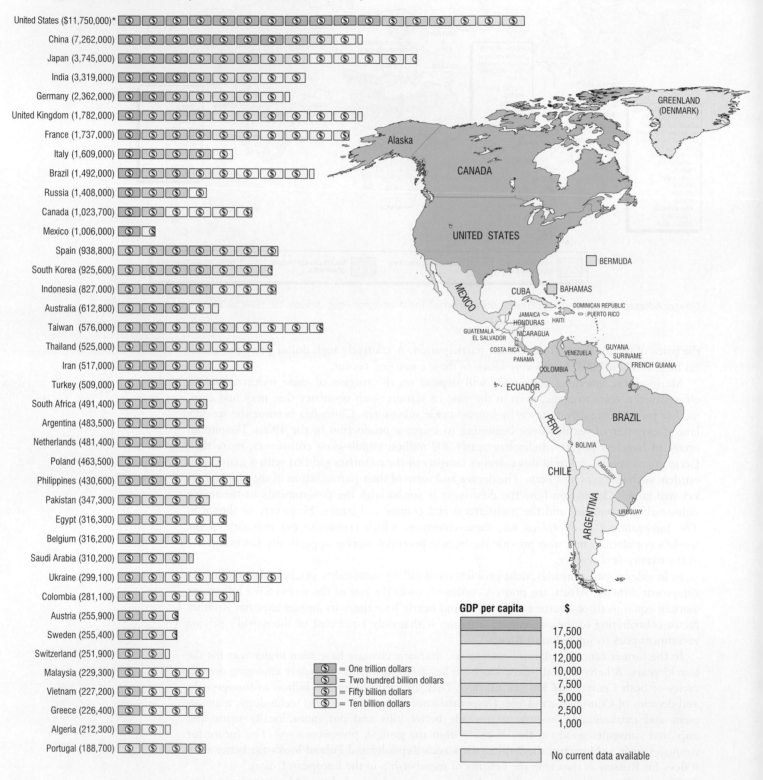

Top World Economies (GDP in million dollars U.S.)

United States ($11,750,000)*

China (7,262,000)

Japan (3,745,000)

India (3,319,000)

Germany (2,362,000)

United Kingdom (1,782,000)

France (1,737,000)

Italy (1,609,000)

Brazil (1,492,000)

Russia (1,408,000)

Canada (1,023,700)

Mexico (1,006,000)

Spain (938,800)

South Korea (925,600)

Indonesia (827,000)

Australia (612,800)

Taiwan (576,000)

Thailand (525,000)

Iran (517,000)

Turkey (509,000)

South Africa (491,400)

Argentina (483,500)

Netherlands (481,400)

Poland (463,500)

Philippines (430,600)

Pakistan (347,300)

Egypt (316,300)

Belgium (316,200)

Saudi Arabia (310,200)

Ukraine (299,100)

Colombia (281,100)

Austria (255,900)

Sweden (255,400)

Switzerland (251,900)

Malaysia (229,300)

Vietnam (227,200)

Greece (226,400)

Algeria (212,300)

Portugal (188,700)

$ = One trillion dollars
$ = Two hundred billion dollars
$ = Fifty billion dollars
$ = Ten billion dollars

GDP per capita $

17,500
15,000
12,000
10,000
7,500
5,000
2,500
1,000

No current data available

Source: Based on *The World Almanac*, 2003.

the product and/or service the company markets, such as the market's ability to buy. For example, a company marketing electrical products (from power generators to appliances) may take into account both general country considerations – such as population, GNP, geography, manufacturing as a percentage of national product, infrastructure and per capita income – and narrower industry-specific considerations of interest to the company and its marketing efforts, such as extent of use of the product, total imports and EU share of these imports.

The discussion that follows is designed to summarize a set of criteria that helps identify foreign markets and screen the most opportune ones for future entry or change of entry mode. Discussed are variables on which information is readily available from secondary sources such as international organizations, individual governments and private organizations or associations.

World Bank and United Nations publications and individual countries' *Statistical Abstracts* provide the starting point for market investigations. The more developed the market, the more data available. Data are available on past developments as well as on projections of broader categories such as population and income. Euromonitor, for example, publishes *World Consumer Income & Expenditure Patterns,* which covers 71 countries around the world.

MARKET CHARACTERISTICS

The main dimensions of a market can be captured by considering variables such as those relating to the population and its various characteristics, infrastructure, geographical features of the environment and foreign involvement in the economy.

Population

The total world population exceeded six billion people in 1999 and is expected to close in on eight billion by 2025. The number of people in a particular market provides one of the most basic indicators of market size and is, in itself, indicative of the potential demand for certain staple items that have universal appeal and are generally affordable. As indicated by the data in Exhibit 4.2, population is not evenly divided among the major regions of the world; Asia holds over half the world's population.

These population figures can be analyzed in terms of marketing implications by noting that countries belonging to the European Union (EU) constitute 85 per cent of the Western European population, and with the expansion of the EU in 2004, the percentage rose to 95. The two largest entities in Asia, China and India, constitute nearly 70 per cent of Asia's population. The greatest population densities are also to be found in Europe, providing the international marketer with a strategically located centre of operation and ready access to the major markets of the world.

Population figures themselves must be broken down into meaningful categories in order for the marketer to take better advantage of them. Since market entry decisions may lie in the future, it is worthwhile to analyze population projections in the areas of interest and focus on their possible implications. Exhibit 4.2 includes United Nations projections that point to a population explosion, but mainly in the developing countries. Northern Europe will show nearly zero population growth for the next 30 years, whereas the population of Africa will triple. Even in the low- or zero-growth markets, the news is not necessarily bad for the international marketer. Those in the 25 to 45 age group, whose numbers are increasing, are among the most affluent consumers of all, having formed family units and started to consume household goods in large quantities as they reach the peak of their personal earnings potential. Early in this century, they are expected to start spending more on leisure goods and health care and related services.[5]

To influence population growth patterns, governments will have to undertake, with the help of private enterprise, quite different social marketing tasks. These will range from promoting and providing incentives for larger families (in Scandinavia, for example) to increased family planning efforts (in Thailand, for example). Regardless of the outcome of such government programmes, current trends will further accelerate the division of world markets into the 'haves' and the 'have-nots'. More adjustment capability will be required on the part of companies that want to market in the developing countries because of lower purchasing power of

EXHIBIT 4.2   World population: Present and the shape of things to come

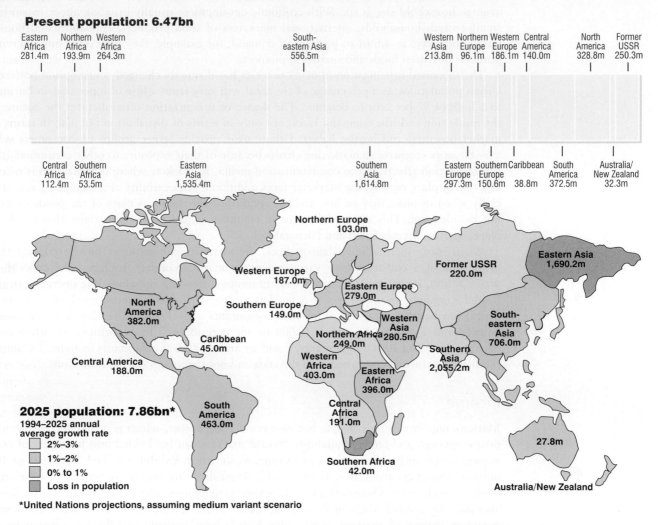

Present population: 6.47bn

Eastern Africa	Northern Africa	Western Africa	South-eastern Asia	Western Asia	Northern Europe	Western Europe	Central America	North America	Former USSR
281.4m	193.9m	264.3m	556.5m	213.8m	96.1m	186.1m	140.0m	328.8m	250.3m

Central Africa	Southern Africa	Eastern Asia	Southern Asia	Eastern Europe	Southern Europe	Caribbean	South America	Australia/New Zealand
112.4m	53.5m	1,535.4m	1,614.8m	297.3m	150.6m	38.8m	372.5m	32.3m

Northern Europe
103.0m

Former USSR
220.0m

Eastern Asia
1,690.2m

Western Europe
187.0m

Eastern Europe
279.0m

North America
382.0m

Southern Europe
149.0m

Western Asia
280.5m

South-eastern Asia
706.0m

Caribbean
45.0m

Northern Africa
249.0m

Central America
188.0m

Western Africa
403.0m

Southern Asia
2,055.2m

Eastern Africa
396.0m

South America
463.0m

Central Africa
191.0m

27.8m

2025 population: 7.86bn*
1994–2025 annual
average growth rate

- 2%–3%
- 1%–2%
- 0% to 1%
- Loss in population

Southern Africa
42.0m

Australia/New Zealand

*United Nations projections, assuming medium variant scenario

Source: Based on *Population Reference Bureau,* 2005 and *U.S. Census Bureau,* 2005. See also **http://www.census.gov**.

individuals and increasing government participation in the marketing of basic products. However, as the life expectancy in a market extends and new target markets become available, international marketers may be able to extend their products' life cycles by marketing them abroad.

Depending on the marketer's interest, population figures can be classified to show specific characteristics of their respective markets. Age distribution and life expectancy correlate heavily with the level of development of the market. Industrialized countries, with their increasing median age and a larger share of the population above 65, will open unique opportunities for international marketers with new products and services. For example, Kimberly-Clark markets its Depend line for those with incontinence problems both in Europe and North America.

Interpretation of demographics will require some degree of experiential knowledge. As an example, which age categories of females should be included in an estimate of market potential for a new contraceptive? This would vary from the very early teens in the developing countries to higher age categories in developed countries, where the maturing process is later.

An important variable for the international marketer is the size of the household. A household describes all the persons, both related and unrelated, who occupy a housing unit.[6] Within the EU, the average household size has shrunk from 2.9 to 2.7 persons in the last 25 years and is expected to decline further.[7] One factor behind the overall growth in households, and the subsequent decline in the average size, has been the increase in the numbers of divorced and sole survivor households. One-person households are most common in Norway and Germany. This compares strikingly with countries such as Colombia, where the average household size is six. With economic development usually bringing about more, but smaller-sized, households, international marketers of food products, appliances and household goods have to adjust to patterns of demand; for example, they may offer single-serving portions of frozen foods and smaller appliances.

The increased urbanization of many markets has distinctly changed consumption patterns. Urban populations as a percentage of the total will vary from a low of 6 per cent in Burundi to a high of 97 per cent in Belgium. The degree of urbanization often dictates the nature of the marketing task the company faces, not only in terms of distribution but also in terms of market potential and buying habits. Urban areas provide larger groups of consumers who may be more receptive to marketing efforts because of their exposure to other consumers (the demonstration effect) and to communication media. In markets where urbanization is recent and taking place rapidly, the marketer faces additional responsibility as a change agent, especially when incomes may be low and the conditions for the proper use of the products may not be adequate. This is especially true in countries where rapid industrialization is taking place, such as Greece, Spain and Portugal.

When using international data sources, the international marketer must recognize that definitions of a construct may vary among the many secondary sources. The concept of urbanization, for example, has different meanings depending on where one operates. In the United Kingdom, an urban area is defined as a place of 10,000[8] or more inhabitants; in Sweden, it is a built-up area with at least 200 inhabitants with no more than 200 metres between houses; and a city or town has 10,000 or more residents.[9] In Mauritius, an urban area between 1000 and 10,000 inhabitants,[10] and an area of 10,000 inhabitants in India.[11] Comparability, therefore, is concerned with the ends and not the means (or the definition).

Income

Markets require not only people but also purchasing power, which is a function of income, prices, savings, and credit availability. World markets can be divided into four tiers of consumers based on broad measures of income, as shown in Exhibit 4.3. Tier 1 consists of 100 million consumers from around the world. Typically, this means consumers in developed markets, such as the Organization for Econonic Cooperation and Development (OECD), but also includes the rich elites in developing markets. Tier 2 consists of the lower-income segments in developed markets, while Tier 3 includes the rising middle-class consumers in emerging markets. Tier 4 is home to the average consumer in developing markets.

EXHIBIT 4.3

World economic pyramid

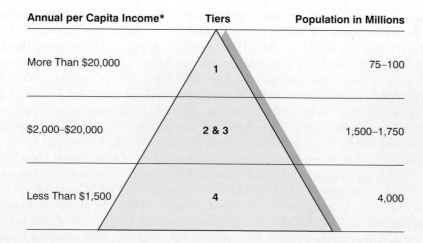

Annual per Capita Income*	Tiers	Population in Millions
More Than $20,000	1	75–100
$2,000–$20,000	2 & 3	1,500–1,750
Less Than $1,500	4	4,000

*Based on purchasing power parity in U.S.$

Source: U.N. World Development Reports.

Apart from basic staple items, for which population figures provide an estimate, income is most indicative of the market potential for most consumer and industrial products and services. For the marketer to make use of information on gross domestic products of various nations, further knowledge is needed on distribution of income. Per capita GDP is often used as a primary indicator for evaluating purchasing power. This figure shows great variation between countries, as indicated by Luxembourg's $62,700 and Ethiopia's $800. The wide use of GDP figures can be explained by their easy availability, but they should nevertheless be used with caution. In industrialized countries, the richest 10 per cent of the population consume 20 per cent of all goods and services, whereas the respective figure for the developing countries may be as high as 50 per cent.[12] In some markets, income distribution produces wide gaps between population groups. The more developed the economy, the more income distribution tends to converge toward the middle class.

The international marketer can use the following classification as a planning guide:

1 *Very low family incomes*. Subsistence economies tend to be characterized by rural populations in which consumption relies on personal output or barter. Some urban centres may provide markets. Example: Cameroon.

2 *Very low, very high family incomes*. Some countries exhibit strongly bimodal income distributions. The majority of the population may live barely above the subsistence level, but there is a strong market in urban centres and a growing middle class. The affluent are truly affluent and will consume accordingly. Examples: India, Mexico.

3 *Low, medium, high family incomes*. Industrialization produces an emerging middle class with increasing disposable income. The very low and very high income classes tend to remain for traditional reasons of social class barriers. Example: Portugal.

4 *Mostly medium family incomes*. The advanced industrial nations tend to develop institutions and policies that reduce extremes in income distribution, resulting in a large and comfortable middle class able to purchase a wide array of both domestic and imported products and services. Example: Denmark.

Although the national income figures provide a general indication of a market's potential, they suffer from various distortions. Figures available from secondary sources are often in US dollars. The per capita income figures may not be a true reflection of purchasing power if the currencies involved are distorted in some way. For example, fluctuations in the value of the US dollar may distort real-income and standard-of-living figures. The goods and services in different countries have to be valued consistently if the differences are to reflect real differences in the volumes of goods produced. The use of purchasing power parities (PPP) instead of exchange rates is intended to achieve this objective. PPPs show how many units of currency are needed in one country to buy the amount of goods and services that one unit of currency will buy in another country. Exhibit 4.4 provides GDP data based on PPPs for selected countries.

In addition, using a monetary measure may not be a proper and all-inclusive measure of income. For example, in developing economies where most of the consumption is either self-produced or bartered, reliance on financial data alone would seriously understate the standard of living. Further, several of the service-related items (for example, protective services and travel), characteristic of the industrialized countries' national income figures, do not exist for markets at lower levels of development.

Moreover, the marketer will have to take into consideration variations in market potential in individual markets. Major urban centres in developing countries may have income levels comparable to those in more developed markets, while rural areas may not have incomes needed to buy imported goods.

In general, income figures are useful in the initial screening of markets. However, in product-specific cases, income may not play a major role and startling scenarios may emerge. Some products, such as motorcycles and television sets in China are in demand regardless of their high price in relation to wages because of their high prestige value. Some products are in demand because of their foreign origin. As an example, European luxury cars have lucrative markets in countries where per capita income figures may be low

EXHIBIT 4.4

Gross domestic product per capita adjusted to purchasing power parities for selected countries, 2009, in £

Highest			Lowest		
1.	Liechtenstein	82,167	227.	Congo DR	202
2.	Qatar	81,898	226.	Burundi	202
3.	Luxembourg	52,462	225.	Liberia	336
4.	Bermuda	47,017	224.	Somalia	403
5.	Norway	39,416	223.	Guinea Bissau	403
6.	Jersey	38,336	222.	Niger	470
7.	Kuwait	36,310	221.	Eritrea	470
8.	Singapore	33,826	220.	Central AR	470
9.	Brunei	33,691	219.	Afghanistan	538
10.	Faroe Islands	32,428	218.	Mozambique	605
11.	United States	31,217	217.	Malawi	605
12.	Andora	30,210	216.	Rwanda	605
13.	Guensey	30,007	215.	Sierra Leone	605
14.	Cayman Islands	30,006	214.	Togo	605
15.	Hong Kong	28,732	213.	Ethopia	605

Source: CIA (2010), 'Country Comparison: GDP – per capita (PPP)', Online. Available from **https://www.cia.gov/library/publications/the-world-factbook/rankorder/2004rank.html** (Accessed 12/5/10).

but there are wealthy consumers who are able and willing to buy them. For example, Mercedes-Benz's target audience in India is families earning 1 million rupees (approximately $30,000). Earnings at that level are enough for a lifestyle to rival that of a European family with an income three times higher due to a much higher level of disposable income.[13] Further, the lack of income in a market may preclude the marketing of a standardized product but, at the same time, provide an opportunity for an adjusted product. A packaged goods company, confronted with considerable disparity in income levels within the same country, can adapt product size or product features. By substituting cheaper parts and materials, successful international marketers can make both consumer and industrial products more affordable in less affluent markets and therefore reach a wider target audience.

Consumption patterns

Depending on the sophistication of a country's data collection systems, economic data on consumption patterns can be obtained and analyzed. The share of income spent on necessities will provide an indication of the market's development level as well as an approximation of how much money the consumer has left for other purchases. Engel's laws[14] provide some generalizations about consumers' spending patterns and are useful generalizations when precise data are not available. They state that as a family's income increases, the percentage spent on food will decrease, the percentage spent on housing and household operations will be roughly constant, and the amount saved or spent on other purchases will increase. Expenditure on food items has been increasing from 2003. Although it was expected to decrease in 2009, it did not because of the global recession (see Exhibit 4.5)[15]

In Western Europe, expenditures on clothing typically account for 5 to 9 per cent of all spending, but in poorer countries the proportion may be lower. In some low-wage areas, a significant proportion of clothing is homemade or locally made at low cost, making comparisons not entirely accurate. Eastern European households spend an inordinate proportion of their incomes on foodstuffs but quite a low proportion on housing. The remaining, less absolutely central areas of consumption (household goods, leisure and transportation) are most vulnerable to short-term cancellation or postponement and thus serve as indicators for the strength of confidence in the market in general.

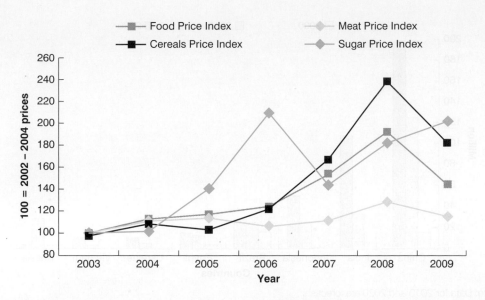

EXHIBIT 4.5

International food prices
indices: 2003–2009

Note: 100 = average export prices for 2002–2004, weighed according to exports' shares of different commodities. Sugar price index refers to index form of the International Sugar Agreement prices with 2002–2004 as base. 2009 figures refer to January–July 2009.

Source: FAO.

In large markets, such as China, India and the United States, marketers need to exercise care in not assuming uniformity across regions. In China, for example, marked differences exist between geographic markets and consumers in urban and rural markets. Nearly 60 per cent of PCs sold find customers in the economically developed east, north and south, especially in the big coastal cities. In the submarket of servers, the share is even higher at 65 per cent. Urban consumers spend 2.5 times more on food and 10 times more on entertainment than their rural counterparts. This does not mean that inland urban markets and rural areas are without opportunity. Massive investments by the central and provincial governments have linked these areas to the coastal ports and export/import markets by multi-lane highways, in their attempt to close some of the income gaps between regions in China.[16]

Data on the growth of a new type of consumer allow a further evaluation of market potential. Exhibit 4.6 shows that a new middle class is developing in emerging market economies as significant proportions of the population rise up from poverty in line with rapid economic growth. The expansion of this middle class not only provides competition for labour and resources, but also enormous potential for global consumer markets. As a result, there will be a gradual shift in the dominance of global consumer markets from advanced economies to emerging market economies.[17] This does not necessarily indicate lack of market potential; replacement markets or the demand for auxiliary products may offer attractive opportunities to the international marketer. Low rates of diffusion should be approached cautiously, because they can signal a market opportunity or lack thereof resulting from low income levels, use of a substitute product, or lack of acceptance.

General consumption figures are valuable, but they must be viewed with caution because they may conceal critical product-form differences; for example, size of appliances may vary per global market. Information about existing product usage can nevertheless provide indirect help to international marketers. As an example, a large number of telephones, and their even distribution among the population or a target group, may allow market research via telephone interviewing.

A problem for marketers in general is inflation; varying inflation rates complicate this problem in international markets. Many of the industrialized countries, such as Germany and Japan, have recently been able to keep inflation rates at single-digit levels, while some have suffered from chronic inflation (Exhibit 4.7). Inflation affects the ability of both industrial customers and consumers to buy and also introduces uncertainty into both the marketer's

Number of households
with annual disposable
income of £3 262–9 785
in selected economies:
2000–2020

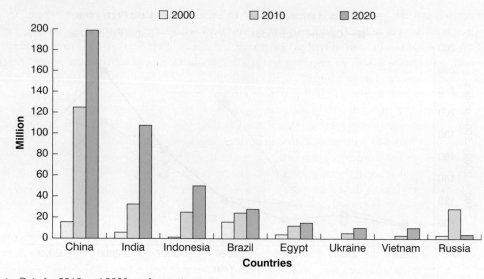

Note: Data for 2010 and 2020 are forecasts.
Euromonitor (2010), 'Emerging Focus: Rising middle class in emerging markets'. Online. Available from:
http://blog.euromonitor.com/2010/03/emerging-focus-rising-middle-class-in-emerging-markets.html

Source: Euromonitor International from national statistics.

Consumer price index
for selected countries

Country	1995	1998	2001	2004
Argentina	3.38	0.92	−1.07	4.42
Australia	4.64	0.85	4.38	2.34
Bangladesh	8.52	6.97	1.39	3.16
Brazil	66.01	3.20	6.86	6.60
Canada	2.17	0.99	2.53	1.83
China (PRC, excl. Hong Kong)	16.90	−0.84	0.34	3.99
Ecuador	22.89	36.10	37.68	2.74
Egypt	15.74	4.18	2.27	11.27
France	1.78	0.67	1.63	2.13
Ghana	59.46	14.62	32.91	12.63
India	10.22	13.23	3.68	3.77
Japan	−0.13	0.66	−0.73	−0.01
Mexico	35.00	15.93	6.36	4.69
Romania	32.24	59.10	34.47	11.88
South Africa	8.68	6.88	5.70	1.39
South Korea	4.50	7.54	4.03	3.61
Turkey	88.11	84.64	54.40	8.60
United States	2.81	1.55	2.83	2.68
United Kingdom	3.41	3.42	1.82	2.96
Venezuela	59.92	35.78	12.53	12.75

Source: Compiled data from *International Financial Statistics* (Washington, DC: International Monetary
Fund, various editions). © International Monetary Fund; **http://www.imf.org**.

planning process and consumers' buying habits. In high-inflation markets, the marketer may have to make changes in the product (more economical without compromising quality), promotion (more rational), and distribution (more customer involvement) to meet customer needs and maintain demand. In response to rapidly escalating prices, a government will often invoke price controls. The setting of maximum prices for products may cause the international marketer to face unacceptable profit situations, future investments may not be made, and production may even have to be stopped.

Another challenge for international marketers is the debt problem. Many of the developing countries are saddled with a collective debt of $1.2 trillion (Exhibit 4.8). Debt crises crush nations' buying power and force imports down and exports up to meet interest payments. For example, the US trade balance with Latin nations has deteriorated from an annual surplus of $6 billion in 1980 to a deficit of $700 billion annually between 2005–2008.[18] To continue growing, many companies are looking at developing nations because of the potential they see 10 to 15 years ahead. Companies from the European Union typically face competition in these regions from entities that are often aided by their government's aid grants, as well as by companies from the rest of the world who do business with the help of government export credits that have interest rates lower than those provided by companies from the European Union.

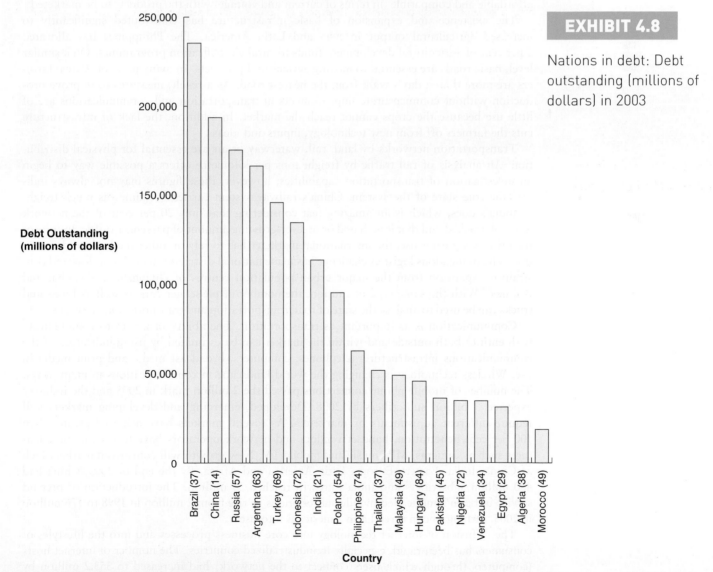

EXHIBIT 4.8

Nations in debt: Debt outstanding (millions of dollars) in 2003

Numbers in parentheses indicate percentages of GDP.

Source: Based on WDI Online, World Bank, accessed January 17, 2006; see also **http://www.worldbank.org**.

Access to these markets can be achieved by helping political leaders provide jobs and by increasing exports. Heinz, for example, operates in many developing countries through joint ventures in which Heinz holds 51 per cent. To sell products in these markets, companies may have to engage in countertrade, either by accepting payment in goods or by supporting customers' efforts in their international marketing.[19] Many industrialized countries, such as Japan, France and the United Kingdom are seeking ways to ease the burden facing debtor nations.

Infrastructure

The availability and quality of an infrastructure is critically important in evaluating marketing operations abroad. Each international marketer will rely heavily on services provided by the local market for transportation, communication and energy, as well as on organizations participating in the facilitating functions of marketing: marketing communications, distributing, information, and financing. Indicators such as steel consumption, cement production, and electricity production relate to the overall industrialization of the market and can be used effectively by suppliers of industrial products and services. As an example, energy consumption per capita may serve as an indicator of market potential for electrical markets, provided evenness of distribution exists over the market. Yet the marketer must make sure that the energy is affordable and compatible (in terms of current and voltage) with the products to be marketed.

The existence and expansion of basic infrastructure has contributed significantly to increased agricultural output in Asia and Latin America. The Philippines has allocated 5 per cent of agricultural development funds to rural electrification programmes. On a similar level, basic roads are essential to moving agricultural products. In many parts of Africa, farmers are more than a day's walk from the nearest road. As a result, measures to improve production without commensurate improvements in transportation and communications are of little use because the crops cannot reach the market. In addition, the lack of infrastructure cuts the farmers off from new technology, inputs and ideas.

Transportation networks by land, rail, waterway or air are essential for physical distribution. An analysis of rail traffic by freight tons per kilometre offers a possible way to begin an investigation of transportation capabilities; however, these figures may not always indicate the true state of the system. China's railway system carries five times as much freight as India's does, which is an amazing feat considering that only 20 per cent of the network is doubletracked and that it is shared by an ever-growing amount of passenger traffic. In spite of the railway's greater use, the international marketer has to rely on other methods of distribution. The tremendous logistics challenge has made national distribution in China slow and constrained expansion from the major urban population centres of Guangzhou, Shanghai and Beijing.[20] With the same type of caution, the number of passenger cars as well as buses and trucks can be used to analyse the state of road transportation and transportation networks.

Communication is as important as transportation. The ability of a firm to communicate with entities both outside and within the market can be estimated by using indicators of the communications infrastructure: telephones, computers, broadcast media and print media in use. Wireless technology is changing the world landscape in communications in many ways. The number of mobile phone connections passed the 2 billion mark in 2005 and the industry expected 3 billion subscribers by 2008. Developed, emerging and developing markets will require different adjustments by marketers. As several markets have achieved greater than 100 per cent penetration, handset vendors and network operators have to provide new features such as cameras, MP3 music and mobile TV. New growth will come from markets such as China, India, Eastern Europe, Latin America and Africa. By the end of 2005, China had 400 million subscribers and India's growth reached 55 million. The introduction of prepaid service in Latin America led mobile subscriptions to rise from 2 million in 1998 to 176 million in 2005, turning one in three Latin Americans into users.[21]

The diffusion of internet technology into core business processes and into the lifestyles of consumers has been rapid, especially in industrialized countries. The number of internet hosts (computers through which users connect to the network) had increased to 353.2 million by 2005, up from 56.2 million in 1999.[22] The total number of people using the internet is difficult to estimate. Estimates in 2008 put the number at nearly 1.5 billion (see Exhibit 4.9). There are

EXHIBIT 4.9   World internet usage and population statistics

World Regions	Population (2008 est.)	Internet Users Dec/31, 2000	Internet Usage, Latest Data	% Population (Penetration)	Usage % of World	Usage Growth % 2000–2008
Africa	955,206,348	4,514,400	**51,065,630**	5.3	3.5	1031.2
Asia	3,776,181,949	114,304,000	**578,538,257**	15.3	39.5	406.1
Europe	800,401,065	105,096,093	**384,633,765**	48.1	26.3	266.0
Middle East	197,090,443	3,284,800	**41,939,200**	21.3	2.9	1176.8
North America	337,167,248	108,096,800	**248,241,969**	73.6	17.0	129.6
Latin America/ Caribbean	576,091,673	18,068,919	**139,009,209**	24.1	9.5	669.3
Oceania/Australia	33,981,562	7,620,480	**20,204,331**	59.5	1.4	165.1
WORLD TOTAL	6,676,120,288	360,985,492	**1,463,632,361**	21.9	100.0	305.5

Notes: (1) Internet usage and world population statistics are for June 30, 2008. (2) Click on each world region name for detailed regional usage information. (3) Demographic (population) numbers are based on data from the US Census Bureau. (4) Internet usage information comes from data published by Nielsen//NetRatings, by the International Telecommunications Union, by local NIC, and other reliable sources. (5) For definitions, disclaimer, and navigation help, please refer to the Site Surfing Guide, now in ten languages. (6) Information in this site may be cited, giving the due credit to **www.internetworldstats.com**. Copyright © 2001 –2008, Miniwatts Marketing Group. All rights reserved worldwide.

Source: **http://www.internetworldstats.com/stats.htm** (Accessed January 31, 2009).

naturally significant differences within regions as well; for example, within the European Union, the Nordic countries have penetration rates of 70 per cent, while new members, such as Poland, are at less than 30 per cent.[23] Given the changes expected in the first years of the twenty-first century, all the estimates indicating explosive growth may be low. The number of users will start evening out around the globe, with new technologies assisting. Computers priced at less than $500 will boost global computer ownership and subsequent online activity. Developments in television, cable, phone, and wireless technologies not only will make the market broader but will also allow for more services to be delivered more efficiently. For example, with the advent of third-generation mobile communications technology, systems will have 100-fold increase in data transfer, allowing the viewing of videos on mobile phones.[24] Television will also become a mainstream internet access method of the future. While the interactive TV market served only 3 million viewers in Europe and North America in 1999, the estimates are for 270 million subscribers by 2009.[25] The growth in international opportunities is leading to a rapid internationalization of internet players.

The careful assessment of infrastructure spells out important marketing opportunities. While 2 billion people in Asia are without electricity and only 16 in 1000 have access to a telephone, the Asian market is the most keenly watched by marketers. According to one estimate, between 1994 and 2000, Asian countries (excluding Japan) spent $1.5 trillion on power, transportation, telecommunications, water supplies and sanitation.[26] The booming middle class in cities such as Bangkok will ensure that cellular phone sales continue at a record pace. With increasing affluence comes an increasing need for energy. General Electric estimates that China will place orders for 168,000 megawatts in additional power-generating capacity, and India more than 70,000 megawatts.

Data on the availability of commercial (marketing-related) infrastructure are often not readily available. Data on which to base an assessment may be provided by government sources, such as Overseas Business Reports; by trade associations, such as the Business Equipment Manufacturers' Association or the Chambers of Commerce; and by trade publications, such as *Advertising Age*. The more extensive the firm's international involvement, the more it can rely on its already existing support network of banks, advertising agencies and distributors to assess new markets.

IMPACT OF THE ECONOMIC ENVIRONMENT ON SOCIAL DEVELOPMENT

Many of the characteristics discussed are important beyond numbers. Economic success comes with a price tag. All the social traumas that were once believed endemic only to the West are now hitting other parts of the world as well. Many countries, including the nations of South East Asia, were able to achieve double-digit growth for decades while paying scant attention to problems that are now demanding treatment: infrastructure limits, labour shortages, demands for greater political freedom, environmental destruction, urban congestion and even the spread of drug addiction.[27]

Due to the close relationship between economic and social development, many of the figures can be used as social indicators as well. Consider the following factors and their significance: share of urban population, life expectancy, number of physicians per capita, literacy rate, percentage of income received by the richest 5 per cent of the population and percentage of the population with access to electricity. In addition to these factors, several other variables can be used as cultural indicators: number of public libraries, registered borrowings, book titles published and number of daily newspapers. The Physical Quality of Life Index (PQLI) is a composite measure of the level of welfare in a country. It has three components: life expectancy, infant mortality and adult literacy rates.[28] The three components of the PQLI are among the few social indicators available to provide a comparison of progress through time in all of the countries of the world.

Differences in the degree of urbanization of target markets in lesser-developed countries influence international marketers' product strategies. If products are targeted only to urban areas, products need minimal adjustments, mainly to qualify them for market entry. However, when targeting national markets, firms may need to make extensive adaptations to match more closely the expectations and the more narrow consumption experiences of the rural population.

In terms of infrastructure, improved access in rural areas brings with it an expansion of non-farm enterprises such as shops, repair services and grain mills. It also changes customs, attitudes and values. As an example, a World Bank study on the impact of rural roads of Yucatán in Mexico found that roads offered an opportunity for enlarging women's role by introducing new ideas, education, medical care and economic alternatives to maize cultivation.[29] In particular, women married later, had fewer children and pursued more non-domestic activities. The same impact has been observed with increased access to radio and television. These changes can, if properly understood and utilized, offer major new opportunities to the international marketer.

As societies attain a certain level of wealth, income becomes less of a factor in people's level of contentment. Emotional well-being may be determined by the quality of social relationships, enjoyment at work, job stability and overall conditions in the country (such as democratic institutions). Countries such as Mexico and Denmark score high on a national well-being index, while Zimbabwe and Russia are among the lowest.[30]

The presence of multinational corporations, which by their very nature are change agents, will accelerate social change. If government control is weak, the multinational corporation bears the social responsibility for its actions. In some cases, governments restrict the freedom of multinational corporations if their actions may affect the environment. As an example, the Indonesian government places construction restrictions (such as building height) on hotels in Bali to avoid the overcrowding and ecological problems incurred in Hawaii when that state developed its tourism sector vigorously.

REGIONAL ECONOMIC INTEGRATION

Economic integration has been one of the main economic developments affecting world markets since World War II. Countries have wanted to engage in economic cooperation to use their respective resources more effectively and to provide larger markets for member-country producers. Some integration efforts have had quite ambitious goals, such as political

EXHIBIT 4.10

Forms of economic integration in regional markets

integration; some have failed as the result of perceptions of unequal benefits from the arrangement or parting of ways politically. Exhibit 4.10, a summary of the major forms of economic cooperation in regional markets, shows the varying degrees of formality with which integration can take place. These economic integration efforts are dividing the world into trading blocs. Of the 32 groupings in existence, some have superstructures of nation-states (such as the European Union), some (such as ASEAN Free Trade Area) are multinational agreements that are currently more political than economic. Some are not trading blocs per se, but work to further them. The Free Trade Area of the Americas (FTAA) is a foreign-policy initiative to further democracy in the hemisphere through incentives to capitalistic development and trade liberalization. Blocs are joining bigger blocs as in the case of the Asia-Pacific Economic Co-operation, which brings partners together from multiple continents (including NAFTA, AFTA and individual countries such as Australia, China, Japan and Russia).[31]

Levels of economic integration

Free Trade Area   The **free trade area** is the least restrictive and loosest form of economic integration among nations. In a free trade area, all barriers to trade among member countries are removed. Goods and services are freely traded among member countries. No discriminatory taxes, quotas, tariffs or other barriers are allowed. Sometimes a free trade area is formed only for certain classes of goods and services. A notable feature of free trade areas is that each member country continues to set its own policies in relation to non-members. This means that each member is free to set any tariffs or other restrictions that it chooses on trade with countries outside of the free trade area. Among such arrangements are the European Free Trade Area (EFTA) and the North American Free Trade Agreement (NAFTA). As an example of the freedom members have in terms of their policies towards non-members, Mexico has signed a number of bilateral free trade agreements with other blocs (the European Union) and nations (Chile) to both improve trade and to attract investment.

Customs Union   The **customs union** is one step further along the spectrum of economic integration. As in the free trade area, members of the customs union dismantle barriers to trade in goods and services among members. In addition, however, the customs union establishes a common trade policy with respect to non-members. Typically, this takes the form of a common external tariff, whereby imports from non-members are subject to the same tariff when sold to any member country. The Southern African Customs Union is the oldest and most successful example of economic integration in Africa.

Common Market   The **common market** amounts to a customs union covering the exchange of goods and services, the prohibition of duties in exports and imports between members,

International Groupings

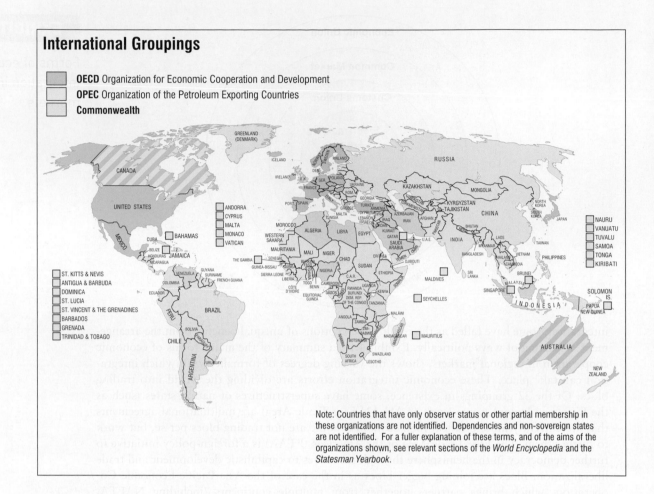

OECD Organization for Economic Cooperation and Development
OPEC Organization of the Petroleum Exporting Countries
Commonwealth

Note: Countries that have only observer status or other partial membership in these organizations are not identified. Dependencies and non-sovereign states are not identified. For a fuller explanation of these terms, and of the aims of the organizations shown, see relevant sections of the *World Encyclopedia* and the *Statesman Yearbook*.

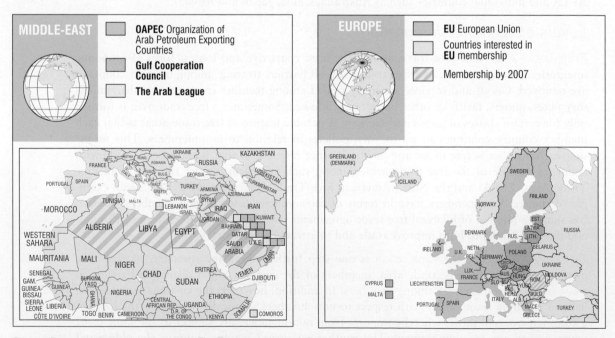

MIDDLE-EAST

OAPEC Organization of Arab Petroleum Exporting Countries
Gulf Cooperation Council
The Arab League

EUROPE

EU European Union
Countries interested in **EU** membership
Membership by 2007

Source: Based on *Statesman Yearbook; The European Union: A Guide for Americans*, 2006, **http://www.eurounion.org/infores/euguide/euguide.htm**; "Afrabet Soup," *The Economist*, February 10, 2001, p. 77, **http://www.economist.com.**

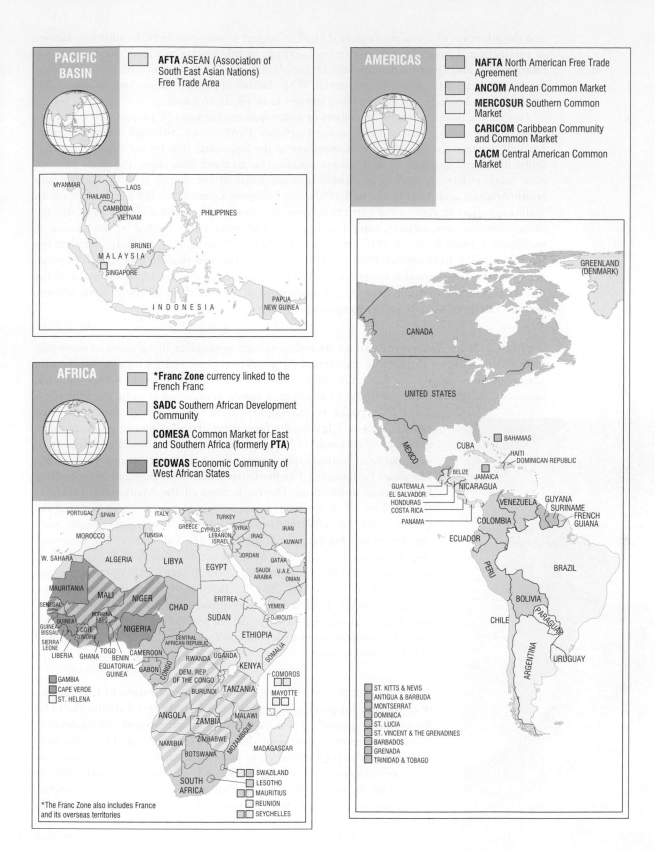

PACIFIC BASIN

AFTA ASEAN (Association of South East Asian Nations) Free Trade Area

MYANMAR
THAILAND — LAOS
CAMBODIA
VIETNAM
PHILIPPINES
BRUNEI
MALAYSIA
SINGAPORE
INDONESIA
PAPUA NEW GUINEA

AFRICA

*Franc Zone currency linked to the French Franc

SADC Southern African Development Community

COMESA Common Market for East and Southern Africa (formerly **PTA**)

ECOWAS Economic Community of West African States

PORTUGAL   SPAIN   ITALY   TURKEY
GREECE   CYPRUS   SYRIA   IRAN
MOROCCO   TUNISIA   LEBANON   IRAQ   KUWAIT
ISRAEL   JORDAN
W. SAHARA   ALGERIA   LIBYA   EGYPT   QATAR   U.A.E.
SAUDI ARABIA   OMAN
MAURITANIA   MALI   NIGER   ERITREA   YEMEN
SENEGAL   CHAD   SUDAN   DJIBOUTI
BURKINA FASO
GUINEA-   GUINEA   CÔTE   NIGERIA   CENTRAL   ETHIOPIA
BISSAU   D'IVOIRE   AFRICAN REPUBLIC   SOMALIA
SIERRA LEONE   GHANA   TOGO   CAMEROON   RWANDA   UGANDA
LIBERIA   BENIN   KENYA
EQUATORIAL   GABON   CONGO   DEM. REP.   COMOROS
GUINEA   OF THE CONGO   MAYOTTE
BURUNDI   TANZANIA

GAMBIA
CAPE VERDE
ST. HELENA

ANGOLA   ZAMBIA   MALAWI
NAMIBIA   ZIMBABWE   MOZAMBIQUE   MADAGASCAR
BOTSWANA
SOUTH AFRICA   SWAZILAND
LESOTHO
MAURITIUS
*The Franc Zone also includes France   REUNION
and its overseas territories   SEYCHELLES

AMERICAS

NAFTA North American Free Trade Agreement

ANCOM Andean Common Market

MERCOSUR Southern Common Market

CARICOM Caribbean Community and Common Market

CACM Central American Common Market

GREENLAND (DENMARK)

CANADA

UNITED STATES

MEXICO
BAHAMAS
CUBA
HAITI
DOMINICAN REPUBLIC
BELIZE   JAMAICA
GUATEMALA
EL SALVADOR   NICARAGUA
HONDURAS
COSTA RICA   VENEZUELA   GUYANA
PANAMA   SURINAME
COLOMBIA   FRENCH GUIANA
ECUADOR

PERU   BRAZIL

BOLIVIA
CHILE   PARAGUAY

ARGENTINA   URUGUAY

ST. KITTS & NEVIS
ANTIGUA & BARBUDA
MONTSERRAT
DOMINICA
ST. LUCIA
ST. VINCENT & THE GRENADINES
BARBADOS
GRENADA
TRINIDAD & TOBAGO

and the adoption of a common external tariff in respect to non-members. In addition, factors of production (labour, capital, and technology) are mobile among members. Restrictions on immigration and cross-border investment are abolished. The importance of factor mobility for economic growth cannot be overstated. When factors of production are mobile, then capital, labour technology may be employed in their most productive uses.

Despite the obvious benefits, members of a common market must be prepared to cooperate closely in monetary, fiscal and employment policies. Furthermore, although a common market will enhance the productivity of members in the aggregate, it is by no means clear that individual member countries will always benefit. Due to these difficulties, the goals of common markets have proved to be elusive in many areas of the world, notably Central and South America and Asia. In the mid-1980s, the European Community (EC) embarked on an ambitious effort to remove the barriers between the then twelve member countries to free the movement of goods, services, capital and people. The process was ratified by the passing of the Single European Act in 1987 with the target date of December 31, 1992, to complete the internal market. In December 1991, the EC agreed in Maastricht that the so-called 1992 process would be a step towards cooperation beyond the economic dimension. While many of the directives aimed at opening borders and markets were completed on schedule, some sectors, such as automobiles, took longer to open up.

Economic Union   The creation of a true economic union requires integration of economic policies in addition to the free movement of goods, services and factors of production across borders. Under an economic union, members will harmonize monetary policies, taxation and government spending. In addition, a common currency is to be used by members. This could be accomplished, de facto, by a system of fixed exchange rates. Clearly, the formation of an economic union requires members to surrender a large measure of their national sovereignty to supranational authorities in communitywide institutions such as the European Parliament. The final step would be a political union calling for political unification. The ratification of the Maastricht Treaty in late 1993 by all of the twelve member countries of the EC created the European Union, effective January 1, 1994. The treaty (jointly with the Treaty of Amsterdam in 1997) set the foundation for economic and monetary union (EMU) with the establishment of the euro (€) as a common currency by January 1, 1999. Sixteen EU countries are currently part of 'Euroland' (Austria, Belgium, Cyprus, Finland, France, Germany, Greece, Ireland, Italy, Luxembourg, Malta, Portugal, Slovakia, Slovenia, Spain and the Netherlands). In addition, moves would be made toward a political union with common foreign and security policy as well as judicial cooperation.[32]

© ROYALTY-FREE/CORBIS

European Integration   The most important implication of the freedom of movement for products, services, people and capital within the EU is the economic growth that is expected to result. Several specific sources of increased growth have been identified. First, there will be gains from eliminating the transaction costs associated with border patrols, customs procedures, and so forth. Second, economic growth will be spurred by the economies of scale that will be achieved when production facilities become more concentrated. Third, there will be gains from more intense competition among European companies. Firms that were monopolists in one country will now be subject to competition from firms in other member countries. The introduction of the euro is expected to add to the efficiencies, especially in terms of consolidation of firms across industries and across countries. Furthermore, countries in Euroland will enjoy cheaper transaction costs and reduced currency risks, and consumers and businesses will enjoy price transparency and increased price-based competition. Marketer reactions to the euro will be discussed further in Chapter 17.

The enlargement of the EU has become one of the most debated issues. In 2004, the EU expanded to 25 members, accepting eight Central European and two Mediterranean countries to the Union. Despite some of the uncertainties about the future cohesiveness of the EU, new nations want to join. Bulgaria and Romania were accepted in 2007, and Turkey's membership is pending. The agreement on the European Economic Area (EEA) extends the Single Market of the EU to three of the four EFTA countries (Iceland, Liechtenstein and Norway, with Switzerland opting to develop its relationship with the EU through bilateral agreements).[33]

The integration has important implications for firms within and outside Europe because it poses both threats and opportunities, benefits and costs. There will be substantial benefits for those firms already operating in Europe. These firms will gain because their operations in one country can now be freely expanded into others and their products may be freely sold across borders. In a borderless Europe, firms will have access to approximately 380 million consumers. Substantial economies of scale in production and marketing will also result. The extent of these economies of scale will depend on the ability of the marketers to find pan-regional segments or to homogenize tastes across borders through promotional activity.

For firms from non-member countries, there are various possibilities depending on the firm's position within the market. Exhibit 4.11 provides four different scenarios with proposed courses of action. Well-established US-based multinational marketers such as H.J. Heinz and Colgate-Palmolive will be able to take advantage of the new economies of scale. For example, 3M plants earlier turned out different versions of the company's products for various markets. Now, the 3M plant in Wales, for example, makes videotapes and video-cassettes for all of Europe. Colgate-Palmolive has to watch out for competitors, like Germany's Henkel, in the brutally competitive detergent market. At the same time, large-scale retailers, such as France's Carrefour and Germany's Aldi group, are undertaking their own efforts to exploit the situation with hypermarkets supplied by central warehouses with computerized inventories. Their procurement policies have to be met by companies like Heinz. Many multinationals are developing pan-European strategies to exploit the emerging situation; that is, they are standardizing their products and processes to the greatest extent possible without compromising local input and implementation.

Company Status	Challenges	Response
Established multinational market/multiple markets	Exploit opportunities from improved productivity Meet challenge of competitors Cater to customers/intermediaries doing same	Pan-European strategy
Firm with one European subsidiary	Competition Loss of niche	Expansion Strategic alliances Rationalization Divestment
Exporter to Europe	Competition Access	European branch Selective acquisition Strategic alliance
No interest	Competition at home Lost opportunity	Entry

Source: Developed from John F. Magee, "1992: Moves Americans Must Make," *Harvard Business Review* 67 (May–June 1989): 78–84.

EXHIBIT 4.11

Proposed company responses to european integration

A company with a foothold in only one European market is faced with the danger of competitors who can use the strength of multiple markets. Furthermore, the elimination of barriers may do away with the company's competitive advantage. For example, more than half of the 45 major European food companies have traditionally been in just one or two of the individual European markets and seriously lag behind broader-based US and Swiss firms. Similarly, automakers PSA and Fiat are nowhere close to the cross-manufacturing presence of Ford and GM. The courses of action include expansion through acquisitions or mergers, formation of strategic alliances, rationalization by concentrating only on business segments in which the company can be a pan-European leader, and finally, divestment.

The term Fortress Europe has been used to describe the fears of many firms about a unified Europe. The concern is that while Europe dismantles internal barriers, it will raise external ones, making access to the European market difficult for other non-EU and US firms. In a move designed to protect European farmers, for example, the EU has occasionally banned the import of certain agricultural goods from the United States. The EU has also called on members to limit the number of American television programmes broadcast in Europe. Finally, many US firms are concerned about the relatively strict domestic content rules passed by the EU. These rules require certain products sold in Europe to be manufactured with European inputs. One effect of the perceived threat of Fortress Europe has been increased direct investment in Europe by US firms. Fears that the EU will erect barriers to US exports and fears of the domestic content rules governing many goods have led many US firms to initiate or expand European direct investment.

North American Integration Although the EU is undoubtedly the most successful and best-known integrative effort, North American integration efforts, although only a few years old, have gained momentum and attention. What started as a trading pact between two close and economically well-developed allies has already been expanded conceptually to include Mexico, and long-term plans call for further additions. However, North American integration is for purely economic reasons; there are no constituencies for political integration.

The ratification of NAFTA created the world's largest free market with 390 million consumers and a total output of $10 trillion, roughly the same size as the EEA.[34] The pact marked a bold departure: Never before have industrialized countries created such a massive free trade area with a developing-country neighbour.

Since Canada stands to gain very little from NAFTA (its trade with Mexico is 1 per cent of its trade with the United States), much of the controversy has centred on the gains and losses for the United States and Mexico. Proponents argue that the agreement will give US firms access to a huge pool of relatively low-cost Mexican labour at a time when demographic trends are resulting in labour shortages in many parts of the United States. At the same time, many new jobs are created in Mexico. The agreement will give firms in both countries access to millions of additional consumers, and the liberalized trade flows will result in higher economic growth in both countries. The top 20 exports and imports between Mexico and the United States are in virtually the same industries, indicating intra-industry specialization and building of economies of scale for global competitiveness.[35] Overall, the corporate view toward NAFTA is overwhelmingly positive.

Opposition to NAFTA centres on issues relating to labour and the environment. Unions in particular worry about job loss to Mexico, given its lower wages and work standards; some estimate that 6 million US workers would be vulnerable to migration of jobs. Similarly, any expansion of NAFTA is perceived as a threat. Distinctive features of NAFTA are the two side agreements that were worked out to correct perceived abuses in labour and the environment in Mexico. The North American Agreement on Labor Cooperation (NAALC) was set up to hear complaints about worker abuse, and the Commission on Environmental Compliance was established to act as a public advocate on the environment. These side agreements have had little impact, however, mainly because the mechanisms have almost no enforcement power.[36]

After a remarkable start in increased trade and investment, NAFTA suffered a serious setback due to a significant devaluation of the Mexican peso in 1995 and its negative impact on trade. Critics argue that too much was expected too fast of a country whose political system and economy were not ready for open markets. In response, advocates argue that there was nothing wrong with the Mexican real economy and that the peso crisis was a political one that would be overcome with time.

Trade among Canada, Mexico and the United States has increased by 50 per cent since NAFTA took effect, exceeding $713 billion in 2004.[37] Reforms have turned Mexico into an attractive market in its own right. Mexico's gross domestic product has been expanding by more than 3 per cent every year since 1989, and exports to the United States have doubled since 1986 to $155.9 billion in 2004. By institutionalizing the nation's turn to open its markets, the free trade agreement has attracted considerable new foreign investment (well over $100 billion since NAFTA began). The United States has benefited from Mexico's success. US exports to Mexico ($110.8 billion) surpass those to Japan at $54.2 billion. While the surplus of $1.3 billion in 1994 had turned to a deficit of $111.5 billion in 2004, these imports have helped Mexico's recovery and will, therefore, strengthen NAFTA in the long term. Furthermore, US imports from Mexico have been shown to have much higher US content than imports from other countries.[38] Cooperation between Mexico and the United States is expanding beyond trade and investment. For example, binational bodies have been established to tackle issues such as migration, border control and drug trafficking.[39]

Among the US industries to benefit are computers, autos and auto parts, petro-chemicals, financial services and aerospace. Aerospace companies such as Boeing, Honeywell, Airbus Industrie and GE Aircraft Engines have recently made Mexico a centre for both parts manufacture and assembly. Aerospace is now one of Mexico's largest industries, second only to electronics, with 10000 workers employed.[40] In Mexico's growth toward a more advanced society, manufacturers of consumer goods will also stand to benefit. NAFTA has already had a major impact on the emergence of new retail chains, many of which were developed to handle new products from abroad.[41] Not only have US retailers, such as Wal-Mart, expanded to and in Mexico, but Mexican retailers, such as Grupo Gigante, have entered the US market.[42] Wal-Mart's use of lower tariffs, physical proximity and buying power are changing the Mexican retail landscape, as shown in *The International Marketplace 4.2*.

Free trade produces both winners and losers. Although opponents concede that the agreement is likely to spur economic growth, they point out that segments of the US economy will be harmed by the agreement. It is likely that wages and employment for unskilled workers in the United States will decrease because of Mexico's low-cost labour pool. US companies have been moving operations to Mexico since the 1960s. The door was opened when Mexico liberalized export restrictions to allow for more so-called maquiladoras, plants that make goods and parts or process food for export to the United States. The supply of labour in the maquiladoras was plentiful, the pay and benefits low, and the work regulations lax by US standards. In the last two decades, maquiladoras evolved from low-end garment or small-appliance assembly outfits to higher-end manufacturing of big-screen TVs, computers and auto parts. The factories shipped $80 billion worth of goods (half of Mexican exports), almost all of it to the United States. However, the arrangement is in trouble. The NAFTA treaty required Mexico to strip maquiladoras of their duty-free status by 2001. Tariff breaks formerly given to all imported parts, supplies, equipment, and machinery used by foreign factories in Mexico now apply only to inputs from Canada, Mexico and the United States. This effect is felt most by Asian factories because they still import a large amount of components from across the Pacific (for example, 97 per cent of components for TVs assembled in Tijuana are imported, most from Asia). There is a lesser effect on Europeans because of Mexico's free trade agreement with the EU, which eliminated tariffs gradually by 2007.[43] Wages have also been rising to $4.38 an hour (up from $2.29 in 1997), resulting in some low-end manufacturers of apparel and toys moving production to Asia.[44] While the Mexican government is eager to attract maquiladora investment, it is also keen to move away from using cheap labour as a central element of competitiveness. Furthermore, many of the companies employing maquiladoras have also come under criticism for their wage practices.[45]

Despite US fears of rapid job loss if companies would send business south of the border, recent studies have declared the job gain or loss almost a washout. The good news is that free

THE INTERNATIONAL **MARKETPLACE 4.2**

NAFTA reshaping retail markets

Wal-Mart saw the promise of the Mexican market in 1991 when it stepped outside the United States for the first time by launching Sam's Clubs in 50–50 partnership with Cifra, Mexico's largest retailer. The local partner was needed to provide operational expertise in a market significantly different in culture and income from Wal-Mart's domestic one. Within months, the first outlet – a bare-bones unit that sold bulk items at just above wholesale prices – was breaking all Wal-Mart records in sales. While tariffs still made imported goods pricey, 'Made in the USA' merchandise also started appearing on the shelves.

After NAFTA took effect in 1994, tariffs tumbled, unleashing pent-up demand in Mexico for US-made goods. The trade treaty also helped eliminate some of the transportation headaches and government red tape that had kept Wal-Mart from fully realizing its competitive advantage. NAFTA resulted in many European and Asian manufacturers setting up plants in Mexico, giving the retailer cheaper access to more foreign brands.

Wal-Mart's enormous buying power has kept it ahead of its Mexican competitors who are making similar moves. Because Wal-Mart consolidates its orders for all goods it sells outside of the United States, it can wring deeper discounts from suppliers than its local competitors. Wal-Mart Mexico has repeatedly exploited NAFTA and other economic forces to trigger price wars. For example, rather than pocket the windfall that resulted when tariffs on Lasko brand floor fans fell from 20 per cent to 2 per cent, price cuts took place equal to the tariff reductions.

Behind Wal-Mart's success are increasingly price-conscious consumers. The greater economic security of NAFTA has helped tame Mexico's once fierce inflation. The resulting price stability has made it easier for Mexican consumers to spot bargains. In addition, Wal-Mart's clean, brightly lit interiors, orderly and well-stocked aisles, and consistent pricing policies are a relief from the chaotic atmosphere that still prevails in many local stores.

Wal-Mart's aggressive tactics have resulted in complaints as well. In 2002, Mexico's Competition Commission was asked to probe into reports that Wal-Mart exerts undue pressure on suppliers to lower their prices. Local retailers, such as Comerci, Gigante, and Soriana, have seen their profits plummet but are forced to provide prices competitive to Wal-Mart's. In addition, they have engaged in aggressive rehauls of their operations. Soriana, for example, took out ads in local newspapers warning about 'foreign supermarkets' when regulators fined a Wal-Mart in Monterrey because a shelf price did not match the price on the checkout receipt.

Mexican retailers are not just playing a defensive game. Gigante has opened nine stores in the Los Angeles area and aims to become the most popular supermarket among California's 11 million Latinos, most of whom are from Mexico and connect with the stores. Latinos boast a collective disposable income of $450 billion a year, with much of it going towards food. 'The big chains gave Gigante the opportunity to come in here', said Steven Soto, head of the Mexican-American Grocers Association, a trade group that represents some 18 000 Latino store managers and owners. 'The chains did not understand how to market to our community'. Given that food tastes are the last things to change with immigrants, Gigante's product choices (e.g., chorizo and carnitas), placements (e.g., produce close by the entrance), and decor have made it a success.

© CORBIS/SYGMA

SOURCES: 'Grocer Grande', *Time Inside Business,* April 2003, A3–A10; 'War of the Superstores', *Business Week,* September 23, 2002, 60; 'How Well Does Wal-Mart Travel?' *Business Week,* September 3, 2001, 82–84; 'How NAFTA Helped Wal-Mart Reshape the Mexican Market', *The Wall Street Journal,* August 31, 2001, A1–A2; and Vijay Govindarajan and Anil K. Gupta, 'Taking Wal-Mart Global: Lessons from Retailing's Giant', *Strategy and Business,* fourth quarter, 1999, 45–56.

trade will create higher-skilled and better-paying jobs in the United States as a result of growth in exports. As a matter of fact, jobs in US exporting firms tend to pay 10 to 15 per cent more than the jobs they have replaced. Losers have been US manufacturers of auto parts, furniture and household glass; sugar, peanut and citrus growers; and seafood and vegetable producers. The US Labor Department has certified 316 000 jobs as threatened or lost due to trade with Mexico and Canada. At the same time, the US economy has added some 20 million jobs in the years since NAFTA. The fact that job losses have been in more heavily unionized sectors has made these losses politically charged. In most cases, high Mexican shipping and inventory costs will continue to make it more efficient for many US industries to serve their home market from US plants. Outsourcing of lower-skilled jobs is an unstoppable trend for developed economies such as the United States. However, NAFTA has given US firms a way of taking advantage of cheaper labour while still keeping close links to US suppliers. Mexican assembly plants get 82 per cent of their parts from US suppliers, while factories in Asia are using only a fraction of that.[46] Without NAFTA, entire industries might be lost to Asia rather than just the labour-intensive portions.

Integration pains extend to other areas as well. Approximately 85 per cent of US– Mexican trade moves on trucks. Under NAFTA, cross-border controls on trucking were to be eliminated by the end of 1995, allowing commercial vehicles to move freely in four US and six Mexican border states. But the US truckers, backed by the Teamsters Union, would have nothing of this, arguing that Mexican trucks were dangerous and exceeded weight limits. The union also worried that opening of the border would depress wages, because it would allow US trucking companies to team up with lower-cost counterparts in Mexico. In 2001, however, the NAFTA Arbitration Panel ruled that Mexican trucks must be allowed to cross US borders and the US Senate approved a measure that allows Mexican truckers to haul cargo provided they meet strict inspection and safety rules.[47]

Countries dependent on trade with NAFTA countries are concerned that the agreement would divert trade and impose significant losses on their economies. Asia's continuing economic success depends largely on easy access to the North American markets, which account for more than 25 per cent of annual export revenue for many Asian countries. Lower-cost producers in Asia are likely to lose some exports to the United States if they are subject to tariffs but Mexican firms are not and may, therefore, have to invest in NAFTA.[48] Similarly, many in the Caribbean and Central America have always feared that the apparel industries of these regions will be threatened as would much-needed investments.

NAFTA may be the first step towards a hemispheric bloc, although nobody expects it to happen anytime soon. It took more than three years of tough bargaining to reach an agreement between the United States and Canada – two countries with parallel economic, industrial and social systems. The challenges of expanding free trade throughout Latin America will be significant. As a first step, Chile was scheduled to join as a fourth member in 1997. However, the membership has not materialized due to US political manoeuvring, and Chile has since entered into bilateral trade agreements with both Canada and Mexico and joined Mercosur as an associate member. This has meant that US marketers are reporting trade deals lost to Canadian competitors, who are free of Chile's 11 per cent tariffs.[49] Overall, many US marketers fear that Latin Americans will start moving closer to Europeans if free trade discussions throughout the hemisphere are not seen to progress. For example, both Mercosur and Mexico have signed free-trade agreements with the EU.[50]

Other economic alliances

Perhaps the world's developing countries have the most to gain from successful integrative efforts. As many of these countries are also quite small, economic growth is difficult to generate internally. Many of these countries have adopted policies of import substitution to foster economic growth. An import substitution policy involves developing industries to produce goods that were formerly imported. Many of these industries, however, can be efficient producers only with a higher level of production than can be consumed by the domestic economy. Their success, therefore, depends on accessible export markets made possible by integrative efforts.

Integration in Latin America Before the signing of the US–Canada Free Trade Agreement, all the major trading bloc activity had taken place elsewhere in the Americas. However, none of the activity in Latin America has been hemispheric; that is, Central America had its structures, the Caribbean nations had theirs, and South America had its own different forms. However, for political and economic reasons, these attempts have never reached set objectives. In a dramatic transformation, these nations sought free trade as a salvation from stagnation, inflation and debt. In response to these developments, Brazil, Argentina, Uruguay and Paraguay set up a common market called Mercosur (Mercado Común del Sur).[51] Despite their own economic challenges and disagreements over trade policy, the Mercosur members and the two associate members, Bolivia and Chile, have agreed to economic-convergence targets similar to those the EU made as a precursor to the euro. These are in areas of inflation, public debt and fiscal deficits. Bolivia, Colombia, Ecuador, Peru and Venezuela have formed the Andean Common Market (ANCOM). Many Latin nations are realizing that if they do not unite, they will become increasingly marginal in the global market. In approaching the EU with a free trade agreement, Mercosur members want to diversify their trade relationships and reduce their dependence on US trade.

The ultimate goal is a free trade zone from Point Barrow, Alaska, to Patagonia under a framework called the **Free Trade Area of the Americas (FTAA)**. The argument is that free trade throughout the Americas would channel investment and technology to Latin nations and give US firms a head start in those markets. Ministerials held since 1994 established working groups to gather data and make recommendations in preparation for the FTAA negotiations and an agreement by 2005. However, by the deadline, the countries involved failed to reach political accord that would have allowed the largest trade zone in the world. The reasons range from failure to reach agreement on freeing trade in agricultural goods to the changed political climate in many Latin American countries.[52] Ideally, the larger countries would have agreed to consider giving smaller and lesser-developed countries more time to reduce tariffs, to open their economies to foreign investment, and to adopt effective laws in areas such as antitrust, intellectual property rights, bank regulation and prohibitions on corrupt business practices. At the same time, the less-developed countries would agree to include labour and environmental standards in the negotiations.[53]

Free market reforms and economic revival up to now have had marketers ready to export and to invest in Latin America. For example, Brazil's opening of its computer market has resulted in Hewlett-Packard establishing a joint venture to produce PCs. In the past, Kodak dealt with Latin America through eleven separate country organizations, but has since streamlined its operations to five 'boundaryless' companies organized along product lines and taking advantage of trading openings, and has created centralized distribution, thereby making deliveries more efficient and decreasing inventory carrying costs.[54]

Integration in Asia Development in Asia has been quite different from that in Europe and in the Americas. While European and North American arrangements have been driven by political will, market forces may force more formal integration on Asian politicians. The fact that regional integration is increasing around the world may drive Asian interest to it for pragmatic reasons. First, European and American markets are significant for the Asian producers, and some type of organization or bloc may be needed to maintain leverage and balance against the two other blocs. Second, given that much of the Asian trade growth is from intraregional trade, having common understandings and policies will become necessary. Future integration will most likely use the frame of the most established arrangement in the region, the Association of South East Asian Nations (ASEAN). Before late 1991, ASEAN had no real structures, and consensus was reached through informal consultations. In October 1991, ASEAN members announced the formation of a customs union called Asean Free Trade Area (AFTA). The ten member countries agreed to reduce tariffs to a maximum level of 5 per cent by 2003 and to create a customs union by 2010. ASEAN has agreed to economic cooperation with China, India, Japan and South Korea.

The Malaysians have pushed for the formation of the East Asia Economic Group (EAEG), which would add Hong Kong, Japan, South Korea and Taiwan to the membership list. This proposal makes sense, because without Japan and the rapidly industrializing countries of the region such as South Korea and Taiwan, the effect of the arrangement would be nominal.

Japan's reaction has been generally negative toward all types of regionalization efforts, mainly because it has the most to gain from free trade efforts. However, part of what has been driving regionalization has been Japan's reluctance to foster some of the elements that promote free trade, for example, reciprocity. Should the other trading blocs turn against Japan, its only resort may be to work toward a more formal trade arrangement in the Asia-Pacific area.

Another formal proposal for cooperation would start building bridges between two emerging trade blocs. Some individuals have publicly called for a US-Japan common market. Given the differences on all fronts between the two countries, the proposal may be quite unrealistic at this time. Negotiated trade liberalization will not open Japanese markets because of major institutional differences, as seen in many rounds of successful negotiations but totally unsatisfactory results. The only solution, especially for the US government, is to forge better cooperation between the government and the private sector to improve competitiveness.[55]

In 1988, Australia proposed the Asia Pacific Economic Cooperation (APEC) as an annual forum to maintain a balance in negotiations. The proposal calls for ASEAN members to be joined by Australia, New Zealand, Japan, South Korea, Canada, Chile, Mexico and the United States. Originally, the model for APEC was not the EU, with its Brussels bureaucracy, but the Organization for Economic Cooperation and Development (OECD), which is a centre for research and high-level discussion. However, APEC has now established an ultimate goal of achieving free trade in the area among its 21 members by 2010.[56]

Economic integration has also taken place on the Indian subcontinent. In 1985, seven nations of the region (India, Pakistan, Bangladesh, Sri Lanka, Nepal, Bhutan and the Maldives) launched the South Asian Association for Regional Cooperation (SAARC). Cooperation has been limited to relatively noncontroversial areas, such as agriculture and regional development and is hampered by political disagreements.

Integration in Africa and the Middle East Africa's economic groupings range from currency unions among European nations and their former colonies to customs unions between neighbouring states. In addition to wanting to liberalize trade among members, African countries want to gain better access to European and North American markets for farm and textile products. Given that most of the countries are too small to negotiate with the other blocs, alliances have been the solution. In 1975, sixteen West African nations attempted to create a megamarket large enough to interest investors from the industrialized world and reduce hardship through economic integration. The objective of the Economic Community of West African States (ECOWAS) was to form a customs union and eventually a common market. Although many of its objectives have not been reached, its combined population of 160 million represents the largest economic entity in sub-Saharan Africa. Other entities in Africa include the Common Market for Eastern and Southern Africa (COMESA), the Economic Community of Central African States (CEEAC), the Southern African Customs Union, the Southern African Development Community (SADC), and some smaller, less globally oriented blocs such as the Economic Community of the Great Lakes Countries, the Mano River Union, and the East African Community (EAC). Most member countries are part of more than one block (for example, Tanzania is a member in both the EAC and SADC). The blocs, for the most part, have not been successful due to small memberships and lack of economic infrastructure to produce goods to be traded within the blocs. Moreover, some of the blocs have been relatively inactive for substantial periods of time while their members endure internal political turmoil or even warfare amongst each other.[57] In 2002, African nations established the African Union (AU) for regional cooperation. Eventually, plans call for a pan-African parliament, a court of justice, a central bank and a shared currency.[58]

Countries in the Arab world have made some progress in economic integration. The Arab Maghreb Union ties together Algeria, Libya, Mauritania, Morocco and Tunisia in northern Africa. The Gulf Cooperation Council (GCC) is one of the most powerful of any trade groups. The per capita income of its six member states (Bahrain, Kuwait, Oman, Qatar, Saudi Arabia and the United Arab Emirates) is in the ninetieth percentile in the world. The GCC was formed in 1980 mainly as a defensive measure due to the perceived threat from the Iran-Iraq war. Its aim is to achieve free trade arrangements with the EU and EFTA. A proposal among GCC members calls for the creation of a common currency by 2010. A strong regional currency would help the GCC become a viable trading bloc, able to compete in the new global environment. Two key elements required to create a common currency are underway: the dismantling of trade barriers among members and the creation of a GCC member bank.[59]

A listing of the major regional trade agreements is provided in Exhibit 4.12.

EXHIBIT 4.12

Major regional
trade agreements

AFTA	**ASEAN Free Trade Area**
	Brunei, Cambodia, Indonesia, Laos, Malaysia, Myanmar, Philippines, Singapore, Thailand, Vietnam
ANCOM	**Andean Common Market**
	Bolivia, Colombia, Ecuador, Peru, Venezuela
APEC	**Asia Pacific Economic Cooperation**
	Australia, Brunei, Canada, Chile, China, Hong Kong, Indonesia, Japan, Malaysia, Mexico, New Zealand, Papua New Guinea, Peru, Philippines, Russia, Singapore, South Korea, Taiwan, Thailand, Vietnam, United States
CACM	**Central American Common Market**
	Costa Rica, El Salvador, Guatemala, Honduras, Nicaragua
CARICOM	**Caribbean Community**
	Antigua and Barbuda, Bahamas, Barbados, Belize, Dominica, Grenada, Guyana, Jamaica, Montserrat, St. Kitts–Nevis, St. Lucia, St. Vincent and the Grenadines, Suriname, Trinidad-Tobago
ECOWAS	**Economic Community of West African States**
	Benin, Burkina Faso, Cape Verde, Gambia, Ghana, Guinea, Guinea-Bissau, Ivory Coast, Liberia, Mali, Mauritania, Niger, Nigeria, Senegal, Sierra Leone, Togo
EFTA	**European Free Trade Association**
	Iceland, Liechtenstein, Norway, Switzerland
EU	**European Union**
	Austria, Belgium, Cyprus, Czech Republic, Denmark, Estonia, Finland, France, Germany, Greece, Hungary, Ireland, Italy, Latvia, Lithuania, Luxembourg, Malta, Netherlands, Poland, Portugal, Slovakia, Slovenia, Spain, Sweden, United Kingdom
GCC	**Gulf Cooperation Council**
	Bahrain, Kuwait, Oman, Qatar, Saudi Arabia, United Arab Emirates
LAIA	**Latin American Integration Association**
	Argentina, Bolivia, Brazil, Chile, Colombia, Cuba, Ecuador, Mexico, Paraguay, Peru, Uruguay, Venezuela
MERCOSUR	**Southern Common Market**
	Argentina, Brazil, Paraguay, Uruguay
NAFTA	**North American Free Trade Agreement**
	Canada, Mexico, United States
SAARC	**South Asian Association for Regional Cooperation**
	Bangladesh, Bhutan, India, Maldives, Nepal, Pakistan, Sri Lanka
SACU	**Southern African Customs Union**
	Botswana, Lesotho, Namibia, South Africa, Swaziland

Note: For information, see **http://www.aseansec.org**; **http://www.apec.org**; **http://www.caricom.org**; **http://www.eurunion.org**; **http://www.mercosur.org.uy**; and **http://www.nafta-sec-alena.org**.

Economic integration and the international marketer

Regional economic integration creates opportunities and potential problems for the international marketer. It may have an impact on a company's entry mode by favouring direct investment, because one of the basic rationales of integration is to generate favourable conditions for local production and intraregional trade. By design, larger markets are created, with potentially more opportunity. Harmonization efforts may result in standardized regulations, which, in turn, affect production and marketing efforts in a positive manner.

Decisions regarding integrating markets must be assessed from four different perspectives: the range and impact of changes resulting from integration, development of strategies to relate to these changes, organizational changes needed to exploit these changes, and strategies to influence change in a more favourable direction.[60]

Effects of Change The first task is to envision the outcome of the change. Change in the competitive landscape can be dramatic if scale opportunities can be exploited in relatively homogeneous demand conditions. This could be the case, for example, for industrial goods, consumer durables such as cameras and watches and professional services. The international marketer will have to take into consideration varying degrees of change readiness within the markets themselves; that is, governments and other stakeholders, such as labour unions, may oppose the liberalization of competition, especially when national champions such as airlines, automobiles, energy, and telecommunications are concerned. However, with deregulation, monopolies have had to transform into competitive industries. In Germany, for example, the price of long-distance calls has fallen 40 per cent, forcing the former monopolist, Deutsche Telekom, to streamline its operations and seek new business abroad. By fostering a single market for capital, the euro is pushing Europe closer to a homogeneous market in goods and services, thereby exerting additional pressure on prices.[61]

Strategic Planning The international marketer will then have to develop a strategic response to the new environment to maintain a sustainable long-term competitive advantage. Those companies already present in an integrated market should fill in gaps in European product/market portfolios through acquisitions or alliances to create a regional or global company. It is increasingly evident that even regional presence is not sufficient and companies need to set their sights on presence beyond that. In industries such as automobiles, mobile communications and retailing, blocs in the twenty-first century may be dominated by two or three giants, leaving room only for niche players. Those with currently weak positions, or no presence at all, will have to create alliances for market entry and development with established firms. General Mills created Cereal Partners Worldwide with Nestlé to establish itself in Europe and to jointly develop new market opportunities in Asia. An additional option for the international marketer is to leave the market altogether if it cannot remain competitive because of new competitive conditions or the level of investment needed. For example, Bank of America sold its operations in Italy to Deutsche Bank after it discovered the high cost of becoming a pan-European player.

Reorganization Whatever changes are made, they will require company reorganization.[62] Structurally, authority will have to become more centralized to execute regional programmes. In staffing, focus will have to be on individuals who understand the subtleties of consumer behaviour programmes across markets and are therefore able to evaluate the similarities and differences between cultures and markets. In developing systems for the planning and implementation of regional programmes, adjustments have to be made to incorporate views throughout the organization. If, for example, decisions on regional advertising campaigns are made at headquarters without consultation with country operations, resentment from the local marketing staff could lead to less-than-optimal execution. The introduction of the euro will mean increased coordination in pricing as compared to the relative autonomy in price setting enjoyed by country organizations in the past. Companies may even move corporate or divisional headquarters from the domestic market to be closer to the customer or centres of innovation. For example, after Procter & Gamble's reorganization, its fabric and home care business unit is headquartered in Brussels, Belgium.

Lobbying International managers, as change agents, must constantly seek ways to influence the regulatory environment in which they have to operate. Economic integration will create its own powers and procedures similar to those of the EU commission and its directives. The international marketer is not powerless to influence both of them; as a matter of fact, a passive approach may result in competitors gaining an advantage or it may put the company at a disadvantage. For example, it was very important for the US pharmaceutical industry to obtain tight patent protection as part of the NAFTA agreement; therefore, substantial time and money were spent on lobbying both the executive and legislative branches of the US government. Often, policymakers rely heavily on the knowledge and experience of the private sector to carry out their own work. Influencing change will therefore mean providing industry information, such as test results, to the policymakers. Many marketers consider lobbying a public relations activity and therefore go beyond the traditional approaches. Lobbying will usually have to take place at multiple levels simultaneously; within the EU, this means the European Commission in Brussels, the European Parliament in Strasbourg, or the national governments within the EU. Marketers with substantial resources have established their own lobbying offices in Brussels, while smaller companies get their voices heard through joint offices or their industry associations. In terms of lobbying, US firms have an advantage because of their experience in their home market; however, for many European firms, lobbying is a new, yet necessary, skill to be acquired. At the same time, marketers operating in two or more major markets (such as the EU and North America) can work to produce more efficient trade through, for example, mutual recognition agreements (MRAs) on standards.

EMERGING MARKETS

Broadly defined, an emerging market is a country making an effort to change and improve its economy with the goal of raising its performance to that of the world's more advanced nations.[63] Improved economies can benefit emerging-market countries through higher personal income levels and better standards of living, more exports, increased foreign-direct investment, and more stable political structures. Developed countries benefit from the development of human and natural resources in emerging markets for increased international trading.

Although opinions on which countries are emerging markets differ, the Big Emerging Markets are China, India, Brazil, Argentina and Indonesia. The data provided in Exhibit 4.13 compares selected emerging markets with each other on dimensions indicating market potential. The biggest emerging markets display the factors that make them strategically important: favourable consumer demographics, rising household incomes and increasing availability of credit, as well as increasing productivity resulting in more attractive prices.[64] As computer-factory workers in China and software programmers in India increase their incomes, they become consumers. The number of people with the equivalent of $10000 in annual income will double, to 2 billion, by 2015 – and 900 million of those newcomers to the consumer class will be in emerging markets. GE, for example, expects to get as much 60 per cent of its revenue growth from emerging markets over the next decade.[65]

Mere size and growth do not guarantee their overall appeal and potential. The growth rates may be consistently higher than in developed markets but they may be subject to greater volatility. For example, Russia, Brazil and Argentina all faced severe financial crises between the years of 1999–2001. Evident in the data is the role of political risk; that is, government interference in entry and market development situations. The Russian government blocked a landmark investment of German engineering company Siemens in OAO Power Machines on antitrust grounds, as the government tightened its control on industries it deems vital to the country's interests. The Russian government has also barred foreign-owned companies from bidding for its oil and metal deposits.[66] In other instances, emerging-market governments have leveraged their position as hosts to foreign investors. The Chinese government has tried to impose their own standards on new technologies, such as EVD for video-disk players and Red Flag Linux for operating systems. The rational behind this 'techno-nationalism' is that China is tired of foreign patent fees for products made and sold domestically (in this case, $4.50 per unit to six Japanese companies that developed the underlying DVD technology).[67]

EXHIBIT 4.13 Market potential of 27 emerging markets, 2008

Countries	Market Size Rank	Index	Market Growth Rate Rank	Index	Market Intensity Rank	Index	Market Consumption Capacity Rank	Index	Commercial Infrastructure Rank	Index	Economic Freedom Rank	Index	Market Receptivity Rank	Index	Country Risk Rank	Index	Overall Index Rank	Index
Hong Kong	25	1	9	35	1	100	1	100	4	96	2	95	1	100	2	88	1	100
China	1	100	1	100	25	9	20	44	18	41	27	1	17	6	13	47	2	89
Singapore	27	1	2	49	10	53	14	53	5	89	5	80	2	84	1	100	3	76
Taiwan	11	5	20	16	7	58	5	81	1	100	4	80	6	30	3	83	4	62
Korea, South	6	11	24	10	6	61	2	92	2	97	7	75	10	19	6	64	5	59
Czech Rep.	23	1	22	15	15	48	4	82	3	96	3	81	9	20	5	65	6	51
Hungary	26	1	25	4	3	68	3	89	7	83	6	75	8	21	9	60	7	48
Mexico	7	11	16	21	9	54	22	29	15	52	9	64	3	83	12	51	8	45
Israel	24	1	27	1	2	72	9	68	8	78	8	70	4	39	7	63	9	45
Poland	15	4	21	16	12	52	7	72	6	85	11	63	16	8	8	60	10	42
India	2	39	3	46	23	22	13	56	24	26	18	43	25	6	16	40	11	40
Russia	3	27	19	19	22	26	12	59	10	63	26	11	19	6	15	41	12	28
Turkey	9	7	8	37	14	48	15	49	14	53	17	45	20	6	19	28	13	25
Malaysia	20	3	14	23	24	19	18	44	9	67	16	46	5	32	11	52	14	25
Chile	21	2	23	14	18	39	24	9	13	55	1	100	12	13	10	60	15	22
Thailand	17	4	10	34	19	39	16	47	17	48	21	32	11	19	17	39	16	22
Argentina	13	5	6	37	5	61	21	33	11	59	14	49	23	2	26	2	17	19
Philippines	12	5	13	23	4	67	19	44	22	23	19	43	13	13	23	18	18	17
Indonesia	5	12	12	25	20	37	10	63	23	30	20	43	21	4	24	15	19	17
Saudi Arabia	14	4	17	21	27	1	8	69	12	56	24	17	14	9	4	65	20	16
Egypt	16	4	7	37	16	45	11	61	21	35	25	16	18	6	20	28	21	16
South Africa	8	7	11	27	13	49	27	1	25	19	10	64	7	22	14	46	22	14
Brazil	4	22	26	4	21	37	25	8	16	49	13	51	27	1	18	32	23	12
Pakistan	10	6	18	20	8	56	6	73	26	18	22	22	26	1	25	9	24	9
Peru	22	2	4	46	17	39	23	24	27	1	12	57	24	2	22	22	25	5
Colombia	19	3	15	22	11	53	26	3	20	40	15	48	22	4	21	23	26	4
Venezuela	18	3	5	41	26	4	17	47	19	41	23	18	15	8	27	1	27	1

Source: **http://globaledge.msu.edu/ResourceDesk/mpi/** (Accessed January 31, 2009).

In Brazil, it took a Dutch telecommunications company six months and eight government agency approvals before obtaining a temporary business licence.[68]

Another concern is the current and future competition from emerging-market companies. Chinese companies have been able to develop powerful global brands in a very short period of time. Some have been developed from the domestic base in a step-by-step manner (e.g., Haier in appliances and Geely in cars) or through acquisitions of existing global brands (such as TCL in TVs and Lenovo in computers).[69] Another concern is based on economic and national security. Companies such as GE, Microsoft, Cisco and Intel all have established R&D operations in China, thereby training foreign scientists and possibly giving the omni-present Chinese government access to proprietary technologies.[70]

Given that emerging markets differ from each other in substantial ways, appropriate strategies have to be developed for each. As shown in Exhibit 4.14, Brazil, China, India and Russia are quite different when measured on marketing-related dimensions. Surveys show that Chinese consumers value convenience, followed by spaciousness and comfort of stores and selection they offer. Carre-four, Wal-Mart and Metro have all done very well in China's new retail environment.[71] In Latin America, however, companies that have tried to export supermarket and hypermarket models from developed markets have faced strong competition from small-scale retailers – the shops, street markets and small independent supermarkets that are an integral part of Latin culture.[72]

A number of strategic choices are available but most of them require recognizing the idio-syncracies of the market. Whatever the strategy, the marketer has to make sure to secure the company's core competencies while being innovative.[73]

Adjust entry strategy

GM entered the Russian market to produce sport utility vehicles (SUVs) in a joint venture with AvtoVAZ, Russia's largest car maker. Russia is one of the eight large markets that will grow substantially in the future. GM chose to use a joint venture to secure a local engineering source to eliminate many of the risks that lead to failure in emerging markets. Since the car, the Niva, is 100 per cent designed in Russia, the cost of engineering is substantially lower than what GM would have had to pay in Europe. Relying completely on local content pro-tects GM from any protective scheme that the government may impose. Controlling the costs allows GM to, in turn, provide a car at the pricing point (approximately $12,000) that con-sumers are willing to pay for a GM branded vehicle. Another benefit of GM's strategy is securing an existing dealer network. An added benefit for GM is its ability to export the Niva to other emerging markets using the Daewoo network (acquired by GM earlier).[74] Dell's suc-cess is based on its customers' approach. However, Dell's practice of selling direct to custom-ers, over the internet or the phone, does not work very well in China. Chinese typically want to lay their hands on computers before they buy them. That means the best way to reach them is via vast retailing operations, the strength of local players Lenovo and Founder Elec-tronics, which both rank ahead of Dell with market shares of 25.7 per cent and 11.3 per cent, respectively. To maintain its core approach, Dell has set up kiosks to demonstrate its SmartPC and other products and allow for orders from these kiosks.[75]

Manage affordability

Volkswagen, which arrived in 1984, and General Motors, which established its operations in 1997, have dominated the Chinese auto markets. However, they are now facing competition offering more economically priced cars. The reason for the shift in purchasing preferences is that the typical buyer has changed. Only a few years ago, the majority of purchases were made by state-owned companies, for whom price was not the critical criterion. Currently, most buyers are individuals who want the best deal for their money. To respond, GM has introduced the $8,000 Chevy Spark but will focus on the higher-end market with its Cadillac line.[76]

Invest in distribution

Kodak has nearly 8,000 photo stores across China, one of the country's largest retail opera-tions. The company taps the desire of many Chinese to run their own businesses while

EXHIBIT 4.14   Marketing contexts for key emerging markets

	Brazil	China	India	Russia
Modes of entry				
	Both greenfield investments and acquisitions are possible. Companies team up with local partners to gain local expertise.	Government permits both greenfield and acquisitions. Acquired companies may have been state-owned and have hidden liabilities. Alliances allow for aligning interests with all levels of government.	Restrictions in some sectors make joint ventures necessary. Red tape hinders companies in sectors where the government does not allow foreign investment.	Both greenfield and acquisitions are possible but difficult. Companies form alliances to gain access to government and local inputs.
Product development/intellectual property rights				
	Local design capability exists. IPR disputes with the United States exist in some sectors.	Imitation and piracy abound. Penalties for violation vary by province and level of corruption.	Some local design capability is available. IPR problems with the United States exist in some industries. Regulatory bodies monitor product quality and fraud.	Strong local design capability but an ambivalent attitude toward IPR. Sufficient regulatory authority exists, but enforcement is patchy.
Supplier base and logistics				
	Suppliers are available with MERCOSUR. A good network of highways, airports, and ports exists.	Several suppliers have strong manufacturing capabilities, but few vendors have advanced technical capabilities. Road network is well developed and port facilities are excellent.	Suppliers are available, but their quality and dependability vary greatly. Roads are in poor condition. Ports and airports are under-developed.	Companies can rely on local companies for basic supplies. The European region has decent logistics networks, trans-Ural does not.
Brand perceptions and management				
	Consumers accept both local and global brands. Global as well as local agencies are present.	Consumers prefer to buy products from American, European, and Japanese companies. Multinational ad agencies dominate.	Consumers buy both local and global brands. Global ad agencies are present, but they have been less successful than locals.	Consumers prefer global brands in automobiles and high tech. Local brands thrive in food and beverages. Some local and global ad agencies are present.

Source: Adapted from Tarun Khanna, Krishna Palepu, and Jayant Sinha, "Strategies that Fit Emerging Markets," *Harvard Business Review* 83 (June 2005), pp. 68, 69.

helping them negotiate setting up their operations. One Kodak campaign offered all of the necessary photo-development equipment, training and a store licence for 99,000 yuan ($12,000). Kodak negotiated a deal with the Bank of China and other big banks to arrange financing for individuals lacking capital. These programmes are part of Kodak's big bet when it bought three debt-laden state enterprises and many of their workers for $1 billion. In return, no other companies in the industry were allowed into China for four years.[77]

Build strong brands

A common characteristic across all emerging markets is the appeal of recognizable brands. While it is easiest for international marketers to extend their global brands to emerging markets, some companies such as Danone acquire companies but continue selling the products under original names. Adding a new quality dimension to well-established brands, consumer loyalty is ensured. Furthermore, this strategy will generate favour among Chinese officials who may not want to see local brands go under. In 2005, Wahaha was honoured as one of 'Most Favourite Chinese Brands' by CCTV. Danone has started making a local water brand Wahaha into a global brand.[78]

DEVELOPING MARKETS

The time may have come to look at the four billion people in the world who live in poverty, subsisting on less than $2,000 a year.[79] Not only is this segment a full two-thirds of the current market place, but it is expected to grow to six billion by 2040. Despite initial skepticism about access and purchasing power, marketers are finding that they can make profits while at the same time having a positive effect on the sustainable livelihoods of people not normally considered potential customers.[80] However, it will require radical departures from the traditional business models; for example, new partnerships (ranging from local governments to non-profits) and new pricing structures (allowing customers to rent or lease rather than buy and providing new financing choices for purchases). Hewlett-Packard has an initiative called World e-Inclusion that, working with a range of global and local partners, aims to sell, lease, or donate a billion dollars worth of satellite-powered computer products and services to markets in Africa, Asia, Eastern Europe, Latin America and the Middle East.[81] To engage with beta communities in Senegal, Hewlett-Packard partnered with Joko, Inc., a company founded by revered Senegalese pop star Youssou n'Dour.

Five elements of success are required for an international marketer to take advantage of and thrive in developing markets.[82]

Research

The first order of business is to learn about the needs, aspirations and habits of targeted populations for whom traditional intelligence gathering may not be the most effective. For example, just because the demand for land lines in developing countries was low, it would have been wrong to assume that little demand for phones existed. The real reasons were that land lines were expensive, subscribers had to wait for months to get hooked up, and lines often went down due to bad maintenance, flood and theft of copper cables. Mobile phones have been a solution to that problem. Subscriptions increased 67 per cent in sub-Saharan Africa in 2004, as compared with 10 per cent in Western Europe.[83]

Creating buying power

Without credit, it is impossible for many of the developing-country consumers to make major purchases. Programmes in microfinance have allowed consumers, with no property as collateral, to borrow sums averaging $100 to make purchases and have retail banking services available to them. Lenders such as GrameenBank in Bangladesh and Compartamos in Mexico have helped millions of families to escape poverty. Excellent payment records (e.g., only

0.56 per cent of the loans are even days late at Compartamos), have started attracting companies such as Citicorp to microfinancing, through underwriting microfinance bonds in markets such as Peru.[84]

Tailoring local solutions

In the product area, companies must combine advanced technology with local insights. Hindustan Lever (part of Unilever) learned that low-income Indians, usually forced to settle for low-quality products, wanted to buy high-end detergents and personal care products, but could not afford them in the quantities available. In response, the company developed extremely low-cost packaging material and other innovations that allowed for a product priced in pennies instead of the $4 to $15 price of the regular containers. The same brand is on all of the product forms, regardless of packaging. Given that these consumers do not shop at supermarkets, Lever employs local residents with pushcarts who take small quantities of the sachets to kiosks.[85]

Improving access

Due to economic and physical isolation of poor communities, providing access can lead to a thriving business. In Bangladesh (with income levels of $200 annually), GrameenPhone Ltd. leases access to wireless phones to villagers. Every phone is used by an average of 100 people and generates $90 in revenue a month – two or three times the revenues generated by wealthier users who own their phones in urban areas. Similarly, Ericsson India, which currently connects 18 villages and 15 small towns in Tamil Nadu through this project, has tied up with various domain experts to offer services and information content which are relevant to its target audience. For example, Ericsson has tied up with Apollo Hospitals to offer Telemedicine and mobile healthcare services. It has also tied up with Bangalore-based Edurite Technologies to offer e-learning services and the local Government to offer e-Governance to Gramjyoti villages and towns.[86] A similar project is the focus of *The International Marketplace 4.3*.

Shaping aspirations

The biggest challenges in developing markets are in providing essential services. In this sense, developing markets can be ideal settings for commercial and technological innovation. With significant demand for mobile handsets in developing countries, both Nokia and Motorola have developed models that sell for as little as $25. They are ideally suited to match consumer demand for inexpensive phones with the features, quality, and brand names consumers want. Emerging low-cost producers from China cannot match the volume or the brand franchises of the global players. While gross margins on these phones may be as little as 15 per cent (as compared with 33 per cent at the high end), the big volumes can establish scale economies that reduce costs even for high-end models.[87] Global marketers are very often the only ones that can realistically make a difference in solving some of the problems in developing markets. Developing new technologies or products is a resource-intensive task and requires knowledge transfer from one market to another. Without multinationals as catalysts, nongovernmental organizations, local governments and communities will continue to flounder in their attempts to bring development to the poorest nations in the world.[88]

The emergence of these markets presents a great growth opportunity for companies. It also creates a chance for business, government and civil society to join together in a common cause to help the aspiring poor to join the world market economy. Lifting billions of people from poverty may help avert social decay, political chaos, terrorism and environmental deterioration that is certain to continue if the gap between the rich and poor countries continues to widen. For example, Coca-Cola has introduced 'Project Mission' in Botswana to launch a drink to combat anaemia, blindness and other afflictions common in poorer parts of the world. The drink, called Vitango, is like the company's Hi-C orange-flavoured drink, but it contains 12 vitamins and minerals chronically lacking in the diets of people in developing countries. The project satisfies multiple objectives for the Coca-Cola Company. First, it could

THE INTERNATIONAL **MARKETPLACE 4.3**

The $100 Laptop

The goal of One Laptop Per Child is to place $100 laptops in the hands of 150 million school children in developing countries. The premise is that computers will spur children to learn and explore outside of a class room, and share discoveries with their families. At the national level, these laptops will improve both public education and the economy in the long term.

To achieve the $100 price, the laptop will be a stripped-down product, usable for basic word-processing, internet, and email. It has no hard drive, instead using flash memory similar to that used in digital cameras. The processor runs at 500MHz. Though spartan, the design is ingenious: each laptop will include a Wi-Fi radio transmitter designed to knit machines into a wireless hub so they can share a connection and pass it on from one computer to another. While the computer has a power cord, it also has an electricity generating crank. The swivelling eight-inch screen is the biggest challenge in terms of cost. To keep the price down, the screen will run in two modes, with a high-resolution monochrome mode for word processing, and a lower-resolution colour mode for internet use. The first versions will be powered by an AMD microprocessor and use an open-source Linux-based operating system provided by Red Hat. All of the systems have to be quite robust given the high heat, dust and moisture conditions in targeted markets.

The laptop will be sold at $100 to governments in countries such as Brazil, Egypt, Nigeria and Thailand, but will also be made available for $200 to the general public. Even at $100 a piece, it is not certain that developing countries can afford the $15 billion to supply 150 million laptops.

At the corporate level, responses vary. AMD, on the one hand, is 'absolutely committed' to the project and it fits with its initiative to bring the internet and computing access to half the world by 2015. It expects the project to be a business for AMD, not just philanthropy. On the other hand, Intel argues that the product's limited programs will not satisfy users. Dell has proposed that it is not feasible to manufacture a $100 computer to meet the company's high standards. The company's argument is that any computer should prepare students for the applications they will be using after they get out of school. Microsoft is supportive of the programme but would like the computer to use its software rather than the open-source alternatives currently proposed. Analysts have suggested that if the final choice is not Microsoft software, the company will launch its own laptop for the developing markets.

SOURCES: 'Intel to Chip in with Low-Cost Rural PC', *Knight Ridder News Service,* January 11, 2006, 1; 'Intel Claims $100 Laptop Will Not Appeal', *Telecomworldwire,* December 12, 2005, 1; 'I'd Like to Teach the World to Type', *Fortune,* November 28, 2005, 63–64; 'The $100 Laptop Moves Closer to Reality', *The Washington Post,* November 14, 2005, B1, B2; and 'The $100 Laptop Moves Closer to Reality', *The Wall Street Journal,* November 14, 2005, B1. See also **www.redhat.com/magazine/014dec05/features/olpc**.

help boost sales at a time when global sales of carbonated drinks are slowing and, second, it will help in establishing relationships with governments and other local constituents that will serve as a positive platform for brand Coca-Cola. The market for such nutritional drinks may be limited, but they are meant to offer Coca-Cola a role of good corporate citizen at a time when being perceived as such is increasingly important for multinational corporations.[89]

SUMMARY

Economic variables relating to the various markets' characteristics – population, income, consumption patterns, infrastructure, geography and attitudes toward foreign involvement in the economy – form a starting point for assessment of market potential for the international marketer. These data are readily available but should be used in conjunction with other, more interpretive data, because the marketer's plans often require a long-term approach. Data on the economic environment produce a snapshot of the past; in some cases, old data are used to make decisions affecting operations two years in the future. Even if the data are recent, they cannot themselves indicate the growth and the intensity of development. Some economies remain stagnant, plagued by natural calamities, internal problems, and lack of export markets, whereas some witness booming economic development.

Economic data provide a baseline from which other more market/product–specific and even experiential data can be collected. Understanding the composition and interrelationships between economic indicators is essential for the assessment of the other environments and their joint impact on market potential. The international marketer needs to understand the impact of the economic environment on social development.

The emergence of economic integration in the world economy poses unique opportunities for and challenges to the international marketer. Eliminating barriers between member markets and erecting new ones vis-à-vis non-members will call for adjustments in past strategies to fully exploit the new situations. In the late 1980s and early 1990s, economic integration increased substantially. The signing of the North American Free Trade Agreement produced the largest trading bloc in the world, whereas the Europeans are moving in their cooperation beyond the pure trade dimension. New trading blocs and the expansion of the existing ones will largely depend on future trade liberalization and political will within and among countries.

As developed markets have matured, marketers are looking at both emerging and developing markets for their future growth. To succeed, marketers will have to be innovative, pioneer new ways of doing business, and outmanoeuvre local competitors, many of them intent on becoming global players themselves.

Key terms

common market	Free Trade Area of the Americas	inflation
customs union	(FTAA)	maquiladoras
debt problem	free trade area	microfinance
economic union	Group of Five	Physical Quality of Life Index (PQLI)
European Union	Group of Seven	political union
factor mobility	Group of Ten	purchasing power parities (PPP)
Fortress Europe	household	Single European Act
	import substitution	urbanization

Questions for discussion

1   Place these markets in the framework that follows.

a.	Indonesia	g.	Turkey	m.	Peru
b.	Mozambique	h.	Spain	n.	Jamaica
c.	India	i.	Singapore	o.	Poland
d.	Bangladesh	j.	Nigeria	p.	United Kingdom
e.	Niger	k.	Algeria	q.	Iraq
f.	Brazil	l.	Zambia	r.	Saudi Arabia

	Income level		
	Low	Middle	High
TRADE STRUCTURE			
Industrial			
Developing			
• Semi-industrial			
• Oil-exporting			
• Primary producing			
• Populous South Asia			
• Least developed			

2   Using available data, assess the market potential for (a) power generators and (b) consumer appliances in (1) the Philippines, (2) Jordan, and (3) Portugal.

3   From the international marketer's point of view, what are the opportunities and problems caused by increased urbanization in developing countries?

4   Comment on this statement: 'A low per capita income will render the market useless'.

5   What can a marketer do to advance regional economic integration?

Internet exercises

1   Compare and contrast two different points of view on expanding trade by accessing the website of The Business Roundtable – an industry coalition promoting increased interaction to and from world markets (**http://www.businessroundtable.org**), and the AFL-CIO, American Federation of Labor–Congress of Industrial Organizations (**http://www.aflcio.org**).

2   Why do marketers engage in major projects in developing countries, such as Hewlett-Packard's e-inclusion project (**http://www.hp.com/e-inclusion/en/index.html**). Outline both the short-term and long-term benefits.

Recommended readings

The Arthur Andersen North American Business Sourcebook. Chicago: Triumph Books, 1994.

Business Guide to Mercosur. London: Economist Intelligence Unit, 1998.

Clement, Norris C. (ed.) *North American Economic Integration: Theory and Practice.* London: Edward Elgar Publications, 2000.

Current issues of *Country Monitor, Business Europe, Business East Europe, Business Asia, Business Latin America, Business China.*

The European Union: A Guide for Americans, 2006 edition. Available at **http://www.eurunion.org/infores/euguide/euguide.htm**.

International Marketing Data and Statistics 2006. London: Euromonitor, 2006.

Marber, Peter. *From Third World to World Class: The Future of Emerging Markets in the Global Economy.* New York: Perseus Books, 1998.

Ohmae, Kenichi. *The Borderless World: Power and Strategy in the Interlinked Economy.* New York: Harper Business, 1999.

Ryans, John K. and Pradeep A. Rau. *Marketing Strategies for the New Europe: A North American Perspective on 1992.* Chicago: American Marketing Association, 1990.

Sueo, Sekiguchi, and Noda Makito (eds). *Road to ASEAN-10: Japanese Perspectives on Economic Integration.* Tokyo: Japan Centre for International Exchange, 2000.

Venables, Anthony, Richard E. Baldwin and Daniel Cohen (eds). *Market Integration, Regionalism and the Global Economy.* Cambridge, England: Cambridge University Press, 1999.

The World in Figures. London: Economist Publications, 2006.

World Development Report 2006. New York: Oxford University Press, 2006.

Yearbook of International Trade Statistics. New York: United Nations, 2006.

Notes

1   Global Business Policy Council, *Globalization Ledger* (Washington, DC: A. T. Kearney, 2000), 3.

2   C. K. Prahalad and Stuart L. Hart, 'The Fortune at the Bottom of the Pyramid', *Strategy and Business,* (first quarter, 2002): 35–47.

3   'African Debt, European Doubt', *Economist,* April 8, 2000, 46.

4   'Who Will Join Europe's Club – and When?' *Economist,* April 8, 2000, 53–54.

5   Rahul Jacob, 'The Big Rise', *Fortune,* May 30, 1994, 74–90.

6   Roger D. Blackwell, Paul W. Miniard, and James F. Engel, *Consumer Behavior* (Mason, OH: Thomson, 2001), 283.

7   *European Marketing Data and Statistics 2001* (London: Euromonitor, 2002), 380.

8   **http://www.defra.gov.uk/rural/ruralstats/rural-defn/Rural_Urban_Introductory_Guide.pdf**

9   **http://www.scb.se/statistik/MI/MI0810/2000I02/MI38SM9601.pdf**

10 **http://docs.google.com/gview?a=v&q=cache:2-gLVoOkiJUJ:earthtrends.wri.org/country_profiles/fetch_profile.php%3Ftheme%3D4%26filename%3Dpop_cou_480.PDF+In+Mauritius,+an+urban+area+between+1,000+and+10,000+inhabitants&hl=en&gl=uk**

11 **http://www.ifpindia.org/Built-Up-Areas-in-India-e-GEOPOLIS.html**

12 The World Bank, *World Development Indicators* (Washington, DC , 2000), 85. See also **http://www.worldbank.org/data/wdi2000**.

13 'In India, Luxury Is Within Reach of Many', *The Wall Street Journal,* October 17, 1995, A17.

14 Named after the German statistician, Ernst Engel. Wikipedia (2010) 'Engel's law'. Online. Available from: **http://en.wikipedia.org/wiki/Engel's_law** (Accessed 27/6/10).

15 London Euromonitor (2008) *International Marketing Data and Statistics* (32nd edn) London . ISBN 9781842644546 1842644548. Online. Available: **http://www.worldcat.org/isbn/1842644548**

16 'Go West Westerners', *Business Week,* November 14, 2005, 60–61; and 'A Booming Coast Breathes New Life into

China's Inland', *The Wall Street Journal,* October 17, 2005, A1, A14.

17 London Euromonitor (2008) *International Marketing Data and Statistics* (32nd edn) London . ISBN 9781842644546 1842644548. Online. Available: **http://www.worldcat.org/isbn/1842644548**

18 **http://www.socialedge.org/blogs/sagar-gubbi/topics/Innovation**

19 Bob Meyer, 'The Original Meaning of Trade Meets the Future in Barter', *World Trade,* January 2000, 46–50.

20 Edward Tse, 'The Right Way to Achieve Profitable Growth in the Chinese Market', *Strategy and Business* (second quarter, 1998): 10–21.

21 'The Mobile Revolution: Global Scale is Critical', *Businessline,* January 10, 2006, 1; Tony Dennis, 'Two Billion Mobile Phone Mark Reached', *The Inquirer,* September 18, 2005, available at **http://www.theinquirer.net**.

22 *Internet Domain Survey,* July 2005, available at **http://www.isc.org**.

23 **http://www.internetworldstats.com/stats9.htm**.

24 'The Mad Grab for Piece of Air', *Business Week,* April 17, 2000, 152–154; and 'Hello, Internet', *Business Week,* May 3, 1999, 170–175.

25 Jesse Berst, 'It's Back: How Interactive TV Is Sneaking Back into Your Living Room', available at **http://www.zdnet.com/anchordesk/story/story_3368.html**. See also, **http://www.visiongain.com**.

26 Rahul Jacob, 'Asian Infrastructure: The Biggest Bet on Earth', *Fortune,* October 31, 1994, 139–150.

27 Global Business Policy Council, *Globalization Ledger* (Washington, DC: A.T. Kearney, April 2000).

28 Ben Crow and Alan Thomas, *Third World Atlas* (Milton Keynes, England: Open University Press, 1984), 85.

29 The World Bank, *World Development Report 1982* (New York: Oxford University Press, 1982), 63.

30 Ed Diener and Eunkook Suh, eds., *Culture and Subjective Well-Being,* (Boston: MIT Press, 2003), chapter 1; and 'In Bhutan, Happiness is King', *The Wall Street Journal,* October 13, 2004, A14.

31 Ilkka A. Ronkainen, 'Trading Blocs: Opportunity or Demise for International Trade?' *Multinational Business Review* 1 (Spring 1993): 1–9.

32 *The European Union: A Guide for Americans* (Washington, DC: Delegation of the European Commission to the United States, 2006), chapter 2. See **http://www.eurunion.org/infores/euguide/euguide.htm**.

33 See **http://secretariat.efta.int**.

34 Gary C. Hufbauer and Jeffrey J. Schott, *NAFTA: An Eight-Year Appraisal* (Washington, DC: Institute for International Economics, 2003), Chapter 1.

35 Sidney Weintraub, *NAFTA at Three: A Progress Report* (Washington, DC: Centre for Strategic and International Studies, 1997), 17–18.

36 John Cavanagh, Sarah Anderson, Jaime Serra and J. Enrique Espinosa, 'Happily Ever NAFTA', *Foreign Policy,* September/ October 2002, 58–65.

37 For annual trade information, see **http://www.census.gov/foreigntrade**.

38 'U.S. Trade with Mexico during the Third NAFTA Year', *International Economic Review* (Washington, DC: International Trade Commission, April 1997): 11.

39 'Fox and Bush, for Richer, for Poorer', *The Economist,* February 3, 2001, 37–38.

40 'Aerospace Suppliers Gravitate to Mexico', *The Wall Street Journal,* January 23, 2002, A17.

41 Laura Heller, 'The Latin Market Never Looked So Bueno', *DSN Retailing Today,* June 10, 2002, 125–126.

42 'Retail Oasis', *Business Mexico,* April 2001, 15.

43 Lara L. Sowinski, 'Maquiladoras', *World Trade,* September 2000, 88–92.

44 'The Decline of the Maquiladora', *Business Week,* April 29, 2002, 59.

45 See, for example, **http://www.crea-inc.org** and **http://www.maquilasolidarity.org**.

46 'Americas: Critics Aside, Nafta Has Been a Boon To Mexico', *The Wall Street Journal,* January 9, 2004, A.11; and 'NAFTA's Scorecard: So Far, So Good', *Business Week,* July 9, 2001, 54–56.

47 'Hogtied', *The Economist,* January 17, 2002, 35.

48 'Localizing Production', *Global Commerce,* August 20, 1997, 1.

49 'Latin America Fears Stagnation in Trade Talks with the United States', *The New York Times,* April 19, 1998, D1.

50 'Mexico, EU Sign Free-Trade Agreement', *The Wall Street Journal,* March 24, 2000, A15.

51 'Latin Lesson', *Far Eastern Economic Review,* January 4, 2001, 109.

52 Gilberto Meza, 'Is the FTAA Floundering?' *Business Mexico,* February 2005, 46–48.

53 'The Americas: A Cautious Yes to Pan-American Trade', *The Economist,* April 28, 2001, 35–36.

54 'Regional Commonalities Help Global Ad Campaigns Succeed in Latin America', *Business International,* February 17, 1992, 47–52; and 'Ripping Down the Walls across the Americas', *Business Week,* December 26, 1994, 78–80.

55 Michael R. Czinkota and Masaaki Kotabe, 'America's New World Trade Order', *Marketing Management* 1 (Summer 1992): 49–56.

56 Robert Scollay, 'The Changing Outlook for Asia-Pacific Regionalism', *The World Economy* 24 (September 2001): 1135–1160.

57 'Afrabet Soup', *The Economist,* February 10, 2001, 77.

58 'Try, Try Again', *The Economist,* July 13, 2002, 41.

59 Josh Martin, 'Gulf States to Adopt a Single Currency', *Middle East,* May 2002, 23–25.

60 Eric Friberg, Risto Perttunen, Christian Caspar, and Dan Pittard, 'The Challenges of Europe 1992', *The McKinsey Quarterly* 21 (no. 2, 1988): 3–15.

61 'Lean, Mean, European', *The Economist,* April 29, 2000, 5–7.

62 Gianluigi Guido, 'Implementing a Pan-European Marketing Strategy', *Long Range Planning* 24 (no. 5, 1991): 23–33.

63 http://www.emdirectory.com.

64 James A. Gingrich, 'Five Rules for Winning Emerging Market Consumers', *Strategy and Business* (second quarter, 1999): 19–33.

65 'GE Pins Hopes on Emerging Markets', *The Wall Street Journal,* March 2, 2005, A3, A10.

66 'Kremlin Blocks Big Acquisition by Siemens AG', *The Wall Street Journal,* April 14, 2005, A14, A16.

67 'China Seeks Its Own High-tech Standards', *CNN.com,* May 27, 2004; and 'Despite Shelving WAPI, China Stands Firm on Chip Tax', *InfoWorld,* April 22, 2004.

68 'In Brazil, Thicket of Red Tape Spoils Recipe for Growth', *The Wall Street Journal,* May 24, 2005, A1, A9.

69 'China's Power Brands', *Business Week,* November 8, 2004, 77–84.

70 'The High-tech Threat from China', *Business Week,* January 31, 2005, 22.

71 'Let the Retail Wars Begin', *Business Week,* January 17, 2005, 44–45.

72 Guillermo D'Andrea, E. Alejandro Stengel, and Anne Goebel-Krstelj, 'Six Truths About Emerging-Market Consumers', *Strategy and Business* 34 (Spring 2004): 58–69.

73 This section builds on Tarun Khanna, Krishna Palepu, and Jayant Sinha, 'Strategies that Fit Emerging Markets', *Harvard Business Review* 83 (June 2005): 63–76 and James A. Gingrich, 'Five Rules for Winning Emerging Market Consumers', *Strategy and Business* (second quarter, 1999): 19–33.

74 'Investing in Russia: A Symbiotic Process', *The Official website of the 8th Annual U.S. Russian Investment Symposium,* June 27, 2001, available at http://www.uris.com.

75 'Tech's Future', *Business Week,* September 27, 2004, 82–89.

76 'GM and VW: How Not to Succeed in China', *Business Week,* May 9, 2005, 94.

77 'Cracking China's Market', *The Wall Street Journal,* January 9, 2003, B1, B4.

78 http://en.wahaha.com.cn/news/company/2005/06/03/wahaha750.html.

79 The World Bank considers $2,000 to be the minimum to sustain a decent life.

80 Dana James, 'B2-4B Spells Profits', *Marketing News,* November 5, 2001, 1, 11–12.

81 http://www.hp.com/e-inclusion/en.

82 This framework is adapted from C. K. Prahalad and Stuart L. Hart, 'The Fortune at the Bottom of the Pyramid', *Strategy and Business,* First Quarter, 2002, 35–47

83 'Cell Phones Reshaping Africa', *CNN.com*, October 17, 2005; 'Calling Across the Divide', *The Economist,* March 12, 2005, 74.

84 'Major victories for micro-finance', *Financial Times,* May 18, 2005, 10. See also http://www.planetfinance.org.

85 Cait Murphy, 'The Hunt for Globalization That Works', *Fortune,* October 28, 2002, 163–176.

86 'And the Winners Are . . .', *The Economist,* September 18, 2004, 17; 'The Digital Village', *Business Week,* June 28, 2004, 60–62; and Arundhati Parmar, 'Indian Farmers Reap Web Harvest', *Marketing News,* June 1, 2004, 27, 31.

87 'Cell Phones for the People', *Business Week,* November 14, 2005, 65.

88 C. K. Prahalad and Allen Hammond, 'Serving the World's Poor, Profitably', *Harvard Business Review,* 80 (September 2002): 48–59

89 'Drinks for Developing Countries', *The Wall Street Journal, November* 27, 2001, B1, B3.

CHAPTER 5

THE POLITICAL AND LEGAL ENVIRONMENT

THE INTERNATIONAL **MARKETPLACE 5.1**

The New Russia: Presentation counts!

Capitalism and communism are fundamentally different both in theory and in practice, as reaffirmed by recent developments in Russia and the former Soviet Union (a federation of communist countries founded in 1922 and dissolved in 1991; also known as the USSR). Capitalism is responsive to consumers because it allows sales success to affect the seller's personal well-being. In contrast, communism prohibits private profit and eliminates any personal incentive for sellers to better satisfy customers. As capitalism comes to formerly communist countries, product presentation takes on a new importance. Russian businesses are warming to western-style packaging.

Under the communist system of the USSR, products had been packed sensibly, but without flair. Companies did not worry about using packaging as a tool to convince consumers that their brand was superior to others. Since the Soviet-era economy had not allowed for brand variety, milk was milk, and salami was salami. Fashionable items like make-up and shoes carried the name of the region in which they were produced – and, usually, only one region specialized in each product. Consumers therefore had no choice but to buy that which was available.

With the collapse of communism came foreign competition and the privatization of manufacturing plants. Now anybody can produce anything and distribute anywhere. As a result, local companies have lost the inherent advantage of being the only producers accessible to Soviet customers. They now have to make their products stand out against rival firms.

A new creativity has surfaced, particularly for consumer products, where Russian firms have the least experience given the scarcity of leisure goods under the Soviet system. This sector is also most susceptible to advertising, as it depends on popular preferences, not basic needs. Today, Red Army Vodka distinguishes itself from competitors by selling its products in bottles shaped like glossy lipstick tubes. Another beverage company, Bravo Premium, plays on the social status of women, creating a 'cocktail in a bottle' targeting exclusively female consumers; served in a slender container made to fit easily in a woman's hand, the drink is named 'Milano', evoking an association with the well-known fashion centre in Italy.

Politics continues to play an important role in brand identity. In the 1990s, Russia experienced a pro-western sentiment that promoted European cultural supremacy over Russia. Many Russians then preferred foreign products over domestic ones, since they were evocative of European standards and traditions. Now, however, a new wave of nationalism sweeps the country. Moscow's Duty Free sells domestically made chocolates called *Schok* with the punchline 'Schok: Now *that's* the Russian way!'

Creative packaging has taken on a role equally crucial to that of actual advertising. Improvements within the packaging industry have happened quickly, and foreign investment has followed. In 2005, Alcan, a Canadian company, spent $55 million to open and equip two packaging plants in the Moscow and St Petersburg areas. Production in both plants will bring additional resources to Russian companies wishing to improve sales through catchy packaging.

Much as most managers would like to ignore them, political and legal factors often play a critical role in international marketing activities. The interpretation and application of regu-lations can sometimes lead to conflicting and even misleading results. Even the best business plans can go awry as a result of unexpected political or legal influences, and the failure to anticipate these factors can be the undoing of an otherwise successful business venture. Exhibit 5.1 ranks the factors that affect a country's investment climate; note that policy uncertainty dominates the concerns of firms. However, variations in political and legal envi-ronments can also offer new opportunities to international marketers, as *The International Marketplace 5.1* shows.

Of course, a single international political and legal environment does not exist. The busi-ness executive must be aware of political and legal factors on a variety of levels. For example, although it is useful to understand the complexities of the host country legal system, such knowledge does not protect against a home country imposed export embargo.

The study of the international political and legal environment must therefore be broken down into several subsegments. Many researchers do this by separating the legal from the po-litical. This separation – although perhaps analytically useful – is somewhat artificial because laws are generally the result of political decisions. Here no attempt will be made to separate legal and political factors, except when such a separation is essential.

Instead, this chapter will examine the political-legal environment from the manager's point of view. In making decisions about his or her firm's international marketing activities, the manager will need to concentrate on three areas: the political and legal circumstances of the home country; those of the host country; and the bilateral and multilateral agreements, trea-ties and laws governing the relations between host and home countries.

HOME COUNTRY POLITICAL AND LEGAL ENVIRONMENT

No manager can afford to ignore the policies and regulations of the country from which he or she conducts international marketing transactions. Wherever a firm is located, it will be affected by government policies and the legal system.

EXHIBIT 5.1

Environmental shortcomings of the investment climate

Source: World Development Indicators 2005, The World Bank Group, Text Figure 5a. **http:// devdata.worldbank.org/ wdi2005/Figures5.htm**, accessed January 6, 2006.

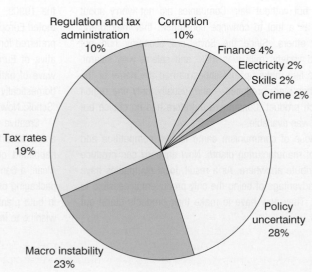

Regulation and tax administration 10%

Corruption 10%

Finance 4%

Electricity 2%

Skills 2%

Crime 2%

Policy uncertainty 28%

Macro instability 23%

Tax rates 19%

Many of these laws and regulations may not be designed specifically to address international marketing transactions, yet they can have a major impact on a firm's opportunities abroad. Minimum wage legislation, for example, affects the international competitiveness of a firm using production processes that are highly labour intensive. The cost of domestic safety regulations may significantly affect the pricing policies of firms in their international marketing efforts. For example, US legislation that created the Environmental Superfund requires payment by chemical firms based on their production volume, regardless of whether the production is sold domestically or exported. As a result, these firms are at a disadvantage internationally when exporting their commodity-type products because they must compete against foreign firms that are not required to make such a payment in their home countries and therefore have a cost advantage.

Other legal and regulatory measures, however, are clearly aimed at international marketing activities. Some may be designed to help firms in their international efforts. The lack of enforcement of others may hurt the international marketer. For instance, many firms are concerned about the lack of safeguards for intellectual property rights in developing countries, an issue discussed later in this chapter.

Another area in which governments may attempt to aid and protect the international marketing efforts of companies is grey market activities. Grey market goods are products that enter markets in ways not desired by their manufacturers. Companies may be hurt by their own products if they reach the consumer via uncontrolled distribution channels such as grey market activities.

Apart from specific areas that result in government involvement, the political environment in most countries tends to provide general support for the international marketing efforts of the country's firms. For example, a government may work to reduce trade barriers or to increase trade opportunities through bilateral and multilateral negotiations. Such actions will affect individual firms to the extent that they affect the international climate for free trade.

Often, however, governments also have specific rules and regulations restricting international marketing. Such regulations are frequently political in nature and are based on the fact that governments believe commerce to be only one objective among others, such as foreign policy and national security. Four main areas of governmental activities are of major concern to the international marketer here: embargoes or trade sanctions, export controls, import controls and the regulation of international business behaviour.

Embargoes and sanctions

The terms trade sanctions and embargoes as used here refer to governmental actions that distort the free flow of trade in goods, services or ideas for decidedly adversarial and political, rather than strictly economic, purposes. Exhibit 5.2 illustrates an EU agreement to impose more sanctions against Zimbabwe.[1] Human rights conditions in the country, as well as the threat of weapons proliferation, are the concerns of the EU countries that help maintain these sanctions in place. Advocates of sanctions regard them as an important weapon of foreign policy. Sceptics question whether sanctions are effective, and whether the costs they impose are worth the benefits.[2]

Trade sanctions were already used in the thirteenth century by the Hansa league, an association of north German merchants with grievances against Norway. Over the years, economic sanctions and embargoes have become an often-used foreign policy tool for many countries. Reasons for the impositions are varied, ranging from human rights to nuclear nonproliferation to terrorism (see the section on terrorism later in this chapter). The range of sanctions imposed can be quite broad. Examples are elimination of credits and prohibition of financial transactions. Typically, the intent is to bring commercial interchange to a complete halt.

The League of Nations set a precedent for the international legal justification of economic sanctions by subscribing to a covenant that provided for penalties or sanctions for breaching its provisions. The members of the League of Nations did not intend to use military or economic measures separately, but the success of the blockades of World War I fostered the opinion that 'the economic weapon, conceived not as an instrument of war but as a means of

EXHIBIT 5.2

More EU sanctions
against Zimbabwe

Source: **http://www.talkzimbabwe.
com/news/117/ARTICLE/4138/
2009-01-22.html** (Accessed
January 31, 2009).

The European Union Thursday indicated that it would impose more sanctions on the Zimbabwean government at the foreign minister's meeting in Brussels, Belgium barely two months after the last set of sanctions was introduced.

This announcement follows on the heels of an announcement last week by Karel Schwarzenberg, Minister of Foreign Affairs of the Czech Republic and President of the Council of the European Union that the EU was mulling further sanctions against President Mugabe's government. He made the announcement during the eighth ministerial troika of the South Africa-European Union Strategic Partnership, held in Kleinmond, South Africa, on 16 January 2009, Jiachi said.

The EU draft did not disclose the names of individuals or companies that will be included on the new list or how many.

The bloc's foreign ministers will also urge 'a probe into whether diamond sales are being used to support (President Mugabe's) government', according to a draft EU paper availed to Reuters news agency.

Said the document: 'The (EU) Council supports action to investigate the exploitation of diamonds from the site of Marange/Chiadzwa and their significance in possible financial support' to the government of President Mugabe according to the document, which will be presented to EU ministers.

The EU draft paper also urges the Kimberley Process – an international certification scheme set up to ensure diamonds do not fund conflict – 'to take action with a view to ensure Zimbabwe's compliance with its Kimberley obligations'.

The World Diamond Council in December raised concern about possible illegal exports of the precious mineral 'for the personal gain of a few'.

The new raft of sanctions coincides with an Extraordinary Summit of the Southern African Development Community (SADC) bloc in Pretoria, South Africa meant to find a peaceful resolution to the Zimbabwean crisis.

This is the second set of sanctions in less than two months. The last set of EU sanctions was imposed on December 8, 2008 exactly a week after former US President George W. Bush issued Executive Order 13469 blacklisting four individuals accused of supporting President Robert Mugabe and his government. The EU added 11 names to a list of some 160 ZANU PF officials banned from entering the bloc.

Usefulness of Sanctions

The usefulness of sanctions as an effective tool in effecting change in Zimbabwe has been questioned by many critics and think tanks.

Global think tank, International Crisis Group, in December 2008 dismissed the effectiveness of sanctions as a helpful tool in effecting change in Zimbabwe.

A report published by the group concluded that sanctions imposed by the West and other forms of pressure are 'unlikely to be productive in the absence of a new approach'.

'Even if the parties find a compromise on ministry allocation and related issues, the creation of two power centres by the GPA suggest that, in the context of their intense mutual distrust, political paralysis would prevent serious action to address the country's problems', read the report.

Cuban Ambassador to Zimbabwe Cosme Espinosa last year urged the people of Zimbabwe to unite against western-imposed sanctions.

'The system of sanctions against a country does not only affect the economy of a country, but also other sectors including health care, and the political well-being of a country among other things', said Espinosa.

Chinese Foreign Minister Yang Jiachi said his government was opposed to further imposition of sanctions against Zimbabwe and expressed confidence in the decisions taken by the SADC and the African Union – guarantors to the Global Political Agreement – signed by the ruling ZANU PF party and the two formations of the opposition Movement for Democratic Change parties.

'We do believe that this issue fundamentally has to be solved by the various elements in Zimbabwe and we believe that the stand taken by the AU, by SADC, are vitally important', said Yang at the end of the last leg of his four-nation African tour this month.

The Zimbabwean government blames sanctions imposed by the West for the current economic crisis in the country.

peaceful pressure, is the greatest discovery and most precious possession of the League'.[3] The basic idea was that economic sanctions could force countries to behave peacefully in the international community.

The idea of the multilateral use of economic sanctions was again incorporated into international law under the charter of the United Nations, but greater emphasize was placed on the enforcement process. Once decided upon, sanctions are mandatory, even though each permanent member of the Security Council can veto efforts to impose sanctions. The charter also allows for sanctions as enforcement action by regional agencies such as the Arab League, and the Organization of African Unity, but only with the Security Council's authorization.

The apparent strength of the United Nations enforcement system soon turned out to be flawed. Stalemates in the Security Council and vetoes by permanent members often led to a shift of emphasize to the General Assembly, which does not have the power to enforce. Further, concepts such as 'peace' and 'breach of peace' are seldom perceived in the same way by all members, and thus no systematic sanctioning policy developed in the United Nations. As a result, sanctions have frequently been imposed unilaterally in the hope of changing a particular country's government, or at least its policies. Unilateral imposition, however, tends to have major negative effects on the firms in the country that is exercising sanctions, since the only result is often a simple shift in trade.

Another key problem with unilateral imposition of sanctions is that they typically do not produce the desired result. Sanctions may make the obtaining of goods more difficult or expensive for the sanctioned country, yet achievement of the purported objective almost never occurs. In order to work, sanctions need to be imposed multilaterally. Only when virtually all nations in which a product is produced agree to deny it to a target can there be a true deprivation effect. Without such denial, sanctions do not have much bite. Yet to get all producing nations to agree can be quite difficult. Typically, individual countries have different relationships with the country subject to the sanctions due to geographic or historic reasons, and therefore cannot or do not want to terminate trade relations.

Yet global cooperation can be achieved. For example, when Iraq invaded Kuwait in August of 1990, virtually all members of the United Nations condemned this hostile action and joined a trade embargo against Iraq. Both major and minor Iraqi trading partners – including many Arab nations – honoured the United Nations trade embargo and ceased trade with Iraq in the attempt to force it to withdraw its troops from Kuwait. Agreements were made to financially compensate those countries most adversely affected by the trade measures. Therefore, when we consider that sanctions may well be the middle ground between going to war and doing nothing, their effective functioning can represent a powerful international policy measure.

One key concern with sanctions is the fact that governments often consider them as being free of cost. However, even though they may not affect the budget of governments, sanctions imposed by governments can mean significant loss of business to firms.

Due to these costs, the issue of compensating the domestic firms and industries affected by these sanctions needs to be raised. Yet, trying to impose sanctions slowly or making them less expensive to ease the burden on these firms undercuts their ultimate chance for success. The international marketing manager is often caught in this political web and loses business as a result. Frequently, firms try to anticipate sanctions based on their evaluations of the international political climate. Even when substantial precautions are taken, firms may still suffer substantial losses due to contract cancellations. However, this can be seen as the cost of one's government's support for an open global trading and investing environment.

Export controls

Many nations have **export control systems**, which are designed to deny or at least delay the acquisition of strategically important goods by adversaries. Most of these systems make controls the exception rather than the rule, with exports taking place independently from politics.

The legal basis for export controls varies across nations. For example, in Germany, armament exports are covered in the so-called War Weapons List, which is a part of the War

Weapons Control Law. The exports of other goods are covered by the German Export List. Dual-use items, which are goods useful for both military and civilian purposes, are then controlled by the Joint List of the European Union.[4]

Laws are passed to control all exports of goods, services and ideas. It is important to note here that an export of goods occurs whenever goods are physically transferred from the exporting nation, for example, the United Kingdom. Services and ideas, however, are deemed exported whenever transferred to a foreign national, regardless of location. Permitting a foreign national from a controlled country to have access to a highly sensitive computer program in the United Kingdom is therefore deemed to be an export. The effect of such a perspective can be major, particularly on universities and for international students.

The Department of Business Enterprise and Regulatory Reform (BERR) is responsible for issuing export licences for specific categories of 'controlled' goods.[5] The determinants for controls are national security, foreign policy, short supply and nuclear nonproliferation.

In order for any export from the United Kingdom to take place, the exporter needs to obtain an export licence. The administering government agencies have, in consultation with other government departments, drawn up a list of commodities whose export is considered particularly sensitive. In addition, a list of countries differentiates nations according to their political relationship with the United Kingdom. Finally, a list of individual firms that are considered to be unreliable trading partners because of past trade-diversion activities exists for each country.

After an export licence application has been filed, government specialists match the commodity to be exported with the commerce control list, a file containing information about products that are either particularly sensitive to national security or controlled for other purposes. The product is then matched with the country of destination and the recipient company. If no concerns regarding any of the three exist, an export licence is issued. Control determinants and the steps in the decision process are summarized in Exhibit 5.3.

This process may sound overly cumbersome, but it does not apply in equal measure to all exports. Most international business activities can be carried out under NLR conditions, which stands for 'no licence required'. NLR provides blanket permission to export. Products can be freely shipped to most trading partners provided that neither the end user nor the end use involved are considered sensitive. However, the process becomes more complicated when products incorporating high-level technologies and countries not friendly to the United Kingdom are involved. The exporter must then obtain an export licence, which consists of written authorization to send a product abroad.

The international marketing repercussions of export controls are important. It is one thing to design an export control system that is effective and that restricts those international business activities subject to important national concerns. It is, however, quite another when controls lose their effectiveness and when one country's firms are placed at a competitive disadvantage with firms in other countries whose control systems are less extensive or even nonexistent.

EXHIBIT 5.3

The U.S. export control system

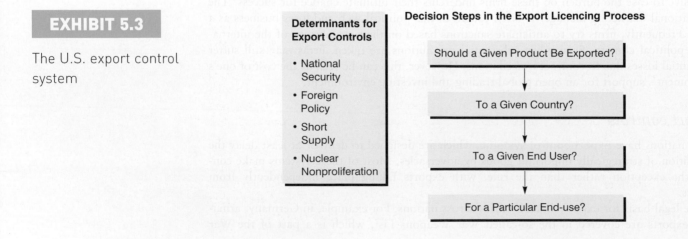

Determinants for Export Controls

- National Security
- Foreign Policy
- Short Supply
- Nuclear Nonproliferation

Decision Steps in the Export Licencing Process

Should a Given Product Be Exported?
↓
To a Given Country?
↓
To a Given End User?
↓
For a Particular End-use?

A new environment for export controls

Today's international environment continues to highlight the importance of export controls. Restricting the flow of materials can be crucial in avoiding the proliferation of weapons of mass destruction; reducing flows of technological knowledge can reduce the sophistication of armaments used by insurgent groups; financial controls can inhibit funding for terrorist training.

Nowadays, the principal focus of export controls rests on the Third World. A number of countries from this region want chemical and nuclear weapons, as well as the technology to make use of them. Even if a country already has dangerous weaponry, export controls can reduce the opportunity for deployment. Libya, for instance, already possesses poisonous gas shells, but can do little with them in the absence of a suitable delivery system. Today's export controls use a 'tactical balance' approach affecting specific hotspots, rather than the 'strategic balance' approach exercised during the era of US–Soviet global deterrence.

Major change has also resulted from the increased foreign availability of high-technology products. In the past decade, the number of participants in the international trade field has grown rapidly. In earlier decades, industrializing countries mainly participated in world trade due to wage-based competition. Today, they are increasingly focused on technology-based competition. As a result, high-technology products are available worldwide from many sources. The broad availability makes any product denial more difficult to enforce. If a nation does control the exports of widely available products, it imposes a major competitive burden on its firms.

Enormous technical progress has also brought about a radical change in computer architecture. Instead of having to replace a personal computer or a workstation with a new computer, one can simply exchange microprocessors or motherboards with new, more efficient ones. Furthermore, today's machines can be connected to more than one microprocessor and users can customize and update configurations almost at will. A user simply acquires additional chips from whomever and uses expansion slots to enhance the capacity of his or her computer.

The question arises as to how much of the latest technology is required for a country to engage in 'dangerous' activity. For example, nuclear weapons and sophisticated delivery systems were developed by the United States and the Soviet Union long before supercomputers became available. Therefore, it is reasonable to assert that researchers in countries working with equipment that is less than state-of-the-art, or even obsolete, may well be able to achieve a threat capability that can result in major destruction and affect world safety.

From a control perspective, there is also the issue of equipment size. Supercomputers and high-technology items used to be fairly difficult to hide and any movement of such products was easily detectable. Nowadays, state-of-the-art technology has been miniaturized. Much leading-edge technological equipment is so small that it can fit into a briefcase, and most equipment is no larger than the luggage compartment of a car. Given these circumstances, it has become difficult to closely supervise the transfer of such equipment.

There is a continuing debate about what constitutes military-use products, civilian-use products, and dual-use products, and the achievement of multilateral agreement on such classifications. Increasingly, goods are of a dual-use nature, meaning that they are commercial products that have potential military applications.[6] Examples are exported trucks that can be used to transport troops, or the exports of supplies to a pesticide factory that, some years later, is revealed to be a poison gas factory.[7] It is difficult enough to define weapons clearly. It is even more problematic to achieve consensus among nations regarding dual-use goods.

Conflicts can result from the desire of nations to safeguard their own economic interests. Due to different industrial structures, these interests vary across nations. For example, Germany, with a strong world market position in machine tools, motors, and chemical raw materials, will think differently about controls than a country such as the United States, which sees computers as an area of its competitive advantage.

The rise in international awareness of the threat of terrorism has led to a renewed importance of global export controls. In recent years, many policies have been targeted to better focus on the dangers of proliferation and terrorist attack. This has helped to differentiate more sharply between those high-tech products that need to be controlled, and those that don't; an overall easing of export control policies in the technology field has resulted.

Import controls

In these countries, either all imports or the imports of particular products are controlled through tariff and non-tariff mechanisms. Tariffs place a tax on imports and raise prices. Non-tariff barriers like voluntary restraint agreements are self-imposed restrictions and cut-backs aimed at avoiding punitive trade actions from the host. Quota systems reduce the volume of imports accepted by a country. The final effect of all these actions is a quantitative reduction of imports.

For the international marketer, such restrictions may mean that the most efficient sources of supply are not available because government regulations restrict importation from those sources. The result is either second-best products or higher costs for restricted supplies. This in turn means that the customer receives inferior service and often has to pay significantly higher prices, and that the firm is less competitive when trying to market its products internationally.

Policymakers are faced with several problems when trying to administer import controls. First, most of the time such controls exact a huge price from domestic consumers. Even though the wide distribution of the burden among many consumers may result in a less obvious burden, the social cost of these controls may be damaging to the economy and subject to severe attack by individuals. However, these attacks are counteracted by pressures from protected groups that benefit from import restrictions. For example, although citizens of the European Union may be forced – because of import controls – to pay an elevated price for all agricultural products they consume, agricultural producers in the region benefit from higher levels of income. Achieving a proper trade-off is often difficult, if not impossible, for the policymaker.

A second major problem resulting from import controls is the downstream change in import composition that results from these controls. For example, if the import of copper ore is restricted, either through voluntary restraints or through quotas, firms in copper-producing countries may opt to shift their production systems and produce copper wire instead, which they then export. As a result, initially narrowly defined protectionist measures may have to snowball in order to protect one downstream industry after another.

A final major problem that confronts the policymaker is that of efficiency. Import controls that are frequently designed to provide breathing room to a domestic industry, either to grow or to recapture its competitive position, often turn out not to work. Rather than improve the productivity of an industry, such controls provide it with a level of safety and a cushion of increased income, yet let the drive for technological advancement fall behind. Alternatively, supply may respond to artificial stimulation and grow far beyond demand.

Regulation of international business behaviour

Home countries may implement special laws and regulations to ensure that the international business behaviour of their firms is conducted within the legal, moral and ethical boundaries considered appropriate. The definition of appropriateness may vary from country to country and from government to government. Therefore, such regulations, their enforcement, and their impact on firms can differ substantially among nations.

Several major areas in which nations attempt to govern the international marketing activities of its firms are boycotts, whereby firms refuse to do business with someone, often for political reasons; antitrust measures, wherein firms are seen as restricting competition; and corruption, which occurs when firms obtain contracts with bribes rather than through performance. Arab nations, for example, have developed a blacklist of companies that deal with Israel. Even though enforcement of the blacklisting has decreased, some Arab customers still demand from their suppliers assurances that the source of the products purchased is not Israel and that the company does not do any business with Israel. The goal of these actions clearly is to impose a boycott on business with Israel.

Boycott measures put firms in a difficult position. Caught in a web of governmental activity, they may be forced to either lose business or pay fines. This is particularly the case if a firm's products are competitive yet not unique, so that the supplier can opt to purchase them elsewhere. Heightening of such conflict can sometimes force companies to withdraw operations entirely from a country.

The second area of regulatory activity affecting international marketing efforts of firms is antitrust laws. These can apply to the international operations of firms as well as to domestic business. In the European Union, for example, the commission watches closely when any firm buys an overseas company, engages in a joint venture with a foreign firm, or makes an agreement with a competing firm. The commission evaluates the effect these activities will have on competition and has the right to disapprove such transactions. However, given the increased globalization of national economies, some substantial rethinking is going on regarding the current approach to antitrust enforcement. One could question whether any country can still afford to define the competition only in a domestic sense or whether competition has to be seen on a worldwide scale. Similarly, one can wonder whether countries will accept the infringement on their sovereignty that results from the extraterritorial application of any nation's law abroad.

There are precedents for making special allowances for international marketers with regard to antitrust laws. In the UK, there is now a provision to exempt from the Competition Act Agreement designed solely to boost exports. In principle, an export agreement among UK producers exclusively to increase exports to non-EU markets is beyond the reach of Article 81.[8] Due to ongoing globalization of production, competition and supply and demand, it would appear that over time the application of antitrust laws to international marketing activities must be revised to reflect global rather than national dimensions.

A third area in which some governments regulate international marketing actions concerns bribery and corruption. Marketers are guided by national and international laws in the sphere of business ethics. The effects of corrupt practices and governmental intervention on international marketing are explored later in this chapter.

HOST COUNTRY POLITICAL AND LEGAL ENVIRONMENT

The host country environment, both political and legal, affects the international marketing operations of firms in a variety of ways. A good manager will understand the country in which the firm operates so that he or she is able to work within the existing parameters and can anticipate and plan for changes that may occur.

Political action and risk

Firms usually prefer to conduct business in a country with a stable and friendly government, but such governments are not always easy to find. Managers must therefore continually monitor the government, its policies, and its stability to determine the potential for political change that could adversely affect corporate operations.

There is political risk in every nation, but the range of risks varies widely from country to country. Political risk is defined as the risk of loss when investing in a given country caused by changes in a country's political structure or policies, such as tax laws, tariffs, expropriation of assets, or restriction in repatriation of profits. For example, a company may suffer from such loss in the case of expropriation or tightened foreign exchange repatriation rules, or from increased credit risk if the government changes policies to make it difficult for the company to pay creditors.[9] In general, political risk is lowest in countries that have a history of stability and consistency. Political risk tends to be highest in nations that do not have this sort of history. In a number of countries, however, consistency and stability that were apparent on the surface have been quickly swept away by major popular movements that drew on the bottled-up frustrations of the population. Three major types of political risk can be encountered: ownership risk, which exposes property and life; operating risk, which refers to interference with the ongoing operations of a firm; and transfer risk, which is mainly encountered when attempts are made to shift funds between countries. Political risk can be

EXHIBIT 5.4   Exposure to political risk

	Loss May Be the Result of:	
Contingencies May Include:	The actions of legitimate government authorities	Events caused by factors outside the control of government
The involuntary loss of control over specific assets without adequate compensation	• Total or partial expropriation • Forced divestiture • Confiscation • Cancellation or unfair calling of performance bonds	• War • Revolution • Terrorism • Strikes • Extortion
A reduction in the value of a stream of benefits expected from the foreign-controlled affiliate	• Nonapplicability of "national treatment" • Restriction in access to financial, labour, or material markets • Controls on prices, outputs, or activities • Currency and remittance restrictions • Value-added and export performance requirements	• Nationalistic buyers or suppliers • Threats and disruption to operations by hostile groups • Externally induced financial constraints • Externally imposed limits on imports or exports

Source: José de la Torre and David H. Neckar, "Forecasting Political Risks for International Operations," in H. Vernon-Wortzel and L. Wortzel, *Global Strategic Management: The Essentials,* 2nd ed. (New York: John Wiley and Sons, 1990), 195. Copyright © 1990 John Wiley and Sons. Reprinted by permission of John Wiley and Sons, Inc.

the result of government action, but it can also be outside the control of government. The type of actions and their effects are classified in Exhibit 5.4.

A major political risk in many countries involves conflict and violent change. A manager will want to think twice before conducting business in a country in which the likelihood of such change is high. To begin with, if conflict breaks out, violence directed toward the firm's property and employees is a strong possibility. Guerrilla warfare, civil disturbances, and terrorism often take an anti-industry turn, making companies and their employees potential targets. For example, in the spring of 1991, Detlev Rohwedder, chairman of the German Treuhand (the institution in charge of privatizing the state-owned firms of the former East Germany), was assassinated at his home in Germany by the Red Army Faction because of his 'representation of capitalism'.

In many countries, particularly in the developing world, coups d'état can result in drastic changes in government. The new government may attack foreign multinational corporations as remnants of the western-dominated colonial past, as has happened in Cuba, Nicaragua and Iran. Even if such changes do not represent an immediate physical threat to firms and their employees, they can have drastic effects. The past few decades have seen such coups in the countries of Ghana, Ethiopia and Venezuela, to name a few. These coups have seriously impeded the conduct of international marketing.

Less dramatic but still worrying are changes in government policies that are caused not by changes in the government itself but by pressure from nationalist or religious factions or discontent with employing foreign workers, as *The International Marketplace 5.2* shows. The aware manager will work to anticipate these changes and plan for ways to cope with them.

THE INTERNATIONAL **MARKETPLACE 5.2**

British unions back reactionary strikes against foreign workers

The strike at the Lindsey Oil Refinery in Lincolnshire and solidarity actions taken throughout the UK, nominally unofficial but fully supported by the unions, represent a dangerous outburst of nationalist sentiment for which the union bureaucracy is wholly responsible. The *World Socialist WebSite* and the Socialist Equality Party unequivocally oppose these actions.

The thousands of workers involved have legitimate grievances and fears for their future. One UK contractor has reportedly shed a third of its workforce at the Lincolnshire site. But these concerns are being manipulated by the union bureaucracy for the most reactionary ends – to promulgate nationalism and economic protectionism as the supposed answer to the worsening crisis of British and world capitalism. The only possible result of such a movement is to pit workers in Britain against their class brothers and sisters in other countries and line British workers up behind their employers in a conflict for the lion's share of markets that are in a state of near collapse.

Far from safeguarding jobs, the unions are encouraging workers to engage in a fratricidal competition for a diminishing pool of jobs that will inevitably involve acceptance of cuts in wages and conditions demanded by the major corporations.

The Lindsey action began when 600 refinery workers walked off the job to protest the arrival of some 100 Italian and Portuguese workers employed by Irem, an Italian subcontractor which had won a £200 million contract from the Total oil company to construct a desulphurization unit. Irem was one of seven subcontractors – five British and two European – which made bids. It is expected to employ a further 300 specialist Italian and Portuguese workers on the project.

The job action has spread nationwide, with up to 3,000 workers at oil refineries, gas terminals and power plants staging sympathy strikes and protest actions in support of the Lindsey workers. In addition, 900 employees at the Sellafield nuclear power plant have voted to walk out Monday.

The central demand being put forward by the unions is encapsulated in the slogan 'British jobs for British workers'. This echoes a speech by Prime Minister Gordon Brown at the 2007 Labour Party conference.

The walkouts are illegal under the anti-union laws brought in by the Conservatives and upheld by the Labour government. Despite their unofficial status, there is no doubt as to who is responsible for the nationalist tenor of the actions. Top officials from Britain's largest trade union, Unite, have addressed the demonstrations and official trade union banners have been prominent at protests and rallies.

Unite issued a statement on January 30 calling for 'a national protest in Westminster' against what it describes as the 'immoral, potentially illegal and politically dangerous practice of excluding UK workers from

some construction projects'. The leader of Unite, Derek Simpson, said that the government 'needs to make it absolutely clear that skilled British workers will not be excluded from construction work at UK plants'.

Bernard McAuley, the regional official most closely associated with the dispute, declared, 'If we lose this battle, our industry will go to the wall . . . We want jobs to be given to local people first'.

Such is the chauvinist character of the union's demands that the dispute has been lauded by the fascist British National Party (BNP), which has hailed the action as 'a great day for British nationalism'.

The trade union leaders have attempted to distance themselves from the BNP, with Trades Union Congress (TUC) General Secretary Brendan Barber stating, 'Unions are clear that the anger should be directed at employers, not the Italian workers'.

These efforts are as transparent as they are cynical. The championing of nationalism and insistence on the supposedly shared interests of British employers and British workers is the very centre of the trade union bureaucracy's perspective. It is responsible for creating the toxic climate in which the BNP can appear on picket lines posing as friends of the 'British worker'.

The slogan 'British jobs for British workers' cannot be interpreted as anything other than a rallying cry against foreign workers. If the unions were to be honest as to their real concerns, their slogan would be 'British contracts for British firms'. With 60 per cent of oil refineries due to be modernized, the Unison union has demanded that contracts be awarded to British firms.

The unions claim that their championing of British companies is a means of defending British jobs. It is not. In reality, the unions' nationalist and class collaborationist programme is responsible for job losses at Lindsey, within the oil refinery industry as a whole and throughout the UK.

For decades the trade unions have insisted that no struggle can be waged to oppose wage cuts and speed up job losses, as such measures are necessary to maintain the profitability and competitiveness of British industry. In the past few months hundreds of thousands of jobs have been shed without a single struggle being mounted by the unions, which have instead offered to accept wage cuts and shorter hours.

The unions have utilized every opportunity, including the situation facing refinery workers, to dragoon the working class behind the very companies that are implementing these cuts.

If one believed the union leaders one would think that the only threat to jobs comes from overseas companies that are employing 'foreign workers'. It is the only issue that exercises them.

The primary and over-riding concern of working people everywhere must be to oppose the spread of nationalism, chauvinism and racism. With the world economy having entered into a slump without parallel since the 1930s, with millions of workers internationally being thrown out of work and losing their livelihoods, the call for workers to defend British employers and British jobs pits them head-long into a fratricidal battle with devastating consequences. It is a recipe for protectionism, trade war and, ultimately, military conflict.

SOURCE: Chris Marsden, 'British unions back reactionary strikes against foreign workers', 1998–2009 *World Socialist WebSite*, **http://www.wsws.org/ articles/2009/feb2009/pers-f02.shtml** (Accessed February 2, 2009).

What sort of changes in policy result from the various events described? The range of possible actions is broad. All of them can affect international marketing operations, but not all are equal in weight. We have learned that companies have to fear violence against employees, and that violence against company property is quite common. In addition, common are changes in policy that take a strong nationalist and antiforeign investment stance. The most drastic steps resulting from such policy changes are usually confiscation and expropriation.

An important governmental action is expropriation, which is the seizure of foreign assets by a government with payment of compensation to the owners. Expropriation has appealed to some countries because it demonstrated nationalism and immediately transferred a certain amount of wealth and resources from foreign companies to the host country. It did have costs to the host country, however, to the extent that it made other firms more hesitant to invest in the country. Expropriation does provide compensation to the former owners. However, compensation negotiations are often protracted and result in settlements that are frequently unsatisfactory to the owners. For example, governments may offer compensation in the form of local, nontransferable currency or may base the compensation on the book value of the firm. Even though firms that are expropriated may deplore the low levels of payment obtained, they frequently accept them in the absence of better alternatives.

The use of expropriation as a policy tool has sharply decreased over time. Apparently, governments have come to recognize that the damage inflicted on themselves through expropriation exceeds the benefits.[10]

Confiscation is similar to expropriation in that it results in a transfer of ownership from the foreign firm to the host country. However, its effects are even harsher in that it does not involve compensation for the firm. Some industries are more vulnerable than others to confiscation and expropriation because of their importance to the host country economy and their lack of ability to shift operations. For this reason, sectors such as mining, energy, public utilities and banking have been targets of such government actions.

Confiscation and expropriation constitute major political risks for foreign investors. Other government actions, however, are nearly as damaging. Many countries are turning from confiscation and expropriation to more subtle forms of control such as domestication. The goal of domestication is the same, to gain control over foreign investment, but the method is different. Through domestication, the government demands partial transfer of ownership and management responsibility and imposes regulations to ensure that a large share of the product is locally produced and a larger share of the profit is retained in the country.

Domestication can have profound effects on the international marketer for a number of reasons. First, if a firm is forced to hire nationals as managers, poor cooperation and communication can result. If the domestication is imposed within a very short time span, corporate operations overseas may have to be headed by poorly trained and inexperienced local managers. Further, domestic content requirements may force a firm to purchase supplies and parts locally, which can result in increased costs, inefficiency and lower-quality products, thus further damaging a firm's competitiveness. Export requirements imposed on companies may also create havoc for the international distribution plan of a corporation and force it to change or even shut down operations in other countries. Finally, domestication will usually shield the industry within one country from foreign competition. As a result, inefficiencies will be allowed to grow due to a lack of market discipline. In the long run, this will affect the international competitiveness of an operation abroad and may become a major problem when, years later, the removal of domestication is considered by the government.

Most businesses operating abroad face a number of other risks that are less dangerous, but probably more common, than the drastic ones already described. Host governments that face a shortage of foreign currency sometimes will impose controls on the movement of capital in and out of the country. Such controls may make it difficult for a firm to remove its profits or investments from the host country. Sometimes, exchange controls are also levied selectively against certain products or companies in an effort to reduce the importation of goods that are considered to be a luxury or unnecessary. Such regulations are often difficult to deal with because they may affect the importation of parts, components, or supplies that are vital for production operations. Restrictions on such imports may force a firm either to alter its production program or, worse yet, to shut down its entire plant. Prolonged negotiations with government officials may be necessary in order to reach a compromise agreement on what constitutes a 'valid' expenditure of foreign currency resources. As the goals of government officials and corporate managers may often be quite different, such compromises, even when they can be reached, may result in substantial damage to the international marketing operations of a firm.

Countries may also raise the tax rates applied to foreign investors in an effort to control the firms and their capital. On occasion, different or stricter applications of the host country's tax codes are implemented for foreign investors. The rationale for such measures is often an apparent underpayment of taxes by such investors, when comparing their payments to those of long-established domestic competitors. Overlooked is the fact that new investors in foreign lands tend to 'overinvest' by initially buying more land, space, and equipment than is initially needed and by spending heavily so that facilities are state-of-the-art. This desire to accommodate future growth and to be highly competitive in the early investment stages will, in turn, produce lower profits and lower tax payments. Yet over time, these investment activities should be very successful, competitive and job-creating. Selective tax increases for foreign investors may result in much-needed revenue for the coffers of the host country, but they can severely damage the operations of the foreign investors. This damage, in turn, may result in decreased income for the host country in the long run.

The international marketing manager must also worry about price controls. In many countries, domestic political pressures can force governments to control the prices of imported products or services, particularly in sectors that are considered to be highly sensitive from a political perspective, such as food or health care. If a foreign firm is involved in these areas, it is a vulnerable target of price controls because the government can play on its people's nationalistic tendencies to enforce the controls. Particularly in countries that suffer from high inflation and frequent devaluations, the international marketer may be forced to choose between shutting down the operation or continuing production at a loss in the hope of recouping that loss once the government chooses to loosen or remove its price restrictions. How a firm can adjust to price controls is discussed in greater detail later in the book.

Managers face political and economic risk whenever they conduct business overseas, but there may be ways to lessen the risk. Obviously, if a new government that is dedicated to the removal of all foreign influences comes into power, a firm can do little. In less extreme cases, however, managers can take actions to reduce the risk if they understand the root causes of the host country policies. Most important is the accumulation and appreciation of factual information about a country's history, political background and culture before making a long-term investment decision. In addition, a high degree of sensitivity by a firm and its employees to country-specific approaches and concerns are important dimensions that help a firm to blend into the local landscape rather than stand out as a foreign object.

Adverse governmental actions are usually the result of a host country's nationalism, desire for independence and opposition to colonial remnants. If a country's citizens feel exploited by foreign firms, government officials are more likely to take antiforeign action. To reduce the risk of government intervention, a firm needs to demonstrate that it is concerned with the host country's society and that it considers itself an integral part of the host country rather than simply an exploitative foreign corporation. Ways to do this include intensive local hiring and training practices, good pay, philanthropy and more societally useful investment. In addition, a company can form joint ventures with local partners to demonstrate a willingness to share its benefits with nationals. Although such actions will not guarantee freedom from risk, they will certainly lessen the exposure to it.

Corporations can also protect against political risk by closely monitoring political developments. Increasingly, private-sector firms offer assistance in such monitoring activities, permitting the overseas corporation to discover potential trouble spots as early as possible and react quickly to prevent major losses. Firms can also take out insurance to cover losses due to political risk. Most industrialized countries offer insurance programmes for their firms doing business abroad. In Germany, for example, Hermes Kreditanstalt provides exporters with insurance. In the United Kingdom, ASPEN covers financial and political risks; Confiscation, Expropriation, Nationalization and Deprivation ('CEND') provides protection against total or partial loss of investments resulting from host government actions. This includes expropriation, forced sale, deprivation of ownership rights or other acts having similar effect.[11]

Usually, insurance policies do not cover commercial risks and, in the event of a claim, cover only the actual loss – not lost profits. In the event of a major political upheaval, however, risk insurance can be critical to a firm's survival.

Clearly, the international marketer must consider the likelihood of negative political factors in making decisions on conducting business overseas. On the other hand, host country political and legal systems can have a positive impact on the conduct of international business. Many governments, for example, encourage foreign investments, especially if they believe that the investment will produce economic and political benefits domestically. Some governments have opened up their economy to foreign investors, placing only minimal constraints on them, in the hope that such policies will lead to rapid economic development. Others have provided for substantial subsidization of new investment activities in the hope that investments will generate additional employment. The international marketer, in his or her investment decision, can and should therefore also pay close attention to the extent and forms of incentives available from foreign governments. Although international marketing decisions should be driven by free market forces, these decisions may change if incentives are offered.

In this discussion of the political environment, laws have been mentioned only to the extent that they appear to be the direct result of political changes. However, each nation has laws regarding marketing, and the international manager must understand their effects on the firm's efforts.

Legal differences and restraints

Countries differ in their laws as well as in their implementation of these laws. For example, the United Kingdom has developed into an increasingly litigious society, in which institutions and individuals are quick to take a case to court. As a result, court battles are often protracted and costly, and simply the threat of a court case can reduce marketing opportunities. In contrast, Japan's legal tradition tends to minimize the role of the law and of lawyers. Some possible reasons include the relatively small number of courts and attorneys; the delays, the costs and the uncertainties associated with litigation; the limited doctrines of plaintiffs' standing and rights to bring class action suits; the tendency of judges to encourage out-of-court settlements; and the easy availability of arbitration and mediation for dispute resolution.

According to JURIST No. 1198, the total number of lawyers in Japan in 1997 was approximately 20000, remarkably small in comparison with 940000 in the US, 82000 in the UK, 111000 in Germany and 35000 in France.[12] However, comparisons can be misleading because officially registered lawyers in Japan perform a small fraction of the duties performed by British lawyers. *The International Marketplace* 5.3 shows how different perceptions and legal practices can lead to substantially different approaches to communication.

Over the millennia of civilization, many different laws and legal systems have emerged. King Hammurabi of Babylon codified a series of judges' decisions into a body of law. Hebrew law was the result of the dictates of God. Legal issues in many African tribes were settled through the verdicts of clansmen. A key legal perspective that survives today is that of theocracy, which has faith and belief as its key focus and is a mix of societal, legal and spiritual guidelines. Examples are Hebrew law and Islamic law (*shari'ah*), which are the result of scripture, prophetic utterances and practices, and scholarly interpretations.[13]

While these legal systems are important to society locally, from an international business perspective the two major legal systems worldwide can be categorized into common law and code law. Common law is based on tradition and depends less on written statutes and codes than on precedent and custom. Common law originated in England and is the system used, for example, in Australia, Canada, Hong Kong, India, Malaysia and South Africa.

THE INTERNATIONAL **MARKETPLACE 5.3**

Sharia law SHOULD be used in Britain, says UK's top judge

The Lord Chief Justice's endorsement of Sharia law has already created huge controversy.

The most senior judge in England yesterday gave his blessing to the use of Sharia law to resolve disputes among Muslims.

Lord Chief Justice Lord Phillips said that Islamic legal principles could be employed to deal with family and marital arguments and to regulate finance.

He declared: 'Those entering into a contractual agreement can agree that the agreement shall be governed by a law other than English law.'

In his speech at an East London mosque, Lord Phillips signalled approval of Sharia principles as long as punishments – and divorce rulings – complied with the law of the land.

But his remarks, which back the informal Sharia courts operated by numerous mosques, provoked a barrage of criticism.

Lawyers warned that family and marital disputes settled by Sharia could disadvantage women or the vulnerable.

Tories said that legal equality must be respected and that rulings incompatible with English law should never be enforceable.

Lord Phillips spoke five months after the Archbishop of Canterbury, Dr Rowan Williams, suggested Islamic law could govern marital law, financial transactions and arbitration in disputes.

The Lord Chief Justice said yesterday of the Archbishop's views: 'It was not very radical to advocate embracing Sharia law in the context of family disputes'.

He added there is 'widespread misunderstanding as to the nature of Sharia law'.

The Archbishop of Canterbury's comments on Sharia law sparked a political storm.

Lord Phillips said: 'Those who are in dispute are free to subject it to mediation or to agree that it shall be resolved by a chosen arbitrator. There is no reason why principles of Sharia law or any other religious code should not be the basis for mediation or other forms of dispute resolution.'

Lord Phillips said that any sanctions must be 'drawn from the laws of England and Wales'. Severe physical punishment – he mentioned stoning, flogging or amputating hands – is 'out of the question' in Britain, he added.

Lord Phillips' speech brought protests from lawyers who fear women could be disadvantaged in supposedly voluntary Sharia deals.

Barrister and human rights specialist John Cooper said: 'There should be one law by which everyone is held to account.

'Well-crafted laws in this country, drawn up to protect both parties including the weak and vulnerable party in matrimonial breakups, could be compromised.'

Resolution, the organization of family law solicitors, said people should govern their lives in accordance with religious principles 'provided that those beliefs and traditions do not contradict the fundamental principle of equality on which Britain's laws are based.'

Spokesman Teresa Richardson said religious law 'must be used to find solutions which are consistent with the basic principles of family law in this country and people must always have redress to the civil courts where they so choose.'

SOURCE: Steve Doughty (2008), 'Sharia law should be used in Britain, says UK's top judge', **http://www.dailymail.co.uk/news/article-1031611/Sharia-law-SHOULD-used-Britain-says-UKs-judge.html** (Accessed February 2, 2009).

On the other hand, code law (**civil law**) is based on a comprehensive set of written statutes. Countries with code law try to spell out all possible legal rules explicitly. Code law is based on Roman law and is found in the majority of the nations of the world, for example, most of the countries in Europe and Asia.[14] In general, countries with the code law system have much more rigid laws than those with the common law system. In the latter, courts adopt precedents and customs to fit the cases, allowing the marketer a better idea of the basic judgment likely to be rendered in new situations.

Although wide in theory, the differences between code law and common law and their impact on the international marketer are not always as broad in practice. For example, many common law countries, including the United Kingdom, have adopted commercial codes to govern the conduct of business.

Host countries may adopt a number of laws that affect a company's ability to market. To begin with, there can be laws affecting the entry of goods, such as tariffs and quotas. Also in this category are antidumping laws, which prohibit below-cost sales of products, and laws that require export and import licencing. In addition, many countries have health and safety standards that may, by design or by accident, restrict the entry of foreign goods. Japan, for example, has particularly strict health standards that affect the import of pharmaceuticals. Rather than accepting test results from other nations, the Japanese government insists on conducting its own tests, which are time consuming and costly. It claims that these tests are necessary to reflect Japanese peculiarities. Yet some importers and their governments see these practices as thinly veiled protectionist barriers.

A growing global controversy surrounds the use of genetic technology. Governments are increasingly devising new rules that affect trade in genetically modified products. For example, Australia introduced a mandatory standard for foods produced using biotechnology, which prohibits the sale of such products unless the food has been assessed by the Australia New Zealand Food Authority.

Other laws may be designed to protect domestic industries and reduce imports. For example, Russia assesses high excise taxes on goods such as cigarettes, automobiles and alcoholic beverages; and provides a burdensome import licencing and quotas regime for alcohol and products containing alcohol to depress Russian demand for imports. In the case of automobiles, combined tariffs, VAT, and excise duties can increase import prices by 70 per cent.[15]

Very specific legislation may also exist to regulate where a firm can advertise or what constitutes deceptive advertising. Many countries prohibit specific claims by marketers comparing their product to that of the competition and restrict the use of promotional devices. Some countries regulate the names of companies or the foreign language content of a product's label. Even when no laws exist, the marketer may be hampered by regulations. For example, in many countries, governments require a firm to join the local chamber of commerce or become a member of the national trade association. These institutions in turn may have internal regulations that set standards for the conduct of business and may be seen as quite confining to the international marketer.

Finally, the enforcement of laws may have a different effect on national and on foreign marketers. For example, the simple requirement that an executive has to stay in a country until a business conflict is resolved may be a major burden for the international marketer.

Influencing politics and laws

To succeed in a market, the international marketer needs much more than business knowhow. He or she must also deal with the intricacies of national politics and laws. Although a full understanding of another country's legal and political system will rarely be possible, the good manager will be aware of the importance of this system and will work with people who do understand how to operate within the system.

Many areas of politics and law are not immutable. Viewpoints can be modified or even reversed, and new laws can supersede old ones. Therefore, existing political and legal restraints do not always need to be accepted. To achieve change, however, there must be some impetus for it, such as the clamours of a constituency. Otherwise, systemic inertia is likely to allow the status quo to prevail.

The international marketer has various options. One approach may be to simply ignore prevailing rules and expect to get away with it. Pursuing this option is a high-risk strategy because of the possibility of objection and even prosecution. A second, traditional option is to provide input to trade negotiators and expect any problem areas to be resolved in multilateral negotiations. The drawback to this option is, of course, the quite time-consuming process involved.

A third option involves the development of coalitions or constituencies that can motivate legislators and politicians to consider and ultimately implement change. This option can be pursued in various ways. One direction can be the recasting or redefinition of issues. Often, specific **terminology** leads to conditioned though inappropriate responses. For example, before China's accession to the World Trade Organization in 2001, the country's trade status with the United States had been highly controversial for many years. The US Congress had to decide annually whether to grant 'Most Favoured Nation' (MFN) status to China. The debate on this decision was always very contentious and acerbic and was often framed around the question of why China deserved to be treated the 'most favoured way'. Lost in the debate was the fact that the term 'most favoured' was simply taken from WTO terminology and indicated only that trade with China would be treated like any other coun-try. Only in late 1999 was the terminology changed from MFN to NTR, or 'normal trade relations'. Even though there was still considerable debate regarding China, the controversy about special treatment had been eliminated.[16]

Beyond terminology, marketers can also highlight the direct linkages and their cost and benefit to legislators and politicians. For example, the manager can explain the employment and economic effects of certain laws and regulations and demonstrate the benefits of change. The picture can be enlarged by including indirect linkages. For example, suppliers, customers and distributors can be asked to participate in delineating to decision makers the benefit of change. Such groups can be quite influential. For example, it has been suggested that it was the community of Indian businesses working as information technology suppliers to US firms that exerted substantial pressure on their government to work toward finding a resolution to the Kashmiri conflict. If so, this is an encouraging example of the benefits of globalization.[17]

Developing such coalitions is not an easy task. Companies often seek assistance in effec-tively influencing the government decision-making process. Such assistance usually is particu-larly beneficial when narrow economic objectives or single-issue campaigns are needed. Typical providers of this assistance are lobbyists. Usually, these are well-connected individu-als and firms that can provide access to policymakers and legislators.

Lobbying firms tend to be located in state, national or regional capitals. Their experience and networks can help in presenting corporate concerns to decision makers. In doing so, new information and insights can be provided to policy makers and decisions can be precipitated more rapidly.

Lobbying is very valuable to the international marketer, as is evidenced by the large num-ber of lobbyists and their high compensation. For example, Brazilian citrus exporters and computer manufacturers have hired legal and public relations firms to provide them with in-formation on relevant legislative activity. The Banco do Brasil lobbied for the restructuring of Brazilian debt and favourable banking regulations.

A key factor in successful lobbying is the involvement of local citizens and companies. Typically, legislators are only willing to take positions on important issues if they are sup-ported by or at least not opposed by their constituents. Therefore, it is important to demon-strate how a particular issue affects a decision maker's domestic constituents. For example, to ward off negative legislation it may be helpful to point out how many jobs are created by a firm's foreign investment, or how export-intensive such an investment can be.

Although representation of the firm's interests to government decision makers and legisla-tors is entirely appropriate, the international marketer must also consider any potential side effects. Major questions can be raised if such representation becomes very strong or is seen as reflecting a conflict of interest. For example, in 2006, former chancellor Schröder of Germany took on the representation of a Russian pipeline corporation. There was substantial concern about the representation, a cause which he had championed and approved as chancellor only months before. There is an unease with revolving door issues of former policy makers work-ing on behalf of clients who were subject to their previous official decisions, or of lobbyists spending large amounts of money to further their cause. Due to the reality or perception of inappropriateness, some countries have passed legislation that restricts lobbying activities.

THE INTERNATIONAL ENVIRONMENT

In addition to the politics and laws of both the home and the host countries, the international marketer must consider the overall international, political and legal environment. Relations between countries can have a profound impact on firms trying to do business internationally.

International politics

The effect of politics on international marketing is determined by both the bilateral political relations between home and host countries and the multilateral agreements governing the relations among groups of countries.

The government-to-government relationship can have a profound effect, particularly if it becomes hostile. For example, there is a sharp conflict in Europe over economic stimulus programmes to member countries. Germany reacted angrily to the EU's request that it increases its allocation to stimulate its economy to €200 billion. The fear from Germany's opponents is that this would lead to its isolation in Europe.[18]

International political relations do not always have harmful effects on international marketers. If bilateral political relations between countries improve, business can benefit. The improvement of political relations with countries of Eastern Europe has opened up new markets for companies from Western Europe.[19] A recent example is the improvement of political relations bweteen China and the UK which will lead to increased UK exports to China.[20]

The international marketer needs to be aware of political currents worldwide and attempt to anticipate changes in the international political environment, good or bad, so that his or her firm can plan for them. Sometimes, however, management can only wait until the emotional fervour of conflict has subsided and hope that rational governmental negotiations will let cooler heads prevail.

International law

International law plays an important role in the conduct of international business. Although no enforceable body of international law exists, certain treaties and agreements respected by a number of countries profoundly influence international business operations. As an example, the World Trade Organization (WTO) defines internationally acceptable economic practices for its member nations. Although it does not deal directly with individual firms, it does influence them indirectly by providing a more stable and predictable international market environment.

In addition to multilateral agreements, firms are affected by bilateral treaties and conventions. The EU, for example, has signed bilateral treaties of political dialogue and cooperation agreement with a wide variety of countries (for example, with Central American countries[21]) and ratified multilateral environment agreements.[22] These agreements generally define the rights of EU firms doing business in the host country. They normally guarantee that the EU firms will be treated by the host country in the same manner in which domestic firms are treated. Although these treaties provide some stability, they can be cancelled when relationships worsen.

The international legal environment also affects the marketer to the extent that firms must concern themselves with jurisdictional disputes. As no single body of international law exists, firms usually are restricted by both home and host country laws. If a conflict occurs between contracting parties in two different countries, a question arises concerning which country's laws will be followed. Sometimes the contract will contain a jurisdictional clause, which settles the matter. If not, the parties to the dispute can follow either the laws of the country in which the agreement was made or those of the country in which the contract will have to be fulfilled. Deciding on the laws to be followed and the location to settle the dispute are two different decisions. As a result, a dispute between a Chinese exporter and a British importer could be resolved in Bejing with the resolution based on British law.

The parties to a business transaction can also choose either arbitration or litigation. Litigation is usually avoided for several reasons. It often involves extensive delays and is very costly. In addition, firms may fear discrimination in foreign countries. Companies therefore tend to prefer conciliation and arbitration because these processes result in much quicker decisions. Arbitration procedures are often spelled out in the original contract and usually provide for an intermediary who is judged to be impartial by both parties. Frequently, intermediaries will be representatives of chambers of commerce, trade associations, or third-country institutions. For example, the rules of the international chamber of commerce in Paris are frequently used for arbitration purposes.

International terrorism and marketing

Terrorism is the systematic use (or threat) of violence aimed at attaining a political goal and conveying a political message. International terrorism seeks to do this across national

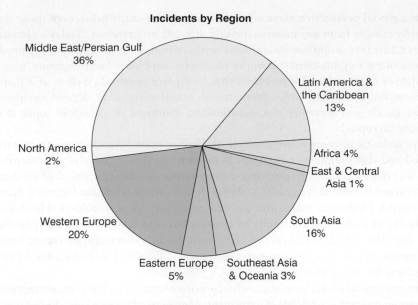

Incidents by Region

- Middle East/Persian Gulf 36%
- Latin America & the Caribbean 13%
- North America 2%
- Africa 4%
- East & Central Asia 1%
- Western Europe 20%
- South Asia 16%
- Eastern Europe 5%
- Southeast Asia & Oceania 3%

EXHIBIT 5.5

Patterns of global terrorism outside the United States

borders.[23] While it has existed for centuries, terrorism's global impact has changed significantly in recent years: improved means of transportation lead to an omnipresence never previously experienced. The rise of terrorist incidents in western nations, often carried out by foreign nationals, brings terrorism to countries once considered immune. Global mass media, meanwhile, have ensured the visibility of terrorist events, spreading fear and creating irrational expectations of localized attacks.

Terrorists direct their strikes at business far more than any other target.[24] Businesses need to be easily accessible and able to conduct transactions with many new persons every day; this introduces a level of vulnerability which is not typically encountered by government offices. Exhibit 5.5 shows the frequency of terrorist attacks in different geographic regions. Bombings are most common, followed by armed assaults, kidnapping, vandalism and hijacking.

While always regrettable, terrorism nevertheless creates new opportunities for firms in a few industries like construction, security and information technology. For most companies, however, terrorism results in reduced revenues or increased costs, and managers must prepare for this. Terrorists intend to affect supply and demand in order to shatter existing economic systems; this brings about both direct and indirect effects. The direct consequences to business are the immediate costs levied on individual firms. While harm is clear to individual firms, from a societal perspective, the direct effects tend to be less consequential than the indirect ones. The latter accumulate over time, and are often not apparent immediately.

The indirect negative consequences of terrorism begin with macroeconomic phenomena, such as the real or perceived decline in per capita income, purchasing power and stock market values. In the wake of a terrorist event, these trends cause a fall in the subjective (perceived) security of the nation. Buyers become uncertain about the state of their nation's economy, and a sharp reduction in demand for both consumer and industrial goods follows – a phenomenon which we call the chill effect.

A further effect on enterprises may be the failures in power, communication, transport and other infrastructure due to actual physical damage incurred at the terrorists' hands. Indirectly, this leads to unpredictable shifts and interruption in the supply of inputs, resources and services. Finally, international terrorism often causes tension between the countries whose citizens or property is involved; the deterioration of transnational relationships can affect foreign buyer and seller attitudes and thus the marketing activities of firms doing business abroad.

One key side-effect of terrorism can be the government policies and laws it brings about. In order to make a country less vulnerable, politicians often enact restrictions on the business environment. New regulations in customs clearance may delay the supply of inputs, increase the administrative burden and require firms to invest in new procedures. Transaction costs generally increase and the commercial environment may be altered in ways that are more harmful to business than the terrorist attack itself might have been.

From a global perspective, these effects are present for many firms, even those that are geographically remote from any location directly affected by terrorism. Today's climate of global commerce involves countless interactions with customers and distributors; producers and marketers often rely on entire networks of diverse suppliers. Such exposure to a variety of factors leaves firms vulnerable to events that take place nearby as well as at a distance. Even firms perceived as having little international involvement may depend on the receipt of imported goods and therefore risk experiencing shortages or delays of input if economies abroad are disrupted.

In the wake of a terrorist event, physical damage must be undone, security arrangements enhanced and risk premiums reassessed. In order to do this effectively, an enterprise must establish its priorities, quantify risk, and outline response scenarios ahead of an actual attack. It is important to note that in today's global climate, firms must aim for more than mere survival. Instead, businesses must offer assured continuity to stakeholders. Flexibility to withstand shock, as well as the continuity of existing business relationships, must be the principal goal of any global firm. In addition to being economically necessary, persistent business activity is a major step in denying terrorists their goals.[25] Exhibit 5.6 shows a model of corporate preparedness for terrorist attack.

There are several obstacles to successful corporate strategy in mitigating terrorism. The first lies in frequent mistakes of global management: Managers of foreign subsidiaries may shunt any terrorism concerns to headquarters. At the same time, executives at headquarters often frame terrorism only in local terms and look to local managers for tackling possible repercussions. As a result, costs incurred from growing precautionary measures cannot be defrayed efficiently throughout the enterprise, and wholesale closure of international operations may follow.

EXHIBIT 5.6   A model of corporate preparedness for terrorism

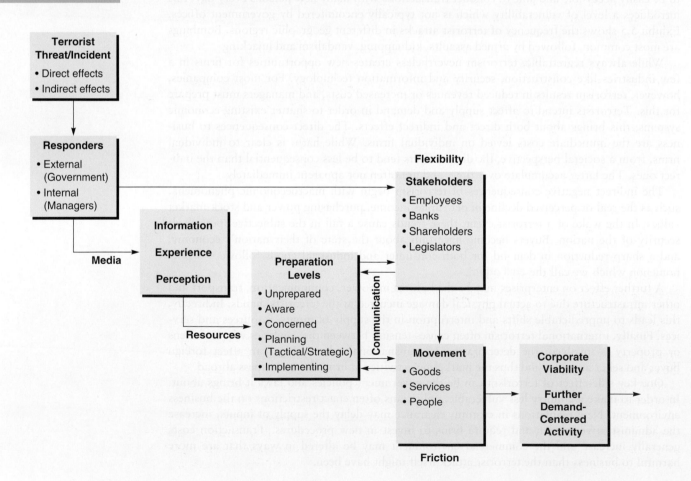

In addition, terrorist risk is difficult to assess in an integrated global economy. If supply chains are complex and multinational, the effects of terrorism can potentially spread across the globe from an initially local focus. For most firms, the costs of averting terrorism are hard to quantify and even harder to justify to key stakeholders. In an era when the mandates of the Sarbanes-Oxley Act (see upcoming section on corporate governance) are straining corporate budgets, top executives put a greater premium on meeting financial performance benchmarks than on addressing vague political risks.

An important consideration is that individual assessment of vulnerability changes based on individual information, experience and perception of an event. Over time, these impressions shift, resulting in potentially faulty managerial decisions. Ironically, the greater the tragedy, the more likely people are to discount it as an aberration, once confidence is restored and normal activities are resumed. Widespread underestimation of the likelihood of future recurrences results. Managers are therefore tempted to rest comfortably in the belief that any future attack will not affect their company and not lead to widespread personal repercussions.

Over time, terrorism will increasingly influence the evaluation and selection of markets, particularly those located abroad. Thus far, for instance, developing nations have proven to be most vulnerable to economic and consumption downturns following terror events.

In a volatile world, marketing managers are the frontline response to business disruption. Although all corporate areas are likely to be affected by terrorist activity, the marketing field, which constitutes a key liaison with the world outside the firm, is likely to be under the most pressure. Marketers deal specifically with the activities of supply and demand that terrorists aim to destroy, and are thus confronted with terrorism on a daily basis. Devising new distribution and logistics avenues in the case of attack, responding with pricing strategies to market dislocations, and communicating the firm's position to buyers and suppliers are all marketing activities.[26]

In some cases, marketers may choose to pursue a strategy of working with customer segments less sensitive to terrorism. For instance, in the months following September 11, marketers in the hotel industry focused their selling efforts on regional rather than national or international business. Oftentimes, sales are perceived to be safer in domestic and thus familiar markets. However, staying domestic is becoming difficult as a long-term strategy in our increasingly globalized world.

Marketers tend to have the clearest understanding of the mutual corporate dependence so critical for effective planning. For example, when determining the need for specific emergency inputs, marketers will not only look for the source of such inputs. They will also be able to analyze the existing relationships and networks, and devise incentives to ensure that the supplier will actually provide goods and services to the firm. Dry runs and simulations can then be used by marketers to develop expectations about long-term effects and to see whether the system works as planned. Without such considerations, a plan for input contingency is akin to identifying the location of petrol stations as the principal remedy for a fuel shortage, without keeping in mind that the stations need to be resupplied to stay open and need to be willing to provide the petrol for a client pulling in.

On the supply side, marketers deal with communication with customers and suppliers, devise campaigns to present information, provide direction and alter any misperceptions. Marketers are the experts who implement steps to address imbalances and create new incentives by changing corporate pricing, packaging or sizing. Goods or services whose price is strongly affected by changing information flows and perceptions of risk are highly susceptible to the indirect consequences of terrorism. Insurance coverage is an example. Actual or perceived terrorist threats tend to create upward pressure on the pricing of particularly vulnerable offerings. Prices may also experience a certain 'stickiness', that is, under conditions of inability to predict the occurrence of terrorism or its indirect effects, once raised, prices may not be decreased. Conversely, firms in certain industries may feel pressure to lower prices in order to induce reluctant buyers to maintain or increase their buying activities. Through their actions, marketers can reverse an emerging softness in demand, rally joint responses, and avoid the occurrence of unintended consequences. With their understanding of the long-term repercussions of terrorism, marketers can also be instrumental in formulating alternative corporate strategies, for example, the shift from an investment-based foreign market expansion to an export-based one.

The continuing efforts of marketers to understand cultural issues are also highly useful for devising terminology and persuasive encouragement. Studies show that there are major cultural differences between, and even within, nations. International marketing, through its linkages via goods, services, ideas and communications, can achieve important assimilations of value systems. Marketers know that culture and values are learned, not genetically implanted. As life's experiences grow more international and more similar, so do values. Therefore, every time international marketing forges a new linkage in thinking and providing for new exchanges of goods or services, new progress is made in shaping a greater global commonality in values. It may well be that international marketing's ability to align global values, and the subsequent greater ease of countries, companies and individuals to build bridges among themselves, may eventually become the field's greatest gift to the world.[27]

ETHICAL ISSUES

Corporate governance, responsibility, intellectual property rights and corruption all fall under the ethical obligations experienced by multinational enterprises today. Whether following the most ethical route in business dealings matters in the long run is, in many ways, a difficult question. Historically, the answer has depended on the environment and outcomes. Nineteenth-century textile mills in the United Kingdom, for instance, flagrantly violated today's standards for workers' rights (including living wages, maximum weekly working hours and safe working conditions). However, they did much to move UK industrialization forward. The growth of trade unions was based on improving the conditions of the workers, especially due to an increasing rise in the employment of women and children.[28]

Today, one issue concerning corporate ethics is the divide between the 'first world' and less developed countries. Should emerging economies follow the same course experienced by Europe and the US in their industrial history? Or should they be aided and, on occasion, forced by developed nations to skip the mishaps of the western experience and industrialize under more stringent modern-day standards?

Restrictions may hinder progress by excessively curbing business practices with ethical requirements. In addition, corporate practices are far from perfect in the world's most advanced countries themselves. Some even claim that a focus on ethics is a thin disguise for protectionism. Finally, globalization raises an interesting concern: when investing abroad, should firms from a developed country with stringent ethical laws be allowed to use looser local principles to their advantage?

The following sections may shed some light on the nature, focus and concerns of the ethical dimension in modern-day businesses abroad.

Corporate governance and responsibility

The relationships among stakeholders that determine and control the strategic direction and performance of an organization are called corporate governance.[29] A system of corporate governance must be established to ensure that decisions are made and interests are represented properly for all stakeholders. The structure, conduct and methods used in the assessment of company behaviour vary dramatically across countries. Key elements of corporate governance, however, remain the transparency of a firm's operations, its financial results, and the principles by which it measures sales, expenses, assets and liabilities.

For some, the overriding objective of corporate governance is to optimize returns to shareholders over time. In order to achieve this, good governance practices focus the attention of the company's board of directors on strategies that ensure corporate growth and increase equity value. In addition, corporate governance frameworks typically protect shareholder rights and ensure their equitable treatment, provide for timely and accurate disclosure of all the company's material matters and ensure the board of directors' accountability to the company and its shareholders.

EXHIBIT 5.7

Comparative corporate
governance regimes

Regime Basis	Characteristics	Examples
Market-based	Efficient equity markets; Dispersed ownership	United States, United Kingdom, Canada, Australia
Family-based	Management & ownership is combined; Family/majority and minority shareholders	Hong Kong, Indonesia, Malaysia, Singapore, Taiwan, France
Bank-based	Government influence in bank lending; Lack of transparency; Family control	Korea, Germany
Government affiliated	State ownership of enterprise; Lack of transparency; No minority influence	China, Russia

Source: Based on J. Tsui and T. Shieh, "Corporate Governance in Emerging Markets: An Asian Perspective," in *International Finance and Accounting Handbook*, 3rd ed., Frederick D. S. Choi, ed. (Hoboken, NJ: Wiley, 2004), 24.424.6.

Others interpret corporate governance as dealing with stakeholders (such as employees, customers, banks, etc.) who are affected by corporate decisions. For them, the providers of capital are only one of various constituencies to satisfy.

The separation of ownership from management, and the various cultural views on stakeholders' identity and significance, all affect corporate governance and lead to different practices across countries, economies, and cultures. Exhibit 5.7 illustrates variants of corporate governance structures classified by regime and ownership. The major factors driving global corporate governance principles and practices are financial market development, the degree of separation between management and ownership, and transparency.

Proponents of a market-based regime emphasize the benefit of forces that result from interplaying supply and demand. Price signals adjust activities instead of government intervention and create an environment of respect for profitability and private property. In exchange for the chance to derive proceeds, investors allocate resources to the most productive and efficient uses. In order for such allocations to take place, however, trust must exist between managers and investors. In return for their financial inputs, managers must provide stakeholders with their best efforts to secure gains on the supplied capital.

In this sense, managers can be seen as marketing their corporate virtue, vision and potential for economic gain to potential investors. It is therefore of vital interest to them that bribery, corruption and obscurity be eliminated, allowing relationships of trust and commitment to be forged between firms and individual sources of money.[30] This takes on additional importance as investment experiences globalization. Transparency must reign not only within a country, but also across borders to foreign business partners.

As firms become increasingly multinational, governments respond by increasing global cooperation to achieve the same principles of taxation and corporate ethics laws across nations. This serves to slowly eliminate tax issues like the shifting of income from high- into low-tax countries, or the shielding of income from taxation by holding profits in tax havens.

Aside from responsibility to stakeholders, corporations are often expected to fulfill certain obligations and exhibit conscientious behaviour towards the societies in which they operate. Such obligations often include environmental safety and efficiency, reasonable working conditions and wages, and concerns about layoffs, healthcare and family care. The European Union has surpassed most of the world in both cultural friendliness to and actual implementation of such programmes. In 1995, the president of the European Commission joined with leading European companies to found CSR Europe, a business network aimed at helping companies integrate corporate social responsibility (CSR) with daily business practices. Meanwhile, *The International Marketplace 5.4* shows that environmental concerns are often important not only for ethical, but also for practical reasons.

THE INTERNATIONAL **MARKETPLACE 5.4**

Does pollution matter?

Economic development in China leads to numerous benefits, such as a rise in GDP and popular welfare levels. However, it has also caused significant environmental challenges. To fuel its rapid industrialization, China consumes record amounts of coal as it builds new factories and energy plants. It has become the world's second largest emitter of greenhouse gases; in the next ten years, it is even expected to surpass the United States, which holds first place.

This may seem like a concern mainly for the Chinese government and for international environmental protection agencies. However, lately the destruction of China's ecosystem has become a threat for multinational corporations as well. A lack of transparent laws concerning the environment has caused instability in the local workforce. The latter, in turn, creates uncertainty about the future and increases the risk faced by any multinational enterprise wishing to enter a developing market. Recent events in rural Huaxi, China, have presented an example.

Factories in Huaxi not only emit dangerous substances into the air, but also discharge harmful chemicals into local water systems. The pollution of waterways, in turn, threatens both the health and lifestyle of local farmers: crops grown with contaminated irrigation become substandard in quality and low in quantity. Local officials, meanwhile, can be bribed into turning a blind eye to polluters to spur economic growth. Such laxity on their part could be viewed as an opportunity for foreign companies: they could now utilize China's resources and cheap labour force without the limits and costs of environmental protection. However, the local populace is increasingly unwilling to live with the environmental decision. A staged sit-in by farmers from Huaxi villages in front of a new factory led to clashes with the police. Yet the persistence of the farmers helped them win, and persuaded the local government to close the factory.

Although the factory in Huaxi belonged to the Chinese government, a multinational firm's manufacturing facility could potentially meet with the same fate. If local interests are capable of manipulating regulations, a multinational's production facility could easily be closed. A sudden change in laws (or their implementation) could threaten the entire input supply structure of an international company, particularly if its international subsidiaries depend on each other for resources and inputs.

Is it therefore better that an international corporation comes into China with stricter environmental laws than those existent in China itself? Should a firm adopt the local culture (including bribing) to be more in tune with local customs? Huaxi proves that even with government support corporations are vulnerable to the concerns of other stakeholders.

SOURCES: Edward Cody, 'For Chinese, Peasant Revolt Is Rare Victory', *Washington Post*, June 13, 2005, **www.washingtonpost.com/wp-dyn/content/article/2005/06/12/AR2005061201531.html** (Accessed January 15, 2006); Cindy Sui, 'China's Economic Development Creating Dire Consequences on Environment', **http://www.petroleumworld.com/story05060305.htm** (Accessed January 15, 2006).

Intellectual property

The development of a new product or technique by a corporation can be a lucrative endeavour, opening the door to a variety of benefits, such as a larger customer base, increased market share, or a reduction in production costs. However, innovation is also a vulnerable process. Statistics regarding the survival rates of new businesses vary from source to source; however, the probability for a new enterprise to fail in the first three years of existence can be as high as 85 per cent.[31] This makes it important that an enterprise be able to recoup its investments into new products, including its research and development costs. However, competitors can make this more difficult if they are able to copy the innovation, thereby reducing the originator's market share and ability to profit. Finally, as 'copycat' enterprises often try to beat the originator through lower prices, they wind up producing inferior products.

The term intellectual property (IP) refers to a legal entitlement of exclusive rights to use an idea, piece of knowledge, or invention. The subject of such legal claims must be a product of the mind – an intangible, but potentially profitable form of property. In the past, intellectual property laws were usually territorial, meaning that the registration and enforcement of rights to certain knowledge had to be pursued separately in each country. Recently, however, IP laws have become increasingly harmonized across nations. TRIPs, or the WTO *Agreement on Trade-Related Aspects of Intellectual Property Rights*, was a significant step in this direction. Adopted in 1994, it introduced intellectual property law into the international trade system for the first time; included were minimum standards for copyrights, appellations of geographic origin, industrial designs, trademarks and even trade secrets. Unlike other international agreements on the subject, TRIPS has powerful enforcement mechanisms (like trade sanctions) at its disposal. Its requirements apply equally to all WTO member states; developing countries are given more time to implement necessary changes. However, the Act's fairness with regards to developing nations and their ability to patent is frequently contested.

Intellectual property is of key concern to various industries. Take music and Apple's iTunes. The European Union has failed to reach a consensus regarding online music copyright laws, which now vary from country to country. The United Kingdom is considered the toughest jurisdiction on copyright infringements; additionally, its musical market differs from most of the world in that nearly one-quarter of its music sales come from independent labels. iTunes therefore had to adjust significantly when entering the EU, first to accommodate for variations in copyright laws across borders, and second to negotiate with the independent artists who define the UK market.

Another more ethically charged issue with intellectual property rights is the availability of medicine. Many life-saving vaccines and remedies were initially developed by private enterprises; examples include the AIDS cocktail and Tamiflu (today's only birdflu-fighting drug). The issue, then, is whether a corporation ought to retain all rights to manufacture the drug, even in times when its supply cannot satisfy world demand, or when its prices are too high for those who need its product. Most patent laws permit, for a limited period of time, a corporation to refuse the manufacture of generic versions for its product. This provides it with the benefit of monopolizing an indispensable commodity.

Multinational corporations have been criticized for exercising this right, particularly in the case of the AIDS cocktail, given the numbers and the typical poverty of those infected with the disease. Cipla, India's third largest drug company, is one of many third-world producers which has offered to make the cocktail at a 'humanitarian price' – one significantly lower than that negotiated by the UN for impoverished African countries. However, three large multinationals (one British, one German and one American) hold the patents for the drugs involved. In South Africa, the country with the largest number of HIV infections, they have filed lawsuits against local generic producers of the cocktail.

Bribery and corruption

In many countries, payments or favours are a way of life, and a 'greasing of the wheels' is expected in return for government services. In the past, it was commom for companies doing business internationally to routinely pay bribes or do favours for foreign officials in order to gain contracts. In the 1970s, major national debates erupted over these business practices to provide ethical and moral leadership, and that contracts won through bribes do not reflect competitive market activity. As a result, countries passed laws to make it a crime for firms to bribe foreign officials for business purposes. For example, the UK passed the Prevention of Corruption Act 1906.

A number of UK firms have complained about the Act, arguing that it hinders their efforts to compete internationally against companies from countries that have no such antibribery laws. The problem is one of ethics versus practical needs and, to some extent, of the amounts involved. For example, it may be difficult to draw the line between providing a generous tip and paying a bribe in order to speed up a business transaction. Many business managers argue that one country should not apply its moral principles to other societies and cultures in which bribery and corruption are endemic. If they are to compete internationally, these managers argue, they must be free to use the most common methods of competition in the host country. Particularly in industries that face limited or even shrinking markets, such stiff competition forces firms to find any edge possible to obtain a contract. This line of argument is based on ethical relativism.

On the other hand, applying different standards to management and firms, depending on whether they do business abroad or domestically, is difficult to envision. In addition, bribes may open the way for shoddy performance and loose moral standards among managers and employees and may result in a spreading of generally unethical business practices. Unrestricted bribery could result in a concentration on how best to bribe rather than on how best to produce and market products. This line of argument is based on ethical universalism.

The international manager must carefully distinguish between reasonable ways of doing business internationally – including compliance with foreign expectations – and outright bribery and corruption. To assist the manager in this task, revisions were made in the 1988 Trade Act to clarify the applicability of the Foreign Corrupt Practices legislation. These revisions clarify when a manager is expected to know about violation of the act, and a distinction is drawn between the facilitation of routine governmental actions and governmental policy decisions. Routine actions concern issues such as obtaining permits and licences, processing governmental papers such as visas and work orders, providing mail and phone services and loading and unloading cargo. Policy decisions refer mainly to situations in which obtaining or retaining contracts is at stake. One researcher differentiates between functional lubrication and individual greed. With regard to functional lubrication, he reports the 'express fee' charged in many countries, which has several characteristics: the amount is small, it is standardized, and it does not stay in the hands of the official who receives it but is passed on to others involved in the processing of the documents. The express service is available to anyone, with few exceptions. By contrast, in the process driven by 'individual greed', the amount depends on the individual official and is for the official's own personal use.[32] Although the facilitation of routine actions is not prohibited, the illegal influencing of policy decisions can result in the imposition of severe fines and penalties.

The issue of global bribery has taken on new momentum. In 1999, the Organization for Economic Cooperation and Development (OECD) (**http://www.oecd.org**) agreed to change the bribery regulations among its member countries not only to prohibit the tax deductibility of improper payments, but to prohibit such payments altogether. Similarly, the World Trade Organization has, for the first time, decided to consider placing bribery rules on its agenda. A good portion of this progress can be attributed to the public work done by Transparency International (TI). This non-profit organization regularly publishes information about the perception of corruption in countries around the globe. In addition, TI also reports on countries whose firms are most and least likely to offer bribes – as shown in Exhibit 5.8.

The EU issued a 'Directive on Statutory Audit' in 2004. This directive (sometimes called 'Europe's SOX', or 'SOX-lite') 'clarifies the duties of statutory auditors, provides for their independence and ethical standards, introduces a requirement for external quality assurance, and

EXHIBIT 5.8

Corruption perception index

	Least Corrupt			Most Corrupt	
Rank	Country	CPI Score	Rank	Country	CPI Score
1	Iceland	9.7	144	Tajikistan	2.1
2	Finland	9.6	151	Angola	2.0
2	New Zealand	9.6	152	Cote d'Ivoire	1.9
4	Denmark	9.5	152	Equatorial Guinea	1.9
5	Singapore	9.4	152	Nigeria	1.9
6	Sweden	9.2	155	Haiti	1.8
7	Switzerland	9.1	155	Myanmar	1.8
8	Norway	8.9	155	Turkmenistan	1.8
9	Australia	8.8	158	Bangladesh	1.7
10	Austria	8.7	158	Chad	1.7

Note: A country's Corruption Perception Index shows the degree of corruption perceived by business people and country analysts. Possible scores range from 10 (very clean) to 0 (highly corrupt). The top ten least corrupt and most corrupt countries are shown above, along with their world ranks and CPI scores.

Source: *Corruptions Perception Index 2005,* Dr. J. Graf for Transparency International, University of Passau, Germany, **http://www.transparency.org**, accessed January 16, 2006.

provides for the public oversight of the audit profession and improved cooperation between oversight bodies in the EU.' It also provides a basis for international cooperation between EU regulators and those in third countries.[33] The UK published the UK Companies Act 2006 – it requires the disclosure of company information and makes provisions for the use of e-communications.[34]

The Acts seem to be effective in changing the way companies operate in the developing world – a fortunate and unexpected side-effect of a law targeting domestic business relations. By requiring corporate directors and CEOs to personally certify their companies' internal controls and by making executives who provide false certifications criminally liable, the law inadvertently led to the emergence of an entire industry of global compliance auditors. These auditors are effective in finding the 'offshore intermediaries' that help companies to sidestep these Acts (which prohibited payoffs to foreign officials). The result has been a sharp increase in the number of companies cleaning up their overseas procedures and self-reporting illegal payments overseas.

A major issue that is critical for international marketers is that of general standards of behaviour and ethics. Increasingly, public concerns are raised about such issues as global warming, pollution and moral behaviour. However, these issues are not of the same importance in every country. What may be frowned on or even illegal in one nation may be customary or at least acceptable in others. For example, cutting down the Brazilian rain forest may be acceptable to the government of Brazil, but scientists, concerned consumers and environmentalists may object vehemently because of the effect of global warming and other climatic changes. The export of tobacco products by developed countries may be legal but results in accusations of exporting death to developing nations. China may use prison labour in producing products for export, but EU law prohibits the importation of such products. Mexico may permit the use of low safety standards for workers, but the buyers of Mexican products may object to the resulting dangers. In the area of moral behaviour, firms are increasingly not just subject to government rules, but are also held accountable by the public at large. For example, issues such as child labour, inappropriately low wages, or the running of sweat shops are raised by concerned individuals and communicated to customers. Firms can then be subject to public scorn, consumer boycotts, and investor scrutiny if their actions are seen as reprehensible, and run the danger of losing much more money than they gained by engaging in such practices.

SUMMARY

The political and legal environment in the home country, the environment in the host country and the laws and agreements governing relationships among nations are all important to the international marketer. Compliance with them is mandatory in order to do business abroad successfully. Such laws can control exports and imports both directly and indirectly and can also regulate the international business behaviour of firms, particularly in the areas of boycotts, antitrust, corruption and ethics.

To avoid the problems that can result from changes in the political and legal environment, the international marketer must anticipate changes and develop strategies for coping with them. Whenever possible, the manager must avoid being taken by surprise and thus not let events control business decisions.

On occasion, the international marketer may be caught between clashing home and host country laws. In such instances, the firm needs to conduct a dialogue with the governments in order to seek a compromise solution. Alternatively, managers can encourage their government to engage in government-to-government negotiations to settle the dispute. By demonstrating the business volume at stake and the employment that may be lost through such governmental disputes, government negotiators can often be motivated to press hard for a settlement of such intergovernmental difficulties. Finally, the firm can seek redress in court. Such international legal action, however, may be quite slow and, even if resulting in a favourable judgment for the firm, may not be adhered to by the government against which the judgment is rendered.

In the final analysis, a firm conducting business internationally is subject to the vagaries of political and legal changes and may lose business as a result. The best the manager can do is to be aware of political influences and laws and strive to adopt them as far as possible.

Key terms

antidumping laws	intellectual property (IP)
boycotts	intellectual property rights
chill effect	lobbyists
code law	operating risk
common law	overinvest
confiscation	ownership risk
corporate governance	political risk
domestication	price controls
Dual-use items	quota systems
embargoes	Sarbanes-oxley Act
Environmental Superfund	tariffs
export control systems	terminology
export licence	theocracy
expropriation	trade sanctions
foreign availability	transfer risk
functional lubrication	voluntary restraint agreements
grey market	

Questions for discussion

1 Discuss this statement: 'High political risk requires companies to seek a quick payback on their investments. Striving for such a quick payback, however, exposes firms to charges of exploitation and results in increased political risk'.

2 How appropriate is it for governments to help drum up business for their companies abroad? Should commerce be completely separate from politics?

3 Discuss this statement: 'The national security that our export control laws seek to protect may be threatened by the resulting lack of international competitiveness of UK firms'.

4 After you hand your passport to the immigration officer in country X, he misplaces it. A small 'donation' would certainly help him find it again. Should you give him money? Is this a business expense to be charged to your company? Should it be tax deductible?

5 Discuss the advantages and disadvantages of common versus code law for the international marketer.

6 What are your views on lobbying efforts by foreign firms?

7 Discuss how changes in technology have affected the effectiveness of UK export control policy.

Internet exercises

1 Summarize the European Union's export licencing policy toward China. (Go to **http://www.fas.org/sgp/crs/row/ RL32870.pdf.**)

2 What are the key components of the anticorruption agreements passed by the European Union, the

Organization of American States and the United Nations? (Go to **http://www.oecd.org** or **http:// www.transparency.org.**)

Recommended readings

Askari, Hossein, John Forrer, Hildy Teegan and Jiawen Yang. *Economic Sanctions: Examining Their Philosophy and Efficacy.* Westport, CT: Praeger Publishers, 2004.

Export Administration Annual Report. Washington, DC: Bureau of Industry and Security, 2006.

IV Global Forum on Fighting Corruption. Washington, DC: Bureau of International Narcotics and Law Enforcement Affairs, US Department of State, June 2005.

Hirschhorn, Eric. *The Export Control Embargo Handbook* (2nd edn). New York: Oceana, 2005.

Hufbauer, Gary C., Jeffrey J. Schott, and Kimberly Ann Elliot. *Economic Sanctions Reconsidered: History and Current Policy,* (3rd edn). Washington, DC: Institute for International Economics, 2005.

McCue, Sarah, *From Farce to Force: Building Profitable E-Commerce Strategies.* Mason, OH: Cengage, 2006.

The OECD Guidelines for Multinational Enterprises. Paris: Organization for Economic Cooperation and Development, 2001.

O'Sullivan, Meghan L. *Shrewd Sanctions: Statecraft and State Sponsors of Terrorism.* Washington, DC: Brookings Institution, 2004.

Notes

1   http://www.talkzimbabwe.com/news/117/ARTICLE/4138/2009-01-22.html

2   Gary Clyde Hufbauer, Jeffrey J. Schott, and Kimberly Ann Elliott, *Economic Sanctions Reconsidered,* 3rd edn (Washington, DC: Institute for International Economics, 2005).

3   Robin Renwick, *Economic Sanctions* (Cambridge, MA: Harvard University Press, 1981), 11.

4   Michael R. Czinkota and Erwin Dichtl, 'Export Controls and Global Changes', *Der Markt* 37, 5 (1996): 148–155.

5   http://www.berr.gov.uk/whatwedo/europeandtrade/strategic-export-control/

6   We are grateful to David Danjczek of Titan Corporation for his helpful comments.

7   E. M. Hucko, *Aussenwirtschaftsrecht-Kriegswaffenkontrollrecht, Textsammlung mit Einführung,* 4th edn (Köln, Germany: Bundesanzeiger, 1993).

8   Utton, M.A., *Market Dominance and Antitrust Policy* (Edward Elgar Publishing, 2003). Online. Available: **http://books.google.co.uk/books?id=hp1oNX6wii4C&pg=PA55&lpg=PA55&dq=exemptions+from+antitrust+laws+in+the+UK&source=web&ots=YoIrG1f2DW&sig=iznfbkPEoEtezqanDLIlvXwvosM&hl=en&sa=X&oi=book_result&resnum=1&ct=result**

9   http://www.investorwords.com (Accessed January 4, 2006).

10 Michael Minor, 'LDCs, TNCs, and Expropriation in the 1980s', *CTC Reporter,* Spring 1988, 53.

11 http://www.aspen-re.com/political_risk.asp

12 http://www.j.u-tokyo.ac.jp/~sota/info/Papers/Sugiyama%20paper.pdf

13 Surya Prakash Sinha, *What Is Law? The Differing Theories of Jurisprudence* (New York: Paragon House, 1989).

14 http://en.wikipedia.org/wiki/Civil_law_(legal_system)

15 *National Trade Estimate Report on Foreign Trade Barriers* (Washington, DC , Office of the United States Trade Representative, 2005), **http://www.ustr.gov** (Accessed January 4, 2006).

16 Michael R. Czinkota, 'The Policy Gap in International Marketing', *Journal of International Marketing,* 8 (no. 1, 2000): 99–111.

17 We are grateful to Professor Ed Soule of Georgetown University for this example.

18 http://www.wsws.org/articles/2008/dec2008/euro-d03.shtml

19 Fischer, M.M. and Johansson, B., 'Opening up international trade in Eastern European countries: Consequences for Aggregate Trade flows in the Rhine-Main-Danube area', *Regional Science: The Journal of the RSAI,* 75, no. 1, 1996, 65–78.

20 http://www.telegraph.co.uk/finance/financetopics/financialcrisis/4434095/Gordon-Brown-pledges-to-double-Britains-exports-to-China.html

21 http://www.delnic.ec.europa.eu/en/eu_and_country/agreements/agreements_ca.htm http://www.delnic.ec.europa.eu/en/docs/Acuerdo_Marco_de_1999.pdf

22 http://ec.europa.eu/environment/international_issues/agreements_en.htm

23 Michael Czinkota, Gary Knight and Peter Liesch, Terrorism and International Business: Conceptual Foundations, in *Terrorism and the International Business Environment,* G. Suder, ed. (Northampton, MA: Edward Elgar, 2004).

24 US Department of State, *Patterns of Global Terrorism 2003* (Washington, DC , 2004).

25 Sheffi Jossi, *The Resilient Enterprise* (Cambridge, MA: MIT Press, 2005).

26 Michael Czinkota, and Gary Knight, 'On the Front Line: Marketers Combat Global Terrorism', *Marketing Management,* May/June 2005, 33–39.

27 Michael R. Czinkota, 'International Marketing and Terrorism Preparedness', testimony before the Congress of the United States, 109th Congress, Committee on Small Business, Washington, DC, November 1, 2005.

28 http://en.wikipedia.org/wiki/Trade_union

29 We are very grateful within this section for input from Professor Michael Moffett of Thunderbird University.

30 Michael R. Czinkota, Illka A. Ronkainen and Bob Donath, *Mastering Global Markets* (Mason, OH: Thomson South-Western, 2004), 362.

31 Robert Sullivan, 'Small Business Start-Up Guide', Chapter 1: Prologue, **http://www.isquare.com/prologue.cfm** (Accessed January 17, 2006).

32 Magoroh Maruyama, 'Bribing in Historical Context: The Case of Japan', *Human Systems Management* 15 (1996): 138–142.

33 http://www.itgovernance.co.uk/corpgov_uk.aspx

34 http://www.wragge.com/corporate_1198.asp

THE INTERNATIONAL MARKETING ENVIRONMENT

Managing the challenge of WTO participation

THAILAND: CONCILIATING A DISPUTE ON TUNA EXPORTS TO THE EC

Tuna is arguably one of the most well-known and abundant of fish, found in large quantities at supermarkets and convenience stores around the world. It is such a popular sight in its canned form that one may have even dissociated it from its origins as a fish, until reminded of the amusing slogan-cum-brand, 'chicken of the sea'. As such, it is safe to say that tuna enjoys as much popularity among consumers as the humble and ubiquitous chicken.

On the production side, easy accessibility and popularity translates into big business, thriving markets and fierce competition. For producers of canned tuna, the fish is their livelihood, an important source of income and an industry of serious economic significance, contributing as it does to the national balance of payments, the employment rate and, subsequently, a productive and healthy social climate.

This is especially true in the case of Thailand, the world's third-largest producer of canned tuna and the largest exporter, accounting for 31 per cent of the global volume of exports. As of 2000, the United States has remained Thailand's biggest export destination, followed by the European Community (EC) and then Canada.[1] Since Thailand's tuna industry is export-oriented, with almost all its production intended for overseas markets, foreign import restrictions and regulations wield considerable impact on its growth and overall dynamism. This is where Thailand encountered difficulties with one of its major trading partners – the EC.

Despite its impressive world ranking, producers of canned tuna in Thailand were convinced that their industry was capable of considerably better performance given more equitable access to the EC market. This inequity existed primarily in the form of a preferential tariff granted by the EC to canned tuna producers from the African, Caribbean and Pacific states (ACP countries), a status consolidated in the Cotonou Agreement (ACP Agreement) of 3 February 2000 between the EC and the ACP countries. While ACP countries were enjoying zero tariffs on tuna imports, other countries such as Thailand were continuing to face an inhibiting tariff of 24 per cent, which was proving detrimental to the legitimate economic interests of Thailand as a major producer of canned tuna. Furthermore, zero import tariffs for ACP countries encouraged investors increasingly to view the ACP countries as a favourable investment destination, in contrast to Thailand, undermining the cost and other comparative advantages that Thailand has to offer.

This case study illustrates the manner in which Thailand raised the issue and challenged the EC tariff within the framework of the Dispute Settlement Understanding (DSU) provided for in the WTO Agreement. There are three major stages to the DSU: consultation between the concerned parties, adjudication by panels and, if necessary, the appellate body, and implementation of the ruling. However, it is not always necessary for every case to follow this trajectory and to be taken to panels. In fact, the preferred path is for members to settle the dispute between themselves, through consultations.[2]

To this end, the DSU provides good offices, conciliation and mediation which may be requested by members if consultations fail to produce an acceptable solution. These options serve as an

Source: World Trade Organization 'Thailand: Conciliating a Dispute on Tuna Exports to the EC'. Online. Available from: **http://www.wto.org/english/res_e/ booksp_e/casestudies_e/case40_e.htm** (Accessed 17/5/10)

intervening step in which an independent third party is engaged to help members resolve the dispute at hand, thereby avoiding panel proceedings which can be the most costly and time-consuming stage of the DSU procedures.

The events concerning this case study span approximately three-and-a-half years, dating back to the conclusion of the ACP Agreement in 2000, followed by the WTO consultation and mediation process and concluding with the EC's new Council Regulation of 5 June 2003. As the first case in WTO history to be settled through mediation, it sets a valuable example for fellow member countries, demonstrating that disputes may be resolved within the WTO without resorting to formal litigation.

Although this is a recent case, it is worth noting that the EC-ACP relationship dates back almost 40 years to 1963. During this time a number of agreements were produced through which the EC granted ACP countries trade benefits on a number of products, including canned tuna. Thus, for this particular product, ACP countries had been enjoying free access to the EC market for almost 30 years prior to the ACP Agreement of 2000. By the mid-1990s, Thailand's tuna industry was increasingly feeling the negative impact of this preferential trading arrangement, as reflected in revenue, investment and opportunity losses.

With the formal establishment of the WTO in 1995 and the entry into force of the GATT 1994 rules came a more favourable climate in which to address such preferential or discriminatory trading relationships in the international arena. One of the basic principles of the WTO legal framework is the MFN (most favoured nation) principle, which states that 'all WTO members are bound to grant to each other treatment as favourable as they give to any other member in the application and administration of import and export duties and charges. A tariff concession made to one member must therefore be extended immediately and unconditionally to all other members'.[3] Thus, with regard to the EC's preferential tariff rates, the legal impetus and the framework within which Thailand could challenge the discriminatory tariff, were in place. It would be up to the concerned parties of Thailand to take up the cause, and to gather the information, personnel and determination necessary to see it through to a satisfactory conclusion.

I. The players

The countries concerned here are Thailand and the Philippines on the one hand and the European Community on the other. The Philippines, as a fellow ASEAN and WTO member facing similar difficulties, joined with Thailand in this landmark attempt to prove that preferential tariffs had long been impairing their economic interests, and to seek appropriate redress or compensation from the EC. For the purposes of this case study, however, the focus will remain on Thailand and its actions, although the term 'complainants' will be used to refer collectively to Thailand and the Philippines when necessary.

Throughout this process, close collaboration and coordination was a vital element between private sector players – that is representatives of the complainants' tuna industries – and their respective governments. In Thailand's case, it was the Ministry of Commerce specifically that provided a strong link between the tuna industry and the Thai permanent mission to the WTO in Geneva, where the mediation took place. At the WTO proceedings, the role of negotiator was assumed by the Thai ambassador to the WTO, who thereby served as the official voice of Thailand.

The Thai tuna industry was represented by Chanintr Chalisarapong, in his capacity as chairman of the Thai Tuna Packers' Group/Thai Food Processors' Association. Chanintr acted as a focal point in consolidating industry data and information, as well as coordinating efforts and cooperation from the private sector side. Since the matter involved issues of international law and practice, lawyers were also hired. Although this was a WTO case, the complainants were challenging the EC, whose headquarters is located in Brussels. Therefore the Thai side chose to engage a law firm based in Brussels, which is where the first round of consultations was also held. Finally, although this case was treated as strictly confidential, no such dispute can exist entirely in a vacuum; therefore, external forces in the form of political pressures from some EC governments had their impact as well.

From the start, the role of each of the major players was well delineated, with each playing to their natural strengths. The major task for the private sector was to provide industry data, information and support in every form possible to the Ministry of Commerce. The Ministry of Commerce, on the other hand, examined the legal and related aspects associated with the negotiation process, as well as providing an official link to Geneva and the WTO proceedings. The Brussels law firm provided in-depth legal counsel and professional backing in writing official submissions, although it did not participate in the actual mediation.

Constructive co-operation between the public and private sectors was a key element for a number of reasons. First, a strong, mutually supportive partnership created a sense of solidarity in a shared pursuit. Second, the government alone would not have been able to allocate the funding necessary for an endeavour of this nature. Therefore, where financial resources were needed, the private sector pooled its funds. Third, the sharing of industry data and information – from sources such as the Customs Bureau, and FAO and EC statistics – enabled the team to build a much stronger case than would otherwise have been possible, which allowed them to maintain consistency and confidence in their positions and arguments throughout the lengthy process. In sum, a vital component of success was the readiness of the affected industry to contribute to its own defence, in terms of funding and manpower.

Of their working relationship with the Thai government Chanintr remarked, 'We launched into the process of seeking redress, confident in our just cause, equipped with the factual tools and reassured by the full support of the government and its willingness to take the lead in negotiations and in lobbying efforts at all levels'. This willingness on the part of the government was matched by the private sector's own efforts: 'When we saw that there was not enough legal expertise in the ministry, we, the private sector, gathered the funding needed to hire a law firm in Brussels. While representatives of the government engaged actively in the negotiations, we continuously provided factual evidence and helped to formulate appropriate ways to respond to the rebuttals and counter-arguments throughout the consultation and mediation processes'.

II. Challenges and the outcome

The initial challenge faced by Thailand was, indeed, how to persuade the EC to enter into discussions on the matter. On 2 March 2000 the EC requested a waiver of its MFN obligations with regard to the ACP Agreement. In the 18 months following the request until the adoption of this waiver, Thailand had on numerous occasions expressed its concerns relating to the implementation of the ACP Agreement and the negative effects that it would have on their canned tuna exports. They received no response.

At the Doha Ministerial Conference, however, a give-and-take situation presented itself. The EC-ACP Agreement could not be extended without the consensus of all WTO members in approving the adoption of the requested waiver. Realizing that Thailand would not concede, the EC agreed to hold consultations with Thailand and the Philippines (the complainants) to examine their differences. In the end, Thailand agreed to concede on the waiver, on condition that their case be taken up in an appropriate forum, with the aim of resolving the conflict of interest.

Thus on 14 November 2001, the day the waiver was adopted, EU Trade Commissioner Pascal Lamy addressed a letter to Manuel A. Roxas, the Philippines Secretary of Trade and Industry, and Adisai Bodharamik, the Thai Minister of Commerce, to express the EC's willingness to enter into full consultations with the Philippines and Thailand. The letter stated that the aim of the consultations would be to 'examine the extent to which the legitimate interests of the Philippines and Thailand are being unduly impaired as a result of the implementation of the preferential tariff treatment for canned tuna originating in ACP countries'.[4] The complainants were not satisfied with the promise of consultations; they had wanted full arbitration. At Thailand's insistence, therefore, the letter also included the option of taking the matter beyond consultations. Since the EC insisted on avoiding arbitration, the parties compromised and decided that, should consultations fail to deliver an acceptable resolution, 'the Community would be open to recourse to the mediation procedure as provided under Art. 5 of the WTO's DSU'.[5] In this manner, the dispute process was initiated.

Shortly afterwards three rounds of consultations were held, the first in Brussels (6–7 December 2001), the second in Manila (29–30 January 2002) and the third in Bangkok (4–5 April 2002). The Ministry of Commerce did not enlist the direct participation of the private sector until the second and third rounds, when the latter contributed to the discussions and negotiations. Although government officials are usually entrusted to do the talking during consultations, in this case Chanintr and other private sector representatives were given the opportunity to provide factual support and to tell their story. Throughout these consultations, complainants demonstrated preparedness and commitment in responding to the numerous rebuttals and arguments springing back and forth between the parties. Nevertheless, as anticipated, a satisfactory solution was not to be had at this stage.

On 4 September 2002 the parties jointly submitted a formal letter to the Director General of the WTO, requesting mediation.

Agreed-upon working procedures were attached to the letter, committing both parties to issue a written submission to the WTO Mediator on 21 October 2002. The written submission would provide a comprehensive picture of the dispute, as well as explain in detail the arguments and positions maintained.

A period of intensive collaboration followed, during which the written submission was drafted. Thailand, the Philippines, their respective governments and the Brussels lawyers held in-depth brainstorming sessions and communicated constantly by email. By the end of that same month, their joint submission was virtually completed. At a meeting with the mediator on 5 November 2002, the WTO ambassadors of each party delivered oral statements in which they presented their main arguments and requests. The mediator alternately called on each party, giving both sides ample opportunities to rebut arguments and to direct questions at one another.

Having alleged economic injury, the major challenge for the complainants was to confirm the merits of their claims, and to convince the mediator that the preferential tariff had substantially negative effects on their tuna industries. The complainants consolidated and analyzed data and worked out a sound methodology by which to make an accurate, quantitative estimate of these adverse economic effects. In doing so, they noted that the EC market – already the largest single market in the world for canned tuna – was continuing to grow and that, while the ACP countries' market share experienced substantial growth in keeping with the expansion of the EC market, the volume imported from Thailand decreased by 46 per cent between 1994 and 2000, according to Chanintr.

The complainants were able to show that this decrease was not due to lack of competitiveness on their part, as exports to other markets in North America, Australia and the Middle East either remained stable or experienced positive growth; if they had lacked competitiveness, they would have experienced similar losses in other markets to which they were exporting. Furthermore, imports from 'non-preferred' countries other than the complainants showed similar downward trends. Even with the advent of the Asian financial crisis in 1997, which drove the Thai currency down to such levels that canned tuna imports from Thailand were even less expensive than usual compared with those of its competitors, Thai export performance vis-à-vis the EC did not improve.

The complainants concluded that the 24 per cent import tariff so distorted the conditions of competition between the complainants and their ACP counterparts that the complainants' products were essentially displaced from the EC market. In such circumstances it would be almost impossible for the complainants to reach their full export potential, and the growth of their canned tuna industries was evidently threatened. According to them, the fact that they managed to maintain a notable EC market presence despite the 24 per cent handicap, while ACP countries were enjoying free access, was in itself a direct testament to the competitiveness and productivity of their industries.

Another challenge related to WTO members' rights and obligations and the difficulty in striking a balance between what one might characterize as a 'legal' versus a 'political' spin on the situation. Legally speaking, Thailand had a solid right to pursue dispute resolution. Politically speaking, however, one must recall that in the WTO there are certain forms of 'positive' discrimination which are acceptable; that is, discrimination in favour of the poorest countries. In the light of this, Thailand argued that, while the preferential tariff was perhaps justifiable in the 1970s as a means of support for least developed countries (LDCs), greatly improved investment and economic situations in the ACP countries by the 1990s no longer warranted it. Thailand did not refute the rationale behind 'positive' discrimination, but maintained that favourable treatment should not be extended to any developing member to the detriment of another developing member.

Once all the arguments and rebuttals had been presented, it was time for the mediator to formulate an advisory opinion as to how the matter should be resolved. This required the mediator to make a thorough examination of the logic and reasoning behind claims made by both parties, for which they consulted with economists. On 20 December 2002, the mediator came out with an advisory opinion that the EC open up a new quota of 25,000 tonnes at a tariff rate of 12 per cent, to be allocated to four beneficiaries: Thailand (for 52 per cent or 13,000 tonnes), Philippines (36 per cent or 9,000 tonnes), Indonesia (11 per cent or 2,750 tonnes) and other third world countries (1 per cent or 250 tonnes).

The mediator's opinion indicated that the merits of the complainants' case had been acknowledged and accepted. The complainants were satisfied by this outcome, but the work was not yet over. The WTO mediation advisory opinion, after all, is not a legal, binding decision. Therefore the EC had every right to reject the advisory opinion and to maintain what had become the status quo as far as imports from the complainants were concerned. Of course, the EC had to take into account that doing so might prompt the complainants to take the case to panel, which would have turned the matter into a fully-fledged legal battle.

Nonetheless, the complainants' actions in this next phase following the advisory opinion would prove every bit as decisive as the mediation itself. Chanintr characterized this phase as a period of 'quiet lobbying' – no small task, as the EC consisted of 15 separate governments, each of which had to be convinced to support the mediator's opinion.

Discreet lobbying required tact and diplomacy. Here again, the close link between the private sector and the government proved indispensable said Chanintr, offering the following comment:

> Through close collaboration our cause was raised everywhere, be it Doha, Brussels or Geneva. Thai ambassadors and officials maintained a constant dialogue, formally or informally, with their EC counterparts everywhere. Of the 15 EC members at the time, Northern Europe supported our cause, as they had no tuna industry of their own to protect. Spain and Portugal, on the other hand, were extremely opposed to the mediator's opinion. In between were France and Italy. We realized that France's opinion carried so much weight among EC constituents that it could have turned the majority vote within the EC either way. Fortunately, our Prime Minister paid an official visit to France at the time and he raised the issue with President Jacques Chirac. He also held discussions with the French Prime Minister and some of his cabinet members. France ended up supporting our case – this was the real turning point. We knew then that our case had achieved success in concrete terms.

These concrete terms were set out in the EU Council Regulation No. 975/2003 of 5 June 2003, in which the tariff rate quota suggested by the mediator was officially adopted. The regulation specifies that the 'tariff quota shall be opened annually for an initial period of five years. Its volume for the first two years shall be fixed as follows: 25,000 tonnes from 1 July 2003 to 30 June 2004, and 25,750 tonnes from 1 July 2004 to 30 June 2005'.[6] The regulation also allowed for a revision in the second year after the tariff quota is opened, so that the volume of the quota could be adapted to the market needs of the EC, if necessary. The regulation entered into force following its publication in the *Official Journal of the European Union*, and is 'binding in its entirety and directly applicable in all [EU] Member States'.[7]

III. Lessons

This case is a good example of how developing country members were able to use their WTO rights to secure more equitable treatment from a developed country trading partner. Once the positive resolution had been reached, EU Trade Commissioner Pascal Lamy travelled to Bangkok to inform Thailand's Minister of Commerce, Adisai Bhodharamik, an indication of continued good relations between the two trading partners. Indeed, Chanintr emphasized that, although the tariff situation was of great importance to its canned tuna industry and national interests, Thailand made a conscious effort to maintain good relations with the EC throughout the proceedings. He said that 'in resorting to the dispute settlement process, we did not seek to confront, but opted for friendly persuasion and understanding. After all, the EC is one of our major trading partners, and a very important consumer not only of Thai tuna but in other sectors as well. We intended to avoid at all costs doing anything that would jeopardize our long-standing and good relationship with the EU'.

On a broader level, it is well accepted that taking action can itself be a sticking point for developing countries wary of investing the time, energy and financial resources in a consultation and mediation process which may not even produce any binding outcomes, let alone taking the matter to panel proceedings. This is often the case for other sectors within Thailand as well. Chanintr nonetheless encourages countries to pursue action if they feel that they have a strong case. An adverse outcome to a dispute is not always a complete loss. The country will at least have made itself heard, which can have positive effects on negotiations in other fora. On the other hand, if the country wins, then the economic returns on the invested time, money and energy will surely come back to it many times over. In Chanintr's opinion, Thailand's main objective was to show the international community that an unfair practice was being directed at the complainants and that they were serious about challenging it.

Regarding obstacles, Chanintr sees them as inevitable and should therefore inspire action rather than inertia. Instead of simply dwelling on them, efforts should be made to overcome obstacles because they are and always will be an inherent part of disputes and negotiations. Above all, this means that economic players must collect data and maintain consistent industry information. Without solid factual evidence, any attempts to make a legal impression would be seriously undermined from the start, as every claim and argument put forth could be challenged or rejected by the opposing side. Certainly, the EC initially rejected just about every argument made by the complainants, but Chanintr reassured Thailand's ambassador to the WTO that the private sector would not back down, and that they would continue to support the government. Another major obstacle is the issue of unity within a given industry or sector, which is often lacking, resulting in poor coordination and teamwork. Therefore, efforts must be made to achieve the level of commitment and the momentum necessary to support the industry throughout the dispute settlement process.

This case sets a precedent for other member countries, demonstrating that even without full court proceedings, a binding result could ultimately be achieved. Though some observers may comment that a 12 per cent tariff is still too high, for Chanintr and his team, 'Compromise was the best outcome, and we are satisfied with the result. We wanted a win–win situation where trade would be managed as fairly as possible. We didn't want to take advantage of our opponent, or to simply turn the tables on them'.

The overriding lesson to take away from this case is that cooperation between a well-represented tuna industry and the Thai government made it possible for the team to overcome obstacles that so often prove to be insurmountable stumbling blocks for other industries or sectors. The public–private sector collaboration utilized in this case sets a positive example for negotiations in other fora. Chanintr emphasized that:

> Government and the private sector working hand in hand can be the best weapon to defend our national interests. The government cannot negotiate effectively without good information and support from the private sector. The two sectors must work together and determine very clearly how much time and resources they have to spend and, if they win, how much the industry will benefit as a whole. Combining strengths made our case more solid, which led to much greater bargaining power. We could not have done it alone.

Questions for discussion

1 Tuna is not just fish – it is an important element of international trade. Discuss the importance of tuna in building economic and political relations in international trade.

2 How important is consultation in solving international disputes? What are its advantages and disadvantages in dispute resolution mechanism?

3 The World Trade Organization's most favoured nation (MFN) principle does not benefit members in the developing countries. How effective was the principle in solving the Thai dispute settlement with the EC?

4 How did the implementation of the preferential tariff treatment for canned tuna originating in ACP countries negatively affect the legitimate interests of the Philippines and Thailand?

Notes

1 Rabobank International, 'The Dynamics of the Thai Tuna Industry', Industrial Note IN 044-222, February 2002, pp. 1–3.

2 Dispute Settlement Training Module, ch. 6, WTO website, http://www.wto.org.

3 Dickson Yeboah, 'Course Material for Intensive Course on Trade Negotiations Skills', *WTO Principles and World Trade Negotiations*, January 2004.

4 Letter from EU Trade Commissioner Pascal Lamy to the Ministers of Commerce of Thailand and the Philippines, 14 Nov. 2001.

5 *Ibid*.

6 Council Regulation (EC) No. 975/2003 of 5 June 2003, opening and providing for the administration of a tariff quota for imports of canned tuna covered by CN codes 1604 14 11, 1604 14 18 and 1604 20 70. Published in the *Official Journal of the European Union*, 7 June 2003.

7 With the addition of ten new member countries to the EU on 1 May 2004, the complainants are set to revisit tariff negotiations with the EU, which provides an opportunity to lower further the 12 per cent rate and to discuss forms of compensation, since new member countries are required to employ the EU tariff, which in some cases is a marked increase from their usual rate.

Fighting poverty through trade

Recently, the World Trade Organization (WTO) announced a resumption of informal talks around the Doha trade negotiations. The Doha talks present the single best opportunity to promote a fair and freer global trading system, and progress in them is a top priority for both the UK and the European Union.

The Department for International Development (DFID) commitment to a successful conclusion to the Doha talks reflects its core belief that trade matters for development. Trade is a powerful engine for growth and can be an important tool for poverty reduction and meeting the Millennium Development Goals. Through Doha, and through other key channels, DFID continues to fight to make trade work for the world's poorest countries.

DOHA AGREEMENT: CRUCIAL FOR THE WORLD'S POOR

The Doha Development Agenda (DDA), which sets out what the WTO talks hope to achieve, could lift millions out of poverty and integrate poorer countries into the global economy. The Agenda would create economic growth, benefiting rich and poor alike. Research from the United Nations Conference on Trade and Development (UNCTAD), the Organization for Economic Cooperation and Development (OECD) and the World Bank indicates that the value of this growth could be tens of billions of dollars in the agriculture and industry sectors alone. This suggests that the more ambitious the outcome of the talks, the greater the gains are likely to be.

The Doha Round commenced in 2001 with a Ministerial Conference in the Qatar capital city that gives the talks their name. DFID continues to work with other UK government departments to ensure that the round delivers on its original development objectives. The main strands of the negotiations relate to industrial goods, agriculture and services, and DFID wants to see developing countries' products in these areas obtain greater access to global markets. Significant cuts in tariffs and subsidies offer the surest way for this to be achieved. Currently, low income countries exporting to the developed world face tariffs that are three to four times higher than those applied to trade between high income countries.

DFID'S DEVELOPMENT PACKAGE: MAKING TRADE WORK

In recent years, progress towards realizing the objectives of the Agenda has not been as swift as originally hoped. The talks' initial deadline of January 01 2005 passed without an agreement having been reached, and in July 2006 the negotiations were suspended because of differences of opinion between six major participating countries on the central issues of increased access to markets for agricultural and industrial products, and cuts in subsidies paid to farmers. If the barriers to trade for the developing world are to be lifted, it is essential that a deal is reached between all members in the talks. A study by the World Bank and the Institute for International Economies showed that the elimination of global trade barriers could lift 300 to 500 million of the world's poor out of poverty.

To help ensure that developing countries really benefit from new trading opportunities created by the Agenda, the UK has produced a development package. This takes account of the specific needs of individual countries, for example safeguarding the livelihoods of West African cotton producers by reducing the support that developed countries give to their own cotton producers. The huge subsidies provided to US cotton farmers have lowered world prices by 9 to 13 per cent, enabling the US to dominate the world market and leading to an increase in poverty in those developing countries where cotton is a major export. The package also calls for a simplification of the complex trading rules that exempt the world's least developed countries from export duties, and a broadening of the exemptions to cover all products being exported.

ECONOMIC PARTNERSHIP AGREEMENTS MUST HELP DEVELOPMENT

As well as through the DDA, another important way in which the DFID is pushing to make trade address poverty is through its work on Economic Partnership Agreements (EPAs). EPAs are trading agreements between the European Union and the 78

African, Pacific and Caribbean (ACP) countries; they are scheduled to take effect from 01 January 2008. It is vital that these agreements bring new trade and development opportunities to, and reflect the concerns of, ACP countries.

DFID is working with the European Commission and all countries involved to ensure that the agreements are development-friendly. In recent months, good progress has been made towards this, with the EU offering 100 per cent free market access to ACP counties, with only rice and sugar being required to undergo a period of adjustment. DFID believes that trade agreements that include full access to European markets and liberal export rules will benefit poor countries and help them share in the world's wealth; over the coming months, EPAs will be a priority of the DFID.

In September 2007, Trade and Development Minister Gareth Thomas attended an EU Development Meeting in Madeira, where he called on the EU and ACPs to focus on the central issue of goods to achieve agreement on the EPAs by the end of the year.

Questions for discussion

1   How effective is the Department for International Development's commitment to the development of trade with developing countries?

2   There are a number of organizations working towards improving trading with developing countries. Discuss the

A GOOD DEAL FOR PRODUCERS IN POOR COUNTRIES

The Fairtrade movement also has a significant role to play in the fight against world poverty. By ensuring higher prices for products from the developing world, greater economic certainty, increased access to global markets, and the empowerment of producers in poor countries, the movement has already benefited some five million people.

Since 1997, DFID has provided nearly £2 million to the Fairtrade Foundation and is discussing further potential support in the future. DFID wants the Foundation to focus on the poorest producers, assess impact more rigorously, expand the number of people benefiting, have an impact on mainstream supermarkets, and be able to sustain itself financially in the long term.

barriers to ensuring that the developing countries get a fair deal when trading with the developed countries.

3   What role does the Fairtrade movement play in the fight against world poverty? What are some of the challenges it faces in fighting against world poverty?

IKEA

IKEA, the world's largest home furnishings retail chain, was founded in Sweden in 1943 as a mail-order company and opened its first showroom ten years later. From its headquarters in Almhult, IKEA has since expanded to worldwide sales of $17.7 billion from 226 outlets in 33 countries. In fact, the second store that IKEA built was in Oslo, Norway. Today, IKEA operates large warehouse showrooms in Sweden, Norway, Denmark, Holland, France, Belgium, Germany, Switzerland, Austria, Canada, the United States, Saudi Arabia, and the United Kingdom. It has smaller stores in Kuwait, Australia, Hong Kong, Singapore, the Canary Islands, and Iceland. A store near Budapest, Hungary, opened in 1990, followed by outlets in Poland, the Czech Republic and the United Arab Emirates in 1991 and Slovakia in 1992, followed by Taiwan in 1994, Finland and Malaysia in 1996, and mainland China in 1998. IKEA first appeared on the internet in 1997 with the World Wide Living Room website. The first store in Russia opened in March of 2000 and in Greece and Israel in 2001. Turkey was added in 2005. Two stores were opened in Japan in 2006. Plans call for opening its first outlet in Ukraine at the end of 2011. The IKEA Group's new organization has three regions: Europe, North America, and Asia and Australia.

The international expansion of IKEA has progressed in three phases, all of them continuing at the present time: Scandinavian expansion, begun in 1963; West European expansion, begun in 1973; and North American expansion, begun in 1976. Of the individual markets, Germany is the largest, accounting for 19 per cent, followed by the US at 16 per cent of company sales. The phases of expansion are detectable in the worldwide sales shares depicted in Exhibit C1.1. 'We want to bring the IKEA concept to as many people as possible', IKEA officials have said. The company estimates that over 1.25 million people visit its showrooms daily. In 2005, nearly 454 million visitors were recorded at IKEA outlets.

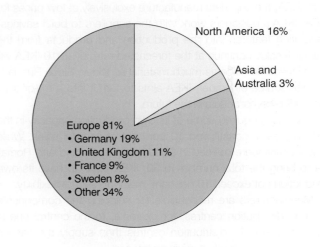

EXHIBIT C1.1   IKEA's worldwide sales expressed as percentages of turnover by market unit

North America 16%

Asia and Australia 3%

Europe 81%
- Germany 19%
- United Kingdom 11%
- France 9%
- Sweden 8%
- Other 34%

THE IKEA CONCEPT

Ingvar Kamprad, the founder, formulated as IKEA's mission to 'offer a wide variety of home furnishings of good design and function at prices so low that the majority of people can afford to buy them'. The principal target market of IKEA, which is similar across countries and regions in which IKEA has a presence, is composed of people who are young, highly-educated, liberal in their cultural values, white-collar workers, and not especially concerned with status symbols.

IKEA follows a standardized product strategy with a universally accepted assortment around the world. Today, IKEA carries an

Sources: This case, prepared by Ilkka A. Ronkainen, is based on Kerry Capell, 'How a Swedish Retailer Became a Global Cult Brand', *Business Week,* November 14, 2005, 96–106; 'Create IKEA. Make Billions, Take Bus', *Fortune,* May 3, 2004, 44; Lisa Margonelli, 'How IKEA Designs Its Sexy Price Tags', *Business 2.0,* October 2002, 108; 'Furnishing the World', *Economist,* November 19, 1994, 79; Richard Norman and Rafael Ramirez, 'From Value Chain to Value Constellation: Designing Interactive Strategy', *Harvard Business Review* 71 (July/August 1993): 65–77; 'IKEA's No-Frills Strategy Extends to Management Style', *Business International,* May 18, 1992, 149–150; Bill Saporito, 'IKEA's Got 'Em Lining Up', *Fortune,* March 11, 1991, 72; Rita Martenson, 'Is Standardization of Marketing Feasible in Culture-Bound Industries? A European Case Study', *International Marketing Review* 4 (Autumn 1987): 7–17; Eleanor Johnson Tracy, 'Shopping Swedish Style Comes to the US', *Fortune,* January 27, 1986, 63–67; Mary Krienke, 'IKEA – Simple Good Taste', *Stores,* April 1986, 58; Jennifer Lin, 'IKEA's US Translation', *Stores,* April 1986, 63; 'Furniture Chain Has a Global View', *Advertising Age,* October 26, 1987, 58; Bill Kelley, 'The New Wave from Europe', *Sales & Marketing Management,* November 1987, 46–48. Updated information available from http://www.ikea.com.

...sortment of thousands of different home furnishings that range from plants to pots, sofas to soup spoons, and wine glasses to wallpaper. The smaller items are carried to complement the bigger ones. IKEA has limited manufacturing of its own but designs all of its furniture. The network of subcontracted manufacturers numbers nearly 1,300 in over 53 countries. The top five purchasing countries are China (18 per cent), Poland (12 per cent), Sweden (9 per cent), Italy (7 per cent), and Germany (6 per cent).

IKEA's strategy is based on cost leadership secured by contract manufacturers, many of whom are in low-labour-cost countries and close to raw materials, yet accessible to logistics links. Extreme care is taken to match manufacturers with products. Ski makers – experts in bent wood – have been contracted to make armchairs, and producers of supermarket carts have been contracted for durable sofas. High-volume production of standardized items allows for significant economies of scale. In exchange for long-term contracts, leased equipment, and technical support from IKEA, the suppliers manufacture exclusively at low prices for IKEA. IKEA's designers work with the suppliers to build savings-generating features into the production and products from the outset. If sales continue at the forecasted rate, by 2010 IKEA will need to source twice as much material as today. Since Russia is a major source of lumber, IKEA aims to turn it into a major supplier of finished products in the future.

IKEA has acquired some of its own production capacity in the last few years, constituting 10 per cent of its total sales. While new facilities were opened in 2000 in Latvia, Poland and Romania to bring the total number to 30, IKEA plans to have its own production not exceed 10 per cent, mainly to secure flexibility.

Manufacturers are responsible for shipping the components to large distribution centres, for example, to the central one in Almhult. These 12 distribution centres then supply the various stores, which are in effect miniwarehouses.

IKEA consumers have to become 'prosumers' – half producers, half consumers – because most products have to be assembled. The final distribution is the customer's responsibility as well. Although IKEA expects its customers to be active participants in the buy–sell process, it is not rigid about it. There is a 'moving boundary' between what consumers do for themselves and what IKEA employees will do for them. Consumers save the most by driving to the warehouses themselves, putting the boxes on the trolley, loading them into their cars, driving home, and assembling the furniture. Yet IKEA can arrange to provide these services at an extra charge. For example, IKEA cooperates with car rental companies to offer vans and small trucks at reasonable rates for customers needing delivery service. Additional economies are reaped from the size of the IKEA outlets; the blue-and-yellow buildings average 300,000 square feet (28,000 square metres) in size. IKEA stores include baby-sitting areas and cafeterias and are therefore intended to provide the value-seeking, car-borne consumer with a complete shopping destination. IKEA managers state that their competitors are not other furniture outlets but all attractions vying for the consumers' free time. By not selling through dealers, the company hears directly from its customers.

Management believes that its designer-to-user relationship affords an unusual degree of adaptive fit. IKEA has 'forced both

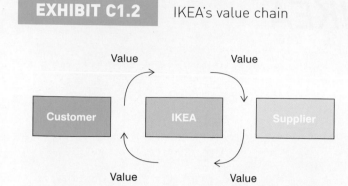

EXHIBIT C1.2   IKEA's value chain

Source: Richard Norman and Rafael Ramirez, "From Value Chain to Value Constellation: Designing Interactive Strategy," *Harvard Business Review* 71 (July/August 1993): 72.

customers and suppliers to think about value in a new way in which customers are also suppliers (of time, labour information and transportation), suppliers are also customers (of IKEA's business and technical services), and IKEA itself is not so much a retailer as the central star in a constellation of services'. Exhibit C1.2 provides a presentation of IKEA's value chain.

Although IKEA has concentrated on company-owned, larger-scale outlets, franchising has been used in areas in which the market is relatively small or where uncertainty may exist as to the response to the IKEA concept. These markets include Hong Kong and the United Arab Emirates. IKEA uses mail order in Europe and Canada but has resisted expansion into the United States, mainly because of capacity constraints.

IKEA offers prices that are 30 to 50 per cent lower than fully assembled competing products. This is a result of large-quantity purchasing, low-cost logistics, store location in suburban areas, and the do-it-yourself approach to marketing. IKEA's prices do vary from market to market, largely because of fluctuations in exchange rates and differences in taxation regimes, but price positioning is kept as standardized as possible. IKEA's operating margins of approximately 10 per cent are among the best in home furnishings. This profit level has been maintained while the company has cut prices steadily. For example, the Klippan sofa's price has decreased by 40 per cent since 1999.

IKEA's promotion is centred on the catalogue. The IKEA catalogue is printed in 47 editions in 24 languages for 33 countries and has a worldwide circulation of well over 160 million copies. The catalogues are uniform in layout except for minor regional differences. The company's advertising goal is to generate word-of-mouth publicity through innovative approaches. The IKEA concept is summarized in Exhibit C1. 3.

IKEA IN THE COMPETITIVE ENVIRONMENT

IKEA's strategic positioning is unique. As Exhibit C1.4 illustrates, few furniture retailers anywhere have engaged in long-term planning or achieved scale economies in production. European

EXHIBIT C1.3   The IKEA concept

Target Market:	"Young people of all ages"
Product:	IKEA offers the same products, which are distinctively Swedish/Scandinavian in design, worldwide. The number of active articles is 9,500. Each store carries a selection of these 9,500, depending on outlet size. The core range is the same worldwide. Most items have to be assembled by the customer. The furniture design is modern and light.
Distribution:	IKEA has built its own distribution network. Outlets are outside the city limits of major metropolitan areas. Products are not delivered, but IKEA cooperates with car rental companies that offer small trucks. IKEA offers mail order in Europe and Canada.
Pricing:	The IKEA concept is based on low price. The firm tries to keep its price-image constant.
Promotion:	IKEA's promotional efforts are mainly through its catalogues. IKEA has developed a prototype communications model that must be followed by all stores. Its advertising is attention-getting and provocative. Media choices vary by market.

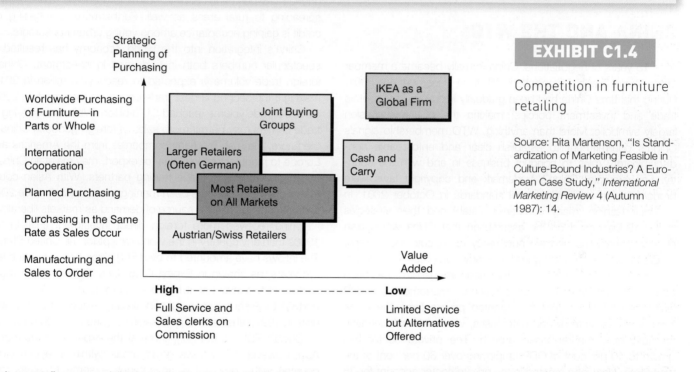

EXHIBIT C1.4

Competition in furniture retailing

Source: Rita Martenson, "Is Standardization of Marketing Feasible in Culture-Bound Industries? A European Case Study," *International Marketing Review* 4 (Autumn 1987): 14.

furniture retailers, especially those in Sweden, Switzerland, Germany and Austria, are much smaller than IKEA. Even when companies have joined forces as buying groups, their heterogeneous operations have made it difficult for them to achieve the same degree of coordination and concentration as IKEA. As customers are usually content to wait for the delivery of furniture, retailers have not been forced to take purchasing risks.

The value-added dimension differentiates IKEA from its competition. IKEA offers limited customer assistance but creates opportunities for consumers to choose (for example, through informational signage), transport, and assemble units of furniture. The best summary of the competitive situation was provided by a manager at another firm: 'We can't do what IKEA does, and IKEA doesn't want to do what we do'.

Questions for discussion

1 What has allowed IKEA to be successful with a relatively standardized product and product line in a business with strong cultural influence? Did adaptations to this strategy in the North American market constitute a defeat to its approach?

2 Which features of the 'young people of all ages' are universal and can be exploited by a global/regional strategy?

3 Is IKEA destined to succeed everywhere it cares to establish itself?

Car financing in China

In China, car financing is a lot like the unification of North and South Korea. Just about everyone wants it to happen. But before that can happen, first you need to sweep away the landmines.

— Mike Dunne, Automotive News

CHINA AND THE WTO

After 15 years of negotiations, China formally became a member of the World Trade Organization (WTO) on December 11, 2001. During this time China had been gradually liberalizing most of its trade and investment policies, making the official admission largely symbolic. More than anything, WTO membership signals China's commitment to establish clear and enforceable non-discriminatory rules to conduct business in and with the country. For example, China's trademark and copyright laws were brought in line with international standards in October 2001. In a similar fashion, many companies established their strategies in the 1990s based on the assumption that China would gain entry into the WTO and are now ready to execute those plans.

Given China's unwillingness to show progress on political reform, the commitment to structural economic reforms has been particularly noteworthy. A constitutional amendment in 1999 legitimized private capital and granted private firms the same legal rights as state-owned enterprises, which laid a foundation for sustained, market-based growth. The private sector has grown to 40 per cent of GDP employing over 30 per cent of the workforce. New jobs created in the private sector account for 38 per cent of all new formal employment, rising to 56 per cent in urban areas. The significance of this is more pronounced given lay-offs in the state-owned enterprise sector.

China has been the fastest growing economy in the last ten years, with annual real GDP growth averaging 10.8 per cent. While average national GDP per capita is $1,000, urban popula-tions (such as those in Shanghai and Guangzhou) enjoy incomes of over $5,000 (a point at which consumption increases dramatically). This has meant that urban households can afford colour TVs (96 per cent have them), phones (76 per cent), and mobile phones (28 per cent). Similar wealth is gradually (albeit slowly) spreading to rural areas as well. Furthermore, purchasing on credit is gaining acceptance among young urban consumers.

China's integration into the world economy has resulted in spectacular numbers both in trade and in investment. China's foreign trade volume is expected to reach $2.5 trillion in 2010, making it the second largest trade country in the world. In 2004, Sino–US trade volume reached $170 billion. While the lowering of trade barriers may permit more sales of foreign goods in China in the future, the rush by many companies from the Americas and Europe to manufacture in China for export, may maintain China's trade imbalance with these trading partners. With Asian countries, however, China has been running a trade deficit since 2000 and will continue to be a source of demand as markets liberalize.

China received more foreign direct investment (FDI) in the 1990s than any country in the world except for the United States. The inflows have amounted to over $60 billion per year in the last five years, as shown in Exhibit C1.5. One of the most popular sectors of this investment has been automobile production (Exhibit C1.6). Planned capacity had already exceeded 2.75 million units in 1999, when actual auto sales reached 565,000 units.

China's FDI has not only come at the expense of the rest of Asia, however. FDI inflows go to areas (within a region and a country) with comparative advantages – some to areas with abundant labour, some to areas with technological skills. With China leading in terms of inward investment flows, it may emerge as a hub for inter-regional demand for goods and services. Countries such as Japan will have to re-orient themselves to focus on research and development, design, software, and high-precision manufactured goods.

Sources: This case was compiled by Ilkka A. Ronkainen using publicly available materials. These include: 'China Now 2nd Largest Auto Market in World After US', Reuters, January 13, 2006, accessed at http://www.reuters. com/news/; 'DaimlerChrysler Plans to Tap into China's Car-Loan Market', *The Wall Street Journal,* November 2, 2005, A8; 'New Cultural Revolution in China: Cars on Credit', *The Wall Street Journal,* August 19, 2004, A11; 'Business Digest', *Far Eastern Economic Review,* February 5, 2004, 23; 'China Clears Car-Financing Ventures', *The Wall Street Journal,* December 30, 2003, A8; 'Motor Nation', *Business Week,* June 17, 2002, 44–45; Gong Zhenzheng, 'Auto Price Wars Start to Rev Up', *China Daily,* January 22, 2002, 5; Joe Studwell, *The China Dream* (Atlantic Monthly Press New York: , 2002), chapter 7, note 29; 'China's Carmakers Flattened by Falling Tariffs', *Business Week,* December 3, 2001; Mike Dunne, 'Car Loans: Ready, Set, Go?' *Automotive News International,* September 1, 2000, 33; 'Why Auto Financing Is Difficult in China', *Access Asia,* November 24, 2001; 'Shanghai Leads in Efforts to Build Personal Credit for Chinese', Xinhua News Agency, July 20, 2000; 'First Auto-Finance Firms to Be Launched in Early 2002', *Access Asia,* December 6, 2001; and Danny Hakim, 'All That Easy Credit Haunts Detroit Now', *The New York Times,* January 6, 2002, section 3, page 1. For further information, see http://www.gmacfs.com and http://www.fordcredit.com.

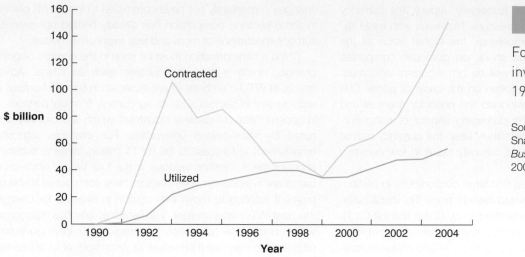

EXHIBIT C1.5

Foreign direct investment in China 1990–2004

Source: "China Data: A Macro Snapshot of China," *The China Business Review,* May–June 2005, 19.

EXHIBIT C1.6   Top 20 foreign-invested enterprises in china by sales

Rank	Foreign-Invested Enterprise	Sales Value (RMB billion)
1	Shanghai Volkswagen Co. Ltd.	56.7
2	Hongfujin Precision Industries (Shenzhen) Co. Ltd.	54.8
3	FAW-Volkswagen Automotive Co. Ltd.	49.0
4	Dafeng Computer (Shanghai) Co. Ltd.	47.8
5	Motorola (China) Electronics Co. Ltd.	38.6
6	Shanghai General Motors Co. Ltd.	34.7
7	Great Wall International Information Products (Shenzhen) Co. Ltd.	29.1
8	Shanghai Hewlett-Packard Co. Ltd.	28.7
9	CNOOC China Co. Ltd.	27.0
10	Dell (China) Co. Ltd.	25.2
11	EMB International Trading (Shanghai) Co. Ltd.	24.3
12	Huaneng Power International, Inc.	23.5
13	Guangzhou Honda Automobile Co. Ltd.	22.3
14	Lenovo (Beijing) Co. Ltd.	17.4
15	West Pacific Petrochemical Co. Ltd., Dalian	15.8
16	Maanshan Iron & Steel Co. Ltd.	15.7
17	Ocean Crown Logistics (Shanghai) Co. Ltd.	15.1
18	Dong Feng Motor Co. Ltd.	13.3
19	Nokia (China) Investment Co. Ltd.	12.8
20	Seagate Technology International (Wuxi) Co. Ltd.	12.7

Sources: "China Data: A Macro Snapshot of China," *The China Business Review,* May–June 2005, 21.

Of economic significance is China's effort to stabilize its currency in the last five years. While officially described as a managed float, the currency (*yuan renminbi*) is effectively pegged to a basket of currencies. This has resulted in China being immune to currency fluctuations that have wreaked havoc among emerging markets such as Mexico, Indonesia, Russia, Brazil and Argentina. However, due to China's increasing foreign exchange reserves, strong capital inflows and current account surplus, as well as pressure from Asian countries (especially Japan), the currency has come under appreciation pressure. However, with trade liberalization due to WTO membership, the higher value of the *renminbi* would aggravate the shock on domestic companies that compete with imports as well as on exporters who must compete in the global market (often on the basis of price). Chinese authorities have acknowledged the need for financial and currency liberalization, but the damaging impact of rising currency in the short term will most likely keep the currency regime of pegging unchanged. This will naturally result in low currency risk for investors.

It has been widely assumed that large corporations in particular from around the world would benefit from the liberalization measures undertaken and committed to by China (Exhibit C1.7). For example, the Motion Picture Association estimated that lifting the barriers to film distribution would result in $80 million in revenues, in addition to another $120 million from sales and rentals of videos (which would no longer be plagued by rampant piracy). Some sectors, such as banking and insurance, are expected to make especially strong moves as markets open up. Foreign insurers can now operate beyond the two cities they were originally limited to and were allowed nationwide access in 2005. Similar liberalization occurred in the retail sector, allowing companies such as Wal-Mart and Carrefour to develop their chains throughout the country. Majority ownership in Chinese companies is now possible, as is the choice of joint venture partners.

As many imports now face no tariff barriers (and the remaining ones are to be eliminated by 2010) or non-tariff barriers (many quotas were eliminated on accession and the rest by 2005), and because trading and distribution rights are now provided, business questions focus on the timetable for change. Most business leaders have been quite realistic in not expecting substantive

changes immediately but have committed to long-term planning. In some sectors, competition has already heated up given consumer expectations of more and less expensive choices.

China's transformation must be seen in the context of political change, which is slow in countries such as China. Adverse effects of WTO membership are expected in terms of output and employment in sectors such as agriculture, financial services and in general 'less-competitive industries' which are typically dominated by state-owned enterprises. For example, agricultural employment is forecast to fall by 11 million, while a substantial share of the 1.7 million workers in the four largest state-owned banks are in jeopardy. These factors have contributed to the government wanting to move with caution in allowing for change in the post-WTO environment. Furthermore, any dramatic change will probably face opposition from regional or local government officials who may see themselves as protectors of local interests.

There are already examples of the challenges to be faced as the WTO agreement is implemented at industrial and regional levels. Companies wanting to exploit the world's largest mobile telecommunications market were promised a 49 per cent stake in domestic operators. But to obtain this, companies have found that waiting periods for official approval are between 270 to 310 days and that any local partner must put up 75 per cent of 1 billion *renminbi* before permission is granted. This will mean that the number of joint-venture partners is considerably smaller than expected, and is possibly limited to state-owned entities. In a similar fashion, banks have found their aspirations dampened. Under the WTO agreement, foreign banks were able to offer *renminbi* banking services to Chinese corporate clients in 2004 and Chinese consumers starting in 2007. New regulations stipulate that foreign banks can only open one branch per year which, given that many are starting from scratch (only 158 branches of foreign banks existed in 2001) and given the tens of thousands of branches currently held by local entities (for example, the Bank of China has 15,200), creates a daunting task. Foreign branches are required to have 1 billion *renminbi* in operating capital to conduct a full range of services, an amount considered discriminatory by those hoping to develop the sector. Exporters have found delays in certifications for their products to enter the China market, especially in areas that are sensitive, such as agriculture.

The expectation is that disputes and problems will emerge but will be solved over time. A parallel can be drawn between the United States and its trading partners (such as the European Union and Canada), which continue to have disagreements within the WTO framework. The extent of the challenges will depend on China's economic health and its ability to absorb the competitive shocks of WTO membership. Of concern for politicians will be the growing gap between the haves and the have-nots (especially the urban and the rural), and the costs of reforming the state sector causing social unrest and challenging the legitimacy of the political structures.

The western world has had a commercial fascination with China for the last 2,000 years. The latest wave of interest started in 1979 with the official opening of China, culminating in the official acceptance of China as the 143rd member of the WTO. Companies will continue to speculate on what sales might be

---

EXHIBIT C1.7   China's WTO obligations

- 2001: After membership, China opened new cities to foreign banks for local currency business.

- 2002: China eliminated restrictions on where foreign law firms may operate and the number of offices that can be opened.

- 2004: Foreign companies permitted to provide health and group insurance to Chinese.

- 2005: U.S. eliminated Chinese textile quotas but adopted measures to prevent import surges.

- 2006: China reduced auto tariffs to 25% from current 80% to 100%.

- 2007: Foreign companies can hold 49% in telecom services (voice) joint ventures.

Source: "China Begins Career as a WTO Member," *The Washington Post*, December 11, 2001, A14.

achieved if only a fraction of the Chinese population would buy their products or services.

China's economic stature will undoubtedly continue to grow. Increased investment will make China a production base for the world as global companies put their best practices to work in the largest emerging market in the world. For the United States, this may mean losses of more than 600,000 jobs and a widening trade deficit with China which, in turn, may result in growing tensions between two world superpowers. At the corporate level, the huge investments have meant that while efforts in China may be profitable, they are not earning their cost of capital (which many multinationals calculate at 15 per cent).

Those companies interested in entering China primarily to exploit its domestic market may have more freedom to do so (such as having control of their own distribution or the ability to provide financing) but will continue to face the same challenges as before the WTO agreement. It is no longer enough to extend products and services (however famous their brand names may be) without adjusting to local market conditions. While foreign players are dominant in sectors such as beverages, film and personal care, local companies still dominate in televisions, refrigerators and washing machines despite the presence of multinational companies. Multinationals may bring their best practices to China, but local firms are quick to copy those practices and with their inherent advantages are able to compete effectively. While some doubt these Chinese companies will be competitive in global markets due to the lack of success factors such as global brands, some companies are already dominant in commodity-based sectors. Qingdao-based appliance maker Haier already has a 40 per cent market share in small refrigerators and is planning to expand its base in the United States to, among other things, learn to be more effective at home. Similarly, Chinese-made cars, such as Geely and Chery, may be exported to the United States as early as 2007.

CHANGES IN THE CHINESE CAR MARKET

A full-scale price war between car makers in China broke out in the first months of 2002. The phenomenon was a result of Chinese consumers' delays in buying cars throughout 2001 as well as increased imports following China's tariff cuts as part of the WTO agreement. The slashing of tariffs in the car sector was the biggest in any sector (from 80 per cent to 50 per cent now and down to 25 per cent by 2006).

Consumers had been waiting for cheaper cars for years, and this dream became a reality through the effects of the WTO agreement. For example, the Buick Sail's pre-WTO price was $13,855 but dropped to $12,040, with further decreases possible as domestic makers lower their prices to maintain competitive advantage. The price war was ignited when Tianjin Automotive Industry Group slashed prices of all of its Xiali compact cars by 9,000 to 23,000 yuan ($1,084–$2,771). More than 3,600 are reported to have been sold during the first four days after the price cut. Chang'an Suzuki, a joint venture between Chongqing-

based Chang'an Motor and Japan's Suzuki Motors, cut its prices by 20 per cent. Analysts estimated that domestic car makers of vehicles priced at less than 150,000 yuan ($18,070) would have to reduce prices, although car makers such as Shanghai General Motors and Shanghai Volkswagen would try to hold on and let dealers engage in price promotions. Even with the price decreases, comparable cars cost far less in Europe, a fact not lost on the Chinese consumer.

Car makers already producing in China are bracing for intense competition. As the Chinese government phases out regulations as to what models to produce, General Motors (GM), Volkswagen (VW), Ford, Honda, and Toyota all plan to launch models aimed at quality- and cost-conscious consumers. With the new market freedoms, car makers will have to focus on customer desires more than ever before.

Eventually, lower prices and wider choice should create a thriving auto industry. Car sales increased from 900,000 units in 2002 and hit the 6-million unit mark by 2006 making China the second largest auto market after the United States. Car sales have been slowing, however, due in part to the central government's crackdown on easy auto credit to help cool an overheating Chinese economy.

CURRENT MARKET STRUCTURE FOR CAR FINANCING IN CHINA

In 2005, most Chinese consumers paid cash for cars, with only 20 per cent financing their purchases. In contrast, US auto purchasers finance between 65 to 93 per cent of all units purchased, depending on the make.

China is still a very small market for auto-financing and for consumer credit in general. There are a number of reasons behind the small market size. Auto-financing was not permitted by the government before 1998. From 1998 to 2004, only four state-owned and two private banks were authorized by the Chinese government to provide loans, with interest rates regulated by the government. These include Bank of China, China's oldest bank, as well as China Construction Bank. These institutions had onerous requirements to gain approval for a loan, including: (1) collateral other than the car (home, deposits at the bank) valued at 100 to 120 per cent of the amount of the loan; (2) a guarantor; (3) proof of income and tax payments (not onerous in and of itself, but many Chinese under-report income and taxes to an extent that verifiable income is insufficient for loan repayment); (4) a marriage certificate (5) an official estimate of the value of the vehicle; and (6) mandated vehicle purchase through an 'approved' retailer. This meant that nearly one-third of car buyers opted to quit the process rather than complete it. Even with the onerous requirements, results have not been promising: since 1998, default rates have ranged from 10 to 30 per cent. Reasons include bad credit checks and disgruntled buyers who refuse to pay off loans after declines in prices for models they had purchased.

In late 2003, the Chinese government granted permission to non-financial and foreign firms to start providing auto-financing operations. The central government saw personal credit as a way to stimulate consumer spending and take some of the burden off the government's traditional means of stimulating the economy, expensive infrastructure projects. By the end of 2005, China had six auto-financing firms, some of which are wholly-owned (e.g., Ford, Toyota and Volkswagen), some joint ventures (e.g., GM with Shanghai Automotive Industry Group, and PSA with the Bank of China). DaimlerChrysler announced its financing operations in late 2005 to boost sales of its Mercedes E-class and Chrysler 300C produced in China.

The infrastructure is not yet fully developed for car financing. Most vehicle regulatory agencies do not allow liens or security interests in autos that are registered for personal use. Laws and regulations are not consistently in place to protect insurance companies when investing in loans or underwriting loan risks. Repossession procedures are not generally codified. Where rules exist, the Public Security Bureau must effect repossession and will decide resale value on repossessed vehicles.

Regional differences are significant. While the industry is still in its infancy, Shanghai is the most advanced both in terms of amounts of consumer credit and the systems in place. For example, GM's venture limited its operations initially to Shanghai, where a credit bureau keeps computer records that shortened credit checks to a few hours. The urban populations of the east will play a major role in the change process because of their increasing wealth and non-traditional attitudes toward buying on credit. Foreign interest in the market for car financing is predicated on the long-term potential of the market, influenced by China's membership in the WTO. While government rules made market entry possible in theory already prior to January 2002, setting up operations is still challenging. Auto-financing companies are only allowed to have one office, which may present logistics challenges. Government rules mandate loans denominated in renminbi (the local currency, 'people's money'). Furthermore, foreign entities can count on local competition from existing and new government-owned institutions as well as private entities. China's banks have more than 10 trillion yuan ($1.2 trillion) in deposits and are eager to put it into use. Yafei Auto Chain General Store – with default rates at less than 2 per cent and 90 per cent regional market share – is a chain of auto dealerships that gets preferential treatment from the Beijing government and enjoys exclusive underwriting support from the China People's Life Insurance Company.

The WTO agreement caused a drop in the tariffs of imported cars from a range of 70 to 80 per cent of the list price to 50 to 60 per cent. By 2006, duties sank another 25 per cent – enough to put cars within the reach of China's upper middle class.

EXPECTED MARKET CHANGES IN CAR FINANCING IN CHINA

All indications are that auto-financing in China in the twenty-first century will be a lucrative business both at the macro level and the micro level. Only a very small share of China's total consumption is made through consumer credit. In an effort to fuel economic growth, Chinese officials have stated that they are working toward percentages of consumption from credit more in line with the western world. Most of the western economies average between 20 per cent and 25 per cent of consumption through consumer credit.

According to the 2004 Gallup survey in China, urban incomes increased 75 per cent between 1997 and 2004, to an annual level of $3,000. GDP per capita in Beijing, Guangzhou, and Shanghai exceeds $5,000. Rural incomes, which are a third of the urban incomes, in comparison, increased only modestly in the same time frame. Most experts agree that automotive purchases generally and automotive finance specifically expand rapidly after crossing the $3,000 per capita GDP threshold.

Consensus estimates for the car financing market – both for personal and business use – are 20 per cent of the expected unit sales. This number is expected to increase by 40 to 60 per cent over a five-year period, resulting in a $3.25 billion market.

All indications are that Chinese consumers' aversion to debt is waning – at least in the cities of the south and east. Estimates for consumer lending in general can be extrapolated from analogous evidence. In 1995, 15,000 individuals in Shanghai borrowed 570 million yuan worth of mortgages. By 2004, 76 per cent of new bank loans went to property, of which 72.8 billion yuan was for personal housing mortgages.

The industry is dependent on accurate and timely information as well as a transparent system of operation. Shanghai Credit Information Services has emerged as a reliable source of credit information for more than 5 million Chinese. Rules for recording liens and repossession and remarketing of vehicles are now in place in Shanghai and Beijing (albeit in their infancy and open to local interpretation).

OPTIONS FOR MARKET ENTRY AND DEVELOPMENT

There are four ways that auto-finance companies can set up in China:

- automakers can launch an auto-financing services subsidiary;

- banks (Chinese) can set up special auto-financing institutions;

- non-banking financial institutions owned by enterprise groups can form an auto-financing company; or

- existing lending consortia can provide financing services for auto companies' sales divisions.

GMAC'S COMPETITIVE POSITION

GMAC and the other financing arms of car makers were at an obvious disadvantage in relation to home-country institutions because the market was reserved for Chinese institutions until January 2002. GMAC previously acted in an advisory capacity to GM's Shanghai JV manufacturing facility, which, in turn, has set up relationships with official government lending institutions (such as China Construction Bank and the Bank of Shanghai).

GMAC's competitive position vis-à-vis the other foreign companies appears to be solid for a number of reasons:

- GM is one of the largest corporate FDI contributors to China in the world and has a substantial partnership with the government;

- GMAC has numerous manufacturing partners to leverage – SGM, Jinbei GM (which produces the Chevrolet S-10 pickup and Blazer SUV), and Wuling (GM has an equity stake in the largest producer of mini-cars for the Chinese market). These partners deliver the second highest number of FDI autos in the market – just behind VW and far ahead of Ford Motor Credit and Peugeot; and

- GMAC has numerous GM-network partners to leverage (Isuzu, Suzuki, Fiat, Fuji Heavy Industries).

GMAC's expertise in auto lending generally and in the following ancillary areas critical to doing business in China should allow for the business to get up and running. It has extensive experience in auto lending in developing markets without efficient infrastructure; for example, it has experience in India, which has no credit bureaus and state involvement in repossession and remarketing. Partnering with other private and quasi-state-run institutions such as Fannie Mae, GMAC subsidiaries (GMAC Mortgage, GMAC Commercial Mortgage and Residential Funding Corporation) have developed expertise in profitable loan securitization, profitable (mortgage) loan servicing, and profitable receivables (purchase and sale), giving them the necessary skills to work together with third parties and governmental units. Finally, market presence in many other countries in the Asia-Pacific region gives GMAC the human resources necessary for China expansion. These offices are staffed with a broad array of third-country expatriates from China and other cultures who have better insight into the Chinese market than do GMAC's US-based staff.

Despite the overwhelming external and internal opportunities, challenges exist as well. Ford's and GM's credit ratings were downgraded by Moody's and Standard & Poor's in 2001, forcing the automakers out of commercial paper and into other, more expensive forms of funding. Their no- or low-interest loans and cheap leases intended to pump up sales since then have threatened the financial health of the car makers' credit arms. For example, GMAC North America's huge success with 0 per cent financing during 2001, Q4's 'Keep America Rolling' and the 2005 'Employee Discount for Everyone', campaigns ate up significant resources. Effectively, GMAC may be out of cash for big market-entry investments and equity investment from the parent company, when GM as a whole faces an unfunded pension liability and reduced cash flow that is critical for reinvestment into future product programmes. Ford Motor Credit is facing even bigger problems given its more aggressive lending practices in the recent past.

IMPLICATIONS FOR GLOBAL OPERATIONS

A car maker's captive financing arm exists for two reasons: to assist in delivering additional cars and trucks to consumers, and to provide a superior return on investment and cash flow to its sole stockholder. While still extremely risky and lacking in short-term profit, the China market is still valued by car makers because of its market potential for sales and because of the potential it displays for their financing arms in terms of auto-finance and mortgages. The question is how to deliver on the promise and the mandate. No company can adopt a wait-and-see attitude any longer.

Questions for discussion

1 Suggest reasons for a company to enter the Chinese market for auto-financing.

2 What is the most prudent mode of entry and market development for a car-financing arm of an auto maker?

3 Where should a company make its moves and with what type of products?

4 What should a company do to influence the positive change in China in its favour?

Part II focuses on the framework of going global. It begins by presenting the overall strategic options and their implementation by the firm, which provides the framework for the subsequent development of the text. This setting of the stage is followed by the development of the knowledge base through marketing research, which ensures that the company not only does things right but also does the right things. Then we concentrate on market entry, primarily through exporting and other low-cost, low-risk international expansion alternatives, followed by the systematic multinational expansion of internationally more experienced firms.

CHAPTER 6
STRATEGIC PLANNING

The case of the white goods industry: Relocation of production and its impact on the industrial structure of the regions affected

The context

The household appliances industry is characterized by a high level of globalization. The globalization of the industry in recent years has been reflected in increasing investments by EU companies in Eastern and South-Eastern European as well as in Asian countries. Nevertheless, the household appliances industry, and in particular the white goods sector, still has a considerable weight in terms of employment levels and production scales in Western European countries such as Italy, Germany, France, Spain, Sweden and the United Kingdom.

In Europe, on the whole, the large household appliances sector still shows an attractive growth rate of + 6.5 per cent a year (over the last 5 years) which represents the average between a growth of almost 2 per cent in Western Europe and more than 14 per cent in Eastern Europe (including Russia and Ukraine). These growth rates are expected due to an increasing consumer demand in Eastern European countries and a substitution market in the West where the choice and purchasing of 'whiteware' will tend to be increasingly influenced by aesthetic components (design and furniture) rather than by the mere function of a product.

The general competitive situation of the European household appliances industry is characterized by stiffer competition. In recent years many Western European countries have seen companies manufacturing household appliances undergo major processes of reorganization and rationalization mainly due to greater competitive pressure on costs, the challenges raised by international markets, changing exchange rates among the world's main currencies, increased costs of raw materials and production factors. These factors were responsible for the relocation of entire production systems, or parts thereof, from the countries of Western Europe and North America to the new EU member states and countries on the periphery of the European Union, such as Turkey, Romania and Russia as well as to China and South America.

Recent and significant cases of restructuring have concerned manufacturers including Electrolux, Whirlpool, Dé Longhi, Zoppas, Candy, Miele and Bosch-Siemens-Household appliances. In the case of Italy, the country with the highest concentration of manufacturers of white goods in the European Union, the industrial crisis has also affected the wealthiest parts of Northern Italy. The enterprises in the household appliances industry which are located in Northern and North-Eastern Italy are transferring their production plants (or parts of them) abroad in order to increase their competitiveness in international markets by reducing production costs. The first effects of these relocation processes are apparent in the North-Eastern Italian economy where there are increasing problems in redeploying workers who lose their jobs and in reorganizing a local economic system that largely depends on the manufacturing sector. These processes of structural change which are affecting major geographical areas with dense industrialization not only in Italy but in all Western European countries raise major challenges for all the actors concerned.

© VARIO IMAGES GMBH & CO.KG/ALAMY

The case of the German white goods industry

According to the German metalworkers' trade union, IG Metall, the constant strides made by the policy of relocation practised by individual groups are having a serious impact on the regions affected. For instance, the threatened closure of Bosch Siemens Hausgeräte GmbH's washing machine factory in Berlin is going ahead, and must be seen against the backdrop of 30 per cent unemployment in the metalworking and electrical goods sector in the city. The compensation for these job losses in industry, which leading politicians had hoped would take the form of fresh employment in the services sector in Berlin, has failed to materialize. So the city remains dependent on the continued existence of its traditional industrial sectors. Moreover, the further migration of industrial jobs away from the capital is heightening its current financial crisis.

The closure of the Nuremberg plant planned by the management of Electrolux would considerably weaken a region that is already structurally weak. The region of Franconia has the lowest rate of industrial jobs in Bavaria. The entertainment industry that used to be settled there (e.g. Grundig) has almost completely disappeared. The loss of tax revenue associated with the further loss of around 1,700 jobs will pose a major problem for the city of Nuremberg.

The Neunkirchen dishwasher plant run by Bauknecht/Whirlpool, which is similarly threatened with closure, is also in a structurally weak region. Industrial activity in the federal state of Saarland used to be dominated by the coal and steel sectors. The region's structural change to new industries (the car and car supplies sectors) has only been partly successful. Saarland suffers from very high unemployment. In this context, the closure of the Neunkirchener plant would be another catastrophe.

The region of Eastern Westphalia, where Miele has based its production, is characterized by an industrial monostructure, i.e., dominated by the kitchen furniture and household goods industry. Miele's management is continuing to back the production sites located there. Any change in this policy would deal the region a fatal blow.

The trade union strategy

German companies cannot compete with cheap foreign producers in terms of prices, since the hourly wages are unbeatable. The only way to achieve a competitive edge is through innovation. Examples of innovations that will soon be viable are computer-controlled appliances for the elderly that are designed to be recycled and the exploration of possible applications involving micro- and nanotechnologies. IG Metall, therefore, is asking for more research and development, crucial for securing the future of production sites. According to IG Metall, R&D synergies should also be sought with the established academic infrastructure. This too would promote the survival of jobs in industry. In view of the current problems faced by the white goods industry, according to IG Metall, an appropriate industrial and structural policy in Germany and at the European level must be applied to alleviate the situation and provide the necessary backing.

SOURCE: Volker Telljohann (2005), 'Coordination or cooperation between trade unions within the EU 25?' **http://www.ucd.ie/indrel/Warwick_Workshop_ Papers/Telljohann05.doc** (Accessed 27/5/09).

GLOBAL MARKETING

Many marketing managers have to face the increasing globalization of markets and competition described in *The International Marketplace 6.1*. The rules of survival have changed since the beginning of the 1980s when Theodore Levitt first coined the phrase *global marketing*.[1] Even the biggest companies in the biggest home markets cannot survive on domestic sales alone if they are in global industries such as cars, banking, consumer electronics, entertainment, pharmaceuticals, publishing, travel services or home appliances. They have to be in all major markets to survive the shakeouts expected to leave three to five players per industry at the beginning of the twenty-first century.[2]

Globalization reflects a business orientation based on the belief that the world is becoming more homogeneous and that distinctions between national markets are not only fading but, for some products, will eventually disappear. As a result, companies need to globalize their international strategy by formulating it across markets to take advantage of underlying market, cost, environmental and competitive factors. This has meant, for example, that Chinese companies (in categories ranging from car parts and appliances to telecommunications) have entered the main markets of the world such as Europe and North America to become global powerhouses.[3] Having a global presence ensures viability against other players in the home market as well.

As shown in Exhibit 6.1, global marketing can be seen as the culmination of a process of international market entry and expansion. Before globalization, marketers utilize a country-by-country multidomestic strategy to a great extent, with each country organization operated as a profit centre. Each national entity markets a range of different products and services targeted to different customer segments, utilizing different marketing strategies with little or no coordination of operations between countries.

However, as national markets become increasingly similar and scale economies become increasingly important, the inefficiencies of duplicating product development and manufacture in each country become more apparent and the pressure to leverage resources and coordinate activities across borders gains urgency. Similarly, the increasing number of customers operating globally, as well as the same or similar competitors faced throughout the major markets, adds to the need for strategy integration.

EXHIBIT 6.1 Global marketing evolution	*Phase 1*	*Phase 2*	*Phase 3*
	Leverage of domestic capabilities: foreign market entry	Expansion of foreign market presence	Coordination of global operations
	Objective: economies of scale	Objective: economies of scope	Objective: exploit synergies throughout network
		Corporate Actions	
	Driven opportunistically, often by approach of distributor or customer	Slower domestic growth creates greater pressure for foreign sales growth	Production of the broadened, new emphasis on full-line service rather than proprietary technology
	Constrained by lack of funding (domestic growth still priority investment), so low cost entry	New lines carried, sales mix broadens and reflects national market	Global account management
	Risk minimized by entering close markets (geographically, culturally, economically)	Search for new customer segments, requiring new management skills	Coordination mechanisms (Global Task Forces)
	Entry based on core products with technical superiority	Countries develop own marketing programs	Learning transferred between countries
		New applications sought	Headquarters introduces global branding, packaging
		Decentralization of R & D, production	Requires common culture
		Regional management reflects foreign experience	

Source: Adapted from Susan P. Douglas and C. Samuel Craig, "Evolution of Global Marketing Strategy: Scale, Scope, and Synergy," *Columbia Journal of World Business* 24 (Fall 1989): 47–58, and George S. Yip, *Total Global Strategy II*, Upper Saddle River, NJ: Pearson, 2002, chapter 1.

It should be noted that global leverage means balancing three interests: global, regional and local. In many cases, the exploitation of commonalities is best executed on a regional basis, given that some differences remain between groups of markets.[4] The same strategic principles apply to developing and implementing global and regional strategy. Naturally, the more a marketer can include the local dimension to efforts in each individual market, the more effective the strategy tends to be.[5] For example, consumers may prefer a global brand that has been adapted to the needs of local usage conditions. While the approach is localized, the global resources of a marketer provide the brand with a winning edge (e.g., in terms of quality or quality perceptions).

Globalization drivers

Both external and internal factors will create the favourable conditions for development of strategy and resource allocation on a global basis. These factors can be divided into market, cost, environmental and competitive factors.[6] Below are examples of globalization drivers.

Market factors The world customer identified by Ernst Dichter more than 40 years ago has gained new meaning today.[7] For example, Kenichi Ohmae has identified consumers in the triad of North America, Europe and the Asia-Pacific region, whom marketers can treat as a single market with similar consumption habits.[8] Over a billion in number, these consumers have similar educational backgrounds, income levels, lifestyles, use of leisure time and aspirations. One reason given for the similarities in their demand is a level of purchasing power (ten times greater than that of the developing markets or even emerging economies) that translates into higher diffusion rates for certain products. Another reason is that developed infrastructures – diffusion of telecommunication and common platforms such as Microsoft Windows and the internet – lead to attractive markets for other goods and services. Emerging and developing markets have been able to leapfrog into the newest technologies, closing significant gaps of the past. Products can therefore be designed to meet similar demand conditions throughout the triad and beyond. These similarities also enhance the transferability of other marketing elements.

At the same time, channels of distribution are becoming more global; that is, a growing number of retailers are now showing great flexibility in their strategies for entering new geographic markets.[9] Some are already world powers (e.g., Benetton and McDonald's), whereas others are pursuing aggressive growth (e.g., Aldi, Toys 'Я' Us, and IKEA). Also noteworthy are cross-border retail alliances, which expand the presence of retailers to new markets quite rapidly. The presence of global and regional channels makes it more necessary for the marketer to rationalize marketing efforts.

Cost factors Avoiding cost inefficiencies and duplication of effort are two of the most powerful globalization cost drivers. A single-country approach may not be large enough for the local business to achieve all possible economies of scale and scope as well as synergies, especially given the dramatic changes in the marketplace. Take, for example, pharmaceuticals. In the 1970s, developing a new drug cost about $16 million and took four years. The drug could be produced in Britain or the United States and eventually exported. Now, developing a drug costs as much as $1 billion and takes as long as 12 years, with competitive efforts close behind. For the leading companies, annual R&D budgets can run to $5 billion. Only global products for global markets can support that much risk.[10] Size has become a major asset, which partly explains the many mergers and acquisitions in industries such as aerospace, pharmaceuticals and telecommunications. The paper industry underwent major regional consolidation between 1998 and 2005, as shown in Exhibit 6.2, as companies from Europe, for example, consolidated their positions in a scale-driven sector.[11] In the heavily contested consumer goods sectors, launching a new brand may cost as much as $100 million, meaning that companies such as Unilever and Procter & Gamble are not going to necessarily spend precious resources on one-country projects.

In many cases, expanded market participation and activity concentration can accelerate the accumulation of learning and experience. General Electric's philosophy is to be first or second in the world in a business or to get out. This can be seen, for example, in its global effort to develop premium computed tomography (CT), a diagnostic scanning system. GE swapped its consumer electronics business with the French Thomson for Thomson's

EXHIBIT 6.2

Consolidation in the
paper industry,
1998–2005

Acquirer	Target	Value	Date Announced
Koch Industries	Georgia-Pacific	$13.2 billion	11/13/05
Chuetsu Pulp & Paper	Mitsubishi Paper	$2.4 billion	1/31/05
Semapa	Portucel	$1.9 billion	7/6/04
Weyerhaeuser	Willamette Industries	$6.2 billion	1/28/02
MeadWestvaco (US)*	Mead (US)*	$3.2 billion	8/29/01
Norske Skogindustrier (Norway)	Fletcher Challenge Paper (New Zealand)	$2.5 billion	4/03/00
Smurfit-Stone (US)	St Laurent Paperboard (Canada)	$1.0 billion	2/23/00
Stora Enso (Finland)	Consolidated Papers (US)	$3.9 billion	2/22/00
International Paper (US)	Champion Int'l (US)	$5.7 billion	2/17/00
Abitibi-Consol. (Canada)	Donohue (Canada)	$4.0 billion	2/11/00
Weyerhaeuser (US)	MacMillan Bloedel (Canada)	$2.3 billion	6/21/99
Int'l Paper (US)	Union Camp (US)	$5.9 billion	11/24/98
Stora (Sweden)*	Enso Oyj (Finland)*	Undisclosed	6/02/98

*Merger of equals

Sources: 'Koch Industries Agrees to Buy Georgia-Pacific', *The Wall Street Journal,* November 14, 2005, A3; 'Paper Merger Attains Size without Adding Huge Debt', *The Wall Street Journal,* August 30, 2001, B4; and 'Stora Enso to Buy Consolidated Papers', *The Wall Street Journal,* February 23, 2000, A3, A8. See also **http://www.storaenso.com**; and Robert Frank, 'The Emerging Global Paper Industry', **http://www.worldleadersinprint.com** (Accessed April 25, 2001).

diagnostic imaging business. At the same time, GE established GE Medical Systems Asia in Tokyo, anchored on Yokogawa Medical Systems, which is 75 per cent owned by GE.

Environmental factors   As shown earlier in this text, government barriers have fallen dramatically in previous years to further facilitate the globalization of markets and the activities of marketers within them. For example, the forces pushing toward a pan-European market are very powerful: The increasing wealth and mobility of European consumers (favoured by the relaxed immigration controls), the accelerating flow of information across borders, the introduction of new products where local preferences are not well established, and the common currency.[12] The resulting removal of physical, fiscal, and technical barriers is also indicative of the changes that are taking place around the world on a greater scale.

At the same time, rapid technological evolution is contributing to the process. For example, Daimler Benz A.G. is able to accomplish its globalization efforts by using new communications methods, such as teleconferencing, intranet, and CAD/CAM links, as well as travel, to manage the complex task of meshing car companies on different continents.[13] Newly emerging markets will benefit from advanced communications by being able to leapfrog stages of economic development. Places that until recently were incommunicado in China, Vietnam, Hungary or Brazil are rapidly acquiring state-of-the-art telecommunications, especially in mobile telephony, that will let them foster both internal and external development.[14]

A new group of global players is taking advantage of today's more open trading regions and newer technologies. 'Mininationals' or 'Born Globals' (newer companies with sales between $200 million and $1 billion) are able to serve the world from a handful of manufacturing bases, compared with having to build a plant in every country as the established multinational corporations once had to do. Their smaller bureaucracies have also allowed these mininationals to move swiftly to seize new markets and develop new products – a key to global success.[15] This phenomenon is highlighted in *The International Marketplace 6.2.*

THE INTERNATIONAL **MARKETPLACE 6.2**

Born global

Exports account for 95 per cent of Cochlear's $40 million sales after a real annual compounded rate of 25 per cent throughout the last ten years. Cochlear is a company specializing in the production of implants for the profoundly deaf. Based in Australia, it maintains a global technological lead through its strong links with hospitals and research units around the world and through its collaborative research with a global network of institutions.

Cochlear is a prime example of small to medium-sized firms that are remaking the global corporation of the future. The term 'mininational' has been coined to reflect their smaller size compared to the traditional multinationals. Sheer size is no longer a buffer against competition in markets where customers are demanding specialized and customized products. With the advent of electronic process technology, mininationals are able to compete on price and quality – often with greater flexibility. By taking advantage of today's more open trading regions, they can serve the world from a handful of manufacturing bases, sparing them from the necessity of building a plant in every country. Developments in information technology have enabled mininationals to both access data throughout most of the world and to run inexpensive and responsive sales and service operations across languages and time zones. An empirical study of exporting firms established in the last ten years found that more than half could be classified as 'Born Globals'.

The smaller bureaucracies of the mininationals allow them to move swiftly in seizing new markets and developing new products, typically in focused markets. In many cases, these new markets have been developed by the mininationals themselves. For example, the decision by many large, multinational corporations to reduce their number of suppliers means that Danish companies, many of which are small and medium-sized enterprises (SMEs), need to expand their core competencies and move beyond simply providing components to identifying system-wide problems and providing solutions[16]. This requires such firms to obtain a greater knowledge of their customers and concentrate on adding value to their products and services. Such an approach demands a strategic approach to marketing and production[17].

The lessons from these new-generation global players are to (1) keep focused and concentrate on being number one or number two in a technology niche; (2) stay lean by having small headquarters to save on costs and to accelerate decision making; (3) take ideas and technologies to and from wherever they can be found; (4) take advantage of employees, regardless of nationality, to globalize thinking; and (5) solve customers' problems by involving them rather than pushing standardized solutions on them. As a result of being flexible, they are better able to weather storms such as the Asian financial crisis by changing emphases in the geographical operations.

SOURCES: Hollesen Svend and Jenster, Per V. (2000), 'The international marketing challenges facing Danish small and medium-sized enterprises', *Strategic Change*, 9(7), 451–459; Gary Knight, Tage Koed Madsen, and Per Servais, 'An Inquiry into Born-Global Firms in Europe and the USA', *International Marketing Review* 21(number 6, 2004): 645–666; Øystein Moen and Per Servais, 'Born Global or Gradual Global? Examining the Export Behavior of Small and Medium-Sized Enterprises', *Journal of International Marketing* 10 (no. 3, 2002): 49–72; Øystein Moen, 'The Born Globals: A New Generation of Small European Exporters', *International Marketing Review* 19 (no. 2, 2002): 156–175; Michael W. Rennie, 'Born Global', *The McKinsey Quarterly* (no. 4, 1993): 45–52; 'Mininationals Are Making Maximum Impact', *Business Week*, September 6, 1993, 66–69; **http://www.cochlear.com**; and **http://www.cisco.com**.

Competitive factors Many industries are already dominated by global competitors that are trying to take advantage of the three sets of factors mentioned earlier. To remain competitive, the marketer may have to be the first to do something or to be able to match or pre-empt competitors' moves. Products are now introduced, upgraded, and distributed at rates unimaginable a decade ago. Without a global network, a marketer may run the risk of seeing carefully researched ideas picked off by other global players. This is what Procter & Gamble and Unilever did to Kao's Attack concentrated detergent, which they mimicked and introduced into the United States and Europe before Kao could react.

With the triad markets often both flat in terms of growth and fiercely competitive, many global marketers are looking for new markets and for new product categories for growth. Nestlé, for example, is setting its sights on consumer markets in fast-growing Asia, especially China, and has diversified into pharmaceuticals by acquiring Alcon and by becoming a major shareholder in the world's number one cosmetics company, the French L'Oréal. Between 1985 and 2000, Nestlé spent $26 billion on acquisitions, and another $18 billion from 2001 to

2002.[18] Since then, the company has focused its acquisitions on the ice-cream and drinks sectors by buying Mövenpick, Powwow, Dreyers and Valio.

Market presence may be necessary to execute global strategies and to prevent others from having undue advantage in unchallenged markets. In response to Caterpillar's growing threat, Komatsu entered into strategic alliances with earth moving manufacturers, for example Dreeser Industries (USA); it also acquired 64 per cent of the shares of Hanomag AG, a German make of earthmoving equipment. To improve its sourcing capabilities, Komatsu purchased a minority equity in FAI s.p.a. an Italian producer of backhoe loaders. It entered into a sourcing alliance with Timberjack of Canada for logging machinery and extended its injection moulding machinery offerings through an alliance with Husky Injection Molding Systems of Canada. It formed a Japanese joint venture with Cybernation Cutting Systems of the United States for producing turnkey cutting systems for fabrication of HVAC ducting and architectural sign components. It formed another alliance in the area of high-speed, high-precision, image processing vision systems for automated inspection of integrated circuits with Cognex Corporation of the United States.[19] In addition, it owns production plants and sales and service units in other countries, mainly the United States, Canada, Mexico, Brazil, the United Kingdom, Germany, Italy, Indonesia, China, Thailand, India and Taiwan.[20]

The outcome The four globalization drivers have affected countries and industrial sectors differently. While some industries are truly globally contested, such as paper and soft drinks, some others, such as government procurement, are still quite closed and will open up as a decades-long evolution. Commodities and manufactured goods are already in a globalized state, while many consumer goods are accelerating toward more globalization. Similarly, the leading trading nations of the world display far more openness than low-income countries, thus advancing the state of globalization in general. The expansion of the global trade arena is summarized in Exhibit 6.3. The size of the market estimated to be global in the early twenty-first century is well over $21 billion, boosted by new sectors and markets that will become available. For example, while financially unattractive in the short to medium term, low-income markets may be beneficial in learning the business climate, developing relationships, and building brands for the future.

EXHIBIT 6.3   The global landscape by industry and market

| | | **Industry** | | |
		Commodities and scale-driven goods	Consumer goods and locally delivered goods and services	Government services
Triad*		Established arena Globalized in 1980s		
Emerging countries†		Growing arena Globally contestable today		
Low-income countries‡		Closed arena Still blocked or lacking significant opportunity		

Country (vertical label on left)

Global ←→ Local

More globalized ↑ / Less globalized ↓ (vertical label on right)

* 30 OECD countries from North America, Western Europe, and Asia; Japan and Australia included
† 70 countries with middle income per capita, plus China and India ($2,000–$20,000)
‡ 100 Countries of small absolute size and low income per capita (< $2,000)

Source: Adapted and updated from Jane Fraser and Jeremy Oppenheim, "What's New about Globalization," *The McKinsey Quarterly* 33 (no. 2, 1997): 173; and Jagdish N. Sheth and Atul Parkatiyar, "The Antecedents and Consequences of Integrated Global Marketing," *International Marketing Review* 18 (no. 1, 2001): 16–29.

Leading companies by their very actions drive the globalization process. There is no structural reason why soft drinks should be at a more advanced stage of globalization than beer and spirits, which remain more local, except for the opportunistic behaviour of Coca-Cola. Similarly, Nike and Reebok have driven their businesses in a global direction by creating global brands, a global customer segment and a global supply chain. By creating a single online trading exchange for all their parts and suppliers, General Motors, Ford, and Daimler-Chrysler created a worldwide market of $240 billion in car components.[21]

THE STRATEGIC PLANNING PROCESS

Given the opportunities and challenges provided by the new realities of the marketplace, decision makers have to engage in strategic planning to match markets with products and other corporate resources more effectively and efficiently, to strengthen the company's long-term competitive advantage. While the process has been summarized as a sequence of steps in Exhibit 6.4, many of the stages can occur simultaneously. Furthermore, feedback as a result of evaluation and control may restart the process at any stage.

It has been shown that for globally committed marketers, formal strategic planning contributes to both financial performance and nonfinancial objectives.[22] These benefits include raising the efficacy of new-product launches, cost reduction efforts, and improving product quality and market share performance. Internally, these efforts increase cohesion and improve on understanding different units' points of view.

Understanding and adjusting the core strategy

The planning process has to start with a clear definition of the business for which strategy is to be developed. Generally, the strategic business unit (SBU) is the unit around which decisions are based. In practice, SBUs represent groupings based on product-market similarities based on (1) needs or wants to be met; (2) end user customers to be targeted or (3) the product or service used to meet the needs of specific customers. For a global marketer such as

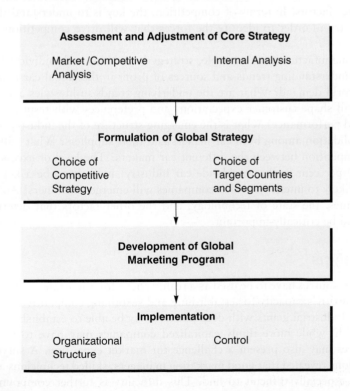

The authors appreciate the contributions of Robert M. Grant in the preparation of this figure.

EXHIBIT 6.4

Global strategy formulation

Kingfisher, the options may be to define the business to be analyzed as the home improvement business, the do-it-yourself business, or the power tool business. Ideally, these SBUs should have primary responsibility and authority in managing their basic business functions.

This phase of the planning process requires the participation of executives from different functions, especially marketing, production, finance, distribution, and procurement. Geographic representation should be from the major markets or regions as well as from the smaller, yet emerging, markets. With appropriate members, the committee can focus on product and markets as well as competitors whom they face in different markets, whether they are global, regional or purely local. Heading this effort should be an executive with highest-level experience in regional or global markets; for example, one global firm called on the president of its European operations to come back to headquarters to head the global planning effort. This effort calls for commitment by the company itself, both in calling on the best talent to participate in the planning effort and later in implementing their proposals.

It should be noted that this assessment against environmental realities may mean a dramatic change in direction and approach. For example, the once-separate sectors of computing and mobile telephony will be colliding and the direction of future products is still uncertain. The computer industry believes in miniaturizing the general-purpose computer, while the mobile-phone industry believes in adding new features (such as photo-messaging, gaming and location-based information) to its existing products.[23] The joint venture between Ericsson and Sony aims at taking advantage of this trend, something that neither party could have done on its own.

Market and competitive analysis

For global marketers, planning on a country-by-country basis can result in spotty worldwide market performance. The starting point for global strategic planning is to understand that the underlying forces that determine business success are common to the different countries that the firm competes in. Planning processes that focus simultaneously across a broad range of markets provide global marketers with tools to help balance risks, resource requirements, competitive economies of scale, and profitability to gain stronger long-term positions.[24] On the demand side this requires an understanding of the common features of customer requirements and choice factors. In terms of competition, the key is to understand the structure of the global industry in order to identify the forces that will drive competition and determine profitability.[25]

For any car manufacturer, for example, strategy begins not with individual national markets, but with understanding trends and sources of profit in the global car market. What are the trends in world demand? What are the underlying trends in lifestyles and transportation patterns that will shape customer expectations and preferences with respect to safety, economy, design and performance? What is the emerging structure of the industry, especially with regard to consolidation among both car makers and their suppliers? What will determine the intensity of competition between the different car makers? The level of excess capacity (currently about 40 per cent in the worldwide car industry) is likely to be a key influence.[26] If competition is likely to intensify, which companies will emerge as winners? An understanding of scale economies, the state of technology, and the other factors that determine cost efficiency is likely to be critically important.

Internal analysis

Organizational resources have to be used as a reality check for any strategic choice, in that they determine a company's capacity for establishing and sustaining competitive advantage within global markets. Industrial giants with deep pockets may be able to establish a presence in any market they wish, while more thinly capitalized companies may have to move cautiously. Human resources may also present a challenge for market expansion. A survey of multinational corporations revealed that good marketing managers, skilled technicians and production managers were especially difficult to find. This difficulty is further compounded when the search is for people with cross-cultural experience to run future regional operations.[27]

At this stage it is imperative that the company assesses its own readiness for the necessary moves. This means a rigorous assessment of organizational commitment to global or regional expansion, as well as an assessment of the product's readiness to face the competitive environment. In many cases this has meant painful decisions of focusing on certain industries and leaving others. For example, Nokia, the world's largest manufacturer of mobile phones, started its rise in the industry when a decision was made at the company in 1992 to focus on digital cellular phones and to sell off dozens of other product lines (such as personal computers, car tyres and toilet tissue). By focusing its efforts on this line, the company was able to bring to market new products quickly, build scale economies into its manufacturing, and concentrate on its customers, thereby communicating a commitment to their needs. Nokia's current 40 per cent market share allows it the best global visibility of and by the market.[28]

Formulating global marketing strategy

The first step in the formulation of global strategy is the choice of competitive strategy to be employed, followed by the choice of country markets to be entered or to be penetrated further.

Choice of competitive strategy In dealing with the global markets, the marketing manager has three general choices of strategies, as shown in Exhibit 6.5: (1) cost leadership, (2) differentiation, or (3) focus.[29] A focus strategy is defined by its emphasize on a single industry segment within which the orientation may be towards either low cost or differentiation. Any one of these strategies can be pursued on a global or regional basis, or the marketer may decide to mix and match strategies as a function of market or product dimensions.

In pursuing cost leadership, the global marketer offers an identical product or service at a lower cost than the competition. This often means investment in scale economies and strict control of costs, such as overheads, research and development, and logistics. Differentiation, whether it is industry-wide or focused on a single segment, takes advantage of the marketer's real or perceived uniqueness on elements such as design or after-sales service. It should be noted, however, that a low-price, low-cost strategy does not imply a commodity situation.[30] Although Japanese and European technical standards differ, mobile phone manufacturers like Motorola and Nokia design their phones to be as similar as possible to hold down manufacturing costs. As a result, they can all be made on the same production line, allowing the manufacturers to shift rapidly from one model to another to meet changes in demand and customer requirements. In the case of IKEA, the low-price approach is associated with clear positioning and a unique brand image focused on a clearly defined target audience of 'young people of all ages'. Similarly, marketers who opt for high differentiation cannot forget the monitoring of costs. One common denominator of consumers around the world is their quest for value for their money. With the availability of information increasing and levels of education improving, customers are poised to demand even more of their suppliers.

Most global marketers combine high differentiation with cost containment to enter markets and to expand their market shares. Flexible manufacturing systems using mostly standard components and total quality management measures that reduce the occurrence of defects, are allowing marketers to customize an increasing amount of their production while at the same time saving on costs. Global activities will in themselves permit the exploitation of scale economies not only in production but also in marketing activities, such as advertising.

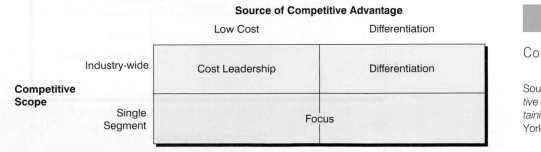

EXHIBIT 6.5

Competitive strategies

Source: Michael Porter, *Competitive Advantage: Creating and Sustaining Superior Performance* (New York: Free Press, 1998), chapter 1.

Country-market choice A global strategy does not imply that a company should serve the entire globe. Critical choices relate to the allocation of a company's resources between different countries and segments.

The usual approach is first to start with regions and further split the analysis by country. Many marketers use multiple levels of regional groupings to follow the organizational structure of the company, e.g., splitting Europe into northern, central and southern regions that display similarities in demographic and behavioural traits. An important consideration is that data may be more readily available if existing structures and frameworks are used.[31]

Various portfolio models have been proposed as tools for this analysis. They typically involve two measures – internal strength and external attractiveness.[32] As indicators of internal strength, the following variables have been used: relative market share, product fit, contribution margin and market presence, which would incorporate the level of support by constituents as well as resources allocated by the company itself. Country attractiveness has been measured using market size, market growth rate, number and type of competitors, and governmental regulation, as well as economic and political stability.

An example of such a matrix is provided in Exhibit 6.6. The 3 × 3 matrix on country attractiveness and company strength is applied to the European markets. Markets in the invest/grow position will require continued commitment by management in research and development, investment in facilities, and the training of personnel and the country level. In cases of relative weakness in growing markets, the company's position may have to be strengthened (through acquisitions or strategic alliances) or a decision to divest may be necessary. For example, by entering into a strategic alliance with Nissan, Renault wanted to establish a strong presence in Asia and North America. The alliance has so far benefited both parties.[33]

In choosing country markets, a company must make decisions beyond those relating to market attractiveness and company position. A market expansion policy will determine the allocation of resources among various markets. The basic alternatives are concentration on a small number of markets and diversification, which is characterized by growth in a relatively large number of markets. Expansion strategy is determined by market-, mix-, and company-related factors, listed in Exhibit 6.7. Market-related factors determine the attractiveness of the market in the first place. With high and stable growth rates only in certain markets, the firm will likely opt for a concentration strategy, which is often the case for innovative products early in their life cycle. If demand is strong worldwide, as the case may be for consumer goods, diversification may be attractive. If markets respond to marketing efforts at increasing rates, concentration will occur. However, when the cost of market share points in any one market becomes too high, marketers tend to begin looking for diversification opportunities.

EXHIBIT 6.6

Example of a market-portfolio matrix

Source: Adapted from Gilbert D. Harrell and Richard O. Kiefer, "Multinational Market Portfolios in Global Strategy Development," *International Marketing Review* 10 (no. 1, 1993): 60–72.

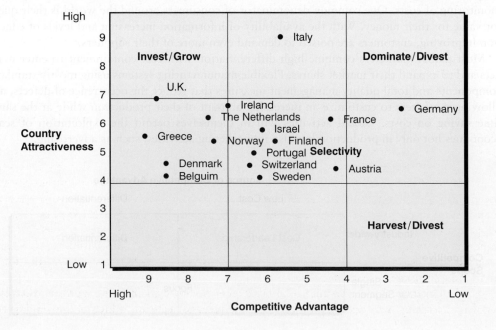

Factor	Diversification	Concentration
MARKET		
Market growth rate	Low	High
Sales stability	Low	High
Sales response function	Decreasing	Increasing
Extent of constraints	Low	High
MARKETING		
Competitive lead time	Short	Long
Spillover effects	High	Low
Need for product adaptation	Low	High
Need for communication adaptation	Low	High
Economies of scale in distribution	Low	High
Program control requirements	Low	High

Sources: Adapted from Igal Ayal and Jehiel Zif, "Marketing Expansion Strategies in Multinational Marketing," *Journal of Marketing* 43 (Spring 1979): 89.

EXHIBIT 6.7

Factors affecting the choice between concentration and diversification strategies

The uniqueness of the product offering with respect to competition is also a factor in expansion strategy. If lead time over competition is considerable, the decision to diversify may not seem urgent. Very few products, however, afford such a luxury. In many product categories, marketers will be affected by spillover effects. Consider, for example, the impact of satellite channels on advertising in Europe or in Asia, where ads for a product now reach most of the market. The greater the degree to which marketing mix elements can be standardized, the more diversification is probable. Overall savings through economies of scale can then be utilized in marketing efforts. Finally, the objectives and policies of the company itself will guide the decision making on expansion. If extensive interaction is called for with intermediaries and clients, efforts are most likely to be concentrated because of resource constraints.

The conventional wisdom of globalization requires a presence in all of the major markets of the world. In some cases, markets may not be attractive in their own right but may have some other significance, such as being the home market of the most demanding customers, thereby aiding in product development, or being the home market of a significant competitor (a pre-emptive rationale). For example, European PC makers, such as Germany's Maxdata, are taking aim at the US market based on the premise that if they can compete with the big multinationals (Dell and Hewlett-Packard) at home, there is no reason why they cannot be competitive in North America as well.[34]

Therefore, for global marketers three factors should determine country selection: (1) the stand-alone attractiveness of a market (e.g., China in consumer products due to its size); (2) global strategic importance (e.g., Finland in shipbuilding due to its lead in technological development in vessel design); and (3) possible synergies (e.g., entry into Latvia and Lithuania after success in the Estonian market, given the market similarities).

Segmentation Effective use of segmentation, that is, the recognition that groups within markets differ sufficiently enough to warrant individual marketing mixes, allows global marketers to take advantage of the benefits of standardization (such as economies of scale and consistency in positioning) while addressing the unique needs and expectations of a specific target group. This approach means looking at markets on a global or regional basis, thereby ignoring the political boundaries that otherwise define markets in many cases. The identification and cultivation of such intermarket segments is necessary for any standardization of marketing programmes to work.[35]

The emergence of segments that span markets is already evident in the world marketplace. Global marketers have successfully targeted the teenage segment, which is converging as a result of common tastes in sports and music fuelled by their computer literacy, travels abroad, and, in many countries, financial independence.[36] Furthermore, a media revolution is creating a common fabric of attitudes and tastes among teenagers. Today, satellite TV and global network concepts such as MTV are both helping create this segment and providing global marketers access to the teen audience around the world. For example, Reebok used a global ad campaign to launch its Instapump line of trainers in Germany, Japan and 137 other countries. Given that teenagers around the world are concerned with social issues, particularly environmentalism, Reebok has introduced a new ecological climbing shoe made from recycled and environmentally sensitive materials. Similarly, two other distinct segments have been detected to be ready for a pan-regional approach. One includes trendsetters who are wealthier and better educated and tend to value independence, refuse consumer stereotypes and appreciate exclusive products. The second one includes Europe's businesspeople who are well-to-do, regularly travel abroad and have a taste for luxury goods.

Despite convergence, global marketers still have to make adjustments in some of the marketing mix elements for maximum impact. For example, while Levi's jeans are globally accepted by the teenage segment, European teens reacted negatively to the urban realism of Levi's US ads. Levi converted its ads in Europe, drawing on images of a mythical America.[37] Similarly, segment sizes vary from one market to another even in cohesive regions such as Europe. The value-oriented segment in Germany accounts for 32 per cent of the grocery sales but only 9 per cent in the United Kingdom and 8 per cent in France.[38]

The greatest challenge for the global marketer is the choice of an appropriate base for the segmentation effort. The objective is to arrive at a grouping or groupings that are substantial enough to merit the segmentation effort (for example, there are nearly 230 million teenagers in Europe, and the Asia-Pacific and the Americas, with the projected growth of the tween and teen market in the EU increasing from £127.72 billion in 2006 to £140.52 billion in 2011, despite an estimated 3 per cent decline in the 12–17-year-old population in that same period.[39]

The possible bases for segmentation are summarized in Exhibit 6.8. Marketers have traditionally used environmental bases for segmentation. However, using geographic proximity, political system characteristics, economic standing or cultural traits as a stand-alone basis may not provide relevant data for decision making. Using a combination of them, however, may produce more meaningful results. One of the segments pursued by global marketers around the world is the middle-class family. Defining the composition of this global middle class is tricky, given the varying levels of development among nations in Latin America and Asia. However, some experts estimate that 25 per cent of the world population enjoy middle-class lives, some 300 million in India alone.[40] Using household income alone may be quite a poor gauge of class. Income figures ignore vast differences in international purchasing

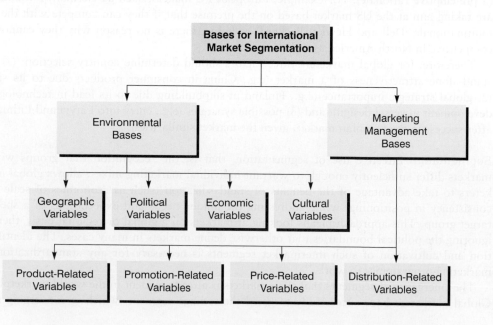

EXHIBIT 6.8

Bases for global market segmentation

Source: Imad B. Baalbaki and Naresh K. Malhotra, "Marketing Management Bases for International Market Segmentation: An Alternate Look at the Standardization/Customization Debate," *International Marketing Review* 10 (no. 1, 1993): 44–19. Reprinted with permission.

power. Chinese consumers, for example, spend less than 5 per cent of their total outlays on rent, transportation and health, while a British family spends 18.9 per cent of their income on housing.[41] Additionally, income distinctions do not reflect education or values – two increasingly important barometers of middle-class status. A global segmentation effort using cultural values is provided in *The International Marketplace 6.3*.

THE INTERNATIONAL **MARKETPLACE 6.3**

Segmenting global markets by cultural values

Three critical factors – nationality, demographics and values – play major roles in determining the nature and evolution of global consumer markets. But their importance relative to one another depends on the product or service category with which marketers are dealing. Core values go much deeper than behaviour or attitude, and they determine, at a basic level, people's choices and desires over the long term. Behaviour changes quickly in response to outside forces of all kinds, including whether a person got a good night's sleep or how long the line is at the grocery store. Although slower to change, attitudes also are prone to external influences. Core values, on the other hand, are intrinsic to a person's identity and inherent beliefs. By appealing to people's inner selves, it's possible to influence their outer selves – their purchase behaviour.

As part of a Roper Reports Worldwide Global Consumer Survey, 1,000 people were interviewed in their homes in each of 35 countries. As part of their responses, they ranked 56 values by the importance they hold as guiding principles in their lives. Among adults, six global values segments emerged, residing in all 35 countries, but to varying degrees in each. Interestingly, the largest values segment across the globe focuses on the material world, while the second largest centres on the soul.

Although most people fall into a particular category, some values cut across many categories and countries. For example, 'protecting the family' ranks in the top 10 for all six groups. All 35 countries rank family in their top five guiding principles, except for Indonesia, which ranks respecting ancestors as number one. All the Asian countries surveyed place family in their top two. Protecting the family was given top value in 22 countries, including the United States. A country-by-country analysis reveals that Great Britain leads the world in wanting to protect the family, Brazil has the most fun seekers, Saudi Arabia ranks first in faith, the Netherlands has the highest percentage worldwide in esteeming honesty, and Korea is the global front-runner in valuing health and fitness.

The research shows that people in different segments generally pursue different activities, buy different products, and use different media. Knowing which segments dominate in a country helps with marketing efforts and enables advertisers to tailor their message to those parts of the population most likely to buy. Profiles of the values segments around the world give marketers the tools to refine their strategies, identify potential consumers, reinforce loyal customer bases, and buffer them against competitive moves.

Segment	Characteristics	Geographics
Strivers	More likely to be men; place more emphasize on material and professional goals	One-third of people in developing Asia; one-quarter in Russia and developed Asia
Devouts	22 per cent of adults; women more than men; tradition and duty are paramount	Africa, Asia, Middle East; least common in Europe
Altruists	18 per cent of adults; larger portion of females; interested in social issues and welfare of society; older	Latin America and Russia
Intimates	15 per cent of population; personal relationships and family take precedence	Europeans and North Americans
Fun seekers	12 per cent of population; youngest group	Disproportionately more in developed Asia
Creatives	10 per cent worldwide; strong interest in education, knowledge, and technology	Europe and Latin America

SOURCE: Tom Miller, 'Global Segments from "Strivers" to "Creatives",' *Marketing News*, July 20, 1998, 11. Reprinted with permission. See also **http://www.nopworld.com**.

It has also been proposed that markets that reflect a high degree of homogeneity with respect to marketing mix variables could be grouped into segments and thereby targeted with a largely standardized marketing strategy. Whether bases related to product, promotion, pricing or distribution are used, their influence should be related to environmentally based variables. Product-related bases include the degree to which products are culture-based, which stage of the life cycle they occupy, consumption patterns and attitudes toward product attributes (such as country of origin), as well as consumption infrastructure (for example, telephone lines for modems). The growth of microwave sales, for example, has been surprising in low-income countries; however, microwaves have become status symbols and buying them more of an emotional issue. Many consumers in these markets also want to make sure they get the same product as available in developed markets, thereby eliminating the need in many cases to develop market-specific products. Adjustments will have to be made, however. Noticing that, for reasons of status and space, many Asian consumers put their refrigerators in their living rooms, Whirlpool makes refrigerators available in striking colours such as red and blue.

With promotion, customers' values and norms set the baseline for global vs regional vs local solutions. The significant emphasize on family relationships among many Europeans and North Americans creates a multiregional segment that can be exploited by consumer-goods and consumer-services marketers (such as car marketers or telecommunications service providers). On the pricing side, dimensions such as customers' price sensitivity may lead the marketer to go after segments that insist on high quality despite high price in markets where overall purchasing power may be low, to ensure global or regional uniformity in the marketing approach. Affordability is a major issue for customers whose buying power may fall short for at least the time being. Offering only one option may exclude potential customers of the future who are not yet part of a targeted segment; companies like Nestlé and Unilever offer an array of products at different price points to attract them and to keep them as they move up the income scale.[42] As distribution systems converge, for example, with the increase of global chains, markets can also be segmented by outlet types that reach environmentally defined groups. For example, manufacturers of children's clothes may look at markets not only in terms of numbers of children but by how effectively and efficiently they can be reached by global chains such as Adams, as opposed to purely local outlets.

Global marketing programme development

Decisions need to be made regarding how best to utilize the conditions set by globalization drivers within the framework of competitive challenges and the resources of the firm. Marketing-related decisions will have to be made in four areas: (1) the degree of standardization in the product offering; (2) the marketing programme beyond the product variable; (3) location and extent of value-adding activities; and (4) competitive moves to be made.

Product offering Globalization is not equal to standardization except in the case of the core product or the technology used to produce the product. The need to localize varies by product. Fashion or fashion products depend for their appeal on sameness. Information technology products are susceptible to power requirements, keyboard configurations (e.g., Europe alone may require 20 different keyboards), instruction-manual language, and warning labels compliant with local regulations.[43] Product standardization may result in significant cost savings upstream. For example, Stanley Works' compromise between French preferences for handsaws with plastic handles and 'soft teeth' and British preferences for wooden handles and 'hard teeth' – to produce a plastic-handled saw with 'hard teeth' – allowed consolidation for production and results in substantial economies of scale. Most car makers have reduced the number of platforms they offer worldwide to achieve greater economies of scale. For example, Toyota has reduced the number of its platforms from 11 to 6. This is not to reduce variety but to deliver it more cost effectively.[44] Shania Twain's double CD *Up!* is an example of catering to multiple segments at the same time: both disks contain the same 19 tracks, but one with the effects pop fans appreciate, and the other with country dimensions. A third disk with 'an Asian, Indian vibe' replaces the country disk in Europe.[45]

EXHIBIT 6.9

Globalization of the marketing mix

Marketing Mix Elements	Adaptation		Standardization	
	Full	Partial	Full	Partial
Product design			C	N
Brand name			C	N
Product positioning		N	C	
Packaging				C/N
Advertising theme		N	C	
Pricing		N		C
Advertising copy	N		C	C
Distribution	N	C		
Sales promotion	N	C		
Customer service	N	C		

Key: C = Coca-Cola; N = Nestlé.

Sources: Adapted from John A. Quelch and Edward J. Hoff, "Customizing Global Marketing," *Harvard Business Review,* May–June 1986 (Boston: Harvard Business School Publishing Division), 61.

Marketing approach Nowhere is the need for the local touch as critical as in the execution of the marketing programme. Uniformity is sought especially in elements that are strategic (e.g., positioning) in nature, whereas care is taken to localize necessary tactical elements (e.g., distribution). This approach has been called glocalization. For example, Unilever achieved great success with a fabric softener that used a common positioning, advertising theme, and symbol (a teddy bear) but differing brand names (e.g., Snuggle, Cajoline, Kuschelweich, Mimosin and Yumos) and bottle sizes. Although the language of its TV commercials varied, the theme ('Adding Vitality to Life') was the same. It has been argued that standardization (globalization) and localization (adaptation) should be viewed as a continuum, with the ultimate strategy being determined by how much is either standardized or localized.[46] For example, if more is standardized the dominant strategy is global. Similarly, if more is localized, the dominant strategy is multicountry (localized). A comparison of the marketing mix elements of two global marketers is given in Exhibit 6.9. Notice that adaptation is present even at Coca-Cola, which is acknowledged to be one of the world's most global marketers.

Location of value-added activities Globalization strives to reduce costs by pooling production or other activities or exploiting factor costs or capabilities within a system. Rather than duplicating activities in multiple, or even all, country organizations, a firm concentrates its activities. Nokia's over 20,000 research & development people work in centres in 12 different countries, including China, Finland, Germany, Hungary and China. The company has also entered into development agreements with operators (such as France Telecom and Vodafone) to bring innovations to market more efficiently.[47] Many global marketers have established R&D centres next to key production facilities so that concurrent engineering can take place every day on the factory floor. To enhance the global exchange of ideas, the centres have joint projects and are in real-time contact with each other.

The quest for cost savings and improved transportation and transfer methods has allowed some marketers to concentrate customer service activities rather than having them present in all country markets. For example, Sony used to have repair centres in all the Scandinavian countries and Finland; today, all service and maintenance activities are actually performed in a regional centre in Stockholm, Sweden. Similarly, MasterCard has teamed up with Mascon Global in Chennai, India, where MasterCard's core processing functions – authorization, clearing and settlement – for worldwide operations are handled.[48]

To show commitment to a given market, both economically and politically, centres may be established in these markets. Philips Electronics has chosen China as their Asian centre for global product research and development.[49]

Competitive moves

A company with regional or global presence will not have to respond to competitive moves only in the market where it is being attacked. A competitor may be attacked in its profit sanctuary to drain its resources, or its position in its home market may be challenged.[50] When Fuji began cutting into Kodak's market share in the United States, Kodak responded by drastically increasing its advertising in Japan, and created a new subsidiary to deal strictly with that market.

Cross-subsidization, or the use of resources accumulated in one part of the world to fight a competitive battle in another, may be the competitive advantage needed for the long term.[51] One major market lost may mean losses in others, resulting in a domino effect. Jockeying for overall global leadership may result in competitive action in any part of the world. This has manifested itself in the form of 'wars' between major global players in industries such as soft drinks, car tyres, computers and mobile phones. The opening of new markets often signals a new battle, as happened in the 1990s in Russia. Given their multiple bases of operation, global marketers may defend against a competitive attack in one country by countering in another country or, if the competitors operate in multiple businesses, countering in a different product category altogether. In the mobile phone category, the winners in the future will be those who can better attack developing and emerging markets with cheaper phones, while providing internet-based devices elsewhere.[52]

In a study of how car makers develop strategies that balance the conflicting pressures of local responsiveness and regional integration in Europe, Japanese marketers were found to practise standardization in model offerings but selectively respond to differences in market conditions by manipulating prices and advertising levels.[53]

Implementing global marketing

The successful global marketers of the future will be those who can achieve a balance between local and regional/global concerns. Marketers who have tried the global concept have often run into problems with local differences. Especially early on, global marketing was seen as a standardized marketing effort dictated to the country organizations by headquarters. For example, when Coca-Cola re-entered the Indian market in 1993, it invested most heavily in its Coke brand, using its typical global positioning, and saw its market leadership slip to Pepsi. Recognizing the mistake, Coke re-emphasized a popular local cola brand (Thums Up) and refocused the Coke brand advertising to be more relevant to the local Indian consumer.[54] To further reduce competition, Coca-Cola acquires local soft-drink brands.

Challenges of global marketing Pitfalls that handicap global marketing programmes and contribute to their suboptimal performance include market-related reasons, such as insufficient research and a tendency to overstandardize, as well as internal reasons, such as inflexibility in planning and implementation.

If a product is to be launched on a broader scale without formal research as to regional or local differences, the result may be failure. An example of this is Lego A/S, the Danish toy manufacturer, which decided to transfer sales promotional tactics successful in the US market unaltered to other markets, such as Japan. This promotion included approaches such as 'bonus packs' and gift promotions. However, Japanese consumers considered these promotions wasteful, expensive, and not very appealing.[55] Going too local has its drawbacks as well. With too much customization or with local production, the marketer may lose its import positioning. For example, when Miller Brewing Company started brewing Löwenbräu under licence in the United States, the brand lost its prestigious import image. Often, the necessary research is conducted only after a product or a programme has failed.

Globalization by design requires a balance between sensitivity to local needs and deployment of technologies and concepts globally. This means that neither headquarters nor independent country managers can alone call the shots. If country organizations are not part of the planning process, or if adoption is forced on them by headquarters, local resistance in the form of the not-invented-here syndrome (NIH) may lead to the demise of the global programme or, worse still, to an overall decline in morale. Subsidiary resistance may stem from resistance to any idea originating from the outside or from valid concerns about the applicability of a concept to that particular market. Without local commitment, no global programme will survive.

Localizing global marketing The successful global marketers of the new century will be those who can achieve a balance between country managers and global product managers at headquarters. This balance may be achieved by a series of actions to improve a company's ability to develop and implement global strategy. These actions relate to management processes, organization structures and overall corporate culture, all of which should ensure cross-fertilization within the firm.[56]

Management processes In the multidomestic approach, country organizations had very little need to exchange ideas. Globalization, however, requires transfer of information not only between headquarters and country organizations but also between/among the country organizations themselves. By facilitating the flow of information, ideas are exchanged and organizational values strengthened. Information exchange can be achieved through periodic meetings of marketing managers or through worldwide conferences to allow employees to discuss their issues and local approaches to solving them. Nestlé, for example, has a Nestlé Nutrition Council, which is composed of ten internationally renowned nutrition scientists whose task is to review current and developing nutrition issues and to advise senior management on their impact upon Nestlé's policies and strategy.[57]

Part of the preparation for becoming global has to be personnel interchange. Many companies encourage (or even require) midlevel managers to gain experience abroad during the early or middle stages of their careers. The more experience people have in working with others from different nationalities – getting to know other markets and surroundings – the better a company's global philosophy, strategy and actions will be integrated locally.

The role of headquarters staff should be that of coordination and leveraging the resources of the corporation. For example, this may mean activities focused on combining good ideas that come from different parts of the company to be fed into global planning. Many global companies also employ world-class advertising and market research staffs whose role should be to consult subsidiaries by upgrading their technical skills, and to focus their attention not only on local issues but also on those with global impact.

Globalization calls for the centralization of decision-making authority far beyond that of the multidomestic approach. Once a strategy has been jointly developed, headquarters may want to permit local managers to develop their own programmes within specified parameters and subject to approval, rather than forcing them to adhere strictly to the formulated strategy. For example, Colgate Palmolive allows local units to use their own ads, but only if they can prove they beat the global 'benchmark' version. With a properly managed approval process, effective control can be exerted without unduly dampening a country manager's creativity.

Overall, the best approach against the emergence of the NIH syndrome is utilizing various motivational policies, such as (1) ensuring that local managers participate in the development of marketing strategies and programmes for global brands; (2) encouraging local managers to generate ideas for possible regional or global use; (3) maintaining a product portfolio that includes local as well as regional and global brands; and (4) allowing local managers control over their marketing budgets so that they can respond to local customer needs and counter global competition (rather than depleting budgets by forcing them to participate only in uniform campaigns). Acknowledging this local potential, global marketers can pick up successful brands in one country and make them cross-border stars. Since Nestlé acquired British sweet manufacturer Rowntree Mackintosh, it has increased its exports by 60 per cent and made formerly local brands, such as After Eight dinner mints, into pan-European hits. When global marketers get their hands on an innovation or a product with global potential, rolling it out in other regions or worldwide is important.

Organization structures Various organization structures have emerged to support the globalization effort. Some companies have established global or regional product managers and their support groups at headquarters. Their tasks are to develop long-term strategies for product categories on a worldwide basis and to act as the support system for the country organizations. This matrix structure focused on customers, which has replaced the traditional country-by-country approach, is considered more effective in today's global marketplace according to companies that have adopted it.

Whenever a product group has global potential, firms such as Royal Dutch Shell and Henkel create strategic-planning units to work on the programmes. These units consist of members from the country organizations that market the products, managers from both global and regional headquarters, and technical specialists.

To deal with the globalization of customers, marketers are extending national account management programmes across countries, typically for the most important customers.[58] In a study of 165 multinational companies, 13 per cent of their revenues came from global customers (revenues from all international customers were 46 per cent). While relatively small, these 13 per cent come from the most important customers who cannot be ignored.[59] British Telecom (BT) for example, distinguishes between international and global customers and provides the global customers with special services, including a single point of contact for domestic and international operations and consistent worldwide service. Executing global account management programmes builds relationships not only with important customers but also allows for the development of internal systems and interaction. It will require, however, a new organizational overlay and demands new ways of working for anyone involved in marketing to global customers. One of the main challenges is in evaluating and rewarding sales efforts. If Nokia sells equipment to Telefonica in Brazil, should the sale be credited to the sales manager in Brazil or to the global account manager for Telefonica? The answer in most cases is to double count the credit.[60]

Corporate culture Corporate culture affects and is affected by two dimensions: the overall way in which the company holds its operations together and makes them a single entity, and the commitment to the global marketplace. 'The Toyota Way', which embodies the Japanese car maker's culture, has five distinct elements:

1 *Kaizen*, the well-known Japanese process of continuous improvement. *Kaizen* is more a frame of mind than a business process. Toyota employees come to work each day determined and committed to become a little better at whatever it is they are doing than they were the day before.

2 *Genchi genbutsu* (GG), which roughly translated means 'go to the source'. Consensus is best built around arguments that are well supported. It also means going to the source of a problem. Western companies are criticized for spending too little time defining what business problem they are facing, and too much time coming up with solutions. GG puts the emphasize the other way round.

3 Toyota employees are encouraged to see problems not as something undesirable, but to view problems positively as a way to help them to improve their performance further. Authority of leaders derives not from hierarchy but from their proficiency as practitioners.

4 Teamwork plays a pivotal role at Toyota. Much of this does not come naturally, and Toyota devotes a lot of time and money to on-the-job training.

5 Respect for other people, not just as people, but also for their skills and the special knowledge that derives from their particular position in the company. Toyota believes that if two people always agree, one of them is superfluous. Different opinions must be expressed, but in a respectful way. Once these values are inculcated into a worker, they guide decision making throughout the day. There is no need to refer matters up the line to ask what to do. Everyone knows what solution should be adopted, so decision making is dramatically speeded up. Japanese colleagues who know the culture well

reach a point of 'emotional fortitude' where their behaviour is entirely consistent with the organization's culture and beliefs. In the West, where individual interests tend to be put before those of any group, it is more difficult for employees to reach this state (i.e., high versus low individualism). [61]

An example of a manifestation of the global commitment is a global identity that favours no specific country (especially the 'home country' of the company). The management features several nationalities, and whenever teams are assembled, people from various country organizations get represented. The management development system has to be transparent, allowing non-national executives an equal chance for the fast track to top management.[62]

Whirlpool's corporate profile states the following: 'Beyond selling products around the world, being a global home-appliance company means identifying and respecting genuine national and regional differences in customer expectations, but also recognizing and responding to similarities in product development, engineering, purchasing, manufacturing, marketing and sales, distribution and other areas.' Companies that exploit the efficiencies from these similarities will outperform others in terms of market share, cost, quality, productivity, innovation and return to shareholders. In truly global companies, very little decision making occurs that does not support the goal of treating the world as a single market. Planning for and execution of programmes take place on a worldwide basis.

THE LOCAL COMPANY IN THE GLOBAL ENVIRONMENT

The global marketplace presents significant challenges but also opportunities for local firms.[63] As global marketers such as Airbus, Toyota, ING Group and Volkswagen expand their presence, there are local companies that must defend their positions or lose out. They can no longer rely on the government to protect or support them. If selling out or becoming a part of a bigger global entity is not an acceptable option, the local marketer will have to build on an existing competitive advantage or adopt a creative growth strategy globally. To counter the significant resources of global marketers (such as powerful brands and sizeable promotional budgets), the local company can compete successfully in the local market by emphasizing the perceived advantages of its product and marketing.[64] More proactively, the local company can pursue its own globalization strategy through segments that have similar features to the local marketer's home market or segments that global marketers have not catered to.

Strategies available to the local company depend on both external and internal realities. The degree and strength of globalization in an industry will determine the pressure that the local marketer will be under. Internally, the extent to which the company's assets are transferable (as opposed to having only local relevance) will determine the opportunity dimension. Exhibit 6.10 provides a summary of the options to be considered.

In markets where a local company has enjoyed government protection, the liberalization of markets as a result of economic integration or WTO membership may mean hardship for the local company. A dodger may have to rethink its entire strategy. With the collapse of communism and introduction of free-market reforms, the Czech carmaker Škoda found its models to be outdated and with little appeal in comparison to western makes that became available for consumers. The company became part of the largest privatization deal in Eastern Europe in its sale to Volkswagen in 1991. Rather than being merged with VW's operations, Škoda has followed VW's formula for success: performance-oriented management, cooperative labour relations, utilitarian marketing and an emphasize on design. It has benefited from wholesale implementation of the latest technologies and working practices and has been able to leapfrog into leaner and more intelligent supply and distribution networks. With sales in 85 countries, Škoda is a leading emerging global brand in one of the most competitive industries.[65]

A defender is a local company that has assets that give it a competitive advantage only in its home market. Ideally, this asset is something that an entering global marketer cannot easily replicate; for example, channel penetration, or a product line that has a strong local

EXHIBIT 6.10

Competitive strategies
for local companies

		Competitive assets	
		Customized to home market	Transferable abroad
Pressures to globalize in the industry	High	**Dodger** Sells out to a global player or becomes part of an alliance	**Contender** Upgrades capabilities to match globals in niches
	Low	**Defender** Leverages local assets in segments where globals are weak	**Extender** Expands into markets similar to home base

Source: Adapted from Niraj Dawar and Tony Frost, "Competing with the Giants: Survival Strategies for Local Companies in Emerging Markets," *Harvard Business Review 77* (March–April 1999): 119–129.

customer franchise. Many believed that small local retailers in Latin America would be swept away with the sector's consolidation and the entry of global players such as Carrefour. This has been the case in developed markets, where small retailers have retained only 10–20 per cent of the consumer packaged-goods market as large retailers have expanded. In Latin America, however, their share has remained at 45–61 per cent, because they are not only meeting the needs of emerging consumers, but in many ways are serving them better. For emerging-market consumers, price is not the determining factor of retailer choice; it is the total cost of purchases (including cost of transportation, time, the burden of carrying purchases and ability to store purchased items).[66] Similarly, the largest retailers in Chile are local family businesses and they have successfully defended themselves against the attempts of foreign retailers to operate in their market.[67]

If a local company's assets are transferable, the company may be able to compete head-on with the established global players worldwide. While Airbus and Boeing have been competing by developing and launching ever-bigger aircraft, the niche for jets that carry 70 to 110 passengers has been left open for others. In the last ten years, the number of regional jet routes has grown 1,000 per cent in Europe and 1,400 per cent in North America. Much of that increase has come from commuter airlines that the majors own or contract with to connect smaller markets with their hubs. The contender that has taken advantage of the increased demand is Brazil's Embraer, which has challenged the market leader, Canada's Bombardier. When demand took off faster than expected, Bombardier could not meet demand, thus opening the door for Embraer. Currently, Brazil's lower labour costs allow Embraer to undercut its competitor on prices.[68]

Extenders are able to exploit their success at home as a platform for expansion elsewhere. This calls for markets or segments that are similar in terms of customer preferences, for example, sizeable expatriate communities. The number of Indians in the UK has increased in the last ten years. This will provide an opportunity for Bollywood to extend its marketing beyond India. Televisa from Mexico, Venevisíon from Venezuela and Globo TV in Brazil have emerged as leading producers and marketers of telenovelas, especially to culturally close markets in Europe.[69] Some local marketers have been seasoned in competing against global players and subsequently extended their market presence to new markets abroad. Jollibee Foods Corporation challenged McDonald's in its home market of the Philippines with its products and services customized to local tastes, and has subsequently expanded its presence to other markets with sizeable Filipino communities, such as Hong Kong. Jollibee now has 24 restaurants operating in seven countries and continues to grow.[70]

Multiple strategies are available to the local marketers when global markets and marketers challenge them. The key is to innovate, rather than imitate, and exploit the inherent competitive advantages over global players.

SUMMARY

Globalization has become one of the most important strategy issues for marketing managers in the last ten years. Many forces, both external and internal, are driving companies to globalize by expanding and coordinating their participation in foreign markets. The approach is not standardization, however. Marketers may indeed occasionally be able to take identical technical and marketing concepts around the world, but most often, concepts must be customized to local tastes. Internally, companies must make sure that country organizations around the world are ready to launch global products and programmes as if they had been developed only for their markets. Firms that are able to exploit commonalities across borders and do so with competent marketing managers in country organizations are able to see the benefits in their overall performance.[71]

Marketing managers need to engage in strategic planning to better adjust to the realities of the new marketplace. Understanding the firm's core strategy (i.e., what business they are really in) starts the process, and this assessment may lead to adjustments in what business the company may want to be in. In formulating global strategy for the chosen business, the decision makers have to assess and make choices about markets and competitive strategy to be used in penetrating them. This may result in the choice of one particular segment across markets or the exploitation of multiple segments in which the company has a competitive advantage. In manipulating and implementing the marketing mix for maximum effect in the chosen markets, the old adage, 'think globally, act locally', becomes a critical guiding principle both as far as customers are concerned and in terms of country organization motivation. While local marketers may have an advantage based on their better understanding of the market, for long-term competitiveness they may also become involved in the global marketplace. This is typically most feasible by exploiting a particular niche in which they have a cost advantage or cultural edge.

Key terms

concentration

contender

cross-subsidization

defender

diversification

dodger

extenders

global account management

glocalization

not-invented-here syndrome (NIH)

triad

Questions for discussion

1 What is the danger in oversimplifying the globalization approach? Would you agree with the statement that 'if something is working in a big way in one market, you better assume it will work in all markets'?

2 In addition to teenagers as a global segment, are there possibly other such groups with similar traits and behaviours that have emerged worldwide?

3 Suggest ways in which a global marketer is better equipped to initiate and respond to competitive moves.

4 Why is the assessment of internal resources critical as early as possible in developing a global strategic plan?

5 What are the critical ways in which the multidomestic and global approaches differ in country-market selection?

6 Outline the basic reasons why a company does not necessarily have to be large and have years of experience to succeed in the global marketplace.

Internet exercises

1 Using the material available at Unilever's website (**http://www.unilever.com**), suggest ways in which Unilever's business groups can take advantage of global and regional strategies due to interconnections in production and marketing.

2 Whirlpool's goal is 'a Whirlpool product in every home, everywhere'. Using its website, **http://www.whirlpool corp.com/about/vision_and_strategy/default.asp**, describe what needs to take place for this vision to become a reality.

Recommended readings

Arnold, David. *Mirage of Global Markets: How Globalizing Companies Can Succeed as Markets Localize.* Englewood Cliffs, NJ: Prentice-Hall, 2003.

Birkinshaw, Julian. *Entrepreneurship in the Global Firm.* Thousand Oaks, CA: Sage Publications, 2000.

The Economist Intelligence Unit. *151 Checklists for Global Management.* New York: The Economist Intelligence Unit, 1993.

Feist, William R., James A. Heely, Min H. Lau and Roy L. Nersesian. *Managing a Global Enterprise.* Westport, CT: Quorum, 1999.

Grant, Robert M. and Kent E. Neupert. *Cases in Contemporary Strategy Analysis.* Oxford, England: Blackwell, 1999.

Grosse, Robert E. (ed.). *Thunderbird on Global Business Strategy.* New York: Wiley Investment, 2000.

Inkpen, Andrew and Kannan Ramaswamy. *Global Strategy: Creating and Sustaining Advantage Across Borders.* Oxford: Oxford University Press, 2005.

Irwin, Douglas A. *Free Trade under Fire.* Princeton, NJ: Princeton University Press, 2002.

Kanter, Rosabeth Moss. *World Class.* New York: Simon & Schuster, 1995.

Lindsey, Brink. *Against the Dead Hand: The Uncertain Struggle for Global Capitalism.* New York: John Wiley & Sons, 2001.

Prahalad, C. K. and Yves L. Doz. *The Multinational Mission: Balancing Local and Global Vision.* New York: Free Press, 1987.

Rosensweig, Jeffrey. *Winning the Global Game: A Strategy for Linking People and Profits.* New York: Free Press, 1998.

Schwab, Klaus, Michael Porter and Jeffrey Sachs. *The Global Competitiveness Report 2001–2002.* Oxford, England: Oxford University Press, 2002.

Scott, Allen J. *Regions and the World Economy: The Coming Shape of Global Production, Competition, and Political Order.* Oxford, England: Oxford University Press, 2000.

Soros, George. *George Soros on Globalization.* New York: Public Affairs, 2002.

Stiglitz, Joseph E. *Globalization and Its Discontents.* New York: W.W. Norton & Co., 2002.

Notes

1   Theodore Levitt, *The Marketing Imagination* (New York: Free Press, 1983), 20–49.

2   Michael R. Czinkota and Ilkka A. Ronkainen, 'A Forecast of Globalization, International Business and Trade: Report from a Delphi Study', *Journal of World Business* 40 (Winter 2005): 111–123.

3   Jonathan Sprague, 'China's Manufacturing Beachhead', *Fortune,* October 28, 2002, I192A–J.

4   Pankaj Ghemawat, 'Regional Strategies for Global Leadership', *Harvard Business Review* 83 (December 2005): 98–108.

5   Bruce Greenwald and Judd Kahn, 'All Strategy is Local', *Harvard Business Review* 83 (September 2005): 94–107.

6   This section draws from George S. Yip, *Total Global Strategy II* (Upper Saddle River, NJ: Prentice Hall, 2002), chapters 1 and 2; Jagdish N. Sheth and Atul Parvatiyar, 'The Antecedents and Consequences of Integrated Global Marketing', *International Marketing Review* 18 (no. 1, 2001): 16–29; George S. Yip, 'Global Strategy . . . In a World of Nations?' *Sloan Management Review* 31 (Fall 1989): 29–41; and Susan P. Douglas and C. Samuel Craig, 'Evolution of Global Marketing Strategy: Scale, Scope, and Synergy', *Columbia Journal of World Business* 24 (Fall 1989): 47–58.

7   Ernst Dichter, 'The World Customer', *Harvard Business Review* 40 (July–August 1962): 113–122.

8   Kenichi Ohmae, *The Invisible Continent: Four Strategic Imperatives of the New Economy* (New York: Harper Business, 2001), chapter 1; Kenichi Ohmae, *The Borderless World: Power and Strategy in the Interlinked Economy* (New York: Harper Business, 1999), chapter 1; and Kenichi

Ohmae, *Triad Power: The Coming Shape of Global Competition* (New York: Free Press, 1985), 22–27.

9   Luciano Catoni, Nora Förisdal Larssen, James Nayor and Andrea Zocchi, 'Travel Tips for Retailers' *The McKinsey Quarterly* 38 (no. 3, 2002): 88–98.

10 Catherine George and J. Michael Pearson, 'Riding the Pharma Roller Coaster', *The McKinsey Quarterly* 38 (no. 4, 2002): 89–98.

11 Nicholas Mockett, 'Global M&A Trands in Paper, Packaging and Printing: 2003–2004', *PriceWaterhouseCoopers Forest & Paper Industry Practice,* available at **http://www.pwc.com/forestry**.

12 Stuart Crainer, 'And the New Economy Winner Is . . . Europe', *Strategy and Business* 6 (second quarter, 2001): 40–47.

13 **http://media.daimler.com/dcmedia/0-921-614216-1-1005770-1-0-0-0-0-1-11700-0-0-1-0-0-0-0-0.html**

14 'Telecommunications', *The Economist,* April 4, 2002, 102.

15 Gary Knight, 'Entrepreneurship and Marketing Strategy: The SME under Globalization', *Journal of International Marketing* 8 (no. 2, 2000): 12–32.

16 Svend Hollesen, S. and Jenster, P.V (2000) 'The international marketing challenges facing Danish small and medium-sized enterprises', *Strategic Change* 9(7), 451–459.

17 *Ibid.*

18 Nestlé data available at **http://www.nestle.com/All_About/Glance/Introduction/Glance+Introduction.htm**; and 'A Dedicated Enemy of Fashion: Nestlé', *The Economist,* August 31, 2002, 51.

19 Yoshino, M.Y. and Rangan, U.S. (1995) *Strategic Alliances: An Entrepreneurial Approach to Globalization*

**http://books.google.co.uk/books?id=QPm5OnFvrE4C
&pg=PA98&lpg=PA98&dq=Komatsu's+response+to
+global+competition&source=bl&ots=DHiCqlZC87&
sig=mskkjQMJGUWapX-MpUTOKSWlkKM&hl=en&ei
=gTUdSrKll8WrjAf78siSDQ&sa=X&oi=book_result
&ct=result&resnum=10#PPR10,M1** (Accessed 27/05/09).

20 Answers.com, 'Komatsu Ltd'. **http://www.answers.com/
topic/komatsu-ltd-adr**

21 '3 Big Carmakers to Create Net Site for Buying Parts',
The Washington Post, February 26, 2000, E1, E8.

22 Myung-Su Chae and John S. Hill, 'Determinants and
Benefits of Global Strategic Planning Formality', *International
Marketing Review* 17 (no. 6, 2000): 538–562.

23 'Computing's New Shape', *The Economist,* November 23,
2002, 11–12.

24 C. Samuel Craig and Susan P. Douglas, 'Configural
Advantage in Global Markets', *Journal of International
Marketing* 8 (no. 1, 2000): 6–26.

25 Michael E. Porter, *Competitive Strategy: Techniques for
Analyzing Industries and Competitors* (New York: Free
Press, 1998), chapter 1.

26 'Europe's Car Makers Expect Tidy Profits', *The Wall Street
Journal,* January 27, 2000, A16.

27 Lori Ioannou, 'It's a Small World After All', *International
Business,* February 1994, 82–88.

28 'Nokia Up in 2005', *Telecommworldwide,* November 22,
2005, 1.

29 Michael Porter, *Competitive Advantage: Creating and
Sustaining Superior Performance* (New York: Free Press,
1998), chapter 1.

30 Robert M. Grant, *Contemporary Strategy Analysis:
Concepts, Techniques, Applications* (Oxford, England:
Blackwell, 2005), chapter 7.

31 George S. Yip, *Total Global Strategy II* (Upper Saddle River,
NJ: Prentice Hall, 2002), chapter 10.

32 The models referred to are GE/McKinsey, Shell International,
and A. D. Little portfolio models.

33 **http://www.negotiationtraining.com.au/articles/
planning-alliances-strategically From "Strategic
Alliances: An Entrepreneurial Approach to
Globalization"** by Michael Y Yoshino, U. Srinivasa Rangan.
Harvard Business Press, 1995**/** (Accessed 27/5/09).

34 Richard Tomlinson, 'Europe's New Computer Game',
Fortune, February 21, 2000, 219–224.

35 Saeed Samiee and Kendall Roth, 'The Influence of Global
Marketing Standardization on Performance', *Journal of
Marketing* 56 (April 1992): 1–17.

36 'Euroteen Market Grabs U.S. Attention', *Marketing News,*
October 22, 2001, 15.

37 'The American Connection', *The Washington Post,* May 25,
2002, E1–E2.

38 Peter N. Child, Suzanne Heywood and Michael Kliger, 'Do
Retail Brands Travel?' *The McKinsey Quarterly* 38 (no. 1,
2002): 73–77.

39 **http://www.marketingcharts.com/interactive/teen-
market-to-surpass-200-billion-by-2011-despite-
population-decline-817/** (Accessed 01/06/09).

40 Aruna Chandra and John K. Ryans, 'Why India Now?'
Marketing Management, March/April 2002, 43–45.

41 **http://www.telegraph.co.uk/news/uknews/1576933/
Britons-spend-one-fifth-of-income-on-homes.html**

42 C.K. Prahalad and Stuart L. Hart, 'The Fortune at the
Bottom of the Pyramid', *Strategy and Business* 7 (first
quarter, 2002): 35–47.

43 Pascal Cagni, 'Think Global, Act European', *Developments
in Strategy and Business,* August 30, 2004, available at
**http://www.strategy-business.com/export/
export.php?article_id=4510703**.

44 Pankaj Ghemawat, 'Regional Strategies for Global
Leadership', *Harvard Business Review* 83 (December 2005):
98–108.

45 'Shania Reigns', *Time,* December 9, 2002, 80–85.

46 Lemark, D. and Wiboon, A. (1997), 'Global business
strategy: A contingency approach'. Online. Available: **http://
findarticles.com/p/articles/mi_qa3674/is_199704/
ai_n8769703/** (Accessed 25/05/09).

47 **http://www.nokia.com/A402785**.

48 Larry Greenemeier, 'Offshore Outsourcing Grows to Global
Proportions', *Information Week,* February 2002, 56–58.

49 'Philips Electronics to Make China One of Three Big
Research Centers', *The Wall Street Journal,* December 20,
2002, B4.

50 W. Chan Kim and R. A. Mauborgne, 'Becoming an Effective
Global Competitor', *Journal of Business Strategy* 8
(January–February 1988): 33–37.

51 Gary Hamel and C. K. Prahalad, 'Do You Really Have a
Global Strategy?' *Harvard Business Review* 63 (July–August
1985): 75–82.

52 'Nokia Widens Lead in Wireless Market While Motorola,
Ericsson Fall Back', *The Wall Street Journal,* February 8,
2000, B8.

53 Andreas F. Grein, C. Samuel Craig and Hirokazu Takada,
'Integration and Responsiveness: Marketing Strategies of
Japanese and European Automobile Manufacturers',
Journal of International Marketing 9 (no. 2, 2001):
19–50.

54 James A. Gingrich, 'Five Rules for Winning Emerging Market
Consumers', *Strategy and Business* (second quarter, 1999):
19–33.

55 Kamran Kashani, 'Beware the Pitfalls of Global Marketing',
Harvard Business Review 67 (September–October 1989):
91–98.

56 George S. Yip, Pierre M. Loewe and Michael Y. Yoshino,
'How to Take Your Company to the Global Market',
Columbia Journal of World Business 23 (Winter 1988):
28–40.

57 **http://www.nestle.com/Resource.axd?Id=602C42FE-
04D6-4669-BEE1-1027492FE5E8**

58 George S. Yip and Tammy L. Madsen, 'Global Account
Management: The New Frontier in Relationship Marketing',
International Marketing Review 13 (no. 3, 1996): 24–42.

59 David B. Montgomery and George S. Yip, 'The Challenge of
Global Customer Management', *Marketing Management,*
Winter 2000, 22–29.

60 Julian Birkinshaw, 'Global Account Management: New Structures, New Tasks', *FT Mastering Management*, 2001, available at **http://www.ftmastering.com/mmo/mmo05_2.htm.**

61 'Teaming with Bright Ideas', *The Economist,* January 19, 2006, 5–6; 'Inculcating Culture', *The Economist,* January 19, 2006, 6; Philip Evans and Bob Wolf, 'Collaboration Rules', *Harvard Business* Review 83 (July–August 2005): 96–104; and Gerard Fairtlough, *The Three Ways of Getting Things Done* (London: Triarchy Press, 2005), chapter 3, section 3.

62 John A. Quelch and Helen Bloom, 'Ten Steps to Global Human Resources Strategy', *Strategy and Business* 4 (first quarter, 1999): 18–29.

63 This section draws from Niraj Dawar and Tony Frost, 'Competing with the Giants: Survival Strategies for Local Companies in Emerging Markets', *Harvard Business Review* 77 (March–April 1999): 119–129; and Güliz Ger, 'Localizing in the Global Village: Local Firms Competing in Global Markets', *California Management Review* 41 (Summer 1999): 64–83.

64 John H. Roberts, 'Defensive Marketing: How a Strong Incumbent Can Protect Its Position', *Harvard Business Review* 83 (November 2005): 150–163.

65 Jonathan Ledgard, 'Škoda Leaps to Market', *Strategy and Business* 10 (Fall 2005): 1–12.

66 Guillermo D'Andrea, E. Alejandro Stengel, and Anne Goebel-Krstelj, '6 Truths About Emerging-Market Consumers', *Strategy and Business* 10 (Spring 2004): 59–69.

67 Bianchi, C. and Mena, J. (2004), 'Defending the local market against foreign competitors: The example of Chilean retailers', *International Journal of Retail & Distribution Management*, 32(10), 495–504.

68 'The Little Aircraft Company That Could', *Fortune,* November 14, 2005, 201–208.

69 Ibsen Martínez, 'Romancing the Globe', *Foreign Policy,* November/December 2005, 48–56.

70 **http://www.jollibee.com.ph/corporate/international.htm**.

71 Sharon O'Donnell and Insik Jeong, 'Marketing Standardization within Global Industries', *International Marketing Review* 17 (no. 1, 2000): 19–33.

CHAPTER 7
MARKETING ORGANIZATION, IMPLEMENTATION AND CONTROL

Nestlé's competitive strategy

Nestlé describes itself as a food, nutrition, health and wellness company. Recently they created Nestlé Nutrition, a global business organization designed to strengthen the focus on their core nutrition business. They believe strengthening their leadership in this market is the key element of their corporate strategy. This market is characterized as one in which the consumer's primary motivation for a purchase is the claims made by the product based on nutritional content.

In order to reinforce their competitive advantage in this area, Nestlé created Nestlé Nutrition as an autonomous global business unit within the organization, and charged it with the operational and profit and loss responsibility for the claim-based business of Infant Nutrition, HealthCare Nutrition and Performance Nutrition. This unit aims to deliver superior business performance by offering consumers trusted, science based, nutrition products and services.

The Corporate Wellness Unit was designed to integrate nutritional value, added in their food and beverage businesses. This unit will drive the nutrition, health and wellness organization across all their food and beverage businesses. It encompasses a major communication effort, both internally and externally, and strives to closely align Nestlé's scientific and R&D expertise with consumer benefits. This unit is responsible for coordinating horizontal, cross-business projects that address current customer concerns as well as anticipating future consumer trends.

Nestlé is a global organization. Knowing this, it is not surprising that international strategy is at the heart of their competitive focus. Nestlé's competitive strategies are associated mainly with foreign direct investment in dairy and other food businesses. Nestlé aims to balance sales between low risk but low growth countries of the developed world and high risk and potentially high growth markets of Africa and Latin America. Nestlé recognizes the profitability possibilities in these high-risk countries, but pledges not to take unnecessary risks for the sake of growth. This process of hedging keeps growth steady and shareholders happy.

When operating in a developed market, Nestlé strives to grow and gain economies of scale through foreign direct investment in big companies. Recently, Nestlé licensed the LC1 brand to Müller (a large German dairy producer) in Germany and Austria. In the developing markets, Nestlé grows by manipulating ingredients or processing technology for local conditions, and employing the appropriate brand. For example, in many European countries most chilled dairy products contain sometimes two to three times the fat content of American Nestlé products and are released under the Sveltesse brand name.

Another strategy that has been successful for Nestlé involves striking strategic partnerships with other large companies. In the early 1990s, Nestlé entered into an alliance with Coca-Cola in ready-to-drink teas and coffees in order to benefit from Coca-Cola's worldwide bottling system and expertise in prepared beverages.

European and American food markets are seen by Nestlé to be flat and fiercely competitive. Therefore, Nestlé is setting its sights on new markets and new business for growth.

In Asia, Nestlé's strategy has been to acquire local companies in order to form a group of autonomous regional managers who know more about the culture of the local markets than Americans or Europeans. Nestlé's strong cash flow and comfortable debt-equity ratio leave it with ample muscle for takeovers. Recently, Nestlé acquired Indofood, Indonesia's largest noodle producer. Their focus will be primarily on expanding sales in the Indonesian market, and in time will look to export Indonesian food products to other countries.

Nestlé has employed a wide-area strategy for Asia that involves producing different products in each country to supply the region with a given product from one country. For example, Nestlé produces soy milk in Indonesia, coffee creamers in Thailand, soybean flour in Singapore, confectionery in Malaysia and cereal in the Philippines, all for regional distribution.

SOURCES: Castelarhost.com (2005), 'Nestlé's Competetive Strategy **http://articles.castelarhost.com/nestle_competitive_strategy.htm**.

© DOMINIC FAVRE/EPA/CORBIS

As companies evolve from purely domestic entities to multinationals, their organizational structure and control systems must change to reflect new strategies. With growth comes diversity in terms of products and services, geographic markets and personnel, leading to a set of challenges for the company. Two critical issues are basic to addressing these challenges: (1) the type of organization that provides the best framework for developing worldwide strategies, while at the same time maintaining flexibility with respect to individual markets and operations; and (2) the type and degree of control to be exercised from headquarters to maximize total effort. Organizational structures and control systems have to be adjusted as market conditions change, as seen in *The International Marketplace 7.1*. While some units are charged with the development of strong global brands, others are charged with local adaptation and creating synergies across programmes.

This chapter will focus on the advantages and disadvantages of the organizational structures available, as well as their appropriateness at various stages of internationalization. A determining factor is where decision-making authority within the organizational structures will be placed. The roles of different entities of the organization need to be defined, including how to achieve collaboration among these units for the benefit of the entire global organization. The chapter will also outline the need for devising a control system to oversee the international operations of the company, emphasizing the control instruments needed in addition to those used in domestic business, as well as the control strategies of multinational corporations. The appropriateness and eventual cost of the various control approaches will vary as the firm expands its international operations. Overall, the objective of the chapter is to study intraorganizational relationships in the firm's attempt to optimize competitive response in areas most critical to its business.

ORGANIZATIONAL STRUCTURE

The basic functions of an organization are to provide (1) a route and locus of decision making and coordination, and (2) a system for reporting and communications. Increasingly, the coordination and communication dimensions have to include learning from the global marketplace through the company's different units.[1] These networks are typically depicted in the organizational chart.

Organizational designs

The basic configurations of international organizations correspond to those of purely domestic ones; the greater the degree of internationalization, the more complex the structures can become. The core building block is the individual company operating in its particular market. However, these individual companies need to work together for maximum effectiveness – thus, the need for organizational design. The types of structures that companies use to manage foreign activities can be divided into three categories based on the degree of internationalization:

1 Little or no formal organizational recognition of international activities of the firm. This category ranges from domestic operations handling an occasional international transaction on an ad hoc basis to separate export departments.

2 International division. Firms in this category recognize the ever-growing importance of international involvement.

3 Global organizations. These can be structured by product, area, function, process or customer.

Hybrid structures may exist as well, in which one market may be structured by product, another by area. Matrix organizations have emerged in large multinational corporations to combine product, regional and functional expertise. As worldwide competition has increased dramatically in many industries, the latest organizational response is networked global organizations in which heavy flows of technology, personnel and communication take place between strategically interdependent units, to establish greater global integration. The ability to identify and disseminate best practices throughout the organization is an important competitive advantage for global companies. For example, in order to share best practices, Renault and Nissan are developing a diesel V6 engine, which equip top of the range vehicles to meet the growing worldwide demand for engines that are powerful and yet fuel and CO_2 efficient.[2] The alliance is also investing around 150 million Euros in the jointly developed TCe petrol engine family, which is expected to account for 85 per cent of Renault's petrol engine sales in 2015[3]. The increasing enthusiasm for outsourcing has put new demands on managing relationships with independent partners. Airbus, for example, streamlined its logistics organization, thereby reducing the number of logistics centres by 90 per cent (from 80 to 8) and creating a network of strong risk-sharing partners and of a reduced number of tier one suppliers, thereby reducing costs and reshaping and consolidating the supply base.[4]

Little or No Formal Organization In the very early stages of international involvement, domestic operations assume responsibility for international marketing activities. The share of international operations in the sales and profits of the corporation is initially so minor that no organizational adjustment takes place. No consolidation of information or authority over international sales is undertaken or is necessary. Transactions are conducted on a case-by-case basis either by the resident expert or quite often with the help of facilitating agents, such as freight forwarders.

As demand from the international marketplace grows and interest within the firm expands, the organizational structure will reflect it. An export department appears as a separate entity. This may be an outside export management company – that is, an independent company that becomes the de facto export department of the firm. This is an indirect approach to international involvement, in that very little experience is accumulated within the firm itself. Alternatively, a firm may establish its own export department, hiring a few seasoned individuals to take full responsibility for international activities. Organizationally, the department may be a sub-department of marketing (as shown in Exhibit 7.1) or may have equal ranking with the various functional departments. This choice will depend on the importance assigned to overseas activities by the firm. Since the export department is the first real step for internationalizing the organizational structure, it should be a fully-fledged marketing

EXHIBIT 7.1

The export department
structure (TAL Apparel)

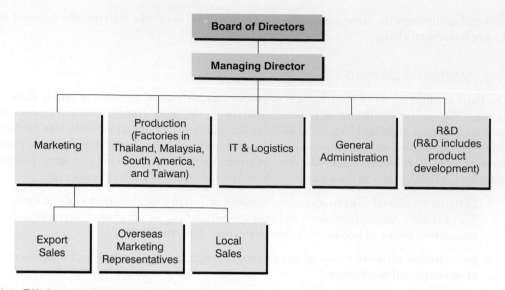

Note: TAL Apparel is based in Hong Kong, with over 100 employees. Its major customers include Marks & Spencer, Goldlion, and Giordano.

Source: Hong Kong Chamber of Commerce.

organization and not merely a sales organization; that is, it should have the resources for market research and market-development activities (such as trade show participation).

Licencing is the international entry mode for some firms. Responsibility for licencing may be assigned to the R&D function despite its importance to the overall international strategy of the firm. A formal liaison among the export, marketing, production and R&D functions should be formed for the maximum utilization of licencing.[5] A separate manager should be appointed if licencing becomes a major activity for the firm.

As the firm becomes more involved in foreign markets, the export department structure will become obsolete. The firm may then undertake joint ventures or direct foreign investment, which require those involved to have functional experience. The firm therefore typically establishes an international division.

Some firms that acquire foreign production facilities pass through an additional stage in which foreign subsidiaries report directly to the president or to a manager specifically assigned this duty. However, the amount of coordination and control that is required quickly establishes the need for a more formal international organization in the firm.

The International Division The international division centralizes in one entity, with or without separate in-corporation, all of the responsibility for international activities, as illustrated in Exhibit 7.2. The approach aims to eliminate a possible bias against international operations that may exist if domestic divisions are allowed to independently serve international customers. In some cases, international markets have been found to be treated as secondary to domestic markets. The international division concentrates international expertise, information flows concerning foreign market opportunities, and authority over international activities. However, manufacturing and other related functions remain with the domestic divisions in order to take advantage of economies of scale.

To avoid situations in which the international division is at a disadvantage in competing for production, personnel and corporate services, corporations need to coordinate between domestic and international operations. Coordination can be achieved through a joint staff or by requiring domestic and international divisions to interact in strategic planning and to submit the plans to headquarters. Further, many corporations require and encourage frequent interaction between domestic and international personnel to discuss common challenges in areas such as product planning. Coordination is also important because domestic operations may be organized along product or functional lines, whereas international divisions are geographically oriented.

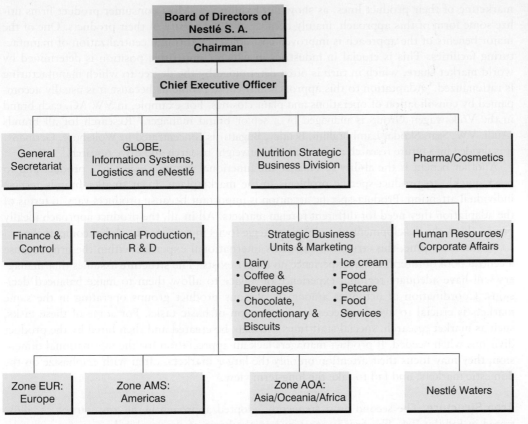

EXHIBIT 7.2

Multinational enterprise organizational structure (Nestlé)

Source: Nestlé 2002. **http://higheredbcs.wiley.com/legacy/college/shenkar/0471383503/pptfigures/ch11.ppt**#301,18, MultinationalEnterprise Organizational Structure.

International divisions best serve firms with few products that do not vary significantly in terms of their environmental sensitivity, and when international sales and profits are still quite insignificant compared with those of the domestic divisions.[6] Companies may outgrow their international divisions as their international sales grow in significance, diversity and complexity. Royal Dutch Shell or Philips, for example, would have never grown to their current prominence by relying on the Dutch market alone.

Global Organizational Structures Global structures have grown out of competitive necessity. In many industries, competition is on a global basis, with the result that companies must have a high degree of reactive capability.

Five basic types of global structures are available:

1 Global product structure, in which product divisions are responsible for all manufacture and marketing worldwide.

2 Global area structure, in which geographic divisions are responsible for all manufacture and marketing in their respective areas.

3 Global functional structure, in which the functional areas (such as production, marketing, finance and personnel) are responsible for the worldwide operations of their own functional areas.

4 Global customer structure, in which operations are structured based on distinct worldwide customer groups.

5 Mixed – or hybrid – structure, which may combine the other alternatives.

Product Structure The product structure is the one that is most used by multinational corporations.[7] This approach gives worldwide responsibility to strategic business units for the marketing of their product lines, as shown in Exhibit 7.3. Most consumer product firms utilize some form of this approach, mainly because of the diversity of their products. One of the major benefits of the approach is improved cost efficiency through centralization of manufacturing facilities. This is crucial in industries in which competitive position is determined by world market share, which in turn is often determined by the degree to which manufacturing is rationalized.[8] Adaptation to this approach may cause problems because it is usually accompanied by consolidation of operations and plant closings. For example, in VW AG, each brand in the Volkswagen Group is managed by a senior brand manager.[9] Research for all brands (Audi, VW, Seat, Skoda, Lamborghini, Bentley, Bugatti) is concentrated in Wolfsburg, Germany. It is divided into future research and mobility, lightweight research and drive research.[10]

Another benefit is the ability to balance the functional inputs needed by a product and to react quickly to product-specific problems in the marketplace. Even smaller brands receive individual attention. Product-specific attention is important because products vary in terms of the adaptation they need for different foreign markets. All in all, the product approach ideally brings about the development of a global strategic focus in response to global competition.

At the same time, this structure fragments international expertise within the firm because a central pool of international experience no longer exists. The structure assumes that managers will have adequate regional experience or advice to allow them to make balanced decisions. Coordination of activities among the various product groups operating in the same markets is crucial to avoid unnecessary duplication of basic tasks. For some of these tasks, such as market research, special staff functions may be created and then hired by the product divisions when needed. If product managers lack an appreciation for the international dimension, they may focus their attention on only the larger markets, often with emphasize on the domestic markets, and fail to take the long-term view.

Area Structure The second most frequently adopted approach is the area structure, illustrated in Exhibit 7.4. The firm is organized on the basis of geographical areas; for example, operations may be divided into those dealing with Europe, the Middle East and Africa. Regional aggregation may play a major role in this structuring; for example, many multinational corporations have located their European headquarters in Brussels, where the EU has its

EXHIBIT 7.3

The global product structure (Kodak)

Source: **http://www.kodak.com/ US/en/corp/aboutKodak/**.

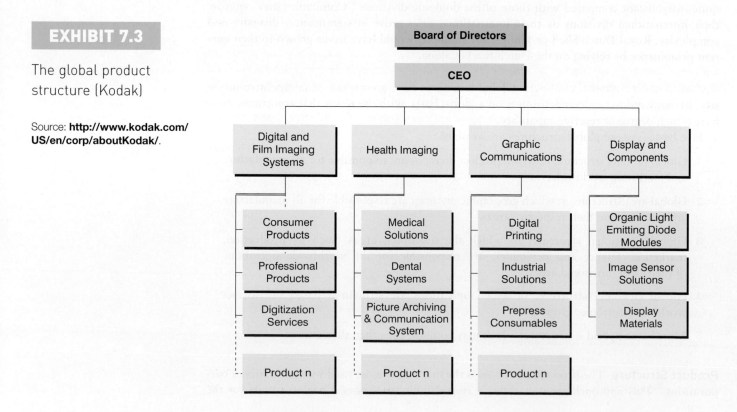

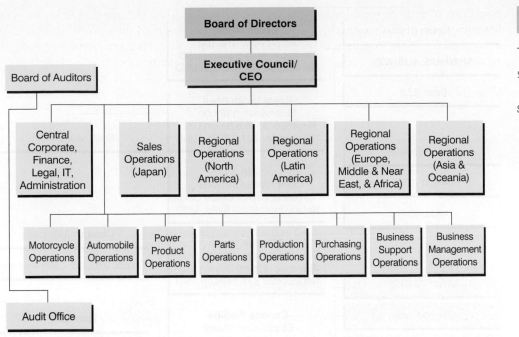

EXHIBIT 7.4

The global area
structure (Honda)

Source: Honda Annual Reports.

headquarters. The driver of the choice can be cultural similarity, such as in the case of Asia, or historic connections between countries, such as in the case of combining Europe with the Middle East and Africa. As new markets emerge, they may first be delegated to an established country organization for guidance with the ultimate objective of having them be equal partners with others in the organization. When Estonia regained its independence and started its transformation to a market economy, many companies assigned their country organization in Finland the responsibility of the Estonian unit's development. In Latvia's case, the Swedish country organization got the job. Since then, the development of new markets such as the 'Stans' (e.g., Kazakhstan and Azerbaijan) has been delegated to country organizations in Russia and Turkey.

The area approach follows the marketing concept most closely because individual areas and markets are given concentrated attention. If market conditions with respect to product acceptance and operating conditions vary dramatically, the area approach is the one to choose. Companies opting for this alternative typically have relatively narrow product lines with similar end uses and end users. However, expertise is most needed in adapting the product and its marketing to local market conditions. Once again, to avoid duplication of effort in product management and in functional areas, staff specialists – for product categories, for example – may be used.

Without appropriate coordination from the staff, essential information and experience may not be transferred from one regional entity to another. If the company expands in terms of product lines, and if end markets begin to diversify, the area structure may also become inappropriate.

Some marketers may feel that going into a global product structure may be too much too quickly and opt, therefore, to have a regional organization for planning and reporting purposes. The objective may also be to keep profit or sales centres of similar size at similar levels in the corporate hierarchy. If a group of countries has small sales compared with other country operations, they can be consolidated into a region. The benefits of a regional operation and regional headquarters are more efficient coordination of programmes across the region (as opposed to globally), a management more sensitized to country-market operations in the region, and the ability for the region's voice to be heard more clearly at global headquarters (as compared to what an individual, especially smaller, country operation could achieve).[11]

Functional Structure Of all the approaches, the functional structure is the most simple from the administrative viewpoint because it emphasizes the basic tasks of the firm – for

The global functional structure (Royal Dutch Shell)

Source: **http://www.answers.com/topic/royal-dutch-shell-plc-adr**

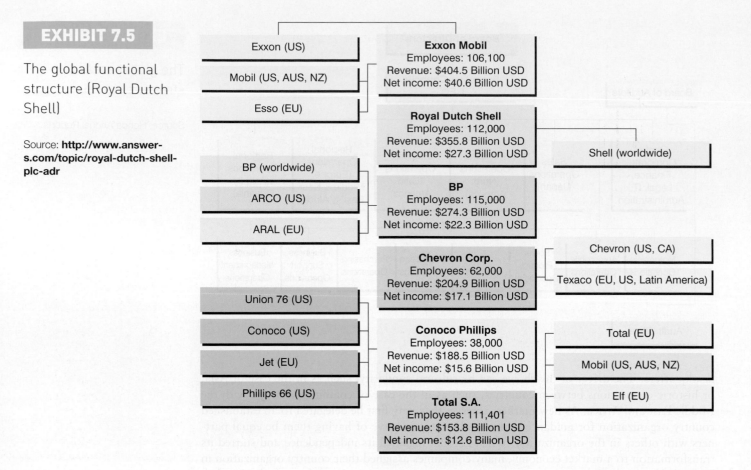

example, manufacturing, sales and research and development. This approach, illustrated in Exhibit 7.5, works best when both products and customers are relatively few and similar in nature. Because coordination is typically the key problem, staff functions have been created to interact between the functional areas. Otherwise, the company's marketing and regional expertise may not be exploited to the fullest extent.

A variation of this approach is one that uses processes as a basis for structure. The process structure is common in the energy and mining industries, where one corporate entity may be in charge of exploration worldwide and another may be responsible for the actual mining operation.

Customer Structure Firms may also organize their operations using the customer structure, especially if the customer groups they serve are dramatically different – for example, consumers versus businesses versus governments. Catering to these diverse groups may require the concentration of specialists in particular divisions. The product may be the same, but the buying processes of the various customer groups may differ. Governmental buying is characterized by bidding, in which price plays a larger role than when businesses are the buyers. However, products and solutions are increasingly developed around capabilities, such as networked communications, that can be used by more than one service or agency.[12] Similarly, in financial institutions, it is important to know whether customers who signed up for one service are already customers for other services being provided by the institution.[13]

Mixed Structure Mixed, or hybrid, organizations also exist. A mixed structure, such as the one in Exhibit 7.6, combines two or more organizational dimensions simultaneously. It permits attention to be focused on products, areas or functions, as needed. This approach may occur in a transitional period after a merger or an acquisition, or it may come about because

EXHIBIT 7.6   The global mixed structure (DaimlerChrysler)

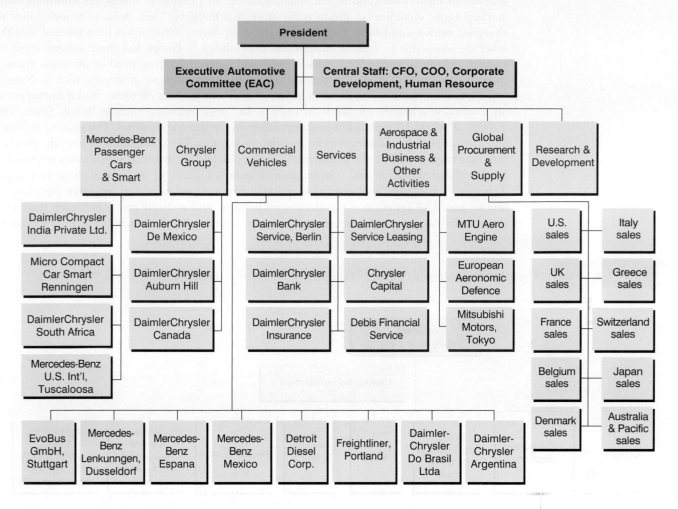

Source: DaimlerChrysler Annual Reports.

of a unique customer group or product line (such as military hardware). It may also provide a useful structure before the implementation of the matrix structure.[14]

Organization structures are, of course, never as clear-cut and simple as they have been presented here. Whatever the basic format, inputs are needed for product, area and function. One alternative, for example, might be an initial product structure that would eventually have regional groupings. Another alternative might be an initial area structure with eventual product groupings. However, in the long term, coordination and control across such structures become tedious.

Matrix Structure   Many multinational corporations – in an attempt to facilitate planning, organizing and controlling interdependent businesses, critical resources, strategies and geographic regions – have adopted the matrix structure.[15] Business is driven by a worldwide business unit (for example, photographic products or commercial and information systems) and implemented by a geographic unit (for example, Europe or Latin America). The geographical units, as well as their country subsidiaries, serve as the 'glue' between autonomous product operations. The global matrix structure provides a three-dimensional linking or overlapping of functions, areas and products. Under this structure, power and responsibility for global operations are shared among product divisions, geographic areas and functional areas.[16]

Organizational matrices integrate the various approaches already discussed, as the Philips example in Exhibit 7.7 illustrates. The product divisions (which are then divided into 60 product groups) have rationalized manufacturing to provide products for continent-wide markets rather than lines of products for individual markets. These product groups adjust to changing market conditions; for example, the components division has been merged into the other divisions due to lack of stand-alone profitability.[17] Philips has three general types of country organizations: In 'key' markets, such as France and Japan, product divisions manage their own marketing as well as manufacturing. In 'local business' countries, such as Nigeria and Peru, the organizations function as importers from product divisions, and if manufacturing occurs, it is purely for the local market. In 'large' markets, such as Brazil, Spain, and Taiwan, a hybrid arrangement is used depending on the size and situation. The product divisions and the national subsidiaries interact together in a matrix-like configuration, with the product divisions responsible for the globalization dimension and the national subsidiaries responsible for local representation and coordination of common areas of interest, such as recruiting. The matrix structure manager has functional, product and resource managers reporting to him or her. The approach is based on team building and multiple command, each team specializing in its own area of expertise. It provides a mechanism for cooperation among country

EXHIBIT 7.7   The global matrix structure (Philips)

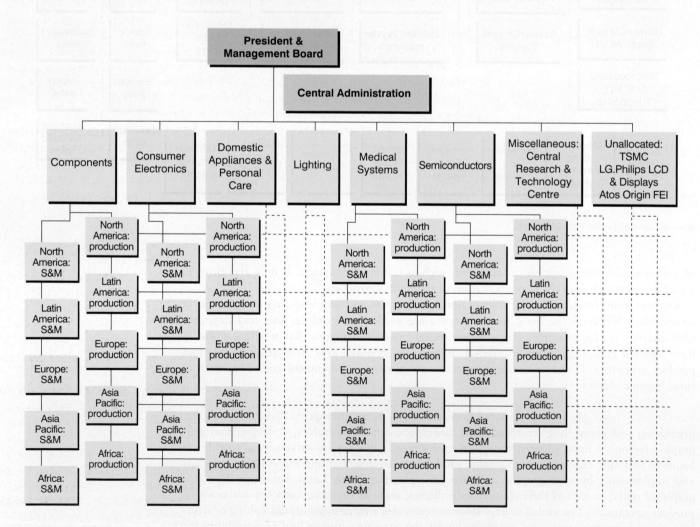

Note: S&M stands for Sales and Marketing.

Source: Philips Annual Reports.

managers, business managers and functional managers on a worldwide basis through increased communication, control and attention to balance in the organization.

The matrices used vary according to the number of dimensions needed. For example, Unilever represents another common organizational structure: the hybrid form. This company operates with three divisional regions, two product segments and five functional segments. Unilever developed and implemented this organizational structure for their company to improve communication and to take advantage of resources that are available to them.[18] The matrix approach helps cut through enormous organizational complexities by building in a provision for cooperation among business managers, functional managers and strategy managers. However, the matrix requires sensitive, well-trained middle managers who can cope with problems that arise from reporting to two bosses – for example, a product line manager and an area manager.

Many companies have found the matrix structure problematic. The dual reporting channel easily causes conflict; complex issues are forced into a two-dimensional decision framework; and even minor issues may have to be resolved through committee discussion.[19] Ideally, managers should solve problems themselves through formal and informal communication; however, physical and psychic distance often make that impossible. Especially when competitive conditions require quick reaction, the matrix, with its inherent complexity, may actually lower the reaction speed of the company. As a result, authority has started to shift in many organizations from area to product, although the matrix may still officially be used. At the same time, approaches to increase collaboration have been focused on, as seen in *The International Marketplace 7.2*.

THE INTERNATIONAL **MARKETPLACE 7.2**

Beyond the matrix

Royal Philips Electronics of the Netherlands is one of the world's biggest electronics companies, as well as the largest in Europe, with 128,000 employees in over 60 countries and sales in 2007 of £28.90 billion. In the past 60 years, it has had three major phases of changes in its organizational structure.

The company was one of the earliest champions of the matrix structure. After World War II, the organizational structure consisted of both national organizations and product divisions. Every division in a given country would report to the head of Philips in that country but also to the division's head at headquarters. This network was loosely held together by coordinating committees designed to resolve any conflicts between the basic reporting structures.

By the 1990s, environmental complexities had rendered the structure inefficient. Accountability and credit were difficult to assign and require. For example, who was to be held responsible for the profit-and-loss account – the country manager or the product head? The subsequent reorganization created a number of units with world-wide responsibility for groups of the company's businesses (e.g., consumer electronics and lighting products). The national offices became subservient to these units, built around products and based at headquarters.

In the last two years, changes have been made that are not necessarily evident in organizational charts. For example, a chief marketing officer has been appointed to help counter criticism of technology and new-product bias at the expense of customer orientation. Under an initiative called 'One Philips', the company has introduced a number of low-key changes. Employees are encouraged to work on cross-cultural and cross-functional teams. New awards have been instituted for employees who have created value for the company by collaborating with others outside their immediate units. Transfers across geographic entities as well as product units are expected as an explicit requirement for advancement. Top executives at Philips have argued that up to 80 per cent of the desired changes will come about through readjustment

of attitudes, the rest from using appropriate incentives, most of them not directly monetary. To accelerate these changes, Philips brought together its top 1,000 managers for a series of workshops designed to find ways to cut through organizational barriers.

SOURCE: 'The Matrix Master', *The Economist,* January 21, 2006, 4. See also **http://www.philips.com**.

Evolution of organizational structures

Companies develop new structures in stages as their product diversity develops and the share of foreign sales increases.[20] At the first stage are autonomous subsidiaries reporting directly to top management, followed by the establishment of an international division. With increases in product diversity and in the importance of the foreign marketplace, companies develop global structures to coordinate subsidiary operations and rationalize worldwide production. As global corporations have faced pressures to adapt to local market conditions while trying to rationalize production and globalize competitive reaction, many have opted for the matrix structure. Ideally, the matrix structure probably allows a corporation to best meet the challenges of global markets: to be global and local, big and small, decentralized with centralized reporting, by allowing the optimizing of businesses globally and maximizing performance in every country of operation.[21] The evolutionary process is summarized in Exhibit 7.8.

Whatever the choice of organizational arrangement may be, the challenge is to stop departments working within themselves rather than working with other departments across the organization. Employee knowledge tends to be fragmented with one unit's experience and know-how inaccessible to other units. Therefore, the wheel gets reinvented at considerable cost to the company and frustration to those charged with tasks. Information technology can be used to synchronize knowledge across even the most complicated and diverse organizations.[22]

EXHIBIT 7.8

Evolution of
international structures

Source: Reprinted by permission of *Harvard Business Review*. From Christopher A. Bartlett, "Building and Managing the Transnational: The New Organizational Challenge," in *Competition in Global Industries,* Michael E. Porter, ed. (Boston: Harvard Business School Press, 1986), 368. Copyright © 1986 by Harvard Business School Publishing Corporation; all rights reserved.

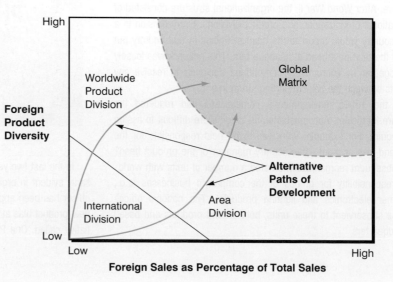

Foreign Sales as Percentage of Total Sales

IMPLEMENTATION

Organizational structures provide the frameworks for carrying out marketing decision making. However, for marketing to be effective, a series of organizational initiatives are needed to develop marketing strategy to its full potential; that is, secure implementation of such strategies at the national level and across markets.[23]

Locus of decision making

Organizational structures themselves do not indicate where the authority for decision making and control rests within the organization, nor will they reveal the level of coordination between units. The different levels of coordination between country units are summarized in Exhibit 7.9. Once a suitable form of structure has been found, it has to be made to work by finding a balance between the centre and the country organizations.

If subsidiaries are granted a high degree of autonomy, the result is termed decentralization. In decentralized systems, controls are relatively loose and simple, and the flows between headquarters and subsidiaries are mainly financial; that is, each subsidiary operates as a profit centre. On the other hand, if controls are tight and if strategic decision making is concentrated at headquarters, the result is termed centralization. Firms are typically neither totally centralized nor totally decentralized. Some functions, such as finance, lend themselves to more centralized decision making, whereas other functions, such as promotional decisions, lend themselves to far less. Research and development is typically centralized in terms of both decision making and location, especially when basic research work is involved. Partly because of governmental pressures, some companies have added R&D functions on a regional or local basis. In many cases, however, variations in decision making are product- and market-based, for example, in Unilever's new organization launched in 2005, managers of global business units are responsible for brand management and product development and managers of regional market development organizations are responsible for sales, trade marketing and media choices.[24]

Allowing maximum flexibility at the country-market level takes advantage of the fact that subsidiary management knows its market and can react to changes quickly. Problems of motivation and acceptance are avoided when decision makers are also the implementers of the strategy. On the other hand, many marketers faced with global competitive threats and opportunities have adopted global strategy formulation, which by definition requires some degree of centralization. What has emerged as a result can be called coordinated decentralization. This means that overall corporate strategy is provided from headquarters, but subsidiaries

Level	Description
5. Central control	No national structures
4. Central direction	Central functional heads have line authority over national functions
3. Central coordination	Central staff functions in coordinating role
2. Coordinating mechanisms	Formal committees and systems
1. Informal cooperation	Functional meetings: exchange of information
0. National autonomy	No coordination between decentralized units, which may even compete in export markets

Level 5 = highest; Level 0 = lowest. Most commonly found levels are 1–4.

EXHIBIT 7.9

Levels of coordination

Source: Norman Blackwell, Jean-Pierre Bizet, Peter Child, and David Hensley, "Creating European Organizations That Work", in *Readings in Global Marketing,* Michael R. Czinkota and Ilkka A. Ronkainen, eds. (London: The Dryden Press, 1995), 376–385.

are free to implement it within the range established in consultation between headquarters and the subsidiaries.

However, moving into this new mode may raise significant challenges. Among these systemic difficulties are a lack of widespread commitment to dismantling traditional national structures, driven by an inadequate understanding of the larger, global forces at work. Power barriers – especially if the personal roles of national managers are under threat of being consolidated into regional organizations – can lead to proposals being challenged without valid reason. Finally, some organizational initiatives (such as multicultural teams or corporate chat rooms) may be jeopardized by the fact that people do not have the necessary skills (e.g., language ability) or that an infrastructure (e.g., intranet) may not exist in an appropriate format.[25]

One particular case is of special interest. Organizationally, the forces of globalization are changing the country manager's role significantly. With profit-and-loss responsibility, oversight of multiple functions, and the benefit of distance from headquarters, country managers enjoyed considerable decision-making autonomy as well as entrepreneurial initiative. Today, however, many companies have to emphasize the product dimension of the product-geography matrix, which means that the power has to shift at least to some extent from country managers to worldwide strategic business unit and product line managers. Many of the previously local decisions are now subordinated to global strategic moves. However, regional and local brands still require an effective local management component. Therefore, the future country manager will have to have diverse skills (such as government relations and managing entrepreneurial teamwork) and wear many hats in balancing the needs of the operation for which the manager is directly responsible with those of the entire region or strategic business unit.[26] To emphasize the importance of the global/regional dimension in the country manager's portfolio, many companies have tied the country manager's compensation to the way the company performs globally or regionally, not just in the market for which the manager is responsible.

Factors affecting structure and decision making

The organizational structure and locus of decision making in multinational corporations are determined by a number of factors. They include (1) the degree of involvement in international operations; (2) the business(es) in which the firm is engaged (in terms, for example, of products marketed); (3) the size and importance of the markets; and (4) the human resource capability of the firm.[27]

The effect of the degree of involvement on structure and decision making was discussed earlier in the chapter. With low degrees of involvement by the parent company, subsidiaries can enjoy high degrees of autonomy as long as they meet their profit targets. The same situation can occur in even the most globally involved companies, but within a different framework.

The firm's country of origin and the political history of the area can also affect organizational structure and decision making. For example, Swiss-based Nestlé, with only 1 to 2 per cent of its sales in the small domestic market, has traditionally had a highly decentralized organization. Moreover, events of the past 90 years, particularly during the two world wars, have often forced subsidiaries of European-based companies to act independently in order to survive.

The type and variety of products marketed will have an effect on organizational decisions. Companies that market consumer products typically have product organizations with high degrees of decentralization, allowing for maximum local flexibility. On the other hand, companies that market technologically sophisticated products display centralized organizations with worldwide product responsibilities.

Going global has recently meant transferring world headquarters of important business units abroad. For example, Philips has moved headquarters of several of its global business units to the United States, including taking its Digital Video Group, Optimal Storage, and Flat Panel Display activities to Silicon Valley.

Apart from situations that require the development of an area structure, the characteristics of certain markets or regions may require separate arrangements for the firm. Upon entry,

AT&T China was made the only one of 20 divisions in the world to be based on geography rather than on product or service line. Furthermore, it was the only one to report directly to the CEO.[28]

The human factor in any organization is critical. Managers, both at headquarters and in the subsidiaries, must bridge the physical and psychic distances separating them. If subsidiaries have competent managers who rarely need to consult headquarters about their problems, they may be granted high degrees of autonomy. In the case of global organizations, subsidiary management must understand the corporate culture because subsidiaries must sometimes make decisions that meet the long-term objectives of the firm as a whole but that are not optimal for the local market.

The networked global organization

No international structure is ideal, and some have challenged the wisdom of even looking for an ideal one. They have called attention to new processes that would, in a given structure, develop new perspectives and attitudes to reflect and respond to complex demands of the opposite forces of global integration and local responsiveness. Rather than a question of which structural alternative is best, the question is thus one of how best to take into account the different perspectives of various corporate entities when making decisions. In structural terms, nothing may change. As a matter of fact, Philips still has its basic matrix structure, yet major changes have occurred in internal relations. The basic change was from a decentralized federation model to a networked global organization; the effects are depicted in Exhibit 7.10. This approach allows for the internal glocalization of strategic planning and implementation.[29]

Companies that have adopted the approach have incorporated three dimensions into their organizations: (1) the development and communication of a clear corporate vision; (2) the effective management of human resource tools to broaden individual perspectives and develop identification with corporate goals; and (3) the integration of individual thinking and activities into the broad corporate agenda.[30] The first dimension relates to a clear and consistent long-term corporate mission that guides individuals wherever they may work in the organization. IBM has established three values for the twenty-first century: dedication to every client's success, innovation that matters (for the company and the world), and trust and personal responsibility in all relationships.[31] The second dimension relates both to developing global managers who can find opportunities in spite of environmental challenges and to creating a global perspective among country managers. The last dimension refers to tackling the 'not-invented-here' syndrome to co-opt possibly isolated, even adversarial managers into the corporate agenda.

For example, in an area structure, units (such as Europe and North America) may operate quite independently, sharing little expertise and information with the others. While they are supposed to build links to headquarters and other units, they may actually be building walls.

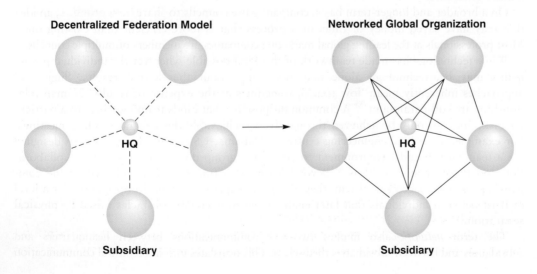

Decentralized Federation Model

HQ

Subsidiary

Networked Global Organization

HQ

Subsidiary

EXHIBIT 7.10

The networked global organization

Source: Reprinted with permission of Thomas Gross, Ernie Turner, and Lars Cederholm, "Building Teams for Global Operations," *Management Review,* June 1987, 34; permission conveyed through Copyright Clearance Centre, Inc.

To tackle this problem, Nissan established four management committees, meeting once a month, to supervise regional operations. Each committee includes representatives of the major functions (e.g., manufacturing, marketing and finance), and the committees (for Japan, Europe and general overseas markets) are chaired by Nissan executive vice presidents based in Japan. The CEO attends the committee meetings periodically but regularly.[32]

The network avoids the problems of duplication of effort, inefficiency and resistance to ideas developed elsewhere by giving subsidiaries the latitude, encouragement and tools to pursue local business development within the framework of the global strategy. Headquarters considers each unit as a source of ideas, skills, capabilities and knowledge that can be utilized for the benefit of the entire organization. This means that the subsidiaries must be upgraded from the role of implementation and adaptation to that of contribution and partnership in the development and execution of worldwide strategies. Efficient plants may be converted into international production centres, innovative R&D units may become centres of excellence (and thus role models), and leading subsidiary groups may be given a leadership role in developing new strategy for the entire corporation.

Centres of excellence can emerge in three formats: charismatic, focused or virtual. Charismatic centres of excellence are individuals who are internationally recognized for their expertise in a function or an area. The objective is primarily to build through an expert, via a mentoring relationship, a capability in the firm that has been lacking. The most common types are focused centres of excellence that are based on a single area of expertise, be it technological or product-based. The centre has an identifiable location from which members provide advice and training. In virtual centres of excellence, the core individuals live and work around the world and keep in touch through electronic means and meetings. The knowledge of dispersed individuals is brought together, integrated into a coherent whole and disseminated throughout the firm.[33]

Promoting internal cooperation

The global marketing entity in today's environment can be successful only if it is able to move intellectual capital within the organization, that is, take ideas and move them around faster and faster.[34]

One of the tools for moving ideas is teaching. For example, Volkswagon AG supports automotive teaching and research, as shown in *the International Marketplace 7.3.*

Another method to promote internal cooperation for global marketing implementation is the use of international teams or councils. In the case of a new product or programme, an international team of managers may be assembled to develop strategy. Although final direction may come from headquarters, the input has included information on local conditions, and implementation of the strategy is enhanced because local managers were involved from the beginning. This approach has worked even in cases that may seem impossible because of market differences.

On a broader and longer-term basis, companies use councils to share best practice, an idea that may have saved money or time, or a process that is more efficient than existing ones. Most professionals at the leading global marketing companies are members of multiple councils.

While technology has made teamwork of this kind possible wherever the individual participants may be, technology alone may not bring about the desired results; 'high-tech' approaches inherently mean 'low touch', sometimes at the expense of results. Human relationships are still paramount.[35] A common purpose is what binds team members to a particular task, and can only be achieved through trust, achievable through face-to-face meetings. For example, at Airbus' engineering centre in Alabama, USA, everything has been designed for a teamwork-friendly environment to encourage group discussions, as well as collaboration and the exchange of ideas.[36] Beyond learning to function effectively within the company's project management system, they also share experiences that, in turn, engender a level of trust between individuals that later enable them to overcome obstacles raised by physical separation.

The term *network* also implies two-way communications between headquarters and subsidiaries and between subsidiaries themselves. This translates into intercultural communication

THE INTERNATIONAL **MARKETPLACE 7.3**

Volkswagen to contribute £3.92 million to Stanford University

nnovation laboratory and automotive research will develop next generation of transportation solutions.

LOS ANGELES – Volkswagen of America announced a contribution of £3.92 million to Stanford University to create the Volkswagen Automotive Innovation Lab (VAIL), on the Stanford University campus, and a new programme for supporting automotive teaching and research.

The VAIL and corresponding CarLab research and teaching programme housed at VAIL, will help to accelerate automotive-related research on campus by increasing the opportunities for collaborations between VW and Stanford and by building a global community of academic and industrial partners committed to the future of automotive research.

'The VAIL will be a solid foundation on which Volkswagen researchers and Stanford scientists will be able to find new ways to explore automotive technology', said Dr Burkhard Huhnke, executive director, Electronics Research Laboratory, Volkswagen of America, Inc. 'The work done at VAIL will help to further develop the future of mobility and autonomous driving that we started with our partnership on the DARPA Grand Challenge vehicles, Stanley and Junior'.

Volkswagen will donate $2 million to Stanford to construct the building housing VAIL and will provide $750,000 a year for five years to fund research and teaching activities in Stanford's CarLab, an interdisciplinary research centre, based at VAIL.

'The success of Junior and Stanley in the DARPA Grand Challenge events show that when Stanford collaborates with great partners in industry, such as Volkswagen, we can create significant new technologies', says Jim Plummer, Dean of Stanford Engineering. 'Transportation is a vital part of life and our goal as engineers is to find innovative ways to meet important human needs'.

Volkswagen and Stanford University's collaboration started with the two highly successful vehicles in the DARPA (Defense Advanced Research Projects Agency) Grand Challenge races with a first place win in the 2005 Grand Challenge and a second place finish at the recent 2007 Urban Challenge event in Victorville, CA.

'The initial focus for VAIL will be vehicle safety, mobility and environmental performance', said Plummer. 'Already signed up for space in the facility are the research groups of computer science and electrical engineering; Professor Sebastian Thrun, leader of the Stanford Racing Team that fielded Junior and Stanley; mechanical engineering Associate Professor Chris Gerdes, whose research group is studying cleaner combustion and advanced vehicle dynamics control; and communication department Professor Clifford Nass, whose research studies the psychology of making cars safer and more enjoyable'.

The VAIL facility will be housed in a new 8,000 square-foot lab located near the corner of Stock Farm Rd and Campus Drive West. The facility will include shared high-bay space with lifts, machinery and composite shops, and meeting rooms. It will also include outdoor test-driving space.

'While the VAIL is the physical home for vehicle research, CarLab is the intellectual community it houses', says Chris Gerdes, director, CarLab. 'The mission of CarLab will be to radically rethink the automobile in order to deliver unprecedented levels of safety and driver and passenger enjoyment'.

'The work done at VAIL and in the CarLab will engage the entire Stanford community and a number of industrial partners and will generate research and teaching opportunities that are both interdisciplinary and real-world in nature', said Plummer. 'We look forward to having a state-of-the-art facility for vehicle research on campus, where students can help develop the next several generations of automotive transportation'.

Founded in 1955, Volkswagen of America, Inc. is headquartered in Auburn Hills, Michigan. It is a subsidiary of Volkswagen AG, headquartered in Wolfsburg, Germany. Volkswagen is one of the world's largest producers of passenger cars and Europe's largest car maker. Volkswagen sells the Rabbit, New Beetle, New Beetle convertible, GTI, Jetta, GLI, Passat, Passat wagon, Eos, and Touareg through approximately 600 independent US dealers. Visit Volkswagen of America online at **vw.com**.

SOURCE: Keyes, S. (2007), 'Volkswagen to contribute $5.75 million to Stanford University', **http://www.media.vw.com/article_display.cfm?article_id=10248** (Accessed 10/06/09).

efforts focused on developing relationships.[37] While this communication can take the form of newsletters or regular and periodic meetings of appropriate personnel, new technologies are allowing marketers to link far-flung entities and eliminate traditional barriers of time and distance. Intranets integrate a company's information assets into a single and accessible system using internet-based technologies such as email, newsgroups, and the World Wide Web. For example, employees at AXA (a UK insurance, investments, pensions and healthcare business) put usability at the heart of its intranet strategy – ensuring the intranet is a practical tool for its 11000 UK-based employees. The aim was to ensure that employees excel professionally by making available the resources they need to acquire new skills and knowledge and by encouraging teamwork and empowerment in the workplace.[38]

The benefits of intranets are:

1   increased productivity, in that there is no longer lag time between an idea and the information needed to implement it;

2   enhanced knowledge capital that is constantly updated and upgraded;

3   facilitated teamwork, enabling online communication at insignificant expense; and

4   incorporation of best practice at a moment's notice by allowing marketing managers and sales personnel to make to-the-minute decisions anywhere in the world.

The technology is increasingly available to create a culture of collaboration both within companies and with pertinent outside constituents.[39]

As the discussion indicates, the networked approach is not a structural adaptation but a procedural one that requires a change in management mentality. Adjustment is primarily in the coordination and control functions of the firm.

The role of country organizations

Country organizations should be treated as a source of supply as much as they are considered a source of demand. Quite often, however, headquarters managers see their role as the coordinators of key decisions and controllers of resources, and perceive subsidiaries as Implementers and adapters of global strategy in their respective local markets. Furthermore, all country organizations may be seen as the same. This view severely limits the utilization of the firm's resources, by not using country organizations as resources and by depriving country managers of possibilities of exercising their creativity.[40]

The role that a particular country organization can play depends naturally on that market's overall strategic importance as well as the competencies of its organization. From these criteria, four different roles emerge (see Exhibit 7.11).

The role of **strategic leader** can be played by a highly competent national subsidiary located in a strategically critical market. The country organization serves as a partner of headquarters in developing and implementing strategy. For example, a strategic leader market may have products designed specifically with it in mind. Nissan's Z-cars have always been designated primarily for the US market, starting with the 240Z in the 1970s to the 370Z introduced in 2008.[41]

EXHIBIT 7.11

Roles for country organizations

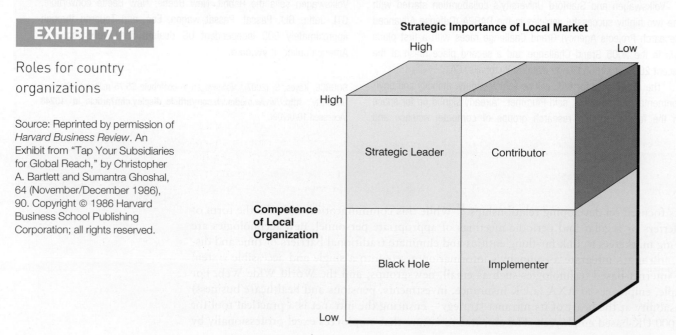

A contributor is a country organization with a distinctive competence, such as product development or regional expertise. Increasingly, country organizations are the source of new products. For example, low-end innovations like Procter & Gamble's liquid Tide are made with a fabric-softening compound developed in Europe. Similarly, country organizations may be assigned as worldwide centres of excellence for a particular product category, for example, ABB Strömberg in Finland for electric drives, a category for which it is a recognized world leader.[42]

The critical mass for the international marketing effort is provided by Implementers. These country organizations may exist in smaller, less-established markets in which corporate commitment to market development is less. The presence in these markets is typically through a sales organization. Although most entities fill this role, it should not be slighted: Implementers provide the opportunity to capture economies of scale and scope that are the basis of a global strategy.

The black hole is a situation that the international marketer has to work out of. A company may be in a 'black hole' situation because it has read the market incorrectly (for example, Philips focused its marketing efforts in the North American market on less-expensive items instead of the up-market products that have made the company's reputation worldwide)[43] or because government may restrict its activities (for example, Citibank being restricted in terms of activities and geography in China). If possible, the marketer can use strategic alliances or acquisitions to change its competitive position. Whirlpool established itself in the European Union by acquiring Philips' white goods' operation, and has used joint ventures to penetrate the Chinese market. If governmental regulations hinder the scale of operations, the firm may use its presence in a major market as an observation post to keep up with developments before a major thrust for entry is executed (for example, with China's WTO membership, the financial services sector should start opening up).

Depending on the role, the relationship between headquarters and the country organization will vary from loose control based mostly on support to tighter control in making sure strategies are implemented appropriately. Yet in each of these cases, it is imperative that country organizations have enough operating independence to cater to local needs and to provide motivation to the country managers. For example, an implementer should provide input in the development of a regional or a global strategy or programme. Strategy formulation should ensure that appropriate implementation can be achieved at the country level.

Good ideas can, and should, come from any country organizations. To take full advantage of this, individuals at the country level have to feel that they have the authority to pursue ideas in the first place and that they can see their concepts through to commercialization.[44] In some cases, this may mean that subsidiaries are allowed to experiment with projects that would not be seen as feasible by headquarters. For example, developing products for small-scale power generation using renewable resources may not generate interest in Honeywell's major markets and subsidiaries but may well be something that one of its developing-country subsidiaries should investigate.

CONTROL

The function of the organizational structure is to provide a framework in which objectives can be met. A set of instruments and processes is needed, however, to influence the behaviour and performance of organization members to meet the goals. Controls focus on actions to verify and correct actions that differ from established plans. Compliance needs to be secured from subordinates through various means of coordinating specialized and interdependent parts of the organization.[45] Within an organization, control serves as an integrating mechanism. Controls are designed to reduce uncertainty, increase predictability and ensure that behaviours originating in separate parts of the organization are compatible and in support of common organizational goals despite physical, psychic and temporal distances.

The critical issue is the same as with organizational structure: What is the ideal amount of control? On the one hand, headquarters needs information to ensure that international activities contribute maximum benefit to the overall organization. On the other hand, controls should not be construed as a code of law and allowed to stifle local initiative.

This section will focus on the design and functions of control instruments available for the international marketer, along with an assessment of their appropriateness. Emphasize will be placed on the degree of formality of controls used.

Types of controls

Most organizations display some administrative flexibility, as demonstrated by variations in the application of management directives, corporate objectives or measurement systems. A distinction should be made, however, between variations that have emerged by design and those that are the result of autonomy. One is the result of management decision, whereas the other has typically grown without central direction and is based on emerging practices. In both instances, some type of control will be exercised. Here, we are concerned only with controls that are the result of headquarters initiative rather than consequences of tolerated practices. Firms that wait for self-emerging controls often find that such an orientation may lead to rapid international growth but may eventually result in problems in areas of product-line performance, programme coordination, and strategic planning.[46]

Whatever the system, it is important in today's competitive environment to have internal benchmarking. Benchmarking relays organizational learning and sharing of best practices throughout the corporate system to avoid the costs of reinventing solutions that have already been discovered. A description of the knowledge transfer process by which this occurs is provided in *The International Marketplace 7.4*.

THE INTERNATIONAL MARKETPLACE 7.4

International best practice exchange

As growing competitive pressures challenge many global firms, strategies to improve the transfer of best practice across geographically dispersed units and time zones becomes critical. The premise is that a company with the same product range targeting the same markets pan-regionally should be able to use knowledge gained in one market throughout the organization. The fact is, however, that companies use only 20 per cent of their most precious resources – knowledge, in the form of technical information, market data, internal know-how, and processes and procedures. Trying to transfer best practices internationally amplifies the problem even more. However, a corporate environment that creates informal cooperation in addition to the more formal, builds the necessary trust – and subsequently the critical mass – to share knowledge.

Copier maker Xerox (formerly Rank Xerox), with over 60 subsidiaries, is working hard to make better use of the knowledge, corporate-wide. A 35-person group identified nine practices that could be applicable throughout the group. These ranged from the way the Australian subsidiary retains customers, to Italy's method of gathering competitive intelligence, to a procedure for handling new major accounts in Spain. These practices were thought to be easier to 'sell' to other operating companies, were considered easy to implement and would provide a good return on investment.

Three countries were much quicker in introducing new products successfully than others. In the case of France, this was related to the training given to employees. The subsidiary gave its sales staff three days of hands-on practice, including competitive benchmarking. Before they attended the course, salespeople were given reading materials and were tested when they arrived. Those remaining were evaluated again at the end of the course, and performance reports were sent to their managers.

The difficult task is to achieve buy-in from the other country organizations. Six months might be spent in making detailed presentations of the best practices to all the companies and an additional three years helping them implement the needed changes. It is imperative that the country manager is behind the proposal in each subsidiary's case. However, implementation cannot be left to the country organizations after the concept has been presented. This may result in the dilution of both time and urgency and with possible country-specific customization that negates comparisons and jeopardizes the success of the change.

With time, these projects become codified into programmes. Focus 500 allows the company's top 500 executives to share information on their interactions with customers and industry partners. Project Library details costs, resources and cycle times of more than 2,000 projects, making it a vital resource in assuring Six Sigma in project management. PROFIT allows salespeople to submit hot selling tips – with cash incentives for doing so.

SOURCES: Philip Evans and Bob Wolf, 'Collaboration Rules', *Harvard Business Review* 83 (July–August 2005): 96–104; Kristine Ellis, 'Sharing Best Practices Globally', *Training*, July 2001, 34–38; Michael McGann, 'Chase Harnesses Data with Lotus Notes', *Bank Systems and Technology* 34 (May 1997): 38; 'Rank Xerox Aims at Sharing Knowledge', *Crossborder Monitor* (September 18, 1996): 8; 'World-Wise: Effective Networking Distinguishes These 25 Global Companies', *Computerworld*, August 26, 1996, 7; See also Xerox Online Fact Book, available at **http://www.xerox.com**.

Three critical features are necessary in sharing best practice. First, there needs to be a device for organizational memory. For example, at Xerox, contributors to solutions can send their ideas to an electronic library where they are indexed and provided to potential adopters in the corporate family. Second, best practice must be updated and adjusted to new situations. For example, best practice adopted by the company's Chinese office will be modified and customized, and this learning should then become part of the database. Finally, best practice must be legitimized. This calls for a shared understanding that exchanging knowledge across units is valued in the organization and that these systems are important mechanisms for knowledge exchange. An assessment of how effectively employees share information with colleagues and utilize the databases can also be included in employee performance evaluations.

In the design of the control system, a major decision concerns the object of control. Two major objects are typically identified: output and behaviour.[47] Output controls consist of balance sheets, sales data, production data, product line growth, or a performance review of personnel. Measures of output are accumulated at regular intervals and forwarded from the foreign operation to headquarters, where they are evaluated and critiqued based on comparisons to the plan or budget. Behavioural controls require the exertion of influence over behaviour after, or ideally before, it leads to action. This influence can be achieved, for example, by providing sales manuals to subsidiary personnel or by fitting new employees into the corporate culture.

To institute either of these measures, corporate officials must decide on instruments of control. The general alternatives are bureaucratic/formalized control or cultural control. Bureaucratic controls consist of a limited and explicit set of regulations and rules that outline desired levels of performance. Cultural controls, on the other hand, are much less formal and are the result of shared beliefs and expectations among the members of an organization. A comparison of the two types of controls and their objectives is provided in Exhibit 7.12. It can be argued that instilling the marketing approach (i.e., customer orientation) will have to rely more on behavioural dimensions since an approach focused on outputs may put undue pressure on short-term profits.[48]

Bureaucratic/Formalized Control The elements of bureaucratic/formalized controls are (1) an international budget and planning system, (2) the functional reporting system, and (3) policy manuals used to direct functional performance. Budgets are short-term guidelines in such areas as investment, cash and personnel, whereas plans refer to formalized long-range

---

EXHIBIT 7.12   Comparison of bureaucratic and cultural control mechanisms

| | Type of Control | | |
Object of Control	Pure Bureaucratic/ Formalized Control	Pure Cultural Control	Characteristics of Control
Output	Formal performance reports	Shared norms of performance	HQ sets short-term performance target and requires frequent reports from subsidiaries
Behaviour	Company policies, manuals	Shared philosophy of management	Active participation of HQ in strategy formulation of subsidiaries

Sources: Peter J. Kidger, "Management Structure in Multinational Enterprises: Responding to Globalization," *Employee Relations,* August 2001, 69–85; and B. R. Baliga and Alfred M. Jaeger, "Multinational Corporations: Control Systems and Delegation Issues," *Journal of International Business Studies* 15 (Fall 1984): 28.

programmes with more than a one-year horizon. The budget and planning process is the major control instrument in headquarters-subsidiary relationships. Although systems and their execution vary, the objective is to achieve the best fit possible with the objectives and characteristics of the firm and its environment.

The budgetary period is typically one year because budgets are tied to the accounting systems of the company. The budget system is used for four main purposes: (1) allocation of funds among subsidiaries; (2) planning and coordination of global production capacity and supplies; (3) evaluation of subsidiary performance; and (4) communication and information exchange among subsidiaries, product organizations and corporate headquarters.[49] Long-range plans, on the other hand, extend over periods of two to ten years, and their content is more qualitative and judgmental in nature than that of budgets. Shorter periods, such as two years, are the norm because of the uncertainty of diverse foreign environments.

Although firms strive for uniformity, this may be comparable to trying to design a suit to fit the average person. The budget and planning processes themselves are formalized in terms of the schedules to be followed.

Control can also be seen as a mechanism to secure cooperation of local units. For example, while a company may grant substantial autonomy to a country organization in terms of strategies, headquarters may use allocation of production volume as a powerful tool to ensure compliance. Some of the ways for headquarters to gain cooperation of country organizations are summarized in Exhibit 7.13. Some of the methods used are formal, such as approval of strategic plans and personnel selection, while some are more informal, including personal contact and relationships as well as international networking.[50]

Since the frequency and types of reports to be furnished by subsidiaries are likely to increase due to globalization, it is essential that subsidiaries see the rationale for the often time-consuming task. Two approaches, used in tandem, can facilitate the process: participation and feedback. Involving the preparers of reports in their ultimate use serves to avoid the perception at subsidiary levels that reports are 'art for art's sake'. When this is not possible, feedback about results and consequences is an alternative. Through this process, communication is also enhanced.

On the behavioural front, headquarters may want to guide the way in which subsidiaries make decisions and implement agreed-upon strategies. European and Japanese multinational companies, relying heavily on manuals for all major functions, tend to be far less formalized than their US counterparts.[51] The manuals are for functions such as personnel policies for recruitment, training, motivation and dismissal. The use of policy manuals as a control instrument correlates with the level of reports required from subsidiaries.

Cultural Control   In European and Japanese companies, less emphasize is placed on formal controls, which are viewed as rigid and too quantitatively oriented. Rather, the emphasize is on corporate values and culture, and evaluations are based on the extent to which an

EXHIBIT 7.13

Securing country-organization cooperation

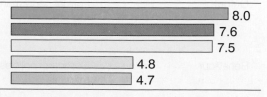

Extent of use of . . .

Approval of local budgets	8.0
Compensation for job performance	7.6
Evaluation of job performance	7.5
Allocation of production capacity/volume	4.8
Financial contribution from HQ	4.7

Among 35 MNCs.
0 to 10 scale (0 = "Never used" and 10 = "Always used")

Source: Henry P. Conn and George S. Yip, "Global Transfer of Critical Capabilities," in *Best Practices in International Business,* Michael R. Czinkota and Ilkka A. Ronkainen, eds. (Mason, OH: South-Western, 2001): 256–274.

individual or entity fits in. Cultural controls require an extensive socialization process, and informal, personal interaction is central to the process. Substantial resources must be spent to train the individual to share the corporate culture, that is, 'the way things are done at the company'.[52] To build common vision and values, managers spend a substantial amount of their first months at Matsushita in what the company calls 'cultural and spiritual training'. They study the company credo, the 'Seven Spirits of Matsushita', and the philosophy of the founder, Konosuke Matsushita. Then they learn how to translate these internalized lessons into daily behaviour and operational decisions. Although more prevalent in Japanese organizations, many western entities have similar programmes, for example, Philips' 'organization cohesion training' and Unilever's 'indoctrination'. This corporate acculturation will be critical to achieve the acceptance of possible transfers of best practice within the organization.[53]

The primary instruments of cultural control are the careful selection and training of corporate personnel and the institution of self-control. The choice of cultural controls rather than bureaucratic controls can be justified if the company enjoys a low turnover rate. Cultural controls are thus applied, for example, when companies offer lifetime or long-term employment, as many Japanese firms do.

In selecting home country nationals and, to some extent, third-country nationals, global companies are exercising cultural control. They assume that these managers have already internalized the norms and values of the company and that they tend to run a country operation with a more global view. In some cases, the use of headquarters personnel to ensure uniformity in decision making may be advisable. Expatriates are used in subsidiaries not only for control purposes but also for initiating change and to develop local talent. Companies control the efforts of management specifically through compensation, promotion and replacement policies.

When the expatriate corps is small, headquarters can exercise control through other means. Management training programmes for overseas managers as well as visits to headquarters will indoctrinate individuals to the company's way of doing things. Similarly, visits to subsidiaries by headquarters teams will promote a sense of belonging. These may be on a formal basis, as for a strategy audit, or less formal – for example, to launch a new product. Some innovative global marketers assemble temporary teams of their best talent to build local skills.

Corporations rarely use one pure control mechanism. Rather, emphasize is placed on both quantitative and qualitative measures. Corporations are likely, however, to place different levels of emphasize on the types of performance measures and on the way the measures are taken. To generate global buy-in, annual bonuses have shifted away from the employee's individual unit and towards the company as a whole. This sends a strong signal in favour of collaboration across all boundaries. Other similar approaches to motivate and generate changes in thinking exist. At BP, for example, individual performance assessments exclude the effects of price of oil and foreign exchange because they are outside the employee's control.[54]

Exercising control

Within most corporations, different functional areas are subject to different guidelines. The reason is that each function is subject to different constraints and varying degrees of those constraints. For example, marketing as a function has traditionally been seen as incorporating many more behavioural dimensions than does manufacturing or finance. As a result, many multinational corporations employ control systems that are responsive to the needs of the function. Yet such differentiation is sometimes based less on appropriateness than on personality. One researcher hypothesized that manufacturing subsidiaries are controlled more intensively than sales subsidiaries because production more readily lends itself to centralized direction, and technicians and engineers adhere more firmly to standards and regulations than do salespeople.[55]

Similarly, the degree of control imposed will vary by subsidiary characteristics, including its location. For example, since Malaysia is an emerging economy in which managerial talent is in short supply, headquarters may want to participate more in all facets of decision making. If a country-market witnesses economic or political turmoil, controls may also be tightened to ensure the management of risk.[56]

In their international operations, multinational corporations place major emphasize on obtaining quantitative data. Although this allows for good centralized comparisons against standards and benchmarks, or cross-comparisons between different corporate units, several drawbacks are associated with the undertaking. In the international environment, new dimensions – such as inflation, differing rates of taxation and exchange rate fluctuations – may distort the performance evaluation of any given individual or organizational unit.

For the global corporation, measuring whether a business unit in a particular country is earning a superior return on investment relative to risk may be irrelevant to the contribution an investment may make worldwide or to the long-term results of the firm. In the short term, the return may even be negative.[57] Therefore, the control mechanism may quite inappropriately indicate reward or punishment. Standardizing the information received may be difficult if the environment fluctuates and requires frequent and major adaptations. Further complicating the issue is the fact that, although quantitative information may be collected monthly, or at least quarterly, environmental data may be acquired annually or 'now and then', especially when crisis seems to loom on the horizon.

To design a control system that is acceptable not only to headquarters but also to the organization and individuals abroad, a firm must take great care to use only relevant data. Major concerns, therefore, are the data collection process and the analysis and utilization of data. Evaluators need management information systems that provide for maximum comparability and equity in administering controls. The more behaviourally-based and culture-oriented controls are, the more care that needs to be taken.

In designing a control system, management must consider the costs of establishing and maintaining it and weigh the costs against the benefits to be gained. Any control system will require investment in a management structure and in systems design. As an example, consider the costs associated with cultural controls: Personal interaction, use of expatriates and training programmes are all quite expensive. Yet these expenses may be justified in savings through lower employee turnover, an extensive worldwide information system and a potentially improved control system.[58] Moreover, the impact goes beyond the administrative component. If controls are erroneous or too time-consuming, they can slow or misguide the strategy implementation process and thus the overall capability of the firm. The result will be lost opportunity or, worse, increased threats. In addition, time spent on reporting takes time away from other tasks. If reports are seen as marginally useful, the motivation to prepare them will be low. A parsimonious design is therefore imperative. The control system should collect all the information required and trigger all the intervention necessary but should not create a situation that resembles the pulling of strings by a puppeteer.

The impact of the environment must also be taken into account when designing controls. First, the control system should measure only dimensions over which the organization has control. Rewards or sanctions make little sense if they are based on dimensions that may be relevant for overall corporate performance but over which no influence can be exerted, for example, price controls. Neglecting the factor of individual performance capability would send wrong signals and severely impede the motivation of personnel. Second, control systems should harmonize with local regulations and customs. In some cases, however, corporate behavioural controls have to be exercised against local customs even though overall operations may be affected negatively. This type of situation occurs, for example, when a subsidiary operates in markets where unauthorized facilitating payments are a common business practice.

Corporations are faced with major challenges to appropriate and adequate control systems in today's business environment. With an increase in local (government) demands for a share in the control of companies established, controls can become tedious, especially if the multinational company is a minority partner. Even in a merger, the backgrounds of the partners may be sufficiently different to cause problems in terms of the controls.

SUMMARY

The structures and control mechanisms needed to operate internationally define relationships between the firm's headquarters and subsidiaries and provide the channels through which these relationships develop. The most fundamental test of organizational design is whether there is a fit with the company's overall marketing strategy and whether it reflects the strengths of the entities within the organization.[59]

International firms can choose from a variety of organizational structures, ranging from a domestic operation that handles ad hoc export orders to a fully-fledged global organization. The choice will depend primarily on the degree of internationalization of the firm, the diversity of international activities, and the relative importance of product, area, function, and customer variables in the process. Whatever the choice of structure may be, implementation of the planned strategies is a critical factor determining success. Companies typically realize only 60 per cent of their strategies' potential value due to factors such as organizations working autonomously and culture blocking execution.[60] To close the strategy-to-performance gap, the buy-in of all units is necessary. Of these, the primary one is the use of subsidiaries as resources, not merely as implementers of headquarters strategy.

The control function is of increasing importance because of the high variability in performance that results from divergent local environments, and the need to reconcile local objectives with the corporate goal of synergism. It is important to grant autonomy to country organizations so that they can be responsive to local market needs, but it is equally important to ensure close cooperation between units.

Control can be exercised through bureaucratic means, emphasizing formal reporting and evaluation of benchmark data. It can also be exercised through a cultural control process in which norms and values are understood by individuals and entities that compose the corporation. Multinational corporations frequently control operations abroad through informal means and rely less on stringent measures.

The execution of controls requires great sensitivity to behavioural dimensions and to the environment. The measurements used must be appropriate and must reflect actual performance rather than marketplace vagaries. Entities should be measured only on factors over which they have some degree of control.

KEY TERMS

area structure

best practice

black hole

budgets

bureaucratic controls

centralization

contributor

coordinated decentralization

cultural controls

customer structure

decentralization

functional structure

implementers

Intranets

matrix structure

mixed structure

plans

process structure

product structure

strategic leader

Questions for discussion

1   Firms differ, often substantially, in their organizational structures even within the same industry. What accounts for these differences in their approaches?

2   Discuss the benefits gained in adopting a matrix approach in terms of organizational structure.

3   What changes in the firm and/or in the environment might cause a firm to abandon the functional approach?

4   Is there more to the 'not-invented-here' syndrome than simply hurt feelings on the part of those who believe they are being dictated to by headquarters?

5   How can systems that are built for global knowledge transfer be used as control tools?

6   'Implementers are the most important country organizations in terms of buy-in for effective global marketing strategy implementation'. Comment.

Internet exercises

1   Improving internal communications is an objective for networked global organizations. Using the website of the Lotus Development Corporation (**http://www.lotus.com**) and its section on case studies, outline how marketers have used the Lotus Domino Express to interactively share information.

2   Using company and product information available on its website, determine why Siemens (**http://www.siemens.com/index.jsp**) has opted for global product/business structures for its organization.

Recommended readings

Bartlett, Christopher and Sumantra Ghoshal. *Managing across Borders*. Cambridge, MA: Harvard Business School Press, 1998.

Bartlett, Christopher and Sumantra Ghoshal. *Transnational Management: Text, Cases, and Readings in Cross-Border Management*. New York: McGraw-Hill, 2000.

Cairncross, Frances. *The Company of the Future*. Cambridge, MA: Harvard Business School Press, 2002.

Chisholm, Rupert F. *Developing Network Organizations: Learning from Practice and Theory*. Boston: Addison-Wesley, 1997.

Doz, Yves, Jose Santos and Peter Williamson. *From Global to Metanational: How Companies Win in the Knowledge Economy*. Cambridge, MA: Harvard Business School Press, 2001.

Galbraith, Jay R. *Designing Organizations: An Executive Guide to Strategy, Structure, and Process Revised*. New York: Jossey-Bass, 2001.

Ghoshal, Sumantra and Christopher Bartlett. *The Individualized Corporation: A Fundamentally New Approach to Management*. New York: Harper Business, 1999.

Govindarajan, Vijay, Anil K. Gupta and C. K. Prahalad. *The Quest for Global Dominance: Transforming Global Presence into Global Competitive Advantage*. New York: Jossey-Bass, 2001.

Govindarajan, Vijay and Robert Newton. *Management Control Systems*. New York: McGraw-Hill/Irwin, 2000.

Kluge, Jurgen, Wolfram Stein and Thomas Licht. *Knowledge Unplugged: The McKinsey & Company Global Survey on Knowledge Management,* London: Palgrave Macmillan, 2002.

McCall, Morgan W. and George P. Hollenbeck. *Developing Global Executives*. Cambridge, MA: Harvard Business School Press, 2002.

Pasternak, Bruce A. and Albert J. Viscio. *The centreless Corporation: A New Model for Transforming our Organization for Growth and Prosperity*. New York: Simon and Schuster, 1998.

Pfeffer, Jeffrey and Robert I. Sutton. *The Knowing-Doing Gap: How Smart Companies Turn Knowledge into Action*. Cambridge, MA: Harvard Business School Press, 1999.

Stewart, Thomas A. *The Wealth of Knowledge: Intellectual Capital and the Twenty-first Century Organization*. New York: Doubleday, 2001.

Notes

1   Lawrence M. Fischer, 'Thought Leader', *Strategy and Business* 7 (fourth quarter, 2002): 115–123.

2   **http://www.easier.com/view/News/Motoring/Renault/article-217095.html**

3   **http://uk.reuters.com/article/motoringAutoNews/idUK127242+17-Feb-2009+RTRS20090217**

4   **http://www.engineeringnews.co.za/article/how-airbus-is-revamping-itself-and-its-flagship-2007-07-20**

5   Michael Z. Brooke, *International Management: A Review of Strategies and Operations* (London: Hutchinson, 1986), 173–174; and 'Running a Licencing Department', *Business International,* June 13, 1988, 177–178.

6   Jay R. Galbraith, *Designing the Global Corporation* (New York: Jossey-Bass, 2000), chapter 3.

7   See, for example, Samuel Humes, *Managing the Multinational: Confronting the Global–Local Dilemma* (London, Prentice Hall, 1993), chapter 1.

8   Vijay Govindarajan, Anil K. Gupta, and C. K. Prahalad, *The Quest for Global Dominance: Transforming Global Presence into Global Competitive Advantage* (New York: Jossey-Bass, 2001), chapters 1 and 2.

9   Volkswagen, 'Annual Report 2008' **http://annualreport2008.volkswagenag.com/corporategovernance/structureandbusinessactivities/structureofthegroup.html**

10 Blocker, A. and Jürgens, U. (2007), 'Changes in the German car design and development sector and the challenge of sustainability'. **http://www.wzb.eu/gwd/wpa/pdf/ bloecker_juergens_gerpisa08.pdf**

11 Philippe Lasserre, 'Regional Headquarters: The Spearhead for Asia Pacific Markets', *Long Range Planning* 29 (February 1996): 30–37; and John D. Daniels, 'Bridging National and Global Marketing Strategies through Regional Operations', *International Marketing Review* 4 (Autumn 1987): 29–44.

12 'Boeing's Defense Unit to Divide Its Operations into 3 Segments', *The Wall Street Journal,* January 28, 2006, A5.

13 'The New Organization', *The Economist,* January 21, 2006, 3–5.

14 Daniel Robey, *Designing Organizations: A Macro Perspective* (Homewood, IL: Irwin, 1982), 327.

15 Christopher A. Bartlett and Sumantra Ghoshal, *Managing across Borders* (Cambridge, MA: Harvard Business School Press, 2002), chapter 10.

16 Miyamoto, K. 'Strategy and organizational structure of global companies'**http://www.worldscibooks.com/etextbook/ 6681/6681_chap01.pdf http://www.worldscibooks.com/business/6681.html**

17 Spencer Chin, 'Philips Shores Up the Dike', *EBN,* October 14, 2002, 4.

18 **http://www.biospace.com/news_story.aspx? NewsEntityId=116413**

19 Milton Harris and Artur Raviv, 'Organization Design', *Management Science* 48 (July 2002): 852–865.

20 John P. Workman, Jr., Christian Homburg, and Kjell Gruner, 'Marketing Organization: Framework of Dimensions and Determinants', *Journal of Marketing* 62 (July 1998): 21–41; and John U. Farley, 'Looking Ahead at the Marketplace: It's Global and It's Changing', in *Reflections on the Futures of Marketing,* Donald R. Lehman and Katherine E. Jocz, eds. (Cambridge, MA: Marketing Science Institute, 1995), 15–35.

21 William Taylor, 'The Logic of Global Business',*Harvard Business Review* 68 (March–April 1990): 91–105.

22 Mohanbir Sawhney, 'Don't Homogenize, Synchronize', *Harvard Business Review* 79 (July–August 2001): 100–108.

23 Ilkka A. Ronkainen, 'Thinking Globally, Implementing Successfully', *International Marketing Review* 13 (no. 3, 1996): 4–6.

24 Jack Neff, 'Unilever Reorganization Shifts P&L Responsibility', *Advertising Age,* February 28, 2005, 13; 'Despite Revamp, Unwieldy Unilever Falls Behind Rivals', *The Wall Street Journal,* January 3, 2005, A1, A5.

25 Russell Eisenstat, Nathaniel Foote, Jay Galbraith, and Danny Miller, 'Beyond the Business Unit', *The McKinsey Quarterly* 37 (no. 1, 2001): 180–195.

26 'Country Managers', *Business Europe,* October 16, 2002, 3; John A. Quelch and Helen Bloom, 'The Return of the Country Manager', *The McKinsey Quarterly* 33 (no. 2, 1996): 31–43; and Jon I. Martinez and John A. Quelch, 'Country Managers: The Next Generation', *International Marketing Review* 13 (no. 3, 1996): 43–55.

27 Rodman Drake and Lee M. Caudill, 'Management of the Large Multinational: Trends and Future Challenges', *Business Horizons* 24 (May–June 1981): 83–91.

28 Joe Studwell, *The China Dream* (New York: Atlantic Monthly Press, 2002), 104–105.

29 Goran Svensson, ''Glocalization' of Business Activities: A 'Glocal Strategy' Approach', *Management Decision* 39 (no. 1, 2001): 6–13.

30 Christopher A. Bartlett and Sumantra Ghoshal, 'Matrix Management: Not a Structure, a Frame of Mind', *Harvard Business Review* 68 (July–August 1990): 138–145.

31 'Big and No Longer Blue', *The Economist,* January 21, 2006, 15; 'Beyond Blue', *Business Week,* April 18, 2005, 68–76.

32 Carlos Ghosn, 'Saving the Business without Losing the Company', *Harvard Business Review* 80 (January 2002): 37–45.

33 Karl Moore and Julian Birkinshaw, 'Managing Knowledge in Global Service Firms', *Academy of Management Executive* 12 (no. 4, 1998): 81–92.

34 Julian Birkinshaw and Tony Sheehan, 'Managing the Knowledge Life Cycle', *Sloan Management Review* 44 (Fall 2002): 75–83.

35 Richard Benson-Armer and Tsun-Yan Hsieh, 'Teamwork across Time and Space', *The McKinsey Quarterly* 33 (no. 4, 1997): 18–27.

36 Reliable Plant (2009), 'Airbus opens engineering centre in Mobile, Alabama' **http://www.reliableplant.com/ Article.aspx?pagetitle=Airbus%20opens% 20engineering%20center%20in% 20Mobile,%20Alabama&articleid=4951**

37 David A. Griffith and Michael G. Harvey, 'An Intercultural Communication Model for Use in Global Interorganizational Networks', *Journal of International Marketing* 9 (no. 3, 2001): 87–103.

38 Kirby, E. (2006), 'Improving intranet usability at AXA' **http://www.allbusiness.com/technology/computer- software-management/4086753-1.html**

39 Linda S. Sanford and Dave Taylor, *Let Go to Grow* (Englewood Cliffs, NJ: Prentice-Hall, 2005), chapter 1.

40 Christopher A. Bartlett and Sumantra Ghoshal, 'Tap Your Subsidiaries for Global Reach', *Harvard Business Review* 64 (November–December 1986): 87–94.

41 Kunz, D (2009) 'New Nissan Z-Series has a lot of zip' **http://abclocal.go.com/kabc/story?section=news/ car_tips&id=6596287**

42 'Percy Barnevik's Global Crusade', *Business Week Enterprise* 1993, 204–211.

43 'A European Electronics Giant Races to Undo Mistakes in the U.S.', *The Wall Street Journal,* January 7, 2004, A1, A10.

44 Julian Birkinshaw and Neil Hood, 'Unleash Innovation in Foreign Subsidiaries', *Harvard Business Review* 79 (March 2001): 131–137; and Julian Birkinshaw and Nick Fry, 'Subsidiary Initiatives to Develop New Markets', *Sloan Management Review* 39 (Spring 1998): 51–61.

45 Vijay Govindarajan and Robert Newton, *Management Control Systems* (New York: McGraw-Hill/Irwin, 2000), chapter 1.

46 Anil Gupta and Vijay Govindarajan, 'Organizing for Knowledge within MNCs', *International Business Review* 3 (no. 4, 1994): 443–457.

47 William G. Ouchi, 'The Relationship between Organizational Structure and Organizational Control', *Administrative Science Quarterly* 22 (March 1977): 95–112.

48 Cheryl Nakata, 'Activating the Marketing Concept in a Global Context', *International Marketing Review* 19 (no. 1, 2002): 39–64.

49 Laurent Leksell, *Headquarters-Subsidiary Relationships in Multinational Corporations* (Stockholm, Sweden: Stockholm School of Economics, 1981), chapter 5.

50 Henry P. Conn and George S. Yip, 'Global Transfer of Critical Capabilities', *Business Horizons* 38 (January/February 1997): 22–31.

51 Arant R. Negandhi and Martin Welge, *Beyond Theory Z* (Greenwich, CT: JAI Press, 1984), 16.

52 Richard Pascale, 'Fitting New Employees into the Company Culture', *Fortune,* May 28, 1994, 28–40.

53 Michael R. Czinkota and Ilkka A. Ronkainen, 'International Business and Trade in the Next Decade: Report from a Delphi Study', *Journal of International Business Studies* 28 (no. 4, 1997): 676–694.

54 'Thinking for a Living', *The Economist,* January 21, 2006, 9–12.

55 R. J. Alsegg, *Control Relationships between American Corporations and Their European Subsidiaries,* AMA Research Study No. 107 (New York: American Management Association, 1971), 7.

56 Ron Edwards, Adlina Ahmad, and Simon Moss, 'Subsidiary Autonomy: The Case of Multinational Subsidiaries in Malaysia', *Journal of International Business Studies* 33 (no. 1, 2002): 183–191.

57 John J. Dyment, 'Strategies and Management Controls for Global Corporations', *Journal of Business Strategy* 7 (Spring 1987): 20–26.

58 Alfred M. Jaeger, 'The Transfer of Organizational Culture Overseas: An Approach to Control in the Multinational Corporation', *Journal of International Business Studies* 14 (Fall 1983): 91–106.

59 Michael Goold and Andrew Campbell, 'Do You Have a Well-Designed Organization?' *Harvard Business Review* 80 (March 2002): 117–124.

60 Michael C. Mankins and Richard Steele, 'Turning Great Strategy into Great Performance', *Harvard Business Review* 83 (July–August 2005): 65–72.

CHAPTER 8
RESEARCH

THE INTERNATIONAL **MARKETPLACE 8.1**

Marketing research findings may vary with the city

Companies rely on marketing research in order to obtain up-to-date and valuable information about their market. International firms, eager to appeal to China's consumer population, search for insight into trends, markets and the best locations. This helps to open up more and better opportunities in a hypercompetitive environment.

Many Chinese consumers see global brands as having higher quality, more financial resources, better marketing and more enhanced R&D than domestic brands. This perception alone puts foreign companies a step above domestic ones. However, knowing what kind of promotions appeal to specific consumer sectors in different locations is essential to convey the right message. Companies must have a clear understanding of which market segment has the greatest opportunities for them specifically – and decide, therefore, prior to entering China, which one to focus resources on.

Typically, foreign companies research and enter the four largest Chinese first-tier cities. These are Shanghai, Shenzhen, Guangzhou and Beijing, with a total population of 45 million.[1] They have well-established infrastructure, high economic development, excellent universities and are leaders in R&D. The dominant consumers in these four cities are characterized by several common dimensions. They are in their thirties, wealthy, well-educated, and with experience in technology. For them, company brand is a matter of pride.

This consumer information, however, is not necessarily reflective of the country as a whole. For instance, many of the third-tier cities are economically much less developed and have less infrastructure

but are growing rapidly. These localities are home to 130 million consumers who are less educated and less technologically educated. Although employees in third-tier cities earn a tenth of what their big-city counterparts do, their high cumulative spending power cannot be ignored. They are not so concerned with luxury and brand names and are very focused on the price and quality of products.

With the exception of Carrefour[2] and Metro and a few other foreign companies, Chinese domestic brands are the only ones targeting third-tier cities. For example, while Nike and Adidas monopolize Shanghai, Beijing, and Guangzhou, Li-Ning Sports Co. Ltd, a Beijing-based sportswear company, targets the smaller cities.

Li-Ning targets younger and older generations who pay more attention to promotions based on frugality and patriotism. Li-Ning offers premium sports shoes at about one-fourth the price of Nike, and with estimated millions of the National Basketball Association (NBA) fans in the country it has plenty of space to expand in the market. The firm targets male high school and university students ages 14 to 30 with active promotions and 'College 3-on-3 plus 1-on-1 challenge basketball games'. For the age group of 45 and over, it emphasizes the value of its product in more price-focused promotions.

The success of its strategy, aided by proper research, is evident in the reported annual sales increase of more than 30 per cent per year since 2001. Li-Ning has 97 per cent of its sales in China, but also works abroad. Therefore it promotes its brand as not only international, but affordable, which is the perfect combination for its market segments in China.

With custom-tailored promotions and a well-researched expansion into the not-yet saturated market of third-tier cities, international marketers may be able to achieve similar growth.

SOURCES: Michael Fielding, 'A Premium Niche; Buyers in China's Lesser Cities Like Giveaways, Promotions; Chinese Niche Market Focuses on Practical', *Marketing News*, October 1, 2005, 18; 'Li Ning: Anything is Possible', *China Daily*, September 13, 2003, **http://www.chinadaily.com.cn**.

Even though most managers recognize the need for domestic marketing research, the single most important cause for failure in the international marketplace is insufficient preparation and information. Major mistakes often occur because the firm and its managers do not have an adequate understanding of the business environment. Hindsight, however, does not lead to an automatic increase in international marketing research. Many firms either do not believe that international market research is worthwhile or face manpower and resource bottlenecks that impede such research. The increase in international marketing practice is also not reflected in the orientation of the articles published in key research journals.[3] Yet building a good knowledge base is a key condition for subsequent marketing success. To do so, one needs to accumulate data and information through research. Two basic forms of research are available to the firm: primary research, where data are collected for specific research purposes, and secondary research, where data that have already been collected are used. This chapter will first outline secondary research issues, focusing primarily on ways to obtain basic information quickly, ensuring that the information is reasonably accurate, and doing so with limited corporate resources. Later, primary research and its ways of answering more in-depth questions for the firm are covered, together with the development of a decision-support system.

DEFINING THE ISSUE

The American Marketing Association (AMA) defines marketing research as 'the function that links the consumer, customer and public to the marketer through information – information used to identify and define marketing opportunities and problems; generate, refine, and evaluate marketing actions; monitor marketing performance; and improve understanding of marketing as a process. Marketing research specifies the information required to address these issues, designs the method for collecting information, manages and implements the data collection process, analyzes the results, and communicates the findings and their implications'.[4]

This very broad statement highlights the fact that research is the link between marketer and market, without which marketing cannot function. It also emphasizes the fact that marketing actions need to be monitored and outlines the key steps of the research process.

Another definition states that marketing research is the 'systematic and objective identification, collection, analysis and dissemination for the purpose of improving decision making related to the identification and solution of problems and opportunities in marketing'.[5] This statement is more specific to research activities for several reasons: It highlights the need for systematic work, indicating that research should be the result of planned and organized activity rather than coincidence. It stresses the need for objectivity and information, reducing the roles of bias, emotions and subjective judgment. Finally, it addresses the need for the information to relate to specific problems. Marketing research cannot take place in a void; rather, it must have a business purpose.

International marketing research must also be linked to the decision-making process within the firm. The recognition that a situation requires action is the factor that initiates the decision-making process. The problem must then be defined. Often, symptoms are mistaken for causes; as a result, action determined by symptoms may be oriented in the wrong direction.

INTERNATIONAL AND DOMESTIC RESEARCH

The tools and techniques of international marketing research are said by some to be exactly the same as those of domestic marketing research, and only the environment differs. However, the environment is precisely what determines how well the tools, techniques and concepts apply to the international market. Although the objectives of marketing research may be the same, the execution of international research may differ substantially from the process of domestic research. As a result, entirely new tools and techniques may need to be developed. The four primary differences are new parameters, new environments, an increase in the number of factors involved, and a broader definition of competition.

New parameters

In crossing national borders, a firm encounters parameters not found in domestic marketing. Examples include duties, foreign currencies and changes in their value, different modes of transportation, international documentation, and port facilities. A firm that has done business only domestically will have had little or no prior experience with these requirements and conditions. Information about each of them must be obtained in order for management to make appropriate business decisions. New parameters also emerge because of differing forms of international operations. For example, a firm can export, it can licence its products, it can engage in a joint venture, or it can carry out foreign direct investment.

New environments

When deciding to go international in its marketing activities, a firm exposes itself to an unfamiliar environment. Many of the assumptions on which the firm was founded and on which its domestic activities were based may not hold true internationally. Firms need to learn about the culture of the host country and its demographics, understand its political system, determine its stability, and appreciate differences in societal structures and language. In addition, they must fully comprehend pertinent legal issues in the host country to avoid operating contrary to local legislation. They should also incorporate the technological level of the society in the marketing plan and understand the economic environment. In short, all the assumptions formulated over the years in the domestic market must be re-evaluated. This crucial point has often been neglected, because most managers were born into the environment of their domestic operations and have subconsciously learned to understand the constraints and opportunities of their business activities. The process is analogous to learning one's native language. Growing up with a language makes speaking it seem easy. Only in attempting to learn a foreign language do we begin to appreciate the complex structure of languages, the need for rules and the existence of different patterns.

Number of factors involved

Going international often means entering into more than one market. As a result, the number of changing dimensions increases geometrically. Even if every dimension is understood, management must also appreciate the interaction between them. Due to the sheer number of factors, coordination of the interaction becomes increasingly difficult. The international marketing research process can help management with this undertaking.

Broader definition of competition

By entering the international market, the firm exposes itself to a much greater variety of competition than existed in the domestic market. For example, when expanding the analysis of an island's food production from a local to an international level, fishery products compete not only with other fishery products but also with meat or even vegetarian substitutes. Similarly, firms that offer labour-saving devices in the domestic marketplace may suddenly face competition from cheap manual labour abroad. Therefore, the firm must, on an ongoing basis, determine the breadth of the competition, track the competitive activities, and, finally, evaluate the actual and potential impact on its own operations.

RECOGNIZING THE NEED FOR RESEARCH

To serve a market efficiently, firms must learn what customers want, why they want it, and how they go about filling their needs. To enter a market without conducting marketing research places firms, their assets, and their entire operation at risk. Even though most firms recognize the need for domestic marketing research, this need is not fully understood for international marketing activities. Often, decisions concerning entry and expansion into overseas markets and the selection and appointment of distributors are made after a cursory subjective assessment of the situation. The research done is less rigorous, less formal, and less quantitative than for domestic marketing activities. Many business executives appear to view foreign market research as relatively unimportant.

A major reason that firms are reluctant to engage in international marketing activities is the lack of sensitivity to differences in consumer tastes and preferences. Managers tend to assume that their methods are both best and acceptable to all others. This is fortunately not true. What a boring place the world would be if it were!

A second reason is a limited appreciation for the different marketing environments abroad. As *The International Marketplace 8.1* shows, international marketing research is essential to company success and growth. Often, managers incorrectly believe that national or geographic boundaries indicate cultural homogeneity. In addition, firms are not prepared to accept that distribution systems, industrial applications and uses, the availability of media, or advertising regulations may be entirely different from those in the home market. Barely aware of the differences, many firms are unwilling to spend money to find out about them.

A third reason is the lack of familiarity with national and international data sources and the inability to use them if obtained. As a result, the cost of conducting international marketing research is seen as prohibitively high and therefore not a worthwhile investment relative to the benefits to be gained.[6] There is wider information collection and more data availability, and the expanding research base also includes more countries than those traditionally researched in marketing, for example, European countries and China. In addition, the internet makes international marketing research much easier and much less expensive. Therefore, growing access to the internet around the world will make research more accessible as well.

Finally, firms often build up their international marketing activities gradually, frequently on the basis of unsolicited orders. Over time, actual business experience in a country or with specific firms may be used as a substitute for organized research.

Yet, international marketing research is important. It permits management to identify and develop strategies for internationalization. This task includes the identification, evaluation and comparison of potential foreign market opportunities and subsequent market selection. Second, research is necessary for the development of a marketing plan. The requirements for successful market entry and market penetration need to be determined. Subsequently, the research should define the appropriate marketing mix for each international market and should maintain continuous feedback in order to fine-tune the various marketing elements. Finally, research can provide management with foreign market intelligence to help it anticipate events, take appropriate action and prepare for global changes.

THE BENEFITS OF RESEARCH

To carry out international research, firms require resources in terms of both time and money. For the typical smaller firm, those two types of resources are its most precious and scarce commodities. To make a justifiable case for allocating resources to international marketing research, management must understand what that value of research will be. This is even more important for international market research than for domestic market research because the cost tends to be higher. The value of research in making a particular decision may be determined by applying the following equation:

$$V(dr) - V(d) > C(r)$$

where

   $V(dr)$ is the value of the decision with the benefit of research;

   $V(d)$ is the value of the decision without the benefit of research;

and

   $C(r)$ is the cost of research.

Obviously, the value of the decision with the benefit of research should be greater than the value of the decision without research, and the value increase should exceed the cost of the research. Otherwise, international marketing research would be a waste of resources. It may be difficult to quantify the individual values because often the risks and benefits are not easy to ascertain. Realistically, companies and their marketing researchers are often quite pragmatic: their research decisions are guided by research objectives, but constrained by resources.[7] The use of decision theory permits a comparison of alternative research strategies.[8]

DETERMINING RESEARCH OBJECTIVES

Research objectives will vary from firm to firm because of the views of management, the corporate mission, and the marketing situation. In addition, the information needs of firms are closely linked with the level of existing international expertise. The firm may therefore wish to start out by determining its internal level of readiness to participate in the global market. This includes a general review of corporate capabilities such as personnel resources and the degree of financial exposure and risk that the firm is willing and able to tolerate. Existing diagnostic tools can be used to compare a firm's current preparedness on a broad-based level.[9] Knowing its internal readiness, the firm can then pursue its objectives with more confidence.

Going international: Exporting

The most frequent objective of international market research is that of foreign market opportunity analysis. When a firm launches its international activities, basic information is needed to identify and compare key alternatives. The aim is not to conduct a painstaking and detailed analysis of the world on a market-by-market basis but instead to utilize a broad-brush approach. Accomplished quickly at low cost, this can narrow down the possibilities for international marketing activities. There are 195 countries in the world,[10] and an evaluation of each one is difficult and time-consuming. There are two ways to evaluate foreign markets, country ranking and clustering, and both should be used. Indexing and ranking countries by their market appeal to a specific business or project is the first step. Clustering countries into similar groups for screening and evaluation is essential for further development and planning of strategies once a specific country is chosen.[11]

Such an approach should begin with a cursory analysis of general market variables such as total and per capita GDP, GDP growth, mortality rates, and population figures. Although these factors in themselves will not provide detailed market information, they will enable the researcher to determine whether the corporation's objectives might be met in those markets. For example, expensive labour-saving consumer products may not be successful in the People's Republic of China because their price may be a significant proportion of the annual salary of the customer, and the perceived benefit to the customer may be only minimal. Such cursory evaluation will help reduce the number of markets to be considered to a more manageable number – for example, from 195 to 25.

Next, the researcher will require information about each individual market for a preliminary evaluation. This information typically identifies the fastest-growing markets, the largest markets for a particular product, market trends, and market restrictions. Although precise and detailed information for each product probably cannot be obtained, it is available for general product categories.

Government restrictions on markets must be also considered. For example, the large population of China would have presented a great market for citrus imports from its relatively close neighbour, Australia. However, due to a citrus canker outbreak in Australia, the importation of its citrus fruit has been prohibited by the Chinese government.[12] A cursory overview will screen markets quickly and reduce the number of markets subject to closer investigation.

At this stage, the researcher must select appropriate markets. The emphasize will shift to focus on market opportunities for a specific product or brand, including existing, latent, and incipient markets. Even though the aggregate industry data have already been obtained,

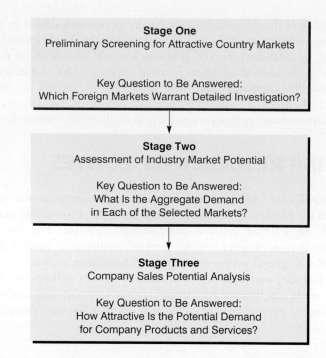

Stage One
Preliminary Screening for Attractive Country Markets

Key Question to Be Answered:
Which Foreign Markets Warrant Detailed Investigation?

Stage Two
Assessment of Industry Market Potential

Key Question to Be Answered:
What Is the Aggregate Demand
in Each of the Selected Markets?

Stage Three
Company Sales Potential Analysis

Key Question to Be Answered:
How Attractive Is the Potential Demand
for Company Products and Services?

general information is insufficient to make company-specific decisions. For example, the market demand for medical equipment should not be confused with the potential demand for a specific brand. In addition, the research should identify demand-and-supply patterns and evaluate any regulations and standards. Finally, a competitive assessment needs to be made that matches markets with corporate strengths and provides an analysis of the best market potential for specific products. Exhibit 8.1 offers a summary of the various stages in the determination of market potential.

Going international: Importing

When importing, firms shift their major focus from supplying to sourcing. Management must identify markets that produce desired supplies or materials or that have the potential to do so. Foreign firms must be evaluated in terms of their capabilities and competitive standing.

The importer needs to know, for example, about the reliability of a foreign supplier, the consistency of its product or service quality, and the length of delivery time. Information obtained through the subsidiary office of a bank or through one's embassy can be very helpful. Information from business rating services and recommendations from current customers are also very useful in evaluating the potential business partner.

In addition, government rules must be scrutinized as to whether exportation from the source country is possible. For example, India may set limits on the cobra handbags it allows to be exported, and laws protecting cultural heritage may prevent the exportation of pre-Columbian artifacts from Latin American countries. The international manager must also analyze domestic restrictions and legislation that may prohibit the importation of certain goods into the home country. Even though a market may exist in France for foreign umbrella handles, for example, quotas may restrict their importation in order to protect domestic industries. Similarly, even though domestic demand may exist for ivory, its importation may be illegal because of worldwide legislation enacted to protect wildlife. Firms must also consider the risks of imports, such as disruption or terrorism. Such occurrences can cause major dislocations in corporate planning and order fulfillment.

Market expansion

Research objectives may include obtaining detailed information for penetrating a market, for designing and fine-tuning the marketing mix, or for monitoring the political climate of a country so that the firm can expand its operation successfully. The better defined the research objective is, the better the researcher will be able to determine the information requirements and thus conserve time and financial resources of the firm.

DETERMINING SECONDARY INFORMATION REQUIREMENTS

Using the research objective as a guide, the researcher will be able to pinpoint the type of information needed. For example, if only general initial market information is required, macro data such as world population statistics will be sufficient. If research is to identify market restraints, then information is required about international accords and negotiations in the WTO. Alternatively, broad product category, production, and trade figures may be desired in order to pinpoint general market activities. For the fine-tuning of a marketing mix, very specific detailed product data may be necessary. This often entails gathering data on both a macro and micro level. On the macro level, these are typically tariff and non-tariff information and data on government trade policy. On the micro level, these tend to be data on local laws and regulations, local standards and specifications, distribution systems and competitive activities.

Sources of data

Secondary data for international marketing research purposes are available from a wide variety of sources. The major ones are briefly reviewed here. In addition, Appendix A to this chapter lists a wide variety of publications and organizations that monitor international issues.

Governments Of all data sources, governments typically have the greatest variety of data available. This information provided by governments addresses either macro or micro issues or offers specific data services. Macro information includes population trends, general trade flows between countries, and world agricultural production. Micro information includes materials on specific industries in a country, their growth prospects, and their foreign trade activities. Specific data services might provide custom-tailored information responding to the detailed needs of a firm. Alternatively, some data services may concentrate on a specific geographic region. More information about selected government publications and research services is presented in Appendix A to this chapter. *The International Marketplace* 8.2 explains some of the information services offered by the European Union.

Most countries have a wide array of national and international trade data available. Increasingly these data are available on the internet, which makes them much more current than ever before. Closer collaboration between governmental statistical agencies also makes the data more accurate and reliable, since it is now much easier to compare data such as bilateral exports and imports to each other. These information sources are often available at embassies and consulates, whose mission includes the enhancement of trade activities. A country's commercial counsellor or commercial attaché can provide the information available from these sources.

International Organizations International organizations often provide useful data for the researcher. The *Statistical Yearbook* produced by the United Nations (UN) contains international trade data on products and provides information on exports and imports by country. Due to the time needed for worldwide data collection, the information is often dated. Additional information is compiled and made available by specialized substructures of the UN. Some of these are the UN Conference on Trade and Development (**http://www.unctad.org**), which concentrates primarily on international issues surrounding developing nations, such as debt and market access; the UN Centre on Transnational Corporations; and the International Trade Centre (**http://www.intracen.org**). The *World Atlas*, published by the World Bank (**http://www.worldbank.org**), provides useful general data on population, growth trends and GDP figures. The World Trade Organization (**http://www.wto.org**) and the

THE INTERNATIONAL **MARKETPLACE 8.2**

Secondary data sources in Europe

With the expanding economic and political union within Europe, official information resources are becoming more centralized. A short sampling of government sources of information helpful to international managers targeting the EU are reviewed below. All of them are accessible through EUROPA (**http://europa.eu.int**), which is the portal site of the European Union.

News

'News' is aimed principally at journalists and other people professionally involved in the information industry. It contains links to the virtual press rooms of the various EU institutions and information on major upcoming events.

Activities

'Activities' sets out the Union's activities by subject, giving an overview of the policies as well as more detailed information for students and professionals.

Institutions

'Institutions' provides a general introduction to each of the institutions and to European decision-making procedures. It also contains links to the institutions' homepages.

The EU at a glance

'The EU at a glance' is aimed at the general public and sets out to provide clear answers to key questions concerning such things as the objectives of the European Union, European citizens' rights and the history of the EU.

Official documents

'Official documents' provides access to the conclusions of European Councils, the General Report on the activities of the European Union, and the Bulletin of the European Union. Other documents, such as the Official Journal, the Treaties, and documents on current legislation and legislation under preparation may be obtained via EUR-Lex.

Services

'Services' is a gateway to various databases, information services, and official publications about the European Union. It also provides access to the latest statistics and the list of information relays in the European Union.

SOURCE: EUROPA – Gateway to the European Union, **http://europa.eu.int/index_en.htm** (Accessed June 8, 2009).

Organization for Economic Cooperation and Development (OECD) (**http://www.oecd.org**) also publish quarterly and annual trade data on their member countries. Organizations such as the International Monetary Fund (**http://www.imf.org**) and the World Bank publish summary economic data and occasional staff papers that evaluate region- or country-specific issues in depth.

Service Organizations A wide variety of service organizations that may provide information include banks, accounting firms, freight forwarders, airlines and international trade consultants. Frequently, they are able to provide data on business practices, legislative or regulatory requirements and political stability as well as basic trade data. Although some of this information is available without charge, its basic intent is to serve as an 'appetiser'. Much of the initial information is quite general in nature; more detailed answers often require an appropriate fee.

Trade Associations Associations such as world trade clubs and domestic and international chambers of commerce (for example, the European Chamber of Commerce in each country) can provide valuable information about local markets. Often, files are maintained on international trade issues and trends affecting international marketers. Useful information can also be obtained from industry associations. These groups, formed to represent entire industry segments, often collect from their members a wide variety of data that are then published in an aggregate form. The information provided is often quite general in nature because of the wide variety of clientele served. It can provide valuable initial insights into international markets, since it permits a benchmarking effort through which the international marketer can establish how it is faring when compared to its competition. For example, an industry summary that indicates firm average exports to be 10 per cent of sales, and export sales growth to take place mainly in Asia, allows a better evaluation of a specific firm's performance by the international marketer.

Directories and Newsletters Many industry directories are available on local, national and international levels. These directories primarily serve to identify firms and to provide very general background information such as the name of the chief executive officer, the address and telephone number, and some information about a firm's products. The quality of a directory depends, of course, on the quality of input and the frequency of updates. Some of the directories are becoming increasingly sophisticated and can provide quite detailed information to the researcher.

Many newsletters are devoted to specific international issues such as international trade finance, international contracting, bartering, countertrade, international payment flows and customs news. Published by banks or accounting firms in order to keep their clientele current on international developments, newsletters usually cater to narrow audiences but can provide important information to the firm interested in a specific area.

Electronic Information Services When information is needed, managers often cannot spend a lot of time, energy or money finding, sifting through and categorizing existing materials. Consider labouring through every copy of a trade publication to find out the latest news on how environmental concerns are affecting marketing decisions in Mexico. With electronic information services, search results can be obtained almost immediately. International online computer database services, numbering in the thousands, can be purchased to supply information external to the firm, such as exchange rates, international news and import restrictions. Most database hosts do not charge any sign-up fee and request payment only for actual use. The selection of initial database hosts depends on the choice of relevant databases, taking into account their product and market limitations, language used and geographical location.

A large number of databases and search engines provide information about products and markets. Many of the main news agencies through online databases provide information about events that affect certain markets. Some databases cover extensive lists of companies in given countries and the products they buy and sell. A large number of databases exist that cover various categories of trade statistics. The main economic indicators of the EU, UN, IMF and OECD are available online. Standards institutes in most of the G8 nations (Canada, France, Germany, Italy, Japan, Russia, United Kingdom and the United States) provide online access to their databases of technical standards and trade regulations on specific products.

In the United Kingdom, the Export Credits Guarantee Department helps exporters of UK goods and services to win business, and UK firms to invest overseas, by providing guarantees, insurance and reinsurance against loss, taking into account the government's wider international policy agenda. Its activities involve underwriting long term loans to support the sale of capital goods, principally for the export of military equipment, but also for aircraft, bridges, machinery and services; it also helps UK companies take part in major overseas projects.[13]

Using data services for research means that researchers do not have to leave their offices, going from library to library to locate the facts they need. Many online services have late-breaking information available within 24 hours. These research techniques are cost-effective as well. Stocking a company's library with all the books needed to have the same amount of data that is available online or with CD-ROM would be too expensive and space-consuming. However, there are also drawbacks. In spite of the ease of access to data on the internet, search engines cover only a portion of international publications. They are also heavily biased toward the English-language. As a result, sole reliance on electronic information may cause the researcher to lose out on valuable input.[14] Electronic databases should therefore be seen as only one important dimension of research scrutiny.

Other Firms Often, other firms can provide useful information for international marketing purposes. Firms appear to be more open about their international rather than their domestic marketing activities. On some occasions, valuable information can also be obtained from foreign firms and distributors.

Evaluating Data

Before obtaining secondary data, the researcher needs to evaluate their appropriateness for the task at hand. As the first step of such an evaluation, the quality of the data source needs to be considered with a primary focus on the purpose and method of the original data collection. Next, the quality of the actual data needs to be assessed, which should include a determination of data accuracy, reliability and recency. Obviously, outdated data may mislead rather than improve the decision-making process. In addition, the compatibility and comparability of the data need to be considered. Since they were collected with another purpose in mind, we need to determine whether the data can help with the issue of concern to the firm. In international research it is also important to ensure that data categories are comparable to each other in order to avoid misleading conclusions. For example, the term *middle class* is likely to have very different implications for income and consumption patterns in different parts of the world. In the UK, the middle class comprises 'wealthy families and individuals with independent incomes from stocks and shares – such as the family portrayed in *The Forsyte Saga* – all those in the professions, including school teachers, and those 'non-manual' employees whose earnings may not have been much higher than those of the skilled working class, but whose employment placed them in the lower middle class'.[15] In contrast, a study by the German Institute for Economic Research (DIW) defined middle class purely from an economic standpoint, according to household income, taking no account of education, occupation or other social indicators. The researchers define the middle class as those whose income falls between 70 and 150 per cent of this median.[16]

Analysing and interpreting secondary data

After the data have been obtained, the researcher must use his or her research creativity to make good use of them. This often requires the combination and cross tabulation of various sets of data or the use of proxy information in order to arrive at conclusions that address the research objectives. A proxy variable is a substitute for a variable that one cannot directly measure. For example, the market penetration of personal music devices, such as the iPod, can be used as an indicator of the number of tracks that can be sold online. Similarly, in an industrial setting, information about plans for new port facilities may be useful in determining future containerization requirements. The level of computerization of a society may also indicate the future need for software.

The researcher must go beyond the scope of the data and use creative inferences to arrive at knowledge useful to the firm. However, such creativity brings risks. Once the analysis and interpretation have taken place, a consistency check must be conducted. The researcher should always cross-check the results with other possible sources of information or with experts.

In addition, the researcher should take another look at the research methods employed and, based on their usefulness, determine any necessary modifications for future projects. This will make possible the continuous improvement of international market research activities and enables the corporation to learn from experience.

Data Privacy The attitude of society towards obtaining and using both secondary and primary data must be taken into account. Many societies are increasingly sensitive to the issue of data privacy, and the concern has grown exponentially as a result of e-business. Readily accessible databases may contain information valuable to marketers, but they may also be considered privileged by individuals who have provided the data. The European Union has passed a number of regulations on privacy and electronic communications. These maintain high standards of data privacy to ensure the free flow of data throughout its member states.

For example, the European Union requires member states to block transmission of data to non-EU countries if these countries do not have domestic legislation that provides for a level of protection judged adequate by the European Union. These laws restrict access to lifestyle information and its use for segmentation purposes. It is particularly difficult for direct marketers to obtain international access to electoral rolls, birth records, or mortgage information.[17] It is important to be aware of the differences in terms of data privacy in each region or country. For example, the EU law permits companies to collect personal data only if the individuals consent to the collection, know how the data will be used, and have access to databases to correct or erase their information. In contrast, there is no general data-protection law in China and very few laws that limit government interference with collection, use and disclosure of personal information.[18] In India too, there is currently no general national data protection law; protection is provided on an uneven basis through sectoral enactments such as the 1993 *Public Financial Institutions Act* and licencing of ISPs under national telecommunications legislation.[19]

In order to settle conflicts between divergent government policies, companies are increasingly likely to encourage global privacy rules for managing information online and to seek international certification to reassure users. Overall, the international marketer must pay careful attention to the privacy laws and expectations in different nations and to possible consumer reactions to the use of data in the marketing effort.

THE PRIMARY RESEARCH PROCESS

Primary research is conducted to fill specific information needs. The research may not actually be conducted by the firm with the need, but the work must be carried out for a specific research purpose. Primary research therefore goes beyond the activities of secondary data collection, which often cannot supply answers to the specific questions posed. Conducting primary research internationally can be complex due to different environments, attitudes and market conditions. Yet, it is precisely because of these differences that such research is necessary. Nonetheless, at this time, marketing research is still mainly concentrated in the industrialized nations of the world. The global marketing research turnover was £15.9 billion in 2005.[20] In addition, over two-thirds of market research turnover was generated in the top five markets: the US (£5.2 billion); the UK (£1.6 billion); France (£1.53 billion); Germany (£1.49 billion) and Japan (£953 million).

Primary research is essential for the formulation of strategic marketing plans. One particular area of research interest is international market segmentation. Historically, firms segmented international markets based on macro variables such as income per capita or consumer spending on certain product categories. Increasingly, however, firms recognize that segmentation variables, such as lifestyles, attitudes, or personality, can play a major role in identifying similar consumer groups in different countries, which can then be targeted across borders. One such group could consist, for example, of educationally elite readers who read *The Financial Times* and *The Economist*. Members in this group are likely to have more in common with one another than with their fellow citizens.[21] Alternatively, in marketing to women, it is important to understand the degree to which they have entered the workforce in a country and how women in different economic segments make or influence purchase decisions. In order to identify these groups and to devise ways of meeting their needs, primary international market research is indispensable.

Determining information requirements

Specific research questions must be formulated to determine precisely the information that is sought. The following are examples of such marketing questions:

- What is the market potential for our furniture in Indonesia?

- How much does the typical Nigerian consumer spend on soft drinks?

- What will happen to demand in Brazil if we raise our product price along monthly inflation levels?

● What effect will a new type of packaging have on our 'green' consumers in Germany, France, and the UK?

Only when information requirements are determined as precisely as possible will the researcher be able to develop a research programme that will deliver a useful product.

Industrial versus consumer research

The researcher must decide whether to conduct research with consumers or with industrial users. This decision will in part determine the size of the universe and respondent accessibility. For example, consumers are usually a very large group and can be reached through interviews at home or through intercept techniques. On the other hand, the total population of industrial users may be smaller and more difficult to reach. Further, cooperation by respondents may be quite different, ranging from very helpful to very limited. In the industrial setting, differentiating between users and decision makers may be much more important because their personality, their outlook and their evaluative criteria may differ widely.

Determining research administration

The major issues in determining who will do the research are whether to use a centralized, coordinated or decentralized approach and whether to engage an outside research service.

Degree of Research Centralization The level of control that corporation headquarters exercises over international marketing research activities is a function of the overall organizational structure of the firm and the nature and importance of the decision to be made. The three major approaches to international research are the centralized, coordinated and decentralized approaches.

The centralized approach clearly affords the most control to headquarters. All research specifications such as focus, thrust and design are directed by the home office and are forwarded to the local country operations for implementation. The subsequent analysis of data again takes place at headquarters. Such an approach can be quite valuable when international marketing research is intended to influence corporate policies and strategy. It also ensures that all international market studies remain comparable to one another. On the other hand, some risks exist. For example, headquarters management may not be sufficiently familiar with the local market situation to be able to adapt the research appropriately. The headquarters' cultural bias may also influence the research activities. Finally, headquarters staff may be too small or insufficiently skilled to provide proper guidance for multiple international marketing research studies.

A coordinated research approach uses an intermediary such as an outside research agency to bring headquarters and country operations together. This approach provides for more interaction and review of the international marketing research plan by both headquarters and the local operations and ensures more responsiveness to both strategic and local concerns. If the intermediary used is of high quality, the research capabilities of a corporation can be greatly enhanced through a coordinated approach.

The decentralized approach requires corporate headquarters to establish the broad thrust of research activities and to then delegate the further design and implementation to the specific countries. The entire research is then carried out locally under the supervision of the specific country operation, and only a final report is provided to headquarters. This approach has particular value when international markets differ significantly, because it permits detailed adaptation to local circumstances. However, implementing research activities on a country-by-country basis may cause unnecessary duplication, lack of knowledge transference and lack of comparable results.

A country's operations may not be aware of research carried out by corporate units in other countries and may reinvent the wheel. This problem can be avoided if a proper intra-corporate flow of information exists so that local units can check whether similar information has already been collected elsewhere within the firm. Corporate units that operate in markets similar to one another can then benefit from the exchange of research findings.

Local units may also develop their own research thrusts, tools and analyzes. A researcher in one country may, for example, develop a creative way of dealing with a non-response problem. This new technique could be valuable to company researchers who face similar difficulties in other countries. However, for the technique to become widely known, systems must be in place to circulate information to the firm as a whole.

Finally, if left to their own devices, researchers will develop different ways of collecting and tabulating data. As a result, findings in different markets may not be comparable and potentially valuable information about major changes and trends may be lost to the corporation.

International marketing research activities will always be carried out subject to the organizational structure of a firm. Ideally, a middle ground between centralization and decentralization will be found, one that permits local flexibility together with an ongoing exchange of information within the corporation. As the extent of a firm's international activities grows, the exchange of information becomes particularly important, because global rather than local optimization is the major goal of the multinational corporation.

Outside Research Services   One major factor in deciding whether or not to use outside research services is, of course, the size of the international operations of a firm. No matter how large a firm is, however, it is unlikely to possess specialized expertise in international marketing research for every single market it currently serves or is planning to serve. Rather than overstretch the capabilities of its staff or assert a degree of expertise that does not exist, a corporation may wish to delegate the research task to outside groups. This is particularly the case when corporate headquarters have little or no familiarity with the local research environment. Exhibit 8.2 provides an example of such a situation. The use of outside research agencies may be especially appropriate for large-scale international marketing research or when highly specialized research skills are required. Increasingly, marketing research agencies operate worldwide, in order to accommodate the research needs of their clients. Exhibit 8.3[22] provides information about the top 25 global research organizations and their international activities.

The selection process for outside research providers should emphasize the quality of information rather than the cost. Low price is no substitute for data pertinence or accuracy.

Before a decision is made, the capabilities of an outside organization should be carefully evaluated and compared with the capabilities available in-house and from competing firms. Although general technical capabilities are important, the prime selection criterion should be previous research experience in a particular country and a particular industry. Some experience is transferable from one industry or country to another; however, the more the corporation's research needs overlap with an agency's past research accomplishment, the more likely it is that the research task will be carried out satisfactorily. Although the research may be more difficult to administer, multinational corporations should consider subcontracting each major international marketing research task to specialists, even if research within one country is carried out by various international marketing research agencies as a result. To have experts working on a problem is usually more efficient than to conserve corporate resources by centralizing all research activities with one service provider, who is only marginally familiar with key aspects of the research. However, if different firms carry out the research, it becomes very important to ensure that data are comparable. Otherwise, the international firm will not be able to transfer lessons learned from one market to another.

Determining the research technique

Selection of the research technique depends on a variety of factors. First, the objectivity of the data sought must be determined. Standardized techniques are more useful in the collection of objective data than of subjective data. *Unstructured data* will require more open-ended questions and more time than structured data. Since the willingness and ability of respondents to spend the time and provide a free-form response are heavily influenced by factors such as culture and education, the prevailing conditions in the country and segments to be studied need to be understood in making these decisions. Whether the data are to be collected in the real world or in a controlled environment also must be decided. Finally, a decision needs

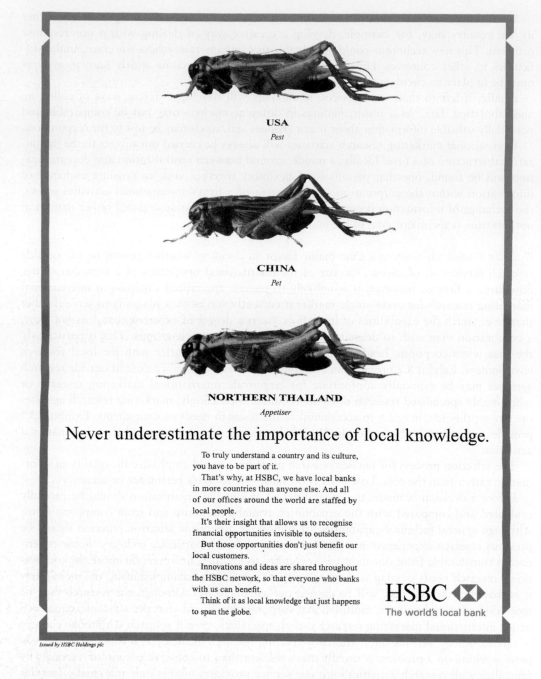

to be made as to whether the research is to collect historical facts or gather information about future developments. This is particularly important for consumer research because firms frequently desire to determine consumers' future intentions to purchase a certain product.

Cultural and individual preferences, which vary significantly among nations, play a major role in determining research techniques. Some managers frequently prefer to gather large quantities of hard data through surveys, which provide numbers that can be manipulated statistically and directly compared to other sets of data. In contrast, other managers prefer the 'soft' approach. For example, much of Japanese-style market research relies heavily on two kinds of information: soft data obtained from visits to dealers and other channel members and hard data about shipments, inventory levels and retail sales.

Once the structure of the type of data sought has been determined, a choice must be made among the types of research instruments available. Each provides a different depth of information and has its unique strengths and weaknesses.

EXHIBIT 8.3   Top 25 global market research firms, 2008

Rank 2008	Rank 2007	Organization Website (www)	Parent Country Headquarters	No. of Countries with Subsidiaries/ Branch Offices[1]	Research Only Full-time Employees[4]	Global Research Revenues[2] (U.S. $, in millions)	% Change From 2007[3]	Revenue From Outside Home Country U.S. $, (Millions)	Per cent of Total
1	1	The Nielsen Company nielsen.com	USA	108	34,516	$ 4,382.2	4.4%	$ 2,344.0	51.2%
2	–	The Kantar Group*	U.K.	80	21,510	3,491.2	3.6	2,722.6	75.3
–	5	*The Kantar Group**	*U.K.*	61	6,950	1,471.9	3.0	1,000.6	66.0
–	3	*Taylor Nelson Sofres Plc.* kantargroup.com	*U.K.*	80	14,560	2,019.3	4.0	1,722.0	82.0
3	2	IMS Health Inc. imshealth.com	USA	76	7,500	2,301.9	1.2	1,487.5	63.9
4	4	GFK SE gfk.com	Germany	57	9,692	1,703.5	5.5	1,389.1	77.3
5	6	Ipsos Group S.A. ipsos.com	France	64	9,094	1,337.8	7.8	1,283.5	89.0
6	7	Synovate synovate.com	U.K.	61	6,746	939.4	2.3	817.3	85.1
7	8	IRI infores.com	USA	8	3,600	708.7	2.3	271.0	37.4
8	9	Westat westat.com	USA	1	1,998	467.4	0.5		
9	10	Arbitron Inc. arbitron.com	USA	2	1,116	338.5	9.0	4.4	1.2
10	11	INTAGE Inc.** intage.co.jp	Japan	3	1,779	320.3	3.7	3.8	1.1
11	12	J.D. Power and Associates* jdpa.com	USA	9	850	266.3	2.2	83.6	30.7
12	14	Maritz Research maritzresearch.com	USA	4	756	224.9	2.6	33.3	14.4
13	16	Opinion Research Corp. opinionresearch.com	USA	5	485	228.4	–0.3	82.4	36.2
14	15	The NPD Group Inc. npd.com		13	1,090	212.2	6.6	57.6	25.5

Rank 2008	Rank 2007	Organization Website (www)	Parent Country Head-quarters	No. of Countries with Subsidiaries/ Branch Offices[1]	Research Only Full-time Employees[4]	Global Research Revenues[2] (U.S. $, in millions)	% Change From 2007[3]	Revenue From Outside Home Country U.S. $, (Millions)	Revenue From Outside Home Country Per cent of Total
15	13	Harris Interactive Inc. harrisinteractive.com	USA	7	899	$ 248.6	10.8%	84.7	38.2
16	17	Video Research Ltd.** videor.co.jp	Japan	3	393	193.1	−2.5	0.2	0.1
17	18	IBOPE Group ibope.com.br	Brazil	12	1,884	123.9	28.3	35.7	22.5
18	20	comScore Inc. comscore.com	USA	5	581	92.7	26.7	16.5	14.1
19	21	Cello Research & Consulting cellogroup.co.uk	U.K.	2	451	90.7	8.9	39.3	39.8
20	22	Market Strategies International marketstrategies.com	USA	3	307	89.7	3.5	14.7	15.9
21	19	Lieberman Research Worldwide lrwonline.com	USA	4	324	87.5	3.0	16.4	18.2
22	–	Mediametrie mediametrie.fr	France	1	515	80.9	5.6	9.4	11.0
23	23	BVA Group bva.com	France	4	742	81.5	3.0	9.0	10.7
24	–	You Gov Plc. Yougov.com	U.K.	9	474	69.7	18.9	58.8	71.0
25	25	Dentsu Research Inc. dentsuresearch.com	Japan	1	163	68.0	0.3	0.2	0.3
		Total			107.465	$18,148.4	3.9%	$10,865.0	57.6%

*Estimated by IR
**For fiscal year ending March 2009.
[1] Includes countries which have subsidiaries with an equity interest or branch offices, or both.
[2] Total revenues that include non-research activities for some companies are significantly higher. This information is given in the individual company profiles.
[3] Rate of growth from year to year has been adjusted so as not to include revenue gains or losses from acquisitions or divestitures. Rate of growth is based on home country currency and includes currency exchange effects.
[4] Includes some non-research employees.

Sources: *Marketing News*, August 30, 2009. **http://www.demoskopia.com.br/TOP252008.html**

Interviews Interviews with knowledgeable persons can be of great value to a corporation desiring international marketing information. Because bias from the individual may be part of the findings, the intent should be to obtain in-depth information rather than a wide variety of data. Particularly when specific answers are sought to very narrow questions, interviews can be most useful.

Focus Groups Focus groups are a useful research tool resulting in interactive interviews. A group of informed persons is gathered for a limited period of time (two to four hours). Usually, the ideal size for a focus group is seven to ten participants. A specific topic is introduced and thoroughly discussed by all group members. Due to the interaction, hidden issues are sometimes raised that would not have been addressed in an individual interview. The skill of the group leader in stimulating discussion is crucial to the success of a focus group. Discussions are often recorded on tape and subsequently analyzed in detail. Focus groups, like in-depth interviews, do not provide statistically significant information; however, they can be helpful in providing information about perceptions, emotions and other non-overt factors. In addition, once individuals are gathered, focus groups are highly efficient in terms of rapidly accumulating a substantial amount of information. With the advances occurring in the communications field, focus groups can also be carried out internationally, with interaction between groups.

When conducting international research via focus groups, the researcher must be aware of the importance of culture in the discussion process. Not all societies encourage frank and open exchange and disagreement among individuals. Status consciousness may result in situations in which the opinion of one is reflected by all other participants. Disagreement may be seen as impolite or certain topics may be taboo.

Observation Observation techniques require the researcher to play the role of a nonparticipating observer of activity and behaviour. Observation can be personal or impersonal – for example, mechanical. Observation can be obtrusive or inobtrusive, depending on whether the subject is aware or unaware of being observed. In international marketing research, observation can be extremely useful in shedding light on practices not previously encountered or understood. This aspect is particularly valuable for the researcher who is totally unfamiliar with a market or market situation, and can be quickly achieved through, for example, participation in a trade mission. Finding employees with personal experience and observations about international markets can be very beneficial for employers.

Observation can also help in understanding phenomena that would have been difficult to assess with other techniques. For example, Toyota sent a group of its engineers and designers to southern California to unobtrusively observe how women get into and operate their cars. They found that women with long fingernails have trouble opening the door and operating various knobs on the dashboard. Based on their observations, Toyota engineers and designers were able to observe the women's plight and redraw some of the automobile exterior and interior designs.[23]

Conducting observations can also have its pitfalls. For example, people may react differently to the discovery that their behaviour has been observed. The degree to which the observer has to be familiarized or introduced to other participants may vary. The complexity of the task may differ due to the use of multiple languages. To conduct in-store research in Europe, for example, store checks, photo audits of shelves and store interviews must be scheduled well in advance and need to be preceded by a full round of introductions of the researchers to store management and personnel. In some countries, such as Belgium, a researcher must remember that four different languages are spoken and their use may change from store to store.

The research instruments discussed so far – interviews, focus groups and observation – are useful primarily for gathering qualitative data. The intent is not to amass data or to search for statistical significance, but rather to obtain a better understanding of given situations, behavioural patterns, or underlying dimensions. The researcher using these instruments must be cautioned that even frequent repetition of the measurements will not lead to a statistically valid result. Yet, statistical validity often is not the major focus of corporate international marketing research. Rather, it is the better understanding, description, and prediction of events that have an impact on marketing decision making. When quantitative data are desired, surveys are appropriate research instruments.

Surveys   Survey research is useful in providing the opportunity to quantify concepts. In the social sciences, the cross-cultural survey is generally accepted as a powerful method of hypothesis testing. Surveys are usually conducted via questionnaires that are administered personally, by mail, or by telephone. Use of the survey technique presupposes that the population under study is able to comprehend and respond to the questions posed. Particularly in the case of mail and telephone surveys, a major precondition is also the feasibility of using the postal system or the widespread availability of telephones. In many countries, only limited records are available about dwellings, their location, and their occupants. In Venezuela, for example, most houses are not numbered but rather are given individual names like 'Casa Rosa' or 'El Retiro'. In some countries, street maps are not even available, for example, in the rural areas. As a result, it becomes virtually impossible to reach respondents by mail.

In other countries, obtaining a correct address may be easy, but the postal system may not function well. The Italian postal service, for example, has suffered from scandals that exposed such practices as selling undelivered mail to paper mills for recycling.

Telephone surveys may also be inappropriate if telephone ownership is rare. In such instances, any information obtained would be highly biased even if the researcher randomizes the calls. In some instances, telephone networks and systems may also prevent the researcher from conducting surveys. Frequent line congestion and a lack of telephone directories, for example, in France.[24] There are also great variations between countries or regions of countries in terms of unlisted telephone numbers (or a user has to request to be an ex-directory number). For example, the percentage of households with unlisted telephone numbers varies widely by country and even city – nearly half of households with a landline in the UK now have an ex-directory number.[25]

Surveys can be hampered by social and cultural constraints. Recipients of letters may be illiterate or may be reluctant to respond in writing. In some nations, entire population segments – for example, women – may be totally inaccessible to interviewers. One must also assess the purpose of the survey in the context of the population surveyed. It has been argued, for example, that one should not rely on consumer surveys for new product development information. Key reasons are the absence of responsibility – the consumer is sincere when spending but not when talking; conservative attitudes – ordinary consumers are conservative and tend to react negatively to a new product; vanity – it is human nature to exaggerate and put on a good appearance; and insufficient information – the research results depend on the product characteristics information that is given to survey participants and that may be incomplete or unabsorbed.[26]

In spite of all these difficulties, however, the survey technique remains a useful one because it allows the researcher to rapidly accumulate a large quantity of data amenable to statistical analysis. Even though quite difficult, international comparative research has been carried out very successfully between nations, particularly if the environments studied are sufficiently similar so that the impact of uncontrollable macrovariables is limited. However, even in environments that are quite dissimilar, in-depth comparative research can be carried out.[27] Doing so may require a country-by-country adjustment of details while preserving the similarity of research thrust. For example, researchers have reported good results in mail surveys conducted simultaneously in Switzerland and the United Kingdom after adjusting the size of the return envelope, outgoing envelope, address style, signature, and cover letter to meet specific societal expectations.[28] With constantly expanding technological capabilities, international marketers will be able to use the survey technique more frequently in the future. Exhibit 8.4 provides an overview of the extent of the technology available to help the international research process.[29]

Designing the questionnaire

Where international marketing research is conducted with questionnaires, these questionnaires should contain questions that are clear and easy to comprehend by the respondents, as

EXHIBIT 8.4   Internet penetration around the globe

World Regions	Population (2008 Est.)	Internet Users Dec. 31, 2000	Internet Users Latest Data	Penetration (% Population)	Users Growth 2000–2008	Users % of Table
Africa	975,330,899	4,514,400	54,171,500	5.6 %	1,100.0 %	3.4 %
Asia	3,780,819,792	114,304,000	657,170,816	17.4 %	474.9 %	41.2 %
Europe	803,903,540	105,096,093	393,373,398	48.9 %	274.3 %	24.6 %
Middle East	196,767,614	3,284,800	45,861,346	23.3 %	1,296.2 %	2.9 %
North America	337,572,949	108,096,800	251,290,489	74.4 %	132.5 %	15.7 %
Latin America/Caribbean	581,249,892	18,068,919	173,619,140	29.9 %	860.9 %	10.9 %
Oceania/Australia	34,384,384	7,620,480	20,783,419	60.4 %	172.7 %	1.3 %
WORLD TOTAL	6,710,029,070	360,985,492	1,596,270,108	23.8 %	342.2 %	100.0 %

Notes: (1) Internet usage and world population statistics are for March 31, 2009. (2) CLICK on each world region name for detailed regional usage information. (3) Demographic (population) numbers are based on data from the US Census Bureau. (4) Internet usage information comes from data published by Nielsen Online, by the International Telecommunications Union, by GfK, local regulators and other reliable sources. (5) For definitions, disclaimer, and navigation help, please refer to the Site Surfing Guide. (6) Information in this site may be cited, giving the due credit to **www.internetworldstats.com**. Copyright © 2001–2009, Miniwatts Marketing Group. All rights reserved worldwide.

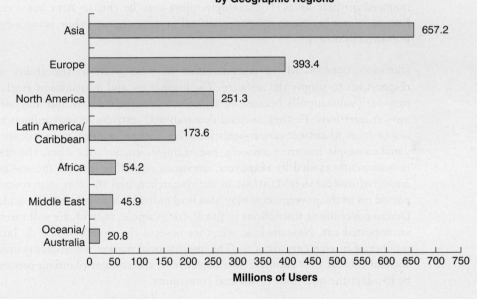

Internet Users in the World by Geographic Regions

Note: Estimated internet users are 1,596,270,108 for March 31, 2009

Source: Internet World Stats **http://www.internetworldstats.com/stats.htm**. (Accessed June 9, 2009).

well as easy for the data collector to administer. Much attention must therefore be paid to question format, content and wording.

Question Format Questions can be structured or unstructured. Structured questions typically allow the respondents only limited choice options. Unstructured (or open-ended) questions permit the capture of more in-depth information, but they also increase the potential for interviewer bias. Even at the cost of potential bias, however, 'the use of open-ended questions appears quite useful in cross-cultural surveys, because they may help identify the frame of reference of the respondents, or may even be designed to permit the respondent to set his own frame of reference'.[30]

Another question format decision is the choice between direct and indirect questions. Societies have different degrees of sensitivity to certain questions. Questions related to the income or age of a respondent may be accepted differently in different countries. The social desirability of answers may also vary. In some cultures, questions about employees, performance, standards and financing are asked directly of a respondent, while in others, particularly in Asia or the Middle East, these questions are thought to be rude and insulting.[31] As a result, the researcher must be sure that the questions are culturally acceptable. This may mean that questions that can be asked directly in some cultures will have to be asked indirectly in others. For example, rather than ask 'How old are you?' one could ask 'In what year were you born?'

The researcher must also be sure to adapt the complexity of the question to the level of understanding of the respondent. For example, a multipoint scaling method, which may be effectively used in a developed country to discover the attitudes and attributes of company executives, may be a very poor instrument if used among rural entrepreneurs. It has been found that demonstration aids are useful in surveys among poorly educated respondents.[32]

The question format should also ensure data equivalence in international marketing research. This requires categories used in questionnaires to be comparatively structured. In a developed country, for example, a white-collar worker may be part of the middle class, whereas in a less-developed country, the same person would be part of the upper class. Before using categories in a questionnaire, the researcher must therefore determine their appropriateness in different environments. This is particularly important for questions that attempt to collect attitudinal, psychographic or lifestyle data, since cultural variations are most pronounced in these areas. For example, pizza may be chic in Asia but a convenience food in Europe,[33] or a bicycle may be recreational in some regions while being a basic mode of transportation in others.[34]

Question Content Major consideration must be given to the ability and willingness of respondents to supply the answers. The knowledge and information available to respondents may vary substantially because of different educational levels and may affect their ability to answer questions. Further, societal demands and restrictions may influence the willingness of respondents to answer certain questions. For various reasons, respondents may also be motivated to supply incorrect answers. For example, in countries where the tax collection system is consistently eluded by taxpayers, questions regarding level of income may deliberately be answered inaccurately. Distrust in the researcher, and the fear that research results may be passed on to the government, may also lead individuals to consistently understate their assets. Due to government restrictions in Brazil, for example, individuals will rarely admit to owning an imported car. Nevertheless, when we observe the streets of Rio de Janeiro, a substantial number of foreign cars are seen. The international market researcher is unlikely to change the societal context of a country. The objective of the content planning process should therefore be to adapt the questions to societal constraints.

Question Wording The impact of culture, for example, language, is of particular importance when wording questions. The goal for the international marketing researcher should be to ensure that the potential for misunderstandings and misinterpretations of spoken or written words is minimized. Cultural differences make this issue an extremely sensitive one in the international marketing research process. As a result, attention must be paid to the translation equivalence of verbal and non-verbal questions that can change in the course of translation. For example, when the term *group discussion* was used in a questionnaire for Russian executives, it was translated to mean 'political indoctrination session'.

The key is to keep questions clear by using simple rather than complex words, by avoiding ambiguous words and questions, by omitting leading questions, and by asking questions in specific terms, thus avoiding generalizations and estimates.[35] To reduce problems of question wording, it is helpful to use a translation-retranslation approach. The researcher formulates the questions, has them translated into the language of the country under investigation, and subsequently has a second translator return the foreign text to the researcher's native language. Through the use of this method, the researcher can hope to detect possible blunders. In addition, it is important that the draft questionnaire be pilot-tested. As demonstrated in *The International Marketplace 8.3* translation mistakes are easy to make. An additional safeguard is the use of alternative wording. Here the researcher uses questions that address the same issue but are worded differently and that resurface at various points in the questionnaire in order to check for consistency in question interpretation by the respondents.

In spite of superb research planning, a poorly designed instrument will yield poor results. No matter how comfortable and experienced the researcher is in international research activities, an instrument should always be pre-tested. Ideally, such a pre-test is carried out with a subset of the population under study. At least a pretest with knowledgeable experts and individuals should be conducted. Even though a pretest may mean delays and additional cost, the risks of poor research are simply too great for this process to be omitted.

THE INTERNATIONAL **MARKETPLACE 8.3**

Survey language

The choice of survey language will be primarily determined by respondents' language proficiencies. In the case of surveying multinational corporations' (MNCs) managerial employees who are likely to possess a sufficient level of English and have been exposed to similar tertiary education in business schools around the world, the use of single-language surveys in English may be adequate. At the same time, research shows that English-language questionnaires lead to significantly less extreme response styles than questionnaires in a respondent's native language, thus underestimating cross-country differences (Harzing, 2006). Especially if both native and non-native English speakers are included in an international survey, survey translation into the respective local language appears crucial.

As many concepts and terms entail culture-specific connotations, their mere direct translation is unlikely to transport the intended meaning. For example, the concept of feedback differs substantially across cultures. Whereas it is usually viewed as a direct, open and formalized process in the US or the UK, many Asian countries regard feedback as a more indirect, anonymous and informal procedure (Hofstede, 1998). Without clearly specifying the intended meaning of the concept in the translated questionnaire, the researcher risks introducing systematic bias. A meaningful translation of the original version of the questionnaire requires a researcher not only to ensure overall conceptual equivalence but also to consider vocabulary, idiomatic and syntactical equivalence (Sekaran, 1983). In this vein, Brislin (1980) has suggested using simple sentence structures as well as clear and familiar wording as much as possible to facilitate translation. In addition, by adding redundancy and necessary context for difficult phrases, the researcher is able to clarify the intended meaning.

The most frequently employed translation technique is back-translation (Brislin, 1970). In this procedure, the original version of the questionnaire is translated into the target language and subsequently translated back into the source language by a second bilingual person. The use of two independent translators increases the chances that the original meaning has been retained, ensures literal accuracy and helps to detect mistakes. However, given the earlier notion that corresponding concepts may not always exist in another language, back-translation does not guarantee overall conceptual equivalence (Peng et al., 1991). Harpaz (2003) identifies two additional translation techniques: bilingual method and committee procedure. The former approach involves sending the original and the translated questionnaire to bilingual individuals and subsequently correcting items based on inconsistencies in their responses. In contrast, in the latter approach a committee consisting of bilingual individuals translates the questionnaire jointly and discusses possible mistakes or difficulties. Finally, to cross-check for possible translation mistakes and to ensure comprehension of the translated questionnaire among respondents, pilot testing is particularly important in international research.

Translation errors are the cause of the greatest number of blunders in international business. So, if you're a company thinking about going global, think about hiring a localization company that offers professional translation services to avoid the embarrassing marketing mishaps of the past.

Here are ten well-known translation errors made by big companies in international research:

1   Mead Johnson Nutritionals had to recall two baby food products because the instructions on how the products were to be prepared had been incorrectly translated from English to Spanish. It was reported by the US Food and Drug Administration that if both products were prepared according to the incorrect Spanish translation they could have caused seizures, irregular heartbeat, renal failure and death.

Obviously this is a blunder no company wants to make and one that could have been avoided with the proper translation. If you're a company thinking about going global take time to research localization companies that offer professional translation services and ensure that the delivery of your marketing message is properly translated for your global market.

2 The Coca-Cola name in China was first read as 'Kekoukela', meaning 'Bite the Wax Tadpole' or 'Female Horse Stuffed with Wax', depending on the dialect. Coke then researched 40,000 characters to find a phonetic equivalent 'kokoukole', translating into 'Happiness in the Mouth'.

3 Frank Perdue's famous chicken slogan, 'It takes a strong man to make a tender chicken' translated in Spanish: 'it takes an aroused man to make a chicken affectionate'.

4 Parker Pen's slogan 'It won't leak in your pocket and embarrass you' translated in Mexico: 'It won't leak in your pocket and make you pregnant'.

5 Colorado brewing company, Coors' 'Turn It Loose' slogan translated in Spanish: 'Suffer from Diarrhea'.

6 Pepsi's 'Come Alive with the Pepsi Generation' slogan translated in Chinese: 'Pepsi Brings Your Ancestors Back from the Grave'.

7 Braniff Airlines launched a new leather first-class seats ad campaign (1977–78) in the Mexican market: 'Fly in Leather' meant 'Fly Naked' (*vuela en cuero*).

8 Dairy Association's huge success with the campaign 'Got Milk?' in Mexico translated to: 'Are You Lactating?'.

9 General Motors' Chevrolet Nova vehicle translated in Spanish in Central and South America as: '*No va*', 'It Doesn't Go'.

10 KFC experienced real problems when the phrase 'finger lickin' good' came out in Chinese as 'eat your fingers off'.

All of these marketing mishaps are examples of how even the smallest translation error can greatly affect the intended marketing message and the consumer's reaction to that message. The hiring of a localization company that offers professional translation services could have saved these big companies a lot of money, time and resources. Fortunately, the examples above were harmless but skipping the proper localization and language research can be very harmful to the public. Rounding off the number one translation error is Mead Johnson Nutritionals, a company that made a very serious mistake.

SOURCES: Articlesbase (2008), 'Ten Global Translation Errors Made by Big Companies', **http://www.articlesbase.com/customer-service-articles/ten-global-translation-errors-made-by-big-companies-533055.html** (Accessed 9/06/09); Reiche, S and Harzing, A (2007), 'Key Issues in International Survey Research', **http://www.harzing.com/intresearch_keyissues.htm** (Accessed 9/06/09).

Developing the sampling plan

To obtain representative results, the researcher must reach representative members of the population under study. Many methods that have been developed in industrialized countries for this purpose are useless abroad. For example, address directories may simply not be available. Multiple families may live in one dwelling. Differences between population groups living, for example, in highlands and lowlands may make it imperative to differentiate these segments. Lack of basic demographic information may prevent the design of a sampling frame. In instances in which comparative research addresses very different areas it may be virtually impossible to match samples.[36]

The international marketing researcher must keep in mind the complexities of the market under study and prepare his or her sampling plan accordingly. Often, samples need to be stratified to reflect different population groups, and innovative sampling methods need to be devised in order to assure representative and relevant responses. For example, a survey concerning grocery shopping habits might require data from housewives in one country, but from maids in another.[37]

Data collection

The international marketing researcher must check the quality of the data collection process. In some cultures, the use of questionnaires is seen as useless by the local population. Instruments are administered primarily to humour the researcher. In such cases, interviewers may cheat quite frequently. Spot checks on the collection procedures are vital to ensure reasonable data quality. A realism check of data should also be used. For example, if marketing research in Italy reports that very little spaghetti is consumed, the researcher should perhaps consider whether individuals responded to their use of purchased spaghetti rather than home-made spaghetti. The data should therefore be compared with secondary information and with analogous information from a similar market in order to obtain a preliminary understanding of data quality.

Analysing and interpreting primary data

Analysis and interpretation of data are required to answer the research questions that were posed initially. The researcher should, of course, use the best tools available and appropriate for analysis. The fact that a market may be in a less-developed country does not preclude the collection of good data and the use of good analytical methods. On the other hand, international researchers should be cautioned against using overly sophisticated tools for unsophisticated data. Even the best of tools will not improve data quality. The quality of data must be matched with the quality of the research tools to achieve appropriately sophisticated analysis and yet not overstate the value of the data. Simple descriptive data analysis tools for quantitative data include the use of Excel to determine frequencies and charts, for example. In contrast, sophisticated inferential tools for quantitative data include the use of SPSS (Statistical Package for Social Scientists) and specific techniques include correlation and regression analyzes.

Presenting research results

The primary focus in the presentation of research results must be communication. In multinational marketing research, communication must take place not only with management at headquarters but also with managers in the local operations. Otherwise, little or no transference of research results will occur, and the synergistic benefits of a multinational operation are lost. To minimize time devoted to reading reports, the researcher must present results clearly and concisely. In the worldwide operations of a firm, particularly in the communication efforts, lengthy data and analytical demonstrations should be avoided. The availability of data and the techniques used should be mentioned, however, so that subsidiary operations can receive the information on request.

The researcher should also demonstrate in the presentation how research results relate to the original research objective and fit with overall corporate strategy. At least schematically, possibilities for analogous application should be highlighted. These possibilities should then also be communicated to local subsidiaries, perhaps through a short monthly newsletter. A newsletter format, ideally distributed through an intranet, can be used regardless of whether the research process is centralized, coordinated or decentralized. The only difference will be the person or group providing the input for the newsletter. It is important to maintain such communication in order for the entire organization to learn and to improve its international marketing research capabilities.

Follow-up and review

Now that the research has been carried out, appropriate managerial decisions must be made based on the research, and the organization must absorb the research. For example, if it has been found that a product needs to have certain attributes to sell well in China, the manager must determine whether the product development area is aware of this finding and the degree to which the knowledge is now incorporated into new product projects. Without such follow-up, the role of research tends to become a mere 'staff' function, increasingly isolated from corporate 'line' activity and lacking major impact on corporate activity. If that is the case, research will diminish and even be disregarded – resulting in an organization at risk.

Research on the Web

The growing use of technology has given rise to new marketing research approaches that allow consumers to be heard more often and permit firms to work much harder at their listening skills. Two primary research approaches are rapidly growing in their use: web-based research and email–based surveys.

The increasing degree to which the World Wide web truly lives up to its name is making it possible for international marketers to use this medium in their research efforts. The technology allows them to reach out in a low-cost fashion and provides innovative ways to present stimuli and collect data. For example, on a website, product details, pictures of products, brands and the shopping environment can be portrayed with integrated graphics and sound – thus bringing the issues to be researched much closer to the respondent. In addition, the behaviour of visitors to a site can be traced and interpreted regarding interest in products, services or information.[38]

Surveys can be administered either through a website or through email. If they are posted on a site, surveys can be of the pop-up nature, where visitors can be targeted specifically. An email survey format eliminates the need for postage and printing. As a result, larger and geographically diverse audiences can be the focus of an inquiry. Research indicates that there is a higher and faster response rate to such electronic inquiries. In addition, the process of data entry can be structured so that responses are automatically fed into data analysis software.[39]

However, it would be too simplistic to assume that the digitalization of survey content is all that it takes to go global on the web. There are cultural differences that must be taken into account by the researcher. Global visitors to a site should encounter research that is embedded in their own cultural values, rituals, and, symbols and testimonials or encouragement should be delivered by culture-specific heroes. For example, a website might first offer a visitor from Korea the opportunity to become part of a product user community.[40]

Web-based surveys enhance a company's ability to interact with its customers by making the survey process easier, cheaper and faster. Widespread and affordable software for producing survey forms enables any company with a website to create its own customized questionnaire.

Customer loyalty can be enhanced by building strong connections through web-based follow-up surveys. Asking customers to evaluate a company's products and services makes them more involved in the product. Inviting customers to work on product planning and asking them to share thought and opinions online results in new ideas and is beneficial to the public perception of a company. Having made a contribution to the development of a company's product, customers are more likely to remain with the company.

The advantages of web-based surveys include faster response rates, easier distribution and reminding of participants to participate. It is also easier to process data, check errors, arrange questions in random order, and include pop-up instructions for selected questions. Web-based surveys allow individuals to respond in their free time, privately and instinctively, and to do so from all over the world. Data can be rapidly analyzed and the overall results can be shown immediately.

Some suggestions for constructing successful web surveys are to include only the most important questions, keep the total number of questions to 30 or fewer, limit the number of screens respondents have to navigate through, keep response time to less than 10 to 15 minutes, inform each respondent of the time needed to complete the survey, and give an incentive to take the survey that directly relates to the company's product respondents are asked to evaluate.[41]

THE INTERNATIONAL INFORMATION SYSTEM

Many organizations have data needs that go beyond specific international marketing research projects. Most of the time, daily decisions must be made, and there is neither time nor money for special research. An information system already in place is needed to provide the decision maker with basic data for most ongoing decisions. Corporations have responded by developing marketing decision support systems. Defined as 'an integrated system of data, statistical analysis, modeling, and display formats using computer hardware and software technology', such a system serves as a mechanism to coordinate the flow of information to corporate managers for decision-making purposes.[42]

To be useful to the decision maker, the system needs various attributes. First, the information must be *relevant*. The data gathered must have meaning for the manager's decision-making process. Second, the information must be *timely*. It is of little benefit to the manager if decision information help that is needed today does not become available until a month from now. To be of use to the international decision maker, the system must therefore feed from a variety of international sources and be updated frequently. For multinational corporations, this means a real-time linkage between international subsidiaries and a broad-based ongoing data input operation.

Third, information must be *flexible* – that is, it must be available in the forms needed by management. A marketing decision support system must permit manipulation of the format and combining of the data. Therefore, great effort must be expended to make diverse international data compatible with and comparable to each other. Fourth, information contained in the system must be *accurate*. This attribute is particularly relevant in the international field because information quickly becomes outdated as a result of major changes. Obviously, a system is of no value if it provides incorrect information that leads to poor decisions. Fifth, the system's information bank must be reasonably *exhaustive*. Because of the interrelationship between variables, factors that may influence a particular decision must be appropriately represented in the information system. This means that the marketing decision support system must be based on a broad variety of factors. Finally, to be useful to managers, the system must be *convenient,* both to use and to access. Systems that are cumbersome and time-consuming to reach and to use will not be used enough to justify corporate expenditures to build and maintain them.

More international information systems are being developed successfully due to progress in computer technology in both hardware and software. To build an information system, corporations use the internal data that are available from divisions such as accounting and finance and also from their subsidiaries. In addition, many organizations put mechanisms in place to enrich the basic data flow. Three such tools are environmental scanning, Delphi studies and scenario building.

Environmental scanning

Any changes in the business environment, whether domestic or foreign, may have serious repercussions on the marketing activities of the firm. Corporations therefore should understand the necessity for tracking new developments and obtaining continuous updates. To carry out this task, some large multinational organizations have formed environmental scanning groups.

Environmental scanning activities are useful to continuously receive information on political, social and economic affairs internationally; on changes of attitudes held by public institutions and private citizens; and on possible upcoming alterations in international markets.

The precision required for environmental scanning varies with its purpose. Whether the information is to be used for mind stretching or for budgeting, for example, must be taken into account when constructing the framework and variables that will enter the scanning process. The more immediate and precise the exercise is to be in its application within the corporation, the greater the need for detailed information. At the same time, such heightened precision may lessen the utility of environmental scanning for the strategic corporate purpose, which is more long-term in its orientation.

Environmental scanning can be performed in various ways. One method consists of obtaining factual input regarding many variables. For example, the US Census Bureau collects, evaluates and adjusts a wide variety of demographic, social and economic characteristics of foreign countries. Estimates for all countries of the world are developed, particularly on economic variables, such as labour force statistics, GDP, and income statistics, but also on health and nutrition variables. Similar factual information can be obtained from international organizations such as the World Bank or the United Nations.

Frequently, corporations believe that such factual data alone are insufficient for their information needs. Particularly for forecasting future developments, other methods are used to capture underlying dimensions of social change. One significant method is content analysis. This technique investigates the content of communication in a society and entails literally counting the number of times preselected words, themes, symbols or pictures appear in a given medium. It can be used productively in international marketing to monitor the social, economic, cultural and technological environment in which the marketing organization is operating.

Corporations can use content analysis to pinpoint upcoming changes in their line of business, and new opportunities, by attempting to identify trendsetting events. For example, the Alaska oil spill by the tanker *Exxon Valdez* resulted in entirely new international concern about environmental protection and safety, reaching far beyond the incident itself.

Environmental scanning is conducted by a variety of groups within and outside the corporation. Frequently, small corporate staffs are created at headquarters to coordinate the information flow. In addition, subsidiary staff can be used to provide occasional intelligence reports. Groups of volunteers are also formed to gather and analyze information worldwide and feed individual analyzes back to corporate headquarters, where they can be used to form the 'big picture'.

Finally, it should be kept in mind that internationally there may be a fine line between tracking and obtaining information and misappropriating corporate secrets. With growing frequency, governments and firms claim that their trade secrets are being obtained and abused by foreign competitors. The perceived threat from economic espionage has led to accusations of government spying networks trying to undermine the commercial interests of companies.[43] Information gatherers must be sensitive to these issues in order to avoid conflict or controversy.

Delphi studies

To enrich the information obtained from factual data, corporations resort to the use of creative and highly qualitative data-gathering methods. Delphi studies are one such method. These studies are particularly useful in the international marketing environment because they are 'a means for aggregating the judgments of a number of ... experts ... who cannot come together physically'.[44] This type of research approach clearly aims at qualitative rather than quantitative measures by aggregating the information of a group of experts. It seeks to obtain answers from those who know instead of seeking the average responses of many with only limited knowledge.

Typically, Delphi studies are carried out with groups of about 30 well-chosen participants who possess particular in-depth expertise in an area of concern, such as future developments in the international trade environment. These participants are asked via mail to identify the major issues in the area of concern. They are also requested to rank their statements according to importance and explain the rationale behind the order. Next, the aggregated information is returned to all participants, who are encouraged to state clearly their agreements or disagreements with the various rank orders and comments. Statements can be challenged, and in another round, participants can respond to the challenges. After several rounds of challenge and response, a reasonably coherent consensus is developed.

The Delphi technique is particularly valuable because it uses the mail or facsimile method of communication to bridge large distances and therefore makes individuals quite accessible at a reasonable cost. It does not suffer from the drawback of ordinary mail investigations: lack of interaction among the participants. One drawback of the technique is that it requires several steps, and therefore months may elapse before the information is obtained. Even though the increasing availability of electronic mail may hasten the process, the researcher must be cautious to factor in the different penetration and acceptance levels of such technology. One should not let the research process be driven by technology to the exclusion of valuable key informants who utilize less sophisticated methods of communication.

Also, substantial effort must be expended in selecting the appropriate participants and in motivating them to participate in this exercise with enthusiasm and continuity. When obtained on a regular basis, Delphi information can provide crucial additions to the factual data available for the marketing information system.

Scenario building

Some companies use scenario analysis to look at different configurations of key variables in the international market. For example, economic growth rates, import penetration, population growth and political stability can be varied. By projecting such variations for medium- to long-term periods, companies can envision completely new environmental conditions.

These conditions are then analyzed for their potential domestic and international impact on corporate strategy.

Of major importance in scenario building is the identification of crucial trend variables and the degree of their variation. Frequently, key experts are used to gain information about potential variations and the viability of certain scenarios.

A wide variety of scenarios must be built to expose corporate executives to multiple potential occurrences. Ideally, even far-fetched variables deserve some consideration, if only to build worst-case scenarios.

Scenario builders also need to recognize the nonlinearity of factors. To simply extrapolate from currently existing situations is insufficient. Frequently, extraneous factors may enter the picture with a significant impact. Finally, in scenario building, the possibility of joint occurrences must be recognized because changes may not come about in an isolated fashion but may be spread over wide regions. An example of a joint occurrence is the indebtedness of developing nations. Although the inability of any one country to pay its debts would not present a major problem for the international banking community, large and simultaneous indebtedness may well pose a problem of major severity. Similarly, given large technological advances, the possibility of 'wholesale' obsolescence of current technology must also be considered. For example, quantum leaps in computer development and new generations of computers may render obsolete the technological investment of a corporation or even a country.

For scenarios to be useful, management must analyze and respond to them by formulating contingency plans. Such planning will broaden horizons and may prepare management for unexpected situations. Familiarization in turn can result in shorter response times to actual occurrences by honing response capability. The difficulty, of course, is to devise scenarios that are unusual enough to trigger new thinking yet sufficiently realistic to be taken seriously by management.[45]

The development of an international information system is of major importance to the multinational corporation. It aids the ongoing decision process and becomes a vital corporate tool in carrying out the strategic planning task. Only by observing global trends and changes will the firm be able to maintain and increase its international competitive position. Many of the data available are quantitative in nature, but attention must also be paid to qualitative dimensions. Quantitative analysis will continue to improve as the ability to collect, store, analyze and retrieve data increases through the use of high-speed computers. Nevertheless, qualitative analysis should remain a major component of corporate research and strategic planning.

SUMMARY

Constraints of time, resources, and expertise are the major inhibitors of international marketing research. Nevertheless, firms need to carry out planned and organized research in order to explore global market alternatives successfully. Such research needs to be closely linked to the decision-making process.

International market research differs from domestic research in that the environment, which determines how well tools, techniques and concepts apply, is different abroad. In addition, the manager needs to deal with new parameters, such as duties, exchange rates and international documentation, a greater number of interacting factors and a much broader definition of the concept of competition.

Given the scarcity of resources, companies beginning their international effort often need to use data that have already been collected – that is, secondary data. Such data are available from governments, international organizations, directories, trade associations, or online databases.

To respond to specific information requirements, firms frequently need primary research. The researcher needs to select an appropriate research technique to collect the information needed. Sensitivity to different international environments and cultures will guide the researcher in deciding whether to use interviews, focus groups, observation, surveys or experimentation as data collection techniques. In addition to traditional data gathering tools, web-based surveys can be faster at bringing better quality results. The same sensitivity applies to the design of the research instrument, where issues such as question format, content and wording are decided. Also, the sampling plan needs to be appropriate for the local environment in order to ensure representative and useful responses.

Once the data have been collected, care must be taken to use analytical tools appropriate for the quality of data collected, so that management is not misled about the sophistication of the research. Finally, the research results must be presented in a concise and useful form so that management can benefit in its decision making, and implementation of the research needs to be tracked.

To provide ongoing information to management, an international information support system is useful. Such a system will provide for the systematic and continuous gathering, analysis and reporting of data for decision-making purposes. It uses a firm's internal information and gathers data via environmental scanning, Delphi studies, or scenario building, thus enabling management to prepare for the future and hone its decision-making skills.

KEY TERMS

content analysis	quantitative data
data equivalence	realism check
direct	research specifications
environmental protection	scenario analysis
foreign market opportunity analysis	social desirability
indirect questions	structured questions
international comparative research	translation-retranslation approach
proxy variable	unstructured (or open-ended) questions
qualitative data	web-based research

Questions for discussion

1   Discuss the possible shortcomings of secondary data.

2   Why would a firm collect primary data in its international marketing research?

3   Discuss the trade-offs between centralized and decentralized international marketing research.

4   How is international market research affected by differences in language?

5   Compare the use of telephone surveys in the United Kingdom and in Egypt.

6   What are some of the crucial variables you would track in an international information system?

7   How has information technology affected international marketing research?

Internet exercises

1   What were the industry and country against which the European Union filed antidumping actions in 2010? (Check **http://www.eubusiness.com/news-eu/wto-trade-dispute.4m0**.)

2   Where would it be most difficult to conduct business due to a high degree of corruption? (Check **http://www.transparency.org**.)

Recommended readings

Baker, Donald I. and Carol D. Terry. *Internet Research,* 2nd edn. Tempe, AZ: Facts on Demand Press, 2004.

Churchill, Gilbert A. and Dawn Iacobucci. *Marketing Research: Methodological Foundations,* 9th edn. Mason, OH: Cengage South-Western, 2005.

Coyle, James. *Internet Resources and Services for International Marketing.* Westport, CT: Oryx, 2002.

Craig, Samuel C. and Susan P. Douglas. *International Marketing Research: Concepts and Methods,* 3rd edn. Chichester: John Wiley and Sons, 2006.

Dobson, Chris. *Introduction to Online Company Research.* Mason, OH: Thomson Texere, 2004.

McCue, Sarah. *Farce to Force: Building Profitable E-Commerce Strategies.* Mason, OH: Thomson Texere, 2006.

Schlein Alan M. *Find It Online, Fourth Edition: The Complete Guide to Online Research,* Temple, AZ: Facts on Demand, 2004.

Notes

1 **http://www.chinahotels.org/travel.html**

2 **http://english.people.com.cn/200301/13/ eng20030113_110000.shtml**

3 Naresh K. Malhotra, Mark Peterson and Susan Bardi Kleiser, 'Marketing Research: A State-of-the-Art Review and Directions for the Twenty-First Century', *Journal of the Academy of Marketing Science* 27 (no. 2, 1999): 160–183.

4 Marketing Definitions, **http://marketingpower.com**, website of the American Marketing Association (Accessed December 5, 2005).

5 Naresh K. Malhotra, *Marketing Research: An Applied Orientation,* 4th edn (Upper Saddle River, NJ: Prentice-Hall, 2003).

6 C. Samuel Craig and Susan P. Douglas, *International Marketing Research,* 3rd edn (Chichester: John Wiley and Sons, 2006).

7 Nina L. Reynolds, 'Benchmarking International Marketing Research Practice in UK Agencies – Preliminary Evidence', *Benchmarking* 7 (no. 5, 2000): 343–359.

8 For an excellent exposition on measuring the value of research, see Gilbert A. Churchill, Jr. and Dawn Iacobucci, *Marketing Research: Methodological Foundations,* 9th ed. (Mason, OH: Cengage South-Western, 2005).

9 For an excellent online diagnostic tool, see Tamer S. Cavusgil's CORE (Company Readiness to Export), Michigan State University, **http://globaledge.msu.edu/diagtools/** (Accessed January 17, 2006).

10 Capitals of every independent country **http:// geography.about.com/od/countryinformation/a/ capitals.htm**

11 Tamer S. Cavusgil, Tunga Kiyak and Sengun Yeniyurt, 'Complementary Approaches to Preliminary Foreign Market Opportunity Assessment: Country Clustering and Country Ranking', *Industrial Marketing Management,* December 24, 2003, 616.

12 'MP Backs Federal Action over China Fruit Trade Stance', *Australian Broadcasting Corporation,* **http://abc.net.au**, September, 15, 2005.

13 **http://www.direct.gov.uk/en/Dl1/Directories/ DG_10011953**

14 Michael R. Czinkota, 'International Information Cross-Fertilization in Marketing: An Empirical Assessment', *European Journal of Marketing,* 34 (2000).

15 **http://chcc.arts.gla.ac.uk/Social_Status/section03/ index.php**

16 Henning, D (2008), 'Germany: The shrinking middle class and the rise of inequality' **http://www.wsws.org/articles/ 2008/mar2008/germ-m22.shtml**

17 Charles A. Prescott, 'The New International Marketing Challenge: Privacy', *Target Marketing* 22 (no. 4, 1999): 29.

18 PHR2004 – People's Republic of China **http://www. privacyinternational.org/article.shtml? cmd%5B347%5D=x-347-83511**

19 Privacy Guide: Asia and the Pacific **http:// www.caslon.com.au/privacyguide6.htm#china**

20 Highlights 2006 **http://www.esomar.org/uploads/pdf/ ESOMAR_Highlights_2006.pdf**

21 Salah S. Hassan and A. Coskun Samli, 'The New Frontiers of Intermarket Segmentation', in *Global Marketing: Perspectives and Cases,* eds. Salah S. Hassan and Roger D. Blackwell (Fort Worth, TX: The Dryden Press, 1994), 76–100.

22 Top 25 global research organizations, 2007 **http:// www.demoskopia.com.br/TOP252007.html** (2007)

23 Michael R. Czinkota and Masaaki Kotabe, 'Product Development the Japanese Way', in *Trends in International Business: Critical Perspectives,* eds. M. Czinkota and M. Kotabe (Oxford, England: Blackwell Publishers, 1998), 153–158.

24 A French Restoration: Utilities and Services **http:// www.howto.co.uk/property/renovation-property-france/utilities_and_services/**

25 Revill, J. (2008) 'Security fears over flood alert' **http:// www.guardian.co.uk/environment/2008/jan/06/ flooding**

26 R. Nishikawa, 'New Product Planning at Hitachi', *Long Range Planning* 22 (1989): 20–24.

27 For an excellent example, see Alan Dubinsky, Marvin Jolson, Masaaki Kotabe and Chae Lim, 'A Cross-National Investigation of Industrial Salespeople's Ethical Perceptions', *Journal of International Business Studies* 22 (1991): 651–670.

28 Tajeddini, K. and Mueller, S.L. (2008), 'Entrepreneurial characteristics in Switzerland and the UK: A comparative study of techno-entrepreneurs', *Journal of International Entrepreneurship* 7 (1), 1–25, **http://www. springerlink.com/content/n467748tq5mv8042/**

29   Internet World Stats **http://www.internetworldstats.com/ stats.htm**

30   Sydney Verba, 'Cross-National Survey Research: The Problem of Credibility', in *Comparative Methods in Sociology: Essays on Trends and Applications,* ed. I. Vallier (Berkeley: University of California Press, 1971), 322–323.

31   Camille P. Schuster and Michael J. Copeland, 'Global Business Exchanges: Similarities and Differences around the World', *Journal of International Marketing* (Number 2, 1999): 63–80.

32   Kavil Ramachandran, 'Data Collection for Management Research in Developing Countries', in *The Management Research Handbook,* eds. N. Craig Smith and Paul Dainty (London: Routledge, 1991), 304.

33   Why pizza is still our favourite food **http:// www.timesonline.co.uk/tol/life_and_style/ food_and_drink/eating_out/article6155848.ece**

34   Tamer S. Cavusgil, Seyda Deligonul, and Attila Yaprak, 'International Marketing as a Field of Study: A Critical Assessment of Earlier Development and a Look Forward', *Journal of International Marketing,* 13 (no. 4, 2005): 1–27.

35   Gilbert A. Churchill, Jr. and Dawn Iacobucci, *Marketing Research: Methodological Foundations,* 9th ed. (Mason, OH: Cengage South-Western, 2005).

36   Kathleen Brewer Doran, 'Lessons Learned in Cross-Cultural Research of Chinese and North American Consumers', *Journal of Business Research,* 55 (2002): 823–829.

37   C. Samuel Craig and Susan P. Douglas, *International Marketing Research,* 3rd edn (Chichester: John Wiley and Sons, 2006).

38   C. Samuel Craig and Susan P. Douglas, 'Conducting International Marketing Research in the Twenty-First Century', *International Marketing Review* 18 (no. 1, 2001): 80–90.

39   Janet Ilieva, Steve Baron and Nigel M. Healey, 'On-line Surveys in Marketing Research: Pros and Cons', *International Journal of Marketing Research* 44 (no. 3, 2002): 361–376.

40   David Luna, Laura A. Peracchio and Maria D. de Juan, 'Cross-Cultural and Cognitive Aspects of WebSite Navigation', *Journal of the Academy of Marketing Science* 30 (no. 4, 2002): 397–410.

41   'Web-based Surveys Help Customers Evolve with Your Products', *ATX Dialogue,* February, 2004, **http:// www.atx.com** (Accessed January 15, 2006).

42   Thomas C. Kinnear and James R. Taylor, *Marketing Research: An Applied Approach,* 5th edn (New York: McGraw-Hill, 1996).

43   Peter Clarke, 'The Echelon Questions', *Electronic Engineering Times,* March 6, 2000, 36.

44   Andre L. Delbecq, Andrew H. Van de Ven and David H. Gustafson, *Group Techniques for Program Planning* (Glenview, IL: Scott, Foresman, 1975), 83.

45   David Rutenberg, 'Playful Plans', Queen's University working paper, 1991.

APPENDIX A

INFORMATION SOURCES FOR MARKETING ISSUES

EUROPEAN UNION

EUROPA
The umbrella server for all
institutions
http://www.europa.eu.int

CORDIS
Information on EU research programmes
http://www.cordis.lu

Council of the European Union
Information and news from the
Council, with sections covering
Common Foreign and Security Policy
(CFSP) and Justice and Home Affairs
http://ue.eu.int

Court of Auditors
Information notes, annual reports, and
other publications
http://www.eca.eu.int

Court of Justice
Overview, press releases, publications,
and full-text proceedings of the court
**http://europa.eu.int/cj/en/
index.htm**

Citizens Europe
Covers rights of citizens of EU member
states
http://www.c-o-e.net

Delegation of the European Commission
to the United States
Press releases, EURECOM:
Economic and Financial News, EU-US
relations, information on EU policies
and Delegation programmes
http://www.eurunion.org

Euro
The Single Currency
http://europa.eu.int/euro

EUDOR (European Union Document
Repository)
Bibliographic database
http://europa.eu.int/eclas

European Agency for the Evaluation of
Medicinal Products
Information on drug approval procedures
and documents of the Committee for
Proprietary Medicinal Products and
the Committee for Veterinary
Medicinal Products
http://www.emea.eu.int

European Bank for Reconstruction and
Development
One Exchange Square
London EC2A 2EH
United Kingdom
http://www.ebrd.com

European Centre for the Development
of Vocational Training
Information on the Centre and contact
information
http://www.cedefop.gr

European Community Information Service
200 Rue de la Loi
1049 Brussels, Belgium
and
2100 M Street NW, 7th Floor
Washington, DC 20037

European Environment Agency
Information on the mission, products and
services, and organizations and staff
of the EEA
http://www.eea.eu.int

European Investment Bank
Press releases and information on
borrowing and loan operations, staff,
and publications
http://www.eib.org

European Monetary Institute
Name: European Central Bank
http://www.ecb.int

EuroStat
**http://europa.eu.int/comm/
eurostat**

European Training Foundation
Information on vocational education and
training programmes in Central and
Eastern Europe and Central Asia
http://www.etf.eu.int

European Union
200 Rue de la Loi
1049 Brussels, Belgium
and
2100 M Street NW 7th Floor
Washington, DC 20037
http://www.eurunion.org

Office for Harmonization in the Internal
Market
Guidelines, application forms, and other
information for registering an EU
trademark
**http://www.oami.eu.int/en/
default.htm**

UNITED NATIONS

http://www.un.org
Conference of Trade and Development
Palais des Nations
1211 Geneva 10
Switzerland
http://unctad.org

Department of Economic and Social
Development
1 United Nations Plaza
New York, NY 10017
http://www.un.org/ecosocdev/

Industrial Development Organization
1660 L Street NW
Washington, DC 20036
     and
Post Office Box 300
Vienna International Center
A-1400 Vienna, Austria
http://www.unido.org

International Trade Centre
UNCTAD/WTO
54–56 Rue de Mountbrillant
CH-1202 Geneva
Switzerland
http://www.intracen.org

United Nations Educational, Scientific and
     Cultural Organization
2 United Nations Plaza, Suite 900
New York, NY 10017
http://www.unesco.org

UN Publications
Room 1194
1 United Nations Plaza
New York, NY 10017
http://unp.un.org

US GOVERNMENT

Agency for International Development
Office of Business Relations
Washington, DC 20523
http://www.usaid.gov

Customs Service
1301 Constitution Avenue NW
Washington, DC 20229
http://www.customs.ustreas.gov

Department of Agriculture
12th Street and Jefferson Drive SW
Washington, DC 20250
http://www.usda.gov

Department of Commerce
Herbert C. Hoover Building
14th Street and Constitution
     Avenue NW
Washington, DC 20230
http://www.commerce.gov

Department of State
2201 C Street NW
Washington, DC 20520
http://www.state.gov

Department of the Treasury
15th Street and Pennsylvania Avenue NW
Washington, DC 20220
http://www.ustreas.gov

Federal Trade Commission
6th Street and Pennsylvania Avenue NW
Washington, DC 20580
http://www.ftc.gov

FedStats
http://www.fedstats.gov

International Trade Commission
500 E Street NW
Washington, DC 20436
http://www.usitc.gov

Small Business Administration
409 Third Street SW
Washington, DC 20416
http://www.sbaonline.sba.gov

US Census Bureau
http://www.census.gov

US Trade and Development Agency
1621 North Kent Street
Rosslyn, VA 22209
http://www.tda.gov

World Fact Book
http://www.odci.gov/cia/
     publications/factbook/index.html

World Trade Centers Association
60 East 42nd Street
Suite 1901
New York, NY 10165
http://www.wtca.org

Council of Economic Advisers
http://www.whitehouse.gov/cea

Department of Defense
http://www.dod.gov

Department of Energy
http://www.energy.gov

Department of Interior
http://www.doi.gov

Department of Labor
http://www.dol.gov

Department of Transportation
http://www.dot.gov

Environmental Protection Agency
http://www.epa.gov

National Trade Data Bank
http://www.stat-usa.gov

National Economic Council
http://www.whitehouse.gov/nec

Office of Management and Budget
http://www.whitehouse.gov/omb

Office of the US Trade Representative
http://www.ustr.gov

Overseas Private Investment
     Corporation
http://www.opic.gov

SELECTED ORGANIZATIONS

Academy for Educational
     Development
1401 New York Avenue NW
Suite 1100
Washington, DC 20005
http://www.aed.org

American Bankers Association
1120 Connecticut Avenue NW
Washington, DC 20036
http://www.aba.com

American Bar Association
Section of International Law
     and Practice
750 N. Lake Shore Drive
Chicago, IL 60611
     and
1800 M Street NW
Washington, DC 20036
http://www.abanet.org/intlaw/
     home.html

American Management Association
440 First Street NW
Washington, DC 20001
http://www.amanet.org

American Marketing Association
311 S. Wacker Drive, Suite 5800
Chicago, IL 60606
http://www.marketingpower.com

American Petroleum Institute
1220 L Street NW
Washington, DC 20005
http://www.api.org

Asia-Pacific Economic Cooperation
     Secretariat
438 Alexandra Road
#41–00, Alexandra Road
Singapore 119958
http://www.apecsec.org.sg

Asian Development Bank
2330 Roxas Boulevard
Pasay City, Philippines
http://www.adb.org

Association of South East Asian
    Nations (ASEAN)
Publication Office
c/o The ASEAN Secretariat
70A, Jalan Sisingamangaraja
Jakarta 11210
Indonesia
http://www.aseansec.org

Better Business Bureau
http://www.bbb.org

Canadian Market Data
http://www.strategis.ic.gc.ca

Chamber of Commerce of the United
    States
1615 H Street NW
Washington, DC 20062
http://www.uschamber.org

Commission of the European
    Communities to the United States
2100 M Street NW
Suite 707
Washington, DC 20037
http://www.eurunion.org

Conference Board
845 Third Avenue
New York, NY 10022
    and
1755 Massachusetts Avenue
NW Suite 312
Washington, DC 20036
http://www.conference-board.org

Deutsche Bundesbank
Wilhelm-Epstein-Str. 14
P.O.B. 10 06 02
D-60006 Frankfurt am Main
http://www.bundesbank.de

Electronic Industries Alliance
2001 Pennsylvania Avenue NW
Washington, DC 20004
http://www.eia.org

Export-Import Bank of the United
    States
811 Vermont Avenue NW
Washington, DC 20571
http://www.exim.gov

Federal Reserve Bank of New York
33 Liberty Street
New York, NY 10045
http://www.ny.frb.org

Gallup Organization
http://www.gallup.com

Greenpeace
http://www.greenpeace.org

Iconoculture
http://iconoculture.com

Inter-American Development Bank
1300 New York Avenue NW
Washington, DC 20577
http://www.iadb.org

International Bank for Reconstruction and
    Development (World Bank)
1818 H Street NW
Washington, DC 20433
http://www.worldbank.org

International Monetary Fund
700 19th Street NW
Washington, DC 20431
http://www.imf.org

International Telecommunication Union
Place des Nations
Ch-1211 Geneva 20
Switzerland
http://www.itu.int

IRSS (Institute for Research in Social Science)
http://www.irss.unc.edu/
    data_archive/home.asp

LANIC (Latin American Network
    Information Center)
http://www.lanic.utexas.edu

Marketing Research Society
111 E. Wacker Drive, Suite 600
Chicago, IL 60601
Michigan State University globalEDGE
http://globaledge.msu.edu/ibrd/ibrd.asp

National Association of Manufacturers
1331 Pennsylvania Avenue
Suite 1500
Washington, DC 20004
http://www.nam.org

National Federation of Independent Business
600 Maryland Avenue SW
Suite 700
Washington, DC 20024
http://www.nfib.org

Organization for Economic Cooperation
    and Development
2 rue Andre Pascal
75775 Paris Cedex Ko, France
    and
2001 L Street NW, Suite 700
Washington, DC 20036
http://www.oecd.org

Organization of American States
17th and Constitution Avenue NW
Washington, DC 20006
http://www.oas.org

The Roper Centre for Public Opinion
    Research
http://www.ropercenter.uconn.edu

Transparency International
Otto-Suhr-Allee 97–99
D-10585 Berlin
Germany
http://www.transparency.org

INDEXES TO LITERATURE

Business Periodical Index
H.W. Wilson Co.
950 University Avenue
Bronx, NY 10452

New York Times Index
University Microfilms International
300 N. Zeeb Road
Ann Arbor, MI 48106
http://www.nytimes.com

Public Affairs Information Service Bulletin
11 W. 40th Street
New York, NY 10018

Wall Street Journal Index
University Microfilms International
300 N. Zeeb Road
Ann Arbor, MI 48106
http://online.wsj.com

DIRECTORIES

American Register of Exporters and Importers
38 Park Row
New York, NY 10038

Arabian Year Book
Dar Al-Seuassam Est. Box 42480
Shuwahk, Kuwait

Directories of American Firms Operating
    in Foreign Countries
World Trade Academy Press
Uniworld Business Publications Inc.
E. 42nd Street
New York, NY 10017

The Directory of International Sources of
    Business Information
Pitman
Long Acre
London WC2E 9AN, England

Encyclopedia of Associations
Gale Research Co.
Book Tower
Detroit, MI 48226

Polk's World Bank Directory
R.C. Polk & Co.
Elm Hill Pike
P.O. Box 1340
Nashville, TN 37202

Verified Directory of Manufacturer's
    Representatives
MacRae's Blue Book Inc.
Broadway
New York, NY 10003

World Guide to Trade Associations
K.G. Saur & Co.
Fifth Avenue
New York, NY 10010

PERIODIC REPORTS, NEWSPAPERS, MAGAZINES

Advertising Age
Crain Communications Inc.
740 N. Rush Street
Chicago, IL 60611
http://www.adage.com

Advertising World
Directories International Inc.
150 Fifth Avenue, Suite 610
New York, NY 10011

Arab Report and Record
84 Chancery Lane
London WC2A 1DL, England
Asian Demographics
http://www.asiandemographics.com

Barron's
University Microfilms International
300 N. Zeeb Road
Ann Arbor, MI 48106
http://online.barrons.com

Business International
Business International Corp.
One Dag Hammarskjold Plaza
New York, NY 10017

Business Week
McGraw-Hill Publications Co.
1221 Avenue of the Americas
New York, NY 10020
http://www.businessweek.com

Commodity Trade Statistics
United Nations Publications
1 United Nations Plaza
Room DC2–0853
New York, NY 10017

Conference Board Record
Conference Board Inc.
845 Third Avenue
New York, NY 10022

*Customs and Border Protection
    Bulletin*
US Customs Service
1301 Constitution Avenue NW
Washington, DC 20229
http://www.cbp.sor

The Dismal Scientist
http://www.economy.com/dismal

The Economist
Economist Newspaper Ltd.
25 St. James Street
London SWIA 1HG, England
http://www.economist.com

Export America
US Department of Commerce
14th Street and Constitution Avenue NW
Washington, DC 20230
http://www.commerce.gov

The Financial Times
Bracken House
10 Cannon Street
London EC4P 4BY, England
http://www.ft.com

Forbes
Forbes, Inc.
60 Fifth Avenue
New York, NY 10011
http://www.forbes.com

Fortune
Time, Inc.
Time & Life Building
1271 Avenue of the Americas
New York, NY 10020
http://www.fortune.com

Global Trade
North American Publishing Co.
401 N. Broad Street
Philadelphia, PA 19108

Industrial Marketing
Crain Communications, Inc.
740 N. Rush Street
Chicago, IL 60611

*International Encyclopedia of the Social
    Sciences*
Macmillan and the Free Press
866 Third Avenue
New York, NY 10022

International Financial Statistics
International Monetary Fund
Publications Unit
700 19th Street NW
Washington, DC 20431
http://www.imf.org

Investor's Daily
Box 25970
Los Angeles, CA 90025

Journal of Commerce
100 Wall Street
New York, NY 10005
http://www.joc.com

Lexis-Nexis Legal Express
    Info Service
http://www.michie.com

Sales and Marketing Management
Bill Communications Inc.
633 Third Avenue
New York, NY 10017
http://salesandmarketing.com

Tomorrow
Global Environment Business
http://www.tomorrow-web.com

Wall Street Journal
Dow Jones & Company
200 Liberty Street
New York, NY 10281
http://online.wsj.com

Pergamon Press Inc.
Journals Division
Maxwell House
Fairview Park
Elmsford, NY 10523

Trade Finance
US Department of Commerce
International Trade Administration
Washington, DC 20230
http://www.commerce.gov

*World Trade Centre Association
    (WTCA) Directory*
60 East 42nd Street
Suite 1901
New York, NY 10048
http://www.wtca.com

Media Guide International: Business/
Professional Publications
Directories International Inc.
150 Fifth Avenue, Suite 610
New York, NY 10011
World Wide web Virtual Law Library
http://www.law.indiana.edu/v-lib

SELECTED TRADE DATABASES

Trade publication references with bibliographic keywords

Agris
Biocommerce Abstracts & Directory
Findex
Frost (short) Sullivan Market
Research Reports
Marketing Surveys Index
McCarthy Press Cuttings Service
Paperchem
PTS F & S Indexes
Trade and Industry Index

Trade publication references with summaries

ABI/Inform
Arab Information Bank
Asia-Pacific
BFAI
Biobusiness
CAB Abstracts
Chemical Business Newbase
Chemical Industry Notes
Caffeeline
Delphes
InfoSouth Latin American
Information System
Management Contents
NTIS Bibliographic Data Base
Paperchem
PIRA Abstract
PSTA
PTS Marketing & Advertising
Reference Service
PTS PromtRapra Abstracts
Textline
Trade & Industry ASAP
World Textiles

Full text of trade publications

Datamonitor Market Reports
Dow Jones News

Euromonitor Market Direction
Federal News Service
Financial Times Business Report
File
Financial Times Fulltext
Globefish
ICC Key Notes Market Research
Investext
McCarthy Press Cuttings Service
PTS Promt
Textline
Trade & Industry ASAP

Statistics

Agrostat (diskette only)
Arab Information Bank
ARI Network/CNS
Comext/Eurostat
Comtrade
FAKT-German Statistics
Globefish
IMF Data
OECD Data
Piers Imports
PTS Forecasts
PTS Time Series
Reuters Monitor
Trade Statistics
Tradstat World Trade Statistics
TRAINS (CD-ROM being developed)
US I/E Maritime Bills of Lading
US Imports for Consumption
World Bank Statistics

Price information

ARI Network/CNS
Chemical Business Newsbase
COLEACP
Commodity Options
Commodities 2000
Market News Service of ITC
Nikkei Shimbun News Database
Reuters Monitor
UPI
US Wholesale Prices

Company registers

ABC Europe Production Europe
Biocommerce Abstracts & Directory
CD-Export (CD-ROM only)
Company Intelligence
D&B Dun's Market Identifiers (USA.)
D&B European Marketing File
D&B Eastern Europe
Dun's Electronic Business Directory

Firmexport/Firmimport
Hoppenstedt Austria
Hoppenstedt Benelux
Hoppenstedt Germany
Huco-Hungarian Companies
ICC Directory of Companies
Kompass Asia/Pacific
Kompass Europe (EKOD)
Mexican Exporters/Importers
Piers Imports
Polu-Polish Companies
SDOE
Thomas Register
TRAINS (CD-ROM being developed)
UK Importers
UK Importers (DECTA)
US Directory of Importers
US I/E Maritime Bills of Lading
World Trade Centre Network

Trade opportunities, tenders

Business
Federal News Service
Huntech-Hungarian Technique
Scan-a-Bid
Tenders Electronic Daily
World Trade Centre Network

Tariffs and trade regulations

Celex
ECLAS
Justis Eastern Europe (CD-ROM only)
Scad
Spearhead
Spicer's Centre for Europe
TRAINS (CD-ROM being developed)
US Code of Federal Regulations
US Federal Register
US Harmonized Tariff Schedule

Standards

BSI Standardline
Noriane/Perinorm
NTIS Bibliographic Data Base
Standards Infodisk ILI (CD-ROM only)

Shipping information

Piers Imports
Tradstat World Trade Statistics
US I/E Maritime Bills of Lading

Others

Fairbase
Ibiscus

THE STRUCTURE OF A COUNTRY COMMERCIAL GUIDE

The following is an example of governmental research made available to firms. Country commercial guides provide a condensed and business-focused overview of business customs, conditions, contacts and opportunities. Using such guides can be of major help in getting started in unfamiliar territory.

Guide for doing business in the US for Hong Kong companies

This guide provides a wealth of user-friendly assistance to SMEs interested in developing business with the US, particularly with respect to the US trade regime, by examining its import and other related regulations, as well as marketing and setting up a business in the US. Its contents cover quotas, import licencing and import restrictions, scheme of customs tariffs, trade measures with respect to anti-dumping, safeguard and IPR issues, customs clearance procedures, payment methods, export controls and dispute settlements, taxes and business insurance, visa and immigration issues, etc.

Chapter 4:   **Trade Measures**

4.1 Anti-dumping Duties and Countervailing Duties

4.2 Safeguards

4.3 IPR Issues

Chapter 5:   **Marking, Labelling and Packing Requirements**

5.1 Marking and Labelling

5.2 Special Labelling and Marking Requirements

5.3 Packing

5.4 Shipping

5.5 Marine and Air Insurance

5.6 Cargo Security

Chapter 6:   **Entry and Customs Clearance**

6.1 Entry Process

6.2 Right to Make Entry

6.3 Invoices

6.4 Clearance Procedures

6.5 Payment of Duties

6.6 Ports of Entry by State

6.7 Regulations on Postal and Sample Shipments

Chapter 7:   **Payment Methods, Export Controls and Dispute Settlement**

7.1 Payment Methods of Goods

7.2 Export Controls

7.3 Dispute Settlement

Chapter 8:   **Appointment of US Sales Agents/Representatives and Setting up Sales Offices/
Subsidiaries**

8.1 Appointing US Sales Agents/Representatives

8.2 Establishing a US Sales Office/Subsidiary

Chapter 9:   **Incorporation of a Business**

9.1 Types of Business Organizations

9.2 Incorporating a Business

9.3 Setting up an Online Business

Chapter 10:   **Taxes and Business Insurance**

10.1 Taxes

10.2 Business Insurance

Chapter 11:   **Employment**

11.1 Employment Procedures

11.2 Employment Regulations and Employer Obligations

Chapter 12:   **Visas and Immigration Issues**

12.1 US Visas

12.2 Working Permits

Chapter 13:   **Sales Promotion in the US**

13.1 Trade Shows

13.2 Trade Magazine Advertising

Source: Hong Kong Trade Development Council (HKTDC) (2010), 'Guide to doing business with US'. Online. Available from: **http://www.hktdc.com/info/mi/bgus/en/** (Accessed 13/5/10).

THE INTERNATIONAL **MARKETPLACE 9.1**

The internationalization of Specsavers

Specsavers was founded in 1984 by Doug and Mary Perkins, who started the business in their spare bedroom on a table-tennis table. The couple had moved to Guernsey after selling a small chain of West Country opticians. In the early 1980s the UK Government deregulated professionals, including opticians, allowing them to advertise their products and services for the first time. They seized the opportunity and opened their first Specsavers, value-for-money, quality eyecare opticians in Guernsey and Bristol, followed shortly afterwards by stores in Plymouth, Swansea and Bath. They aimed to offer a wide range of stylish, fashionable glasses at affordable prices for everyone. They wanted the company to be seen as trustworthy an optician as a local independent but with the huge buying power of a national company that meant savings could be passed on to the customer.

The company has grown rapidly since, thriving with its joint venture partnership approach to eyecare. It hit the milestone of 100 stores in July 1988, 200 in 1993, 300 in 1995, 400 in 2000, 500 in 2003, 600 in 2004 and 700 in 2005. The first Netherlands store opened in 1997, the first Swedish in 2004, and 2005 saw the first in Denmark and Norway. In 2006 the first store was opened in Spain, and in 2007 the company began supplying in Australia whilst opening the first store in Finland. In January 2008 Dame Mary Perkins opened the 1000th store in Roosendaal, Holland, followed by the launch of the first three Specsavers stores in Australia in March. By July 2009 there were 173 in Australia plus 24 in New Zealand.

For the past eight years it has been voted Britain's most-trusted brand of opticians by *Reader's Digest*. The current straplines 'Number One Choice For Eye Tests' and 'Number One Choice For Contact Lenses' reflect its position as market leader. Specsavers' range includes Tommy Hilfiger, Red or Dead, fcuk, Bench, Quiksilver, Roxy, Jasper Conran and Missoni, as well as the market leading Osiris designer brand.

Our frames are developed using the latest innovative manufacturing and design techniques from the highest quality components and raw materials available. The full range of over 2,000 size and colour options is structured around a comprehensive features and benefits pricing structure, starting from £25 through to £169. Our own lens manufacturing laboratories – three of the largest in Europe – supply the latest high-tech lenses in volume at the lowest possible cost. All Specsavers frames come with free Single Vision Pentax lenses as standard.

Specsavers is also the retail market leader in contact lenses, with its own brand of easyvision monthly and daily disposable lenses, and has also driven the use of continuous-wear lenses. Currently one out of every three UK contact lens wearers chooses Specsavers. Furthermore, Specsavers is the largest provider of home-delivery contact lenses in Europe through its Lensmail service.

Specsavers is bringing its core offers to its rapidly expanding hearing service, which is now doing for hearing what the retailer has already achieved in optics – dramatically reducing prices and waiting times and making audiology services more accessible for everyone.

© ROBERT CONVERY/ALAMY

Specsavers is already the largest retail dispenser of digital hearing aids in the UK and offers a hearing service from over 400 locations.

The company continues to expand. From just two staff working at that table-tennis table, there are now more than 500 based at Specsavers' headquarters in Guernsey and around 26,000 worldwide. The company has more than 1390 stores across the Channel Islands, UK, Ireland, the Netherlands, Scandinavia, Spain, Australia and New Zealand.

SOURCE: Specsavers (2010), 'History'. Online. Available from: **http://www.specsavers.co.uk/about/history** (Accessed 10/5/10).

As *The International Marketplace 9.1* shows, participation in the international marketplace is within the grasp of even small firms. It can be very rewarding and may turn out to be the key to prosperity for both corporations and employees. Firms that export grow faster, are more productive, and have employees who tend to earn more.[1] Even though some firms go international from the start, most of them do so gradually. New activities in an unfamiliar environment increase a firm's risk. Therefore, companies must prepare their activities and adjust to the needs and opportunities of international markets in order to become long-term participants.

This chapter discusses the activities that take place within the firm preparing to enter the international market. It focuses on the basic stimuli for internationalization and on the internal and external change agents that activate these stimuli. The concerns and preoccupations of firms as they begin their international marketing operations are discussed. Finally expansion strategies, such as franchising, licencing and foreign direct investment are presented. Exhibit 9.1 provides a model of the international entry and expansion process. It shows what triggers and inhibits international expansion and outlines the subsequent discussion of this chapter.

STIMULI TO INTERNATIONALIZE

In most business activities, one factor alone rarely accounts for any given action. Usually a mixture of factors results in firms taking steps in a given direction. This is true of internationalization; there are a variety of stimuli both pushing and pulling firms along the international path. Exhibit 9.2 lists the major motivations to go international, differentiated into proactive

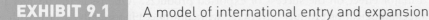

EXHIBIT 9.1 A model of international entry and expansion

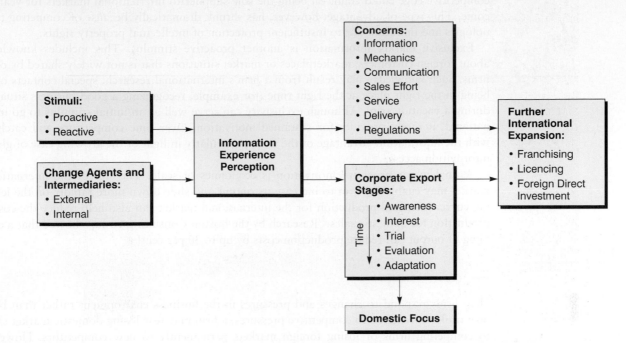

Proactive Stimuli	Reactive Stimuli
• Profit advantage	• Competitive pressures
• Unique products	• Overproduction
• Technological advantage	• Declining domestic sales
• Exclusive information	• Excess capacity
• Economies of scale	• Saturated domestic markets
• Market size	• Proximity to customers and ports

EXHIBIT 9.2

Why firms go international

and reactive motivations. Proactive motivations represent stimuli to attempt strategic change. Reactive motivations influence firms that respond to environmental shifts by changing their activities over time. In other words, proactive firms go international because they want to, while reactive ones go international because they have to.

Proactive stimuli

Profits are the strongest catalyst to become involved in international marketing. Management may perceive international sales as a potential source of higher profit margins or of added-on profits. Of course, the perceived profitability from going international may not match actual profitability because of such factors as high start-up costs, sudden shifts in exchange rates or insufficient market research.

A second major stimulus results either from unique products or a technological advantage. A firm's goods or services may not be widely available from international competitors or may offer technological advances in a specialized field. Uniqueness can provide a competitive edge and result in major business success abroad. Again, real and perceived advantages should be differentiated. Many firms believe that theirs are unique products or services, even though, on a global level, this may not be the case. The intensity of marketing's interaction with the research and development function, as well as the level of investment into R&D, has been shown to have a major effect on the success of exported products.[2] One issue to consider is how long such a technological or product advantage will continue. Historically, a firm with a competitive edge could count on being the sole supplier to international markets for years to come. This type of advantage, however, has shrunk dramatically because of competing technologies and imitation due to insufficient protection of intellectual property rights.

Exclusive market information is another proactive stimulus. This includes knowledge about foreign customers, marketplaces or market situations that is not widely shared by other firms. Such knowledge may result from a firm's international research, special contacts or by being in the right place at the right time (for example, recognizing a good business situation during a vacation trip). Although exclusivity can serve well as an initial stimulus to go international, it rarely provides for sustained motivation. Over time competitors will catch up with the information advantage of the firm, particularly in light of the growing ease of global information access.

A final major proactive motivation is economies of scale. The size of the international market may enable the firm to increase its output and slide down more rapidly on the learning curve. Increased production for the international market can also help reduce the cost of production for domestic sales.[3] Research by the Boston Consulting Group showed that a doubling of output can reduce production costs by up to 30 per cent!

Reactive stimuli

Here firms respond to changes and pressures in the business environment rather than blaze new trails. In reaction to competitive pressures, a firm may fear losing domestic market share to competing firms or losing foreign markets permanently to new competitors. However, insufficient preparation may result in a hasty market entry and a quick withdrawal.

Overproduction is a major reactive motivation. Historically, during downturns in the domestic business cycle, markets abroad provided an ideal outlet for high inventories. Such market expansion often does not represent commitment by management, but rather a temporary safety-valve activity. Instead of developing an international marketing perspective by adjusting the marketing mix to needs abroad, firms stimulate export sales with short-term price cuts.[4] As soon as the domestic market demand returns to previous levels, international marketing activities are curtailed or even terminated. Firms that have used such a strategy once may encounter difficulties when trying it again, because many foreign customers are not interested in temporary or sporadic business relationships. The lessons learned, and the increased synchronization of the major industrial economies, may well decrease the importance of this motivation over time.

Stable or declining domestic sales, whether measured in sales volume or market share also stimulate firms. Products marketed by the firm domestically may be in the declining stage of the product life cycle. Firms may opt to prolong the life by expanding the market. In the past, such efforts often met with success in developing nations because their customers only gradually reached a level of need already attained by customers in industrialized nations. Increasingly, however, global lag times are quite short. Nevertheless, developing nations often still have very good use for products for which the demand in the industrialized world is already on the decline. This holds particularly true for high-technology items that are outdated by the latest innovations. Such 'just-dated' technology – for example, slightly obsolete medical equipment – can be highly useful to economic development and offer vast progress.

Excess capacity can be a powerful motivation. If equipment is not fully utilized, international expansion can help achieve broader distribution of fixed costs. Alternatively, if all fixed costs are assigned to domestic production, the firm can penetrate international markets with a pricing scheme that focuses mainly on variable costs. Such a strategy may result in the offering of products abroad at a cost lower than at home, which may trigger dumping charges. In the long run, fixed costs recovery needs to ensure the replacement of production equipment used for international marketing activities.

The stimulus of a saturated domestic market is similar to that of declining domestic sales. Again, firms can use the international market to prolong the life cycle of their product and of their organization.

A final major reactive motivation is proximity to customers and ports. Physical closeness to foreign markets can encourage the international activities of a firm. In Europe, due to geographical closeness of countries, many firms find themselves going international. For example, a European company operating in the heart of Belgium needs to go only 50 miles to be in multiple foreign markets.

In this context, the concept of psychic or psychological distance needs to be understood. Geographic closeness to foreign markets may not necessarily translate into real or perceived closeness to the foreign customer. Sometimes cultural variables, legal factors and other societal norms make a foreign market that is geographically close seem psychologically distant. For example, UK firms perceive the US to be much closer psychologically than Europe due to similarity of language. Two major issues frame the context of psychological distance. First, some of the distance seen by firms is based on perception rather than reality. For example, German firms may view the Austrian market simply as an extension of their home market due to so many superficial similarities. However, the attitudes and values of managers and customers may vary substantially between markets. Too much of a focus on the similarities may let the firm lose sight of the differences. Many Canadian firms have incurred high costs in learning this lesson when entering the United States.[5] At the same time, closer psychological proximity does make it easier for firms to enter markets. Therefore, for firms new to international marketing, it may be advantageous to begin this new activity by entering the psychologically closer markets first in order to gather experience before venturing into markets that are farther away.[6]

Overall, the more successful international firms are motivated by proactive – that is, firm-internal – factors. The motivations of firms do not seem to shift dramatically over the short term but are rather stable. For the reader who seeks involvement in international markets and searches for good corporate opportunities, an important consideration should be whether a firm is proactive or reactive.

CHANGE AGENTS

Someone or something within the firm must initiate change and shepherd it through to implementation. This intervening individual or variable is here called a change agent. change agents in the internationalization process are shown in Exhibit 9.3.

Internal change agents

The type and quality of management is key to a firm's international activities. Dynamic management is important when firms take their first international steps. Over the long term, management commitment and management's perceptions and attitudes are also good predictors of export success.[7] Key also are the international experience and exposure of management.[8] Managers who have lived abroad, know foreign languages, or are particularly interested in foreign cultures are likely, sooner rather than later, to investigate whether international

Internal	External
• Enlightened management	• Demand
• New management	• Other firms
• Significant internal event	• Domestic distributors
	• Banks
	• Chambers of commerce
	• Governmental activities
	• Export intermediaries
	– Export management companies
	– Trading companies

EXHIBIT 9.3

Change agents in the internationalization process

marketing opportunities would be appropriate for their firm. Managerial urge reflects the desire, drive and enthusiasm towards international marketing activities. This enthusiasm can exist simply because managers like to be part of a firm that operates internationally. They may like international travel – for example, to call on a major customer in the Bahamas during a cold winter month. Similarly, the urge to internationalize may simply reflect entrepreneurial zeal – a desire for continuous market growth and expansion.[9]

This conclusion has largely been formulated by reverse deduction: The managers of firms that are unsuccessful or inactive in the international marketplace usually exhibit a lack of commitment to international marketing. International markets cannot be penetrated overnight – to succeed in them requires substantial market development activity, market research and the identification of and response to new market factors. Therefore, a high level of commitment is crucial to endure setbacks and failure. It is important to involve all levels of management early on in the international planning process. Any international venture must be incorporated into the firm's strategic management process. A firm that sets no strategic goals is less likely to achieve long-term success.[10]

It is also important to establish a specific structure in which someone has the responsibility for international activities. Without such responsibility, the focus necessary for success is lost. Just one person assigned part-time can explore international opportunities successfully.

Another major change agent is a significant internal event. The development of a new product that can be useful abroad can serve as such an event, as can the receipt of new information about current product uses. As an example, a manufacturer of hospital beds learned that beds it was selling domestically were being resold in a foreign country. Further, the beds sold abroad for more than twice the price they were fetching at home. This new information triggered a strong interest by the company's management to enter international markets.

In small and medium-sized firms (firms with fewer than 250 employees), the initial decision to go international is usually made by the chief executive officer (CEO), with substantial input from the marketing department. The implementation of this decision usually becomes primarily the responsibility of marketing personnel. The strategic evaluation of international marketing activities is typically carried out again by the CEO of the firm. This makes the CEO and the marketing department the leading internal change agents.

External change agents and intermediaries

The primary outside influence on a firm's decision to go international is foreign demand. Inquiries from abroad and other expressions of demand have a powerful effect on initial interest in entering the international marketplace. Unsolicited international orders are one major factor that encourages firms to begin exporting. Through their websites, firms can easily become unplanned participants in the international market. Customers from abroad can visit the site and place an international order, even though a firm's plans may have been strictly domestic. Of course, a firm can choose to ignore foreign interest and lose out on new markets. Alternatively, it can unexpectedly find itself an exporter.[11] We call such firms **accidental exporters**. While good fortune may have initiated the export activity, over the longer term the firm must start planning how to systematically increase its international expansion or, at least, how to make more of these 'accidents' happen.

Another major change agent may actually be a competitor. Just as firms respond to competitive pressures from other companies, statements by executives from competing firms may serve as change agents. Therefore, formal and informal meetings among managers from different firms at trade association meetings, conventions or business roundtables often trigger major change.

Domestic distributors also initiate change. To increase their international distribution volume, they encourage purely domestic clients to participate in the international market. This is true not only for exports but also for imports.

Banks and other service firms, such as accountants, can alert domestic clients to international opportunities. Although these service providers have historically followed their major multinational clients abroad, increasingly they are establishing a foreign presence and then urging domestic clients to expand their market reach.

Chambers of commerce and other business associations that interact with firms locally can frequently heighten international marketing interests. These organizations function as secondary intermediaries, by sponsoring the presence and encouragement of other managers. They can also provide valuable information about local markets.

Government efforts on the national or local level can also serve as a major change agent. In light of the contributions exports make to growth, employment and tax revenue, governments are active in encouraging and supporting exports. In the United Kingdom, the Department for Business, Innovation and Skills (which replaced the Department of Trade and Industry) is particularly involved in export promotion.

Corporate export stages

For many firms, internationalization is a gradual process, particularly in small markets. However, firms may very well be born global, founded for the explicit purpose of marketing abroad because the domestic economy is too small to support their activities. It appears that in some countries more than a third of exporting firms commenced their export activities within two years of establishment.[12] Such start-up or innate exporters play a growing role in an economy's international trade involvement.

In addition, firms with a strong e-commerce focus may also be gaining rapid global exposure due to the ease of outreach and access. Such rapid exposure, however, should not be confused with actual internationalization, since it may often take a substantial amount of time to translate exposure into international business activities and strategic corporate acceptance.

In most instances today, firms begin their operations in the domestic market. From their home location, they gradually expand, and, over time, some of them become interested in the international market. The development of this interest typically appears to proceed in several stages as shown in Exhibit 9.4.

In each one of these stages, firms are measurably different in their capabilities, problems and needs.[13] Initially, the vast majority of firms are not even aware of the international marketplace. Frequently, management will not even fill an unsolicited export order. Should unsolicited orders or other international market stimuli continue over time, however, a firm may gradually become aware of international market opportunities. While such awareness is unlikely to trigger much business activity, it can lead management to gradually become interested in international activities. Eventually, firms will answer inquiries, participate in export counselling sessions, attend international trade fairs and seminars and even begin to fill unsolicited export orders.

Prime candidates among firms to make this transition from aware to interested are those companies that have a track record of domestic market expansion. In the next stage, the firm gradually begins to explore international markets. Management is willing to consider the feasibility of exporting. In this trial or exploratory stage, the firm begins to export systematically, usually to psychologically close countries. However, management is still far from being committed to international marketing activities.

After some export activity, typically within two years of the initial export, management is likely to conduct an evaluation of its export efforts. Key questions concern the fulfilment of expectations. Are our products as unique as we thought they were, and are we making enough money on our exports? If a firm is disappointed with its international performance it

EXHIBIT 9.4

Key corporate export stages

- Awareness
- Interest
- Trial
- Evaluation
- Adaptation

may withdraw from these activities. Alternatively, it can continue as an experienced small exporter. Success can also lead to the process of export adaptation. Here a firm is an experienced exporter to a particular country and adjusts its activities to changing exchange rates, tariffs and other variables. Management is ready to explore the feasibility of exporting to additional countries that are psychologically farther away. Frequently, this level of adaptation is reached once export transactions comprise 15 per cent of overall sales volume. Planning for export marketing becomes incorporated into the strategy of the firm.

The population of exporting firms within these stages does not remain stable. Research evidence has generally shown that in any given year, 15 per cent of exporters will stop exporting by the next year, while 10 per cent of non-exporters will enter the foreign market. The most critical junctures for the firm are the points at which it begins or ceases exporting.[14]

As can be expected, firms in different stages are faced with different problems. Firms at an export awareness stage are primarily concerned with operational matters such as information flow and the mechanics of carrying out international business transactions. They understand that a totally new body of knowledge and expertise is needed and try to acquire it. Companies that have already had some exposure to international markets begin to think about tactical marketing issues such as communication and sales effort. Finally, firms that have reached the export adaptation phase are mainly strategy- and service-oriented. They worry about longer-range issues such as service delivery and regulatory changes. One can recognize that increased sophistication in international markets translates into increased application of marketing knowledge on the part of firms. The more they become active in international markets, the more firms recognize that a marketing orientation is internationally just as essential as it is in the domestic market.

Intermediaries

Firms who choose to export their products may do so in a number of different ways. They may export directly, use export intermediaries such as export management companies or trading companies, or harness the technology of the internet to engage in e-commerce. They can also sell to a domestic firm that in turn sells abroad. For example, many products sold to multinational corporations are used as input for their global sales.

Market intermediaries specialize in bringing firms or their goods and services to the global market. Often, they have detailed information about the competitive conditions in certain markets or they have personal contacts with potential buyers abroad. They can also evaluate credit risk, call on customers abroad, and manage the physical delivery of the product. Two key intermediaries are export management companies and trading companies.

Export management companies

Export management companies (EMCs) are domestic firms that perform international marketing services as commission representatives or as distributors for several other firms. Most EMCs are quite small. They are frequently formed by one or two principals with experience in international marketing or in a particular geographic area.

EMCs have two primary forms of operation. They either take title to goods and operate internationally on their own account, or they perform services as agents. As an agent, an EMC is likely to have a contractual relationship, which specifies exclusivity agreements and sales quotas. In addition, price arrangements and promotional support payments are agreed on.[15] Since EMCs often serve a variety of clients, their mode of operation may vary from client to client and from transaction to transaction. An EMC may act as an agent for one client, whereas for another client, or even for the same one on a different occasion, it may operate as a distributor.

For the export management company concept to work, both parties must recognize the delegation of responsibilities, the costs associated with these activities, and the need for information sharing and cooperation. On the manufacturer's side, use of an EMC is a major channel commitment. This requires a thorough investigation of the intermediary, a willingness to cooperate on a prolonged basis and proper rewards. The EMC in turn must adopt a flexible approach to the export relationship. As access to the internet is making customers increasingly sophisticated, export management companies must ensure that they continue to deliver true added value. They must acquire, develop and deploy resources, such as new knowledge about foreign markets or about export processes, in order to lower their client firm's export-related transaction costs.[16] The EMC must show that the service is worth the cost.

Trading companies

Another major intermediary is the trading company. The concept was originated by the European trading houses such as the Fuggers and was soon formalized by the monarchs. Hoping to expand their power and wealth, kings chartered traders with exclusive trading rights and protection by the naval forces in exchange for tax payments. Today, the most famous trading companies are the *sogoshosha* of Japan. Names like Sumitomo, Mitsubishi, Mitsui and C. Itoh have become household words around the world. These general trading companies play a unique role in world commerce by importing, exporting, countertrading, investing and manufacturing. Due to their vast size, they can benefit from economies of scale and survive on very low profit margins.

Four major reasons have been given for the success of the Japanese *sogoshosha*. First, these firms are organized to gather, evaluate and translate market information into business opportunities. By making large investments in their information systems, these firms have developed a strategic information advantage. Second, their vast transaction volume provides them with cost advantages. For example, they can negotiate preferential transportation rates. Third, these firms serve large markets around the world and have transaction advantages. They can benefit from unique opportunities, such as barter trade in which they exchange goods for goods. Finally, *sogoshosha* have access to vast quantities of capital, both within Japan and in the international capital markets. With their financial advantage they can carry out transactions that are larger and riskier than is feasible for other firms.

For many decades, the emergence of trading companies was commonly believed to be a Japan-specific phenomenon. Over time, however, prodded by government legislation, successful trading companies have also emerged in countries as diverse as Brazil, South Korea and Turkey. Export trading company (ETC) legislation designed to improve the export performance of small and medium-sized firms permits bank participation in trading companies and reduces the antitrust threat to joint export efforts. Businesses are encouraged to join together to export or offer export services.

Bank participation in ETCs was intended to allow better access to capital. The relaxation of antitrust provisions in turn was to enable firms to share the cost of international market entry. As an example, in case a warehouse is needed to support foreign-market penetration, one firm alone does not have to bear all the costs.

Export trading companies seem to offer major benefits to UK firms wishing to penetrate international markets. As of June 2009, there were 18,500 registered ETCs.[17] They have not been used very extensively. By 2006, only 80 individual ETCs had been certified by the US Department of Commerce. Yet these certificates covered more than 3,000 firms, mainly because various trade associations had applied for certification for all of their members.[18]

Firms participating in trading companies by joining or forming them need to consider the difference between product- and market-driven activities. Firms have a tendency to use a trading company to dispose of their existing merchandise. International success, however, depends primarily on market demand. Trading companies must therefore accomplish a balance between the demands of the market and the supply of the members in order to be successful. Information must be collected on the needs and wants of foreign customers. It must then be disseminated to participating firms and help must be provided in implementing change. Otherwise, lack of responsiveness to market demand will limit international success.

E-COMMERCE

Many companies increasingly choose to market their products internationally through e-commerce, the ability to offer goods and services over the web. *The International Marketplace 9.2* highlights the rapid growth of e-commerce. There are a variety of ways in

THE INTERNATIONAL **MARKETPLACE 9.2**

Global digital economy: m-commerce, e-commerce and e-payments

E-commerce is now an important part of the economy, particularly in the developed markets. While e-commerce is still in its infancy in many emerging markets, this is set to change in the coming years especially in China. In 2008 China had the highest number of internet users in the world, overtaking the USA. E-commerce growth in the USA remains strong however, with China also offering significant opportunities for those operating in the e-commerce space.

Worldwide the number of internet users has now reached around 1.4 billion and billions will be spent by consumers during 2008 on online retail. While the economic slowdown will most likely curb e-commerce growth somewhat over the next couple of years, particularly spending on online advertising, there is evidence that so far the online retail market has remained steady due mostly to the lower prices offered via online shopping.

Internet banking has slowly become more popular around the world, with 30 per cent or more of internet users utilizing such services in some markets. However many online banking websites have at least one potential design weakness that could leave users vulnerable to cyber attacks. Improved bank security measures over the last couple of years, such as the introduction of home chip and pin devices is helping to combat this issue.

In the next few years the total entertainment and publishing industry (including offline and online) is expected to be worth more than $2 trillion – driven in particular by a wave of growth in online video games, gambling, music, social networking/user generated content and online video. In recent times sales of digital music, mostly via the internet, have increased by more than 30 per cent; in contrast sales of CDs and DVDs continue to decline. Online video consumption is also beginning to produce promising results and

---

TABLE 9.1   Comparison of popular websites in different markets – 2008

Market

Japan	USA	United Arab Emirates	Germany
Google sites	Google sites	Google sites	Google sites
Yahoo! sites	Yahoo! sites	Yahoo! sites	Yahoo! sites
Microsoft sites	Microsoft sites	Microsoft sites	Microsoft sites
Wikipedia sites	Wikipedia sites	Wikipedia sites	Wikipedia sites
Rakuten Inc	AOL	Maktoob	eBay
FC2 inc	Fox Interactive Media	Bayt	United-internet sites
NTT Group	eBay	Gulf News	AOL
GMO Internet Group	Amazon sites	Amazon sites	ProSiebenSat1 sites
Livedoor	Time Warner – excluding AOL	CNET download.com	Verlagsgruppe Georg von Holtzbrinck
Nifty Corporation	Ask Network	Souq	Arcandor AG
Amazon sites	New York Times Digital	AME Info	T-Online sites
Apple Inc	Apple Inc	United Arab Emirates University	Deutsche Telekom
NEC Corporation	Viacom Digital	Ma7room.com	Vodafone Group
Sony Online	Glam Media	UAE Women Network	Otto Gruppe

Source: BuddeComm based on various industry sources, 2008

advertisers have begun to seriously take note. Pay-to-own download-ing is particularly popular and new business models in this area are expected to emerge over the next few years. Travel and adult content services are also popular with more growth expected ahead.

Mobile commerce is potentially important for a wide range of industries, including telecommunications, IT, finance, retail and the media, as well as for end-users. It will work best in those areas where it can emphasize the core virtue of mobile networks – conven-ience. However while there are good applications, the technologies and business models to date have not been well suited to mass mar-ket applications. The regulatory environment has also held this mar-ket up. This is beginning to change as banks and merchants collaborate with mobile operators. Applications around contactless cards using Near Field Communications are also being developed around the world. Focus has also turned to the developing markets, where mobile phones are being viewed as an opportunity to reach the masses that would not otherwise use m-payment or m-banking services.

In countries such as Kenya and India, national mobile banking systems are thriving and they are literally popping up around the world as well. In Kenya, three million out of Vodafone's ten million subscribers are using mobile banking services and Vodafone is rap-idly rolling the service out in other countries as well.

SOURCE: Wansink, K. (2008), 'Global Digital Economy: M-Commerce, E-Commerce and E-Payments', **http://www.budde.com.au/Research/2008-Global-Digital-Economy-M-Commerce-E-Commerce-E-Payments.html** (Accessed 18/06/09).

which companies can market their products over the internet. One key option is the devel-opment of corporate websites. As discussed previously, many companies initially become exporters because of unsolicited international orders. In order to encourage more orders from foreign consumers, companies should accept international means of payment and have the ability to ship their product internationally. In addition, companies need to con-sider the ever-growing population of non–English speakers on the web. Websites should be offered in several different languages. However, having a website translated and kept up to date may be costly and time-consuming. If the site is well developed, it will naturally lead to the expectations that order fulfilment will be of equal calibre. Therefore, any World Wide Web strategy has to be tied closely to the company's overall growth strategy in world markets.

Companies can also enter e-commerce by exporting through a variety of business-to-consumer and business-to-business forums. For example, consumers and businesses alike can sell their products on the online auction site eBay (**http://www.ebay.com**). Businesses who would like to target the Chinese market can use China's Alibaba (**http://www.alibaba.com**), whose slogan is 'Global trade starts here'. Alibaba, in particular, targets small and medium-sized businesses who would like to export to China, and Chinese businesses looking to expand domestically. In 2008, Alibaba International had a transaction volume of RMB3.0 billion, with close to 38.1 million registered users.[19]

There are a variety of new concerns if a firm uses e-commerce to export. Due to interna-tional time differences, firms must be ready to provide 24-hour order taking and customer support service, have the regulatory and customs-handling expertise to deliver internation-ally, and have an understanding of global marketing environments for the further develop-ment of business relationships. Many companies choose to use the capabilities of air carriers such as UPS, DHL and FedEx, who offer a range of support services such as order fulfilment, delivery, customs clearance and supply chain management. There are some legal concerns for e-businesses, such as export control laws, especially if they market strategically important products or software. Firms must also consider privacy, security and intellectual property regulations. The EU's privacy measures differ from place to place. EU privacy measures are much more stringent than those of China and thus may impact Chinese com-panies looking to do business in Europe. Comprehensive legal protection for the privacy of citizens has become a major focus of the Chinese legislature, given the rapid development of the internet, the ease of the dispersion of large amounts of data and other issues.[20] Further-more, companies need to be able to protect their customers from identity theft and other online scams.

As the global penetration of the internet grows, e-commerce will become an even more important venue for commercial activity. It can be expected that countries will implement more laws concerning business transactions over the internet, and that the international community as a whole will develop standards, either outside or inside the World Trade Organization, for conducting e-commerce.

LICENCING AND FRANCHISING

Licencing and franchising are market expansion alternatives used by all types of firms, large and small. They offer flexibility and reflect the needs of the firm and the market. A small firm, for example, may take up licencing to use a foreign business concept or to expand without much capital investment. A multinational corporation may use the same strategy to rapidly enter foreign markets in order to take advantage of new conditions and foreclose opportunities for its competition.

Licencing

Under a licencing agreement, one firm, the licensor, permits another to use its intellectual property in exchange for compensation designated as a royalty. The recipient firm is the licensee. The property might include patents, trademarks, copyrights, technology, technical know-how or specific marketing skills. For example, a firm that has developed new packaging for liquids can permit other firms abroad to use the same process. Licencing therefore amounts to exporting and importing intangibles.

Assessment of licencing As an international entry strategy, licencing requires neither capital investment nor knowledge or marketing strength in foreign markets. Royalty income provides an opportunity to obtain an additional return on research and development investments already incurred. Licencing offers a proven concept that reduces the risk of R&D failures, the cost of designing around the licensor's patents, or the fear of patent infringement litigation. Furthermore, ongoing licencing cooperation and support enables the licensee to benefit from new developments.

Licencing reduces the exposure to government intervention and terrorism, since the licensee is typically a local company. It allows a firm to test a foreign market without major investment of capital or management time. It can also pre-empt a market for the competition, especially if the licensor's resources permit full-scale involvement only in selected markets. A final reason for growing licencing activities is the increase in global protection of intellectual property rights, which makes companies more willing to transfer proprietary knowledge internationally.[21] A strong foreign partner then becomes a local force with a distinct interest in rooting out unlicenced activities.

Licencing is not without disadvantages. It leaves most international marketing functions to the licensee. As a result, the licensor gains only limited expertise. Moreover, the initial toehold in the foreign market may not be a foot in the door. In exchange for the royalty, the licensor may create its own competitor not only in the markets for which the agreement was made but also in third markets.

Licencing has come under criticism from supranational organizations, such as the United Nations Conference on Trade and Development (UNCTAD). It has been alleged that licencing lets multinational corporations capitalize on older technology. Such technology, however, may be in the best interest of the recipient. Guinness Brewery, for example, in order to produce Guinness Stout in Nigeria, licensed equipment that had been used in Ireland at the turn of the twentieth century. This equipment had additional economic life in Nigeria because it presented a good fit with local needs.

Principal issues in negotiating licencing agreements The key issues in negotiating licencing agreements include the scope of the rights conveyed, compensation, licensee compliance, dispute resolution and the term and termination of the agreement.[22] Clear agreements reduce trouble down the road.

The rights conveyed are product and/or patent rights. Defining their scope involves specifying the technology, know-how, or show-how to be included, the format and guarantees. An example of format specification is an agreement on whether manuals will be translated into the licensee's language.

Compensation issues may be heavily argued. The licensor wants to cover (1) transfer costs, which are all variable costs incurred in transferring technology to a licensee and all ongoing costs of maintaining the agreement; (2) R&D costs incurred in researching and developing the licensed technology; and (3) opportunity costs incurred in the foreclosure of other sources of profit, such as exports or direct investment. To cover these costs, the licensor wants a share of the profits generated from the use of the licence.

Compensation can take the form of running royalties, such as 5 per cent of the licensee sales, and/or up-front payments, service fees and disclosure fees (for proprietary data). Sometimes, government regulations restrict royalty payments. In such instances, the know-how transferred can be capitalized and payments can be profits or dividends.

Licensee compliance in the agreement should address: (1) export control regulations, (2) confidentiality of the intellectual property and technology provided and (3) record keeping and provisions for licensor audits. Finally, the term, termination and survival of rights must be specified.

Trademark licencing **Trademark licencing** permits use of the names or logos of designers, literary characters, sports teams and movie stars on merchandise such as clothing. British designer Laura Ashley started the first major furniture licencing programme. Sports Direct first acquired a licence for the Dunlop brand for sports and leisure goods in various countries as part of the acquisition of Dunlop Slazenger Group Holdings Limited in 2004.[23] The licensors can obtain large revenues with little effort, whereas the licensees can produce a branded product that consumers will recognize immediately. Fees can range between 7 and 12 per cent of net sales for merchandising licence agreements.[24]

Both licensor and licensee may run into difficulty if the trademark is used for a product too far removed from the original success or if the licenced product casts a shadow on the reputation of the licensor. In licencing a trademark, consumer perceptions have to be researched to understand the effect on the brand's position.

Franchising

In franchising, a parent company (the franchiser) grants another, independent entity (the franchisee) the right to do business in a specified manner. This right can take the form of selling the franchiser's products or using its name, production, preparation, and marketing techniques, or its business approach. The major forms of franchising are manufacturer-retailer systems (such as car dealerships), manufacturer-wholesaler systems (such as soft drink companies) and service firm-retailer systems (such as lodging services and fast food outlets). Product/trade franchising emphasizes the product or commodity to be sold, while business format franchising focuses on ways of doing business.

Franchising's origins are in Bavaria, but it has been adopted by various types of businesses in many countries. Franchises exist across many different industries, but the ones perhaps most visible to consumers are in the restaurant and food service industry. For example, 24 per cent of British and 30 per cent of French franchisers are active outside their home countries.[25] In Vietnam one can encounter several Asian-owned franchises such as the South Korea-based Burger Khan, Thailand's Five Star Chicken and Japan's Lotto Burger.[26]

The typical reasons for the international expansion of franchise systems are market potential, financial gain and saturated domestic markets. From a franchisee's perspective, the franchise is beneficial because it reduces risk by implementing a proven concept. In Malaysia, for example, the success rate in the franchise business is 90 per cent, compared to a 20 per cent success rate of all new businesses.[27]

From a government perspective, franchising does not replace exports or export jobs. From a recipient-country view, franchising requires little outflow of foreign exchange and the bulk of the profit generated remains within the country.[28]

One key franchising concern is the need for standardization, without which many of the benefits of the transferred know-how are lost. Typically, such standardization will include the use of a common business name, similar layout, and similar production or service processes. Apart from leading to efficient operations, all of these factors will also contribute to a high degree of international recognizability. Standardization, however, does not mean 100 per cent uniformity. Adjustments in the final product need to take local market conditions into account. For example, fast-food outlets in Europe often need to serve beer and wine to be attractive to the local clientele. In order to enter the Indian market, where cows are considered sacred, McDonald's has developed non-beef burgers.

Another issue is the protection of the total business system that a franchise offers. Once a business concept catches on, local competition may emerge quite quickly with an imitation of the product, the general style of operation and even with a similar name.

Selection and training of franchisees present another concern. Although the local franchisee knows the market best, the franchiser still needs to understand the market for product adaptation purposes and operational details. There may be complications in selecting appropriate advertising media, effective copy testing, effective translation of the franchiser's message and the use of appropriate sales promotion tools. Exhibit 9.5 summarizes research findings regarding the challenges faced in international franchising.

To encourage better-organized and more successful growth, many companies turn to the master franchising system, wherein foreign partners are selected and awarded the rights to a large territory in which they in turn can sub-franchise. As a result, the franchiser gains market expertise and an effective screening mechanism for new franchises, while reducing costly mistakes.[29]

EXHIBIT 9.5

Key challenges to international franchising

Source: Edwards, W. (2008), 'International Expansion: Do opportunities outweigh Challenges?' **http://www.franchise.org/Franchise-News-Detail.aspx?id=37992** (Accessed 18/06/09).

1 Expanding outside your home country efficiently and cost-effectively: Without a plan and priorities you can find yourself spending lots of money with little result.

2 Defining the benefits, risks, opportunities and challenges: What are the specific benefits for your franchise? What are the resources needed for your franchise that you have or have to add and when? What will this effort take away from your home country growth?

3 Defining the time and cost it will take to succeed outside your home country: That all important financial model that shows your investment and expected return over time.

4 Protecting your brand and intellectual property: An up-front investment in trademarks is essential to maintain your brand value.

5 The added cost of training and support across many times zones: Budget for this up front and include it in your initial master franchise fee.

6 Deciding where to take your franchise to get the best return on your investment.

7 Picking the right master franchisees: The most difficult and time-consuming task of all in the global development of your franchise and the task most often not done properly. Take your time to find, evaluate and conduct due diligence on master-franchise candidates.

8 How will your franchise go global? Master franchising to one company per country? Area or province franchising larger countries such as China, Germany and the United States? Direct franchising which means more up-front investment on your part but more control and more profits long term? Maybe your franchise will use more than one of these market-entry structures. Take time to evaluate what each development method means to your franchise in terms of up-front investment and long-term return.

9 While in the past developed countries franchises were the only ones going global, in recent years we have seen a flood from developing countries, for example, Indian, Chinese, South African and Latin American franchisors also entering world markets. Now there is competition with these companies in many countries.

FOREIGN DIRECT INVESTMENT

Foreign direct investment represents international investment flows which acquire properties and plants. The international marketer makes such investments to create or expand a long-term interest in an enterprise with some degree of control. Portfolio investment in turn focuses on the purchase of stocks and bonds internationally. Portfolio investment is of primary concern to the international financial community.

Foreign direct investment has grown rapidly and has clearly become a major avenue for international market entry and expansion. In a study to investigate where 150 MNCs would invest in 2010, Asia emerged as the top region of interest for multinationals seeking to expand abroad, with almost half of the companies surveyed planning to increase their investments in the region over the coming year; this was followed by Europe, where more than one-quarter of companies plan to increase investments; interest in Latin American investment ranked third; North America and the Middle East tied in fourth place; and Africa ranked sixth. Despite some of the most difficult economic conditions for generations, the UK maintains its position as the number one destination for foreign investors in Europe, and second in the world. It is seen as an attractive commercial destination by more nations than ever before. In 2009, 53 countries have invested in the UK, with investment projects from India increasing by 44 per cent in the past year to become the UK's second largest source – 108 FDI projects. The USA remains the first source of investment – which this year rose by 30 per cent to 621 projects. Other nations providing increased investment into the UK this year were Italy (up 45 per cent), France (up 15 per cent), Canada (up 25 per cent) and The Gulf (up 25 per cent).[30]

Major foreign investors

The United Nations defines multinational corporations as 'enterprises which own or control production or service facilities outside the country in which they are based'.[31] This definition makes all foreign direct investors multinational corporations. Yet large corporations are the key players. Exhibit 9.6 lists the 40 largest corporations around the world. They come from a wide variety of countries, depend heavily on their international sales, and, in terms of sales, are larger than many countries. As these firms keep growing, they appear to benefit from greater abilities to cope with new, unfamiliar situations.[32] Yet it also appears that there is an optimal size that, when exceeded, increases the costs of operations.[33]

Many of the large multinationals operate in well over 100 countries. For some, their original home market accounts for only a fraction of their sales. For example, the Dutch company Philips, Swedish SKF, and Swiss Nestlé sell less than 5 per cent of their total sales in their home country. In some firms, even the terms *domestic* and *foreign* have fallen into disuse. Others are working to consider issues only from a global perspective. For example, in management meetings of ABB (Asea Brown Boveri), individuals get fined $100 every time the words *foreign* and *domestic* are used.

Through their investment, multinational corporations bring economic vitality and jobs to their host countries and often pay higher wages than the average domestically oriented firms.[34]

At the same time, however, trade follows investment. This means that foreign direct investors often bring with them imports on an ongoing basis. The flow of imports in turn may contribute to the weakening of a nation's international trade position.

Reasons for foreign direct investment

Firms expand internationally for a wide variety of reasons. The major determinants are marketing and cost factors, an attractive investment climate and the ability to overcome trade barriers.

Marketing factors   Marketing considerations and the corporate desire for growth are major causes for the increase in foreign direct investment. Even large domestic markets limit growth, which typically means greater responsibilities and more pay for those who

EXHIBIT 9.6

World's forty largest corporations

Rank	Company	Country	Revenues ($ millions)	Profits ($ millions)
1	Wal-Mart Stores	United States	287,989	10,267
2	BP	UK	285,059	15,371
3	Exxon Mobil	United States	270,772	25,330
4	Royal Dutch/Shell Group	United States	268,690	18,183
5	General Motors	United States	193,517	2,805
6	DaimlerChrysler	Germany	176,687	3,067
7	Toyota Motor	Japan	172,616	10,898
8	Ford Motor	United States	172,233	3,487
9	General Electric	United States	152,866	16,819
10	Total	France	152,609	11,955
11	Chevron	United States	147,967	13,328
12	ConocoPhillips	United States	121,663	8,129
13	AXA	France	121,606	3,133
14	Allianz	Germany	118,937	2,735
15	Volkswagen	Germany	110,648	842
16	Citigroup	United States	108,276	17,046
17	ING Group	Netherlands	105,886	7,422
18	Nippon Telegraph & Telephone	Japan	100,545	6,608
19	American Intl Group	United States	97,987	9,731
20	Intl Business Machines	United States	96,293	8,430
21	Siemens	Germany	91,493	4,144
22	Carrefour	France	90,381	1,724
23	Hitachi	Japan	83,993	479
24	Assicurazioni Generali	Italy	83,267	1,635
25	Matsushita Electric Industrial	Japan	81,077	544
26	McKesson	United States	80,514	−156
27	Honda Motor	Japan	80,486	4,523
28	Hewlett-Packard	United States	79,905	3,497
29	Nissan Motor	Japan	79,799	4,766
30	Fortis	Netherlands	75,518	4,177
31	Sinopec	China	75,076	1,268
32	Berkshire Hathaway	United States	74,382	7,308
33	ENI	Italy	74,227	9,047
34	Home Depot	United States	73,094	5,001
35	Aviva	UK	73,025	1,936
36	HSBC Holdings	UK	72,550	11,840
37	Deutsche Telekom	Germany	71,988	5,763
38	Verizon Communications	United States	71,563	7,830
39	Samsung Electronics	Korea	71,555	9,419
40	State Grid	China	71,290	694

Sources: FT Global 500 2009, **http://media.ft.com/cms/8289770e-4c79-11de-a6c5-00144feabdc0. pdf** (Accessed June 18, 2009).

contribute to it. Corporations therefore seek wider market access in order to maintain and increase their sales. This objective can be achieved most quickly through acquisitions abroad.

Corporations also attempt to obtain low-cost resources and ensure their sources of supply. Finally, once the decision is made to invest internationally, the investment climate plays a major role. Firms will seek to invest where their investment is most protected and has the best chance to flourish.

Foreign direct investment permits corporations to circumvent current barriers to trade and operate abroad as a domestic firm, unaffected by duties, tariffs or other import restrictions. For example, research on Japanese foreign direct investment in Europe found that a substantial number of firms have invested there in order to counteract future trade friction.[35]

Customers may insist on domestic goods and services, as a result of nationalistic tendencies, as a function of cultural differences or for strategic planning and security purposes.[36] Having the origin of a product associated with a specific country may also bring positive effects with it, particularly if the country is known for the particular product category. An investment in a Swiss dairy firm by a cheese producer is an example.

Firms have been categorized as resource seekers, market seekers and efficiency seekers.[37] Resource seekers search for either natural resources or human resources. Natural resources typically are based on mineral, agricultural or oceanographic advantages. Companies seeking human resources typically search for either low-cost labour or highly skilled labour. The value of labour resources may change over time and lead to corporate relocations. For example, in the 1980s, many non-European firms invested in the low-wage countries of Portugal, Spain and Greece. The major political changes of the 1990s, however, shifted the investment interest to Hungary, the former East Germany and the Czech Republic, where wages were even lower. As *The International Marketplace 9.3* shows, new investors may be able to take advantage of resource and market conditions that are quite different from the ones encountered by established investors.

Corporations primarily in search of better opportunities to enter and expand within markets are market seekers. Particularly when markets are closed or access is restricted, corporations have a major incentive to invest rather than export. Efficiency seekers attempt to obtain the most economic sources of production. They frequently have affiliates in multiple markets with highly specialized product lines or components and exchange their production in order to maximize the benefits to the corporation. The reasons why firms engage in foreign investment can change over time.

A second major cause for the increase in foreign direct investment is the result of derived demand, which is the result of the move abroad by established customers. Large multinational firms like to maintain their established business relationships and, therefore, frequently encourage their suppliers to follow them abroad. As a result, a few initial investments can lead to a series of additional investments. For example, advertising agencies may move to service foreign affiliates of their domestic clients. Similarly, engineering firms, insurance companies and law firms may provide their services abroad. Some suppliers invest abroad out of fear that their clients might find better sources abroad and therefore begin to import the products or services they currently supply.

Government incentives Governments are under pressure to provide jobs for their citizens. Foreign direct investment can increase employment and income. For example, foreign companies making direct investments in Slovenia may apply for financial grants. The purpose of the Invitation for Applications is to boost attractiveness of Slovenia as a location for foreign direct investment by lowering entry (start-up) costs to the investors whose investment will have a positive impact on new employment, knowledge and technology transfer, facilitation of balanced regional development, and will foster alliances between foreign investors and Slovenian companies.[38] Increasingly, state and local governments promote investment by sending out investment missions or opening offices abroad in order to inform local businesses about the beneficial investment climate at home.

Government incentives are mainly of three types: fiscal, financial and nonfinancial. Fiscal incentives are specific tax measures designed to attract the foreign investor. They typically

THE INTERNATIONAL **MARKETPLACE 9.3**

Foreign car companies in China

DETROIT, Jan. 4 – Automotive executives expect that non-Chinese Asian car companies will have the greatest success in China in the future, according to the results of an annual global survey of automotive leaders by KPMG LLP, the US audit, tax and advisory firm.

The auto execs also see China continuing to be a major region for foreign investment. They continue to see a growing domestic market to sell cars to a population that is becoming more affluent.

'Asian consumers, particularly those in China, are viewed as the most important source of industry growth', said Betsy Meter, a partner in KPMG's automotive practice. 'The demand in Asian countries will go up significantly in coming years, with a burgeoning economy and increasing consumer wealth. Automotive companies recognize the opportunity that awaits'.

The KPMG survey is based on interviews with 140 senior executives at vehicle manufacturers and automotive suppliers from around the globe. Companies based in North America, Great Britain, France, Germany, Sweden, India, China, Korea and Japan are represented in the study. KPMG has released an annual survey of automotive executives expressing their views on the state of the industry since 1999.

What manufacturers will succeed in China? Forty-two per cent of the Auto execs felt that other Asian companies (non-Chinese firms) were seen as most likely to succeed, followed by Chinese companies (23 per cent), European companies (16 per cent) and North American companies (15 per cent).

Although lower production and manufacturing costs are still seen as one motive to invest in China, the main reason voiced by respondents for making such investment has undergone a significant shift. This year, 52 per cent of respondents now say that the main incentive to invest in the country's auto industry is to sell to Chinese consumers, who are becoming wealthier. That's up sharply from last year when 45 per cent held that view. Similarly, only 30 per cent of respondents this year said the main reason to invest was to export out of China, down from 35 per cent a year ago.

The KPMG survey also found that fears of overcapacity in China are rising. Last year 52 per cent of the executives thought there was some overcapacity and this year 62 per cent feel so. Those who believe there is more than 10 per cent overcapacity rose from 24 per cent last year to 38 per cent in 2005. A majority of respondents still expect the total number of foreign vehicle manufacturers in China to shrink within five years, but they believe more companies are expected to survive the shakeout than respondents in last year's survey.

When asked about whether they expect the levels of profitability to increase in the Chinese auto industry, 59 per cent expect levels to increase over the next five years, but a considerable number, 26 per cent, are still suspect of potential profits.

SOURCE: The Auto Channel, 'Non-Chinese Asian car makers seen as having most success in growing Chinese market, KPMG survey finds'. Online. Available from: **http://www.theautochannel.com/news/2006/01/04/204666.html**   (Accessed 18/06/09).

---

consist of special depreciation allowances, tax credits or rebates, special deductions for capital expenditures, tax holidays and other reductions of the tax burden on the investor. Financial incentives offer special funding for the investor by providing land or buildings, loans, loan guarantees or wage subsidies. Nonfinancial incentives consist of guaranteed government purchases; import quotas and local content requirements; special protection from competition through tariffs and investments in infrastructure facilities.

Incentives may slightly alter the advantage of a region. By themselves, they are unlikely to spur an investment decision if proper market conditions do not exist. Consequently, when individual states or regions within a country offer special incentives to foreign direct investors, they may be competing against each other for a limited pie rather than increasing the size of the pie. Furthermore, a question exists about the extent to which new jobs are actually created by foreign direct investment. Since many foreign investors import equipment, parts and even personnel, the expected benefits in terms of job creation may often be either less than initially envisioned or only temporary. One additional concern arises from domestic firms already in existence. Since their 'old' investment typically does not benefit from incentives designed to attract new investment, established firms may feel disadvantaged when competing against the newcomer.

A perspective on foreign direct investors

Foreign direct investors, and particularly multinational corporations, are viewed with a mixture of awe and dismay. Governments and individuals praise them for bringing capital, economic activity, employment and for transferring technology and managerial skills. These actions encourage competition, market choice and competitiveness.

At the same time, investment may lead to dependence. Just as the establishment of a corporation can create all sorts of benefits, its disappearance can also take them away again. Very often, international direct investors are accused of draining resources from their host countries. By employing the best and the brightest, they are said to deprive domestic firms of talent, thus causing a brain drain. Once they have hired locals, multinational firms are often accused of not promoting them high enough.

By raising money locally, multinationals can starve smaller capital markets. By bringing in foreign technology, they are viewed either as discouraging local technology development or as perhaps transferring only outmoded knowledge. By increasing competition, they are declared the enemy of domestic firms. There are concerns about foreign investors' economic and political loyalty toward their host government, and a fear that such investors will always protect only their own interests and those of their home governments. In addition, due to their sheer size, which sometimes exceeds the financial assets of the government, foreign investors can be viewed with suspicion.

Clearly, a love–hate relationship frequently exists between governments and the foreign investor. Corporate experts may be more knowledgeable than government employees. Particularly in developing countries, this knowledge advantage may offer opportunities for exploitation. There seems to be a distinct 'liability of foreignness' affecting both firms and governments.

An array of guidelines for international corporate behaviour has been published by organizations such as the United Nations, the Organization for Economic Cooperation and Development and the International Labour Organization. They address the behaviour of foreign investors in such areas as employment practices, consumer and environmental protection, political activity and human rights. While the social acceptability of certain practices may vary among nations, the foreign investor should transfer the best business practices across nations. The multinational firm should be a leader in improving standards of living around the world. It will be managerial virtue, vision and veracity combined with corporate openness, responsiveness, long-term thinking and truthfulness that will determine the degrees of freedom and success of global business in the future.[39]

Types of ownership

A corporation's ownership choices can range from 100 per cent ownership to a minority interest. The different levels of ownership will affect corporate flexibility, ability to control business plans and strategy, and exposure to risk. Some firms appear to select specific foreign ownership structures based on their experience with similar structures in the past.[40] In other words, they tend to keep using the same ownership model. However, the ownership decision should be a strategic response to corporate needs or a consequence of government regulation.

Full ownership   Many firms prefer to have 100 per cent ownership. Sometimes, this is the result of ethnocentric considerations, based on the belief that no outside entity should have an impact on management. At other times, the issue is one of principle.

To make a rational decision about the extent of ownership, management must evaluate how important total control is for the success of its international marketing activities. Often, full ownership may be a desirable, but not a necessary, prerequisite for international success. At other times, interdependencies between local operations and headquarters may require total control. Since the international environment is quite hostile to full ownership by multi-national firms it is important to determine whether these reasons are important enough to warrant a sole ownership policy or whether the needs of the firm can be accommodated with other arrangements.

Commercial activities under the control of foreigners are frequently believed to reflect the wishes, desires and needs of headquarters abroad much more than those of the domestic economy. Governments fear that domestic economic policies may be counteracted by such firms, and employees are afraid that little local responsibility and empathy exist at headquarters. A major concern is the 'fairness' of profit repatriation, or transfer of profits, and the extent to which firms reinvest into their foreign operations. Governments often believe that transfer pricing mechanisms are used to amass profits in a place most advantageous for the firm and that, as a consequence, local operations often show very low levels of performance. By reducing the foreign control of firms, they hope to put an end to such practices.

Ownership can be limited either through outright legal restrictions or through measures designed to make foreign ownership less attractive – such as limitations on profit repatriation. The international marketer is therefore frequently faced with the choice of either accepting a reduction in control or of losing the opportunity to operate in the country.

General market instability can also serve as a major deterrent to full ownership of foreign direct investment. Instability may result from political upheavals or changes in regimes. More often, it results from threats of political action, complex and drawn-out bureaucratic procedures and the prospect of arbitrary and unpredictable alterations in regulations after the investment decision has been made.[41]

Joint ventures   Joint ventures are collaborations of two or more organizations for more than a transitory period.[42] The partners share assets, risks and profits, though equality of partners is not necessary. The partners' contributions to the joint venture can vary widely and can consist of funds, technology, know-how, sales organizations or plant and equipment.

Advantages of joint ventures   The two major reasons for joint ventures are governmental and commercial. Government restrictions are designed to reduce the extent of control that foreign firms can exercise over local operations. As a basis for defining control, most countries have employed percentage levels of ownership. Over time, the thresholds of ownership that define control have decreased as it became apparent that even small, organized groups of stockholders may influence control of an enterprise. At the same time, many countries also recognize the competitive benefits of foreign direct investment and permit more control of local firms by foreign entities.

Equally important to the formation of joint ventures are commercial considerations. Joint ventures can pool resources and lead to a better outcome for each partner than if they worked individually. This is particularly the case when each partner has a specialized advantage in areas that benefit the joint venture. For example, a firm may have new technology available, yet lack sufficient capital to carry out foreign direct investment on its own. By linking efforts with a partner, the technology can be used more quickly and market penetration is easier. Similarly, if one of the partners has an already established distribution system, a greater volume of sales can be achieved more rapidly.

Joint ventures also permit better relationships with local organizations – government, local authorities or labour unions. If the local partner can bring political influence to the undertaking, the new venture may be eligible for tax incentives, grants and government support and may be less vulnerable to political risk. Negotiations for certifications or licences may be easier with authorities. Relationships with the local financial establishment may enable the joint venture to tap local capital markets. The greater experience – and therefore greater familiarity – with the culture and environment of the local partner may enable the joint venture to be more aware of cultural sensitivities and to benefit from greater insights into changing market conditions and needs.

Disadvantages of joint ventures Problem areas in joint ventures, as in all partnerships, involve implementing the concept and maintaining the relationship. Joint venture regulations are often subject to substantial interpretation and arbitrariness. Major problems can arise due to conflicts of interest, problems with disclosure of sensitive information and disagreement over how profits are to be shared; these are typically the result of a lack of communication and planning before, during and after the formation of the venture. In some cases, managers are interested in launching the venture but are too little concerned with actually running the enterprise. In other instances, managers dispatched to the joint venture by the partners may feel differing degrees of loyalty to the venture and its partners.[43] The joint venture may, for example, identify a particular market as a profitable target, yet the headquarters of one of the partners may already have plans for serving this market, plans that would require competing against its own joint venture. Reconciling such conflicts of loyalty is one of the greatest human resource challenges for joint ventures.[44]

Strategic alliances One special form of joint ventures consists of strategic alliances or partnerships, which are arrangements between two or more companies with a common business objective. They are more than the traditional customer–vendor relationship, but less than an outright acquisition. The great advantage of such alliances is their ongoing flexibility, since they can be formed, adjusted and dissolved rapidly in response to changing conditions. In essence, strategic alliances are networks of companies, which collaborate in the achievement of a given project or objective. Partners for one project may well be fierce competitors for another.

Alliances can range from information cooperation in the market development area to joint ownership of worldwide operations. For example, Mamut and Validis (UK-based integrated software solutions and internet services for SMEs and on-demand, data checking service for financial accounts firms, respectively) have entered into a strategic alliance to offer an innovative accounting service to SME customers as part of the Mamut Business Platform. Mamut and Validis will enhance their offering by tailoring the service to meet individual country-specific accounting requirements and legislation. This will reduce the costs associated with localized work in individual markets, enabling the companies to differentiate their offering and ensuring the service can be rolled out rapidly.[45]

Market development is one reason for the growth in such alliances. In Japan, Motorola is sharing chip designs and manufacturing facilities with Toshiba to gain greater access to the Japanese market. Another focus is spreading the cost and risk inherent in production and development efforts. Hitachi and Texas Instruments have teamed up to develop the next generation of memory chips. The costs of developing new jet engines are so vast that they force aerospace companies into collaboration; one such consortium was formed by Britain's Rolls Royce, Motoren-und-Turbinen Union from Germany, Fiat of Italy, Japanese Aero Engines and United Technologies' Pratt & Whitney division. Some alliances are also formed to block or co-opt competitors.[46] For example, Intermind Corporation, the French leader in personalized information delivery for the web and other electronic networks, announced a comprehensive set of marketing and distribution partnerships for the European market with key distributors, software vendors, consulting firms and media partners in Europe, including The Kinnevik Group in Scandinavia, Internet2000 in Germany, Trio Information System in Sweden, Groupe GFI in France, Centrum Systemow Teleinformatycznych TP.S.A. in Poland and Global One, a joint venture between Deutsche Telekom, France Telecom and Sprint.[47]

Companies must carefully evaluate the effects of entering such a coalition, particularly with regards to strategy and competitiveness. The most successful alliances are those that match the complementary strengths of partners to satisfy a joint objective. Often the partners have different product, geographic, or functional strengths, which the alliance can build on in order to achieve success with a new strategy or in a new market. They can then either operate jointly as equals or have one partner piggyback by making use of the other's strengths. Firms also can have a reciprocal arrangement whereby each partner provides the other with access to its market. Manchester United and the New York Yankees sell each others' licensed products and develop joint sponsorship programmes. International airlines have started to share hubs, coordinate schedules and simplify ticketing. Star Alliance (joining airlines such as Lufthansa and United) and Oneworld (British Airways and American Airlines) provide worldwide coverage for their customers both in the travel and shipping communities.

In a management contract, the supplier brings together a package of skills that will provide an integrated service to the client without incurring the risk and benefit of ownership. The activity is quite different from other contractual arrangements because people actually move and directly implement the relevant skills and knowledge in the client organization.[48]

Management contracts have clear benefits for the client. They can provide organizational skills that are not available locally, expertise that is immediately available rather than built up and management assistance in the form of support services that would be difficult and costly to replicate locally. In addition, the outside involvement is clearly limited. When a turnkey project is online, the system will be totally owned, controlled and operated by the customer. As a result, management contracts are seen by many governments as a useful alternative to foreign direct investment and the resulting control by non-domestic entities.

Similar advantages exist for the supplier. The risk of participating in an international venture is substantially lowered because no equity capital is at stake. At the same time, a significant amount of operational control can be exercised. Being on the inside represents a strategic advantage in influencing decisions. In addition, existing know-how that has been built up with significant investment can be commercialized. Frequently, the impact of fluctuations in business volume can be reduced by making use of experienced personnel who otherwise would have to be laid off. Accumulated service knowledge and comparative advantage should be used internationally. Management contracts permit a firm to do so.

In a dynamic business environment, alliances must be able to adjust to market conditions. Any agreement should therefore provide for changes in the original concept so that the venture can grow and flourish. In light of growing international competition and the rising cost of innovation in technology, strategic alliances are likely to continue their growth in the future.

Government consortia One form of cooperation takes place at the industry level and is typically characterized by government support or even subsidization. Usually, it is the reflection of escalating cost and a governmental goal of developing or maintaining global leadership in a particular sector. A new drug, computer, or telecommunication switch can cost more than $1 billion to develop and bring to market. To combat the high costs and risks of research and development, research consortia have emerged in Europe, Japan and the United States. These consortia pool their resources for research into technologies ranging from artificial intelligence and electric car batteries to semiconductor manufacturing.

The European Union has several megaprojects to develop new technologies, under the names BRITE, COMET, ESPRIT, EUREKA, RACE and SOKRATES. Japanese consortia have worked on producing the world's highest-capacity memory chip, and other advanced computer technologies. On the manufacturing side, the formation of Airbus Industries secured European production of commercial jets. The consortium, now backed by the European Aeronautic Defence and Space Company (EADS), which emerged from the link-up of the German DaimlerChrysler Aerospace AG, the French Aerospatiale Matra, and CASA of Spain has become a prime global competitor.[49]

SUMMARY

Most companies become gradually involved in international markets, though some are born global. A variety of internal and external factors expose them to the international market. Employees and management serve as particularly important change agents. After becoming aware of international marketing opportunities, companies progress through the corporate export stages, and may choose to retreat to a purely domestic focus or to increase the scope of their international activities through a variety of different means.

Firms may employ third parties, such as export management companies or trading companies, or they may break into the global marketplace using the technology of the internet. If a firm wants to establish an international presence it can also license its products, open global franchises, or directly invest into a region of the world. These expansion alternatives involve varying degrees of risk, and varying degrees of control that a company may exercise over its international ventures. Firms' involvement in international markets may also be legally limited by the extent to which a country allows foreign ownership of assets. Companies looking to go abroad need to consider a variety of factors – such as mechanics, corporate structure, strategic goals, logistics, cost and regulations – before they expand.

Key terms

accidental exporters

born global

brain drain

complementary strengths

derived demand

e-commerce

efficiency seekers

exploratory stage

export adaptation

export trading company (ETC)

financial incentives

fiscal incentives

franchising

innate exporters

joint ventures

licencing

management contract

market seekers

master franchising system

nonfinancial incentives

opportunity costs

piggyback

portfolio investment

profit repatriation

psychological distance

r&d costs

research consortia

resource seekers

safety-valve activity

strategic alliances

sogoshosha

trademark licencing

transfer costs

Questions for discussion

1 Discuss the difference between a proactive and a reactive firm.

2 Discuss the impact of the internet and e-commerce in making a firm global.

3 What is meant by the term 'born global'?

4 Why might a firm choose to retreat to a domestic focus?

5 Explain the difference between franchising, licencing and foreign direct investment, in terms of ownership, control and risk.

6 From a government standpoint, what kind of investment is most beneficial to a country?

7 Discuss the benefits and drawbacks of strategic partnerings at the corporate level.

Internet exercises

1 What programmes does the Export-Import Bank (**http://www.exim.gov**) offer that specifically benefit small businesses trying to export? What benefits can be derived from each?

2 Use the United Nations Conference on Trade and Development FDI Database (available under the Statistics option at **http://www.unctad.org/Templates/StartPage.asp?intItemID=2068**) to summarize the foreign direct investment profile of a country or region of your choice.

Recommended readings

Barkoff, Rupert M. *Fundamentals of Franchising*. American Bar Association, 2005.

Blair, Roger D. and Francine Lafontaine. *The Economics of Franchising*. London: Cambridge University Press, 2005.

Export Yellow Pages. Washington, DC: US Department of Commerce, 2005–06 Edition.

International Trade Centre. *World Directory of Importer's Associations*. Geneva: ITC, 2002.

Johnson, Thomas. *Export/Import Procedures and Documentation*. New York: American Management Association, 2002.

Ohmae, Kenichi. *The Next Global Stage: The Challenges and Opportunities in Our Borderless World*. Philadelphia: Wharton School Publishing, 2005.

Ott, Ursula. *International Joint Ventures*. New York: Macmillan, 2006.

Reuer, Jeffrey. *Strategic Alliances: Theory and Evidence*. London: Oxford University Press, 2004.

Notes

1 Howard Lewis III and J. David Richardson, *Why Global Commitment Really Matters!* (Washington, DC: Institute for International Economics, 2001).

2 Tiger Li, 'The Impact of the Marketing-R&D Interface on New Product Export Performance: A Contingency Analysis', *Journal of International Marketing* 7 (no. 1, 1999): 10–33.

3 Michael L. Ursic and Michael R. Czinkota, 'An Experience Curve Explanation of Export Expansion', in *International Marketing Strategy: Environmental Assessment and Entry Strategies* (Fort Worth, TX: The Dryden Press, 1994), 133–141.

4 C. P. Rao, M. Krishna Erramilli and Gopala K. Ganesh, 'Impact of Domestic Recession on Export Marketing Behaviour', *International Marketing Review* 7 (1990): 54–65.

5 Shawna O'Grady and Henry W. Lane, 'The Psychic Distance Paradox', *Journal of International Business Studies* 27 (no. 2, 1996): 309–333.

6 Aviv Shoham and Gerald S. Albaum, 'Reducing the Impact of Barriers to Exporting: A Managerial Perspective', *Journal of International Marketing* 3 (4, 1995): 85–105.

7 Michael R. Czinkota, 'US Exporters in the Global Marketplace: An Analysis of the Strengths and Vulnerabilities of Small and Medium-Sized Manufacturers', Testimony before the 107th Congress of the United States, House of Representatives, Committee on Small Business, Washington, DC, April 24, 2002.

8 Shaoming Zou and S. Tamer Cavusgil, 'The GMS: A Broad Conceptualization of Global Marketing Strategy and Its Effect on Firm Performance', *Journal of Marketing,* October 2002, 40–56.

9 Yoo S. Yang, Robert P. Leone and Dana L. Alden, 'A Market Expansion Ability Approach to Identify Potential Exporters', *Journal of Marketing* 56 (January 1992): 84–96.

10 S. Tamer Cavusgil and Shaoming Zou, 'Marketing Strategy–Performance Relationship: An Investigation of the Empirical Link in Export Marketing Ventures', *Journal of Marketing* 58 (no. 1, 1994): 1–21.

11 Michael R. Czinkota, 'Export Promotion: A Framework for Finding Opportunity in Change', *Thunderbird International Business Review,* May–June 2002, 315–324.

12 Oystein Moen and Per Servais, 'Born Global or Gradual Global? Examining the Export Behavior of Small and Medium-Sized Enterprises', *Journal of International Marketing* 10 (no. 3, 2002): 49–72.

13 Masaaki Kotabe and Michael R. Czinkota, 'State Government Promotion of Manufacturing Exports: A Gap Analysis', *Journal of International Business Studies* (Winter 1992): 637–658.

14 Andrew B. Bernard and J. Bradford Jensen, *Exceptional Exporter Performance: Cause Effect or Both,* Census Research Data Centre, Pittsburgh, Carnegie Mellon University, 1997.

15 Daniel C. Bello and Nicholas C. Williamson, 'Contractual Arrangement and Marketing Practices in the Indirect Export Channel', *Journal of International Business Studies* 16 (Summer 1985): 65–82.

16 Mike W. Peng and Anne Y. Ilinitch, 'Export Intermediary Firms: A Note on Export Development Research', *Journal of International Business Studies* 3 (1998): 609–620.

17 British Exporters (2009), 'Publishers of British Exporters Online and CD-ROM'. Online. Available from: **www.exportuk.co.uk/** (Accessed 18/06/09).

18 Shirley Hooker, Office of Export Trading Companies, US Department of Commerce, Washington, DC, January 19, 2006.

19 Alibaba.com announces full 2008 results with revenues up 39% **www.abnnewswire.net/press/en/60346/ Alibabacom_Limited_HKG:1688_Announces_Full_ Year_2008_Results_With_Revenue_Up_39.html**

20 Du, Y. and Murphy, M. 'Data protection and privacy issues in China', **www.hg.org/article.asp?id=5340** (Accessed 18/06/09).

21 Farok J. Contractor and Sumit K. Kundu, 'Franchising versus Company-Run Operations: Modal Choice in the Global Hotel Sector', *Journal of International Marketing* 6 (no. 2, 1998): 28–53.

22 Martin F. Connor, 'International Technology Licencing', Seminars in International Trade, National Centre for Export-Import Studies, Washington, DC.

23 Tennis Warehouse (2009), 'Slazenger rackets'. Online. Available from: **http://tt.tennis-warehouse.com/ showthread.php?t=246211** (Accessed 18/06/09).

24 Pamela M. Deese and Sean Wooden, 'Managing Intellectual Property in Licencing Agreements', *Franchising World* 33 (September 2001): 66–67.

25 Josh Martin, 'Profitable Supply Chain Supporting Franchises', *Journal of Commerce,* Global Commerce Section (March 11, 1998): 1C.

26 George W. Russell, 'Into the Frying Pan', *Asian Business* 37 (October 2001): 28–29.

27 Leonard N. Swartz, 'International Trends in Retailing', Arthur Andersen, December 1999.

28 Farok J. Contractor, 'Economic and Environmental Reasons for the Continuing Growth in Alliances and Interfirm Cooperation', in *Emerging Issues in International Business Research,* eds. M. Kotabe and P. Aulakh (Northampton, MA: Elgar Publishing, 2002).

29 Marko Grünhagen and Carl L. Witte, 'Franchising as an Export Product and Its Role as an Economic Development Tool for Emerging Economies', *Enhancing Knowledge Development in Marketing,* vol. 13, eds. W. Kehoe and J. Lindgren Jr. (Chicago: American Marketing Association, 2002), 414–415.

30 Williams, L. (2009) 'View from the top' fDi Magazine, from The Financial Times Ltd, June/July 2009 issue (www.fdiintelligence.com) **www.fdimagazine.com/news/ fullstory.php/aid/2934/View_from_the_top.html** (Accessed 18/06/09).

31 *Multinational Corporations in World Development* (New York: United Nations, 1973), 23.

32 Bernard L. Simonin, 'Transfer of Marketing Know-How in International Strategic Alliances: An Empirical Investigation of the Role and Antecedents of Knowledge Ambiguity', *Journal of International Business Studies* 30 (3, 1999): 463–490.

33 Lenn Gomes and Kannan Ramaswamy, 'An Empirical Examination of the Form of the Relationship between Multinationality and Performance', *Journal of International Business Studies* 30 (no. 1, 1999): 173–188.

34 Howard Lewis III and David Richardson, *Why Global Commitment Really Matters!* (Washington, DC: Institute for International Economics, 2001).

35 Detlev Nitsch, Paul Beamish and Shige Makino, 'Characteristics and Performance of Japanese Foreign Direct Investment in Europe', *European Management Journal* 13 (3, 1995): 276–285.

36 Michael R. Czinkota, 'From Bowling Alone to Standing Together', *Marketing Management,* March/April 2002, 12–16.

37 Jack N. Behrman, 'Transnational Corporations in the New International Economic Order', *Journal of International Business Studies* 12 (Spring-Summer 1981): 29–42.

38 UKTI Today, 'Record results for UK FDI', Online. Available from: **http://www.ukinvest.gov.uk/United-Kingdom/ 103545/en-TW.html** (Accessed 18/06/09).

39 Michael R. Czinkota, 'Success of Globalization Rests on Good Business Reputations', *The Japan Times,* October 12, 2002, 19.

40 Prasad Padmanabhan and Kang Rae Cho, 'Decision Specific Experience in Foreign Ownership and Establishment Strategies: Evidence from Japanese Firms', *Journal of International Business Studies* 30 (1, 1999): 25–44.

41 Isaiah Frank, *Foreign Enterprise in Developing Countries* (Baltimore: Johns Hopkins University, 1980).

42 W. G. Friedman and G. Kalmanoff, *Joint International Business Ventures* (New York: Columbia University Press, 1961).

43 Holton, R.H. (1981), 'Making international joint ventures work', in Otterbeck. L. (ed.) *The Management of Headquarters: Subsidiary Relations in Multinational Corporations,* pp. 255–267 (London: Gower).

44 Oded Shenkar and Shmuel Ellis, 'Death of the 'Organization Man': Temporal Relations in Strategic Alliances', *The International Executive* 37 (6, November/December 1995): 537–553.

45 Hanoa, E. and Holness, S. (2007), 'Mamut and Validis enter into a strategic alliance'. Online. Available from: **www.mamut.com/uk/about/press/pressreleases/ det.asp?id=5918** (Accessed 18/06/09).

46 Jordan D. Lewis, *Partnerships for Profit: Structuring and Managing Strategic Alliances* (New York: Free Press, 1990), 85–87.

47 Newswire (2009), 'Intermind Corporation announces European Strategic alliances', **www.prnewswire.co.uk/ cgi/news/release?id=19836** (Accessed 18/0609).

48 Lawrence S. Welch and Anubis Pacifico, 'Management Contracts: A Role in Internationalization?' *International Marketing Review* 7 (1990): 64–74.

49 **www.eads.com** (Accessed November 13, 2002).

BBQ donut – internationalization strategy by coincidence

© GMBH, HÖRSTEL

THE INNOVATIVE IDEA

It was one of the hot summer days in 2002 in the south of Germany. Sebastian Schmitt and his friends had a barbecue on one of the German lakes. They were dreaming up the idea that it would be 'cool' to have a barbecue on a boat in the middle of the lake instead of the border of the lake. Mr Schmitt thought it should be a kind of an island, where people could barbecue just while they are floating on the lake.

STARTING AN ENTREPRENEURIAL BUSINESS

At this time, Mr Schmitt was still a student, just planning to start his Master's thesis. He used this opportunity and described in his thesis the usefulness of the island. He called the idea of having a barbecue on a boat in the middle of the lake the 'bbq-donut®'

and described how it could be used, especially in both leisure areas and for entertainment. While he was developing a model of the bbq-donut®, he was taking part in different competitions. Feedback from these competitions was very positive and he used the feedback to perfect his idea. The business plan of bbq-donut® was well-written. The bbq-donut® was awarded 'the best business plan of Baden-Württemberg' by McKinsey & Company.. Consequently, the plan easily attracted interest from potential investors who assured him of financing for the project. The financing was carried out in the same year.

Within a short time, the engineer Sebastian Schmitt, inventor and developer of bbq-donut®, launched his own company, called 'artthink GmbH & Co. KG', [1] headquartered in Stuttgart, Germany. artthink GmbH & Co. KG now develops and sells the bbq-donut® products. Sebastian Schmitt has all the German and international industrial property rights, as well as legal rights and patent. The name 'bbq-donut®' became a worldwide registered and protected brand.

THE PRODUCT

A maximum of nine people can barbecue while they are floating. The charcoal grill is in the middle of the Donut. The official type designation of the product means 'a float – which is a kind of a sport boat'. The bbq-donut® was the first system to be registered as a boat, and has a boat licence. Customers can buy either a basic model (from €14,500) or a loaded model (€23,500).

Hotels and leisure parks as well as different organizations that arrange trips on inland water can rent the bbq-donut®. For those who intend to buy the bbq-donuts®, they should run a boat rental company and rent it out by the hour. The target group is anyone who has a direct access to water, for example, owners of lakes, leisure parks, hotels, boat rental companies.

CHALLENGES AT THE BEGINNING

The project was fairly new, and had neither market experience nor customer experience. However, the bbq-donut® can be used anywhere, is an absolute eye-catcher and an effective customer magnet: whether for barbecue parties on the water, as an advertising platform at your next trade fair or as special extra seating in your business.

GLOBAL ENTREPRENEURSHIP

There were good chances for success on the global market in the leisure industry. The entry markets were Germany, Switzerland and Austria followed by planned merchandising for Southern Europe, Africa and USA.

The customer analysis showed a very big potential on the American market, especially in leisure parks. After some experience with the product and services on the European market, the company decided to approach the US market. The US market was interesting because of its size and the openness towards innovative product concepts. They decided to licence-out the right for production and the sales.

In the meanwhile, the company was selling its products in more than 20 countries all over the world, from Portugal, Russia, South Africa, China and Dubai. How was it possible to develop these markets so fast? There was no strategic concept based on this expansion, it was by coincidence. The ground work for 'internationalization by coincidence' was the heavy presence in the German media because of the extraordinary idea and design of the bbq-donut® and the participation in exhibitions in Germany. The foreign business partners were introduced to the bbq-donut® mainly through trade shows and exhibitions.

Questions for discussion

1   Is it possible to systemize the market entry mode 'Internationalization by coincidence'?

2   Name the existing possibilities for the market entry and the market proposition.

3   What was the purpose of entering the US market soon after foundation of the company? What do you think about the 'Life Time Management' of the product?

Notes

1   More details about the company and the product can be obtained from: http.www.artthink.de or www.bbq-donut.de

MORE READING

http://themantuary.wordpress.com/2008/05/19/
bbq-donut/http://www.gizmag.com/the-floating-
restaurant-table/9330/http://www.digitaltrends.com/
lifestyle/bbq-donut-floating-grill/

Source: This case was prepared by Helmut Kohlert.

Polar-adidas

INTRODUCTION

On Sunday, April 3, 2005, in a downtown hotel in Erlangen, Germany, Mr Jorma Kallio, managing Director of Polar Electro Oy, a Finnish family-owned manufacturer of heart rate monitors, was preparing his opening speech to a group of some 100 Polar Electro employees and partners. He was in central Germany for an internal launch of a partnership between Polar Electro and adidas, the second largest sporting goods manufacturer in the world. The next day, on the premises of the expansive headquarters complex of adidas in Herzogenaurach, the partnership and 'Project Fusion', the world's first completely integrated training system, would be introduced to marketing and sales personnel. The project had been under development for the last year and a half and kept confidential – only some 40 people within Polar Electro knew about it. Project Fusion was a new, complete solution for runners to be launched in 2006, consisting of adidas shoes with built-in electronics, running textiles that had built-in sensors, and watch-type sports computers that would display such information as heart rate data, speed and distance to the runner (see Exhibit C2.1). The electronics technology was provided by Polar, but the textiles and shoes would be sold as premium adidas-branded goods.

Mr. Kallio was convinced that the partnership with adidas would be very beneficial for his company. First of all, becoming a trusted partner of adidas, an icon in sporting goods, was like a top-grade seal of approval for Polar. Polar would certainly benefit from the great brand equity that adidas owned. The majority of consumers around the world have heard of adidas, but just a selected few were aware of Polar. The adidas partnership would certainly raise consumer awareness of the Polar brand, something that Polar needed if it was to achieve its ambitious goals of both growing its sports-related business and extending from the core of serious sports into lifestyle applications. Second, the partnership could give a boost to the distribution of Polar goods. While Polar was represented through some 35,000 retailers in 50 countries, the channel power of adidas could not be ignored by wholesalers or retailers. Third, there was certainly a lot to learn from a successful company like adidas, be it in concept development or marketing processes.

There were some concerns, however. First, the sheer difference in size between the two companies: Polar's sales in 2004 had been 170 million euros, whereas adidas sales exceeded 5 billion euros, making it 30 times the size of Polar. The track record of alliances in general is not great and significant size differences between partners can cause difficulties in the relationship sooner or later. As an example, when adidas could appoint five people to a certain part of the project, Polar could afford two at most. Executives who were to implement the partnership, such as Christian Franke, Director of Brand Marketing at Polar, would have a lot on their plates. Another concern was the ability of Polar to perform in the relationship. Even though Kallio had full confidence in the capabilities of his managers, the fact that Polar was engaged in the development of very demanding high-tech electronics, whereas adidas would be responsible for shoes and textiles, was a factor that might bring surprises. His concern was that if there were unexpected difficulties in the development of electronics, the schedule of introducing new, jointly-developed products with adidas might turn out to be frighteningly tight. A large company could hire an additional twenty R&D engineers if there were unexpected challenges in the development work, but for a company of Polar's size that would be financially an extreme solution. In terms of the classic risk of enabling and creating a future competitor, Kallio did not see it very relevant in this very case. He had full confidence in the partner, largely thanks to the solid personal relationship that existed between Kallio and key executives at adidas. Referring to the key executives in both of the companies, Kallio said: 'We all understand and in fact love sports, so we talk the same language – that is a great starting point for the relationship'.

This case was authored by Hannu Seristö of the Helsinki School of Economics and Ilkka A. Ronkainen. For further information on the companies and their strategies, see http://www.adidas-polar.com; http://www.polarfi/polar/channels/eng/; http://www.adidas-group.com/en/home/welcome.asp; and http://www.nokia.com.

ABOUT PARTNERSHIP AGREEMENTS

The agreement with adidas comprised a joint development of technology for endeavours such as 'Project Fusion'. Polar is responsible for providing the sensor, but joint work is needed particularly in fusing the textiles and sensor technology, which inevitably means shared engineering and industrial design. In shared engineering, a challenging issue typically is to decide

EXHIBIT C2.1

Press release on the launch of project fusion

Helsinki/Herzogenaurach—August 4, 2005
adidas and Polar introduce the world's first completely integrated training system

Polar Electro, the innovative leader in heart rate monitoring, and adidas, one of the world's leading sports brands, have formed a partnership that will introduce the world's first completely integrated training system. Called "Project Fusion," it seamlessly integrates Polar heart rate and speed and distance monitoring equipment into adidas apparel and footwear.

The integration simplifies use and increases comfort, allowing the products to become part of the athlete. Included in the project are the adidas adiStar Fusion range of apparel (t-shirts, long sleeve shirts, bras, women's tops), the adidas adiStar Fusion shoe, Polar's s3™ Stride Sensor, The Polar WearLink™ transmitter, and The Polar RS800™ Running Computer.

How does it work? Special fibers bonded onto adidas tops work in conjunction with Polar's WearLink™ technology to eliminate the need for a separate chest strap to monitor heart rate. Just snap the tiny Polar WearLink connector onto the front of the shirt and go. The data are sent to the Polar RS 800™ wrist-mounted running computer, which easily displays and records all information in real time. Simply put, your shirt talks to your running computer.

The adiStar Fusion shoe has a strategically placed cavity in the midsole which can house the very light Polar s3™ Stride Sensor, making it easier to use, more comfortable and more consistently accurate than top-of-shoe systems. And you won't even know it's there when your shoe is talking to your running computer.

Information like speed and distance, chronograph functions, along with heart rate, are also shown on the RS800™ in real time. And when the workout is over, all data can be downloaded onto a computer so workouts can be easily managed and analyzed, meaning the whole system talks to you.

"The great thing about the system is that it's so easy to use," says Michael Birke, adidas Running Business Unit Manager. "By putting all the best equipment into one package, it's made training simpler, more comfortable and more precise. The system is greater than the sum of its parts."

"An athlete can train more effectively with the right objective information," says Marco Suvilaakso, Running Segment Manager for Polar Electro. "This system caters to the individual, with precise and personalized feedback."

Purchasing the entire system—Polar RS 800™, Polar s3™ Stride Sensor, adiStar Fusion top, and adiStar Fusion shoe—will be around 640 Euros/680 Dollars. The products are available as separate pieces as well, and available in Spring of 2006.

which partner owns the jointly-created intellectual property. Also, as 'Project Fusion' is a complete package, or solution, the industrial design has to be coordinated in terms of form and appearance. Rights concerning the design issues should normally be covered in partnership agreements.

Partnership agreements need to address the issues of exclusivity; that is, can certain technologies or solutions be offered to other companies beyond the main partners? Normally it is not recommended to lock oneself into one partner only, since it would compromise one's flexibility or stand-alone capability. On the other hand, exclusivity given to a partner is bound to enhance commitment and trust in the relationship.

The second part of the agreement deals with joint marketing efforts. Channels where there is joint presence and sales efforts have to be specified, including complementary marketing efforts (i.e., whereby Polar uses the adidas distribution system to get its products to the world marketplace). A considerable benefit for Polar is that adidas controls globally 145 flagship stores, such as adidas Originals Georgetown in Washington, D.C., Performance Store Abasto in Buenos Aires, adidas Concept Store Nevski in St Petersburg, and adidas Originals Sydney. As for promotion, the choice of media for shared appearance and, for instance, joint websites (such as http://www.adidas-polar.com) are important issues to address in the agreement.

In implementation, the management of the partnership should be clarified in the agreement. Whether there is, for example, a steering board composed of members from both partners, and who will serve as its chairperson, are some of the questions to settle. Also, determination of areas of responsibilities between the partners and the sharing of costs and revenues is normally a standard clause in an agreement of this sort. Finally, the agreements normally should address issues like the term and termination procedures of the partnership, and the settlement of disputes.

THE GROWTH OF POLAR ELECTRO OY

The origins of the Finnish sports instruments producer Polar Electro can be traced back to the need of cross-country skiing coaches for a device to measure an athlete's heart rate during training sessions in the field, as opposed to this being possible only in a laboratory environment. There were no light, portable devices available, only large expensive laboratory equipment. Promoted by this need, professor Säynäjäkangas of the technology faculty at Oulu University started development work on technology that would make such measurements possible. Work was done partly with colleagues at the Oulu University, and eventually a company called Polar Electro was founded in Oulu in 1977, with Säynäjäkangas as the owner. The first heart rate monitor (HRM) was a battery-powered device that measured the heart rate from a fingertip. By 1982, the technology had advanced to the point that the first wireless heart rate monitor was ready. The first computer interface was introduced in 1984. The zone feature was launched in 1987, which was a predecessor to the so-called OwnZone feature of today. The principle is that the suitable intensity levels of training may vary daily due to factors such as fatigue, illness, or jetlag, and the athlete should check the right intensity levels before each training session.

In the 1980s, Polar Electro sought cooperation with top-level competitive athletes and world-class trainers and coaches. Relationships with leading universities and research institutes in the area of sports medicine were established. The target customers for Polar technology were competitive national and Olympic level athletes. From the very beginning the company was compelled to take a global look at the markets, because the chosen niche was narrow. Domestic market sales would have been in hundreds of units during the early years.

During this era, Polar Electro was first and foremost a technology company that conducted research, developed new technological solutions and started to build manufacturing capacity for the large-scale production of heart rate monitors. Early on, the company benefited from financial support for promising high-technology start-ups in developing regions by Finnish government agencies. Products were sold mostly under other brands, through private label arrangements, particularly in the US market, which was then the key market for Polar Electro. Marketing to the masses existed only in long-term plans.

By the end of the 1980s, Polar Electro had grown to a company of one hundred employees with annual sales of almost 20 million dollars.

At this point, the target market was broadened from the original devices aimed at competitive top-level athletes. The first steps to the so-called fitness market were taken in 1987. New models were developed for ordinary people who wanted to monitor the intensity of training, through heart rate measurement, while they were exercising. The Polar brand became a focus of development in 1989. Polar's target was defined as being 'anyone with a heart'. Indeed, the company provided an HRM for race horses, which they continue to provide to this day.

Throughout the 1990s, Polar started to put more emphasize on marketing, partly driven by increasing competitive pressures. The heart rate monitor business had caught the attention of some big firms and entrepreneurs, all hoping to challenge Polar in this potentially sizeable business area. Large players like the US watchmaker Timex and the Japanese electronics company Casio started to work on HRM products, and in Europe such companies as Sigma from Germany and Cardiosport from the UK introduced comparable HRMs. However, in terms of features, technology, quality, and even production costs, Polar was able to maintain its lead of a couple of years in this race. The building of an extensive international dealer network became the key focus of marketing efforts.

The key products by Polar in the 1990s comprised specific models for runners, cyclists and fitness users. Two special product groups were developed: Team Systems, to be used in the training of football or ice-hockey teams; and Educational Systems that were used in the physical education classes of school children, mostly in the United States, where the Federal Government provided support for schools that adopted innovative equipment to improve the quality of physical education. The largest product category for Polar was fitness, because the products appealed to many different kinds of users. Several trailblazing technologies were introduced at this time, including the first integrated one-piece transmitter of heart rate measures in 1992; coded transmission of heart rate measures (from the chest transmitter unit to the wristwatch unit) in 1995; the first HRM combined with a bicycle computer, which had speed, cadence and altitude measurement in 1996; personalized OwnZone training intensity zone and OwnCal energy consumption solutions in 1997; and the Polar fitness test in 1999, which provided a very accurate estimate of physical condition, even when measured while the person is not exercising but simply lying down for about five minutes.

Polar Electro has used aggressive patenting policy to protect its inventions and intellectual property. In 2000, the company introduced a soft and very user-friendly textile transmitter belt to replace the traditional rather hard plastic model. The launch of a speed and distance measurement device in 2004 brought a new dimension to running computers: a pod attached to the running shoe measures acceleration and sends the information to the wrist unit with an accuracy of 99 per cent. Now runners can see on their wrist units not only their heart rate and training intensity information, but also their real-time pace or speed and the distance covered. Competitors to this speed-and-distance technology include GPS-based running computers by the US company Garmin and by Nike, developed with the Dutch electronics firm Philips. Outdoor computers were also launched in 2004. These wristwatch type devices have an electronic compass, barometer, altimeter, thermometer, and various watch and diary functions in addition to the advanced heart rate measurement features.

Polar spends some 10 per cent of its sales on research and development, which takes place mostly in Oulu. The company benefits from the supply of high-quality engineers from the University of Oulu. Oulu is a city with a concentration of high-tech companies, particularly in the area of electronics (Nokia, the world's largest mobile phone manufacturer, has a significant R&D and manufacturing presence in the city). The company also maintains collaborative ties with well-known institutes, such as Cooper Institute in Dallas, Texas, and leading universities in the areas of cardiology and sports medicine.

After-sales service is an essential component of the HRM business. The devices are rather complicated pieces of technology, and consumers often need support in installing software updates or setting up data transfer between the devices and the PC. These computers are also very personal objects, literally close to the heart, and consumers typically want support immediately if they have a problem in the use of the equipment. The objective is to provide an answer to consumers' or retailers' questions within 24 hours, anywhere in the world. Competitors have not been able to match Polar's level in after-sales service, making Polar users very loyal customers.

Industrial design has been a focus in the last two years. The design and looks of the products were somewhat soulless until a new generation of more fashionable and colourful models was launched in 2004. In particular, female consumers were targeted with specific light and colourful fitness computers. Polar received international recognition for its improved design in 2004, when its new outdoor computer AXN 500 received an award in the German IF design competition.

Today, Polar Electro sees its mission as providing people with the best solution to achieve their personal well-being, sports and performance goals. The company exists to improve people's quality of life by generating innovative, high-quality, and user-friendly products. The Polar brand's essence is captured in the statement that 'Polar is the leading brand and the true partner in improving human health and well-being through its understanding of personal physiology and the environment'. Physiology refers to the monitoring of heart, and the environment refers to the measurement of altitude, direction, speed, distance and temperature.

Most of Polar's €170 million in sales come from Western Europe and the United States, while the Asian market represents a very small share of business. Volume production is in the Far East, while the R&D and the manufacturing of the most advanced premium models remain in Oulu. Some 1,700 people work in Finland and in the 15 wholly-owned foreign marketing subsidiaries in the key world markets.

Polar may be a household name for competitive athletes and the most active exercisers, but the average consumer does not really know the brand. Potential markets include millions of people that could need and want a heart rate monitor. Driving this potential is an increasing realization by individuals, societies and national economies that if people exercise more and are in better physical condition, the result is fewer health problems and lower consequent costs to the society. Populations particularly in Western Europe and Japan are ageing, and the elderly want to stay active and healthy to lead rewarding lives after retirement. Obesity is increasingly a problem, particularly in North America, but also in Western Europe and possibly soon in many Asian countries as well. Competition in the future is more in the area of marketing rather than in the pure development of technology. Design, trends, and fashion are becoming an essential part of this business, making HRMs a lifestyle product.

POLAR MARKETING

The heart rate monitor consists of two parts: the transmitter and the receiver. The transmitter is worn around one's chest, as close to the heart as possible to ensure accurate sensing of the heart beat. Modern generation transmitters, provided only by Polar, are soft fabric belts where the sensors, or electrodes, are woven into the fabric, and the signal is sent to the receiver through a separate little unit that is snapped onto the belt. The fabric transmitters are much more comfortable to use than the old versions. The retail cost of a transmitter is in the region of 40 euros.

The receiver is like a sports wristwatch that functions mainly as the display for measured information. The receiver typically has heart rate measurement functions, watch and chronometer functions, and a variety of other features. The simplest models display only time and the current heart rate, whereas the most advanced models have several test features; a training diary and training programme features; measure air pressure, altitude and temperature; have compass functions; and display speed and distance information. The case of the receiver is typically made of different grades of plastics, but some expensive models are made of steel or titanium.

The basic heart rate monitors by Polar cost about 60 euros in retail, whereas the most advanced models with a titanium case can cost close to 500 euros. The cheapest heart rate monitors in the market, often by Asian manufacturers, can be bought for as little as 20 euros, but these are typically of poor quality, poor usability, and with no product support nor real warranty.

Polar heart rate monitors are distributed through sporting goods stores, specialty stores, department stores, and in some cases catalogue sellers and online stores. The products are so rich in features that the expertise and professionalism of the sales personnel is a key factor in the sales process. As a result, Polar has committed significant resources to the training of sales people throughout the channel.

Polar provides extensive online support for its products. Software can be downloaded from the Polar website, and consumers can create their own training programmes and diaries on the global website (http://www.polar.fi).

OTHER PARTNERSHIPS

In early 2004, a technology and marketing partnership between Nokia and Polar was made public. Polar offers a few heart rate monitor models that have the capability to communicate with a certain Nokia mobile phone, model 5140. This compatibility allows the user to transmit training data from the wrist computer to the mobile phone, and again send it via mobile phone network, for instance, to the PC of one's coach. So, for instance, a distance-runner who is training in the warm conditions of South Africa in January can easily send his daily training session information for analysis by his trainer in Northern Europe in order to get instructions for the following day's training. Nokia and Polar were very visible in a joint marketing campaign, with the theme 'Training Mates', during the 2004 Tour de France.

A key product that had Nokia compatibility is the running computer model S625X. It was launched in the summer of 2004 and was a great success from the very beginning. The S625X has a speed-and-distance feature that is based on acceleration technology. Acceleration data are turned into information on distance covered and speed or pace of the runner, and then displayed on the wrist receiver. The accuracy is very high, with error rates of less than 1 per cent (i.e., when running 10 kilometers, the error in the distance information is expected to be less than 100 meters). Runners love it and media have praised it. Even though the product is relatively expensive (€400), it appears that S625X is becoming one of the most successful running computers Polar has ever made.

GROWTH PROSPECTS OF POLAR

Polar Electro has many of the ingredients to grow and become a truly significant global company. It has a solid technological basis,

processes in place, and very capable personnel. In its own niche market, it is the world market leader. However, it has to acknowledge its limited resources: there are numerous potential new business areas and an abundance of ideas, but the development of completely new products takes millions of euros. Brand marketing is obviously very important in the future, but doing that with a real impact can easily consume tens of millions of euros per year. Asia is undoubtedly the market for the future, as in almost every business, but the question is how to go there, since it appears to be quite different from Europe and North America: what products (adapted or not), which features, which markets (alone or with partners, or through which channels), are some of the key questions. Moreover, the human resources might turn out to be a challenge – there are limitless opportunities, but the current managers may not be able to handle all the new issues simultaneously. Both the owners and the management see the numerous avenues for growth, but there are a multitude of factors to assess when choosing the right path to follow.

In terms of financial benefits, it is perhaps too early to assess the value of these partnerships. For one thing, the measurement of inputs and outputs is not that simple. For instance, how do you measure accurately the management effort that has been put into the partnerships, and whether that effort could have been used more effectively somewhere else?

Mr. Kallio was convinced that the adidas partnership was very valuable for Polar especially in the long term. Some questions remained, however. How can a relatively small company make sure that it can perform in a relationship with a significantly larger partner like adidas, and not let the partner down? How can Polar make sure that it gets most of the possible value out of the partnership – for instance, through learning from a more experienced company? How about assessing the inputs and outputs – how should Polar measure whether the relationship is producing value to the company?

Questions for discussion

1   How does the alliance with adidas fit with Polar's growth objectives?

2   What are the pros and cons of having a company like adidas as an alliance partner?

3   By 2012, what is the likely outcome of this alliance (e.g., will Polar become part of adidas)?

Parker Pen Company

Parker Pen Company, the manufacturer of writing instruments based in Janesville, Wisconsin, has always been one of the world's best-known companies in its field. George Safford Parker had patented his first fountain pen in 1889, and founded Parker Pen Company in 1892, marketing Parker pens as the best writing instruments. The idea of pens as status symbols dates back to the 1920s, when a Parker Pen manager argued that if people bought cars as status symbols, they could purchase high-priced pens as ones as well. As the business expanded its product line, market presence was also increased. In 1903, Parker's first overseas distributorship was established in Scandinavia through a shopkeeper in Copenhagen. In 1953, Parker Pen opened a 226,000-square-foot state-of-the-art facility in Janesville and manufacturing plants in France and Mexico. International marketing activities extended the company to 154 countries by the 1980s.

In early 1984, the company launched a global marketing campaign in which everything was to have 'one look, one voice', and with all planning to take place at headquarters. Everything connected with the selling effort was to be standardized. This was a grand experiment of a widely debated concept. A number of international companies were eager to learn from Parker's experiences.

Results became evident quickly. In February 1985, the globalization experiment was ended, and most of the masterminds of the strategy either left the company or were fired.

GLOBALIZATION

Globalization is a business initiative based on the conviction that the world is becoming more homogeneous and that distinctions between national markets are not only fading but, for some products, they will eventually disappear. Some products, such as Coca-Cola and Levi's, have already proven the existence of universal appeal. Coke's 'one sight, one sound, one sell' approach is a legend in the world of global marketers. Other companies have some products that can be 'world products', and some that cannot and should not be. For example, if cultural and competitive differences are less important than their similarities, a single advertising approach can exploit these similarities to stimulate sales everywhere, and at far lower cost than if campaigns were developed for each individual market.

Compared with the multidomestic approach, globalization differs in three basic ways:

1 The global approach looks for similarities between markets. The multidomestic approach ignores similarities.

2 The global approach actively seeks homogeneity in products, image, marketing, and advertising message. The multidomestic approach produces unnecessary differences from market to market.

3 The global approach asks, 'Should this product or process be for world consumption?' The multidomestic approach, relying solely on local autonomy, never asks the question.

Globalization requires many internal modifications as well. Changes in philosophy concerning local autonomy, concern for local operating results rather than corporate performance, and local strategies designed for local – rather than global – competitors are all delicate issues to be solved. By design, globalization calls for centralized decision-making; therefore, the 'not-invented-here' syndrome becomes a problem. This can be solved by involving those having to implement the globalization strategy at every possible stage as well as keeping lines of communication open.

GLOBALIZATION AT PARKER PEN COMPANY

In January 1982, James R. Peterson became the president and CEO of Parker Pen. At that time, the company was struggling, and global marketing was one of the key measures to be used to revive the company. While at R.J. Reynolds, Peterson had been impressed with the industry's success with globalization. He wanted for Parker Pen nothing less than the writing instrument equivalent of the Marlboro man.

For the previous few years, a weak dollar had lulled Parker Pen into a false sense of security. About 80 per cent of the company's sales were abroad, which meant that when local currency profits were translated into dollars, big profits were recorded.

The market was changing, however. The Japanese had started marketing inexpensive disposable pens with considerable success through mass marketers. Brands such as Paper Mate, Bic, Pilot and Pentel each had greater sales, causing Parker's

EXHIBIT C2.2

Ads for Parker's global campaign

Source: Joseph M. Winski and Laurel Wentz, "Parker Pen: What Went Wrong?" *Advertising Age,* June 2, 1986, 1, 60.

overall market share to plummet to 6 per cent. Parker Pen, meanwhile, stayed with its previous strategy and continued marketing its top-of-the-line pens through department stores and stationery stores. Even in this segment, Parker Pen's market share was eroding because of the efforts of A.T. Cross Company and Montblanc of Germany.

Subsidiaries enjoyed a high degree of autonomy in marketing operations, which resulted in broad and diverse product lines and 40 different advertising agencies handling the Parker Pen account worldwide.

When the dollar's value skyrocketed in the 1980s, Parker's profits plunged and the loss of market share became painfully evident.

Peterson moved quickly upon his arrival. He trimmed the payroll, chopped the product line to 100 (from 500), consolidated manufacturing operations and ordered an overhaul of the main plant to make it a state-of-the-art facility. Ogilvy & Mather was hired to take sole control of Parker Pen advertising worldwide. The logic behind going with one agency instead of the 40 for-

merly employed was cost savings and the ability to coordinate strategies on a worldwide basis. Among the many agencies terminated was Lowe Howard-Spink in London, which had produced some of the best advertising for Parker Pen's most profitable subsidiary. The immediate impact was a noticeable decline in employee morale and some expressed bitterness at the subsidiary being dictated to although it had been cross-subsidizing the American operations over the years.

A decision was also made to go aggressively after the low end of the market. The company would sell an upscale line called Premier, mainly as a positioning device. The biggest profits were to come from a roller-ball pen called Vector, selling for $2.98. Plans were drawn to sell an even cheaper pen called Itala – a disposable pen never thought possible at Parker.

Three new managers, to be known as Group Marketing, were brought in. All three had extensive marketing experience, most of it in international markets. Richard Swart, who became marketing vice president for writing instruments, had handled 3M's image advertising worldwide and taught company managers the ins and outs of marketing planning. Jack Marks became head of writing instruments advertising. At Gillette, he had orchestrated the worldwide marketing of Silkience hair-care products.

Carlos Del Nero, brought in to be Parker's manager of global marketing planning, had gained broad international experience at Fisher-Price. The concept of marketing by centralized direction was approved.

The idea of selling pens the same way everywhere did not sit well with many Parker subsidiaries and distributors. Pens were indeed the same, but markets, they believed, were different: France and Italy fancied expensive fountain pens; Scandinavia was a ballpoint market. In some markets, Parker could assume an above-the-fray stance; in others it had to get into the trenches and compete on price. Nonetheless, headquarters communicated to them all:

Advertising for Parker Pens (no matter model or mode) will be based on a common creative strategy and positioning. The worldwide advertising theme, 'Make Your Mark With Parker', has been adopted. It will utilize similar graphic layout and photography. It will utilize an agreed-upon typeface. It will utilize the approved Parker logo/design. It will be adapted from centrally supplied materials.

Swart insisted that the directives were to be used only as 'starting points' and that they allowed for ample local flexibility. The subsidiaries perceived them differently. The UK subsidiary, especially, fought the scheme all the way. Ogilvy & Mather London strongly opposed the 'one world, one brand, one advertisement' dictum. Conflict arose, with Swart allegedly shouting at one of the meetings: 'Yours is not to reason why; yours is to implement'. Local flexibility in advertising was out of the question (see Exhibit C2.2).

The London-created 'Make Your Mark' campaign was launched in October 1984. Except for language, it was essentially the same: long copy, horizontal layout, illustrations in precisely the same place, the Parker logo at the bottom, and the tag line or local equivalent in the lower right-hand corner. Swart once went to the extreme of suggesting that Parker ads avoid long copy and use just one big picture.

Problems arose on the manufacturing side. The new $15 million plant broke down repeatedly. Costs soared, and the factory turned out defective products in unacceptable numbers. In addition, the new marketing approach started causing problems. Although Parker never abandoned its high-end position in foreign markets, its concentration on low-priced, mass distribution products in the United States caused dilution of its image and ultimately losses of $22 million in 1985. Conflict was evident internally, and the board of directors began to turn against the concept of globalization.

In January 1985, Peterson resigned. Del Nero left the company in April; Swart was fired in May, Marks in June. When Michael Fromstein became CEO of the company, he assembled the company's country managers in Janesville and announced: 'Global marketing is dead. You are free again'.

EPILOGUE

After nearly a century in Janesville, Wisconsin, the Writing Instrument Group was acquired for $100 million in 1986 in a leveraged management buyout by Parker UK managers and investors. Headquarters were moved to Newhaven, England, and the privately-held company returned to many of its old traditions of innovation and quality. Advertising was returned to Lowe.

In 1993, the company was acquired by Gillette and made part of the company's Stationery Products Group, and in 2000, Newell Rubbermaid acquired the business including the Paper Mate, Parker, Waterman and Liquid Paper brands to make their Office Products Group the world leader in writing instruments with 3,000 different products.

Questions for discussion

1 Was the proposed globalization strategy for Parker Pen flawed or merely plagued by implementation challenges?

2 What marketing miscalculations were made by the advocates of globalization at Parker Pen?

3 Parker Pen has since become part of two major global-brand powerhouses. What are the benefits and drawbacks of being part of a larger entity in the global marketing environment?

Teva Pharmaceuticals Ltd

INTRODUCTION

To understand the success of Teva Pharmaceuticals Ltd (Teva), the largest and most successful pharmaceutical company of generics in the world, we must start not with the history of the company itself, but rather with the culture of the country in which the company was founded. While in most cases this would not be of determining importance, it is our belief that in Teva's case it played a significant role in the company's success throughout the years.

What we now know as Teva did not exist until the 1970s. Prior to that, Israel had a number of small local pharmaceutical companies providing services to the local market of the newly established state. These companies had been started by Jewish immigrants who migrated to the British Mandate of Palestine in the 1930s..

After World War II and the founding of the State of Israel in 1948, the Arab League instituted an economic embargo with any company doing business in or with Israel. This included pharmaceutical companies, which did not want to lose business in the Arab nations and thus refrained from selling or licencing their medicines to Israel. As a result, Israeli companies could call on a legal loophole that provided them with the ability to legally copy the formulas in case they made efforts in good faith to try to obtain a licencing agreement. For many pharmaceutical companies, this was a threat which left them with no option but to grant a licence or be passed over, and see their medicines sold without any commercial benefit to them.

With few natural resources, Israelis had no option but to develop the skills necessary to squeeze every drop of value of what was available to them. This daring became known as 'chutzpa' (unbelievable gall or audacity). Moreover, this culture was augmented by the 'think outside the box' and 'the decision is yours' attitude that was (and is still) a part of the fighting doctrine in the Israel Defence Forces. All in all, Israelis thought that assertiveness and daring would carry the day in order to survive. This culture allowed Israel to develop from thin air an almost total independence with regards to weapons. An unforeseen consequence was that some of the know-how and daring 'spilled-over' into the private sector. This allowed the country to develop things as varied as drip irrigation, the mobile telephone, the firewall that protects computers from intruders and also the pharmaceutical industry.

THE BEGINNING

Teva can trace its roots to the beginning of the twentieth century. 'Salomon, Levine & Elstein' (SLE), a wholesale drug manufacturer and distributor based in Jerusalem, was the first pharmaceutical company to serve as a provider of medicines for the first four decades of the twentieth century. During the early 1930s, immigrants from Germany came to the British Mandate of Palestine escaping Nazi anti-Semitism and brought with them the skills necessary to set up what would be the foundation of Israel's pharmaceutical and chemical industries. One such immigrant founded a small drug manufacturing company which he named Teva ('Nature').

Due to the Arab boycott installed by the Arab League in 1945 to punish those companies who had been thinking about or were actually trading with Israel, Israelis had to think of different ways to circumvent this embargo for the country's and their own survival. In the case of the pharmaceutical industry, about 20 small family-owned drug distributors and manufacturers already existed. By the late 1950s, these companies fulfilled the needs of the country's population, which was close to two million. Nevertheless, due to the boycott, the drug companies could not legally obtain licences for the production of medicines developed by western drug companies. Instead, they resorted to 'compulsory licencing' in which a country, who had tried to legally obtain a licence but could not, would nonetheless obtain it through this loophole.

By the 1950s, these small companies started consolidating. SLE acquired Assia, one of the small pharmaceuticals. One of its employees, Eli Hurvitz, would change the way the pharmaceutical company would look like in Israel and the rest of the world. In 1968, he acquired Teva, another company already listed in the Tel Aviv Stock Exchange since 1951, and Ikapharm in 1980. SLE changed the name of the company to Teva Pharmaceuticals Ltd. (Teva) in 1976, the year when Eli Hurvitz became CEO of the company. By this time, Teva was already worth over 22.57m EUR.

It is curious to note that, had it not been for the Arab boycott, maybe Israel would have never developed her own pharmaceutical and technology capabilities. To paraphrase Abba Eban, Foreign Minister of Israel in the 1980s: 'The Arabs never missed an opportunity to help Israel launch an industry'.

GROWING UP

No other event in Teva's history was as decisive as the 'Billion Dollar Theory'. In the late 1980s, Eli Hurvitz, asked his managers why Teva could not become a 'Billion Dollar' company, and if so, how would they go about it?

In the late 80s, Eli Hurvitz had hired Dr Joseph Aleksandrowicz to lead the strategic planning unit of Teva. This was to be the first in a series of innovative moves by Hurvitz. No other Israeli company to that point had ever considered planning strategically. Most companies at the time were either owned, or at least partly owned, by Koor Industries Ltd, a conglomerate of industries owned by the 'Histadrut', the largest of the worker's unions (these companies were more concerned with maintaining employment benefits than turning out a profit. For them the notion of strategic planning was as foreign as profits). Furthermore, one of the most innovative actions to be taken by Dr. Aleksandrowicz was to hire professors from the top US business schools to come to Israel and help establish an in-house management training programme. This was very unusual in Israel at that time, when being a career officer was a prerequisite for obtaining a senior management position.

The most important conclusion to come out of this strategic exercise was the focused approach Teva took from that point on. Teva decided to develop only pharmaceuticals and to penetrate a large market in order to reach the 'Billion Dollar' goal which it knew could not be reached solely by selling in the Israeli market exclusively.

FIRST STEPS IN THE INTERNATIONAL MARKET

Teva began its international expansion in the United States, when it struck a deal with W.R. Grace, a major American chemical conglomerate. Here again, 'chutzpa' played a major role in getting Teva a deal which would have been impossible to obtain if it were anything but an Israeli company. Chief Financial Officer Dan Suesskind said, 'When we got together with W.R. Grace we said to them, "We are willing to contribute to the partnership whatever we have, but money we don't ship over the ocean, of this you have enough in the US" That's how we got to this arrangement' … Teva was able to secure 100 per cent financing by Grace and still maintain a 50 per cent share of its business, an incredible business feat by any measure.

In addition, the company entered the US market right after the enactment of the Hatch-Waxman Act in 1984. The Act resulted in an increase in penetration of generic medicines from 13 per cent of the total number of prescriptions in 1983 to more than 50 per cent in 2006, all of which would amount to a significant discount to the consumer and insurance companies. Furthermore, the company knew how to take advantage of the newly passed Abbreviated New Drug Application (ANDA) process which enabled generic medicines to obtain FDA approval in a fraction of the time it had taken the innovative company in earlier processes. In addition, the Act contained two provisions.

The first was one that guaranteed a 180-day exclusivity period in which only the generic brand and the innovative company could market the product.

The second one allowed companies to challenge existing patents before they actually expired, thus expanding the number of products they could develop once the patents expired or were successfully challenged in court.

To the company's benefit, Teva also pioneered the use of computers to mine the databases of the US patent office to systematically search for patents that were about to expire, or could be challenged. This practice, not usually in use, became a potent weapon in Teva's marketing arsenal. Teva became so proficient at filing ANDA petitions that in the eyes of many of its competitors they had become a serial ANDA filer. We must also note that Teva used the US legal system quite successfully to block many of its competitors.

DEVELOPING COMPETITIVE ADVANTAGE

Teva recognized that the days of the 'mom and pop' pharmacies were coming to an end. They began focusing on large national chains. At the time, Teva filled a vacuum that had either not been identified or simply ignored by large wholesalers. It enabled the large chain to streamline its costs by sourcing most of its products from a single supplier. In addition to providing a wide range of products, Teva also provided inventory management systems. It offered its customers volume-based discounts and pricing bundles which were less relevant to the local pharmacy, but were of significant importance to a chain looking to squeeze every dollar out of its existing supply chain.

Teva also continued to focus on providing its products at an acceptable price. With everyone saying 'the Chinese are coming', Teva moved to neutralize price as the sole differentiating factor. The company went back and analyzed its own supply chain and streamlined it to the point that no other supplier was able to compete on the basis of price alone. Teva went further and agreed to give any customer a credit if it could be proved that a similar product was being offered to them by a competitor. In Hurvitz' words, 'No one takes market share away from Teva, no one!'

MERGERS & ACQUISITIONS

Since 1985, Teva has executed M&A transactions totaling over 16.14 billion EUR. The last company to be acquired by Teva was Barr Pharmaceuticals, Inc. for 6.30 million EUR. This puts Teva at the top of the pharmaceutical M&A charts. As Hurvitz stated, 'the market needs consolidation, globally. The more commoditized the market, the more this is true. And in this industry, the smaller players are the price leaders…. Mathematically we have a problem: we are already large. Today we are 20 per cent of the [US] market. How far can we go?' Many acknowledged the need for consolidation among generic companies. In the US, the top four firms controlled less than 50 per cent of the market and the next

PART III

EXPORT MARKETING MIX

10 **Product adaptation**

11 **Export pricing**

12 **Marketing communications**

13 **Distribution management**

Cases

art III focuses on the company that is considering whether to fill an unsolicited export order, on the manager who wants to find out how the current product line can be marketed abroad, and on the firm searching for ways to expand its currently limited international activities. It concentrates on low-cost, low-risk international expansion, which permits a firm to enter the global market without an extraordinary commitment of human and financial resources. The reader will share the concerns of small and medium-sized firms that need international marketing assistance most and that supply the largest employment opportunity, before progressing to the advanced international marketing activities described in Part 4.

CHAPTER 10
PRODUCT ADAPTATION

In Spain, Pepsi becomes 'Pesi'

After responding to local pronunciation of 'Pecsi' in Argentina, campaign goes to Europe

In America many Spanish speakers can pronounce the brand's name more easily and phonetically without that pesky second 'P', and the phenomena has arrived in Spain. In a new commercial-within-a-commercial, hunky Spanish soccer star Fernando Torres gets fed up when the director keeps correcting the way he says 'Pesi' on camera.

After the English-speaking director yells 'Cut' through 189 takes, Mr. Torres rips the letter 'P' from a Pepsi sign behind him and boldly tells the director that in his neighbourhood, it's called 'Pesi'.

This approach was a big hit, although somewhat controversial, in Argentina last year when Pepsi humorously renamed the brand 'Pecsi' in keeping with Argentine accents. Now Pepsi is parsing different Spanish accents, adopting the 'Pesi' spelling in Spain without the Argentine 'C'.

In Argentina, the challenge for the brand's agency, BBDO, was to do a price comparison with Coca-Cola to emphasize Pepsi's lower price during the depths of the global economic crisis last year. The message was that in a tough economy, Pepsi costs one peso less than Coke, so you can either save money by drinking Pepsi, or save by drinking Pecsi.

'Changing Pepsi to Pecsi was a way of gaining closeness [to the consumer] and transcending a mere value message', said Ramiro Rodriguez Cohen, a BBDO Argentina creative director.

Pepsi also created a Pecsipedia for Argentine slang that more than 1,500 people contributed to.

'This campaign is based on a universal insight: Pepsi is pronounced in many different ways, as was reflected in the BBDO Argentina campaign', said a spokewoman for Pepsi's agency in Spain, Contrapunto BBDO.

In Spain, the execution is different. In addition to the TV spot with Mr. Torres, Contrapunto BBDO also created a 'making of' version that tells the whole narrative: Mr. Torres, a famous player who used to play for the Atletico Madrid soccer team, was hired to make a blockbuster Pepsi commercial, set in a space ship that's surrounded by monsters and princesses. But the story changes dramatically when he takes his linguistic stand and becomes a true hero, defending his neighbourhood and the way people speak there.

Both videos are on the website lodigascomolodigas.com (Spanish for 'You say it like you say it'), which was created by Spanish agency La Despensa and attracted more than 200,000 visitors in the first two weeks.

Another video on the site introduces the Comando Pesi, a team charged with going first to Mr. Torres' neighbourhood and then to other parts of Spain to see how they pronounce the soft drink's name and what other local expressions they use. Their local words and idioms will be added to the Real Pesipedia Española, which sounds like a spoof of the Real Academia Española, Spain's conservative body responsible for establishing the rules governing the usage of the Spanish language.

As in Argentina, the overall message in Spain is, 'Do you say 'Pepsi' or 'Pesi'? If you say 'Pepsi,' it's correct. If you say 'Pesi,' it's even better. It doesn't matter how you say it, you are saving either way'.

With all the buzz in Latin America about the Pecsi campaign, BBDO Argentina's Mr. Cohen said he's heard consumers in other Spanish-speaking countries like Mexico and Venezuela also have trouble with the standard pronunciation of Pepsi. 'We are very proud that the success of the campaign in Argentina allows the concept to be applied in other parts of the world', he said.

A Pepsi spokesman at the company's New York headquarters said that other than Argentina and Spain, 'There currently are no plans to use similar advertising in other Spanish-speaking markets'.

SOURCE: Valentina Vescovi and Aixa Rocca (2010), 'In Spain, Pepsi Becomes 'Pesi''. Online. Available from: **http://adage.com/globalnews/article?article_id=141916** (Accessed 13/5/10).

Since meeting and satisfying customer needs and expectations is the key to successful marketing, research findings on market traits and potential should be used to determine the optimal degree of customization needed in products and product lines relative to incremental cost of the effort. Even if today's emerging market trends allow this assessment to take place regionally or even globally, as seen in *The International Marketplace 10.1*, both regulations and customer behaviour differences require that they and the severity of their impact be taken into consideration. Adapting to new markets should be seen not only in the context of one market but also as to how these changes can contribute to operations elsewhere. A new feature for a product or a new line item may have applicability on a broader scale, including the market that originated the product.[1]

Take the Boeing 737, for example. Due to saturated markets and competitive pressures, Boeing started to look for new markets in the Middle East, Africa and Latin America for the 737 rather than kill the programme altogether. To adjust to the idiosyncrasies of these markets, such as softer and shorter runways, the company redesigned the wings to allow for shorter landings and added thrust to the engines for quicker takeoffs. To make sure that the planes would not bounce even if piloted by less experienced captains, Boeing redesigned the landing gear and installed low-pressure tyres to ensure that the plane would stick to the ground after initial touchdown. In addition to becoming a success in the intended markets, the new product features met with approval around the world and made the Boeing 737 the best-selling commercial jet in history.

This chapter is concerned with how the international marketer should adjust the firm's product offering to the marketplace, and it discusses the influence of an array of both external and internal variables. A delicate balance has to be achieved between the advantages of standardization and those of localization to maximize export performance. The challenge of intellectual property violation will be focused on as a specialty topic. International marketers must be ready to defend themselves against theft of their ideas and innovations.

PRODUCT VARIABLES

The core of a firm's international operations is a product or service. This product or service can be defined as the complex combination of tangible and intangible elements that distinguishes it from the other entities in the marketplace, as shown in Exhibit 10.1. The firm's success depends on how good its product or service is and on how well the firm is able to differentiate the product from the offerings of competitors. Products can be differentiated by their composition, by their country of origin, by their tangible features such as packaging or quality, or by their augmented features such as warranty. Further, the positioning of the product in consumers' minds (for example, Volvo's reputation for safety) will add to its perceived value. The core product – for example, the ROM BIOS component of a personal computer or the recipe for a soup – may indeed be the same as or highly similar to those of competitors, leaving the marketer with the other tangible and augmented features of the product with which to achieve differentiation.

EXHIBIT 10.1

Elements of a product

Source: Adapted from Philip Kotler
Marketing Management, 11th ed.,
408. © 2003. Reprinted by
permission of Pearson Education,
Inc., Upper Saddle River,
New Jersey .

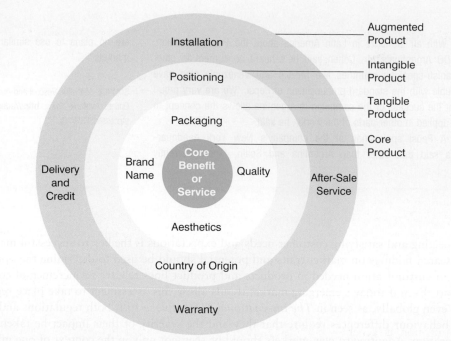

To the potential buyer, a product is a complete cluster of value satisfactions. A customer attaches value to a product in proportion to its perceived ability to help solve problems or meet needs. This will go beyond the technical capabilities of the product to include intangible benefits sought. The country of origin has strong influence on consumer perceptions. In Latin America, for example, great value is placed on imported products, for example, purchasing a pair of pyjamas.[2] If packaging is localized, then the product may no longer have the appeal that motivates customers to choose the product over others, especially over local competitors. In some cases, customer behaviour has to be understood from a broader perspective. For example, while Chinese customers may view Japanese products quite positively regarding their quality, historic animosity toward Japan may prevent them from buying Japanese goods or cause them to prefer goods from other sources.[3] Given such dramatic variation from market to market, careful assessment of product dimensions is called for.

Standardization versus adaptation

The first question, after the internationalization decision has been made, concerns the product modifications that are needed or warranted. A firm has four basic alternatives in approaching international markets: (1) selling the product as in the international marketplace; (2) modifying products for different countries and/or regions; (3) designing new products for foreign markets; and (4) incorporating all the differences into one flexible product design and introducing a global product. Different approaches for implementing these alternatives exist. For example, a firm may identify only target markets where products can be marketed with little or no modification. A large consumer products marketer may have in its product line for any given markets global products, regional products, and purely local products. Some of these products developed for one market may later be introduced elsewhere, including the global marketer's 'home' market.

The overall advantages and drawbacks of standardization versus adaptation are summarized in Exhibit 10.2. The benefits of standardization – that is, selling the same product worldwide – are cost savings in production and marketing. In addition to these economies of scale, many point to economic integration as a driving force in making markets more unified. As a response to integration efforts around the world, especially in Europe, many international marketers are indeed standardizing many of their marketing approaches, such as branding and packaging, across markets. Similarly, having to face the same competitors in the major

Factors Encouraging Standardization	Factors Encouraging Adaptation
• Economies of scale in production	• Differing use conditions
• Economies in product R&D	• Government and regulatory influences
• Economies in marketing	• Differing consumer behaviour patterns
• "Shrinking" of the world marketplace/economic integration	• Local competition
• Global competition	• True to the marketing concept

EXHIBIT 10.2

Standardization versus adaptation

markets of the world will add to the pressure of having a worldwide approach to international marketing. However, in most cases, demand and usage conditions vary sufficiently to require some changes in the product or service itself.

Coca-Cola, Levi's jeans, and Colgate toothpaste have been cited as evidence that universal product and marketing strategy can work. Yet the argument that the world is becoming more homogenized may actually be true for only a limited number of products that have universal brand recognition and minimal product knowledge requirements for use.[4] Although product standardization is generally increasing, there are still substantial differences in company practices, depending on the products marketed and where they are marketed. As shown in Exhibit 10.3, industrial products such as steel, chemicals and agricultural equipment tend to be less culturally grounded and warrant less adjustment than consumer goods. Similarly, marketers in technology-intensive industries such as scientific instruments or medical equipment find universal acceptability for their products.[5] Within consumer products, luxury goods and personal care products tend to have high levels of standardization while food products do not.

Adaptation needs in the industrial sector may exist even though they may not be overt. As an example, capacity performance is seen from different perspectives in different countries. Typically, the performance specifications of a German product are quite precise; for example, if a German product is said to have a lifting capacity of 1,000 kilograms, it will perform precisely up to that level. Buyers of Japanese machine tools have also found that these tools will perform at the specified levels, not beyond them. Technology gaps in industrial markets may require adaptation to bridge them, at least for the short term.[6]

Consumer goods generally require product adaptation because of their higher degree of cultural grounding. The amount of change introduced in consumer goods depends not only on

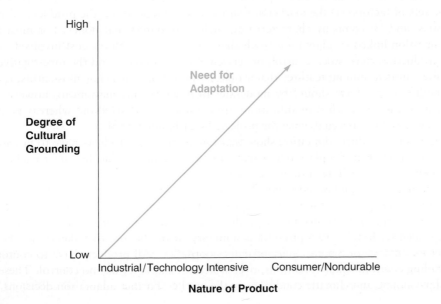

EXHIBIT 10.3

Strategic adaptation to foreign markets

Sources: Adapted from W. Chan Kim and R. A. Mauborgne, "Cross-Cultural Strategies," *Journal of Business Strategy* 7 (Spring 1987): 31; and John A. Quelch and Edward J. Hoff, "Customizing Global Marketing," *Harvard Business Review* 64 (May–June 1986): 92–101.

cultural differences but also on economic conditions in the target market. Low incomes may cause pressure to simplify the product to make it affordable in the market. For example, Unilever learned that low-income Indians, usually forced to settle for low-quality products, wanted to buy high-end detergents and personal care products but could not afford them in the available formats. In response, the company developed extremely low-cost packaging material and other innovations that allowed the distribution of single-use sachets, at very cheap prices. Having the same brand on both product formats builds long-term loyalty for the company.[7]

Beyond the dichotomy of standardization and adaptation exist other approaches. The international marketer may design and introduce new products for foreign markets in addition to the firm's relatively standardized 'flagship' products and brands. Some of these products developed specifically for foreign clients may later be introduced elsewhere, including in the domestic market. For example, IKEA introduced sleeper sofas in the United States to cater to local tastes but has since found demand for the concept in Europe as well.

Even companies that are noted for following the same methods worldwide have made numerous changes in their product offerings. Coca-Cola introduces 30 to 40 new products per year, the majority of which are never marketed outside the country of introduction.[8] Although Colgate toothpaste is available worldwide, the company also markets some products locally, such as a spicy toothpaste formulated especially for the Middle East. McDonald's serves abroad the same menu of hamburgers, soft drinks and other foods that it does in the United States, and the restaurants look the same. But McDonald's has also tried to tailor its product to local styles; for example, in Japan, the chain's trademark character, known as Ronald McDonald in the United States, is called Donald McDonald because it is easier to pronounce that way. Menu adjustments include beer in Germany and wine in France, mutton burgers in India, and rye-bread burgers in Finland.

Increasingly, companies are attempting to develop global products by incorporating differences regionally or worldwide into one basic design. This is not pure standardization, however. To develop a standard in the home market, for example, and use it as a model for other markets is dramatically different from obtaining inputs from the intended markets and using the data to create a standard. What is important is that adaptability is built into the product around a standardized core. The international marketer attempts to exploit the common denominators, but local needs are considered from product development to the eventual marketing of the product. Car manufacturers like VW and Nissan may develop basic models for regional, or even global, use, but they allow for substantial discretion in adjusting the models to local preferences.

Factors affecting adaptation

In deciding the form in which the product is to be marketed abroad, the firm should consider three sets of factors: (1) the market(s) that have been targeted; (2) the product and its characteristics; and (3) company characteristics, such as resources and policy. For most firms, the key question linked to adaptation is whether the effort is worth the cost involved – in adjusting production runs, stock control, or servicing, for example – and the investigative research involved in determining features that would be most appealing. For most firms, the expense of modifying products should be moderate. In practice, this may mean, however, that the expense is moderate when modifications are considered and acted on, whereas modifications are considered but rejected when the projected cost is substantial.

Studies on product adaptation show that the majority of products have to be modified for the international marketplace one way or another. Changes typically affect packaging, measurement units, labelling, product constituents and features, usage instructions, and, to a lesser extent, logos and brand names.[9]

There is no panacea for resolving questions of adaptation. Many firms are formulating decision-support systems to aid in product adaptation, and some consider every situation independently. Exhibit 10.4 provides a summary of the factors that determine the need for either mandatory or discretionary product adaptation. All products have to conform to the prevailing environmental conditions, over which the marketer has no control. These relate to legal, economic and climatic conditions in the market. Further adaptation decisions are made

EXHIBIT 10.4   Factors affecting product-adaptation decisions

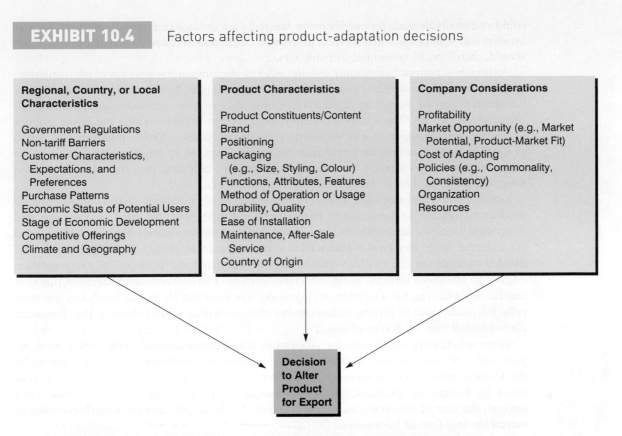

Regional, Country, or Local Characteristics	Product Characteristics	Company Considerations
Government Regulations Non-tariff Barriers Customer Characteristics, Expectations, and Preferences Purchase Patterns Economic Status of Potential Users Stage of Economic Development Competitive Offerings Climate and Geography	Product Constituents/Content Brand Positioning Packaging (e.g., Size, Styling, Colour) Functions, Attributes, Features Method of Operation or Usage Durability, Quality Ease of Installation Maintenance, After-Sale Service Country of Origin	Profitability Market Opportunity (e.g., Market Potential, Product-Market Fit) Cost of Adapting Policies (e.g., Commonality, Consistency) Organization Resources

Decision to Alter Product for Export

Source: Adapted from V. Yorio, *Adapting Products for Export* (New York: Conference Board, 1983), 7.

to enhance the exporter's competitiveness in the marketplace. This is achieved by matching competitive offers, catering to customer preferences, and meeting demands of local distribution systems.

The adaptation decision will also have to be assessed as a function of time and market involvement. The more exporters learn about local market characteristics in individual markets, the more they are able to establish similarities and, as a result, standardize their marketing approach, especially across similar markets. This market insight will give the exporters legitimacy with the local representatives in developing a common understanding of the extent of standardization versus adaptation.[10]

THE MARKET ENVIRONMENT

Government regulations

Government regulations often present the most stringent requirements. Some of the requirements may serve no purpose other than political (such as protection of domestic industry or response to political pressures). Due to the sovereignty of nations, individual firms need to comply but can influence the situation by lobbying, directly or through their industry associations, for the issue to be raised during trade negotiations. Government regulations may be spelled out, but firms need to be ever vigilant in terms of changes and exceptions.

Sweden was the first country in the world to enact legislation against most aerosol sprays on the grounds that they may harm the atmosphere. The ban, which came into effect on January 1, 1979, covered thousands of hair sprays, deodorants, air fresheners, insecticides, paints, waxes and assorted sprays that use Freon gases as propellants. It does not apply to certain medical sprays, especially those used by people who suffer from asthma. The Swedish government, which has one of the world's most active environmental protection departments, was the first to take seriously warnings by scientists that continued release of these chemicals could eventually degrade the earth's ozone layer. As a matter of fact, certain markets, such as Sweden and California, often serve as precursors of changes to come in broader markets and should, therefore, be monitored by marketers.

Although economic integration usually reduces discriminatory governmental regulation, some national environmental restrictions may stay in place. For example, a ruling by the European Court of Justice let stand Danish laws that require returnable containers for all beer and soft drinks. These laws seriously restrict foreign brewers, whose businesses are not on a scale large enough to justify the logistics system necessary to handle returnables.[11] A poll of 4,000 European companies found that burdensome regulatory requirements (e.g., need to ensure that products confirm to national requirements) affecting exports made the United Kingdom the most difficult market to trade with in the EU.[12]

Government regulations are probably the single most important factor contributing to product adaptation and, because of bureaucratic red tape, often the most cumbersome and frustrating factor to deal with. In some cases, government regulations have been passed and are enforced to protect local industry from competition from abroad. In early 2000, the EU decided to limit the use of older commercial aircraft that have 'hush kit' mufflers on their engines to cut down airplane noise. US marketers saw a two-dimensional threat in this new regulation: what the EU was really trying to do was keep out US goods (hush kits are typically US made) and, in forcing airlines to buy new aircraft, to direct them to buy European Airbus rather than US Boeing planes.[13]

Some government regulations for adaptation may be controversial both within the company and with some of its constituents, including home governments. Google was forced by the Chinese government to establish a new site, Google.cn, the contents of which are censored by Google in accordance with government preferences. Although a warning label informs the user of the arrangement, the company has been criticized for its collaboration to curtail the free flow of information.[14]

Non-tariff barriers

Non-tariff barriers include product standards, testing or approval procedures, subsidies for local products, and bureaucratic red tape. The non-tariff barriers affecting product adjustments usually concern elements outside the core product. For example, France requires the use of the French language in any offer, presentation, or advertisement whether written or spoken, in instructions for use, and in specification or guarantee terms for goods or services, as well as for invoices and receipts.

As non-tariff barriers are usually in place to keep foreign products out and/or to protect domestic producers, getting around them may be the toughest single problem for the international marketer. The cost of compliance with government regulations is high. For certain exports to the European Union, a typical machine manufacturer can expect to spend between $50,000 and $100,000.[15] As an example, Mack International has to pay $10,000 to $25,000 for a typical European engine certification. Brake system changes to conform with other countries' regulations run from $1,500 to $2,500 per vehicle. Wheel equipment changes will cost up to $1,000 per vehicle. Even with these outlays and the subsequent higher price, the company is still able to compete successfully in the international marketplace.

Small companies with limited resources may simply give up in the face of seemingly arbitrary harassment. For example, product testing and certification requirements have made the entry of many foreign companies into Japanese markets quite difficult, if not impossible.[16] Japan requires testing of all pharmaceutical products in Japanese laboratories, maintaining that these tests are needed because the Japanese may be physiologically different from people in the rest of the world. Similarly, foreign ski products were kept out because Japanese snow was somehow unique. Many exporters, rather than try to move mountains of red tape, have found ways to accommodate Japanese regulations. Japanese media, for example, visited Chinese export food factories and quality supervision institutions as China sought mutual trust on the food trade after dumpling poisoning.[17]

With a substantial decrease in tariff barriers, non-tariff forms of protectionism have increased. On volume alone, agriculture dominates the list. The EU have fought over beef produced with the aid of hormones. Although it was declared safe for consumption by UN health authorities, the Europeans have banned the importation of such beef and demand appropriate labelling as a precondition for market entry. In a similar debate, an international trade agreement was reached in 2000 that requires the labelling of genetically modified food in the world market.

One way to keep a particular product or producer out of a market is to insist on particular standards. Since the EU chose ISO 9000 as a basis to harmonize varying technical norms of its member states, some of its trading partners have accused it of erecting a new trade barrier against outsiders.[18] ISO 9000, created by the International Organization for Standardization (ISO), is a set of technical standards designed to offer a uniform way of determining whether manufacturing plants and service organizations implement and document sound quality procedures. The ISO itself does not administer or regulate these standards; that job is left to the 158 countries[19] that have voluntarily adopted them. Audit and certification services are provided by independent certification bodies, which are generally controlled by the IAF (International Accreditation Forum) through their national accreditation body members.[20] The feeling that ISO registration is a trade barrier comes from the Europeans' earlier start and subsequent control of the programme. Of the 670,399 registrations made by 2005, Europe accounts for 326,895, while North American companies have reached 49,962.[21]

There is no legal requirement to adopt the standards; however, many agree that these guidelines are already determining what may be sold to and within the EU and increasingly around the world. This is especially true for products for which there are safety or liability issues, or that require exact measurements or calibration, such as medical or exercise equipment.

The International Organization for Standardization also issued the first standards on environmental management, the ISO 14000 series in 1996. The standards, which basically require that a firm design an environmental management system, do provide benefits for the adopters such as substantial efficiencies in pollution control (e.g., packaging) and a better public image.[22] However, these standards can also serve as a non-tariff barrier if advanced nations impose their own requirements and systems on developing countries that often lack the knowledge and resources to meet such conditions.

Customer characteristics, expectations and preferences

The characteristics and behaviour of intended customer groups are as important as governmental influences on the product adaptation decision. Even when the benefits sought are quite similar, the physical characteristics of customers may dictate product adaptation. Quaker Oats' extension of the Snapple soft drink product to Japan suffered from lack of fit on three dimensions: the glass bottles the drink comes in are almost twice the size that Japanese customers are used to; the product itself was too sweet for the palate; and the Japanese did not feel comfortable with the sediment that characteristically collects at the bottom of the bottle.[23] Tefal, the world leader in cookware, makes available pans with detachable handles in Japan enabling storage in the traditionally tighter spaces of Japanese kitchens. The general expectation is that products are economical in purchase, use and maintenance.[24] Franchising, the success of which is based on the use of standard products and product lines around the world, is vulnerable to market-specific characteristics and preferences, as shown in *The International Marketplace 10.2*.

Product decisions of consumer-product marketers are especially affected by local behaviour, tastes, attitudes and traditions – all reflecting the marketer's need to gain customers' approval. This group of variables is critical in that it is the most difficult to quantify but is nevertheless essential in making a go/no-go decision. The reason why European DIY firms have failed to penetrate the Asian market is because of the different approaches to DIY.[25]

Three groups of factors determine cultural and psychological specificity in relation to products and services: consumption patterns, psychosocial characteristics and general cultural criteria. The types of questions asked in Exhibit 10.5 should be answered and systematically recorded for every product under consideration. Use of the list of questions will guide the international marketer through the analysis, ensuring that all the necessary points are dealt with before a decision is made.

THE INTERNATIONAL **MARKETPLACE 10.2**

Undercover journalist revealed food chain trouble

Months of undercover investigations by journalists have been the basis of the current labour problem at Pizza Hut, McDonald's and KFC, a report in the *New Express* reveals here in a translation by ESWN, called 'McWages in China'.

The detailed report is, for sure, going to cause the companies involved more trouble and might signal a strategy more companies will have to face. Only after the journalists filed official complaints did the labour authorities reluctantly decide to investigate the reports.

This woman is 43-years-old. She claimed to have been laid off from her previous job and her husband had died from cancer. She worked at KFC and earned 4.7 RMB per hour. At first, KFC told her to sign a full-time contract. Then they wanted her to sign a part-time contract. This woman worked at least seven hours per day. She had never taken Lunar New Year off in eight years. However, she is coming up to ten years of employment and KFC does not intend to renew the contract with her.

According to the law, any employee who works for ten years cannot be dismissed.

This woman was in tears: 'KFC claims to have helped so many impoverished students and hardship cases in China. I am a single mother and I need this job to feed my family. On the last week at the end of my eighth year contract, I received a rating of 100 for my work. Now they are saying that I am too old and they won't renew my contract'.

The strategy of the companies when they smelled trouble looks dubious at best: they reissued new backdated contracts. That does not sound like a company who is complying with the law.

The temperature has been rising for the foreign food chains that have come under scrutiny for the – according to an investigation – breaking of the labour law.

China Hearsay has a 'seen it, done it' approach to the case and paints the standard procedure for this kind of cases. I have to argue against it, since this does not look like a standard operation. This is real politics and the managers in charge of this crisis have reason enough to feel the beginning of a panic.

First, for Chinese standards this looks like a pretty well-organized action. It was very clear after the trade union started to organize WalMart and Foxconn against the will of the companies, they could not just go back to their offices and continue drinking tea. This looks like the plan for the moment and if I would be working at KFC, Pizza

© ROB CRANDALL/ALAMY

Hut or McDonald's, I would take this very seriously. This does not go away by itself.

Second, it is part of a policy shift on several levels. Until a few years ago, almost anything you did to encourage economic growth was okay and nobody really bothered about the negative side-effects. The different governmental institutions (and for the time being the trade union ACFTU is still one of them) are building a case, both for their bosses upstairs, but also for the Chinese citizens.

So, what is to be done? Raising the salaries over the minimum wages, paying the wrongly not-paid wages and deeply, deeply apologize for mistakes being made. And set up a trade union of course. Again: this is not going over by itself.

Next, this is going to be a successful action on the part of the government and the trade unions. There is no way this can be written up by the state media without being a resounding success. That will cost some money, but will have consequences for other foreign companies too who will be next. In the long run, okay the very long run, it will also have consequences for the Chinese companies, since the Chinese workers know they will get support when they ask for their legal rights.

SOURCE: Tuinstra, Fons, 'Undercover journalist revealed food chain trouble', *China Herald*, April 07, 2007 souhttp://www.chinaherald.net/labels/pizzahut.html.

As Brazilians are rarely breakfast eaters, Dunkin' Donuts is marketing doughnuts in Brazil as snacks and desserts and for parties. To further appeal to Brazilians, the company makes doughnuts with local fruit fillings like papaya and guava. Campbell Soup Company failed in Brazil with its offerings of vegetable and beef combinations, mainly because Brazilians prefer the dehydrated products of competitors such as Knorr and Maggi; Brazilians could use these

I   Consumption Patterns

  A   Pattern of Purchase

    1   Is the product or service purchased by relatively the same consumer income group from one country to another?

    2   Do the same family members motivate the purchase in all target countries?

    3   Do the same family members dictate brand choice in all target countries?

    4   Do most consumers expect a product to have the same appearance?

    5   Is the purchase rate the same regardless of the country?

    6   Are most of the purchases made at the same kind of retail outlet?

    7   Do most consumers spend the same amount of time making the purchase?

  B   Pattern of Usage

    1   Do most consumers use the product or service for the same purpose or purposes?

    2   Is the product or service used in different amounts from one target area or country to another?

    3   Is the method of preparation the same in all target countries?

    4   Is the product or service used along with other products or services?

II   Psychosocial Characteristics

  A   Attitudes toward the Product or Service

    1   Are the basic psychological, social, and economic factors motivating the purchase and use of the product the same for all target countries?

    2   Are the advantages and disadvantages of the product or service in the minds of consumers basically the same from one country to another?

    3   Does the symbolic content of the product or service differ from one country to another?

    4   Is the psychic cost of purchasing or using the product or service the same, whatever the country?

    5   Does the appeal of the product or service for a cosmopolitan market differ from one market to another?

  B   Attitudes toward the Brand

    1   Is the brand name equally known and accepted in all target countries?

    2   Are customer attitudes toward the package basically the same?

    3   Are customer attitudes toward pricing basically the same?

    4   Is brand loyalty the same throughout target countries for the product or service under consideration?

III   Cultural Criteria

    1   Does society restrict the purchase and/or use of the product or service to a particular group?

    2   Is there a stigma attached to the product or service?

    3   Does the usage of the product or service interfere with tradition in one or more of the targeted markets?

Source: Adapted from Stuart Henderson Britt "Standardizing Marketing for the International Market," *Columbia Journal of World Business* 9 (Winter 1974): 40–32. Copyright © 1974 Columbia Journal of World Business. Reprinted with permission.

© BASSEM TELLAWI/ASSOCIATED PRESS

products as soup starters but still add their own flair and ingredients. The only way of solving this problem is through proper customer testing, which can be formidably expensive for a company interested only in exports.

Often, no concrete product changes are needed, only a change in the product's **positioning**. Positioning refers to consumers' perception of a brand as compared with that of competitors' brands, that is, the mental image that a brand, or the company as a whole, evokes. For example, Gillette has a consistent image worldwide as a masculine, hardware, sports-oriented company. A brand's positioning, however, may have to change to reflect the differing lifestyles of the targeted market. Coca-Cola has renamed Diet Coke in many countries Coke Light, and subtly shifted the promotional approach from 'weight loss' to 'figure maintenance'. Coca-Cola positioned its product as a soft drink that would help people feel and look their best rather than one solely centred around weight loss. The company hoped that consumers would perceive these characteristics just by looking at the product's graphics regardless of the name it bore.

On occasion, market realities may cause a shift in the product's positioning. Panda, a Northern European chocolate and confectionery maker, had to place its liquorice products in the United Kingdom in healthcare stores after finding traditional channels at British daily-goods retailers blocked by competition.

Health- and beauty-care products often rely on careful positioning to attain a competitive advantage. Timotei shampoo, which is Unilever's brand leader in that category, has a natural-looking image with a focus on mildness and purity. Because people around the world have different hair, Timotei's formula varies, but it always has the same image. The selling of 'lifestyle' brands is common for consumer goods for which differentiation may be more difficult. Lifestyles may be more difficult for competitors to copy, but they are also more susceptible to changes in fashion.[26]

Even the export of TV culture, which is considered by many as a local product, can succeed abroad if concepts are adjusted to reflect local values. By 2006, *Muppets* were being seen in over 140 countries, including 20 co-productions reflecting local languages, customs, and educational needs. The Russian version of *Sesame Street* is 70 per cent locally produced and features Aunt Dasha, a quintessential Russian character who lives in a traditional cottage and spouts folklore and homespun wisdom. In China, new characters were added for local colour (such as Little Berry, 'Xiao Mei'). The creators of the joint Israeli–Palestinian production, called *Sesame Stories*, hope that the exploits of Dafi, a purple Israeli Muppet, and Haneen, an orange Palestinian one, will help teach mutual respect and understanding by exposing children to each other's culture and breaking down stereotypes.[27] When the Arab satellite network MBC started broadcasting the *Simpsons*, 'Al Shamsoon' had replaced Homer's Duff beer with soda, hot dogs with Egyptian beef sausages, donuts with cookies called kahk, and Moe's Bar had been written out completely.[28]

Economic development

Management must take into account the present stage of economic development of the overseas market. As a country's economy advances, buyers are in a better position to buy and to demand more sophisticated products and product versions. With broad country considerations in mind, the firm can determine potentials for selling certain kinds of products and services. This means managing affordability in a way that makes the marketer's products accessible. For example, C&A, an apparel retailer from Holland, has been able to build a successful business in Latin American countries because it offers reasonable-quality goods at various price points – the best $10, $20, $30 dresses on the market. In Brazil, two-thirds of its sales are to families with incomes below $8,000 per year.[29]

In some cases, the situation in a developing market may require **backward innovation**; that is, the market may require a drastically simplified version of the firm's product due to lack of purchasing power or usage conditions. They have to be simple and capable of operating in harsh environments. India's TVS Electronics, for example, has developed a new all-in-one business machine designed especially for small shopkeepers in developing markets. It is part cash register, part computer, and able to tolerate heat, dust and power outages.[30]

Buying power will affect packaging in terms of size and units sold in a package. In developing markets, products such as cigarettes and razor blades are often sold by the piece so that consumers with limited incomes can afford them. Soft drink companies have introduced four-can packs in Europe, where cans are sold singly even in large stores. On the other hand, products oriented to families, such as food products, appear in larger sizes in developing markets where families tend to be on the whole larger than in developed markets.

Economic conditions may change rapidly, thus warranting change in the product or the product line. During the Asian currency crisis, McDonald's replaced french fries with rice in its Indonesian restaurants due to cost considerations. With the collapse of the local rupiah, potatoes, the only ingredient McDonald's imports to Indonesia, quintupled in price. In addition, a new rice and egg dish was introduced to maintain as many customers as possible despite the economic hardship.[31]

Competitive offerings

Monitoring competitors' product features, as well as determining what has to be done to meet and beat them, is critical. Competitive offerings may provide a baseline against which the firm's resources can be measured – for example, what it takes to reach a critical market share in a given competitive situation. An analysis of competitors' offerings may reveal holes in the market or suggest avoiding certain market segments. To familiarize the strategies of the enemy you must learn how they think. The same applies to competitors. Familiarize yourself with their products and sales process. This may seem a big expense, but the strategic information you gather will enable you to position yourself to capture a greater share of the market.[32]

In many markets, the international marketer is competing with global players and local manufacturers and must overcome traditional purchasing relationships and the certainty they provide. What is needed is a niche-breaking product that is adjusted to local needs. TeleGea has had success in Japan because its technology (which has been adjusted to support Asian languages) automates the service-fulfilment process for telecom companies, cutting their delivery costs by more than 30 per cent.[33]

Climate and geography

Climate and geography will usually have an effect on the total product offering: the core product; tangible elements, mainly packaging; and the augmented features. Some products, by design, are vulnerable to the elements. Marketing of chocolate products is challenging in hot climates, which may restrict companies' options. Cadbury Schweppes has its own display cases in shops, while Toblerone has confined its distribution to air-conditioned outlets. Nestlé's solution was to produce a slightly different Kit Kat chocolate wafer for Asia with reduced fat content to raise the candy's melting point. The international marketer must consider two, sometimes contradictory, aspects of packaging for the international market. On the one hand, the product itself has to be protected against longer transit times and possibly for longer shelf life; on the other hand, care has to be taken that no non-allowed preservatives are used. One firm experienced this problem when it tried to sell Colombian guava paste in the United States. As the packaging could not withstand the longer distribution channels and the longer time required for distribution, the product arrived in stores in poor condition and was promptly taken off the shelves. If a product is exposed to a lot of sunshine and heat as a result of being sold on street corners, as may be the case in developing countries, marketers are advised to use special varnishing or to gloss the product wrappers. Without this, the colouring may fade and make the product unattractive to the customer.

PRODUCT CHARACTERISTICS

Product characteristics are the inherent features of the product offering, whether actual or perceived. The inherent characteristics of products and the benefits they provide to consumers in the various markets make certain products good candidates for standardization, others not. Consumer nondurables, such as food products, generally show the highest amount of sensitivity towards differences in national tastes and habits. Consumer durables, such as cameras and home electronics, are subject to far more homogeneous demand and more predictable adjustment (for example, adjustment to a different technical system in television sets and videotape recorders). Industrial products tend to be more shielded from cultural influences. However, substantial modifications may sometimes be required – in the telecommunications industry, for example – as a result of government regulations and restraints.

Product constituents and content

The international marketer must make sure products do not contain ingredients that might be in violation of legal requirements or religious or social customs. When religion or custom determines consumption, ingredients may have to be replaced in order for the product to be acceptable. In Islamic countries, for example, animal fats have to be replaced by ingredients such as vegetable shortening. In deference to Hindu and Muslim beliefs, McDonald's 'Maharaja Mac' is made with mutton in India.

Digital technology is making it easy and inexpensive to substitute product placements in country or region-specific versions of the same movie. Dr Pepper's logo appeared on a refrigerator in the US version of *Spiderman 2*, whereas overseas the logo belonged to Mirinda, a fruit-flavoured soft drink brand that Pepsico markets outside the United States.[34]

Branding

Brand names convey the image of the product or service. The term brand refers to a name, term, symbol, sign, or design used by a firm to differentiate its offerings from those of its competitors. Brands are one of the most easily standardized items in the product offering; they may allow further standardization of other marketing elements such as promotional items. The brand name is the vocalizable part of the brand, the brand mark the non-vocalizable part (for example, Camel's 'camel'). According to the American Marketing Association (AMA), a brand is a 'name, term, sign, symbol, or design, or a combination of them, intended to identify the goods and services of one seller or group of sellers and to differentiate them from those of competition'. The term *trademark* refers to the legally protected part of the brand, indicated by the symbol ®. Increasingly, international markets have found their trademarks violated by counterfeiters who are illegally using or abusing the brand name of the marketer.

The international marketer has a number of options in choosing a branding strategy. The marketer may choose to be a contract manufacturer to a distributor (the generics approach) or to establish national, regional, or worldwide brands. The use of standardization in branding is strongest in culturally similar markets; for example, for UK marketers this means the US and China. Standardization of product and brand do not necessarily move hand in hand; a regional brand may well have local features, or a highly standardized product may have local brand names.[35]

The establishment of worldwide brands is difficult; how can a consumer marketer establish world brands when it sells more than 400 brands in more than 150 countries, most of them under different names? This is Unilever's situation. Many companies have, however, massive standardization programmes of brand names, packaging, and advertising.[36] Standardizing names to reap promotional benefits can be difficult, because a particular name may already be established in each market and the action may raise objections from local constituents. Despite the opposition, globalizing brands presents huge opportunities to cut costs and achieve new economies of scale.[37]

The psychological power of brands is enormous. Brands are not usually listed on balance sheets, but they can go further in determining success than technological breakthroughs by allowing the marketer to demand premium prices.[38] Brand loyalty translates into profits despite the fact that favoured brands may not be superior by any tangible measure. New brands may be very difficult and expensive to build, and as a result, the company may seek a tie-in with something that the customer feels positively towards.

Brand names often do not travel well. Semantic variations can hinder a firm's product overseas. Even the company name or the trade name should be checked out. For instance, Mirabell, the manufacturer of the genuine Mozart Kugel (a chocolate ball of marzipan and nougat), initially translated the name of its products as 'Mozart balls' but has since changed the name to the 'Mozart round'.[39] Most problems associated with brands are not as severe but require attention nevertheless. To avoid problems with brand names in foreign markets, Catchword conducts an informal linguistic review to weed out names with obvious pronunciation issues or problematic meanings.[40] NameLab suggests these approaches:[41]

1 Translation. Little Pen Inc. would become La Petite Plume, S.A., for example.

2 Transliteration. This requires the testing of an existing brand name for connotative meaning in the language of the intended market. Toyota's MR2 brand faced a challenge in French-speaking countries due to the pronunciation of 'MR2' and emphasized the Spyder designation to defuse the connotation. In other instances, positive connotations are sought, as shown in *The International Marketplace 10.3.*

3 Transparency. This can be used to develop a new, essentially meaningless brand name to minimize trademark complexities, transliteration problems, and translation complexities. (Sony is an example.)

4 Transculture. This means using a foreign-language name for a brand. Vodkas, regardless of where they originate, should have Russian-sounding names or at least Russian lettering, whereas perfumes should sound French.

Brands are powerful marketing tools; for example, the chemicals and natural ingredients in any popular perfume retailing for $140 an ounce may cost less than $3.

Packaging

Packaging serves three major functions: protection, promotion and user convenience. The major consideration for the international marketer is making sure the product reaches the ultimate user in the form intended. Packaging will vary as a function of transportation mode, transit conditions and length of time in transit. Due to longer time that products spend in channels of distribution, firms in the international marketplace, especially those exporting food products, have had to use more expensive packaging materials and/or more expensive transportation modes. The solution of food processors has been to utilize airtight, reclosable containers that reject moisture and other contaminants.

Pilferage is a problem in a number of markets and has forced companies to use only shipping codes on outside packaging.[42] With larger shipments, containerization has helped alleviate the theft problem. An exporter should anticipate inadequate, careless, or primitive loading methods. The labels and loading instructions should be not only in English but also in the market's language as well as in symbols.

The promotional aspect of packaging relates mostly to labelling. The major adjustments concern bilingual legal requirements, as in the case of Canada (French and English), Belgium (French and Flemish), and Finland (Finnish and Swedish). Even when the same language is spoken across markets, nuances will exist requiring labelling adaptation. Ace Hardware's Paint Division had to be careful in translating the word 'plaster' into Spanish. In Venezuela, *friso* is used, while Mexicans use *yeso*. In the end, *yeso* was used for the paint labels, because the word was understood in all of Latin America.[43] Governmental requirements include more informative labelling on products. Inadequate identification, failure to use the needed languages, or inadequate or incorrect descriptions printed on the labels may cause problems. If in doubt, a company should study competitors' labels.

User convenience is a priority in packaging decisions. Containers need to be strong enough to withstand the logistics challenge, yet must open easily for the consumer. Nestlé, for example, has packaging teams around the world working on improvements and market-specific

THE INTERNATIONAL **MARKETPLACE 10.3**

When there is more to a name

Products in Asia often carry brand names that are translated from their original names. They are either direct translations (which result in a different-sounding but same-meaning name in the local language) or phonetic (which result in the same sound but likely different meaning). Given the globalization of markets, marketers not only need to decide whether to translate their brand names but also must consider the form, content, style, and image of such translations.

In Europe and the Americas, brand names such as Coca-Cola and Sharp have no meaning in themselves, and few are even aware of the origins of the name. But to Chinese-speaking consumers, brand names include an additional dimension: meaning. Coca-Cola means 'tasty and happy' and Sharp stands for 'treasure of sound'.

Chinese and western consumers share similar standards when it comes to evaluating brand names. Both appreciate a brand name that is catchy, memorable and distinct, and says something indicative of the product. But, because of cultural and linguistic factors, Chinese consumers expect more in terms of how the names are spelled, written and styled and whether they are considered lucky. When Frito-Lay introduced Cheetos in the Chinese market, it did so under a Chinese name that translates as 'Many Surprises'; in Chinese *qi duo* – roughly pronounced 'chee-do'.

Other similar examples include:

> BMW "宝马•"—precious horse
>
> Benz "奔驰•"—speedy : fast speed
>
> Budweiser "百威"—hundreds of power and influence
>
> Heineken "喜力"—happy and powerful
>
> Rejoice "•飘柔"—waving and softening
>
> Windows "•视窗"—a window of vision
>
> J&J "•强生"—strong life
>
> Gucci "古姿"—classic pose
>
> Ikea "宜家"—pleasant home
>
> Canon "佳能"—perfect capability
>
> Ricoh "理光"—neatening light

A name is like a work of art, and the art of writing (*shu fa* – calligraphy) has had a long tradition all over Asia. Reading Chinese relies more on the visual processes, whereas reading English is dominated by

(A hundred happy things)

(Treasure of sound)

USED WITH PERMISSION OF PEPSICO; USED WITH PERMISSION OF SHARP. PEPSI AND THE PEPSI GLOBE DESIGN ARE REGISTERED TRADEMARKS OF PEPSICO, INC.

phonological processes (affecting, for example, the processing of features such as font style and colour). A name has to look good and be rendered in appealing writing, thereby functioning like a logo or trademark. Companies will consequently have to take into account this dimension of Chinese and Chinese-based languages such as Korean, Japanese and Vietnamese when they create corporate and brand names and related communications strategies.

In a study of Fortune 500 companies in China and Hong Kong, the vast majority of marketers were found to localize their brand names using, for the most part, transliteration (such as that used by Cheetos).

SOURCES: Nader Tavassoli and Jin K. Han, 'Auditory and Visual Brand Identifiers in Chinese and English', *Journal of International Marketing* 10 (no. 2, 2002): 13–28; F. C. Hong, Anthony Pecotich and Clifford J. Schultz, 'Brand Name Translation: Language Constraints, Product Attributes, and Consumer Perceptions in East and South East Asia', *Journal of International Marketing* 10 (no. 2, 2002): 29–45; June N.P. Francis, Janet P.Y. Lam and Jan Walls, 'The Impact of Linguistic Differences on International Brand Name Standardization', *Journal of International Marketing* 10 (no. 1, 2002): 98–116; Eugene Sivadas, 'Watching Chinese Marketing, Consumer Behavior', *Marketing News*, July 20, 1998, 10; 'The Puff, the Magic, the Dragon', *The Washington Post*, September 2, 1994, B1, B3; and 'Big Names Draw Fine Line on Logo Imagery', *South China Morning Post*, July 7, 1994, 3.

adjustments. Some are as simple as deeper indentations in the flat end of candy wrappers in Brazil making opening them easier, or deeper notches on single-serve packages of Nescafé in China. A new glue was introduced for Smarties tubes in the United Kingdom to ensure a louder clicking sound when opened.[44]

Package aesthetics must be a consideration in terms of the promotional role of packaging. This mainly involves the prudent choice of colours and package shapes. African nations, for example, often prefer bold colours, but flag colours may be alternately preferred or disallowed. Red is associated with death or witchcraft in some countries. Colour in packaging may be faddish. White is losing popularity in industrialized countries because name brands do not want to be confused with generic products, usually packaged in white. Black, on the other hand, is increasingly popular and is now used to suggest quality, excellence and 'class'. Package shapes may serve an important promotional role as well. When Grey Goose, a French brand of vodka, researched its international market entry, the development of the bottle took centre stage. The company finally settled on a tall (taller than competition) bottle that was a mélange of clear glass, frosted glass, a cutaway of geese in flight, and the French flag.[45]

Package size varies according to purchasing patterns and market conditions. For instance, a six-pack format for soft drinks may not be feasible in certain markets because of the lack of refrigeration capacity in households. Quite often, consumers with modest or low discretionary purchasing power buy smaller sizes or even single units in order to stretch a limited budget. For example, the smallest size of laundry detergent available in Latin American supermarkets is 500 grams, while sizes as small as 150 grams may be in demand (and carried by small retailers).[46] The marketer also has to take into consideration perceptions concerning product multiples. In the West, the number 7 is considered lucky, whereas 13 is its opposite. In Japan, the ideogram for the number 4 can also be read as 'death'. Therefore, consumer products in multiples of four have experienced limited sales. On the other hand, 3 and 5 are considered lucky numbers. Similarly, 4 is the unluckiest number in Chinese and 2, 6 and 8 the luckiest.[47]

Marketers are wise to monitor packaging technology developments in the world marketplace. A major innovation was in aseptic containers for fruit drinks and milk. Tetra Pak International, the $6.5 billion Swedish company, converted 40 per cent of milk sales in Western Europe to its aseptic packaging system, which keeps perishables fresh for five months without refrigeration. Today, it markets its technologies in over 160 countries.[48]

Finally, the consumer mandate for marketers to make products more environmentally friendly also affects the packaging dimension, especially in terms of the 4 Rs: redesign, reduce, recycle and reuse. The EU has strict policies on the amounts of packaging waste that are generated and the levels of recycling of such materials.[49] Depending on the packaging materials (20 per cent for plastics and 60 per cent for glass), producers, importers, distributors, wholesalers and retailers are held responsible for generating the waste. In Germany, which has the toughest requirements, all packaging must be reusable or recyclable and packaging must be kept to a minimum needed for proper protection and marketing of the product. Exporters to the EU must find distributors who can fulfil such requirements and agree how to split the costs of such compliance.

Appearance

Adaptations in product styling, colour, size and other appearance features are more common in consumer marketing than in industrial marketing. Colour plays an important role in the way consumers perceive a product and marketers must be aware of the signal being sent by the product's colour.[50] Colour can be used for brand identification – for example, the yellow of Hertz, red of Avis and green of British Petroleum (BP). It can be used for feature reinforcement; for example, Honda adopted the colour black to give its motorcycles a Darth Vader look, whereas Rolls Royce uses a dazzling silver paint that denotes luxury. Colours communicate in a subtle way in developed societies; they have direct meaning in more traditional societies. For instance, in the late 1950s, when Pepsi Cola changed the colour of its coolers and vending machines from deep regal blue to light ice blue, the result was catastrophic in South East Asia. Pepsi had a dominant market share, which it lost to Coca-Cola because light blue is associated with death and mourning in that part of the world. IKEA has found that Latin families prefer bold colours to the more subdued Scandinavian preferences, and want to display numerous pictures in elaborate frames.[51] The only way companies can protect themselves against incidents of this kind is through thorough on-site testing.

Method of operation or usage

The product as it is offered in the domestic market may not be operable in the foreign market. One of the major differences faced by appliance manufacturers is electrical power systems. In some cases, variations may exist even within a country, such as Brazil. An exporter can learn about these differences through local government representatives or various trade publications such as the UK's Trade and Investment site.[52] However, exporters should determine for themselves the adjustments that are required by observing competitive products or having their product tested by a local entity.

Many complicating factors may be eliminated in the future through standardization efforts by international organizations and by the conversion of most countries to the metric system. When Canada adopted the metric system in 1977–1978, many companies were affected. For example, Perfect Measuring Tape Company in Toledo had to convert to metric if it wanted to continue selling disposable paper measuring tape to textile firms in Canada. Once the conversion was made, the company found an entire world of untapped markets. It was soon shipping nearly 30 per cent of its tape to overseas markets as disparate as Australia and Zimbabwe.[53] A similar situation occurred when the UK refused to join the single currency. The first three years of experience with the single currency witnessed a strong pound–weak euro pattern that cost British-based manufacturers in terms of lower profits and reduced market share. This affected multinational companies, given the high price of the pound sterling in euro terms, and the problems that this has brought to companies like Honda and Toyota, which have been using the UK as an export platform toward Europe. This trend will be maintained as a structural aspect of the UK environment as long as it remains outside the euro zone.[54]

Products that rely heavily on the written or spoken language have to be adapted for better penetration of the market. For example, SPSS, Inc., the marketer of statistical software, localizes Windows for German, English, Kanji and Spanish. Producing software in the local language has also proven to be a weapon in the fight against software piracy.

An exporter may also have to adapt the product to different uses. MicroTouch Systems, which produces touch-activated computer screens for video poker machines and ATMs, makes a series of adjustments in this regard. Ticket vending machines for the French subway need to be waterproof, since they are hosed down. Similarly, for the Australian market, video poker screens are built to take a beating because gamblers there take losing more personally than anywhere else.[55]

The international marketer should be open to ideas for new uses for the product being offered. New uses may substantially expand the market potential of the product. For example, Turbo Tek, Inc., which produces a hose attachment for washing cars, has found that foreign customers have expanded the product's functions. In Japan, Turbo-Wash is used for cleaning bamboo, and the Dutch use it to wash windows, plants, and the sidings of their houses.[56] To capture these phenomena, observational research, rather than asking direct questions, may be the most appropriate approach. This is especially true in emerging and developing markets, in order to understand how consumers relate to products in general and to the marketer's offer in particular.

Quality

Many western exporters must emphasize quality in their strategies because they cannot compete on price alone. Many new exporters compete on value in the particular segments they have chosen. In some cases, producers of cheaper Asian products have forced international marketers to re-examine their strategies, allowing them to win contracts on the basis of technical advantage. To maintain a position of product superiority, exporting firms must invest in research and development for new products as well as manufacturing methods. For example,

Sargent and Burton, a small Australian producer of high-technology racing boats, invested in CAD/CAM technology to develop state-of-the-art racing boats that have proven successful in international competition against sophisticated overseas entries.[57]

Increasingly, many exporters realize that they have to meet international quality standards to compete for business abroad and to win contracts from multinational corporations. Foreign buyers, especially in Europe, are requiring compliance with international ISO 9000 quality standards. For example, German electronics giant Siemens requires ISO compliance in 50 per cent of its supply contracts and is encouraging other suppliers to conform. This has helped eliminate the need to test parts, which saves time and money. However, many exporters still have grave misgivings about the certification process and its benefits.[58]

Many exporters may overlook the importance of product quality, especially when entering a developing market. If manufacturers of room air conditioners, for example, Weiss Technik, who plan to market their most up-to-date air conditioners in China should realize that many Chinese buyers want a more sophisticated product than the standard unit sold in Europe. In China, it is a major purchase, and therefore often a status symbol. The Chinese also want special features such as remote control and an automatic air-sweeping mechanism.[59]

Service

When a product sold overseas requires repairs, parts, or service, the problem of obtaining, training and holding a sophisticated engineering or repair staff is not easy. If the product breaks down, and the repair arrangements are not up to standard, the image of the product will suffer. In some cases, products abroad may not even be used for their intended purpose and may thus require modifications not only in product configuration but also in service frequency. Snow ploughs exported from Europe, for example, from Germany and the UK, are used to remove sand from driveways in Saudi Arabia. Closely related to servicing is the issue of product warranties. In consumer goods markets, wide variations occur in warranty policies and practices between products, firms and industries. The protective facet of warranties carefully delimits the responsibility of the manufacturer for post-sale product performance and quality and hence stabilizes the firm's future costs and profits.[60] Offering warranty implies additional costs in the form of warranty servicing cost. Product reliability has a serious impact on the warranty servicing cost. As such, effective management of product reliability must take into account the link between warranty and reliability.[61] As such, warranties are not only instructions to customers about what to do if the product fails within a specified period of time, but are also effective promotional tools.

Country-of-origin effects

The country of origin of a product, typically communicated by the phrase 'Made in (country)', has a considerable influence on the quality perceptions of a product. The manufacture of products in certain countries is affected by a built-in positive or negative sterotype of product quality. These stereotypes become significant when important dimensions of a product category are also associated with a country's image.[62] For example, if an exporter has a positive match of quality and performance for its exports, the country of origin should be a prominent feature in promotional campaigns. If there is a mismatch, the country of origin may have to be hidden through the adoption of a carefully crafted brand name (e.g., a Hong Kong-based apparel company chose the name Giordano), or the product sold with the help of prestigious partners whose image overshadows concerns about negative country-of-origin perceptions. This issue may be especially important to emerging countries, which need to increase exports, and for importers, who source products from countries different from those where they are sold.[63] In some markets, however, there may be a tendency to reject domestic goods and embrace imports of all kinds.

When the country of origin does matter to consumers, it is in the exporter's best interest to monitor consumers' perceptions. For example, many consumers around the world perceive Nokia as a Japanese brand, which does not have a negative impact on the company despite the incorrect appropriation, and has led to no action by Nokia. In contrast, consumers may prefer local products to foreign ones. For example, UK consumers prefer domestic products to those originating from specific foreign countries, and these preferences are linked to consumer ethnocentrism.[64] As a result, country of origin leads to consumer bias.[65]

Some products have fared well in the international marketplace despite negative country-of-origin perceptions. For example, Belarus tractors (manufactured both in Belarus and Russia) have fared well in Europe not only because of their reasonable price tag but also because of their ruggedness. Only the lack of an effective network has hindered the company's ability to penetrate western markets to a greater degree.[66]

Country-of-origin effects lessen as customers become more informed. In addition, as more countries develop the necessary bases to manufacture products, the origin of the products also becomes less important. This can already be seen with so-called hybrid products (for example, a European multinational company manufacturing the product in Malaysia). The argument has been made that with the advent of more economic integration, national borders become less important.[67] However, many countries have started strategic campaigns to improve their images to promote exports and in some cases to even participate in joint promotional efforts. In some cases, this means the development of new positive associations rather than trying to refute past negative ones.[68]

French and Italian trade and consumer groups are lobbying the European Union to require mandatory place-of-origin labels on all clothing, footwear and other goods imported into the European Union.[69] The issue has become a sensitive one for high-end European fashion houses that are starting to make products overseas in low-cost countries.[70] In 2008 the UK's Food Standards Agency produced a country-of-origin labelling guidance.[71]

COMPANY CONSIDERATIONS

Product adaptation is an international marketing tool that serves a variety of strategic needs. In addition to the need to cater to market differences and to compete effectively with others in these markets, the role of product adaptation is also to reach internal goals more effectively.[72]

The issue of product adaptation most often climaxes in the question 'Is it worth it?' The answer depends on the firm's ability to control costs, correctly estimate market potential, and finally, secure profitability, especially in the long term. The costs of product adaptation may be recouped through higher export performance. Arguments to the contrary exist as well. While new markets, such as those in central Europe, may at present require product adaptation, some marketers may feel that the markets are too small to warrant such adjustments and may quite soon converge with Western European ones, especially in light of their EU membership. Sales of a standard product may be smaller in the short term, but long-term benefits will justify the adoption of this approach.[73] However, the question that used to be posed as 'Can we afford to do it?' should now be 'Can we afford not to do it?'

The decision to adapt should be preceded by a thorough analysis of the market. Formal market research with primary data collection and/or testing is warranted. From the financial standpoint, some firms have specific return-on-investment levels to be satisfied before adaptation (for instance, 25 per cent), whereas some let the requirement vary as a function of the market considered and also the time in the market – that is, profitability may be initially compromised for proper market entry.

Most companies aim for consistency in their marketing efforts. This translates into the requirement that all products fit in terms of quality, price, and user perceptions. An example of where consistency may be difficult to control is in the area of warranties. Warranties can be uniform only if the use conditions do not vary drastically and if the company is able to deliver equally on its promise anywhere it has a presence.

A critical element of the adaptation decision has to be human resources; that is, individuals to make the appropriate decisions. Individuals are needed who are willing to make risky decisions and who know about existing market conditions. Many companies benefit from having managers from different (types of) countries, giving them the experience and the expertise to make decisions between standardization and adaptation.

PRODUCT COUNTERFEITING

Counterfeit goods are any goods bearing an unauthorized representation of a trademark, patented invention, or copyrighted work that is legally protected in the country where it is marketed. Precisely because counterfeiting is illegal, it is difficult to measure accurately its extent. The OECD estimates that the international trade in counterfeit and pirated items amounts to about £137.64 billion annually – the equivalent of 2 per cent of world commerce.[74] Hardest hit are the most innovative, fastest-growing industries, such as computer software, pharmaceuticals and entertainment. It is estimated that criminal games copying and other illegal activities cost the videogames industry in excess of £750 million a year.[75] Globally, the piracy rate went up from 38 per cent in 2007 to 41 per cent in 2008. The global rate rose for the second year in a row because PC shipments grew fastest in high-piracy rate countries.[76]

The monetary value of unlicensed software ('losses' to software vendors) grew by more than £3,493 billion (11 per cent) to £36,302 billion from 2007 to 2008, although half of that growth was the result of changing exchange rates. Excluding the effect of exchange rates, losses grew by 5 per cent to £34,383 billion. The legitimate software market grew by 14 per cent.[77]

The lowest-piracy countries are the United States, Japan, New Zealand and Luxembourg, all near 20 per cent. In contrast, the highest-piracy countries are Armenia, Bangladesh, Georgia and Zimbabwe, all over 90 per cent. The highest-piracy regions are Central and Eastern Europe, with a regional average of 67 per cent, and Latin America (65 per cent). The lowest regions are North America (21 per cent) and the European Union (35 per cent).[78]

The practice of product counterfeiting has spread to high-technology products and services from the traditionally counterfeited products: high-visibility, strong brand name consumer goods. In addition, previously the only concern was whether a company's product was being counterfeited; now, companies have to worry about whether the raw materials and components purchased for production are themselves real.[79] The European Union estimates that trade in counterfeit goods now accounts for 2 per cent of total world trade. The International Chamber of Commerce estimates the figure at 5–7 per cent. In general, countries with lower per capita incomes, higher levels of corruption in government, and lower levels of involvement in the international trade community tend to have higher levels of intellectual property violation.[80] Exhibit 10.6 summarizes the extent of counterfeits in different industries.[81]

Counterfeiting problems require different courses of action. Counterfeit products that originate overseas and that are marketed in the European Union should be stopped by the

Value of counterfeits in relation to total turnover	%
Copyright industry (motion picture videos, business software, music recordings)	40
Computer software	35
Audio-video	25
Textiles and clothing	22
Toys	12
Perfumes	10
Watches	5
Automotive industry – parts	5–10

Source: ETH Zurich (2009), 'Problem-analysis report on counterfeiting and illicit trade', **http://www.bridge-project.eu/data/File/BRIDGE%20WP05%20%20Anti-Counterfeiting%20 Problem%20Analysis.pdf** (23/11/09).

EXHIBIT 10.6

Estimates of value of counterfeits in different industries

customs barrier. Due to the highly organized nature of counterfeiting and piracy, the response to it must be as coordinated as possible. Counterfeits often enter the EU through the countries where there is no intellectual property protection and once the goods are in the EU they may circulate freely. Within member states, competent national authorities responsible for combating this must be in regular contact with each other and their actions must be synchronized. They must be in permanent contact with relevant private sector bodies. Since counterfeiting and piracy are often cross-border activities, better cooperation between member states is a must.[82] Enforcement has been problematic because of the lack of adequate personnel and the increasingly high-tech character of the products. When an infringement occurs overseas, action can be brought under the laws of the country in which it occurs. The sources of the largest number of counterfeit goods are China, Brazil, Taiwan, Korea and India, which are a problem to the legitimate owners of intellectual property on two accounts: the size of these countries' own markets and their capability to export. For example, Nintendo estimates its annual losses to video-game piracy at $700 million, with the origin of the counterfeits mainly in China. China, Korea, Brazil, Mexico, Spain and Paraguay are listed as the greatest contributing nations to piracy of the company's products. Nintendo suggests, for example, that 'Chinese customs officials must stop shipments of game copiers and other infringing products out of China, and China should work in the coming year to eliminate barriers to its enforcement laws', and that 'the Spanish government implement laws protecting the creative copyright industry and enact laws against internet piracy'.[83] Countries in Central America and the Middle East are typically not sources but rather markets for counterfeit goods. Counterfeiting is a pervasive problem in terms not only of geographic reach but of the ability of the counterfeiters to deliver products, and the market's willingness to buy them, as shown in *The International Marketplace 10.4*.

The first task in fighting intellectual property violation is to use patent application or registration of trademarks or mask works (for semiconductors). The rights granted by a patent, trademark, copyright, or mask work registration in the United Kingdom confer no protection in a foreign country. There is no such thing as an international patent, trademark or copyright. Although there is no shortcut to worldwide protection, some advantages exist under treaties or other international agreements. These treaties, under the World Intellectual Property Organization (WIPO), include the Paris Convention for the Protection of Industrial Property, the Patent Cooperation Treaty, the Berne Convention for the Protection of Literary and Artistic Works, and the Universal Copyright Convention, as well as regional patent and trademark offices such as the European Patent Office. Applicants are typically granted international protection throughout the member countries of these organizations.[84]

After securing valuable intellectual property rights, the international marketer must act to enforce, and have enforced, these rights. Four types of action against counterfeiting are legislative action, bilateral and multilateral negotiations, joint private sector action, and measures taken by individual companies, as shown in Exhibit 10.7. It is essential that all the parties interact to gain the most effect.

The international marketer has to understand the different legislations in order to prevent trade in counterfeits, as highlighted in *The International Marketplace 10.5*.

A number of private-sector joint efforts have emerged in the battle against counterfeit goods. In 1978, the International Anti-Counterfeiting Coalition was founded to lobby for stronger legal sanctions worldwide. The coalition consists of 375 members. The International Chamber of Commerce established the Counterfeit Intelligence and Investigating Bureau in London, which acts as a clearing house capable of synthesizing global data on counterfeiting.

In today's environment, companies are taking more aggressive steps to protect themselves. The victimized companies are losing not only sales but also goodwill in the longer term if customers believe they have the real product rather than a copy of inferior quality. In addition to the normal measures of registering trademarks and copyrights, companies are taking steps in product development to prevent knockoffs of trademarked goods. For example, new authentication materials in labelling are extremely difficult to duplicate. Some companies, such as Disney, have tried to legitimize offenders by converting them into authorized licensees. These local companies would then be a part of the fight against counterfeiters, because their profits would be the most affected by fakes.

THE INTERNATIONAL **MARKETPLACE 10.4**

What countries made Nintendo's rampant piracy list this year?

Every year, Nintendo documents the worst countries in the world in terms of rampant Nintendo game piracy, issuing a report to the US Trade Representative requesting help. What countries made the list this year?

Nintendo issues the annual report to the Office of the US Trade Representative as part of the Special 301 process, which asks for input from the public to underscore areas of concern. So where is piracy rampant this year? For the most part, the list contains the usual suspects. Brazil, China, Korea, Mexico and Paraguay all return to the list this year, perhaps indicating that the US government didn't do enough in those areas last year, instead focusing on less important things, like electing a new president, fighting an ongoing war and dealing with the failing economy. Priorities, people!

So what has changed? Hong Kong, present on the list last year, has been removed completely, so apparently everything is okay there now. Good job! In its place? Spain. I freaking knew it. They've been way too quiet in Spain lately.

Check out Nintendo's country-by-country report below.

PEOPLE'S REPUBLIC OF CHINA: China continues to be the hub of production for counterfeit Nintendo video game products. The number of online shopping sites in China selling infringing Nintendo products is increasing, and help is needed by the government to curtail the growth of these illegal marketplaces. These products are sold both inside China and to the world, including our key market in the United States. Chinese customs officials must stop shipments of game copiers and other infringing products out of China, and China should work in the coming year to eliminate barriers to its enforcement laws.

REPUBLIC OF KOREA: Internet piracy in Korea continues to increase, as does the availability of devices that get around product security and allow for the play of illegal Nintendo software. A massive customs raid of 10 premises that resulted in the seizure of more than 75,000 game copiers at the beginning of 2009 is a positive sign the government is serious about enforcement. Nintendo is pleased with Korea's consistent customs seizures, and courts are now starting to hold distributors of circumvention devices, such as game copiers, accountable. The Korea-US free trade agreement is important to all intellectual property rights holders.

BRAZIL: Federal anti-piracy actions are not reducing piracy in Brazil, and local enforcement efforts are weak. Efforts to prosecute for piracy are virtually non-existent. Customs and border control agents failed to seize a single shipment of Nintendo video game products in Brazil in 2008. Internet piracy is increasing with no legal infrastructure in place to respond to the threat it poses to rights holders. High tariffs and taxes also constitute market barriers for legitimate video game products.

MEXICO: Anti-piracy actions by the Mexican government in 2008 were wholly inadequate. The Mexican government must recognize the seriousness of the piracy problem and start using existing enforcement tools. Mexico's participation in negotiating the Anti-Counterfeiting Trade Agreement is encouraging, but enforcement efforts need to move forward now. The willingness of Mexican customs and Mexican postal service workers to be trained by trademark owners was a positive sign in 2008.

SPAIN: The availability of game-copying devices in Spain is alarming. Internet sites offering game-copying devices and illegal Nintendo software are widespread and must be addressed. Nintendo asks that the Spanish government implement laws protecting the creative copyright industry and enact laws against internet piracy. Nintendo considers education a priority in its fight against piracy in the European Union. Customs authorities play an important role in enforcing intellectual property rights, and Nintendo is seeing positive signs in

© JEREMY SUTTON-HIBBERT/ALAMY

this area. Nintendo is pleased about recent steps taken by the Spanish National Police against distributors of game copiers.

PARAGUAY: Corruption continues to hamper anti-piracy efforts. Nintendo's anti-piracy actions in Paraguay show that illegal goods are imported and also locally produced. Border controls are key to decreasing piracy, and the revised criminal code will increase penalties against those distributing circumvention devices in Paraguay.

SOURCE: Fahy, M. (2009) 'What countries made Nintendo's rampant piracy list this year?' **http://kotaku.com/5160062/what-countries-made-nintendos-rampant-piracy-list-this-year** (Accessed 23/11/09).

EXHIBIT 10.7

Measures to combat counterfeiting

Source: Ilkka A. Ronkainen, "Protecting Intellectual Property Rights: Public and Private Sector Interaction," working paper, Georgetown University, February 2006.

	Public Sector	Private Sector
Legislative	TRIPS Section 301 Action	Input to Trade Negotiation Lobbying
Cooperation and Liaison	Conventions	Industry Organizations
Enforcement	Customs Services Task Forces	Task Forces Private Investigation
Prevention	Education	Education/Publicity Strategic Alliances Marketing Strategy Assessment and Application

Many companies maintain close contact with the government and the various agencies charged with helping them. Computer makers and company attorneys regularly conduct seminars on how to detect pirated software and hardware. Other companies retain outside investigators to monitor the market and stage raids with the help of law enforcement officers. There are global piracy and counterfeiting consultants. It is predicted that in 2009 global counterfeiting of pharmaceuticals will grow to £91 billion worldwide and China alone will produce over 200,000,000,000 counterfeit cigarettes.[85] Britain is on the front line, both as Europe's prime target for counterfeiters (medicine prices are high compared with most other EU countries) and as a staging post between producers in the Far East and the medicine-hungry buyers of the United States. However, most people in the UK are largely unaware of the scale of the problem: a study in 2007 by the University of London's School of Pharmacy found that only 19 per cent of Britons felt there was a growing risk from counterfeit medicines, compared with 74 per cent of Europeans as a whole.[86]

The issue of intellectual property protection will become more important in international trade. It is a different problem from what it was a decade ago, when the principal victims were manufacturers of designer items. Today, the protection of intellectual property is crucial in high technology. The ease with which technology can be transferred and the lack of adequate protection of the developers' rights in certain markets make this a serious problem.[87]

Enforcement of intellectual property rights

Over the last decade, the counterfeiting and piracy phenomenon has risen to very dangerous dimensions and has become one of the most devastating problems facing world business.

With direct links to organized crime, counterfeiters have become extremely skilled entrepreneurs operating on a global scale. Counterfeiters make expert use of current technology and trade and succeed in producing every imaginable type of fake. Where previously only luxury goods, fashion and music and film products fell victim, nowadays counterfeiting affects foodstuffs, cosmetics, hygiene products, medicine and spare parts of cars, toys and various types of technical and electronic equipment.

As a result, the danger to our health and safety increases, while at the same time consumers are often not aware that when they buy a fake product there is a good chance that at least part of the money will go to organized crime or child labour.

Within the EU there are already a number of legal instruments in place, such as the Enforcement Directive, but in order to make them more effective the EU is seeking stronger administrative cooperation between authorities at all levels in the fight against piracy and counterfeiting.

On September 2008 the Council adopted a Resolution on a comprehensive EU anti-counterfeiting and anti-piracy plan. This Resolution endorsed the need to step up the fight against fake goods and called for the creation of a European observatory on counterfeiting and piracy.

The new European observatory on counterfeiting and piracy is coordinated by the European Commission and brings together representatives from member states' administrations, private industry and consumer organizations to improve efforts to combat a rising problem that threatens consumer health and safety, business, jobs and national and local economies.

The observatory is a pan-European platform that will collect key data related to counterfeiting and piracy; it will also identify and share best practices, and help to raise public awareness.

European counterfeiting and piracy observatory: Frequently asked questions

Why do we need an observatory?

Over the past ten years the global explosion in counterfeiting and piracy has become one of the most devastating problems facing world business. Twenty years ago, counterfeiting might have been regarded as a problem chiefly for the manufacturers of expensive handbags. But nowadays, counterfeiters have broadened their manufacture to include not only fake electrical appliances, car parts and toys, but also medicines – a development which could have potentially disastrous results (see MEMO/08/299).

International trade in counterfeit and pirated goods is estimated to have reached USD 200 billion in 2005. Clearly, action is required.

On 25 September 2008, the Competitiveness Council adopted a Resolution on a comprehensive EU anti-counterfeiting and anti-piracy plan (see IP/08/1416). This Resolution endorsed the need to step up the fight against counterfeiting and piracy and called for the creation of a European counterfeiting and piracy observatory.

The European Commission is pleased to announce the launch of the observatory on 2 April 2009, at a high level conference on counterfeiting and piracy. The overall goal of the observatory is to produce continuous, objective assessments and up-to-date research that lead to exchange of best practice and knowledge gathering among policymakers, industry experts and enforcement bodies.

What do we mean by an 'observatory'?

The structure of the observatory will be light and flexible. Each member state of the EU will have a delegate alongside key private sector representatives. The day-to-day operation of the observatory will be run by the Commission services. The work of the observatory will be shaped on the basis of a series of regular meetings where the representatives will jointly discuss the work and output of the observatory and how to best tackle the problems at hand.

The observatory will provide a forum for discussions between members of the European Parliament, member states, businesses, experts on intellectual property rights, researchers, enforcement bodies to analyze problems and shape best practice improvements. As a result it aims to become a recognized source of knowledge on counterfeiting and piracy and a central resource for enforcers.

What will be the observatory's main tasks?

The observatory will boost the fight against counterfeiting and piracy by:

1 **Obtaining better information including figures about the size of the problem**

Broad facts about the damage caused by counterfeiting and piracy are fairly well known, but more detailed figures based on solid evidence have been more difficult to assemble. This is partly due to the clandestine nature of the problem, but also because national authorities and businesses affected by the problem have not collected information in a systematic and uniform way. Some base their figures on the number of incidents, some in terms of volume, and some in terms of value; some collect only information from where the goods originate; and some group products in very broad categories while the others clearly specify them.

At present, the most robust figures indicating the scale of the problem are based on customs seizures of counterfeit/pirated goods at EU borders. Unfortunately, infringements at the borders only depict a part of the picture and as a result, infringers are seemingly able to keep one step ahead of the law.

It is necessary to understand why some products, sectors, member states and geographic areas within the EU are more vulnerable than others. Comprehensive and comparable figures will help to establish priorities and programmes and facilitate more focused enforcement.

2   Better cooperation between enforcement authorities

Due to the highly organized nature of counterfeiting and piracy, the response to it must be as coordinated as possible. Counterfeits often enter the EU through the countries where there is no intellectual property protection and once the goods are in the EU they may circulate freely. Within member states, competent national authorities responsible for combating this must be in regular contact with each other and their actions must be synchronized. They must be in permanent contact with relevant private sector bodies. Since counterfeiting and piracy are often cross-border activities, better cooperation between member states is a must.

3   Exploring and spreading successful private sector strategies

Through regular contacts, the observatory will gather information on successful anti-counterfeiting and piracy strategies and successful measures undertaken by the private sector. It will outline how businesses have managed to prevent and disrupt infringing acts; how they have coped with multiple jurisdictions and recovered damages; how they have learned from the difficulties they have encountered while enforcing their rights through traditional civil, criminal, administrative enforcement mechanisms and how we can all learn more from any alternative enforcement procedures being used.

4   Raising public awareness

Consumers are often not aware that when they buy a fake product there is a good chance that at least part of the money will go to organized crime or child labour. In many cases, fake goods are made under slavish conditions, often by children under ten years of age. Not to mention the widely reported stories from countries where fake cough medicines, life-saving drugs or even contaminated milk have killed hundreds of people and sickened thousands more. Therefore, it is essential that consumers are duly informed about the risks and dangers of buying counterfeit and pirated goods as well as the effect on society as a whole.

The observatory will aim to identify successful public awareness campaigns, strategies and initiatives within member states and to communicate successful approaches.

SOURCE: European Commission, Enforcement of intellectual property rights, **http://ec.europa.eu/internal_market/iprenforcement/index_en.htm**; EUROPA, European Counterfeiting and Piracy Observatory: Frequently Asked Questions **http://europa.eu/rapid/pressReleasesAction.do?reference=MEMO/09/146&format=HTML&aged=0&language=EN&guiLanguage=en**.

SUMMARY

Marketers may routinely exaggerate the attractiveness of international markets, especially in terms of their similarity. Despite the dramatic impact of globalization as far as market convergence is concerned, distances, especially cultural and economic, challenge the marketer to be vigilant.[88] The international marketer must pay careful attention to variables that may call for an adaptation in the product offering. The target market will influence the adaptation decision through factors such as government regulation and customer preferences and expectations. The product itself may not be in a form ready for international market entry in terms of its brand name, its packaging or its appearance. Some marketers make a conscious decision to offer only standardized products; some adjust their offerings by market.

Similar to the soft drink and packaged-goods marketers that have led the way, the newest marketers of world brands are producing not necessarily identical products but recognizable products. As an example, the success of McDonald's in the world marketplace has been based on variation, not on offering the same product worldwide. Had it not been for the variations, McDonald's would have limited its appeal unnecessarily and would have been far more subject to local competitors' challenges.

Firms entering or participating in the international marketplace will find it difficult to cope with the conflicting needs of the domestic and international markets. They will be certain to ask whether adjustments in their product offerings, if the marketplace requires them, are worthwhile. There are, unfortunately, no magic formulas for addressing the problem of product adaptation. The answer seems to lie in adopting formal procedures to assess products in terms of the markets' and the company's own needs.

The theft of intellectual property – ideas and innovations protected by copyrights, patents and trademarks – is a critical problem for many industries and countries, accelerating with the pace of globalization.[89] Governments have long argued about intellectual property protection, but the lack of results in some parts of the world has forced companies themselves to take action on this front.

Key terms

augmented features

backward innovation

brand

core product

mandatory/discretionary product adaptation

mandatory

Questions for discussion

1   Comment on the statement 'It is our policy not to adapt products for export'.

2   What are the major problems facing companies, especially smaller ones, in resolving product adaptation issues?

3   How do governments affect product adaptation decisions of firms?

4   Are standards like those promoted by the International Organization for Standardization (see **http://www.iso.ch**) a hindrance or an opportunity for exporters?

5   Is any product ever the same everywhere it is sold?

6   Propose ways in which intellectual property piracy could be stopped permanently.

Internet exercises

1   How can marketers satisfy the 4 Rs of environmentally correct practice? See, for example, the approaches proposed by the Duales System Deutschland (**www.gruener-punkt.de**).

2   The software industry is the hardest hit by piracy. Using the website of the Business Software Alliance (**http://www.bsa.org**), assess how this problem is being tackled.

Recommended readings

Arnold, David. *The Mirage of Global Markets: How Globalizing Companies Can Succeed as Markets Localize*. Englewood Cliffs, NJ: Prentice-Hall, 2003.

Czinkota, Michael R., Ilkka A. Ronkainen and Bob Donath. *Mastering Global Markets: Strategies for Today's Trade Globalist*. Mason, OH: Cengage South-Western, 2004.

Gorchels, Linda. *The Product Manager's Handbook: The Complete Product Management Resource*. New York: McGraw-Hill, 2005.

Keegan, Warren J. and Charles S. Mayer. *Multinational Product Management*. Chicago: American Marketing Association, 1977.

Lasalle, Diane and Terry A. Britton. *Priceless: Turning Ordinary Products into Extraordinary Experiences*. Boston, MA: Harvard Business School Press, 2002.

Levitt, Theodore. *The Marketing Imagination*. New York: Free Press, 1986.

Lorenz, C. *The Design Dimension: Product Strategy and the Challenge of Global Markets*. New York: Basil Blackwell, 1996.

Nelson, Carl A. *Exporting: A Manager's Guide to the Export Market*. Mason, OH: Thomson South-Western, 1999.

Papadopoulos, Nicolas and Louise A. Heslop. *Product-Country Images*. Binghamton, NY: International Business Press, 1993.

Renner, Sandra L. and W. Gary Winget. *Fast-Track Exporting*. New York: AMACOM, 1991.

Rodkin, Henry. *The Ultimate Overseas Business Guide for Growing Companies*. Homewood, IL: Dow Jones–Irwin, 1990.

Tuller, Lawrence W. *Exporting, Importing, and Beyond: How to 'Go Global' with Your Small Business*. Avon, MA: Adams Media Corporation, 1997.

Urban, Glen L. and John Hauser. *Design and Marketing of New Products*. Englewood Cliffs, NJ: Prentice-Hall, 1993.

Notes

1   Jeffrey E. Garten, 'Globalization without Tears: A New Social Compact for CEOs', *Strategy and Business* (fourth quarter, 2002): 36–45.

2   Rahman, O., Zhu, X. and Wing-sun, L. (2008), 'A study of the pyjamas purchasing behaviour of Chinese consumers in Hangzhou, China', *Journal of Fashion Marketing and Management*, 12(2), 217–231.

3   Jill G. Klein, Richard Ettenson and Marlene Morris, 'The Animosity Model of Foreign Product Purchase: An Empirical Test in the People's Republic of China', *Journal of Marketing* 62 (January 1998): 89–100.

4   Thomas L. Friedman, *The Lexus and the Olive Tree: Understanding Globalization* (New York: Anchor Books, 2000), chapters 3 and 15.

5   S. Tamer Cavusgil and Shaoming Zou, 'Marketing Strategy–Performance Relationship: An Investigation of the Empirical Link in Export Market Ventures', *Journal of Marketing* 58 (January 1994): 1–21.

6   Jean L. Johnson and Wiboon Arunthanes, 'Ideal and Actual Product Adaptation in US Exporting Firms', *International Marketing Review* 12 (number 3, 1995): 31–46.

7   Dana James, 'B2–4B Spells Profits', *Marketing News,* November 5, 2001, 1, 11–12.

8   'Star Power', *Fortune,* February 6, 2006, 61.

9   Jean-Noël Kapferer, *Survey among 210 European Brand Managers* (Paris: Euro-RSCG, 1998).

10 Carl A. Sohlberg, 'The Perennial Issue of Adaptation or Standardization of International Marketing Communication: Organizational Contingencies and Performance', *Journal of International Marketing* 10 (no. 3, 2002): 1–21.

11 'EU/Country Briefing', *Business Europe,* April 21, 1999, 9–11.

12 'Trading Places', *The Economist,* November 22, 2001, 58.

13 'US and EU at Odds over Jet Noise', *The Washington Post,* January 19, 2000, E1, E10.

14 'Google Under the Gun', *Time,* February 13, 2006, 53–54; 'Microsoft Revises Policy on Shutting Down Blogs', *The Wall Street Journal,* February 1, 2006, B10; and 'Here Be Dragons', *The Economist,* January 28, 2006, 59.

15 Erika Morphy, 'Cutting the Cost of Compliance', *Export Today* 12 (January 1996): 14–18.

16 James D. Southwick, 'Addressing Market Access Barriers in Japan through the WTO: A Survey of Typical Japan Market Access Issues and the Possibility to Address Them through WTP Dispute Resolution Procedures', *Law and Policy in International Business* 31 (Spring 2000): 923–976.

17 Xinhua (2008), 'Chinese Export Food Factories Open to Japanese Media'. Available **http://english.cri.cn/2946/2008/03/21/1221@336633.htm** (Accessed 18/08/09).

18 Davis Goodman, 'Thinking Export? Think ISO 9000', *World Trade,* August 1998, 48–49.

19 Wikipedia, 'International Organization for Standardization, members' **http://en.wikipedia.org/wiki/International_Organization_for_Standardization#Members**

20 Galloway, J. (2009), 'Joint Accreditation System of Australia and New Zealand' **http://www.jas-anz.com.au/images/stories/Documents/Policies/policy7-08.pdf**

21 *ISO Survey 2004,* available at **http://www.iso.ch**.

22 Enrique Sierra, 'The New ISO 14000 Series: What Exporters Should Know', *Trade Forum* (no. 3, 1996): 16–31.

23 Kirk Loncar, 'Look Before You Leap', *World Trade,* June 1997, 92–93.

24 Drew Martin and Paul Herbig, 'Marketing Implications of Japan's Social-Cultural Underpinnings', *Journal of Brand Management* 9 (January 2002): 171–179.

25 **http://ccc.qbook.tv/content/view/45/62/**

26 Jennifer Aaker, 'Dimensions of Measuring Brand Personality', *Journal of Marketing Research* 34 (August 1997): 347–356.

27 **http://www.sesameworkshop.org**.

28 'The Simpsons Exported to Middle East – Minus Bacon, Beer', *ABC News,* October 18, 2005.

29 James A. Gingrich, 'Five Rules for Winning Emerging Market Consumers', *Strategy and Business* (second quarter, 1999): 35–42.

30 'Tech's Future', *Business Week,* September 27, 2004, 82–89.

31 'Holding the Fries – At the Border', *Business Week,* December 14, 1998, 8.

32 Design Chef (2009), 'Know and Monitor Your Competition', **http://www.designchefdirectory.com/tips/monitor-competition.htm**(Accessed 14/10/09).

33 'Exporting to Survive', *Time Global Business,* September 2002, A20–A22.

34 'Dubbing in Product Plugs', *The Wall Street Journal,* December 6, 2004, B1, B5.

35 Robert Gray, 'Local on a Global Scale', *Marketing,* September 27, 2001, 22–23.

36 Jean-Noël Kapferer, 'Is There Really No Hope for Local Brands?' *Journal of Brand Management* 9 (January 2002): 163–170.

37 Alan Mitchell, 'Few Brands Can Achieve a Truly Global Presence', *Marketing Week,* February 7, 2002, 32–33.

38 'The Best Global Brands', *Business Week,* August 5, 2002, 92–108.

39 'Mozart's Genius Extends to Selling Lederhosen in Japan', *The Wall Street Journal Europe,* January 6, 1992, Section 1.1.

40 Catchword, 'Speaking Globally'. **http://www.catchwordbranding.com/capabilities/global-linguistics-testing.php** (Accessed 16/11/09).

41 NameLab, Inc. (**http://www.namelab.com**).

42 Barry M. Tarnef, 'How to Protect Your Goods in Transit without Going Along for a Ride', *Export Today* 9 (May 1993): 55–57.

43 Jesse Wilson, 'Are Your Spanish Translations Culturally Correct?' *Export Today* 10 (May 1994): 68–69.

44 'The Perils of Packaging: Nestlé Aims for Easier Openings', *The Wall Street Journal,* November 17, 2005, B1, B5.

45 Dan McGinn, 'Vodka with Punch', **http://mbajungle.com**, September/October 2002, 34–36.

46 Guillermo D'Andrea, E. Alejandro Stengel and Anne Goebel-Krstelj, 'Six Truths About Emerging-Market Consumers', *Strategy and Business* 34 (Spring 2004): 58–69.

47 China travel.com 'Chinese lucky numbers'. Available **http://www.chinatravel.com/facts/traditions-and-custom/chinese-lucky-numbers.htm** (Accessed 16/11/09).

48 **http://www.tetrapak.com**.

49 'Waste Not', *Business Europe,* February 20, 2002, 4.

50 Thomas J. Madden, Kelly Hewett and Martin S. Roth, 'Managing Images in Different Cultures: A Cross-National Study of Color Meanings and Preferences', *Journal of International Marketing* 8 (no. 4, 2000): 90–107.

51 'How the Swedish Retailer Became a Global Cult Brand', *Business Week,* November 14, 2005, 96–106.

52 Department for Business Innovation and Skills (BIS), 'UK Trade and Investment' **http://www.uktradeinvest.gov.uk/** (Accessed 16/11/09).

53 'Why Don't We Use the Metric System?' *Fortune,* May 29, 2000, 56–57.

54 Lees, F. And Maurer, L. (2002), 'American Companies Should Prepare for the UK Entering the Euro System', *Review of Business*, Vol. 23. Available at: **http://www.questia.com/googleScholar.qst;jsessionid=LBwKvxBmsj17TxZV2vrKFTQ875vqLhrm1WMc3nDXxMClxRcwXjw6!-689845967!-368539431?docId=5002079929**

55 Carla Kruytbosch, 'The Minds behind the Winners', *International Business,* January 1994, 56–70.

56 'Awash in Export Sales', *Export Today* 5 (February 1989): 11.

57 Ian Wilkinson and Nigel Barrett, 'In Search of Excellence in Exports: An Analysis of the 1986 Australian Export Award Winners', paper given at the Australian Export Award presentations, Sydney, November 28, 1986.

58 Thomas H. Stevenson and Frank C. Barnes, 'Fourteen Years of ISO 9000: Impact, Criticisms, Costs and Benefits', *Business Horizons* 44 (May/June 2001): 45–51.

59 'Keeping Cool in China', *The Economist,* April 6, 1996, 73–74.

60 Anderson, E. (2005), 'The protective dimension of product warranty policies and practices', *Journal of Consumer Affairs*, 7(2), 111–120.

61 Murthy, D. (2006), 'Product warranty and reliability', *Annals of Operations Research*, 143(1), March, 133–146.

62 Martin S. Roth and Jean B. Romeo, 'Matching Product Category and Country Image Perceptions: A Framework for Managing Country-of-Origin Effects', *Journal of International Business Studies* 23 (third quarter, 1992): 477–497.

63 Warren J. Bilkey and Erik Nes, 'Country-of-Origin Effects on Product Evaluations', *Journal of International Business Studies* 13 (Spring–Summer 1982): 88–99.

64 Balabanis, G. and Diamantopoulos, A. (2004), 'Domestic country bias, country-of-origin effects, and consumer ethnocentrism: A multidimensional unfolding approach', *Journal of the Academy of Marketing Science*, 32(1), 80–95.

65 Daye, D. and VanAuken, B. (2008), 'Branding: The country of origin effect'. Online **http://www.brandingstrategyinsider.com/2008/03/branding-the-co.html** (Accessed 19/11/09).

66 Johny K. Johansson, Ilkka A. Ronkainen and Michael R. Czinkota, 'Negative Country-of-Origin Effects: The Case of the New Russia', *Journal of International Business Studies* 25 (first quarter, 1994): 1–21.

67 Johny K. Johansson, 'Determinants and Effects of the Use of "Made In" Labels', *International Marketing Review* 6 (1989): 47–58.

68 Philip Kotler and David Gertner, 'Country as Brand, Product and Beyond: A Place Marketing and Brand Management Perspective', *Journal of Brand Management* 9 (April 2002): 249–261.

69 Nuthall, K. (2007), 'MEPS call for country-of-origin labelling on all clothing and footwear imports', **http://www.internationalnewsservices.com/articles/36-archive/11763-meps-call-for-country-of-origin-labelling-on-all-eu-clothing-and-footwear-imports** (Assessed 19/11/09).

70 'Push for "Made In" Tags Grows in EU', *The Wall Street Journal,* November 7, 2005, A6; and 'Breaking a Taboo, High Fashion Starts Making Goods Overseas', *The Wall Street Journal,* September 27, 2005, A1, A10.

71 Food Standards Agency, 'Country of origin labelling guidance'. Online. **http://www.food.gov.uk/multimedia/pdfs/originlabelling.pdf** (Accessed 19/11/09).

72 Roger J. Calantone, Daekwan Kim, Jeffrey B. Schmidt and S. Tamer Cavusgil, 'The Influence of Internal and External Firm Factors on International Product Adaptation Strategy and Export Performance: A Three-Country Comparison', *Journal of Business Research* 59 (number 2, 2006): 176–185.

73 Arnold Schuh, 'Global Standardization as a Success Formula for Marketing in Central Eastern Europe', *Journal of World Business* 35 (Summer 2000): 133–148.

74 European Commission (2007), 'Keeping better guard on intellectual property'. Online **http://ec.europa.eu/enterprise/library/ee_online/art34_en.htm** (Accessed 23/11/09).

75 ELSPA (2009), 'Court of Appeal Copyright Clarification Welcomed', **http://www.elspa.com/?i=8171&s=1111&f=49** (Accessed 23/11/09).

76 Business Software Alliance (2008), 'Sixth Annual BSA-IDC Global Software Piracy Study', **http://global.bsa.org/globalpiracy2008/studies/globalpiracy2008.pdf** (Accessed 23/11/09).

77 Business Software Alliance (2008), 'Sixth Annual BSA-IDC Global Software Piracy Study', **http://global.bsa.org/globalpiracy2008/studies/globalpiracy2008.pdf** (Accessed 23/11/09).

78 Ibid.

79 Ilkka A. Ronkainen, 'Imitation as the Worst Kind of Flattery: Product Counterfeiting', *Trade Analyst* 2 (July–August 1986): 2.

80 Sanyal, R. (2005), 'Determinants of Bribery in International Business: The Cultural and Economic Factors', *Journal of Business Ethics,* 59(1/2), 139–145.

81 ETH Zurich (2009), 'Problem-analysis report on counterfeiting and illicit trade', **http://www.bridge-project.eu/data/File/BRIDGE%20WP05%20%20Anti-Counterfeiting%20Problem%20Analysis.pdf** (Accessed 23/11/09).

82 EUROPA (2009), 'European Counterfeiting and Piracy Observatory: Frequently Asked Questions', **http://europa.eu/rapid/pressReleases Action.do?reference=MEMO/09/146&format=HTML&aged=0&language=EN&guiLanguage=en** (Accessed 23/11/09).

83 Slashdot (2009) 'Nintendo asks for government help to fight piracy', **http://games.slashdot.org/article.pl?sid=09/02/26/1118217** (Accessed 23/11/09).

84 **http://www.wipo.org**

85 Global Piracy & Counterfeiting Consultants, 'America's watchdog warns the world about Chinese counterfeit pharmaceuticals & cigarettes', **http://gp-cc.com/pressrelease.htm** (Accessed 30/11/09).

86 Global Piracy & Counterfeiting Consultants, 'Counterfeit medicines: the pills that kill', **http://gp-cc.com/pressrelease.htm** (Accessed 30/11/09).

87 Michael G. Harvey and Ilkka A. Ronkainen, 'International Counterfeiters: Marketing Success without the Cost and the Risk', *Columbia Journal of World Business* 20 (Fall 1985): 37–45.

88 Pankaj Ghemawat, 'Distance Still Matters: The Hard Reality of Global Expansion', *Harvard Business Review* 79 (September 2001): 137–147.

89 Kenneth Cukier, 'In Defence of Creativity', *RSA Journal,* December 2005, 18–21.

CHAPTER 11
EXPORT PRICING

THE INTERNATIONAL **MARKETPLACE 11.1**

Jean-Claude Trichet leads European team to press China on freeing yuan to rise

Top European officials will press China this weekend to allow its currency to rise against the euro, amid political fears that the euro's strength could undermine Europe's recovery from its worst recession in decades.

European Central Bank President Jean-Claude Trichet, Luxembourg prime minister and finance minister Jean-Claude Juncker and European Economic Commissioner Joaquin Almunia are due to meet this Sunday with top officials from China's central bank and finance ministry in Nanjing, where they will lobby for a stronger Chinese yuan.

European officials made a similar excursion to China two years ago, with little result. The yuan – whose value China links to the US dollar – has risen only about 7 per cent against the euro since then.

China's Deputy Foreign Minister, Zhang Zhijun, reiterated his country's currency policy last Tuesday, saying China will keep the yuan 'basically stable around reasonable, balanced levels'. Such statements suggest that the visitors are unlikely to win China's agreement to allow a faster appreciation of the yuan.

That might not matter as much as European officials think, analysts say. Despite the high-profile appeal, many economists and business leaders say Europe's exports may depend less on the euro's exchange rate than on China's ability to deliver economic growth and support a revival in world trade volumes.

Global demand is three to four times more powerful than exchange rates in determining exports, says Silvio Peruzzo, economist

at Royal Bank of Scotland in London. So if the euro appreciates 5 per cent and global trade expands by an equal rate, the net effect for the eurozone would be an extra one percentage point of gross domestic product, he says.

A higher yuan would be 'nice to have', said Volker Treier, chief economist at the German Chambers of Industry and Commerce, since it would make European-made products more competitive on price against Chinese goods. However, 'right now the demand side is the more decisive one'.

JPMorgan economists also say global demand for European goods is a more important determinant of the eurozone's exports than currency rates, and estimate it would take a very large rise in the euro's level to prevent strong export growth over the next few quarters.

Business leaders agree. 'The volume to be generated throughout the upturn is more important than the exchange-rate hurdle', noted Karl Haeusgen, chief executive of HAWE Hydraulik SE, an engineering company based in Munich.

And in the specific case of China, the exchange rate 'is less of a problem' than in other markets, he said, because customers there are willing to pay a premium for technology.

The euro's steady rise has not scared off other German exporters, either, especially those in specialized engineering products that are less sensitive to price fluctuations than cheap, mass-produced goods.

'The product is the focus, not the currency', said Dagmar Bollin-Flade, chief executive of Christian Bollin Armaturenfabrik GmbH, one of Frankfurt's oldest businesses producing specialty valves for the petrochemical industry and power plants.

Last year, the Bollin firm, which makes over 350,000 different kinds of shut-off valves, was able to ink deals in China despite the high euro. Demand from China has tapered off since, she said, but that was due more to changes in the structure of Chinese power plants than the euro.

A higher yuan and robust Chinese demand would be best, 'but if I had to make a choice, demand is more important', said Gernot Nerb, head of industry research at the IFO Institute for Economic Research. IFO's closely-watched survey of German companies has shown a rise in export expectations, thanks to demand in China and other emerging economies like Brazil, Mr Nerb said.

EU officials say they want to make the case that a stronger yuan is good for both China and Europe. According to people within the European Commission, the three officials are preparing presentations for the Chinese that model the potential effects of a stronger yuan, including restraining domestic inflation in China.

The yuan is now set at around 6.85 to the US dollar, so when the greenback declines against other floating currencies like the euro, China's currency declines with it, making Chinese products cheaper in global markets. The euro passed the key $US1.50 threshold earlier this week, hitting a 15-month high against the US dollar.

China still makes up only a small share of total eurozone exports at €43 billion (£39 billion) this year through August, trailing the UK and the US. But unlike eurozone exports to the US and the UK, which are down more than 20 per cent from last year, the region's exports to China have held steady. Economists say they should resume firm growth soon. The Organization for Economic Cooperation and Development expects China's economy to expand more than 10 per cent next year, three times faster than global GDP.

SOURCE: Poon, T. and Cohen, A. (2009), 'Jean-Claude Trichet leads European team to press China on freeing yuan to rise', *The Wall Street Journal*, **http://www.theaustralian.com.au/business/news/jean-claude-trichet-leads-european-team-to-press-china-on-freeing-yuan-to-rise/story-e6frg90x-1225804530508.**

This chapter will focus on the pricing decision from the exporter's point of view: the setting of export price, terms of sale and terms of payment. The setting of export prices is complicated by factors such as increased distance from the markets, currency fluctuations, governmental policies such as duties and typically longer and different types of channels of distribution. In spite of new factors influencing the pricing decision, the objective remains the same: to create demand for the marketer's offerings and to do so profitably in the long term. In achieving this, financing arrangements for export transactions are critical for two reasons: to secure sales and to combat various types of risk. Two special considerations in export pricing – leasing and dumping – are discussed at the end of this chapter. Foreign market pricing (by subsidiaries) and intracompany transfer pricing, that is, pricing for transactions between corporate entities, will be discussed in Chapter 17.

PRICE DYNAMICS

Price is the only element of the marketing mix that is revenue generating; all the others are costs. It should therefore be used as an active instrument of strategy in the major areas of marketing decision making, as seen in *The International Marketplace 11.1*. Price serves as a means of communication with the buyer by providing a basis for judging the attractiveness of the offer. It is a major competitive tool in meeting and beating close rivals and substitutes. Competition will often force prices down, whereas intracompany financial considerations have an opposite effect. Prices, along with costs, will determine the sustainability of a firm's advantage.

Price should not be determined in isolation from the other marketing mix elements. It may be used effectively in positioning the product in the marketplace. The feasibility range for price setting established by demand, competition, costs and legal considerations may be narrow or wide in a given situation (for example, the pricing of a commodity versus an innovation). Regardless of how narrow the gap allowed by these factors, however, pricing should never be considered a static element. The marketer's ultimate goal is to make the customer as inelastic as possible; that is, the customer should prefer the marketer's offer even at a price premium.

Similarly, pricing decisions cannot be made in isolation from the other functions of the firm. Effective financial arrangements can significantly support the marketing programme if they are carefully formulated between the finance and marketing areas. Sales are often won or lost on the basis of favourable credit terms to the buyer. With large numbers of competent firms active in international markets, financing packages – often put together with the help of governmental support – have become more important. Customers abroad may be prepared to accept higher prices if they can obtain attractive credit terms.

A summary of international pricing situations is provided as a matrix in Exhibit 11.1. Pricing challenges – such as pricing for a new market entry, changing price either as an attack strategy or in response to competitive changes, and multiple-product coordination in cases of related demand – are technically the same as problems encountered in domestic markets. The scope of these pricing situations will vary according to the degree of foreign involvement and the type of market encountered.

In first-time pricing, the general alternatives are (1) skimming, (2) following the market price, and (3) penetration pricing. The objective of skimming is to achieve the highest possible contribution in a short time period. For an exporter to use this approach, the product has to be unique, and some segments of the market must be willing to pay the high price. As more segments are targeted and more of the product is made available, the price is gradually lowered. The success of skimming depends on the ability and speed of competitive reaction.

If similar products already exist in the target market, market pricing can be used. The final customer price is determined based on competitive prices, and then both production and marketing must be adjusted to the price. This approach requires the exporter to have a thorough knowledge of product costs, as well as confidence that the product life cycle is long enough to warrant entry into the market. It is a reactive approach and may lead to problems if sales volumes never rise to sufficient levels to produce a satisfactory return. Although firms typically use pricing as a differentiation tool, the international marketing manager may have no choice but to accept the prevailing world market price.

When penetration pricing is used, the product is offered at a low price intended to generate volume sales and achieve high market share, which would compensate for a lower per-unit return. One company found, for example, that a 20 per cent reduction in average pricing roughly doubled the demand for its product.[1] This approach typically requires mass markets, price-sensitive customers, and decreasing production and marketing costs as sales volumes increase. The basic assumption of penetration pricing is that the lower price will increase sales, which may not always be the case. This approach can also be used to discourage other marketers from entering the market.

Price changes are called for when a new product is launched, when a change occurs in overall market conditions (such as a change in the value of the billing currency), or when there is a change in the exporter's internal situation, such as costs of production. An exporter may elect not to change price even though the result may be lower profitability. However, if a

Pricing Situation	International Involvement		
	Exporting	Foreign-Market Pricing	Intracompany Pricing
First-Time Pricing			
Changing Pricing			
Multiple-Product Pricing			

EXHIBIT 11.1

International pricing situations

Sources: Elements of the model adopted from Howard Forman and Richard A. Lancioni, "International Industrial Pricing Strategic Decisions and the Pricing Manager: Some Key Issues," *Professional Pricing Society*, October 9, 1999, at **http://www.pricingsociety.com/pdf-4-index/international-industrial-pricing.pdf**; and Helmut Becker, "Pricing: An International Marketing Challenge," in International Marketing Strategy, eds. Hans Thorelli and Helmut Becker (New York: Pergamon Press, 1980): 203–215.

decision is made to change prices, related changes must also be considered. For example, if an increase in price is required, it may at least initially be accompanied by increased promotional efforts. Price changes usually follow changes in the product's stage in the life cycle. As the product matures, more pressure will be put on the price to keep the product competitive despite increased competition and less possibility of differentiation.

With multiple-product pricing, the various items in the line may be differentiated by pricing them appropriately to indicate, for example, an economy version, a standard version, and the top-of-the-line version. One of the products in the line may be priced to protect against competitors or to gain market share from existing competitors. The other items in the line are then expected to make up for the lost contribution of such a 'fighting brand'.

Although foreign market pricing and intracompany pricing are discussed later in conjunction with global pricing challenges, they do have an impact on the exporter as well. For example, distributors in certain markets may forgo certain profit margins in exchange for exclusivity. This may mean that the exporter will have to lower prices to the distributor and take less profit to ensure sales and to remain competitive, or, if the market conditions warrant it, to move into more direct distribution.[2] Similarly, the exporter, in providing products to its own sales offices abroad, may have to adjust its transfer prices according to foreign exchange fluctuations. Exporters with operations across multiple diverse markets will have to align and coordinate prices to minimize problems such as grey-market imports.[3]

THE SETTING OF EXPORT PRICES

In setting the export price, a company can use a process such as the one summarized in Exhibit 11.2. The setting of export price is influenced by both internal and external factors, as well as their interaction.[4] Internal factors include the company's philosophy, goals and objectives; the costs of developing, producing and marketing the export product; and the nature of the exporter's product and industry. External factors relate to international markets in general or to a specific target market in particular and include such factors as customer, regulatory, competitive, and financial (mainly foreign exchange) characteristics. The interaction of these elements causes pricing opportunities and constraints in different markets. For example, company management may have decided to challenge its main foreign competitor in the competitor's home market. Regulation in that market requires expensive product adaptation, the cost of which has to be absorbed now for the product to remain competitive.

As in all marketing decisions, the intended target market will establish the basic premise for pricing. Factors to be considered include the importance of price in customer decision making (in particular, the ability to pay), the strength of perceived price-quality relationships, and potential reactions to marketing-mix manipulation by marketers. For example, an exporter extending a first-world product to an emerging market may find its potential unnecessarily limited and thus opt for a new version of a product that costs a fraction of the original version. Customers' demands will also have to be considered in terms of support required by the intermediary. The marketing mix must be planned to match the characteristics of the target market. Pricing will be a major factor in determining the desired brand image as well as the distribution channels to be used and the level of promotional support required. Conversely, mix elements affect pricing's degrees of freedom. If the use of specialty channels is needed to maintain product positioning, price will be affected.

Pricing policies follow from the overall objectives of the firm for a particular target market and involve general principles or rules that a firm follows in making pricing decisions.[5] Objectives include profit maximization, market share, survival, percentage return on investment, and various competitive policies such as copying competitors' prices, following a particular competitor's prices, or pricing so as to discourage competitors from entering the market. For example, an exporter entering a new market may allow wholesalers and retailers above-normal profit margins to encourage maximum sales volume, geographic distribution, and loyalty. Loctite Corporation (a wholly owned subsidiary of Henkel KGaA, Germany), in marketing adhesives for industrial uses, requires a highly technical selling effort from distributors and uses higher-than-average compensation packages to secure their services. These

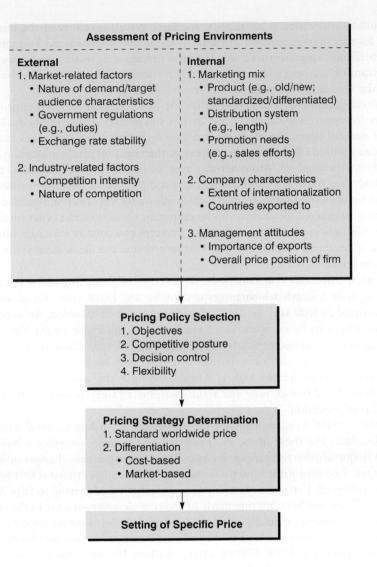

Assessment of Pricing Environments

External
1. Market-related factors
   - Nature of demand/target audience characteristics
   - Government regulations (e.g., duties)
   - Exchange rate stability
2. Industry-related factors
   - Competition intensity
   - Nature of competition

Internal
1. Marketing mix
   - Product (e.g., old/new; standardized/differentiated)
   - Distribution system (e.g., length)
   - Promotion needs (e.g., sales efforts)
2. Company characteristics
   - Extent of internationalization
   - Countries exported to
3. Management attitudes
   - Importance of exports
   - Overall price position of firm

Pricing Policy Selection
1. Objectives
2. Competitive posture
3. Decision control
4. Flexibility

Pricing Strategy Determination
1. Standard worldwide price
2. Differentiation
   - Cost-based
   - Market-based

Setting of Specific Price

EXHIBIT 11.2

Stages in setting of export prices

Sources: Elements of model adopted from Matthew Myers, S. Tamer Cavusgil, and Adamantios Diamantopoulos, "Antecedents and Actions of Export Pricing Strategy: A Conceptual Framework and Research Propositions," *European Journal of Marketing* 36 (numbers 1/2, 2002): 159–189; Barbara Stöttinger, "Strategic Export Pricing: A Long and Winding Road," *Journal of International Marketing* 9 (no. 1, 2001): 40–63; S. Tamer Cavusgil, "Pricing for Global Markets," *Columbia Journal of World Business* 31(Winter 1996): 66–78; and Alfred R. Oxenfeld, "Multistage Approach to Pricing," *Harvard Business Review* 38 (July/August 1960): 120–132.

types of demands are common especially in the early stages of the export effort and may have to be satisfied to gain market penetration. They should be phased out later on, however, with sales volume increases making up for the difference.[6]

Where and how decisions are made is also an important part of an exporter's pricing policy. The degree to which the pricing decision should be localized is a function of competitive conditions and economic conditions, such as inflation. The more dissimilarity and uncertainty a market displays, the more local pricing decision has to be pushed. The inherent conflicts between local sales (focused on volume generation) and upper management (focused on profitability) have to be settled as well.[7] This is especially true in terms of pricing flexibility; in other words, the willingness to adjust prices under certain circumstances, such as competitive changes or currency fluctuations.

Export pricing strategy

The general price-setting strategies in international marketing are (a) a standard worldwide price and (2) dual pricing, which differentiates between domestic and export prices. Two approaches exist within each of these general strategies: cost-based, which is relatively simple to establish and implement, and market-based, in which the focus is on customer demand and competition. In general, the more involved the company is in exports, the more likely they are to use market-driven methods, whereas those new to exports prefer the cost-driven methods.

The **standard worldwide price** may be the same price regardless of the buyer (if foreign product or foreign marketing costs are negligible) or may be based on average unit costs of fixed, variable, and export-related costs. Uniform pricing is advisable when customers worldwide are aware of the prices charged, and when there is little chance of differentiating the product or the service to warrant price differences.

In **dual pricing**, domestic and export prices are differentiated and two approaches to pricing products for export are available: cost-driven and market-driven methods. If a cost-based approach is decided upon, the marketer can choose between the **cost-plus method** and the **marginal cost method**. The cost-plus strategy is the true cost, fully allocating domestic and foreign costs to the product. Although this type of pricing ensures margins, the final price may be so high that the firm's competitiveness is compromised. This may cause some exporters to consider a flexible cost-plus strategy, which allows for variations in special circumstances.[8] Discounts may be granted, depending on the customer, the size of the order or the intensity of competition. Changes in prices may also be put into effect to counter exchange rate fluctuations. Despite these allowances, profit is still a driving motive and pricing is more static as an element of the marketing mix.

The marginal cost method considers the direct costs of producing and selling products for export as the floor beneath which prices cannot be set. Fixed costs for plants, R&D and domestic overhead as well as domestic marketing costs are disregarded. An exporter can thus lower export prices to be competitive in markets that otherwise might have been beyond access. On certain occasions, especially if the exporter is large, this may open a company to dumping charges, because determination of dumping may be based on average total costs, which are typically considerably higher. A comparison of the cost-oriented methods is provided in Exhibit 11.3. Notice how the rigid cost-plus strategy produces the highest selling price by full-cost allocation.

Market-differentiated pricing calls for export pricing according to the dynamic conditions of the marketplace. For these firms, the marginal cost strategy provides a basis, and prices may change frequently due to changes in competition, exchange rate changes or other environmental changes. The need for information and controls becomes crucial if this pricing alternative is to be attempted. Exporters are likely to use market-based pricing to gain entry or better penetration in a new market, ignoring many of the cost elements, at least in the short term.

While most exporters, especially in the early stages of their internationalization, use cost-plus pricing, it usually does not lead to desired performance.[9] It typically leads to pricing too high in weak markets and too low in strong markets by not reflecting prevailing market

EXHIBIT 11.3

Export pricing alternatives

Production Costs	Standard	Cost Plus	Marginal Cost
Materials	2.00	2.00	2.00
Fixed costs	1.00	1.00	0.00
Additional foreign product costs	0.00	0.10	0.10
Production overhead	0.50	0.50	0.00
Total production costs	3.50	3.60	2.10
U.S. marketing costs	1.50	0.00	0.00
General and administrative	0.75	0.75	0.00
Foreign marketing	0.00	1.00	1.00
Other foreign costs	0.00	1.25	1.25
Subtotal	5.75	6.60	4.35
Profit margin (25%)	1.44	1.65	1.09
Selling price	7.19	8.25	5.44

Source: Adapted from Lee Oster, "Accounting for Exporters," *Export Today* 7 (January 1991): 28–33.

conditions. However, as experience is accumulated, the process allows for more flexibility and is more market-driven. Care has to be taken, however, that the cost of implementing a pricing-adaptation strategy does not outweigh the advantages of having a more adapted price.[10]

Interestingly, exporters have been found to differ in their pricing approaches by their country of origin. For example, Korean firms price more competitively in international markets than domestically, while EU firms seem to consider costs and profits more in setting their export prices.[11]

Overall, exporters see the pricing decision as a critical one, which means that it is typically taken centrally under the supervision of top-level management. In addition to product quality, correct pricing is seen as the major determinant of international marketing success.[12]

Export-related costs

In preparing a quotation, the exporter must be careful to take into account and, if possible, include unique export-related costs. These are in addition to the normal costs shared with the domestic side. They include the following:

1 The cost of modifying the product for foreign markets.

2 Operational costs of the export operation: personnel, market research, additional shipping and insurance costs, communications costs with foreign customers and overseas promotional costs.

3 Costs incurred in entering the foreign markets: tariffs and taxes; risks associated with a buyer in a different market (mainly commercial credit risks and political risks); and risks from dealing in other than the exporter's domestic currency – that is, foreign exchange risk.

The combined effect of both clear-cut and hidden costs results in export prices that far exceed domestic prices. The cause is termed price escalation. In the case of Geochron, the marketer of world time indicators, the multilayered distribution system with its excessive markups makes the price of a $1,300 clock exceed $3,800 in Japan.[13]

Four different export scenarios are compared with a typical domestic situation in Exhibit 11.4. The first case is relatively simple, adding only the CIF (cost, insurance, freight) and tariff charges. The second adds a foreign importer and thus lengthens the foreign part of the distribution channel. In the third case, a value-added tax (VAT), such as those used within the European Union, is included in the calculations. This is imposed on the full export selling price, which represents the 'value added' to or introduced into the country from abroad. In Italy, for example, where most food items are taxed at 2 per cent, processed meat is taxed at 18 per cent because the government wants to use the VAT to help reduce its trade deficit. The fourth case simulates a situation typically found in less-developed countries where distribution channels are longer. Lengthy channels can easily double the landed (CIF) price.

Complicating price escalation in today's environment may be the fact that price increases are of different sizes across markets. If customers are willing to shop around before purchasing, the problem of price differentials will make distributors unhappy and could result in a particular market's being abandoned altogether.

Price escalation can be overcome through creative strategies, depending on what the demand elasticities in the market are. Typical methods, such as the following, focus on cost cutting:

1 Reorganize the channel of distribution. The example in Exhibit 11.5, based on import channels for spaghetti and macaroni in Japan, shows how the flow of merchandise through the various wholesaling levels has been reduced to only an internal wholesale distribution centre, resulting in savings of 25 per cent and increasing the overall potential for imports. Shortening of channels may, however, bring about other costs such as demands for better discounts if a new intermediary takes the role of multiple previous ones.

2 Adapt the product. The product itself can be reformulated by including less expensive ingredients or unbundling costly features, which can be made optional. Remaining

| **EXHIBIT 11.4** | Export price escalation |

International Marketing Channel Elements and Cost Factors	Domestic Wholesale-Retail Channel	CASE 1 Same as Domestic with Direct Wholesale Import CIF/Tariff	CASE 2 Same as 1 with Foreign Importer Added to Channel	CASE 3 Same as 2 with VAT Added	CASE 4 Same as 3 with Local Foreign Jobber Added to Channel
Manufacturer's net price	6.00	6.00	6.00	6.00	6.00
+ Insurance and shipping cost (CIF)	—	2.50	2.50	2.50	2.50
= Landed cost (CIF value)	—	8.50	8.50	8.50	8.50
+ Tariff (20% on CIF value)	—	1.70	1.70	1.70	1.70
= Importer's cost (CIF value + tariff)	—	10.20	10.20	10.20	10.20
+ Importer's margin (25% on cost)	—	—	2.55	2.55	2.55
+ VAT (16% on full cost plus margin)	—	—	—	2.04	2.04
= Wholesaler's cost (= importer's price)	6.00	10.20	12.75	14.79	14.79
+ Wholesaler's margin (33 1/3% on cost)	2.00	3.40	4.25	4.93	4.93
+ VAT (16% on margin)	—	—	—	79	79
= Local foreign jobber's cost (= wholesale price)	—	—	—	—	20.51
+ Jobber's margin (33 1/3% on cost)	—	—	—	—	6.84
+ VAT (16% on margin)	—	—	—	—	1.09
= Retailer's cost (= wholesale or jobber price)	8.00	13.60	17.00	20.51	28.44
+ Retailer's margin (50% on cost)	4.00	6.80	8.50	10.26	14.22
+ VAT (16% on margin)	—	—	—	1.64	2.28
= Retail price (what consumer pays)	12.00	20.40	25.50	32.41	44.94
Percentage price escalation over domestic		70%	113%	170%	275%
Percentage price escalation over Case 1			25%	59%	120%
Percentage price escalation over Case 2				27%	76%
Percentage price escalation over Case 3					39%

Source: Helmut Becker, "Pricing: An International Marketing Challenge," in *International Marketing Strategy*, eds. Hans Thorelli and Helmut Becker (New York: Pergamon Press, 1980), 215.

features, such as packaging, can also be made less expensive. If price escalation causes price differentials between markets, the product can be altered to avoid cross-border price shopping by customers. For example, Geochron alters its clocks' appearance from one region to another.

3   Use new or more economical tariff or tax classifications. In many cases, products may qualify for entry under different categories that have different charges levied against them. The marketer may have to engage in a lobbying effort to get changes made in existing systems, but the result may be considerable savings. For example, in response to the US Customs Service's ruling that multipurpose vehicles were light trucks and, therefore, subject to 25 per cent tariffs (and not the 2.5 per cent levied on passenger cars), Britain's Land Rover had to argue that its $75,000+ luxury vehicle, the Range

EXHIBIT 11.5   Distribution adjustment to decrease price escalation

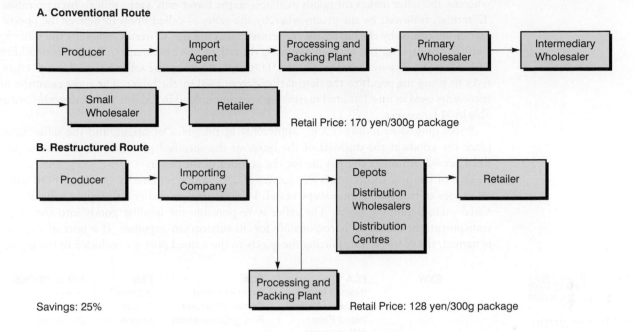

A. Conventional Route

Producer → Import Agent → Processing and Packing Plant → Primary Wholesaler → Intermediary Wholesaler

→ Small Wholesaler → Retailer

Retail Price: 170 yen/300g package

B. Restructured Route

Producer → Importing Company → Depots / Distribution Wholesalers / Distribution Centres → Retailer

Processing and Packing Plant

Savings: 25%

Retail Price: 128 yen/300g package

Source: From *International Marketing Strategy: Readings*, 1st edition by Michael R. Czinkota. ©1994. Reprinted with permission of South-Western, a division of Cengage Higher Education: **http://www.thomsonrights.com**.

Rover, was not a truck. When the United States introduced a luxury tax (10 per cent of the part of a car's price that exceeded $33,000), Land Rover worked closely with the US Internal Revenue Service to establish that its vehicles were trucks (since trucks were free of such tax). Before it got its way, however, it had to make slight adjustments in the vehicle, since the IRS defines a minimum weight for trucks at 6,000 lbs. Land Rover's following-year model weighed in at 6,019 lbs.[14]

4   Assemble or produce overseas. In the longer term, the exporter may resort to overseas sourcing or eventually production. Through foreign sourcing, the exporter may accrue an additional benefit to lower cost: duty drawbacks. An exporter may be refunded up to 99 per cent of duties paid on imported goods when they are exported or incorporated in articles that are subsequently exported within five years of the importation.[15]

If the marketer is able to convey a premium image, it may then be able to pass the increased amounts to the final price.

Appropriate export pricing requires the establishment of accounting procedures to assess export performance. Without such a process, hidden costs may bring surprises. For example, negotiations in the Middle Eastern countries or Russia may last three times longer than the average domestic negotiations, dramatically increasing the costs of doing business abroad. Furthermore, without accurate information, a company cannot combat phenomena such as price escalation.

TERMS OF SALE

The responsibilities of the buyer and the seller should be spelled out as they relate to what is and what is not included in the price quotation and when ownership of goods passes from seller to buyer. Incoterms are the internationally accepted standard definitions for terms of sale set by the International Chamber of Commerce (ICC) since 1936. The Incoterms 2000 (for the next ten years) went into effect on January 1, 2000, with significant revisions to better reflect changing transportation technologies and the increased use of electronic communications.[16] Although the same terms may be used in domestic transactions, they gain new meaning in the international arena. The terms are grouped into four categories, starting with the terms whereby the seller makes the goods available to the buyer only at the seller's own premises (the 'E'-terms), followed by the group whereby the seller is called upon to deliver the goods to a carrier appointed by the buyer (the 'F'-terms). Next are the 'C'-terms, whereby the seller has to contract for carriage but without assuming the risk of loss or damage to the goods or additional costs after the dispatch, and finally the 'D'-terms, whereby the seller has to bear all costs and risks to bring the goods to the destination determined by the buyer. The most common of the Incoterms used in international marketing are summarized in Exhibit 11.6. Incoterms are available in 31 languages.

Prices quoted *ex-works (EXW)* apply only at the point of origin, and the seller agrees to place the goods at the disposal of the buyer at the specified place on the date or within the fixed period. All other charges are for the account of the buyer.

One of the new Incoterms is *free carrier (FCA)*, which replaced a variety of FOB terms for all modes of transportation except vessel. FCA (named inland point) applies only at a designated inland shipping point. The seller is responsible for loading goods into the means of transportation; the buyer is responsible for all subsequent expenses. If a port of exportation is named, the costs of transporting the goods to the named port are included in the price.

EXHIBIT 11.6

Selected trade terms (Incoterms)

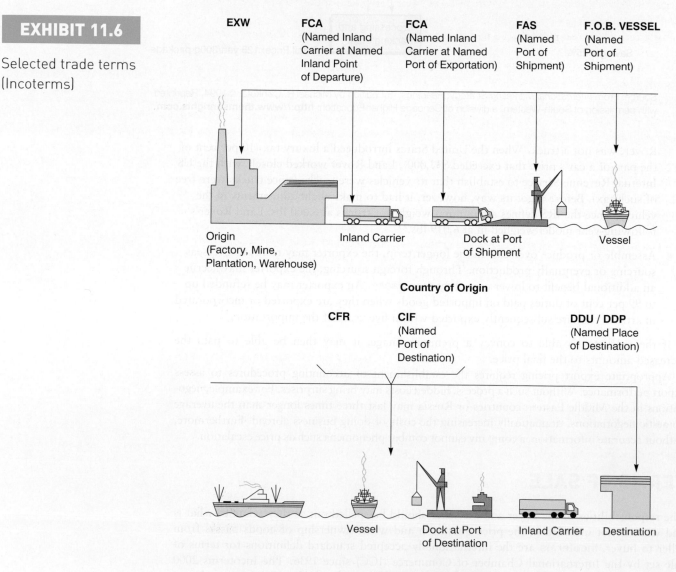

Free alongside ship (FAS) at a named port of export means that the exporter quotes a price for the goods, including charges for delivery of the goods alongside a vessel at the port. The seller handles the cost of unloading and wharfage; loading, ocean transportation and insurance are left to the buyer.

Free on board (FOB) applies only to vessel shipments. The seller quotes a price covering all expenses up to, and including, delivery of goods on an overseas vessel provided by or for the buyer.

Under *cost and freight (CFR)* to a named overseas port of import, the seller quotes a price for the goods, including the cost of transportation to the named port of debarkation. The cost of insurance and the choice of insurer are left to the buyer.

With cost, insurance and freight (*CIF*) to a named overseas port of import, the seller quotes a price including insurance, all transportation, and miscellaneous charges to the point of debarkation from the vessel. If other than waterway transport is used, the terms are *CPT* (carriage paid to) or *CIP* (carriage and insurance paid to).

With *delivered duty paid (DDP)*, the seller delivers the goods, with import duties paid, including inland transportation from import point to the buyer's premises. With *delivered duty unpaid (DDU)*, only the destination customs duty and taxes are paid by the consignee. Ex-works signifies the maximum obligation for the buyer; delivered duty paid puts the maximum burden on the seller.

Careful determination and clear understanding of terms used, and their acceptance by the parties involved, are vital if subsequent misunderstandings and disputes are to be avoided not only between the parties but also within the marketer's own organization.[17]

These terms are also powerful competitive tools. The exporter should therefore learn what importers usually prefer in the particular market and what the specific transaction may require. An inexperienced importer may be discouraged from further action by a quote such as ex-plant Jessup, Maryland, whereas CIF Helsinki will enable the Finnish importer to handle the remaining costs because they are incurred in a familiar environment.

Increasingly, exporters are quoting more inclusive terms. The benefits of taking charge of the transportation on either a CIF or DDP basis include the following: (1) exporters can offer foreign buyers an easy-to-understand 'delivered cost' for the deal; (2) by getting discounts on volume purchases for transportation services, exporters cut shipping costs and can offer lower overall prices to prospective buyers; (3) control of product quality and service is extended to transport, enabling the exporter to ensure that goods arrive with the buyer in good condition; and (4) administrative procedures are cut for both the exporter and the buyer.[18] These benefits are highlighted in *The International Marketplace 11.2*.

When taking control of transportation costs, however, the exporter must know well in advance what impact the additional costs will have on the bottom line. If the approach is implemented incorrectly, exporters can be faced with volatile shipping rates, unexpected import duties, and restive customers. Most exporters do not want to go beyond the CIF quotation because of uncontrollables and unknowns in the destination country. Whatever terms are chosen, the programme should be agreed to by the exporter and the buyer(s) rather than imposed solely by the exporter.

Freight forwarders are useful in determining costs, preparing quotations and making sure that unexpected changes do not cause the exporter to lose money. Freight forwarders are useful to the exporter not only as facilitators and advisors but also in keeping down some of the export-related costs. Rates for freight and insurance provided to freight forwarders may be far more economical than to an individual exporter because of large-volume purchases, especially if export sales are infrequent. Some freight forwarders can also provide additional value-added services, such as taking care of the marketer's duty-drawback receivables.

TERMS OF PAYMENT

Export credit and terms add another dimension to the profitability of an export transaction. The exporter has in all likelihood already formulated a credit policy that determines the degree of risk the firm is willing to assume and the preferred selling terms. The main objective is to meet the importer's requirements without jeopardizing the firm's financial goals. The

THE INTERNATIONAL **MARKETPLACE 11.2**

Penetrating foreign markets by controlling export transport

Companies that once sought short-term customers to smooth out recessions are searching for every means to get an edge over rivals in foreign markets. To achieve that, they are increasingly concerned about controlling quality and costs at every step, including the transportation process.

International transport costs are far higher than domestic shipping expenses. International ocean transport typically accounts for 4 to 20 per cent of the product's delivered cost but can reach as high as 50 per cent for commodity items. That makes transport a factor in situations in which a single price disadvantage can cause a sale to be lost to a competitor.

Most companies continue to abdicate responsibility for export shipping – either because they lack sophistication or simply because they do not want to be bothered. Increasingly, however, companies like Deere & Co. are paying for, controlling, and often insuring transport from their factories either to foreign ports or to the purchasing companies' doorsteps. This means that they are shipping on a DDP basis.

Deere exports premium-quality farm and lawn equipment worldwide. For years, it has insisted on overseeing transportation because it boosts sales, cuts costs and ensures quality. 'We have a long-term relationship with our dealers. It is in our best interest to do the transport job', says Ann Salaber, an order control manager in the export order department.

One goal of Deere's approach to transportation is to ensure that equipment is delivered to customers in good condition – a factor that Deere considers central to its image as a quality producer. The goal is to avoid cases like the one in which an inexperienced customer insisted on shipping a tractor himself. The tractor was unwittingly put on a ship's deck during a long, stormy sea voyage and arrived in terrible shape.

The process also helps when Deere tractor windows are inadvertently broken during transport. As Deere closely monitors the tractors, it can quickly install new windows at the port and avoid the huge cost of flying replacements to a customer as far away as Argentina.

Cost is an important consideration as well. Depending on where a $150,000 combine is shipped, transport costs can range between $7,500 and $30,000 or between 5 and 20 per cent of delivered cost. Deere's ability to buy steamship space in volume enables it to reduce transport costs by 10 per cent. That in turn enables it to cut the combine's delivered cost by between $750 and $3,000. 'That adds up', says Salaber. Due to those savings, 'you do not have to discount so much, and Deere gets more profit'.

SOURCES: Toby B. Gooley, 'Incoterms 2000: What the Changes Mean to You', *Logistics Management and Distribution Report* 39 (January 2000): 49–51; 'How Badly Will the Dollar Whack the US?' *Business Week*, May 5, 1997; Gregory L. Miles, 'Exporter's New Bully Stick', *International Business*, December 1993, 46–49; **http://www.iccwbo.org**; and **http://www.deere.com**.

exporter will be concerned over being paid for the goods shipped and will therefore consider the following factors in negotiating terms of payment: (1) the amount of payment and the need for protection; (2) terms offered by competitors; (3) practices in the industry; (4) capacity for financing international transactions; and (5) relative strength of the parties involved.[19] If the exporter is well established in the market with a unique product and accompanying service, price and terms of trade can be set to fit the exporter's desires. If, on the other hand, the exporter is breaking into a new market or if competitive pressures call for action, pricing and selling terms should be used as major competitive tools. Both parties have their own concerns and sensitivities; therefore, this very basic issue should be put on the negotiating table at the very beginning of the relationship.

The basic methods of payment for exports vary in terms of their attractiveness to the buyer and the seller, from cash in advance to open account or consignment selling. Neither of the extremes will be feasible for longer-term relationships, but they do have their use in certain situations. For example, in the 1999–2000 period very few companies were exporting into Russia except on a cash-in-advance basis, due to the country's financial turmoil. A marketer may use multiple methods of payment with the same buyer. For example, in a distributor relationship, the distributor may purchase samples on open account, but orders have to be paid for with a letter of credit. These methods are depicted in the risk triangle presented in Exhibit 11.7.

The most favourable term to the exporter is cash in advance because it relieves the exporter of all risk and allows for immediate use of the money. It is not widely used,

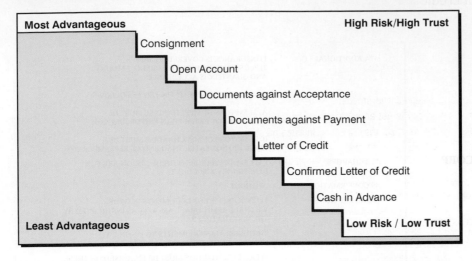

BUYER'S PERSPECTIVE

SELLER'S PERSPECTIVE

Most Advantageous — High Risk/High Trust

- Consignment
- Open Account
- Documents against Acceptance
- Documents against Payment
- Letter of Credit
- Confirmed Letter of Credit
- Cash in Advance

Least Advantageous — Low Risk / Low Trust

EXHIBIT 11.7

Methods of payment for exports

Source: Adapted from Chase Manhattan Bank, *Dynamics of Trade Finance* (New York: Chase Manhattan Bank, 1984), 5.

however, except for smaller, first-time transactions or situations in which the exporter has reason to doubt the importer's ability to pay. Cash-in-advance terms are also found when orders are for custom-made products, because the risk to the exporter is beyond that of a normal transaction. In some instances, the importer may not be able to buy on a cash-in-advance basis because of insufficient funds or government restrictions.

A letter of credit is an instrument issued by a bank at the request of a buyer. The bank promises to pay a specified amount of money on presentation of documents stipulated in the letter of credit, usually the bill of lading, consular invoice and a description of the goods.[20] Letters of credit are one of the most frequently used methods of payment in international transactions.

Letters of credit can be classified among three dimensions:

1 Irrevocable versus revocable. An irrevocable letter of credit can neither be cancelled nor modified without the consent of the beneficiary (exporter), thus guaranteeing payment. According to the new rules drawn by the International Chamber of Commerce, all letters of credit are considered irrevocable unless otherwise stated.[21]

2 Confirmed versus unconfirmed. In the case of a US exporter, a US bank might confirm the letter of credit and thus assume the risk, including the transaction (exchange) risk. The single best method of payment for the exporter in most cases is a confirmed, irrevocable letter of credit. Banks may also assume an advisory role but not assume the risk; the underlying assumption is that the bank and its correspondent(s) are better able to judge the credibility of the bank issuing the letter of credit than is the exporter.

3 Revolving versus non-revolving. Most letters of credit are non-revolving, that is, they are valid for the one transaction only. In case of established relationships, a revolving letter of credit may be issued.

Exhibit 11.8 provides an example of a letter of credit.

The letter of credit provides advantages to both the exporter and the importer, which explains its wide use. The approach substitutes the credit of the bank for the credit of the buyer and is as good as the issuing bank's access to dollars. In custom-made orders, an irrevocable letter of credit may help the exporter secure pre-export financing. The importer will not need to pay until the documents have arrived and been accepted by the bank, thus giving an additional float. The major caveat is that the exporter has to comply with all the terms of the letter of credit.[22] For example, if the documents state that shipment is made in crates measuring 4 × 4 × 4 and the goods are shipped in crates measuring 4 × 3 × 4, the bank will not honour the letter of credit. If there are changes, the letter of credit can be amended to ensure payment. Importers have occasionally been accused of creating discrepancies to slow down the payment process or to drive down the agreed-upon price.[23] In some cases, the

EXHIBIT 11.8 Letter of credit

NPS WORLD TRADE BANCORP

NINA PINTA SANTA MARIA

0556 29PNBPUS33APIIL6264190547
1756 20BOTKSGXAXX0607854525

          * THE BANK OF ERATOSTHENES
          * LISBON, PORTUGAL

          700 02

:27   /SEQUENCE OF A/1
:40A   /FORM OF DOCU: IRREVOCABLE
:20   /DOCUMENTARY: 655-210-482267
:31C   DATE OF ISSUE: APR 29 2006
:31D   /DATE AND PLA: OCT 21 2006

                              USA

:50   /APPLICANT: :JPP ALTO DURO PTE LTD
                              RUA CASTILHO, 70
                              LISBON,
                              PORTUGAL 2-DTR 1350-058

:59   /BENEFICIARY::   WORKS PLASTIQUE INTERNATIONAL
                              2345 MILLWOOD CIRCLE
                              CHARLOTTE, NORTH CAROLINA 21261
                              U.S.A

:32B/VAL/AMOUNT   : USD ****************39,100.00

:41D/AVAILABLE WD   : ANY BANK
                              BY NEGOTIATION

:42C DRAFTS AT...   :SIGHT FOR FULL INVOICE COST AND MARKED
                              AS BEING DRAWN UNDER THIS CREDIT.

:42D/DRAWEE: :ISSUING BANK

:43P/PARTIAL SHIP   :ALLOWED

:44TTRANSSSHIPMENT   :ALLOWED

44A: LOADING ON BOARD/DISPATCH/TAKING
                              IN CHARGE AT/FROM....
                              ANY EUROPEAN PORT

:48B/FOR TRANSPORT   :LISBON

:44C/LATEST DATE   :SEP 30 2006

:45A/DESCRIPTION   :43 M/TONS "NAVIGATOR" 4 HOLES PREE-PUNCHED

                              CNF

:46A/DOCUMENTS RE   :1) SIGNED COMMERCIAL INVOICES IN QUADRUPLICATE.
                              2) FULL SET (3/3) CLEAN ON BOARD OCEAN BILLS OF LADING MADE
                              OUT TO ORDER OF SHIPPER AND BLANK ENDORSED
                              MARKED "FREIGHT PREPAID" AND NOTIFY APPLICANT.

                              3) PACKING LIST IN QUADRUPLICATE

:47A/ADDITIONAL   C   1) INSURANCE IS COVERED BY BUYER.
                              2) PLUS ORMINUS 10 PCT ON CREDIT AMOUNT
                              AND QUANTITY IS ACCEPTABLE

                              3) SHIPMENT MUST BE EFFECTED AS FOLLOWS:

                              A) 21.5M/TONS OF MERCHANDISE MUST BE
                              EFFECTED NOT LATER THAN END OF JUNE 2006.

                              B) 21.5M/TONS OF MERCHANDISE MUST BE
                              EFFECTED NOT LATER THAN END OF SEPTEMBER 2006.

:71B/CHARGES   : ALL BANK CHARGES OUTSIDE LISBON ARE FOR
                              BENEFICIARY'S ACCOUNT.

:49/CONFIRMATION   :WITHOUT

78/INSTRUCTIONS   1) UPON RECEIPT OF DOCUMENTS IN ORDER,
                              WE SHALL REMIT DRAFT AMOUNT AS INSTRUCTED BY
                              THE NEGOTIATING BANK.

                              2) COURIER ALL DOCUMENTS TO U.S. IN TWO
                              CONSECUTIVE LOTS.

                              3) EACH NEGOTIATION MUST BE ENDORSED ON THESE
                              REVERSE OF THIS CREDIT

                              4) NEGOTIATING BANK MUST CERTIFY COMPLIANCE WITH
                              ALL TERMS OF CONDITIONS OF THIS CREDIT.

27/BANK INFO   (THIS CREDIT IS SUBJECT TO UCP 1993 REVISION
                              PUBLICATION NO.500).

MAC : FA11B280 CHK   :66A-358B077C2

SW99091O557094-2000

Note: The parties and transactions depicted are fictitious examples and are not intended to represent any known institution or activity.

exporter must watch out for fraudulent letters of credit, especially in the case of less-developed countries. In these cases, exporters are advised to ship only on the basis of an irrevocable letter of credit, confirmed by their bank, even after the credentials of the foreign contact have been established.

With the increasing amount of e-commerce, things will have to change. Solutions include online issuance and status reporting on letters of credit, creating a worldwide network of electronic trade hubs, and offering a smart card that will allow participating companies to transact financial business online.[24] For example, TradeCard is an online service for B2B (business-to-business) exchanges. Once an exporter and importer have agreed on the terms, the buyer creates an electronic purchase order, which specifies the terms and conditions. Once it is in electronic format, the seller formally agrees to the contract. The purchase order is stored in TradeCard's database. The system then creates both a commercial invoice and a packing list, and a promise of payment is included with the invoice for the seller. A third-party logistics provider sends proof of delivery electronically to TradeCard, which then debits the buyer's account and credits the seller's account.[25] Trade portals now support document creation and transmission, and make it possible for all parties to the transaction to exchange information on the same secure site.

The letter of credit is a promise to pay but not a means of payment. Actual payment is accomplished by means of a draft, which is similar to a personal cheque. Like a cheque, it is an order by one party to pay another. Most drafts are documentary, which means that the buyer must obtain possession of various shipping documents before obtaining possession of the goods involved in the transaction. Clean drafts – orders to pay without any other documents – are mainly used by multinational corporations in their dealings with their own subsidiaries and in well-established business relationships.

In documentary collection situations, the seller ships the goods, and the shipping documents and the draft demanding payment are presented to the importer through banks acting as the seller's agent. The draft, also known as the bill of exchange, may be either a sight draft or a time draft (Exhibit 11.9). A sight draft documents against payment and is payable on presentation to the drawee, that is, the party to whom the draft is addressed. A time draft documents against acceptance and allows for a delay of 30, 60, 90, 120 or 180 days. When a time draft is drawn on and accepted by a bank, it becomes a banker's acceptance, which is sold in the short-term money market. Time drafts drawn on and accepted by a business firm become trader's acceptances, which are normally not marketable. A draft is presented to the drawee, who accepts it by writing or stamping a notice of acceptance on it. With both sight and time drafts, the buyer can effectively extend the period of credit by avoiding receipt of the goods. A date draft requires payment on a specified date, regardless of the date on which the goods and the draft are accepted by the buyer.

To illustrate, an exporter may have a time draft accepted by HSBC for $1 million to be paid in 90 days. Like many exporters who extend credit for competitive reasons, the firm may have immediate need for the funds. It could contact an acceptance dealer and sell the acceptance at a discount, with the rate depending on the market rate of interest. If the annual interest rate was 6 per cent, for example, the acceptance could be sold for $985,222 ($1 million divided by 1.015).

EXHIBIT 11.9   Documentary collection

NPS WORLD TRADE BANCORP	customer draft
NINA PINTA SANTA MARIA	

Tenor	Date
90 Days Date	April 29, 2006

Pay to the order of	Amount
NPS World Trade Bancorp	$100,000

Amount in words	
One Hundred Thousand and no/100 dollars	

To	Firm Name
NPS World Trade Bancorp	

Drawn Under _____   Authorized Signature _____

Note: The parties and transactions depicted are fictitious examples and are not intended to represent any known institution or activity.

Even if the draft is not sold in the secondary market, the exporter may convert it into cash by discounting. To discount the draft simply means that the draft is sold to a bank at a discount from face value. If the discounting is with recourse, the exporter is liable for the payment to the bank if the importer defaults. If the discounting is without recourse, the exporter will not be liable even if the importer does not pay the bank. Discounting without recourse is known as factoring or, in the case of higher credit risk and longer-term receivables, forfaiting.

The normal manner of doing business in the domestic market is open account (open terms). The exporter selling on open account removes both real and psychological barriers to importing. However, no written evidence of the debt exists, and the exporter has to put full faith in the references contacted. Worst of all, there is no guarantee of payment. If the debt turns bad, the problems of overseas litigation are considerable. Bad debts are normally easier to avoid than to rectify. In emerging countries, importers will usually need proof of debt in the application to the central bank for hard currency, which will not allow them to deal on an open-account basis. It may be more expedient to send the documents through a bank via direct collections, which can reduce the process by several days or even weeks.[26] For more involved marketers with units abroad, internal transactions are normally handled on an open-account basis.

The most favorable term to the importer is consignment selling, which allows the importer to defer payment until the goods are actually sold. This approach places all the burden on the exporter, and its use should be carefully weighed against the objectives of the transaction. If the exporter wants entry into a specific market through specific intermediaries, consignment selling may be the only method of gaining acceptance by intermediaries. The arrangement will require clear understanding as to the parties' responsibilities – for example, which party is responsible for insurance until the goods have actually been sold. If the goods are not sold, returning them will be costly and time-consuming; for example, there is getting through customs or paying, avoiding paying, or trying to get refunds on duties. Due to its burdensome characteristics, consignment is not widely used.

GETTING PAID FOR EXPORTS

The exporter needs to minimize the risk of not being paid if a transaction occurs. The term commercial risk refers primarily to the insolvency of, or protracted payment default by, an overseas buyer. Commercial defaults, in turn, usually result from deterioration of conditions in the buyer's market, fluctuations in demand, unanticipated competition, or technological changes. These naturally emerge domestically as well, but the geographic and cultural distances in international markets make them more severe and more difficult to anticipate. In addition, non-commercial or political risk is completely beyond the control of either the buyer or the seller. For example, the foreign buyer may be willing to pay but the local government may use every trick in the book to delay payment as far into the future as possible.

These challenges must be addressed through actions by either the company itself or support systems. The decision must be an informed one, based on detailed and up-to-date information in international credit and country conditions. In many respects, the assessment of a buyer's creditworthiness requires the same attention to credit checking and financial analysis as for domestic buyers; however, the assessment of a foreign private buyer is complicated by some of the following factors:

1 Credit reports may not be reliable.

2 Audited reports may not be available.

3 Financial reports may have been prepared according to a different format.

4 Many governments require that assets be annually re-evaluated upward, which can distort results.

5 Statements are in local currency.

6 The buyer may have the financial resources in local currency but may be precluded from converting to dollars because of exchange controls and other government actions.

More than one credit report should be obtained (from sources such as the two in Exhibit 11.10), and it should be determined how each credit agency obtains its reports. They may use the same correspondent agency, in which case it does the exporter no good to obtain the same information from two sources and to pay for it twice. Exhibit 11.11 provides a summary of the major sources of credit information. Private-sector companies (such as Dun & Bradstreet, Amadeus and Europages) also provide the needed credit information. Local credit reporting agencies, such as Profancresa in Mexico, may also provide regional services (in this case, throughout Latin America). With the growth of e-commerce, a company may want to demonstrate its creditworthiness to customers and suppliers in a rapid and secure fashion. The Coface Group (in the Americas) introduced the '@rating' system, available on the World Wide Web and designed to assess a company's performance in paying its commercial obligations.[27]

Beyond protecting oneself by establishing creditworthiness, an exporter can match payment terms to the customer. In the short term, an exporter may require payment terms that guarantee payment. In the long term, the best approach is to establish a relationship of mutual trust, which will ensure payment even if complications arise during a transaction.[28] Payment terms need to be stated clearly and followed up effectively. If prompt payment is not stressed and enforced, some customers will assume they can procrastinate.

Should a default situation occur in spite of the preparatory measures discussed above, the exporter's first recourse is the customer. Communication with the customer may reveal a misunderstanding or error regarding the shipment. If the customer has financial or other concerns or objections, rescheduling the payment terms may be considered. Third-party intervention through a collection agency may be needed if the customer disputes the charges. For example, the Total Credit Management Group, a cooperative of leading credit and collection companies in 46 countries, can be employed. Only when further amicable demands are unwarranted should an attorney be used.[29]

MANAGING FOREIGN EXCHANGE RISK

Unless the exporter and the importer share the same currency (as is the case in the 13 countries of Euroland), exchange rate movements may harm one or the other of the parties. If the price is quoted in the exporter's currency, the exporter will get exactly the price it wants but may lose some sales due to lack of customer orientation. If the exporter needs the sale, the invoice may be in the importer's currency, and the exchange risk will be the burden of the exporter. Some exporters, if they are unable to secure payment in their own currency, try to minimize the risk by negotiating shorter terms of payment, such as 10 or 15 days. Exchange risks may be a result of an appreciating or depreciating currency or result from a revaluation or devaluation of a currency by a central bank. Assume that a UK importer bought $250,000 or €208,750 worth of goods from a German company, which agreed to accept British pounds for payment in 90 days. At the time of the quotation, the exchange rate for $1 was €0.835, whereas at the time of payment, it had changed to €0.820. This means that the German exporter, instead of receiving €208,750, winds up with €206,250.

Two types of approaches to protect against currency-related risk are proposed: (1) risk shifting, such as foreign currency contractual hedging, and/or (2) risk modifying, such as manipulating prices and other elements of a marketing strategy.

When invoicing in foreign currencies, an exporter cannot insulate itself from the problems of currency movements, but it can at least know how much it will eventually receive by using the mechanism of the forward exchange market. In essence, the exporter gets a bank to agree to a rate at which it will buy the foreign currency the exporter will receive when the importer makes payment. The rate is expressed as either a premium or a discount on the current spot rate. A fixed rate allows the exporter to budget effectively without currency fluctuations eroding profit margins.[30] The risk still remains if the exchange rate does not move as anticipated, and the exporter may be worse off than if it had not bought forward. Although forward contracts are the most common foreign currency contractual hedge, other financial instruments

EXHIBIT 11.10

Providers of international credit information

EXHIBIT 11.11   Sources of international credit information

	Response Time	Service Offerings	Presence	Remarks
Dun & Bradstreet **http://www.dnb.com**	Many non-subscription-based reports, in electronic copies, readily available for U.S. customers by online purchase; shipment delays on printed reports depending on location; non-U.S. customers can access online database by subscription; certain delays on customized information	• Credit information, both standardized and customized • Country risk reports for 132 countries available online, costing $350 on the average	8,000 employees worldwide (including all other D&B business), covering 100 million companies in 214 countries	Core strength in small and medium-size enterprises, with 80% of active files in its U.S. database being small companies with less than 10 staff; industry standard, with the largest worldwide company coverage
FCIB-NACM **http://www.fcibglobal.com**	Same day for already-available reports (excluding shipment); customized credit reports can take from a few days to three weeks; no online database	• Country risk reports cost $100 each for members and $125 for non-members • Credit reports • Business credit magazines • Seminars and conferences for export groups	Two main offices in the United States and UK, with country representatives in Europe, Canada, Mexico, and China	Services focus on exports business; membership costs $840, fees for industry-focus export groups range from $125 to $515
@rating **http://www.cofacerating.com**	Online focus, instantaneous access of information	• Free online check of company's reliability and financial soundness • Free country risk assessment and rating • Fee-based information reports • Fee-based @rating quality labeling service	Presence in 99 countries, 5 continents, covering 41 million companies	Most efficient and least costly resource, but analysis may lack depth; aim to become standard web-based rating system, supported by the EU
International Company Profiles **http://www.ita.doc.gov**	About 10 days of processing time, depending on complexity of information and availability from existing database; no online service, thus adding delays from shipment, depending on location	• Company background check, including financial status, management profile, and company potential • $500–700 for each company report	151 international offices in 85 countries, with 1,800 employees	Focus on serving small and mid-sized companies in the United States; analysis is U.S.-centric because service provider is part of U.S. Department of Commerce
Local Credit Agencies or Trade Councils	Varies	• Focus on information of local companies	Locally	Quality varies, with limited scope in international marketing
Bank Reports	Slower	Company background	None (client)	Limited in scope

Source: Interviews with company and organization personnel, February 2006.

and derivatives, such as currency options and futures, are available. An option gives the holder the right to buy or sell foreign currency at a prespecified price on or up to a prespecified date. The difference between the currency options market and the forward market is that the transaction in the former gives the participant the right to buy or sell, whereas a transaction in the forward market entails a contractual obligation to buy or sell. This means that if an exporter does not have any or the appropriate amount of currency when the contract comes due, it would have to go into the foreign exchange markets to buy the currency, potentially exposing itself to major losses if the currency has appreciated in the meanwhile. The greater flexibility in the options contract makes it more expensive, however. The currency futures market is conceptually similar to the forward market; that is, to buy futures on the British pound sterling implies an obligation to buy in the future at a prespecified price. However, the minimum transaction sizes are considerably smaller on the futures market. Forward quotes apply to transactions of $1 million or more, whereas on the futures market transactions will typically be well below $100,000. The market, therefore, allows relatively small firms engaged in international trade to lock in exchange rates and lower their risk. Forward contracts, options and futures are available from banks and the London Stock Exchange.

European Union exporters have faced both high and low values of the dollar with respect to other currencies in the past ten years: low values in the early to mid-1990s, high values since then until early 2002, and lower values of as much as 30 per cent from then on. When the exporter's domestic currency is weak, strategies should include stressing the price advantage to customers and expanding the scale and scope of the export operation. Sourcing can be shifted to domestic markets and the export price can be subjected to full-costing. However, under the opposite scenario, the exporter needs to engage in non-price competition, minimizing the price dimension as much as possible. Costs should be reduced by every means, including enhancing productivity. At this time, the exporter should prioritize efforts to markets that show the greatest returns. Marketers may also attempt to protect themselves by manipulating leads and lags in export and import payments or receivables in anticipation of either currency revaluations or devaluations. This, however, will require thorough market knowledge and leverage over overseas partners. Alternatives available to marketers under differing currency conditions are summarized in Exhibit 11.12.

Whatever the currency movements are, the marketer needs to decide how to adjust pricing to international customers in view of either a more favourable or a less favourable domestic currency rate. A European exporter, during a strong euro, has three alternatives. First, making no change in the euro price would result in a less favourable price in foreign currencies and, most likely, lower sales, especially if no corrective marketing steps are taken. Second, the export price could be decreased in conjunction with increases in the value of the euro to maintain stable export prices in foreign currencies. This first alternative is an example of pass-through, while the second alternative features the absorption approach; that is, the increase in the price is absorbed into the margin of the product, possibly even resulting in a loss. For pass-through to work, customers have to have a high level of preference for the exporter's product. In some cases, exporters may have no choice but to pass most of the increase to the customer due to the cost structure of the firm. Exporters using the absorption approach have as their goal long-term market-share maintenance, especially in a highly competitive environment.

EXHIBIT 11.12

Exporter strategies under varying currency conditions

Weak	Strong
1 Stress price benefits	1 Nonprice competition
2 Expand product line	2 Improve productivity/cost reduction
3 Shift sourcing to domestic market	3 Sourcing overseas
4 Exploit all possible export opportunities	4 Prioritize exports
5 Cash-for-goods trade	5 Countertrade with weak currency countries
6 Full-costing	6 Marginal-cost pricing
7 Speed repatriation	7 Slow collections
8 Minimize expenditure in local currency	8 Buy needed services abroad

Source: Adapted from S. Tamer Cavusgil, "Unraveling the Mystique of Export Pricing," *Business Horizons* 31 (May–June 1988): 54–63.

EXHIBIT 11.13

Absorption versus pass-through: Japanese and German automarketer behaviour

Model	Real Dollar Appreciation	Real Retail Price Change in U.S. Market
Honda Civic 2-Dr. Sedan	39%	−7%
Nissan 200 SX 2-Dr.	39	−10
Toyota Cressida 4-Dr.	39	6
BMW 320i 2-Dr. Sedan	42	−8
BMW 733i 4-Dr. Sedan	42	−17
Mercedes 300 TD Sta. Wgn.	42	−39

Source: Joseph A. Gagnon and Michael M. Knetter, "Markup Adjustment and Exchange Rate Fluctuations: Evidence from Panel Data on Automobile Exports," *Journal of International Money and Finance* 14 (no. 2, 1995): 289–310. Copyright © 1995, with permission from Elsevier.

The third alternative is to pass through only a share of the increase, maintaining sales if possible while at the same time preserving profitability. According to a study on exporter responses to foreign-exchange rate changes over the period of 1973 to 1997, Japanese exporters have the highest tendency to dampen the effects of exchange-rate fluctuations in foreign-currency export prices in both directions by adjusting their home-currency prices.[31] Furthermore, Japanese exporters put a larger emphasize on stabilizing the foreign currency prices of their exports during a weak yen than when the yen is strong. German exporters display completely the opposite behaviour. The data in Exhibit 11.13 for German and Japanese auto exports support these findings for the period, when the dollar appreciated against the German mark and the Japanese yen.

The strategic response depends on market conditions and may result in different strategies for each market or product. Destination-specific adjustment of mark-ups in response to exchange-rate changes have been referred to as pricing-to-market.[32] For example, a mark-up change will be more substantial in a price-sensitive market and/or product category. In addition, the exporter needs to consider the reactions of local competitors, who may either keep their prices stable (hoping that price increases in imports will improve their position) or increase their prices along with those of imports in search of more profits. If the exporter faces a favourable domestic currency rate, pass-through means providing international customers with a more favourable price, while absorption means that the exporter keeps the export price stable and pockets a higher level of profits.

Some exporters prefer price stability to the greatest possible degree and allow mark-ups to vary in maintaining stable local currency prices. Honda, for example, maintains its price to distributors as long as the spot exchange rate does not move more than plus or minus 5 per cent from the rate in effect when the quote was made. If the movement is an additional 5 percentage points in either direction, Honda and its distributors will share the costs or benefits. Beyond that the price will have to be renegotiated to bring it more in line with current exchange rates and the economic and competitive realities of the market.[33] During times of exchange-rate gains, rather than lower the price, some exporters use other support tools (such as training and trade deals) with their distributors or customers, on the premise that increasing prices after a future currency swing in the opposite direction may be difficult.

Beyond price manipulation, other adjustment strategies exist. They include the following:

1 Market refocus. If lower values of the target market currencies make exporting more difficult by, for example, making collection times longer, marketers may start looking at other markets for growth. In some cases, the emphasize may switch to the domestic market, where market share gain at the expense of imports may be the most efficient way to grow. Currency appreciation does not always lead to a dire situation for the exporter. Domestic competitors may depend very heavily on imported components and may not be able to take advantage of the currency-related price pressure on the exporter. The manufacturing sectors of Indonesia, Malaysia, Philippines and Thailand use over 30 per cent imported parts and raw materials in the production process.[34]

2 Streamlined operations. The marketer may start using more aggressive methods of collection, insisting on letters of credit and insurance to guarantee payments. Some have
   tightened control of their distribution networks by cutting layers or taking over the
   responsibility from independent intermediaries. On the product side, marketers may
   focus on offerings that are less sensitive to exchange-rate changes.

3 Shift in production. Especially when currency shifts are seen as long-term, marketers
   will increase direct investment. With the high value of the yen, Japanese companies
   shifted production bases to lower-cost locations or closer to final customers. Matsushita
   Electric, for example, moved a substantial share of its production to South East Asian
   countries, while earthmoving-equipment maker Komatsu entered into an agreement
   with Linde AG of Germany on global collaboration in the production and marketing of
   forklift trucks and related products[35]. Remaining units in Japan will focus on research
   and development, design, software and high-precision manufactured goods.[36]

SOURCES OF EXPORT FINANCING

Except in the case of larger companies that may have their own financing entities, most international marketers assist their customers abroad in securing appropriate financing. Export
financing terms can significantly affect the final price paid by buyers. Consider, for example,
two competitors for a $1 million sale. Exporter A offers an 8 per cent interest rate over a ten-
year payment period, while B offers 9 per cent for the same term. Over the ten years, the difference in interest is $55,000. In some cases, buyers will award a contract to the provider of
cheaper credit and overlook differences in quality and price.

Financing assistance is available from both the private and the public sectors. The international marketer should assess not only domestic programmes but also those in other countries. For example, Japan and Taiwan have import financing programmes that provide
exporters with added potential in penetrating these significant markets.[37]

Commercial banks

Commercial banks the world over provide trade financing depending on their relationship with
the exporter, the nature of the transaction, the country of the borrower, and the availability of
export insurance. This usually means that financing assistance is provided only to first-rate
credit risks, leaving many EU exporters to report major problems in enlisting assistance from
EU commercial banks. Furthermore, some EU banks do not see international trade finance as
part of their core competence. Although the situation has improved, exporters still continue to
complain about lack of export financing as it pertains to developing countries, financing high
technology, or lending against foreign receivables. Many exporters complain that banks will
not deal with them without a guarantee from the banks, such as property and/or equipment.

However, as the share of international sales and reach of companies increases, banking relationships become all the more important, a fact that is also noted by banks themselves. Many
banks offer enhanced services, such as electronic services, which help exporters monitor and
expedite their international transactions to customers who do a certain amount of business
with them. As with all suppliers, the more business done with a bank, the higher the level of
service, usually at a better price. As the relationship builds, the more comfortable bankers feel
about the exporter's business and the more likely they will go out of their way to help, particularly with difficult transactions. It is clear that the development of an effective credit policy
requires teamwork between the company's marketing and finance staffs and its bankers.

In addition to using the types of services a bank can provide as a criterion of choice, an
exporter should assess the bank's overseas reach.[38] This is a combination of the bank's own
network of facilities and correspondent relationships. While money-centre banks can provide
the greatest amount of coverage through their own offices and staff, they still use correspondents in regions outside the main banking or political centres of foreign markets. For example,
HSBC has a worldwide network of 8,000 branches in more than 100 countries.

Some banks have formed alliances to extend their reach to markets that their customers are entering. Regional banks which have no intention of establishing branches abroad, rely only on strong alliances with, or ownership by, foreign banks. Foreign banks can provide a competitive advantage to exporters because of their home-country connections and their strong global networks. For example, Commerzbank, Germany's third-largest private-sector bank, has branches in the Far East, Latin America, South America and Eastern Europe to support its international trade financing activities.[39] Regardless of the arrangement, the bank's own branches or correspondents play an important role at all stages of the international transaction, from gathering market intelligence about potential new customers to actually processing payments. Additional services include reference checks on customers in their home markets and suggestions for possible candidates to serve as intermediaries.

Forfaiting and factoring

Forfaiting provides the exporter with cash at the time of the shipment. In a typical forfait deal, the importer pays the exporter with bills of exchange or promissory notes guaranteed by a leading bank in the importer's country. The exporter can sell them to a third party at a discount from their face value for immediate cash. The sale is without recourse to the exporter, and the buyer of the notes assumes all the risks. The discount rate takes into account the buyer's creditworthiness and country, the quality of the guaranteeing bank and the interest cost over the term of the credit.

The benefits to the exporter are the reduction of risk, simplicity of documentation (because the documents used are well-known in the market), and 100 per cent coverage, which official sources such as export–import banks do not provide. In addition, forfaiting does not involve either content or country restrictions, which many of the official trade financing sources may have.[40] The major complaints about forfaiting centre on availability and cost. Forfaiting is not available where exporters need it most, that is, the high-risk countries. Furthermore, it is usually a little more expensive than public sources of trade insurance.

Certain companies, known as factoring houses, may purchase an exporter's receivables for a discounted price (2 to 4 per cent less than face value). Factors not only buy receivables but also provide the exporter with a complete financial package that combines credit protection, accounts-receivable bookkeeping, and collection services to take away many of the challenges that come with doing business overseas.[41] Arrangements are typically with recourse, leaving the exporter ultimately liable for repaying the factor in case of a default. Some factors accept export receivables without recourse but require a large discount.

The industry is dominated by a dozen major players, most of which are subsidiaries of major banks. One leader is the CIT Group, 44 per cent owned by Dai-Ichi Kangyo Bank of Japan, which has won the President's 'E' Award for its excellence in export service.[42] However, with the increase in companies looking for factoring services, independent factors are also emerging. Factors can be found through the Commercial Finance Association or through marketing facilitators whose clients use factors.

Although the forfaiting and factoring methods appear similar, they differ in three significant ways: (1) factors usually want a large percentage of the exporter's business, while most forfaiters work on a one-shot basis; (2) forfaiters work with medium-term receivables (over 180 days to 5 years), while factors work with short-term receivables; and (3) factors usually do not have strong capabilities in the developing countries, but since forfaiters usually require a bank guarantee, most are willing to deal with receivables from these countries. Furthermore, forfaiters work with capital goods, factors typically with consumer goods.[43]

Official trade finance[44]

Official financing can take the form of either a loan or a guarantee, including credit insurance. In a loan, the government provides funds to finance the sale and charges interest on those funds at a stated fixed rate. The government lender accepts the risk of a possible default. In a guarantee, a private sector lender provides the funds and sets the interest rate, with the government assuring that it will reimburse the lender if the loan is unpaid. The government is providing not funds but rather risk protection. The programmes provide assurance that the governmental agency will pay for a major portion of the loss should the foreign buyer default on payment. The advantages are significant: (1) protection in the riskiest part of an exporter's business (foreign sales receivables); (2) protection against political and commercial risks over which the exporter does not have control; (3) encouragement to exporters to make competitive offers by extending terms of payment (4) broadening of potential markets by minimizing exporter risks; (5) the possibility of leveraging exporter accounts receivable; and (6) through the government guarantee, the opportunity for commercial banks to remain active in the international finance arena.[45]

Because credit has emerged as an increasingly important component in export selling, governments of most industrialized countries have established entities that insure credit risks for exports. Officially supported export credit agencies (ECAs), such as the French Coface or German Hermes, are organizations whose central purpose is to promote national trade objectives by providing financial support for national exports. ECAs benefit from varying degrees of explicit or implicit support from national governments. Some ECAs are divisions of government trade missions. Other ECAs operate as autonomous or even private institutions, but most require a degree of recourse to national government support.

One of the greatest impediments small businesses experience in attempting to fulfill export orders is a lack of working capital to build necessary inventory for the export order. The ability to offer financing or credit terms is often critical in competing for, and winning, export contracts. Increasingly, foreign buyers expect suppliers to offer open account or unsecured credit terms rather than requiring letters of credit, which may be expensive. Yet for small exporters, extending credit terms to foreign customers may represent an unacceptable risk, especially when the exporter's bank is unwilling to accept foreign receivables as collateral for working lines of credit. The solution is export credit insurance, wherein, for a reasonable premium, an institution (e.g., an insurance company or an ECA) guarantees payment to the seller if the buyer defaults. The short-term credit-insurance business is dominated by five major players, which account for more than 75 per cent of the world market: Coface, Euler, Gerling, Hermes and NCM.[46]

Banks also guarantee to provide repayment protection for private-sector loans to creditworthy buyers of EU goods and services. The fee schedule is determined by country risk and repayment terms of the transaction. Medium-term guarantees (not to exceed seven years) are typically used by commercial banks that do not want exposure in a certain country or that have reached their internal exposure limit in a given country. For long-term guarantees, projects are usually large and commercial banks may not want such exposure for long periods of time in one country or in a particular industry sector.

In addition to country-specific entities, the exporter will find it worthwhile to monitor the activities of multilateral institutions such as the United Nations and the World Bank Group as well as regional development banks (such as the Inter-American Development Bank and the Asian Development Bank). They specialize in financing investment activities and can provide valuable leads for future business activity.

PRICE NEGOTIATIONS

The final export price is negotiated in person or electronically. Since pricing is the most sensitive issue in business negotiations, the exporter should be ready to discuss price as part of a comprehensive package and should avoid price concessions early on in the negotiations.[47]

An importer may reject an exporter's price at the outset in the hopes of gaining an upper hand or obtaining concessions later on. These concessions include discounts, an improved product, better terms of sales/payment, and other possibly costly demands. The exporter should prepare for this by obtaining relevant information on the target market and the customer, as well as by developing counterproposals for possible objections. For example, if the importer states that better offers are available, the exporter should ask for more details on such offers and try to convince the buyer that the exporter's total package is indeed superior. In the rare case that the importer accepts the initial bid without comment, the exporter should make sure the extended bid was correct by checking the price calculations and the Incoterm used. Furthermore, competitive prices should be revisited to ascertain that the price reflects market conditions accurately.

During the actual negotiations, pricing decisions should be postponed until all of the major substantive issues have been agreed upon. Since quality and reliability of delivery are the critical dimensions of supplier choice (in addition to price), especially when long-term export contracts are in question, the exporter may want to reduce pressure on price by emphasizing these two areas and how they fit with the buyer's needs.

LEASING

Trade liberalization around the world is expected to benefit lessors both through expected growth in target economies and through the eradication of country laws and regulations hampering outside lessors. For the marketing manager who sells products such as printing presses, computers, forklift trucks and machine tools, leasing may allow penetration of markets that otherwise might not exist for the firm's products if the firm had to sell them outright. Balance-of-payment problems have forced some countries to prohibit or hinder the purchase and importation of equipment into their markets; an exception has been made if the import is to be leased. In developing countries, the fact that leased products are serviced by the lessor may be a major benefit because of the shortage of trained personnel and scarcity of spare parts. At present, leasing finances over $40 billion in new vehicles and equipment each year in developing countries. The main benefit for the lessor is that total net income, after charging off pertinent repair and maintenance expenses, is often higher than it would be if the unit was sold.

In today's competitive business climate, traditional financial considerations are often only part of the asset-financing formula. Many leasing companies have become more than a source of capital, developing new value-added services that have taken them from asset financiers to asset managers or forming relationships with others who can provide these services. In some cases, lessors have even evolved into partners in business activities. El Camino Resources, Ltd, targets high-growth, technology-dependent companies such as internet providers and software developers for their hardware, software and technical services needs, including e-commerce as well as internet and intranet development.[48]

DUMPING

Inexpensive imports often trigger accusations of dumping – that is, selling goods overseas for less than in the exporter's home market or at a price below the cost of production, or both. Dumping ranges from predatory dumping to unintentional dumping. Predatory dumping refers to a tactic whereby a foreign firm intentionally sells at a loss in another country in order to increase its market share at the expense of domestic producers, which amounts to an international price war. Unintentional dumping is the result of time lags between the dates of sales transaction, shipment and arrival. Prices, including exchange rates, can change in such a way that the final sales price turns out to be below the cost of production or below the price prevailing in the exporter's home market. It has been argued that current dumping laws, especially in the United States, do not adequately take into account such developments as floating exchange rates, which make dumping appear to be more widespread.[49]

International Trade Commission finds that domestic industry is being, or is threatened with being, materially injured by the imports. The remedy is an antidumping duty equal to the dumping margin. International agreements and EU law provide for countervailing duties, which may be imposed on imports that are found to be subsidized by foreign governments and which are designed to offset the advantages imports would otherwise receive from the subsidy. The WTO reports a total of 212 antidumping measures taken in 2004 (with the European Union and the United States in the lead with over 25 actions each), whereas the total number five years earlier was 84.[50] As more developing and emerging markets are reducing tariffs to comply with WTO agreements, they are switching to antidumping penalties to protect domestic players.

Governmental action against dumping and subsidized exports violating WTO rules may result in hurting the very industries seeking relief. In some cases, dumping suits have strong competitive motivations; for example, to discourage an aggressive competitor by accusing it of selling at unfair prices. Antidumping and unfair subsidy suits have led in some cases to formal agreements on voluntary restraints, whereby foreign producers agree that they will supply only a certain percentage of the EU market. For example, the European Union on October 6, 2006 'approved' a European Commission proposal to impose final dumping duties (on top of normal duties) of 16.5 per cent and 10 per cent, respectively, on European imports of certain leather footwear from China and Vietnam for a two-year period beginning October 5, 2006.[51]

To minimize the risk of being accused of dumping (as well as to be protected from dumping), the marketer can focus on value-added products and increase differentiation by including services in the product offering. For example, if the company operates in areas made sensitive by virtue of the industry (such as electronics) or by the fact that local competition is economically vulnerable yet powerful with respect to the government, it may seek to collaborate with local companies in gaining market access.[52]

SUMMARY

The status of price has changed to that of a dynamic element of the marketing mix. This has resulted from both internal and external pressures on business firms. Management must analyze the interactive effect that pricing has on the other elements of the mix, and how pricing can assist in meeting the overall goals of the marketing strategy.

The process of setting an export price must start with the determination of an appropriate cost baseline, and should include variables such as export-related costs to avoid compromising the desired profit margin. The quotation needs to spell out the respective responsibilities of the buyer and the seller in getting the goods to the intended destination. The terms of sale indicate these responsibilities but may also be used as a competitive tool. The terms of payment have to be clarified to ensure that the exporter will indeed get paid for the products and services rendered. Facilitating agents such as freight forwarders and banks are often used to absorb some of the risk and uncertainty in preparing price quotations and establishing terms of payment.

Exporters also need to be ready to defend their pricing practices. Competitors may petition their own government to investigate the exporter's pricing to determine the degree to which it reflects costs and prices prevailing in the exporter's domestic market.

Key terms

absorption

antidumping duty

banker's acceptance

cash in advance

commercial risk

consignment selling

cost-plus method

countervailing duties

discounting

documentary collection

draft

dual pricing

duty drawbacks

factoring

forfaiting

forward exchange market

futures

Incoterms

letter of credit

marginal cost method

market pricing

market-differentiated pricing

open account

option

pass-through

penetration pricing

predatory dumping

price escalation

price manipulation

pricing-to-market

skimming

standard worldwide price

unintentional dumping

value-added tax (VAT)

Questions for discussion

1 Propose scenarios in which export prices are higher/lower than domestic prices.

2 What are the implications of price escalation?

3 Discuss the use of the currency of quotation as a competitive tool.

4 Argue for the use of more inclusive shipping terms from the marketing point of view.

5 Suggest different importer reactions to a price offer and how you, as an exporter, could respond to them.

6 Who is harmed and who is helped by dumping?

Internet exercises

1 Assess the international trade financing commitment of different commercial banks, such as HSBC (**http://www.hsbc.co.uk/1/2/**), Barclays Bank (**http://group.barclays.com/Home**) and Banque Paribas (**http://www.bnpparibas.com/**).

2 The International Trade Administration monitors cases filed against US exporters on charges of dumping, to assist them

in the investigations and their subsequent defence. Using their data on such cases (**http://ia.ita.doc.gov/intro/index.html**), focus on a few countries (e.g., EU, Canada, South Africa, Japan) and assess what industries seem to come under the most ITA scrutiny.

Recommended readings

Contino, Richard M. and Tony Valmis (eds). *Handbook of Equipment Leasing: A Deal Maker's Guide*. New York: AMACOM, 1996.

Czinkota, Michael R., Ilkka A. Ronkainen and Marta Ortiz-Buonafina. *Export Marketing Imperative*. Mason, OH: Cengage South-Western, 2004.

Hinkelman, Edward G. *A Short Course in International Payments*. New York: World Trade Press, 2002.

Jackson, John H. and Edwin A. Vermulst (eds). *Anti-dumping Law and Practice*. Ann Arbor: University of Michigan Press, 1990.

Jagoe, John R. and Agnes Brown. *Pricing Your Products for Export & Budgeting for Export*. Minneapolis, MN: The Export Institute, 1998.

Johnson, Thomas E. *Export/Import Procedures and Documentation*. New York: AMACOM, 2002.

Lowell, Julia and Loren Yager. *Pricing and Markets: US. and Japanese Responses to Currency Fluctuations*. Santa Monica, CA: Rand Corporation, 1994.

Monroe, Kent B. *Pricing: Making Profitable Decisions*. New York: McGraw-Hill, 2003.

Nagle, Thomas T. and Reed K. Holden. *The Strategy and Tactics of Pricing: A Guide to Profitable Decision Making*. Englewood Cliffs, NJ: Prentice-Hall, 2002.

Palmer, Howard. *International Trade Finance and Pre-Export Finance*. London: Euromoney Publications, 1999.

Ramberg, Jan. *ICC Guide to Incoterms*. Paris: ICC Publishing, Inc., 2000.

US Department of the Treasury. *A Basic Guide to Importing*. New York: McGraw-Hill, 1996.

Venedikian, Harry M. and Gerald A. Warfield. *Export-Import Financing*. New York: John Wiley & Sons, 1996.

Woznick, Alexandra and Edward G. Hinkelman. *A Basic Guide to Exporting*. New York: World Trade Press, 2000.

Notes

1 James A. Gingrich, 'Five Rules for Winning Emerging Market Consumers', *Strategy and Business* (second quarter, 1999), 35–46.

2 David Arnold, 'Seven Rules of International Distribution', *Harvard Business Review* 78 (November/December 2000): 131–137.

3 Matthew Myers, S. Tamer Cavusgil and Adamantios Diamantopoulos, 'Antecedents and Actions of Export Pricing Strategy: A Conceptual Framework and Research Propositions', *European Journal of Marketing* 36 (numbers 1/2, 2002): 159–189.

4 Matthew B. Myers and S. Tamer Cavusgil, 'Export Pricing Strategy-Performance Relationship: A Conceptual Framework', *Advances in International Marketing* 8 (1996): 159–178.

5 Howard Forman and Richard A. Lancioni, 'International Industrial Pricing Strategic Decisions and the Pricing Manager: Some Key Issues', Professional Pricing Society, October 9, 1999, at **http://www.pricingsociety.com/pdf-4-index/international-industrial-pricing.pdf**

6 John A. Boyd, 'How One Company Solved Its Export Pricing Problems', *Small Business Forum*, Fall 1995, 28–38.

7 Matthew Myers, 'The Pricing of Export Products: Why Aren't Managers Satisfied with the Results', *Journal of World Business* 32 (number 3, 1997): 277–289.

8 S. Tamer Cavusgil, 'Unraveling the Mystique of Export Pricing', *Business Horizons* 31 (May–June 1988): 54–63.

9 Thomas T. Nagle and Reed K. Holden, *The Strategy and Tactics of Pricing: A Guide to Profitable Decision Making* (Englewood Cliffs, NJ: Prentice-Hall, 2002), chapter 3.

10 Luis Felipe Lages and David B. Montgomery, 'Effects of Export Assistance on Pricing Strategy Adaptation and Export Performance', *MSI Reports*, issue 3, 2004, 67–88.

11 Méjean, I. and Schwellnus, C. (2009), 'Price convergence in the European Union: Within firms or composition of firms?' **http://www.sciencedirect.com/science?_ob= ArticleURL&_udi=B6V6D-4VS40FS-2&_user= 605157&_rdoc=1&_fmt=&_orig=search&_sort=d&_ docanchor=&view=c&_searchStrId=1115635909&_ rerunOrigin=google&_acct=C000031258&_version= 1&_urlVersion=0&_userid=605157&md5= 2693fe880e6b4520ff7c390d5ba31b1a**

12 Barbara Stöttinger, 'Strategic Export Pricing: A Long and Winding Road', *Journal of International Marketing* 9 (no. 1, 2001): 40–63.

13 'Keeping Time with the Global Market', *World Trade*, December 1999, 82–83.

14 'What's in a Name', *Economist*, February 2, 1991, 60.

15 Al D'Amico, 'Duty Drawback: An Overlooked Customs Refund Program', *Export Today* 9 (May 1993): 46–48. See also **http://www.cbp.gov**.

16 International Chambers of Commerce, *Incoterms 2000* (Paris: ICC Publishing, 2000). See also **http://www.iccwbo.org**.

17 Kevin Reilly, 'Exporters Must Ensure Coordination of Incoterms and Documentary Requirements for LC Payment', *Business Credit* 107 (number 6, 2005): 48–50.

18 Alexandra Woznik and Edward G. Hinkelman, *A Basic Guide to Exporting* (Novate, CA: World Trade Press, 2000), chapter 10.

19 'Getting Paid: Or What's a Transaction For?' *World Trade*, September 1999, 42–52; and Chase Manhattan Bank, *Dynamics of Trade Finance* (New York: Chase Manhattan Bank, 1984): 10–11.

20 David K. Eiteman, Arthur I. Stonehill and Michael H. Moffett, *Multinational Business Finance* (Reading, MA: Addison-Wesley, 2002), 460–488.

21 International Chamber of Commerce, *Uniform Customs and Practice for Documentary Credits* (New York: ICC Publishing Corp., 2002).

22 Vincent M. Maulella, 'Payment Pitfalls for the Unwary', *World Trade*, April 1999, 76–79.

23 Erika Morphy, 'Form vs. Format', *Export Today*, 15 (August 1999): 47–52.

24 Erika Morphy, 'Paper's Last Stand', *Global Business*, May 2001, 36–39.

25 'Ready Cash?' *Global Business*, September 2000, 45. See also **http://www.tradecard.com**.

26 Tom Beube, 'Cashing in on China', *World Trade*, October 2005, 64–66.

27 **http://www.cofacerating.com**.

28 Michael S. Tomczyk, 'How Do You Collect When Foreign Customers Don't Pay?' *Export Today* 9 (November–December 1993): 33–35.

29 James Welsh, 'Covering Your Bets on Credit and Collections', *World Trade*, February 1999, 28–29; and Ron Siegel and Mark Stoyas, 'Foreign Collections', *Export Today* 11 (April 1995): 44–46.

30 Guido Schultz, 'Foreign Exchange Strategies for Coping with Currency Volatility', *World Trade*, January 2005, 10.

31 Saied Mahdavi, 'Do German, Japanese, and US Export Prices Asymmetrically Respond to Exchange Rate Changes?' *Contemporary Economic Policy* 18 (January 2000): 70–81.

32 Paul R. Krugman, 'Pricing-to-Market When the Exchange Rate Changes', in S. W. Arndt and J. D. Robinson (eds), *Real-Financial Linkages among Open Economies* (Cambridge, MA: MIT Press, 1987), 49–70.

33 Michael H. Moffett, 'Harley Davidson: Hedging Hogs', in Michael R. Czinkota, Ilkka A. Ronkainen and Michael H. Moffett, *International Business 2003 Update* (Mason, OH: Cengage, 2003), 634–637.

34 'Competitive Exports, Sky High Imports', *Financial Mail*, October 2, 1998, 19.

35 'Komatsu Ltd', *International Directory of Company Histories*. The Gale Group, Inc, 2006. Answers.com 09 Jan. 2010. **http://www.answers.com/topic/komatsu-ltd-adr** (Accessed 9/1/10).

36 Chi Lo, 'Asia's Competitive Endgame: Life after China's WTO Entry', *The China Business Review*, January–February 2002, 22–36.

37 See, for example, **http://www.jetro.org**.

38 'How to Choose a Trade Bank', *World Trade*, April 2004, 20.

39 **http://www.commerzbank.com**.

40 Lawrence W. Tuller, 'Beyond the LC', *Export Today*, 12 (August 1996): 70–74.

41 Daniel S. Levine, 'Factoring Pays Off', *World Trade*, September 1998, 79–80.

42 Ray Pereira, 'International Factoring', *World Trade*, December 1999, 68–69.

43 Mary Ann Ring, 'Innovative Export Financing', *Business America*, January 11, 1993, 12–14.

44 The authors acknowledge the assistance of Craig O'Connor of the Export-Import Bank of the United States.

45 'EXIM-Bank Program Summary', in *Export-Import Bank of the United States* (Washington, DC: EXIM Bank, 1985), 1; updated for 2006.

46 Robert Frewen, 'Are Your International Credit Terms Cutting Your Throat?' *World Trade*, January 2001, 71–73.

47 Claude Cellich, 'Business Negotiations: Making the First Offer', *International Trade Forum* 14 (no. 2, 2000): 12–16.

48 **http://www.elcamino.com**.

49 Paul Magnusson, 'Bring Anti-Dumping Laws Up to Date', *Business Week*, July 19, 1999, 45.

50 **http://www.wto.org**.

51 AAFA 'EU Anti-Dumping Cases' **http://www.appareland footwear.org/LegislativeTradeNews/EUAntiDumping Cases.asp** (Accessed 9/1/10).

52 Delener Nejdet, 'An Ethical and Legal Synthesis of Dumping: Growing Concerns in International Marketing', *Journal of Business Ethics* 17 (November 1998): 1747–1753.

CHAPTER 12
MARKETING COMMUNICATIONS

THE INTERNATIONAL **MARKETPLACE 12.1**

Why should I trust you?

Trust is a critical factor in any type of a relationship because without trust there is no relationship at all. In the wake of mistrust of consumers by such organizations as Enron, one would forgive consumers for not trusting businesses.

Trust has been seen as an important aspect in business success. This is particularly important in global marketing where an organization faces different cultures. Contracts gained can easily be lost if there is not trust among the parties concerned. Being able to trust the global marketer is seen as an important factor in the establishment of long-term relationships.

What do we mean by trust? There are three forms of trust, namely: personal trust, collective trust and institutional. Personal trust is based on our initial knowledge of the business partner. 'It may also depend on characteristics of group such as an ethnic group, kinship, or in bilateral (business) relationships based on knowledge of each other'. There may not be written contracts but relationships based on trust 'are governed by informal norms and rules'. This is quite important in some cultures, especially in developing economies. In such cases, the potential business partner must strive to build relationships with the locals, for example, through influential friends or relations.

In contrast collective trust refers 'to shared norms and mutual business conventions, which differ across sectors or business groups and play an important role in shaping business relationships'. The group as a whole trusts the business partner when they value the reputation of the business partner. The difference between personal trust and collective trust is that the former is based on personal knowledge of the business partner, whereas in the latter trust is based on the reputation of the business partner. In developing collective trust the business partner has to develop a good reputation.

In institutional trust the scope of trust extends beyond both 'the number of people we know personally' and the reputation of the commercial partner to the 'use of "anonymous" sources in business relationships (such as new partners, or consultants for business assistance)'. These are seen as legal safeguards in case the other two types of trust fail. This form is prevalent in developed economies. It is built on the premise that for a business to succeed it must be both customer-centred and that the relationship should be mutually beneficial. If an organization wants to win at the expenses of customers, the relationship is unstable and it will ultimately lose the trust of the customer in it as an institution. This is what happened to Enron. It focused on profits and ignored the importance of being customer-focused. 'As it shifted its belief systems, Enron ceased to believe in being trustworthy, and thus became unworthy of trust'. A marketing truth is that 'true success in a capitalist system rests on trust'.

It is apparent from the above that the global marketer should be able to build the right form of trust, as different cultures prefer different forms of trust. It is clear that trust forms the foundation for effective communication and contributes to long-term business relationships.

SOURCES: Becton, C., Wysocki, A. and K. Kepner, 'Building Teamwork and the Importance of Trust in a Business Environment'. Online. Available: **http://edis.ifas.ufl.edu/HR018** (Accessed 12/04/09). Kautonem, T., Chepurenko, A, Malieva, E. and U. Venesaar (2003) 'Does Trust Matter? – Cross Cultural View On Entrepreneurship In Different Trust Milieus'. Online. Available: **http://66.102.9.104/search?q=cache:2YIWrY54fW4J:www.rwi-essen.de/pls/portal30/docs/FOLDER/TRUST/DOWNLOADS_TRUST/DOESTRUSTMATTER.PDF+Does+trust+matter+in+international+marketing%3F&hl=en&ct=clnk&cd=4&gl=uk** (Accessed 05/04/09). Green, C. H (2007) 'What Should Enron Have Taught Us?'. Online. Available: **http://trustedadvisor.com/articles/19/** (Accessed 15/04/09).

Effective communication is particularly important in international marketing because of the geographic and psychological distances that separate a firm from its intermediaries and customers. By definition, communication is a process of establishing a 'commonness' of thought between a sender and a receiver.[1] This process extends beyond the conveying of ideas to include persuasion and thus enables the marketing process to function more effectively and efficiently. Ideally, marketing communication is a dialogue that allows organizations and consumers to achieve mutually satisfying exchange agreements. This definition emphasizes the two-way nature of the process, with listening and responsiveness as integral parts. A relationship has to be established from the beginning and deepened over time. Trust is an important element in international marketing, as seen in *The International Marketplace 12.1*.

This chapter will include an overview of the principles of marketing communications in international markets. As face-to-face, buyer–seller negotiations are possibly the most fundamental marketing process,[2] guidelines for international business negotiations are discussed first. Second, the chapter will focus on the management of the international communications mix from the exporter's point of view. Because the exporter's alternatives may be limited by the entry mode and by resources available, the tools and the challenges are quite different from those of the multinational entity. We discuss the promotional approaches used by global marketers in Chapter 18.

THE MARKETING COMMUNICATIONS PROCESS

As shown in the communications model presented in Exhibit 12.1, effective communication requires three elements – the sender, the message and the receiver – connected by a message channel. The process may begin with an unsolicited inquiry from a potential customer or as a planned effort by the marketer. Whatever the goal of the communications process, the sender needs to study receiver characteristics before encoding the message in order to achieve maximum impact. Encoding the message simply means converting it into symbolic form that is properly understood by the receiver. This is not a simple task, however. For example, if an e-commerce site's order form asks only for typical UK-type address information, such as a post code, and does not include anything for other countries, the would-be buyer abroad will interpret this as unwillingness to do business outside the United Kingdom. Similarly, if an export price is quoted on an ex-works basis (which includes only the cost of goods sold in the price), the buyer may not be interested in or be able to take responsibility for the logistics process and will go elsewhere.

The message channel is the path through which the message moves from sender (source) to receiver. This link that ties the receiver to the sender ranges from sound waves conveying the human voice in personal selling to transceivers or intermediaries such as print and broadcast media. Although technological advances (for example, video conferencing and the internet) may have made buyer–seller negotiations more efficient, the fundamental process and its

EXHIBIT 12.1

The marketing communications process

Source: Adapted from Terence A. Shimp, *Advertising, Promotion, and Supplemental Aspects of Integrated Marketing Communications* (Mason, OH: South-Western, 2003), 82. Reprinted by permission.

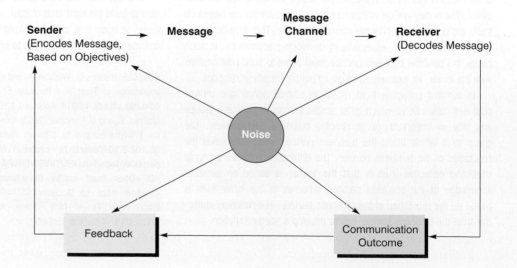

purpose have remained unchanged. Face-to-face contact is still necessary for two basic reasons. The first is the need for detailed discussion and explanation, and the second is the need to establish the rapport that forms the basis of lasting business relationships. Technology will then support in the maintenance of the relationship.

The message channel also exists in mass communications. Complications in international marketing may arise if a particular medium does not reach the targeted audience, which is currently the case for internet communications, for example, due to varying online penetration rates around the world.[3] Other examples of complications are the banning of advertising for certain product categories, such as for cigarettes in most of Europe, and the fact that some marketing practices may not be allowed, such as direct selling in China.

Once a sender has placed a message into a channel or a set of channels and directed it to the intended destination, the completion of the process is dependent on the receiver's decoding – that is, transforming the message symbols back into thought. If there is an adequate amount of overlap between sender characteristics and needs reflected in the encoded message, and receiver characteristics and needs reflected in the decoded message, the communications process has worked.

A message moving through a channel is subject to the influence of extraneous and distracting stimuli, which interfere with the intended accurate reception of the message. This interference is referred to as noise. In the international marketing context, noise might be a bad telephone connection, failure to express a quotation in the inquirer's system of currency and measurement, or lack of understanding of the recipient's environment – perhaps having only an English-language website. For example, a UK company received a message from its Thai client complaining of an incomplete delivery: an order of 85,000 units was four short! When the UK company shipped in bulk, the number of units was estimated by weight. In Thailand, however, labour is cheap and materials expensive, allowing the client to hand-count shipments. The solution was to provide a slight overage in each shipment without incurring a major expense but achieving customer satisfaction.[4] Similarly, a valid inquiry from overseas may not be considered seriously by an international marketer because of noise consisting of low-quality paper, grammatical errors or a general appearance unlike domestic correspondence.

The international marketer should be most alert to cultural noise. The lack of language skills may hinder successful negotiations, whereas translation errors may render a promotional campaign or brochure useless. Similarly, non-verbal language and its improper interpretation may cause problems. While eye contact in Europe may be direct, the cultural style of the Japanese may involve markedly less eye contact.[5]

The success of the outcome is determined by how well objectives have been met in generating more awareness, a more positive attitude, or increased purchases. For example, the development of sales literature in the local language and reflective of the product line offered may result in increased inquiries or even more sales. While call centres abroad may provide significant cost savings, their use has to be benchmarked against customer-service standards, expectations and overall goodwill towards the company.[6]

Regardless of whether the situation calls for interpersonal or mass communications, the collection and observation of feedback is necessary to analyze the success of the communications effort. The initial sender–receiver relationship is transposed, and interpretative skills similar to those needed in developing messages are needed. To make effective and efficient use of communications requires considerable strategic planning. Examples of concrete ways in which feedback can be collected are inquiry cards and toll-free numbers distributed at trade shows to gather additional information. Similarly, the internet allows marketers to track traffic flows and to install registration procedures that identify individuals and track their purchases over time.[7]

INTERNATIONAL NEGOTIATIONS

When international marketers travel abroad to do business, they are frequently shocked to discover the extent to which the many variables of foreign behaviour and custom complicate their efforts.[8] Given that most negotiations are face-to-face, they present one of the most obvious and immediate challenges to be overcome. This means that international marketers have to adjust their approaches to establishing rapport, information exchange, persuasion, and concession making if they are to be successful in dealing with their clients and partners, such as intermediaries.[9] The consequences of failure are quickly seen in profits not realized and increases in non-recoverable expenses, as well as decreased motivation of the international negotiators.[10]

The two biggest dangers faced in international negotiations are parochialism and stereotyping. Parochialism refers to the misleading perception that the world of business is becoming ever more American and that everyone will behave accordingly. This approach leads to stereotyping in explaining remaining differences. Stereotypes are generalizations about any given group, both positive and negative. For example, a positive stereotype has a clear influence on decisions to explore business options, whereas a negative stereotype may lead to a request to use a low-risk payment system, such as a letter of credit.[11] In a similar fashion, seemingly familiar surroundings and situations may lull negotiators into a false sense of security. This may be true for a UK negotiator in China or Malaysia thinking that the same language leads to the same behavioural patterns, or even in a far-off market if the meeting takes place in a hotel belonging to a large multinational chain.

The level of adjustment depends on the degree of cultural familiarity the parties have and their ability to use that familiarity effectively. For example, in China, the ideal negotiator is someone who has an established relationship with the Chinese and is trusted by them.[12] This is especially true in making the initial contact or stepping in if problems emerge. However, the Chinese may be less effective in leading a negotiation. Where the Chinese are often willing to make an exception for visitors, they will expect ethnic Chinese to accept the Chinese way of doing things. The ideal team would, therefore, include a non-Chinese who understands the culture and an ethnic-Chinese individual. Together, the two can play 'good guy–bad guy' roles and resist unreasonable demands.[13] If neither party is familiar with the counterpart's culture, outside facilitators should be employed.

With the increased use of the internet, the question arises as to its use in international negotiations. Using the e-dimension does allow the exporter to overcome distances, minimize social barriers (e.g., age, gender, status), obtain instant feedback, negotiate from a home base, and do so with a number of parties simultaneously. However, it cannot be used in isolation, given the critical role of building trust in negotiations. Additionally, its extensive use may restrict much of the interaction to focusing mostly on price. The internet is effective in the exchange of information and for possible clarification during the course of the process.[14] It should be noted that technology is only gradually making its way to such use; lack of the necessary tools and mind-set may challenge the internet's use for this purpose.

Stages of the negotiation process

The process of international business negotiations can be divided into five stages: the offer, informal meetings, strategy formulation, negotiations and implementation.[15] Which stage is emphasized and the length of the overall process will vary dramatically by culture. The negotiation process can be a short one, with the stages collapsing into one session, or a prolonged endeavour taking weeks. The differences between Northern and Southern Europe highlight this. Northern Europe, with its Protestant tradition and indoor culture, tends to emphasize the technical, the numerical and the tested. Careful pre-negotiation preparations are made. For example, bargaining is not a typical behaviour in Hungary and they like to have a lot of background information. Southern Europe, with its Catholic background and open-air lifestyle, tends to favour personal networks, social contexts and flair. Meetings in the South are often longer, but the total decision process may be faster.[16] As a French business manager put it, 'in France we are less formal than the Brits at the start of a relationship, but over time, we don't tend to become as informal as the British will'.[17] This shows that the rules of protocol are formal to begin with and informal once the business relationship has been established.

The offer stage allows the two parties to assess each other's needs and degree of commitment. The initiation of the process and its progress are determined to a great extent by background factors of the parties (such as objectives) and the overall atmosphere (for example, a spirit of cooperativeness). As an example, buyers may be sceptical of an exporter who is focused on short-term gains or that leaves immediately when the business environment turns sour.

After the buyer has received the offer, the parties meet to discuss the terms and get acquainted. In many parts of the world (Asia, the Middle East and Africa), informal meetings may often make or break the deal. Foreign buyers may want to ascertain that they are doing business with someone who is sympathetic and whom they can trust. For example, the UK attaches considerable importance to building strong business relationships with Kuwait.[18] In some cases, it may be necessary to utilize facilitators (such as consultants or agents) to establish the contact.

Both parties have to formulate strategies for formal negotiations. This means not only careful review and assessment of all the factors affecting the deal to be negotiated but also preparation for the actual give-and-take of the negotiations. For example, no matter how thoroughly the firm has prepared, or how successful it has been in entering and penetrating a foreign market, a review will be needed to make sure that optimum results are achieved.[19] In contrast, Chinese negotiators are happier when they achieve outcome parity. This is evidence that cultural values (e.g., harmonious relationships for the Chinese) create the environment in which negotiation tactics are selected.[20] Thus, managers should consciously and carefully consider competitive behaviours of clients and partners. It is imperative to realize that public-sector needs may not necessarily fit into a mould that the marketer would consider rational, especially in the case of governmental buyers. Negotiators may not necessarily behave as expected; for example, the negotiating partner may adjust behaviour to the visitor's culture.

The actual face-to-face negotiations and the approach used in them will depend on the cultural background and business traditions prevailing in different countries. The most commonly used are the competitive and collaborative approaches.[21] In a competitive approach, the negotiator is concerned mainly about a favourable outcome at the expense of the other party, while in the collaborative approach focus is on mutual needs, especially in the long term. For example, an exporter accepting a proposal that goes beyond what can be realistically delivered (in the hopes of market entry or renegotiation later) will lose in the long term. To deliver on the contract, the exporter may be tempted to cut corners in product quality or delivery, eventually leading to conflict with the buyer.

The choice of location for the negotiations also plays a role in the outcome. Many negotiators prefer a neutral site. This may not always work, for reasons of resources or parties' perceptions of the importance of the deal. The host does enjoy many advantages, such as lower psychological risk due to familiar surroundings. Guests may run the risk of cultural shock and being away from professional and personal support systems. These pressures are multiplied if the host chooses to manipulate the situation with delays or additional demands. Visiting teams are less likely to walk out; as a matter of fact, the pressure is on them to make concessions. However, despite the challenges of being a guest, the visitor has a chance to see firsthand the counterpart's facilities and resources, and to experience culture in that market. In addition, visiting a partner, present or potential, shows commitment to the effort.[22]

Negotiator characteristics (e.g., gender, race, or age) may work for or against the exporter in certain cultures. It is challenging to overcome stereotypes, but well-prepared negotiators can overcome these obstacles or even make them work to their advantage. For example, a female negotiator may use her uniqueness in male-dominated societies to gain better access to decision makers.[23] It may be easier for a Westerner to interact with younger Chinese for the simple reason that their educational backgrounds, behavioural styles and objectives are more similar than those of the old cadres.[24]

How to negotiate in other countries[25]

A combination of attitudes, expectations and habitual behaviour influences negotiation style. Although some of the following recommendations may go against the approach used at home, they may allow the negotiator to adjust to the style of the host-country negotiators.

1   *Team assistance.* Using specialists will strengthen the team substantially and allow for all points of view to be given proper attention. Further, observation of negotiations can be valuable training experience for less-experienced participants. Whereas western teams may average two to four people, a Chinese negotiating team may consist of up

to ten people.[26] In the context of negotiation, the need to preserve or develop an atmosphere of trust is also hypothesized as being part of the decision-making system of the individual.[27] Even if there are intragroup disagreements during the negotiations, it is critical to show one face to the counterparts and handle issues within the team privately, outside the formal negotiations.

2 *Traditions and customs*. For newcomers, status relations and business procedures must be carefully considered with the help of consultants or local representatives. For example, in highly structured societies, such as Korea, great respect is paid to age and position.[28] It is prudent to use informal communication to let counterparts know, or ask them about, any prestigious degrees, honours or accomplishments by those who will be facing one another in negotiations. What seem like simple rituals can cause problems. No first encounter in Asia is complete without an exchange of business cards. Both hands should be used to present and receive cards, and respect should be shown by reading them carefully.[29] One side should be translated into the language of the host country.

3 *Language capability*. Ideally, the international marketing manager should be able to speak the customer's language, but that is not always possible. A qualified individual is needed as part of a marketing team to ensure that nothing gets lost in the translation, literally or figuratively. Whether the negotiator is bilingual or an interpreter is used, it might be a good gesture to deliver the first comments in the local language to break the ice. The use of interpreters allows the negotiator longer response time and a more careful articulation of arguments. If English is being used, a native speaker should avoid both jargon and idiomatic expressions, avoid complex sentences, and speak slowly and enunciate clearly.[30] An ideal interpreter is one who briefs the negotiator on cultural dimensions, such as body language, before any meetings. For example, sitting in what may be perceived as a comfortable position in Europe may be seen by the Chinese as showing a lack of control of one's body and, therefore, of one's mind.

4 *Determination of authority limits*. Negotiators from Western Europe are often expected to have full authority when they negotiate in the Far East, although their local counterparts seldom if ever do. Announcing that the negotiators do not have the final authority to conclude the contract may be perceived negatively; however, if it is used as a tactic to probe the motives of the buyer, it can be quite effective. It is important to verify who does have that authority and what challenges may be faced in getting that decision. In negotiating in Russia, for example, the international marketer will have to ascertain who actually has final decision-making authority – the central, provincial, or local government – especially if permits are needed.

5 *Patience*. In many countries, such as China, business negotiations may take three times the amount of time that they do in Western Europe. Showing impatience in countries such as Brazil or Thailand may prolong negotiations rather than speed them up. Also, Western European executives tend to start relatively close to what they consider a fair price in their negotiations, whereas Chinese negotiators may start with 'unreasonable' demands and a rigid posture.[31]

6 *Negotiation ethics*. Attitudes and values of foreign negotiators may be quite different from those that a US marketing executive is accustomed to. Being tricky can be valued in some parts of the world, whereas it is frowned on elsewhere. For example, western negotiators may be taken aback by last-minute changes or concession requests by Russian negotiators.[32]

7 *Silence*. To negotiate effectively abroad, a marketer needs to read correctly all types of communication. Western European businesspeople often interpret inaction and silence as a negative sign. As a result, Japanese executives tend to expect that they can use silence to get them to lower prices or sweeten the deal. Finns may sit through a meeting expressionless, hands folded and not moving much. There is nothing necessarily negative about this; they show respect to the speaker with their focused, dedicated listening.[33]

8 *Persistence.* Insisting on answers and an outcome may be seen as a threat by negotiating partners abroad. In some markets, negotiations are seen as a means of establishing long-term commercial relations, not as an event with winners and losers. Western European negotiators are likely to refer to written agreements and expertise during the negotiations as a function of their national culture, whereas Asians may focus more on relationship commitment. Confrontations are to be avoided because minds cannot be changed at the negotiation table; this has to be done informally. Face is an important concept throughout the Far East.

9 *Holistic view.* Concessions should be avoided until all issues have been discussed, so as to preclude the possibility of granting unnecessary benefits to the negotiation partners. Concessions traditionally come at the end of bargaining. This is especially true in terms of price negotiations. If price is agreed on too quickly, the counterpart may want to insist on too many inclusions for that price.

10 *The meaning of agreements.* What constitutes an agreement will vary from one market to another. In many parts of the world, legal contracts are still not needed; as a matter of fact, reference to legal counsel may indicate that the relationship is in trouble. For the Chinese, the written agreement exists mostly for the convenience of their western partners and represents an agenda on which to base the development of the relationship.[34]

When a verbal agreement is reached, it is critical that both parties leave with a clear understanding of what they have agreed to. This may entail only the relatively straightforward act of signing a distributor agreement, but in the case of large-scale projects, details must be explored and spelled out. In contracts that call for cooperative efforts, the responsibilities of each partner must be clearly specified. Otherwise, obligations that were anticipated to be the duty of one contracting party may result in costs to another. For example, foreign principal contractors may be held responsible for delays that have been caused by the inability of local subcontractors (whose use might be a requisite of the client) to deliver on schedule.

MARKETING COMMUNICATIONS STRATEGY

The international marketing manager has the responsibility of formulating a communications strategy for the promotion of the company and its products and services. The basic steps of such a strategy are outlined in Exhibit 12.2.

Few, if any, firms can afford expenditures for promotion that is done as 'art for art's sake' or only because major competitors do it. The first step in developing communications strategy is therefore assessing what company or product characteristics and benefits should be communicated to the export market. This requires constant monitoring of the various environments and target audience characteristics. For example, Volvo has used safety and quality

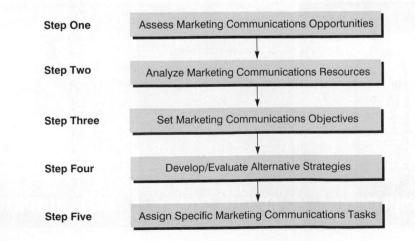

Step One	Assess Marketing Communications Opportunities
Step Two	Analyze Marketing Communications Resources
Step Three	Set Marketing Communications Objectives
Step Four	Develop/Evaluate Alternative Strategies
Step Five	Assign Specific Marketing Communications Tasks

EXHIBIT 12.2

Steps in formulating marketing communications strategy

Source: Framework adapted from Wayne DeLozier, *The Marketing Communication Process* (New York: McGraw-Hill, 1976), 272.

as its primary themes in its worldwide promotional campaigns since the 1950s. This approach has provided continuity, repetition and uniformity in positioning Volvo in relation to its primary competitors: Mercedes-Benz (prestige) and BMW (sportiness).

Absolut, which is owned by the Swedish government, was exported to the US market in 1979 with no introductory promotion by its distributor, Carillon Importers Ltd. At the time, import vodka sales were almost nonexistent and Absolut's brand name unknown. With a very small budget ($750,000) and the capability to do only print advertising, Carillon's agency TBWA set about establishing brand awareness. Since then the ads have featured a full-page shot of the bottle and a two-word headline.[35] Absolut is now the third largest international premium spirit and is available in 125 markets. Absolut currently comprises the following products within the same quality framework: Absolut Vodka, introduced in 1979; Absolut Peppar (1986); Absolut Citron (1988); Absolut Kurant (1992); Absolut Mandrin (1999); Absolut Vanilia (2003).[36] In the UK, Smirnoff dominates the market with 40 per cent while Absolut takes around 5 per cent.[37] Vodkas are now the largest category in the distilled spirits business, with Absolut ruling the high-class vodka crowd. Certain rules of thumb can be followed in evaluating resources to be allocated for export communications efforts. A sufficient commitment is necessary, which means a relatively large amount of money. The exporter has to operate in foreign markets according to the rules of the marketplace, which in the UK, for example, means high promotional costs – perhaps 30 per cent of exports or even more during the early stage of entry. With heavily contested markets, the level of spending may even have to increase.

Due to monetary constraints that most exporters face, promotional efforts should be concentrated on key markets. For example, European liquor marketers traditionally concentrate their promotional efforts on Great Britain, which is considered the world capital of the liquor trade. A specific objective might be to spend more than the closest competitors do in the

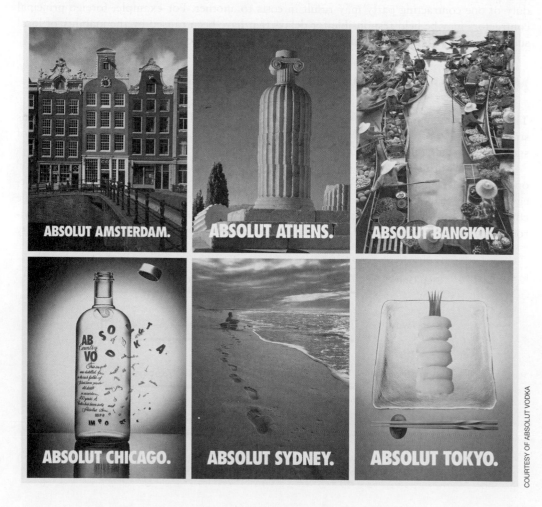

Western European market. In some cases, an exporter will have to limit this to one country, even one area, at a time to achieve set goals with the available budget. International campaigns require patient investment; the market has to progress through awareness, knowledge, liking, preference and favourable purchase intentions before payback begins. Payback periods of one or two years cannot be realistically expected. For many exporters, a critical factor is the support of the intermediary. Whether a distributor is willing to contribute a $3 million media budget or a few thousand pounds makes a big difference. In some cases, intermediaries take a leading role in the promotion of the product in a market. In the case of Absolut, for example, Maxxium UK has been credited with the creative advertising widely acknowledged as a primary reason for the brand's success. In most cases, however, the exporter should retain some control of the campaign rather than allow intermediaries or sales offices a free hand in the various markets operated. Although markets may be dissimilar, common themes and common objectives need to be incorporated into the individual campaigns. For example, Duracell, the world leader in alkaline batteries, provides graphics – such as logos and photos – to country operations. Although many exporters do not exert pressure to conform, overseas distributors take advantage of annual meetings to discuss promotional practices with their head office counterparts.

Alternative strategies are needed to spell out how the firm's resources can be combined and adapted to market opportunities. The tools the international marketer has available to form a total communications programme for use in the targeted markets are referred to as the promotional mix. They consist of the following:

1 *Advertising:* Any form of nonpersonal presentation of ideas, goods or services by an identified sponsor, with predominant use made of *mass* communication, such as print, broadcast or electronic media, or *direct* communication that is pinpointed at each business-to-business customer or ultimate consumer using computer technology and databases.

2 *Personal selling:* The process of assisting and persuading a prospect to buy a good or service or to act on an idea through use of person-to-person communication with intermediaries and/or final customers.

3 *Publicity:* Any form of nonpaid, commercially significant news or editorial comment about ideas, products or institutions.

4 *Sales promotion:* Direct inducements that provide extra product value or incentive to the sales force, intermediaries or ultimate consumers.

5 *Sponsorship:* The practice of promoting the interests of the company by associating it with a specific event (typically sports or culture) or a cause (typically a charity or a social interest).

The use of these tools will vary by company and by situation. Although all Suzuki motorcycles are on allocation in overseas markets, their promotion focuses on post-purchase reinforcement. Owners, in turn, become a powerful promotional tool for Suzuki through word-of-mouth communication. The company also sells 'motor clothes', illustrated in catalogues. Copies are made for overseas dealers, who cannot afford to translate and reprint them, and they pass them on to their customers with notes that not all items are available or permissible in their markets.[38]

The choice of tools leads to either a push or a pull emphasize in marketing communications. Push strategies focus on the use of personal selling. Despite its higher cost per contact, personal selling is appropriate for the international marketing of industrial goods, which have shorter channels of distribution and smaller target populations than do consumer goods. Governmental clients are typically serviced through personal selling efforts. Some industries, such as pharmaceuticals, traditionally rely on personal selling to service the clientele.

On the other hand, pull strategies depend on mass communications tools, mainly advertising. Advertising is appropriate for consumer-oriented products with large target audiences and long channels of distribution. Of its promotional budget, Absolut has traditionally spent up to 85 per cent on print media in the United Kingdom, with the balance picked up by outdoor advertising, mainly billboards. The base of the advertising effort has been formed by magazines such as *Sports Illustrated, Vanity Fair, Business Week, Rolling Stone, Esquire,*

Time and *Newsweek*. However, starting with 2006, the company's online spending is increasing to 20 per cent of the annual media budget, with the new domain building an online community and more interactive content.

No promotional tool should be used in isolation or without regard to the others; hence, we see a trend toward integrated marketing communications. Promotional tools should be coordinated according to target market and product characteristics, the size of the promotional budget, the type and length of international involvement and control considerations. As an example, industrial purchasing decisions typically involve eight to eleven people. As a salesperson may not reach all of them, the use of advertising may be necessary to influence the participants in the decision-making process. In addition, steps must be taken to have information readily available to prospects who are interested in the exporter's products. This can be achieved with the development of a website and participating in trade shows.

Exhibit 12.3 provides an example of an advertising campaign for a disk-drive exporter. While the company's ads in its home market focus on product benefits and technical

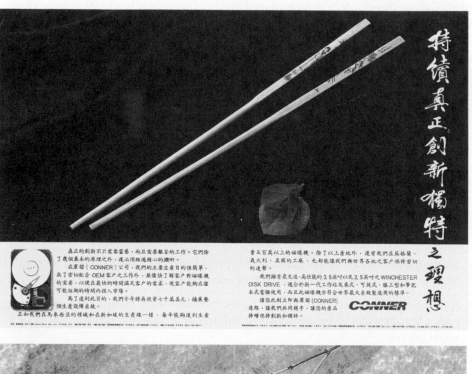
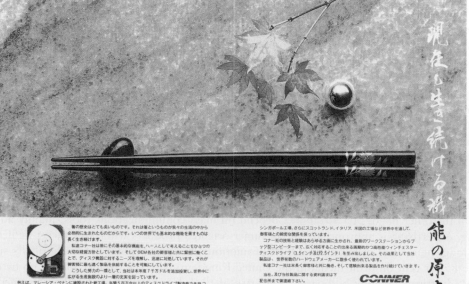

excellence, the approach taken in Asia was much softer. Under the theme 'Unique ideas are often the most enduring', the objective was to increase original equipment makers' awareness of the company's products and the fact that it designed them in close cooperation with its customers. The Chinese ad pictured bone Chinese chopsticks on black cloth, while the Japanese version showed enamelled Japanese (pointed) chopsticks on a marble slab to appeal to different aesthetics.

Finally, specific marketing communications tasks must be assigned, which may require deciding on a division of labour with foreign intermediaries or with other exporters for cooperative communications efforts. For example, Volkswagen does not manufacture motor vehicles in the UK but exports them to the UK. It cooperates closely with its distributors in the marketing of its products. In addition, it uses the internet to advertise its products.[39]

In cases in which the locally-based intermediaries are small and may not have the resources to engage in promotional efforts, the exporter may suggest dealer-participatory programmes. In exchange for including the intermediaries' names in promotional material without any expense to them – for example, in announcing a sweepstakes – the exporter may request increased volume purchases from the intermediaries.

COMMUNICATIONS TOOLS

The main communications tools used by exporters to communicate with the foreign marketplace from their domestic base are business and trade journals, directories, direct advertising, the internet, trade fairs and missions, and personal selling. If the exporter's strategy calls for a major promotional effort in a market, it is advisable either to use a domestic agency with extensive operations in the intended market or to use a local agency and work closely with the company's local representatives in media and message choices.

Since the promoter–agency relationship is a close one, it may be helpful if the exporter's domestic agency has an affiliate in the target foreign market. The management function and coordination can be performed by the agency at home, while the affiliate can execute the programme as it seems appropriate in that market. An exporter, if it has a sufficient budget, may ask its domestic agency to set up a branch overseas. Some exporters, especially those that have a more significant presence overseas, leave the choice of the agency to local managers. If a local agency is to be chosen, the exporter must make sure that coordination and cooperation between the agency and the exporter's domestic agency can be achieved. Whatever the approach used, the key criterion must be the competence of the people who will be in charge of the creation and implementation of the promotional programmes.

Business/trade journals and directories

Many varied business and trade publications, as well as directories, are available to the exporter. These include *Business Week, Fortune, The Economist* and *Financial Times,* which are standard information sources worldwide. Extensions of these are their regional editions; for example, *The Asian Wall Street Journal* or *Business Week – Europe.* Trade publications can be classified as (1) horizontal, which cater to a particular job function cutting across industry lines, such as *Purchasing World* or *Industrial Distribution;* and (2) vertical, which deal with a specific industry, such as *Chemical Engineering* or *International Hospital Supplies.* These journals are global, regional or country-specific in their approaches. Many UK-based publications are available in other European language editions.

Directories provide a similar tool for advertising efforts. Many markets feature exporter yellow pages, some of which offer online versions in addition to the traditional print ones. For example, *The Exporter's Guide* offers UK firms a means to promote their businesses worldwide at no cost (if they just want to be listed), and at low cost for an advertisement or link to their email or homepage. Some of the directories are country-specific.

The two main concerns when selecting media are effectiveness in reaching the appropriate target audience(s) and efficiency in minimizing the cost of doing so, measured in terms of cost per thousand. If the exporter is in a position to define the target audience clearly (for example, in terms of demographics or product-related variables), the choice of media will be easier. In addition, consideration should be given to how well a given medium will work with the other tools the exporter wishes to employ. For example, advertisements in publications and directories may have the function of driving customers and prospects to the exporter's website.[40]

In deciding which publications to use, the exporter must apply the general principles of marketing communications strategy. Coverage and circulation information is available from Standard Rate & Data Service (**http://www.srds.com**). SRDS provides a complete list of international publications (more than 100,000 media properties in all) in the International Section of the *Business Publication,* and audit information is provided for countries such as Italy, France, Austria, Switzerland, Germany, Mexico and Canada. Outside these areas, the exporter has to rely on the assistance of publishers or local representatives. Actual choices are usually complicated by lack of sufficient funds and concern over the information gap. The simplest approach may be to use UK publishers, in which the exporter may have more confidence in terms of rates and circulation data. Before advertising is placed in an unfamiliar journal, the marketer should analyze its content and overall quality of presentation.

Direct marketing

The purpose of direct marketing is to establish a relationship with a customer in order to initiate immediate and measurable responses.[41] This is accomplished through direct-response advertising, telemarketing and direct selling.

Direct mail is by far the dominant direct-response medium, but some advertising is also placed in mass media, such as television, magazines and newspapers. Direct mail can be a highly personalized tool of communication if the target audience can be identified and defined narrowly. Ranging from notices to actual samples, it allows for flexibility in the amount of information conveyed and in its format. Direct mail is directly related in its effectiveness to the availability and quality of the mailing lists. Mailing lists may not be available around the world in the same degree that they are in, say, the United Kingdom. However, more and better lists are surfacing in Asia, Latin America and the Middle East. In addition, reliable, economical, global postal services have become available.[42]

Even when mailing lists are available, they may not be as up-to-date or as precise as the international marketer would desire. In China, for example, lists are available to send literature directly to factories, ministries, professional societies, research institutes and universities. However, such mailings can be extremely costly and produce few results. An effective and efficient direct-mail campaign requires extensive market-by-market planning of materials, format and mode of mailing.

Catalogues are typically distributed to overseas customers through direct mail, although many catalogues have online versions as well. Their function is to make the exporter's name known, generate requests for further information, stimulate orders and serve as a reminder between transactions. Catalogues are particularly useful if a firm's products are in a highly specialized field of technology and if only the most highly qualified specialists are to be contacted. In many markets, especially the developing ones, people may be starving for technology information and will share any mailings they receive. Due to this unsatisfied demand, a very small investment can reach many potential end users.

The growing mail-order segment is attracting an increasing number of foreign entrants to markets previously dominated by local firms. However, because consumers are wary of sending orders and money to an unknown company overseas, the key to market penetration is a local address. In Japan, L.L. Bean, the US outdoor clothing merchandiser, works through McCann Direct, the specialized direct-marketing division of McCann-Erickson Hakuhodo Inc., Japan's largest foreign advertising agency. Bean places ads for its catalogues in Japanese media, orders for catalogues are sent to McCann Direct, and McCann Direct then forwards the addresses to Bean's headquarters in Maine, where all the orders for catalogues or goods are filled.[43] Despite the economic promise of emerging markets such as China, India and Russia, the development of direct marketing is constrained by negative attitudes towards western business practices and problems with distribution networks and marketing support systems, as well as bureaucratic obstacles.[44]

Traditional direct mail is undergoing major change. New types of mail services (e.g., Global Express Mail) enable companies to deal with their customers more efficiently when customers buy through catalogues or electronic means. New electronic media will assume an increasing share in the direct-response area. However, direct marketing will continue to grow as a function of its targetability, its measurability, and the responsiveness of consumers to direct marketing efforts.

In the past, marketers thought that country-specific offices were almost essential to bringing their companies closer to overseas customers. Now, with functioning telecommunication systems and deregulation in the industry, telemarketing (including sales, customer service and help-desk-related support) is flourishing throughout the world. A growing number of countries in Latin America, Asia and Africa are experiencing growth in this area as consumers are becoming more accustomed to calling toll-free numbers and more willing to receive calls from marketers.

In Europe, companies are using this service to publicize their assigned local phone numbers on television or print ads, direct mailings, catalogues, or websites, and the calls are then routed to a call centre. The number and location of such call centres will depend on a variety of issues, such as what the distribution area of the product is, what the costs of operation are, how important local presence is, and how important certain capabilities are, such as language and the ability to handle calls from various time zones.[45] Argentina, Brazil and Costa Rica are choices for Central and Latin American call centre operations, India and the Philippines for Asia, while Belgium, Holland, Ireland, Portugal and some of the new EU countries are leading locations in Europe (Exhibit 12.4).[46] If only one centre is used in Europe, for example, access to a multilingual workforce is a major factor in selecting the location. When a call comes in, the name of the country in which the call originates is displayed above the switchboard so that it can be taken by an operator who speaks the language(s) native to that country. Some of the developments in the industry are highlighted in *The International Marketplace 12.2*.

Call centre activity has developed more slowly in emerging markets than it has in Europe, mostly because of infrastructural reasons and cultural resistance to the new form of communicating with business.[47] However, new technologies are helping to overcome such resistance. Database marketing allows the creation of an individual relationship with each customer or prospect. For example, a call centre operator will know a customer's background with the company or overall purchasing habits. Care has to be taken not to violate privacy regulations or sensitivities. The development of the needed databases through direct mail or the internet will advance the use of telemarketing.

EXHIBIT 12.4

An example of an international call centre

Situations responsible for job outsourcing to India

Was it only the dot-com bust or the 9/11 incidents that caused outsourcing? It was due to the increased ease in communication and the emergence of a cosmopolitan culture around the world, and a fast disappearing of regional barriers. India has benefited though offshore outsourcing, which is a product of this fast-moving globalization. Below are four major factors that made India a target for offshore outsourcing.

Government policies and backing

India has written its success story not in spite of the chaotic, robust democracy, but because of it. Decades of Socialist Democracy and affirmative action have allowed the participation of the poorest, for whom education is the only way out. This mindset has led to increased schooling and import-substitution, and produced generations of entrepreneurs who had to develop indigenous product. That self-reliance is helping India now.

Liberalization has taken root in India and the government has steadily lowered interest rates, eased up foreign exchange restrictions, and freed banks from their social obligations. The governments within India, at the centre as well as in certain states, have realized that India has stumbled upon a goldmine and seem determined to mine this gold. As a result, a renewed support from the government is forthcoming.

With the rupee fully convertible, Indian businesses are now free to invest anywhere. Simultaneously, credit banking has lead to a consumer boom and a new and confident India has emerged even as old problems persist.

Social

Education has always been important in India and the status of its citizens has been heavily weighed on the terms of this parameter. Being a society driven by casteism, knowledge has been the easiest way to emerge out of the limitations of caste to a great extent. In fact the highest place in the caste hierarchy has been given to the Pundits or Brahmans because they were the knowledgeable and educated ones, much above the kings and nobles. The Brahman did not have any worldly possessions yet he was the one everyone had to bow before because he was empowered with knowledge.

Carrying on from this tradition, Indians are proud to involve themselves in careers that require education. They enjoy and take pride in the status of knowledge workers. For decades maids and drivers and other labourers have gone overseas to look for employment, but they have never been able to show pride in the work. Many never disclosed the nature of their work and on the strength of the foreign currency earned tried to gain social respect. But outsourcing, especially

from the IT field, has touched the balance between respectability and riches. Given this respectability the learned group strove towards getting these jobs. These jobs became more preferable than the few respected government jobs that were available. The growing middle class that had gained respect over the years found this the best way out, for they had now the choice of not being forced into what they considered lowly jobs.

Outsourcing solved a lot of those problems. The not-so-rich parent no longer had to dole out lots of cash to send his child overseas, nor did he have to get separated from him for years. The jobs were coming home and all kinds of people with various levels of qualifications could now get these coveted jobs. The pay may not be as high as in the foreign lands but it surely was enough to make him live life king-size back home among appreciative relatives and a support system.

Economic

The economic factor has been greatly highlighted in this issue. Even though it is indeed a major factor in the process, analysts have been overlooking the other very important factors. It is true that if it were not due to economic reasons outsourcing would have never happened. It works both ways for the people who outsource as well as for those that take up the jobs. Cutting costs has been the major concern of companies who are faced not only with recession but also with growing competition. Coupled with that is the growing stature of a fussy and smart consumer who wants the best for the least. Development of easy transportability and service delivery has given the consumer a global market and he is willing to make the best of it. This has made it imperative for companies to deliver to the demands of the consumer.

Developed nations have had a good per capita income. Their workforce is used to the high wages and is therefore unwilling to comply with lower wages.

Language

Even as a certain part of the Indian think tank described the gaining popularity of English as a medium of education, a hangover of British slavery, Indians continued to learn the language because it had already become a status symbol. Also some states who felt Hindi, the national language, had been imposed upon them preferred the use of English to connect them to the other parts of India; and English, which was stipulated to be phased out as the official language of the government, refused to step down. Moreover, English was gaining global acceptance and Indians were unwilling to limit themselves. With this background, when IT happened and English became the lingua franca of the internet, India smoothly fitted in. It had the largest population of English-speaking people among the third world countries. China and Japan which had technologically challenged the US and raced ahead in manufacturing could not do a repeat performance, as its populace had never mastered foreign languages. India is a multi-language society and many speak at least three languages. As a society they are very comfortable with a multi-lingual system and schools all over India follow the three-language formula envisaged by former Prime Minister, Rajiv Gandhi. This was done with the intention of national integration.

SOURCE: Mapsofindia (2009), 'Situations Responsible for Job Outsourcing to India'. Online. Available from: **http://www.mapsofindia.com/outsourcing-to-india/reasons-for-outsourcing.html** (Accessed 13/5/10).

Some exporters see the use of call centres as a preliminary step to entering an international market with a deeper presence such as a sales office.

Internet[48]

Having a website is seen as necessary if for no other reason than image; lack of a web presence may convey a negative image to the various constituents of the marketer. The website should be linked to the overall marketing strategy and not just be there for appearance's sake. This means having a well-designed and well-marketed site.[49] Quality is especially critical if customers use the website to find more information or clarification, as triggered by the exporter's other communications efforts such as advertisements or telemarketing efforts.

Having a web presence will support the exporter's marketing communications effort in a number of ways. First, it allows the company to increase its presence in the marketplace and to communicate its overall mission and information about its marketing mix. Second, the internet will allow 24-hour access to customers and prospects. Providing important information during decision making can help the customer clarify the search. The potential interactivity of the website (e.g., in providing tailor-made solutions to the customer's concerns) may provide a competitive advantage as the customer compares alternative sites. For example, the website for apparel marketer Lands' End allows consumers to identify their body type and then mix and match clothing items that suit them.[50] Interactivity is also critical when the site is designed, in determining what features to include (e.g., should sites adjust to different dialects of a language in a region?).

Third, the internet can improve customer service by allowing customers to serve themselves when and where they choose. This is an area where an exporter's web presence can reduce overall communications costs in the most significant way. Naturally, the exporter must have the necessary capacity to serve all interested customers through the website, especially if there is an increase in interest and demand. An important dimension of customer service is after-sales service to solve consumer problems and to facilitate the formation of consumer groups. A web forum where customers can exchange news and views on product use will not only facilitate product research, but will also build loyalty among consumers.

The fourth advantage is the ability of the exporter to gather information, which has its uses not only in research but also in database development for subsequent marketing efforts. While the data collected may be biased, they are also very inexpensive to collect. If the data are used to better cater to existing customers, then data collected through internet interaction are the best possible.

The fifth advantage of the internet is the opportunity to actually close sales. This function is within the realm of e-commerce. It will require a significant commitment on the part of the exporter in terms of investment in infrastructure to deliver not only information but also the product to the customer. E-commerce is discussed in more detail in Chapter 13.

In addition to communications with customers, the internet provides the possibility to communicate with internal constituents. Exporters may have part of their websites set up with detailed product and price information that only their agents, representatives or distributors have access to. Especially when changes are called for, this is an efficient way of communicating about them without having to mail or fax each and every overseas party.

Websites can also be used in the recruitment of intermediaries and partners. Fair Play Partners uses its site to promote an effective job market for people in mid and later lives.[51]

Internet strategy is not restricted to the exporter's own website. The exporter needs to determine with which portals, such as AOL (**http://www.aol.com**) or Yahoo! (**http://www.yahoo.com**), or with what type of hyperlinks with related products or services, such as internet International Business Exchange (**http://www.imex.com**), to negotiate for banner advertising on those sites.

The challenges faced by exporters in internet-based communications are related to the newness of the medium and the degree to which adjustments need to be made for each market served. A very large portion of the world population has yet to adopt the internet, and its users have a distinct profile. In some cases this might match the exporter's intended target market (such as for online music); however, in many cases internet diffusion has yet to reach the targeted customer.

While English-only websites can deliver information and support to some international customers, having local-language sites and registering with local search engines demonstrate appropriate market and cultural sensitivity. The choice of languages will depend on the target audience. The most popular languages are French, Spanish, German, Japanese and Chinese. For some, a dialect must be specified; for example, Spanish has three main variants: European, Mexican and South American. The exporter needs also to determine which pages have to be modified. Pages that emphasize marketing, sales and corporate identity are normally the ones chosen.[52]

While the exporter's local websites may (and for global product or service offerings, should) be quite similar in terms of aesthetics, adjustments should also be made for such dimensions as depth of product line and level of market presence. Customers who are familiar with the internet may access information about products and services before purchasing them and may visit sites in several countries. Second-generation technology is increasing the interactivity of advertising on the web. Given that individuals around the world have different information needs, varying levels of company and product familiarity, and different user capabilities, exporters can adjust their websites' content and develop paths tailored to each group of customers or even to an individual customer. Overall, the incorporation of the internet into the exporter's marketing strategy will enhance market orientation, marketing competence and eventually marketing performance.[53]

Marketers using the web as an advertising medium will need to be concerned about market-by-market differences in regulations. For example, Germany sued Benetton (**http://www.benetton.com**) for 'exploiting feelings of pity' with one of its 'United Colours of Benetton' campaigns.[54] Finally, online communications strategy should also include provisions for technological development. Hand-held devices such as mobile phones and video iPods may present a new media opportunity provided that consumers are willing to watch entertainment, and the advertising that supports it, on a small screen.[55]

Trade shows and missions

Marketing goods and services through trade shows is a European tradition that dates back at least as far as AD 1240. After sales force costs, trade shows are one of the most significant cost items in marketing budgets. Although they are usually associated with industrial firms, some consumer-products firms are represented as well. Typically, a trade show is an event at which manufacturers, distributors and other vendors display their products or describe their services to current and prospective customers, suppliers, other business associates and the press.[56] The International Automotive Services Industries Show and the International Coal Show, for example, run eight hours a day for three days, plus one or two preview days, and register 25,000 attendees. In the consumer goods area, expositions are the most common type of show. Tickets are usually sold; typical expositions include home/garden, boat, auto, stereo and antiques. Although a typical trade show or typical participant does not exist, an estimated $75,000 is allocated for each show, and the median manufacturer or distributor attends nine or ten shows annually. The number of days spent at trade shows averages 2.4, and the hours per day are 8.6.[57]

Whether an exporter should participate in a trade show depends largely on the type of business relationship it wants to develop with a particular country. More than 16,000 trade shows create an annual $50 billion in business worldwide.[58] A company looking only for one-time or short-term sales might find the expense prohibitive, but a firm looking for long-term involvement may find the investment worthwhile. Arguments in favour of participation include the following:

1 Some products, by their very nature, are difficult to market without providing the potential customer a chance to examine them or see them in action. Trade fairs provide an excellent opportunity to introduce, promote and demonstrate new products. Auto shows, such as the ones in Geneva and Tokyo, feature 'concept' cars to gauge industry and public opinion. Recently, many of these new models have been environmentally friendly, such as being 90 per cent recyclable. The world's premier mobile telephony event, 3GSM World Congress, has nearly 1,000 marketers showcasing their latest mobile products, services and solutions.[59]

2 An appearance at a show produces goodwill and allows for periodic cultivation of contacts. Beyond the impact of displaying specific products, many firms place strong emphasize on 'waving the company flag' against competition. This facet also includes morale boosting of the firm's sales personnel and distributors.

3 The opportunity to find an intermediary may be one of the best reasons to attend a trade show. A show is a cost-effective way to solicit and screen candidates to represent the firm, especially in a new market. Copylite Products of Ft Lauderdale used the CeBIT computer-and-automation show in Hannover, Germany, to establish itself in Europe. The result was a distribution centre in Rotterdam and six distributors covering eight countries. Its $40,000 investment in the trade show has reaped millions in new business.[60]

4 Attendance is one of the best ways to contact government officials and decision makers, especially in China. For example, participation in the Chinese Export Commodities Fair, which is held twice a year in Guangzhou, China, is 'expected' by the host government.

5 Trade fairs provide an excellent chance for market research and collecting competitive intelligence. The exporter is able to view most rivals at the same time and to test comparative buyer reactions. Trade fairs provide one of the most inexpensive ways of obtaining evaluative data on the effectiveness of a promotional campaign.

6 Exporters are able to reach a sizeable number of sales prospects in a brief time period at a reasonable cost per contact. According to research by Hannover Messe, more than 86 per cent of all attendees represent buying influences (managers with direct responsibility for purchasing products and services). Of equal significance is the fact that trade show visitors are there because they have a specific interest in the exhibits.[61] Similarly, suppliers can be identified. One US apparel manufacturer at the International Trade Fair for Clothing Machinery in Cologne paid for its participation by finding a less expensive thread supplier.[62]

On the other hand, the following are among the reasons cited for nonparticipation in trade fairs:

1 High costs. These can be avoided by participating in events sponsored by the UK Department of Trade and Industry or exhibiting at UK trade centres or export development offices. An exporter can also lower costs by sharing expenses with distributors or representatives. Further, the costs of closing a sale through trade shows are estimated to be much lower than for a sale closed through personal representation.

2 Difficulty in choosing the appropriate trade fairs for participation. This is a critical decision. Because of scarce resources, many firms rely on suggestions from their foreign distributors on which fairs to attend and what specifically to exhibit. Caterpillar, for example, usually allows its foreign dealers to make the selections for themselves. In markets where conditions are more restricted for exporters, such as China, Caterpillar in effect serves as the dealer and thus participates itself.

3 For larger exporters with multiple divisions there is the problem of coordination. Several divisions may be required to participate in the same fair under the company banner. Similarly, coordination is required with distributors and agents if joint participation is desired, which requires joint planning.

Trade show participation is too expensive to be limited to the exhibit alone. A clear set of promotional objectives would include targeting accounts and attracting them to the show with pre-show promotions using mailings, advertisements in the trade journals, or website information. Contests and giveaways are effective in attracting participants to the company's exhibition area. Major customers and attractive prospects often attend, and they should be acknowledged, for example, by arranging for a hospitality suite.[63] Finally, a system is needed to evaluate post-show performance and to track qualified leads.

Exporters may participate in general or specialized trade shows. General trade fairs are held in Hannover, Germany (see *The International Marketplace 12.3*) and Milan, Italy. An example of a specialized one is Retail Solutions, a four-day trade show on store automation held in London. Participants planning to exhibit at large trade shows may elect to do so independently or as part of a national pavilion. For small and medium-sized companies the benefit of a group pavilion is in both cost and ease of the arrangements. These pavilions are often part of governmental export-promotion programmes. Even foreign government assistance may be available; for example, the Japanese External Trade Organization (JETRO) helps non-Japanese companies participate in the country's two largest trade shows.

Other promotional events that the exporter can use are trade missions, seminar missions, solo exhibitions, video/catalogue exhibitions and virtual trade shows. **Trade missions** can be UK-specialized trade missions or industry-organized, government-approved (IOGA) trade missions, both of which aim at expanding the sales of UK goods and services and the establishment of agencies and representation abroad. The UK Department of Trade and Industry is actively involved in assistance of both types. **Seminar missions** are events in which eight to ten firms are invited to participate in a one- to four-day forum, during which the team members conduct generic discussions on technological issues — that is, follow a soft-sell approach. This is followed up by individual meetings with end users, government agencies, research institutions and other potentially useful contacts. Individual firms may introduce themselves to certain markets by proposing a technical seminar there. Synopses of several alternative proposed lectures, together with company details and the qualifications of the speakers, must be forwarded to the proper body, which will circulate the proposals to interested bodies and coordinate all the arrangements. The major drawback is the time required to arrange for such a seminar, which may be as much as a year. **Solo exhibitions** are generally limited to one, or at the most, a few product themes and are held only when market conditions warrant them. Philips' approach is the Philips Electronics Circus, which features three interconnected tents equipped with the company's latest technology. The idea is to let consumers experience the latest technology, thus helping to boost brand recognition and sales.[64] **Video/catalogue exhibitions** allow exporters to publicize their products at low cost. They consist of 20 to 35 product presentations on videotapes, each lasting five to ten minutes. They provide the advantage of actually showing the product in use to potential customers. **Virtual trade shows** enable exporters to promote their products and services over the internet and to have electronic presence without actually attending a trade show.[65] Trade leads and international sales interests are collected and forwarded by the sponsor to the companies for follow-up. The information stays online for 365 days for one flat fee. The virtual trade zone is promoted heavily and buyers are given a chance to review company information for possible contact.[66]

Personal selling

Personal selling is the most effective of the promotional tools available to the marketer; however, its costs per contact are high. The average cost of sales calls may vary from $200 to $1,100, depending on the industry and the product or service. Personal selling allows for immediate feedback on customer reaction as well as information on markets.

The exporter's sales effort is determined by the degree of internationalization in its efforts, as shown in Exhibit 12.5. As the degree of internationalization advances, so will the exporter's own role in carrying out or controlling the sales function.

Indirect exports When the exporter uses indirect exports to reach international markets, the export process is externalized; in other words, the intermediary, such as an EMC, will

THE INTERNATIONAL **MARKETPLACE 12.3**

At the fair

CeBIT is the Olympic Games of industrial exposition. With more than 4,000,000 square feet (360,000 square metres) of indoor exhibition space and over 6,000 exhibitors, the Hannover-based event is ten times as large as most trade shows anywhere in the world. It is superbly organized, with its own train station, post office, over 30 restaurants and 600 permanent staff. While the range of exhibits covers everything available in information technology and communications, the 2005 fair focused particularly on mobile services, digital lifestyle, IT Security and IT outsourcing services.

The sheer magnitude of the fair and the technology displayed there are impressive, but are not necessarily the most significant aspects of the event. Rather, it is the opportunity it presents for people from everywhere in the world to view the latest developments and learn an incredible amount about their potential. Most important, it provides the opportunity to meet hundreds of people who can become invaluable future resources, if not necessarily direct sources of future business. More than 474,000 visitors attended in 2005, including 128,500 from abroad (21,400 from Asia, 4,100 from the Americas, 4,500 from Africa, and 1,300 from the Asia-Pacific region). Over 11,000 journalists from 70 countries cover the event annually.

A total of 6,300 exhibitors from 70 countries booked space for 2006, of which 1,700 exhibitors were from the Asia-Pacific region. The worldwide participation numbers are significant, especially considering that, in addition to Hannover, regional CeBIT fairs are also available for exhibitors in Istanbul, Long Beach, New York, Shanghai and Sydney. CeBIT 2007 was attended by 6,153 exhibitors from 77 different countries, and it attracted 480,000 visitors (an increase of more than 10 per cent compared with 2006).

In 2003, the fair was preceded for the first time by a summit meeting of the industry's key decision makers and influencers. 'ICT World Forum @ CeBIT 2003' brought together many of the world's leading players in the information technology and telecommunications industries to discuss new trends and formulate new strategies. This forum continues to provide a meeting place for the international elite of the ICT world.

SOURCES: Press releases available at **http://presse.messe.de**; 'Hannover Fair 2002 Delivers As Expected', *Control Engineering* 49 (May 2002): 17; 'Hannover's Trade Fair: The Week of the Widget', *The Washington Post,* April 29, 1996, A13; Valerio Giannini, 'The Hannover Messe', *Export Today* 9 (July–August 1993): 29–32; **http://www.cebit.de**; and **http://www.ictwf.com**.

© DEUTSCHE MESSE AG

EXHIBIT 12.5

Levels of exporter
involvement in
international sales

Type of Involvement	Target of Sales Effort	Level of Exporter Involvement	Advantage/ Disadvantage
Indirect exports	Home-country–based intermediary	Low	+ No major investment in international sales − Minor learning from/ control of effort
Direct exports	Locally-based intermediary	Medium	+ Direct contact with local market − Possible gatekeeping by intermediary
Integrated exports	Customer	High	+ Generation of market-specific assets − Cost/risk

Source: Framework adapted from Reijo Luostarinen and Lawrence Welch, *International Operations of the Firm* (Helsinki, Finland: Helsinki School of Economics, 1990), chapter 1.

take care of the international sales effort. While there is no investment in international sales by the marketer, there is also no, or very little, learning about sales in the markets that buy the product. The sales effort is basically a domestic one directed at the local intermediary. This may change somewhat if the marketer becomes party to an ETC with other similar producers. Even in that case, the ETC will have its own sales force and exposure to the effort may be limited. Any learning that takes place is indirect; for example, the intermediary may advise the marketer of product adaptation requirements to enhance sales.

Direct exports At some stage, the exporter may find it necessary to establish direct contact with the target market(s), although the ultimate customer contact is still handled by locally based intermediaries, such as agents or distributors. Communication with intermediaries must ensure both that they are satisfied with the arrangement and that they are equipped to market and promote the exporter's product appropriately. Whatever the distribution arrangement, the exporter must provide basic selling aid communications, such as product specification and data literature, catalogues, the results of product testing, and demonstrated performance information – everything needed to present products to potential customers. In some cases, the exporter has to provide the intermediaries with incentives to engage in local advertising efforts. These may include special discounts, push money, or cooperative advertising. Cooperative advertising will give the exporter's product local flavour and increase the overall promotional budget for the product. However, the exporter needs to be concerned that the advertising is of sufficient quality and that the funds are spent as agreed.

For the marketer–intermediary interaction to work, four general guidelines have to be satisfied:[67]

1 Know the sales scene. Often what works in the exporter's home market will not work somewhere else. This is true especially in terms of compensation schemes. In US firms, incentives and commission play a significant role, while in most other markets salaries are the major share of compensation. The best way to approach this is to study the salary structures and incentive plans in other competitive organizations in the market in question.

2 Research the customer. Customer behaviour will vary across markets, meaning the sales effort must adjust as well. ECA International, which sells marketing information worldwide based on a membership concept (companies purchase memberships to both participate in information gathering and receive appropriate data), found that its partners' sales forces could not sell the concept in Asia. Customers wanted instead to purchase information piece by piece. Only after research and modification of the sales effort was ECA able to sell the membership idea to customers.

3   Work with the culture. Realistic objectives have to be set for the salespeople based on their cultural expectations. This is especially true in setting goals and establishing measures such as quotas. If either of these is set unrealistically, the result will be frustration for both parties. Cultural sensitivity also is required in situations where the exporter has to interact with the intermediary's sales force – in training situations, for example.[68] In some cultures, such as those in Asia, the exporter is expected to act as a teacher and more or less dictate how things are done, while in some others, such as in Northern Europe, training sessions may be conducted in a seminar-like atmosphere of give and take.

4   Learn from your local representatives. If the sales force perceives a lack of fit between the marketer's product and the market, as well as inability to do anything about it, the result will be suboptimal. A local sales force is an asset to the exporter, given its close contact with customers. Beyond daily feedback, the exporter is wise to undertake two additional approaches to exploit the experience of local salespeople. First, the exporter should have a programme by which local salespeople can visit the exporter's operations and interact with the staff. If the exporter is active in multiple markets of the same region, it is advisable to develop ways to put salespeople in charge of the exporter's products in different markets to exchange ideas and best practice. Naturally, it is in the best interest of the exporter also to make regular periodic visits to markets entered.

An approach that requires more commitment from the exporter is to employ its own sales representatives, whose main function is to represent the firm abroad to existing and potential customers and to seek new leads. It is also important to sell with intermediaries, by supporting and augmenting their efforts. This type of presence is essential at some stage of the firm's international involvement. Other promotional tools can facilitate foreign market entry, but eventually some personal selling must take place. A cooperative effort with the intermediaries is important at this stage, in that some of them may be concerned about the motives of the exporter in the long term. For example, an intermediary may worry that once the exporter has learned enough about the market, it will no longer need the services of the intermediary. If these suspicions become prevalent, sales information may no longer flow to the exporter in the quantity and quality needed.

Integrated exports In the final stage of export-based internationalization, the exporter internalizes the effort through either a sales office in the target market or a direct contact with the buyer from home base. This is part of the exporter's perceived need for increased customer relationship management, where the sales effort is linked to call-centre technologies, customer-service departments, and the company's website. This may include also automating the sales force as seen in *The International Marketplace 12.4*. Advancements in 3G networks, VoIP (voice-over-internet protocol), and dual-mode handsets will bring new opportunities to account management, and real-time reporting tools will enable managers to gain insight into the sales process like nothing previously seen.

The establishment of a sales office does not have to mean an end to the use of intermediaries; the exporter's salespeople may be dedicated to supporting intermediaries' sales efforts. At this stage, expatriate sales personnel, especially those needed to manage the effort locally or regionally, may be used. The benefits of expatriates are their better understanding of the company and its products, and their ability to transfer best practice to the local operation. With expatriate management, the exporter can exercise a high amount of control over the sales function. Customers may also see the sales office and its expatriate staff as a long-term commitment to the market. The challenges lie mostly in the fit of the chosen individual to the new situation. The cost of having expatriate staff is considerable, approximately 2.5 times the cost at home, and the availability of suitable talent may be a problem, especially if the exporting organization is relatively small.[69]

The role of personal selling is greatest when the exporter sells directly to the end user or to governmental agencies, such as foreign trade organizations. Firms selling products with high price tags (such as the Airbus) or companies selling to monopolies (such as Seagrams liquor to certain Northern European countries, where all liquor sales are through state-controlled

THE INTERNATIONAL **MARKETPLACE 12.4**

Automating the sales force

Dataram Corp. saw its sales shriveling and its distributor-based sales struggling to meet the needs of a rapidly changing market. To survive, Dataram executives decided the company had to go directly to its worldwide customers. However, with only a few in-house sales representatives and inadequate mechanisms to track leads and service customers, the Princeton, New Jersey–based supplier of storage and memory products for high-end computers faced an uphill battle against formidable odds.

The most critical decision in Dataram's change of approach was to automate its sales force. The company's sales representatives and managers worldwide now are equipped with Dell notebook computers listing vital information about their clients and the company's products and services. The system is used to manage database marketing activity, such as lead generation and tracking, trade shows, telemarketing, advertising tracking, product support and customer service. Management can also spot emerging trends, avert impending disasters and forecast sales with the help of the system. 'When a sales rep can answer a question in 15 minutes instead of three days, the company is perceived as a consultant as much as a vendor', say company officials. Recruiting salespeople may be easier when a company can offer state-of-the-art support. Futhermore, if turnover takes place, important customer information is not lost but preserved in the database.

Sales Force automation (SFA), like anything else in marketing, is subject to the realities of the international environment: borders, time zones, languages, and cultures. Sales professionals may see their customer accounts as proprietary and may not be willing to share information for fear of losing their leverage. Furthermore, in markets in which personal relationships drive sales practices, such as in Latin America, technological wizardry may be frowned upon. Representatives in every country may want to do things slightly differently, which means that a system that can be localized is needed. This localization may be as comprehensive as complete language translations or as minor as changing address fields in the database. Another issue to be considered is cost – hardware costs are higher in Europe, and telecommunications costs have to be factored in. Finally, with transoceanic support needs, the company may want to look for local support or invest in keeping desk personnel on board at off-hours.

A significant concern is the cost. The cost of SFA software varies per company size and per bundle. For example, The Soffront Sales Force Automation includes: Soffront Sales, Soffront Mobile Sales, Soffront Multi-Channel Contract Centre, Soffront Knowledge Management for Sales, Soffront Business Rules for Sales and Soffront Customization Tools. However, according to a recent study, automated companies have realized sales increases of 10 to 30 per cent, and in some cases as much as 100 per cent.

Complaints are also heard. While initial reactions to the use of technology are normally high, six months after implementation some companies report negative job-related perceptions by salespeople, some even going so far as to reject the technology. Poor results are especially likely when salespeople feel that their jobs or roles are being threatened. These facts need to be incorporated into the implementation plan of any SFA programme.

SOURCES: 'How Sales Teams Should Use CRM', *Customer Relationship Management* 10 (February 2006): 30–35; Cheri Speier and Viswanath Venkatesh, 'The Hidden Minefields in the Adoption of Sales Force Automation Techniques', *Journal of Marketing* 66 (July 2002): 98–111; 'Increasing Sales Force Performance', *Industrial Distribution,* July 2002, 30; Kathleen V. Schmidt, 'Why SFA Is a Tough Sell in Latin America', *Marketing News,* January 3, 2000; Steven Barth, 'Building a Global Infrastructure', *World Trade,* April 1999, S8–S10; Eric J. Adams, 'Sales Force Automation: The Second Time Around', *World Trade,* March 1996, 72–74; 'Risky Business', *World Trade,* December 1995, 50–51; and 'Power Tool', *World Trade,* November 1993, 42–44. See also **http://www.dataram.com**, **http://www.soffront.com**.

outlets) must rely heavily on person-to-person communication, oral presentations, and direct-marketing efforts. Many of these firms can expand their business only if their markets are knowledgeable about what they do. This may require corporate advertising and publicity generation through extensive public relations efforts.

Whatever the sales task, effectiveness is determined by a number of interrelated factors. One of the keys to personal selling is the salesperson's ability to adapt to the customer and the selling situation.[70] This aspect of selling requires cultural knowledge and empathy; for example, in the Middle East, sales presentations may be broken up by long discussions of topics that have little or nothing to do with the transaction at hand. The characteristics of the buying task, whether routine or unique, have a bearing on the sales presentation. The exporter may be faced by a situation in which the idea of buying from a foreign entity is the biggest obstacle in terms of the risks perceived. If the exporter's product does not provide a clear-cut relative advantage over that of competitors, the analytical, interpersonal skills of the salesperson are needed to assist in the differentiation. A salesperson, regardless of the market, must have a thorough knowledge of the product or service. The more the salesperson is able to apply that knowledge to the particular situation, the more likely it is that he or she will obtain a positive result. The salesperson usually has front-line responsibility for the firm's customer relations, having to handle conflict situations such as the parent firm's bias for domestic markets and thus the possibility that shipments of goods to foreign clients receive low priority.

SUMMARY

Effective communication is essential in negotiating agreements. To maximize the outcome of negotiations with clients and partners from other cultural backgrounds, international marketers must show adjustment capability to different standards and behaviours. Success depends on being prepared and remaining flexible, whatever the negotiation style in the host country.

Effective and efficient communication is needed for the dual purpose of (1) informing prospective customers about the availability of products or services and (2) persuading customers to opt for the marketer's offering over those of competitors. Within the framework of the company's opportunities, resources, and objectives, decisions must be made about whether to direct communications to present customers, potential cus-

tomers, the general public, or intermediaries. Decisions must be made on how to reach each of the intended target audiences without wasting valuable resources. A decision also has to be made about who will control the communications effort: the exporter, an agency, or local representatives. Governmental agencies are the best sources of export promotion support, which is essential in alleviating the environmental threats perceived by many exporters.

The exporting international marketer must also choose tools to use in the communications effort. Usually, two basic tools are used: (1) mass selling through business and trade journals, direct mail, the internet, trade shows and missions; and (2) personal selling, which brings the international marketer face-to-face with the targeted customer.

Key terms

customer relationship management	pull strategies
database marketing	push strategies
decoding	seminar missions
encoding	solo exhibitions
feedback	telemarketing
integrated marketing communications	telemarketing
noise	trade missions
outcome	video/catalogue exhibitions
promotional mix	virtual trade shows

Questions for discussion

1 What is potentially harmful in going out of one's way to make clients feel comfortable by playing down status distinctions such as titles?

2 Discuss this statement: 'Lack of foreign-language skills puts UK negotiators at a disadvantage'.

3 Compare and contrast the usefulness to a novice exporter of elements of the promotional mix.

4 Why do exporters usually choose UK-based services when placing advertisements to boost export sales specifically?

5   Some exporters report that they value above all the broad exposure afforded through exhibiting at a trade show, regardless of whether they are able to sell directly at the event. Comment on this philosophy.

6   What specific advice would you give to an exporter who has used domestic direct marketing extensively and wishes to continue the practice abroad?

Internet exercises

1   The success of CeBIT in Hannover has prompted Deutsche Messe AG to market the CeBIT concept outside Germany using the slogan 'CeBIT Worldwide Events'. Using **http://www.cebit.de**, suggest a rationale for this.

2   Will the availability of Better Business Framework on the internet add to its ability to 'offer UK firms a means to promote their businesses worldwide' and 'attract appropriate foreign customers'? The service is available at **http://www.dti.gov.uk/index.html**.

Recommended readings

Butler, David. *Bottom-Line Call Centre Management: Creating a Culture of Accountability and Excellent Customer Service.* New York: Butterworth-Heineman, 2004.

Handbook of International Direct and E-Marketing. London: Kogan Page Ltd., 2001.

Hodge, Sheida. *Global Smarts: The Art of Communicating and Deal Making Anywhere in the World.* New York: John Wiley and Sons, 2000.

Jagoe, John R. and Agnes Brown. *Export Sales and Marketing Manual.* Washington, DC: Export Institute, 2001.

Monye, Sylvester O. *The Handbook of International Marketing Communications.* Malden, MA: Blackwell Publishers, 2000.

Reedy, Joel, Shauna Schullo and Kenneth Zimmerman. *Electronic Marketing.* Mason, OH: Cengage South-Western, 2003.

Schuster, Camille P. and Michael J. Copeland. *Global Business: Planning for Sales and Negotiations.* Mason, OH: Cengage/South-Western, 1997.

Shimp, Terence A. *Advertising, Promotion, and Supplemental Aspects of Integrated Marketing Communications.* Mason, OH: Cengage South-Western, 2006.

Thompson, Keith. *Sales Automation Done Right.* Mississauga, ON: SalesWay Press, 2005.

Tussie, Diane, (ed.). *The Environment and International Trade Negotiations.* London: St. Martin's Press, 1999.

Zeff, Robbin Lee and Brad Aronson. *Advertising on the internet.* New York: John Wiley and Sons, 1999.

Zimmerman, Jan and Hoon Meng Ong. *Marketing on the internet.* New York: Maximum Press, 2002.

Notes

1   Wilbur Schramm and Donald F. Roberts, *The Process and Effects of Mass Communications* (Urbana: University of Illinois Press, 1971), 12–17.

2   John L. Graham and Persa Economou, 'Introduction to the Symposium on International Business Negotiations', *Journal of International Business Studies* 29 (no. 4, 1998): 661–663.

3   Joel Reedy, Shauna Schullo and Kenneth Zimmerman, *Electronic Marketing* (Mason, OH: South-Western, 2003), chapter 17.

4   'What's Working for Other American Companies', *International Sales & Marketing,* November 22, 1996, 5.

5   George Field, Hotaka Katahira and Jerry Wind, *Leveraging Japan: Marketing to the New Asia* (Hoboken, NJ: Jossey-Bass, 1999), chapter 10.

6   'Overseas Call Centres Can Cost Firms Goodwill', *Marketing News,* April 15, 2004, 21; and 'Lost in Translation', *The Economist,* November 29, 2003, 58.

7   John A. Quelch and Lisa R. Klein, 'The internet and International Marketing', *Sloan Management Review* 38 (Spring 1996): 60–75.

8   Terence Brake, Danielle Walker and Thomas Walker, *Doing Business Internationally: The Guide to Cross-Cultural Success* (New York: McGraw-Hill Trade, 1994), chapters 1 and 2.

9   Courtney Fingan, 'Table Manners', *Global Business,* July 2000, 48–52.

10 Nina Reynolds, Antonis Simintiras and Efi Vlachou, 'International Business Negotiations: Present Knowledge and Direction for Future Research', *International Marketing Review* 20 (number 3, 2003): 236–261.

11 Nurit Zaidman, 'Stereotypes of International Managers: Content and Impact on Business Interactions', *Group and Organization Management* 25 (March 2000): 45–66.

12 Xiaohua Lin and Stephen J. Miller, 'Negotiation Approaches: Direct and Indirect Effect of National Culture', *International Marketing Review* 20 (number 3, 2003): 286–303.

13 Arnold Pachtman, 'Getting to 'Hao! *International Business,* July/August 1998, 24–26.

14 Claude Cellich, 'FAQ . . . About Business Negotiations on the internet', *International Trade Forum,* 15 (no. 1, 2001): 10–11.

15 Pervez N. Ghauri, 'Guidelines for International Business Negotiations', *International Marketing Review* 4 (Autumn 1986): 72–82.

16 Palhegyi Kristina (2010) 'Negotiating business in a moderately high-context culture'. Online. Available from: **http://www.filolog.com/crosscultureNegotiation.html** (Accessed 15/04/09).

17 Gottschalk, Andrew (2009) 'Negotiating with the British: From across the waters'. Online. Available from: **http://www.medius-associates.com/public_downloads/ articles/Negotiating_with_the_British.pdf** (Accessed 15/04/09).

18 **http://dti.gov.uk/about/dti-ministerial-team/ pages31380.html**

19 Cateora, P.R. and P.N. Ghauri. *International Marketing* (Maidenhead, McGraw-Hill Publishing, 2002), reproduced with the kind permission of the McGraw-Hill publishing companies.

20 Catherine H. Tinsley and Madan M. Pillutla, 'Negotiating in the United States and Hong Kong', *Journal of International Business Studies* 29 (no. 4, 1998): 711–728.

21 Claude Cellich, 'Negotiations for Export Business: Elements for Success', *International Trade Forum* 9 (no. 4, 1995): 20–27.

22 Jackie Mayfield, Milton Mayfield, Drew Martin and Paul Herbig, 'How Location Impacts International Business Negotiations', *Review of Business* 19 (Winter 1998): 21–24.

23 'Stay-at-Home' Careers?' *Global Business,* January 2001, 62.

24 Rajesh Kumar and Verner Worm, 'Social Capital and the Dynamics of Business Negotiations Between the Northern Europeans and the Chinese', *International Marketing Review* 20 (number 3, 2003): 262–285.

25 Framework for this section adapted from John L. Graham and Roy A. Herberger, Jr., 'Negotiators Abroad – Don't Shoot from the Hip', *Harvard Business Review* 61 (July– August 1983): 160–168.

26 Sally Stewart and Charles F. Keown, 'Talking with the Dragon: Negotiating in the People's Republic of China', *Columbia Journal of World Business* 24 (Fall 1989): 68–72.

27 Zarkada-Fraser, A. and Fraser, C. 'Moral decision making in international sales negotiations', *Journal of Business & Industrial Marketing*, 16 (no. 4, 2001): 274–293.

28 Frank L. Acuff, 'Just Call Me Mr. Ishmael', *Export Today* 11 (July 1995): 14–15.

29 Andrea Kirby, 'Doing Business in Asia', *Credit Management,* October 2002, 24–25.

30 Kathy Schmidt, 'How to Speak So You're Open to Interpretation', *Presentations* 13 (December 1999): 126–127.

31 Berry J. Kesselman and Bryan Batson, 'China: Clause and Effect', *Export Today* 12 (June 1996): 18–26.

32 Ilkka A. Ronkainen, 'Project Exports and the CMEA', in *International Marketing Management*, Erdener Kaynak (ed.) (New York: Praeger, 1984), 305–317.

33 Richard D. Lewis, *When Cultures Collide* (London: Nicholas Brealey Publishing, 2000), chapter 17.

34 Y. H. Wong and Thomas K. Leung, *Guanxi: Relationship Marketing in a Chinese Context* (Binghamton, NY: Haworth Press, 2001), chapter 3.

35 Richard W. Lewis, *Absolut Book: The Absolut Vodka Advertising Story* (New York: Journey Editions, 1996); and Richard W. Lewis, *Absolut Sequel: The Absolut Advertising Story Continues* (New York: Periplus Editions, 2005). For the latest ads in the series, see **http://www.absolut.com**.

36 The DrinkShop.com (2010) 'Producer Information'. Online. Available from: **http://www.thedrinkshop.com/products/ nlpdetail.php?prodid=628** (Accessed 15/4/09).

37 Attwood, K. (2007) 'Diageo demonstrates Absolut conviction'. *The Independent*, 13 March 2007 Online. Available from: **http://www.independent.co.uk/news/ business/news/diageo-demonstrates-absolut-conviction-440014.html** (Accessed 15/4/09).

38 Suzuki G.B. (2009) 'Suzuki on-road promotions'. Online. Available from: **http://www.suzuki-gb.co.uk/promos/ promo.php?id=000019** (Accessed 19/4/09).

39 **http://www.volkswagen.co.uk/home**

40 Sean Callahan, 'McCann-Erickson Offers B-to-B Clients the World', *Business Marketing,* January 2000, 35.

41 *The Handbook of International Direct and E-Marketing* (London: Kogan Page Ltd., 2001), chapter 1.

42 Hope Katz Gibbs, 'Mediums for the Message', *Export Today* 15 (June 1999): 22–27.

43 Deborah Begum, 'U.S. Retailers Find Mail-Order Happiness in Japan', *World Trade,* 13 (May 1996): 22–25.

44 William McDonald, 'International Direct Marketing in a Rapidly Changing World', *Direct Marketing* 61 (March 1999): 44–47.

45 Hope Katz Gibbs, 'It's Your Call', *Export Today* 13 (May 1997): 46–51. For examples, see Brendan Reid, 'Call Centre Showcase', *Call Centre Magazine* 15 (March 2002): 40–41. See also **http://www.callcenterops.com**.

46 Sam Bloomfield, 'Reach Out and Touch Someone Far, Far Away', *World Trade,* April 1999, 80–84.

47 Melanie May, 'The World is DM's Oyster', *Marketing Direct,* December 2005, 38–43.

48 For a discussion on marketing on the internet, see K. Douglas Hoffman, Michael R. Czinkota, Peter R. Dickson, Patrick Dunne, Abbie Griffith, Michael D. Hutt, John H. Lindgren, Robert F. Lusch, Ilkka A. Ronkainen, Bert Rosenbloom, Jagdish N. Sheth, Terence A. Shimp, Judy A. Siguaw, Penny M. Simpson, Thomas W. Speh and Joel E. Urbany, *Marketing: Best Practices* (Mason, OH: South-Western, 2003), chapter 15.

49 P. Rajan Varadarajan and Manjit Yadav, 'Marketing Strategy and the internet', *Academy of Marketing Science* 30 (Fall 2002): 296–312.

50 'International in Internet Closes U.S. Lead', *Marketing News,* February 14, 2000, 7.

51 **http://www.fairplaypartnership.org. uk/currentinitiatives age.html**

52 Gerry Dempsey, 'A Hands-On Guide for Multilingual WebSites', *World Trade,* September 1999, 68–70.

53 V. Kanti Prasad, K. Ramamurthy and G. M. Naidu, 'The Influence of Internet-Marketing Integration on Marketing Competencies and Export Performance', *Journal of International* Marketing 9 (no. 4, 2001): 82–110.

54 Lewis Rose, 'Before You Advertise on the Net – Check the International Marketing Laws', *Bank Marketing,* May 1996, 40–42.

55 'Marketers Aim New Ads at Video iPod Users', *The Wall Street Journal,* January 31, 2006, B1.

56 Thomas V. Bonoma, 'Get More Out of Your Trade Shows', *Harvard Business Review* 61 (January–February 1983): 137–145.

57 'It's Show Time', *Marketing News,* August 15, 2005, 9. See also, **http://www.exhibitsurveys.com**.

58 Kathleen V. Schmidt, 'Trading Plätze', *Marketing News,* July 19, 1999, 11.

59 **http://www.3gsmworldcongress.com**.

60 Richard B. Golik, 'The Lure of Foreign Trade Shows', *International Business,* March 1996, 16–20.

61 **http://www.messe.de/27711** for 'Trade Shows as a B2B Communication Tool'.

62 'IMB '97 a Hit: Cologne Show Draws 30,000 Manufacturers from 100 Countries', *Apparel Industry Magazine,* August 1997, 16–26.

63 Bob Lamons, 'Involve Your Staff in Trade Shows for Better Results', *Marketing News,* March 1, 1999, 9–10.

64 'Philips under the Big Top', *Advertising Age,* December 1, 2003, 3, 36.

65 Liz Lee-Kelley, David Gilbert, and Nada F. Al-Shehabi, 'Virtual Exhibitions; An Exploratory Study of Middle East Exhibitors' Dispositions', *International Marketing Review* 21 (number 6, 2004): 634–644.

66 **http://www.ahead-bs.com/**

67 Charlene Solomon, 'Managing an Overseas Sales Force', *World Trade,* April 1999, S4–S6.

68 Sergio Román and Salvador Ruiz, 'A Comparative Analysis of Sales Training in Europe: Implications for International Sales Negotiations', *International Marketing Review* 20 (number 3, 2003): 304–326.

69 For a detailed discussion of the expatriate phenomenon, see Michael R. Czinkota, Ilkka A. Ronkainen and Michael H. Moffett, *International Business* (Mason, OH: South-Western, 2005), chapter 19.

70 Lisa Bertagnoli, 'Selling Overseas Complex Endeavor', *Marketing News,* July 30, 2001, 4.

CHAPTER 13
DISTRIBUTION
MANAGEMENT

Managing channel conflict is a key issue for mobile retail distribution

With direct retail sales accounting for some 30 per cent of the total by 2009, or US$ 46 billion worldwide, the challenge for operators, vendors and content providers is how to deliver mass market services in the most effective way. 'Probably the main enabler for this is communication, both vertical – to and from the supplier, and horizontal – between the different channels', says the report's lead author Richard Jesty. By clearly communicating its goals and objectives, and then underpinning these with guidelines such as service level agreements, mobile value chain players can help to manage the potential disruption of traditional 'bricks and mortar' retail channels by the newer forms of distribution.

A powerful driver for this trend towards direct forms of retailing is the increasing importance of mobile content in the merchandising mix over the coming years. Informa Telecoms & Media estimates that around 95 per cent of mobile content is distributed directly today – for example by premium SMS or direct response to a call centre. To reach a mass market audience, mobile value chain players need to get a balance between this kind of direct delivery and indirect delivery via distributors and retailers. The critical factor here for all players is how to put mobile services such as games or music in front of consumers on the high street or in a shopping mall.

One way of doing this is to set up multimedia kiosks in retail stores so that consumers can 'browse and buy' online using a touchscreen and then download content to their phone via a short range link such as Bluetooth. Another way is to distribute mobile content in a pre-packaged form so that consumers can pick it up in a self-service environment from a supermarket or high street store.

'We're seeing an emerging trend for music and games to be offered on removable memory cards which can be used in mobile phones – but it's still early days for this kind of product', comments Richard Jesty.

This new breed of distribution channels includes developments such as installing multimedia terminals in convenience stores, or offering mobile prepaid top-up services through bank cash machines. This trend has channel management implications for vendors and operators, since the commercial terms offered to each type of channel will need to be appropriate to each trading environment. There are also implications for the technical infrastructure and service platform, because service delivery can take place instore, via direct mail or via over-the-air downloading.

Equally, the increase in importance of packaged software being sold through supermarkets and other national chains will call for a new supply channel involving logistics and distribution specialists, and requiring a new range of value added services from these players.

The new strategic report from Informa Telecoms & Media (Mobile Distribution and Retail 2005) is published this month, and covers the mobile distribution and retail industries worldwide, bringing together Informa Telecoms and Medis's latest forecasts which are based on its ongoing programme of research amongst key players in the mobile business. A feature of this research is the online survey of telecoms professionals worldwide. In addition, a number of case studies of leading edge practice are presented, illustrating current themes and trends in the market, along with selected profiles of leading players.

SOURCE: Mobile Europe (2005) 'Managing channel conflict is a key issue for mobile retail distribution' **http://www.mobileeurope.co.uk/news_wire/ 111051/Managing_channel_conflict_is_a_key_issue_for_mobile_retail_ distribution.html** (13/1/10)

Channels of distribution provide the essential linkages that connect producers and customers. The links are intracompany and extracompany entities that perform a number of functions. Optimal distribution systems are flexible and are able to adjust to market conditions over both the short and long terms. In general, companies use one or more of the following distribution systems: (1) the firm sells directly to customers through its own field sales force or through electronic commerce; (2) the company operates through independent **intermediaries**, usually at the local level; or (3) the business depends on an outside distribution system that may have regional or global coverage.

A channel of distribution should be seen as more than a sequence of marketing institutions connecting producers and consumers; it should be a team working toward a common goal.[1] Too often intermediaries are mistakenly perceived as temporary market-entry vehicles and not the partners with whom marketing efforts are planned and implemented. The intermediary is often the de facto marketing arm of the producer/originator. In today's marketing environment, being close to customers, be they the final consumer or intermediary and solving their problems, are vital to bringing about success. For example, when an office supplier superstore has established a joint venture in a foreign country, there is a need to dispatch employees to the country subsidiary to educate that division on the special needs of a superstore. If this partnership is compromised, the result is channel conflict, as seen in *The International Marketplace 13.1*.

Since most marketers cannot or do not want to control the distribution function completely, structuring channel relationships becomes a crucial task. The importance of this task is further compounded by the fact that the channel decision is the most long-term of the marketing mix decisions in that, once established, it cannot easily be changed. In export marketing, a new dimension is added to the task: the export channel decision, in addition to making market-specific decisions. An experienced exporter may decide that control is of utmost importance and choose to perform tasks itself and incur the information collection and adaptation costs. An infrequent exporter, on the other hand, may be quite dependent on experienced intermediaries to get its product to markets. Whether export tasks are self-performed or assigned to export intermediaries, the distribution function should be planned so that the channel will function as one rather than as a collection of different or independent units.

The decisions involved in the structuring and management of the export channel of distribution are discussed first, including an evaluation of a distribution challenge presented by parallel imports. The chapter will end with a discussion of the steps needed in preparation for e-commerce. Logistics issues will be discussed in detail in Chapter 16.

CHANNEL STRUCTURE

A generalization of channel configurations for consumer and industrial products as well as services is provided in Exhibit 13.1. Channels can vary from direct, producer-to-consumer types to elaborate, multilevel channels employing many types of intermediaries, each serving a particular purpose. For example, Canadian software firms enter international markets by exporting directly from Canada (40 per cent), by opening their own sales offices (14 per cent), by entering into cooperative arrangements with other exporters (15 per cent), by using a local distributor or a value-adding reseller (13 per cent), or by a mixture of modes (17 per cent).[2] British firms, on the other hand, exported directly in 60 per cent of the cases, 8 per cent opened a foreign sales office, 5 per cent used an agent, and the remainder entered a cooperative export effort such as piggybacking, in which the exporter uses another company's channel to enter a foreign market.[3] Software makers use the internet to communicate with foreign counterparts and to find new partners. Firms also derive substantial benefits from delivering value-added services to users over the internet.[4] However, the internet has limited capability to substitute for personal sales.

Channel configurations for the same product will vary within industries, even within the same firm, because national markets quite often have unique features. This may mean dramatic departures from accepted policy for a company. For example, to reach the British market, which is dominated by a few retailers such as Tesco, Asda, J. Sainsbury's and Morrisons, marketers such as Heinz may have to become suppliers to these retailers' private-label programmes in addition to making their own efforts.[5] A firm's international market

EXHIBIT 13.1   Channel configuration

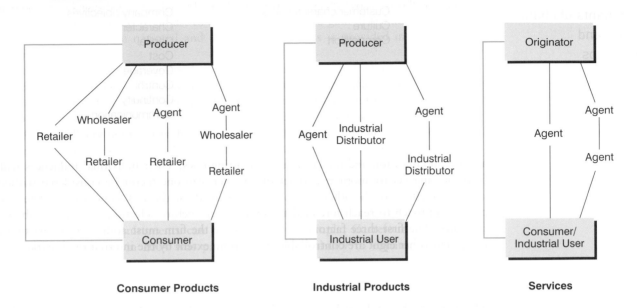

Consumer Products   **Industrial Products**   **Services**

experience will also cause variation in distribution patterns. AMPAK, a manufacturer of packaging machinery, uses locally-based distributors in markets where it is well established. Others are entered indirectly by using domestically based intermediaries: either by using the services of trading companies or through selling to larger companies, which then market the products alongside their own.

The connections made by marketing institutions are not solely for the physical movement of goods. They also serve as transactional title flows and informational communication flows. Rather than unidirectional, downward from the producer, the flows are usually multi-directional, both vertical and horizontal. As an example, the manufacturer relies heavily on the retailer population for data on possible changes in demand. Communications from retailers may be needed to coordinate a cooperative advertising campaign instituted by a manufacturer. The three flows – physical, transactional and informational – do not necessarily take place simultaneously or occur at every level of the channel. Agent intermediaries, for example, act only to facilitate the information flow; they do not take title and often do not physically handle the goods. Similarly, electronic intermediaries, such as amazon.com, have to rely on facilitating agents to perform the logistics function of their operation.

As only a few products are sold directly to ultimate users, an international marketer has to decide on alternative ways to move products to chosen markets. The basic marketing functions of exchange, physical movement, and various facilitating activities must be performed, but the marketer may not be equipped to handle them. Intermediaries can therefore be used to gain quick, easy and relatively low-cost entry to a targeted market.

CHANNEL DESIGN

The term *channel design* refers to the length and the width of the channel employed.[6] Length is determined by the number of levels or different types of intermediaries. In the case of consumer products, the most traditional is the producer–wholesaler–retailer–customer configuration. Channel width is determined by the number of institutions of each type in the channel. An industrial goods marketer may grant exclusive distribution rights to a foreign entity, whereas a consumer goods marketer may want to use as many intermediaries as possible to ensure intensive distribution.

Channel design is determined by factors that can be summarized as the 11 Cs, listed in Exhibit 13.2. These factors are integral to both the development of new marketing channels

significant investment, but is necessary to ensure customer trust through superior execution of marketing programs. In developing markets, the lack of available intermediaries encourages the integration of distribution functions but requires direct investment in the market.[20]

Cost

Closely related to the capital dimension is cost – that is, the expenditure incurred in maintaining a channel once it is established. Costs will naturally vary over the life cycle of a relationship with a particular channel member, as well as over the life cycle of the products marketed. An example of the costs involved is promotional money spent by a distributor for the marketer's product. A cooperative advertising deal between the international marketer and the intermediary would typically split the costs of the promotional campaign executed in the local market.

Costs will vary in terms of the relative power of the manufacturer vis-à-vis its intermediaries. The number of European retailers accounting for 75 per cent of consumer sales has decreased from 132 in 1980 to 40 in 2005. This consolidation includes not only large retailers such as Ahold and Migros but also smaller retailers that have joined forces to form buying groups. One of the most significant is Expert Global, which has a total of 7,400 participating retailers in 22 European, North American, South American and Pacific countries. The concentrated distribution systems being developed by these giants are eroding the marketing strength of manufacturers, which lay in their networks of distribution depots that delivered direct to stores. Now, retailers want delivery to their central distribution centres. In addition, they are pushing stockholding costs to manufacturers by demanding more frequent deliveries, in smaller, mixed loads, with shorter delivery time.[21]

Costs may also be incurred in protecting the company's distributors against adverse market conditions. Some manufacturers help their distributors maintain competitive prices through subsidies when the exchange rate of the home country causes pricing problems. Extra financing aid can be extended to distributors that have been hit with competitive adversity. Such support, although often high in monetary cost, will pay back manyfold through a smoother manufacturer–distributor relationship.

Coverage

The term *coverage* is used to describe both the number of areas in which the marketer's products are represented and the quality of that representation. Coverage is therefore two-dimensional, in that horizontal coverage and vertical coverage need to be considered in channel design. The number of areas to be covered depends on the dispersion of demand in the market and also on the time elapsed since the product's introduction to the market. Three different approaches are available:

1 Intensive coverage, which calls for distributing the product through the largest number of different types of intermediaries and the largest number of individual intermediaries of each type.

2 Selective coverage, which entails choosing a number of intermediaries for each area to be penetrated.

3 Exclusive coverage, which involves only one entity in a market.

Generally, intensive and selective coverage call for longer channels using different types of intermediaries, usually wholesalers and agents. Exclusive distribution is conducive to more direct sales. For some products, such as ethnic or industrial products, customers are concentrated geographically and allow for more intensive distribution with a more direct channel. A company typically enters a market with one local distributor, but as volume expands, the distribution base often has to be adjusted. The advantages of a single distributor are listed in Exhibit 13.7.

Expanding distribution too quickly may cause problems. Benetton, one of Italy's major exporters of clothing, had planned to have 1,000 stores in the United States by 1990. The plan was abandoned because of concerns about oversaturation of certain urban areas and over-projection of retail sales. Rather, more emphasize is being put on customer service, and the

EXHIBIT 13.7

Advantages of a single
distributor

1 One corporate presence eliminates confusion among buyers and local officials.

2 The volume of business that results when exports are consolidated will attract a larger/more qualified distributor. The distributor will thus have greater influence in its local business community.

3 Communication is less plagued by noise. This will have a positive effect in many areas, from daily information flows to supervising and training.

4 More effective coordination of the sales and promotional effort can be achieved through mutual learning.

5 Logistics flows are more economical.

6 A stronger presence can be maintained in smaller markets, or markets in which resources may dictate a holding mode, until more effective penetration can be undertaken.

7 Distributor morale and the overall principal–intermediary relationship are better through elimination of intrabrand competition.

Source: Adapted from Business International Corporation, *201 Checklists: Decision Making in International Operations* (New York: Business International Corporation, 1980), 26–27.

number of stores in major North American cities was 84 in 2006.[22] Similarly, expanding distribution from specialty outlets to mass distribution may have an impact on the product's image and the after-sales service associated with it. The impact on channel relations may be significant if existing dealers perceive loss of sales as a result of such a move. This may be remedied by keeping the product lines in mass-distribution outlets different, or possibly developing a different brand for the new channels.

Control

The use of intermediaries will automatically lead to loss of some control over the marketing of the firm's products.[23] The looser the relationship is between the marketer and intermediaries, the less control the marketer can exert. The longer the channel, the more difficult it becomes for the marketer to have a final say in pricing, promotion and the types of outlets in which the product will be made available.

In the initial stages of internationalization or specific market entry, an intermediary's specialized knowledge and working relationships are needed, but as exporters' experience base and sales in the market increase, many opt to establish their own sales offices. Use of intermediaries provides quick entry using an existing system in which complementary products provide synergistic benefits. Furthermore, payments are received from one entity rather than from multiple customers.

The issue of control correlates heavily with the type of product or service being marketed. In the case of industrial and high-technology products, control will be easier to institute because intermediaries are dependent on the marketer for new products and service. Where the firm's marketing strategy calls for a high level of service, integrated channels are used to ensure that the service does get performed.[24] Later on, an exporter may want to coordinate programmes across markets on a regional basis, which is much easier if the channel is controlled.

The marketer's ability and willingness to exercise any type of power – whether reward, coercive, legitimate, referent, or expert – determines the extent of control. The exercise of control causes more incidents of conflict in channels of distribution than any other activity in the relationship. This points to the need for careful communication with foreign intermediaries about the marketer's intentions and also the need for certain control measures. These might include the marketer's need to be the sole source of advertising copy or to be in charge of all product-modification activities. Generally, the more control the marketer wishes to have, the more cost is involved in securing that control.

Continuity

Channel design decisions are the most long-term of the marketing mix decisions. Utmost care must therefore be taken in choosing the right type of channel, given the types of intermediaries available and any environmental threats that may affect the channel design.

Nurturing continuity rests heavily on the marketer because foreign distributors may have a more short-term view of the relationship. For example, Japanese wholesalers believe that it is important for manufacturers to follow up initial success with continuous improvement of the product. If such improvements are not forthcoming, competitors are likely to enter the market with similar, lower-priced products, and the wholesalers of the imported product will turn to the Japanese suppliers.

Continuity is also expressed through visible market commitment. Industries abroad may be quite conservative; distributors will not generally support an outsider until they are sure it is in the market to stay. Such commitments include sending in technical or sales personnel or offering training, and setting up wholly-owned sales subsidiaries from the start – and staffing them with locals to help communicate that the company is there for the long term.[25] Investment in distributors may be literal (resulting in co-ownership in the future) or abstract (resulting in more solid commitment in the relationship).

Communication

Communication provides the exchange of information that is essential to the functioning of the channel. Communication is an important consideration in channel design, and it gains more emphasize in international distribution because of various types of distances that may cause problems. In the buyer–seller relationships in international markets, the distance that is perceived to exist between a buyer and a seller has five aspects, all of which are amplified in the international setting:[26]

1. Social distance: the extent to which each of the two entities in a relationship is familiar with the other's ways of operating.

2. Cultural distance: the degree to which the norms, values or working methods between the two entities differ because of their separate national characteristics.

3. Technological distance: the differences between the product or process technologies of the two entities.

4. Time distance: the time that must elapse between establishing contact or placing an order and the actual transfer of the product or service involved.

5. Geographical distance: the physical distance between the locations of the two entities.

All these dimensions must be considered when determining whether to use intermediaries and, if they are to be used, what types to use.

Communication, if properly utilized, will assist the international marketer in conveying the firm's goals to the distributors, in solving conflict situations, and in marketing the product overall. Communication is a two-way process that does not permit the marketer to dictate to intermediaries. Cases are well known in which the marketer is not able to make the firm's marketing programme functional. Prices may not be competitive; promotional materials may be obsolete or inaccurate and not well received overall. This may be compounded if the exporter tries to transplant abroad procedures and programmes used domestically.[27] Solving these types of problems is important to the welfare of both parties.

Channels of distribution, because of their sequential positioning of the entities involved, are not conducive to noiseless communication. The marketer must design a channel and choose intermediaries that guarantee good information flow. Proper communication involves not only the passage of information between channel members but also a better understanding of each party's needs and goals. This can be achieved through personal visits, exchange of personnel, or distribution advisory councils. Consisting of members from all channel participants, advisory councils meet regularly to discuss opportunities and problems that may have arisen.

SELECTION OF INTERMEDIARIES

Once the basic design of the channel has been determined, the international marketer must begin a search to fill the defined roles with the best available candidates, and must secure their cooperation.

Types of intermediaries

Two basic decisions are involved in choosing the type of intermediaries to serve a particular market. First, the marketer must determine the type of relationship to have with intermediaries. The alternatives are distributorship and agency relationship. A distributor will purchase the product and will therefore exercise more independence than agencies. Distributors are typically organized along product lines and provide the international marketer with complete marketing services. Agents have less freedom of movement than distributors because they operate on a commission basis and do not usually physically handle the goods. This, in turn, allows the marketer control to make sure, for example, that the customer gets the most recent and appropriate product version. In addition to the business implications, the choice of type will have legal implications in terms of what the intermediary can commit its principal to and the ease of termination of the agreement.

Second, the international marketer must decide whether to utilize indirect exporting, direct exporting, or integrated distribution in penetrating a foreign market.[28] Indirect exporting requires dealing with another domestic firm that acts as a sales intermediary for the marketer, often taking over the international side of the marketer's operations. The benefits, especially in the short term, are that the exporter can use someone else's international channels without having to pay to set them up. But there may be long-term concerns in using this strategy if the marketer wants to actively and aggressively get into the markets itself. Indirect exporting is only practised by firms very early on in their internationalization process. With direct exporting, the marketer takes direct responsibility for its products abroad by either selling directly to the foreign customer or finding a local representative to sell its products in the market. The third category of export marketing strategy, integrated exporting, requires the marketer to make an investment in the foreign market for the purpose of selling its products in that market or more broadly. This investment could be the opening, for example, of a German or EU sales office, a distribution hub, or even an assembly operation or manufacturing facility. Although the last set of strategies indicates longer-term commitment to a market, it is riskier than the first two because the marketer is making a major financial investment. For example, if the exporter moves from an agency agreement to a sales office, its costs for that market are now fixed costs (i.e., will be incurred even if no sales are made) instead of the previous variable costs. Setting up even a modest office may be expensive.[29] The cost of an office manager and a secretary can easily reach €80,000, while a full-scale sales office may cost €400,000 on an annual basis. Real estate costs can be substantial if the office is in a main business district.

The major types of intermediaries are summarized in Exhibit 13.8. Care should be taken to understand conceptual differences that might exist from one market to another. For example, a commissionario may sell in his or her own name (as a distributor would) but for an undisclosed principal (an agency concept). Similarly, a del credere agent guarantees the solvency of the customer and may therefore be responsible to the supplier for payment by the customer.[30]

The respective strengths and weaknesses of various export intermediary types were discussed in Chapter 9.

Sources for finding intermediaries

Firms that have successful international distribution attest to the importance of finding top representatives.[31] This undertaking should be held in the same regard as recruiting and hiring within the company, because an ineffective foreign distributor can set an exporter back years; it is almost better to have no distributor than a bad one in a major market.

EXHIBIT 13.8

International channel
intermediaries

Agents		
Foreign (Direct)		**Domestic (Indirect)**
Brokers		Brokers
Manufacturer's representatives		Export agents
Factors		EMCs
Managing agents		Webb-Pomerene associations
Purchasing agents		Commission agents
Distributors		
Distributors/dealers		Domestic wholesalers
Import jobbers		EMCs
Wholesalers/retailers		ETCs
		Complementary marketing

Sources: Peter B. Fitzpatrick and Alan S. Zimmerman, *Essentials of Export Marketing* (New York: American Management Association, 1985), 20; Bruce Seifert and John Ford, "Export Distribution Channels," *Columbia Journal of World Business* 24 (Summer 1989): 16; and **http://www.export.gov**.

The approach can be either passive or active. Foreign operations for a number of smaller firms start through an unsolicited order; the same can happen with foreign distribution. Distributors, wherever they are, are always on the lookout for product representation that can be profitable and status enhancing. The initial contact may result from an advertisement or from a trade show the marketer has participated in.

The marketer's best interest lies in taking an active role. The marketer should not simply use the first intermediary to show an interest in the firm. The choice should be the result of a careful planning process. The exporter should start by gaining an understanding of market conditions in order to define what is expected of an intermediary and what the exporter can offer in the relationship. At the same time, procedures need to be set for intermediary identification and evaluation.[32] The exporter does not have to do all of this independently; both governmental and private agencies can assist the marketer in locating intermediary candidates.

Governmental agencies UK Trade & Investment has various services that can assist firms in identifying suitable representatives abroad. UK Trade & Investment, with its team of expert advisers located across the globe, can help you fulfil your international ambitions. It can assist you at all stages of the business planning cycle, from inception to completion.[33] The government also provides a mechanism by which the marketer can indicate its interest in international markets. *The UK Export Buyers Guide* is a directory that includes information and displays advertisements on companies interested in exporting.

Private sources The easiest approach for the firm seeking intermediaries is to consult trade directories. Country and regional business directories such as Kompass (Europe), Bottin International (worldwide), Nordisk Handelskalendar (Northern Europe), and the Japan Trade Directory are good places to start. Company lists by country and line of business can be secured from Dun & Bradstreet, Reuben H. Donnelly or Kellysearch. Telephone directories, especially the yellow page sections or editions, can provide distributor lists. Although not detailed, these listings will give addresses and an indication of the products sold.

The firm can solicit the support of some of its facilitating agencies, such as banks, advertising agencies, shipping lines and airlines. All these have substantial international information networks and can put them to work for their clients. The services available will vary by agency, depending on the size of its foreign operations. Banks usually have the most extensive networks through their affiliates and correspondent banks. Similarly, the exporter may solicit

EXHIBIT 13.9

Del Monte Fresh Produce Company has a royalty-free perpetual licence to use the Del Monte trademark in connection with the production, manufacture, sale and distribution of prepared foods and beverages in over 100 countries throughout Europe, Africa and the Middle East. Del Monte has operated in Europe for over 75 years and is the premier brand associated with fruit-based or fruit-derived products and is the leading brand for canned fruit and pineapple in many Western European markets. Del Monte has had a presence in the United Kingdom, the largest market, since 1926 and is perceived to be a quality brand with high consumer awareness. Del Monte has a reputation with both consumers and retailers for value, quality and reliability.

© STUDIOMODE/ALAMY

Del Monte Fresh Produce Company only picks fruit once it has reached the moment of perfect ripeness. The fruit is then packed within hours with the utmost care to prevent damage and ensure that each and every can and prepared snack of Del Monte fruit contains the freshest, tastiest, juiciest fruit – delivering a taste of sunshine in every bite.

Strict quality controls are implemented at every stage of the operation to ensure that the consumer can always rely on consistent high quality product in every Del Monte item.

Products available only in Europe, the Middle East and Africa.

Source: **http://www.freshdelmonte.com/products-prepared.aspx**

the help of associations or chambers of commerce. For example, interest in China may warrant contacting British Chambers of Commerce in Beijing, Hong Kong or Shanghai.

The marketer can take an even more direct approach by buying space to solicit representation. Advertisements typically indicate the type of support the marketer will be able to give to its distributor. An example of an advertisement for intermediaries placed in a trade medium is provided in Exhibit 13.9. For example, Regent Medical, a leading exporter of surgical gloves, may advertise for intermediaries in magazines such as *International Hospital Supplies* or on websites such as **http://www.hospitalmanagement.com**. Trade fairs are an important forum to meet potential distributors and to get data on intermediaries in the industry.

Increasingly, marketers are using their own websites to attract international distributors and agents. The marketer may also deal directly with contacts from previous applications, launch new mail solicitations, use its own sales organization for the search, or communicate with existing customers to find prospective distributors. The latter may happen after a number of initial (unsolicited) sales to a market, causing the firm to want to enter the market on a

EXHIBIT 13.10

Sources for locating
foreign intermediaries

1 Distributor inquiries

2 Home government (e.g., UK Trade & Investment)

   Trade opportunities programme

   Commercial service international contacts

   Country directories of international contacts

   Agent/distributor service

   International company profile

3 Host government

   Representative offices

   Import promotion efforts

4 Trade sources

   Magazines, journals

   Directories

   Associations and Chambers of Commerce

   Banks, advertising agencies, carriers

5 Field sales organizations

6 Customers

7 Direct-mail solicitation/contact of previous applicants

8 Trade fairs

9 Websites

10 Independent consultants

more formal basis. If resources permit, the international marketer can use outside service agencies or consultants to generate a list of prospective representatives.

The purpose of using the sources summarized in Exhibit 13.10 is to generate as many prospective representatives as possible for the next step, screening.

Screening intermediaries

In most firms, the evaluation of candidates involves both what to look for and where to go for the information. At this stage, the international marketer knows the type of distributor that is needed. The potential candidates must now be compared and contrasted against determining criteria. Although the criteria to be used vary by industry and by product, a good summary list is provided in Exhibit 13.11 Especially when various criteria are being weighed, these lists must be updated to reflect changes in the environment and the marketer's own situation. Some criteria can be characterized as determinant, in that they form the core dimensions along which candidates must perform well, whereas some criteria, although important, may be used only in preliminary screening. This list should correspond closely to the exporter's own determinants of success – all the things that have to be done better to beat out competition.

Before signing a contract with a particular agent or a distributor, international marketers should satisfy themselves on certain key criteria. A number of these key criteria can be easily quantified, thereby providing a solid base for comparisons between candidates, whereas others are qualitative and require careful interpretation and confidence in the data sources providing the information.

Characteristics	Weight	Rating
Goals and strategies	–	–
Size of the firm	–	–
Financial strength	–	–
Reputation	–	–
Trading areas covered	–	–
Compatibility	–	–
Experience in products/with competitors	–	–
Sales organization	–	–
Physical facilities	–	–
Willingness to carry inventories	–	–
After-sales service capability	–	–
Use of promotion	–	–
Sales performance	–	–
Relations with local government	–	–
Communications	–	–
Overall attitude/commitment	–	–

EXHIBIT 13.11

Criteria for choosing an international distributor

Performance The financial standing of the candidate is one of the most important criteria, as well as a good starting point. This figure will show whether the distributor is making money and is able to perform some of the necessary marketing functions such as extension of credit to customers and risk absorption. Financial reports are not always complete or reliable, or they may lend themselves to interpretation differences, pointing to a need for third-party opinion. Many Latin American intermediaries lack adequate capital, a situation that can lead to more time spent managing credit than managing marketing strategy. Therefore, at companies like Xerox, assessment focuses on cash flow and the intermediary's ability to support its operations without outside help.[34]

Sales are another excellent indicator. What the distributor is presently doing gives an indication of how he or she could perform if chosen to handle the international marketer's product. The distributor's sales strength can be determined by analysing management ability and the adequacy and quality of the sales team. If the intermediary is an importer or wholesaler, its ability to provide customer service to the next channel level is a critical determinant of future sales.

The distributor's existing product lines should be analyzed along four dimensions: competitiveness, compatibility, complementary nature and quality. Quite often, international marketers find that the most desirable distributors in a given market are already handling competitive products and are therefore unavailable. In that case, the marketer can look for an equally qualified distributor handling related products. The complementary nature of products may be of interest to both parties, especially in industrial markets, where ultimate customers may be in the market for complete systems or one-stop shopping. The quality match for products is important for product positioning reasons; a high-quality product may suffer unduly from a questionable distributor reputation. The number of product lines handled gives the marketer an indication of the level of effort to expect from the distributor. Some distributors are interested in carrying as many products and product lines as possible to enhance their own standing, but they have the time and the willingness to actively sell only those that bring the best compensation. At this time, it is also important to check the candidate's physical facilities for handling the product. This is essential particularly for products that may be subject to quality changes, such as food products. The assessment should also include the candidate's marketing materials, including a possible website, for adequacy and appropriateness.

The distributor's market coverage must be determined. The analysis of coverage will include not only how much territory, or how many segments of the market, are covered, but also how well the markets are served. Again, the characteristics of the sales force and the number of sales offices are good quantitative indicators. To study the quality of the distributor's market coverage, the marketer can check whether the sales force visits executives, engineers and operating people or concentrates mainly on purchasing agents. In some areas of the world, the marketer has to make sure that two distributors will not end up having territorial overlaps, which can lead to unnecessary conflict.

Professionalism   The distributor's reputation must be checked. This rather abstract measure takes its value from a number of variables that all should help the marketer forecast fit and effectiveness. The distributor's customers, suppliers, facilitating agencies, competitors and other members of the local business community should be contacted for information on the business conduct of the distributor in such areas as buyer–seller relations and ethical behaviour. This effort will shed light on variables that may be important only in certain parts of the world; for example, variables such as political clout, which is essential in certain developing countries.

The marketer must acknowledge the distributor as an independent entity with its own goals. The distributor's business strategy must therefore be determined, particularly what the distributor expects to get from the relationship and where the international marketer fits into those plans. As a channel relationship is long term, the distributor's views on future expansion of the product line or its distribution should be clarified. This phase will also require a determination of the degree of help the distributor would need in terms of price, credit, delivery, sales training, communication, personal visits, product modification, warranty, advertising, warehousing, technical support, and after-sales service. Leaving uncertainties in these areas will cause major problems later.

Finally, the marketer should determine the distributor's overall attitude in terms of cooperation and commitment to the marketer. An effective way of testing this, and weeding out the less interested candidates, is to ask the distributor to assist in developing a local marketing plan or to develop one. This endeavour will bring out potential problem areas and will spell out which party is to perform the various marketing functions.[35]

A criteria list is valuable only when good data are available on each and every criterion. Although the initial screening can take place at the firm's offices, the three to five finalists should be visited. No better method of assessing distributors exists than visiting them, inspecting their facilities, and interviewing their various constituents in the market. A number of other critical data sources are important for firms without the resources for on-site inspection. The distributor's suppliers or firms not in direct competition can provide in-depth information. A bona fide candidate will also provide information through a local bank.

The distributor agreement

When the international marketer has found a suitable intermediary, a foreign sales agreement is drawn up.[36] The agreement can be relatively simple, but given the numerous differences in the market environments, certain elements are essential. The checklist presented in Exhibit 13.12 is the most comprehensive in stipulating the nature of the contract and the respective rights and responsibilities of the marketer and the distributor.

Contract duration is important, especially when an agreement is signed with a new distributor. In general, distribution agreements should be for a specified, relatively short period (one or two years). The initial contract with a new distributor should stipulate a trial period of either three or six months, possibly with minimum purchase requirements. Duration should be determined with an eye on the local laws and their stipulations on distributor agreements. These will be discussed later in conjunction with distributor termination.

Geographic boundaries for the distributor should be determined with care, especially by smaller firms. Future expansion of the product market might be complicated if a distributor claims rights to certain territories. The marketer should retain the right to distribute products independently, reserving the right to certain customers. For example, many marketers maintain a dual distribution system, dealing directly with certain large accounts. This type of arrangement should be explicitly stated in the agreement. Trans-shipments, sales to customers outside the agreed-upon territory or customer type, have to be explicitly prohibited to prevent the occurrence of parallel importation.

EXHIBIT 13.12

Elements of a distributor
agreement

A   Basic components

1   Parties to the agreement

2   Statement that the contract supersedes all previous agreements

3   Duration of the agreement (perhaps a three- or six-month trial period)

4   Territory:

(a)   exclusive, non-exclusive, sole

(b)   manufacturer's right to sell direct at reduced or no commission to local government and old customers

5   Products covered

6   Expression of intent to comply with government regulations

7   Clauses limiting sales forbidden by UK export controls

B   Manufacturer's rights

1   Arbitration:

(a)   if possible, in the manufacturer's country

(b)   if not, before international Chamber of Commerce or using the London Court of Arbitration rules

(c)   definition of rules to be applied (e.g., in selecting the arbitration panel)

(d)   assurance that award will be binding in the distributor's country

2   Jurisdiction that of the manufacturer's country (the signing completed at home); if not possible, a neutral site such as Sweden or Switzerland

3   Termination conditions (e.g., no indemnification if due notice given)

4   Clarification of tax liabilities

5   Payment and discount terms

6   Conditions for delivery of goods

7   Non-liability for late delivery beyond manufacturer's reasonable control

8   Limitation on manufacturer's responsibility to provide information

9   Waiver of manufacturer's responsibility to keep lines manufactured outside the United Kingdom (e.g., licensees) outside of covered territory

10   Right to change prices, terms and conditions at any time

11   Right of manufacturer or agent to visit territory and inspect books

12   Right to repurchase stock

13   Option to refuse or alter distributor's orders

14   Training of distributor personnel in the United Kingdom subject to:

(a)   practicality

(b)   costs to be paid by the distributor

(c)   waiver of manufacturer's responsibility for UK immigration approval

C   Distributor's limitations and duties

1   No disclosure of confidential information

2   Limitation of distributor's right to assign contract

3   Limitation of distributor's position as legal agent of manufacturer

EXHIBIT 13.12

Continued

4   Penalty clause for late payment

5   Limitation of right to handle competing lines

6   Placement of responsibility for obtaining customs clearance

7   Distributor to publicize designation as authorized representative in defined area

8   Requirement to move all signs or evidence identifying distributor with manufacturer if relationship ends

9   Acknowledgment by distributor of manufacturer's ownership of trademark, trade names, patents

10   Information to be supplied by the distributor:

   (a)   sales reports

   (b)   names of active prospects

   (c)   government regulations dealing with imports

   (d)   competitive products and competitors' activities

   (e)   price at which goods are sold

   (f)   complete data on other lines carried (on request)

11   Information to be supplied by distributor on purchasers

12   Accounting methods to be used by distributor

13   Requirement to display products appropriately

14   Duties concerning promotional efforts

15   Limitation of distributor's right to grant unapproved warranties, make excessive claims

16   Clarification of responsibility arising from claims and warranties

17   Responsibility of distributor to provide repair and other services

18   Responsibility to maintain suitable place of business

19   Responsibility to supply all prospective customers

20   Understanding that certain sales approaches and sales literature must be approved by manufacturer

21   Prohibition of manufacture or alteration of products

22   Requirement to maintain adequate stock, spare parts

23   Requirement that inventory be surrendered in event of a dispute that is pending in court

24   Prohibition of transshipments

Source: Adapted from 'Elements of a Distributor Agreement', *Business International,* March 29, 1963, 23–24. Some of the sections have been changed to reflect the present situation.

The payment section of the contract should stipulate the methods of payment as well as how the distributor or agent is to draw compensation. Distributors derive compensation from various discounts, such as the functional discount, whereas agents earn a specific commission percentage of net sales (such as 15 per cent). Given the volatility of currency markets, the agreement should also state the currency to be used. The international marketer also needs to make sure that none of the compensation forwarded to the distributor is in violation of the Foreign Corrupt Practices Act or the OECD guidelines. A violation occurs if a payment is made to influence a foreign official in exchange for business favours, depending on the nature of the action sought. So-called grease or facilitating payments, such as a small fee to expedite paperwork through customs, are not considered violations.[37]

Product and conditions of sale need to be agreed on. The products or product lines included should be stipulated, as well as the functions and responsibilities of the intermediary in terms of carrying the goods in inventory, providing service in conjunction with them, and promoting them. Conditions of sale determine which party is to be responsible for some of the expenses involved, which will in turn have an effect on the price to the distributor. These conditions include credit and shipment terms.

Effective means of communication between the parties must be stipulated in the agreement if a marketer–distributor relationship is to succeed. The marketer should have access to all information concerning the marketing of his or her products in the distributor's territory, including past records, present situation assessments, and marketing research concerning the future. Communication channels should be formal for the distributor to voice formal grievances. The contract should state the confidentiality of the information provided by either party and protect the intellectual property rights (such as patents) involved.

CHANNEL MANAGEMENT

A channel relationship can be likened to a marriage in that it brings together two independent entities that have shared goals. For the relationship to work, each party must be clear about its expectations and openly communicate changes perceived in the other's behaviour that might be contrary to the agreement. The closer the relationship is to a distribution partnership, the more likely marketing success will materialize. Conflict will arise, ranging from small grievances (such as billing errors) to major ones (rivalry over channel duties), but it can be managed to enhance the overall channel relationship. In some cases, conflict may be caused by an outside entity, such as grey markets, in which unauthorized intermediaries compete for market share with legitimate importers and exclusive distributors. Nevertheless, the international marketer must solve the problem.

The relationship has to be managed for the long term. An exporter may in some countries have a seller's market situation that allows it to exert pressure on its intermediaries for concessions, for example. However, if environmental conditions change, the exporter may find that the channel support it needs to succeed is not there because of the manner in which it managed channel relationships in the past.[38] Firms with harmonious relationships are typically those with more experience abroad and those that are proactive in managing the channel relationship. Harmonious relationships are also characterized by more trust, communication, and cooperation between the entities and, as a result, by less conflict and perceived uncertainty.[39]

As an exporter's operations expand, the need for coordination across markets may grow. Therefore, the exporter may want to establish distributor advisory councils to help in reactive measures (e.g., how to combat parallel importation) or proactive measures (e.g., how to transfer best practice from one distributor to another). Naturally, such councils are instrumental in building *esprit de corps* for the long-term success of the distribution system.

Factors in channel management

An excellent framework for managing channel relationships is shown in Exhibit 13.13. The complicating factors that separate the two parties fall into three categories: ownership; geographic, cultural and economic distance; and different rules of law. Rather than lament their existence, both parties need to take strong action to remedy them. Often, the major step is acknowledgment that differences do indeed exist, followed by measures to build mutual trust.[40]

In international marketing, manufacturers and distributors are usually independent entities. Distributors typically carry the products of more than one manufacturer and judge products by their ability to generate revenue without added expense. The international marketer, in order to receive disproportionate attention for its concerns, may offer both monetary and psychological rewards.

Distance can be bridged through effective two-way communication. This should go beyond normal routine business communication to include innovative ways of sharing

EXHIBIT 13.13

Performance problems
and remedies when
using overseas
distributors

Source: Adapted from Philip
J. Rosson, "Success Factors in
Manufacturer–Overseas Distributor
Relationships in International
Marketing," in *International
Marketing Management,* ed.
Erdener Kaynak (New York:
Praeger, 1984), 91–107.

High Export Performance Inhibitors	Bring	Remedy Lies in
Separate Ownership	• Divided Loyalties • Seller–Buyer Atmosphere • Unclear Future Intentions	Offering good incentives, helpful support schemes, discussing plan frankly, and interacting in a mutually beneficial way
Geographic, Economic, and Cultural Separation	• Communication Blocks • Negative Attitudes toward Foreigners • Physical Distribution Strains	Making judicious use of two-way visits, establishing a well-managed communication program, including distributor advisory council
Different Rules of Law	• Vertical Trading Restrictions • Dismissal Difficulties	Full compliance with the law, drafting a strong distributor agreement

pertinent information. The international marketer may place one person in charge of distributor-related communications or put into effect an interpenetration strategy – that is, an exchange of personnel so that both organizations gain further insight into the workings of the other.[41] Cross-cultural differences in people's belief systems and behaviour patterns have to be acknowledged and acted on for effective channel management. For example, in markets where individualism is stressed, local channel partners may seek arrangements that foster their own self-interest and may expect their counterparts to watch out for themselves. Conflict is seen as a natural phenomenon. In societies of low individualism, however, a common purpose is fostered between the partners.[42]

Economic distance manifests itself in exchange rates, for example. Instability of exchange rates can create serious difficulties for distributors in their trading activities, not only with their suppliers but also with their domestic customers. Manufacturers and distributors should develop and deploy mutually acceptable mechanisms that allow for some flexibility in interactions when unforeseen rate fluctuations occur.[43] For example, a company can institute a system of risk sharing in which it will maintain a single foreign currency price as long as the spot exchange rate does not move beyond a mutually agreed-upon rate. Should that happen, the company and the distributor will share the costs or benefits of the change.

Laws and regulations in many markets may restrict the manufacturer in terms of control. For example, in the European Union, the international marketer cannot prevent a distributor from re-exporting products to customers in another member country, even though the marketer has another distributor in that market. EU law insists on a single market where goods and services can be sold throughout the area without restriction. In 1998, VW was fined €94 million and in 2000 GM €45 million for taking steps to limit intra-EU imports. Even monitoring parallel imports may be considered to be in restraint of trade.

Most of the criteria used in selecting intermediaries can be used to evaluate existing intermediaries as well. If not conducted properly and fairly, however, evaluation can be a source of conflict. In addition to being given the evaluation results in order to take appropriate action, the distributor should be informed of the evaluative criteria and should be a part of the overall assessment process. Again, the approach should be focused on serving mutual benefits. For example, it is important that the exporter receive detailed market and financial performance data from the distributor. Most distributors identify these data as the key sources of power in distribution and may, therefore, be inherently reluctant to provide them in full detail. The exchange of such data is often the best indicator of a successful relationship.[44]

A part of the management process is channel adjustment. This can take the form of channel shift (eliminating a particular type of channel), channel modification (changing individual members while leaving channel structure intact), or role or relationship modification (changing functions performed or the reward structure) as a result of channel evaluation. The need for channel change should be well established and not executed hastily because it will cause a major distraction in the operations of the firm. Some companies have instituted procedures that require executives to consider carefully all of the aspects and potential results of change before execution.

Grey markets

Grey markets, or parallel importation, refer to authentic and legitimately manufactured trademark items that are produced and purchased abroad but imported or diverted to the market by bypassing designated channels.[45] The IT industry estimates that grey market sales of IT products account for over €28.85 billion in revenue each year, collectively costing IT manufacturers up to €3.61 billion annually in lost profits.[46] Grey marketed products vary from inexpensive consumer goods (such as chewing gum) to expensive capital goods (such as excavation equipment). The phenomenon is not restricted to the United States; Japan, for example, has witnessed grey markets because of the high value of the yen and the subsidization of cheaper exports through high taxes. Japanese marketers thus often found it cheaper to go to Los Angeles to buy export versions of Japanese-made products. Grey markets are not a fringe phenomenon either; for example, 93 per cent of the mobile phone market in Laos is furnished through sourcing or smuggling from Thailand.

A case history of the phenomenon is provided in Exhibit 13.14, which shows the flow of Seiko watches through authorized and unauthorized channels. Seiko is a good example of a

EXHIBIT 13.14   Seiko's authorized and unauthorized channels of distribution

- - - → Broken arrows denote the flow of Seiko watches through authorized channels of distribution.
——→ Solid arrows denote the flow of Seiko watches through unauthorized channels of distribution.

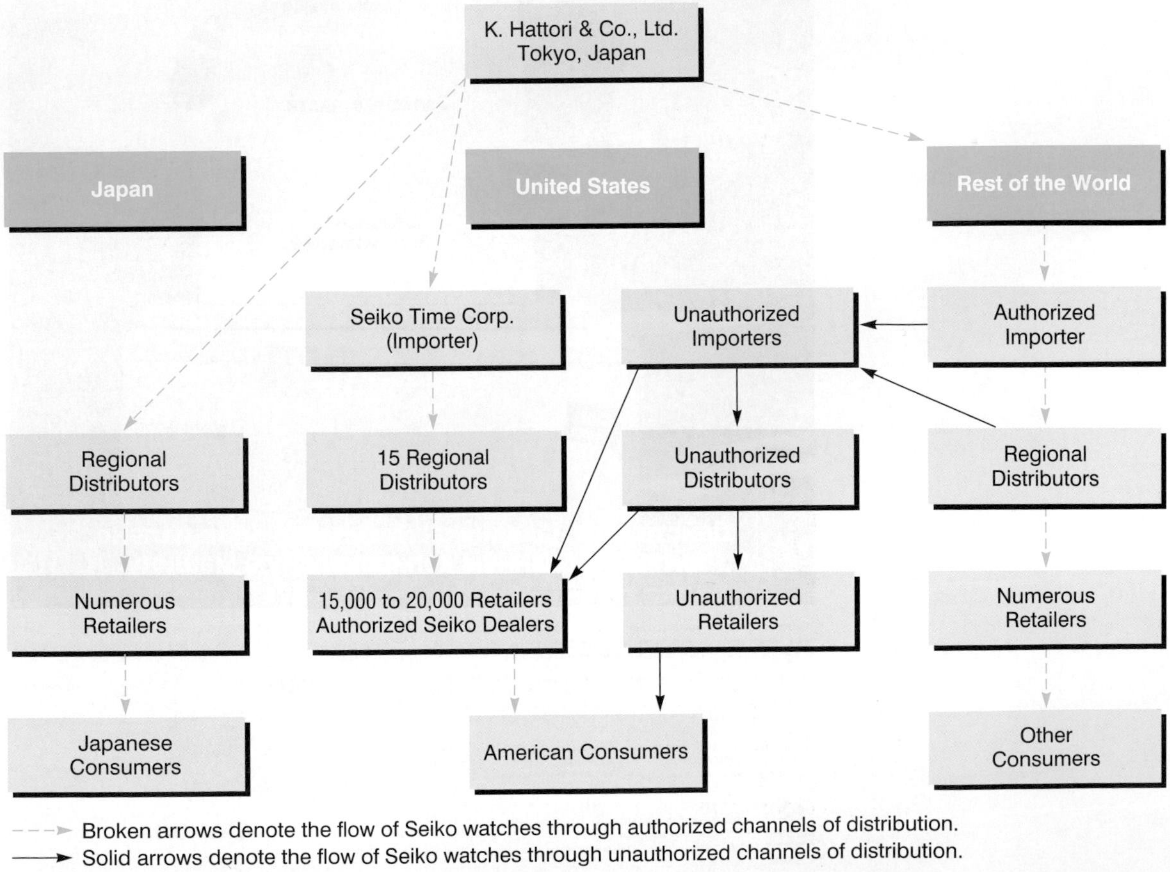

Source: Jack Kaikati, "Parallel Importation: A Growing Conflict in International Channels of Distribution," Symposium on Export-Import Interrelationships, Georgetown University, November 14–15, 1985.

typical grey market product in that it carries a well-known trademark. Unauthorized import-ers, such as Progress Trading Company in New York, and retailers, such as Kmart or Gem of the Day, buy Seiko watches around the world at advantageous prices and then sell them to consumers at substantial discounts over authorized Seiko dealers. Seiko has fought back, for example, by advertising warnings to consumers against buying grey market watches on the grounds that these products may be obsolete or worn-out models and that consumers might have problems with their warranties. Many grey marketers, however, provide their own war-ranty-related service and guarantee watches sold through them. Since watches have strong commercial potential online due to the power of their brand identities, grey-market watch websites are having the most impact on higher-priced watch lines selling for €800 retail. Authorized retailers are being forced to take bigger discounts to keep from losing sales.[47]

Various conditions allow unauthorized resellers to exist. The most important are price segmentation and exchange rate fluctuations. Competitive conditions may require the interna-tional marketer to sell essentially the same product at different prices in different markets or to different customers.[48] As many products are priced higher in, for example, the United Kingdom, a grey marketer can purchase them in Europe or the Far East and offer discounts

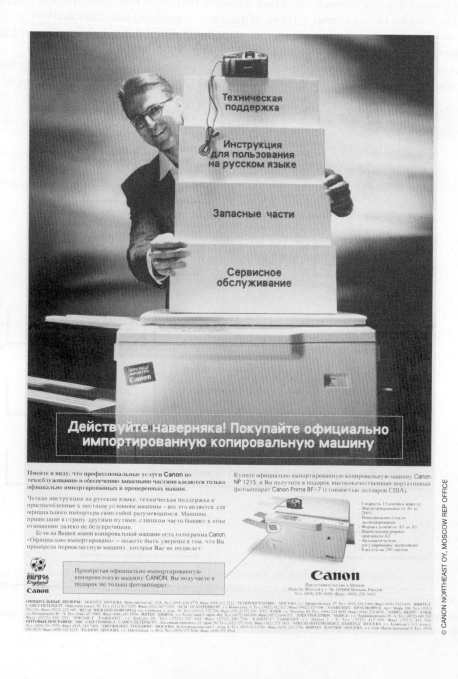

THE INTERNATIONAL **MARKETPLACE 13.3**

Country of origin and grey markets

Since the Russian currency crisis of 1998, global oil prices have fuelled a boom that has not only replenished government coffers, but also boosted wages across the board and given many Asian, European and North American marketers reason to look at the market. While expenditures by businesses and consumers tend to be modest by international standards, the buyers are extremely quality aware and brand conscious. Making erroneous assumptions in this regard may be costly, as Canon found with its operations.

As part of a strategic initiative to relocate products and transfer technology, Canon moved the production of its basic model 1215 copier to China. One of the world's leading manufacturers of cameras, optical products, imaging equipment and computer peripherals, Canon believes in being an organization that undertakes optimal production activities worldwide. It does so through its 120 subsidiaries around the globe.

The change of country of origin from Japan to China was not expected to affect buyers. However, in Russia, Canon found quite the opposite to be true. In many high-technology product categories, both Russian trade and retail customers divided products into three categories: 'white' ones, made in Europe or the United States, the best made and subsequently premium priced; 'red' ones, assembled in Russia and considered with suspicion; and 'yellow' ones, from Asia and rated somewhere in between red and white. However, in China's case, the perception among Russians has traditionally been that technology flows there from Russia but not vice versa, and that nothing interesting in terms of technology can originate from China.

The problem was identified relatively quickly – within three months of the change in source of supply – and the sourcing was redirected back to Japan. However, in the meantime, many intermediaries in Dubai, Hong Kong and Singapore identified an opportunity and offered Russian customers 'made in Japan' versions of the same product while the official channel was stuck with the 'made in China' counterparts.

In a worst-case scenario, Canon would have been forced to sell the copiers at any price. However, it undertook the following campaign, which resulted in the swift sale of all the Chinese-made copiers:

1 It developed an 'officially imported' hologram, which was attached to every Canon product acquired through official channels in Russia.

2 It offered to profile dealers as authorized resellers through a dealer-participatory campaign in which their names were included in the advertisements.

3 It offered final customers a premium, a Canon BP-7 camera.

The accompanying advertisement appeared in Russian trade magazines to deliver this message. It portrays the hologram and states the following benefits of buying from official dealers (while implicitly warning readers not to buy from other sources): technical support and training, Russian-language instructions and manuals, product support and local service.

SOURCES: Example courtesy of Jouko Tuominen, Oy Canon Ab, 'To Russia with Love: The Multinationals' Song', *Business Week*, September 16, 2002, 54; and 'Laptops from Lapland', *The Economist*, September 6, 1997, 67–68; **http://www.canon.com**.

---

between 10 and 40 per cent below list price when reselling them in the UK market. Exchange rate fluctuations can cause price differentials and thus opportunities for grey marketers. For example, during the Asian financial crisis, grey marketers imported Caterpillar, Deere and Komatsu construction and earth-moving equipment no longer needed for halted projects in markets such as Thailand and Indonesia – and usually never used – for as little as 60 per cent of what dealers paid wholesale.[49]

However, in these cases, the grey market goods typically cost more than those usually available through authorized suppliers. In other cases, if there are multiple production sites for the same product, grey markets can emerge due to negative perceptions about the country of origin, as seen in the case highlighted in *The International Marketplace 13.3*.

Grey market flows have increased as current barriers to trade are being eliminated. The European Union has significant parallel importation due to significant price differentials in ethical drugs, which are in turn the result of differences in regulation, insurance coverage, medical practice and exchange rates. Of the fifteen member countries, only Denmark grants manufacturers the freedom to price their ethical drugs. The share of parallel trade is estimated at 15 per cent and is expected to grow since the European Commission is supporting the practice.[50]

Opponents and supporters of the practice disagree on whether the central issue is price or trade rights. Detractors typically cite the following arguments: (1) the grey market unduly hurts the legitimate owners of trademarks; (2) without protection, trademark owners will have little incentive to invest in product development; (3) grey marketers will 'free ride' or take unfair advantage of the trademark owners' marketing and promotional activities; and (4) parallel imports can deceive consumers by not meeting product standards or their normal expectations of after-sale service. The bottom line is that grey market goods can severely under-cut local marketing plans, erode long-term brand images, eat up costly promotion funds, and sour manufacturer–intermediary relations.

Proponents of parallel importation approach the issue from an altogether different point of view. They argue for their right to 'free trade' by pointing to manufacturers that are both over-producing and overpricing in some markets. The main beneficiaries are consumers, who benefit from lower prices and discount distributors, with whom some of the manufacturers do not want to deal and who have now, because of grey markets, found a profitable market niche.

Grey markets attract consumers with high price sensitivities. However, given the price–quality inference, quality may become a concern for the consumer, especially if they do not have relevant information about the brand and the intermediary. In addition, risk aversion will have a negative influence on consumers' propensity to buy grey-market goods. The likelihood of obtaining a counterfeit version, a deficient guarantee, or no service are foremost concerns.[51]

The solution for the most part lies with the contractual relationships that tie businesses together. In almost all cases of grey marketing, someone in the authorized channel commits a diversion, thus violating the agreements signed. One of the standard responses is therefore disenfranchisement of such violators. This approach is a clear response to complaints from the authorized dealers who are being hurt by transshipments. Tracking down offenders is quite expensive and time-consuming, however. Some of the grey marketers can be added to the authorized dealer network if mutually acceptable terms can be reached, thereby increasing control of the channel of distribution.[52]

A one-price policy can eliminate one of the main reasons for grey markets. This means choosing the most efficient of the distribution channels through which to market the product, but it may also mean selling at the lowest price to all customers regardless of location and size. A meaningful one-price strategy must also include a way to reward the providers of other services, such as warranty repair, in the channel.

Other strategies have included producing different versions of products for different markets. For example, some electronics-goods companies are designing products so they will work only in the market for which they are designated. Some of the latest printers from Hewlett-Packard do not print if they are fed ink cartridges not bought in the same region as the printer. Nintendo's handheld game machines are sold in Europe with power adaptors that do not work in China.[53] Some companies have introduced price incentives to consumers. Hasselblad, the Swedish camera manufacturer, offers rebates to purchasers of legally imported, serial-numbered camera bodies, lenses and roll-fill magazines. Many manufacturers promote the benefits of dealing with authorized dealers (and, thereby, the dangers of dealing with grey market dealers). For example, Rolex's message states that authorized dealers are the only ones who are capable of providing genuine accessories and who can ensure that the customer gets an authentic product and the appropriate warranty. Many pharmaceutical companies, such as Glaxo SmithKline, have embarked on educational and promotional campaigns to call attention to buying drugs from abroad from internet pharmacies.[54]

Termination of the channel relationship

Many reasons exist for the termination of a channel relationship, but the most typical are changes in the international marketer's distribution approach (for example, establishing a sales office), or a (perceived) lack of performance by the intermediary. On occasion, termination may result from either party not honouring agreements; for example, by selling outside assigned territories and initiating price wars.[55]

Channel relationships go through a life cycle. The concept of an international distribution life cycle is presented in Exhibit 13.15. Over time, the manufacturer's marketing capabilities

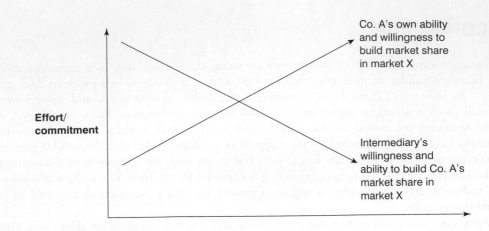

Effort/
commitment

Co. A's own ability
and willingness to
build market share
in market X

Intermediary's
willingness and
ability to build Co. A's
market share in
market X

EXHIBIT 13.15

International distribution
life cycle

Source: Framework courtesy of
Professors David Arnold, Harvard
Business School, and Professor
John Quelch, London Business
School.

increase while a distributor's ability and willingness to grow the manufacturer's business in that market decreases. When a producer expands its market presence, it may expect more of a distributor's effort than the distributor is willing to make available. Furthermore, with expansion, the manufacturer may want to expand its product line to items that the distributor is neither interested in nor able to support. In some cases, intermediaries may not be interested in growing the business beyond a certain point (e.g., due to progressive taxation in the country) or as aggressively as the principal may expect (i.e., being more of an order-taker than an order-getter). As a marketer's operations expand, it may want to start to coordinate operations across markets for efficiency and customer-service reasons or to cater to global accounts – thereby needing to control distribution to a degree that independent intermediaries are not willing to accept, or requiring a level of service that they may not be able to deliver.

Independent distributors do remain long-run representatives of originators under certain circumstances. Some markets may not be considered strategic (e.g., due to size) or they may be culturally challenging (e.g., Saudi Arabia). The distributors may carry product lines that are complementary thus enhancing the originator's efforts, and they may act more as partners by sharing information, or undertaking originator-specific projects in their or nearby markets to become 'indispensable'.[56]

If termination is a result of such a structural change, the situation has to be handled carefully. The effect of termination on the intermediary has to be understood, and open communication is needed to make the transition smooth. For example, the intermediary can be compensated for investments made, and major customers can be visited jointly to assure them that service will be uninterrupted.

Termination conditions are one of the most important considerations in the distributor agreement, because the just causes for termination vary and the penalties for the international marketer may be substantial. Just causes include fraud or deceit, damage to the other party's interest, or failure to comply with contract obligations concerning minimum inventory requirements or minimum sales levels. These must be spelled out carefully because local courts are often favourably disposed towards local businesses. In some countries, termination may not even be possible. In the EU and Latin America, terminating an ineffective intermediary is time-consuming and expensive. One year's average commissions are typical for termination without justification. A notice of termination has to be given three to six months in advance. In Austria, termination without just cause and/or failure to give notice of termination may result in damages amounting to average commissions for between 1 and 15 years.

The time to think about such issues is before the overseas distribution agreement is signed. It is especially prudent to find out what local laws say about termination and to check what type of experience other firms have had in the particular country. Careful preparation can allow the exporter to negotiate a termination without litigation. If the distributor's performance is unsatisfactory, careful documentation and clearly defined performance measures may help show that the distributor has more to gain by going quietly than by fighting.

E-COMMERCE

Increasingly, various marketing constituents are seeing the web not only as a communication tool but as a builder of interactive relationships and as a device to sell products and services.[57] As shown in Exhibit 13.16, e-commerce, the ability to offer goods and services over the web (both business to consumer [B2C] and business to business [B2B]) is expected to reach significant compound annual growth rates in the next few years around the world. While the United States accounts for the majority of e-commerce activity, the non-US portion is expected to grow substantially in the next few years, with the expansion of e-commerce markets in Asia. Total e-commerce spending is expected to rise from $2.5 trillion in 2004 to $8.5 trillion in 2009.[58] The biggest engine of growth for B2B e-commerce is expected to be global transactions.

Many companies willing to enter e-commerce will not have to do it on their own. Hub sites (also known as virtual malls, e-marketplaces or digital intermediaries) will bring together buyers, sellers, distributors and transaction payment processors in one single marketplace, making convenience the key attraction. With 1,400 of them in place,[59] entities such as Priceline.com (**http://www.priceline.com**), eBay (**http://www.ebay.com**), Shoplet (**http://www.shoplet.com**), Quadrem (**http://www.quadrem.com**), and ECnet (**http://www.ecnet.com**) are leading the way.

As soon as customers have the ability to access a company through the internet, the company itself has to be prepared to provide 24-hour order taking and customer service, to acquire the regulatory and customs-handling expertise to deliver internationally, and to develop an in-depth understanding of marketing environments for the further development of the business relationship. The instantaneous interactivity of users' experience will also be translated into an expectation of expedient delivery of answers and products ordered.

The challenges faced in terms of response and delivery capabilities can be overcome by outsourcing services or by building international distribution networks. Air express carriers

EXHIBIT 13.16	Internet usage statistics

	The Internet Big Picture					
	World Internet Users and Population Statistics					
World regions	Population (2009 est.)	Internet users Dec. 31, 2000	Internet users latest Data	Penetration (% population)	Growth % 2000–2009	Users % of table
Africa	991,002,342	4,514,400	**67,371,700**	6.8	1,392.4	3.9
Asia	3,808,070,503	114,304,000	**738,257,230**	19.4	545.9	42.6
Europe	803,850,858	105,096,093	**418,029,796**	52.0	297.8	24.1
Middle East	202,687,005	3,284,800	**57,425,046**	28.3	1,648.2	3.3
North America	340,831,831	108,096,800	**252,908,000**	74.2	134.0	14.6
Latin America/Caribbean	586,662,468	18,068,919	**179,031,479**	30.5	890.8	10.3
Oceania/Australia	34,700,201	7,620,480	**20,970,490**	60.4	175.2	1.2
WORLD TOTAL	6,767,805,208	360,985,492	**1,733,993,741**	**25.6**	380.3	100.0

Notes: (1) Internet Usage and World Population Statistics are for September 30, 2009. (2) Click on each world region name for detailed regional usage information. (3) Demographic (population) numbers are based on data from the US Census Bureau. (4) Internet usage information comes from data published by Nielsen Online, by the International Telecommunications Union, by GfK, local Regulators and other reliable sources. (5) For definitions, disclaimer, and navigation help, please refer to the Site Surfing Guide. (6) Information in this site may be cited, giving the due credit to www.internetworldstats.com. Copyright © 2001–2009, Miniwatts Marketing Group. All rights reserved worldwide.

Source: **http://www.internetworldstats.com/stats.htm**

such as DHL, FedEx and UPS offer full-service packages that leverage their own internet infrastructure with customs clearance and email shipment notification. If a company needs help in order fulfilment and customer support, logistics centres offer warehousing and inventory management services as well as same-day delivery from in-country stocks. DHL, for example, has eight express logistics centres and 287 strategic parts centres worldwide, with key centres in Bahrain for the Middle East, Brussels for Europe, and Singapore for Asia-Pacific. Some companies elect to build their own international distribution networks. Both QVC, a televised shopping service, and amazon.com, an online retailer of books and consumer goods, have distribution centres in Britain and Germany to take advantage of the European internet audience and to fulfill more quickly and cheaply the orders generated by their websites.

Transactions and the information they provide about the buyer allow for greater customization and for service by region, by market, or even by individual customer. One of the largest online sellers, Dell Computers, builds a Premier Page for its corporate customers with more than 400 employees, which is linked to the customer's intranet and thus allows approved employees to configure PCs, pay for them and track their delivery status. Premier Pages also provide access to instant technical support and Dell sales representatives. Presently there are 5,000 companies with such service, and $5 million worth of Dell PCs are ordered every day.[60]

Although English has long been perceived as the lingua franca of the web, the share of non-English speakers worldwide increased to 65 per cent in 2006. It has also been shown that web users are three times more likely to buy when the offering is made in their own language.[61] However, not even the largest of firms can serve all markets with a full line of their products. Getting a website translated and running is an expensive proposition and, if done correctly, time-consuming as well. If the site is well developed, it will naturally lead to expectations that order fulfilment will be of equal calibre. Therefore, any worldwide web strategy has to be tied closely with the company's overall growth strategy in world markets.

A number of hurdles and uncertainties are keeping some companies out of global markets or preventing them from exploiting these markets to their full potential. Some argue that the World Wide Web does not live up to its name, since it is mostly a tool for the the developed countries. Yet, as internet penetration levels increase in the near future, due to technological advances, improvements in many countries' web infrastructures and customer acceptance, e-business will become truly global. As a matter of fact, in some cases emerging markets may provide a chance to try out new approaches, because the markets and the marketers in them are not burdened by history, as seen in *The International Marketplace 13.4*.

The marketer has to be sensitive to the governmental role in e-commerce. No real consensus exists on the taxation of e-commerce, especially in the case of cross-border transactions. While the United States and the EU have agreed not to impose new taxes on sales through the internet, there is no uniformity in the international taxation of transactions.[62] Other governments believe, however, that they have something to gain by levying new e-taxes. Until firm legal precedents are established, international marketers should be aware of their potential tax liabilities and prepare for them, especially if they are considering substantial e-commerce investments. One likely scenario is an e-commerce tax system that closely resembles sales taxes at physical retail outlets. Vendors will be made responsible for collecting sales taxes and forwarding them to the governments concerned, most likely digitally. Another proposal involves the bit-tax, a variation of the internet access tax.

In addition, any product traded will still be subject to government regulations.[63] For example, a company can be fined if it exports to a country on the sanctions list due to its sponsorship of terrorism.

Governments will also have to come to terms with issues related to security, privacy and access to the internet.[64] The private sector argues for the highest possible ability to safeguard its databases, to protect cross-border transmission of confidential information, and to conduct secure financial transactions using global networks. This requires an unrestricted market for encryption products that operate globally. However, some governments fear that

US, Google and China square off over Internet

Google's threat to quit China over censorship and hacking intensified Sino-US frictions on Wednesday as Washington said it had serious concerns and demanded an explanation from Beijing.

China has not made any significant comment since Google, the world's top search engine, said it will not abide by censorship and may shut its Chinese-language google.cn website because of attacks from China on human rights activists using its Gmail service and on dozens of companies, including Adobe Systems.

Chinese authorities were 'seeking more information on Google's statement', the Xinhua news agency reported in English, citing an unnamed official from China's State Council Information Office, the government arm of the country's propaganda system.

Friction over the internet now seems sure to stoke tensions between the United States and China, joining friction over climate change, trade, human rights and military ambition.

With China the largest lender to the United States, holding $800 billion (£491.5 billion) in Treasury bills, these internet tensions will make steering this vast, fast-evolving relationship all the more tricky, especially with the US Congress in an election year.

'China has been taking a harder line', said Shi Yinhong, an expert on relations with the United States at Renmin University in Beijing. 'The next few months are going to see some turbulence in China-US relations. We may see some tactical concessions from China, but the general trend isn't towards compromise'.

China has said it does not sponsor hacking.

Pressing China for an explanation, US Secretary of State Clinton said: 'The ability to operate with confidence in cyberspace is critical in a modern society and economy.

'We have been briefed by Google on these allegations, which raise very serious concerns', Clinton said in Honolulu.

Chinese industry analysts said the issue had snowballed beyond Google and its problems.

'If this becomes heavily politicized, and there are signs that it is, and people in the Chinese government say, "This is good. It serves you right, and we won't bow our heads to the United States", then there'll be no way out', said Xie Wen, a former executive in China for Yahoo and other big internet companies, who is now a prominent industry commentator.

'The impact on China's image will gradually also affect the enthusiasm of investors', he added. 'It's not the pure economic losses – a billion or so – it's the deteriorating environment'.

Tensions Over Internet

China's policy of filtering and restricting access to websites has been a frequent source of tension with the United States and tech companies, such as Google and Yahoo Inc.

Google's announcement suggested the recent intrusions were more than isolated hacker attacks.

'These attacks and the surveillance they have uncovered – combined with the attempts over the past year to further limit free speech on the web – have led us to conclude that we should review the feasibility of our business operations in China', Google's chief legal officer David Drummond said in a statement posted on the company's blog.

Some 20 other companies were also attacked by unknown assailants based in China, said Google. RBC Capital Markets analyst Stephen Ju said the move was a turnaround for Google. 'Just about every earnings call recently has been that they are focused on the long-term growth opportunities for China and that they are committed'.

Shares of Google dipped 1.3 per cent although an executive described China as 'immaterial' to its finances. Shares in Baidu, Google's main rival in China, surged 7 per cent.

A Google spokesperson said the company was investigating the attack and would not say whether the company believed Chinese authorities were involved.

US President Barack Obama, during a visit to China in November, told an online town hall that he was 'a big supporter of non-censorship'.

China Silent, No Backdown Seen

After the Google announcement, searches on its google.cn search engine turned up images and sites previously blocked, including pictures from the 1989 crackdown on pro-democracy protests in Beijing.

Other searches remained restricted, carrying messages warning users that some content was blocked.

China's ruling Communist Party, wary of the internet becoming an uncontrolled forum for the country's 360 million internet users, is unlikely to allow Google to avoid repercussions.

'Hostile western forces have never abandoned their strategic schemes to westernize and divide us, and they are stepping up ideological and cultural infiltration', the Party's chief propaganda official, Li Changchun, wrote last month.

If google.cn, launched in 2006, shuts down, Beijing could seek to restrict access to Google's main search engine, which can also do searches in Chinese, although China's 'firewall' of internet filters blocks many users from opening up the results.

'The general tendency over the past year has been to accuse foreigners of having a Cold War mentality and being anti-China', said Rebecca MacKinnon, an expert on the Chinese internet at the Open Society Institute.

'How exactly they are going to react to this, I cannot anticipate, but it's likely that it will not be pretty'.

SOURCE: Oreskovic, A. and Buckley, C. (2010) 'US, Google and China square off over internet' **http://uk.news.yahoo.com/22/20100113/tts-uk-google-china-ca02f96.html** (12/1/10)

---

encryption will enable criminals and terrorist organizations to avoid detection and tracking. Therefore, a strong argument is made in favour of limiting the extent of encryption.

Privacy issues have grown exponentially as a result of e-business. The European Union has a directive that introduced high standards of data privacy to ensure the free flow of data throughout its 25 member states. Each individual has the right to review personal data, correct them and limit their use. But more importantly, the directive also requires member states to block transmission of data to countries, including the United States, if those countries' domestic legislation does not provide an adequate level of protection. The issue between the United States and the EU will most likely be settled by companies, such as IBM, adopting global privacy policies for managing information online and getting certified by groups, such as Better Business Bureaus or TRUSTe, that are implementing privacy labeling systems to tell users when a site adheres to their privacy guidelines.[65] A register of such companies will also then have to be developed.

A related concern is the content of material on the internet. While freedom of information across international lines is encouraged and easily achieved, some countries (such as China and Saudi Arabia) regulate information and others have quotas on domestically produced broadcasting. Regulations on advertising are also implemented.

For industries such as music and motion pictures, the internet is both an opportunity and a threat.[66] It provides a new and efficient method of distribution and customization of products. At the same time, it can be a channel for intellectual property violations, through unauthorized postings on websites from which protected material can be downloaded. In addition, the music industry is concerned about a shift in the balance of economic power: if artists can deliver their works directly to customers via technologies such as MP3, what will be the role of labels and distributors? Many labels have switched to digital music and seen their profits increase with the new distribution mode.[67]

28 For a discussion of the basic forms, see **http://www.export.gov/exportbasics/index.asp**.

29 'It Could Be Worse', *International Business,* April 1996, 8.

30 Peter B. Fitzpatrick and Alan S. Zimmerman, *Essentials of Export Marketing* (New York: American Management Association, 1985), 43.

31 S. Tamer Cavusgil, Poh-Lin Yeoh and Michel Mitri, 'Selecting Foreign Distributors: An Export Systems Approach', *Industrial Marketing Management* 24 (Winter 1995): 297–304.

32 'Five Steps to Finding the Right Business Partners Abroad', *World Trade,* March 1999, 86–87.

33 UK Trade and Investment (2010) 'Preparing to trade' **www.uktradeinvest.gov.uk/ukti/appmanager/ukti/ourservices?_nfls=false&_nfpb=true&_pageLabel= preparing_to_trade** (Accessed 12/1/10).

34 Joseph V. Barks, 'Penetrating Latin America', *International Business,* February 1996, 78–80.

35 Keysuk Kim and Changho Oh, 'On Distributor Commitment in Marketing Channels for Industrial Products: Contrast between the United States and Japan', *Journal of International Marketing* 10 (no. 1, 2002): 72–97.

36 For a detailed discussion, see International Chambers of Commerce, *The ICC Model Distributorship Contract* (Paris: ICC Publishing, 2002), chapters 1–3; **http://www.iccwbo.org**.

37 Michael G. Harvey and Ilkka A. Ronkainen, 'The Three Faces of the Foreign Corrupt Practices Act: Retain, Reform or Repeal', in *1984 AMA Educators' Proceedings* (Chicago: American Marketing Association, 1984), 290–294.

38 Gary L. Frazier, James D. Gill and Sudhir H. Kale, 'Dealer Dependence Levels and Reciprocal Actions in a Channel of Distribution in a Developing Country', *Journal of Marketing* 53 (January 1989): 50–69.

39 Leonidas C. Leonidou, Constantine S. Katsikeas, and John Hadjimarcou, 'Building Successful Export Business Relationships: A Behavioral Perspective', *Journal of International Marketing* 10 (no. 3, 2002): 96–115.

40 Chun Zhang, S. Tamer Cavusgil and Anthony S. Roath, 'Manufacturer Governance of Foreign Distributor Relationships: Do Relational Norms Enhance Competitiveness in the Export Market?' *Journal of International Business Studies* 34 (number 6, 2003): 550–580.

41 Bert Rosenbloom, *Marketing Channels: A Management View* (Mason, OH: South-Western, 2003), Chapter 9.

42 Sudhir H. Kale and Roger P. McIntyre, 'Distribution Channel Relationships in Diverse Cultures', *International Marketing Review* 8 (1991): 31–45.

43 Constantine S. Katsikeas and Tevfik Dalgic, 'Importing Problems Experienced by Distributors: The Importance of Level-of-Import Development', *Journal of International Marketing* 3 (no. 2, 1995): 51–70.

44 David Arnold, 'Seven Rules of International Distribution', *Harvard Business Review* 78 (November–December 2000): 131–137.

45 Ilkka A. Ronkainen and Linda van de Gucht, 'Making a Case for Gray Markets', *Journal of Commerce,* January 6, 1987, 13A.

46 **http://www.agmaglobal.org**.

47 Jeff Prine, 'Time On-Line, the New Global Grey Market', *Modern Jeweler,* November 1998, 45–48.

48 Frank V. Cespedes, E. Raymond Corey and V. Kasturi Rangan, 'Gray Markets: Causes and Cures', *Harvard Business Review* 66 (July–August 1988): 75–82.

49 'the Earth Is Shifting under Heavy Equipment', *Business Week,* April 6, 1998, 44.

50 Peggy E. Chaudry and Michael G. Walsh, 'Managing the Gray Market in the European Union: The Case of the Pharmaceutical Industry', *Journal of International Marketing* 3 (no. 3, 1995): 11–33; and 'Parallel Trade and Comparative Pricing of Medicines: Poor Choice for Patients', *Pfizer Forum,* 1996.

51 Jen-Hung Huang, Bruce C.Y. Lee and Shu Hsun Ho, 'Consumer Attitude toward Gray Market Goods', *International Marketing Review* 21 (number 6, 2004): 598–614.

52 For a comprehensive discussion on remedies, see Robert E. Weigand, 'Parallel Import Channel – Options for Preserving Territorial Integrity', *Columbia Journal of World Business* 26 (Spring 1991): 53–60; and S. Tamer Cavusgil and Ed Sikora, 'How Multinationals Can Counter Grey Market Imports', *Columbia Journal of World Business* 23 (Winter 1988): 75–85.

53 'Electronics with Borders: Some Work Only in the US', *The Wall Street Journal,* January 17, 2005, B1, B5.

54 See, for example, Glaxo SmithKline, *Importation,* available at **http://us.gsk.com/health/downloads/importation.pdf**.

55 Hong Liu and Yen Po Wang, 'Co-ordination of International Channel Relationships', *Journal of Business and Industrial Marketing* 14 (no. 2, 1999): 130–150.

56 David Arnold, *The Mirage of Global Markets* (Upper Saddle River, NJ: Prentice-Hall, 2003), 149–150.

57 Anna Morgan-Thomas and Susan Bridgewater, 'internet and Exporting: Determinants of Success in Virtual Export Channels', *International Marketing Review* 21 (numbers 4/5, 2004): 393–408.

58 **http://www.idc.com**.

59 'Shopping for a Marketplace', *Global Business,* February 2001, 36–37.

60 Eryn Brown, 'Nine Ways to Win on the web', *Fortune,* May 24, 1999, 112–125.

61 Hope Katz Gibbs, 'Taking Global Local', *Global Business,* December 1999, 44–50.

62 Christia Victor and Wen-Jang Jih, 'Fair or Not? The Taxation of E-Commerce', *Information Systems Management* 23 (number 1, 2006): 68–73.

63 Aldo Forgione, 'The Good, the Bad, the Ugly: The Frontiers of Internet Law', *Journal of Internet Law* 9 (July 2005): 25–31.

64 'E-Commerce Firms Start to Rethink Opposition to Privacy Regulation as Abuses, Anger Rise', *The Wall Street Journal,* January 6, 2000, A24.

65 Amy Zuckerman, 'Order in the Courts?' *World Trade,* September 2001, 26–28.

66 'Music Piracy Poses a Threat to Regional Artists', *The Wall Street Journal,* June 4, 2002, B10.

67 'Warner Music's Earnings Surge 92% on Digital Sales, Lower Costs', *The Wall Street Journal,* February 15, 2006, B3.

PART III EXPORT MARKETING MIX

Dr Eris: Cosmetics from Poland

Dr Irena Eris is famous in Poland. In 1999 the Business Centre Club honoured her with the title Business Woman of the Decade, in 2003 she was recognized for the creation of an internationally competitive Polish brand, and in 2004 she was placed on the list of influential women in Polish history that had changed the course of events, overcome stereotypes and initiated new thinking. In 2005 she received the Economic Award from the President of Poland.

It all started in 1982 when Dr Eris, who holds a PhD from the Faculty of Pharmacology at Berlin's Humboldt University, inherited the equivalent of six small Fiat cars. With this inheritance, in 1983 she and her husband opened a cottage workshop producing nourishing facial cream. The first cosmetic products were mixed in a makeshift machine made by a local locksmith friend.

THE POLISH COSMETICS MARKET

With its population of 40 million people, Poland is the eighth largest country in Europe. Its per capita consumption is only one-fifth of the average of the pre-2004 European Union (EU) member countries. The key competitive factors are price, quality and brand recognition. Packaging and advertising have become increasingly important. Poles tend to be risk averse when choosing everyday cosmetics. They prefer to buy a known brand from a known store. Purchasing decisions are determined by company reputation and brand recognition.

Poland has long traditions in the production of cosmetics. Max Faktor – born in Lódź, Poland, during the 1870s – became the founder of modern make-up, creating the global Max Factor brand. Helena Rubinstein, a Polish immigrant to the United States, is one of the biggest names in facial care. In the Communist era, Poland was by far the largest cosmetics producer in the former socialist countries. The cosmetics of Pollena and Nivea were cherished by women and men of all ages. Poland was also a large market for cosmetics. Most of the cosmetics products were affordably priced. Only 5 per cent represented luxury products, most of them imported. The collapse of the Council for Mutual Economic Assistance (CMEA) market at the beginning of the 1990s caused the market for Polish cosmetics to stagnate. Existing procurement and distribution networks in the domestic and foreign Soviet Bloc markets were dismantled. Market positions in the big Russian market and in the other markets of Central and Eastern Europe were lost.

Today, the cosmetics industry in Poland employs approximately 19,000 people. It has remained a key employer in a volatile labour market, but the transition process to a market-led economy has caused enormous job losses. The 'shock therapy' approach to the privatization of state-owned enterprises led to the mushrooming of small domestic cosmetics companies; by the end of 2005 there were more than 470. Less than 15 per cent of these employed more than 50 people. International cosmetics manufacturers were quick to enter the Polish cosmetics industry via acquisition of former state-owned companies or greenfield investment. They have big production capacity, premier facilities, established retail clout and high brand recognition.

In the last 10 years the production of cosmetics in Poland has experienced steady annual growth (see Exhibit C3.1). In 2002 the market was valued at 1.85 billion Polish Zloty (PLN), the equivalent of US$450 million at the current exchange rate. The value of Polish cosmetics exports in 2002 was US$291 million, representing almost 10 per cent growth over 2001. More than two-thirds of all exports went to former CMEA markets and about 30 per cent to the European Union member countries. The major importers were Russia (18 per cent of the total value of Polish exports), Hungary (14 per cent), Lithuania (12 per cent), Ukraine (11 per cent), Germany (8 per cent) and the United Kingdom (7 per cent). Avon Cosmetics, Miraculum, Cussons Group, Kolastyna, Ziaja, Dr Irena Eris, Polena Ewa and L'Oréal are the biggest exporters.

Cosmetics imports come from Germany (23 per cent), France (21 per cent), the United Kingdom (17 per cent), and Italy and

EXHIBIT C3.1   Market size, US$ million

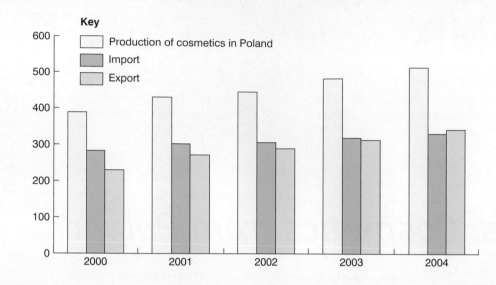

Key
- Production of cosmetics in Poland
- Import
- Export

Spain (6 per cent each). Imported cosmetics sell at a price premium and enjoy high brand recognition.

Cosmetics manufacturers in Poland can be divided into four groups:

1 Producers owned by the Pollena conglomerate, owned by foreign investors (Beiersdorf, Cussons Group and Unilever). They develop and introduce new products in the Polish market and upgrade the acquired cosmetic products.

2 Formerly state-owned cosmetics manufacturers, privatized and functioning independently (Pollena Ewa and Miraculum).

3 A large group of Polish private cosmetics firms established in the 1980s and 1990s (Inter-Fragrances, Dr Irena Eris Cosmetics Laboratories, Kolastyna, Soraya, Dax Cosmetics, Dermika and Ziaja).

4 New factories built by global cosmetics companies (Johnson & Johnson, L'Oréal, Avon and Oriflame).

The strong domestic producers have established positions in the skin and body care product market segment and control about two-thirds of this market. The market leader is Beiersdorf-Lechia with almost a 30 per cent share, followed by Johnson & Johnson (8 per cent), Unilever (7 per cent), Kolastyna (6.5 per cent), and Dr Irena Eris (5 per cent).

The facial care cosmetics market segment is dominated by Dr Irena Eris (16 per cent), followed by Ziaja (10 per cent), Oceanic (9 per cent), and Cussons (8 per cent). All foreign facial care brands have positioned themselves in the middle or premium sector of the market. For example, the US firm Johnson & Johnson dominates the mid-market with 45 per cent market share, while the French Garnier with its brand L'Oréal leads in the premium sector with more than 50 per cent market share. The market pressure from foreign brands has pushed most of the Polish

facial care brands into the low-price mass markets. The self-tanning cosmetics segment is dominated by L'Oréal with 27.5 per cent, Beiersdorf with 25.3 per cent, and Dr Irena Eris with 12.2 per cent market share.

Premium cosmetics brands are sold via specialized networks of stores such as Empik, Galeria Centrum, Ina Centre and French Sephora. The medium- and low-priced cosmetics are distributed via hypermarket and supermarket chains, drug stores and specialty stores. Companies such as Avon, Oriflame, and Amway use direct selling. The largest distributor of cosmetics is Polbita, a privately owned company established in 1990. Polbita owns 20 per cent of the cosmetics distribution system in Poland. Its store chain Drogeria Natura has more than 330 retail outlets.

Since 1988 almost all global and international cosmetics brands have entered the Polish market. They seek new market development and expansion. The best recognized foreign brands are: Christian Dior, Guerlain, Yves Saint Laurent, Yves Rocher, L'Oréal, Laboratories Paris, Lancôme, Paloma Picasso, Guy Laroche, Giorgio Armani, Cacharel, Coty, Elizabeth Arden, Pierre Robert, Colgate Palmolive, Nivea, Jean Pierresand, Vichy Laboratories, Jade, Max Factor, Revlon, Maybelline, Biotherm, Givenchy, Nino Cerruti, Margaret Astor and Rimmel. They have all set up their own exclusive stores and beauty salons. Aggressive advertising, new product development, and simultaneous product introduction in Paris and Warsaw reinforce their premium market position.

The ongoing process of market liberalization and EU enlargement has been favourable for the growing market presence of foreign cosmetics brands in Poland. The variety of products and services has led to a much greater consumer choice. This has increased the competitive pressure on Polish brands that are mostly too small to compete against global multinationals. One manager of a Polish medium-sized cosmetics company stated:

'Small and medium-sized cosmetics companies do not have enough market power. I cannot see how they can compete successfully against the multinationals after the EU enlargement. It is unlikely that the Polish government will protect us. It will not provide financial help for consolidation. Foreign giants will have no problem pushing us out of business. There will be more products, but Polish brands will gradually disappear'.

Nevertheless, domestically-owned cosmetics companies in Poland have been increasingly trying to gain market presence in the EU markets. Some managers believe that the EU enlargement can provide more opportunities for export and participation in partnerships with other cosmetics firms from the wider Europe.

THE COMPANY

Dr Irena Eris Cosmetic Laboratories was set up in socialist Poland in 1982 with a monthly production output of 3,000 packages. Demand for Eris cosmetics constantly increased and the company expanded its operations rapidly.

The transition period with its diverse economic and political reforms created new opportunities for business growth. The increased productivity and profitability of the company in the early 1990s led to the launch of a new plant. Dr Eris reinvested most of the company profits in product innovation and new technologies.

Presently, the company employs 350 employees and produces 300 types of products grouped into several product lines. The monthly output is approximately 1,000,000 units. All company cosmetics products meet the quality standards of the European Union and the US Food and Drug Administration. Dr Irena Eris holds ISO 9001 (since 1996) and Environment Management ISO 14001 (since 2001). Those certificates guarantee that its cosmetics are of global quality and their production is environmentally friendly.

Dr Eris's focus is on innovation and R&D. Its R&D investment in 2004 was 3.4 per cent of company turnover, growing to 4.6 per cent in 2005. A large team of dermatologists, allergy specialists, biologists and molecular biologists works on various projects at the company's Centre for Science and Research set up in 2001 (see Exhibit C3.2). R&D is the core of the company's strategy to develop scientifically advanced products.[1] Consumers who are interested in scientifically created cosmetics are the main targets.

Scientific research and innovative solutions are key to the brand positioning strategy of Dr Irena Eris. All products are original and based on in-company research. This makes them distinctive and more difficult for competitors to copy. In the mid-1990s, Dr Eris was the first in Europe to propose the use of vitamin K in cosmetics. More recently, it was the first company in the world to test and use the innovative complex FitoDHEA – folacin in its products.

Brand image

The brand image of Dr Irena Eris is built on respect for people, stressing their individual nature and the importance of cooperation. The brand development strategy reflects the value of interpersonal relationships within the company and with its clients. The brand value of Dr Irena Eris is based on its holistic approach to the individual specific needs and preferences of customers. It offers an individual skin care programme for home use and for use in specialized professional salons and spa hotels.

The brand has also gained international recognition. In 2005 it was nominated to the 2005 Beauty Awards for the best

---

EXHIBIT C3.2   Structure of the R&D department

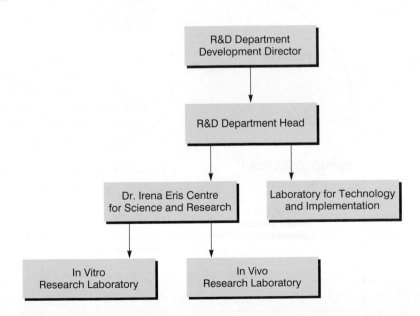

Source: Dr. Irena Eris Cosmetics Laboratories.

cosmetics introduced in the UK market. It was also awarded the Gold Glamour award by the British edition of *Glamour*.

The target segments of Dr Irena Eris span all age groups. Users are women who prioritize cosmetic efficiency based on research. They wish to use high-quality products that are modern and pleasant to use. There are different segments (see Exhibit C3.3).

The company targets the economy segment with mass products. The premium segment is reached with innovative products. The dermocosmetics segment is served with health and hygienic products. Specialized products are designed for the professional segment. These segments are reached via 20,000 retail points of sale for widely distributed products and 1,000 points of sale for products destined for limited distribution via pharmacies, beauty salons and centres.

Diversification

The company has diversified into related activities. Following the success of a four-star Spa Hotel, Dr Irena Eris, in Krynica Zdrój in Poland, it has invested in a second Spa Hotel, Dr Irena Eris Wzgórza Dylewskie, in Wysoka Wieś near Ostróda, which is to be completed in the first half of 2006. The Spa Hotels offer a comprehensive, tailor-made skin treatment and revitalizing programme. Skin treatment is complemented by a range of health improvement packages including exercises, massage, spa therapy and physical activities. The spa hotel concept promotes Dr Eris as a modern lifestyle brand.

Moreover, the brand Dr Irena Eris has been extended to the franchise chain Dr Irena Eris Cosmetics Institutes. There are 22 of them established in the largest Polish cities. Such institutes were also opened in Moscow, Russia, and Bogota, Colombia. It is

projected that ten new Institutes will serve clients in Poland and abroad by 2007. The Institutes offer several basic company treatments based on the Dr Irena Eris Professional Programme. The treatments are carried out using preparations from the company's own specialized line of cosmetics. They are exclusively used in beauty salons (Prosystem). The therapy is complemented by a line of products for subsequent home care (Prosystem home care). The treatments are selected individually and preceded by obligatory skin diagnosis by dermatologists partnering with Dr Irena Eris Cosmetic Institutes. The personnel of the Institutes consists of beauty therapists trained at the company's own centre.

Marketing communications

The marketing communications strategy of Dr Irena Eris is consistent with its strategic focus on innovation. It is the Polish company with the highest advertising expenditure. In Poland the company advertises on national and regional state-owned and private TV channels, on billboards, and in fashion and women's magazines. Advertising and PR activities in the key international markets are generally standardized but adapted to the local language. Private TV channels are mostly used for the firm's international advertising campaigns. Next come advertisements in fashion magazines and in-store promotions. The company has strengthened its position in the professional segment by developing close relationships with leading business customers and participating in international fairs.

Dr Irena Eris Cosmetic Laboratories donates PLN500,000 worth of products and money for charitable causes. It is a key contributor to the Always Healthy and Active Club programmes

---

EXHIBIT C3.3

Market segments and company brands

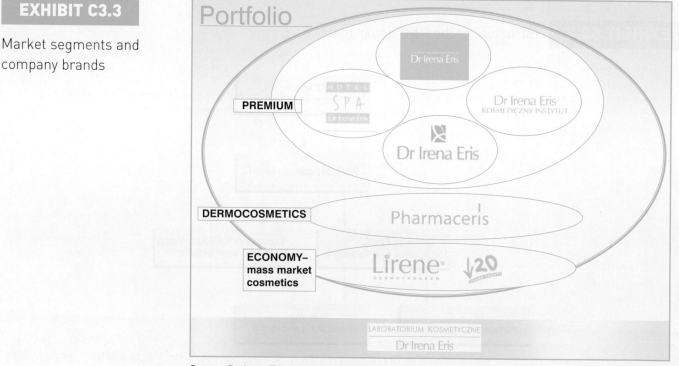

Source: Dr. Irena Eris Cosmetic Laboratories.

set up to meet the needs of seven million adult Polish women. The programme aims to increase the knowledge of mature women about health-related issues, and improve their general health and quality of life. In 2001, Dr Eris was awarded the Summa Bonitas award from the foundation Zdążyć z pomocą for its corporate social responsibility.[2]

The 2004 sales of Dr Irena Eris Cosmetics Laboratories were PLN97.6 million (€24 million) from domestic and export sales. This was 15 per cent growth compared with the results in 2003. In 2004 after-tax profit was PLN7 million.

Internationalization

Most of the initial attempts to go international were driven by opportunities based on personal contacts. In 1989 the company started exporting its products. The debut was made in the vast US market. The large Polish community in the US formed a formidable basis for foreign market expansion. Personal relationships and contacts were of foremost importance. Currently, Dr Eris cosmetics are available in over 1,000 specialized US salons.

After tapping into the US market, Dr Eris turned her sights on neighbouring Germany and the former CMEA markets. Geographic proximity, low psychic distance, and previously strong positions of Polish cosmetics in these markets proved helpful with market entry and penetration.

Dr Irena Eris has developed its international presence systematically since the mid-1990s. Direct exporting has been the preferred mode of foreign market entry. Management has recognized the benefits of economies of scope and uses various sources of information in support of foreign market expansion. The firm works with a range of exclusive distributors. In 2004 Dr Irena Eris products were introduced to the British market via the retailer Boots. The growth of exports has been substantial and in 2004 the company recorded an increase of international sales by 40 per cent. By 2006 the products of Dr Irena Eris were available in 24 countries around the globe. They are sold in beauty shops, pharmacies, supermarkets and beauty salons. Major markets are the United States, Lithuania, Russia, the Czech Republic, Hungary, the Slovak Republic, the Ukraine, Germany, Tasmania, Taiwan and Singapore.

Franchising has been used for the company's international growth in the form of cosmetics institutes. Apart from the two franchise operations in Moscow and Bogota, an expansion of franchise operations is planned across Europe.

Questions for discussion

1 What does the future hold for Polish small- and medium-sized cosmetics manufacturers? Do you agree with the statement of the Polish manager?

2 What should Dr Irena Eris Cosmetics Laboratories do to secure its future as market leader in the facial cosmetics segment in the Polish market?

3 Explain the internationalization of Dr Irena Eris Cosmetics Laboratories in the United States.

Notes

1 More details about the research programme can be obtained from: http://www.drirenaeris.pl/badania/en/badania.php and http://www.drirenaeris.pl/en/kosmetyki_skladniki.php.

2 For more information, see http://www.businessweek.com/magazine/content/04_19/b3882011.htm.

Source: This case was developed by Svetla T. Marinova and Marin A. Marinov. It is intended to be used as a basis for classroom discussion rather than to illustrate either effective or ineffective handling of a business situation. The authors acknowledge the assistance of Dr Irena Eris and her personal assistant Ms Aleksandra Trzcinska in developing the case.

Imaginarium

At the beginning of March 2001, Félix Tena was reviewing the internationalization process of his young company. Tena was the president and majority shareholder of Step Two, S.A., a company with headquarters in Zaragoza, Spain, that owned and operated Imaginarium, a retail chain of educational toy stores.

At the end of 2000, the chain consisted of 168 toy stores, 54 of which were owned and operated by Imaginarium, while 114 were franchised. There were 120 stores in Spain, and the other 48 were located in nine different countries. In the 2000 fiscal year, which had ended on January 31st, 2001, company sales had amounted to approximately €34 million, with after tax profits of €2.4 million.[1]

BACKGROUND

After studying business administration in Spain, Tena had continued his studies in the United States. This had allowed him to witness first-hand the American way of life and of doing business.

Upon his return to Spain he launched Publijuego, a small business venture in the educational toy sector. His first product was a board game similar to Monopoly, where the streets of a real city appeared on a board. This generated two sources of income, because he sold the individual board games to end users, and also the advertising space to different local businesses whose brands or retail emblems appeared on the board of the game. Tena subsequently sold 50 per cent of Publijuego to some Italian partners, but the partnership was not successful, and the company was wound up in 1990.

At that time, Tena observed that mass merchandisers were becoming increasingly important players in the Spanish toy market. The market had been formerly dominated by small, independent, specialized toy stores which sold toys throughout the year.

Toys 'R' Us, the 'category killer', had opened its first store in Spain in Barcelona in 1991, and traditional small independent toy stores were fast disappearing from the Spanish retail scene. The mass merchandisers were changing the toy retail game by concentrating their sales efforts around the high Christmas season, when they temporarily allocated significant sales floor space to toys. They only bought and sold toys they knew would be backed by strong national TV campaigns. They all sold the same manufacturer-branded toys, and the main sales pitch was low prices. Toys received the same retail marketing treatment as any

other packaged consumer product. No one seemed to place any importance on identifying and promoting the educational role that toys, as children's companions, should play.

This situation made a strong impact on Tena and he began to wonder whether anything could be done to change it. Perhaps he could find a different range or collection of toys that would transmit or contribute something new for children: imagination, relationships, opportunities to play with their parents, far from fads and from cartoon characters. He felt that children should be active participants rather than mere spectators.

IMAGINARIUM: A NEW BUSINESS CONCEPT

In November 1992, Tena decided to embark on a new entrepreneurial business venture by opening his first Imaginarium retail outlet in Zaragoza's old town district.[2] It was considered 'a pilot store'. The functional and decorative designs were created locally in Zaragoza, Spain.

Tena admitted that when developing this new business idea, some details about the retail toy trade in other countries had served as inspiration. But the overall Imaginarium business concept was the result of an original process and included full details of lighting, shelving, size and distribution of the retail store, range of toys offered, and so on.

The opening of the first pilot store implied a strategic change for Tena. As he put it, 'I was no longer a manufacturer and seller of toys, but I had become a purchaser and a retailer. All the toys I sold in my store were bought from other manufacturers, after a very careful process of choice and selection'. In order to do his toy procurement, he took advantage of his extensive knowledge and contacts in the toy industry. He also attended specialized international toy trade shows. The product range was chosen according to a system. On the one hand, he wanted to offer toys for children aged between birth and eight or nine years; on the other hand, he defined a certain number of content and activity areas: pre-school, games, music and theatre, dolls, manual work, science and nature, professions, movement, and so forth. An attempt was made to include toys at several price points or price levels within each cell or section of the toy matrix thus defined.

When preparing the opening of the first pilot store, Tena already had a clear idea that this one was going to be the first store of a retail chain. According to this idea, Tena already had set up separate 'headquarters' with a team of two or three other people.[3] It was Tena's objective to help children learn, imagine and discover. Some months later, this objective was summarized in what was to become the company's mission statement: 'Imaginarium: making a joyful contribution to the human development of boys and girls throughout the world'.

Fine-tuning the new business concept

Early in 1993, Tena came across a Disney University leaflet announcing a one-week seminar soon to be held at the Disney Centre in Florida.

This seminar helped him fine-tune his idea of the store and the business along the following lines:

- 'Business involves putting on a show on a stage'.

- 'Customers should receive more than they expect to receive'.

- 'Customers should feel an emotional experience'.

- 'Customers are our guests'.

Another idea that occurred to Tena was that, in order to create a chain of retail stores that could easily be reproduced and multiplied, all the design details and operating procedures would have to be highly standardized. This required the preparation of highly detailed operating manuals that also reflected the 'philosophy' or 'concept' of the Imaginarium business.

In 1993, Tena decided to franchise Imaginarium, maintaining that almost all decisions would be made at company headquarters. This manifested itself in the merchandising details of the retail stores, the logistics operations, and the operating manuals prepared for the franchisees. The product range offered, shelving and display stands in the Imaginarium stores were all determined in advance. Toys were not supplied in answer to orders placed at the discretion of the store managers or franchisees, but by means of automatic restocking procedures.

Opening the next four stores

Based on the experience acquired in the pilot store in Zaragoza, Tena introduced some improvements in the model, and in September 1993 he proceeded to open four new stores: two in Madrid, and two in Barcelona. All of them were owned and operated by Imaginarium, and each one of them required an investment of about € 90,000.[4]

These efforts crystallized some of the conceptual and operational details that defined the character of Imaginarium. For instance, shop attendants were defined as 'juególogas' ('toyologues' or toy experts, with a scientific connotation). They had to be able to advise parents about the toys they sold, and to look upon the children with an educator's understanding. The company therefore adopted very specific hiring policies, and many of the 'toyologues' were graduates in education, psychology, sociology or related fields. The company provided them and their 'guests' with data cards on each toy, containing detailed information regarding its use, recommended child age, the kinds of

child-development benefits generated by that particular toy, and so on. Each toy purchased was wrapped, including a label with the name of the recipient child and a lollipop.

With a few exceptions, Imaginarium stores only sold toys manufactured according to its specifications, and under its own trademark and packaging. Generally speaking, it was not possible to find exactly the same toy anywhere else.

After the success of the 1993 openings, Tena was convinced that the store layout and overall business concept was sound. The subsequent evolution of the company's sales figures and forecasts shown below would seem to prove him right.[5]

Sales revenue (in million euros)
2000: 22.5
2001: 33.6 (as budgeted)
2002: 42.5 (forecast)

Note: Fiscal year ending on January 31 of the indicated year.

Opening of the first franchised stores

In 1994 Imaginarium opened seven new toy stores: five owned and operated by the company and two franchised. Quite spontaneously, people who had seen the first stores phoned the company requesting a licence to open a franchised store. Tena thought this was terrific because it would allow him to grow faster. It would allow him to negotiate with his toy suppliers better terms of prices, exclusivity rights, etc. By growing fast, he might be able to pre-empt potential future competitors.

At the end of 1994 the British venture-capital company 3i (Investors in Industry) bought 35 per cent of the shares of Step Two, S.A. At that time Tena thought he might be able to eventually open a total of about 60 toy stores throughout Spain. He was wrong, however, as this figure was exceeded in 1998, and doubled by 1999.

Opening the first stores abroad

In 1996, a Colombian entrepreneur applied for the master franchise for Colombia. Another entrepreneur requested the master franchise for Portugal.

Tena decided he would make master franchise agreements in some countries, provided the applicant appeared to be enthusiastic, and had sufficient financial resources and market knowledge to assure the opening of a number of toy stores by himself, or to subfranchise.

Tena decided that his first priority would be to expand his chain of educational toy stores in Southern Europe. In 1999 he opened his first three stores in France. Seven more were opened in 2000. Out of these ten, nine were owned and operated by Imaginarium, and one was franchised. In Italy, four stores were opened in 2000. Only one was franchised.

Tena also decided that his second priority would be Latin America. By the end of 2000, he had signed master franchise agreements with local entrepreneurs in Colombia (5 toy stores),

Venezuela (5), Dominican Republic (2), Mexico (1), El Salvador (1) and Argentina (2).

The company was planning to open 25 new stores outside Spain in 2001, and a further 63 stores in 2002, thereby increasing the number of countries with Imaginarium stores to 18 by the end of 2002.

THE PRODUCT DEPARTMENT

At the beginning of 2001, an external observer of the Imaginarium business would probably say that the Imaginarium business model and process started in the product department. Its manager was 35, and she was one of the few pioneers who had worked with Tena since his days at Publijuego.

Her vision was based on very few market surveys, a lot of personal observation and lots of common sense. She took into account the age of target children, making sure the toys were educational, that the children would play with them, and were not sexist or racist or violent. Increasingly, toy manufacturers sent samples, which were stored in the 'sample file' shelves in the product department, organized according to the same thematic sections in Imaginarium stores.

At the beginning of each year, right after the Christmas high season, she would attend a certain number of international toy trade shows. She insisted on the fact that their toys would always carry the Imaginarium brand, and (with very few exceptions) they were to be exclusively sold at Imaginarium stores. They developed and launched two toy collections per year, in Spring–Summer and in Autumn–Winter. Each collection was made up of about 1,200 SKUs (stock keeping units). For the year 2000 collection, Imaginarium had some 110 different suppliers.

THE EXPANSION AND PROJECTS DEPARTMENT

This department's mission was to open new stores. Imaginarium might proactively open a new store, in a particular location, either fully owned or franchised. Alternatively, they might be reactive, when an entrepreneur requested a licence to open a franchised store in a particular location. A strict, standardized eight-stage selection process had been set up for selecting future franchisees. The company's business know-how was transmitted by means of initial training courses, refresher courses, operation manuals and ongoing communications and assistance.

Imaginarium insisted upon the fact that all stores were run and attended by specially qualified personnel (the 'toyologues'). They were also given ongoing training to make sure that they were able to advise guests regarding the ideal product for each boy or girl. They had to be able to transmit the fundamental idea of the company's culture and mission in their day-to-day work: 'To cheerfully contribute to the human development of children throughout the world in fun and creative ways'.

OPERATIONS AND LOGISTICS

The operations department serviced each store as soon as it was ready to open. Stores were located in expensive premium locations. Therefore they were designed without a backroom or a storeroom. All available products were on the sales floor.

Toy manufacturers sent their orders to a central warehouse in Zaragoza. Most Imaginarium toy stores were staffed from about 8:30 a.m. to 10:30 p.m. At the close of each day's sales, each store sent out automatic sales records to Zaragoza, where restocking orders were prepared, loaded on a truck, and shipped in a few hours. In most cases, the restocking merchandise arrived early in the morning, in time to be placed on the shelves by the time the store opened again in the morning. Resupply to stores located in France or Italy would normally take place every two or three days, and might take two days to reach their destination. Supplies were shipped to Latin America by full container load, every two weeks, consigned to the master franchisee.

An IT department supported all business and logistics operations.

IMAGINARIUM'S MARKETING STRATEGY

A clear business concept, retail store design and locations, capable and devoted retail store attendants, exclusive and branded products, and reasonable prices seemed to be the factors that drove Imaginarium's expansion, with limited media advertising.

The company spent a substantial proportion of its marketing funds producing and mailing two catalogues per year, mostly to Club Imaginarium members, as described below.

In August 1999 the company launched its first webpage, but by late 2000 it was reconsidering its internet strategy. It was clear to Imaginarium management that its goal was to promote multichannel sales, while including a high content of corporate values in each of the different sales channels. However, management had doubts as to whether the strategy was the right one. In particular, it worried about the potential negative reaction of franchised store owners who might dislike the fact that the company would start taking orders online. Tena insisted that the marketing department should develop a multichannel sales model where internet sales would actually enhance sales in the Imaginarium bricks-and-mortar stores.

Also, questions were raised regarding the strategic relationships between the store expansion strategy, the internet strategy and the relational marketing strategy, as developed by means of Club Imaginarium (Exhibit C3.4).

CLUB IMAGINARIUM

Club Imaginarium was created with the initial purpose of having a 'guest database' and of doing 'something special'. Its first members were registered in 1993. By early 2001, almost 400,000 families had registered. Registration cards were only available at

EXHIBIT C3.4 Evolution of imaginarium retail stores, 1992–2000

	1992	1993	1994	1995	1996	1997	1998	1999	2000	Total
Spain	1	4	11	22	32	50	67	96	119	119
Abroad:					3	6	14	27	49	49
Portugal					2	5	11	18	19	19
Colombia					1	1	2	3	5	5
Venezuela							1	2	5	5
Dominican Republic								1	2	2
France								3	10	10
Italy									4	4
Mexico									1	1
El Salvador									1	1
Argentina									2	2
Total number of stores in operation	1	4	11	22	35	56	81	123	168	168
Number of new countries with stores	1	1	1	1	3	3	4	6	10	10
Total number of company's own stores	1	4	9	15	20	26	31	38	54	54
Total number of franchise stores			2	7	15	30	50	85	114	114
Total number of own stores + franchise stores	1	1	11	22	35	56	81	123	168	168

The total of 168 stores includes those opened on December 31, 2000. The heading "Total number of company's own stores" includes the stores run directly by the franchiser Step Two, S.A., in Spain, plus the company's own stores in France and Italy. The heading "Total number of franchise stores" includes the franchise stores in Spain, France, and Italy, as well as the master franchisers' own stores in Portugal, Colombia, Venezuela, Mexico, El Salvador, and Argentina, plus the subfranchised stores in these six countries.

Imaginarium stores, and registration required the signature of at least one of the parents.

Membership is awarded to a family. From the registration card, information is stored in the data base including names, addresses, birthdates, genders, postal address, telephone number and e-mail address.

Up to 2001, membership or loyalty cards had not been issued to members of Club Imaginarium. Therefore, no distinction was made in the Imaginarium stores between occasional 'guests' and registered members of the Club.

However, active Club members were identified when they went to an Imaginarium store in response to an invitation. Such invitations announced the opening of a new store or offered a free birthday gift on condition of making a minimum purchase. Club members were also informed that they could pick up a free copy of the new seasonal toy catalogue. On such occasions, Club members received a coded coupon which, if redeemed or used, allowed the company to know who had actively responded or participated.

Imaginarium did not register its Club members' transactions (purchases), but could conclude which Club members were the most active and participated in the various activities and events to which they were invited. The information thus gathered enabled the company to decide whether or not to include the

EXHIBIT C3.5 Step two, S.A., profit and loss account at 31 January 2001 (in Euros)

Income	33,592,942
Expenses	−29,996,474
Operating profit	3,596,468
Financial expenses and others	−510,423
Profits from ordinary activities	3,086,045
Extraordinary profits	65,080
Profits before tax	3,151,125
Corporate tax	−714,621
Fiscal-year profits	2,436,504

Step Two parent-company figures. They do not include the subsidiaries in Italy, France, and Switzerland, sales on the internet, or franchise-store sales.

'lapsed' or less active Club members in the types of promotional activities that entailed higher unit costs for the company, such as mailing to them the product catalogues twice every year. 'Lapsed' Club members could be 'restored' if they participated again in some activities or events.

According to the marketing manager of Imaginarium, 'The more guests join the Club, the more they'll come to a store, the more they'll buy from us, and the more they will remember Imaginarium when they have to choose a toy store to buy from. The Club is of vital importance for managing our relationships with our members'.

However, the managers of Imaginarium had for some time been giving thought to the idea of launching a loyalty card or a similar system or mechanism that would allow them to track and register the specific toy purchases made by each family member of the Club.

Such a loyalty card could be a multisponsor card, such as Travel Club, or it could be an exclusive Imaginarium card.[6] After consulting with companies specializing in such matters, the marketing manager of Imaginarium came to the conclusion that issuing and operating their own loyalty card could cost up to about 2 to 3 per cent of Imaginarium turnover. This cost would include the cost of issuing and mailing the cards themselves, some incentives to be granted to members using the cards, and the administrative costs (maintaining the database, telephone operators to solve any incidents, mailings, e-mails, etc.).

Questions for discussion

1   In planning the future of his company, Felix Tena asked himself the following questions:

- At what speed should the business expand in terms of new stores?
- Where should they be located?
- Should the company open more stores of its own, or should it give priority to franchised stores?
- In the latter option, should the company grant individual franchises, or rather, should agreements be reached with master franchises?
- Given that the company already had educational toy stores open in ten countries, should they now concentrate on and aim at further penetrating these countries? Or rather, should they expand to other national markets?
- What role should the internet play in the company's future development?
- How should they go about developing better relationships with the some 400,000 families, who are already members of Club Imaginarium?

Notes

1   During the period December 2000–January 2001, the rate of exchange was around 0.9 US dollars per 1 euro.
2   The first Imaginarium store was opened in the area popularly known as 'The Tube'. It was an area with very narrow streets, equipped with old and somewhat dilapidated buildings. It was far from what would normally be considered a prime shopping area.
3   Another indication of Tena's intention to open a chain of franchised toy stores was the fact that in 1992, he opened a franchise store for a clothing and accessories chain. This allowed him to acquire first-hand experience in managing a franchised store. This clothing store was subsequently sold.
4   The euro currency was not actually launched until 1999. This figure is given here as the equivalent amount in euros of the former Spanish pesetas invested. In January 1999, the euro was formally launched with an exchange rate of 1 euro = 1.19 US dollars. Subsequently, the exchange rate fell to about 1 euro = 0.90 US dollars in early 2001.
5   These are the sales figures of the parent company Step Two, S.A. They do not include the sales of the subsidiaries in Italy and France, online sales, or the downstream sales of the retail franchisees.
6   This was a Spanish loyalty card similar to Air Miles, with multiple sponsor, such as a supermarket chain, a telephone company, a chain of gas stations, or a leading Spanish bank. It was estimated that it would cost Imaginarium about 1 per cent on retail sales.

Source: This is a condensed version of the case 'Imaginarium', prepared by Laureano Berasategui under the supervision of Professors Lluis G. Renart and Francesc Parés, as a basis for class discussion, rather than to illustrate either an effective or ineffective handling of an administrative situation. The complete version of the case (IESE code M-1173-E) is available from IESE Publishing, 08034 Barcelona, Spain, iesep@iesep.com. Both the original case and the present condensed version are Copyright © IESE, and cannot be further reproduced, stored in a retrieval system, used in a spreadsheet, or transmitted in any form or by any means – electronic, mechanical, photocopying, recording or otherwise – without the permission of IESE. The complete version of this case was the joint recipient of the prize in the 'Marketing' category, in the 2004 edition of the European Case Writing Competition, organized every year by the European Foundation for Management Development (EFMD), Brussels, Belgium.

Joemarin Oy

Finland's first customers in the sailboat business are generally believed to have been the Vikings. More recently, ships and boats were exported as partial payment for World War II reparations. This long tradition in building sailboats is due, no doubt, to Finland's proximity to the sea, long coastline and its 60,000 lakes. Among luxury sailing yachts, the Swan boats of Nautor Oy and the Finnclippers of Fiskars Oy are internationally known and admired. There are, however, over 100 other boat builders in Finland that turn out 10,000 sailing yachts yearly.

Although most of the Finnish sailboat companies are situated on the coast, for obvious reasons, Joemarin Oy is located in the town of Joensuu, roughly 450 kilometres northeast of Helsinki. Joemarin was founded in the town that lends part of its name to the company because of the efforts of Kehitysaluerahasto, which is the Development Area Foundation of the Finnish government. Kehitysaluerahasto provided a loan of 4 million Finnish marks to Joemarin, a privately owned company, to start its operations in the Joensuu area because of the town's high rate of unemployment.

The present product line consists of three types of fibreglass sailboats. The Joemarin 17 is a coastal sailing yacht with a new design approach (Exhibit C3.6). This approach is to provide a craft that enables a family to make weekend and holiday cruises in coastal waters and also offers exciting sailing. The sailboat is very fast. The Finnish Yacht Racing Association stated in its test in which the Joemarin 17 was judged to be the best in her class: 'She is delicate, lively, spacious, and easy to steer. She is well balanced and has a high-quality interior. She is especially fast on the beat and lively to handle in a free wind'.

The Joemarin 17, a small day cruiser with berths for two adults and two children, has a sail area of 130 square feet, weighs half a ton, and has an overall length of a little over 17 feet. The hull is made of glass-reinforced plastic (GRP), and the mast and boom are made of aluminum. The boat has a drop keel that is useful when negotiating shallow anchorages or when lifting the boat on a trailer for transportation. The layout of the boat is shown in Exhibit C3.7.

The Joemarin 34 is a relatively large motor sailer that sleeps seven people in three separate compartments. The main saloon contains an adjustable dining table, a complete galley, and a navigator's compartment. The main saloon is separated from the fore cabin by a folding door. The aft cabin, which is entered by a separate companionway, contains a double berth, wardrobe, wash basin and lockers. The toilet and shower are situated between the fore cabin and the main saloon. The boat has a sail area of 530 square feet, weighs about five tons, and has an overall length of 33 feet 9 inches. A significant feature of the craft is that she is equipped with a 47 horsepower diesel engine.

The Joemarin 34 has the same design approach as the 17. She is well appointed, with sufficient space for seven people to live comfortably. An important feature is that the three separate living compartments allow for considerable privacy. In addition, however, the modern hull is quite sleek, making her an excellent sailing yacht.

The Joemarin 36 was designed for a different purpose. Whereas the 17 and 34 are oriented towards a family approach to sailing – combining the features of safety and comfortable accommodation with good sailing ability – the 36 is first and foremost a sailing craft. It does have two berths, a small galley, and toilet facilities, but the emphasize is on sailing and racing rather than comfort. The boat has a sail area of 420 square feet, weighs a little less than four tons, and has an overall length of 35 feet 10 inches. The boat is also equipped with a small (7 horsepower) diesel engine for emergency power situations. The Joemarin 36 is a traditional Swedish design and, therefore, is directed almost solely at the Swedish market.

The company was established in order to manufacture sailboats for export. The Finnish sailboat market is small because of the short sailing season. Nevertheless, the company has been successful in marketing the 17 in Finland, although this was difficult in the beginning because of the lack of boat dealers. To circumvent this problem, Joemarin persuaded a number of new car dealers throughout the country to handle the Joemarin 17 on an agency basis. This involved the company providing one boat to each car dealer, who placed it in the showroom. The dealer then marketed the sailboats for a 15 per cent sales commission.

Although many people scoffed at this idea, the system produced reasonable sales and also made the company known throughout Finland. This contributed to an arrangement with one of the largest cooperative wholesale–retail operations in Finland.

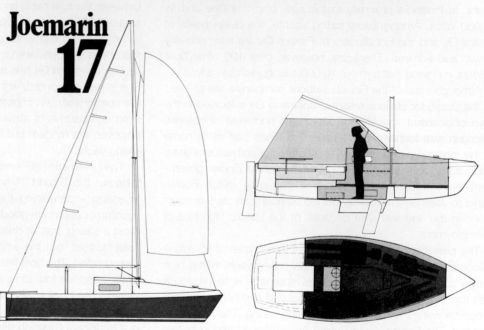

Like most cooperatives, this organization began with agricultural products; however, the product range of the company now includes virtually every conceivable consumer product. The present contract states that the cooperative will purchase 80 Joemarin 17 boats per year for the next three years.

The Swedish market is served by a selling agent, although this representative has not been particularly effective. Because Sweden is also the home of many sailboat builders, the company has tried to market only the 36 in that country. In Denmark, France, Holland, Germany and the United Kingdom, Joemarin has marketed the 34 through importers. These importers operate marinas in addition to new sailboat dealerships. They purchase the boats from Joemarin for their own accounts and mark up the price by about 20 per cent. In return for exclusive marketing rights in their respective countries, they agree to purchase a minimum number

(usually three or four) of the 34 design per year. None of these importers is interested in marketing the 17 or the 36; the shipping cost for the 17 is too high compared with the value of the boat, and there is little customer interest in the 36.

Joemarin is planning to introduce a new sailboat. Whereas the present products were designed by people in the company who were relatively unknown (to the customers), the hull of the new sailboat has been designed by an internationally known boat designer. The cost of these design services was a $30,000 initial fee plus a $3,000 royalty fee to be paid for each boat produced. The new sailboat, the Joemarin 29, has an interior quite similar to that of the Joemarin 34. This is not unexpected because the same Joemarin people designed the interiors and decks of both sailboats.

The new boat is a motor sailer that sleeps six people in three separate compartments, is 28 feet 9 inches long, weighs 4 tons,

EXHIBIT C3.8 Joemarin sales

	Last Year			Present Year		
	No.	Average Price[a]	Revenue	No.	Average Price[a]	Revenue
J/M-17	200	13,500	2,700,000	240	14,850	3,564,000
J/M-29	—	—	—	—	—	—
J/M-34	30	162,000	4,860,000	36	178,000	6,408,000
J/M-36	4	94,500	378,000	5	103,950	519,750
			7,938,000			10,491,750

[a] All prices are manufacturer's prices; prices and revenues are in euros: € 1.00 = U.S. $1.20.

and has a joined cabin space and a separate aft cabin, small galley, toilet and shower facilities, and a 12 horsepower diesel engine. Because of a new construction technique that greatly reduces the amount of fibreglass required, the variable costs to construct the boat are only 60 per cent of the costs for the 34. With a preliminary selling price of €97,500, the Joemarin 29 is receiving favourable attention, and the company is concerned that sales may have an adverse effect on sales of the 34.

The company categorizes the marketing expenses as fixed costs because allocating these expenses to specific products is difficult. The major element of the programme is participation in international boat shows in London, Paris, Hamburg, Amsterdam, Copenhagen and Helsinki. The initial purpose of participating in these shows was to locate suitable importers in the target markets; however, this effort is maintained in order to support the marketing programmes of the importers. The importers are also

supported by advertising in the leading yachting magazines in the national markets. Joemarin's personal selling effort consists primarily of servicing the importers and agents and staffing the exhibitions at the boat shows. Most of the sales promotion costs are the result of the elaborate sales brochures that the company has developed for each boat. These brochures are printed in four colours on three folded pages of high-quality paper. The costs are greatly increased, however, by having to print a relatively small number of each brochure in Finnish, French, English, German and Swedish. The brochures are provided to the agents and importers and are used at the boat shows.

The company is in the process of preparing its production and marketing plan for the coming year in order to arrange financing. The president is strongly committed to the continued growth of the company, and the market indications suggest that there is a reasonably strong demand for the 17 in Finland and

EXHIBIT C3.9 Joemarin profit statement for present year

	In €	As a Percentage of Sales
Sales revenue	10,491,750[a]	
Variable costs (direct labour and materials)	6,755,000	65.0%
Fixed costs:		
Production (building expenses, production management salaries)	472,500	4.5
Product design costs (salaries, prototypes, testing, consultants)	661,500	6.4
Administration costs (salaries, insurance, office expenses)	324,000	3.1
Marketing costs (salaries, advertising, boat shows, sales promotion, travel expenses)	1,142,000	11.0
Total fixed costs	2,600,000	25.0%
Profit before taxes	1,136,750	10.0

[a] All prices are manufacturer's prices; prices and revenues are in euros; 1.00 € = U.S. $1.20.

EXHIBIT C3.10   Shipping costs for Joemarin 36 to Sweden, and for Joemarin 29 and 34 to other countries

Country	Present Exchange Rates in €	Expected Inflation Rates	Estimated Freight and Insurance Costs per Boat
Denmark	Danish Kroner = 0.1340	2.2%	€ 6,750
France	€	1.8	€ 9,500
Holland	€	2.1	€ 8,500
Sweden	Swedish Kroner = 0.1078	1.3	€ 5,000
United Kingdom	English Pound = 1.4716	2.0	€11,000
Germany	€	2.1	€ 8,500
Finland	€	1.1	—

SOURCE: Eurostat Newsrelease, January 19, 2006.

for the 34 in most of the other national markets. The sales results of the previous and present years are shown in Exhibit C3.8; the profit statement for the present year is shown in Exhibit C3.9.

The main problem in developing the plan for next year is determining the price for each sailboat in each market. In previous years, Joemarin had established its prices in Finnish marks, on an ex-factory basis. Management has become convinced, however, that it must change the terms of its prices in order to meet competition in the foreign markets. Thus, the company has decided to offer CIF prices to its foreign customers in the currency of the foreign country. The use of truck ferries between Finland and Sweden, Denmark and Germany is expected to make this pricing approach more competitive.

Joemarin would also like to assure its agents and importers that the prices will remain in effect for the entire year, but the financial manager is concerned about the possible volatility of exchange rates because of the varying rates of inflation in the market countries. The present exchange rates, the expected inflation rates in the market countries, and the estimated costs to ship the Joemarin 36 to Stockholm and the Joemarin 29 and 34 to the other foreign marinas are shown in Exhibit C3.10.

A second difficulty in pricing the product line in Joemarin is to establish a price for the 29 that will reflect the value of the boat but will not reduce the sales of the 34. There are three schools of thought concerning the pricing of motor sailers. The predominant theory is that price is a function of the overall length of the sailboat. A number of people, however, believe that the overall weight of the craft is a much more accurate basis. The third opinion argues that price is a function of the special features and equipment. Exhibit C3.11, which was prepared by a Swiss market research firm, shows the relationship between present retail prices and the length of new motor sailers in the West European market.

EXHIBIT C3.11   Retail price in the European market of sailing yachts as a function of overall length

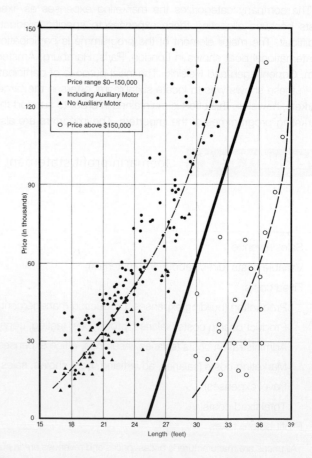

Price range $0–150,000
- ● Including Auxiliary Motor
- ▲ No Auxiliary Motor
- ○ Price above $150,000

Note: All yachts to the right of the bold dividing line are priced above 150,000.

Questions for discussion

1 Determine the optimal manufacturer's selling price in the Finnish market for the four Joemarin sailboats for the coming year.

2 Determine the CIF prices for the Joemarin 36 to the final customer in Sweden for the coming year. The agent's commission is 15 per cent of the final selling price, and the final selling price should be in Swedish kroner.

3 Recommend a course of action for the company to take in regard to the Joemarin 36.

4 Determine the CIF prices, in the foreign currencies, for the Joemarin 29 and 34 to the importers in Denmark, France, Holland, the United Kingdom and Germany for the coming year.

5 Develop a production and marketing plan for Joemarin for the coming year. What steps can the company take to ensure that the plan is in line with the demand for its products in its foreign markets?

Source: This case was prepared by James H. Sood of the American University. Reprinted with permission.

IV THE GLOBAL MARKETING MIX

Part IV deals with global marketing activities. The core marketing concerns of the beginning internationalist and the multinational corporation are the same. Yet experienced marketers face challenges and opportunities that are different from those encountered by new entrants. They are able to expend more resources on international marketing efforts than are small and medium-sized firms. In addition, their perspective can be more globally oriented. Multinational corporations also have more impact on individuals, economies and governments. Therefore, they are much more subject to public scrutiny and need to be more concerned about repercussions of their activities. Yet their very size often enables them to be more influential in setting international marketing rules.

CHAPTER 14
GLOBAL PRODUCT MANAGEMENT AND BRANDING

THE INTERNATIONAL **MARKETPLACE 14.1**

Are global brands the way to go?

Pressure is on marketing managers to develop global approaches that increase growth and profit potential, while at the same time maintaining local appeal. If these two seemingly opposite demands could be coupled and the goal of being 'global locally' met, one of the greatest challenges facing marketers could be solved. The cost of developing global programmes is high in terms of intellectual and monetary investment, and the marketing challenges are commensurate. Externally, customer behaviour similarities may not be sufficient. Internally, country management may object to cross-border efforts as an incursion to decision making.

In the last few years, the global/local controversy has been most evident in branded consumer products. A number of companies have engaged in brand pruning efforts with the aim of reducing brand portfolios to manageable sizes. Preference has naturally been given to global brands given their prominent positions. (For example, according to Unilever executives, three-quarters of the company's business comes from 25 global brands.) Many local brands are being evaluated according to their potential as global candidates or as examples of best practice that could be applied elsewhere. The bottom line for global companies is that there aren't enough resources to go around for managing scores of local brands that are not truly different.

Global brands, like any facet of global marketing, are supposed to benefit from the scale and the scope that having a presence in multiple markets brings. As global retailers gain more power, marketers may feel more pressure to have brands that can travel with their customers. Another justification for a global presence is fuelled by the increasing similarity that consumers are displaying in terms of their consumption habits and preferences. It has also been argued that global brands are perceived to be more value-added for the consumer, either through better quality (as a function of worldwide acceptance) or by enhancing the consumer's self-perception as being cosmopolitan, sophisticated and modern.

Internally, global branding can be seen as a tool to tighten organizational relationships using the transfer of best practice in brand management, as well as programmes like brand stewardship through brand management teams at headquarters or designated centres of excellence. Concentrating resources and efforts on a limited number of brands should bring about improved results. For example, Unilever has singled out six brands for special attention in the personal care category, all of which have shown double-digit growth in recent years.

While the level and effects of globalization can be disputed, the critical question is whether a brand's image will carry over effectively to other markets. Efforts to standardize brand names by eliminating local brand names have met with consumer hostility, and globally branded items introduced into product lines have not always received enthusiastic support of country managers. Consumers' behaviour may have converged, but some markets continue to have their own idiosyncrasies that can prove fatal to globalization efforts. The ability of a global product to penetrate individual markets is determined to

some extent by the product category in question. Global brands may have more success in high-profile, high-involvement categories, while consumers may still give local brands preference in purchasing everyday products.

SOURCES: Johny K. Johansson and Ilkka A. Ronkainen, 'The Esteem of Global Brands', *Journal of Brand Management* 12 (number 5, 2005): 339–354; and Johny K. Johansson and Ilkka A. Ronkainen, 'Are Global Brands the Right Choice for Your Company?' *Marketing Management,* March/April, 2004, 53–56.

Developing and managing a product portfolio in the global marketplace is both a great challenge and an attractive opportunity. While market conditions may warrant changes in individual product features, products and product lines should be managed for the greatest possible effect globally, regionally and locally as shown in *The International Marketplace 14.1*. Global and regional products have to utilize best practice across borders, while local products should be monitored for possible use in other markets.

This chapter is divided into two parts to highlight these issues. The first part will focus on how the product development process can take into account the globalization of markets without compromising dimensions considered essential by local markets. To a large extent this means that the process is market-driven rather than determined by cost or convenience of manufacture. For example, Germany's Volkswagen operated for years under the philosophy that one car was good enough for the whole world. Similarly, Japanese product-development engineers fought against the concept of a third row of seats for a sport utility vehicle.

The second half of the chapter features a discussion of product management, especially how marketers can utilize resources on a worldwide basis to exploit opportunities in product markets. Unilever, one of the world's largest food companies, often has to take a local view, given differences in the daily diet. Similarly, detergent formulas may have to differ between markets because washing habits, machines, clothes and water quality vary. However, many strategic product decisions, such as branding, will benefit from worldwide experience and exposure applied to the local context. Some categories cross national borders quite well, such as ice cream, tea, and personal wash products, and translate to opportunities with a standard approach.[1] Unilever owns more than 400 brands as a result of acquisitions, however, the company focuses on what are called the 'billion-dollar brands', 13 brands which each achieve annual sales in excess of €1 billion. Unilever's top 25 brands account for more than 70 per cent of sales.[2] The brands fall almost entirely into two categories: Food and Beverages, and Home and Personal Care.[3]

GLOBAL PRODUCT DEVELOPMENT

Product development is at the heart of the global marketing process. New products should be developed, or old ones modified, to cater to new or changing customer needs on a global or regional basis. At the same time, corporate objectives of technical feasibility and financial profitability must be satisfied.

To illustrate, Black & Decker, manufacturer of power tools for do-it-yourself household repairs, has done some remodelling of its own. Previously, the company was the consummate customizer: the Italian subsidiary made tools for Italians, the British subsidiary for the British. At the same time, Japanese power tool makers, such as Makita Electric Works Ltd, saw the world differently. Makita was Black & Decker's first competitor with a global strategy. Makita management did not care that Germans prefer high-powered, heavy-duty drills and that UD consumers want everything lighter. They reasoned that a good drill at a low price will sell anywhere in the world. Using this strategy, Makita effectively cut into Black & Decker's market share. As a result, Black & Decker unveiled 50 new models – each standardized for world production. The company's current objective is to 'establish itself as the preeminent global manufacturer and marketer' in its field.[4]

With competition increasingly able to react quickly when new products are introduced, worldwide planning at the product level provides a number of tangible benefits. A firm that adopts a worldwide approach is better able to develop products with specifications compatible on a worldwide scale. A firm that leaves product development to independent units will incur greater difficulties in transferring its experience and technology.

In many global corporations, each product is developed for potential worldwide usage and unique market requirements are incorporated whenever technically feasible. Some design their products to meet the regulations and other key requirements in their major markets and then, if necessary, smaller markets' requirements are met on a country-by-country basis. For example, Nissan develops lead-country models that can, with minor changes, be made suitable for local sales in the majority of markets. For the remaining situations, the company also provides a range of additional models that can be adapted to the needs of local segments. Using this approach, Nissan has been able to reduce the number of basic models from 48 to 28.[5] This approach also means that the new product can be introduced concurrently into all the firm's markets. Companies like Sony and Xerox develop most of their products with this objective in mind.

Some markets may require unique approaches to developing global products. At Gillette, timing is the only concession to local taste. Emerging markets, such as Eastern Europe and China, are first weaned on less-expensive products before they are sold the latest versions.[6] In a world economy where most of the growth is occurring in emerging markets, the traditional approach of introducing a global product may keep new products out of the hands of consumers due to their premium price. As a result, Procter & Gamble works out what consumers in various countries can afford and then develops products they can pay for. For example, in Brazil, the company introduced a diaper called Pampers Uni, a less-expensive version of its mainstream product. The strategy is to create price tiers, generating brand loyalty early and then encouraging customers to trade up as their incomes and desire for better products grow.[7]

The main goal of the product development process, therefore, is not to develop a standard product or product line but to build adaptability into products and product lines that are being developed to achieve worldwide appeal. To accomplish the right balance, marketers need to develop basic capability for capturing consumer information within their country organizations. If consumers are willing to talk about their preferences, traditional approaches such as focus groups and interviews work well. Procter & Gamble, for example, generates Chinese consumer information using a 30-person market research team.[8]

The product development process

The product development process begins with idea generation. Ideas may come from within the company – from the research and development staff, sales personnel, or almost anyone who becomes involved in the company's efforts. Intermediaries may suggest ideas because they are closer to the changing, and often different, needs of international customers. In franchising operations, franchisees are a source of many new products. For example, the McFlurry, McDonald's ice cream dessert, was the brainchild of a Canadian operator.[9] Competitors are a major outside source of ideas. A competitive idea from abroad may be modified and improved to suit another market's characteristics.

For a number of companies, especially those producing industrial goods, customers provide the best source of ideas for new products.[10] Many new commercially important products are initially thought of and even prototyped by users rather than originators. They tend to be developed by lead users – companies, organizations, or individuals who are ahead of trends or have needs that go beyond what is available at present. For example, a car company in need of a new braking system may look for ideas at racing teams or even at the aerospace industry, which has a strong incentive to stop its vehicles before they run out of runway.[11] Of the 30 products with the highest world sales, 70 per cent trace their origins to manufacturing and marketing (rather than laboratories) via customer input.[12] Many companies work together with complementary-goods producers in developing new solutions; Renault and Nissan established an alliance to achieve profitable growth for both companies. With the increased diffusion of the internet, chat rooms about products and features will become an important source of information pertinent to product development and adjustment. For example, Sony set up a website to support hackers who are interested in exploring and developing new types of games that could be played on the Sony PlayStation. In the field of industrial products, users are invited to use toolkits to design products and services that fit their own needs precisely.[13]

For some companies, procurement requisitions from governments and supranational organizations (for example, the United Nations) are a good source of new product ideas. When the United Nations Children's Fund (UNICEF) was looking for containers to transport temperature-sensitive vaccines in tropical climates, Igloo Corporation noticed that the technology from its picnic coolers could be used and adapted for UNICEF's use.[14] Facilitating agents, such as advertising agencies or market research organizations, can be instrumental in scanning the globe for new ideas.

Most companies develop hundreds of ideas every year; for example, 3M may have 1,000 new product ideas competing for scarce development funds annually. Product ideas are screened on market, technical and financial criteria: Is the market substantial and penetrable, can the product be mass produced, and if the answer to both of these questions is affirmative, can the company produce and market it profitably? Too often, companies focus on understanding only the current demand of the consumer. A repositioning of the concept may overcome an initial negative assessment; for example, in countries with no significant breakfast habit, cereal marketers present their products as snacks. Procter & Gamble created the perception that dandruff – traditionally a nonissue for the Chinese – is a social stigma and offered a product (Head & Shoulders anti-dandruff shampoo) to solve the problem. Today, P&G controls more than half the shampoo market in China.[15]

A product idea that at some stage fails to earn a go-ahead is not necessarily scrapped. Most progressive companies maintain data banks of 'miscellaneous opportunities'. Often, data from these banks are used in the development of other products. One of the most famous examples concerns 3M. After developing a new woven fabric some 50 years ago, 3M's Commercial Office Supply Company did not know what to do with the technology. Among the applications rejected were seamless brassiere cups and disposable nappies. The fabric was finally used to make surgical and industrial masks.

All the development phases – idea generation, screening, product and process development, scale-up and commercialization – should be global in nature with inputs into the process from all affected markets. If this is possible, original product designs can be adapted easily and inexpensively later on. The process has been greatly facilitated through the use of computer-aided design (CAD). Some companies are able to design their products so that they meet most standards and requirements around the world, with minor modifications on a country-by-country basis. The product development process can be initiated by any unit of the organization, in the parent country or abroad. If the initiating entity is a subsidiary that lacks technical and financial resources for implementation, another entity of the firm is assigned the responsibility. Most often this is the parent and its central R&D department.

Global companies may have an advantage in being able to utilize resources from around the world. Otis Elevator Inc.'s product for high-rises, the Elevonic, is a good example of this. The elevator was developed by six research centres in five countries. Otis' group in Farmington, Connecticut, handled the systems integration, Japan designed the special motor drives that make the elevators ride smoothly, France perfected the door systems, Germany handled the electronics, and Spain took care of the small-geared components. The international effort saved more than $10 million in design costs and cut the development cycle from four years to two.[16]

Even though the product development activity may take place in the parent country, all the affected units actively participate in development and market planning for a new product. For example, a subsidiary would communicate directly with the product division at the headquarters level and also with the international staff, who could support the subsidiary on the scene of the actual development activity. This often also involves the transfer of people from one location to another for such projects. For example, when Fiat wanted to build a car specifically for emerging markets, the task to develop the Palio was given to a 300-strong team which assembled in Turin, Italy. Among them were 120 Brazilians, ranging from engineers to shop-floor workers, as well as Argentines, Turks and Poles.[17]

The activities of a typical global programme are summarized in Exhibit 14.1. The managing unit has prime responsibility for accomplishing: (1) single-point worldwide technical development and design of a new product that conforms to the global design standard and global manufacturing and procurement standards, as well as transmittal of the completed design to each affected unit; (2) all other activities necessary to plan, develop, originate, introduce and support the product in the managing unit, as well as direction and support to affected units to ensure that concurrent introductions are achieved; and (3) integration and coordination of all global programme activities.

The affected units, on the other hand, have prime responsibility for achieving: (1) identification of unique requirements to be incorporated in the product goals and specifications as well as in the managing unit's technical effort; (2) all other activities necessary to plan, originate, introduce and support products in affected units; and (3) identification of any nonconcurrence with the managing unit's plans and activities.

During the early stages of the product development process, the global emphasize is on identifying and evaluating the requirements of both the managing unit and the affected units and incorporating them into the plan. During the later stages, the emphasize is on the efficient development and design of a global product with a minimum of configuration differences and on the development of supporting systems capabilities in each of the participating units. The result of the interaction and communication is product development activity on a global basis, as well as products developed primarily to serve world markets. For example, Fiat's Palio is designed for the rough roads of the Brazilian interior rather than the smooth motorways of Italy. The car was also deliberately overengineered, because market research revealed that customers' future preferences were developing that way.

This approach effectively cuts through the standardized-versus-localized debate and offers a clear-cut way of determining and implementing effective programmes in several markets simultaneously. It offers headquarters the opportunity to standardize certain aspects of the product while permitting maximum flexibility, whenever technically feasible, to differing market conditions. For instance, in terms of technical development, members of subsidiaries' staffs take an active part in the development processes to make sure that global specifications are built into the initial design of the product.[18]

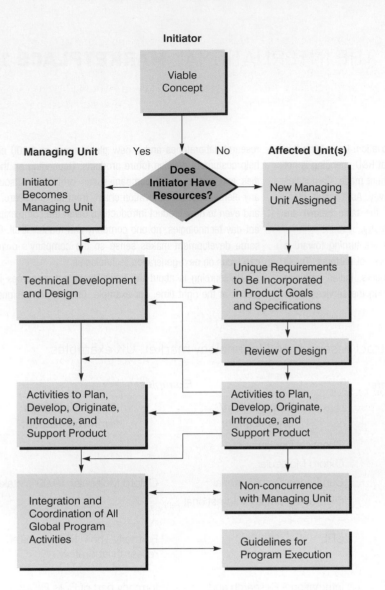

Initiator

Managing Unit   Yes   No   **Affected Unit(s)**

EXHIBIT 14.1

Global program
management

Source: Ilkka A. Ronkainen,
"Product Development in the
Multinational Firm," *International
Marketing Review* 1 (Winter 1983):
24–30.

The process has to be streamlined in terms of duration as well. In industries characterized by technological change, coming to market nine to twelve months late can cost a new product half its potential revenues. To cut down on development time, companies like NEC and Canon use multidisciplinary teams that stay with the project from start to finish, using a parallel approach towards product launch. Designers start to work before feasibility testing is over; manufacturing and marketing begin gearing up well before the design is finished. Such teams depend on computer systems for designing, simulating, and analysing products. Toyota Motor Company estimates that it will, sometime in the future, develop a new automobile in one year (its RAV4 mini sport utility vehicle was brought to market in 24 months), whereas some of its competitors may spend as much as five years on the process.[19]

The challenge today is that no internal R&D effort can possibly predict, evaluate and cover all possible configurations. Taking these new realities to heart, companies need to systematically tap into the capabilities of external knowledge and skills leaders, not just for state-of-the-art products but also for the continuous innovation and evolution of ideas (as argued in *The International Marketplace 14.2*).[20] At Procter & Gamble, the 'connect-and-develop' model's objective is to identify promising ideas around the world, and apply the company's own R&D, manufacturing, and marketing capabilities to them to create better and cheaper products, faster.[21] A total of 45 per cent of the initiatives in the company's product development portfolio have key elements from external constituents.

THE INTERNATIONAL **MARKETPLACE 14.2**

Outsourcing innovation

The next step in outsourcing may be innovation. Underlying this phenomenon is a growing consensus that R&D spending is not generating enough return on the investment made. Companies can either cut costs or increase R&D productivity. As a result, little-known companies (such as those shown in the table below) are emerging as new powers in the technology industry.

At the minimum, most leading companies are turning toward a model of innovation that employs global networks of partners. These can include EU chipmakers, Taiwanese engineers, Indian software developers and Chinese factories. IBM is offering the services of its research laboratories and a new global team of 1,200 engineers to help customers develop future products. Depending on their capabilities and needs, many companies can profitably outsource almost any elements in the innovation chain, from basic research to testing, and even to new-product introduction. Given the complexities of present-day technologies, no one company can master it all. Outsourcing some development makes sense so the company's own engineers can focus on next-generation technologies.

Outsourcing is about the flexibility to put resources in the right places at the right time. For example, using a pre-designed platform

Types of new entrants in the contract research and technology market: UK examples

	Types of new entrants:	Examples:	
		Name of firm/ organization:	Related/affiliated firm/organization:
1.	New firm types:	Chemical Design	
		Oxford Molecular	
		Cambridge Combinatorial	Oxford Molecular 19.99% stake
		Oxford Asymmetry International	
2.	Spin-offs:	–	–
2.1	Spin-offs (from manufacturing and service firms)	CRL	Formerly Thorn EMI's central research laboratory
		International Research and Development	formerly part of Rolls Royce Industrial Power
2.2	Spin-offs (from universities)	Aston Molecules	Aston University, Birmingham
		Bradford University Research	Bradford University, Bradford
3.	Diversification:	BSI	Has over 250 research staff working on basic and applied R&D
4.	Government privatization:	ADAS	Former government agency for agricultural R&D and laboratory and consultancy services
		AEA Technology	Formerly the UK Atomic Energy Authority
		LGC	Formerly the Laboratory of the Government Chemist

Source: Centre for Research on Innovation and Competition (CRIC), Manchester Institute of Innovation Research (MIoIR) (2007) 'Outsourcing of Research and Development'. Online. Available from: **http://www.cric.ac.uk/cric/compprojects/project-4.htm** (Accessed 16/2/10).

can cut 70 per cent of development costs off a new model. As a rule of thumb, it takes $10 million and 150 staff to develop a new mobile phone from scratch.

The danger of outsourcing R&D is creating competition. Motorola hired BenQ from Taiwan to design and manufacture mobile phones. Subsequently, BenQ started selling its phones in China under its brand name. Companies try to draw the line between mission-critical R&D and commodity work. What will be outsourced is routine, computer-like, spec-sheet based tasks, while work that entails artistry, creativity and empathy with the customer will be performed at home. Motorola has announced that it will keep R&D spending at around 10 per cent for the long term. Lucent has plans to keep its R&D staff at 9,000. However, most companies' new hiring will occur at their own labs abroad in China, India and Eastern Europe. Some marketers are making their own R&D and design efforts a competitive tool; for example, each iPod has 'Designed in California' etched on its back panel.

SOURCES: Nitin Nohria, 'Feed R&D – or Farm it Out', *Harvard Business Review* 83 (July/August 2005): 17–27; 'Outsourcing Innovation', *Business Week*, March 21, 2005, 84–90; James B. Quinn, 'Outsourcing Innovation: The New Engine of Growth', *Sloan Management Review* 41 (number 4, 2000): 13–29; Centre for Research on Innovation and Competition (CRIC) (2007), 'Outsourcing of Research and Development'. Online. Available from **http://www.cric.ac.uk/cric/compprojects/project-4.htm.**

Firms using worldwide product management are better able to develop products that can be quickly introduced into any market.[22] Foreign market introduction can take the form of either production or marketing abroad. In general, the length of the lag will depend on (1) the product involved, with industrial products having shorter lags because of their more standardized general nature; (2) degree of newness; (3) customer characteristics – both demographics and psychographics; (4) geographic proximity; (5) firm-related variables – the number and type of foreign affiliations as well as overall experience in global marketing and (6) degree of commitments of resources.

Many companies allow and encourage their research centres to devote part of their time purely to their own endeavours. These initiatives are both effective for the motivation of the local personnel and incubators for future regional and global products. For example, the current research and development activities of consumer-product companies, which tend to be centralized near world headquarters, will have to shift to take into account the increasing numbers of customers who live in emerging markets.

The location of R&D activities

In the past, many corporations located most of their product development operations within the parent corporation. However, a significant number of companies have started using foreign-based resources to improve their ability to compete internationally. At Asea Brown Boveri, for example, 80 per cent of research was carried out in the company's Swiss, Swedish and German offices only a few years ago, but now it is only half of the total. The company has established new research units in countries such as India and China to stay closer to markets to meet customer needs.[23] Dutch electronics giant Philips has 15 research-and-development centres in China as part of the company's strategies aiming at satisfying demand for its products (such as low-end mobile phones) in China, India, Africa, South America and Eastern Europe. These centres are integrated with the efforts of the R&D centres in Europe and the company's Innovation Campus in India.[24] While many endeavours may be set to deal with the local markets or similar regions, solutions may find broader acceptance in the world marketplace. For example, Campbell's R&D centre in Hong Kong was initially set up to adjust the company's product offering to the Chinese market. It has since acquired a new role of transferring product concepts developed for the Asian market to the Americas and Europe, due to an increasing interest in ethnic foods. Savi Technology, a provider of real-time solutions for managing supply chains, established its R&D Centre for IT Logistic Excellence in Singapore, because the city-state is a major starting point for many supply chains and Savi's major customers operate from there.[25]

Investments for R&D abroad are made for four general reasons: (1) to aid technology transfer from parent to subsidiary; (2) to develop new and improved products expressly for foreign markets; (3) to develop new products and processes for simultaneous application in world markets of the firm; and (4) to generate new technology of a long-term exploratory nature. The commitment of the firm to international operations increases from the first type of investment to the third and fourth, in which there is no or little bias toward headquarters performing the job.[26]

A survey of 209 multinationals in Europe, Japan and North America shows that the trend towards internationalization of R&D is growing. The Japanese have the lowest degree of internationalization in their R&D efforts compared to their European and North American counterparts; the Europeans give their country operations abroad more responsibilities in product development.[27] In most cases, companies want to be closer to the customers they intend to serve. In some industries, such as pharmaceuticals, having localized R&D efforts is necessary due to heavy regulatory efforts by local or regional governments.

In truly global companies, the location of R&D is determined by the existence of specific skills, as seen in *The International Marketplace 14.3*. Placing R&D operations abroad may

THE INTERNATIONAL **MARKETPLACE 14.3**

Centres of excellence

Local markets are absorbing bigger roles as marketers scan the world for ideas that will cross borders. The consensus among marketers is that many more countries are now capable of developing products and product solutions that can be applied on a worldwide basis. This realization has given birth to centres of excellence. A centre of excellence is defined as an organizational unit that incorporates a set of capabilities that have been identified as an important source of value creation with the explicit intention that these capabilities be leveraged by and/or disseminated to other parts of the firm.

Colgate-Palmolive has set up centres of excellence around the world, clustering countries with geographic, linguistic or cultural similarities to exploit the same marketing plans. Unilever is extending the innovation centres it opened for personal care products to its food businesses, starting with ice cream. In addition to innovation centres for oral care in Milan and hair care in Paris, there are now similar centres for developing product ideas, research, technology and marketing expertise for ice cream products in Rome, Hamburg, London and Paris; and in Bangkok for the Asian market.

Countries have an edge if there is strong local development in a particular product category, such as hair care in France and Thailand, creating an abundance of research and development talent. Local management or existing products with a history of sensitivity to the core competence also helps win a worldwide role for a country unit. For example, ABB Strömberg in Finland was assigned as a worldwide centre of excellence for electric drivers, a category for which it is a recognized world leader.

Volkswagen's centres of excellence have been established with one main objective: to put quality back at the centre of its strategy, for example, engines, engineering and developing common platforms. Centres of excellence do not necessarily have to be focused on products or technologies. Corning has established a centre for marketing excellence where sales and marketing staff from all Corning's businesses, from glass to television components to electronic communications displays, will be able to find help with marketing intelligence, strategies, new product lines and e-business. Procter & Gamble has six development hubs that are focused on finding products and technologies that are specialties of their regions. The China hub looks for new high-quality materials and cost innovations, while the India hub seeks out local talent in the sciences to solve problems, using tools such as computer modelling.

Whatever the format, centres of excellence have as the most important tasks to leverage and/or to transfer their current leading-edge capabilities, and to continually fine-tune and enhance those capabilities so that they remain state-of-the-art. Centres of excellence provide country organizations a critical tool by which to develop subsidiary-specific advantages to benefit the entire global organization.

SOURCES: Larry Huston and Nabil Sakkab, 'Connect and Develop: Inside Procter & Gamble's Model for Innovation', *Harvard Business Review* 84 (March 2006): 58–66; Tony Frost, Julian Birkinshaw and Prescott Ensign, 'Centres of Excellence in Multinational Corporations', *Strategic Management Journal* 23 (November 2002): 997–1018; Karl J. Moore, 'A Strategy for Subsidiaries: Centres of Excellence to Build Subsidiary-Specific Advantages', *Management International Review* 41 (third quarter, 2001): 275–290; Erin Strout, 'Reinventing a Company', *Sales and Marketing Management* 152 (February 2000): 86–92; Karl Moore and Julian Birkinshaw, 'Managing Knowledge in Global Service Firms: Centres of Excellence', *Academy of Management Executive* 12 (November 1998): 81–92; Laurel Wentz, 'World Brands', *Advertising Age International*, September 1996, i1–i21; 'Ford to Merge European, North American Car Units', *The Washington Post*, April 22, 1994, G1–2; 'Percy Barnevik's Global Crusade', *Business Week Enterprise* 1993, 204–211; **http://www.colgate.com**; **http://www.abb.com**; **http://www.ford.com**; **http://www.pg.com**; and **http://www.corning.com**.

also ensure access to foreign scientific and technical personnel and information, either in industry or at leading universities. The location decision may also be driven by the unique features of the market, for example, technical, social, aesthetic values, technological innovations and design skill. The UK government has created a regulatory and business framework which actively encourages home-grown and inward investments.[28] It offers an environment where all companies are treated equally, regardless of ownership, with the result that no other member state in the EU is home to as many manufacturers of vehicles – cars, trucks and buses – as the UK.[29] Working with the most demanding customers (on issues such as quality) will give companies assurance of success in broader markets.[30]

Given the increasing importance of emerging and developing markets, many marketers believe that an intimate understanding of these new consumers can be achieved only through proximity. Consequently, Unilever has installed a network of innovation Centres in 19 countries, many of which are emerging markets (such as Brazil, China and Thailand). Hewlett-Packard's eInclusion division, which focuses on rural markets, established a branch of its HP Labs in India charged with developing products and services explicitly for that market.[31]

R&D centres are seen as highly desirable investments by host governments. Developing countries are increasingly demanding R&D facilities as a condition of investment or continued operation, to the extent that some companies have left countries where they saw no need for the added expense. Countries that have been known to have attempted to influence multinational corporations are Japan, India, Brazil and France. The Chinese government has maintained a preference for foreign investors who have promised a commitment to technology transfer, especially in the form of R&D centres; Volkswagen's ability to develop its business in China is largely due to its willingness to do so. Some governments, such as Canada, have offered financial rewards to multinational corporations to start or expand R&D efforts in host markets. In addition to compliance with governmental regulation, local R&D efforts can provide positive publicity for the company involved. Internally, having local R&D may boost morale and elevate a subsidiary above the status of merely a manufacturing operation.[32]

In companies that still employ multidomestic strategies, product development efforts amount to product modifications – for example, making sure that a product satisfies local regulations. Local content requirements may necessitate major development input from the affected markets. In these cases, local technical people identify alternate, domestically available ingredients and prepare initial tests. More involved testing usually takes place at a regional laboratory or at headquarters.

The organization of global product development

The product development activity is undertaken by specific teams, whose task is to subject new products to tough scrutiny at specified points in the development cycle, to eliminate weak products before too much is invested in them and to guide promising prototypes from labs to the market.[33] Representatives of all the affected functional areas serve on each team to ensure the integrity of the project. A marketing team member is needed to assess the customer base for the new product, engineering to make sure that the product can be produced in the intended format, and finance to keep costs under control. An international team member should be assigned a permanent role in the product development process and not simply called in when a need arises. Organizational relationships have to be such that the firm's knowledge-based assets are easily transferable and transferred.[34]

In addition to having international representation on each product development team, some multinational corporations hold periodic meetings of purely international teams. A typical international team may consist of five members, each of whom also has a product responsibility (such as cable accessories) as well as a geographical responsibility (such as the Far East). Others may be from central R&D and domestic marketing planning. The function of international teams is to provide both support to subsidiaries and international input to overall planning efforts. A critical part of this effort is customer input before a new product design is finalized. This is achieved by requiring team members to visit key customers throughout the process. A key input of international team members is the potential for universal features that can be used worldwide as well as unique features that may be required for individual markets.

Such multi-disciplinary teams maximize the payoff from R&D by streamlining decision making; that is, they reduce the need for elaborate reporting mechanisms and layers of committee approvals. With the need to slash development time, reduce overall material costs and trim manufacturing processes, these teams can be useful. For example, in response to competition, Honeywell set up a multi-disciplinary 'tiger team' to build a thermostat in twelve months rather than the usual four years.[35]

Challenges to using teams or approaches that require cooperation between R&D centres are often language and cultural barriers. For example, theoretically thinking European engineers may distrust their more pragmatic US counterparts. National rivalries may also inhibit the acceptance by others of solutions developed by one entity of the organization. Many companies have solved these problems with increased communication and exchange of personnel.[36]

With the costs of basic research rising and product life cycles shortening, many companies have joined forces in R&D. However, a problem expressed by firms outsourcing their research or technical requirements was that although they may formally receive all the codified knowledge associated with the project, they would not gain more tacit elements associated with the process. Managers were also concerned that although the external partner may competently deliver a piece of technological knowledge, at the end of the project they may also share this knowledge with other competitors. Firms have come to acknowledge that technological knowledge is not a simple one-way flow of resources; collaboration involves sharing of future (unknown) complementary knowledge 'assets'. New knowledge fields may only be developed by combining complementary knowledge sources from a variety of different contributors. The decision involves an important 'matching' process to see whether a project to gain new technological knowledge is viable.[37]

The testing of new product concepts

The final stages of the product development process will involve testing the product in terms of both its performance and its projected market acceptance. Depending on the product, testing procedures range from reliability tests in the pilot plant to mini-launches, from which the product's performance in world markets will be estimated. Any testing will prolong full-scale commercialization and increase the possibility of competitive reaction. Further, the cost of test marketing is substantial – on average, $1 to $1.5 million per market.

Because of the high rate of new product failure (estimated at 67–95 per cent[38] and usually attributed to market or marketing reasons), most companies want to be assured that their product will gain customer acceptance. They therefore engage in testing or a limited launch of the product. This may involve introducing the product in one country – for instance, Belgium or Ireland – and basing the go-ahead decision for the rest of Europe on the performance of the product in that test market. Some countries are emerging as test markets for global products. Brazil is a test market used by Procter & Gamble and Colgate before rollout into the Latin American market. Unilever uses Thailand as a test market for the Asian market.

In many cases, companies rely too much on instinct and hunch in their marketing abroad, although in domestic markets they make extensive use of testing and research. Lack of testing has led to a number of major product disasters over the years. The most serious blunder is to assume that other markets have the same priorities and lifestyles as the domestic market. After a failure in introducing canned soups in Italy in the 1960s, Campbell Soup Company repeated the experience by introducing them in Brazil in 1979. Research conducted in Brazil after the failure revealed that women fulfill their roles as homemakers in part by such tasks as making soups from scratch. A similar finding had emerged in Italy more than 20 years earlier. However, when Campbell was ready to enter the Eastern and Central European markets in the 1990s, it was prepared for this and was careful to position the product initially as a starter or to be kept for emergencies.

Other reasons for product failure are a lack of product distinctiveness, unexpected technical problems and mismatches between functions.[39] Mismatches between functions may occur not only between, for example, engineering and marketing, but within the marketing function as well. Engineering may design features in the product that established distribution channels or selling approaches cannot exploit. Advertising may promise the customer something that the other functions within marketing cannot deliver.

The trend is toward a complete testing of the marketing mix. All the components of the brand are tested, including formulation, packaging, advertising and pricing. Test marketing is indispensable because pre-launch testing is an artificial situation; it tells the researcher what people say they will do, not what they will actually do. Test marketing carries major financial risks, which can be limited only if the testing can be conducted in a limited area. Ideally, this would utilize localized advertising media – that is, broadcast and print media to which only a limited region would be exposed. However, localized media are lacking even in developed markets such as Western Europe.

Due to expensive, risky or even impossible, test marketing in Eastern Europe and else where, researchers have developed three research methods to cope with the difficulty. Laboratory test markets are the least realistic in terms of consumer behaviour over time, but this method allows the participants to be exposed to television advertisements, and their reactions can be measured in a controlled environment. Microtest marketing involves a continuous panel of consumers serviced by a retail grocery operated by the research agency. The panelists are exposed to new products through high-quality colour print ads, coupons and free samples. Initial willingness to buy and repeat buying are monitored. Forced distribution tests are based on a continuously reporting panel of consumers, but they encounter new products in normal retail outlets. This is realistic, but competitors are immediately aware of the new product. An important criterion for successful testing is to gain the cooperation of key retailing organizations in the market. Mars Confectionery, which was testing a new chocolate malted-milk drink in the UK, could not get distribution in major supermarkets for test products. As a result. Mars changed its approach and focused its marketing on the home delivery market.[40] Faced with a similar fate, Panda, a small liquorice maker from Finland, repositioned its product and sold it through health-care stores in the UK.

The global product launch[41]

The impact of an effective global product launch can be great, but so can the cost of one that is poorly executed. High development costs as well as competitive pressures are forcing companies to rush products into as many markets as possible. However, at the same time, a company can ill afford new products that are not effectively introduced, marketed and supported in each market the company competes in.

A global product launch means introducing a product into countries in three or more regions within a narrow time frame. To achieve this, a company must undertake a number of measures. The country managers should be involved in the first stage of product strategy formulation to ensure that local and regional considerations are part of the overall corporate and product messages. More important, intercountry coordination of the rollout preparations will ultimately determine the level of success in the introduction. A product launch team (consisting of product, marketing, manufacturing, sales, service, engineering and communication representatives) can also approach problems from an industry standpoint, as opposed to a home country perspective, enhancing product competitiveness in all markets.

Adequate consideration should be given to localization and translation requirements before the launch. This means that the right messages are formulated and transmitted to key internal and external audiences. Support materials have to take into account both cultural and technical differences. The advantage of a simultaneous launch is that it boosts the overall momentum and attractiveness of the product by making it immediately available in key geographic markets.

Global product launches typically require more education and support of the sales channel than do domestic efforts or drawn-out efforts. This is due to the diversity of the distribution channels in terms of the support and education they may require before the launch.

A successfully executed global launch offers several benefits. First, it permits the company to showcase its technology in all major markets at the same time. Setting a single date for the launch functions as a strict discipline to force the entire organization to gear up quickly for a successful worldwide effort. A simultaneous worldwide introduction also solves the 'lame duck' dilemma of having old models available in some markets while customers know of the existence of the new product. If margins are most lucrative at the early stages of the new product's life cycle, they should be exploited by getting the product to as many markets as possible from the outset. With product development costs increasing and product life cycles shortening, marketers have to consider this approach seriously. An additional benefit of a worldwide launch may be added publicity to benefit the marketer's efforts, as happened with the introductions worldwide of Microsoft's Windows 95, 98, 2000 and XP versions.

MANAGEMENT OF THE PRODUCT AND BRAND PORTFOLIO

Most marketers have a considerable number of individual items in their product portfolios, consisting of different product lines, that is, grouping of products managed and marketed as a unit. The options for a particular portfolio (or multiple portfolios) are to expand geographically to new markets or new segments and add to existing market operations through new product lines or new product business. The marketer will need to have a balanced product and market portfolio – a proper mix of new, growing and mature products to provide a sustainable competitive advantage.[42]

The assessment of the product portfolio will have to take into account various interlinkages both external and internal to the firm. Geographic interlinkages call attention to market similarities, especially to possibilities of extending operations across borders. Product-market interlinkages are manifested in common customers and competitors. Finally, the similarities in present-day operations should be assessed in terms of product lines, brands and brand positionings. As a result of such an analysis, Mars has stayed out of the US chocolate milk market, despite a product-company fit, because the market is dominated by Hershey and Nestlé. However, it has entered this particular market elsewhere, such as Europe.

Analysing the product portfolio

The specific approach chosen and variables included will vary by company, according to corporate objectives and characteristics as well as the nature of the product market. A product portfolio approach based on growth rates and market share positions allows the analysis of business entities, product lines or individual products. Exhibit 14.2 represents the product-market portfolio of Company A, which markets the same product line in several countries. The company is a leader in most of the markets in which it has operations, as indicated by its relative market shares. It has two cash cows (United States and Canada), four stars

EXHIBIT 14.2

Example of a product-market portfolio

Source: Adapted from Jean-Claude Larréché, "The International Product-Market Portfolio," in *1978 AMA Educators' Proceedings* (Chicago: American Marketing Association, 1978), 276.

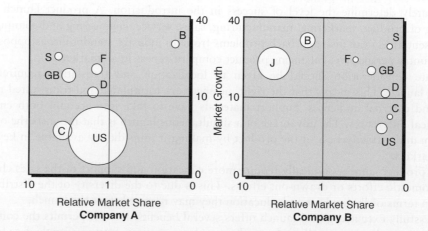

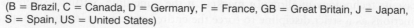

(B = Brazil, C = Canada, D = Germany, F = France, GB = Great Britain, J = Japan, S = Spain, US = United States)

(Germany, Great Britain, France and Spain), and one 'problem child' (Brazil). In the mature US market, Company A has its largest volume but only a small market share advantage compared with competition. Company A's dominance is more pronounced in Canada and in the EU countries.

At the same time, Company B, its main competitor, although not a threat in Company A's major markets, does have a commanding lead in two fast-growing markets: Japan and Brazil. As this illustration indicates, an analysis should be conducted not only of the firm's own portfolio but also of competitors' portfolios, along with a projection of the firm's and the competitors' future international products – market portfolios. Building future scenarios based on industry estimates will allow Company A to take remedial long-term action to counter Company B's advances. In this case, Company A should direct resources to build market share in fast-growing markets such as Japan and Brazil.

In expanding markets, any company not growing rapidly risks falling behind for good. Growth may mean bringing out new items or lines or having to adjust existing products. In the last ten years, General Motors has invested over $5 billion in the Brazilian car market, which is the eighth largest in the world. While production capacity of the world's two dozen carmakers is more than double the expected demand of 1.1 million cars and all makers were initially losing money, GM, with its investments and new models, has positioned itself to take advantage of significant growth rates projected for the future. Volkswagen and Fiat have seen their market shares fall, mainly because they have been milking the market with old models: Volkswagen with the 20-year-old Golf and Fiat with the Uno, which dates back to 1984.[43] GM is not going to be left unchallenged, however. With its strategic alliance with Chrysler, Fiat, for example, is hoping to regain lost ground through access to Chrysler's distribution network and suppliers and a 35 per cent equity stake in Chrysler.[44] The United Auto Workers Union (UAW) own 55 per cent of the new Chrysler Group. The rest is split between the US Treasury and Canadian Government at 8 per cent and 2 per cent, respectively.[45]

Portfolios should also be used to assess market, product, and business interlinkages.[46] This effort will allow the exploitation of increasing market similarities through corporate adjustments in setting up appropriate strategic business units (SBUs), and the standardization of product lines, products and marketing programmes.

The presentation in Exhibit 14.3 shows a market-product-business portfolio for a food company, such as Nestlé or Unilever. The interconnections are formed by common target markets served, sharing of research and development objectives, use of similar technologies, and the benefits that can be drawn from sharing common marketing experience. The example indicates possibilities within regions and between regions; frozen foods both in Europe and the United States and ice cream throughout the three mega-markets. Such assessments are integral in preparing future strategic outlines for different groups or units. For example, at Nestlé, ice cream was identified as an area of global development since the company already had a presence in a number of market areas and had identified others for their opportunity.

Advantages of the product portfolio approach The major advantages provided by the product portfolio approach are as follows:

1 A global view of the competitive structure, especially when longer-term considerations are included.

2 A guide for the formulation of a global marketing strategy based on the suggested allocation of scarce resources between product lines.

3 A guide for the formulation of marketing objectives for specific markets based on an outline of the role of each product line in each of the markets served – for example, to generate cash or to block the expansion of competition.

4 A convenient visual communication goal, achieved by integrating a substantial amount of information in an appealingly simple format including assessment of interlinkages between units and products.

EXHIBIT 14.3

Example of market-product-business portfolio

Source: Adapted from Susan P. Douglas and C. Samuel Craig, "Global Portfolio Planning and Market Interconnectedness," *Journal of International Marketing 4* (no. 1, 1996): 93–110.

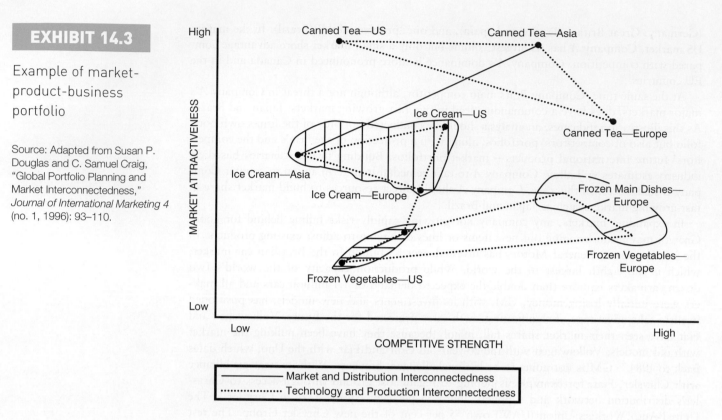

Before making strategic choices based on such a portfolio, the global marketer should consider the risks related to variables such as entry mode and exchange rates; management preferences for idiosyncratic objectives, such as concentrating on countries with similar market characteristics; and marketing costs. For example, the cost of entry into one market may be less because the company already has a presence there in another product category and the possibility exists that distribution networks may be shared. Similarly, ideas for new products and marketing programmes can be leveraged across geographies based on both market characteristics and company position in those markets.[47]

The portfolio assessment also needs to be put into a larger context. The Korean market and Korean carmakers may not independently warrant urgent action on the part of the leading companies. However, as part of the global strategic setting in the auto industry, both the market and its companies become critically important. Indonesia is now the third largest car market in South East Asia after Thailand, where an estimated 485,000 cars were sold, as compared to 620,000 cars sold in Thailand in 2008.[48] Increased demand could reach 1.3 million by 2010, hence Indonesia has attracted car manufacturers. Similarly, Korea, along with China and Japan, is one of the three most important vehicle markets in Asia and can be considered an ideal platform for exporting to other parts of the continent. While Korean carmakers, such as Daewoo and Samsung Motors, were heavily in debt, acquiring them would carry some benefits. GM wanted to acquire Daewoo to attain the top-producer position in the world. Renault, which wanted to acquire Samsung, saw synergistic benefits in that Samsung relies heavily on technology from Nissan, acquired by Renault earlier. There were also other indirect benefits; whoever acquired Daewoo would gain the number-one spot in Poland, long deemed crucial for tapping growth in Central Europe.[49] Renault acquired a 70 per cent stake in Samsung, and GM completed the deal for Daewoo in late 2002 and uses its low-cost automobiles to supplement its line up in Asia and Europe. Today, Renault Samsung Motors (henceforth RSM) maintains a good position within the Korean automotive market, with its SM5 vehicle continuing to hold its ground against competitors. Also, RSM is in the phase of changing its products from a Nissan-based architecture to a Renault-based one. For example, the next generation of Megane will take over the Nissan Sylphy as the base for SM3. Also, according to the development trend of the Renault-Nissan Alliance, petrol engines will continue to be provided by Nissan, whereas diesel engines will be provided by Renault.[50]

Disadvantages of the product portfolio approach

The application of the product portfolio approach has a number of limitations. International competitive behaviour does not always follow the same rules as in the firm's domestic market; for example, the major local competitor may be a government-owned firm whose main objective is to maintain employment. With European integration, many believed that the continent's £12.67 billion appliance business would consolidate into a handful of companies. Whirlpool was the major non-EU company that wanted to take advantage of the emerging opportunity and was expected to gain 20 per cent of the market. Whirlpool Europe reported fourth-quarter sales of £60.13 million, a 2 per cent increase from the prior year and an operating profit of £12.03 million during the fourth quarter compared with £1.27 million reported in the previous year period. The company expects full-year 2010 industry unit shipments to be approximately equal to 2009 levels.[51]

The relationship between market share and profitability may be blurred by a number of factors in the marketing environment. Government regulations in every market will have an impact on the products a company can market. Product lines offered will also be affected by various local content laws – those stipulating that a prescribed percentage of the value of the final product must be manufactured locally. Market tastes have an important impact on product lines. These not only may alter the content of a product but also may require an addition in a given market that is not available elsewhere. The Coca-Cola Company has market leadership in a product category unique to Japan: coffee-flavoured soft drinks. The market came into existence some 20 years ago and grew rapidly, eventually accounting for 10 per cent of soft drink sales. The beverage is packaged like any other soft drink and is available through vending machines, which dispense hot cans in the winter and cold servings during warm weather.

The fact that global firms produce the same products in different locations may have an impact on consumer perceptions of product risk and quality. If the product is produced in an emerging country, for example, the global marketer has to determine whether a well-known brand name can compensate for the concern a customer might feel. The situation may be more complicated for retailers importing from independent producers in developing nations under the retailer's private labels. In general, country-of-origin effects on product perceptions are more difficult to determine since the introduction of hybrid products.

Managing the brand portfolio

Branding is one of the major beneficiaries of a well-conducted portfolio analysis. Brands are important because they shape customer decisions and, ultimately, create economic value. Brand is a key factor behind the decision to purchase in both consumer and business-to-business situations. A worldwide study by Euro RSCG Worldwide (2009) found that brand quality and service are the driving forces behind consumer purchase decisions in the current economy. Compared to February 2008, nearly 25 per cent more consumers polled reported that they buy based on quality, not price. It is interesting to note that customers look for value. The same study noted that 'there is a tremendous opportunity for marketers to resonate with consumers by communicating brand value as a core commitment to quality, tradition and customer service. The key is to break through consumer anxiety and reassure customers that they are making intelligent purchase decisions for themselves, their families and the community at large'.[52]

Brands are a major benefit to the customer as well. They simplify everyday choices, reduce the risk of complicated buying decisions, provide emotional benefits and offer a sense of community. In technology (e.g., computer chips), where products change at an ever-increasing pace, branding is critical – far more so than in packaged goods, where a product may be more understandable because it stays the same or very similar over time. 'Intel Inside', which derived from Intel's ad agency recommending 'Intel, the Computer Inside' and the Japanese operation's 'Intel In It', increased the company's brand awareness from 22 per cent to 80 per cent within two years of its introduction.[53]

The benefit of a strong brand name is, in addition to the price premium that awareness and loyalty allow, the ability to exploit the brand in a new market or a new product category. In a global marketplace, customers are aware of brands even though the products themselves may not be available. This was the case, for example, in many of the former Soviet Republics, before their markets opened up. Starbucks has relied on the strength of its brand in breaking into new markets, including Vienna, Europe's café capital.[54]

Global marketers have three choices of branding within the global, regional and local dimensions: brands can feature the corporate name, have family brands for a wide range of products or product variations, or have individual brands for each item in the product line. With the increase in strategic alliances, co-branding, in which two or more well-known brands are combined in an offer, has also become popular. Examples of these approaches include Heinz, which has a policy of using its corporate name in all its products, Procter & Gamble, which has a policy of stand-alone products or product lines, and Nestlé, which uses a mixture of Nestlé and Nes-designated brands and stand-alones. In the case of marketing alliances, the brand portfolio may be a combination of both partners' brands. General Mills' alliance with Nestlé in cereals, Cereal Partners Worldwide, features General Mills brands such as Trix and Nestlé brands such as Chocapic.[55]

Market power is usually in the hands of brand-name companies that have to determine the most effective use of this asset across markets. The value of brands can be seen in recent acquisitions where prices have been many times over the book value of the company purchased. Nestlé, for example, paid five times the book value for Rowntree, the owner of such brands as Kit Kat and After Eight. Many of the world's leading brands command high brand equity values, in other words, the price premium the brand commands times the extra volume it moves over what an average brand commands.[56]

An example of global rankings of brands is provided in Exhibit 14.4. This Interbrand-sponsored study rates brands on their value and their strength. Each ranked brand had to be global in nature, deriving 20 per cent or more of sales from the home market. The brand value has been determined using publicly available financial information and market analysis. Brand strength is scored using seven attributes: market, stability, leadership, support, trend, geography and protection. GE has introduced the tagline 'Imagination at work', across all its marketing communications, and it has set up a number of co-branding and co-marketing agreements with other known brands as a means of leveraging its brand value and ensuring that the GE umbrella covers more. The dot coms have also shown an improvement from 2008, apart from eBay which remained at 46. Google increased from 10 to 7, Amazon from 58 to 43 and Yahoo from 65 to 64. Of the top 100 global brands in terms of value, 38 are European, 9 Asian, 1 Canadian and the rest (52) US-based. This analysis looks at brands, not companies, which means that companies that are all one brand have a better chance of being featured. An assessment has also been made of the portfolio brands; and the only ones that made it into the top 100 are L'Oréal (44), Nestle (58) and Johnson & Johnson (80).[57]

Brand strategy decisions

The goal of many marketers currently is to create consistency and impact, both of which are easier to manage with a single worldwide identity.[58] **Global brands** are a key way of reaching this goal. Global brands are those that reach the world's mega-markets and are perceived as the same brand by consumers and internal constituents.[59] While some of the global brands are completely standardized, some elements of the product may be adapted to local conditions. These adjustments include brand names (e.g., Ariel, Allways and Wella), positioning (e.g., Ford Fiesta as a small car in Germany but a family vehicle in Portugal), or product versions sold under the same brand name (e.g., 9–13 different types of coffee sold under the Nescafé name in Europe alone).[60]

Consumers all over the world associate global brands with three characteristics and evaluate their performance on them when making purchase decisions.[61] First, global brands carry

EXHIBIT 14.4

World's most valuable brands

Rank 2009	Rank 2008	Employer	2009 Brand value ($ millions)	2008 Brand value ($ millions)	Per cent change (%)	Country of ownership
1	1	Coca-Cola	68,734	66,667	3	US
2	2	IBM	60,211	59,031	2	US
3	3	Microsoft	56,647	59,007	−4	US
4	4	GE	47,777	53,086	−10	US
5	5	Nokia	34,864	35,942	−3	Finland
6	8	McDonald's	32,275	31,049	4	US
7	10	Google	31,980	25,590	25	US
8	6	Toyota	31,330	34,050	−8	Japan
9	7	Intel	30,636	31,261	−2	US
10	9	Disney	28,447	29,251	−3	US
11	12	Hewlett-Packard	24,096	23,509	2	US
12	11	Mercedes-Benz	23,867	25,577	−7	Germany
13	14	Gillette	22,841	22,069	4	US
14	17	Cisco	22,030	21,306	3	US
15	13	BMW	21,671	23,298	−7	Germany
16	16	Louis Vuitton	21,120	21,602	−2	France
17	18	Marlboro	19,010	21,300	−11	US
18	20	Honda	17,803	19,079	−7	Japan
19	21	Samsung	17,518	17,689	−1	S. Korea
20	24	Apple	15,443	13,724	12	US
21	22	H&M	15,375	13,840	11	Sweden
22	15	American Express	14,971	21,940	−32	US
23	26	Pepsi	13,706	13,249	3	US
24	23	Oracle	13,699	13,831	−1	US
25	28	Nescafe	13,317	13,055	2	Switzerland
26	29	Nike	13,179	12,672	4	US
27	31	SAP	12,106	12,228	−1	Germany
28	35	Ikea	12,004	10,913	10	Sweden
29	25	Sony	11,953	13,583	−12	Japan
30	33	Budweiser	11,833	11,438	3	Belgium
31	30	UPS	11,594	12,621	−8	US
32	27	HSBC	10,510	13,143	−20	Britain
33	36	Canon	10,441	10,876	−4	Japan
34	39	Kellogg's	10,428	9,710	7	US
35	32	Dell	10,291	11,695	−12	US

Source: *Business Week* (2009), '100 Best Global Brands'. http://bwnt.businessweek.com/interactive_reports/best_global_brands_2009/

a strong quality signal suggested by their success across markets. Part of this is that great brands often represent great ideas and leading-edge technological solutions. Second, global brands compete on emotion catering to aspirations that cut across cultural differences. Global brands may cater to needs to feel cosmopolitan, something that local brands cannot deliver. Global brands may also convey that their user has reached a certain status both professionally and personally. This type of recognition represents both perception and reality, enabling brands to establish credibility in markets.[62] The third reason consumers choose global brands is involvement in solving social problems linked to what they are marketing and how they conduct their business. Expectations that global marketers use their monetary and human resources to benefit society are uniform from developed to developing markets.

There are three main implications for the marketing manager to consider: (1) Don't hide globality. Given the benefits of globality, marketers should not be shy in communicating this feature of a brand. Creatively, this may mean referring to the leadership position of the brand around the world or referring to the extent of innovation or features that are possible only for a brand with considerable reach. Marketers intent on scaling down their brand portfolios and focusing on global offerings are able to invest in more marketing muscle and creative effort behind the sleeker set of offerings. (2) Tackle home-country bias. One of the marketing mantras is 'being local on a global scale'. Since some markets feature substantial preference for home-grown brands, it is imperative to localize some features of the marketing approach, possibly including even the brand name. One approach could be that a brand has a consistent global positioning but the name varies according to country language. For example, Vauxhall (UK) is called Opel in Germany. Many global brands have already localized to neutralize the home-country effect. (3) Satisfy the basics. Global brands signal quality and aspiration. However, taking a global approach to branding is not in itself the critical factor. What is critical is creating differentiation and familiarity as well as the needed margins and growth. The greater esteem that global brands enjoy is not sufficient in itself for pursuing this strategy. However, this dimension may tip the balance in ultimate strategy choice. At the same time, it is evident that globality should not be pursued at the cost of alienating local consumers by pre-emptively eliminating purely local brands or converging them under a global brand.[63]

Branding is an integral part of the overall identity management of the firm.[64] Global brands need to achieve a high degree of consistency in their delivery of customer service and how it is communicated across all consumer points of touch. Therefore, it is typically a centralized function to exploit to the fullest the brand's assets as well as to protect the asset from dilution by, for example, extending the brand to inappropriate new lines. The role of headquarters, strategic business unit management, global teams, or global managers charged with a product, is to provide guidelines for the effort without hampering local initiative at the same time.[65] The 'glocal' dimension can only be achieved by giving regional and local managers the power to interpret and express the message. An example of this effort is provided in *The International Marketplace 14.4*. In addition to the use of a global brand name from the very beginning, many marketers are consolidating their previously different brand names (often for the same or similar products) with global or regional brand names. For example, Mars replaced its Treets and Bonitas names with M&M worldwide and renamed its best-seller, Marathon, with the Snickers name it uses in North and South America. The benefits in global branding are in marketing economies and higher acceptance of products by consumers and intermediaries. The drawbacks are in the loss of local flavour, especially when a local brand is replaced by a regional or global brand name. At these times, internal marketing becomes critical to instill ownership of the global brands in the personnel of the country organizations.[66]

An example of a brand portfolio is provided in Exhibit 14.5. It indicates four levels of brands at Nestlé: worldwide corporate and strategic brands, regional strategic brands and local brands. The worldwide brands are under the responsibility of SBU and general management, which establish a framework for each in the form of a planning policy document. These policies lay out the brand's positioning, labelling standards, packaging features and other related marketing mix issues, such as a communications platform. The same principle applies to regional brands, where guidelines are issued and decisions made by SBU and regional management. Among the 7,500 local brands are 700 local strategic brands, such as Chambinho in Brazil, which are monitored by the SBUs for positioning and labelling standards. Nestlé is consolidating its efforts behind its corporate and strategic brands. This is taking place in various ways. When Nestlé acquired Rowntree, which had had a one-product one-brand policy, it added its corporate name to some of the products, such as Nestlé Kit Kat. Its refrigerated products line under the Chambourcy brand is undergoing a name change to Nestlé. Some of the products that do not carry the corporate name feature a Nestlé Seal of

THE INTERNATIONAL **MARKETPLACE 14.4**

Development and management of a global brand

One of the biggest implications of globalization for companies seeking to expand to foreign shores is the task of balancing standardization with customization. From a branding perspective, this issue assumes even more significance. When some of the world's biggest brands expand beyond their home markets, they are tempted to repeat their tried and tested formula in the new market as well. In fact this has been the path followed by many brands. The assumption in such a case is that customers would be eager to consume the great brand because of its authenticity, heritage and associations. But this tendency is gradually changing as global companies are learning about the unique needs of the customers in different markets along with the pressures of lifestyle, economic and cultural conditions.

A case in point is the success of global brands in the Indian market. One of the booming economies in Asia, India offers tremendous opportunities to global companies. A brief look at the Indian landscape will prove why – an estimated 1.2 million affluent households that is expanding at 20 per cent a year, 40 million middle income households (earnings of £12,916 to £29,064 adjusted for PPP) growing at 10 per cent a year, more than 110 million households with earnings of £4,844 to £12,916 (adjusted for PPP) and more than 70 per cent of the population below the age of 36. It is no wonder then, that global brands are making a bee line to the Indian market to grab a share of the growing pie.

This alluring face of the Indian business landscape has another facet to it and that is the presence of highly discerning and demanding customers. In spite of the booming economy and the increasing disposable income, Indian consumers are very cautious and clear in their priorities. Consumers are still not ready to splurge on branded goods at premium prices. Added to this is a growing number of Indian brands that offer superior quality at affordable prices. In such a scenario, global brands can win only if they attune themselves to the local conditions.

Unilever is a classic example of a global brand which has pioneered serving the locals with products that address the local sensitivities. Unilever's Indian subsidiary Hindustan Lever Limited (HLL) has been the leader in recognizing the tremendous opportunity lying at the bottom of the pyramid-customer base that aspires to consume products but in smaller quantities and at lesser prices. HLL literally invented the shampoo sachets – small plastic packets of shampoo for less than INR 1 (£.014). This became such a rage among the rural consumers that many other brands started offering products such as detergent, coffee and tea powder, coconut oil and tooth paste in sachets. Even though the unit price was higher, rural consumers were able to afford to purchase the smaller quantity at their convenience.

Nokia is another example of a global mobile brand. Nokia also recognized the growing importance of rural customers in the Indian

© DAVID PEARSON/ALAMY

mobile telephone market which grew from a mere 300,000 subscribers in 1996 to a whopping 55 million subscribers in 2004. Nokia introduced its dust-resistant keypad, anti-slip grip and an inbuilt flash light. These features, albeit small, appealed to a specific target of truck drivers initially and then to a broader segment of rural consumers. These features endeared Nokia to the Indian consumer as Nokia displayed a genuine commitment in responding to local customer needs.

These examples clearly endorse the glocalization route to winning customers in diverse markets. Glocalization – maintaining the brand logo, the key message and the underlying philosophy and localizing the brand elements to offer customers an authentic local feel – is

increasingly becoming the preferred business model for global brands. By extending the unique brand experience through customized channels and offerings, global brands seem to have found a middle path where they can maintain the global brand aura and still appeal to the customers in the authentic local way!

SOURCE: Roll, M. (2010), 'Glocalization, global marketing, branding, Unilever, Hindustan Lever, Nokia'. **http://www.venturerepublic.com/resources/ Glocalization_global_marketing_branding_Unilever_Hindustan_Lever_ Nokia.asp** (Accessed 16/2/10).

Guarantee on the back. About 40 per cent of the company's sales come from products covered by the corporate brand.[67] L'Oréal is managed independently due to the fact that Nestlé is only a 26.4 per cent owner in the corporation that in itself markets brands such as Maybelline, Helena Rubinstein, Garnier and SoftSheen-Carson.[68]

Carefully crafted brand portfolios allow marketers to serve defined parts of specific markets. At Whirlpool, the Whirlpool brand name will be used as the global brand to serve the broad middle market segment, while regional and local brands will cover the others. For example, throughout Europe, the Bauknecht brand is targeted at the upper end of the market seeking a reputable German brand. Ignis and Laden are positioned as price value brands, Ignis Europe-wide, Laden in France. This approach applies to Whirlpool's other markets as well: in Latin America, Consul is the major regional brand.[69]

The brand portfolio needs to be periodically and regularly assessed. A number of global marketers are focusing their attention on 'A' brands with the greatest growth potential. By continuing to dispose of non-core brands, the marketer can concentrate on the global ones and reduce production, marketing, storage and distribution costs. It is increasingly difficult for the global company to manage purely local brands. The surge of private label products has also put additional pressure on 'B' brands.[70]

However, before disposing of a brand, managers need to assess it in terms of current sales, loyalty, potential and trends. For example, eliminating a local brand that may have a strong and loyal following, has been created by local management, and shows potential to be extended to nearby markets is not necessarily in the best interests of the company. Three approaches for purely local brands may work: a penetration price approach, a cultural approach positioning the product as a true defender of local culture, and a 'chameleon' approach, in which the brand tries not to look local.[71] The number-one chewing gum brand in France for the past 25 years has been Cadbury Schweppes' Hollywood.

Private brand policies

The emergence of strong intermediaries has led to the significant increase in private brand goods, that is, the intermediaries' own branded products or 'store brands'. Two general approaches have been used: umbrella branding, where a number of products are covered using the same brand (often the intermediary's name), and separate brand names for individual products or product lines.

With price sensitivity increasing and brand loyalty decreasing, private brand goods have achieved a significant penetration in many countries. The overall penetration of private brand goods in the United Kingdom is 42 per cent, in Germany 38 per cent, in Finland 25 per cent and in France 31 per cent.[72] Over the past 20 years, private brand sales in the United States have averaged 14 per cent of supermarket sales. As both the trade and consumers become more sophisticated, private brands' market share is expected to reach UK levels in many parts of Europe and the world.

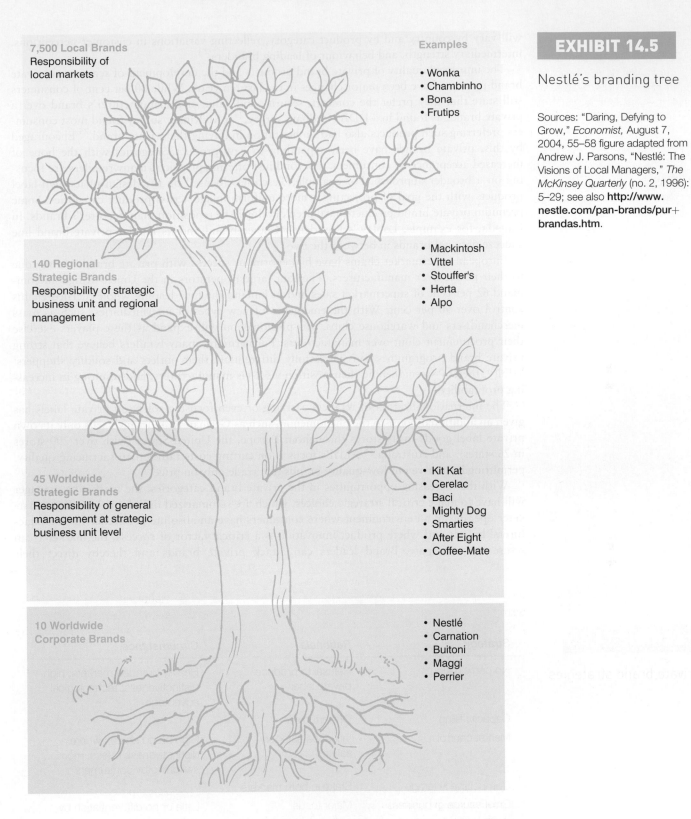

7,500 Local Brands
Responsibility of
local markets

**140 Regional
Strategic Brands**
Responsibility of strategic
business unit and regional
management

**45 Worldwide
Strategic Brands**
Responsibility of general
management at strategic
business unit level

**10 Worldwide
Corporate Brands**

Examples

- Wonka
- Chambinho
- Bona
- Frutips

- Mackintosh
- Vittel
- Stouffer's
- Herta
- Alpo

- Kit Kat
- Cerelac
- Baci
- Mighty Dog
- Smarties
- After Eight
- Coffee-Mate

- Nestlé
- Carnation
- Buitoni
- Maggi
- Perrier

EXHIBIT 14.5

Nestlé's branding tree

Sources: "Daring, Defying to
Grow," *Economist*, August 7,
2004, 55–58 figure adapted from
Andrew J. Parsons, "Nestlé: The
Visions of Local Managers," *The
McKinsey Quarterly* (no. 2, 1996):
5–29; see also **http://www.
nestle.com/pan-brands/pur+
brandas.htm**.

While private brand success can be shown to be affected strongly by economic conditions
and the self-interest of retailers who want to improve their bottom lines through the contribution of private label goods, new factors have emerged to make the phenomenon more long-
lived and significant in changing product choices worldwide. The level of private brand share

will vary by country and by product category, reflecting variations in customer perceptions, intermediary strength, and behaviour of leading branders.[73]

The improved quality of private brand products and the development of segmented private brand products have been major changes in the last ten years. While 60 per cent of consumers still state that they prefer the comfort, security and value of a manufacturer's brand over a private brand, as found in a DDB Needham survey,[74] a McKinsey survey found most consumers preferring such products also had no hesitation in buying the private brand.[75] Encouraged by this, private brands have been expanding to new product categories with the hope of increased acceptance by consumers.[76] Beyond just offering products, many retailers are focusing on a broader approach. For example, Tesco has focused on the design of its own-label products with the goal of projecting a more uniform image across product categories. Some premium private brand products have been developed to reposition manufacturer's brands. In Canada, for example, Loblaw's President's Choice brand and its regular private brand line squeeze national brands in between the two.

European supermarket chains have had enormous success with private brands mainly due to their power over manufacturers. The four largest operators in the United Kingdom command 62 per cent of supermarket sales and in Finland the four leading wholesaler-led chains control over 90 per cent. With the emergence of new types of intermediaries, such as mass merchandisers and warehouse clubs, this phenomenon will expand as these players exercise their procurement clout over manufacturers. Furthermore, many retailers believe that strong private brand programmes can successfully differentiate their outlets and solidify shoppers' loyalty, thereby strengthening their position vis-à-vis manufacturers, and resulting in increasing profitability.[77]

The internationalization of retailers carrying or even focusing solely on private labels has given an additional boost to the phenomenon, such as German ALDI, which sells only its own private label goods in its stores throughout Europe, the United States (with over 700 stores in 26 states), and Australia.[78] ALDI's focus is on cutting costs rather than sacrificing quality, permitting it to drive out low-quality brands that trade only on price.

With the increasing opportunities in the private brand categories, the marketing manager will have to make critical strategic choices, which are summarized in Exhibit 14.6. If the marketer operates in an environment where consumers have an absolute preference for manufacturers' brands and where product innovation is a critical factor of success, the marketer can refuse to participate. Brand leaders can attack private brands and thereby direct their

---

EXHIBIT 14.6

Private brand strategies

Strategy	Rationale	Circumstance
No participation	Refusal to produce private label	Heavily branded markets; high distinctiveness; technological advantage
Capacity filling	Opportunistic	
Market control	Influence category sales	High brand shares where distinctiveness is less; more switching by consumers
Competitive leverage	Stake in both markets	
Chief source of business	Major focus	Little or no differentiation by consumers
Dedicated producer	Leading cost position	

Sources: Adapted from Sabine Bonnot, Emma Carr, and Michael J. Reyner, "Fighting Brawn with Brains," *The McKinsey Quarterly* 40 (no. 2, 2000): 85–92; and François Glémet and Rafael Mira, "The Brand Leader's Dilemma," *The McKinsey Quarterly* 33 (no. 2, 1993): 4.

ambitions on smaller competitors, which often may be local-only players. The argument for strategic participation is that since the phenomenon cannot be eliminated, it is best to be involved. For example, Nestlé sells ice cream called Grandessa for ALDI through a newly acquired unit called Scholler.[79] Reasons include capacity filling, economies of scale, improved relationships with trade, and valuable information about consumer behaviour and costs. The argument that profits from private brand manufacture can be used for promotion of the manufacturer's own brands may be eliminated by the relatively thin margins and the costs of having to set up a separate private brand manufacturing and marketing organization. Participation in the private brand category may, however, be inconsistent with the marketer's global brand and product strategy by raising questions about quality standards, by diluting management attention, and by affecting consumers' perception of the main branded business. Many marketers pursue a mixture of these strategies as a function of marketing and market conditions. Wilkinson Sword, for example, produces private brand disposable razors for the most dominant chain in Finland, the K-Group, thereby enabling it to compete on price against other branded products (especially the French Bic) and increasing its share of shelf space.

SUMMARY

The global product planning effort must determine two critical decisions: (1) how and where the company's products should be developed, and (2) how and where the present and future product lines should be marketed.

In product development, multinational corporations are increasingly striving toward finding common denominators to rationalize worldwide production. This is achieved through careful coordination of the product development process by worldwide or regional development teams. No longer is the parent company the only source of new products. New product ideas emerge throughout the system and are developed by the entity most qualified to do so.

The global marketer's product line is not the same worldwide. The standard line items are augmented by local items or localized variations of products to better cater to the unique needs of individual markets. External variables such as competition and regulations often determine the final composition of the line and how broadly it is marketed.

Global marketers will also have to determine the extent to which they will use one of their greatest assets, brands, across national markets. Marketers will have to choose among global brands, regional brands and purely local approaches as well as forgoing their own branding in favour of becoming a supplier for private brand efforts of retailers. Efficiencies of standardization must be balanced with customer preferences and internal issues of motivation at the country-market level.

Key terms

computer-aided design (CAD)

forced distribution tests

global brands

laboratory test markets

lead users

microtest marketing

Questions for discussion

1 How can a company's product line reflect the maxim 'think globally, act locally'?

2 Will a globally oriented company have an advantage over a multidomestic, or even a domestic, company in the next generation of new product ideas?

3 What factors should be considered when deciding on the location of research and development facilities?

4 What factors make product testing more complicated in the international marketplace?

5 What are the benefits of a coordinated global product launch? What factors will have to be taken into consideration before the actual launch?

6 Argue for and against the use of the corporate name in global branding.

Internet exercises

1 Using the list of the world's leading brands (available at **http://www.interbrand.com**), evaluate why certain brands place high, some lower. Speculate on the future of, for example, the dot coms.

2 Using the Mach3 as an example, evaluate how the different country websites of Gillette (accessible through **http://www.gillette.com**) support its worldwide brand effort.

Recommended readings

Aaker, David A. *Building Strong Brands*. New York: The Free Press, 1996.

Aaker, David and Erich Joachimsthaler. *Brand Leadership: The Next Level of Brand Revolution*. New York: The Free Press, 2000.

Bedbury, Scott. *A Brand New World: Eight Principles for Achieving Brand Leadership in the 21st Century*. New York: Viking Press, 2002.

Cooper, Robert G. *Product Leadership: Creating and Launching Superior New Products.* New York: Perseus Books, 2000.

Cooper, Robert G. *Winning at New Products: Accelerating the Process from Idea to Launch*. New York: Perseus Books, 2001.

Deschamps, Jean-Philippe and P. Raganath Nayak. *Product Juggernauts: How Companies Mobilize to Generate a Stream of Market Winners*. Boston: Harvard Business School Press, 1995.

Gorchels, Linda. *The Product Manager's Handbook: The Complete Product Management Resource*. New York: McGraw-Hill, 2000.

Gregory, James R. and Jack G. Wiechman. *Branding across Borders: A Guide to Global Brand Marketing*. New York: McGraw-Hill, 2001.

Kapferer, Jean-Noël. *The New Strategic Brand Management: Creating and Sustaining Brand Equity Long Term*. New York: Kogan Page, 2004.

Keller, Kevin L. *Strategic Brand Management: Building, Measuring, and Managing Brand Equity*. Upper Saddle River, NJ: Prentice Hall, 2002.

Kitcho, Catherine. *High Tech Product Launch*. Mountain View, CA: Pele Publications, 1999.

Kotabe, Masaaki. *Global Sourcing Strategy: R&D, Manufacturing, and Marketing Interfaces*. Greenwich, CT: Greenwood Publishing Group, 1992.

Macrae, Chris. *The Brand Chartering Handbook*. Harlow, England: Addison-Wesley, 1996.

Ries, Laura and Al Ries. *The 22 Immutable Laws of Branding: How to Build a Product or Service into a World-Class Brand*. New York: Collins, 2002.

Schmitt, Bernd and Alexander Simonson. *Marketing Aesthetics: The Strategic Management of Brands, Identity and Image*. New York: The Free Press, 1997.

Notes

1 *Introducing Unilever,* available at **http://www.unilever.com**.

2 Wikipedia 'Unilever' **http://en.wikipedia.org/wiki/Unilever** (Accessed 3/2/10).

3 Wikipedia 'Unilever' **http://en.wikipedia.org/wiki/Unilever** (Accessed 3/2/10).

4 Black & Decker's Vision Statement is available at **http://www.bdk.com/**. See also 'Black & Decker's Gamble on 'Globalization,' *Fortune,* May 14, 1984, 40–48.

5 'The Zen of Nissan', *Business Week,* July 22, 2002, 18–20.

6 'Blade-runner', *The Economist,* April 10, 1993, 68.

7 Bill Saporito, 'Behind the Tumult at P&G', *Fortune,* March 7, 1994, 74–82.

8 Edward Tse, 'Competing in China: An Integrated Approach', *Strategy and Business* 3 (fourth quarter, 1998): 45–52.

9 Ben Van Houten, 'Foreign Interpreter', *Restaurant Business,* November 1, 1999, 32.

10 Eric von Hippel, *The Sources of Innovation* (Oxford, England: Oxford University Press, 1997), chapter 1.

11 Eric von Hippel, Stefan Thomke, and Mary Sonnack, 'Creating Breakthroughs at 3M', *Harvard Business Review* 77 (September–October 1999): 47–57.

12 'Could America Afford the Transistor Today?' *Business Week,* March 7, 1994, 80–84.

13 Eric von Hippel and Ralph Katz, 'Shifting Innovation to Users via Toolkits', *Management Science* 48 (July 2002): 821–833.

14 David DeVoss, 'The $3 Billion Question', *World Trade,* September 1998, 34–39.

15 Edward Tse, 'The Right Way to Achieve Profitable Growth in the Chinese Market', *Strategy & Business* 3 (second quarter, 1998): 10–21.

16 'The Stateless Corporation', *Business Week,* May 14, 1990, 98–106; see also 'The World of Otis', available at **http://www.otis.com**.

17 'A Car Is Born', *Economist,* September 13, 1997, 68–69.

18 Ilkka A. Ronkainen, 'Product Development in the Multinational Firm', *International Marketing Review* 1 (Winter 1983): 24–30.

19 Durward K. Sobek, Jeffrey K. Liker, and Allen C. Ward, 'Another Look at How Toyota Integrates Product Development', *Harvard Business Review* 76 (July–August 1998): 36–49.

20 James B. Quinn, 'Outsourcing Innovation: The New Engine of Growth', *Sloan Management Review* 41 (number 4, 2000): 13–29.

21 Larry Huston and Nabil Sakkab, 'Connect and Develop: Inside Procter & Gamble's Model for Innovation', *Harvard Business Review* 84 (March 2006): 58–66.

22 Georges LeRoy, *Multinational Product Strategies: A Typology for Analysis of Worldwide Product Innovation Diffusion* (New York: Praeger, 1976), 1–3.

23 'ABB Opens R&D Centre in Beijing', *China Business Daily News,* April 4, 2005; and Imperial and ABB Set to Pool R&D Expertise', *Professional Engineering* 17 (number 21, 2004): 45.

24 '8 Multinationals Found R&D Centres in Shanghai', *China Business Daily News,* May 27, 2005.

25 'Savi Launches Global R&D Centre in Singapore', *Transportation & Distribution,* July 2002, 16.

26 Robert Ronstadt, 'International R&D: The Establishment and Evolution of Research and Development Abroad by US Multinationals', *Journal of International Business Studies* 9 (Spring–Summer 1978): 7–24.

27 Guido Reger, 'Internationalization of Research and Development in Western European, Japanese, and North American Multinationals', *International Journal of Entrepreneurship and Innovation Management* 2 (nos. 2/3, 2002): 164–185.

28 Darling, A. (2006) 'Show of strength from UK Industry'. Online. Available from: **http://www.thefreelibrary.com/ Show+of+strength+from+UK+industry%3B+ BIRMINGHAM+POST+MOTOR+WEEK+Trade... -a0148443198** (Accessed 16/2/10).

29 Department of Trade and Industry 'Success and Sustainability in the UK Automotive Industry'. Online. Available from **http://www.berr.gov.uk/files/file29165.pdf** (Accessed 8/2/10).

30 Michelle Fellman, 'Auto Researchers' Focus on Customers Can Help Drive Sales in Other Industries', *Marketing News,* January 4, 1999, 12.

31 C. K. Prahalad and Allen Hammond, 'Serving the World's Poor, Profitably', *Harvard Business Review* 80 (September 2002): 48–57; see also, **http://www.hp.com/hpinfo/ globalcitizenship/gcreport/socialinvest/einclusion.html**.

32 Lester C. Krogh, 'Managing R&D Globally: People and Financial Considerations', *Research & Technology Management* 14 (July–August 1994): 25–28.

33 Rajesh Sethi, Daniel Smith, and C. Whan Park, 'Cross-Functional Product Development Teams, Creativity, and the Innovativeness of New Consumer Products', *Journal of Marketing Research* 38 (February 2001): 73–85.

34 Julian Birkinshaw, 'Managing Internal R&D Networks in Global Firms – What Sort of Knowledge Is Involved?' *Long Range Planning* 35 (June 2002): 245–267.

35 'Manufacturers Strive to Slice Time Needed to Develop Products', *The Wall Street Journal,* February 23, 1988, 1, 24.

36 Gloria Barczak and Edward McDonough III, 'Leading Global Product Development Teams', *Research Technology Management* 46 (number 6, 2003): 14–22.

37 Centre for Research on Innovation and Competition (2007) 'Outsourcing of Research and Development'. Online. Available from: **http://www.cric.ac.uk/cric/compprojects/ project-4.htm** (Accessed 16/2/10).

38 A.C. Nielsen, 'New-Product Introduction – Successful Innovation/Failure: Fragile Boundary', *A.C. Nielsen BASES,* June 24, 1999, 1; Robert G. Cooper and Elko J. Kleinschmidt, 'New Product Processes at Leading Industrial Firms', *Industrial Marketing Management* 14 (May 1991): 137–147; and David S. Hopkins, 'Survey Finds 67% of New Products Fail', *Marketing News,* February 8, 1986, 1.

39 Eric Berggren and Thomas Nacher, 'Introducing New Products Can Be Hazardous to Your Company', *The Academy of Management Executive* 15 (August 2001): 92–101.

40 Laurel Wentz, 'Mars Widens Its Line in U.K.', *Advertising Age,* May 16, 1988, 37.

41 Veronica Wong, 'Antecedents of International New Product Rollout Timeliness', *International Marketing Review* 19 (no. 2, 2002): 120–132; Robert Michelet and Laura Elmore, 'Launching Your Product Globally', *Export Today* 6 (September 1990): 13–15; and Laura Elmore and Robert Michelet, 'The Global Product Launch', *Export Today* 6 (November–December 1990): 49–52.

42 George S. Day, 'Diagnosing the Product Portfolio', *Journal of Marketing* 41 (April 1977): 9–19.

43 'Even Rivals Concede GM Has Deftly Steered Road to Success in Brazil', *The Wall Street Journal,* February 25, 1999, A1, A8.

44   Chrysler LLC, (2009) 'Fiat Group, Chrysler Group LLC and Cerberus Capital Management L.P. Announce Plans for a Global Strategic Alliance'. Online. Available from: **http://www.chrysler.co.uk/pressreleases/20-01-09.html** (Accessed 8/2/10).

45   BBC (2009) 'Fiat and Chrysler create alliance'. Online. Available from **http://news.bbc.co.uk/1/hi/7839542.stm** (Accessed 16/2/09).

46   Susan P. Douglas and C. Samuel Craig, 'Global Portfolio Planning and Market Interconnectedness', *Journal of International Marketing* 4 (no. 1, 1996): 93–110.

47   C. Samuel Craig and Susan P. Douglas, 'Configural Advantage in Global Markets', *Journal of International Marketing* 8 (no. 1, 2000): 6–26.

48   Global Intelligence Alliance (2010) 'Booming Indonesia automobile market to attract more investments in 2010'. Online. Available from: **http://www.globalintelligence.com/insights-analysis/asia-news-update/asia-news-update-january-1-2010/** (Accessed 16/2/10).

49   'Will Renault Go for Broke in Asia?' *Business Week,* February 28, 2000; and 'Ford, GM Square Off over Daewoo Motor: The Question Is Why?' *The Wall Street Journal,* February 14, 2000, A1, A13.

50   Absolute Astronomy (2009) 'Renault Samsung Motors'. Online. Available from: **http://www.absoluteastronomy.com/topics/Renault_Samsung_Motors** (Accessed 16/2/10).

51   Whirlpool (2009) 'Whirlpool Corporation Reports Fourth-Quarter and Full-Year 2009 Results'. Online. Available from: **http://phx.corporate-ir.net/phoenix.zhtml?c=97140&p=RssLanding&cat=news&id=1381606** (Accessed 16/2/10).

52   Taragan.com (2009), 'Euro RSCG Worldwide Study Unveils How Consumers Define "Value" in 2009 and Beyond'. Online. Available from **http://blog.taragana.com/pr/euro-rscg-worldwide-study-unveils-how-consumers-define-value-in-2009-and-beyond-1850/** (Accessed 16/2/10). credit: The Gaea Times (**http://gaeatimes.com**)

53   Tobi Elkin, 'Intel Inside at 10', *Advertising Age,* April 30, 2001, 4, 31.

54   'Starbucks: Keeping the Brew Hot', *Business Week Online,* August 6, 2001.

55   **http://www.nestle.com/our_brands/breakfast_cereals/overview/breakfast+cereals.htm**.

56   David A. Aaker, *Managing Brand Equity: Capitalizing on the Value of a Brand Name* (New York: Free Press, 1995), 21–33.

57   *Business Week* (2009) '100 Best Global Brands'. Online. Available from: **http://bwnt.businessweek.com/interactive_reports/best_global_brands_2009/** (Accessed 16/2/10).

58   'Global Brands', *Business Week,* August 1, 2005, 45–46.

59   Johny K. Johansson and Ilkka A. Ronkainen, 'Are Global Brands the Right Choice for Your Company?' *Marketing Management,* March/April, 2004, 53–56.

60   Jean-Noël Kapferer, 'The Post-Global Brand', *Journal of Brand Management* 12 (number 5, 2005): 319–324.

61   Douglas B. Holt, John A. Quelch and Earl L. Taylor, 'How Global Brands Compete', *Harvard Business Review* 82 (September 2004): 68–75.

62   Interbrand, *Going Global: Global Branding-Risks and Rewards* (New York: Interbrand, October 2005): 1–7, available at **http://www.interbrand.com**.

63   Johny K. Johansson and Ilkka A. Ronkainen, 'The Esteem of Global Brands', *Journal of Brand Management* 12 (number 5, 2005): 339–354.

64   Bernd Schmitt and Alexander Simonson, *Marketing Aesthetics: The Strategic Management of Brands, Identity, and Image* (New York: Free Press, 1997), chapter 1.

65   David Aaker and Erich Joachimsthaler, 'The Lure of Global Branding', *Harvard Business Review* 77 (November/December 1999): 137–144; for an interesting application, see Anand P. Raman, 'The Global Brand Face-Off', *Harvard Business Review* 81 (June 2003): 35–45.

66   Colin Mitchell, 'Selling the Brand Inside', *Harvard Business Review* 80 (January 2002): 99–105.

67   Andrew J. Parsons, 'Nestlé: The Visions of Local Managers', *The McKinsey Quarterly* 36 (no. 2, 1996): 5–29.

68   Richard Tomlinson, 'L'Oreal's Global Makeover', *Fortune,* September 30, 2002, 141–146.

69   Ilkka A. Ronkainen and Ivan Menezes, 'Implementing Global Marketing Strategy: An Interview with Whirlpool Corporation', *International Marketing Review* 13 (no. 3, 1996): 56–63.

70   'Unilever's Goal: Power Brands', *Advertising* Age, January 3, 2000, 1, 12; and 'Why Unilever B-Brands Must Be Cast Aside', *Marketing,* June 10, 1999, 13.

71   Jean-Noël Kapferer, 'Is There Really No Hope for Local Brands?' *Journal of Brand Management* 9 (January 2002): 163–170.

72   Private Label Manufacturers Association; available at **http://www.plmainternational.com/plt/plten.html**.

73   David Dunne and Chakravarthi Narasimhan, 'The New Appeal of Private Labels', *Harvard Business Review* 77 (May–June 1999): 41–52; and John A. Quelch and David Harding, 'Brands versus Private Labels', *Harvard Business Review* 74 (January–February 1996): 99–109.

74   'Shoot Out at the Check-Out', *The Economist,* June 5, 1993, 69–72.

75   François Glémet and Rafael Mira, 'The Brand Leader's Dilemma', *The McKinsey Quarterly* 33 (no. 2, 1993): 3–15.

76   'Like My Pants? Pssst, They're Wal-Mart', *The Wall Street Journal,* September 3, 2002, B1.

77   Varun Mudgil, 'The Big Two Build on Private Label', *Retail World,* July 22, 2002, 3.

78   Alan Treadgold, 'ALDI – A Four-Letter Word That Promises Fierce Competition', *Retail World,* August 16, 2002, 6; see also **http://www.aldi.vs**.

79   'Nestlé Set to Enter Euro Own-Label Market', *Marketing Week,* August 9, 2001, 7.

CHAPTER 15
GLOBAL
SERVICES

Africa banks on mobile phones

Most working people in Ghana do not exist, at least not in the records of any trustworthy bank: The taxi drivers stash their salaries beneath floor mats and the market women tie their earnings up in the waistlines of their wrapper-skirts.

They are the 'un-banked' – potential customers but for now invisible, lost among the 80 per cent of Africans who do their banking in tin cans and waist packs. They do not keep the sort of accounts one can present to a loan officer.

African ladies on mobile phones

© CHARLES STURGE / ALAMY

Africa's economy of cash handovers and stowed-away savings has long been a hindrance to the continent's economic growth, as well as a cause and excuse to deny credit to its poor.

But now, at a time when 10 million Ghanaians own a phone, the world's banks, mobile phone networks and aid agencies are coming here to flip one thing into the other – to tweak a few features on a sim card, circumvent some regulations, and *voila*. The ordinary pre-paid mobile phone becomes something not unlike a checking account – a way to text money from person to person throughout this intricate economy.

'It's the next big gold rush,' said Michael Amankwah, CEO of Core-Net, a Ghanaian ATM manufacturer whose business, the chief executive freely admits, 'is going to take a big hit', when mobile phone banking takes hold. 'It's the future of transactions and payments here.'

Already, telecom companies in Kenya and South Africa are shuffling millions of dollars in rands and shillings a day, as customers text along their excess income – perhaps to help an ailing but faraway relative buy medicine, or to pay workers harvesting a distant farm.

In March, the continent's largest mobile phone network, MTN, announced plans to bring their Mobile Money service to 21 nations – they'll even throw in an MTN-branded debt card. In Cote d'Ivoire, French telecom giant Orange is hammering out a similar programme, and in eight East African nations, including the Democratic Republic of the Congo, the British firm Monitise, which is not a telecoms firm, will do the same.

'This is a way to include quite a number of people who are outside the reach of the financial system,' said David Andah, executive secretary of Ghana's Microfinance Institutions Network. 'I'm talking about that woman on the beach selling fish. People who are not linked up at all.'

Analysts expect similar programmes to take off in most African countries within a year. They forecast that several hundred million of Africa's least connected traders, farmers and labourers will be brought into the banking system within three to five years.

For the small towns and unreachable villages that have sent generations of talented youths and natural resources to the booming cities, this is an especially big deal. The technology should ease the path of remittances home, and make it easier for agriculturalists to operate multiple, far-apart farms.

Those lucky enough to procure a micro-loan will be able to receive payments without travelling for hours. Those hopeful enough to apply for a loan will be able to bring to the counter some evidence of their income, if only in text messages.

And in the capitals of each new country where mobile banking takes off, governments face the enticing option of taxing millions more petty purchases a day, in all the impractical corners where bureaucrats seldom go.

'As the cash-less society grows, the consequences are going to be pretty heavy,' said Ghana Manager Kofi Kufuor, of Afric Xpress, a company that helps Ghanaians pay their bills and transfer money via text messages. 'This is a lot of money we are talking about.'

And a lot of people: 'You have 6.1 billion people on this planet, out of which only one and half, two billion have an account,' said Prateek Shrivastava, head international strategist for Monitise. 'Billions are going to be interested.'

Yet, out of those billions of people – whose infinitesimal transactions were once so extraneous to the world's financial institutions – nobody stands to benefit quite like Africa's increasingly powerful telecom companies, the conglomerates who built this continent's cellular towers and enable its calls.

'These guys are going to be more powerful than Google, more powerful than Microsoft, within the locality in which they operate,' Amankwah said. 'Already, telecoms move more money than the banks. And they have control over the channels – it's their sim card. You're using their network.'

'These guys are going to be kings.'

SOURCE: Hinshaw, D. (2009) Africa banks on cell phones'. **http://www.globalpost. com/dispatch/ghana/090527/africa-looks-cell-phone-banking**.

International services marketing is a major component of world business. As *The International Marketplace 15.1* shows, services can be crucial globally. This chapter will highlight marketing dimensions that are specific to services, with particular attention given to their international aspects. A discussion of the differences between the marketing of services and of goods will be followed by insights on the role of services in the United States and in the world economy. The chapter will explore the opportunities and new problems that have arisen from the increase in international services marketing, focusing particularly on the worldwide transformations of industries as a result of profound changes in the environment and in technology. The strategic responses to these transformations by both governments and firms will be described. Finally, the chapter will outline the initial steps that firms need to undertake in order to offer services internationally – and will look at the future of international services marketing.

DIFFERENCES BETWEEN SERVICES AND GOODS

We rarely contemplate or analyze the precise role of services in our lives. Services often accompany goods, but they are also, by themselves, an increasingly important part of our economy, domestically and internationally. One writer has contrasted services and products

Services as a portion of gross domestic product

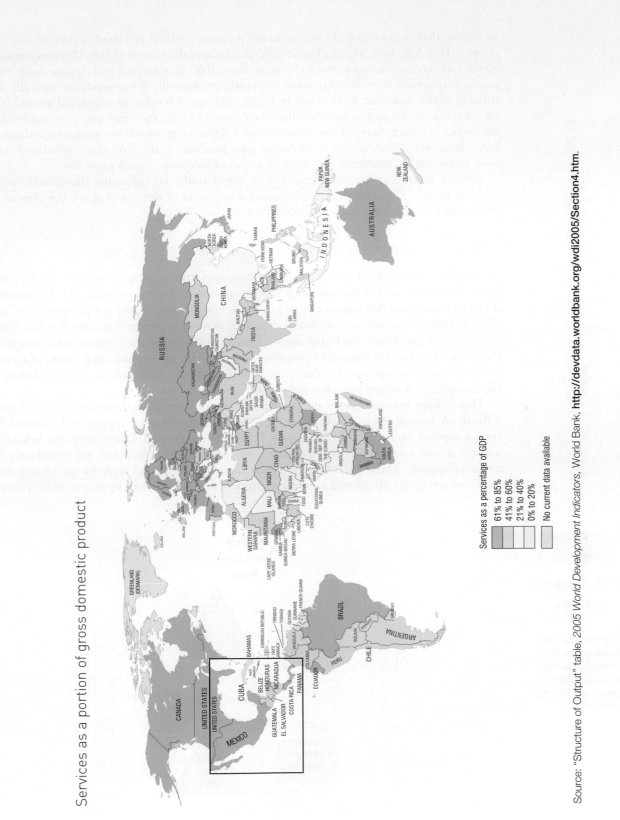

Services as a percentage of GDP

61% to 85%
41% to 60%
21% to 40%
0% to 20%
No current data available

Source: "Structure of Output" table, 2005 World Development Indicators, World Bank, **http://devdata.worldbank.org/wdi2005/Section4.htm.**

by stating that 'a good is an object, a device, a thing; a service is a deed, a performance, an effort'.[1] This definition, although quite general, captures the essence of the difference between goods and services. Services tend to be more intangible, personalized and custom-made than goods. Services are also often marketed differently from goods. While goods are typically distributed to the customer, services can be transferred across borders or originated abroad, and the service provider can be transferred to the customer or the customer can be transferred to the service territory. Services also typically use a different approach to customer satisfaction. It has been stated that 'service firms do not have products in the form of pre-produced solutions to customers' problems; they have processes as solutions to such problems'.[2]

Services are the fastest-growing sector of world trade, far outpacing the growth in the trade of goods. These major differences add dimensions to services that are not present in goods and thus call for a major differentiation.

Linkage between services and goods

Services may complement goods; at other times, goods may complement services. Offering goods that are in need of substantial technological support and maintenance may be useless if no proper assurance for service can be provided. For this reason, the initial contract of sale often includes important service dimensions. This practice is common in aircraft sales. When an aircraft is purchased, the buyer often contracts not only for the physical good – namely, the plane – but also for training of personnel, maintenance service, and the promise of continuous technological updates. Similarly, the sale of computer hardware is critically linked to the availability of proper servicing and software.

This linkage between goods and services can make international marketing efforts quite difficult. A foreign buyer, for example, may wish to purchase helicopters and contract for service support over a period of ten years. If the sale involves a UK firm, both the helicopter and the service sale will require an export license. Such license, however, are issued only for an immediate sale. Therefore, over the ten years, the seller will have to apply for an export licence each time service is to be provided. As the issuance of a licence is often dependent on the political

EXHIBIT 15.1

Tangible and intangible offerings of airlines

Source: Adapted from G. Lynn Shostack, "Breaking Free from Product Marketing," in *Services Marketing,* ed. Christopher H. Lovelock (Englewood Cliffs, NJ: Prentice-all,1984), 40.

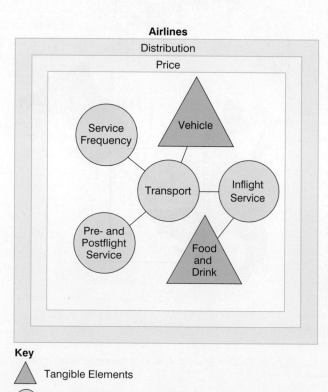

climate, the buyer and seller are haunted by uncertainty. As a result, sales may be lost to firms in countries that can unconditionally guarantee the long-term supply of support services.

Services can be just as dependent on goods. For example, an airline that prides itself on providing an efficient reservation system and excellent linkups with rental cars and hotel reservations could not survive without its airplanes. As a result, many offerings in the marketplace consist of a combination of goods and services. A graphic illustration of the tangible and intangible elements in the market offering of an airline is provided in Exhibit 15.1.

The simple knowledge that services and goods interact, however, is not enough. Successful managers must recognize that different customer groups will frequently view the service/goods combination differently. The type of use and usage conditions will also affect evaluations of the market offering. For example, the intangible dimension of 'on-time arrival' by airlines may be valued differently by college students than by business executives. Similarly, a 20-minute delay will be judged differently by a passenger arriving at her final destination than by one who has just missed an overseas connection. As a result, adjustment possibilities in both the service and the goods area can be used as strategic tools to stimulate demand and increase profitability. For different offerings, service and goods elements may vary substantially. The marketer must identify the role of each and adjust all of them to meet the desires of the target customer group.

Stand-alone services

Services do not always come in unison with goods. Increasingly, they compete against goods and become an alternative offering. For example, rather than buy an in-house computer, the business executive can contract computing work to a local or foreign service firm. Similarly, the purchase of a car (a good) can be converted into the purchase of a service by leasing the car from an agency.

Services may also compete against each other. As an example, a store may have the option of offering full service to consumers who purchase there or of converting to the self-service format. With automated checkout services, consumers may self-serve all activities such as selection, transportation, packaging and pricing.

Services differ from goods most strongly in their intangibility: They are frequently consumed rather than possessed. Even though the intangibility of services is a primary differentiating criterion, it is not always present. For example, publishing services ultimately result in a tangible good, namely, a book or an article. Similarly, construction services eventually result in a building, a subway or a bridge. Even in those instances, however, the intangible component that leads to the final product is of major concern to both the producer of the service and the recipient of the ultimate output because it brings with it major considerations that are not traditional to goods.

One major difference concerns the storing of services. Because of their nature, services are difficult to inventory. If they are not used, the 'brown around the edges' syndrome tends to result in high services perishability. Unused capacity in the form of an empty seat on an airplane, for example, becomes nonsaleable quickly. Once the plane has taken off, selling an empty seat is virtually impossible – except for an inflight upgrade from standard to first class – and the capacity cannot be stored for future usage. Similarly, the difficulty of keeping services in inventory makes it troublesome to provide service backup for peak demand. Constantly maintaining service capacity at levels necessary to satisfy peak demand would be very expensive. The marketer must therefore attempt to smooth out demand levels through price or promotion activities in order to optimize the use of capacity.

For many service offerings, the time of production is very close to or even simultaneous with the time of consumption. This fact points toward close customer involvement in the production of services. Customers frequently either service themselves or cooperate in the delivery of services. As a result, the service provider often needs to be physically present when the service is delivered. This physical presence creates both problems and opportunities, and it introduces a new constraint that is seldom present in the marketing of goods. For example, close interaction with the customer requires a much greater understanding of and emphasize on the cultural dimension. A good service delivered in a culturally unacceptable fashion is doomed to failure. Sensitivity to culture, beliefs and preferences is imperative in the services industry. In some instances, the need to be sensitive to diverse customer groups in domestic markets can greatly assist a company in preparing for international market expansion. A common pattern of internationalization for service businesses is therefore to develop stand-alone business systems in each country. At the same time, however, some services have become 'de-localized' as advances in modern technology have made it possible for firms to de-link production and service processes and switch labour-intensive service performance to countries where qualified, low-cost labour is plentiful.

The close interaction with customers also points towards the fact that services often are custom-made. This contradicts the desire of a firm to standardize its offering; yet at the same time, it offers the service provider an opportunity to differentiate the service from the competition. The concomitant problem is that in order to fulfill customer expectations, service consistency is required. As with anything offered in real time, however, consistency is difficult to maintain over the long run. The human element in the service offering therefore takes on a much greater role than in the offering of goods. Errors can enter the system, and non-predictable individual influences can affect the outcome of the service delivery. The issue of quality control affects the provider as well as the recipient of services. Efforts to increase such control through uniformity may sometimes be seen by customers as a reduction in service choices. The quality perception of service customers is largely determined by the behaviour of the employees they contact. Customer-contact workers are therefore a key internal group whose skills must be addressed systematically through internal marketing, which takes place between firms and employees. The target groups of internal marketing are managers and employees of all levels who handle customer concerns. They must first be convinced that complaints contain business opportunities rather than dangers, and must therefore be handled in a positive and proactive manner. Second, achievement-based rewards should be established to create complaint management incentives for employees.[3]

Buyers have more problems in observing and evaluating services than goods. This is particularly true when a shopper tries to choose intelligently among service providers. Even when sellers of services are willing and able to provide more market transparency where the details of the service are clear, comparable, and available to all interested parties, the buyer's problem is complicated: Customers receiving the same service may use it differently and service quality may vary for each delivery. Since production lines cannot be established to deliver an identical service each time, and the quality of a service cannot be tightly controlled, the problem of service heterogeneity emerges, meaning that services may never be the same from one delivery to another.[4] For example, a teacher's advice, even if it is provided on the same day by the same person, may vary substantially depending on the student. Over time, even for the same student, the counselling may change. As a result, service offerings are not directly comparable, which makes quality measurements quite challenging. Therefore, the reputation of the service provider plays an overwhelming role in the customer choice process.

Services often require entirely new forms of distribution. Traditional channels are often multi-tiered and long and therefore slow. They often cannot be used because of the perishability of services. A weather news service, for example, either reaches its audience quickly or rapidly loses its value. As a result, direct delivery and short distribution channels are often required. When they do not exist – which is often the case domestically and even more so internationally – service providers need to be distribution innovators in order to reach their market.

All these aspects of services exist in both international and domestic settings. Their impact, however, takes on greater importance for the international marketer. For example, because of the longer distances involved, service perishability that may be an obstacle in domestic business becomes a barrier internationally. Similarly, the issue of quality control for international services may be much more difficult to deal with due to different service uses, changing expectations and varying national regulations.

As services are delivered directly to the user, they are frequently much more sensitive to cultural factors than are products. Sometimes their influence on the individual may even be considered with hostility abroad. For example, the showing of western films in cinemas or television in developing countries is often attacked as an imposition of western culture. National leaders who place strong emphasize on national cultural identity frequently denounce foreign services and attempt to hinder their market penetration. Even dimensions which one thinks to be highly standardized around the globe may need to be adapted.

Similarly, services are subject to many political vagaries occurring almost daily. Yet coping with these changes can become the service provider's competitive advantage.

THE ROLE OF INTERNATIONAL SERVICES IN THE WORLD ECONOMY

The rise of the service sector is a global phenomenon. Services contribute an average of more than 60 per cent to the gross national product of industrial nations. Services are also rapidly moving to the forefront in many other nations as well, accounting for 70 per cent in Mexico, 65 per cent in South Africa and about 46 per cent in Thailand.[5] Even in the least developed countries, services typically contribute at least 45 per cent of GDP. With growth rates higher than other sectors such as agriculture and manufacturing, services are instrumental in job creation in these countries.[6] Exhibit 15.2 shows the importance of the service sector across the world. Within these countries, the names of such firms as American Express, McDonald's, Club Med, Thomas Cook, Mitsubishi and Hilton have become widely familiar. The linkage between growth of services and gender is interesting. As Exhibit 15.3 demonstrates, countries with a high share of the population employed in services tend to have the highest participation of women in the labour market.

Country	Services as Percentage of GDP	Percentage of Workforce in Services
United States	78.3%	83%
Canada	68.7	74
Brazil	50.6	66
Australia	69.6	70
Japan	73.5	70
Kenya	65.1	n/a
European Union	70.1	66.9
Austria	66.3	67
Belgium	74	74.2
Denmark	73.8	79
Finland	66.5	70
France	76.1	71.5
Germany	70.3	63.8
Greece	71.7	68
Ireland	49	63
Italy	69.1	63
Luxembourg	83.1	86
The Netherlands	73.5	73
Portugal	65.9	60
Spain	67.9	64.4
Sweden	69.7	74
United Kingdom	72.9	79.5

Sources: *The World Factbook* 2005, **http://www.cia.gov**, accessed January 26, 2006.

EXHIBIT 15.2

Services across the world

EXHIBIT 15.3   High employment in services goes hand-in-hand with high employment for women: employment/population ratios in services and for women, 2002, percentages

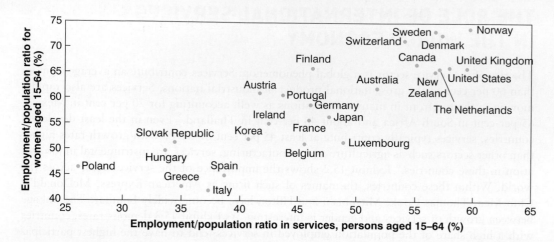

Source: "Growth in Services: Fostering Employment, Productivity and Innovation," Organisation for Economic Co-Operation and Development, Paris, 2005.

GLOBAL TRANSFORMATION OF SERVICES

The rapid rise in international services marketing has been the result of major shifts in the business environment and innovations in technology. One primary change in the past decade has been the reduction of governmental regulation of services. The deregulatory movement began in the US in the mid-1970s, beginning with a decision to reduce government interference in the marketplace, in the hope that this would enhance competitive activity. As a consequence, some service sectors have benefited, and others have suffered from the withdrawal of government intervention. The primary deregulated industries have been transportation, banking, and telecommunications. As a result, new competitors participate in the marketplace. Regulatory changes were initially thought to have primarily domestic effects, but they have rapidly spread internationally. For example, the 1984 deregulation of AT&T has given rise to the deregulation of Japan's telecommunications monopoly, NT&T. European deregulation followed in the mid-1990s.

Similarly, deregulatory efforts in the transportation sector have had international repercussions. New air carriers have entered the market to compete against established trunk carriers, and have done so sucssesfully by pricing their services lower both nationally and internationally. In doing so, these airlines also affected the regulatory climate abroad. Obviously, a British airline can count only to a limited extent on government support to remain competitive with new low-priced fares offered by other carriers also serving the British markets. As a result, the deregulatory movement has spread internationally and has fostered the emergence of new competition and new competitive practices. As many of these changes result in lower prices, demand has been stimulated, leading to a rise in the volume of international services trade.

Another major change has been the decreased regulation of service industries by their industry groups. For example, business practices in fields such as healthcare, law and accounting are becoming more competitive and aggressive. New economic realities require firms in these industries to search for new ways to attract market share. International markets are one frequently untapped possibility for market expansion and have therefore become a prime target for such service firms.

Technological advancement is another major factor in increasing service trade. Progress in technology offers new ways of doing business and permits businesses to expand their horizons internationally. For example, Volkswagen uses one major computer system to carry out its new car designs. This practice not only lowers expenditures on hardware but also permits better utilization of existing equipment and international design collaboration, by allowing design groups in different time zones to use the equipment around the clock. This development could, however, take place only after advances in data transmission procedures.

In a similar fashion, more rapid transmission of data has permitted financial institutions to expand their service delivery through a worldwide network. Again, were it not for advances in technology, such expansion would rarely have been possible or cost-effective.

Another result of these developments is that service industry expansion has not been confined to the traditional services that are labour-intensive and could therefore have been performed better in areas of the world where labour possesses a comparative advantage because of lower prices. Rather, technology-intensive services are the sunrise industries of the new century. Increasingly, firms can reconfigure their service delivery in order to escape the location-bound dimension. Banks, for example, can offer their services through automatic teller machines or telephone banking. Consultants can advise via video conferences, and teachers can teach the world through multimedia classrooms. Physicians can perform operations in a distant country if proper computer linkages can drive roboticized medical equipment.

As a result, many service providers have the opportunity to become truly global marketers. To them, the traditional international market barrier of distance no longer matters. Knowledge, the core of many service activities, can offer a global reach without requiring a local presence. Service providers therefore may have only a minor need for local establishment, since they can operate without premises. You don't have to be there to do business! The effect of such a shift in service activities is major. Insurance and bank buildings in the downtowns of the world may soon become obsolete. Talented service providers see the demand for their performance increase while less capable ones will suffer from increased competition. Most important, consumers and society have a much broader range and quality of service choices available, and often at a lower cost.

INTERNATIONAL TRADE PROBLEMS IN SERVICES

Together with the increasing importance of service marketing, new problems have beset the service sector. Even though many of these problems have been characterized as affecting mainly the negotiations between nations, they are of sufficient importance to the firm in its international activities to merit a brief review.

Data collection problems

The data collected on service trade are quite poor. Service transactions are often 'invisible' statistically as well as physically. The fact that governments have precise data on the number of trucks exported, down to the last bolt, but little information on reinsurance flows, reflects past governmental inattention to services.

Only recently have policymakers recognized that the income generated and the jobs created through the sale of services abroad are just as important as income and jobs resulting from the production and exportation of goods. As a result, many governments are beginning to develop improved measuring techniques for the services sector. For example, the UK government has improved its estimates of services by covering more business, professional and technical services and incorporating improved measurement of telecommunications services and insurance services. New data are also developed on travel and passenger fares, foreign students' expenditures in the United Kingdom, repairs and alterations of equipment, and non-interest income of banks.

It is easy to imagine how many data collection problems are encountered in countries lacking elaborate systems and unwilling to allocate funds for such efforts. The gathering of information is, of course, made substantially more difficult because services are intangible and therefore more difficult to measure and to trace than goods. The lack of service homogeneity does not make the task any easier. In an international setting, of course, an additional major headache is the lack of comparability between services categories as used by different national statistical systems. For example, gas and electricity production and distribution may be classified as goods by some governments and classified as services/utilities by others.

Insufficient knowledge and information has led to a lack of transparency. As a result, governments have great difficulty gauging the effect of service transactions internationally or influencing service trade. Consequently, international services negotiations progress only slowly, and governmental regulations are often put into place without precise information as to their repercussions on actual trade performance.

Regulations and service trade negotiations

Typical obstacles to services trade can be categorized into two major types: barriers to entry and problems in performing services. Governments often justify barriers to entry by referring to national security and economic security. For example, the impact of banking on domestic economic activity is given as a reason why banking should be carried out only by nationals or indeed be operated entirely under government control. Sometimes, the protection of service users is cited, particularly of bank depositors and insurance policyholders. Some countries claim that competition in societally important services is unnecessary, wasteful, and should be avoided. Another justification for barriers is the frequently used infant industry argument: 'With sufficient time to develop on our own, we can compete in world markets'. Often, however, this argument is used simply to prolong the ample licencing profits generated by restricted entry. Impediments to services consist of either tariff or non-tariff barriers. Tariff barriers typically restrict or inhibit market entry for the service provider or consumer, while non-tariff barriers tend to impede service performance. Yet, defining a barrier to service marketing is not always easy. For example, Germany gives an extensive written examination to prospective accountants (as do most countries) to ensure that licenced accountants are qualified to practice. Naturally, the examination is given in German.

Even if barriers to entry are nonexistent or can be overcome, service companies have difficulty in performing effectively abroad once they have achieved access to the local market. One reason is that rules and regulations based on tradition may inhibit innovation. A more important reason is that governments aim to pursue social or cultural objectives through national regulations. Of primary importance here is the distinction between discriminatory and nondiscriminatory regulations. Regulations that impose larger operating costs on foreign service providers than on the local competitors, that provide subsidies to local firms only, or that deny competitive opportunities to foreign suppliers are a proper cause for international concern. The discrimination problem becomes even more acute when foreign firms face competition from government-owned or government-controlled enterprises, which are discussed in more detail in Chapter 17, 'Global Pricing'. On the other hand, nondiscriminatory regulations may be inconvenient and may hamper business operations, but they offer less opportunity for international criticism.

For example, barriers to services destined for the EU market result mainly from regulatory practices. The fields of banking, insurance and accounting provide some examples. These industries are regulated at both federal and state levels, and the regulations often pose formidable barriers to potential entrants from abroad. The chief complaint of foreign countries is not that the European Union discriminates against foreign service providers but rather that the European Union places more severe restrictions on them than do other countries. These barriers are, of course, a reflection of the decision-making process within the EU domestic economy and are unlikely to change in the near future. A coherent approach toward international commerce in services is hardly likely to emerge from the disparate decisions of agencies such as the European Medicine Agency (EMEA), the European Food Safety Authority (EFSA) or the Community Fisheries Control Agencey (CFCA).

All these regulations make it difficult for the international service marketer to penetrate world markets. At the governmental level, services frequently are not recognized as a major facet of world trade or are viewed with suspicion because of a lack of understanding, and barriers to entry often result. To make progress in tearing them down, much educational work needs to be done. At the Geneva Ministerial in 2008 the Doha Round came very close to a framework agreement on tariff cuts for industrial goods and agricultural exports and a comprehensive package of farm reform in developed countries.[7] This package would have gone further than any previous multilateral trade agreement.[8] It would have removed almost all remaining tariffs between developed countries for industrial goods and would have included a proportionate contribution from large emerging economies such as Brazil, China and India.[9] Unfortunately, the meeting broke down over a disagreement between exporters of agricultural bulk commodities and countries with large numbers of subsistence farmers on the precise terms of a 'special safeguard measure' to protect farmers from surges in imports. At this time, the future of the Doha Round is uncertain.[10]

CORPORATIONS AND INVOLVEMENT IN INTERNATIONAL SERVICES MARKETING

Services and e-commerce

Electronic commerce has opened up new horizons for global services reach and has drastically reduced the meaning of distance. For example, when geographic obstacles make the establishment of retail outlets cumbersome and expensive, firms can approach their customers via the World Wide Web. Government regulations that might be prohibitive to a transfer of goods may not have any effect on the international marketing of services. In addition, regardless of size, companies are finding it increasingly easy to appeal to a global marketplace. The internet can help service firms develop and transitional economies overcome two of the biggest tasks they face: gaining credibility in international markets and saving on travel costs. Little-known firms can become instantly 'visible' on the internet. Even a small firm can develop a polished and sophisticated web presence and promotion strategy. Customers are less concerned about geographic location if they feel the firm is electronically accessible. An increasing number of service providers have never met their foreign customers except 'virtually', online.[11]

Nonetheless, several notes of caution must be kept in mind. First, the penetration of the internet has occurred at different rates in different countries. There are still many businesses and consumers who do not have access to electronic business media. Unless they are to be excluded from a company's focus, more traditional ways of reaching them must be considered. Also, firms need to prepare their internet presence for global visitors. For example, the language of the internet is English – at least as far as large corporations are concerned. Yet, many of the visitors coming to Websites either may not have English as their first language or may not speak English at all.

Many companies do not permit any interaction on their websites, thus missing out on feedback or even order placement from visitors. Some websites are so culture-bound that they often leave their visitors bewildered and disappointed. Yet over time, increasing understanding about doing business in the global marketplace will enable companies to be more refined in their approach to their customers.

Services and academia[12]

In the context of international services, it makes sense to briefly review the position of higher education. Academia has staunchly resisted accepting the notion of being part of any services 'sector'. University chancellors, deans, and professors from around the world consistently assure the trade community that the problems they face are so specific and unique that wholesale approaches to anything in higher education would be heresy. However, academia is not exempt from influence by the same factors as other global services, such as demand and supply.

The terrorist attacks of September 11, 2001, have had a long term effect on the direction and extent of international student mobility. Today's heightened security environment has imposed new scrutiny and reporting requirements. New bureaucratic processes thus lead to more visa denials and to substantial delays in visa interviews; the delays often conflict with time sensitive academic admission requirements. Universities have found it difficult to restructure their time frames for international students in order to accommodate the realities and needs of national concerns. In addition, disenchantment with studying in the United States – for reasons of direct policy disagreements, cultural concerns and a greater desire to stay at home – have contributed to the fall in international enrolment at British institutions.

Attacks on certain races had a similar effect on Australian education, which has seen its revenue from education falling.[13]

However, private, profit-oriented developments in the higher education sector keep blossoming. The electronic learning market around the world is surging in its impact. In 2009, the worldwide market for e-learning was 21.8 billion EUR, the demand is growing by 12.8 per cent and the revenues will reach 40 billion EUR by 2014.[14]

Typical international services

Although many firms are already active in the international service arena, others often do not perceive their existing competitive advantage. Numerous services have great potential for internationalization.

Financial institutions can offer some functions very competitively in the international field of banking services. Increased mergers and acquisitions on a global basis have led to the emergence of financial giants in Europe, Japan and the United States. With the increased reach made possible by electronic commerce, they can develop direct linkages to clients around the world, offering tailor-made financial services and reduction in intermediation cost.

Another area with great international potential is construction, design and engineering services. Economies of scale work not only for machinery and material but also for areas such as personnel management and the overall management of projects. Particularly for international projects that are large scale and long term, the experience advantage could weigh heavily in favour of seasoned firms. The economic significance of these services far exceeds their direct turnover because they encourage subsequent demand for capital goods. For example, having an engineering consultant of a certain nationality increases the chances that contracts for the supply of equipment, technology, and know-how will be won by an enterprise of the same nationality, given the advantages enjoyed in terms of information, language and technical specification.[15]

Firms in the fields of legal and accounting services can aid their domestic clients abroad through support activities; they can also aid foreign firms and countries in improving business and governmental operations. In computer and data services, international potential is growing rapidly. Knowledge of computer operations, data manipulations, data transmission and data analysis are insufficiently exploited internationally by many small and medium-sized firms. For example, India is increasingly participating in the provision of international data services. Although some aspects of the data field are high-technology intensive, many operations still require skilled human service input. The coding and entering of data often has to be performed manually because appropriate machine-readable forms may be unavailable or not usable. Because of lower wages, Indian companies can offer data-entry services at a rate much lower than in more industrialized countries. As a result, data are transmitted in raw form to India where they are encoded on a proper medium and returned to the ultimate user. To some extent, this transformation can be equated to the value-added steps that take place in the transformation of a raw commodity into a finished product. Obviously, using its comparative advantage for this labour-intensive task, India can compete in the field of international services. In 2004–2005, revenue from software and service exports from India reached $17.2 billion; this is a growth of 34.5 per cent from the previous year. However, after a dream run for years, India's export revenues from software and services industry is expected to see just 4–7 per cent growth this fiscal year and the downturn is likely to continue till mid-2010.[16] The UK and the US remain dominant customers, although India is also gaining ground in new markets like Germany, Japan and Singapore.[17]

Many opportunities exist in the field of teaching services. Both the academic and the corporate education sectors have concentrated their work in the domestic market. Yet the teaching of knowledge is in high global demand and offers new opportunities for growth. Technology allows teachers to go global via video conferences, e-mail office hours, and internet-relayed teaching materials. Removing the confinement of the classroom may well trigger the largest surge in learning that humankind has ever known.

Management consulting services can be provided by firms to institutions and corporations around the globe. Of particular value is management expertise in areas where firms possess global leadership, be it in manufacturing or process activities. For example, companies with highly refined transportation or logistics activities can sell their management experience abroad. Yet consulting services are particularly sensitive to the cultural environment, and their use varies significantly by country and field of expertise.

All domestic service expenditures funded from abroad by foreign citizens also represent a service export. This makes tourism an increasingly important area of services trade. For example, every foreign visitor who spends foreign currency in a country contributes to an improvement in that nation's current account. The natural resources and beauty offered by so many countries have already made tourism one of the most important services trade components. Exhibit 15.4 shows the top 10 tourism destinations, tourism earners and tourism spenders.

A proper mix in international services might also be achieved by pairing the strengths of different partners. For example, information technology expertise from one country could be combined with financial resources from another. The strengths of both partners can then be used to obtain maximum benefits.

Combining international advantages in services may ultimately result in the development of an even newer and more drastic comparative lead. For example, if a firm has an international head start in such areas as high technology, information gathering, information processing and information analysis, the major thrust of its international service might not rely on providing these service components individually but rather on enabling clients, based on all resources, to make better decisions. If better decision-making is transferable to a wide variety of international situations, that in itself might become the overriding future competitive advantage of the firm in the international market.

Starting to market services internationally

For many firms, participation in the internet will offer the most attractive starting point in marketing services internationally. Setting up a website will allow visitors from any place on the globe to view the offering. Of course, the most important problem will be communicating the existence of the site and enticing visitors to visit. For that, very traditional advertising and communication approaches often need to be used. In some countries, for example, rolling billboards announce websites and their benefits. Overall, however, we need to keep in mind that not everywhere do firms and individuals have access to or make use of the new e-commerce opportunities.

For services that are delivered mainly in the support of or in conjunction with goods, the most sensible approach for the international novice is to follow the path of the good. For years, many large accounting and banking firms have done so by determining where their major multinational clients have set up new operations and then following them. Smaller service

EXHIBIT 15.4

World tourism: The top ten

Rank	Tourism destination	Tourism earners	Tourism spenders
1	France	United States	United States
2	Spain	Spain	Japan
3	United States	France	Germany
4	Italy	Italy	United Kingdom
5	China	Germany	France
6	United Kingdom	United Kingdom	Italy
7	Austria	China	Spain
8	Mexico	Austria	China
9	Germany	Turkey	Canada
10	Canada	Greece	Mexico

Sources: World Travel & Tourism Council, Executive Summary: *The 2005 Travel & Tourism Economic Research/Travel & Tourism: Sowing the Seeds of Growth,* **http://www.wttc.org**, 2003 Data, accessed January 26, 2006.

marketers who cooperate closely with manufacturing firms can determine where the manufacturing firms are operating internationally. Ideally, of course, it would be possible to follow clusters of manufacturers in order to obtain economies of scale internationally while, at the same time, looking for entirely new client groups abroad.

For service providers whose activities are independent from goods, a different strategy is needed. These individuals and firms must search for market situations abroad that are similar to the domestic market. Such a search should concentrate in their area of expertise. For example, a design firm learning about construction projects abroad can investigate the possibility of rendering its design services. Similarly, a management consultant learning about the plans of a foreign country or firm to computerize operations can explore the possibility of overseeing a smooth transition from manual to computerized activities. What is required is the understanding that similar problems are likely to occur in similar situations.

Another opportunity consists in identifying and understanding points of transition abroad. Just as US society has undergone change, foreign societies are subject to a changing domestic environment. If, for example, new transportation services are introduced, an expert in containerization may wish to consider whether to offer service to improve the efficiency of the new system.

Leads for international service opportunities can also be gained by staying informed about international projects sponsored by domestic organizations, as well as international organizations such as the United Nations, the International Finance Corporation, or the World Bank. Very frequently, such projects are in need of support through services. Overall, the international service marketer needs to search for familiar situations or similar problems requiring similar solutions in order to formulate an effective international expansion strategy.

Strategic implications of international services marketing

To be successful, the international service marketer must first determine the nature and the aim of the service offering – that is, whether the service will be aimed at people or at things, and whether the service act in itself will result in tangible or intangible actions. Exhibit 15.5 provides examples of such a classification that will help the marketer to better determine the position of the services effort.

During this determination, the marketer must consider other tactical variables that have an impact on the preparation of the service offering. The measurement of services capacity and delivery efficiency often remains highly qualitative rather than quantitative. In the field of communications, the intangibility of the service reduces the marketer's ability to provide samples. This makes communicating the service offer much more difficult than communicating an offer for a good. Brochures or catalogues explaining services often must show a 'proxy' for the service in order to provide the prospective customer with tangible clues. A cleaning service, for instance, can show a picture of an individual removing rubbish or cleaning a window. Yet the picture will not fully communicate the performance of the service. Due to the different needs and requirements of individual consumers, the marketer must pay very close attention to the two-way flow of communication. Mass communication must often be supported by intimate one-on-one follow-up.

The role of personnel deserves special consideration in the international marketing of services. Because the customer interface is intense, proper provisions need to be made for training personnel both domestically and internationally. Major emphasize must be placed on appearance. The person delivering the service – rather than the service itself – will communicate the spirit, value and attitudes of the service corporation. The service person is both the producer and the marketer of the service. Therefore, recruitment and training techniques must focus on dimensions such as customer relationship management and image projection as well as competence in the design and delivery of the service.[18]

This close interaction with the consumer will also have organizational implications. Whereas tight control over personnel may be desired, the individual interaction that is required points toward the need for an international decentralization of service delivery. This,

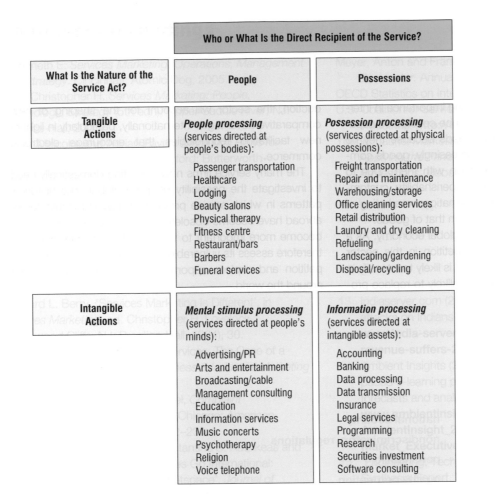

Who or What Is the Direct Recipient of the Service?		
What Is the Nature of the Service Act?	**People**	**Possessions**
Tangible Actions	**People processing** (services directed at people's bodies): Passenger transportation Healthcare Lodging Beauty salons Physical therapy Fitness centre Restaurant/bars Barbers Funeral services	**Possession processing** (services directed at physical possessions): Freight transportation Repair and maintenance Warehousing/storage Office cleaning services Retail distribution Laundry and dry cleaning Refueling Landscaping/gardening Disposal/recycling
Intangible Actions	**Mental stimulus processing** (services directed at people's minds): Advertising/PR Arts and entertainment Broadcasting/cable Management consulting Education Information services Music concerts Psychotherapy Religion Voice telephone	**Information processing** (services directed at intangible assets): Accounting Banking Data processing Data transmission Insurance Legal services Programming Research Securities investment Software consulting

EXHIBIT 15.5

Understanding the service act

Source: Christopher H. Lovelock and Jochen Wirtz, *Services Marketing: People, Technology, Strategy,* 5th ed., 15. © 2005. Reprinted by permission of Pearson Education, Inc., Upper Saddle River, NJ.

in turn, requires both delegation of large amounts of responsibility to individuals and service 'subsidiaries' and a great deal of trust in all organizational units. This trust, of course, can be greatly enhanced through proper methods of training and supervision. Sole ownership also helps strengthen trust. Research has shown that service firms, in their international expansion, tend greatly to prefer the establishment of full-control ventures. Only when costs escalate and the company-specific advantage diminishes will service firms seek out shared-control ventures.[19]

The areas of pricing and financing require special attention. As services cannot be stored, much greater responsiveness to demand fluctuation must exist, and, therefore, much greater pricing flexibility must be maintained. At the same time, flexibility is countered by the desire to provide transparency for both the seller and the buyer of services in order to foster an ongoing relationship. The intangibility of services also makes financing more difficult. Frequently, even financial institutions with large amounts of international experience are less willing to provide financial support for international services than for products. The reasons are that the value of services is more difficult to assess, service performance is more difficult to monitor, and services are difficult to repossess. Therefore, customer complaints and difficulties in receiving payments are much more troublesome for a lender to evaluate for services than for products.

Finally, the distribution implications of international services must be considered. Usually, short and direct channels are required. Within these channels, closeness to the customer is of overriding importance in order to understand what the customer really wants, to trace the use of the service, and to aid the consumer in obtaining a truly tailor-made service.

The growth of logistics as a field has brought to the forefront three major concepts: the systems concept, the total cost concept and the trade-off concept. The systems concept is based on the notion that materials-flow activities within and outside of the firm are so extensive and complex that they can be considered only in the context of their interaction. The systems concept stipulates that some components may have to work suboptimally to maximize the benefits of the system as a whole. The goal is to provide the firm, its suppliers, and its customers, both domestic and foreign, with the benefits of synergism expected from the coordinated application of size.

In order for the systems concept to work, information flows and partnership trust are instrumental. Logistics capability is highly information dependent, since information availability is key to planning and to process implementation. Long-term partnership and trust are required in order to forge closer links between firms and managers.

A logical outgrowth of the systems concept is the development of the total cost concept. To evaluate and optimize logistical activities, cost is used as a basis for measurement. The purpose of the total cost concept is to minimize the firm's overall logistics cost by implementing the systems concept appropriately.

Implementation of the total cost concept requires that the members of the system understand the sources of costs. To develop such understanding, a system of activity-based costing has been developed, which is a technique designed to more accurately assign the indirect and direct resources of an organization to the activities performed based on consumption.[1] In the international arena, the total cost concept must also incorporate the consideration of total after-tax profit, by taking the impact of national tax policies on the logistics function into account. The objective is to maximize after-tax profits rather than to minimize total cost.

The trade-off concept, finally, recognizes the linkages within logistics systems that result from the interaction of their components. For example, locating a warehouse near the customer may reduce the cost of transportation. However, the new warehouse will lead to increased storage costs and more inventory. Managers can maximize performance of logistics systems only by formulating decisions based on the recognition and analysis of such trade-offs. Consider a manufacturer building several different goods. The goods all use one or both of two parts, A and B, which the manufacturer buys in roughly equal amounts. Most of the goods produced use both parts. The unit cost of part A is $7, of part B, $10. Part B has more capabilities than part A; in fact, B can replace A. If the manufacturer doubles its purchases of part B, it qualifies for a discounted $8 unit price. For products that incorporate both parts, substituting B for A makes sense to qualify for the discount, since the total parts cost is $17 using A and B, but only $16 using Bs only. Part B should therefore become a standard part for the manufacturer. But departments building products that only use part A may be reluctant to accept the substitute part B because, even discounted, the cost of B exceeds that of A. Use of the trade-off concept will solve the problem.[2]

SUPPLY CHAIN MANAGEMENT

The integration of these three concepts has resulted in the new paradigm of supply chain management, which encompasses the planning and management of all activities involved in sourcing and procurement, conversion and logistics. It also includes coordination and collaboration with channel partners, which can be suppliers, intermediaries, third party service providers and customers. In essence, supply chain management integrates supply and demand management within and across companies.[3]

Advances in information technology have been crucial to progress in supply chain management. Consider the example of Gestamp (Spain's leading supplier of metal components for car manufacturers), which used electronic data interchange technology to integrate inbound and outbound logistics between suppliers and customers. The company reports increased manufacturing productivity, reduced investment needs, increased efficiency of the billing process and led to a lower rate of logistic errors across the supply process after implementing a

EXHIBIT 16.1   The international supply chain

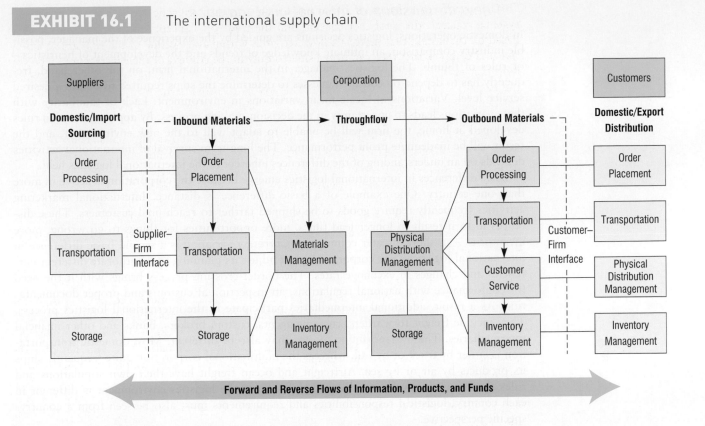

supply chain management system.[4] Globalization has opened up supplier relationships for companies outside the buyer's domestic market; however, the supplier's ability to provide satisfying goods and services will play the most critical role in securing long-term contracts. In addition, the physical delivery of goods often can be old-fashioned and slow. Nevertheless, the use of such strategic tools will be crucial for international managers to develop and maintain key competitive advantages. An overview of the international supply chain is shown in Exhibit 16.1.

THE IMPACT OF INTERNATIONAL LOGISTICS

Logistics costs comprise between 10 and 30 per cent of the total landed cost of an international order.[5] International firms experience ongoing increases in their logistics cost. Surging fuels costs show no signs of dropping. Globalization has stretched the length of the value chain. Transportation providers have boosted their prices, both to offset fuel costs but also as a result of growing demand for their services and constraints in capacity. Increased security requirements for freight also have increased costs.[6]

Close collaboration with suppliers is required in order to develop a just-in-time inventory system, which in turn may be crucial to maintain manufacturing costs at a globally competitive level. Yet without electronic data interchange, such collaborations or alliances are severely handicapped. While most industrialized countries can offer the technological infrastructure for such computer-to-computer exchange of business information, the application of such a system in the global environment may be severely restricted. Often, it is not just the lack of technology that forms the key obstacle to modern logistics management, but rather the entire business infrastructure, ranging from ways of doing business in fields such as accounting and inventory tracking, to the willingness of businesses to collaborate with one another.

The new dimensions of international logistics

In domestic operations, logistics decisions are guided by the experience of the manager, possible industry comparison, an intimate knowledge of trends and the development of heuristics – or rules of thumb. The logistics manager in the international firm, on the other hand, frequently has to depend on educated guesses to determine the steps required to obtain a desired service level. Variations in locale mean variations in environment. Lack of familiarity with these variations leads to uncertainty in the decision-making process. By applying decision rules developed at home, the firm will be unable to adapt well to the new environment, and the result will be inadequate profit performance. The long-term survival of international activities depends on an understanding of the differences inherent in the international logistics field.

Basic differences in international logistics emerge because the corporation is active in more than one country. One example of a basic difference is distance. International marketing activities frequently require goods to be shipped farther to reach final customers. These distances in turn result in longer lead times, more opportunities for things to go wrong, more inventories – in short, greater complexity. Currency variation is a second basic difference in international logistics. The corporation must adjust its planning to incorporate different currencies and changes in exchange rates. The border-crossing process brings with it the need for conformance with national regulations, an inspection at customs and proper documentation. As a result, additional intermediaries participate in the international logistics process. They include freight forwarders, customs agents, custom brokers, banks and other financial intermediaries. The transportation modes may also be different. Most domestic transportation is either by truck or by rail, whereas the multinational corporation quite frequently ships its products by air or by sea. Airfreight and ocean freight have their own stipulations and rules that require new knowledge and skills. Since the logistics environment is different in each country, logistical responsibilities and requirements must also be seen from a country-specific perspective.

INTERNATIONAL TRANSPORTATION ISSUES

International transportation is of major concern to the international firm because transportation determines how and when goods will be received. The transportation issue can be divided into three components: infrastructure, the availability of modes and the choice of modes.

Transportation infrastructure

In industrialized nations, firms can count on an established transportation network. Internationally, however, major infrastructural variations may be encountered. Some countries may have excellent inbound and outbound transportation systems but weak transportation links within the country as shown in *The International Marketplace 16.2*. This is particularly true in former colonies, where the original transportation systems were designed to maximize the extractive potential of the countries. In such instances, shipping to the market may be easy, but distribution within the market may represent a very difficult and time-consuming task.

The international marketer must therefore learn about existing and planned infrastructures abroad. In some countries, for example, railroads may be an excellent transportation mode, far surpassing the performance of trucking, whereas in others, the use of railroads for freight distribution may be a gamble at best. The future routing of pipelines must be determined before any major commitments are made to a particular location if the product is amenable to pipeline transportation. The transportation methods used to carry cargo to seaports or airports must also be investigated. Mistakes in the evaluation of transportation options can prove to be very costly. One researcher reported the case of a food processing firm that built a pineapple cannery at the delta of a river in Mexico. Since the pineapple plantation was located upstream, the company planned to float the ripe fruit down to the cannery on barges. To its dismay, the firm discovered that at harvest time the river current was far too strong for barge traffic. Since no other feasible alternative method of transportation existed, the plant was closed, and the new equipment was sold for a fraction of its original cost.[7]

THE INTERNATIONAL **MARKETPLACE 16.2**

China's logistics industry: Rapid change ahead

China is a developing country when it comes to logistics, but one that is currently opening up to foreigners and expanding rapidly. China's economy largely depends on trade, and its exports rose 35 per cent in 2005. The expansion of trade signals a need for increased improvements in transportation and logistics areas. The vice-minister of the National Development and Reform Commission, Ou Xinqian, stated that China's logistics industry will soon be transformed from its current 'initial' state to a more 'well-developed' one.

The Chinese government is pouring money into the process and encourages investors to do the same. Zhou Keren of the Chinese Foreign Affairs Commission reported the start-up of 20 logistics companies in November of 2004 and their continual successful operation. The growing improvement in China's logistics is not only attracting local companies but the big international corporations as well.

Major conglomerates such as DHL, UPS and FedEx are looking at China as a place of possible expansion and increased revenue. DHL estimates its revenues from China to be 50 per cent higher in 2005 when compared to the year before. Foreign companies are having a good impact on local logistics providers (currently there are 730,000 registered in China) by forcing local firms to compete and therefore have the same technological standards. These local firms have a lot to catch up with, as the foreign logistics providers are not taking a moment's break but instead are coming out with new services to offer customers. New options such as temperature-controlled warehouses and parts distribution from foreign firms are rapidly increasing.

The costs of logistics are much higher in China than they are in the United States. A recent statistic shows China's logistics expense is 21 per cent of its GDP while it is nearly half of that in developed countries. Much of this can be attributed to poor transportation means – roads and railways. The second drawback is corruption, as most of the transactions are handled by several middlemen who often demand something extra in order to speed up the transaction. This problem became visible to the outside world in April 2005 when the former deputy director of Beijing's transport department was convicted for bribery and embezzlement. Yet many international companies look at China as a place with opportunity for growth, development, and – most important – revenue.

SOURCES: Helen Atkinson, 'China's New Logistics Choices', *Journal of Commerce*, May 9, 2005; 'Logistics Industry Moving Forward', *China Daily*, May 19, 2005.

Extreme variations also exist in the frequency of transportation services. For example, a particular port may not be visited by a ship for weeks or even months. Sometimes, only carriers with particular characteristics, such as small size will serve a given location. All of these infrastructural concerns must be taken into account in the initial planning of the firm's transportation service.

Availability of modes

Even though goods are shipped abroad by rail or truck, international transportation frequently requires ocean or airfreight modes, which many corporations only rarely use domestically. In addition, combinations such as land bridges or sea bridges frequently permit the transfer of freight among various modes of transportation, resulting in intermodal movements. The international marketer must understand the specific properties of the different modes in order to use them intelligently.

Ocean shipping Water transportation is a key mode for international freight movements. An interruption of ocean-based transportation can have quite serious consequences for an economy. Three types of vessels operating in ocean shipping can be distinguished by their service: liner service, bulk service and tramp or charter service. Liner service offers regularly scheduled passage on established routes. Bulk service mainly provides contractual services for individual voyages or for prolonged periods of time. Tramp service is available for irregular routes and is scheduled only on demand.

In addition to the services offered by ocean carriers, the type of cargo a vessel can carry is also important. Most common are conventional (break bulk) cargo vessels, container ships and roll-on-roll-off vessels. Conventional cargo vessels are useful for oversized and unusual cargoes but may be less efficient in their port operations. It is a reflection of the premium assigned to speed and ease of handling that has caused a decline in the use of general cargo vessels and a sharp increase in the growth of container ships. These carry standardized containers that greatly facilitate the loading and unloading of cargo and intermodal transfers. Very large ships can carry 5000 standard containers. What a flood of goods! A key concern is to reduce the time the ship has to spend in port, where money is spent but little income generated. Roll-on-roll-off (RORO) vessels are essentially oceangoing ferries. Trucks can drive onto built-in ramps and roll off at the destination. Another vessel similar to the RORO vessel is the LASH (lighter aboard ship) vessel. LASH vessels consist of barges stored on the ship and lowered at the point of destination. These individual barges can then operate on inland waterways, a feature that is particularly useful in shallow water.

The availability of a certain type of vessel, however, does not automatically mean that it can be used. The greatest constraint in international ocean shipping remains the lack of ports and port services. For example, modern container ships cannot serve some ports because the local equipment is unable to handle the resulting traffic. This problem is often found in developing countries, where local authorities lack the funds to develop facilities. In some instances, governments purposely limit the development of ports to impede the inflow of imports. Increasingly, however, nations recognize the importance of appropriate port structures and are developing such facilities in spite of the heavy investments necessary. If such investments are accompanied by concurrent changes in the overall infrastructure, transportation efficiency should, in the long run, more than recoup the original investment. Exhibit 16.2 shows the bustling shipping in Shanghai, which is one of the largest ports in the world.

EXHIBIT 16.2   Shanghai Harbour, China

© GILLES SABRE/CORBIS

Large investments in infrastructure are usually necessary to produce results. Selective allocation of funds to transportation tends to only shift bottlenecks to some other point in the infrastructure. If these bottlenecks are not removed, the consequences may be felt in the overall economic performance of the nation. For many products, quick delivery is essential because of required high levels of industry responsiveness to orders. From a regional perspective, maintaining adequate facilities is therefore imperative in order to remain on the list of areas and ports served by international carriers. Investment in leading-edge port technology can also provide an instrumental competitive edge and cause entire distribution systems to be reconfigured to take advantage of possible savings.

Air shipping Airfreight is available to and from most countries. This includes the developing world, where it is often a matter of national prestige to operate a national airline. The tremendous growth in international airfreight is shown in Exhibit 16.3. The total volume of airfreight in relation to the total volume of shipping in international business remains quite small. Yet 40 per cent of the world's manufactured exports by value travel by air.[8] Clearly, high-value items are more likely to be shipped by air, particularly if they have a high **density**, that is, a high weight-to-volume ratio.

Airlines make major efforts to increase the volume of airfreight by developing better, more efficient ground facilities, introducing airfreight containers, and marketing a wide variety of special services to shippers. In addition, some airfreight companies have specialized and become partners in the international logistics effort.

From the shipper's perspective, the products involved must be amenable to air shipment in terms of their size. In addition, the market situation for any given product must be evaluated. For example, airfreight may be needed if a product is perishable or if, for other reasons, it requires a short transit time. The level of customer service needs and expectations can also play a decisive role. The shipment of an industrial product that is vital to the ongoing operations of a customer may be much more urgent than the shipment of packaged consumer products.

Choice of transport modes

The international marketer must make the appropriate selection from the available modes of transportation. This decision, of course, will be heavily influenced by the needs of the firm and its customers. The manager must consider the performance of each mode on four dimensions: transit time, predictability, cost and non-economic factors.

Transit time The period between departure and arrival of the carrier varies significantly between ocean freight and airfreight. The 45-day transit time of an ocean shipment can be

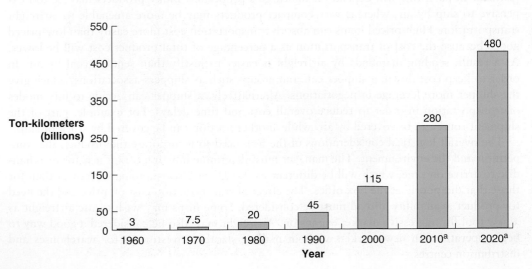

EXHIBIT 16.3

International airfreight, 1960–2020

Source: *Civil Aviation Statistics of the World* (Montreal: ICAO), http://www.icao.org; and Airbus Industries Global Market Forecast, 2004–2023, http://www.airbus.com, accessed November 22, 2005.

reduced to 12 hours if the firm chooses airfreight. The length of transit time will have a major impact on the overall operations of the firm. A short transit time may reduce or even eliminate the need for an overseas depot. Also, inventories can be significantly reduced if they are replenished frequently. As a result, capital can be freed up and used to finance other corporate opportunities. Transit time can also play a major role in emergency situations. If the shipper is about to miss an important delivery date because of production delays, a shipment normally made by ocean freight can be made by air.

Perishable products require short transit times. Rapid transportation prolongs the shelf life in the foreign market. For products with a short life span, air delivery may be the only way to enter foreign markets successfully. International sales of cut flowers have reached their current volume only as a result of airfreight. At all times, the international marketing manager must understand the interactions between different components of the logistics process and their effect on transit times. Unless a smooth flow can be assured throughout the entire supply chain, bottlenecks will deny any timing benefits from specific improvements. For example, Levi Strauss, the blue jeans manufacturer, offered customers in some of its stores the chance to be measured by a body scanner to get custom-made jeans. Less than an hour after such measurement, a Levi factory began to cut the jeans of the customer's choice. Unfortunately, it then took ten days to get the finished product to the customer.[9]

Predictability Providers of both ocean and airfreight service wrestle with the issue of **reliability**. Both modes are subject to the vagaries of nature, which may impose delays. Yet because reliability is a relative measure, the delay of one day for airfreight tends to be seen as much more severe and 'unreliable' than the same delay for ocean freight. However, delays tend to be shorter in absolute time for air shipments. As a result, arrival time via air is more predictable. This attribute has a major influence on corporate strategy. Due to the higher predictability of airfreight, inventory safety stock can be kept at lower levels. Greater predictability can also serve as a useful sales tool for foreign distributors, who are able to make more precise delivery promises to their customers. If inadequate harbour facilities exist, airfreight may again be the better alternative. Finally, merchandise shipped via air is likely to suffer less loss and damage from exposure of the cargo to movement. Therefore, once the merchandise arrives, it is more likely to be ready for immediate delivery – a facet that also enhances predictability.

Cost A major consideration in choosing international transportation modes is the cost factor. International transportation services are usually priced on the basis of both **cost of the service** provided and the **value of the service** to the shipper. As a result of the high value of the products shipped by air, airfreight is often priced according to the value of the service. In this instance, of course, price becomes a function of market demand and the monopolistic power of the carrier.

The international marketer must decide whether the clearly higher cost of airfreight can be justified. In part, this will depend on the cargo's properties. Bulky products may be too expensive to ship by air, whereas very compact products may be more amenable to airfreight transportation. High-priced items can absorb transportation cost more easily than low-priced goods because the cost of transportation as a percentage of total product cost will be lower. As a result, sending diamonds by airfreight is easier to justify than sending coal by air. In order to keep cost down, a shipper can join groups such as shippers-associations, which give the shipper more leverage in negotiations. Alternatively, a shipper can decide to mix modes of transportation in order to reduce overall cost and time delays. For example, part of the shipment route can be covered by air, while another portion can be covered by truck or ship.

The overall logistical considerations of the firm need to incorporate the product, the competition and the environment. The manager must determine how important it is for merchandise to arrive on time, which will be different for DVDs of Oscar-nominated movies than for those that did poorly at the box office. The effect of transportation cost on price and the need for product availability abroad must be considered. Some firms may wish to use airfreight as a new tool for aggressive market expansion. Airfreight may also be considered a good way to begin operations in new markets without making sizeable investments for warehouses and distribution centres.

EXHIBIT 16.4

Loading a bulldozer on a plane

Source: Shipping by airfreight has really taken off in the past 20 years. Even large and heavy items, such as this bulldozer, are shipped to their destination by air.

Although costs are the major consideration in mode choice, an overall perspective must be employed. The manager must factor in all corporate activities that are affected by mode choice and explore the total cost effects of each alternative. The final selection of a mode will depend on the importance of different modal dimensions to the markets under consideration. A useful overall comparison between different modes of transportation is provided in Exhibit 16.5.

Non-economic factors Often, non-economic dimensions will enter into the selection process for a proper form of transportation. The transportation sector, nationally and internationally, both benefits and suffers from heavy government involvement. Carriers may be owned or

Characteristics of Mode	Mode of Transportation				
	Air	Pipeline	Highway	Rail	Water
Speed (1 = fastest)	1	4	2	3	5
Cost (1 = highest)	1	4	2	3	5
Loss and Damage (1 = least)	3	1	4	5	2
Frequency* (1 = best)	3	1	2	4	5
Dependability (1 = best)	5	1	2	3	4
Capacity† (1 = best)	4	5	3	2	1
Availability (1 = best)	3	5	1	2	4

EXHIBIT 16.5

Evaluating transportation choices

*Frequency: number of times mode is available during a given time period.
† Capacity: ability of mode to handle large or heavy goods.
Source: Ronald H. Ballou, *Business Logistics: Supply Chain Management*, 5th ed. © 2004. Reprinted by permission of Prentice Hall, Upper Saddle River, NJ.

heavily subsidized by governments. As a result, governmental pressure is exerted on shippers to use national carriers, even if more economical alternatives exist. Such preferential policies are most often enforced when government cargo is being transported. Restrictions are not limited to developing countries. For example, some countries may require that all government cargo and all official government travellers use national flag carriers when available.

For balance-of-payments reasons, international quota systems of transportation have been proposed. The United Nations Commission on International Trade and Development (UNCTAD), for example, has recommended a 40/40/20 treaty whereby 40 per cent of the traffic between two nations is allocated to vessels of the exporting country, 40 per cent to vessels of the importing country, and 20 per cent to third-country vessels (40/40/20). However, stiff international competition among carriers and the price sensitivity of customers frequently render such proposals ineffective, particularly for trade between industrialized countries.

THE INTERNATIONAL SHIPMENT

International shipments usually involve not just one carrier but multiple types of carriers. The shipment must be routed to the port of export, where it is transferred to another mode of transportation – for example, from truck or rail to vessel. Documentation for international shipments is universally perceived as so complicated, especially by smaller firms, that it can be a trade barrier. Recognizing the impact both in terms of time and money that documentation can have, trading regions such as the European Union have greatly simplified their required documentation for shipments.

Documentation

In the most simple form of exporting, the only documents needed are a bill of lading and an export declaration. In most countries, these documents are available either from the government or from transportation firms. For example, an export declaration can be obtained in the United Kingdom from the Business Link British Chamber of Commerce (**http://www.businesslink.gov.uk/bdotg/action/detail?type=RESOURCES&itemId=1077787688**).

Most exports fit under a general licence, which is a generalized authorization consisting simply of a number to be shown on the documents. Certain goods and data require a special validated licence for export, as discussed in Chapter 5. For importation, the basic documents are a bill of lading and an invoice. Exhibit 16.6 provides a summary of the main documents used in international shipments.

The bill of lading is the most important document to the shipper, the carrier and the buyer. It acknowledges receipt of the goods, represents the basic contract between the shipper and the carrier, and serves as evidence of title to the goods for collection by the purchaser. Various types of bills of lading exist. The inland bill of lading is a contract between the inland carrier and the shipper. Bills of lading may be negotiable instruments in that they may be endorsed to other parties (order bill) or may be non-negotiable (straight). The shipper's export declaration states proper authorization for export and serves as a means for governmental data collection efforts.

The packing list, if used, lists in some detail the contents, the gross and net weights, and the dimensions of each package. Some shipments, such as corrosives, flammables, and poisons, require a shipper's declaration for dangerous goods. When the international marketer is responsible for moving the goods to the port of export, a dock receipt (for ocean freight) or a warehouse receipt (if the goods are stored) is issued before the issuance of the bill of lading. Collection documents must also be produced and always include a commercial invoice (a detailed description of the transaction), often a consular invoice or pro-forma invoice (required by certain countries for data collection purposes), and a certificate of origin (required by certain countries to ensure correct tariffs). Insurance documents are produced when stipulated by the transaction. In certain countries, especially in Latin America, two

A   Documents Required by the U.S. Government

  1   Shipper's export declaration

  2   Export licence

B   Commercial Documents

  1   Commercial invoice

  2   Packing list

  3   Inland bill of lading

  4   Dock receipt

  5   Bill of lading or airway bill

  6   Insurance policies or certificates

  7   Shipper's declaration for dangerous goods

  8   Vessel loading observation inspection

C   Import Documents

  1   Import licence

  2   Foreign exchange licence

  3   Certificate of origin

  4   Consular invoice

  5   Customs invoice

  6   Customs notification

EXHIBIT 16.6

Documentation for an international shipment

Source: Dun & Bradstreet, *Exporter's Encyclopedia* (New York: Dun & Bradstreet, 1985); and **http://www.fsa.usda.gov**., accessed November 14, 2005.

additional documents are needed. An import licence may be required for certain types or amounts of particular goods, while a foreign exchange licence allows the importer to secure the needed hard currency to pay for the shipment. The exporter has to provide the importer with the data needed to obtain these licences from governmental authorities and should make sure, before the actual shipment, that the importer has indeed secured the documents.

Two guidelines are critical in dealing with customs anywhere in the world: sufficient knowledge or experience in dealing with the customs service in question and sufficient preparation for the process. Whatever the required documents, their proper preparation and timing is of crucial importance, particularly since the major terrorist attacks of 2001. Many governments expect detailed information about cargo well in advance of its arrival in port. Improper or missing documents can easily delay payment or cause problems with customs.

Assistance with international shipments

Several intermediaries provide services in the physical movement of goods. One very important distribution decision an exporter makes is the selection of an international freight forwarder. Such an international freight forwarder acts as an agent for the marketer in moving cargo to an overseas destination. Independent freight forwarders are regulated. The forwarder advises the marketer on shipping documentation and packing costs and will prepare and review the documents to ensure that they are in order. Forwarders will also book the space aboard a carrier. They will make necessary arrangements to clear outbound goods with customs and, after clearance, forward the documents either to the customer or to the paying bank. A customs broker serves as an agent for an importer with authority to clear inbound goods through customs and ship them on to their destination. These functions are performed for a fee. Customs brokers are often regulated by their national customs service.

INTERNATIONAL INVENTORY ISSUES

Inventories tie up a major portion of corporate funds. As a result, capital used for inventory is not available for other corporate opportunities. Since annual inventory carrying costs (the expense of maintaining inventories) can easily comprise up to 25 per cent or more of the value of the inventories themselves, proper inventory policies should be of major concern to the international marketing manager. Just-in-time inventory policies minimize the volume of inventory by making it available only when it is needed for the production process. Firms using such a policy will choose suppliers on the basis of their delivery and inventory performance. Proper inventory management may therefore become a determining variable in obtaining a sale.

In deciding the level of inventory to be maintained, the international marketer must consider three factors: the order cycle time, desired customer service levels and the use of inventories as a strategic tool.

Order cycle time

The total time that passes between the placement of an order and the receipt of the merchandise is referred to as order cycle time. Two dimensions are of major importance to inventory management: the length of the total order cycle and its consistency. In international marketing, the order cycle is frequently longer than in domestic business. It comprises the time involved in order transmission, order filling, packing and preparation for shipment, and transportation. Order transmission time varies greatly internationally depending on whether telephone, fax, mail, or electronic order placement is used in communicating. The order filling time may also be increased because lack of familiarity with a foreign market makes the anticipation of new orders more difficult. Packing and shipment preparation require more detailed attention. Finally, of course, transportation time increases with the distances involved. As a result, total order cycle time can frequently approach a hundred days or more. Larger inventories may have to be maintained both domestically and internationally to bridge these time gaps.

Consistency, the second dimension of order cycle time, is also more difficult to maintain in international marketing. Depending on the choice of transportation mode, delivery times may vary considerably from shipment to shipment. This variation requires the maintenance of larger safety stocks in order to be able to fill demand in periods when delays occur.

The international marketer should attempt to reduce order cycle time and increase its consistency without an increase in total costs. This objective can be accomplished by altering methods of transportation, changing inventory locations, or improving any of the other components of the order cycle time, such as the way orders are transmitted. By shifting order placement from mail to telephone or to electronic data interchange (EDI), for example, a firm can reduce the order cycle time substantially.

Customer service levels

The level of customer service denotes the responsiveness that inventory policies permit for any given situation. Customer service is therefore a management-determined constraint within the logistics system. A customer service level of 100 per cent could be defined as the ability to fill all orders within a set time – for example, three days. If within these three days only 70 per cent of the orders can be filled, the customer service level is 70 per cent. The choice of customer service level for the firm has a major impact on the inventories needed. In their domestic operations, companies frequently aim to achieve customer service levels of 95 to 98 per cent. Often, such 'homegrown' rules of thumb are then used in international inventory operations as well.

Managers may not realize that standards determined heuristically and based on competitive activity in the home market are often inappropriate abroad. Different locales have country-specific customer service needs and requirements. Service levels should not be oriented primarily around cost or customary domestic standards. Rather, the level chosen for use internationally should be based on customer expectations encountered in each market. These expectations are dependent on past performance, product desirability, customer sophistication, the competitive status of the firm and whether a buyers' or sellers' market exists.

High customer service levels are costly and the goal should not be the highest customer service level possible, but rather an acceptable level. Different customers have different priorities. Some will be prepared to pay a premium for speed. In industrial marketing, for example, even an eight-hour delay may be unacceptable for the delivery of a crucial product component, since it may mean a shutdown of the production process. Other firms may put a higher value on flexibility and another group may see low cost as the most important issue. Flexibility and speed are expensive, so it is wasteful to supply them to customers who do not value them highly. The higher prices associated with higher customer service levels may reduce the competitiveness of a firm's product.

Inventory as a strategic tool

International inventories can be used by the international corporation as a strategic tool in dealing with currency valuation changes or hedging against inflation. By increasing inventories before an imminent devaluation of a currency, instead of holding cash, the corporation may reduce its exposure to devaluation losses. Similarly, in the case of high inflation, large inventories can provide an important inflation hedge. In such circumstances, the international inventory manager must balance the cost of maintaining high levels of inventories with the benefits accruing to the firm from hedging against inflation or devaluation. Many countries, for example, charge a property tax on stored goods. If the increase in tax payments outweighs the hedging benefits to the corporation, it would be unwise to increase inventories before a devaluation.

Despite the benefits of reducing the firm's financial risk, inventory management must still fall in line with the overall corporate market strategy. Only by recognizing the trade-offs, which may result in less than optimal inventory policies, can the corporation maximize the overall benefit.

INTERNATIONAL STORAGE ISSUES

Although international logistics is discussed as a movement or flow of goods, a stationary period is involved when merchandise becomes inventory stored in warehouses. Heated arguments can arise within a firm over the need for and utility of warehousing internationally. On the one hand, customers expect quick responses to orders and rapid delivery. Accommodating the customer's expectation may require locating many distribution centres around the world. On the other hand, warehousing space is expensive. In addition, the larger volume of inventory increases the inventory carrying cost. The international marketer must consider the trade-offs between service and cost to determine the appropriate levels of warehousing.

Storage facilities

One important location decision is how many distribution centres to have and where to locate them. The availability of facilities abroad will differ from the domestic situation. For example, whereas public storage is widely available in some countries, such facilities may be scarce or entirely lacking in others. The standards and quality of facilities abroad may also often not be comparable to those offered at home. As a result, the storage decision of the firm is often accompanied by the need for large-scale, long-term investments. Despite the high cost, international storage facilities should be established if they support the overall marketing effort. In many markets, adequate storage facilities are imperative in order to satisfy customer demands and to compete successfully.

Once the decision is made to utilize storage facilities abroad, the warehouse conditions must be carefully analyzed. In some countries, warehouses have low ceilings. Packaging developed for the high stacking of products is therefore unnecessary. In other countries, automated warehousing is available. Proper bar coding of products and the use of package dimensions acceptable to the warehousing system are basic requirements. In contrast, in warehouses still stocked manually, weight limitations will be of major concern.

To optimize the logistics system, the marketer should analyse international product sales and then rank products according to warehousing needs. An ABC analysis classifies products that are most sensitive to delivery time as 'A' products. 'A' products would be stocked in all distribution centres, and safety stock levels would be kept high. Products for which immediate delivery is not urgent are classified as 'B' products. They would be stored only at selected distribution centres around the world. Finally, 'C' products for which short delivery time is not important, or for which there is little demand, are stocked only at headquarters. Should an urgent need for delivery arise, airfreight could be considered for rapid shipment. Classifying products through such an ABC analysis enables the international marketer to substantially reduce total international warehousing requirements and still maintain acceptable service levels.

Outsourcing

For many global firms the practice of outsourcing, which refers to the shifting of traditional corporate activities to parties outside the firm and often outside the country – is on the increase. Firms in the United Kingdom outsource to India, in Germany outsource to Hungary and in France to Algeria. The decisive factors for choosing to outsource are the desire to reduce and control operating costs, to improve company focus, to gain access to world-class capabilities and to free internal resources for other purposes.[10]

Our research into the future of outsourcing indicates continued growth and expansion of this practice.[11] An increasing portion of high-end, high value added services will be sourced from low labour cost but high labour skilled countries. The internationalization of the back office functions of multinational corporations will continue to grow. However, even sophisticated services will quickly move to low-cost locations. To remain competitive, firms in developed economies must change their strategy to focus on their ability to manage, coordinate and define the interfaces between suppliers and customers. The challenge will be to effectively train the workers in the emerging markets to carry out their tasks, but to stay ahead of them in the ability to take on global coordination.

More manufacturing jobs will move to emerging markets. Firms will face the challenge to retain first-mover advantages through continued innovation. When cost pressures force firms to source globally, some will locate their own plants abroad, while others will outsource the needed inputs. Sourcing from abroad through independent suppliers on a contractual basis will have long-term consequences on the processes, competence and capabilities of firms. In comparing the outsourcing networks of Japanese and UK companies, there is key concern that UK companies will gradually sever their value chain. In search of cost efficiency, they will increase their dependence on foreign suppliers for products that become technologically more sophisticated. The creation of new technology is a gradual and painstaking learning process of continual adjustment and refinement, as new productive methods are tested and adapted in light of a company's accumulated experience. Thus, overreliance on acquisitions and new technologies from other firms may not result in the same sustainable competitive advantage available through internal development. The manufacturing shift abroad may, therefore, shift current technology, design and process advantages.[12] As some say, 'It helps to develop and hang on to the blueprints'.

The International Marketplace 16.3 explains how firms can make use of outsourcing providers.

Foreign trade zones

The existence of foreign trade zones can have a major effect on the international logistician, since production cost advantages may require a reconfiguration of storage, processing and

THE INTERNATIONAL MARKETPLACE 16.3

Rio Tinto signs legal services outsourcing agreement with CPA Global

London, UK – 18 June 2009: Rio Tinto today announced that it has entered into a legal services outsourcing agreement with CPA Global that is projected to save Rio Tinto up to 20 per cent annually in legal costs.

Under the agreement, CPA Global, one of the world's leading providers of outsourced legal support services, are providing a team of lawyers in India to support Rio Tinto's in-house legal function on a global basis.

Initially, the work undertaken by CPA Global includes contract review and drafting, legal research and document review. However, it is anticipated that the scope of work will expand to cover other routine legal services work traditionally handled in-house by Rio Tinto or shared amongst the company's panel of law firms.

Rio Tinto's managing attorney, Leah Cooper, said: 'We took a long hard look at our internal costs and the amount we were spending with outside counsel and saw an opportunity to make significant changes to the way we deliver legal services to the group. We have developed a ground-breaking legal model with CPA Global that will generate tremendous savings and serve the business without compromising quality.

'By shifting work to CPA Global our internal team will be freed up to get involved in some of the more complex and challenging legal matters, which in the past might have been sent to outside counsel at significant cost.

'As more of our standard legal work is filtered though to CPA Global, we will have more time to lift our heads up from the day-to-day reactive delivery of legal services and focus on being more pro-active. We will have more time to spend with the business, develop stronger relationships and understand what we can do to prevent legal issues developing in the first place with a stronger focus on prevention rather than cure'.

Andrew Loach, CPA Global's vice-president, legal support services, said: 'We are delighted to have been appointed as Rio Tinto's legal services outsourcing partner. Rio Tinto have really done their homework on this and recognized that there is a better, more cost efficient way of structuring your legal services work, without sacrificing quality or security.'

Bhaskar Bagchi, CPA Global's country head – India, added: 'CPA Global's India team will serve as an extension of Rio Tinto's internal legal department. They are hand-picked, well trained legal professionals who will work on a whole range of Rio Tinto legal matters from across the globe.'

Commenting on the choice of CPA Global, Rio Tinto's Leah Cooper said: 'CPA Global provided us with fresh thinking about how to unlock real savings on our legal costs without altering the level of service we offered our internal clients. What we particularly liked about CPA Global was that they are legal outsourcing specialists, not generalists, with a global size and scale.'

SOURCE: CPA Global (2009) 'Rio Tinto signs legal services outsourcing agreement with CPA Global'. CPA Global (2009) 'Rio Tinto signs legal services outsourcing agreement with CPA Global'. **http://www.cpaglobal.com/media_centre/press_releases/0145/rio_tinto_signs_legal_services** (Accessed 26/2/10)

---

distribution strategies. Trade zones are considered, for purposes of tariff treatment, to be outside the customs territory of the country within which they are located. They are special areas and can be used for warehousing, packaging, inspection, labelling, exhibition, assembly, fabrication, or trans-shipment of imports without burdening the firm with duties.[13] Trade zones can be found at major ports of entry and also at inland locations near major production facilities. For example, China has agreed free trade zones with the UK and a listing of these trade zones can be found at **http://www.cbbc.org/market_intelligence/presense/trade_zone.html**.

Foreign trade zones are designed to exclude the impact of duties from the location decision. This is done by exempting merchandise in the foreign trade zone from duty payment. The international firm can therefore import merchandise, store it in the foreign trade zone and process, alter, test, or demonstrate it – all without paying duties. If the merchandise is subsequently shipped abroad (that is, re-exported), no duty payments are ever due. Duty payments become due only if and when the merchandise is shipped into the country from the foreign trade zone.

One country that has used trade zones very successfully for its own economic development is China. Through the creation of *special economic zones* in which there are no tariffs, substantial tax incentives, and low prices for land and labour, the government has attracted many foreign investors bringing in investment. These investors have brought new equipment, technology and managerial know-how and have therefore substantially increased the local economic prosperity.

Both parties to the arrangement benefit from foreign trade zones. The government maintaining the trade zone achieves increased employment. The firm using the trade zone obtains a spearhead in or close to the foreign market without incurring all of the costs customarily associated with such an activity. As a result, goods can be reassembled and large shipments can be broken down into smaller units. Goods can also be repackaged when packaging weight becomes part of the duty assessment, and can also be given domestic 'made-in' status if assembled in the foreign trade zone. Whenever use of a trade zone is examined, however, the marketer must keep the stability of rules, and the additional cost of storage, handling and transportation in mind before making a decision.

INTERNATIONAL PACKAGING ISSUES

Packaging is instrumental in getting the merchandise to the ultimate destination in a safe, maintainable and presentable condition. Packaging that is adequate for domestic shipping may be inadequate for international transportation because the shipment will be subject to the motions of the vessel on which it is carried. Added stress in international shipping also arises from the transfer of goods among different modes of transportation. Exhibit 16.7 provides examples of some sources of stress that are most frequently found in international transportation.

The responsibility for appropriate packaging rests with the shipper of goods. According to the UK Carriage of Goods by Sea Act of 1992, neither the carrier nor the ship shall be responsible for loss or damage arising or resulting from insufficiency of packing.[14] The shipper must therefore ensure that the goods are prepared appropriately for international shipping. This is important because it has been found that 'the losses that occur as a result of breakage, pilferage, and theft exceed the losses caused by major maritime casualties, which include fires, sinkings and collision of vessels. Thus, the largest of these losses is a preventable loss'.[15]

Packaging decisions must take into account differences in environmental conditions – for example, climate. When the ultimate destination is very humid or particularly cold, special provisions must be made to prevent damage to the product. The task becomes even more challenging when one considers that, in the course of long-distance transportation, dramatic changes in climate can take place.

EXHIBIT 16.7   Stresses in intermodal movement

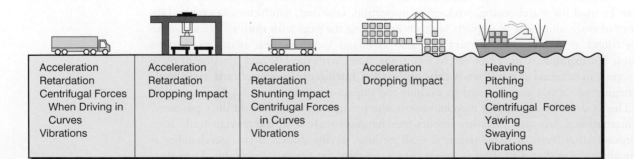

| Acceleration Retardation Centrifugal Forces When Driving in Curves Vibrations | Acceleration Retardation Dropping Impact | Acceleration Retardation Shunting Impact Centrifugal Forces in Curves Vibrations | Acceleration Dropping Impact | Heaving Pitching Rolling Centrifugal Forces Yawing Swaying Vibrations |

Note: Each transportation mode exerts a different set of stresses and strains on containerized cargoes. The most commonly overloaded are those associated with ocean transport.

Source: Reprinted with permission from *Handling and Shipping Management,* September 1980 issue, p. 47; and David Greenfield, "Perfect Packing for Export," Copyright © 1980, Penton Publishing, Cleveland, OH.

Packaging issues need to be closely linked to overall strategic plans. The individual responsible for international packaging should utilize transportation modes as efficiently as possible. This requires appropriate package design, which takes into account the storage properties of the product.

The weight of packaging must be considered, particularly when airfreight is used, since the cost of shipping is often based on weight. At the same time, packaging material must be sufficiently strong to permit stacking in international transportation. Another consideration is that, in some countries, duties are assessed according to the gross weight of shipments, which includes the weight of packaging. Obviously, the heavier the packaging, the higher the duties will be.

The shipper must pay sufficient attention to instructions provided by the customer for packaging. Requests by the customer that the weight of any one package should not exceed a certain limit, or that specific package dimensions should be adhered to, are usually made for a reason. Often they reflect limitations in transportation or handling facilities at the point of destination.

Although the packaging of a product is often used as a form of display abroad, international packaging can rarely serve the dual purpose of protection and display. Therefore, double packaging may be necessary. The display package is for future use at the point of destination; another package surrounds it for protective purposes.

One solution to the packaging problem in international logistics has been the development of intermodal containers – large metal boxes that fit on trucks, ships, railroad cars and airplanes – and ease the frequent transfer of goods in international shipments. In addition, containers offer greater safety from pilferage and damage. Of course, if merchandise from a containerized shipment is lost, frequently the entire container has been removed. Developed in different forms for both sea and air transportation, containers also offer better utilization of carrier space because of standardization of size. The shipper therefore may benefit from lower transportation rates.

Container traffic is heavily dependent on the existence of appropriate handling facilities, both domestically and internationally. In addition, the quality of inland transportation must be considered. If transportation for containers is not available and the merchandise must be removed and reloaded, the expected cost reductions may not materialize.

In some countries, rules for the handling of containers may be designed to maintain employment. For example, exporters to the US should be aware that US union rules obligate shippers to withhold containers from firms that do not employ members of the International Longshoreman Association for loading and unloading containers within a 50-mile radius of Atlantic or Gulf ports. Such restrictions can result in an onerous cost burden.

Overall, close attention must be paid to international packaging. The customer who ordered and paid for the merchandise expects it to arrive on time and in good condition. Even with replacements and insurance, the customer will not be satisfied if there are delays. This dissatisfaction will usually translate directly into lost sales.

MANAGEMENT OF INTERNATIONAL LOGISTICS

Since the very purpose of a multinational firm is to benefit from system synergism, a persuasive argument can be made for the coordination of international logistics at corporate headquarters. Without coordination, subsidiaries will tend to optimize their individual efficiency but jeopardize the overall performance of the firm.

Centralized logistics management

A significant characteristic of the centralized approach to international logistics is the existence of headquarters staff that retains decision-making power over logistics activities affecting international subsidiaries. Such an approach is particularly valuable in instances where corporations have become international by rapid growth and have lost the benefit of a cohesive strategy.

If headquarters exerts control, it must also take the primary responsibility for its decisions. Clearly, ill will may arise if local managers are appraised and rewarded on the basis of performance they do not control. This may be particularly problematic if headquarters staff suffer from a lack of information or expertise.

To avoid internal problems both headquarters staff and local logistics management should report to one person. This person, whether the vice-chairman for international logistics or the chairman of the firm, can then become the final arbiter to decide the firm's priorities. Of course, this individual should also be in charge of determining appropriate rewards for managers, both at headquarters and abroad, so that corporate decisions that alter a manager's performance level will not affect the manager's appraisal and evaluation. Further, this individual can contribute an objective view when inevitable conflicts arise in international logistics coordination. The internationally centralized decision-making process leads to an overall logistics management perspective that can dramatically improve profitability.

Decentralized logistics management

When a firm serves many international markets that are diverse in nature, total centralization would leave the firm unresponsive to local adaptation needs. If each subsidiary is made a profit centre in itself, each one carries the full responsibility for its performance, which can lead to greater local management satisfaction and to better adaptation to local market conditions. Yet often such decentralization deprives the logistics function of the benefits of coordination. For example, whereas headquarters, referring to its large volume of total international shipments, may be able to extract bottom rates from transportation firms, individual subsidiaries by themselves may not have similar bargaining power. The same argument also applies to the sourcing situation, where the coordination of shipments by the purchasing firm may be much more cost-effective than individual shipments from many small suppliers around the world.

Once products are within a specific market, however, increased input from local logistics operations should be expected and encouraged. At the very least, local managers should be able to provide input into the logistics decisions generated by headquarters. Ideally, within a frequent planning cycle, local managers can identify the logistics benefits and constraints existing in their particular market and communicate them to headquarters. Headquarters can then either adjust its international logistics strategy accordingly or can explain to the manager why system optimization requires actions different from the ones recommended. Such a justification process will greatly help in reducing the potential for animosity between local and headquarters operations.

Contract logistics

While the choice is open to maintain either centralized or decentralized in-house logistical management, a growing preference among international firms is to outsource, which means to employ outside logistical expertise. Often referred to as contract or third-party (3PL) logistics, it is a rapidly expanding industry. Most companies have outsourced at least one major logistics function such as customs clearance, transportation management, freight payment, warehouse management, shipment tracking, or other transportation-related functions. The main thrust behind the idea is that individual firms are experts in their industry and should therefore concentrate only on their operations. Third-party logistics providers, on the other hand, are experts solely at logistics, with the knowledge and means to perform efficient and innovative services for those companies in need. The goal is improved service at equal or lower cost.

Logistics providers' services vary in scope. For instance, some may use their own assets in physical transportation, while others subcontract out portions of the job. Certain other providers are not involved as much with the actual transportation as they are with developing systems and databases or consulting on administrative management services. In many instances, the partnership consists of working closely with established transport providers such as ParcelForce (UK), Sealane, Eddie Stobart, Federal Express or UPS. The concept of improving service, cutting costs, and unloading the daily management onto willing experts is driving the momentum of contract logistics.

One of the greatest benefits of contracting out the logistics function in a foreign market is the ability to take advantage of an existing network, complete with resources and experience. The local expertise and image are crucial when a business is just starting up. The prospect of newly entering a region such as Europe with different regions, business formats and languages can be frightening without access to a seasoned and familiar logistics provider.

One of the main arguments levelled against contract logistics is the loss of the firm's control in the supply chain. Yet contract logistics does not and should not require the handing over of control. Rather, it offers concentration on one's specialization – a division of labour. The control and responsibility toward the customer remain with the firm.

THE SUPPLY CHAIN AND THE INTERNET

Many firms still use their websites as a marketing and advertising tool without expanding them to order-taking capabilities. That is changing rapidly. Global net e-commerce revenue is expected to surpass the $1 trillion mark by 2012.[16]

Companies wishing to enter e-commerce do not have to do so on their own. Hubsites (also known as virtual malls or digital intermediaries) bring together buyers, sellers, distributors and transaction payment processors in a single marketplace, making convenience the key attraction. The future is also growing brighter for hubs in the consumer-to-consumer market, where companies like eBay are setting high standards of profitability.

When customers have the ability to access a company through the internet, a company itself has to be prepared for 24-hour order-taking and customer service, and to have the regulatory and customs-handling expertise for international delivery. The instantaneous interactivity that users experience will also be translated into an expectation of expedient delivery of answers and products ordered. As internet penetration levels increase in the near future due to technological advances, improvements in many countries' web infrastructures, and customer acceptance, e-business will become truly global.

Some companies elect to build their own international distribution networks. Both QVC, a televised shopping service, and amazon.com, an online retailer of books, have distribution centres in Britain and Germany to take advantage of the European internet audience and to fulfil more quickly and cheaply the orders generated by their websites. Transactions and the information they provide about the buyers also allow for more customization and service by region, market, or even individual customer.

For industries such as music and motion pictures, the internet is both an opportunity and a threat. The web provides a new, efficient method of distribution and customization of products. Apple corporation uses the web for both e-commerce and logistics purposes. The video iPod is a clever example of improved distribution techniques. Instead of making a trip to a store to purchase an audio CD a customer can now log into his web account at iTunes, download the music and/or video files onto his computer, and then upload the files to the iPod, making the distribution aspect of logistics quicker and more efficient by giving the customer partial control of the process.

At the same time, the web can be a channel for intellectual property violation through unauthorized posting and downloading on other sites. For example, film production companies are concerned with the increasing piracy of DVDs. One of the reasons why it is so difficult to stop theft of intellectual property is because it is simple to download films illegally from various online sources. Currently companies lose tens of billions of pounds in sales each year due to such theft.

LOGISTICS AND SECURITY

Firms worldwide have been exposed to the vicissitudes of terrorism, which often aims to disrupt the flow of supply and demand in order to damage economic systems. Governments are devoting major efforts to improved security measures such as the screening of shipments and shippers. International marketers may therefore have to redesign the movements of goods and services. Although a great portion of international transactions can today be conducted via e-mail or on the web, products still need to get to where the customers are. Companies require movement and storage of products to occur with the fewest number of impediments so that products reach customers on time.

Logistics systems are often the targets of attacks. These systems are the true soft spots of vulnerability for both nations and firms. In most instances, the containers are secured by nothing more than a low cost seal that can be easily broken. Similar to imported merchandise, exported products also need to be protected by companies as they leave the country in order to prevent terrorists from contaminating shipments with the goal of destroying foreign markets together with the reputations of the exporting firms.

Security measures instigated by governments will affect the ability of firms to efficiently plan their international shipments. There is now more uncertainty and less control over the timing of arrivals and departures. There is also a much greater need for internal control and supervision of shipments. Cargo security will increasingly need not only to ensure that nothing goes missing, but also that nothing has been added to the shipment.[17]

Security measures for international shipments affect the ability of firms to efficiently plan their distributions. Increased inspections of containers used in international shipping, new security programmes to protect ports, and other new protective policies are decreasing the efficiency and effectiveness of international shipping and logistics. In consequence, the costs of value chain and supply chain activities have increased substantially. There is now more uncertainty and less control over the timing of arrivals and departures. Companies may be inclined to produce more essential products themselves instead of relying on outside producers to deliver those products on time.

Similarly, costs may rise if companies should choose to purchase goods from suppliers located in close proximity, or from suppliers which are more familiar – and therefore apparently safer – in order to reduce their vulnerability. Companies may also increase their inventory holdings (especially when inventory comes from an international producer) in hope of protecting against delays caused by sudden heightened security measures against terrorism.[18] Holding more inventory or drawing goods from more than one source will increase the ability to meet the customer's demand at times when an outside producer is unable to deliver on time. Flexibility of supply chains is therefore a necessity when logistics security is at risk from terrorism.[19]

Firms with a just-in-time regimen are exploring alternative management strategies, because the process of moving goods has become more expensive. Some firms are considering replacing international shipments with domestic ones, where transportation via truck would replace transborder movement and eliminate the use of vulnerable international transportation. Further down the line are planning scenarios in which firms consider redesigning their logistics strategies to incorporate the effects of substantial and long-term interruptions of supplies and operations.

Another important security problem for logistics is shipping piracy. Even though pirates are often seen as legends from the past, piracy is very much a part of today's shipping security concerns. The twenty-first century freebooters are highly organized and heavily armed. Annual cargo crime losses for 2008 were estimated at £155 million.[20]

Indonesian and Somali shores are the most treacherous areas of the world, as they are the primary choices for modern pirates.[21] Recent piracy maps completed by the International Chamber of Commerce can be seen at their website.[22] Companies conducting business in the surrounding areas have to face higher costs due to security measures undertaken to prevent severe cargo losses. In order to protect their revenues, export companies have been installing electric fences on their cargo ships. In spite of large corporate investments to build security, new attacks happen daily.

RECYCLING AND REVERSE LOGISTICS

By using logistics, the international marketer can play an increasingly important role in allowing the firm to operate in an environmentally conscious way. Environmental laws,

THE INTERNATIONAL MARKETPLACE 16.4

How safe is your luggage?

More travellers than ever are arriving on holiday without their luggage, with up to 10 air passengers losing their bags on every flight, figures showed last night.

British Airways was nominated the worst performing of all Europe's major airlines and is forecast to lose a record 1.3 million bags this year.

One in every 35 passengers on BA flights lost luggage between April and June and a continued baggage crisis at Heathrow is expected to exacerbate the problem throughout the summer peak.

A BA spokesman admitted the airline's performance was not acceptable. 'Our baggage performance has not been good enough. Improving this is a top priority'. He said that unlike Amsterdam Schiphol and Charles De Gaulle (the hubs for KLM and Air France), which operate at 80 per cent capacity, Heathrow was performing at its maximum, leaving no leeway should things go wrong.

BA attributes some of the problems to a government restriction of only one piece of hand luggage on flights to and from Britain. Other European carriers still allow two.

Willie Walsh, the chief executive of BA, and other airline chiefs met Ruth Kelly, the Transport Secretary, last week in an attempt to have this overturned. BA claims the restrictions mean 23,000 bags a day go through a system designed for 18,000. It has admitted a backlog of 20,000 bags but baggage workers claim it is closer to 40,000.

BA has drafted in volunteers from Gatwick and its head office to help clear the backlog and luggage has been sent to Milan to be sorted.

Passengers have trouble contacting BA's baggage retrieval line. Readers of *The Daily Telegraph* complain of emails going unanswered and misleading baggage tracking information.

Have you ever wondered what happens to all of those missing bags, once they are finally located? Many never find their way home. Instead, they are likely to end up at the Unclaimed Baggage Centre, located in Scottsboro, Alabama, in the United States. Unofficially known as 'the lost luggage capital of the world', the UBC sells items that have been recovered from virtually every airline worldwide. So if it means a great deal to you to locate a special item lost during your travels, you may just want to book a trip to Alabama. Just be sure to keep a close eye on your bags.

SOURCES: Starner-Smith (2007) 'Airlines losing millions of bags a year'. **http://www.telegraph.co.uk/news/uknews/1559201/Airlines-losing-millions-of-bags-a-year.html**; Safe Travel (2010) 'Airlines and lost luggage'. Online. Available from: **http://www.safetravel.co.uk/LostLuggageAtAirports.html** (Accessed 1/3/10).

---

expectations and self-imposed goals set by firms are difficult to adhere to without a logistics orientation that systematically takes these concerns into account. Since laws and regulations differ across the world, the firm's efforts need to be responsive to a wide variety of requirements. One logistics orientation that has grown in importance due to environmental concerns is the development of reverse distribution systems. Such systems are instrumental in ensuring that the firm not only delivers the product to the market, but also can retrieve it from the market for subsequent use, recycling or disposal. To a growing degree, the ability to develop such reverse logistics is a key determinant for market acceptance and profitability.

Traditionally businesses have focused on forward logistics even though product returns, an example of reverse logistics, have always been a fact of business life. With the growth of direct-to-consumer internet sales, the reverse supply chain has exploded, amounting to over $100 billion per year – greater than the GDP of two-thirds of the world's countries! Industries facing the highest return volume are magazine/book publishing (50 per cent), catalogue retailers (18 to 35 per cent) and greeting card companies (20 to 30 per cent).[23] Just the disposal of returned merchandise alone can result in major headaches and costs.

Similar to forward logistics, reverse logistics require quality information and processes, and the ability to track both at all times. Reverse logistics, however, is also a complex customer service, inventory control, information management, cost accounting, and disposal process. Customers don't want to wait weeks before charges are removed from their credit cards, and returned goods idling in warehousing cause both higher carrying costs and the risk of obsolescence and shrinkage.

Reverse logistics management is highly specialized. Return and reclamation rates vary drastically between industries such as cosmetics or pharmaceuticals. The objectives of successful reverse logistics are the same: recovering the greatest value possible from returns, maintaining customer loyalty, controlling costs and harvesting information to help reduce future returns. Successful reverse logistics greatly affects a company's bottom line. Idle electronic and computer parts in inventory lose 12 per cent of value each month. Conversely, efficient management of returns can reduce companies' annual logistics costs by as much as 10 per cent.

Society is beginning to recognize that retrieval should not be restricted to short-term consumer goods, such as bottles. Rather, it may be even more important to devise systems that enable the retrieval and disposal of long-term capital goods, such as cars, refrigerators, air conditioners and industrial goods, with the least possible burden on the environment. Increasingly, governments establish rules that hold the manufacturer responsible for the ultimate disposal of the product at the end of its economic life. In Germany, for example, car manufacturers are required to take back their used vehicles for dismantling and recycling. The design of such long-term systems across the world may well be one of the key challenges and opportunities for the logistician and will require close collaboration with all other functions in the firm, such as design, production and sales.

On the transportation side, logistics managers will need to expand their involvement in carrier and routing selection. Shippers of oil or other potentially hazardous materials are increasingly expected to ensure that the carriers used have excellent safety records and use only double-hulled ships. Society may even expect corporate involvement in choosing the route that the shipment will travel, preferring routes that are far from ecologically important and sensitive zones.

In the packaging field, environmental concerns are also growing on the part of individuals and governments. Increasingly, it is expected that the amount of packaging materials used is minimized and that the materials used are more environmentally friendly.

Companies need to learn how to simultaneously achieve environmental and economic goals. Esprit, the apparel maker, and The Body Shop, screen all their suppliers for environmental and socially responsible practices. ISO 14000 is a standard specifically targeted at encouraging international environmental practices by evaluating companies both at the organization level (management systems, environmental performance and environmental auditing) and at the product level (life-cycle assessment, labelling and product standards).[24] From the environmental perspective, those practices are desirable that bring about fewer shipments, less handling and more direct movement. Such practices are to be weighed against optimal efficiency routings, including just-in-time inventory and quantity discount purchasing. For example, even though a just-in-time inventory system may connote highly desirable inventory savings, the resulting cost of frequent delivery, additional highway congestion and incremental air pollution also need to be factored into the planning horizon. Firms will need to assert leadership in such trade-off considerations in order to provide society with a better quality of life.

SUMMARY

Competitiveness depends on cost efficiency. International logistics and supply chain management are of major importance because distribution comprises between 10 and 30 per cent of the total landed cost of an international order.

International logistics is concerned with the flow of materials into, through, and out of the international corporation and includes materials management as well as physical distribution. The logistician must recognize the total systems demands of the firm in order to develop trade-offs between various logistics components. By taking a supply chain perspective, the marketing manager can develop logistics systems that are highly customer-focused and very cost-efficient. Implementation of such a system requires close collaboration between all members of the supply chain.

International logistics differs from domestic activities in that it deals with greater distances, new variables, and greater complexity because of country-specific differences.

The international marketer needs to understand transportation infrastructures in other countries and modes of transportation such as ocean shipping and airfreight. The choice among these modes will depend on the customer's demands and the firm's transit time, predictability and cost requirements. In addition, non-economic factors such as government regulations weigh heavily in this decision.

Inventory management is another major consideration. Inventories abroad are expensive to maintain yet often crucial for international success. The marketer must evaluate requirements for order cycle times and customer service levels in order to develop an international inventory policy that can also serve as a strategic management tool.

The marketer must also deal with international storage issues and determine where to locate inventories. International warehouse space will have to be leased or purchased and decisions made about utilizing foreign trade zones.

International packaging is important because it ensures arrival of the merchandise at the ultimate destination in safe condition. In developing packaging requirements, the marketer must consider environmental concerns as well as climate, freight and handling conditions.

International logistics management is growing in importance. The marketer must consider the benefits and the drawbacks that the information technology revolution has brought to supply chain and logistics activities. Increasingly, better implementation of change in logistics is key to defining a firm's competitiveness.

Security concerns have also greatly affected the planning and implementation of the logistics interface. In previous decades many governmental efforts were devoted to speeding up transactions across borders. Now national security concerns are forcing governments to construct new barriers to entry and conduct new inspections. Distribution and logistics are also susceptible to indirect effects of terrorism that may arise when, for instance, companies choose to hold more inventory because of the fear of not receiving shipments in time due to terrorist attacks. Flexibility of supply chains to allow for disruptions caused by terrorism is therefore a necessary component of conducting business in this day and age. Companies also will have to think about the need to build reverse logistics systems, when customer returns and recycling activities make such systems a necessity.

Key terms

ABC analysis	materials management
bill of lading	physical distribution
bulk service	piracy
certificate of origin	reliability
consular invoice or pro-forma invoice	reverse distribution systems
container ships	shipper's declaration for dangerous goods
cost of the service	shipper's export declaration
currency variation	supply chain management
customs broker	systems concept
density	third-party (3PL) logistics
foreign exchange licence	total cost concept
import licence	trade-off concept
international freight forwarder	tramp service
inventory carrying costs	transportation modes
liner service	value of the service

Questions for discussion

1   What kind of transportation issues should a logistics manager consider when a firm is going international?

2   Why should customer service levels differ internationally? Is it, for example, ethical to offer a lower customer service level in developing countries than in industrialized countries?

3   How can an improved logistics infrastructure contribute to the economic development of China?

4   What are the major differences between centralized and decentralized logistics management?

5   What options are available for securing logistics systems from terrorism?

6   What steps can logisticians take to make their efforts more environmentally friendly?

Internet exercises

1   What type of information is available to exporters? Go to **http://www.hmrc.gov.uk/businesses/**. Give examples of links that an exporter would find helpful and explain why.

2   Determine the length of transit time a shipment takes between two international destinations. What else should you know before making a shipping decision? Go to **http://www.apl.com** and click on 'Schedules'.

Recommended readings

Anderson, David. *Mass Customization: The Ultimate Supply Chain Management and Lean Manufacturing Strategy*. London: CIM, 2003.

Christopher, Martin. *Logistics and Supply Chain Management* (3rd edn), London: Financial Times, 2005.

Coyle, John J., Edward J. Bardi and Robert A. Novak. *Transportation*. Mason, OH: Thomson/South-Western, 2005.

Gourdin, Kent. *Global Logistics Management*. Oxford: Blackwell Publishing, 2006.

Monczka, Robert, Robert B. Handfield and Robert J. Trent. *Purchasing and Supply Chain Management* (3rd edn), Mason, OH: Cengage/South-Western, 2005.

Schechter, Damon, and Gordon F. Sander. *Delivering the Goods: The Art of Managing Your Supply Chain*. New York: John Wiley & Sons, 2003.

Simchi-Levi, David, Philip Kaminsky and Edith Simchi-Levi. *Designing & Managing the Supply Chain: Concepts, Strategies, and Case Studies* (2nd edn), Boston: McGraw-Hill, 2003.

Stauss, Bernd, and Wolfgang Seidel. *Complaint Management*. Mason, OH: Cengage/South-Western, 2005.

Notes

1   Bernard LaLonde and James Ginter, 'Activity-Based Costing: Best Practices', *Paper #606,* The Supply Chain Management Research Group, Ohio State University, September 1996.

2   Toshiro Hiromoto, 'Another Hidden Edge: Japanese Management Accounting', in *Trends in International Business: Critical Perspectives,* ed. M. Czinkota and M. Kotabe (Oxford, England: Blackwell, 1998), 217–222.

3   Council of Supply Chain Management Professionals, **http://www.cscmp.org/website/aboutcscmp/definitions/definitions.asp** (Accessed January 9, 2006).

4   Accenture Global, **http://www.accenture.com/global/services/by_subject/supply_chain_mgmt/client_successes/enhancedmanagement.htm** (Accessed January 9, 2006).

5   Richard T. Hise, 'The Implications of Time-Based Competition on International Logistics Strategies', *Business Horizons,* September/October 1995, 39–45.

6   Tonya Vinas, 'IW Value-Chain Survey: A Map of the World', *Industry Week*, September 1, 2005, **http://www.industryweek.com/readarticle.aspx?articleid=10629&sectionid=11&cid=knc-iwtraf#** (Accessed January 9, 2006).

7   David A. Rick, *Blunders in International Business,* 4th edn (Oxford, England: Blackwell, 2006).

8   **http://www.iata.org** (Accessed November 15, 2005).

9   'Survey: E-Management', *The Economist,* November 11, 2000, 36.

10   Top Ten Outsourcing Survey, The Outsourcing Institute, **www.outsourcing.com** (Accessed January 30, 2006).

11   Michael R. Czinkota and Ilkka A. Ronkainen, 'A Forecast of Globalization, International Business and Trade: Report from a Delphi Study', *Journal of World Business* 40 (2005), 111–123.

12   Kotabe Masaaki, 'Efficiency vs. Effectiveness Orientation of Global Sourcing Strategy: A Comparison of U.S. and Japanese Multinational Companies', *Academy of Management Executive* 12 (number 4, 1999), 107–119.

13   Patriya S. Tansuhaj and George C. Jackson, 'Foreign Trade Zones: A Comparative Analysis of Users and Non-Users', *Journal of Business Logistics* 10 (1989): 15–30.

14   Office of Public Sector Information 'Carriage of Goods by Sea Act 1992'. Online. Available from: **http://www.opsi.gov.uk/Acts/acts1992/ukpga_19920050_en_1** (Accessed 26/2/10).

15   Charles A. Taft, *Management of Physical Distribution and Transportation,* 7th edn (Homewood, IL: Irwin, 1984), 324.

16   Report Buyer (2008) '2008 Global Broadband – M-Commerce, E-Commerce & E-Payments'. Online. Available from: **http://www.reportbuyer.com/telecoms/misc_telecoms/2008_global_broadband_m_commerce_e_commerce_e_payments.html** (Accessed 26/2/10).

17   Michael Czinkota and Gary Knight, 'Managing the terrorist threat', European Business Forum, **http://www.ebfonline.com/main_feat/in_depth.asp?id=526** (Accessed December 8, 2005).

18   Michael R. Czinkota, 'International Marketing and Terrorism Preparedness', testimony before the Congress of the United States, 109th Congress, Washington, DC, November 1, 2005.

19   Yossi Sheffi and James B. Rice Jr., 'A Supply Chain View of the Resilient Enterprise', *MIT Sloan Management Review*, 47 (number 1, 2005), 41–48.

20   Eye For Transport (2009) 'Global recession will lead to increased cargo crime, says TAPA'. Online. Available from: **http://www.eyefortransport.com/content/global-recession-will-lead-increased-cargo-crime-says-tapa** (Accessed 1/3/10).

21   Chilli, K. (2010) 'Pirate Attacks in the Modern World'. Online. Available from: **http://ezinearticles.com/?Pirate-Attacks-in-the-Modern-World&id=1381729** (Accessed 1/3/10).

22   International Chamber of Commerce, Piracy Report, **http://www.icc-ccs.org/prc/piracyreport.php** (Accessed December 8, 2005).

23   Bob Trebelcock, 'Seven Deadly Sins of Reverse Logistics', *Logistics Management,* June 2002.

24   Haw-Jan Wu and Steven C. Dunn, 'Environmentally Responsible Logistics Systems', *International Journal of Physical Distribution and Logistics Management* 2 (1995): 20–38.

17. Rajeev Batra, 'Marketing Issues and Challenges in Transitional Economies', Journal of International Marketing 5, no. 4 (1997): 95-114.

18. http://www.panohub.yahoo.com/telecoms/.

19. http://www.eyefortravel.com/.

20. Michael R. Czinkota, Peter R. Dickson, Patrick Dunne, Abbie Griffin, Michael H. Hutt, Bala V. Balachandran, John M. Gattorna, and the American Marketing Association, Marketing: Best Practices, 2nd ed. (Mason, OH: Thomson/South-Western, 2004).

21. Michael Minor, Gary Willett and the Market Planner, 'Pricing Success Stories', http://www.abcdonline.com/main_nav/m_depth.asp?id=626.

22. Bernard LaLonde, 'International Marketing and Purchasing Procedures', Journal of Business Logistics (United States) 23, no. 1 (2002).

CHAPTER 17
GLOBAL PRICING

Shifting profits across borders: 'Transfer pricing' is the biggest tax avoidance

In recent days the Tax Gap series of articles (*The Guardian* newspaper) has identified secrecy, complex organizational structures, tax havens and profit hungry accountancy firms as the key ingredients of the tax avoidance industry. They all come together in the biggest tax avoidance scheme of all, known as 'transfer pricing'. The name of the game is to shift profits to low tax jurisdictions and avoid taxes in countries where corporations have substantial trading operations.

Globalization has enabled a computer microchip company to design its products in country A, manufacture in B, test in C, hold patents in D and assign marketing rights to a subsidiary in country E. Such a structure gives corporations huge discretion in allocating costs to each country and shifting profits through internal trade. Around 60 per cent of the world trade consists of transfers internal to multinational corporations. This gives them numerous opportunities for shifting profits across borders.

There are international rules on transfer pricing, but they all rely on notions of 'costs' which are highly malleable. Tax rules require companies to use 'arm's length' or normal commercial prices to transfer goods and services, but such prices are not always easy to find. Many markets are thin and often dominated by the same multinationals.

Transfer pricing is also big business. Ernst & Young, a major accountancy firm, markets its services with the statement that 'suc-cessfully managing business and tax issues related to transfer pricing involves much more than documentation compliance. Transfer pricing affects almost every aspect of an MNE and can significantly impact its worldwide tax burden. Our ... professionals help MNEs address this burden ... with leading solutions. Our multidisciplinary team helps MNEs develop transfer pricing strategies, tax effective solutions, and controversy management approaches that best fit their objectives'.

Tax authorities believe that multinationals manipulate the import and export prices to avoid taxes. China is an interesting case. It has enticed foreign capital by offering low taxes and other incentives. Foreign Direct Investment (FDI) has flooded in. Despite the perks, over 70 per cent of multinational companies claim to be making losses. If so, why do they insist on making investment in China?

Christian Aid estimates that developing countries may be losing over £107 billion of tax revenues a year, primarily through transfer pricing strategies. As a result, governments are unable to provide security, healthcare, education, sanitation facilities, clean water, transport and other essentials. Millions of people are sent to a premature death.

Rather than giving credence to prices cooked up by companies, tax authorities should develop their own benchmarks. A related approach is a system of 'formulary apportionment' where companies are taxed on the basis of their economic activity and income within a particular geographic jurisdiction rather than arbitrary allocation of costs to geographical areas.

Tax authorities lack the resources to combat the tax avoidance industry. Ernst & Young alone employs over 900 professionals to sell transfer pricing schemes.

Governments need to mobilize the public. Companies should be required to publish a table showing their sales, purchases, profits, assets, liabilities, taxes and employees in each country of their operations. Upon seeing that there are substantial sales and little profit, or large profit and very few employees in a jurisdiction, the public would know that some transfer pricing games have been played. Corporate tax returns should be publicly available. Companies should publish details of transfer prices actually used. The public may be horrified to learn that companies have priced flash bulbs at £215.53 each, pillow cases at £608.81 each and a ton of sand at £1,355.09, when the average world trade price was £0.44, £0.42 and £7.51 respectively. Armed with this information people can decide to boycott the exploitative companies. Those devising abusive pricing structures should be held personally liable.

SOURCE: Sikka, P. (2009) 'Shifting profits across borders: "Transfer pricing" is the biggest tax avoidance'. Online. Available from: **http://www.guardian. co.uk/commentisfree/2009/feb/11/taxavoidance-tax** (Accessed 1/3/10).

Successful pricing is a key element in the marketing mix. Many executives believe that developing a pricing capability is essential to business survival, and rank pricing as second only to the product variable in importance among the concerns of marketing managers.[1] This chapter will focus on price setting by multinational corporations that have direct inventories in other countries. This involves the pricing of sales to members of the corporate family as well as pricing within the individual markets in which the company operates. With increased economic integration and globalization of markets, the coordination of pricing strategies between markets becomes more important. At the same time, marketers may have to develop creative solutions to respond to financial crises, or to buyers who want to attach strings to their purchases (due to the size of the deal, or because they may not have the traditional means with which to pay for their purchases).

TRANSFER PRICING

Transfer pricing, or intracorporate pricing, is the pricing of sales to members of the extended corporate family. With rapid globalization and consolidation across borders, estimates have up to two-thirds of world trade taking place between related parties, including shipments and transfers from parent company to affiliates as well as trade between alliance partners.[2] This means that transfer pricing has to be managed in a world characterized by different tax rates, different foreign exchange rates, varying governmental regulations, and other economic and social challenges, as seen in *The International Marketplace 17.1*. Allocation of resources among the various units of the multinational corporation requires the central management of the corporation to establish the appropriate transfer price to achieve the following objectives:

1 Competitiveness in the international marketplace.

2 Reduction of taxes and tariffs.

3 Management of cash flows.

4 Minimization of foreign exchange risks.

5 Avoidance of conflicts with home and host governments.

6 Internal concerns such as goal congruence and motivation of subsidiary managers.[3]

Intracorporate sales can so easily change the consolidated global results that they compose one of the most important ongoing decision areas in the company. This is quite a change from the past when many executives dismissed internal pricing as the sole responsibility of the accounting department and as a compliance matter. Transfer pricing, when viewed from a company-wide perspective, enhances operational performance (including marketing), minimizes the overall tax burden, and reduces legal exposure both at home and abroad.[4] According to an annual survey, the portion of multinationals citing transfer pricing as the most important issue in terms of taxation has grown from one-half to two-thirds, and at the subsidiary level this importance is even more pronounced.[5]

Transfer prices can be based on costs or on market prices.[6] The cost approach uses an internally calculated cost with a percentage markup added. The market price approach is based on an established market selling price and the products are usually sold at that price minus a discount to allow some margin of profit for the buying division. In general, cost-based prices are easier to manipulate because the cost base itself may be any one of these three: full cost, variable cost or marginal cost.

Factors that have a major influence on intracompany prices are listed in Exhibit 17.1. Market conditions in general, and those relating to the competitive situation in particular, are typically mentioned as key variables in balancing operational goals and tax considerations. In some markets, especially in the Far East, competition may prevent the international marketer from pricing at will. Prices may have to be adjusted to meet local competition with lower labour costs. This practice may provide entry to the market and a reasonable profit to the affiliate. However, in the long term, it may also become a subsidy to an inefficient business. Further, tax and customs authorities may object because underpricing means that the seller is earning less income than it would otherwise receive in the country of origin and is paying duties on a lower base price on entry to the destination country.

Economic conditions in a market, especially the imposition of controls on movements of funds, may require the use of transfer pricing to allow the company to repatriate revenues.

A new dimension is emerging with the increase in e-commerce activity. Given a lack of clear understanding and agreement of tax authorities on taxation of electronic transfer pricing activities, companies have to be particularly explicit on how pricing decisions are made to avoid transfer-price audits.[7]

International transfer pricing objectives may lead to conflicting objectives, especially if the influencing factors vary dramatically from one market to another. For example, it may be quite difficult to perfectly match subsidiary goals with the global goals of the multinational corporation. Specific policies should therefore exist that would motivate subsidiary managers to avoid making decisions that would be in conflict with overall corporate goals. If transfer pricing policies lead to an inaccurate financial measure of the subsidiary's performance, this should be taken into account when a performance evaluation is made.

EXHIBIT 17.1

Influences on transfer pricing decisions

1 Market conditions in target countries

2 Competition in target countries

3 Corporate taxes at home and in target countries

4 Economic conditions in target countries

5 Import restrictions

6 Customs duties

7 Price controls

8 Exchange controls

9 Reasonable profit for foreign affiliates

Source: Compiled from Robert Feinschreiber, *Transfer Pricing Handbook* (New York: John Wiley & Sons, 2002), chapter 1 ("Business Facets of Transfer Pricing"); and Jane O. Burns, "Transfer Pricing Decisions in U.S. Multinational Corporations," *Journal of International Business Studies* 11 (Fall 1980): 23–39.

Use of transfer prices to achieve corporate objectives

Three philosophies of transfer pricing have emerged over time: (1) cost-based (direct cost or cost-plus); (2) market-based (discounted 'dealer' price derived from end market prices); and (3) arm's-length price, or the price that unrelated parties would have reached on the same transaction. The rationale for transferring at cost is that it increases the profits of affiliates, and their profitability will eventually benefit the entire corporation. In most cases, cost-plus is used, requiring every affiliate to be a profit centre. Deriving transfer prices from the market is the most marketing-oriented method because it takes local conditions into account. Arm's-length pricing is favoured by many constituents, such as governments, to ensure proper intracompany pricing. However, the method becomes difficult when sales to outside parties do not occur in a product category. Additionally, it is often difficult to convince external authorities that true negotiation occurs between two entities controlled by the same parent. Generally tax authorities will honour agreements among companies provided those agreements are commercially reasonable and the companies abide by the agreements consistently.[8]

The effect of environmental influences in overseas markets can be alleviated by manipulating transfer prices at least in principle. High transfer prices on goods shipped to a subsidiary and low ones on goods imported from it will result in minimizing the tax liability of a subsidiary operating in a country with a high income tax. The European Union is, taken as a whole, a high tax area. In 2007, the last year for which detailed data are available, the average tax of the 27 member countries was 39.8 per cent of GDP, 12 points higher than those recorded in Japan and the US. Belgium, France, Italy and Austria all had a tax ratio to in excess of 40% in 2007. On the whole, the overall tax ratio ranges from 29.4 per cent in Romania to 48.7 per cent in Denmark. The UK tax ratio was 29.7 per cent. Countries can cut their rates, thereby giving multinationals a reason to report higher profits outside of their home markets. On the other hand, a higher transfer price may have an effect on the import duty, especially if it is assessed on an *ad valorem* basis. Exceeding a certain threshold may boost the duty substantially when the product is considered a luxury and will have a negative impact on the subsidiary's competitive posture. Adjusting transfer prices for the opposite effects of taxes and duties is, therefore, a delicate balancing act.

Transfer prices may be adjusted to balance the effects of fluctuating currencies when one partner is operating in a low-inflation environment and the other in one of rampant inflation. Economic restrictions such as controls on dividend remittances and allowable deductions for expenses incurred can also be blunted. For example, if certain services performed by corporate headquarters (such as product development or strategic planning assistance) cannot be charged to the subsidiaries, costs for these services can be recouped by increases in the transfer prices of other product components. A subsidiary's financial and competitive position can be manipulated by the use of lower transfer prices. Start-up costs can be lowered, a market niche carved more quickly, and long-term survival guaranteed. Ultimately, the entire transfer price and taxation question is best dealt with at a time when the company is considering a major expansion or restructuring of operations. For example, if it fits the overall plan, a portion of a unit's R&D and marketing activities could be funded in a relatively low tax jurisdiction.

Transfer pricing problems grow geometrically as all of the subsidiaries with differing environmental concerns are added to the planning exercise, calling for more detailed intracompany data for decision making. Further, fluctuating exchange rates make the planning even more challenging. However, to prevent double taxation and meet arm's-length requirements, it is essential that the corporation's pricing practices be uniform. Many have adopted a philosophy that calls for an obligation to maintain a good-citizen fiscal approach (that is, recognizing the liability to pay taxes and duties in every country of operation and to avoid artificial tax-avoidance schemes) and a belief that the primary goal of transfer pricing is to support and develop commercial activities.[9] Some companies make explicit mention of this obligation of good citizenship in their corporate codes of conduct.

Transfer pricing challenges

Transfer pricing policies face two general types of challenges. The first is internal to the multinational corporation and concerns the motivation of those affected by the pricing policies of the corporation. The second, an external one, deals with relations between the corporation and tax authorities in both the home country and the host countries.

Performance measurement Manipulating intracorporate prices complicates internal control measures and, without proper documentation, will cause major problems. If the firm operates on a profit centre basis, some consideration must be given to the effect of transfer pricing on the subsidiary's apparent profit performance and its actual performance. To judge a subsidiary's profit performance as not satisfactory when it was targeted to be a net source of funds can easily create morale problems. The situation may be further complicated by cultural differences in the subsidiary's management, especially if the need to subsidize less-efficient members of the corporate family is not made clear. An adjustment in the control mechanism is called for to give appropriate credit to divisions for their actual contributions. The method may range from dual bookkeeping to compensation in budgets and profit plans. Regardless of the method, proper organizational communication is necessary to avoid conflict between subsidiaries and headquarters.

Taxation Transfer prices will by definition involve the tax and regulatory jurisdictions of the countries in which the company does business, as is pointed out in *The International Marketplace 17.1*. Sales and transfers of tangible properties and transfers of intangibles such as patent rights and manufacturing know-how are subject to close review and to determinations about the adequacy of compensation received. This quite often puts the multinational corporation in a difficult position. UK authorities may think the transfer price is too low, whereas it may be perceived as too high by the foreign entity, especially if a less-developed country is involved. UK companies are guided by the Inland Revenue Guides to Corporation Tax.

The starting point for testing the appropriateness of transfer prices is a comparison with *comparable uncontrolled* transactions, involving unrelated parties. Uncontrolled prices exist when (1) sales are made by members of the multinational corporation to unrelated parties; (2) purchases are made by members of the multinational corporation from unrelated parties; and (3) sales are made between two unrelated parties, neither of which is a member of the multinational corporation. In some cases, marketers have created third-party trading where none existed before. Instead of selling 100 per cent of the product in a market to a related party, the seller can arrange a small number of direct transactions with unrelated parties to create a benchmark against which to measure related-party transactions.

If this method does not apply, the *resale* method can be used. This usually applies best to transfers to sales subsidiaries for ultimate distribution. The arm's-length approximation is arrived at by subtracting the subsidiary's profit from an uncontrolled selling price. The appropriateness of the amount is determined by comparison with a similar product being marketed by the multinational corporation.

The *cost-plus* approach is most applicable for transfers of components or unfinished goods to overseas subsidiaries. The arm's-length approximation is achieved by adding an appropriate markup for profit to the seller's total cost of the product.[10] The key is to apply such markups consistently over time and across markets.

The two methods focused on profits are based on the *functional analysis approach*. The functional analysis measures the profits of each of the related companies and compares them with the proportionate contribution to total income of the corporate group or comparable multinational marketers. It addresses the question of what profit would have been reported if the intercorporate transactions had involved unrelated parties. Understanding the functional inter-relationships of the various parties (that is, which entity does what) is basic to determining each entity's economic contribution via-à-vis total income of the corporate group.

Such comparisons, however, are not always possible even under the most favourable circumstances and may remain burdened with arbitrariness.[11] Comparisons are impossible for products that are unique or when goods are traded only with related parties. Adjusting price comparisons for differences in the product mix, or for the inherently different facts and circumstances surrounding specific transactions between unrelated parties, undermines the reliance that can be placed on any such comparisons.

PRICING WITHIN INDIVIDUAL MARKETS

Pricing within the individual markets in which the company operates is determined by (1) corporate objectives; (2) costs; (3) customer behaviour and market conditions; (4) market structure; and (5) environmental constraints.[12] Since all these factors vary among the countries in which the multinational corporation might have a presence, the pricing policy is under pressure to vary as well. With price holding a position of importance with customers, a market-driven firm must be informed and sensitive to customer views and realities.[13] This is especially critical for those marketers wanting to position their products as premium alternatives.

Although many global marketers emphasize non-price methods of competition, they rank pricing high as a marketing tool overseas, even though the non-domestic pricing decisions are made at the middle management level in a majority of firms.[14] Pricing decisions also tend to be made more at the local level, with coordination from headquarters in more strategic decision situations.[15] With increased trade liberalization and advanced economic integration, this coordination is becoming more important.

Corporate objectives

Global marketers must set and adjust their objectives, both financial (such as return on investment) and marketing-related (such as maintaining or increasing market share), based on the prevailing conditions in each of their markets. Pricing may well influence the overall strategic moves of the company as a whole. This is well illustrated by the decision of many foreign-based companies, carmakers for example, to begin production in the United States rather than to continue exporting. To remain competitive in the market, many have had to increase the dollar component of their output. Apart from trade barriers, many have had their market shares eroded because of higher wages in their home markets, increasing shipping costs, and unfavourable exchange rates. Market share very often plays a major role in pricing decisions in that marketers may be willing to sacrifice immediate earnings for market share gain or maintenance. This is especially true in highly competitive situations; for example, during a period of extremely high competitive activity in Japan in the mainframe sector, the local Fujitsu's one-year net income was only 5 per cent of sales, compared with IBM's 12.7 per cent worldwide and 7.6 per cent in Japan. In the longer term, situations of this type may require cross-subsidization from other geographic units.

Pricing decisions will also vary depending on the pricing situation. The basics of first-time pricing, price adjustment, and product line pricing as discussed earlier apply to pricing within non-domestic situations as well. For example, companies such as Kodak and Xerox, which introduce all of their new products worldwide within a very short time period, have an option of either skimming or penetration pricing. If the product is an innovation, the marketer may decide to charge a premium for the product. If, however, competition is keen or expected to increase in the near future, lower prices may be used to make the product more attractive to the buyers and the market less attractive to the competition. The Korean conglomerates (such as Daewoo, Goldstar, Hyundai and Samsung) were able to penetrate and capture the low end of many consumer goods markets in both the United States and Europe based on price competitiveness over the past ten years (as shown in Exhibit 17.2). In the last few years, Chinese marketers have used similar pricing strategies to establish market positions. For example, Shanghai-based SVA Group sells LCD and plasma TV sets through channels such as Costco and Target at prices that are 30 per cent below those of Panasonic from Japan.[16]

For the most part, the Koreans have competed in the world marketplace, especially against the Japanese, on price rather than product traits, with the major objective of capturing a foothold in various markets. However, substantial strides in production technology and relentless marketing have started to make Korean products serious competitors in the medium to high price brackets as well.[17] In many cases, Koreans have been able to close the price gap and, in some cases, they have abandoned certain segments altogether. For example, in the compact refrigerator market, the Chinese have taken over.[18]

EXHIBIT 17.2   The price edge game

Product	Korean Brand				Japanese Brand				Chinese Brand
	1985	1996	2000	2006	1985	1996	2000	2006	2006
Subcompact autos	Excel/Accent (Hyundai)				Sentra (Nissan)				Chery QQ
	$5,500	$9,079	$9,699	$12,455	$7,600	$11,499	$11,649	$13,200	$7,500
DVD Videocassette recorders	Samsung				Toshiba				
	$270	$260	$120	$99	$350	$430	$199	$119	N/A
Compact refrigerators	Goldstar				Sanyo				Haier
	$149	$150	$149	$149	$265	$180	$99	$159	$128
13-inch colour televisions	Samsung				Hitachi/ SONY				
	$148	$179	$170	$130	$189	$229	$180	$140	N/A
Microwave ovens	Goldstar				Toshiba				
	$149	$120	$130	$95	$180	$140	$130	$100	N/A

SOURCE: Originally published in L. Helm, "The Koreans Are Coming," *Business Week*, December 23, 1985, 46–52; direct manufacturer/retailer inquiries, December 1996, March 2000, and February 2006. In the absence of information/availability, a similar make/model has been used based on *Consumer Reports* data.

Price changes may be frequent if the company's objective is to undersell a major competitor. A marketer may, for example, decide to maintain a price level 10 to 20 per cent below that of a major competitor; price changes would be necessary whenever the competitor made significant changes in its prices. Price changes may also be required because of changes in foreign exchange rates.

With longer-term unfavourable currency changes, marketers have to improve their efficiency and/or shift production bases. For example, Japanese car manufacturers transplanted more manufacturing into the United Kingdom to ensure that yen–pound changes did not have as sharp an impact as they once did. Furthermore, design and production was improved so that profitability could be maintained even at 80 or 85 yen to the pound. The strategy is to cut prices when the value of the yen is more than the pound.

Product line pricing occurs typically in conjunction with positioning decisions. The global marketer may have a premium line as well as a standard line and, in some cases, may sell directly to retailers for their private label sales. Products facing mass markets have keener competition and smaller profit margins than premium products, which may well be priced more liberally because there is less competition. For example, for decades, Caterpillar's big ticket items virtually sold themselves. However, environmental factors, such as the economic depression and budget deficit, resulted in fewer large-scale highway and construction projects. The company was forced to expand to smaller equipment to remain competitive globally.

Costs

Costs are frequently used as a basis for price determination largely because they are easily measured and provide a floor under which prices cannot go in the long term. These include procurement, manufacturing, logistics and marketing costs, as well as overheads. Quality at an affordable price drives most procurement systems. The decision to turn to offshore suppliers may often be influenced by their lower prices, which enable the marketer to remain competitive.[19] Locating manufacturing facilities in different parts of the world may lower various costs, such as labour or distribution costs, although this may create new challenges. While a market may be attractive as far as labour costs are concerned, issues such as productivity, additional costs (for instance, logistics), and political risk will have to be factored in. Furthermore, a country may lose its attraction due to increasing costs (for example, the average industrial wage rose 110 per cent in Korea in the 1990s), and the marketer may have to start the cycle anew by going to new markets (such as Indonesia or Vietnam).

Varying inflation rates will have a major impact on the administration of prices, especially because they are usually accompanied by government controls. The task of the parent company is to aid subsidiaries in their planning to ensure reaching margin targets despite unfavourable market conditions. Most experienced companies in the emerging markets generally have strong country managers who create significant value through their understanding of the local environment. Their ability to be more agile in a turbulent environment is a significant competitive advantage. Inflationary environments call for constant price adjustments; in markets with hyperinflation, pricing may be in a stable currency such as the euro with daily translation into the local currency. In such volatile environments, the marketer may want to shift supply arrangements to cost-effective alternatives, pursue rapid inventory turnovers, shorten credit terms, and make sure contracts have appropriate safety mechanisms against inflation (e.g., choice of currency or escalator clause).

The opposite scenario may also be encountered; that is, prices cannot be increased due to economic conditions. Inflation has been kept in check in developed economies for a number of reasons. Globalization has increased the number of competitors, and the internet has made it easy for customers to shop for the lowest prices. Big intermediaries, such as Tesco and Carrefour are demanding prices at near cost from their suppliers. In Europe, the advent of the euro has made prices even more transparent.[20] A survey of executives from 134 countries revealed that 59 per cent of the respondents did not expect to be able to raise prices in the coming year.[21] Strategies for thriving in disinflationary times may include (1) target pricing, in which efficiencies are sought in production and marketing to meet price-driven costing; (2) value pricing, to move away from coupons, discounts and promotions to everyday low prices; (3) stripping down products, to offer quality without all the frills; (4) adding value by introducing innovative products sold at a modest premium (accompanied by strong merchandising and promotion) but perceived by customers to be worth it; and (5) getting close to customers by using new technologies (such as the internet and EDI) to track their needs and company costs more closely.[22]

Internally, controversy may arise in determining which manufacturing and marketing costs to include. For example, controversy may arise over the amounts of research and development to charge to subsidiaries or over how to divide the costs of a pan-regional advertising campaign when costs are incurred primarily on satellite channels and viewership varies dramatically from one market to the next.

Demand and market factors

Demand will set a price ceiling in a given market. Despite the difficulties in obtaining data on foreign markets and forecasting potential demand, the global marketer must make judgements concerning the quantities that can be sold at different prices in each foreign market. The global marketer must understand the price elasticity of consumer demand to determine appropriate price levels, especially if cost structures change. A status-conscious market that insists on products with established reputations will be inelastic, allowing for far more pricing freedom than a market where price-consciousness drives demand. Many European companies have regarded Japan as a place to sell premium products at premium prices. With the increased information and travel that globalization has brought about, status-consciousness is being replaced by a more practical consumerist sensibility: top quality at competitive prices.

The marketer's freedom in making pricing decisions is closely tied to customer perceptions of the product offering and the marketing communication tied to it. Toyota is able to outsell Chevys, which are identical and both produced by NUMMI Inc., which is a joint venture between Toyota and GM, even though its version (the Corolla) is priced $2,000 higher on the average. Similarly, Korean automakers have had a challenging time in shedding their image as a risky purchase. For example, consumers who liked the Hyundai Santa Fe said they would pay $10,000 less because it was a Hyundai.[23]

Hyundai has made major inroads into improving quality perceptions with its ten-year drivetrain warranty policy (which is very expensive, however).

Prices have to be set keeping in mind not only the ultimate consumers but also the intermediaries involved. The success of a particular pricing strategy will depend on the willingness of both the manufacturer and the intermediary to co-operate. For example, if the marketer wants to undercut its competition, it has to make sure that retailers' margins remain adequate and competitive to ensure appropriate implementation. At the same time, there is enormous pressure on manufacturers' margins from the side of intermediaries who are growing in both size and global presence. These intermediaries, such as French Carrefour and British Marks & Spencer, demand low-cost, direct-supply contracts, which many manufacturers may not be willing or able to furnish.[24] The only other option may be to resort to alternate distribution modes, which may be impossible.

Market structure and competition

Competition helps set the price within the parameters of cost and demand. Depending on the marketer's objectives and competitive position, it may choose to compete directly on price or elect for non-price measures. If a pricing response is sought, the marketer can offer bundled prices (e.g., value deals on a combination of products) or loyalty programmes to insulate the firm from a price war. Price cuts can also be executed selectively rather than across the board. New products can be introduced to counter price challenges. For example, when Japanese Kao introduced a low-priced diskette to compete against 3M, rather than drop its prices 3M introduced a new brand, Highland, that effectively flanked Kao's competitive incursion. Simply dropping the price on the 3M brand could have badly diluted its image. On the non-price front, the company can opt to fight back on quality by adding and promoting value-adding features.[25]

If a company's position is being eroded by competitors who focus on price, the marketer may have no choice but to respond. For example, IBM's operation in Japan lost market share in mainframes largely because competitors undersold the company. A Japanese mainframe was typically listed at 10 per cent less than its IBM counterpart, and it frequently carried an additional 10 to 20 per cent discount beyond that. This created an extremely competitive market. IBM's reaction was to respond in kind with aggressive promotion of its own, with the result that it began regaining its lost share. Motorola and Nokia, the leading mobile phone makers, are facing tough conditions in the Korean market. In addition to being competitive in price and quality, local companies such as Samsung and Goldstar are quick to come up with new models to satisfy the fast-changing needs of consumers while providing better after-sales service, free of charge or at a marginal price, than the two global players.[26] In a market known for its ethnocentric consumers, the locals have won the battle.

In some cases, strategic realignment may be needed. To hold on to its eroding worldwide market share, Caterpillar has strived to shrink costs and move away from its old practice of competing only by building advanced, enduring machines and selling them at premium prices. Instead, the company has cut prices and has used strategic alliances overseas to produce competitive equipment to better suit local and regional needs.

Some marketers can fend off price competition by emphasizing other elements of the marketing mix, even if they are at an absolute disadvantage in price. Singer Sewing Machine Co., which gains nearly half its $500 million in non-US sales from developing countries, emphasizes its established reputation, product quality and liberal credit terms, as well as other services (such as sewing classes), rather than compete head-on with lower-cost producers.[27] At $40 to $60, jeans are not affordable to the masses in developing countries. Arvind Mills, the world's fifth-largest denim maker, introduced 'Ruf & Tuf' jeans – a ready-to-make kit of jeans components priced at $6 which could be assembled inexpensively by a local tailor.[28]

The pricing behaviour of a global marketer may come under scrutiny in important market sectors, such as automobiles or retailing. If local companies lose significant market share to outsiders as a result of lower prices, they may ask for government interference against alleged dumping. Wal-Mart resigned from Mexico's National Retailers Association to protest an ethics code that members approved prohibiting price comparisons in ads by their members (on the basis of negative publicity for other retailers). Since ad campaigns are the key to Wal-Mart's 'everyday low prices' strategy, it had no choice but to leave the organization.[29]

Environmental constraints

Governments influence prices and pricing directly as well. In addition to the policy measures, such as tariffs and taxes, governments may also elect to directly control price levels. Once under price controls, the global marketer has to operate as it would in a regulated industry. Setting maximum prices has been defended primarily on political grounds: It stops inflation and an accelerating wage-price spiral, and consumers want it. Supporters also maintain that price controls raise the income of the poor. Operating in such circumstances is difficult. Achieving change in prices can be frustrating; for example, a company may wait 30 to 45 days for an acknowledgment of a price-increase petition.

To fight price controls, multinational corporations can demonstrate that they are getting an unacceptable return on investment and that, without an acceptable profit opportunity, future investments will not be made and production perhaps will be stopped. These have been the arguments of European and US pharmaceutical marketers in China.[30] Cadbury Schweppes sold its plant in Kenya because price controls made its operation unprofitable. At one time, Coca-Cola and PepsiCo withdrew their products from the shelves in Mexico until they received a price increase. Pakistani milk producers terminated their business when they could not raise prices, and Glaxo Wellcome, a pharmaceutical manufacturer, cancelled its expansion plans in Pakistan because of price controls.

In general, company representatives can cite these consequences in arguing against price controls: (1) the maximum price often becomes the minimum price if a sector is allowed a price increase, because all businesses in the sector will take it regardless of cost justification; (2) the wage-price spiral advances vigorously in anticipation of controls; (3) labour often turns against restrictions because they are usually accompanied by an income policy or wage restrictions; (4) non-inflationary wage increases are forestalled; (5) government control not only creates a costly regulatory body but also is difficult to enforce; (6) authorities raise less in taxes because less money is made; and (7) a government may have to bail out many companies with cheap loans or make grants to prevent bankruptcies and unemployment.[31] Once price controls are invoked, management will have to devote much time to resolving the many difficulties that controls present. The best interest of multinational corporations is therefore served by working with governments, especially in the developing countries, to establish an economic policy centred on a relatively free market without price controls. This means, for example, that pharmaceutical firms need to convince governments that their products greatly benefit the public and that their prices are reasonable. If the companies can point to R&D focused on solving local challenges, the argument can be made more convincingly.

DEALING WITH FINANCIAL CRISES

A series of currency crises have shaken all emerging markets in the last ten years. The devaluation of the Mexican peso in 1994, the Asian crisis of July 1997, the Russian ruble collapse of August 1998, the fall of the Brazilian real in January 1999, the Argentine default in 2001 and the 2008/9 global financial crises, have all provided a spectrum of emerging market economic failures, each with its own complex causes and challenging outlooks.

Causes of the crises

Both the Mexican and Thai cases of currency devaluation led to regional effects in which international investors saw Mexico and Thailand as only the first domino in a long series of failures to come. The reasons for the crises were largely in three areas allowing comparison: corporate socialism, corporate governance, and banking stability and management. In 1997, business liabilities exceeded the capacities of government to bail businesses out, and practices such as lifetime employment were no longer sustainable. Many firms in the Far East were often controlled by families or groups related to the governing party of the country. The interests of stockholders and creditors were secondary in an atmosphere of cronyism. With the speculative investments made by many banks failing, banks themselves had to close, severely hampering the ability of businesses to obtain the necessary capital financing needed for operations. The pivotal role of banking liquidity was the focus of the International Monetary Fund's bail-out efforts.

The Asian crisis had global impact. What started as a currency crisis quickly became a region-wide recession.[32] The slowed economies of the region caused major reductions in world demand for many products, especially commodities. World oil markets, copper markets and agricultural products all saw severe price drops as demand kept falling. These changes were immediately noticeable in declined earnings and growth prospects for other emerging economies. The problems of Russia and Brazil were reflections of those declines. In Argentina, the government defaulted on its debt, blocked Argentines from paying obligations to foreigners, and stopped pegging the peso to the US dollar.[33]

The 2007–2009 financial crisis had its roots in the US housing market, where a boom in the housing sector was driving the economy to a new level. A combination of low interest rates and large inflows of foreign funds helped to create easy credit conditions where it became quite easy for people to take home loans. As more and more people took home loans, the demands for property increased and fuelled the home prices further. As there was enough money to lend to potential borrowers, the loan agencies started to widen their loan disbursement reach and relaxed the loan conditions (giving loans to people on low incomes (subprime loans), but where interests were slightly higher than the prime loans. Unfortunately this boom came to a close. Overbuilding of houses led to an oversupply of houses, thereby limiting demand. House prices fell drastically; subprime investments were unprofitable and risky. Lending companies were in trouble as loan values were higher than the cost of houses and loans were written off. This spread to global banks and brokerages which had to write off an estimated £342 billion in subprime losses, with the largest hits taken by Citigroup (£36.8 billion) and Merrill Lynch (£34.9 billion). A little over half of these losses, or £173.7 billion, have been suffered by US-based firms, £151.7 billion by European firms and a relatively modest £16 billion by Asian ones. Some global banks filed for bankruptcy, for example. What is worse is the fact that the losses suffered by banks in the subprime mess have directly affected their money market the world over.[34]

Governments and central banks are trying every trick in the book to stabilize the markets. They have pumped hundreds of billions of pounds into their money markets to try and unfreeze their inter-bank and credit markets. Large financial entities have been nationalized, for example, Lloyds Bank and Northern Rock Bank. The US government has set aside $700 billion to buy the 'toxic' assets like CDOs that sparked off the crisis. Central banks have got together to coordinate cuts in interest rates. None of this has stabilized the global markets so far. However, it is hoped that proper monitoring and controlling of the money market will eventually control the situation.[35]

Effects of the Crises

The collapse of the ruble in Russia and of Russia's access to international capital markets brought into question the benefits of a free-market economy, long championed by the advocates of western-style democracy. While Russia is the sixth-most populous nation, a nuclear power, and the holder of a permanent seat in the Security Council of the United Nations, its economic status is in many ways that of a developing country. There is a growing middle class, particularly in the largest cities. Some Russian businesses had revealed glimmerings of respect for shareholders, staff and customers. Higher standards were encouraged by a growing international business presence. Many of these positive changes were put into jeopardy.

In Brazil, similar effects were felt. A total of 30 million consumers left the middle class. Many of the free-trade experiments within Mercosur were being re-evaluated or endangered, especially by Brazilian moves in erecting tariff barriers. Many of the key sectors, such as automobiles, were hit by layoffs and suspended production. In Argentina, the supply of most foreign-made goods was choked off.

The financial crisis of 2007–2009 has resulted in the collapse of large financial institutions, the 'bail out' of banks by national governments and downturns in stock markets around the world. The collapse of a global housing bubble, which peaked in the US in 2006, caused the values of securities tied to real estate pricing to plummet thereafter, damaging financial institutions globally.[36] The global recession has resulted in a sharp drop in international trade, rising unemployment and slumping commodity prices. In December 2008, the National Bureau of Economic Research (NBER) declared that the United States had been in recession since December 2007. Several economists have predicted that recovery may not appear until 2011 and that the recession will be the worst since the Great Depression of the 1930s. The conditions leading up to the crisis, characterized by an exorbitant rise in asset prices and associated boom in economic demand, are considered a result of the extended period of easily available credit, inadequate regulation and oversight, or increasing inequality.[37]

Consumer and marketer responses

Changes in the economic environment affect both consumers and marketers. Consumer confidence is eroded and marketers have to weigh their marketing strategies carefully. Some of these adjustments are summarized in Exhibit 17.3.

Recessions have an impact on consumer spending. For example, the 30 million Brazilians who, as a result of the real crisis, were no longer able to consume in a middle-class tradition were also lost to many marketers, such as McDonald's. Rather than buying hamburgers, they would consume more traditional and therefore less expensive meals. Similarly, some consumption may turn not only toward local alternatives but even to generics. Especially hard hit may be big-ticket purchases, such as cars, furniture and appliances, that may be put on long-term hold.

Marketers' responses to these circumstances have varied from abandoning markets to substantially increasing their efforts. While Daihatsu pulled out of Thailand, GM decided to stay, with a change in the car model to be produced and reduced production volume. Returning to a market having once abandoned it may prove to be difficult. For example, distribution channels may be blocked by competition, or suspicion about the long-term commitment of a returnee may surface among local partners. Manipulating the marketing mix is also warranted. Imported products are going to be more expensive, sometimes many times what the local versions cost. Therefore, emphasizing the brand name, the country of origin and other benefits may convince the consumer of a positive value-price relationship. Adaptive positioning means recasting the product in a new light rather than changing the product itself. For example, Michelin changed its positioning from 'expensive, but worth it' to 'surprisingly affordable' in Asian markets affected by the crisis.[38] If the perceived prices are too high, the product and/or its packaging may have to be changed by making the product smaller or the number of units in a pack fewer. For example, Unilever reduced the size of its ice-cream packs, making them cheaper, and offers premiums in conjunction with the purchase of soap products (for example, buy three, get one free).[39] Nike's approach in Asia is described in *The International Marketplace 17.2.*

While marketers from Europe and North America may be faced by these challenges, local companies may have an advantage, not only at home but in international markets as well. Their lower prices give them an opportunity to expand outside their home markets or aggressively pursue expansion in new markets. Similarly, companies with sourcing in markets hit by currency crises may be able to benefit from lower procurement costs.

The most interesting approach in the face of challenges is to increase efforts in building market share. This is achieved by investing more due to decreasing competition (which results from some competitors leaving). This strategy is naturally based on the premise that the market will rebound in the foreseeable future, thus rewarding investments made earlier.

EXHIBIT 17.3

Consumer and marketer adjustment to financial crisis

Consumer Adjustment to Financial Hardship	Marketer Adjustment to Financial Hardship
General reactions • Reduce consumption and wastefulness • More careful decision making • More search for information	**Marketing-mix strategies** • Withdraw from weak markets • Fortify in strong markets • Acquire weak competitors • Consider youth markets • Resale market for durables
Product adjustments • Necessities rather than luxuries • Switch to cheaper brands or generics • Local rather than foreign brands • Smaller quantities/packages	**Product strategies** • Prune weak products • Avoid introducing new products in gaps • Flanker brands • Augment products with warranties • Adaptive positioning
Price adjustments • Life-cycle costs—durability/value emphasize on economical prices	**Pricing strategies** • Improve quality while maintaining price • Reduce price while maintaining quality • Consider product life-cycle pricing
Promotion adjustments • Rational approach • Reduced attraction to gifts • Information rather than imagery	**Promotion strategies** • Maintain advertising budget • Focus on print media • Assurances through rational appeals • Expert endorsements • Advisory tone • Customer loyalty programs • Train sales force to handle objections
Shopping adjustments • Increased window shopping • Preference for discount stores • Fewer end-of-aisle purchases	**Distribution strategies** • Location is critical • Sell in discount and wholesale centres • Prune marginal dealers • Alternative channels

SOURCE: Compiled from Swee Hoon Ang, Siew Meng Leong, and Philip Kotler, "The Asian Apocalypse: Crisis Marketing for Consumers and Businesses," *Long Range Planning* 33 (February 2000): 97–119.

PRICING COORDINATION

The issue of standard worldwide pricing has been mostly a theoretical one because of the influence of the factors already discussed. However, coordination of the pricing function is necessary, especially in larger, regional markets such as the European Union, especially after the introduction of the euro. With the increasing level of integration efforts around the world, and even discussion of common currency elsewhere, control and coordination of global and regional pricing takes on a new meaning.

With more global and regional brands in the global marketer's offering, control in pricing is increasingly important. Of course, this has to be balanced against the need for allowing subsidiaries latitude in pricing so that they may quickly react to specific market conditions.

Studies have shown that foreign-based multinational corporations allow their US subsidiaries considerable freedom in pricing. This has been explained by the size and unique features

THE INTERNATIONAL **MARKETPLACE 17.2**

Just do it (even in a crisis)

Nike's international revenues have gradually grown to be the majority of the company's $13.7 billion annual turnover. Asia's share of the total is $1.6 billion, or 13 per cent. Asia is Nike's third largest market in terms of revenue and number one location in terms of manufacturing. While growth in Asia has been robust recently (for example, 20 per cent in 2004), there have been some challenging times as well.

When the Asian financial crisis sapped the purchasing power in many communities, Nike started targeting teens living in the region's rural and suburban areas with a range of 'entry-level' footwear. The Nike Play Series line, launched in India, Indonesia, Singapore and Thailand, retailed for $25, roughly half of most Nike shoes and far less than the $150 charged for its top-range products.

Asian kids in rural areas might be playing sports with no shoes at all, so they cannot relate to Nike's high-end products. Nike Play Series was created to introduce them to the concept of different shoes for different sports. Even among those who purchase luxury products, sales fell 30 per cent during the crisis in markets hardest hit.

Ads for the new product line used the slogan 'It's My Turn' and depicted young Asian athletes (such as Singaporean soccer star Alvin Patrimonio) alongside images of major sports stars. Nike also built branded Play Zones in new or refurbished urban centres in Singapore, Kuala Lumpur, Bangkok, Manila and Johor Bahru. Each included a multicourt facility where kids play everything from badminton to basketball, highlighted by 'event days' with tournaments. In rural areas, Nike donated equipment such as basketball hoops and soccer goal posts to raise the profile of the Nike Play Series.

The experience in Asia has enabled Nike to transfer experiences to new product categories and new markets. For example, Nike launched a lower-priced shoe line in Wal-Mart stores using the Starter brand.

SOURCE: 'Nike Finds a Way to Go to Wal-Mart', *Advertising Age*, March 21, 2005, 1; 'How Nike Got Its Game Back', *Business Week*, November 4, 2002, 129; Normandy Madden 'Nike Sells $25 Shoe Line in Recession-Hit Region', *Advertising Age*, November 1999, 17. See also **http://www.nikebiz.com**.

of the market. Further, it has been argued distances create a natural barrier against arbitrage practices that would be more likely to emerge in Europe, although even with the common currency, different rules and standards, economic disparities, and information differences may make deal-hunting difficult.[40] However, recent experience has shown that pricing coordination has to be worldwide because parallel imports will surface in any markets in which price discrepancies exist, regardless of distances. Marketers who mainly sell to organizational customers, such as Nokia to telecommunications operators, have started using standard worldwide pricing.

THE EURO AND MARKETING STRATEGY

On January 1, 1999, the euro (€) was officially launched by the European Union and it became the one and only currency of the 16 nations in the eurozone, or Euroland, January 1, 2008. (Please note that of the 27 EU member states, only 16 countries have adopted the euro as their official currency). Although the early focus was largely on managing the operational aspects of converting to the use of the euro for all business activities (such as preparing to account for sales and purchasing in euros as well as transforming internal accounting for areas such as R&D budgeting), the strategic issues are the most significant for the future.

In the longer term all firms will need to re-examine the positioning of their businesses. The potential advantages of a single-currency Europe (such as a more competitive market, both internally and externally) have been widely expounded, but the threats to businesses of all nationalities, sizes and forms have not been so widely discussed. The threats are many. As barriers to the creation of a single domestic market are eliminated, more production and operating strategy decisions will be made on the basis of true-cost differentials (proximity to specific inputs, materials, immobile skills, or niche customers, for example). Consolidation will be the norm for many business units whose existence was in some way perpetuated by

EXHIBIT 17.4

The Eurozone area

| EU Eurozone (16) | EU states obliged to join the Eurozone (9) | EU state with an opt-out on Eurozone participation (1 - UK) | EU state planning to hold a referendum on the euro (1 - Denmark) | States outside the EU with issuing rights (3) | Other non-EU users (4)

Source: Wikipedia (2010), 'Eurozone'. Online. Available from: **http://en.wikipedia.org/wiki/Eurozone** (Accessed 14/5/10).

the uses of different currencies. This restructuring will have lasting effects on the European business landscape. For example, many marketers are streamlining their operations throughout Euroland and eliminating overlapping entities, such as distribution facilities.[41]

The euro will push national markets closer together. First and foremost in this area is the transparency to consumers of a single currency and a single cross-border price. The euro combined with the growing use of e-business, for example, will allow consumers in Barcelona to surf the web for the cheapest source of fresh seafood delivered from anywhere within the EU27. Although theoretically possible before, the quotation of prices by individual currency and complexity of payment often posed a barrier – somewhat real, somewhat imagined – to cross-border purchasing. This barrier no longer exists, as consumers are now able to demand the highest quality product and service at the lowest price from businesses throughout the European community.

A more troublesome result is pricing, both within the firm and to the marketplace. Within the firm, the transfer prices between business units of the firm, whether in-country or cross-border, will now be held to an even more rigorous standard of no differentiation. Transfer prices internationally, however, are one of the key factors in how firms reposition profits in order to reduce their global tax burdens. Without this veil of differences in currency of denomination, any differences in transfer prices across multinational units will be even more apparent (and will not be allowed).

EXHIBIT 17.5

Countries which have adopted the Euro

	State	Adopted	Population	Exceptions
	Austria	1 January 1999	8,356,707	
	Belgium	1 January 1999	10,741,048	
	Cyprus	1 January 2008	801,622	Northern Cyprus
	Finland	1 January 1999	5,325,115	
	France	1 January 1999	64,105,125	New Caledonia / French Polynesia / Wallis and Futuna
	Germany	1 January 1999	82,062,249	
	Greece	1 January 2001	11,262,539	
	Ireland	1 January 1999	4,517,758	
	Italy	1 January 1999	60,090,430	Campione d'Italia
	Luxembourg	1 January 1999	491,702	
	Malta	1 January 2008	412,614	
	Netherlands	1 January 1999	16,481,139	Aruba / Netherlands Antilles
	Portugal	1 January 1999	10,631,800	
	Slovakia	1 January 2009	5,411,062	
	Slovenia	1 January 2007	2,053,393	
	Spain	1 January 1999	45,853,045	
	Eurozone		328,597,348	

SOURCE: Wikipedia (2010) 'Eurozone'. Online. Available from: **http://en.wikipedia.org/wiki/Eurozone** (Accessed 14/5/10)

The single currency has made prices completely transparent for all buyers. If discrepancies are not justifiable due to market differences such as consumption preferences, competition, or government interference, parallel importation may occur. The simplest solution would be to have one euro price throughout the market. However, given the huge differences of up to 100 per cent (as shown in Exhibit 17.6), that solution would lead to significant losses in sales and profits, as a single price would likely be closer to the lower-priced countries' level. The recommended approach is a pricing corridor that considers existing country-specific prices while optimizing the profits at a pan-European level.[42] As described in *The International Marketplace 17.3*, such a corridor defines the maximum and minimum prices that country organizations can charge – enough to allow flexibility as a result of differences in price elasticities, competition and positioning, but not enough to attract parallel imports that may start at price differences of 20 per cent and higher.[43] This approach moves pricing authority away from country managers to regional management and requires changes in management systems and incentive structures.

In terms of specific pricing approaches, marketers should aim to lower prices as slowly as possible, especially for less price-sensitive customers. Alternatives include developing selective offers to price-sensitive customers using discounts and long-term contracts – measures that put considerably less downward pressure on prices across all customers. In addition, marketers can enhance the value of product and service offerings selectively, and thereby maintain price differentials across Europe.[44]

Multinational customers, such as Coca-Cola or IBM, like to drive hard bargains with their suppliers, seeking low and consistent prices worldwide. This can become a problem when some suppliers provide steep discounts in emerging markets such as China, while keeping

EXHIBIT 17.6   Price differentials across European consumer goods markets

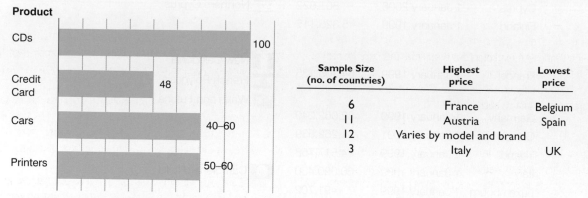

Per cent difference between highest and lowest

Product		
CDs		100
Credit Card		48
Cars		40–60
Printers		50–60

Sample Size (no. of countries)	Highest price	Lowest price
6	France	Belgium
11	Austria	Spain
12	Varies by model and brand	
3	Italy	UK

Source: Adapted from Johan Ahlberg, Nicklas Garemo, and Tomas Nauclér, "The Euro: How to Keep Your Prices Up and Your Competitors Down," *The McKinsey Quarterly* 35 (no. 2, 1999): 112–118.

prices higher in developed markets. Marketers should make sure that price differences reflect differences in quality or in the services provided. Many industrial companies try to coordinate pan-regional purchasing in Europe by empowering an individual or department to do so. However, many of them still have national structures whereby country organizations retain considerable say-so in what is bought. Marketers can take advantage of this separation of decision-making power and influence.

COUNTERTRADE

The Australian government declared that it would only purchase military equipment from the United States if the US Navy and Marine Corps would buy lollipops from an Australian firm, Allen Sweets Ltd.[45] General Motors exchanged automobiles for a trainload of strawberries. As explained in *The International Marketplace 17.4*, countertrade can be used to expand business opportunities. Or a nation may swap physicians in exchange for oil. All these are examples of countertrade activities carried out around the world.

Countertrade is a sale that encompasses more than an exchange of goods, services, or ideas for money. In the international market, countertrade transactions 'are those transactions which have as a basic characteristic a linkage, legal or otherwise, between exports and imports of goods or services in addition to, or in place of, financial settlements'.[46] Historically, countertrade was mainly conducted in the form of barter, which is a direct exchange of goods of approximately equal value, with no money involved. These transactions were the very essence of business at times when no money – that is, a common medium of exchange – existed or was available or accepted. Money permits greater flexibility in trading activities. However, we see returns to the barter system as a result of economic circumstances.

Countertrade transactions have therefore always arisen when economic circumstances have encouraged a direct exchange of goods over the use of money. Conditions that support such business activities are lack of money, lack of value of money, lack of acceptability of money as an exchange medium, or greater ease of transaction by using goods. However, the shrinking of established markets and the existence of a substantial product surplus are also conditions that foster countertrade.

These same reasons prevail in today's resurgence of countertrade activities. Throughout the past decades, the use of countertrade has steadily increased. In 1972, countertrade was used by only 15 countries. By 1983, the countries conducting countertrade transactions numbered 88, and by 2004 the number was 130.[47] Officials of the General Agreement on Tariffs

THE INTERNATIONAL **MARKETPLACE 17.3**

Coordinating prices in integrating markets

Price differentials can survive across individual European Union markets only if marketers act decidedly. This calls for centralizing pricing authority and establishing 'pricing corridors'. Some marketers may have to pull out of low-margin markets where price increases cannot be sustained.

Future European price levels will be markedly lower than current ones, and firms must take quick action to avoid seeing prices fall to the lowest level prevailing in marginal markets. This is due to the large differentials that existed and continue to exist among EU member states. Prices in markets such as Portugal and Spain are often significantly lower than those in northern Europe markets, where consumers can afford much larger margins and where costs are higher. The differentials can range from 30 per cent for natural yogurt to as much as 200 per cent for pharmaceuticals. Even among northern nations, a 2001 European Commission study found that consumers in the United Kingdom were paying 66 per cent more for the exact same car model as their counterparts in the Netherlands.

Parallel imports into affluent markets will force prices down as buyers simply go to the cheapest available source for their goods. If manufacturers leave it to market forces, prices may go down to the lowest level. For example, Portugal may influence prices in Germany through parallel imports. The parallel market in pharmaceuticals is worth $1 billion in the United Kingdom alone.

In order to avoid this, manufacturers must compromise now between the current policy of individually optimized prices and a uniform European price. Such a compromise will be possible because, even after the 1992 phenomenon and the introduction of the euro, Europe has not become a homogeneous market. Consumer habits will adjust gradually, allowing certain price differentials to be retained and defended.

Some experts recommend that manufacturers set up a European pricing corridor dropping high prices somewhat and raising low ones, creating a sustainable differential among markets in member states. The corridor would be much narrower for easily transportable items like photographic film than for heavy ones such as industrial machinery.

These changing market conditions imply a new focus on centralized price setting for Europe. The price corridor will be set by the head office, with local subsidiaries free to set prices within it. This approach runs contrary to the prevailing corporate culture, which is based on decentralization.

Manufacturers ought to consider pulling out of poorer markets where price hikes cannot be sustained. It is better to lose a small percentage of sales rather than see turnover, margins and profits plummet. So far, however, there appears to be little movement toward more centralized pricing. Some experts are concerned by the lack of urgency apparently felt by many European executives, who seem content to wait and see what happens.

Indeed, a number of European industrialists argue that large price differences can be maintained in Europe through product differentiation. Simpler products could be sold into less-prosperous markets, whereas more elaborate items might go to those markets that are able to afford them.

In at least one industry – pharmaceuticals – executives fear that neither pricing corridors nor product differences will prevent prices from falling to the lowest level. In markets such as France, Spain and Portugal, prices for drugs are already very low because of national reimbursement schemes.

'We are sandwiched between the European Commission, which is determined to eliminate all trade barriers at whatever cost, and some national governments that are keeping pharmaceutical products artificially low,' comments an executive at a major European drug maker. 'In practice, the Commission has absolutely no control over the prices set by national governments.' Pharmaceutical firms, which have heavy research and development costs, say they need high margins if they are to continue investing and competing with Japanese and US companies. However, if countries such as France, which accounts for a substantial part of the European drug market, continue to keep prices low, customers from other countries will simply buy their supplies in those markets. Manufacturers may well find themselves locked in an untenable position in an industry in which specifications are standardized, products cannot be differentiated, and suppliers cannot withdraw from the market for ethical reasons.

Studies have shown, however, that marketers can increase their profitability by coordinating their pricing, especially when conditions are unfavourable in terms of small markets and high levels of competition.

SOURCE: Mahmut Parlar and Kevien Weng, 'Coordinating Pricing and Production Decisions in the Presence of Price Competition', *European Journal of Operational Research* 170 (number 1, 2006): 211–236; 'Common Good', *The Economist – A Survey of European Business and the Euro,* December 1, 2001, 8–10; 'Cure-All Wanted', *The Economist – A Survey of European Business and the Euro,* December 1, 2001, 13–14; 'Car Prices in Britain Are Still the Highest in Europe', *Independent,* February 20, 2001, 11; Stephen A. Butscher, 'Maximizing Profits in Euroland', *Journal of Commerce,* May 5, 1999, 5; 'Pricing in Post 1992 EC: Expert Urges Fast Action to Protect Margins', *Business International,* August 24, 1992, 267; and **http://europa.eu.int/euro/quest**.

THE INTERNATIONAL **MARKETPLACE 17.4**

Countertrade and expansion of business opportunities

The Brazilian government has suggested a barter deal to South Korea's major shipbuilders and the state-run oil developer KNOC (Korea National Oil Corp).

The arrangement essentially has Korea, the world's largest shipbuilders, providing Brazil with drill ships or floating production, storage, and offloading platforms in return for stakes in its oil fields in the Santos area, which KNOC would manage.

The barter plan was proposed by the South American nation when the two countries held summit talks in Brazil this past November.

China has inked an agreement with ESolar Inc. of Pasadena (CA) to build a series of solar thermal power plants in China. It's one of the largest renewable energy plants of its kind, with a total capacity of 2,000 megawatts.

Under terms of the deal ESolar agreed to a countertrade, i.e. they will construct their power plant receivers in China, rather than in the US. However, ESolar will retain control of the intellectual property behind the technology's design and operation.

ESolar relies on a sophisticated software system and imaging technology to control 176,000 small mirrors that form arrays at its standard 46-megawatt power plant. The software positions the mirrors to create a virtual parabola to focus the sun on the receiver tower.

The mirrors' dimensions – each about the size of a television screen – allow ESolar to make and install them cheaply and use less land for the power plant.

International tourists are now counted each year in tens of millions, and tourism is today the largest single industry on earth. Huge investments have been made globally in hotels catering to foreign visitors. With the economic difficulties affecting these countries, the problem is how to fill hotel rooms to the point where these investments remain viable.

Many national tourism authorities are using countertrade to expand their business opportunities. For example:

- Canadian farmers supplying barley to a US customer were offered trips to Las Vegas in exchange.

- A chain of spa hotels has been constructed in Hungary by an Italian company with partial payment in vacations and holidays at the hotels.

- To pay for gas piped from Russia, Turkey has considered setting up tourist parks with hotel complexes in Yalta and Baku.

- Cuba has set up a tourist enterprise, Cubanacan SA, to develop organized tours, seaside vacations and congresses. The hard currency earnings will pay for the foreign expertise to increase hotel capacity and occupancy.

- Cuba also signed contracts with certain countries to construct eight hotels at Varadero, in exchange for sugar, tobacco and nickel.

- India has offered tourism packages on its list of exports available for countertrade deals.

- Egypt once paid for television receivers, supplied by a Japanese company, with tourism for Japanese nationals.

The major advantage of this form of countertrade is that it gives these countries the opportunity to sell their tourism in western countries where they do not possess effective marketing access.

SOURCE: *Barter News* (2009) 'Barter On The Big Stage – Ships For Oil'. **http://www.barternews.com/barter_on_the_big_stage_ships_for_oil.htm**; *Barter News* (2009) 'A Look At Countertrade In Tourism'. **http://www.barternews.com/a_look_at_countertrade_in_tourism.htm**; *Barter News* (2009) 'China Uses Countertrade In Solar Deal With U.S. Company'. **http://www.barternews.com/countertrade.htm**.

---

and Trade (GATT) claimed that countertrade accounts for around 5 per cent of the world trade.[48] The UK's Department of Trade and Industry has suggested 15 per cent, while numerous scholars believe it to be closer to 30 per cent, with east–west trade having been as high as 50 per cent in some trading sectors of Eastern European and Third World Countries.[49]

Why countertrade?

Many countries are deciding that countertrade transactions are more beneficial to them than transactions based on financial exchange alone. A primary reason is that world debt crises and exchange rate volatility have made ordinary trade financing very risky. Many in the developing world cannot obtain the trade credit or financial assistance necessary to afford desired imports. Heavily indebted nations, faced with the possibility of not being able to afford imports at all, resort to countertrade to maintain product inflow.

The use of countertrade permits the covert reduction of prices and therefore allows firms and governments to circumvent price and exchange controls. Particularly in commodity markets with operative cartel arrangements, such as oil or agriculture, this benefit may be very useful to a producer. For example, by using oil as a countertraded product for industrial equipment, a surreptitious discount (by using a higher price for the acquired products) may expand market share. In a similar fashion, the countertrading of products masks dumping activities.[50]

Countertrade is also often viewed by firms and nations alike as an excellent mechanism to gain entry into new markets. When a producer believes that marketing is not its strong suit, or that international competition is too strong, it often sees countertrade as useful. The producer often hopes that the party receiving the goods will serve as a new distributor, opening up new international marketing channels and ultimately expanding the original market. Conversely, markets with little cash can provide major opportunities for firms if they are willing to accept countertrade. A firm that welcomes countertrade welcomes new buyers and sets itself apart from the competition.

Countertrade also can provide stability for long-term sales. For example, if a firm is tied to a countertrade agreement, it will need to source the product from a particular supplier, whether or not it wants to do so. This stability is often highly valued because it eliminates, or at least reduces, vast swings in demand and thus allows for better planning.

Under certain conditions, countertrade can ensure the quality of an international transaction. In instances where the seller of technology is paid in output produced by the technology delivered, the seller's revenue depends on the success of the technology transfer and maintenance services in production. Therefore, the seller is more likely to be dedicated in the provision of services, maintenance and general technology transfer.[51] In such instances, the second part of the transaction serves as a 'hostage' that induces both trading partners to fulfil their contractual obligations. Particularly under conditions of limited legal protection, countertrade can be equated to an exchange of hostages that ensures that all parties involved live up to their agreement.[52]

In spite of all these apparent benefits of countertrade, there are strong economic arguments against this activity. These arguments are based mainly on efficiency grounds. As economist Paul Samuelson stated, 'Instead of there being a double coincidence of wants, there is likely to be a want of coincidence; so that, unless a hungry tailor happens to find an undraped farmer, who has both food and a desire for a pair of pants, neither can make a trade'.[53] Instead of trade balances being settled on a multilateral basis, with surpluses from one country being balanced by deficits with another, countertrade requires that accounts be settled on a country-by-country or even transaction-by-transaction basis. Trade then results only from the ability of two parties or countries to purchase specified goods from one another rather than from competition. As a result, uncompetitive goods may be marketed. In consequence, the ability of countries and their industries to adjust structurally to more efficient production may be restricted. Countertrade can therefore be seen as eroding the quality and efficiency of production and as lowering world consumption. These economic arguments notwithstanding, however, countries and companies see countertrade as an alternative that may be flawed but worthwhile to undertake. As far as the unilateral focus is concerned, it may well be that this restriction can be removed through electronic commerce. With growing ease of reach, it may well become possible to create an online global barter economy that addresses itself to those transactions that cannot be conducted on regular financial terms.

TYPES OF COUNTERTRADE

Under the traditional types of barter arrangements, goods are exchanged directly for other goods of approximately equal value. However, simple barter transactions are less often used today.

Increasingly, participants in countertrade have resorted to more sophisticated versions of exchanging goods that often also include some use of money. Exhibit 17.7 provides an overview of the different forms of countertrade that are in use today. One refinement of simple barter is the counterpurchase, or parallel barter, agreement. The participating parties sign two separate contracts that specify the goods and services to be exchanged. Frequently, the exchange is not of precisely equal value; therefore, some amount of cash will be involved. However, because an exchange of goods for goods does take place, the transaction can rightfully be called barter.

Another common form of countertrade is the buyback, or compensation, arrangement. One party agrees to supply technology or equipment that enables the other party to produce goods with which the price of the supplied products or technology is repaid. One example of such a buyback arrangement is an agreement entered into by Levi Strauss and Hungary. The company transferred the know-how and the Levi's trademark to Hungary. A Hungarian firm

EXHIBIT 17.7   Classification of forms of countertrade

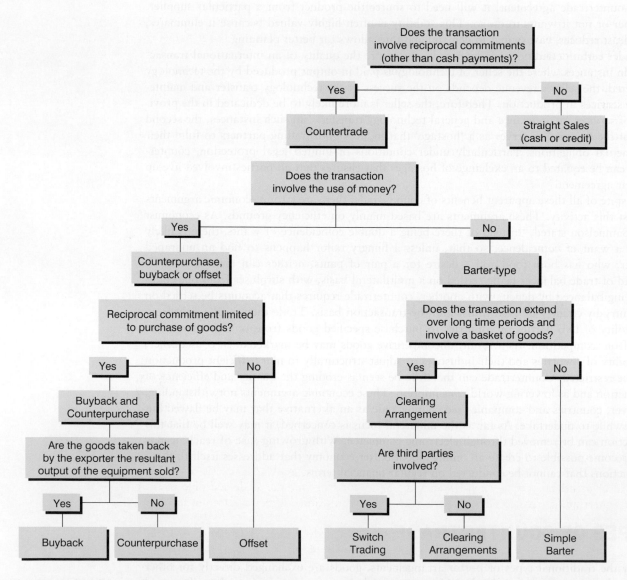

Source: Adapted from Jean-François Hennart, "Some Empirical Dimensions of Countertrade," *Journal of International Business Studies* 21 (no. 2, 1990): 245.

began producing Levi's products and marketing some of them domestically. The rest are marketed abroad by Levi Strauss, in compensation for the know-how.

A more refined form of barter, aimed at reducing the effect of the immediacy of the transaction, is called clearing arrangements. Here, clearing accounts are established in which firms can deposit and withdraw the results of their countertrade activities. These currencies merely represent purchasing power, however, and are not directly withdrawable in cash. As a result, each party can agree in a single contract to purchase goods or services of a specified value. Although the account may be out of balance on a transaction-by-transaction basis, the agreement stipulates that over the long term, a balance in the account will be restored. Frequently, the goods available for purchase with clearing account funds are tightly stipulated. In fact, funds have on occasion been labelled 'horseradish clearing funds'. Additional flexibility can be given to the clearing account by permitting switch-trading, in which credits in the account can be sold or transferred to a third party. Doing so can provide creative intermediaries with opportunities for deal making by identifying clearing account relationships with major imbalances and structuring business transactions to reduce them.

Another key form of barter arrangement is called offset, which is the industrial compensation mandated by governments when purchasing defence-related goods and services in order to offset or counterbalance the effect of this purchase on the balance of payments. Offsets can include co-production, licences production, subcontractor production, technology transfer, or overseas investment. Typically, in order to secure the sale of military equipment, the selling companies have to offset the cost of the arms through investment in non-related industries. The offsets frequently reach or exceed the price of the defence equipment, to the delight of the buyer, but often to the chagrin of the home country government of the selling firms. According to Andy Thomis, chief executive of Cohort plc, other countries actively conduct offsetting whereas the UK seems more reluctant. What the UK does in terms of offset, it does so with a lack of enthusiasm.

With the increasing sophistication of countertrade, the original form of straight barter is used less today. The most frequently completed forms of countertrade are counterpurchase, buyback agreements and, due to continued major military expenditures around the world, offsets.

PREPARING FOR COUNTERTRADE

Early on in the countertrade process a firm needs to decide whether it wishes to use an outside countertrade intermediary or keep the management of the transaction in-house. Assistance from intermediaries can be quite expensive but relieves the firm of the need to learn a new expertise. Exhibit 17.8 provides a summary of the advantages and disadvantages of carrying out countertrade transactions versus outsourcing them. If companies carry out countertrade transactions in-house, the profitability of countertrade can be high. However, developing an in-house capability for handling countertrade should be done with great caution.

First, the company needs to determine the import priorities of its products to the country or firm to which it is trying to sell. Goods that are highly desirable and necessary for a country mandating countertrade are less likely to be subject to countertrade requirements than imports of goods considered luxurious and unnecessary. As a next step, the company needs to incorporate possible countertrade cost into the pricing scheme. It is quite difficult to increase the price of goods once a 'cash-deal' price has been quoted and a subsequent countertrade demand is presented.

At this stage, the most favoured countertrade arrangement from the buyer's perspective should be identified. To do this, the company needs to determine the goals and objectives of the countertrading parties. These can consist of import substitution, preservation of hard currency or export promotion.

The next step is to match the strengths of the firm with current and potential countertrade situations. The company should explore whether any internal needs can fulfil a countertrade contract. This may mean that raw materials or intermediate products currently sourced from other suppliers could now be obtained from the countertrade partner. However, this assessment should not be restricted to the corporation itself. A firm may be able to use its

Organizing for
countertrade: In-house
versus third parties

Advantages	Disadvantages
In-House	
• More profitable	• Accounting and legal expertise required
• Customer contact	• Reselling problems
• Greater control	• Recruitment and training costs
• More flexibility	• Less objectivity
• More learning	• Unexpected risks and demands for countertrade
Third Parties	
• Export specialists	• May be expensive
• Customer contacts	• Distanced from customer
• Reselling contacts	• Less flexibility
• Legal and accounting expertise	• Less confidentiality
• More objectivity	• Less learning

SOURCE: Adapted from Charles W. Neale, David D. Shipley, and J. Colin Dodds, "The Countertrading Experience of British and Canadian Firms," *Management International Review* 31 (no. 1, 1991): 33.

distribution capabilities or its contacts with customers and suppliers to help with counter-trade transactions. Based on the notion that the supplier benefits from the export taking place due to the countertrade, main contractors may demand that major suppliers participate in disposing of the countertraded goods. As a result, even companies that do not see themselves as international marketers may suddenly be confronted with countertrade demands.

At this point, the company can decide whether it should engage in countertrade transactions. The accounting and taxation aspects of the countertrade transactions should be considered because they can often be quite different from current procedures. The use of an accounting or tax professional is essential to comply with difficult and obscure tax regulations.

Next, all of the risks involved in countertrade must be assessed. This means that the goods to be obtained need to be specified, the delivery time for these goods needs to be determined, and the reliability of the supplier and the quality and consistency of the goods need to be assessed. It is also useful to explore the impact of countertrade on future prices, both for the price of the specific goods obtained and for the world market price of the category of goods. For example, a countertrade transaction may appear to be quite profitable at the time of agreement. Months or even years may pass before the transaction is actually consummated, however, and world market prices can change. The effect of the countertrade transaction itself on market price should also be considered. Large-volume transactions may affect established prices. Such a situation not only may affect the profitability of a transaction but also can result in possible legal actions by other suppliers of similar products who feel injured.

When evaluating the countertraded products, it is useful to determine the impact of the countertraded products on the sales and profits of other complementary product lines currently marketed by the firm. Any repercussions from outside groups should also be investigated. Such repercussions may consist of antidumping actions brought about by competitors or reactions from totally unsuspected quarters.

Using all of the information obtained, the company can finally evaluate the length of the intended relationship with the countertrading partner and the importance of this relationship for future plans and goals. These parameters will be decisive for the final action because they may form constraints overriding short-term economic effects. Overall, management needs to remember that, in most instances, a countertrade transaction should remain a means for successful international marketing and not become an end in itself.

SUMMARY

I n a world of increasing competition, government regulation, accelerating inflation and widely fluctuating exchange rates, global marketers must spend increasing amounts of time planning pricing strategy. Since pricing is the only revenue-generating element of the marketing mix, its role in meeting corporate objectives is enhanced. However, it comes under increasing governmental scrutiny as well, as evidenced by intracompany transfer pricing.

The three philosophies of transfer pricing that have emerged over time are cost-based, market-based and arm's-length. Transfer pricing concerns are both internal and external to the company. Internally, manipulating transfer prices may complicate control procedures and documentation. Externally, problems arise from the tax and regulatory entities of the countries involved.

Pricing decisions are typically left to the local managers; however, planning assistance is provided by the parent company. Pricing in individual markets comes under the influence of environmental variables, each market with its own unique set. This set consists of corporate objectives, costs, customer behaviour and market conditions, market structure and environmental constraints.

Economic crises have hit many of the world's emerging markets in the last twelve years. In such a challenging environment, effective marketing planning and implementation take on additional significance. While withdrawal may be a feasible alternative, the consequences have to be assessed against the company's global operations. Marketers have found ways to grow market share even under such adverse circumstances.

The individual impact of these environmental variables and their interaction must be thoroughly understood by the global marketer, especially if regional or even worldwide, coordination is attempted. Control and coordination are becoming more important with increasing economic integration.

Corporations use countertrade as a competitive tool to maintain or increase market share. The complexity of these transactions requires careful planning in order to avoid major corporate losses. Management must consider how the acquired merchandise will be disposed of, what the potential for market disruptions is and to what extent the countertraded goods fit with the corporate mission.

Key terms

arm's-length price

barter

buyback

clearing arrangements

counterpurchase

countertrade

offset

price elasticity of consumer demand

switch-trading

Questions for discussion

1   Comment on the pricing philosophy, 'Sometimes price should be wrong by design'.

2   The standard worldwide base price is most likely looked on by management as full-cost pricing, including an allowance for manufacturing overhead, general overhead and selling expenses. What factors are overlooked?

3   In combating price controls, multinational corporations will deal with agency administrators rather than policymakers. How can they convince administrators that price relief is fair to the company and also in the best interest of the host country?

4   Which elements of pricing can be standardized?

5   Using the price differences presented in Exhibit 17.6 as a base, argue why such price differences will stay in place even with the euro.

6   Discuss the advantages and drawbacks of countertrade.

Internet exercises

1   The European Union promotes the benefits of the euro as a common currency for the 12 EU nations that have adopted it (see **http://europa.eu.int/comm/economy_finance/ euro/our_currency_en.htm**). What are possible disadvantages of it?

2   Compare the services of the Global Offset and Countertrade Organization (**http://www.countertrade.org**) and the Asia-Pacific Countertrade Association (**http://www.apca.net**).

Recommended readings

Brauer, Juergen. *Arms Trade and Economic Development: Theory and Policy in Offsets*. Oxford: Routledge, 2005.

Bureau of Industry and Security, U.S. Department of Commerce. *Offsets in Defense Trade, 10th Annual Report*. Washington DC: January 2006.

Carrero Caldreon, Jose Manuel (ed.) *Advance Pricing Agreements: A Global Analysis*. Cambridge, MA: Kluwer Law International, 1999.

Chabot, Christian N. *Understanding the Euro: The Clear and Concise Guide to the New Trans-European Currency*. New York: McGraw-Hill, 1998.

Dolan, Robert J. and Hermann Simon. *Power Pricing: How Managing Price Transforms the Bottom Line*. New York: Free Press, 1997.

Feinschreiber, Robert. *Transfer Pricing Handbook*. New York: John Wiley & Sons, 2002.

Levin, Jay. *A Guide to the Euro*. Boston: Houghton Mifflin, 2002.

Nagle, Thomas T. and Reed K. Holden. *The Strategy and Tactics of Pricing: A Guide to Growing More Profitably*. New York: Pearson, 2005.

Tang, Y.W. *Current Trends and Corporate Cases in Transfer Pricing*. Westport, CT: Quorum Books, 2002.

Zurawicki, Leon. *International Countertrade*. New York: Pergamon Press, 2003.

Notes

1   Shantanu Dutta, Mark Bergen, Daniel Levy, Mark Ritson and Mark Zbaracki, 'Pricing as a Strategic Capability', *Sloan Management Review* 43 (Spring 2002): 61–66; and Saeed Samiee, 'Elements of Marketing Strategy: A Comparative Study of U.S. and Non-U.S. Based Companies', *International Marketing Review* 1 (Summer 1982): 119–126.

2   Victor H. Miesel, Harlow H. Higinbotham and Chun W. Yi, 'International Transfer Pricing: Practical Solutions for Intercompany Pricing', *International Tax Journal* 28 (Fall 2002): 1–22.

3   Wagdy M. Abdallah, 'How to Motivate and Evaluate Managers with International Transfer Pricing Systems', *Management International Review* 29 (1989): 65–71.

4   Sherif Assef and Surjya Mitra, 'Making the Most of Transfer Pricing', *Insurance Executive*, Summer 1999, 2–4.

5   Ernst & Young, *Transfer Pricing 2005–2006 Global Surveys* (New York: Ernst & Young, November 2005), available at **http://www.ey.com**.

6   Robert Feinschreiber, *Transfer Pricing Handbook* (New York: John Wiley & Sons, 2002), chapter 2 'Practical Aspects of Transfer Pricing'.

7   Wagdy Abdallah, 'Global Transfer Pricing of Multinationals and E-Commerce in the 21st Century', *Multinational Business Review* 10 (Fall 2002): 62–71.

8   Erika Morphy, 'Spend and Tax Politics', *Export Today* 15 (April 1999): 50–56.

9   Michael P. Casey, 'International Transfer Pricing', *Management Accounting* 66 (October 1985): 31–35.

10   Robert B. Stack, Maria de Castello and Natan J. Leyva, 'Transfer Pricing in the United States and Latin America', *Tax Management International Journal* 31 (no. 1, 2002): 24–43.

11   Victor H. Miesel, Harlow H. Higinbotham and Chun W. Yi, 'International Transfer Pricing: Practical Solutions for Intercompany Pricing – Part II', *International Tax Journal* 29 (Winter 2003): 1–23.

12   Kent B. Monroe, *Pricing: Making Profitable Decisions* (New York: McGraw-Hill, 2003), 12.

13   Douglas W. Vorhies, Michael Harker and C. P. Rao, 'The Capabilities and Performance Advantages of Market-Driven Firms', *European Journal of Marketing* 33 (nos. 11/12, 1999): 1171–1202.

14   Saeed Samiee, 'Pricing in Marketing Strategies of U.S.- and Foreign-Based Companies', *Journal of Business Research* 15 (March 1987): 17–30.

15   For an example of pricing processes by multinational marketers, see John U. Farley, James M. Hulbert and David Weinstein, 'Price Setting and Volume Planning by Two European Industrial Companies: A Study and Comparison of Decision Processes', *Journal of Marketing* 44 (Winter 1980): 46–54.

16   'The China Price', *Business Week*, December 6, 2004, 102–112.

17 'Ford, GM Square Off over Daewoo Motor; The Question Is: Why?' *The Wall Street Journal*, February 14, 2000, A1, A13.

18 Jonathan Sprague, 'Haier Reaches Higher', *Fortune*, September 16, 2002, 43–46.

19 Mark Bernstein, 'Expanding Capacity While Facing Global Pricing Puts Cummins' Supply Chain to the Test', *World Trade*, February 2006, 34–36.

20 'The Price Is Wrong', *The Economist*, May 25, 2002, 59.

21 'Global Survey of Business Executives: Inflation and Pricing', *The McKinsey Quarterly*, February 20, 2006; available at **http://www.mckinseyquarterly.com.**

22 'Stuck!' *Business Week*, November 15, 1993, 146–155.

23 'Hyundai Gets Hot', *Business Week*, December 17, 2001, 84–86.

24 Richard Tomlinson, 'Who's Afraid of Wal-Mart?' *Fortune*, June 26, 2000, 58–62.

25 Akshay R. Rao, Mark E. Bergen and Scott Davis, 'How to Fight a Price War', *Harvard Business Review* 78 (March–April 2000): 107–116.

26 'Domestic Electronic Products Overtaking Foreign Goods', *Korea Times*, May 12, 1996, 8.

27 Louis Kraar, 'How to Sell to Cashless Buyers', *Fortune*, November 7, 1988, 147–154.

28 C. K. Prahalad and Stuart L. Hart, 'The Fortune at the Bottom of the Pyramid', *Strategy and Business* 7 (first quarter, 2002): 35–47.

29 'Wal-Mart Quits Retailers Group', *Advertising Age*, October 21, 2002, 16.

30 Wang Yuguan and Jiang Song, 'China: A Future Star for Foreign Pharma Companies', *Pharmaceutical Executive*, August 1999, 78–87.

31 Victor H. Frank, 'Living with Price Control Abroad', *Harvard Business Review* 63 (March–April 1984): 137–142.

32 Pam Woodall, 'Survey: East Asian Economies: Six Deadly Sins', *Economist*, March 7, 1998, S12–14.

33 'The Long Road Back: A Survey of Argentina', *The Economist*, June 5, 2004, 1–12.

34 The Indian Blogger (2009), 'Reasons for global recession: In plain simple English'. Online. Available from: **http://www.theindianblogger.com/problems/reasons-for-global-recession-in-plain-simple-english/** (Accessed 2/3/10).

35 *Ibid*.

36 Wikipedia, 'Global economic crises 2007–2009'. Online. Available from: **http://en.wikipedia.org/wiki/Financial_crisis_of_2007%E2%80%932010** (Accessed 2/3/10).

37 Wikipedia, 'Late-2000s recession'. Online. Available from: **http://en.wikipedia.org/wiki/Late-2000s_recession** (Accessed 2/3/10).

38 Swee Hon Ang, Siew Meng Long and Philip Kotler, 'The Asian Apocalypse: Crisis Marketing for Consumers and Businesses', *Long Range Planning* 33 (February 2000): 97–119.

39 'Asia's Sinking Middle Class', *Far Eastern Economic Review*, April 9, 1998, 12–13.

40 'Borders and Barriers', *The Economist – A Survey of European Business and the Euro*, December 1, 2001, 10–11.

41 'One Currency – But 15 Economies', *Business Week*, December 31, 2001, 59.

42 'Even After Shift to Euro, One Price Won't Fit All', *The Wall Street Journal Europe*, December 28, 1998, 1.

43 Stephen A. Butscher, 'Maximizing Profits in Euroland', *Journal of Commerce*, May 5, 1999, 5.

44 Johan Ahlberg, Nicklas Garemo and Tomas Nauclér, 'The Euro: How to Keep Your Prices Up and Your Competitors Down', *The McKinsey Quarterly* 35 (no. 2, 1999): 112–118.

45 Travis K. Taylor, 'Using Offsets in Procurement as an Economic Development Strategy', Working Paper for presentation at the International Conference on Defence Offsets and Economic Development, Alfred University, College of Business, September 2002.

46 'Current Activities of International Organizations in the Field of Barter and Barter-like Transactions', *Report of the Secretary General*, United Nations, General Assembly, 1984, 4.

47 Hew, David, 'What is Offset, Countertrade, and Structured Finance', Asia-Pacific Countertrade Association, 2004, **http://www.apca.net.**

48 Wikipedia (2009), 'Counter trade', Online. Available from: **http://en.wikipedia.org/wiki/Counter_trade** (Accessed 2/3/10).

49 Wikipedia (2009), 'Counter trade'. Online. Available from: **http://en.wikipedia.org/wiki/Counter_trade** (Accessed 2/3/10).

50 Dorothy A. Paun, Larry D. Compeau and Dhruv Grewal, 'A Model of the Influence of Marketing Objectives on Pricing Strategies in International Countertrade', *Journal of Public Policy and Marketing* 16 (no. 1, 1997): 69–82.

51 Rolf Mirus and Bernard Yeung, 'Why Countertrade? An Economic Perspective', *The International Trade Journal* 7 (no. 4, 1993): 409–433.

52 Chong Ju Choi, Soo Hee Lee and Jai Boem Kim, 'A Note on Countertrade: Contractual Uncertainty and Transaction Governance in Emerging Economies', *Journal of International Business Studies* 30 (no. 1, 1999): 189–202.

53 Paul Samuelson, Economics, 11th edn (New York: McGraw-Hill, 1980), 260.

CHAPTER 18
GLOBAL PROMOTIONAL STRATEGIES

THE INTERNATIONAL **MARKETPLACE 18.1**

Coca-Cola's sponsorship of 2010 FIFA World Cup in South Africa – A great opportunity to grow sales in Africa

The relationship between financial scope and sporting success is frequently the subject of debate in the media; the involvement of major investors in football clubs, the re-tendering of TV rights and the question as to what extent a gold medal in a fringe sport can be marketed, are all issues which are keenly discussed. The financial framework has long become a relevant aspect of sports coverage in terms of ensuring sporting competitiveness. The majority of the population recognizes the great importance of sponsors and partners for sport today. For example, over 90 per cent of the German population between 14 and 69 years of age regard sponsorship as important. In view of limited state funding, the vast majority assume that sports can only be successfully sponsored when companies also get involved. In this regard, sponsors are seen as sporting partners and their involvement is regarded as essential. Consequently, sponsorship activities are extremely well accepted.

'This year's FIFA World Cup Trophy Tour by Coca-Cola is bigger and better than ever before', Coca-Cola's head of worldwide sports and entertainment marketing, Emmanuel Seuge, said recently. 'The first Trophy Tour in 2006 was a huge success and we're delighted that we're going to give even more fans the chance to get close to the real trophy. We're especially looking forward to taking the trophy to every single country in Africa', added Seuge.

At a recent industry gathering, Ahmet C. Bozer, who is President of Coca-Cola's Eurasia and Africa region, believes that the FIFA World Cup in South Africa will be a great opportunity to grow the popularity of the company's brands locally.

Eurasia and Africa is a growth engine for Coca-Cola as the region accounts for approximately 15 per cent of Coca's unit case volume (3.5 billion unit cases in 90 countries and £550 million operating income).

Coca-Cola, which dominates the local markets for soda, water and juices, is expecting to strengthen again when the World Cup kicks off in June next year. The company's main soda products in Eurasia and Africa, for instance, have seen a 7 per cent growth each year for the past 3 years.

Bozer argues that the region has a high potential with 54 per cent of the world's teenagers and 47 per cent of the world's population all located there. Besides, the region is rich in terms of resources with 80 per cent of the world's oil and 70 per cent of the world's gas. In addition, the region has an impressive urbanization growth combined with an emerging middle class.

Overall soft drink per capita consumption in Eurasia and Africa is recorded at 27 ko, which is below the global average of 85 ko, said Bozer. However, some countries are above that average, including South Africa. But there is a lot of potential for per capita development in Eurasia and Africa markets. He expects the World Cup will play a vital role in industry volume growth for soft drinks. For the region, he expects that by 2020 it will double, spurred by the growth of soda drinks.

Scheduling a World Cup to suit broadcasters in all key markets is impossible. While the matches will kick off at an ideal time for the European market, the lucrative emerging markets in Asia will get night-time games and, consequently, brands targeting the latter region may find it harder to reach their objectives. When the 2002 World Cup was hosted by South Korea and Japan, cumulative TV viewing figures in Asia reached 11.1bn. Four years ago, when Germany staged the tournament, the figure dipped by nearly 2bn.

However, brands with a focus on Africa are set to prosper. For years, Puma has used its sponsorship of the Cameroon team, and star player Samuel Eto'o, to spearhead its marketing, and, although not an official sponsor, has pinpointed the first World Cup on the African continent as a key event. The brand has sold products in South Africa for nearly 30 years and, while Africa accounts for only a fraction of its revenues, it aims to boost sales dramatically during and after the tournament. If qualification goes as expected, Puma could also gain exposure via Africa's other leading teams, including Ghana, Ivory Coast, Senegal, Tunisia and Egypt.

The first World Cup in Africa is a step into the unknown for FIFA, but all the indicators suggest South Africa 2010 will prove to be a carnival for fans and sponsors alike. The success of the event will also be an indication of the importance of players in sponsorship like Coca-Cola. Coca-Cola has been involved in sports sponsorship since the 1928 Olympics but has had a formal association with FIFA since 1974 and an official sponsorship of FIFA World Cup that began in 1978. Coca-Cola has had stadium advertising at every FIFA World Cup since 1950.

SOURCE: Crammer, C. (2009) 'The Social Context of Sponsorship'. Online. Available from: **http://www.sportfive.com/index.php?id=630** (Accessed 15/03/10); FLEXNEWS (2009) 'Coca-Cola's Sponsorship of 2010 FIFA World Cup in South Africa – A Great Opportunity to Grow Sales in Africa'. Online. Available from: **http://www.flex-news-food.com/pages/26096/Coca/coca-colas-sponsorship-2010-fifa-world-cup-south-africa—great-opportunity-grow-sales-africa.html** (Accessed 15/03/10); Kemp, E. (2009) 'Coca-Cola, Sony Ericsson and other sponsors prepare for FIFA 2010 World Cup in Africa'.

Online. Available from: **http://www.marketingmagazine.co.uk/news/911702/Coca-Cola-Sony-Ericsson-sponsors-prepare-FIFA-2010-World-Cup-Africa/** (Accessed 15/03/10).

The general requirements of effective marketing communications apply to the global marketer as well; however, the environments and the situations usually are more numerous and call for coordination of the promotional effort. Increasingly, marketers opt for varying degrees of pan-regional and integrative approaches to take advantage of similarities in markets they serve, as seen in *The International Marketplace 18.1*. All possible points of touch that the customer has with the marketer's brands have to be incorporated into the communications plan.

The technology is in place for global communication efforts, but difficult challenges still remain in the form of cultural, economic, ethnic, regulatory and demographic differences in the various countries and regions. Standardization of any magnitude requires sound management systems and excellent communication to ensure uniform strategic and tactical thinking of all the professionals in the overseas marketing chain.[1] One marketer has suggested the development of a worldwide visual language that would be understandable and that would not offend cultural sensitivities.

This chapter will analyze the elements to be managed in promotional efforts in terms of environmental opportunities and constraints. A framework is provided for the planning of promotional campaigns. Although the discussion focuses mostly on advertising, other elements of the promotion mix, especially sales promotion and publicity, fit integrally into the planning model. Naturally, all of the mass selling methods have to be planned in conjunction with personal selling efforts. For example, personal selling often relies on updated direct e-mailing lists and promotional materials sent to prospects before the first sales call.

PLANNING PROMOTIONAL CAMPAIGNS

The planning for promotional campaigns consists of the following seven stages, which usually overlap or take place concurrently, especially after the basics of the campaign have been agreed on:

1 Determine the target audience.

2 Determine specific campaign objectives.

3 Determine the budget.

4 Determine media strategy.

5 Determine the message.

6 Determine the campaign approach.

7 Determine campaign effectiveness.[2]

The actual content of these stages will change by type of campaign situation; compare, for example, a local campaign for which headquarters provides support versus a global corporate image campaign.

The target audience

Global marketers face multiple audiences beyond customers. The expectations of these audiences have to be researched to ensure the appropriateness of campaign decision making. Consider the following publics with whom communication is necessary: suppliers, intermediaries, government, the local community, bankers and creditors, media organizations, shareholders and employees. Each can be reached with an appropriate mix of tools. A multinational corporation that wants to boost its image with the government and the local community may sponsor events. One of the approaches available is cause-related marketing, in which the company, or one of its brands, is linked with a cause such as environmental protection or children's health. For example, Unilever's Funfit Programme for its Persil washing powder brand in Europe creates resource packs for teachers to help boost children's fitness through physical education lessons. Microsoft launched a website in Singapore to further the use of information technology. For every page hit within the site, Microsoft donated one cent to three local charities. This type of activity can benefit a brand but must be backed by a genuine effort within the company to behave responsibly.[3]

Some campaigns may be targeted at multiple audiences. For example, British Airways' 'Manhattan Landing' campaign (in which Manhattan Island takes to the air and lands in London) was directed not only at international business travellers but also at employees, the travel industry and potential stockholders (the campaign coincided with the privatization of the airline). Once the repositioning was achieved, the airline focused on establishing its global stature with the 'Face' campaign and switched later to service enhancements with 'Sweet Dreams'.[4] As companies such as airlines become more internationally involved, target audience characteristics change. Today, American Airlines, which enjoys a huge domestic market, services 40 countries (130 with its alliance partners), generating a third of passenger miles compared with virtually none in 1980.[5]

An important aspect of research is to determine multimarket target audience similarities. If such exist, pan-regional or global campaigns can be attempted. Grey Advertising checks for commonalities in variables such as economic expectations, demographics, income and education. Consumer needs and wants are assessed for common features. An increasing number of companies are engaging in corporate image advertising in support of their more traditional tactical product-specific and local advertising efforts.[6] Especially for multidivisional companies, an umbrella campaign may help either to boost the image of lesser-known product lines or make the company itself be understood correctly or perceived more positively. Companies may announce repositioning strategies through image campaigns to both external and internal constituents. GE's campaign, branded Ecomagination, is a company-wide initiative to push environmentally-friendly products (as shown in Exhibit 18.1). The plan is to double company revenues from eco-safe products to $20 billion by 2010. To go beyond the campaign, each of GE's 11 business units are to come up with at least five big environmental ideas capable of generating $100 million of revenue within the next three to five years.[7] Canon has used the approach to reposition itself as an information technology specialist instead of just a manufacturer of office automation machines, and as a serious contender to Xerox in the high end of the market.[8] Costs may also be saved in engaging in global image campaigning, especially if the same campaign or core concepts can be used across borders.

EXHIBIT 18.1   An example of a corporate image campaign

Our latest cleaner coal technology will markedly reduce emissions compared to traditional coal plants while taking advantage of a plentiful, domestic fossil fuel. Which means cleaner air for everyone to breathe. Who would have thought coal could be so beautiful?

imagination at work

Source: General Electric. see also **http://www.ge.com/ecomagination**.

In some cases the product may be standard across markets but the product's positioning, and subsequently marketing communication, has to change. For example, Mars is a meal substitute in Britain but an energizer in continental Europe. The Ford Fiesta is a small car for the German market, but a family car in Portugal.[9] Audience similarities are more easily found in business markets.

Campaign objectives

Nothing is more essential to the planning of international promotional campaigns than the establishment of clearly defined, measurable objectives. These objectives can be divided into overall global and regional objectives as well as local objectives. The objectives that are set at the local level are more specific and set measurable targets for individual markets. These objectives may be product- or service-related or related to the entity itself. Typical goals are to increase awareness, enhance image and improve market share in a particular market. Whatever the objective, it has to be measurable for control purposes.

While Tradeteam (United Kingdom) was awarded the European Transport Company of the Year 2010 in Brussels on February 11,[10] an award of the UK's top favourite transport company in the same month went to EFM.[11] Tradeteam currently operates the AURORA OMS. This system can be modified to run alongside a customer's existing technology. AURORA provides full visibility of orders and delivery. More importantly perhaps, it provides a valuable tool in the assessment of the profit and sales performance of every outlet.[12]

Local objectives are typically developed as a combination of headquarters (global or regional) and country organization involvement. Basic guidelines are initiated by headquarters, whereas local organizations set the actual country-specific goals. These goals are subject to headquarters approval, mainly to ensure consistency. Although some campaigns, especially global ones, may have more headquarters' involvement than usual, local input is still quite important, especially to ensure appropriate implementation of the subsequent programmes at the local level.

The budget

The promotional budget links established objectives with media, message and control decisions. Ideally, the budget would be set as a response to the objectives to be met, but resource constraints often preclude this approach. Many marketers use an objective task method but realities may force compromises between ideal choices and resources available.[13] As a matter of fact, available funds may dictate the basis from which the objective task method can start. Furthermore, advertising budgets should be set on a market-by-market basis because of competitive differences across markets. When it comes to global image campaigns, for example, headquarters should provide country organizations with extra funds for their implementation.

Budgets can also be used as a control mechanism if headquarters retains final budget approval. In these cases, headquarters decision makers must have a clear understanding of cost and market differences to be able to make rational decisions.

In terms of worldwide top ad spending, Exhibit 18.2 shows that although the US is the biggest adspender (£11,677 million), its growth was lower than that of Russia or Brazil (92 per cent and 80 per cent respectively). The figures also show that Japan has the lowest adspend growth of 6 per cent. On the whole, there was a decrease in ad spending in 2009 although the spend increased from 2010.[14]

Media strategy

Target audience characteristics, campaign objectives and the budget form the basis for the choice between media vehicles and the development of a media schedule. The major factors determining the choice of the media vehicles to be used are (1) the availability of the media in a given market; (2) the product or service itself; and (3) media habits of the intended audience.

Media availability Media spending varies dramatically around the world, as seen in Exhibit 18.3. In absolute terms, the United States spends more money on advertising than most of the

EXHIBIT 18.2

Top ten contributors to global ad spend growth between 2007 and 2010

Country	Growth (£ million)	Growth (%)
USA	11,677	9.9
China	6,716	63.5
Russia	5,439	92.1
Brazil	5,089	79.6
UK	3,827	22.8
India	2,283	52.2
Japan	1,526	5.7
South Korea	1,418	21.6
South Africa	1,364	47.7
Philippines	1,340	56.6

Source: http://www.marketingcharts.com/television/ad-spend-forecast-as-west-slows-down-developing-markets-to-propel-growth-5107/zenithoptimedia-top-10-contributing-countries-regions-to-ad-spend-growth-2007-2010-june-2008jpg/

other major advertising nations combined. Other major spenders are China, Russia, Brazil and the United Kingdom.

The economic decline has affected most parts of the world, but some have been hit harder than others. One region that seems to be holding its own is Asia Pacific (APAC). Although consumer confidence in APAC has declined in recent months, those declines have generally not been as steep as in Europe or North America. Main media, defined by Nielsen as free to air TV, newspapers and magazines, increased 13 per cent in 2008, while all other media (radio, outdoor, pay TV, cinema and other) posted an 8 per cent increase for the year.[15]

In 2008, three markets recorded declines in ad spend versus 2007. These were Taiwan (−11 per cent), South Korea (−8 per cent) and Thailand (−4 per cent). In contrast, five countries showed solid double-digit growth. These were India (29 per cent), Indonesia (19 per cent), China (17 per cent), Malaysia (12 per cent) and Philippines (11 per cent).[16]

The media available to the international marketer in major ad markets are summarized in Exhibit 18.4. Cinema advertising is important in countries such as India and Nigeria. Until a few years ago, the prevailing advertising technique used by the Chinese consisted of outdoor

EXHIBIT 18.3

Worldwide advertising spend forecasts (global advertising recession 2009, minor recovery in 2010–11, 2007–11)

	Year-on-year change (%)				
	2007	2008	2009	2010	2011
Worldwide	**6.8**	**1.3**	**−8.5**	**1.6**	**4.3**
North America	2.7	−3.7	−10.3	−2.4	1.5
Western Europe	6.0	−1.1	−9.2	0.2	2.6
Asia Pacific	6.5	3.2	−5.0	4.7	6.3
Central & Eastern Europe	23.9	12.5	−15.3	3.4	9.8
Latin America	16.3	14.5	0.2	7.5	7.9
Africa/Middle East/Row	24.8	22.4	−9.3	16.0	10.6

Note: Interpretation: Percentage change is comparison of stated year and previous year, spend covers major media (newspapers, magazines, television, radio, cinema, outdoor, internet).

Source: ZenithOptimedia (July 2009). **http//:www.DigitalStrategyConsulting.com**.

boards and posters found outside factories today. The internet is well on the way to establishing itself as a complementary advertising medium worldwide and will constitute 15 per cent of total global advertising growth by 2011. Internet advertising constitutes 9 per cent of advertising in Sweden and is expected to increase to 12 per cent. China accounts for half of the Asia-Pacific region's internet advertising, the internet usage will constitute 77 per cent of its projected growth and its expenditure on advertising will continue to grow as highlighted in Exhibit 18.5. In addition to PCs, mobile phones and interactive TV will become delivery mechanisms.

The breakdown by media in Exhibit 18.4 points to the enormous diversity in how media are used in a given market. These figures do not tell the whole story, however, which emphasizes the need for careful homework on the part of the international manager charged with media strategy. As an example, Brazil has five television networks, but one of them – TV Globo – corners 50 per cent of all television advertising spending. Throughout Latin America, the tendency is to allocate half or more of total advertising budgets to television, with the most coveted spots on prime-time soap operas that attract viewers from Mexico to Brazil. In general, advertising in Latin America requires flexibility and creativity. Inflation rates have caused advertising rates to increase dramatically in countries like Argentina. In Mexico, advertisers can use the 'French Plan', which protects participating advertisers from price increases during the year and additionally gives the advertiser two spots for the price of one. For these concessions, the advertiser must pay for the year's entire advertising schedule by October of the year before.

The major problems affecting global promotional efforts involve conflicting national regulations. Even within the EU there is no uniform legal standard. Conditions do vary from country to country, and ads must comply with national regulation. Most European countries either observe the Code of Advertising Practice of the International Chamber of Commerce or have their guidelines based on it.[17] Some of the regulations include limits on the amount of time available for advertisements; for example, in Italy, the state channels allow a maximum of 12 per cent advertising per hour and 4 per cent per week, and commercial stations allow 18 per cent per hour and 15 per cent per week. Furthermore, the leading Italian stations do not guarantee audience delivery when spots are bought. Strict separation between programmes and commercials is almost a universal requirement, preventing a sponsored programme style, as in some countries. Restrictions on items such as comparative claims and gender stereotypes are prevalent; for example, Germany prohibits the use of superlatives such as 'best'.

Until now, with few exceptions, most nations have been very successful in controlling advertising that enters their borders. When commercials were not allowed on the state-run

---

EXHIBIT 18.4

Advertising share by medium: Worldwide (internet ad expenditure set to overtake magazine spend in 2009, 2007–11)

| | Advertising spend share (%) | | | | |
	2007	2008	2009	2010	2011
Television	37.3	38.0	38.6	39.3	39.2
Newspapers	26.9	25.1	23.4	22.2	21.2
Internet	**8.7**	**10.5**	**12.6**	**13.8**	**15.1**
Magazines	12.2	11.6	10.5	9.9	9.7
Radio	8.0	7.7	7.6	7.4	7.2
Outdoor	6.5	6.7	6.8	6.9	7.0
Cinema	0.5	0.5	0.5	0.5	0.6

Note: Interpretation: Not all countries itemize spend by media channel, so are not included.

Source: ZenithOptimedia: **http://www.zenithoptimedia.com**, 16/3/10; **http://www.DigitalStrategy Consulting.com**

stations, advertisers in Belgium had been accustomed to placing their ads on the Luxembourg station. Radio Luxembourg has traditionally been used to beam messages to the United Kingdom. Currently, however, approximately half of the homes in Europe have access to additional television broadcasts through either cable or direct satellite, and television will no longer be restricted by national boundaries. The implications of this to global marketers are significant. The viewer's choice will be expanded, leading to competition among government-run public channels, competing state channels from neighbouring countries, private channels, and pan-European channels.[18] This means that marketers need to make sure that advertising works not only within markets but across countries as well. As a consequence, media buying will become more challenging.

Product influences Marketers and advertising agencies are currently frustrated by wildly differing restrictions on how products can be advertised. Agencies often have to produce several separate versions to comply with various national regulations. Consumer protection in general has dominated the regulatory scene both in the European Union and the United States.[19] Changing and standardizing these regulations, even in an area like the EU, is a long and difficult process. While some countries have banned tobacco advertising altogether (e.g., France), some have voluntary restriction systems in place. For example, in the United Kingdom, tobacco advertising is not allowed in magazines aimed at very young women, but it is permitted in other women's magazines. Starting in 2003, tobacco companies were required to print vivid pictures of lung cancer victims and diseased organs on cigarette packets sold in the United Kingdom. The EU has developed union-wide regulation and has banned all forms of cross-border tobacco advertising from 2005. This means no tobacco advertising in print, as well as on radio, the internet and Formula One racing. Existing regulations ban TV advertising. Tobacco marketers would be allowed to advertise on cinema, poster and billboard sites, but can still be banned by national laws.[20] A summary of product-related regulations found in selected European countries is provided in Exhibit 18.5. Tobacco products, alcoholic beverages and pharmaceuticals are the most heavily regulated products in terms of promotion.

However, the manufacturers of these products have not abandoned their promotional efforts. Altria Group (formerly Philip Morris) engages in corporate image advertising using its cowboy spokesperson. Some European cigarette manufacturers have diversified into the entertainment business (restaurants, lounges, cinemas) and named them after their cigarette brands. AstraZeneca, a leading global pharmaceutical, funded a TV campaign run by the French Migraine Association, which discussed medical advances but made no mention of the

EXHIBIT 18.5

Advertising spend forecasts: Only internet grows (advertising forecasts show only internet advertising continues growing, 2007–11)

	Spend ($m)				
	2007	*2008*	*2009*	*2010*	*2011*
All media	**486,532**	**492,067**	**450,110**	**457,192**	**467,733**
Television	181,322	186,822	173,625	179,508	186,929
Newspapers	130,744	123,748	105,533	101,499	101,019
Internet	**42,281**	**51,601**	**56,797**	**63,124**	**72,085**
Magazines	59,475	56,886	47,373	45,490	46,161
Radio	38,697	37,853	34,036	33,676	34,515
Outdoor	31,730	32,764	30,469	31,568	33,384
Cinema	2,283	2,394	2,278	2,427	2,641

Note: Interpretation: Not all countries itemize spend by media channel, so are not included.

Source: http://www.netimperative.com/news/2009/august/worldwide-advertising-spend-forecasts; http://www.DigitalStrategyConsulting.com

company. Novo Nordisk has set up an internet page on diabetes separate from its home page and established the World Diabetes Foundation awareness group.[21]

Certain products are subject to special rules. In the United Kingdom, for example, advertisers cannot show a real person applying an underarm deodorant; the way around this problem is to show an animated person applying the product. What is and is not allowable is very much a reflection of the country imposing the rules. Explicit advertisements of contraceptives are commonplace in Sweden, for example, but far less frequent in most parts of the world. A number of countries have varying restrictions on advertising of toys; Greece bans them altogether, and Belgium restricts their use before and after children's programming.

Beyond the traditional media, the international marketer may also consider **product placement** in films, TV shows, games, or websites. Although there is disagreement about the effectiveness of the method beyond creating brand awareness,[22] products from makers such as BMW, Omega, Nokia and Heineken have been placed in films to help both parties to the deal: to create a brand definition for the product and a dimension of reality for the film. The estimated size of the product-placement market is driven partly by the success of reality television and by a more empowered consumer who can skip traditional ads with the touch of a button.[23]. In China, for example, most commercials on Chinese state-run television are played back-to-back in ten-minute segments, making it difficult for any 30-second ad to be singled out. Placing products in soap operas, such as 'Love Talks', has been found to be an effective way to get to the burgeoning middle class in the world's most populous country.[24] Some marketers have started to create stand-alone entertainment vehicles around a brand, such as the BMW film series on the internet.[25] Calls have been made to ban product placements, or at the very least clearly disclose them in credits. The European Commission will allow product placement in fiction (not in news or factual material), and requires clear labelling.[26]

Audience characteristics

A major objective of media strategy is to reach the intended target audience with a minimum of waste. As an example, Amoco Oil Company wanted to launch a corporate image campaign in China in the hope of receiving drilling contracts. Identifying the appropriate decision makers was not difficult because they all work for the government. The selection of appropriate media proved to be equally simple because most of the decision makers overseeing petroleum exploration were found to read the vertical trade publications: *International Industrial Review, Petroleum Production,* and *Offshore Petroleum.*

If conditions are ideal, and they seldom are in international markets, the media strategist would need data on (1) media distribution, that is, the number of copies of the print medium or the number of sets for broadcast; (2) media audiences; and (3) advertising exposure. For instance, an advertiser interested in using television in Brazil would like to know that the top adult TV programme is 'O Clone', with an average audience share of 48 per cent and a 30-second ad rate of $71,000. In markets where more sophisticated market research services are available, data on advertising perception and consumer response may be available. In many cases, advertisers have found circulation figures to be unreliable or even fabricated.

Global media

Media vehicles that have target audiences on at least three continents and for which the media buying takes place through a centralized office are considered to be **global media**.[27] Global media have traditionally been publications that, in addition to the worldwide edition, have provided advertisers the option of using regional editions. For example, *Time Europe* covers the Middle East, Africa and, since 2003, Latin America. An Asian edition (*Time Asia*) is based in Hong Kong and a Canadian edition (*Time Canada*) is based in Toronto. The South Pacific edition, covering Australia, New Zealand and the Pacific Islands, is based in Sydney. Different editions enable advertisers to reach a particular country, continent, or the world. In print media, global vehicles include dailies such as *International Herald Tribune,* weeklies such as *The Economist,* and monthlies such as *National Geographic.* Included on the broadcast side are BBC Worldwide TV, CNN, the Discovery Channel and MTV. The

Discovery Channel reaches more than 600 million subscribers in 160 countries in 35 languages through Discovery Channel–Europe, Discovery Channel–Latin America/Iberia, Discovery Channel–Asia, Discovery Canada, Discovery New Zealand and several other language-tailored networks. The argument that global media drown out local content is not borne out in fact.[28] MTV as a global medium is profiled in *The International Marketplace 18.2*, and shows that one country's MTV looks very little like another's. While Italy, for example, is stylish and features food shows, Japan is very techie featuring a lot of wireless products.

Advertising in global media is dominated by major consumer ad categories, particularly airlines, financial services, telecommunications, automobiles and tobacco. The aircraft industry represents business market advertisers. In choosing global media, media buyers consider the three most important media characteristics: targetability, client-compatible editorial and editorial quality.[30] Some global publications have found that some parts of the globe are more appealing to advertisers than others; for example, some publications have eliminated editions in Africa (due to lack of advertising) and in Asia and Latin America (due to financial crises).

In broadcast media, pan-regional radio stations have been joined by television as a result of satellite technology. The pan-European satellite channels, such as Sky Channel and Super Channel, were conceived from the very beginning as advertising media. Many are sceptical about the potential of these channels, especially in the short term, because of the challenges of developing a cross-cultural following in Europe's still highly nationalistic markets.[31] Pan-European channels have had to cut back, whereas native language satellite channels like Tele 5 in France and RTL Plus in Germany have increased their viewership. The launch of STAR TV (see Exhibit 18.6) has increased the use of regional advertising campaigns in Asia. While this medium is still regarded as a corporate advertising vehicle, it has nonetheless attracted the interest of consumer goods manufacturers as well.[32] The alternative showing the most immediate promise is cable channels that cater to universal segments with converging tastes, such as MTV, Animal Planet or the Cartoon Network, all of which feature both local content and localized versions of foreign content.

The internet provides the international marketer with a global medium. One simple way of getting started is to choose a few key languages for the website. For example, Gillette decided to add German and Japanese to its Mach3 website after studying the number of internet users in those countries.[33] If the marketer elects to have a global site and region-specific sites (e.g., organized by country), they all should have a similar look, especially in terms of the level of sophistication. Another method is to join forces with internet service providers. Samsung has gained more global brand value than any other brand ranked over the last five years. A big contributor has been Samsung's bold internet-marketing strategy, which had the company enter into long-term contracts with 425 high-traffic websites (such as *PC Magazine*), negotiating for top banner position (as shown in Exhibit 18.7). Samsung now has right of first refusal for the position in perpetuity, and delivers a lower-cost internet buy than its competitors in the consumer-electronics sector.[34]

The promotional message

The creative people must have a clear idea of the characteristics of the audience expected to be exposed to the message. In this sense, the principles of creating effective advertising are the same as in the domestic marketplace. The marketer must determine what the consumer is really buying – that is, the customer's motivations. These will vary, depending on the following:

1   The diffusion of the product or service into the market. For example, to penetrate Third World markets with business computers is difficult when few potential customers know how to type, or with internet advertising when the infrastructure is lacking.

2   The criteria on which the customer will evaluate the product. For example, in traditional societies, advertising the time-saving qualities of a product may not be the best approach, as Campbell Soup Company learned in Italy, Brazil and Poland, where women felt inadequate as homemakers if they did not make soups from scratch.

THE INTERNATIONAL **MARKETPLACE 18.2**

The world wants its MTV!

MTV has emerged as a significant global medium, with more than 627 million[29] households in 167 countries subscribing to its services. The reason for its success is simple – MTV offers consistent, high-quality programming that reflects the tastes and lifestyle of young people.

Its balance of fashion, film, news, competitions and comedy wrapped in the best music and strong visual identity has made it 'the best bet to succeed as a pan-European thematic channel, with its aim to be in every household in Europe', according to *Music Week,* Britain's leading music trade paper. Given that 79 per cent of the channel's viewers are in the elusive 16–34 age group, MTV is a force as an advertising medium for those who want to closely target their campaigns. MTV has proven to be the ultimate youth marketing vehicle for companies such as Wrangler, Wrigleys, Braun, Britvic, Levi Strauss, Pepsi, Pentax and many others. Although many knockoffs have been started around the world, the enormous cost of building a worldwide music video channel will most likely protect MTV.

MTV's best response to threats from competition has been to make programming as local as possible. Its policy of 70 per cent local content has resulted in some of the network's more creative shows, such as Brazil's month-long Rockgol which pitted musicians against record industry executives and Russia's Twelve Angry Viewers, a talk show focused on the latest videos.

Digital compression allows the number of services offered on a satellite feed to be multiplied. The network will use the new capacity to complement pan-regional programming and playlists, customizing them to local tastes in key areas. For example, MTV Asia has launched MTV India to have five hours of India-specific programming during the 24-hour satellite feed to the subcontinent.

Owned by CBS Corporation, MTV's global network consists of the following entities:

- **MTV Europe** reaches 43 territories (124 million households), 24 hours a day in stereo, via satellite, cable and terrestrial distribution. The station acquires its own video clips, drawing from the domestic markets in individual European countries to discover bands making an international sound. It has its own team of VJs presenting shows specially tailored for the European market. The channel's programming mix reflects its diverse audience, with coverage of music, style, news, movie information, comedy, and more. MTV Europe has five local programming feeds and five local advertising windows – UK/ Ireland; MTV Central: (Austria, Germany and Switzerland); MTV European (76 territories, including France and Israel); MTV Southern (Italy); and MTV Nordic (Sweden, Norway and others). It was launched on August 1, 1987.

- **MTV USA** is seen 24 hours a day on cable television in over 85 million US television homes. Presented in stereo, MTV's

overall on-air environment is unpredictable and irreverent, reflecting the cutting-edge spirit of rock 'n' roll that is the heart of its programming. Through its graphic look, VJs, music news, promotions, interviews, concert tour information, specials and documentaries, as well as its original strip programming, MTV has become an international institution of pop culture and the leading authority on rock music since it launched on August 1, 1981.

- **MTV Asia** was launched on September 15, 1991. MTV Asia reaches over 138 million households in 21 territories. Programming is tailored to the musical tastes, lifestyles and sensibilities of Asian audiences in three regions: MTV Mandarin, MTV South East Asia and MTV India. Although MTV Japan was originally launched in October 1984 under a licencing agreement, it was reintroduced in 2001 as a wholly-owned entity of MTV Networks International. The 24-hour music television channel and website feature original Japanese-language programming and reach 2.8 million households.

- **MTV Latin America** reaches 28 million households in 21 countries and territories. The network features a mix of US and Latin music, regional production, music and entertainment news, artist interviews, concert coverage and specials.

- **MTV Brazil** was launched in 1990 and is a joint venture of MTVNetworks and Abril S.A., Brazil's leading magazine publisher. The Portuguese-language network, viewed in 16 million households, is broadcast via UHF in São Paulo and via VHF in Rio de Janeiro.

- **MTV Russia,** launched in September 1998, is a free over-the-air service reaching more than 20 million homes in major cities. The entity was established with BIZ Enterprises in a multiyear licencing agreement. In 2000, MTV Networks International gained an equity position in MTV Russia. Programming includes music videos from Russian and international artists, as well as coverage of social issues relevant to Russian youth.

SOURCES: 'MTV's Passage to India', *Fortune,* August 9, 2004, 116–125; Claudia Penteado, 'MTV Breaks New Ground', *Advertising Age Global,* March 2002, 8; 'MTV's World', *Business Week,* February 18, 2002, 81–84; 'MTV Asia's Hit Man', *Advertising Age Global,* December 2001, 10; 'Focus: Trends in TV', *Advertising Age International,* January 11, 1999, 33; 'MTV Fights Back from Nadir to Hit High Notes in India', *Advertising Age International,* March 30, 1998, 10; 'High Tech helps MTV Evolve', *World Trade,* June 1996, 10; 'Will MTV Have to Share the Stage?' *Business Week,* February 21, 1994, 38; and **http://www.mtv.com.**

EXHIBIT 18.6 Example of a pan-regional medium

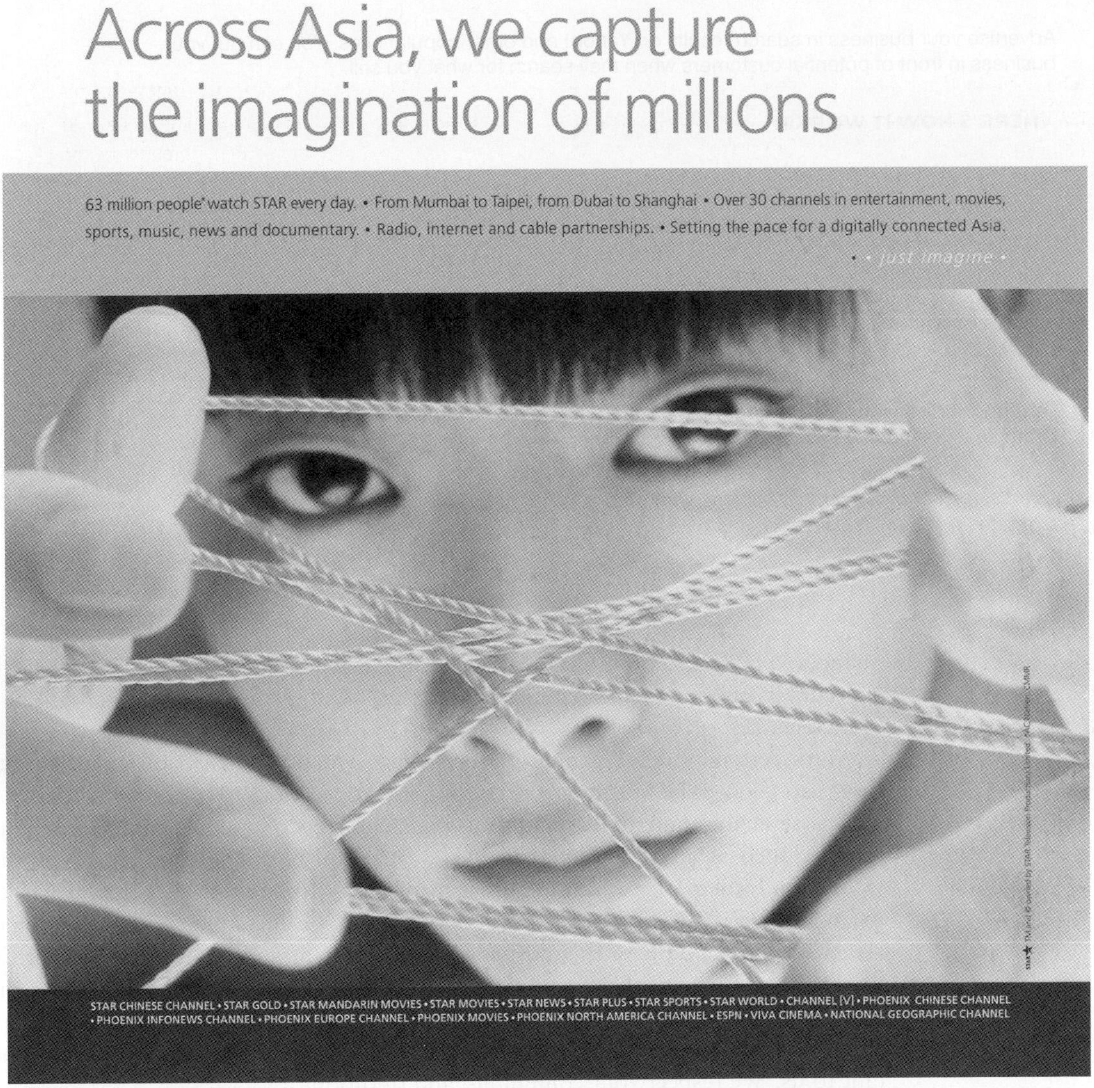
Across Asia, we capture the imagination of millions
63 million people* watch STAR every day. • From Mumbai to Taipei, from Dubai to Shanghai • Over 30 channels in entertainment, movies, sports, music, news and documentary. • Radio, internet and cable partnerships. • Setting the pace for a digitally connected Asia.
• • just imagine •
STAR TM and © owned by STAR Television Productions Limited *AC Nielsen CMMR
STAR CHINESE CHANNEL • STAR GOLD • STAR MANDARIN MOVIES • STAR MOVIES • STAR NEWS • STAR PLUS • STAR SPORTS • STAR WORLD • CHANNEL [V] • PHOENIX CHINESE CHANNEL • PHOENIX INFONEWS CHANNEL • PHOENIX EUROPE CHANNEL • PHOENIX MOVIES • PHOENIX NORTH AMERICA CHANNEL • ESPN • VIVA CINEMA • NATIONAL GEOGRAPHIC CHANNEL

Source: Courtesy of STAR Group Limited.

3 The product's positioning. For example, Parker Pen's upscale market image around the world may not be profitable enough in a market that is more or less a commodity business. The solution is to create an image for a commodity product and make the public pay for it – for example, the positioning of Perrier in the United States as a premium mineral water.

The ideal situation in developing message strategy is to have a world brand – a product that is manufactured, packaged, and positioned the same around the world. Companies that have been successful with the global approach have shown flexibility in the execution of the campaigns. The idea may be global, but overseas subsidiaries then tailor the message to suit local market conditions and regulations. Executing an advertising campaign in multiple markets requires a balance between conveying the message and allowing for local

EXHIBIT 18.7   Online advertising

Sponsored Search

Advertise your business in search results on Yahoo! and other popular sites. You can put your business in front of potential customers when they search for what you sell.

Getting Started with Search Engine Marketing
Learn search marketing essentials in a free webinar. Register today

Source: **http://advertising.yahoo.com/smallbusiness/ysm**. Reproduced with permission of Yahoo! Inc. ©2010 Yahoo! Inc. YAHOO and the YAHOO! logo are registered trademarks of Yahoo! Inc.

nuances. The localization of global ideas can be achieved by various tactics, such as adopting a modular approach, localizing international symbols and using international advertising agencies.[35]

Marketers may develop multiple broadcast and print ads from which country organizations can choose the most appropriate for their operations. This can provide local operations with cost savings and allow them to use their budgets on tactical campaigns (which may also be developed around the global idea). Localization means adapting your products and services for a local market that is different from yours. It requires more than translation, and will mean completely tailoring your product or service, business plan and marketing efforts to the target audience. Many of the most successful companies sell more than half of their products overseas and many of the most visited websites have some level of localization. In addition to breaking the language barriers, it willl also have a psychological effect on your potential foreign customers making them feel you care about them. It is a way of saying 'You are important to us. We respect your community and traditions'.[36]

Product-related regulations will affect advertising messages as well. When General Mills Toy Group's European subsidiary launched a product line related to G.I. Joe-type war toys and soldiers, it had to develop two television commercials, a general version for most European countries and another for countries that bar advertisements for products with military or violent themes. As a result, in the version running in Germany, Holland and Belgium, Jeeps replaced the toy tanks, and guns were removed from the hands of the toy soldiers. Other countries, such as the United Kingdom, do not allow children to appear in advertisements.

Marketers may also want to localize their international symbols. Some of the most effective global advertising campaigns have capitalized on the popularity of pop music worldwide and used well-known artists in the commercials, such as Pepsi's use of Tina Turner. In some versions, local stars have been included with the international stars to localize the campaign. Aesthetics plays a role in localizing campaigns. The global marketer does not want to chance the censoring of the company's ads or risk offending customers. For example, even though importers of perfumes into Saudi Arabia want to use the same campaigns as are used in Europe, they occasionally have to make adjustments dictated by moral standards. In one case, the European version shows a man's hand clutching a perfume bottle and a woman's hand seizing his bare forearm. In the Saudi Arabian version, the man's arm is clothed in a dark suit sleeve, and the woman's hand is merely brushing his hand.

The use of one agency – or only a few agencies – ensures consistency. The use of one agency allows for coordination, especially when the global marketer's operations are decentralized. It also makes the exchange of ideas easier and may therefore lead, for example, to wider application of a modification or a new idea. For example, BP uses Ogilvy & Mather for its largely corporate-image-based advertising. Companies such as Procter & Gamble and Unilever have each of their global brands under a single agency, such as Pampers handled by Saatchi & Saatchi, and Old Spice by Wieden + Kennedy (as shown in *The International Marketplace 18.3*).[37]

The environmental influences that call for these modifications, or in some cases totally unique approaches, are culture, economic development and lifestyles. It is quite evident that customers prefer localized to foreign-sourced advertising.[38] Of the cultural variables, language is most apparent in its influence on promotional campaigns. The European Union alone has eleven languages: English, Finnish, French, German, Dutch, Danish, Italian, Greek, Spanish, Swedish and Portuguese. Advertisers in the Arab world have sometimes found that the voices in a TV commercial speak in the wrong Arabic dialect. The challenge of language is often most pronounced in translating themes. For example, Coca-Cola's worldwide theme 'Can't Beat the Feeling' is the equivalent of 'I Feel Coke' in Japan, 'Unique Sensation' in Italy, and 'The Feeling of Life' in Chile. In Germany, where no translation really worked, the original English language theme was used. One way of getting around this is to have no copy or very little copy and to use innovative approaches, such as pantomime. Using any type of symbolism will naturally require adequate copy testing to determine how the target market perceives the message.

THE INTERNATIONAL **MARKETPLACE 18.3**

Rethinking agency partners

Procter & Gamble Co. shifted global advertising duties for its Old Spice brand to Wieden + Kennedy, an independent ad firm based in Portland, Oregon, from Publicis Groupe's Saatchi and Saatchi for advertising and Starcom MediaVest for media planning and buying.

The account shift was the latest example of a small ad firm winning a big account at the expense of a global ad firm. Recently, Wieden and other small firms, such as Miami agency Crispin Porter + Bogusky, have won accounts with global marketers such as Coca-Cola and Volkswagen AG. A growing number of marketers believe small independents are more adept than bigger firms at using untraditional marketing methods that do not depend heavily on TV ads. Some also see smaller firms as better equipped to react to a rapidly changing media landscape because they are not bogged down by bureaucracy and the potential conflicts that abound in bulky conglomerates.

P&G said Wieden was given the account because of its extensive work on brands that target 'young men'. 'They know the male consumer very well', said Tami Jones, a spokeswoman for P&G. The Old Spice brand is sold in 30 markets around the world.

P&G also awarded media buying and planning duties in North America to Wieden. The move is a break from P&G's past practice of hiring different agencies to handle its creative work and its media planning and buying duties. P&G says Wieden will be given the media duties on a 'test' basis in North America. Publicis Groupe's Starcom Mediavest will continue to handle media planning and buying on the brand outside of North America.

The fragmentation of audiences among an array of media options is forcing marketers to put less emphasize on traditional media such as TV and more on new media such as websites, video on demand, cable TV, email, or iPod. Marketers are increasingly asking their marketing communications partners to include both creative and media placement recommendations. Having both under one roof makes things easier and more coordinated.

SOURCES: 'Agencies Rethink Wall Between Creative, Media', *The Wall Street Journal*, March 1, 2006, B3; and 'P&G Moves Old Spice Account to Small Independent Ad Firm', *The Wall Street Journal*, February 9, 2006, B7.

The stage of economic development – and therefore the potential demand for and degree of awareness of the product – may vary and differentiate the message from one market to another. Whereas developed markets may require persuasive messages (to combat other alternatives), a developing market may require a purely informative campaign. Campaigns may also have to be dramatically adjusted to cater to lifestyle differences in regions that are demographically quite similar. For example, N.W. Ayer's Bahamas tourism campaign for the European market emphasized clean water, beaches and air. The exceptions are in Germany, where it focuses on sports activities and in the United Kingdom, where it features humour.

The campaign approach

Many multinational corporations are staffed and equipped to perform the full range of promotional activities. In most cases, however, they will rely on the outside expertise of advertising agencies and other promotions-related companies such as media-buying companies and specialty marketing firms. In the organization of promotional efforts, a company has two basic decisions to make: (1) what type of outside services to use and (2) how to establish decision-making authority for promotional efforts.

Outside services   Of all the outside promotion-related services, advertising agencies are by far the most significant. A list of the world's top 25 agencies and agency groups is given in Exhibit 18.8. Size is typically measured in terms of revenue and billings. Billings are the cost of advertising time and space placed by the agency plus fees for certain extra services, which are converted by formula to correspond to media billings in terms of value of services performed. Agencies do not receive billings as income; in general, agency income is approximately 15 per cent of billing.

Agencies form world groups for better coverage. One of the largest world holding groups, WPP Group, includes such entities as Ogilvy & Mather, J. Walter Thompson, Young & Rubicam and Grey. Smaller advertising agencies have affiliated local agencies in foreign markets.

The choice of an agency will largely depend on the quality of coverage the agency will be able to give the multinational company. Global marketing requires global advertising, according to proponents of the globalization trend. The reason is not that significant cost savings can be realized through a single worldwide ad campaign but that such a global campaign is inseparable from the idea of global marketing. Some predict that the whole industry will be concentrated into a few huge multinational agencies. Agencies with networks too small to compete have become prime takeover targets in the creation of worldwide mega-agencies. Many believe that local, mid-sized agencies can compete in the face of globalization by developing local solutions and/or joining international networks.[39]

Although the forecast that six large agencies will eventually place most international advertising may be exaggerated, global marketing is the new wave and is having a strong impact on advertising. Major realignments of client–agency relationships have occurred due to mergers and to clients' reassessment of their own strategies toward more global or regional approaches.

Advertising agencies have gone through major geographic expansion in the last eight years. The leader is McCann-Erickson, with advertising running in 130 countries, compared with 72 in 1991. In 2004, it handled the most international assignments of any group (a total of 61 accounts with 1,295 assignments).[40] Some agencies, such as DDB Worldwide, were domestically focused in the early 1990s but have been forced to rethink with the globalization of their clients. As a result, DDB Worldwide had doubled its country presence to 99 by 2002.[41] New markets are also emerging, and agencies are establishing their presence in them. China's $30 billion ad market has competitors from around the world, including the WPP Group, which has 5,500 employees in 13 joint ventures.[42]

A presentation of agency–client relationships is provided in Exhibit 18.9. The J. Walter Thompson agency, which serves 87 countries worldwide, has 28 accounts that it serves in more than ten countries including Kimberly-Clark, Nestlé, and Unilever. On the client side, Unilever assigns more business on an international basis than any other global marketer, working with eight agency networks from four holding groups. In a study of 40 multinational marketers, 32.5 per cent are using a single agency worldwide, 20 per cent are using two, 5 per cent

EXHIBIT 18.8

World's top 25 marketing organizations (ranked by worldwide revenue in 2009)

Rank	Agency	Worldwide revenue (£)
1	WPP	9.06 billion
2	Omnicom Group	8.90 billion
3	Interpublic Group of Cos	4.63 billion
4	Publicis Groupe	4.60 billion
5	Dentsu	2.20 billion
6	Aegis Group	1.66 billion
7	Havas	1.54 billion
8	Hakuhodo DY Holdings	1.04 billion
9	MDC Partners	389.27 million
10	Asatsu-DK	335.20 million
11	Alliance Data Systems (Epsilon)	332.39 million
12	Media Consulta	284.58 million
13	Microsoft Corp	272.34 million
14	Photon Group	254.96 million
15	Carlson Marketing	244.40 million
16	Cheil Worldwide	226.40 million
17	IBM Corp (IBM Interactive)	208.70 million
18	Sapient Corp (Sapient Interactive)	203.81 million
19	Inventive Health (inventive Communications)	186.61 million
20	Grupo ABC (ABC Group)	186.41 million
21	STW Group	170.43 million
22	LBi International	160.64 million
23	Clemenger Group	159.17 million
24	Cossette Communication Group	158.71 million
25	George P. Johnson Co	158.51 million

Source: http://adage.com/agencyfamilytrees09/#worlds_top_50_agency_companies

are using three, 10 per cent are using four, and 32.5 per cent are using more than four agencies. Of the marketers using only one or two agencies, McCann-Erickson was the most popular with 17 per cent of the companies.[43] While global media reviews (to consolidate all business to a single agency) are popular, most large companies typically use more than one agency, with the division of labour usually along product lines. For example, Matsushita Electric Industrial Company, an innovator in the consumer electronics industry, uses two major agencies. Dentsu handles everything involving portables, audio and television. Grey Advertising handles the hi-fi area, the Technics label and telephone products. Panasonic has a small agency for primarily non-consumer items. Marketers are choosing specialized interactive shops over full-service agencies for internet advertising. This is largely for pragmatic reasons due to conflicts, agencies' uneven coverage of the world (especially in emerging markets), and the marketers' own inability to make decisions from headquarters work on a global scale.[44]

The main concern arising from the use of mega-agencies is conflict. With only a few giant agencies to choose from, the global marketer may end up with the same agency as the main competitor. The mega-agencies believe they can meet any objections by structuring their companies as rigidly separate, watertight agency networks (such as the Interpublic Group) under the umbrella of a holding group. Following that logic, Procter & Gamble, a client of Saatchi &

EXHIBIT 18.9 Worldwide agency–client relationships

Agency Networks (columns):

- Arnold Worldwide
- Bartle Bogle Hegarty
- BBDO Worldwide
- DDB Worldwide
- Dems
- Euro RSCG Worldwide
- Fallon Worldwide
- Foote Cone & Belding Worldwide
- Grey Worldwide
- Hakuhodo
- JWT
- Leo Burnett Worldwide
- Lowe Worldwide
- McCann Erickson Worldwide
- Ogilvy & Mather Worldwide
- Publicis
- Saatchi & Saatchi
- TBWA Worldwide
- United Network
- Y & R Advertising

Rank	Marketer	Dots/Assignments
1	Unilever	580
2	Procter & Gamble Co.	309
3	Nestle	290
4	Altria Group	220
5	L'Oreal	201
6	Johnson & Johnson	191
7	Diageo	175
8	Pfizer	165
9	Novartis	159
10	Kimberly-Clark Corp.	158
11	Mattel	156
12	PepsiCo	151
13	Ford Motor Co.	135
14	GlaxoSmithKline	134
15	General Mills	128
16	Mars Inc.	121
17	Coca-Cola Co.	114
18	Sanofi-Aventis	107
19	Siemens	98
20	Tchibo Holding	97
21	Reckitt Benckiser	96
22	Royal Dutch Shell Group of Cos.	92
23	Cadbury Schweppes	92
24	Motorola	90
25	Henkel	88

Note: Ranking based on total assignments the advertisers awarded the agency networks in this report.
SOURCE: Reprinted with permission from the November 14, 2005, issue of *Advertising Age*. Copyright, Crain Communications Inc., 2006.

Saatchi, and Colgate-Palmolive, a client of Ted Bates, should not worry about falling into the same network's client base. However, when the Saatchi & Saatchi network purchased Ted Bates, Colgate-Palmolive left the agency.

Despite the globalization trend, local agencies will survive as a result of governmental regulations. In Peru, for example, a law mandates that any commercial aired on Peruvian television must be 100 per cent nationally produced. Local agencies also tend to forge ties with foreign agencies for better coverage and customer service and thus become part of the general globalization effort. A basic fear in the advertising industry is that accounts will be taken away from agencies that cannot handle world brands. An additional factor is contributing to the fear of losing accounts. In the past, many multinational corporations allowed local subsidiaries to make advertising decisions entirely on their own. Others gave subsidiaries an approved list of agencies and some guidance. Still others allowed local decisions subject only to headquarters' approval. Now the trend is toward centralization of all advertising decisions, including those concerning the creative product.

Decision-making authority The alternatives for allocating decision-making authority range from complete centralization to decentralization. With complete centralization, the headquarters level is perceived to have all the right answers and has adequate power to impose its suggestions on all of its operating units. Decentralization involves relaxing most of the controls over foreign affiliates and allowing them to pursue their own promotional approaches.

Of 40 multinational marketers, 26 per cent have centralized their advertising strategies, citing as their rationale the search for economies of scale, synergies and brand consistency. Xerox's reason is that its technology is universal and opportunities abound for global messages. Centralization is also occurring at the regional level. GAZ (Russian) and Magna's (Canadian) Opel division in Europe is seeking to unify its brand-building efforts with central direction. A total of 34 per cent of the companies favour decentralization with regional input. This approach benefits from proximity to market, flexibility, cultural sensitivity and faster response time. FedEx allows local teams to make advertising decisions as needed. The majority of marketers use central coordination with local input. While Ford Motor Company conceives brand strategy on a global level, ad execution is done at the regional level, and retail work is local.[45] However, multinational corporations are at various stages in their quest for centralization. Procter & Gamble and Gillette generally have an approved list of agencies, whereas Quaker Oats and Johnson & Johnson give autonomy to their local subsidiaries but will veto those decisions occasionally.

The important question is not who should make decisions but how advertising quality can be improved at the local level. Gaining approval in multinational corporations is an interactive approach using coordinated decentralization. This nine-step programme, which is summarized in Exhibit 18.10, strives for development of common strategy but flexible execution. The approach maintains strong central control but at the same time capitalizes on the greatest asset of the individual markets: market knowledge. Interaction between the central authority and the local levels takes place at every single stage of the planning process. The central authority is charged with finding the commonalities in the data provided by the individual market areas. This procedure will avoid one of the most common problems associated with acceptance of plans – the NIH syndrome (not invented here) – by allowing for local participation by the eventual implementers.

A good example of this approach was Eastman Kodak's launch of its Ektaprint copier-duplicator line in eleven separate markets in Europe. For economic and organizational reasons, Kodak did not want to deal with different campaigns or parameters. It wanted the same ad graphics in each country, accompanied by the theme 'first name in photography, last word in copying'. Translations varied slightly from country to country, but the campaign was identifiable from one country to another. A single agency directed the campaign, which was more economical than campaigns in each country would have been and was more unified and identifiable through Europe. The psychological benefit of association of the Kodak name with photography was not lost in the campaign.

Agencies are adjusting their operations to centrally run client operations. Many accounts are now handled by a lead agency, usually in the country where the client is based. More and more

EXHIBIT 18.10

Coordinated approach to pan-regional campaign development

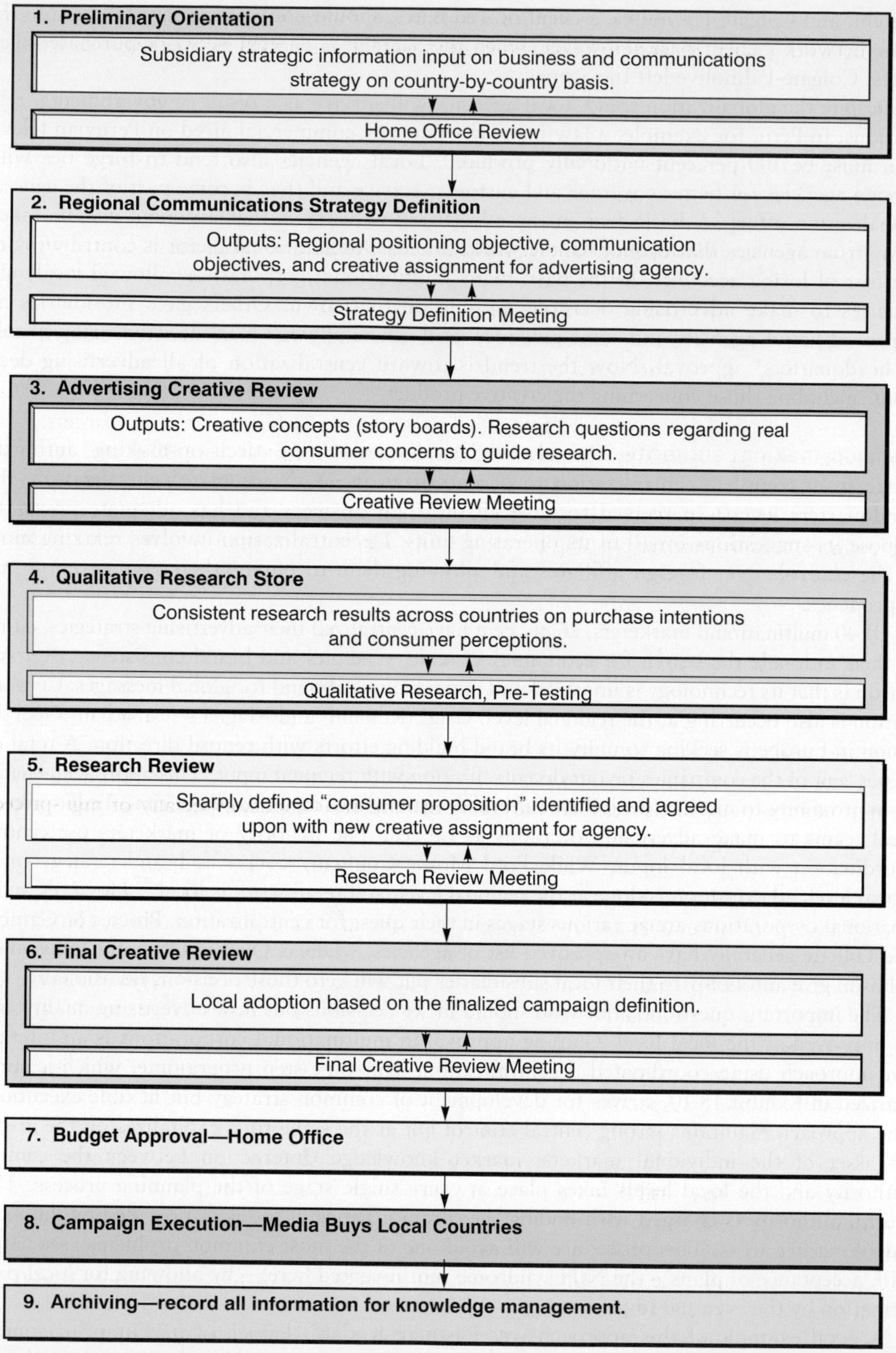

1. Preliminary Orientation

Subsidiary strategic information input on business and communications strategy on country-by-country basis.

Home Office Review

2. Regional Communications Strategy Definition

Outputs: Regional positioning objective, communication objectives, and creative assignment for advertising agency.

Strategy Definition Meeting

3. Advertising Creative Review

Outputs: Creative concepts (story boards). Research questions regarding real consumer concerns to guide research.

Creative Review Meeting

4. Qualitative Research Store

Consistent research results across countries on purchase intentions and consumer perceptions.

Qualitative Research, Pre-Testing

5. Research Review

Sharply defined "consumer proposition" identified and agreed upon with new creative assignment for agency.

Research Review Meeting

6. Final Creative Review

Local adoption based on the finalized campaign definition.

Final Creative Review Meeting

7. Budget Approval—Home Office

8. Campaign Execution—Media Buys Local Countries

9. Archiving—record all information for knowledge management.

Source: Jae H. Pae, Saeed Samiee, and Susan Tai, "Global Advertising Strategy: The Moderating Role of Brand Familiarity and Execution Style," *International Marketing Review* 19 (no. 2, 2002): 176–189; Clive Nancarrow and Chris Woolston, "Pre-Testing International Press Advertising," *Qualitative Market Research: An International Journal* (1998): 25–38; and David A. Hanni, John K. Ryans, Jr., and Ivan R. Vernon, "Coordinating International Advertising: The Goodyear Case Revisited for Latin America," *Journal of International Marketing* 3 (no. 2, 1995): 83–98.

agencies are moving to a strong international supervisor for global accounts. This supervisor can overrule local agencies and make personnel changes. Specialty units have emerged as well.

Measurement of advertising effectiveness

John Wanamaker reportedly said, 'I know half the money I spend on advertising is wasted. Now, if I only knew which half'. Whether or not advertising effectiveness can be measured, most companies engage in the attempt. Measures of advertising effectiveness should range from pre-testing of copy appeal and recognition, to post-testing of recognition, all the way to sales effects. The measures most used are sales, awareness, recall, executive judgement, intention to buy, profitability and coupon return, regardless of the medium used.[46]

The technical side of these measurement efforts does not differ from that in the domestic market, but the conditions are different. Very often, syndicated services, such as A.C. Nielsen, are not available to the global marketer. If available, their quality may not be at an acceptable level. Testing is also quite expensive and may not be undertaken for the smaller markets. The biggest challenge to advertising research will come from the increase of global and regional campaigns. Comprehensive and reliable measures of campaigns for a mass European market, for example, are difficult because audience measurement techniques and analysis differ for each country. Advertisers are pushing for universally accepted parameters to compare audiences in one country to those in another.

OTHER PROMOTIONAL ELEMENTS

Personal selling

Advertising is often equated with the promotional effort; however, a number of other efforts are used to support advertising. The marketing of industrial goods, especially of high-priced items, requires strong personal selling efforts. In some cases, personal selling may be truly global; for example, Airbus and Boeing salespeople engage in sales efforts around the world from their domestic bases. However, most personal selling is done by the subsidiaries, with varying degrees of headquarters' involvement. In cases in which personal selling constitutes the primary thrust of the corporate promotional effort and in which global customer groups can be identified, unified and coordinated sales practices may be called for. When distribution is intensive, channels are long, or markets have tradition-oriented distribution, headquarters' role should be less pronounced and should concentrate mostly on offering help and guidance.[47] A pivotal role is played by the field sales manager as the organizational link between headquarters and the salespeople.[48]

Eastman Kodak developed a line-of-business approach to allow for standardized strategy throughout a region.[49] In Europe, one person is placed in charge of the entire programme in each country, with responsibility for all sales and service teams. Typically, each customer is served by three representatives, each with a different responsibility. Sales representatives maintain ultimate responsibility for the account; they conduct demonstrations, analyze customer requirements, determine the right type of equipment for each installation, and obtain the orders. Service representatives install and maintain the equipment and retrofit new product improvements to existing equipment. Customer service representatives are the liaison between sales and service. They provide operator training on a continuing basis and handle routine questions and complaints. Each team is positioned to respond to any European customer within hours.

The training of the salesforce usually takes place in the national markets, but global corporations' headquarters will have a say in the techniques used. For instance, when Kodak introduced the Ektaprint line, sales team members were selected carefully. US personnel could be recruited from other Kodak divisions, but most European marketing personnel had to be recruited from outside the company and given intensive training. Sales managers and a select group of sales trainers were sent to the Rochester, New York, headquarters for six weeks of training. They then returned to Europe to set up programmes for individual countries so that future teams could be trained there. To ensure continuity, all the US training materials were translated into the languages of the individual countries. To maintain a unified programme and overcome language barriers, Kodak created a service language consisting of 1,200 words commonly found in technical information.

Foreign companies entering the Japanese market face challenges in establishing a sales-force. Recruitment poses the first major problem, since well-established, and usually local, entities have an advantage in attracting personnel. Many have, therefore, entered into joint ventures or distribution agreements to obtain a salesforce. Companies can also expect to invest more in training and organizational culture-building activities than in the United States. These may bring long-term advantages in fostering loyalty to the company.[50]

Sales promotion

Sales promotion has been used as the catch-all term for promotion that does not fall under advertising, personal selling or publicity. Sales promotion directed at consumers involves such activities as couponing, sampling, premiums, consumer education and demonstration activities, money-off packs, point-of-purchase materials and direct mail. The use of sales promotions as alternatives and as support for advertising is increasing worldwide. The appeal is related to several factors: cost and clutter of media advertising, simpler targeting of customers compared with advertising, and easier tracking of promotional effectiveness (for example, coupon returns provide a clear measure of effectiveness).

The success of Tang, Kraft Foods' pre-sweetened powder juice substitute in Latin America, is for the most part traceable to successful sales promotion efforts. One promotion involved trading Tang pouches for free popsicles from Kraft Foods' Brazilian subsidiary. The company also placed coupons for free groceries in Tang pouches. In Puerto Rico, General Foods ran Tang sweepstakes. In Argentina, in-store sampling featured Tang pitchers and girls in orange Tang dresses. Decorative Tang pitchers were a hit throughout Latin America. Sales promotion directed at intermediaries, also known as trade promotion, includes activities such as trade shows and exhibitions, trade discounts and cooperative advertising.

For sales promotion to be effective, the campaign planned by manufacturers, or their agencies, must gain the support of the local retailer population. Coupons from consumers, for example, have to be redeemed and sent to the manufacturer or to the company handling the promotion. A.C. Nielsen tried to introduce pence-off coupons in Chile and ran into trouble with the nation's supermarket union, which notified its members that it opposed the project and recommended that coupons not be accepted. The main complaint was that an intermediary, like Nielsen, would unnecessarily raise costs and thus the prices to be charged to consumers. Also, some critics felt that coupons would limit individual negotiations because Chileans often bargain for their purchases.

Global marketers are well advised to take advantage of local or regional opportunities. In Brazil, petrol delivery people are used to distribute product samples to households by companies such as Nestlé, Johnson & Johnson and Unilever. The delivery people are usually assigned to the same district for years and have, therefore, earned their clientele's trust. For the marketers, distributing samples this way is not only effective, it is very economical: they are charged three pence for each unit distributed. The petrol companies benefit as well in that their relationship with customers is enhanced through these 'presents'.[51]

Sales promotion tools fall under varying regulations, as can be seen from Exhibit 18.11. A particular level of incentive may be permissible in one market but illegal in another. The Northern European countries present the greatest difficulties in this respect because every promotion has to be approved by a government body. In France, a gift cannot be worth more than 4 per cent of the retail value of the product being promoted, making certain promotions virtually impossible. Although competitions are allowed in most of Europe, to insist on receiving proofs of purchase as a condition of entry is not permitted in Germany.

Regulations such as these make truly global sales promotions rare and difficult to launch. Although only a few multinational brands have been promoted on a multiterritory basis, the approach can work. In general, such multicountry promotions may be suitable for products such as soft drinks, liquor, airlines, credit cards and jeans, which span cultural divides. Naturally, local laws and cultural differences have to be taken into account at the planning stage.

EXHIBIT 18.11

Regulations regarding premiums, gifts, and competitions in selected countries

Country	Category	No Restrictions or Minor Ones	Authorized with Major Restrictions	General Ban with Important Exceptions	Almost Total Prohibition
Australia	Premiums	X			
	Gifts	X			
	Competitions			X	
Austria	Premiums				X
	Gifts			X	
	Competitions			X	
Canada	Premiums	X			
	Gifts	X			
	Competitions			X	
Denmark	Premiums			X	
	Gifts		X		
	Competitions			X	
France	Premiums	X			
	Gifts		X		
	Competitions	X			
Germany	Premiums				X
	Gifts			X	
	Competitions			X	
Hong Kong	Premiums	X			
	Gifts	X			
	Competitions	X			
Japan	Premiums			X	
	Gifts			X	
	Competitions			X	
Korea	Premiums			X	
	Gifts			X	
	Competitions			X	
United Kingdom	Premiums	X			
	Gifts	X			
	Competitions			X	
United States	Premiums	X			
	Gifts	X			
	Competitions	X			
Venezuela	Premiums			X	
	Gifts			X	
	Competitions			X	

Source: Jean J. Boddewyn, *Premiums, Gifts, and Competitions*, 1988, published by International Advertising Association, 342 Madison Avenue, Suite 2000, NYC, NY 10017. Reprinted with permission.

Although many of the promotions may be funded centrally, they will be implemented differently in each market so that they can be tied with the local company's other promotional activities. For example, Johnson & Johnson Vision Care offered trials of its one-day Acuvue contact lens throughout Europe, Africa and the Middle East. The aim was to deliver the brand message of 'Enhancing Everyday Experiences' and encourage consumers to book a sight test. The venue was a road-show event that adapted well to local market conditions. Professional lens fitters offered on-the-spot trials at gyms, sports clubs and leisure centres. The programme was devised and tested in Germany, and has since been executed in 18 different countries. The creative materials were translated into 14 languages and a virtual network using intranets ensured that all offices shared information and best practice.[52]

In the province of Québec in Canada, advertisers must pay a tax on the value of the prizes they offer in a contest, whether the prize is a trip, money or a car. The amount of the tax depends on the geographical extent of the contest. If it is open only to residents of Québec, the tax is ten per cent; if open to all of Canada, three per cent; if worldwide, one per cent. Subtle distinctions are drawn in the regulations between a premium and a prize. As an example, the Manic soccer team was involved with both McDonald's and Provigo Food stores. The team offered a dollar off the price of four tickets, and the stubs could be cashed for a special at McDonald's. Provigo was involved in a contest offering a year's supply of groceries. The Manic-McDonald's offer was a premium that involved no special tax; Provigo, however, was taxed because it was involved in a contest. According to the regulation, a premium is available to everyone, whereas a prize is available to a certain number of people among those who participate. In some cases, industries may self-regulate the use of promotional items.

Public relations

Image – the way a multinational corporation relates to and is perceived by its key constituents – is a bottom-line issue for management. Public relations is the marketing communications function charged with executing programmes to earn public understanding and acceptance, which means both internal and external communication. The function can further be divided into proactive and reactive forms.

Internal public relations   Internal communication is especially important in multinational corporations to create an appropriate corporate culture.[53] The Japanese have perfected this in achieving a *wa* (we) spirit. Everyone in an organization is, in one way or another, in marketing and will require additional targeted information on issues not necessarily related to his or her day-to-day functions. A basic part of most internal programmes is the employee publication produced and edited typically by the company's public relations or advertising department and usually provided in both hard-copy and electronic formats. Some have foreign-language versions. More often, as at ExxonMobil, each affiliate publishes its own employee publication. The better this vehicle can satisfy the information needs of employees, the less they will have to rely on others, especially informal sources such as the grapevine. Audiovisual media in the form of emails, films, videotapes, slides and videoconferencing are being used, especially for training and indoctrination purposes. Some of the materials that are used internally can be provided to other publics as well; for example, booklets, manuals and handbooks are provided to employees, distributors and visitors to the company.

External public relations   External public relations (also known as marketing public relations) is focused on the interactions with customers. In the *proactive* context, marketers are concerned about establishing global identities to increase sales, differentiate products and services and attract employees. These activities have been seen as necessary to compete against companies with strong local identities. External campaigns can be achieved through the use of corporate symbols, corporate advertising, customer relations programmes and publicity. For example, Black & Decker's corporate logo, which is in the shape and colour of an orange hexagon, is used for all B&D products. Specific brand books are developed to guide marketing personnel worldwide on the proper use of these symbols to ensure a consistent global image. Exhibit 18.12 depicts an agricultural marketing publication, *The Furrow*, in three different language versions. Total circulation is 1.5 million in 14 languages in more than 115 countries.

Publicity, in particular, is of interest to the multinational corporation. Publicity is the securing of editorial space (as opposed to paid advertising) to further marketing objectives. Since it is editorial in content, the consuming public perceives it as more trustworthy than advertising. A good example of how publicity can be used to aid in advertising efforts was the introduction by Princess Lines of a new liner, the *Royal Princess*. Because of its innovative design and size, the *Royal Princess* was granted substantial press coverage, which was especially beneficial in the travel and leisure magazines. Such coverage does not come automatically but has to be coordinated and initiated by the public relations staff of the company.

Unanticipated developments in the marketplace can place the company in a position that requires *reactive* public relations, including anticipating and countering criticism. The criticisms range from general ones against all multinational corporations to more specific ones. They may be based on a market; for example, doing business with prison factories in China. They may concern a product; for example, Nestlé's practices of advertising and promoting infant formula in developing countries where infant mortality is unacceptably high. They may centre on conduct in a given situation; for example, Union Carbide's perceived lack of response in the Bhopal disaster. The key concern is that, if not addressed, these criticisms can lead to more significant problems, such as the internationally orchestrated boycott of Nestlé's products. The six-year boycott did not so much harm earnings as it harmed image and employee morale.

Crisis management is becoming more formalized in companies, with specially assigned task forces ready to step in if problems arise. In general, companies must adopt policies that will allow them to effectively respond to pressure and criticism, which will continue to surface. Crisis management policies should have the following traits: (1) openness about corporate activities, with a focus on how these activities enhance social and economic performance; (2) preparedness to utilize the tremendous power of the multinational corporation in a

EXHIBIT 18.12

External media:
The Furrow

Source: Courtesy of Deere & Co.,
Moline, IL, USA; **http://www.
johndeere.com**.

responsible manner and, in the case of pressure, to counter criticisms swiftly; (3) integrity, which often means that the marketer must avoid not only actual wrongdoing but the mere appearance of it; and (4) clarity, which will help ameliorate hostility if a common language is used with those pressuring the corporation.[54] The marketer's role is one of enlightened self-interest; reasonable critics understand that the marketer cannot compromise the bottom line.

Complicating the situation often is the fact that groups in one market criticize what the marketer is doing in another market. For example, the Interfaith Centre on Corporate Responsibility urged Colgate-Palmolive to stop marketing Darkie toothpaste under that brand name in Asia because of the term's offensiveness elsewhere in the world. Darkie toothpaste was sold in Thailand, Hong Kong, Singapore, Malaysia and Taiwan and was packaged in a box that featured a likeness of Al Jolson in blackface.[55] Colgate-Palmolive redid the package and changed the brand name to Darlie.

With growing and evolving interactive technology, consumers can find or initiate topics of interest on the web and engage in online discussions that strongly affect their and others' views. This new form of communication, consumer-generated media (CGM), is growing at 30 per cent per year. While these media can take multiple forms, the most prominent are online bulletin boards, blogs, podcasts and websites for consumers to post complaints and compliments. Social media marketing is also an increasing area which businesses should not ignore, as highlighted in Exhibit 18.13. The challenges for the global marketer include the new media's limitless reach, fast diffusion of news, and its very expressive and influential nature. To leverage CGM to the marketer's advantage, someone in the company needs to be put in charge of the phenomenon: to monitor the relevant information and then disseminate the important findings and take action when needed.[56] Some marketers are incorporating consumer-generated content into their promotion mixes. For example, Ford and Mercedes Benz encourage drivers to send digital photos of themselves living the Ford/Mercedes-Benz lifestyle for posting on the company's website.[57]

The public relations function can be handled in-house or with the assistance of an agency. The use and extent of public relations activity will vary by company and the type of activity needed. Product-marketing PR may work best with a strong component of control at the local level and a local PR firm, while crisis management – given the potential for worldwide adverse impact – will probably be controlled principally from a global centre.[58] This has meant that global marketers funnel short-term projects to single offices for their local expertise while maintaining contact with the global agencies for their worldwide reach when a

---

EXHIBIT 18.13

Social networking still the no. 1 growth area in online marketing. Change in online marketing usage/spending* in 2009 according to US small businesses, by tactic (% of respondents)

	More	About the same	Less	Do not use
Social networking	25%	33%	5%	37%
Email (current clients)	22%	33%	6%	40%
Email (potential clients)	21%	30%	5%	45%
Company website	20%	33%	9%	38%
E-commerce	13%	20%	8%	60%
Blogging	12%	12%	6%	70%
Search engine	11%	27%	8%	54%
Online display	8%	24%	8%	60%
Online video	5%	11%	6%	77%
Podcasting	3%	8%	6%	83%
Mobile devices	2%	9%	6%	82%

Note: numbers may not add up to 100% due to rounding. *Time or money.

Source: Ostrow, A (2009) 'Social networking still the No 1 growth area in online marketing', http://mashable.com/2009/01/12/social-networking-online-marketing/

universal message is needed. Some global corporations maintain public relations staffs in their main offices around the world, while others use the services of firms that are part of large worldwide agency groups such as Weber Shandwick (Interpublic Group of Companies), Fleishman Hillard (Omnicom Group), or Hill & Knowlton (WPP Group).

Sponsorship marketing

Sponsorship involves the marketer's investment in events or causes. Sponsorship funds world-wide are directed for the most part at sports events (both individual and team sports) and cultural events (both in the popular and high-culture categories). Examples range from Coca-Cola's sponsorship of the 2004 Olympic Games in Athens and MasterCard's sponsorship of 2006 World Cup Soccer in Germany, to Visa's sponsoring of Eric Clapton's tour, Ford's sponsoring of the Montreux Detroit Jazz Festival and Coca-Cola's sponsorship of the 2010 World Cup in South Africa. Sponsorship of events such as the Olympics is driven by the desire to be associated with a worldwide event that has a positive image, global reach and a proven strategic positioning of excellence. The rising costs of sponsorship and the difficulty of establishing return on the investment has forced some marketers to bow out; for example, IBM after Sydney in 2000, and Xerox after Athens in 2004.[59]

The challenge is that an event may become embroiled in controversy, thus hurting the sponsors' images as well. Furthermore, in light of the high expense of sponsorship, marketers worry about ambush marketing by competitors. Ambush marketing is the unauthorized use of an event without the permission of the event owner. For example, an advertising campaign could suggest a presumed sponsorship relationship. During the Atlanta Olympic Games in 1996, some of the sponsors' competitors garnered a higher profile than the sponsors themselves. For example, Pepsi erected stands outside venues and plastered the town with signs. Nike secured substantial amounts of air time on radio and TV stations. Fuji bought bill-boards on the route from the airport into downtown Atlanta. None of the three contributed anything to the International Olympic Committee during this time.[60] In London in 2012, total costs are estimated to be $7 billion, and big sponsors may expect to pay as much as $80 million apiece. The ambush-marketing provisions of the London Olympics Bill will prohibit the use of terms such as 'gold', 'summer', and '2012' in advertisements by non-sponsors.[61]

Cause-related marketing is a combination of public relations, sales promotion and corporate philanthropy. This activity should not be developed merely as a response to a crisis, nor should it be a fuzzy, piecemeal effort to generate publicity; instead, marketers should have a social vision and a planned long-term social policy. For example, in Casanare, Colombia, where it is developing oil interests, British Petroleum invests in activities that support its business plan and contribute to the region's development. This has meant an investment of $10 million in setting up a loan fund for entrepreneurs, giving students technical training, supporting a centre for pregnant women and nursing mothers, working on reforestation, building aqueducts, and helping to create jobs outside the oil industry.[62] Examples of IBM's contributions to local communities are provided in *The International Marketplace 18.4*. Cisco Systems' Networking Academy is an example of how a marketer can link philanthropic strategy, its competitive advantage, and broader social good. To address a chronic deficit in IT job applicants, the company created The Network Academy concept whereby it contributes networking equipment to schools. Cisco now operates 10,000 academies in secondary schools, community colleges and community-based organizations in 150 countries. As the leading player in the field, Cisco stands to benefit the most from this improved labour pool. At the same time, Cisco has attracted worldwide recognition for this programme, boosted its employee morale and partner goodwill, as well as generated a reputation for leadership in philanthropy.[63]

Increasingly, the United Nations is promoting programmes to partner multinationals and NGOs (non-governmental organizations) to tackle issues such as healthcare, energy and biodiversity. For example, Merck and GlaxoSmithKline have partnered with UNICEF and the World Bank to improve access to AIDS care in the hardest hit regions of the world.[64]

THE INTERNATIONAL **MARKETPLACE 18.4**

Expanding the social vision: Global community relations

A recent Roper survey found that 92 per cent of the respondents feel it is important for marketers to seek out ways to become good corporate citizens, and they are most interested in those who get involved in environmental, educational and health issues. Many are worried that globalization has brought about a decline in corporate conduct and responsibility. However, many marketers have seen it as completely the opposite. Community relations is, as one chief executive put it, 'food for the soul of the organization'. It has become a strategic aspect of business and a fundamental ingredient for the long-term health of the enterprise. As a global company, IBM has a network of staff responsible for corporate responsibility throughout the 152 countries of operation. Major initiatives that address environmental concerns, support programmes for the disabled, and support education reform have been pioneered by IBM around the world.

IBM's policy of good corporate citizenship means accepting responsibility as a participant in community and national affairs and striving to be among the most-admired companies in its host countries. IBM sponsors Worldwide Initiatives in Volunteerism, a $1 million-plus programme to fund projects worldwide and promote employee volunteerism. In Thailand, for example, IBM provides equipment and personnel to universities and donates money to the nation's wildlife fund and environmental protection agency. The firm is one of only two companies with a US-based parent to win the Garuda Award, which recognizes significant contributions to Thailand's social and economic development.

As part of its long-term strategy for growth in Latin America, IBM is investing millions of dollars in an initiative that brings the latest technology to local schools. IBM does not donate the computers (they are bought by governments, institutions and other private firms), but it does provide the needed instruction and technological support. Some 800,000 children and 10,000 teachers have benefited from the programme in ten countries. IBM Latin America's technology-in-education initiative is a creative combination of marketing, social

responsibility, and long-term relationship building that fits in with the company's goal of becoming a 'national asset' in Latin American countries. In Venezuela, IBM teamed with the government to bring computers to the K–12 environment to enhance the learning process through technology.

Increased privatization and government cutbacks in social services in many countries offer numerous opportunities for companies to make substantive contributions to solving various global, regional and local problems. Conservative governments in Europe are welcoming private-sector programmes to provide job training for inner-city youth, to meet the needs of immigrants, and to solve massive pollution problems. And in Eastern and Central Europe, where the lines between the private and public sectors are just now being drawn, corporations have a unique opportunity to take a leadership role in shaping new societies. IBM Germany provided computer equipment and executive support to clean the heavily polluted River Elbe, which runs through the Czech Republic and Germany into the North Sea.

James Parkel, director of IBM's Office of Corporate Support Programs, summarizes the new expectations in the following way: 'Employees don't want to work for companies that have no social conscience, customers don't want to do business with companies that pollute the environment or are notorious for shoddy products and practices, and communities don't welcome companies that are not good corporate citizens. Many shareholder issues are socially driven.'

SOURCES: Michael E. Porter and Mark R. Kramer, 'The Competitive Advantage of Corporate Philanthropy', *Harvard Business Review* 80 (December 2002): 56–68; Roger L. Martin, 'The Virtue Matrix: Calculating the Return on Corporate Responsibility', *Harvard Business Review* 80 (March 2002): 68–75; Bradley K. Googins, 'Why Community Relations Is a Strategic Imperative', *Strategy and Business* (third quarter, 1997): 64–67; 'Consumers Note Marketers' Good Causes: Roper', *Advertising Age*, November 11, 1996, 51; Paul N. Bloom, Pattie Yu Hussein, and Lisa R. Szykman, 'Benefiting Society and the Bottom Line', *Marketing Management,* Winter 1995, 8–18; and **http://www.ibm.com**.

SUMMARY

As global marketers manage the various elements of the promotions mix in differing environmental conditions, decisions must be made about channels to be used in

communication, the message, who is to execute or help execute the programme, and how the success of the endeavour is to be measured. The trend is toward more harmonization of strategy, at the same time allowing for flexibility at the local level and early incorporation of local needs into the promotional plans.

The effective implementation of the promotional programme is a key ingredient in the marketing success of the firm. The promotional tools must be used within the opportunities and constraints posed by the communications channels as well as by the laws and regulations governing marketing communications.

Advertising agencies are key facilitators in communicating with the firm's constituent groups. Many marketers are realigning their accounts worldwide in an attempt to streamline their promotional efforts and achieve a global approach.

The use of other promotional tools, especially personal selling, tends to be more localized to fit the conditions of the individual markets. Decisions concerning recruitment, training, motivation and evaluation must be made at the affiliate level, with general guidance from headquarters.

An area of increasing challenge for global marketers is public relations. Global entities, by their very design, draw attention to their activities. The best interest of the marketer lies in anticipating problems with both internal and external constituencies and managing them, through communications, to the satisfaction of all parties. Community relations and cause-related marketing play important roles in this process.

Key terms

ambush marketing

cause-related marketing

consumer-generated media (CGM)

corporate image advertising

global media

product placement

Questions for discussion

1 MasterCard sponsors the World Cup and Visa the Olympics. Who gets the 'better deal', since the expense of sponsorship is about the same for both?

2 Comment on the opinion that 'practically speaking, neither an entirely standardized nor an entirely localized advertising approach is necessarily best'.

3 What type of adjustments must advertising agencies make as more companies want 'one sight, one sound, one sell' campaigns?

4 Assess the programmed management approach for coordinating international advertising efforts.

5 Discuss problems associated with measuring advertising effectiveness in foreign markets.

6 What is the role of community relations for a global marketer? How can the marketer treat even the anti-globals as customers?

Internet exercises

1 The FIFA World Cup is a marketing platform from which a company can create awareness, enhance its image and foster goodwill. FIFA offers sponsors a multitude of ways to promote themselves and their products in conjunction with the FIFA World Cup as well as other FIFA Events. Using FIFA's website (**http://www.fifa.com**), assess the different ways a sponsor can benefit from this association. Assess FIFA's attempts to curb ambush marketing.

2 A company wishing to engage in global markets through the internet has to make sure that its regional/local websites are of the same calibre and consistent with its global site. Using Procter & Gamble as an example (**http://www.pg.com/ company/who_we_are/globalops..html**), evaluate whether its various sites abroad satisfy these criteria.

Recommended readings

Anholt, Simon. *Another One Bites the Grass: Making Sense of International Advertising*. New York: John Wiley & Sons, 2000.

Bly, Robert W. *Advertising Manager's Handbook*. New York: Aspen Publishers, 2002.

Burnett, Leo. *Worldwide Advertising and Media Fact Book*. Chicago, IL: Triumph Books, 1994.

De Mooij, Marieke K. *Global Marketing and Advertising: Understanding Cultural Paradoxes*. San Francisco: Sage Publications, 2005.

Grey, Anne-Marie and Kim Skildum-Reid. *The Sponsorship Seeker's Toolkit*. New York: McGraw-Hill, 2002.

Jones, John Philip. *International Advertising: Realities and Myths*. San Francisco: Sage Publications, 1999.

Monye, Sylvester O. (ed.). *The Handbook of International Marketing Communications*. Cambridge, MA: Blackwell Publishers, 2000.

Moses, Elissa. *The $100 Billion Allowance: How to Get Your Share of the Global Teen Market*. New York: John Wiley & Sons, 2000.

Niefeld, Jaye S. *The Making of an Advertising Campaign: The Silk of China*. Englewood Cliffs, NJ: Prentice Hall, 1989.

Peebles, Dean M. and John K. Ryans. *Management of International Advertising: A Marketing Approach*. Boston: Allyn & Bacon, 1984.

Roberts, Mary-Lou and Robert D. Berger. *Direct Marketing Management*. Englewood Cliffs, NJ: Prentice Hall, 1999.

Schultz, Don E. and Philip J. Kitchen. *Communicating Globally: An Integrated Marketing Approach*. New York: McGraw-Hill, 2000.

Shimp, Terence A. *Advertising, Promotion, and Supplemental Aspects of Integrated Marketing Communications*. Mason, OH: Thomson/South-Western, 2006.

Zenith Media. *Advertising Expenditure Forecasts*. London: Zenith Media, December 2005.

Notes

1 Carl Arthur Sohlberg, 'The Perennial Issue of Adaptation or Standardization of International Marketing Communication: Organizational Contingencies and Performance', *Journal of International Marketing* 10 (no. 3, 2002): 1–21.

2 Framework adapted from Dean M. Peebles and John K. Ryans, *Management of International Advertising: A Marketing Approach* (Boston: Allyn & Bacon, 1984), 72–73.

3 'Why P&G Is Linking Brands to Good Causes', *Marketing*, August 26, 1999, 11; and 'Microsoft's Singapore Site Ties Page Views to Charity', *Advertising Age International*, October 1999, 4.

4 'The Material Years 1982–1992', *Marketing*, July 4, 2002, 22–23.

5 http://www.aa.com.

6 'Corporate Campaigns Attract Bigger Slices of Advertising Pie', *Advertising Age International,* March 8, 1999, 2.

7 Jonah Bloom, 'GE: The Marketing Giant Lights Up with Imagination', *Creativity,* October 2005, 63; and Matthew Creamer, 'GE Sets Aside Big Bucks to Show Off Some Green', *Advertising Age,* May 9, 2005, 7

8 William J. Holstein, 'Canon Takes Aim at Xerox', *Fortune,* October 14, 2002, 215–220.

9 Jean-Noël Kapferer, 'The Post-Global Brand', *Journal of Brand Management* 12 (number 5, 2005): 319–324.

10 MMM Business Media (2010), 'European Transport Company of the Year 2010'. Online. Available from: **http://195.207.63.119/teuforum2010//index.aspx?id=CONTACT** (Accessed 15/3/10).

11 TPi (2010), EFM is 'Favourite Freight Company' at TPi Awards'. Online. Available from: **http://www.etnow.com/news/2010/2/efm-is-favourite-freight-company-at-tpi-awards**

12 Tradeteam (2010), 'Services'. Online. Available from: **http://www.tradeteam.com/services.php** (Accessed 15/3/10).

13 J. Enrique Bigne, 'Advertising Budget Practices: A Review', *Journal of Current Issues and Research in Advertising* 17 (Fall 1995): 17–32.

14 Marketingcharts (2010), 'Ad Spend Forecast: As West Slows Down, Developing Markets to Propel Growth'. Online. Available from: **http://www.marketingcharts.com/television/ad-spend-forecast-as-west-slows-down-developing-markets-to-propel-growth-5107/zenithoptimedia-top-10-contributing-countries-regions-to-ad-spend-growth-2007-2010-june-2008jpg/** (Accessed 16/3/10).

15 The Nielsen Company (2010), 'Weathering the Storm: Asia Pacific Ad Spend Holds its Own'. Online. Available from: **http://blog.nielsen.com/nielsenwire/global/weathering-the-storm-asia-pacific-ad-spend-holds-its-own/** (Accessed 16/3/10).

16 Andrews, A. and Mason, R. (2008), 'Global advertising to tumble £14.3 bn'. Online. Available from: **http://www.telegraph.co.uk/finance/newsbysector/mediatechnologyandtelecoms/3659492/Global-advertising-spend-to-tumble-21bn.html** (Accessed 16/3/10).

17 **http://www.iccwbo.org/home/statements_rules/rules/1997/advercod.asp**.

18 European Media: Flirtation and Frustration', *The Economist,* December 9, 1999, 85–86.

19 Ross D. Petty, 'Advertising Law in the United States and European Union', *Journal of Public Policy and Marketing* 16 (Spring 1997): 2–13.

20 'Tobacco Advertising: European Commission Takes Action Against Two Noncompliant EU Member States', *European Commission Press Releases,* February 1, 2006.

21 'Pushing Pills: In Europe, Prescription-Drug Ads Are Banned', *The Wall Street Journal,* March 15, 2002, B1.

22 Pola B. Gupta and Kenneth R. Lord, 'Product Placement in Movies: The Effect of Prominence and Mode on Audience Recall', *Journal of Current Issues and Research in Advertising* 20 (Spring 1998): 47–60.

23 'Value of Product Placement Market Exploded 30.5% to $3.46 Billion in 2004', *PQ Media,* March 29, 2005, available at **http://www.pqmedia.com/press-product-placement.html.**

24 'Chinese TV Discovers Product Placement', *The Wall Street Journal,* January 26, 2000, B12.

25 Hank Kim, 'Madison Avenue Melds Pitches and Content', *Advertising Age,* October 7, 2002, 1, 14–16.

26 'Lights, Camera, Brands', *The Economist,* October 29, 2005, 61–62.

27 'Global Media', *Advertising Age International,* February 8, 1999, 23.

28 Benjamin Compaine, 'Global Media', *Foreign Policy,* November/December 2002, 20–28.

29 GBC (2009), Core Competence Award Commended (2009): MTV Networks. Online. Available from: **http://www.gbcimpact.org/itcs_node/0/0/award/1932** (Accessed 17/3/10).

30 David W. Stewart and Kevin J. McAuliffe, 'Determinants of International Media Buying', *Journal of Advertising* 17 (Fall 1988): 22–26.

31 'Eurosport Posts Big Victory: First Profit Since Rocky Start', *Advertising Age International,* March 30, 1998, 17.

32 Michael Cooper, 'TV: The Local Imperative', *Campaign,* April 21, 2000, 44–45.

33 'The internet', *Advertising Age International,* June 1999, 42.

34 'Global Brands', *Business Week Online Extra,* August 1, 2005, available at **www.businessweek.com/@@cEj1BIYQQAOKkwIA/magazine/content/05_31/b3945098.htm**.

35 'Global Marketing Campaigns with a Local Touch', *Business International,* July 4, 1988, 205–210.

36 MarketingLocalization.com (2010) 'Why localization?' Online. Available from: **http://www.marketinglocalization.com/Why-Localization/** (Accessed 17/03/10).

37 R. Craig Endicott, 'Global Marketing', *Advertising Age,* November 14, 2005, 17; and Jack Neff, 'P&G Flexes Muscle for Global Branding', *Advertising Age,* June 3, 2002, 53.

38 Jae H. Pae, Saeed Samiee and Susan Tai, 'Global Advertising Strategy: The Moderating Role of Brand Familiarity and Execution Style', *International Marketing Review* 19 (no. 2, 2002): 176–189.

39 'So What Was the Fuss About?' *The Economist,* June 22, 1996, 59–60.

40 'Global Accounts Ranks Unilever First', *Advertising Age,* September 9, 2002, 16. See also **http://www.mccann.com**.

41 Laurel Wentz and Sasha Emmons, 'AAI Charts Show Yearly Growth, Consolidation', *Advertising Age International,* September 1996, 1–33. See also **http://www.ddb.com**.

42 'China's $30 Billion Ad Market Catching Up to Western Markets', *Ad Age China,* March 1, 2006, available at **http://china.adage.com**.

43 'U.S. Multinationals', *Advertising Age International,* June 1999, 39.

44 Richard Linnett, 'Global Media Reviews Not So Worldly', *Advertising Age,* August 19, 2002, 1, 32.

45 'Centralization', *Advertising Age International,* June 1999, 40.

46 Debra A. Williamson, 'ARF to Spearhead Study on Measuring web Ads', *Advertising Age,* February 10, 1997, 8; and Gerard J. Tellis and Doyle L. Weiss, 'Does TV Advertising Really Affect Sales? The Role of Measures, Models, and Data Aggregation', *Journal of Advertising* 24 (Fall 1995): 1–12.

47 John S. Hill, Richard R. Still, and Unal O. Boya, 'Managing the Multinational Sales Force', *International Marketing Review* 8 (1991): 19–31.

48 Artur Baldauf, David W. Cravens and Nigel F. Piercy, 'Examining the Consequences of Sales Management Control Strategies in European Field Sales Organizations', *International Marketing Review* 18 (no. 5, 2001): 474–508.

49 Joseph A. Lawton, 'Kodak Penetrates the European Copier Market with Customized Marketing Strategy and Product Changes', *Marketing News,* August 3, 1984, 1, 6. See also Changes', *Marketing News,* August 3, 1984, 1, 6. See also **http://www.kodak.com**.

50 Robert B. Money and John L. Graham, 'Salesperson Performance, Pay, and Job Satisfaction: Tests of a Model Using Data Collected in the United States and Japan', *Journal of International Business Studies* 30 (no. 1, 1999): 149–172.

51 'Fuel and Freebies', *The Wall Street Journal,* June 10, 2002, B1, B6.

52 Robert McLuhan, 'Face to Face with Global Consumers', *Marketing,* August 22, 2002, 34.

53 Tim R. V. Davis, 'Integrating Internal Marketing with Participative Management', *Management Decision* 39 (no. 2, 2001): 121–138.

54 Oliver Williams, 'Who Cast the First Stone?' *Harvard Business Review* 62 (September–October 1984): 151–160.

55 'Church Group Gnashes Colgate-Palmolive', *Advertising Age,* March 24, 1986, 46.

56 Christopher Hart and Pete Blackshaw, 'Internet Inferno', *Marketing Management,* January/February 2006, 19–25; and Christopher Hart and Pete Blackshaw, 'Communication Breakdown', *Marketing Management,* November/December 2005, 24–30.

57 Allison Enright, 'Spin (Out of) Control', *Marketing News,* February 15, 2006, 19–20.

58 Michael Carberry, 'Global Public Relations', keynote speech at Public Relations Association of Puerto Rico's Annual Convention, San Juan, September 17, 1993.

59 Rich Thomaselli, 'No Fun in Games', *Advertising Age,* August 9, 2004, 1, 21.

60 'Olympic Torch Burns Sponsors' Fingers', *Financial Times,* December 13, 1999, 6.

61 'War Minus the Shooting', *The Economist,* February 18, 2006, 62–63.

62 Bradley K. Googins, 'Why Community Relations Is a Strategic Imperative', *Strategy and Business* 2 (third quarter, 1997): 64–67.

63 Michael E. Porter and Mark R. Kramer, 'The Competitive Advantage of Corporate Philanthropy', *Harvard Business Review* 80 (December 2002): 56–68. See also **http://www.cisco.com/web/about/ac227/about_cisco_corp_citi_net_academies.html**.

64 'Business Scales World Summit', *The Wall Street Journal,* August 28, 2002, A12, A13.

CAREERS IN INTERNATIONAL MARKETING

A career in international marketing does not consist only of jet-setting travel between Rome, London and Paris. Globalists need to be well versed in the specific business functions and may wish to work at summer internships abroad, take language courses, and travel not simply for pleasure but to observe business operations abroad and to gain a greater understanding of different peoples and cultures. Taking on and successfully completing an international assignment is seen by managers as crucial for the development of professional, managerial and intercultural skills and is highly likely to affect career advancement.[1]

FURTHER TRAINING

One option for the student on the road to more international involvement is to obtain further in-depth training by enrolling in graduate business school programmes that specialize in international business education. A substantial number of universities around the world specialize in training international managers. In addition, as the world becomes more global, more organizations are able to assist students interested in studying abroad or in gathering foreign work experience.

Apart from individual universities and their programmes for study abroad, many non-profit institutions stand ready to help and to provide informative materials. Exhibit 18A.1 provides information about programmes and institutions that can help with finding an international job.

EMPLOYMENT WITH A LARGE FIRM

One career alternative in international marketing is to work for a large multinational corporation. These firms constantly search for personnel to help them in their international operations. For example, a Procter & Gamble recruiting advertisement published in a university's student newspaper is reproduced in Exhibit 18A.2.

Many multinational firms, while seeking specialized knowledge like languages, expect employees to be firmly grounded in the practice and management of business. They rarely will hire a new employee at the starting level and immediately place him or her in a position of international responsibility. Usually, a new employee is expected to become thoroughly familiar with the company's internal operations before being considered for an international position. The reason a manager is sent abroad is that the company expects him or her to reflect the corporate spirit, to be tightly wed to the corporate culture, and to be able to communicate well with both local and corporate management personnel. In this liaison position, the manager will have to be exceptionally sensitive to both headquarters and local operations. As an intermediary, the expatriate must be empathetic and understanding, and yet fully prepared to implement the goals set by headquarters.

It is very expensive for companies to send an employee overseas. Typically, the annual cost of maintaining a manager overseas is about three times the cost of hiring a local manager. Companies want to be sure that the expenditure is worth the benefit they will receive, even though certainty is never possible.

Even if a position opens up in international operations, there is some truth in the saying that the best place to be in international business is on the same floor as the chairman at headquarters. Employees of firms that have taken the international route often come back to headquarters to find only a few positions available for them. Such encounters lead, of course, to organizational difficulties, as well as to financial pressures and family problems, all of which may add up to significant executive stress. This is because family re-entry creates anxiety. Because 25 per cent of expatriates quit within one year of their return, companies are paying increasing attention to the spouses and children of employees. For this reason about 15 per cent of Fortune 500 firms offer support for children of employees relocated abroad.[2]

EXHIBIT 18A.1

Websites useful in gaining international employment

Advancing Women
P.O. Box 6642
San Antonio, TX 78209 USA
(210) 822-8087
Website: **http://www.advancingwomen.com/
networks/intlinks.html**
Provides international networking contacts for women.

AVOTEK Headhunters
Nieuwe Markt 54
6511 XL Nijmegen,
NETHERLANDS
Telephone: (31) 24 3221367
Fax: (31) 24 3240467
Website: **http://www.avotek.n1**
Lists websites and addresses of jobs and agencies worldwide.
Offers sale publications and other free reference materials.

Council Exchanges
Council on International Educational Exchange
633 3rd Avenue
New York, NY 10017
USA
Telephone: (212) 822-2600
Fax: (212) 822-2649
Website: **http://www.ciee.org**
Paid work and internships overseas for college students
and recent graduates. Also offers international volunteer
projects, as well as teaching positions.

Datum Online
91 Charlotte Street
London W1P 1LB
UK
Telephone: 44 171 255 1313/1314/1320
Fax: 44 (0) 171 255 1316
E-mail: admin@datumeurope.com
http://www.datumeurope.com/
Online database providing all the resources to find IT, sales,
and accountancy jobs across Europe.

Dialogue with Citizens
Internal Market Directorate General
MARKT A/04, C107 03/52
European Commission
Rue de la Loi, 200
B-1049 Brussels
BELGIUM
Telephone: (011) 322 299 5804
Fax: (011) 322 295 6695
Website: **http://ec.europa.eu/youreurope/nav/en/
citizens/home.html**

Factsheets on EU citizens' rights regarding residence,
education, working conditions and social security, rights as

a consumer, and ways of enforcing these rights, etc.
Easy-to-use guides that give a general outline of EU
citizens' rights and the possibilities offered by the European
Single Market. A Signpost Service for citizens' practical
problems.

Ed-U-Link Services
PO Box 2076
Prescott, AZ 86302
USA
Telephone: (520) 778-5581
Fax: (520) 776-0611
Website: **http://www.edulink.com/
JobOpeningsMain.html**
Provides listings of and assistance in locating teaching jobs
abroad.

80 Days
Website: **http://www.80days.com**
Links to Websites with job listings worldwide, including
volunteer work and teaching English as a foreign language.
Has special section on Europe.

The Employment Guide's Careerweb
150 West Brambleton Avenue
Norfolk, VA 23510
USA
Telephone: (800) 871-0800
Fax: (757) 616-1593
Website: **http://www.employmentguide.com**
Online employment source with international listings,
guides, publications, etc.

Escape Artist
EscapeArtist.com Inc.
Suite 832–1245
World Trade Center
Panama
Republic of PANAMA
Fax: (011) 507 317 0139
Website: **http://www.escapeartist.com**
Website for U.S. expatriates. Contains links on overseas
jobs, living abroad, offshore investing, free magazine, etc.

EuroJobs
Heathefield House
303 Tarring Rd.
Worthing
West Sussex BN115JG
UK
Telephone: 44 (0) 1260 223144
Fax: 44 (0) 1260 223145
E-mail: medialinks@eurojobs.com
http://www.eurojobs.com

Lists vacant jobs all over Europe. Also includes the possibility of submitting CV to recruiters; employment tips and other services.

EURopean Employment Services—EURES
Employment and Social Affairs Directorate General
EMPL A/03, BU33 02/24
European Commission
Rue de la Loi, 200
B-1049 Brussels
BELGIUM
Telephone: (011) 322 299 6106
Fax: (011) 322 299 0508 or 295 7609
Website: **http://europa.eu.int/eures**
Aims to facilitate the free movement of workers within the 17 countries of the European Economic Area. Partners in the network include public employment services, trade unions, and employer organizations. The Partnership is coordinated by the European Commission. For citizens of these 17 countries, provides job listings, background information, links to employment services, and other job-related websites in Europe.

Expat Network
International House
500 Purley Way
Croydon
Surrey CRO 4NZ
UK
Telephone: (44) 20 8760 5100
Fax: (44) 20 8760 0469
Website: **http://www.expatnetwork.com**
Dedicated to expatriates worldwide, linking to overseas jobs, country profiles, healthcare, expatriate gift and bookshop, plus in-depth articles and industry reports on issues that affect expatriates. Over 5,000 members. Access is restricted for non-members.

Federation of European Employers (FedEE)
Superla House
127 Chiltern Drive
Surbiton
Surrey, KT5 8LS
UK
Telephone: (44) 20 8339 4134
Fax: (44) 13 5926 9900
Website: **http://www.fedee.com**
FedEE's European Personnel Resource Centre is the most comprehensive and up-to-date source of pan-European national pay, employment law, and collective-bargaining data on the web.

HotJobs.com
Hotjobs.com, Ltd.
406 West 31st Street
New York, NY 10001
USA
Telephone: (212) 699-5300
Fax: (212) 944-8962

Website: **http://hotjobs.yahoo.com**
Contains international job listings, including Europe.

Jobpilot
75 Cannon Street
London EC4N 5BN
UK
Telephone: (44) 20 7556 7044
Fax: (44) 20 7556 7501
Website: **http://www.jobpilot.com**
"Europe's unlimited career market on the internet."

Jobs.ac.uk
University of Warwick
Coventry CV4 7AL
UK
Telephone: 44 (0) 24 7657 2839
Fax: 44 (0)24 7657 2946
http://www.jobs.ac.uk/
Search jobs in science, research, academic, and related employment in the UK and abroad.

Monster.com
TMP Worldwide Global Headquarters
1633 Broadway
33rd Floor
New York, NY 10019
USA
Telephone: 1 800 MONSTER or (212) 977-4200
Fax: (212) 956-2142
Website: **http://www.monster.com**
Global online network for careers and working abroad. Career resources (including message boards and daily chats). Over 800,000 jobs.

Organization of Women in International Trade
Website: **http://www.owit.org**
Offers networking and opportunities in international trade. Has chapters worldwide.

OverseasJobs.com
AboutJobs.com Network
12 Robinson Road
Sagamore Beach, MA 02562
USA
Telephone: (508) 888-6889
Website: **http://www.overseasjobs.com**
Job seekers can search the database by keywords or locations and post a resume online for employers to view.

PlanetRecruit.com
PlanetRecruit Ltd.
Alexandria House
Covent Garden
Cambridge CB1 2HR
UK
Telephone: (44) 87 0321 3660
Fax: (44) 87 0321 3661
Website: **http://www.planetrecruit.com**

One of the world's largest UK and international recruitment networks. Features accounting and finance, administrative and clerical, engineering, graduate and trainee, IT, media, new media and sales, marketing and public-relations jobs from about 60 countries.

The Riley Guide
Margaret F. Dikel
11218 Ashley Drive
Rockville, MD 20852
USA
Telephone: (301) 984-4229
Fax: (301) 984-6390
Website: **http://www.rileyguide.com**
It is a directory of employment and career information sources and services on the internet, providing instruction for job seekers and recruiters on how to use the internet to their best advantage. Includes a section on working abroad, including in Europe.

SCI-IVS USA
814 NE 40th Street
Seattle, WA 98105
USA
Telephone: (206) 545-6585
Fax: (206) 545-6585
Website: **http://www.sci-ivs.org**
Through various non-commercial partner organizations worldwide and through SCI international, national, and regional branch development, the U.S. branch of SCI participates in the SCI network which exchanges over 5,000 volunteers each year in short-term (2–4 week) international group workcamps and in long-term (3–12 months) volunteer postings in over 60 countries.

Transitions Abroad Online: Work Abroad
PO Box 1300
Amherst, MA 01004-1300
Telephone: (800) 293-0373 or (413) 256-3414
Fax: (413) 256-0373

Website: **http://www.transitionsabroad.com**
Contains articles from its bimonthly magazine; a listing of work abroad resources (including links); lists of key employers, internship programs, volunteer programs, and English-teaching openings.

Vacation Work Publications
9 Park End Street
Oxford, OXI 1HJ
UK
Website: **http://www.vacationwork.co.uk**
Lists job openings abroad, in addition to publishing many books on the topic. Has an information exchange section and a links section.

Upseek.com
Telephone: (877) 587-5627
Website: **http://www.upseek.com**
A global search engine that empowers job seekers in the online job search market. Provides job opportunities from the top career and corporate sites with some European listings.

Women in the Academy of International Business
Centre for International Business Studies
Mays Business School, Texas A&M University
College Station, TX 77843
USA
Website: **http://cibs.tamu.edu/waib**
Encourages networking, mentoring and research by linking women faculty, administrators and Ph.D. students in international business studies.

WWOOF International
PO Box 2675
Lewes BN7 1RB,
UK
Website: **http://www.wwoof.org**
WWOOF International is dedicated to helping those who would like to work as volunteers on organic farms internationally.

Source: European Union, **http://www.eurunion.org.**

EMPLOYMENT WITH A SMALL OR MEDIUM-SIZED FIRM

A second alternative is to begin work in a small or medium-sized firm. Some of these firms have only recently developed an international outlook, and the new employee will arrive on the 'ground floor'. Initial involvement will normally be in the export field – evaluating potential foreign customers, preparing quotes, and dealing with mundane activities such as shipping and transportation. With a very limited budget, the export manager will only occasionally visit foreign markets to discuss marketing strategy with foreign distributors. Most of the work will be done by email, by fax, or by telephone. The hours are often long because of the need to reach contacts overseas, for

example, during business hours in Hong Kong. Yet the possibilities for implementing creative business methods are virtually limitless, and the contribution made by the successful export manager will be visible in the firm's growing export volume.

Alternatively, international work in a small firm may involve importing – finding new low-cost sources for domestically sourced products. Decisions often must be based on limited information, and the import manager is faced with many uncertainties. Often, things do not work out as planned. Shipments are delayed, letters of credit are cancelled, and products may not arrive in the form and shape anticipated. Yet the problems are always new and offer an ongoing challenge.

As a training ground for international marketing activities, there is probably no better place than a smaller firm. Ideally, the person

EXHIBIT 18A.2

Advertisement recruiting new graduates for employment in international operations

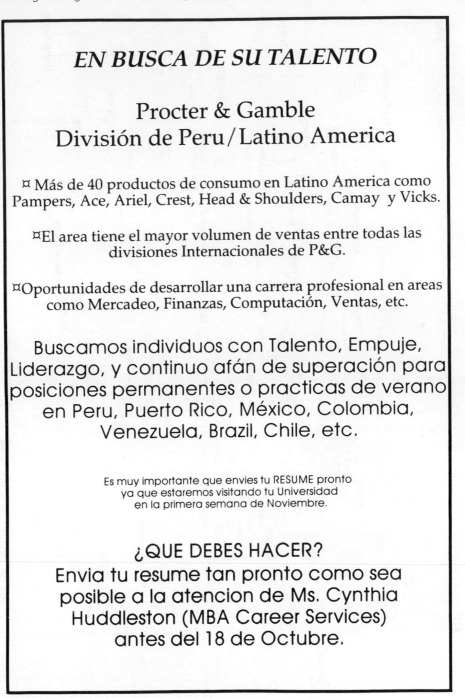

EN BUSCA DE SU TALENTO

Procter & Gamble
División de Peru/Latino America

¤ Más de 40 productos de consumo en Latino America como Pampers, Ace, Ariel, Crest, Head & Shoulders, Camay y Vicks.

¤El area tiene el mayor volumen de ventas entre todas las divisiones Internacionales de P&G.

¤Oportunidades de desarrollar una carrera profesional en areas como Mercadeo, Finanzas, Computación, Ventas, etc.

Buscamos individuos con Talento, Empuje, Liderazgo, y continuo afán de superación para posiciones permanentes o practicas de verano en Peru, Puerto Rico, México, Colombia, Venezuela, Brazil, Chile, etc.

Es muy importante que envies tu RESUME pronto ya que estaremos visitando tu Universidad en la primera semana de Noviembre.

¿QUE DEBES HACER?
Envia tu resume tan pronto como sea posible a la atencion de Ms. Cynthia Huddleston (MBA Career Services) antes del 18 de Octubre.

Source: The Procter & Gamble Company. Used by permission.

EXHIBIT 18A.3

The cost per diem in the world's major business cities (in U.S. dollars)

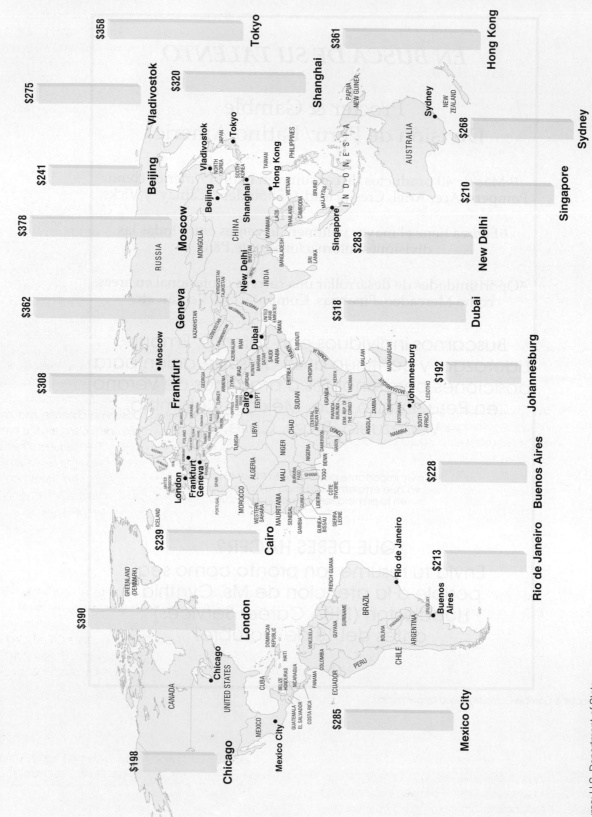

Source: U.S. Department of State,
January 2006; **http://www.state.gov/travel**, accessed January 19, 2006.

with some experience may find work with an export trading or export-management company, concentrating virtually exclusively on the international arena.

OPPORTUNITIES FOR WOMEN IN GLOBAL FIRMS

As firms become more involved in global business activities, the need for skilled global managers is growing. Concurrent with this increase in business activity is the ever growing presence and managerial role of women in international business.

The number of women who manage international businesses is very low. The reason for the low participation of women in global management roles seems to have been the assumption that because of the subservient roles of women in Japan, Latin America and the Middle East, neither local nor expatriate women would be allowed to succeed as managers. The error is that expatriates are not seen as local women, but rather as 'foreigners who happen to be women', thus solving many of the problems that would be encountered by a local woman manager.

There appear to be some distinct advantages for a woman in a management position overseas. Among them are the advantages of added visibility and increased access to clients. Clients tend to assume that 'expatriate women must be excellent, or else their companies would not have sent them'.

It also appears that companies that are larger in terms of sales, assets, income and employees send more women overseas than smaller organizations. Further, the number of women expatriates is not evenly distributed among industry groups. Industry groups that utilize greater numbers or percentages of women expatriates include banking, electronics, petroleum, publishing, diversified corporations, pharmaceuticals and retailing and apparel.

For the future, it is anticipated that the upward trend previously cited reflects increased participation of women in global management roles in the future.

SELF-EMPLOYMENT

A third alternative is to hang up a consultant's shingle or to establish a trading firm. Many companies are in dire need of help for their international marketing effort and are quite prepared to part with a portion of their profits to receive it. Yet in-depth knowledge and broad experience are required to make a major contribution to a company's international marketing effort or to run a trading firm successfully. Specialized services that might be offered by a consultant include international market research, international strategic planning, or, particularly desirable, beginning-to-end assistance in international market entry or international marketing negotiations.

The up-front costs in offering such a service are substantial and are not covered by turnover but rather have to be covered by profits. Yet the rewards are there. For an international marketing expert, the hourly chargeable rate typically is as high as $400 for experienced principals and $150 for staff. Whenever international travel is required, overseas activities are often billed at the daily rate of $3,000 plus expenses. When trading on one's own, income and risk can be limitless. Even at these relatively high rates, solid groundwork must be completed before all the overhead is paid. The advantage is the opportunity to become a true international entrepreneur. Consultants and owners of trading firms work at a higher degree of risk than employees, but with the opportunity for higher rewards.

International marketing is complex and difficult, yet it affords many challenges and opportunities. 'May you live in interesting times' is an ancient Chinese curse. For the international marketer, this curse is a call to action. Observing changes and analyzing how best to incorporate them into one's plans are the bread and butter of the international marketer. The frequent changes are precisely what makes international marketing so fascinating. It must have been international marketers who were targeted by the old Indian proverb 'When storms come about little birds seek to shelter, while eagles soar'. May you be an eagle!

Recommended readings

Hult, G.T.M. and E.C. Lashbrooke, Jr. *Study Abroad: Perspective and Experiences from Business School*. Vol. 13. St. Louis: 2003.

Kocher, Eric and Nina Segal. *International Jobs: Where They Are and How to Get Them*. 6th edn. Phoenix, AZ: Perseus Books Group, 2004.

Lauber, Daniel and Kraig Rice. *International Job Finder: Where the Jobs Are Worldwide*. River Forest, IL: Planning/Communications, 2003.

Goldsmith, Marshall, Warren G. Bennis, John O'Neil, Cathy Greenberg, Maya Hu-Chan and Alastair Roberston. *Global Leadership: The Next Generation*. London: Financial Times Prentice Hall, 2004.

Notes

1   Gunter K. Stahl, Edwin L. Miller and Rosalie L. Tung, 'Toward the Boundaryless Career: A Closer Look at the Expatriate Career Concept and the Perceived Implications of an International Assignment', *Journal of World Business* 37 (2002): 216–227.

2   Joann S. Lublin, 'To Smooth a Transfer Abroad, a New Focus on Kids', *The Wall Street Journal,* January 26, 1999, B1, B14.

Oil for food

BACKGROUND

Prior to World War I, the small Middle Eastern area of present-day Kuwait was an autonomous district of Ottoman Iraq. Thereafter, it fell under British rule, and later became a sovereign emirate. Iraq never recognized Kuwaiti independence, blaming the authority of the Kuwaiti Emir on British colonialist intervention.

Feeling threatened by Shi'ite Iran during the war of the 1980s, Kuwait allied itself with Iraq. By the time the war ended, Iraq had incurred a $14 billion debt to Kuwait.

Iraq had hoped to repay its debts with oil revenues, encouraged by OPEC oil production cuts that caused oil prices to soar. Charging that it had performed a service by acting as a buffer against Iran, Iraq demanded absolution of its war debts altogether. Iraq also accused Kuwait of 'slant drilling' into adjacent Iraqi oil fields. Kuwait disagreed and increased oil production, thereby lowering world prices and depriving Iraq of expected large profits.

The Iran–Iraq war had resulted in the destruction of almost all Iraqi port facilities on the Persian Gulf, inhibiting its use of the key trade route. Uncertain about peace on the Iranian border in the future, many in Iraq's government felt that the country's security could only be assured through greater control of the coast. Kuwaiti territory's historic ties to Iraq, allegedly destroyed by imperialist British intervention, as well as Kuwait's 'economic warfare' in the oil fields, were President Hussein's primary justifications for the invasion of Kuwait.

Iraq also had grievances against the Saudi government, not the least of which were war debts. Geographic vastness and a small population would make Saudi Arabia unable to repel any Iraqi invasion.

On August 2, 1990, Iraq invaded Kuwait and began what would go down in history as the First Gulf War. The invasion brought the Iraqi army within easy striking distance of Saudi Arabia's most valuable oil fields. Iraq's belligerence towards Israel and its poor human rights record were now enhanced by the threat it posed to Saudi Arabia, a country of great strategic interest to the United States. If Iraq were to control Saudi oil fields, it would have a dangerously large share of the world's oil supply. The United States was firmly opposed to Iraq's invasion of Kuwait. It led a coalition force of approximately thirty nations, mandated by the United Nations, to attack the invaders in January 1991. A decisive victory was won within days, driving Iraqi forces back across their domestic border.

ECONOMIC SANCTIONS

Once military peace was restored, the United Nations imposed economic sanctions on Iraq. The conditions for repeal included a weapons inspection regime. The sanctions amounted to a full trade embargo. Exhibit C4.1 shows how Iraq's crude oil production plummeted due to the export prohibition. Due to the lack of income, the influx of items like food, medicines, and construction materials necessary to maintain the country's infrastructure all but stopped. This proved to be one of the toughest and most comprehensive such policies in history. A report by UNICEF in 1998 found that they resulted in an increase of 90,000 civilian deaths per year due to malnutrition, absence of medication and easily preventable disease. The sanctions' humanitarian impact soon became so notorious that several UN representatives in Iraq resigned in protest.

IMPROVING PRODUCT FLOW

The 'Oil for Food' programme was established as a counterweight to the impact of economic sanctions on Iraq's civilians, as well as a means to increase global oil supply. Exhibit C4.2 illustrates how global oil demand grew during these years. Starting in December 1996, Iraq was permitted to resume exports of crude oil at a 'fair market price', so designated by the UN; the condition

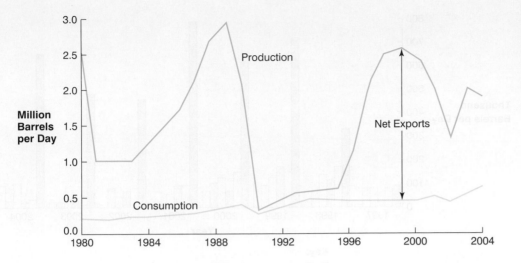

EXHIBIT C4.1

Iraq's oil production and consumption, 1980–2005

Note: Production includes crude oil, lease condensate, natural gas liquids, ethanol, and refinery gain.

Source: http://www.eia.doe.gov, accessed January 3, 2006.

was that sales proceeds be used for humanitarian purposes only – namely, the purchase of medicines, vaccines and food items.

The first shipments of food arrived in Iraq in March 1998; at that time, some 60 per cent of Iraq's 26 million population were fully dependent on its rations. With the programme's aid, the welfare of individual Iraqis began to improve significantly: the population's health, plummeting under the sanctions regime, began to recover with the influx of new medicines. In just five years, immunization campaigns sharply cut the incidence of preventable disease. The occurrence of illnesses like malaria and diphtheria fell by as much as 90 per cent in some areas. In the north, there was a 56 per cent reduction in chronic childhood malnutrition, and both children and adults saw their daily calorific intake increase by 83 per cent. Finally, effective programmes for school feeding, water rehabilitation and landmine deactivation were established.

EXHIBIT C4.2

Year	World Oil Demand (average?), Thousand Barrels per Day
1996	71,500
1997	73,308
1998	74,032
1999	75,789
2000	76,880
2001	77,656
2002	78,357
2003	79,890
2004	82,473

Source: http://www.eia.doe.gov/emeu/ipsr/source4.html, accessed January 3, 2006.

THE ISSUE

In spite of the relief the programme provided to Iraqis, eventually several shortcomings in its method and administration came to light. A key problem was the United Nations' lack of experience in administering business ventures. According to UN Secretary-General Kofi Annan, it was 'one of the largest, most complex and most unusual tasks' ever undertaken by the organization. One of the programme's positive effects was, however, that it spurred Mr Annan to vow systemwide reforms to prevent the recurrence of its many mishaps.

SELLING THE OIL

A basic assumption of the programme was that Iraq itself, and not the UN, would choose its oil buyers. This empowered it with economic leverage, which it used to attempt a reversal of the sanctions. Sales were made to companies and individuals whose native countries were perceived as friendly to Iraq, and, preferably, as capable of easing sanctions through the UN Security Council. Russian and French oil corporations therefore became frequent purchasers of Iraqi crude oil. However, as Exhibit C4.3 illustrates, the United States remained by far the greatest importer of Iraqi crude.

In the meantime, companies whose countries of origin were out of favour with the Iraqi government were subject to the denial, or at least the reduction, of allocated oil supplies. At the beginning, there was hope of persuading the United States to soften its attitude towards the sanctions regime, and significant allocations were granted to US businesses. However, when no change took place in the US government's agenda, allocations that Iraq had previously reserved for the United States went to other traders.

Corporations that benefited from Iraq's favours were often little-known traders who wanted to sell their allocated crude oil to world-class corporations with greater logistical and marketing

Oil imports from Iraq, by country

Source: http://www.eia.doe. gov, accessed January 3, 2006.

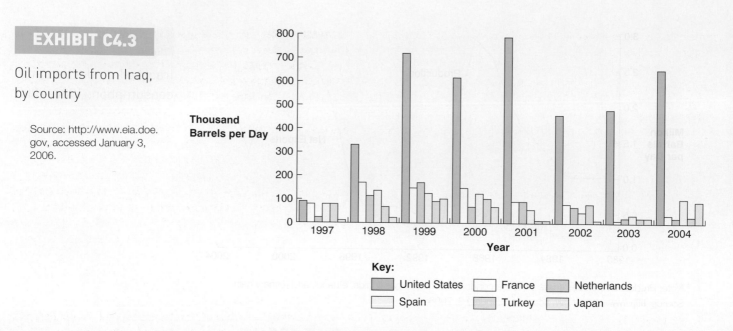

Thousand Barrels per Day

Year

Key:
☐ United States ☐ France ☐ Netherlands
☐ Spain ☐ Turkey ☐ Japan

ability. They used little-known intermediary companies, which bought their oil supplies and resold them to customers in the world market. Technically, this transaction was no longer under the auspices of the Oil-for-Food programme, being the business of the intermediary rather than the original company. The intermediary sold its oil at a premium above the UN's official price, and then used the premium for side-payments in order to remain a preferred trader. These layers of participants between the extraction and end-use of Iraq's crude resulted in transactions where it was nearly impossible to trace all the participants of a particular contract.

In 2000, Iraq started to demand forbidden surcharges of 10 to 30 per cent on every barrel of oil, since world oil prices made such increases possible. Within two years this scheme created $229 million in illicit income for the Iraqi government.

Every contracting customer was advised of the surcharge requirement even though UN rules made such payments illegal. Companies often disguised their payments by funneling them through offshore bank accounts or labelling them as legitimate expenses (such as 'commissions' or 'loading fees'). In spite of universal market recognition that Iraqi crude oil could not be purchased without a surcharge, a disclaimer came to be included as standard assurance in contracts that the surcharges had, supposedly, not been paid.

BUYING THE GOODS

In a parallel development with the above, fees or 'kickbacks' were paid to Iraq by the vendors of humanitarian goods. Here, too, it was up to Iraq to select the companies from which it would purchase, using revenue gained from sales of oil. In total, the Iraqi government was able to obtain $1.55 billion of unlawful revenue through this procedure.

OIL FOR FOOD

In 1999 Iraq tried to recoup the cost of transporting humanitarian goods from the Persian Gulf to inland areas. However, such payment was not approved by UN officials. The Iraqi government asked the contractors themselves to make transportation payments, which were routed directly to a bank account the government itself controlled. Given the lucrative market some of these foodstuff and pharmaceutical producers saw in Iraq, many were willing to pay.

By 2000, Iraq had instituted a broader policy of a general 10 per cent kickback on top of the inland transport fees. Dubbed the 'after-sales-service' fee, this payment was a requirement for goods to be permitted to enter Iraq. The UN contractors, meanwhile, could not receive any payments from the UN until their goods had reached Iraqi destinations.

After-sales-service provisions were incorporated into corporate contracts in order to create the illusion of inflated prices; this permitted contractors to recover from the UN the money they had essentially used as bribes to the Iraqi government. By the programme's end, the contracts of more than 2,200 companies had contained inland transport charges, after-sales-service charges, or both.

THE BANKING ISSUE

The Banque National de Paris, S.A. ('BNP'), a French bank, had been selected by the Security Council to manage the third-party oil revenue account. Under its services agreement with the United Nations, it was required to confirm all letters of credit issued by other banks under the programme. However, it was permitted itself to issue letters of credit on behalf of private oil buyers; its relations with companies financing these particular letters were not restricted. BNP and its affiliates issued 75 per cent of all the letters of credit involved in the programme's oil purchases.

Once oil transactions were financed through BNP, the bank's loyalties became divided between the UN's interest to promote transparency in the programme, and the interests of its private clients. Often, the latter wanted to maintain the confidentiality of their business, and specifically requested that BNP not disclose the nature or participants of their transactions.

THE INVESTIGATION

An Independent Inquiry Committee (IIC), chaired by Paul Volcker (former Chairman of the US Federal Reserve under Jimmy Carter and Ronald Reagan), spent one and a half years investigating the flaws that turned 'the mother of all UN humanitarian programmes' into a way for Saddam Hussein's regime to siphon off $1.8 billion dollars. More than 2,000 companies doing business under the Oil-for-Food initiative were involved in bribes and kickbacks, which benefited a government internationally renowned for human rights violations. However, the IIC's fifth and final report came with the following disclaimer: 'Identification of a particular company's contract as having been the subject of an illicit payment does not necessarily mean that such company – as opposed to an agent or secondary purchaser with an interest in the transaction – made, authorized, or knew about an illicit payment'.

Questions for discussion

1   Can anything be done in the future to prevent such corruption? Could anything have been done at the start of the programme to equip the UN for its role as intermediary?

2   How should prices have been set to prevent the tampering? Were they real market prices if contractors had been willing to pay more for Iraqi oil?

3   Discuss the ethics of the banking issue in this situation.

Sources

Independent Inquiry Committee into the UN Oil-for-Food Programme, 'Report on Programme Manipulation – October 27, 2005'.

'The United Nations Oil-for-Food Programme: Focus on Humanitarian Relief'. **http://www.un.org/News/dh/iraq/oip/human_relief.htm** (Accessed November 8, 2005).

UN News Centre, 'After Final Oil-for-Food Report, Annan Calls for States to Act, Pledges UN Reforms'. **http://www.un.org/apps/news/story.asp?NewsID=16386&Cr=iraq&Crl=oil** (Accessed November 8, 2005).

UN Press Release, 'Head of Oil-for-Food Inquiry Calls for Wide-Ranging Reform within United Nations', October 27th, 2005. **http://www.un.org/News/Press/docs/2005/ik524.doc.htm** (Accessed November 8, 2005).

'UN Defends Its Anti-Corruption Efforts'. *San Francisco Chronicle*, January 19, 2005; and **http://www.un.org/News/dh/iraq/shashi-19jan.htm** (Accessed November 8, 2005).

Blood free diamonds

The ancient Greeks called diamonds the tears of the gods. Today, we know that natural diamonds consist of highly compressed carbon molecules. They have become a symbol of beauty, power, wealth and love. Nevertheless, diamonds and the diamond trade are plagued by a sad reality: the exploitation of people for diamond extraction and the use of diamond profits to fund terrorist activity and rebel groups.

Trade in diamonds is highly profitable. The stones are small, readily converted to cash, easily transportable, not detectable by dogs, nor do they set off any metal detectors. Unfortunately, this makes them an easy target for money laundering activities by terrorist and rebel groups. In addition, their high value encourages some diamond producing countries to employ means of extraction that may violate human rights. Consider the case in Botswana where a rich diamond deposit was discovered on the land belonging to a tribal group, the Bushmen. The government forcibly resettled all 2,500 of them.

THE DIAMOND PRODUCTION PROCESS: FROM MINE TO MARKET

Diamonds are mined in several different ways: in open pits, underground, in alluvial mines (mines located in ancient creek beds where diamonds were deposited by streams), and in coastal and marine mines. Despite advances in technology, diamond excavation remains a labour-intensive process in most areas of the world. Over 156 million carats of diamonds are mined annually (one carat is the equivalent of 0.2 grams).

Once diamonds have been excavated, they are sorted, by hand, into grades. While there are thousands of categories and subcategories based on size, quality, colour and shape, there are two broad categories of diamonds – gem grade and industrial grade. On average, close to 60 per cent of the annual production is of gem quality. In addition to jewelry, gem quality stones are used for collections, exhibits and decorative art objects. Industrial diamonds, because of their hardness and abrasive qualities, are often used in the medical field, in space programmes and for diamond tools.

After the diamonds have been sorted, they are transported to one of the world's four main diamond trading centres – Antwerp, Belgium, which is the largest; New York, USA; Tel Aviv, Israel; and Mumbai, India. Daily, between five and ten million individual stones pass through the Antwerp trading centre. After they have been purchased, the diamonds are sent off to be cut, polished and/or otherwise processed. Five countries currently dominate the diamond processing industry – India, which is the largest (processing 9 out of every 10 diamonds); Israel; Belgium; Thailand; and the United States, with China emerging as a new processing centre. Finally, the polished diamonds are sold by manufacturers, brokers and dealers to importers and wholesalers all over the world, who in turn, sell to retailers. The total timeframe from the time of extraction to the time at which the diamond is sold to the end consumer is called the 'pipeline', and it usually takes about 2 years.

THE NOT SO DAZZLING SIDE OF THE DIAMOND TRADE

While women across the world may want a diamond on their finger, the industry's sparkling reputation has been tarnished. Reports have shown that profits from the diamond trade have financed deadly conflicts in African nations such as Angola, Sierra Leone, Congo, Cote d'Ivoire and Liberia. In addition, reports by the *Washington Post* and Global Witness (**http://www.globalwitness.org**), a key organization in monitoring the global diamond trade, revealed that Al Qaeda used smuggled diamonds from Sierra Leone, most likely obtained via Liberia, to fund its terrorist activities. Diamonds that have been obtained in regions of the world plagued by war and violence are called 'conflict diamonds' or 'blood diamonds'.

The use of diamonds for illicit activities has been widespread. During the Bush War of Angola in 1992, Jonas Savimbi, the head of a rebel movement called UNITA (National Union for the Total Independence of Angola), extended his organization into the vast diamond fields of the country. In less than one year, UNITA's diamond-smuggling network became the largest in the world – netting hundreds of million dollars a year with which they purchased weapons. Diamonds were also a useful tool for buying

Source: This case was prepared by Daria Cherepennikova under the supervision of Professor Michael R. Czinkota of Georgetown University.

friends and supporters, and could be used as a means for stock-piling wealth.

Soon warring groups in other countries like Sierra Leone, Liberia and the Democratic Republic of Congo adopted the same strategy. For example, the RUF (Revolutionary United Front) in Sierra Leone, a group that achieved international notoriety for hacking off the arms and legs of civilians and abducting thousands of children and forcing them to fight as soldiers, controlled the country's alluvial diamond fields and used them to fund their activities.

According to current diamond industry estimates, conflict diamonds make up between 2 and 4 per cent of the annual global production of diamonds. However, human rights advocates disagree with that number. They argue that up to 20 per cent of all diamonds on the market could be conflict diamonds.

THE KIMBERLEY PROCESS

Diamonds are generally judged on the 'Four Cs': cut, carat, colour and clarity; some have recently pushed for the addition of a 'fifth C': conflict. On November 5, 2002, representatives from 52 countries, along with mining executives, diamond dealers, and members from advocacy groups, met in Interlaken, Switzerland, to sign an agreement that they hoped would eliminate conflict diamonds from international trade. The agreement was called the Kimberley Process and took effect on January 1, 2003.

The Kimberley Process is a United Nations-backed certification plan created to ensure that only legally mined rough diamonds, untainted by conflicts, reach established markets around the world. According to the plan, all rough diamonds passing through or into a participating country must be transported in sealed, tamper-proof containers and must be accompanied by a government-issued certificate guaranteeing the container's contents and origin. Customs officials in importing countries are required to certify that the containers have not been tampered with and are instructed to seize all diamonds that do not meet the certification requirements.

The agreement also stipulates that only those countries that subscribe to the new rules will be able to trade legally in rough diamonds. Countries that break the rules will be suspended and their diamond trading privileges will be revoked. Furthermore, individual diamond traders who disobey the rules will be subject to punishment under the laws of their own countries.

CRITICS SPEAK OUT

Several advocacy groups have voiced concerns that the Kimberley Process remains open to abuse, and that it will not be enough to stop the flow of conflict diamonds. Many worry that bribery and forgery are inevitable and that corrupt government officials will render the scheme inoperable. Even those diamonds with certified histories attached may not be trustworthy. Alex Yearsley of Global Witness predicts that firms will 'be a bit more careful with their invoices' as a result of the implementation of the Kim-

berley Process, but warns, 'if you're determined, you can get around this process'. His organization urges governments to implement stricter policies of internal control, for the diamond industry to publicize names of individuals in companies found to be involved in the conflict trade, and for the United Nations to consider implementing sanctions against diamonds from Côte d'Ivoire.

Government organizations also voiced concerns in a 2002 report: 'The period after rough diamonds enter the first foreign port until the final point of sale is covered by a system of voluntary industry participation and self-regulated monitoring and enforcement. These and other shortcomings provide significant challenges in creating an effective scheme to deter trade in conflict diamonds'.

Government organizations and policy groups are not the only ones bringing the problem of conflict diamonds to light. Rapper Kanye West released a song entitled 'Diamonds from Sierra Leone' after hearing about the atrocities of conflict diamonds in Africa. 'This ain't Vietnam still/People lose hands, legs, arms for real', he raps. A Hollywood film *Blood Diamond*, starring Leonardo DiCaprio, also features an ethical dilemma about buying and trading diamonds.

NEW TECHNOLOGIES OFFER SOLUTIONS

Recently, a number of new technologies have emerged that, if adopted by the diamond industry worldwide, could change the way that diamonds are produced, traded and sold. Several companies in developed countries, using machines produced by Russian scientists, have been able to make industrial and gem-grade diamonds artificially. In terms of industrial-grade diamonds, which constitute at least 40 per cent of all annual diamond production, this could mean tremendous cost savings for industries using industrial diamonds and the elimination of conflict diamonds from industrial uses. For gem-grade diamonds the viability of synthetic diamonds is questionable. Because of marketing campaigns by industry leader DeBeers Diamond Group, most consumers still feel that diamond gems are natural pieces of art and a rarity of nature. They are unwilling to trade that image for the mass-production view of synthetic diamonds.

Another emerging technology is laser engraving. Lasers make it possible to mark diamonds – either in their rough or cut stage – with a symbol, number or bar code that can help to permanently identify that diamond. Companies who adopt the technology have an interesting marketing opportunity to create diamond brands. Intel, a manufacturer of computer chips, launched a mass marketing campaign 'Intel Inside' to create brand awareness in the previously homogenous market where computer chips were a commodity. Consumers have positive associations with computers using Intel chips – and may only consider computers that have 'Intel inside'. Likewise, establishing brand awareness and building brand equity could add value to diamonds and help increase consumer comfort and confidence.

Sirius Diamonds, a Vancouver-based cutting and polishing company, now microscopically laser-engraves a polar bear logo and an identification number on each gem it processes. Another company, 3Beams Technologies of the United States, is currently working on a system to embed a bar code inside a diamond (as opposed to on its surface) which would make it much more difficult to remove.

Another option is the 'invisible fingerprint' invented by a Canadian security company called Identex. The technology works by electronically placing an invisible information package on each stone. The fingerprint can include any information that the producer desires such as the mine source and production date. The data can only be read by Identex's own scanners. Unfortunately, if the diamond is recut, the fingerprint will be lost, although it can be reapplied at any time. Though this represents a major drawback

to the technology, the recutting of a diamond is expensive and typically reduces its size and value. The technology's creators believe that it will soon become an industry standard because it is a quick and cost-effective way to analyze a stone. The technology may supplement or even replace paper certification.

Lastly, processes are being developed to read a diamond's internal fingerprint – its unique sparkle and combination of impurities. The machine used to do this is called a Laser Raman Spectroscope (LRS). A worldwide database could identify a diamond's origin and track its journey from the mine to end consumer. However, creation of such a database requires large investments for equipment to cope with the volume of diamonds. Such investment will only happen if customers are willing to pay for such identification.

Questions for discussion

1   In light of the conflict diamond issue, would you buy a diamond? Why or why not?

2   As a diamond retailer, what options do you have to ensure that the diamonds you sell are not conflict diamonds?

3   As a diamond producer, what steps can you take to prevent conflict diamonds from entering your supply chain?

4   Do you think the diamond industry as a whole has an ethical responsibility to combat the illicit trade in diamonds?

Sources

'A Crook's Best Friend'. *The Economist*, January 4, 2003.

'Conflict and Security; Conflict Diamonds Are Forever'. *Africa News*, November 8, 2002.

Cowell, Alan. '40 Nations in Accord on "Conflict Diamonds."' *The New York Times*, November 6, 2002.

DeBeers Group. **http://www.debeersgroup.com** (accessed February 13, 2006).

Duke, Lynne. 'Diamond Trade's Tragic Flaw'. *Washington Post*, April 29, 2001.

Finlayson, David. 'Preserving Diamond's Integrity'. *Vancouver Sun*, December 23, 2002.

Fowler, Robert R. 'Final Report of the UN Panel of Experts on Violations of Security Council Sanctions Against UNITA'. (S/2000/203) March 10, 2000.

Jha, Amarendra. 'Diamond Pact Hits Surat Cutters'. *The Times of India*, December 28, 2002.

Jones, Lucy. 'Diamond Industry Rough to Regulate; Central African Republic Works to Monitor Gem Trade'. *The Washington Times*, August 22, 2002.

'Making It Work: Why the Kimberley Process Must Do More to Stop Conflict Diamonds'. Global Witness, November 2005.

Olson, Donald W. 'Diamond, Industrial and Gemstones'. *U.S. Survey Minerals Yearbook*, 2004. **http://minerals.usgs.gov/minerals/pubs/** (Accessed February 23, 2006).

Reeker, Philip T. 'Implementing the Kimberley Process'. January 2, 2003. **http://www.diamonds.net** (Accessed February 22, 2006).

Rory M. O'Ferrall. 'De Beers O'Ferrall Calls Kimberley End of Beginning'. December 2, 2002. **http://www.diamonds.net** (Accessed February 22, 2006).

Smillie, Ian. 'The Kimberley Process: The Case for Proper Monitoring'. Partnership Africa Canada, September 2002. **http://www.partnershipafricacanada.org** (Accessed March 28, 2003).

Sparshott, Jeffrey. 'WTO Targets "Conflict Diamonds."' *The Washington Times*, March 1, 2003.

Watson, Andrea. 'Tribes Face Death in Diamond Bonanza'. *Sunday Express*, January 17, 2006.

'U.S.: Blood Diamond Plan Too Soft'. *Associated Press Online*, June 18, 2002.

The F-18 Hornet Offset

I n May 1992, the Finnish government's selection of the F/A-18 Hornet over the Swedish JAS-39 Gripen, the French Mirage 2000–5, and fellow American F-16 to modernize the fighter fleet of its air force was a major boost to McDonnell Douglas (MDC) in an otherwise quiet market. The deal would involve the sale of 57 F-18 Cs and 7 F-18 Ds at a cost of FIM 9.5 billion (approximately $2 billion). The Finnish version would have an 'F' for 'fighter' (rather than F/A) because the attack dimension is not included. Deliveries would take place between 1995 and 2000. Armaments would add another $1 billion to the deal.

Winning the contract was critical since MDC had been on the losing side of two major aircraft competitions in the United States in 1991. In addition, one of its major projects with the US Navy had been terminated (the A-12), and the government of the Republic of Korea had changed its mind to buy F-16 aircraft after it already had an agreement with MDC for F/A-18 Hornets.

However, the $3 billion was not earned without strings attached. Contractually, McDonnell Douglas and its main sub-contractors (Northrop, General Electric and General Motors' subsidiary Hughes), the 'F-18 Team', were obligated to facilitate an equivalent amount of business for Finnish industry over a ten-year period (1992–2002) using various offset arrangements.

OFFSETS

Offsets are various forms of industrial and business activities required as a condition of purchase. They are an obligation imposed on the seller in major (most often military hardware) purchases by or for foreign governments to minimize any trade imbalance or other adverse economic impact caused by the outflow of currency required to pay for such purchases. In wealthier countries, they are often used for establishing infrastructure. Two basic types of offset arrangements exist: direct and indirect (as seen in Exhibit C4.4). Although offsets have long been associated only with the defence sector, there are now increasing demands for offsets in commercial sales where the government is the purchaser or user.

From 1993 to 2004, 513 offset agreements totalling $77.2 billion were reported by US defence exporters. Sales of aerospace defence systems made up 84 per cent of all export contracts, totalling $64.8 billion. The average term for completing the offset agreements was 78–84 months. The agreements were concluded with a total of 41 nations, with 65.1 per cent attributed to European nations. Although the average offset requirement is 99.1 per cent for Europe, many countries require 100 per cent. Outside of Europe, the overall requirement is 46.6 per cent; however, there are exceptions, such as South Africa's 116.7 per cent average.

Direct offset consists of product-related manufacturing or assembly either for the purposes of the project in question only or for a longer-term partnership. The purchase, therefore, enables the purchaser to be involved in the manufacturing process. Various Spanish companies produce dorsal covers, rudders, aft fuselage panels, and speed brakes for the F/A-18s designated for the Spanish Air Force. In addition to co-production arrangements, licenced production is prominent. Examples include Egypt producing US M1-A1 tanks, China producing MDC's MD-82 aircraft, and Korea assembling the F-16 fighter. An integral part of

Sources: This case study was written by Ilkka A. Ronkainen and funded in part by a grant from the Business and International Education Program of the US Department of Education. The assistance of the various organizations cited in the case is appreciated. Special thanks to David Danjczek, past chair of the Global Offset and Countertrade Association. For more information, see **http://www.boeing.com/defense-space/military/fa18/fa18.htm**; **http://geae.net/geenginecenter/service_militaryavi.html**; **http://www.northgrum.com**; **http://www.hughes.com**.

EXHIBIT C4.4　The offset process

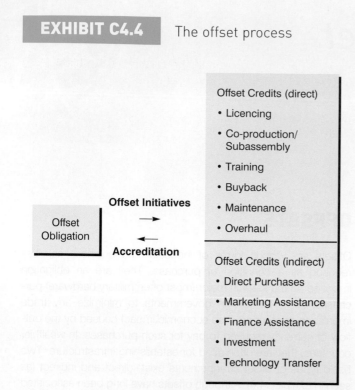

Offset Obligation

Offset Initiatives →

← **Accreditation**

Offset Credits (direct)
- Licencing
- Co-production/ Subassembly
- Training
- Buyback
- Maintenance
- Overhaul

Offset Credits (indirect)
- Direct Purchases
- Marketing Assistance
- Finance Assistance
- Investment
- Technology Transfer

these arrangements is the training of the local employees. Training is not only for production/assembly purposes but also for maintenance and overhaul of the equipment in the longer term. Some offsets have buyback provisions; that is, the seller is obligated to purchase output from the facility or operations it has set up or licenced. For example, Westland takes up an agreed level of parts and components from the Korean plant that produces Lynx Helicopters under licence. In practice, therefore, direct offsets amount to technology transfer.

Indirect offsets are deals that involve products, investments and so forth that are not to be used in the original sales contract but will satisfy part of the seller's 'local' obligation. Direct purchases of raw materials, equipment or supplies by the seller or its suppliers from the offset customer country present the clearest case of indirect offsets. These offset arrangements are analogous to counterpurchases and switch trading. Sellers faced with offset obligations work closely with their supplier base, some having goals of increasing supplier participation in excess of 50 per cent. Teamwork does make the process more effective and efficient. There are various business activities taking place and procurement decisions being made by one of the sellers or its suppliers without offset needs that others may be able to use as offset credit to satisfy an indirect obligation.

Many governments see offsets as a mechanism to develop their indigenous business and industrial sectors. Training in management techniques may be attractive to both parties. The upgrading of skills may be seen by the government as more critical for improving international competitiveness than efforts focused only on hardware. For the seller, training is relatively inexpensive, but it provides good credits because of its political benefit.

An important dimension of the developmental effort will relate to exports. This may involve the analysis of business sectors showing the greatest foreign market potential, improving organizational and product readiness, conducting market research (e.g., estimating demand or assessing competition), identifying buyers or partners for foreign market development, or assisting in the export process (e.g., company visits, support in negotiations and reaching a final agreement, facilitating trial/sample shipments, handling documentation needs).

Sales are often won or lost on the availability of financing and favourable credit terms to the buyer. Financing packages put together by one of the seller's entities, if it is critical in winning the bid, will earn offset credits.

Buyer nations focusing on industrial development and technology transfer have negotiated contracts that call for offsetting the cost of their purchases through investments. Saudi Arabian purchases of military technology have recently been tied to sellers' willingness to invest in manufacturing plants, defence-related industries, or special-interest projects in the country. British Aerospace, for example, has agreed to invest in factories for the production of farm feed and sanitary ware.

Most often, the final offset deal includes a combination of activities, both direct and indirect vis-à-vis the sale, and no two offset deals are alike. With increasing frequency, governments may require 'pre-deal counterpurchases' as a sign of commitment and ability to deliver should they be awarded the contract. Some companies, such as United Technologies, argue that there is limited advantage in carrying out offset activities in advance of the contract, unless the buyer agrees to a firm commitment. While none of the bidders may like it, buyers' market conditions give them very little choice to argue. Even if a bidder loses the deal, it can always attempt to sell its offset credits to the winner or use the credits in conjunction with other sales that one of its divisions may have. Some of the companies involved in the bidding in Finland maintain offset accounts with the Finnish government.

McDonnell's deal with the Finnish Air Force

The F/A-18 Hornet is a twin-engine, twin-tail, multimission tactical aircraft that can be operated from aircraft carriers or from land bases (see Exhibit C4.5). It is both a fighter (air-to-air) and an attack (air-to-ground) aircraft. McDonnell Aircraft Company, a division of MDC, is the prime contractor for the F/A-18. Subcontractors include General Electric for the Hornet's smokeless F404 low bypass turbofan engines, Hughes Aircraft Company for the APG-73 radar, and Northrop Corporation for the airframe. Approximately 1,100 F/A-18s have been delivered worldwide. Although it has been in use by the United States since 1983, it has been (and can continue to be) upgraded during its operational lifetime. Furthermore, it had proven its combat readiness in the Gulf War.

Only since June 1990 has the F/A-18 been available to countries that are not members of the North Atlantic Treaty Organization (NATO). The change in US government position resulted from the rapidly changed East–West political situation. The attractive

Prime contractor	McDonnell Douglas
Principal subcontractor	Northrop Corporation
Type	Single- (C) and two-seat (D), twin-turbofan for fighter and attack missions
Power Plant	Two General Electric F404-GE-402 (enhanced performance engine)
Thrust	4,800 kp each (approx.)
Afterburning thrust	8,000 kp each (approx.)
Dimensions	
Length	17.07 m
Span	11.43 m
Wing area	37.16 m^2
Height	4.66 m
Weights	
Empty	10,455 kg
Normal takeoff	16,650 kg
Maximum takeoff	22,328 kg
Wing loading	450 kg/m^2
Fuel (internal)	6,435 litre (4,925 kg)
Fuel (with external tanks)	7,687 litre
Armament	
Cannon	One General Electric M61A-1 Vulcan rotary-barrel 20-mm
Missiles	Six AIM-9 Sidewinder air-to-air
	Four AIM-7 Sparrow
	Six AIM-120 AMRAAM
Radar	AN/APG-73 multi-mode air-to-air and air-to-surface
Performance	
Takeoff distance	430 m
Landing distance	850 m
Fighter-mission radius	> 740 km
Maximum speed	1.8 Mach (1,915 km/h) at high altitude
	1.0 Mach at intermediate power
Service ceiling	15,240 m
Payload	7,710 kg
Used since	1983
Expected manufacturing lifetime	2000+
Users	USA, Australia, Canada, Spain, Switzerland, and Kuwait
Ordered quantity	1,168

deals available in neutral countries such as Switzerland and Finland helped push the government as well. When the Finnish Air Force initiated its programme in 1986, MDC was not invited to (and would not have been able to) offer a bid because of US government restrictions. Finland is prohibited by World War II peace accords from having attack aircraft, hence the designation F-18.

THE FINNISH GOVERNMENT POSITION

The Finnish government's role in the deal had two critical dimensions: one related to the choice of the aircraft, the other related to managing the offset agreement in a fashion to maximize the benefit to the country's industry for the long term.

Selecting the fighter

In 1986, the Finnish Air Force (FAF) decided to replace its ageing Swedish-made Drakens and Soviet-made MIG-21s, which made up three fighter squadrons. At that time, the remaining service life of these aircraft was estimated to be 15 years, calling for the new squadrons to be operational by the year 2000 and to be up-to-date even in 2025. Finland, due to its strategic geographic location, has always needed a reliable air defence system. The position of neutrality adopted by Finland had favoured split procurement between Eastern and Western suppliers until the collapse of the Soviet Union in December 1991 made it politically possible to purchase fighters from a single Western supplier.

The first significant contacts with potential bidders were made in 1988, and in February 1990, the FAF requested proposals from the French Dassault-Breguet, Sweden's Industrigruppen JAS, and General Dynamics in the United States for 40 fighters and trainer aircraft. In January 1991, the bid was amended to 60 fighters and seven trainers. Three months later, MDC joined the bidding, and by July 1991, binding bids were received from all four manufacturers.

During the evaluative period, the four bidders tried to gain favour for their alternative. One approach was the provision of deals for Finnish companies as 'pre-deal counterpurchases'. For example, General Dynamics negotiated for Vaisala (a major Finnish electronics firm) to become a subcontractor of specialty sensors for the F-16. Before the final decision, the Swedish bidder had arranged for deals worth $250 million for Finnish companies, the French for over $100 million, and General Dynamics for $40 million. MDC, due to its later start, had none to speak of. Other tactics were used as well. The Swedes pointed to long ties that the countries have had, and especially to the possibilities to develop them further on the economic front. As a matter of fact, offsets were the main appeal of the Swedish bid since the aircraft itself was facing development cost overruns and delays. The French reminded the Finnish government that choosing a European fighter might help in Finland's bid to join the European Union (EU) in 1995. Since the FAF preferred the US AMRAAM missile system for its new fighters, the US government cautioned that its availability depended on the choice of the fighter. The companies themselves also worked on making their bid sweeter: Just before the official announcement, General Dynamics improved its offer to include 67 aircraft for the budgeted sum and a guarantee of 125 per cent offsets; that is, the amount of in-country participation would be 125 per cent of the sale price paid by the Finnish government for the aircraft.

After extensive flight testing both in the producers' countries and in Finland (especially for winter conditions), the Hornet was chosen as the winner. Despite the high absolute cost of the aircraft (only 57 to be bought versus 60), the Hornet's cost-effectiveness relative to performance was high. The other alternatives were each perceived to have problems: The JAS-39 Gripen had the teething problems of a brand-new aircraft; the Mirage's model 2000-5 has not yet been produced; and the F-16 may be coming to the end of its product life cycle. The MIG-29 from the Soviet Union/Russia was never seriously in the running due to the political turmoil in that country. Some did propose purchasing the needed three squadrons from the stockpiles of the defunct East Germany (and they could have been bought quite economically), but the uncertainties were too great for a strategically important product.

Working out the offsets

Typically, a specific committee is set up by the government to evaluate which arrangements qualify as part of the offset. In Finland's case, the Finnish Offset Committee (FOC) consists of five members with the Ministries of Defence, Foreign Affairs, and Industry and Trade represented. Its task is to provide recommendations as to which export contracts qualify and which do not. The Technical Working Group was set up to support its decision making, especially in cases concerning technology transfer. From 1977 to 1991, the procedures and final decisions were made by the Ministry of Defence; since then, the responsibility has been transferred to the Ministry of Trade and Industry (see Exhibit C4.6). The transfer was logical given the increased demands and expectations on the trade and technology fronts of the F/A-18 deal.

When the committee was established in 1977 in conjunction with a major military purchase, almost all contracts qualified until an export developmental role for offsets was outlined. The Finnish exporter is required to show that the offset agreement played a pivotal role in securing its particular contract.

Two different approaches are taken by the government to attain its developmental objective. First, the government will not make available (or give offset credit for) counterpurchasing goods that already have established market positions unless the counterpurchaser can show that the particular sale would not have materialized without its support (e.g., through distribution or financing). Second, the government will use compensation 'multipliers' for the first time. While previous deals were executed on a one-on-one basis, the government now wants, through the use of multipliers, direct purchases to certain industries or types of companies. For example, in the case of small or medium-sized companies, a multiplier of two may be used; that is, a purchase of $500,000 from such a firm will satisfy a $1 million share of the counterpurchaser's requirement. Attractive multipliers also may be used that may generate long-term export opportunities or support Finland's indigenous arms or other targeted industry. Similarly, the seller may also insist on the use of multipliers. In the case of technology transfer, the seller may request a high multiplier because of the high initial cost of research and development that may have gone into the technology licenced or provided to the joint venture as well as its relative importance to the recipient country's economic development.

Finnish industry is working closely with the government on two fronts. The Finnish Industrial Offset Consortium (FINDOC) was established to collaborate with the Finnish Foreign Trade

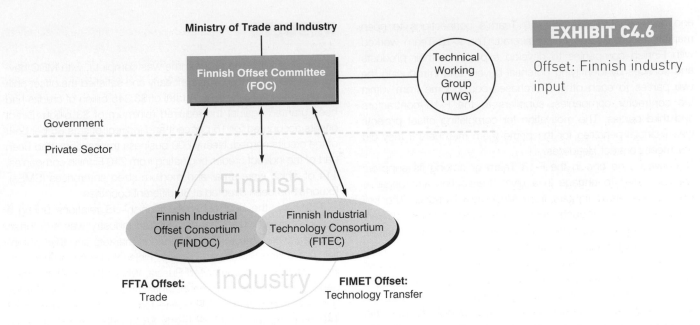

Association (a quasi-governmental organization) on trade development. FINDOC's 21 members represent 15 main business areas (e.g., aircraft, shipbuilding, pulp and paper machinery, and metal and engineering) and are among the main Finnish exporters. Their consortium was set up to take advantage of offset opportunities more efficiently and to provide a focal point for the F-18 Team's efforts. For example, MDC and FINDOC arranged for a familiarization trip to the United States for interested Finnish businesses in the autumn of 1992. For those companies not in FINDOC, it is the task of the FFTA to provide information on possibilities to benefit from the deal. The Finnish Industrial Technology Consortium (FITEC) was established to facilitate technology transfer to and from the Finnish metal and engineering industries.

THE F-18 TEAM'S POSITION

The monies related to offset management and associated development are not generally allowed as a separate cost in the sales contract. Profit margins for aircraft sales are narrow, and any additional costs must be watched closely. Extraordinary demands by the buyer make bidding more challenging and time-consuming. For example, the customer may want extensive changes in the product without changes in the final price. Switzerland wanted major alterations made to the airframe and additional equipment, which made its total cost per plane higher than the price in Finland. In the experience of high-tech firms, the add-on for direct offsets ranges from 3 to 8 per cent, which has to be incorporated into the feasibility plans. Offsets have to make good business sense and, once agreed to be successfully executed.

Competing for the deal

In accepting the offer to bid for the FAF deal, the F-18 Team believed it had only a 5 per cent chance to win the deal but, given its size, decided to go ahead. From the time it received a request to bid from the FAF, MDC had three months to prepare its proposal. The only main negative factor from the short preparation time was MDC's inability to arrange for 'prepurchase' deals and generate goodwill with the constituents.

After two fact-finding missions to Finland, MDC established an office in Helsinki in August 1991. The decision to have a full-time office in Finland (compared to the competitors whose representatives were in Helsinki two days a week on the average) was made based on the experiences from Korea and Switzerland. MDC's approach was to be ready and able to help the customer in terms of information and be involved with all the constituents of the process, such as the testing groups of the FAF, the Ministry of Defence (owners of the programme), and the Parliament (supporters of the programme).

Beyond the technical merits of the Hornet, MDC's capabilities in meeting the pending offset obligations were a critical factor in winning the deal. MDC had by 1992 a total of 100 offset programmes in 25 countries with a value of $8 billion, and its track record in administering them was excellent. Another factor in MDC's favour was its long-term relationship with Finnair, the national airline. Finnair's aircraft have predominantly come from MDC, from the DC-2 in 1941 to the MD-11 aircraft delivered in 1991.

Satisfying the offset obligation

Offset deals are not barter where the seller and the buyer swap products of equal value over a relatively short time period. The F-18 Team members had to complete the offset programme by the year 2002 through a number of different elements including marketing assistance, export development, technology transfer, team purchases and investment financing. One of the major beneficiaries of the offset arrangement was Patria Finnavitec, the only major aircraft manufacturer in Finland. Patria Finnavitec assembled the 57 C-versions in Finland

and also counted on the F-18 Team's connections to open markets for its Redigo trainer aircraft. The F-18 Team worked with Finnish companies to develop exports for their products and services by identifying potential buyers and introducing the two parties to each other. Purchases could come from within the contractor companies, suppliers to the F-18 contractors and third parties. The motivation for completing offset projects was financial penalties for the prime team members if they did not meet contract deadlines.

However, no one in the F-18 Team or among its suppliers was obligated to engage in a given transaction just because Finland purchased fighters from McDonnell Douglas. The key point was that products must meet specifications, delivery dates and price criteria to be successfully sold in any market. After an appropriate purchase had taken place, the F-18 Team received offset credit based on the Finnish-manufactured content of the transaction value as approved by the Finnish Offset Committee. For example, when Finnyards won the bid to build a passenger ferry for the Danish Stena Line, Northrop received offset credits due to its role in financing Finnyard's bid.

The offset obligations were not limited to the United States. The team had offset partners all over the world because the members operate worldwide. Furthermore, given the long time frame involved, there were no pressing time constraints on the members to earn offset credits.

Since 1992, the MDC office in Helsinki has had two officers: one in charge of the aircraft, the other focused in offsets. Due to the worst recession in recent Finnish history, the response to the offset programme was unprecedented, and the office was inundated with requests for information and deals.

RESULTS

By October 2002 the programme was complete, with MDC having delivered all of the 64 aircraft early and satisfied the offset obligations ahead of schedule. A total of $3.345 billion of credits had been granted against the required minimum of $3 billion. Direct offsets accounted for 15 per cent and indirect offsets 85 per cent of the credits earned. Nearly 600 business transactions had been part of the indirect credits originating from 210 Finnish companies, 114 of which were small and medium-sized enterprises (SMEs). Exports had been directed at 30 different countries.

Politically, the deal enhanced Finnish–US relations during a period of spectacular changes. Finnish industry was supported at a time when major shifts occurred in markets and their potential. The United States had become Finland's fourth largest trading partner, having surpassed Russia. While FINDOC companies generated, as expected, a substantial share (48 per cent) of the business transactions, SMEs benefited as well. They generated 140 projects, for a total of nearly $500 million in sales. Some broke into world markets as a result of the offset deal.

Exports accounted for nearly two-thirds of the indirect offset credits. However, significant activity also centred on technology transfer and investments. Aker Finnyards received technology transfers to allow it to move into the hovercraft market where it has already delivered its prototype vessel for the Finnish Navy. SMEs benefited through marketing assistance programmes (which constituted 10 per cent of the total credits). Groups of SME managers were able to use the facilities of General Electric Trading in New York while getting accustomed to the US business climate and establishing relationships with intermediaries and clients.

Questions for discussion

1   Why would the members of the F-18 Team, McDonnell Douglas, Northrop, General Electric and Hughes, agree to such a deal rather than insist on a money-based transaction?

2   After the deal was signed, many Finnish companies expected that contracts and money would start rolling in by merely calling up McDonnell Douglas. What are the fundamental flaws of this thinking?

3   Why do seller governments typically take an unsupportive stance on countertrade arrangements?

4   Comment on this statement: 'Offset arrangements involving overseas production that permit a foreign government or producer to acquire the technical information to manufacture all or part of a UK-origin article, trade short-term sales for long-term loss of market position'.

Recommended readings

'Countertrade's Growth Continues'. *BarterNews* 27 (1993): 54–55.

'Offsets in the Aerospace Industry'. *BarterNews* 27 (1993): 56–57.

'Investing, Licencing, and Trading Conditions Abroad: Saudi Arabia'. *Business International,* May 15, 1990, 5.

Jakubik, Maria, Irina Kabirova, Tapani Koivunen, Päivi Lähtevänoja and Denice Stanfors. *Finnish Air Force Buying Fighters.* Helsinki School of Economics, September 24, 1993.

State Audit Office. *Offsets in the Procurement of Hornet Fighters.* Helsinki, Finland: Edita, 1999, chapter 1.

US Department of Commerce. *Offsets in Defense Trade Tenth Study.* Washington, DC: Bureau of Industry and Security, December 2005, overview.

GLOSSARY

ABC analysis A classification of products and warehousing system based on sensitivity to delivery time; those most sensitive to delivery time are classified as 'A' products; those less sensitive as 'B', and those least sensitive as 'C' products.

absorption A pricing approach in which foreign currency appreciation/depreciation is not reflected (either entirely or partially) in the target market price.

accidental exporters Firms which become international due to unsolicited orders, such as those placed via a website, requiring export; unplanned participation in the international market.

acculturation Adjusting and adapting to a specific culture other than one's own.

agent An intermediary for the distribution of goods who earns a commission on sales. *See also* distributor.

ambush marketing The unauthorized use of an event without the permission of the event owner; for example, an advertising campaign that suggests a sponsorship relationship.

analysis Collecting data and using various quantitative and qualitative techniques of marketing research to investigate an issue.

antidumping duty A duty imposed on imports alleged to be 'dumped' – or sold at less than fair market value – on a domestic marketplace.

antidumping laws Laws prohibiting below-cost sales of products.

area structure An approach to organization based on geographical areas.

area studies Environmental briefings and cultural orientation programmes; factual preparation for living or working in another culture.

arm's-length price A basis for intracompany transfer pricing: The price that unrelated parties would have arrived at for the same transaction.

augmented features Elements added to a core product or service that serve to distinguish it from competing products or services.

back-translation The translation of a foreign language version back to the original language by a person different from the one who made the first translation; an approach used to detect omissions and avoid language blunders.

backward innovation Simplifying a product or service due to lack of purchasing power or usage conditions.

banker's acceptance A method of payment for exported goods: When a time draft, with a specified term of maturity, is drawn on and accepted by a bank, it becomes a banker's acceptance, which is sold in the short-term money market. *See also* documentary collection; discounting.

barriers to entry Obstacles to trade created by governments and market conditions.

barter Exchange of goods for other goods of equal value.

best practice An idea which has saved money or time, or a process that is more efficient than existing ones; best practices are usually established by councils appointed by a company.

bilateral negotiations Trade agreements carried out mainly between two nations.

bill of lading A document that acknowledges receipt of the goods, represents the basic contract between the shipper and the carrier, and serves as evidence of title to the goods for collection by the purchaser; required for export.

black hole A situation that the international marketer has to work his/her way out of; a company may be in a 'black hole' because it has read the market incorrectly or because government may restrict its activities.

born global Newly founded firm that, from its inception, is established as an international business.

boycotts Refusing to purchase from or trade with a company because of political or ideological differences.

brain drain Foreign direct investors attracting the best and brightest employees from a domestic firm; said to be depriving domestic firms of talent.

brand Name, term, symbol, sign or design used by a firm to differentiate its offerings from those of its competitors.

budgets Short-term financial guidelines in such areas as investment, cash and personnel. *See also* plans.

built environment The structures created by human activities; most evident in cities.

bulk service Ocean freight service that mainly provides contractual services for individual voyages for prolonged periods of time.

bureaucratic controls A limited and explicit set of regulations and rules that outline desired levels of performance. *See also* cultural controls.

buyback A form of countertrade: A compensation arrangement whereby one party agrees to supply technology or equipment that enables the other party to produce goods with which the price of the supplied technology or equipment is repaid.

cash in advance A method of payment for exported goods: The most favourable term to the exporter; not widely used, except for smaller, custom orders, or first-time transactions, or situations in which the exporter has reason to doubt the importer's ability to pay.

cause-related marketing Marketing that links a company or brand with a cause, such as environmental protection or children's health.

centralization When a firm maintains tight controls and strategic decision making is concentrated at headquarters. *See also* coordinated decentralization.

certificate of origin A document required by certain countries to ensure correct tariffs are paid.

change agent The introduction into a culture of new products or ideas or practices, which may lead to changes in consumption.

chill effect A sharp reduction in demand for both consumer and industrial goods due to buyer uncertainty about the state of their nation's economy.

clearing arrangements Clearing accounts for deposit and withdrawal of results of countertrade activities.

climate A natural feature that has profound impact on economic activity within a place.

code law A comprehensive set of written statutes; countries with code law try to spell out all possible legal rules explicitly; it is based on Roman law and found in a majority of nations.

commercial risk Term referring primarily to an overseas buyer suspected of insolvency or protracted payment default.

commissionario An intermediary for the distribution of goods who may sell in its own name (as a distributor would), but for an undisclosed principal (an agency concept).

common law Based on tradition and depends less on written statutes and codes than on precedent and custom.

common market Goods and services, including labour, capital and technology, are freely exchanged among member countries; restrictions are removed on immigration and cross-border investment; member countries adopt common trade policies with nonmembers.

complementary strengths The abilities an organization brings when working with another. These abilities should cancel the weaknesses of the partner and the two do together what they could not do separately.

computer-aided design (CAD) A combination of hardware and software that allows for the design of products.

concentration A market expansion policy characterized by focusing on and developing a small number of markets. *See also* diversification.

confiscation Transfer of ownership from a foreign firm to the host country without compensation to the owner.

consignment selling A method of payment that allows the importer to defer payment until the imported goods are actually sold.

consular invoice A document required by certain countries for data collection purposes, to track exports/imports.

consumer-generated media (CGM) Online bulletin boards, blogs, podcasts and other websites at which consumers can post product complaints and compliments.

container ships Cargo vessels that carry standardized containers, which greatly facilitate the loading and unloading of cargo and intermodal transfers.

contender A local company whose assets are transferable, allowing it to compete head-on with established global players worldwide.

content analysis A research technique investigating the content of communication in a society; for example, counting the number of times preselected words, themes, symbols or pictures appear in a given medium.

contributor A role of a country organization; a subsidiary with a distinctive competence, such as product development or regional expertise.

control mechanisms Tools to monitor environmental forces, competitors, channel participants and customer receptiveness; includes short-term control tools and long-term control tools, such as auditing.

coordinated decentralization Overall corporate strategy is provided from headquarters (centralized decision making) but subsidiaries are free to implement it within the range established in consultation between headquarters and the subsidiaries.

core product Product or service in its simplest, generic state; other tangible and augmented features may be added to distinguish a core product or service from its competitors.

corporate governance The relationships among stakeholders used to determine and control the strategic direction and performance of an organization.

corporate image advertising An umbrella marketing communications plan to make the company itself be correctly understood or perceived more positively.

cost of service The amount the shipper is allowed to charge the recipient based on how much it costs to despatch the products.

cost-plus method A pricing strategy based on the true cost of a product (inclusive of domestic and foreign marketing costs).

counterpurchase A form of countertrade that is a parallel barter agreement: The participating parties sign two separate contracts that specify goods and services to be exchanged (some cash may be exchanged to compensate for differences in value).

countertrade Transactions in which purchases are tied to sales and sales to purchases.

countervailing duties A duty imposed on imports alleged to be priced at less than fair market value, due to subsidization of an industry by a foreign government.

cross-subsidization The use of resources accumulated in one part of the world to compete for market share in another part of the world.

cultural assimilator A programme in which trainees must respond to scenarios of specific situations in a particular country.

cultural controls Informal rules and regulations that are the result of shared beliefs and expectations among the members of an organization. *See also* bureaucratic controls.

cultural convergence The growing similarity of attitudes and behaviours across cultures.

cultural knowledge Broad, multifaceted knowledge acquired through living in a certain culture.

cultural universals Characteristics common to all cultures, such as body adornments, courtship, etiquette, family gestures, joking, mealtimes, music, personal names, status differentiation and so on.

culture An integrated system of learned behaviour patterns that are distinguishing characteristics of members of any given society.

currency flows Transfer of capital across national boundaries.

currency variation Changes in exchange rates which can affect the purchases and profitability of the international firm.

customer involvement The degree of participation of the recipient in the production of a service.

customer relationship management Exporter's strategy to increase perceived attention to the foreign customer through call-centre technologies, customer-service departments and the company's website.

customer structure An approach to organization that is based on the customer groups that are served – for example, consumers versus businesses versus governments.

customs broker An agent for an importer with authority to clear inbound goods through customs and ship them on to their destination.

customs union Nation members of customs unions agree to set aside trade barriers and also establish common trade policies with nonmember nations.

data equivalence A consideration that ensures comparative structure in survey questions by taking into account cultural variations.

database marketing Promotional tool combining telemarketing with data on the purchasing habits of a customer; allows the creation of an individual relationship with each customer or prospect.

database marketing A form of direct marketing in which database information (developed through direct mail or the Internet) allows the creation of an individual relationship with each customer or prospect.

debt problem Developing countries can be burdened with loans from international sources or other countries, which can crush a nation's buying power and force imports down and exports up to meet interest payments.

decentralization When a firm grants its subsidiaries a high degree of autonomy; controls are relatively loose and simple. *See also* coordinated decentralization.

decoding The process by which the receiver of a message transforms an 'encoded' message from symbols into thought.

defender A local company that has assets that give it a competitive advantage only in its home market.

del credere agent An intermediary for the distribution of goods who guarantees the solvency of the customer and may therefore be responsible to the supplier for payment by the customer.

density Weight-to-volume ratio of a good; high-density goods are more likely to be shipped as air freight, rather than ocean freight.

deregulation Reduction of governmental involvement in the marketplace.

derived demand Business opportunities resulting from the move abroad by established customers and suppliers.

direct exporting A distribution channel in which the marketer takes direct responsibility for his/her products abroad by either selling directly to the foreign customer or finding a local representative to sell its products in the market. *See also* indirect exporting.

direct/indirect questions In designing a survey questionnaire, the degree of societal sensitivity must be taken into account when determining the directness or indirectness of questions.

discounting When a time draft, a method of payment for exported goods with a specified term of maturity, is drawn on and accepted by a bank, it may be converted into cash by the exporter by discounting; the draft is sold to a bank at a discount from face value. *See also* banker's acceptance.

discretionary product adaptation Conforming a product or service to meet prevailing social, economic and climactic conditions in the market.

discriminatory regulations Rules and laws that impose larger operating costs on foreign firms than on local competitors, that provide subsidies to local firms only, or that deny competitive opportunities to foreign suppliers. Nondiscriminatory regulations may be inconvenient and may hamper business operations, but they offer less opportunity for international criticism.

distribution culture Existing channel structures and philosophies for distribution of goods.

distributor An intermediary that purchases goods for resale through its own channels. *See also* agent.

diversification A market expansion policy characterized by growth in a relatively large number of markets. *See also* concentration.

documentary collection A method of payment for exported goods: The seller ships the goods and the shipping documents and the draft demanding payment are presented to the importer through a bank acting as the seller's agent; the draft, also known as the bill of exchange, may be a sight draft or a time draft.

dodger A local company that sells out to a global player or becomes part of an alliance.

domestication Gaining control over the assets of a foreign firm by demanding partial transfer of ownership and management responsibility to the host country.

draft A method of payment for exported goods: Similar to a personal cheque; an order by one party to pay another; 'documentary' drafts must be accompanied by specified shipping documents; 'clean' drafts do not require documentation; also known as the 'bill of exchange'. *See also* documentary collection.

dual pricing Differentiation of domestic and export prices.

dual-use items Goods that are useful for both military and civilian purposes.

duty drawbacks A refund of up to 99 per cent of duties paid on imports when they are re-exported or incorporated into articles that are subsequently exported within five years of the importation.

e-commerce E-commerce is the buying and selling of goods and services using electronic media, for example, the Internet.

economic blocs Groups of nations that integrate economic and political activities.

economic union Integration of economic policies among member countries; monetary policies, taxation and government spending are harmonized.

economies of scale Production condition where an increase in the quantity of the product results in a decrease of the production cost per unit.

efficiency seekers Firms that attempt to obtain the most economic sources of production in their foreign direct investment strategy.

embargoes Governmental actions that terminate the free flow of trade in goods, services, or ideas, imposed for adversarial and political purposes.

encoding The process by which a sender converts a message into a symbolic form that will be properly understood by the receiver.

environmental protection A major force shaping the relationship between the developed and developing world; being environmentally responsible may help a company to build trust and improve its image, but may be contradictory to a developing nation's need to expand into undeveloped areas and exploit its resources.

Environmental Superfund A fund to cover the costs of domestic safety regulations, made up from fees imposed on US chemical manufacturers, based upon volume of production.

ethnocentrism The belief that one's own culture is superior to others.

European Union Effective January 1, 1994; formed by the ratification of the Maastricht Treaty; set the foundation for economic and monetary union among member countries and the establishment of the euro, a common currency.

exchange rates Price of a currency expressed in units of another currency, e.g., yen per euro.

experiential knowledge Knowledge acquired only by being involved in a culture other than one's own.

exploratory stage A stage in which a firm begins to explore the feasibility of exporting or otherwise engaging in international trade.

export adaptation An experienced export firm with the ability to adjust its activities to keep pace with changing exchange rates, tariffs and other variables in the international market.

export control systems Governmental policy designed to deny or at least delay the acquisition of strategically important goods by adversaries.

export licence Written authorization to send a product abroad.

export trading company (ETC) Legal construct designed to encourage small and medium-sized companies to participate in the international marketplace.

expropriation Seizure of foreign assets by a government with payment of compensation to the owners.

extender A company that is able to exploit its success at home as a platform for expansion elsewhere; this calls for markets or segments that are similar in terms of customer preferences.

facilitating payments Small fees paid to expedite paperwork through customs; also called 'grease;' not considered in violation of the Foreign Corrupt Practices Act or OECD guidelines.

factor mobility The loosening of restrictions on the trade of capital, labour and technology among nations.

factoring A trade financing method; companies known as factoring houses may purchase an exporter's receivables for a discounted price; factors also provide the exporter with a complete financial package combining credit protection, accounts-receivable bookkeeping and collection services.

factual information Objective knowledge of a culture obtained from others through communication, research and education.

feedback Responses to communications that seek to generate awareness, evoke a positive attitude, or increase purchases; collection and analysis of feedback is necessary to analyse the success of communication efforts.

field experience Placing a trainee in a different cultural environment for a limited time; for example, living with a host family of the nationality to which the trainee will be assigned.

financial incentives Special funding legislated by governments to attract foreign investments.

fiscal incentives Special funding legislated by governments to attract foreign investments.

focus groups Eight to twelve consumers representing the proposed target market audience, brought together to discuss motivations and behaviour.

forced distribution tests A group of consumers reports on new products they encounter in normal retail outlets. *See also* laboratory test markets; microtest marketing.

foreign affiliate A US firm of which foreign entities own at least 10 per cent.

foreign availability High-technology products that are available worldwide, from many sources.

foreign direct investment Capital funds that flow from abroad; company is held by noncitizens; foreign ownership is typically undertaken for longer-term participation in an economic activity.

foreign exchange licence A licenve that may be required by certain countries for an importer to secure the needed hard currency to pay for an import shipment; the exporter has to provide the importer with the data needed to obtain these licences from governmental authorities and should make sure that the importer has indeed secured the documents.

foreign market opportunity analysis Basic information needed to identify and compare key alternatives when a firm plans to launch international activities.

forfaiting A trade financing technique; the importer pays the exporter with bills of exchange or promissory notes guaranteed by a leading bank in the importer's country; the exporter can sell them to a third party at a discount from their face value for immediate cash.

Fortress Europe Term expressing the fear that unified European nations will raise barriers to trade with other nations, including setting rules about domestic content and restricting imports.

forward exchange market A method used to counter challenges in currency movements; the exporter enters into an agreement for a rate at which it will buy the foreign currency at a future date; the rate is expressed as either a premium or a discount on the current spot rate.

franchising A business model in which a parent company (the franchiser) grants another, independent entity (the franchisee) the right to do business in a specified manner. This right can take the form of selling the franchiser's products or using its name, production, preparation and marketing techniques, or its business approach.

free trade area The least restrictive and loosest form of economic integration among nations; goods and services are freely traded among member countries.

Free Trade Area of the Americas (FTAA) A proposed free trade zone reaching from Point Barrow, Alaska, to Patagonia; negotiations and an agreement planned for 2005.

functional lubrication Bribes that are not imposed by individual greed, but that serve to 'grease the wheels' of bureaucratic processes; amounts tend to be small, the 'express fee' is standardized and the money is passed along to the party in charge of processing a document.

functional structure An approach to organization that emphasizes the basic tasks of the firm – for example, manufacturing, sales, and research and development.

futures A method used to counter problems of currency movements; in the currency futures market, for example, a buyer agrees to buy futures in British pound sterling, which implies an obligation to buy in the future at a prespecified price. *See also* option.

geologic characteristics The characteristics of a place relating to its natural attributes.

global account management Account programmes extended across countries, typically for the most important customers, to build relationships.

global brands Brands that reach the world's mega-markets and are perceived as the same brand by consumers and internal constituents.

global linkages The worldwide network of trade connections that binds together countries, institutions and individuals.

global media Media vehicles that have target audiences on at least three continents.

glocalization Building in organizational flexibility to allow for local/regional adjustments in global strategic planning and implementation; uniformity is sought in strategic elements such as positioning of a product; care is taken to localize tactical elements, such as distribution.

grey market Distribution channels uncontrolled by producers; goods may enter the marketplace in ways not desired by their manufacturers.

Group of Five Five industrialized nations regarded as economic superpowers: The United States, United Kingdom, France, Germany and Japan.

Group of Seven Seven industrialized nations regarded as economic superpowers: The United States, United Kingdom, France, Germany, Japan, Italy and Canada.

Group of Ten Ten industrialized nations regarded as economic superpowers: The United States, United Kingdom, France, Germany, Japan, Italy, Canada, the Netherlands, Belgium and Sweden.

high context cultures Cultures in which the context is at least as important as what is actually said; for example, Japan and Saudi Arabia have cultures in which what is not said can carry more meaning than what is said.

household All the persons, both related and unrelated, who occupy a housing unit.

hydrology Rivers, lakes and other bodies of water influence the kinds of economic activities that occur in a place.

implementation The actual carrying out of the planned marketing activity.

implementors A role of a country organization; although implementors are usually placed in smaller, less-developed countries, they provide the opportunity to capture economies of scale and scope that are the basis of a global strategy.

import licence A licence that may be required by certain countries for particular types or amounts of imported goods.

import substitution A policy that requires a nation to produce goods that were formerly imported.

Incoterms Internationally accepted standard definitions for terms of sale, covering variable methods of transportation and delivery between country of origin and country of destination, and set by the International Chamber of Commerce (ICC) since 1936.

in-depth studies Market research tools that gather detailed data used to study consumer needs across markets.

indirect exporting A distribution channel that requires dealing with another domestic firm that acts as a sales intermediary for the marketer, often taking over the international side of the marketer's operations. *See also* direct exporting.

infant industry Relatively new firms are sometimes seen as deserving of protection which allows the industry to 'grow up' before having to compete with 'adult' global industries.

inflation The increase in consumer prices compared with a previous period.

infrastructures Economic, social, financial and marketing support systems, from housing to banking systems to communications networks.

innate exporters Start-up exporters; firms founded for the express purpose of marketing abroad; also described as 'born global'.

intangibility Cannot be seen, touched, or held. A key difference between goods and services.

integrated distribution An export marketing strategy in which the marketer makes an investment into the foreign market for the purpose of selling its products.

integrated exporting An export marketing strategy in which the marketer takes direct responsibility for its products abroad by either selling directly to the foreign customer or finding a local representative to sell its products in the market.

integrated marketing communications Coordinating various promotional strategies according to target market and product characteristics, the size of budget, the type of international involvement and control considerations.

intellectual property (IP) A legal entitlement of exclusive rights to use an idea, piece of knowledge or invention.

intellectual property rights Safeguarding rights by providing the originators of an idea or process with a proprietary compensation, at least, in order to encourage quick dissemination of innovations.

intermediaries Independent distributors of goods, operating primarily at a local level. *See also* distributor; agent.

international comparative research Research carried out between nations, particularly those with similar environments, where the impact of uncontrollable macrovariables is limited.

international freight forwarder An agent who provides services in moving cargo to an overseas destination; independent freight forwarders are regulated in the United States and should be certified by the Federal Maritime Commission.

international marketing The process of planning and conducting transactions across national borders to create exchanges that satisfy the objectives of individuals and organizations.

interpretive knowledge Knowledge that requires comprehensive fact finding and preparation, and an ability to appreciate the nuances of different cultural traits and patterns.

intranet A company network that integrates a company's information assets into a single and accessible system using Internet-based technologies such as email, newsgroups and the World Wide Web.

inventory carrying costs The expense of maintaining inventories.

joint ventures Collaborations of two or more organizations for more than a transitory period, in which the partners share assets, risks and profits.

Kyoto Protocol An international contract signed in 1997 that calls for reductions in the emissions of carbon dioxide and five other greenhouse gases.

laboratory test markets Participants are exposed to a product and their reactions measured in a controlled environment. *See also* microtest marketing; forced distribution tests.

lead users Companies, organizations or individuals who are ahead of trends or have needs that go beyond what is available at the present time.

letter of credit A method of payment for exported goods: an instrument issued by a bank at the request of a buyer; the bank promises to pay a specified amount of money on presentation of documents stipulated in the letter of credit, usually the bill of lading, consular invoice and a description of the goods.

licensing An agreement in which one firm (the licensor) permits another firm (the licensee) to use its intellectual property in exchange for compensation designated as a royalty.

liner service Ocean freight service that offers regular scheduled passage on established routes.

lobbyists Well-connected individuals and firms that help companies influence the governmental decision-making process by providing access to policymakers and legislators.

low context cultures Cultures in which most information is contained explicitly in words; for example, North American cultures.

management contract An agreement where the supplier brings together a package of skills that will provide for the ongoing operation of the client's facilities.

maquiladoras Mexican plants that make goods and parts or process food for export to the United States.

marginal cost method A pricing strategy that considers only the direct cost of producing and selling products for export as the floor beneath which prices cannot be set; overhead costs are disregarded, allowing an exporter to lower prices to be competitive in markets that otherwise might not be accessed.

market pricing Determining the initial price of a product by comparison with competitors' prices.

market seekers Firms that search for better opportunities for entry and expansion in their foreign direct investment strategy.

market transparency Clarity of the offering made to the customer; transparency in service delivery is often difficult to ensure, because services may be customized to individual needs.

market-differentiated pricing Export pricing based on the dynamic, changing conditions of each marketplace.

marketing 'An organization function and a set of processes for creating, communicating and delivering value to customers, and for managing customer relationships in ways that benefit the organization and its stake-holders' (American Marketing Association).

master franchising system A system wherein foreign partners are selected and awarded the franchising rights to territory in which they, in turn, can subfranchise.

materials management The timely movement of raw materials, parts and supplies into and through a firm.

matrix structure An approach to organization based on the coordination of product and geographic dimensions of planning and implementing strategy.

microfinance Programmes in developing markets that allow consumers, with no property as collateral, to borrow sums averaging $100 to make purchases and to have access to retail banking services.

microtest marketing A panel of consumers is exposed to new products through a retail grocery operated by a research agency. *See also* laboratory test markets; forced distribution tests.

mixed structure An approach to organization that combines one or more possible structures (see product, functional, process and customer structures); also called a hybrid structure.

multilateral negotiations Trade agreements carried out among a number of nations.

national security Protecting the welfare – economic, cultural, or military – of a nation's people; tariffs, barriers to entry and other obstacles to trade often are established to ensure such protection.

noise Extraneous and distracting stimuli that interfere with the communication of a message.

nondiscriminatory regulations Rules and laws that may be inconvenient and hamper business operations, but that are imposed in an even-handed manner, without discriminating between local and foreign suppliers.

nonfinancial incentives Support such as guaranteed government purchases; special protection from competition through tariffs; import quotas and local content requirements designed to attract foreign investments.

non-tariff barriers Barriers to trade that are more subtle than tariff barriers; for example, these barriers may be government or private-sector 'buy domestic' campaigns, preferential treatment of domestic bidders over foreign bidders, or the establishment of standards that are not common to foreign goods or services.

not-invented-here syndrome (NIH) Local resistance or decline in morale caused by the perception that headquarters is not sensitive to local needs.

offset A form of countertrade: Industrial compensation mandated by governments when purchasing defence-related goods and services in order to equalize the effect of the purchase on the balance of payments.

open account A method of payment, also known as open terms; exporter selling on open account removes both real and psychological barriers to importing; however, no written evidence of the debt exists and there is no guarantee of payment.

operating risk Exposing ongoing operations of a firm to political risk in another nation.

opportunity costs Costs resulting from the foreclosure of other sources of profit, such as exports or direct investment; for example, when licencing eliminates options.

option A method used to counter challenges in currency movements; gives the holder the right to buy or sell foreign currency at a prespecified price on or up to a prespecified date. *See also* futures.

outcome The results of meeting objectives that seek to generate awareness, evoke a positive attitude, or increase purchases.

overinvest Tendency in the initial acquisition process to buy more land, space and equipment than is needed immediately to accommodate future growth.

ownership risk Exposing property and life to political risk in another nation.

parallel importation Authentic and legitimately manufactured trademark items that are produced and purchased abroad but imported or diverted to the markets by bypassing designated channels; also called 'grey market'.

pass-through A pricing approach in which foreign currency appreciation/depreciation is reflected in a commensurate amount in the target market price.

Pax Romana 'The Roman Peace', referring to the common coinage, trading activities and communication networks established and protected throughout a vast empire.

penetration pricing Introducing a product at an initial low price to generate sales volume and achieve high market share.

perishability The rapidity with which a service or good loses value or becomes worthless; unused capacity in the form of an empty seat on an airplane, for example, quickly becomes nonsaleable.

physical distribution The movement of a firm's finished product to its customers.

Physical Quality of Life Index (PQLI) A composite measure of the level of welfare in a country, including life expectancy, infant mortality and adult literacy rates.

piggyback In a joint venture, one partner can piggyback by making use of the other's strengths.

piracy A contemporary security concern for shipping; annual cargo crime losses are estimated at $30–50 billion internationally.

place Distribution policy covers the place variable of the marketing mix and has two components: channel management and logistics management.

planning The blueprint generated to react to and exploit the opportunities in the marketplace, involving both long-term strategies and short-term tactics.

plans Formalized long-range financial programmes with more than a one-year horizon. *See also* budget.

political risk Term referring to a factor beyond the control of an exporter or importer; for example, a foreign buyer may be willing to pay but the local government may delay methods of payment.

political risk The risk of loss when investing in a given country caused by changes in a country's political structure or policies, such as tax laws, tariffs, expropriation of assets or restriction in repatriation of profits.

political union Unification of policies among member nations and establishment of common institutions.

population The human element of the environment.

portfolio investment An international investment flow that focuses on the purchase of stocks and bonds.

positioning The presentation of a product or service to evoke a positive and differentiated mental image in the consumers' perception.

predatory dumping Dumping – or selling goods overseas for less than in the exporter's home market or at a price below the cost of production, or both – that is termed 'predatory' because it is used deliberately to increase the exporter's market share and undermine domestic industries.

price The revenue-generating element of the marketing mix.

price controls Government regulations that set maximum or minimum prices; governmental imposition of limits on price changes.

price elasticity of consumer demand Adjusting prices to current conditions: for example, a status-conscious market that insists on products with established reputations will be inelastic, allowing for more pricing freedom than a price-conscious market.

price escalation The higher cost of a product resulting from the costs of exporting and marketing in a foreign country.

price manipulation Adjusting prices of exported goods to compensate for changing currency rates.

pricing-to-market Destination-specific adjustment of mark-ups in response to exchange-rate changes. *See also* pass-through; absorption.

process structure An approach to organization that uses processes as a basis for structure; common in the energy and mining industries, where one entity may be in charge of exploration worldwide and another may be responsible for the actual mining operation.

product placement Creating brand awareness by arranging to have a product shown or used in visual media such as films, television, games or websites.

product policy Covers all the elements that make up the good, service or idea that is offered by the marketer, including tangible (product) and intangible (service) characteristics.

product structure An approach to organization that gives worldwide responsibility to strategic business units for the marketing of their product lines.

profit repatriation Transfer of business gains from a local market to another country by the foreign direct.

promotion tools Communications policy uses promotion tools such as advertising, sales promotion, personal selling and publicity to interact with customers, middlemen and the public.

promotional mix The tools an international marketer has available to form a total communications programme for use in a targeted market: advertising, personal selling, publicity, sales promotion and sponsorship.

proxy variable A substitute for a variable that one cannot directly measure.

psychological distance Perceived distance from a firm to a foreign market, caused by cultural variables, legal factors and other societal norms; a market that is geographically close may seem to be psychologically distant.

pull strategies Promotional strategies in a targeted market relying primarily on mass communication tools, mainly advertising; appropriate for consumer-oriented products with large target audiences and long channels of distribution.

purchasing power parities (PPP) A measure of how many units of currency are needed in one country to buy the amount of goods and services that one unit of currency will buy in another country.

push strategies Promotional strategies in a targeted market relying primarily on personal selling; higher cost per contact, but appropriate for selling where there are shorter channels of distribution and smaller target populations.

qualitative data Data is gathered to better understand situations, behavioural patterns and underlying dimensions.

quality perception The evaluative impression that customers develop of a service, largely determined by the behaviour of the employees that they contact.

quantitative data Data is amassed to assess statistical significance; surveys are appropriate research instruments.

quota systems Control of imports through quantitative restraints.

R&D costs Costs resulting from the research and development of licensed technology.

realism check A step in the analysis of data in which the researcher determines what facts may have inadvertently skewed the responses; for example, if Italian responders report that very little spaghetti is consumed in Italy, the researcher may find that the responders were distinguishing between store-bought and homemade spaghetti.

reference groups A person or group of people that significantly influences an individual's attitude and behaviour.

regulatory practices The primary source of barriers to services destined for the US market; fields such as banking, insurance and accounting are regulated at both federal and state levels, often posing formidable barriers to entrants from abroad.

reliability The vagaries of nature can impose delays on transportation services; these delays tend to be shorter in absolute time for air shipments, which are considered more predictable.

research consortia Joint industry efforts in the research and development of new products to combat the high costs and risks of innovation; often supported by governments.

research specifications In the centralized approach to coordinating international marketing, specifications such as focus, thrust and design are directed by the home office to the local country operations for implementation.

resource seekers Firms that search for either natural resources or human resources in their foreign direct investment strategy.

reverse distribution systems Logistics that ensure that a firm can retrieve its goods from the market for subsequent use, recycling or disposal.

safety-valve activity The use of overseas sales as a way to balance inventories or compensate for overproduction in the short term.

Sarbanes-Oxley Act Law enacted in the United States in 2002, in the wake of major corporate corruption scandals (such as Enron and WorldCom), intended to protect investors by improving the accuracy and reliability of corporate disclosures.

scenario analysis Evaluating corporate plans under different conditions, such as variations in economic growth rates, import penetration, population growth and political stability over medium- to long-term periods.

self-reference criterion The unconscious reference to one's own cultural values in comparison to other cultures.

seminar missions Promotional event in which eight to ten firms are invited to participate in a one- to four-day forum; a soft-sell approach aimed at expanding sales abroad.

sensitivity training An approach based on the assumption that understanding and accepting oneself is critical to understanding a person from another culture.

service capacity Ability to supply service on demand, including the planning of backup during peak periods; similar to an inventory of goods.

service consistency Uniformity or standardization in the offering of a service; unlike products, services are often subject to individual influences and the need to customize to satisfy unique customer interactions.

shipper's declaration for dangerous goods Required for shipments such as corrosives, flammables and poisons.

shipper's export declaration A document that states proper authorization for export and serves as a means for governmental data collection efforts.

Single European Act Ratified in 1987 by twelve European countries to free the exchange of goods, services, capital and people among member countries.

skimming Offering a product at an initial high price to achieve the highest possible sales contribution in a short time period; as more market segments are identified, the price is gradually lowered.

social desirability Actions or wishes triggered by the expectation or preferences of one's human environment.

social stratification The division of a particular population into classes.

sogoshosha Large Japanese trading companies, such as Sumitomo, Mitsubishi, Mutsui and C. Itoh.

soils Variations in the soils found in different geographic regions (and their interactions with climate) have a profound impact on agricultural prodution.

solo exhibitions Promotional event, generally limited to one or a few product themes and held only when market conditions warrant them; aimed at expanding sales abroad.

standard worldwide price A price-setting strategy in which a product is offered at the same price regardless of the geography of the buyer.

strategic alliances A special form of joint ventures, consisting of arrangements between two or more companies with a common business objective. They are more than the traditional customer–vendor relationship, but less than an outright acquisition.

strategic leader A role of a country organization; a highly competent national subsidiary located in a strategically critical market.

structured/unstructured questions In a survey questionnaire, structured questions typically allow the respondent only limited options, as potential responses to unstructured (or open-ended) questions permit the capture of more in-depth information, but they also increase the potential for interviewer bias.

supply chain management An integration of the three major concepts of the logistics in which a series of value-adding activities connect a company's supply side with its demand side. *See also* systems concept; total cost concept; and trade-off concept.

switch-trading Credits in a clearing account (established for countertrading) can be sold or transferred to a third party.

systems concept One of three major concepts of the logistics of international management, based on the notion that materials-flow activities within and outside of the firm are so extensive and complex that they can be considered only in the context of their interaction. *See also* total cost concept and trade-off concept.

tariffs Import control mechanisms that raise prices through placement of a tax.

telemarketing Promotional tool that is growing worldwide as customers become more accustomed to calling toll-free numbers and more willing to receive calls from marketers.

terminology Specific designations or definitions of terms, used by trade bodies (such as the WTO) or in trade agreements; these terms can often have unintended or distorted applications in political discourse.

terrain The geology of a place expressed in terms of its regional characteristics; terrain plays a role in population, resources, travel and trade.

theocracy A legal perspective that holds faith and belief as its key focus and is a mix of societal, legal and spiritual guidelines.

third-party (3PL) logistics The outsourcing of logistical management, which is a rapidly expanding industry.

total cost concept One of three major concepts of the logistics of international management, in which cost is used as a basis for measurement; the purpose of the total cost concept is to minimize the firm's overall logistics cost by implementing the systems concept appropriately. *See also* systems concept and trade-off concept.

trade deficit A trade deficit occurs when a country imports more goods and services than it exports.

trade missions A promotional event aimed at expanding sales abroad; may be a country-specific, industry-organized, or government-approved event. *See also* seminar missions.

trade sanctions Governmental actions that inhibit the free flow of trade in goods, services or ideas, imposed for adversarial and political purposes.

trademark licensing The ownership of the name or logo of a designer, literary character, sports team, or film star, for example, which can be used on merchandise.

trade-off concept One of three major concepts of the logistics of international management, which recognizes that linkages within logistics systems lead to interactions; for example, locating a warehouse near the customer may reduce the cost of transportation, but requires investment in a new warehouse. *See also* systems concept and total cost concept.

tramp service Ocean freight service that is available for irregular routes and is scheduled only on demand.

transfer costs Costs incurred in negotiating licensing agreements; all variable costs resulting from transfer of a technology to a licensee and all ongoing costs of maintaining the agreement.

transfer risk Exposing the transfer of funds to political risk across international borders.

translation-retranslation approach Reducing problems in the wording of questions by translating the question into a foreign language and having a second translator return the foreign text to the researcher's native language.

transportation mode Choices among air freight and ocean freight, pipeline, rail and trucking.

triad The megamarkets of North American, Europe and Asia-Pacific.

unintentional dumping Dumping – or selling goods overseas for less than in the exporter's home market or at a price below the cost of production, or both – that is termed 'unintentional' because the lower price is due to currency fluctuations.

urbanization Descriptions of urbanization range from densely-populated cities to built-up areas to small towns with proclaimed legal limits.

value of service How much a good is desired relative to other goods.

value-added tax (VAT) A tax on the value added to goods and services charged as a percentage of price at each stage in the production and distribution chain.

video/catalogue exhibitions Promotional tool coordinating product presentations from several companies in one catalogue or video; aimed at expanding sales abroad.

virtual trade shows Electronic promotional tool enabling exporters to promote their products and services over the Internet and to have an electronic presence without actually attending an overseas trade show; aimed at expanding European sales abroad.

voluntary restraint agreements Non-tariff import control mechanisms consisting of self-imposed restrictions and cutbacks aimed at avoiding punitive trade actions from a host.

web-based research Surveys and other data collection techniques administered using the resources of the Internet.

INDEX